COMPUTER FUNDAMENTALS

Concepts, Systems and Applications

D.P. NAGPAL

S Chand And Company Limited

(ISO 9001 Certified Company)

S Chand And Company Limited

(ISO 9001 Certified Company)

Head Office: Block B-1, House No. D-1, Ground Floor, Mohan Co-operative Industrial Estate, New Delhi – 110 044 | Phone: 011-66672000

Registered Office: A-27, 2nd Floor, Mohan Co-operative Industrial Estate, New Delhi – 110 044 Phone: 011-49731800

www.**schandpublishing.com**; e-mail: **info@schandpublishing.com**

Branches

Ahmedabad : Ph: 27542369, 27541965; ahmedabad@schandpublishing.com
Bengaluru : Ph: 22354008, 22268048; bangalore@schandpublishing.com
Bhopal : Ph: 4274723, 4209587; bhopal@schandpublishing.com
Bhubaneshwar : Ph: 2951580; bhubaneshwar@schandpublishing.com
Chennai : Ph: 23632120; chennai@schandpublishing.com
Guwahati : Ph: 2738811, 2735640; guwahati@schandpublishing.com
Hyderabad : Ph: 40186018; hyderabad@schandpublishing.com
Jaipur : Ph: 2291317, 2291318; jaipur@schandpublishing.com
Jalandhar : Ph: 4645630; jalandhar@schandpublishing.com
Kochi : Ph: 2576207, 2576208; cochin@schandpublishing.com
Kolkata : Ph: 23357458, 23353914; kolkata@schandpublishing.com
Lucknow : Ph: 4003633; lucknow@schandpublishing.com
Mumbai : Ph: 25000297; mumbai@schandpublishing.com
Nagpur : Ph: 2250230; nagpur@schandpublishing.com
Patna : Ph: 2260011; patna@schandpublishing.com
Ranchi : Ph: 2361178; ranchi@schandpublishing.com
Sahibabad : Ph: 2771238; info@schandpublishing.com

First Edition 1999
Subsequent Editions and Reprints 1999, 2004, 2008, 2009, 2010, 2013, 2014
Revised Edition 2015
Reprints 2017, 2018
Reprint 2020

ISBN: 978-81-219-2388-0 **Product Code:** H3CFA50COMP10ENZX15R

PRINTED IN INDIA

By Vikas Publishing House Private Limited, Plot 20/4, Site-IV, Industrial Area Sahibabad, Ghaziabad – 201 010 and Published by S Chand And Company Limited, A-27, 2nd Floor, Mohan Co-operative Industrial Estate, New Delhi – 110 044

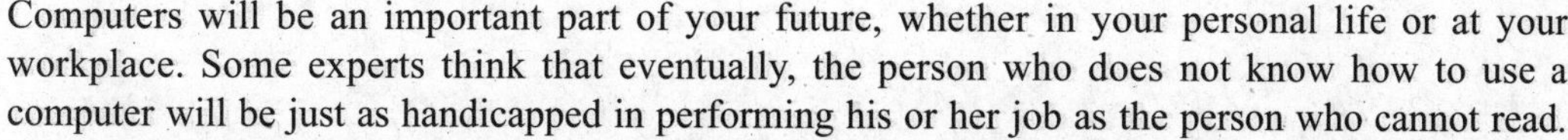

PREFACE TO THE REVISED EDITION

Computers will be an important part of your future, whether in your personal life or at your workplace. Some experts think that eventually, the person who does not know how to use a computer will be just as handicapped in performing his or her job as the person who cannot read.

In this revised edition, most of chapters have been updated thoroughly with the latest technology. However, few chapters 'Internet Protocol Version 6', 'Cryptography', 'Secure Communications', 'Virtulization and Security', 'Cloud Computing and its Security' have been added, which make this book all the more resourceful for the readers and students.

To become a computer literate, you should not only know who uses computers, but also how and where they can be used; the kinds of tasks they perform, how they affect your society and economy, and how to use them in your own life and career. If you are taking this course to familiarize yourself with the world of computers, **Computer Fundamentals** serves as an interesting and informative guide in your journey to computer literacy. If you intend to become a computer professional, this book will give you the broad-based background you will need to pursue more advanced course-work in the' area.

This book caters to all categories of students. On the one hand, it helps the students to pass the examination and on the other it satisfies the intellectual curiosity of brilliant' students. This book also serves as a basic references volume and is suitable for self study for those who have little or no background knowledge of the subject. It covers the material of the Computer Fundamentals or Information Technology Course of BCA, MCA, B.Tech, M.Tech, MIT, MBA, BCA, CCNA, AMIE, CA and all other examinations where Computer Fundamentals or Information Technology forms a subject.

I would like to thank my family, friends and colleagues for their frank comments and enthusiasm for the book.

All valuable suggestions for improvement will be highly appreciated and gratefully acknowledged by the author.

AUTHOR

CONTENTS IN BRIEF

CONTENTS

INTRODUCTION

Almost all of us are involved, in some fashion, with computers on a daily basis. They are in the cars we drive, the televisions we watch, the clocks that tell us the time, the microwave ovens that heat up food and, of course, in the machines that populate many of our desktops. Without computers, life would certainly be a lot different. Computers, however, are relatively new on the human scene. We can measure civilization in thousands of years and the industrial revolution in hundreds. Yet computers have only been around for tens of years. This relative newcomer has been quick to take hold, dig in, and proliferate.

Most people know that a computer is a fast calculator, but it is much more than that. It is a machine which performs fast calculations plus performs burdensome chores such as choosing, copying, moving, comparing and performing other operations on alphabetic, numeric and other symbols which represent data (raw material of information).

A computer may be defined as a machine that can solve problems by accepting data, performing certain operations and presenting the results of those operations under the direction of detailed step-by-step instructions. Such a set of sequenced instructions, which cause a computer to perform particular operations is called a *program*.

Computer Science is the study of the operating principles of computers, computer programming languages and algorithms for solving theoretical as well as practical problems. It involves the development and use of devices for processing information. Information in one form is presented to the device (input information) and information in another form is required from it (output information). This process of conversion of raw material into the finished product is nothing but data processing. Data processing may be defined as the process of transforming data (raw material of information) into useful information by the computer.

1.1 CHARACTERISTICS OF COMPUTERS

A computer is an intelligent amplifier that performs the above mentioned operations in a faster, accurate and efficient way. Thus, it frees humans to use their time in matters involving creativity & judgement. The characteristics possessed by computers can be listed as follows:

1.1.1 Speed

A computer can add and subtract numbers, compare letters to determine alphabetic sequence, move and copy numbers and letters. As such, there is nothing profound in these operations. What is significant is the speed with which computers carry out these operations. This speed varies from a few microseconds (millionth of a second) to nanoseconds (billionth of a second). For instance, a small computer can evaluate investment decisions by performing hundreds of thousands of machine operations in a second.

1.1.2 Accuracy

Computers are very accurate. They can perform their hundreds of thousands of operations with great accuracy as their circuits have no mechanical parts to wear and malfunction. They can run errorless for days at a time.

1.1.3 Reliability

Computer output is generally very reliable, subject to the condition that the input data entering the computer should be correct and the program of instructions should be reliable and correct. Incorrect input data and unreliable programs give us computer errors and wrong results. Hence, the phrase GARBAGE IN-GARBAGE OUT (GIGO).

1.1.4 Provides a Capability that Would Otherwise be Impossible

Because computers can operate on data at such phenomenal speeds, they can produce results that would simply not be feasible otherwise. For example, computers can be used to provide management with up-to-the-minute figures on all aspects of its business. With this information, managers can make more meaningful decisions.

Similarly, computers enable companies to provide customers with instantaneous services, such as airline flight availability and charge account status. The result is that these companies can offer far more customer services than would be possible without the computer.

1.1.5 Storage Capability

Because various computer media can store millions of characters of data in a condensed form, there are tremendous savings in the storage area required to maintain the vital records necessary in a business environment.

1.1.6 Intangible Benefits

There are many companies that utilize computers for intangible benefits such as flexibility, ability to accommodate growth, and the psychological factor that may give them a competitive edge in attracting consumers to buy their products or services.

1.1.7 Reduced Cost

With the ever-increasing advances being made in the state of the art, the cost of computer equipment has dropped drastically over the years. Hardware costs have been decreasing at an estimated annual rate of 25 percent. Thus, companies that at one time could not justify the cost of acquiring their own computer system may now find it not only feasible to acquire a system, but cost-effective as well.

1.2 TECHNOLOGICAL EVOLUTION OF COMPUTERS

As soon as humans domesticated animals and started to carry on trade with other people, they needed a system to keep track of numbers. First, people counted on their fingers; then, they cut notches on sticks, counted stones, and even tied knots in ropes. The abacus—a rudimentary, first computing device—is generally thought to be on Chinese origin, but it actually evolved in different cultures at about the same time. This simple device, which uses beads to represent digits and wires to hold places, is still used today.

Early in the 17th century, Wilhelm Schickard, a professor of astronomy, mathematics, and Hebrew at Turbingen, Germany, designed an ingenious machine to add, subtract, and to some degree, multiply and divide numbers into the hundreds. Unfortunately, before the device was half completed, the factory where it was housed burned. Schickard and his entire family died of the plague before he could construct another model. Much later, a master mechanic recreated the instrument from Schickard's old letters and rough models. Had this invention been available to subsequent innovators, it could have changed the history of computers entirely.

The evolution of computing devices did proceed, although slowly, even without Schickard's clever machine as prototype. But first, an interesting thing was happening with numbers.

In the 1600s, John Napier, a Scotsman, discovered a way to manipulate numbers for multiplication and subtraction of other numbers. The series of numbers and their relationships were called *logarithms*. By placing the numbers on ivory rods (called *Napier's bones*), solutions to complex problems could be found relatively quickly by matching logarithms and then adding or subtracting the appropriate numbers. Robert Bissaker's invention of the slide rule around 1650 replaced Napier's ivory rods.

Blaise Pascal, a French mathematician and philosopher interested in the branch of mathematics known as probability theory, invented the first mechanical digital calculator that could perform addition and subtraction on whole numbers. Although this machine was an improvement over time-consuming manual calculations, it was not as technically advanced as Schickard's computing device. The Pascaline, developed around 1642, was a dismal financial failure. First, Pascal was the only person who could repair it. Second, it was cheaper to have people complete the calculations; and, third, workers feared being replaced by the Pascaline, thereby losing their jobs. Regardless, Pascal's gear-driven, decimal counting wheel was used until the electronic calculator made it obsolete. A programming language, Pascal, was later named to honour his contributions.

Later, Gottfried Wilhelm von Leibniz, a German mathematician who along with Sir Isaac Newton co-invented calculus, produced the stepped-wheel calculator. This device, created in 1673, resembled a combination slide rule and meat grinder and could perform all four arithmetic functions—addition, subtraction, multiplication, and division. The Leibniz wheel was an improvement on Pascal's calculator; however, it was not particularly reliable and never became widely used. It did impress Peter the Great, however, who sent one to the Emperor of China to convince him of Germany's technology and to increase trade between the East and West.

In 1804, Frenchman Joseph Marie Jacquard built an automated punched-card machine that was used to operate weaving looms. Jacquard's invention showed that data could be coded on cards; the cards could be joined to create a series of instructions; and these instructions could automate the weaving. Programmable instructions proved to be a concept of great importance for modern computers.

In 1822, a British inventor and mathematician, Charles P. Babbage, designed an all-purpose problem-solving machine, the difference engine, that had a mechanical memory to store results. The Royal Astronomical Society encouraged Babbage with government grants, and his design grew more complex as revisions occurred to him. The grants ceased in 1834, but undaunted, Babbage proposed a more elaborate computing machine, the analytical engine. Although the power from six steam engines would have been required to run the analytical engine and it would have occupied the length of a football field, Babbage's steam-powered machine would have computed mathematical tables and logarithms automatically. Data would have been entered by using punched cards, and the machine could have been programmed to change operating procedures. Regrettably, the analytical engine was never built; however, this concept was a mechanical predecessor of the modern-day computer.

For his contributions, Babbage earned the title, 'father of the computer;' however, he also invented the speedometer, locomotive cow catcher, and the first reliable life-expectancy (actuarial) tables for the insurance profession.

Babbage had a confidante and partner, Augusta Ada, Countess of Lovelace and daughter of poet Lord Byron. Lady Lovelace understood Babbage's ideas, recognized their great value, and in the 1840s, wrote scientific papers explaining his ideas to others. She even suggested using a binary rather than decimal system for storage. Lady Lovelace is sometimes thought of as 'the first programmer' because she refined the design of the analytical engine by including the automatic repetition of a series of calculations. This looping procedure is extremely valuable to today's programmers.

In the 1850s, George Boole, a self-taught English mathematician, realized that complex mathematical problems could be solved by reducing them to a series of affirmatively-or negatively-answered questions. The binary system of 1s for positive answers and 0s for negative could thus be implemented. This theory of Boolean logic became fundamental to the design of computer circuitry.

In the 1880s, Dr. Herman Hollerith built the first electromechanical, punched-card, data-processing machine. Hollerith, whose father-in-law was a census official, suggested that his machine could tabulate and sort census information by using the 80-column punched cards that he also invented.

Using his tabulating equipment, Hollerith processed the 1890 United States census information pertaining to 63,056,000 people in one-third the time required to count 50,262,000 people in 1880. He then founded the Tabulating Machine Company, one of many companies that eventually merged to become IBM.

After Hollerith's discoveries, there was a lag in creativity in the computer field. Progress was being made, but nothing spectacular was reported.

Then, in 1927 at Massachusetts Institute of Technology (MIT), Vannevar Bush and his colleagues created an electromechanical machine that solved simple differential equations. By 1931, the machine had been modified and perfected to solve more complex equations. The differential analyzer carried out calculations by the rotation of various shafts. Although it resembled a giant dishpan with steel rods sticking out, it was a good analog computing device.

George Stibitz, a research mathematician at Bell Telephone Laboratory, tinkered with the idea that Boolean logic provided a natural language for electromechanical circuits. His device, created in 1937 from batteries, flashlight bulbs, wire, and tobacco-can strips of metal, controlled the on and off flow of electricity called the *Complex Number Calculator*, the machine added binary numbers—a basic requirement for all future digital computers. In 1940, Stibitz and his colleague, Samuel Williams, demonstrated how using this device with teletype machines could send calculations over a distance of 250 miles.

In lowa in 1939, John Atanasoff and Clifford Berry collaborated to build the Atanasoff-Berry Computer (the ABC). The ABC was the world's first general-purpose, electronic, digital computer; but even though its purpose was to solve simultaneous linear algebraic equations, it did not generate a lot of interest in the scientific community. When Dr. Atanasoff contacted IBM about his machine, the company said that they would never be interested in an electronic computing machine.

In 1941, in the midst of World War II, Konrad Zuse built the first operational general-purpose computer for Germany. His machine used binary logic even though Zuse had not heard of George Boole. To assist the German war effort, Zuse proposed an updated model using vacuum tubes instead of electromechanical relays to increase operational speed a thousandfold. He suggested to Adolph Hitler that the new machine could be used by the military to compare and evaluate aircraft designs and to break war time codes. Hitler refused funding saying that the war would be over before the two years Zuse needed to finish the machine.

Fortunately for the Allies, the Polish secret service smuggled a replica of the Enigma, a German message-scrambling device, to the British. Alan Turing, an eccentric English genius, began to work at unravelling the mysteries of the Enigma. In 1943, Turing and his colleagues capitalized on the vacuum-tube technology that Zuse had wanted to pursue. The British machine built to counteract Enigma was called Colossus; it could process 25,000 characters per second. In 1950, Turing also constructed the Automatic Computing Engine (ACE), which some touted as the first programmable, digital computer. Because of the secrecy involved with most of Turing's projects, his contributions were not acknowledged until after his death.

Most industries in the United States rallied to support the war effort. Thomas J. Watson, president of IBM, offered to supply thousands of punch-card sorting machines. His plans also included Howard Aiken, a Harvard mathematician. Aiken wanted to build a general-purpose, programmable computer similar to the one Babbage had proposed.

Aiken completed the first automatic, sequence-controlled calculator, Mark-I, in 1944. It calculated by using electromechanical relays (*i.e.*, electricity rather than muscles), effectively replacing Hollerith's gear mechanism.

The Mark-I was not a small machine. At 51 feet long and 8 feet high, it contained over 750,000 parts and was strung with 500 miles of wires. It used paper tape input and required 3,000 telephone relays that made loud clicking noises when operating. Output was on punched cards; calculations of 23-digit numbers took only three seconds. Six months of manual calculations could be completed in one day. With these calculation capabilities, the Mark-I and its successors aided the military in computing ballistics data.

Technology now was advancing rapidly, and many people worked on similar ideas simultaneously. John Mauchly, a physicist on the staff at the University of Pennsylvania's Moore School of Engineering, visited Atanasoff in Iowa in 1941, when the ABC Computer was still in its prototype stages of construction. The possible applications of the machine interested and impressed Mauchly.

In 1942, Mauchly and another Moore School colleague, J. Presper Eckert, submitted a proposal to the government to build a machine that would compute artillery firing tables. On April 9, 1943, the government granted the Moore School a $400,000 contract to build the Electronic Numerical Integrator and Computer (ENIAC).

At 80 feet long by 18 feet high, ENIAC was twice as big as the Mark-I. Instead of gears or mechanical relays, the 30-ton ENIAC contained over 100,000 electronic components, including 17,468 vacuum tubes. Although the vacuum tubes took up a lot of space, their use increased the speed of calculations by a thousandfold. The ENIAC operated on the decimal system which allowed the punched-card output to be read easily by humans. A major drawback, however, was the extreme difficulty in changing programs or operations because instructions had to be manually wired into the circuitry.

The ENIAC was put into operation at Aberdeen Proving Ground, Maryland, in 1947. Although too late for service in wartime, it was used for calculations in weather forecasting, wind tunnel designs, ballistics tables, and cosmic-ray study. Since it took the operators as long as two days to manually replug the wires involved in changing instructions, the ENIAC was not an efficient general-purpose computer.

Mauchly and Eckert claimed the ENIAC was the first general-purpose, electronic, digital computer, but on October 19, 1973, a court settlement declared that the Atanasoff-Berry Computer was entitled to that honor.

The ENIAC was obsolete almost before it was completed, and Mauchly and Eckert planned a successor called the Electronic Discrete Variable Automatic Computer (EDVAC). Completed in 1949, EDVAC stored its instructions electronically and used the binary system of coding instructions and input.

The EDVAC was one of the first two stored-program computers. It consisted of five units: arithmetical; central control; memory; input; and output. The improvements over the ENIAC included reduction of the number of tubes, increased memory, easier use, and a simpler, faster way to set up additional problems.

The development of the stored-program concept used in EDVAC has been claimed by many; however, the definitive paper outlining this and other differences in the computer's design features has been credited to John von Neumann, the special consultant hired by the Moore School for the EDVAC project. John von Neumann was a mathematical genius with a photographic memory. His paper 'First Draft of a Report on the EDVAC' presented in the mid-1940s served as a blueprint for future stored-program computers.

Also in 1949, Englishman Maurice V. Wilkes of Cambridge incorporated the von Neumann stored-program concept into the Electronic Delay Storage Automatic Computer (EDSAC). The EDSAC was available a few months before the EDVAC and was, therefore, awarded the title of the first stored-program computer.

At Harvard around 1949, An Wang, founder of Wang Laboratories developed magnetic-core memories. Subsequently, Jay Forrester at MIT discovered a way to organize magnetic-core memories into a grid, providing a more practical application than the previous serial connections. Computers became not only faster, but also more reliable and capable of containing larger memories.

In 1951, Mauchly and Eckert formed their own company to create a commercially usable general-purpose computer—UNIVAC I. When Mauchly and Eckert fell upon hard times, Remington Rand bought their company and completed it. UNIVAC-I was designed specifically for business data-processing applications, and it was the first general-purpose computer used commercially. Previously, computers had been used solely for scientific or military applications. The U.S. Census Bureau immediately installed UNIVAC-I and used it for more than twelve years. In Louisville, Kentucky in 1954, General Electric Company processed the first computerized payroll using a UNIVAC-I.

It wasn't long before other companies including Burroughs (now called UNISYS), Honeywell, IBM, and others realized the commercial value of computers and began offering their own.

From 1950 to 1952, people in the U.S. Navy and at the Digital Computer Lab at MIT developed the Whirlwind, another vacuum tube, stored-program computer. The Whirlwind simulated high-performance trainer aircraft contained self-diagnostics, and performed 50,000 operations per second; however, it was only about 85 percent accurate. During the early 1950s, the military used it for air surveillance.

Other innovators appeared on the scene in the late 1950s. Both Jack Kilby, at Texas Instruments, and Robert Noyce, at Fairchild Semiconductor, discovered that resistors, capacitors, and transistors could be made simultaneously from the same semiconductor material. Any number of transistors could be etched on silicon; the integrated circuit, christened the 'chip', was developed and refined. These 1959 discoveries were mass produced in 1962 and were included in 1964 computers.

The 1960s also brought the arrival of Gene Amdahl's revolutionary IBM System/360 series of mainframe computers—the first general-purpose, digital computers using integrated circuit technology. Because they were a 'family' of computers and used compatible software, the series was a valuable addition to growing companies. Later, in his own company, Amdahl built a competitive computer that was faster, less expensive, and smaller in size.

The miniaturization of components developed through various technological innovations, coupled with the success of the commercial use of computers, led Ken Olsen and his Digital Equipment Corporation (DEC) to the production of the first minicomputer, the PDP-1, in 1963. Less expensive than a mainframe, the minicomputer was for use by small companies.

At the other end of the spectrum, computers were becoming more powerful. In fact, the ILLIAC-IV was a supercomputer, first used at the Ames Research Center in 1972, for solving aerodynamic problems that were too large and complicated for other systems.

Other supercomputers were being developed too. In 1976, Seymour Cray's Cray-1 super computer was delivered to Los Alamos Scientific Laboratory in New Mexico, and a Control Data Corporation CYBER-205 was used by the Meteorological Service in the United Kingdom for weather predictions.

Meanwhile, advances were being made in the field of programming languages. High-level, English-like programming languages began to be developed in the mid-1950s. John Backus and a group of IBM engineers developed FORTRAN (FORmula TRANslator) as the first problem-oriented, algebraic programming language. Its orientation, therefore, was more toward mathematicians and scientists.

By 1959, Rear Admiral Grace Murray Hopper was instrumental in developing COBOL (Common Business Oriented Language) as the first programming language designed for business data processing. Hopper also helped to invent the UNIVAC-I's compiler, a program that could translate other programs into machine language—the 1s and 0s that the computer 'understands'.

Dr. John Kemeny, a mathematics professor at Dartmouth, and his colleague, Dr. Thomas Kurtz, developed the computer language BASIC (Beginner's All-purpose Symbolic Instruction Code) in 1965. They later presented a version called True BASIC, which uses structured programming techniques to make programs easier to read, debug, and update. Today, numerous high-level languages are in use, including Pascal, C, and Logo.

By 1970, Intel had created a memory chip that could store a kilobit of information. A kilobit translates roughly into 25 five-letter words. Another innovation at Intel came from Ted Hoff, who in 1970 further improved the integrated circuit by compressing twelve chips into four. The arithmetic and logic functions of several chips could be contained on one chip, called a microprocessor. Hoff's microprocessor, called the Intel 4004 ('forty-oh-four'), made the development of the small computer, or microcomputer, a reality.

The first hobbyist microcomputer became available in 1975. H. Edward Roberts, an electrical engineer who is now generally known as the 'father of the microcomputer' designed the Altair 8800. It sold in kit form for approximately $395 and required some electronics knowledge to assemble. To the buyer, the novelty of owning a computer far outweighed the inconvenience of a memory that could hold only 256 bits.

Competition for the Altair 8800 appeared in 1977 from the TRS-80 Model 1 by Tandy Radio Shack and the Personal Electronic Transactor (PET) by Commodore Business Machines.

Many microcomputer companies have come and gone, but one of the great rags-to-riches stories is Apple Computer, Inc., founded by Steven Jobs and Stephen Wozniak. Apple Computer's first headquarters was a garage.

Wozniak, the technical expert, made a micro-computer that was affordable and small enough for both individuals and owners of small businesses. Because he knew very little about circuitry or coding, Jobs provided the marketing impetus for the small company. Since the first commercial Apple computers went on sale in 1977, their popularity has increased.

In 1981, Adam Osborne introduced a truly portable microcomputer, Osborne-1. It weighed only 24 pounds, had memory capacity of 64 kilo-bytes, and cost approximately $1,795. Osborne-1 could be manufactured in just over one hour, using only 40 screws to put together the easy-to-assemble parts.

As microcomputers gained popularity, many companies introduced their own versions—not only for hobbyists and small-business users, but also for the entire business community.

1.3 BRIEF HISTORY OF COMPUTERS

Ever since the mankind started to carry on trade with other people, they felt the need of a system to keep track of the numbers. They used different ways to do so and started evolving tools. The earlier computing devices such as Abacus were created to serve the same purpose. Let us have a look at the major milestones which led to present day computers.

3000 BC	***The Abacus—a rudimentary first computing device developed***
AD 700-900	Europeans started using **Hindu-Arabic math**
1600	Hindu-Arabic math became popular in Europe
1614	John Napier introduced **logarithms**

Fig. 1.1 The abacus

1642	Blaise Pascal, a French Mathematician and experimental Physicist, built the first mechanical digital calculator, **Pascaline**, that could perform addition and subtraction on whole numbers
1822	Charles Babbage, Professor of Mathematics at Cambridge University, considered as 'Father of computers', invented **difference engine** with mechanical memory to store results
1840s	Augusta Ada, 'The first Programmer' suggested **binary data** storage rather than the decimal
1850s	George Boole, a self taught English Mathematician, realized that complex mathematical problems could be solved by reducing them to a series of affirmatively or negatively answered questions. The binary system of 1s for positive answers and 0s for negative ones could thus be implemented. This theory of Boolean logic became fundamental to the design of computer circuitry
1880s	Dr. Herman Hollerith, a Statistician, was employed by the Census Bureau, which was falling far behind in its ability to provide census reports. To find a solution to the census problem, Hollerith developed a punched card that would contain data coded in form of punched holes. Hollerith then built tabulating machine that could read the cards and process the data.
1939	The **first prototype electronic computer** was conceived by Dr. John Vincent Atanasoff, a Professor of Physics and Mathematics at Iowa State College. Atanasoff teamed up with Clifford Berry, his graduate assistant, and began to build the first electronic computer. They called it the 'Atanasoff-Berry Computer', or ABC. The ABC used vacuum tubes for storage and arithmetic-logic function. The ABC was designed for the special purpose of solving systems of simultaneous equations.
1940s	Von Neumann presented a paper, outlining the stored **program concept**.

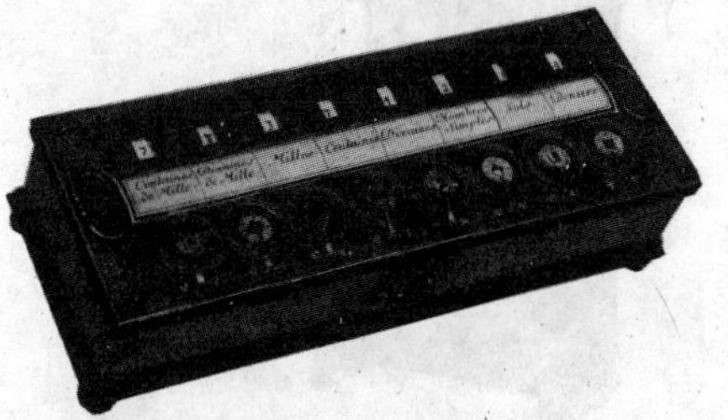

Fig. 1.2 Pascaline

Fig. 1.3 A replica of Babbage's difference engine (Analytical Engine)

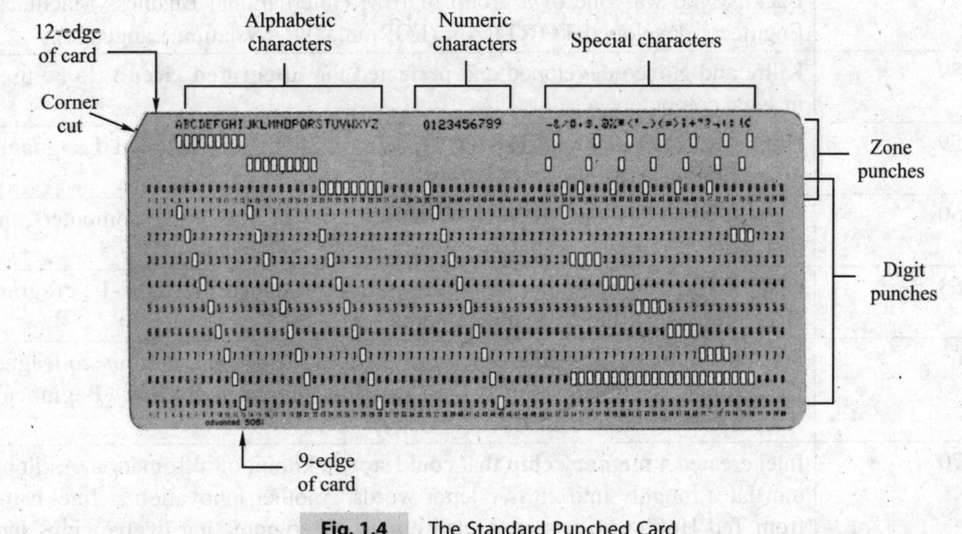

Fig. 1.4 The Standard Punched Card

1944	Aiken built the **Mark I**, the first automatic, sequence controlled calculator; used by military to compute ballistics data.
1947	Mauchly and Eckert built **ENIAC** (ENIAC is an acronym for Electronic Numeric Integrator And Calculator). It was a second general purpose electronic digital computer.

Fig. 1.5 Tabulating Machine

1949	Englishman Maurice V. Wilkes of Cambridge built **EDSAC** (Electronic Delayed Storage Automatic Computer), the first stored program computer.
1949	Mauchly, Eckert and Von Neumann built **EDVAC** (Electronic Discrete Variable Automatic Computer), the second stored program computer.
1949	At Harvard, An Wang, founder of Wang Laboratories developed **magnetic-core memories**.
1949	Jay Forrester at MIT organized **magnetic-core memory** to be more efficient.
1950	Turing built the **ACE** (Automatic Computing Engine), which can be considered the first programmable digital computer.
1950s	Read Admiral (Retd.) Grace Hopper developed **UNIVAC-I** Compiler.
1951	Mauchly and Eckert built the first computer, designed and sold commercially—**UNIVAC-I** (Universal Automatic Computer).
1957	Backus who was one of a group of IBM (International Business Machines) Engineers developed **FORTRAN** (FORmula TRANslation Language).
1959	Kilby and Noyce developed and perfected the **integrated circuit**, to be used in later computers.
1959	Hopper developed the **COBOL** (**Com**mon **B**usiness **O**riented **L**anguage) programming language.
1960s	Gene Amdahl designed **IBM System/360** series of Mainframe computers, the first general purpose digital computers to use integrated circuits.
1963	Olsen with Digital Equipment Corporation produced the **PDP-1** (**P**rogram **D**ata **P**rocessor), the first minicomputer.
1965	Dr. John Kemeny, a Mathematics Professor at Dartmouth, and his colleague, Dr. Thomas Kurtz, developed the Computer language **BASIC** (**B**eginner's **A**ll-purpose **S**ymbolic **I**nstruction **C**ode).
1970	Intel created a **memory chip** that could store a kilobit of information. A kilobit translates roughly into 25 five-letter words. Another innovation at Intel came from Ted Hoff, who has integrated circuit by compressing twelve chips into four. The arithmetic and logic functions of several chips could be contained on one chip, called microprocessor. Hoffs microprocessor was called the Intel 4004 ('forty-oh-four').
1972	The 'Floppy' Disk—A **floppy disk** is a data storage medium that is composed of a disk of thin, flexible ('floppy') magnetic storage medium sealed in a square or rectangular.

1974	The Ethernet Computer Networking—**Ethernet** is a physical and data link layer technology for local area networks (LANs). *Ethernet* was invented by engineer Robert Metcalfe.
1975	H. Edward Roberts, an electrical engineer who is now generally known as the 'Father of the Microcomputer' designed the first **Micro Computer**.
1976	Seymour Cray's **CRAY-I** Super Computer was delivered to Los Alamos Scientific Laboratory in New Mexico.
1977	Stephen Wozniak, the technical expert, and Steven Jobs designed and built the first **Apple Micro Computer**.
1979	VisiCalc Spreadsheet Software—**VisiCalc** was the first spreadsheet program available for personal computers.
1979	WordStar Software—**WordStar** was a text-based word processing program, meaning that it worked with files that were essentially text, with markup language-like formatting.
1980s	Lower-cost computer systems—**Personal computers** intended for home use were produced. New program products introduced.
1981	IBM computers were sold commercially as 'personal computers'. Microsoft has invented **MS-DOS** computer operating System.
1983	Apple Lisa Computer—The first home computer with **Graphical User Interface** (GUI).
1984	Apple Macintosh Computer—The more affordable home computer with a **GUI**.
1985	Microsoft has come out with the Windows Operating System.
1991	Tim Berns-Lee created the World Wide Web at C.E.R.N. in Switzerland. The **European Organization for Nuclear Research** (French: Organisation européenne pour la recherche nucléaire), known as **CERN**.

1.4 THE FIVE GENERATIONS OF COMPUTERS

Since the 1940s, advances in computers have come rapidly. The general trends have been faster processing, smaller size, more storage capacity, and lower cost. We typically look at modern computer development in terms of generations elements of which are shown in Fig. 1.6.

First—Vacuum Tube

Second—Transistor

Third and Fourth—IC

Fourth—Microprocessor

Fig. 1.6 Generations of Computer Components

1.4.1 First Generation—1940–1956: Vacuum Tubes

The first computers used vacuum tubes for circuitry and magnetic drums for memory, and were often enormous, taking up entire rooms. A magnetic drum, also referred to as drum, is a metal cylinder coated with magnetic iron-oxide material on which data and programs can be stored. Magnetic drums were once used as a primary storage device but have since been implemented as auxiliary storage devices.

The tracks on a magnetic drum are assigned to channels located around the circumference of the drum, forming adjacent circular bands that wind around the drum. A single drum can have up to 200 tracks. As the drum rotates at a speed of up to 3,000 rpm, the device's read/write heads deposit magnetized spots on the drum during the write operation and sense these spots during a read operation. This action is similar to that of a magnetic tape or disk drive.

They were very expensive to operate and in addition to using a great deal of electricity, generated a lot of heat, which was often the cause of malfunctions. First generation computers relied on machine language to perform operations, and they could only solve one problem at a time. Machine languages are the only languages understood by computers. While easily understood by computers, machine languages are almost impossible for humans to use because they consist entirely of numbers. Computer Programmers, therefore, use either high level programming languages or an assembly language programming. An assembly language contains the same instructions as a machine language, but the instructions and variables have names instead of being just numbers.

Programs written in high level programming languages retranslated into assembly language or machine language by a compiler. Assembly language program retranslated into machine language by a program called an assembler (assembly language compiler).

Every CPU has its own unique machine language. Programs must be rewritten or recompiled, therefore, to run on different types of computers. Input was based on punch card and paper tapes, and output was displayed on printouts.

The UNIVAC and ENIAC computers are examples of first-generation computing devices. The UNIVAC was the first commercial computer delivered to a business client, the U.S. Census Bureau in 1951.

Acronym for Electronic Numerical Integrator And Computer, the world's first operational electronic digital computer, developed by Army Ordnance to compute World War II ballistic firing tables. The ENIAC, weighing 30 tons, using 200 kilowatts of electric power and consisting of 18,000 vacuum tubes,1,500 relays, and hundreds of thousands of resistors, capacitors, and inductors, was completed in 1945. In addition to ballistics, the ENIAC's field of application included weather prediction, atomic-energy calculations, cosmic-ray studies, thermal ignition, random-number studies, wind-tunnel design, and other scientific uses. The ENIAC soon became obsolete as the need arose for faster computing speeds.

General features of these computers were:

1. Electronic circuitry used vacuum tubes.
2. Punched cards used for feeding information.
3. Punched cards and paper used for getting results.
4. Magnetic tapes were used for external storage.
5. Oriented towards batch processing, where the entire machine is dedicated to a particular job until completed.
6. Human operators had to set switches.
7. Development of machine language and assembly language.
8. Typical computers: UNIVAC-I, IBM 650, BURROUGHS 220.

1.4.2 Second Generation—1956-1963: Transistors

Transistors replaced vacuum tubes and ushered in the second generation computer. Transistor is a device composed of semiconductor material that amplifies a signal or opens or closes a circuit. Invented in 1947 at Bell Labs, transistors have become the key ingredient of all digital circuits, including computers. Today's **latest microprocessor** contains tens of millions of microscopic transistors.

Prior to the invention of transistors, digital circuits were composed of vacuum tubes, which had many disadvantages. They were much larger, required more energy, dissipated more heat, and were more prone to failures. It's safe to say that without the invention of transistors, computing as we know it today would not be possible.

The transistor was invented in 1947 but did not see widespread use in computers until the late 50s. The transistor was far superior to the vacuum tube, allowing computers to become smaller, faster, cheaper, more energy-efficient and more reliable than their first-generation predecessors. Though the transistor still generated a great deal of heat that subjected the computer to damage, it was a vast improvement over the vacuum tube. Second-generation computers still relied on punched cards for input and printouts for output.

Second-generation computers moved from cryptic binary machine language to symbolic, or assembly, languages, which allowed programmers to specify instructions in words. High-level programming languages were also being developed at this time, such as early versions of COBOL and FORTRAN. These were also the first computers that stored their instructions in their memory, which moved from a magnetic drum to magnetic core technology.

The first computers of this generation were developed for the atomic energy industry.

The transistors, invented by Bell Telephone Laboratories in 1948, formed the basis for the second generation of computers. Through use of the transistor, these computers were much faster, more reliable and more versatile than first generation computers. Some principle characteristics of second generation were:

1. Electronic circuitry characterized by the use of transistors.
2. Punched cards and magnetic tape used for input of data.
3. Punched cards and paper used for output.
4. Magnetic core storage, *i.e.*, magnetic tape used for external storage.
5. Oriented towards far more versatile types of applications in which multiple users were capable of using the machine concurrently.
6. Human operators handled punched cards.
7. Development of high-level languages FORTRAN, COBOL, BASIC, PL/1 and others.
8. Typical computers: IBM 1400 series and 7000 series, Control Data 3600, General Electric 635, and Honeywell 200.

1.4.3 Third Generation—1964-1971: Integrated Circuits

The development of the integrated circuit was the hallmark of the third generation of computers. Transistors were miniaturized and placed on silicon chips, called semiconductors, which drastically increased the speed and efficiency of computers.

A non-metallic chemical element in the carbon family of elements, Silicon—atomic symbol 'Si'—is the second most abundant element in the earth's crust, surpassed only by oxygen. Silicon does not occur un-combined in nature. Sand and almost all rocks contain silicon combined with oxygen, forming silica. When silicon combines with other elements, such as iron, aluminium or potassium, a silicate is formed. Compounds of silicon also occur in the atmosphere, natural waters, many plants and in the bodies of some animals.

Silicon is the basic material used to make computer chips, transistors, silicon diodes and other electronic circuits and switching devices because its atomic structure makes the element an ideal semiconductor. Silicon is commonly doped, or mixed, with other elements, such as boron, phosphorous and arsenic, to alter its conductive properties.

A chip is a small piece of semi conducting material (usually silicon) on which an integrated circuit is embedded. A typical chip is less than ¼-square inches and can contain millions of electronic components (transistors). Computers consist of many chips placed on electronic boards called printed circuit boards. There are different types of chips. For example, CPU chips (also called microprocessors) contain an entire processing unit, whereas memory chips contain blank memory.

Semiconductor is a material that is neither a good conductor of electricity (like copper) nor a good insulator (like rubber). The most common semiconductor materials are silicon and germanium. These materials are then doped to create an excess or lack of electrons.

Computer chips, both for CPU and memory, are composed of semiconductor materials. Semiconductors make it possible to miniaturize electronic components, such as transistors. Not only does miniaturization mean that the components take up less space, it also means that they are faster and require less energy.

Instead of punched cards and printouts, users interacted with third generation computers through keyboards and monitors and interfaced with an operating system, which allowed the device to run many different applications at one time with a central program that monitored the memory. Computers for the first time became accessible to a mass audience because they were smaller and cheaper than their predecessors.

A summary of main features of this generation of computers is as follows:

1. Electronic circuitry characterized by micro-electronic, or integrated circuits which although microscopic in size, contained the equivalent of many transistors.
2. Monitors and keyboards were introduced for data input and output.
3. Punched cards began losing their prominence as the input or output device.
4. Magnetic disks used for external storage.
5. Designed around sophisticated operating systems capable of handling several jobs concurrently.
6. A concept of computer 'families' was introduced.
7. More high-level language including RPG (Report Program Generator) and PASCAL were developed. Heavy emphasis was laid on applications-oriented languages—FORTRAN and COBOL.
8. Typical computers: IBM System/360.

1.4.4 Fourth Generation—1971—Present: Microprocessors

The microprocessor brought the fourth generation of computers, as thousands of integrated circuits we rebuilt onto a single silicon chip. A silicon chip that contains a CPU. In the world of personal computers, the terms microprocessor and CPU are used interchangeably. At the heart of all personal computers and most workstations sits a microprocessor. Microprocessors also control the logic of almost all digital devices, from clock radios to fuel-injection systems for automobiles.

Three basic characteristics differentiate microprocessors:

1. **Instruction Set:** The set of instructions that the microprocessor can execute.
2. **Bandwidth:** The number of bits processed in a single instruction.
3. **Clock Speed:** Given in megahertz (MHz), the clock speed determines how many instructions per second the processor can execute.

In both cases, the higher the value, the more powerful the CPU. For example, a 32-bit microprocessor that runs at 50 MHz is more powerful than a 16-bit microprocessor that runs at 25 MHz.

What in the first generation filled an entire room could now fit in the palm of the hand. The Intel 4004 chip, developed in 1971, located all the components of the computer—from the central processing unit and memory to input/output controls—on a single chip.

Abbreviation of central processing unit, and pronounced as separate letters. The CPU is the brains of the computer. Sometimes referred to simply as the processor or central processor, the CPU is where most calculations take place. In terms of computing power, the CPU is the most important element of a computer system.

On large machines, CPUs require one or more printed circuit boards. On personal computers and small workstations, the CPU is housed in a single chip called a microprocessor.

Two typical components of a CPU are:

1. The **Arithmetic Logic Unit (ALU)**, which performs arithmetic and logical operations.
2. The **Control Unit**, which extracts instructions from memory and decodes and executes them, calling on the ALU when necessary.

In 1981 IBM introduced its first computer for the home user, and in 1984 Apple introduced the Macintosh. Microprocessors also moved out of the realm of desktop computers and into many areas of life as more and more everyday products began to use microprocessors.

As these small computers became more powerful, they could be linked together to form networks, which eventually led to the development of the Internet. Fourth generation computers also saw the development of GUI's, the mouse and handheld devices.

The significant distinction for the fourth generation is the development of Large-Scale Integration (LSI) and Very Large Scale Integration (VLSI). LSI placed several thousand transistors onto a single chip. VLSI placed several hundred thousand transistors onto a single chip. These developments were followed by creation of microprocessors. Let us consider characteristics of fourth generation:

1. Further miniaturization in which complete circuits are reduced to virtually microscopic sizes. Hundreds of circuits may be placed on a chip of the size of a pinhead.
2. Further refinement of input and output devices.
3. Introduction of microcomputers.
4. Magnetic disks became the primary means of external storage.
5. Further sophistication of operating systems capable of virtual storage, in which the machine can operate as if its main storage were several times its actual size.
6. The beginning of broad use of special software for managing large data bases.
7. Fourth generation languages emerged and application software for microcomputers became popular.
8. Typical computers: IBM System/370, BURROUGHS B7700 and HP3000.

1.4.5 Fifth Generation—Present and Beyond: Artificial Intelligence

Fifth generation computing devices, based on artificial intelligence, are still in development, though there are some applications, such as voice recognition, that are being used today.

Artificial Intelligence is the branch of computer science concerned with making computers behave like humans. The term was coined in 1956 by John McCarthy at the Massachusetts Institute of Technology. Artificial intelligence includes:

1. **Games Playing:** Programming computers to play games such as chess and checkers.

2. **Expert Systems:** Programming computers to make decisions in real-life situations (for example, some expert systems help doctors diagnose diseases based on symptoms).
3. **Natural Language:** Programming computers to understand natural human languages.
4. **Neural Networks:** Systems that simulate intelligence by attempting to reproduce the types of physical connections that occur in animal brains.
5. **Robotics:** Programming computers to see and hear and react to other sensory stimuli.

Currently, no computers exhibit full artificial intelligence (that is, are able to simulate human behaviour). The greatest advances have occurred in the field of games playing. The best computer chess programs are now capable of beating humans. In May, 1997, an IBM super-computer called Deep Blue defeated world chess champion Gary Kasparov in a chess match.

In the area of robotics, computers are now widely used in assembly plants, but they are capable only of very limited tasks. Robots have great difficulty identifying objects based on appearance or feel, and they still move and handle objects clumsily.

Natural-language processing offers the greatest potential rewards because it would allow people to interact with computers without needing any specialized knowledge. You could simply walk up to a computer and talk to it. Unfortunately, programming computers to understand natural languages has proved to be more difficult than originally thought. Some rudimentary translation systems that translate from one human language to another are in existence, but they are not nearly as good as human translators.

There are also voice recognition systems that can convert spoken sounds into written words, but they do not understand what they are writing; they simply take dictation. Even these systems are quite limited—you must speak slowly and distinctly.

In the early 1980s, expert systems were believed to represent the future of artificial intelligence and of computers in general. To date, however, they have not lived up to expectations. Many expert systems help human experts in such fields as medicine and engineering, but they are very expensive to produce and are helpful only in special situations.

Today, the hottest area of artificial intelligence is neural networks, which are proving successful in a number of disciplines such as voice recognition and natural-language processing.

There are several programming languages that are known as AI languages because they are used almost exclusively for AI applications. The two most common are LISP and Prolog. The name **LISP** derives from '**LIS**t **P**rocessing'.

1.5 CATEGORIES OF COMPUTERS

Computers can be classified into two categories:

1. Classification according to the logic used 2. Classification according to size.

1.5.1 Classification According to the Logic Used

1.5.1.1 Analog Computers

These computers recognize data as a continuous measurement of a physical property. Their output is usually in the form of readings on dials or graphs. Voltage, pressure, speed and temperature are some physical properties that can be measured in this way.

Example:

(*i*) A Service Station gasoline pump contains an analog processor that connects fuel flow measurements into quantity and price values.

(*ii*) Automobile speedometer, etc.

1.5.1.2 Digital Computers

These are high speed programmable electronic devices that perform mathematical calculations, compare values, and store the results. They recognize data by counting discrete signals representing either a high ('on') or low ('off') voltage state of electricity. Numbers, alphabets and special symbols can all be reduced to representation by 1s and 0s.

Example:

(*i*) Personal computers.

(*ii*) Score board that directly counts discrete values such as the time left to play and the score of each team.

Digital computers are further grouped into two categories:

1. **General purpose digital computers:** The digital computers which can theoretically be used for any type of application are called general purpose digital computers. For instance, the computers that are used for payroll, graphs, analysis, account, banking system, etc.
2. **Special purpose digital computers:** These are those digital computers which are made and used for a specific job. For instance, the computer installed in automobiles to control fuel, ignition instrument and braking systems.

1.5.1.3 Hybrid Computers

Hybrid computers combine the best features of analog and digital computers. They have the speed of analog computers and the accuracy of digital computers. They are usually used for special problems in which input data derived from measurements is converted into digits and processed by computer. Consider the hybrid computer used in producing iron ore pellets for steelmaking. It controls manufacturing and prepares production data on inventory and costs. The computer accepts data both from sensors within the production area and from conventional Input/Output (I/O) devices.

As production starts, data on the materials used in manufacturing goes into the computer for analysis. The computer uses the data to establish operating standards. Sensors report on all aspects of manufacturing, and the computer converts these measurements into numeric equivalents. The computer ensures that all operations are within limits and quickly notes exceptions.

Using the production data, the computer plans for future manufacturing and distributes existing inventories, activities which require the computer to compute digital data and produce reports for management. The hybrid computer is perfectly suited to this application. The computer can act like an analog computer, converting measurements into numeric input. It can act as a digital computer, processing stored data for management.

1.5.2 Classification According to Size

There are both large and small computers.

1.5.2.1 Large Computer Systems

They have been traditionally divided into three main categories:

1. **Super Computers:** A super computer is generally characterized as being the fastest, most powerful and most expensive computer. One of the most powerful super computer today, The Cray-2 is set up in a C-shape, is not as tall as a person and is small enough to fit in the space of a large business desk. Supercomputers have large memories and high processing speeds; they can process up to billion instructions per second. They are used for processing very large files and performing large-scale mathematical calculations. In fact, supercomputers are used for such intense computing that they are enclosed in frames containing liquid coolant to prevent them from melting down.

Most supercomputers have two characteristics in common. One is the ability to recover automatically from failures. Also, unlike conventional computers, which have a single processor which processes one instruction at a time, supercomputers have multiple processors (or CPUs) that process multiple instructions at a time; this is known as parallel processing. Some applications to which parallel processing is ideally suited are resource optimization, image processing, graphics, and financial portfolio analysis.

Fault-tolerant computer use a backup mechanism to automatically isolate and reconfigure hardware that fails during system operation. Companies that require highly reliable computer systems use fault-tolerant computers. For example, European bank use fault-tolerant systems because of their reliability and their ability to process huge volumes of data. In the US, the Securities and Exchange Commission also uses fault-tolerant computers to analyse massive amounts of financial data that U.S. corporations submit to the commission. The White House has recently installed four high-security fault-tolerant computers for a wide variety of applications.

Supercomputers are widely used in scientific applications such as aerodynamic design and simulation, processing of geological data, processing of data regarding genetic coding and collecting and processing weather data.

2. **Mainframe Computers:** A mainframe computer is usually slower, less powerful and less expensive than supercomputers.

   Mainframes process data at several million instructions per second (MIPS). More than 1,000 remote workstations can be accommodated by a typical mainframe computer.

   A technique that allows many people at terminals to access the same computer at one time is called **time sharing**.

   Mainframes are used by banks and many businesses to update inventory, etc.

3. **Minicomputer:** Minicomputers are smaller than mainframe, general purpose computers, and give computing power without adding the prohibitive expenses associated with larger systems.

   The minicomputer's size prevents it from being portable but it can be moved more easily than a mainframe.

   Minicomputer integrates commercial and technical operations better than the more powerful computers. It is generally easier to use.

   Minicomputers are well adapted for functions such as accounting, word processing, data base management, statistical packages for social sciences, Computer Aided Design (CAD) and Numerical Analysis etc.

1.5.2.2 Small Computer Systems

They have been divided into four categories:

1. **Microcomputers:c**A microcomputer is the smallest, least expensive of all the computers. The prefix 'micro' refers mainly to the physical size of the computer and its circuitry, rather than its capabilities.

   The essential differences between microcomputers and mainframe or minicomputers are that microcomputers have smallest memory and less power, are physically smaller and permit fewer peripherals to be attached. Microcomputers are also called **personal computers**.

2. **Laptops and Notebooks:** Laptops and notebooks provide mobile computing technology. These are computers that are battery-operated and hence can be used any time and anywhere. Laptop computers are small enough to fit on the lap of a user; notebook computers are even smaller. The primary differences between a laptop and a notebook are size and weight.

Notebooks are smaller than laptops and weigh less. However, both are equipped with powerful microprocessors, graphic capabilities, adequate memory size, and mouse-driven input. Some laptops and notebooks even have fase capabilities, CD-ROM drives, and optical storage devices and can be linked to various input and output devices.

3. **Hand-Held Computers:** Hand-held computers are even smaller than notebooks. They are primarily used to collect field data. For example, archaeologists at a dig site in Jordan use hand-held computers to gather information about centuries-old artifacts. The New York city transit police use hand-held computers to apprehend criminals, when a suspect is apprehended, a police officer uses a hand-held computer to do a back-ground check on the individual. Each hand-held computer holds more than 1,200 records and provides police officers with timely, and sometimes life-saving information.
4. **Pen-Based Computing:** Pen-based computing refers to portable computers that use an electronic writing pad and a light-sensitive Eelectronic pen, thus freeing users from the constraints of a keyboard. When the user writes on the pad, the writing is converted into digital input and stored in a file in the computer. Pen-based computing is becoming increasingly popular because most people are comfortable using a pen. It is particularly useful for sales and service representatives, insurance agents, retail suppliers, delivery people, inventory clerks, and health care providers, who are often on the move.

1.6 COMPUTER LIMITATIONS

Computers are very good at what they do, but there are many tasks that they can't do. They can't do anything unless they are first programmed with specific instructions. Computers can't decide how they are to be programmed or provide their own input; they can't interpret the data they generate; they can't implement any decisions that they suggest; and they think.

Computers can be programmed to store recipes, but they can't decide to fix dinner. They can keep track of scientific data, but they can't conceive or express the ideas for continued research. Their memories can contain the contents of encyclopedias, but only humans can decide what to do with that knowledge.

The computer is one of the most powerful tools ever developed. But we have all read articles similar to the one about the man who was treated for pneumonia and then charged by the hospital's computer for the use of the delivery room and nursery. Such 'computer failures' may be amusing, but most of such foul-ups happen because people fail to consider some basic computer limitations. Without reliable programs and sound logic, no computer system will perform adequately.

The computer does what it's programmed to do Eitalic and nothing else. This doesn't mean that it must be stupid. A clever program can be written to direct the computer to store the results of previous decisions. Then, by using the program's branching ability, the computer may be able to modify its behavior according to the success or failure of past decisions. But a program that has operated flawlessly for months can suddenly produce nonsense. Perhaps some rare combination of events has presented the system with a situation for which there's no programmed course of action. Or perhaps the course of action provided by the programmer contains an error that's just being discovered. Of course, a reliable program that's supplied with incorrect data may also produce nonsense.

The computer can only process jobs which can be expressed in a finite number of steps leading to a specific goal. Each step must be clearly defined. If the steps in the solution cannot be precisely stated, the job cannot be done. This is why the computer may not be helpful to people in areas where subjective evaluations are important. For example, it may not be able to tell a sales manager if a new product will be successful. The market decision may hinge on educated guesses about future social, political, technological, and economic changes. But the computer can tell the manager how the product will fare under assumed price, cost, and sales volume conditions. These assumed values can be fed into the computer. An analysis program can then manipulate them in response to a series of 'what if' questions to project the effects that the manager's questions will have no profits.

Even if program steps are finite and understood, there are still some tasks whose execution could take millions of years, even on a supercomputer. Joseph Weizenbaum, a computer scientist at MIT, has observed that a program could be written to try every legal chess move in a given situation. Every response to a move could then be evaluated, and the subsequent moves and countermoves could all be identified until the computer found a move which, if suitably pursued, would guarantee a win. Weizenbaum notes that this program would certainly be finite, but the time needed to execute it would be unimaginably large. Although in principle the computer could do the job, in practice it cannot. The term **combinatorial explosion** is used for this type of problem where a finite number of steps generates an impossibly large number of computer operations.

1.7 THE IMPACT OF COMPUTERS ON SOCIETY

Even when you don't see them, computers are usually working behind the scenes—where you go to school, shop, work, or transact business. Some computers are responsible for your leisure enjoyment and entertainment; others are found in government operations and professions such as medicine and law. Let us have a brief idea of the impact of computer usage on various sectors of our society.

1.7.1 Business and Industry

In business, computers are being used for many data processing tasks such as word processing, filing, assembling numbers and facts associated with general office functions like accounting, payroll processing and personnel record keeping.

With advances in computer technology, the industrial sector has progressed remarkably in terms of:

1. New efficient methods of production
2. Optimal Usage of available resources
3. Greater efficiency
4. Better quality of products
5. Reduction in cost of production, and
6. Improved safety & reliability

1.7.2 Health Care

Computers are also being used for planning and control purposes by health-care professionals. Computer equipment is used to monitor pulse rate, blood pressure and other vital signs. This leads to correct and fast diagnosis. Medical researchers are using computers as a tool in their search for cures of deadly diseases like Cancer and AIDS.

1.7.3 Education

Education system is making use of computers on a large scale. Computers bring to the educational process such attributes as untiring patience and round-the-clock availability. Their use leads to improved student performance in thinking logically, formulating problem-solving procedures, and understanding relationships. For example, business students gain a better understanding of relationships as they introduce changes in economic variables and then see how these changes affect office—simulated business operations.

1.7.4 Humanities

In recent years, computer usage has increased in people having interests in history, literature, music, graphics, arts and other branches of humanities.

They use it to:

1. ease manuscript preparation
2. translate texts from one natural language to another
3. conduct studies that would otherwise be impractical
4. apply artistic talents to a new medium, and
5. discover significant stylistic patterns in text.

1.7.5 Science and Technology

Thousands of scientific applications are processed daily on the computers. One of the most important daily activity is weather forecasting, which involves solution of mathematical equations using world-wide data about air pressure, temperature, humidity and other values. Our weather department has one of the most powerful computers for this task, the Super Computer.

1.7.6 Recreation and Entertainment

Our entertainment and pleasure-time pursuits have also been affected by computerization. For instance, electronic pianos contain digital computers. Musical instruments can also be linked to a personal computer, thereby creating a variety of sounds. For example:

1. In movies, computer generated graphics gives freedom to designers so that special effects, and even imaginary characters can play a part in making movies, videos, and commercials.
2. In sports, computers compile statistics, sell tickets, create training programs and diets for athletes, and suggest game plan strategies based on the competitor's past performance.
3. In restaurants, almost every one has eaten food where the clerk enters an order by indicating choices on a rather unusual looking cash register, the device directly enters the actual data into a computer, and calculates the cost and then prints a receipt.

1.7.7 Government

Various departments of our Government use computers for their planning, control and law enforcement activities. To name a few—Traffic, Tourism, Information & Broadcasting, Education, Railways, Aviation and many others.

1.7.8 Defence

There are many uses computers in Defence such as:

1. Controlling UAV or unmanned air-crafts an example is Predator. If you have cable I would recommend watching the shows 'Future Weapons' and 'Modern Marvels'. The show future weapon gives an entire hour to the predator.
2. They are also used on Intercontinental Ballistic Missiles (ICBMs) that uses GPS and Computers to help the missile get to the target.
3. Computers are used to track incoming missiles and help slew weapons systems onto the incoming target to destroy them.
4. Computers are used in helping the military find out where all their assets are (Situational Awareness) and in Communications/Battle Management Systems.
5. Computers are used in the logistic and ordering functions of getting equipments to and around the battlefield.
6. Computers are used in tanks and planes and ships to target enemy forces, help run the platform and more recently to help diagnose any problems with the platforms.
7. Computers help design and test new systems.

1.7.9 Sports

In today's technologically growing society, computers are being used in nearly every activity.

1.7.10 Recording Information

Official statistics keepers and some scouts use computers to record statistics, take notes and chat online while attending and working at a sports event.

1.7.11 Analyzing Movements

The best athletes pay close attention to detail. Computers can slow recorded video and allow people to study their specific movements to try to improve their tendencies and repair poor habits.

1.7.12 Writers

Many sportswriters attend several sporting events a week, and they take their computers with them to write during the game or shortly after while their thoughts are fresh in their mind.

1.7.13 Scoreboard

While some scoreboards are manually updated, most professional sports venues have very modern scoreboards that are programmed to update statistics and information immediately after the information is entered into the computer.

1.8 INFORMATION TECHNOLOGY ENABLED SERVICES (ITES)

Information technology enabled services, or ITES, is a form of outsourced service which has emerged due to involvement of IT in various fields such as banking and finance, telecom, insurance, etc. Some of the examples of ITES are medical transcription, back-office accounting, insurance claim, credit card processing and many more.

Firms usually from developed countries outsource such services to countries like India, China and Philippines in order to gain from large talent pool and low labor cost.

Apart from the reasons like cost cutting, focus on core job and leverage the expertise of Business Process Outsourcing (BPO) company, one major reason for outsourcing IT enables services is to eliminate resource related constraints and reduce IT staff.

Few IT enabled services are given below:

- **BPO**—Business Process Outsourcing.
- **KPO**—Knowledge Process Outsourcing.
- **BTO**—Business Transformation Outsourcing is transformation of client's business by value adding and providing end to end IT and BPO solutions.
- **HRO**—Human Resource Outsourcing is the outsourcing of HR functions like hiring, payroll etc to another company.
- **BPM**—Business Process Management is an approach to make an organization more effective, efficient and flexible to adapt changes.
- **RPO**—Research Process Outsourcing–Companies looking for data on research outsource it to other companies.
- **MBPO**—Medical Business Process Outsourcing is the outsourcing of medical functions like billing, forms processing, transcription etc.

All these are offshoots of IT enabled services and are fast growing niches. They require certain skill sets in an employee. There are examples of doctors, CA, MBAs and domain experts who have joined these specialized BPO projects and carved a growing and unorthodox career.

BPO is the fastest growing sector of IT enabled services however it has its own set of challenges, attrition being the top most which we will discuss in next section. Employees leave organizations to move to a new job with higher package. This results in slower promotions for people who keep on hopping jobs.

Call center outsourcing has created lakhs of jobs which should be treated as a long term career due to the immense growth opportunities that they provide. Promotion every 1.5–2 years is feasible and lots of people working in BPOs have got fast promotions. Rags to riches stories are abundant in the BPO industry.

1.9 BUSINESS PROCESS OUTSOURCING (BPO)

Business process outsourcing (BPO) is the practice of outsourcing non core functions like call center to a third party vendor. It is however not limited to call centers only and has extended to outsourcing of back office work, HR, marketing etc.

BPO that is contracted outside a company's country is called **offshore outsourcing**. BPO that is contracted to a company's neighboring (or nearby) country is called **near shore outsourcing**.

Often the business processes are **information technology**—based, and are referred to as **ITES-BPO**. Knowledge Process Outsourcing (KPO) and Legal Process Outsourcing (LPO) are some of the sub-segments of business process outsourcing industry.

India is chosen as the preferred market place for outsourcing due to low costs and second largest English speaking population. Most of the business is outsourced from countries like US, UK, Australia and European countries.

BPO success story in India has motivated other countries to setup this industry. Philippines, China and Eastern European countries are also being seen as the other preferred destinations behind India.

1.9.1 Advantages

Three main reasons why organizations choose to outsource their business are:

1. **Low costs:** Organizations are able to save on an average 40% by outsourcing.
2. **Focus on core activities:** Companies are able to invest their time and energy on their core activities (*e.g.*, banking, manufacturing, provide services like ISP).
3. **Benefit from expertise of ITES Companies:** They are able to implement the best practices learnt from other accounts.

1.9.2 Future of Outsourcing

Indian ITES industry has grown over 900% in the last 10 years and is expected to grow further. NASSCOM has predicted humongous 1 crore (10 million) jobs in the IT and ITES industry by the year 2020.

More than 25 lakh (2.5 million) people are already working and growing professionally in the IT and ITES industry.

BPO jobs have a lot to offer because of which so many aspirants have chosen them. Fat salary package is one of the reasons. This industry also offers fast growth and numerous opportunities for promotions.

Besides, academic excellence is not a prerequisite in this industry. Undergraduates and graduates in any field can join this industry. Although there are certain projects which require specialization, in general call centers hire people from diverse educational backgrounds.

Companies have also been hiring from campuses. Campus hiring was a norm in the IT industry and ITES has followed the same to achieve the required numbers.

There are numerous examples of people from diverse backgrounds getting tremendous growth in the industry. Young, old, highly educated, undergraduates, experienced, fresher, etc., there is nothing that can stop you from making it big in the BPOs if you really want to succeed.

1.9.3 BPO Services

BPO services cover a wide range of services that BPO industry caters to. Broadly BPO services can be divided into 5 categories:

1. Call Centers
2. Data Processing
3. BFSI—Banking, Financial Servies and Insurance
4. Healthcare
5. LPO—Legal Outsourcing

Categories like data processing, BFSI and healthcare are KPO businesses.

1.9.3.1 Call Centers

Call Centers use various mediums like-phone calls, email and chat to provide 3 types of supports:

- Technical Support in case of an ISP, Hardware manufacturer and software (Firewall, antivirus etc.) companies.
- Customer Service for common queries related to order status, 'How to' questions, account status etc.
- Outbound sales to sell products and services like credit cards, mortgage, telecom and ISP plans, mobile services etc.
- Airlines book and sell tickets through their call centers. Customers can call for any changes required to be made or for information.
- Public sector companies also use call centers to cater to their customers' needs.

1.9.3.2 Data Processing

As the name suggests Data processing is the set of actions performed on data to achieve the end results. It includes:

- Data entry
- Digitization of books (e-books)
- Digitization of recordings
- Conversion from one document type to another *e.g.*, Word to pdf, html to word etc

1.9.3.3 BFSI-Banking, Financial Services and Insurance

BFSI includes:

- Bank reconciliation
- Credit cards
- Stock broking
- Insurance policy sales
- Changes in policy
- Private or corporate banking
- Settlement of trades
- Financial statements
- Verification and issuance of policies
- Policy withdrawals/loans
- Premium payments and modifications

1.9.3.4 Healthcare Outsourcing

Healthcare includes:

- Healthcare policy administration
- Billing

❒ Financial administration
❒ Forms processing
❒ Transcription

1.9.3.5 LPO

LPO includes:

❒ Legal document review
❒ Research and writing
❒ Contract management
❒ Patent and trademark renewals
❒ Drafting legal documents
❒ Patent Analytics and Patent Research

1.9.4 Benefits and Limitations

The main advantage of BPO is the way in which it helps increase a company's flexibility. However, several sources have different ways in which they perceive organizational flexibility. In early 2000s BPO was all about cost efficiency, which allowed a certain level of flexibility at the time. Due to technological advances and changes in the industry (specifically the move to more service-based rather than product-based contracts), companies who choose to outsource their back-office increasingly look for time flexibility and direct quality control. Business process outsourcing enhances the flexibility of an organization in different ways:

Most services provided by BPO vendors are offered on a fee-for-service basis, using business models such as Remote In-Sourcing or similar software development and outsourcing models. This can help a company to become more flexible by transforming fixed into variable costs. A variable cost structure helps a company responding to changes in required capacity and does not require a company to invest in assets, thereby making the company more flexible. Outsourcing may provide a firm with increased flexibility in its resource management and may reduce response times to major environmental changes.

Another way in which BPO contributes to a company's flexibility is that a company is able to focus on its core competencies, without being burdened by the demands of bureaucratic restraints. Key employees are herewith released from performing non-core or administrative processes and can invest more time and energy in building the firm's core businesses. The key lies in knowing which of the main value drivers to focus on—customer intimacy, product leadership, or operational excellence. Focusing more on one of these drivers may help a company create a competitive edge.

A third way in which BPO increases organizational flexibility is by increasing the speed of business processes. Supply chain management with the effective use of supply chain partners and business process outsourcing increases the speed of several business processes, such as the throughput in the case of a manufacturing company.

Finally, flexibility is seen as a stage in the organizational life cycle: A company can maintain growth goals while avoiding standard business bottlenecks. BPO therefore allows firms to retain their entrepreneurial speed and agility, which they would otherwise sacrifice in order to become efficient as they expanded. It avoids a premature internal transition from its informal entrepreneurial phase to a more bureaucratic mode of operation.

A company may be able to grow at a faster pace as it will be less constrained by large capital expenditures for people or equipment that may take years to amortize, may become outdated or turn out to be a poor match for the company over time.

Although the above-mentioned arguments favor the view that BPO increases the flexibility of organizations, management needs to be carful with the implementation of it as there are issues, which work against these advantages. Among problems, which arise in practice are: A failure to meet service levels, unclear contractual issues, changing requirements and unforeseen charges, and a dependence on the BPO which reduces flexibility. Consequently, these challenges need to be considered before a company decides to engage in business process outsourcing.

A further issue is that in many cases there is little that differentiates the BPO providers other than size. They often provide similar services, have similar geographic footprints, leverage similar technology stacks, and have similar Quality Improvement approaches.

1.9.5 Threats

Risk is the major drawback with Business Process Outsourcing. Outsourcing of an Information System, for example, can cause security risks both from a communication and from a privacy perspective. For example, security of North American or European company data is more difficult to maintain when accessed or controlled in the Sub-Continent. From a knowledge perspective, a changing attitude in employees, underestimation of running costs and the major risk of losing independence, outsourcing leads to a different relationship between an organization and its contractor.

Risks and threats of outsourcing must therefore be managed, to achieve any benefits. In order to manage outsourcing in a structured way, maximizing positive outcome, minimizing risks and avoiding any threats, a Business continuity management (BCM) model is set up. BCM consists of a set of steps, to successfully identify, manage and control the business processes that are, or can be outsourced.

1.10 KNOWLEDGE PROCESS OUTSOURCING (KPO)

Knowledge Process Outsourcing (KPO) is outsourcing of work which requires special skills, experience, education and qualification. Few examples are Finance and accounting (F&A), Investment banking (IB), market research, data services related projects.

It is considered to be an extension of BPO. Initially BPO was thought to be 'call centres' only however that perception has changed with the increase in knowledge services related projects. Knowledge services industry is high revenue earning as it requires special skills. Most of the BPO companies have knowledge service projects and are planning to increase revenue and growth in this industry. MBAs, Lawyers, Chartered Accountant, B Com/M Com, Civil Engineers or architects, Doctors, BSc/MSc, PhDs degree holders can join KPO.

India is the preferred destination for knowledge services due to availability of large pool of professionals with required qualifications apart from other reasons like low costs and quality services.

1.10.1 Services

Companies provide following services through Knowledge service unit:

- Financial accounting
- Financial statements
- Financial analysis
- Website designing
- Search engine optimization
- Payroll processing
- Research on Investment
- Market research data analysis
- Content management

1.11 LEGAL PROCESS OUTSOURCING (LPO)

Legal outsourcing, also known as legal process outsourcing (LPO) refers to the practice of a law firm or corporation obtaining legal support services from an outside law firm or legal support services company (LPO provider). When the LPO provider is based in another country the practice is called offshoring and involves the practice of outsourcing any activity except those where personal presence or contact is required *e.g.*, appearances in court and face-to-face negotiations. When the LPO provider is based in the same country the practice of outsourcing includes agency work and other services requiring a physical presence such as court appearances. This process is one of the incidents of the larger movement towards outsourcing. The most commonly offered services have been agency work, document review, legal research and writing, drafting of pleadings and briefs, and patent services.

A lawyer in countries like US/UK would typically charge between $100–400 per hour. Law practicing companies in India do the same work at a much less cost.

India has been a preferred location for Legal outsourcing. Its large English speaking population and US/UK law graduates are advantages for this industry.

This industry has generated lot of jobs in India and has forced the lawyers in US/UK and few other countries to cut down on their exorbitant fees. This has not only helped the Law companies located in US/UK but the common man as well. Indian law is based on English common law and is considered to be one of the most well researched laws. This gives companies in the US/UK another reason to outsource their work to India.

The concept of legal process outsourcing is based on the division of labour principle, prevalent in law firms, where various time consuming and onerous processes like due diligence are delegated to paralegals, document reviewers or interns. This allows the firm to address the various legal issues that arise on a daily basis while being able to streamline productivity.

The process involves a contract, with due consideration, between both firms. The following are the various methods by which the process could be initiated:

- ❒ **Direct Contract:** This is the most straight forward means of establishing contact. The firm needing legal services directly approaches the legal process outsourcing vendor.
- ❒ **Managed Outsourcing:** This is a case where the firm establishes contact with a legal process outsourcing vendor and retains a traditional law firm to coordinate the vendor's activities and to ensure quality control.
- ❒ **Required Outsourcing:** This form of outsourcing occurs when the firm mandates a certain level of outsourcing in the legal process, either to reduce costs or to fulfill statutory requirements.
- ❒ **Multi-sourcing:** This involves segregating the work assigned to LPO providers in order to reduce risk and take advantage of each provider's strengths. This approach is helpful is cases where expertise is required on matters of jurisdiction and merits. Having more than one provider 'on deck' also allows a service recipient to obtain more favorable pricing. On the other hand, multi-sourcing can be more complicated than other approaches. Successfully managing multiple, competing providers requires strong and effective governance procedures.

1.11.1 Services

Services offered in the industry are:

- ❒ Legal document review
- ❒ Contract management
- ❒ Drafting legal documents
- ❒ Research and writing
- ❒ Patent and trademark renewals
- ❒ Patent Analytics and Patent Research

1.11.2 Reasons

Among the leading proponents of this process have been corporate clients concerned with rising legal expenses. The legal departments of corporations began using the services of such providers. Soon these corporations began to pressure their legal representatives to outsource certain legal processes to cut costs.

1.11.3 Advantages

Most firms and corporations outsource primarily to save cash, and this is considered the biggest advantage for legal outsourcing. While an attorney in major legal markets such as the US may charge from $150 to $500 per hour when performing rote services, legal process outsourcing firms generally charge a small fraction of that price. It has attracted major corporations to outsource specific work outside their legal departments. Many destinations for outsourcing have benefited from the upsurge in bankruptcies and litigations that have occurred in the wake of the Global Financial Crisis.

LPO firms in India had predicted an annual growth of 200% due to recession related litigation and the increased need to save costs in the US. Their expectations have not been met. The major reason for this is that US lawyers themselves have started looking at alternative fee structures due to the recession and job losses. In spite of setbacks, the LPO industry has seen growth of about 40–60% in the last year. Although some areas of practice, such as real estate, have drastically collapsed due to the recession, some areas such as litigation, document review, and corporate compliance have gained ground, resulting in business directed to LPO firms in India.

1.12 CALL CENTRE

A call center or call centre is a physical place where customer and other telephone calls are handled by an organization, usually with some amount of computer automation. Typically, a call center has the ability to handle a considerable volume of calls at the same time, to screen calls and forward them to someone qualified to handle them, and to log calls. Call centers are used by mail-order catalog organizations, telemarketing companies, computer product help desks, and any large organization that uses the telephone to sell or service products and services.

A call centre is operated through an extensive open workspace for call centre agents, with work stations that include a computer for each agent, a telephone set/headset connected to a telecom switch, and one or more supervisor stations. It can be independently operated or networked with additional centres, often linked to a corporate computer network, including mainframes, microcomputers and LANs. Increasingly, the voice and data pathways into the centre are linked through a set of new technologies called Computer Telephony Integration (CTI).

A contact centre, also known as customer interaction centre is a central point of any organization from which all customer contacts are managed. Through contact centres, valuable information about company are routed to appropriate people, contacts to be tracked and data to be gathered. It is generally a part of company's customer relationship management (CRM). Today, customers contact companies by telephone, email, online chat, fax, and instant message.

Call centre technology is subject to improvements and innovations. Some of these technologies include speech recognition software to allow computers to handle first level of customer support, text mining and natural language processing to allow better customer handling, agent training by automatic mining of best practices from past interactions, support automation and many other technologies to improve agent productivity and customer satisfaction. Automatic lead selection or lead steering is also intended to improve efficiencies, both for inbound and outbound campaigns, whereby inbound calls are intended to quickly land with the appropriate agent to handle the task, whilst minimizing wait times and long lists of irrelevant options for people calling in, as well as for outbound calls, where lead selection allows management to designate what type of leads go to which agent based on factors including skill, socioeconomic factors and past performance and percentage likelihood of closing a sale per lead.

The concept of the Universal Queue standardizes the processing of communications across multiple technologies such as fax, phone, and email whilst the concept of a Virtual queue provides callers with an alternative to waiting on hold when no agents are available to handle inbound call demand.

A typical call centre telephone has no hand-set, phone is for headset use only.

Premise-based Call Centre Technology: Historically, call centres have been built on PBX equipment that is owned and hosted by the call centre operator. The PBX might provide functions such as Automatic Call Distribution, Interactive Voice Response, and skills-based routing. The call centre operator would be responsible for the maintenance of the equipment and necessary software upgrades as released by the vendor.

Virtual Call Centre Technology: With the advent of the Software as a service technology delivery model, the virtual call centre has emerged. In a virtual call centre model, the call centres operator does not own, operate or host the equipment that the call centre runs on. Instead, they subscribe to a service for a monthly or annual fee with a service provider that hosts the call centre telephony equipment in their own data centre. Such a vendor may host many call centres on their equipment. Agents connect to the vendor's equipment through traditional PSTN telephone lines, or over Voice over IP. Calls to and from prospects or contacts originate from or terminate at the vendor's data centre, rather than at the call centre operator's premise. The vendor's telephony equipment then connects the calls to the call centre operator's agents.

Virtual Call Centre Technology allows people to work from home, instead of in a traditional, centralised, call centre location, which increasingly allows people with physical or other disabilities that prevent them from leaving the house, to work.

Cloud Computing for Call Centres: Cloud computing for call centres extends cloud computing to Software as a service, or hosted, on-demand call centres by providing application programming interfaces (APIs) on the call centre cloud computing platform that allow call centre functionality to be integrated with cloud-based Customer relationship management, such as Salesforce.com or Oracle CRM and leads management and other applications.

The APIs typically provide programmatic access to two key groups of features in the call centre platform:

Computer Telephony Integration (CTI) APIs provide developers with access to basic telephony controls and sophisticated call handling on the call centre platform from a separate application.

Configuration APIs provide programmatic control of administrative functions of the call centre platform which are typically accessed by a human administrator through a Graphical User Interface (GUI).

1.12.1 Various Call Centre Models

Some variations of call centre models are listed below:

- **Contact centre:** Supports interaction with customers over a variety of media, including but not necessarily limited to telephony, e-mail and internet chat.
- **Inbound call centre:** Exclusively or predominantly handles inbound calls (calls initiated by the customer).
- **Outbound call centre:** One in which call centre agents make outbound calls to customers or sales leads.
- **Blended call centre:** Combining automatic call distribution for incoming calls with predictive dialling for outbound calls, it makes more efficient use of agent time as each type of agent (inbound or outbound) can handle the overflow of the other.
- **Telephone answering service:** A more personalised version of the call centre, where agents get to know more about their customers and their callers; and therefore look after calls just as if based in their customers office.

REVIEW QUESTIONS

Multiple Choice Questions

1. Which generation of computers is covered by the period 1964–77?
(*a*) First (*b*) Second (*c*) Third (*d*) Fourth

2. Which of the following belongs to the first generation of computer?
(*a*) AC (*b*) IBM 1401 (*c*) IBM 8090 (*d*) UNIVAC

3. What hardware was used by first generation computers?
(*a*) Transistors (*b*) Valves (*c*) VLSI (*d*) ICs

4. A collection of eight bits is called:
(*a*) Byte (*b*) Word (*c*) Record (*d*) File

5. A typical modern computer uses:
(*a*) LSI chips (*b*) Vacuum tubes (*c*) Valves (*d*) All the above

6. Which is the most powerful type of computers?
(*a*) Microcomputer (*b*) Minicomputer
(*c*) Mainframe computer (*d*) Super computer

7. The first electronic digital computer contained:
(*a*) Electronic valves (*b*) Vacuum tubes
(*c*) Transistors (*d*) Semiconductor memory

8. The first computer made available for commercial use was:
(*a*) Mark-I (*b*) ENIAC (*c*) EDSAC (*d*) UNIVAC

9. The first computer used to store a program
(*a*) EDSAC (*b*) ENIAC (*c*) EDVAC (*d*) ACE

10. Who is called the 'grandfather' of the computer?
(*a*) Blaise Pascal (*b*) Charles Babbage
(*c*) Joseph Jacquard (*d*) Dr. Herman Hollerith

11. The first mechanical computer designed by Charles Babbage was called:
(*a*) Abacus (*b*) Processor (*c*) Calculator (*d*) Analytical Engine

12. The fifth generation digital computer will be:
(*a*) Extremely cheap (*b*) Very expensive
(*c*) Versatile (*d*) Artificially intelligent

13. Who was the father of Punched Card Processing?
(*a*) J. Presper Eckert (*b*) Charles Babbage
(*c*) Dr. Herman Hollerith (*d*) Blaise Pascal

14. The transistorized computer circuits were introduced in the:
(*a*) First generation (*b*) Second generation (*c*) Third generation (*d*) Fourth generation

15. The third generation of computers covers the period:
(*a*) 1971–1982 (*b*) 1982–1994 (*c*) 1959–1964 (*d*) 1965–1971

16. The first machine to successfully perform long services of arithmetic and logical operations was
(*a*) EDSAC (*b*) UNIVAC-I (*c*) Mark-I (*d*) ENIAC

17. Which is true for the digital computer?
(*a*) It is less accurate than the analog computer
(*b*) It represents the decimal numbers through a string of binary digits

(*c*) It is used primarily in scientific applications
(*d*) Both (*a*) and (*c*)

18. Super computers are primarily useful for:
(*a*) Input-output intensive processing (*b*) Data-retrieval operations
(*c*) Mathematical-intensive scientific applications (*d*) All of the above

19. The first electronics computer in the world was:
(*a*) UNIVAC (*b*) EDVAC (*c*) ENIAC (*d*) All of the above

20. First generation computers are characterised by
(*a*) Vaccum tubes and magnetic drum (*b*) Minicomputers
(*c*) Magnetic tape and transistors (*d*) All of the above

21. What was the computer conceived by Babbage?
(*a*) Analytical Engine (*b*) Arithmetic Machine (*c*) Donald Knuth (*d*) All of the above

ANSWERS

Multiple Choice Questions

1. (*c*) **2.** (*d*) **3.** (*b*) **4.** (*a*) **5.** (*a*) **6.** (*d*) **7.** (*a*) **8.** (*d*)
9. (*a*) **10.** (*b*) **11.** (*d*) **12.** (*d*) **13.** (*c*) **14.** (*b*) **15.** (*d*) **16.** (*c*)
17. (*b*) **18.** (*c*) **19.** (*c*) **20.** (*a*) **21.** (*a*)

QUESTIONS

1. If computers are so accurate, why is the phrase 'garbage in-garbage out' associated with their use. Discuss.

2. Describe the characteristics that delineate the first and second generations of computers.

3. Compare the distinctions between third and fourth generation computers.

4. What innovation or invention led to today's computers? Discuss.

5. What is a Computer System? Describe different components of a computer system.

6. How do the computers differ in size and logic used?

7. What is the difference between analog and digital computers?

8. Large computer systems are grouped into which three categories? Give details.

9. What are characteristics of a microcomputer?

10. Discuss and give example of computer usage by different sectors of our society.

11. Do you think computers are superior to human beings? Discuss.

12. What is a hybrid computer? Explain in brief.

13. Discuss the limitations of computers.

14. Write an explanatory note on 'The impact of computers on society'.

15. What do you understand by the terms 'Hardware', 'Software', and 'Liveware'?

16. What are the main types of Software?

17. What is the function of Operating System?

18. Discuss the advantages and disadvantages of using computers?

19. Explain briefly the major innovations of first generation computers.

20. Write a note on evolution of computers.

21. Write short note on Information Technology Enabled Services.

22. What is Business Process Outsourcing? Discuss.

23. What are the advantages of Business Process Outsourcing and its future?

24. What are Knowledge Process Outsourcing and its services? Discuss.

25. What are Legal Process Outsourcing and its advantages? Discuss.

26. Write short note on Call Centre.

2

BASIC COMPUTER ORGANIZATION

2.1 BASIC OPERATIONS OF COMPUTERS

The **basic operations of computers** have not changed much over the years. It is the technology used to accomplish those operations which have changed. In 1950s, it took a roomful of vacuum tubes and equipment to perform the tasks that are now completed by a single chip, no bigger than a child's thumbnail. Advances in semiconductor technology have reduced the size of the chip. Depending on conditions, a semiconductor can serve as a conductor (allowing the transmission of electricity) or as an insulator (inhibiting the transmission of electricity).

One complete electronic semiconductor circuit contained on a small piece of silicon is called as **Integrated Circuit** (IC). Large-Scale Integration (LSI) and Very Large Scale Integration (VLSI) technology have drastically increased the number of complete circuits residing on a small piece of silicon. An IC, also called a chip is used for design of both logic and memory circuitry. Its compactness and tremendous power have put the computer into almost every aspect of today's world. Let us have an overview of basic **components of the computer hardware**.

2.2 CENTRAL PROCESSING UNIT (CPU)

Every things computer does is controlled by its **Central Processing Unit** (CPU). The CPU is the **brains of the computer**. Sometimes referred to simply as the **central processor** or **Nerve Centre** or **heart**, but more commonly called **processor**, the CPU is where most calculations take place. In terms of computing power, the CPU is the most important element of a computer system. It add and compare its data in chipA CPU or Processors of all computers, whether micro, mini or mainframe must have three element or parts primary storage, arithmetic logic unit (ALU), and control unit. **Control Unit** (CU)—decodes the program instruction. CPU chip used in a computer is partially made out of Silica. on other words silicon chip used for data processing are called **Micro Processor**.

Central processing unit (CPU) is the central component of the PC. Sometimes it is called as processor. It is the brain that runs the show inside the PC. All work that is done on a computer is performed directly or indirectly by the processor. Obviously, it is one of the most important components of the PC. It is also, scientifically, not only one of the most amazing parts of the PC, but one of the most amazing devices in the world of technology. The processor plays a significant role in the following important aspects of your computer system:

- **Performance:** The processor is probably the most important single determinant of system performance in the PC. While other components also playa key role in determining performance, the processor's capabilities dictate the maximum performance of a system. The other devices only allow the processor to reach its full potential.
- **Software Support:** Newer, faster processors enable the use of the latest software. In addition, new processors such as the Pentium with MMX Technology, enable the use of specialized software not usable on earlier machines.

- **Motherboard Support:** The processor that decides to use in your system will be a major determining factor in what sort of chipset we must use, and hence what motherboard you buy. The motherboard in turn dictates many facets of. The system's capabilities and performance.
- **Reliability and Stability:** The quality of the processor is one factor that determines how reliably your system will run. While most processors are very dependable, some are not. This also depends to some extent on the age of the processor and how much energy it consumes.
- **Energy Consumption and Cooling:** Originally processors consumed relatively little power compared to other system devices. Newer processors can consume a great deal of power. Power consumption has an impact on everything from cooling method selection to overall system reliability.

The CPU is the component of a computer system with the circuitry to control the interpretation and execution of instructions. It performs the process part of INPUT-PROCESS-OUTPUT cycle.

In a microcomputer, the components of the CPU are mounted on the main circuit board, called the 'motherboard'. A microprocessor chip contains the circuits and special storage locations called **registers**—needed to perform the arithmetic-logic and control functions.

The various components on the main circuit board of the personal computer processor unit are linked together by sets of parallel electrical conducting lines called **buses**. Different collections of these internal bus lines are used for different purposes and are given different names. These internal buses also provide an electrical interconnection between processor components and the interface devices used with peripheral equipment.

A number of factors determine the performance characteristics of all microprocessor systems. The processing capabilities of these systems depend upon:

2.2.1 Microprocessor Used

A microprocessor chip can be of:

1. 8 bit
2. 16 bit
3. 8/16 bit
4. 16/32 bit
5. 32/32 bit

These chips differ from one another in their data handling and addressing capabilities. For instance, an 8 bit machine retrieves from storage, manipulates and processes 8 bit bytes of data at a time. Whereas in a 8/16 chip, data paths are only 8 bits wide but data are processed 16 bits at a time. The 32/32 machines are the latest powerful super microprocessors. The 32/32 bit chips have 32 bits wide internal and 32 bits wide external data paths.

In *computer architecture*, **64 bit computing** is the use of processors that have *datapath* widths, *integer* size, and *memory addresses* widths of 64 bits (eight *octets*). Also, 64 bit *CPU* and *ALU architectures* are those that are based on *registers*, *address buses*, or *data buses* of that size. From the software perspective, 64 bit computing means the use of *code* with 64 bit virtual memory addresses.

In 2003 they were introduced to the (previously *32 bit*) mainstream *personal computer* arena in the form of the *x86-64* and 64 bit *PowerPC* processor architectures and later in 2012 even in processors that were before mainly used in *smartphones, tablet computers*, and embedded systems with the introduction of the *AArch64* processor architectures in ARMv8 and on September 10, 2013 with the introduction of the 64 bit ARMv8 *Apple A7 SOC*, powering the *iPhone 5s*.

A 64 bit register can store 264 (over 18 *quintillion* or 1.8 × 1019) different values. Hence, a processor with 64 bit memory addresses can directly access 264 bytes of byte-addressable memory.

Without further qualification, a **64 bit computer architecture** generally has integer and addressing *registers* that are 64 bits wide, allowing direct support for 64 bit data types and addresses. However, a CPU might have external *data buses* or *address buses* with different sizes from the registers, even larger (the 32 bit Pentium had a 64 bit data bus, for instance). The term may also refer to the size of low-level data types, such as 64 bit *floating-point* numbers.

2.2.2 Clock Speed

There are two cycles that occur during the processing of each program instruction. These are instruction cycle and execution cycle. These cycles are syncronized by a specific number of electrical pulses produced by an electronic clock that is built into the processor. Therefore, the speed with which an instruction is executed is also directly related to the chip's clock speed, *i.e.*, the number of pulses it uses each second. Cycle time is the time required to execute a basic operation.

2.2.3 Primary Storage Capacity

The more the data and program segments can be kept in primary storage, the fewer time-consuming disk operations be necessary. This speeds up the processing.

2.2.4 Instruction Sets

Every microprocessor has the built-in ability to respond to a particular set of machine instructions.

2.3 MAIN COMPONENTS OF CPU

The main components of a Central Processing Unit are:

1. Arithmetic and Logic Unit (ALU)
2. Control Unit
3. Primary Storage Unit.

2.3.1 Arithmetic and Logic Unit

The **Arithmetic and Logic Unit** (ALU) is that part of CPU where actual data processing occurs. All calculations (mathematical) and all comparisons (logic function) take place in this unit.

Every arithmetic step requires at least two numbers and then it produces a result. Multiplication, for example, uses a multiplicand and a multiplier to get a product. Although every ALU must be able to manage the two data words and the result, different processing and storage techniques are used in different models (Fig. 2.1).

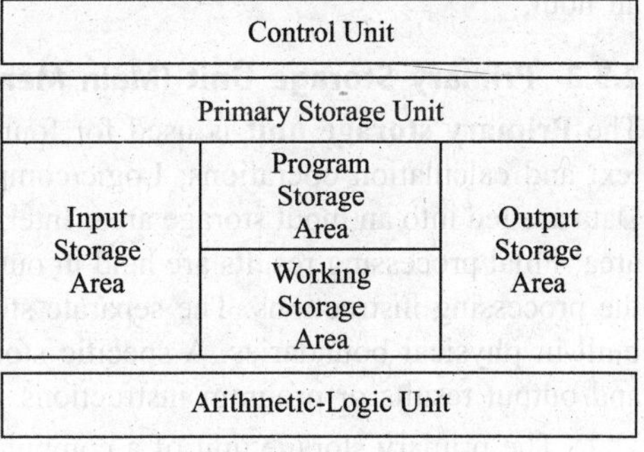

Fig. 2.1 Block diagram

In addition to arithmetic functions, the ALU also performs logic functions. A logic function is one where numbers or conditions are compared to each other. Circuits in the ALU are generally used to compare two numbers by subtracting one from the other. The sign (negative or positive) and the value of the difference tell the processor that the first number is equal to, less than, or greater than the second number. Alphabetic data may also be compared according to an assigned order sequence.

2.3.2 Control Unit

The Control Unit interprets any instruction it receives from memory and directs the sequences of events necessary to execute the instruction. Control unit uses a system clock which synchronizes all tasks by sending out electrical pulses. The clock speed (the number of pulses or cycles per second) is measured in megahertz (MHz) and is the main element in determining the speed of the processor. Computer speed is also measured by the number of instructions completed per second, or millions of instructions per second (MIPS). **Hertz** is the unit of frequency that measures the number of cycles per second in a periodic signal; a megahertz is equal to one million hertz. All things being equal, an 8 MHz processor will do things twice as fast as a 4 MHz processor.

Other factors also affect processing speed; the instruction set is one. An **instruction set** consists of the group of commands available to the CPU which determines the basic computer operations (arithmetic, logic, and storage and retrieval functions) that can be performed. A CPU is designed with an instruction set that the control unit uses to direct and coordinate the computer's operations.

Each instruction takes a specific number of system clock cycles to complete. The same instruction may take ten clock cycles to complete on one processor but only five clock cycles on another. So even though both of these processors are running at 8 MHz, one takes twice as long to complete the same instruction.

Computer speed is also measured by the number of instructions completed per second, or **millions of instructions per second (MIPS)**. This measurement is usually how large computer systems, such as minicomputers, mainframes, and supercomputers, are compared. Typical speeds for minicomputers are in the 5–10 MIPS range. Mainframe computers generally perform in the 20–50 MIPS range but the range can go to more than 100 MIPS. Supercomputers execute instructions from approximately 200 MIPS and up. Some microprocessors, such as the Interl 80386, can execute 3–4 MIPS. Most microprocessors, such as the Intel 80386, can execute 3–4 MIPS. Most microprocessors, however, run at less than one MIPS and are usually classified only by their system clock speeds. A typical micro-computer can execute an instruction, such as adding two numbers, in a few milliseconds. Mainframes and supercomputers can execute in the microsecond and nanosecond ranges.

The difference between a millisecond and a microsecond may seem to be insignificant; however, it is roughly the same as the difference between one minute and one day, or one hour and one month. Just think of how much more you can accomplish in a month than you can in an hour.

2.3.3 Primary Storage Unit (Main Memory)

The **Primary storage unit** is used for four activities—Input/output operations; Manipulation of text and calculation operations; Logic/comparision operations; Storage and retrieval operations. Data are fed into an input storage area; Intermediate processing results are held in working storage area; Final processing results are held in output storage area, and a program storage area contains the processing instructions. The separate storage locations used for these four tasks do not have built-in physical boundaries. A specific storage location can hold input data in one application and output results or program instructions in another.

The primary storage unit of a computer has many small storage areas. Each storage area is assigned an address—an identification (*e.g.*, a label, name or number) that designates a particular location in storage or any other data source. There are 65,536 or more storage locations in the primary storage sections of most PCs. The address in one such computer may be numbered from 00000 to 65,536 (or more). In a storage location each character is represented by a string of adjacent binary numbers (0s and 1s) that are treated as a unit. This unit or set of binary digits, or bits is called a byte. A typical byte consists of a grouping of 8 bits.

Primary storage may take one of the three forms:

1. Magnetic Core Memory
2. Semiconductor Memory
3. Bubble memory

2.4 TYPES OF COMPUTER MEMORY

2.4.1 Magnetic Core Memory

Magnetic core memory consists of small magnetic cores with wires running through them. Electric current flows through the wires and depending on the direction of the current flow, electricity magnetizes the core in different directions. The direction of magnetization indicates certain data representation to the CPU. However, since this form of memory is bulky, it has given way to newer technologies, such as semiconductor memories.

2.4.2 Semiconductor Memory

All computers made today use semiconductor elements in their primary storage units. This type of memory is made by 'etc.hing' electronic circuits onto a silicon chip. The two most common forms of semiconductor memory are:

1. Random Access Memory (RAM)
2. Read-Only Memory (ROM)

2.4.2.1 Random Access Memory (RAM)

This is that part of primary storage where data and program instructions are held temporarily while being manipulated or executed. It is called Random Access Memory because any of the locations on a chip can be randomly selected and used to directly store and retrieve data and instructions. RAM is volatile; *i.e.*, it depends on a steady supply of electricity and when the power is shut off, everything stored is lost.

RAM chips may be classified as dynamic or static.

Dynamic RAM chip: The storage cell circuits in dynamic RAM chips contain:

1. A transistor that acts like a mechanical on-off light switch.
2. A capacitor that is capable of storing an electric charge.

Depending on the switching action of the transistor, capacitor either contains no charge (0 bit) or does hold a charge (1 bit). The charge on the capacitor tends to leak 'off', therefore, provision is made to 'regenerate' the storage charge. Thus a dynamic RAM chip provides volatile storage.

Static RAM chip: It also provides volatile storage, but as long as it is supplied with power, it needs no special regenerator circuits to retain the stored data. Static RAM chips are more complicated and take up more space than dynamic RAM chips because they require more transistors and other devices to store a bit of data. Therefore, static RAMs are used in specialized applications while dynamic RAMs are used in primary storage section.

Every processor has a primary storage section (general purpose storage section) that holds the active programs, and data being processed. In addition to this, many processors also have built-in specialized storage elements that are used for specific processing and control purposes. One element used during processing operations is a high speed **buffer memory (cache memory)** which is both fast and expensive per character stored, as compared to primary storage. This high speed circuitry serves as a 'scratch pad' to temporarily store data and instructions that are likely to be retrieved many times during processing, thereby improving the processing speed. Data may be transferred automatically between the buffer and primary storage. Cache memory is used in large as well as small computers.

2.4.2.2 Read Only Memory (ROM)

Read **O**nly **M**emory, *i.e.*, **ROM** chip retains the stored data when the power supply is cut. So, unlike RAM chips, ROM chips are non-volatile. ROM chip may contain microprogram control instructions that cause the machine to perform certain operations such as starting the computer or instructions to the entire operating system. ROM chip can only be read, it does not accept any input data or instructions from the users. The actual contents of ROM are set by the manufacturers and they are unchangeable and permanent. ROM is mainly of three types:

Programmable **R**ead **O**nly **M**emory **(PROM)** allows a chip to be programmed by the user for converting critical and lengthy operations into microprograms that are fused into a chip. Once, they are in a hardware form, they can be executed at a very high speed. Once operations have been written into a PROM chip, they cannot be altered.

Erasable **P**rogrammable **R**ead **O**nly **M**emory **(EPROM)** can be erased and reprogrammed. It needs to be removed from the processor and exposed to ultraviolet light for some time before it can accept any new contents.

Electrically **E**rasable and **P**rogrammable **R**ead **O**nly **M**emory **(EEPROM)** can be reprogrammed with special electrical pulses.

To illustrate the use of RAM and ROM, let's look at how they might be used in a typical microcomputer. The primary storage unit is represented as the cube in Fig. 2.2 (*a*). The cube is composed of two parts, RAM and ROM. ROM is shown as the thin portion along the top of the cube. When the computer is first turned on, ROM performs predetermined instructions, such as checking the system for errors. Notice that nothing is contained in RAM at this point.

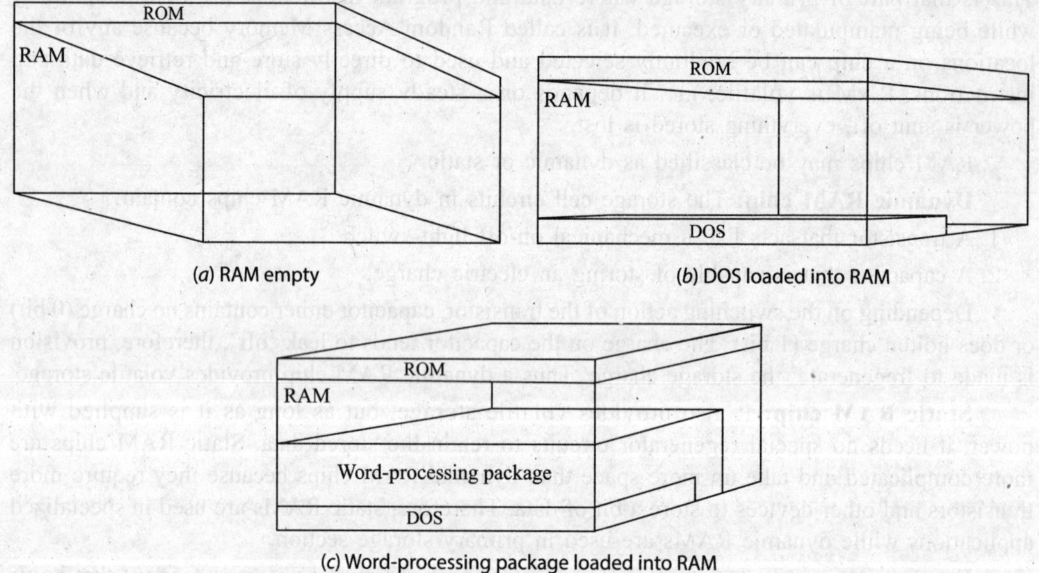

(*a*) RAM empty

(*b*) DOS loaded into RAM

(*c*) Word-processing package loaded into RAM

Fig. 2.2 An example of RAM and ROM use in a microcomputer

Before a computer can be used, it must have operating instructions. The software that provides these instructions is called the **Operating System (OS)**. The typical microcomputer operating system resides on a disk and is referred to as a **Disk Operating System (DOS)**. DOS must be transferred, or loaded, into RAM. Figure 2.2 (*b*) shows the part of RAM that is occupied by DOS.

Now, let's say you want to write a letter. The computer needs programming instructions in the form of an application package that directs the computer to function as a word processor. This word-processing package also has to be loaded into RAM. Once it has been loaded, it is ready to use. These application programs usually take a lot of memory space [Fig. 2.2 (*c*)]. Remember, though, that RAM is volatile. If you turn the computer off now, primary storage will contain only ROM and again look like Fig. 2.2 (*a*).

The amount of primary storage is very important in determining the capabilities of the computer. The more primary storage available means that more instructions and data can be loaded into the computer. Many applications require a specific amount of memory; if the computer doesn't have that amount, the application package cannot be used. Most computers have provisions for either adding individual RAM chips to the main circuit board or adding RAM cards. A RAM card is a group of integrated circuits already assembled on a printed circuit board. It can be plugged into the main circuit board of a computer to increase the amount of RAM.

2.4.3 Bubble Memory

One attempt to overcome the volatility of RAM was the development of bubble memory. **Bubble memory** is built on a thin piece of the mineral garnet where certain sections are polarized (subjected to a magnetic field) to produce bubble-like areas. Data are represented by the presence or absence of these bubbles. Bubble memory is nonvolatile, but it is not used as widely as semiconductor memory because it is slower and more expensive.

2.4.4 Special-Purpose Memories

The two types of special-purpose memories in the computer are registers and buffers. These memories are vital to moving data in an out of primary storage and to processing the data. The CPU uses them to improve the computer's overall performance. Figure 2.3 shows the interconnections of the components of the CPU with these special memories.

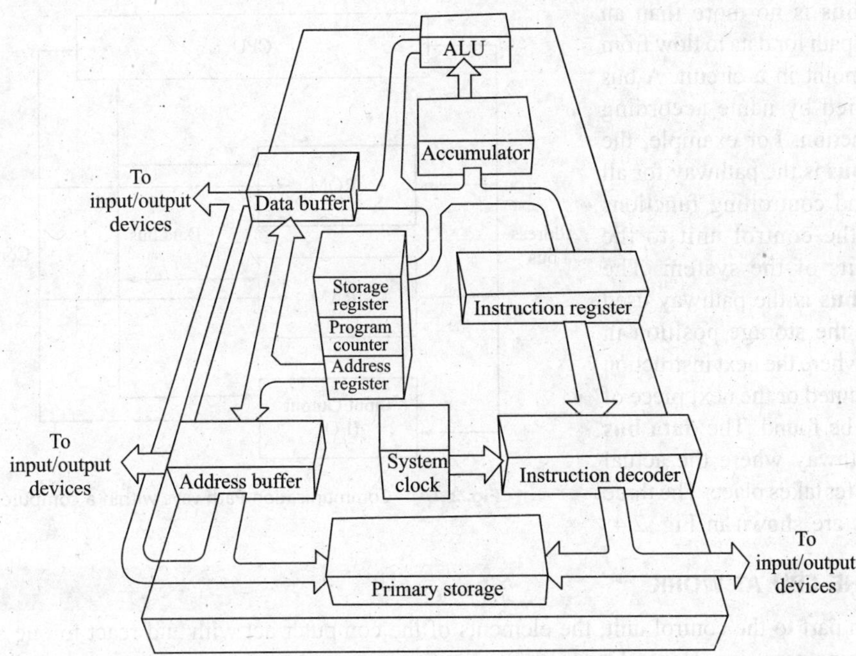

Fig. 2.3 Arrows show the movement of data or instructions between registers and buffers within the CPU

A **register** holds an instruction or data that are to be worked on immediately. It is part of the CPU and can hold only one piece of data at a time. Because registers are part of the CPU, the transfer of data in and out of primary storage is a very high-speed operation. In fact, the size and number of these registers help determine the overall speed of the computer. The names and functions of the registers used most often are:

- ❒ Accumulator—Stores the result of the last processing step of the ALU
- ❒ Instruction register—Holds an instruction in the control unit before it is decoded

- ❒ Address register—Holds the location of the next piece of data
- ❒ Storage register—Holds data on the way to or from primary storage
- ❒ Program counter—Holds the location of the next instruction to be executed

A **buffer**, another temporary holding space for data, may be part of the CPU, or it may be built into devices used to input or output data. Unlike a register, a buffer can hold more than one piece of data at a time. The buffer acts as an intermediary *between* the CPU and any input or output device. Input and output devices operate at much slower rates than the CPU, so it is necessary to have a temporary holding place for larger amounts of data. For example, a printer cannot print data as fast as the CPU can send them. Therefore, with no place to temporarily store the data, the CPU would be idly waiting for the printer to catch up. The CPU's operating speed would be reduced to the rate of the particular output device. Using a buffer allows the data to be stored temporarily, thereby freeing the CPU to do other tasks.

2.5 COMMUNICATION PATHWAYS

The ALU, the control unit, and the primary storage unit must have a way to communicate:

- ❒ Control bus
- ❒ Address bus
- ❒ Data bus

These links among and within the various units are called **buses**.

A **bus** is no more than an electrical path for data to flow from point to point in a circuit. A bus is classified by name according to its function. For example, the **control bus** is the pathway for all timing and controlling functions sent by the control unit to the other units of the system. The **address bus** is the pathway used to locate the storage position in memory where the next instruction to be executed or the next piece of data will be found. The **data bus** is the pathway where the actual data transfer takes place. The three bus paths are shown in Fig. 2.4.

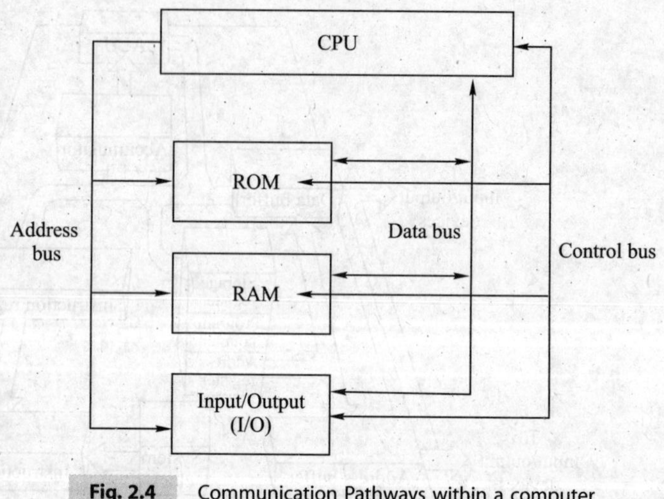

Fig. 2.4 Communication Pathways within a computer

2.6 THE CPU AT WORK

Thanks in part to the control unit, the elements of the computer act with and react to one another with amazing precision. Depending on the instruction executed, certain computer components may or may not be used. In one instance, the instruction executed may involve computations within the ALU, while another simply looks into and displays the contents of some memory location.

Regardless of the actual instruction, the computer goes through two basic cycles to execute it: **instruction cycle** and **execution cycle**. The instruction cycle is made up of two distinct steps: **fetch** and **decode**.

In general, during the instruction cycle, the fetch step locates an instruction in memory and sends it to the control unit. During the decode step, the instruction is decoded and sent to the ALU along with any necessary data. During the execution cycle, the instruction is executed by the ALU, and the result is stored in the accumulator until needed. The program counter is incremented to identify the location of the next instruction to be executed, and the instruction-execution sequence of operations is repeated for the next instruction and continues until the program ends. It may seem like a long process to fetch, decode, and execute a single instruction, but it is actually done in less than a blink of an eye—and it takes only about 200 milliseconds (.2 second) to blink an eye!

2.7 VON-NEUMANN ARCHITECTURES

Von Neumann Architecture also known as the *Von Neumann model*, the computer consisted of a CPU, memory and I/O devices. The program is stored in the memory. The CPU fetches an instruction from the memory at a time and executes it.

Thus, the instructions are executed sequentially which is a slow process. Neumann machine are called control flow computer because instruction are executed sequentially as controlled by a program counter. To increase the speed, parallel processing of computer have been developed in which serial CPU's are connected in parallel to solve a problem. Even in parallel computers, the basic building blocks are Neumann processors.

The von Neumann architecture is a design model for a stored-program digital computer that uses a processing unit and a single separate storage structure to hold both instructions and data. It is named after mathematician and early computer scientist John von Neumann. Such a computer implements a universal Turing machine, and the common 'referential model' of specifying sequential architectures, in contrast with parallel architectures (Fig. 2.5).

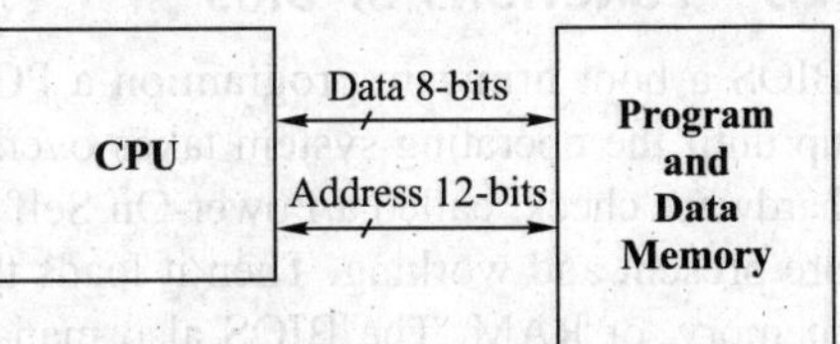

Fig. 2.5

One shared memory for instructions (program) and data with one data bus and one address bus between processor and memory. Instructions and data have to be fetched in sequential order (known as the Von Neuman Bottleneck), limiting the operation bandwidth. Its design is simpler than that of the Harvard architecture. It is mostly used to interface to external memory.

2.8 BIOS (BASIC INPUT/OUTPUT SYSTEM)

A **BIOS** (Basic Input/Output System) Short for ROM BIOS, or System BIOS is an electronic set of instructions that a computer uses to successfully start operating. The BIOS is located on a chip inside of the computer and is designed in a way that protects it from disk failure. The main function of the BIOS is to give instructions for the **Power-On Self Test (POST)**.

This self test ensures that the computer has all of the necessary parts and functionality needed to successfully start itself, such as use of memory, a keyboard and other parts. If errors are detected during the test, the BIOS instructs the computer to give a code that reveals the problem. Error codes are typically a series of beeps heard shortly after startup.

The BIOS also works to give the computer basic information about how to interact with some critical components, such as drives and memory that it will need to load the operating system. Once the basic instructions have been loaded and the self-test has been passed, the computer can proceed with loading the operating system from one of the attached drives. Computer users can often make certain adjustments to the BIOS through a configuration screen on the computer. The setup screen is typically accessed with a special key sequence during the first moments of startup. This setup screen often allows users to change the order in which drives are accessed during startup and control the functionality of a number of critical devices. Features vary among individual BIOS versions.

We can also use flash-memory cards to hold BIOS information. This allows users to update the BIOS version on computers after a vendor releases an update. This system was designed to solve problems with the original BIOS or to add new functionality. Users can periodically check for updated BIOS versions, as some vendors release a dozen or more updates over the course of a product's lifetime. Mother board (System) BIOS, Video adapter firmware (BIOS), Drive controller firmware (BIOS), Modem Card firmware (BIOS), Network adapter board. BIOS, SCSI adapter BIOS. The mother board BIOS provides routines to support motherboard features. BIOS ROM chips for major sub systems of computer such as video and drive control must also be included.

Actually BIOS can be placed in between the computer and external devices as its name tells it is used for reading the keystroke, displaying values on screen, Reading and writing to and from floppy and hard disks etc.

The keyboard is assigned the port number 60, which is known to BIOS. BIOS reads this port and data from keyboard goes to computer.

2.9 FUNCTIONS OF BIOS

BIOS a boot firmware program on a PC which controls the computer from the time you start It up until the operating system takes over. When you turn on a PC, the BIOS first conduct a basic hardware check, called a Power-On Self Test (POST), to determine whether all of the attachments are present and working. Then it loads the operating system into your computer's random access memory, or RAM. The BIOS also manages data flow between the computer's operating system and attached devices such as the hard disk, video card, keyboard, mouse, and printer. The BIOS stores the date, the time, and your system configuration information in a battery-powered, non-volatile memory chip, called a CMOS (Complementary Metal Oxide Semiconductor) after its manufacturing process. The main functions of the BIOS are:

1. BIOS power on self Test (POST)
2. Bootstrap loader
3. BIOS Setup utility program
4. System service routines

1. BIOS Power on Self Test (POST): While booting the system, BIOS first performs POST. It is a built-in diagnostic program that checks hardware to ensure that everything is present and is working properly. Then additional tests are done during booting. The POST takes very less time to run and if there is no problem, it is difficult to notice that it is running. Actually the monitor even had not activated to see the problem (if there), so speaker is used. When a PC is turned on, there are beeping sounds and if there is some problem in machine, system stopped without booting up. These beep patterns depends on the maker of BIOS and used to diagnose many hardware problems of PC. As the POST tests all important components of system, POST boot errors are fatal. BIOS send the detail of problems to special I/O address (usually 80h). A special debugging card is put to ISA slot to accept debugging codes that BIOS sends to it. The place where POST stops and find a problem can be seen by displaying the codes from card.

2. Bootstrap Loader: To boot the operating system. The BIOS contains a program known as bootstrap loader whose responsibility is to search and start the operating system boot program. Then the boot program of operating system controls the computer system and boots the operating system. The boot sequences for Award BIOS software are:

- ❐ Test the CPU
- ❐ Initialize support chips
- ❐ Initialize the keyboard
- ❐ ROM BIOS test
- ❐ CMOS RAM test
- ❐ Memory test
- ❐ Cache initialization
- ❐ Initialize the vector table

- ❒ CMOS RAM check sum
- ❒ Keyboard initialization
- ❒ Video circuit test
- ❒ Video memory test
- ❒ DMA Controller test
- ❒ PIC tests
- ❒ EISA mode test
- ❒ Enable EISA slots
- ❒ Check memory size
- ❒ Memory test
- ❒ Check EISA memory
- ❒ Mouse initialization
- ❒ Cache initialization
- ❒ Shadow RAM setup
- ❒ Floppy test
- ❒ Hard drive test
- ❒ Serial/parallel port test
- ❒ Initialize math coprocessor
- ❒ Boot speed
- ❒ POST loop
- ❒ Security/Password information
- ❒ Write to CMOS RAM
- ❒ Initialize adapter ROM
- ❒ Set up the time
- ❒ Boot the system and control given to INT 19 boot loader.

3. BIOS Setup Utility Program: A non-volatile memory (NVRAM) is used to store information about the computer system. During installation of a system, the user run BIOS setup program and enter the correct parameters. The settings of memory, disk types and other settings are stored in NVRAM and not in BIOS chip itself. To construct NVRAM, the material required is CMOS (Complementary metal oxide semiconductor). These CMOS chips are very efficient storage devices as they store and maintain data on very low values of current. The system's configurations therefore are also termed as CMOS settings, which we can set using BIOS set up program. The BIOS reads the parameters from CMOS RAM as and when required.

CMOS settings can be maintained by battery backup either by using capacitor or by a battery built into NVRAM chip. This chip also has system clock. If there is no battery, the setting remains for short period of time and we need to reset the system. With it there is loss of BIOS password which protects BIOS set up program.

To clear the CMOS RAM contents, two methods used are:

(*i*) By using clear CMOS jumper.

(*ii*) By holding down enter key during booting of the system.

For Pentium III motherboards, different set ups are there in AMI BIOS. These are:

- ❒ **Standard CMOS Setup:** It is used to set time date, hard disk type, type of floppy drive, type of monitor and keyboard.
- ❒ **Advanced CMOS Setup:** It is used to set typematic rate and delay, above 1 MB memory test, memory test tick sound, click <Del> message display, system boot up sequence etc.
- ❒ **Advanced Chipset Setup:** It is used to set features of chipset.
- ❒ **Power Management Setup:** It is used to control power conservation options.
- ❒ **PCI/Plug and Play Setup:** It is used to set options of PCI bus and that of plug and play devices.
- ❒ **Peripherals Setup:** It is used to control options related to I/O controllers.
- ❒ **CPU Configuration Setup:** This setup is used to select the types of CPU installed in the motherboard. In AMI BIOS, the settings are auto as it automatically finds out the type of CPU in the computer system.
- ❒ **System Service Routines:** The BIOS provides various software routines (subprograms) that can be called by higher-level software such, as DOS, Windows, or their applications, to

perform different tasks. Virtually every task that involves accessing the system hardware has traditionally been controlled using one or more of the BIOS programs (although many newer operating systems now bypass the BIOS for improved performance). This includes actions like reading and writing from the hard disk, processing information received from devices, etc.

BIOS services are accessed using software interrupts, which are similar to the hardware interrupts except that they are generated inside the processor by programs instead of being generated outside the processor by hardware devices. One thing that this use of interrupts does is to allow access to the BIOS without knowing where in memory each routine is located.

Normally, to call a software routine you need to know its address. With interrupts, a table called an interrupt *vector table* is used that bypasses this problem. When the system is started up, the BIOS puts addresses into this table that represent where its routines are located for each interrupt it responds to. Then, when DOS or an application wants to use a BIOS routine, it generates a software interrupt. The system processes the interrupt, looks up the value in the table, and jumps to the BIOS routine automatically. DOS itself and application programs can also use this interrupt vector table.

2.10 PARALLEL SYSTEMS

Parallel Processing Systems are designed to speed up the execution of programs by dividing the program into multiple fragments and processing these fragments simultaneously. Such systems are multiprocessor systems also known as tightly coupled systems. Parallel systems deal with the simultaneous use of multiple computer resources that can include a single computer with multiple processors, a number of computers connected by a network to form a parallel processing cluster or a combination of both.

Parallel computing is an evolution of serial computing where the jobs are broken into discrete parts that can be executed concurrently. Each part is further broken down to a series of instructions. Instructions from each part execute simultaneously on different CPUs.

Parallel systems are more difficult to program than computers with a single processor because the architecture of parallel computers varies accordingly and the processes of multiple CPUs must be coordinated and synchronized. Several models for connecting processors and memory modules exist, and each topology requires a different programming model. The three models that are most commonly used in building parallel computers include synchronous processors each with its own memory, asynchronous processors each with its own memory and asynchronous processors with a common, shared memory. Flynn has classified the computer systems based on parallelism in the instructions and in the data streams. These are:

1. Single instruction stream, single data stream (SISD).
2. Single instruction stream, multiple data stream (SIMD).
3. Multiple instruction streams, single data stream (MISD).
4. Multiple instruction stream, multiple data stream (MIMD).

The above classification of parallel computing system is focused in terms of two independent factors: the number of data streams that can be simultaneously processed, and the number of instruction streams that can be simultaneously processed. Here 'instruction stream' we mean an algorithm that instructs the computer what to do whereas 'data stream' (*i.e.*, input to an algorithm) we mean the data that are being operated upon.

Even though Flynn has classified the computer 'systems into four types based on parallelism but only two of them are relevant to parallel computers. These are SIMD and MIMD computers.

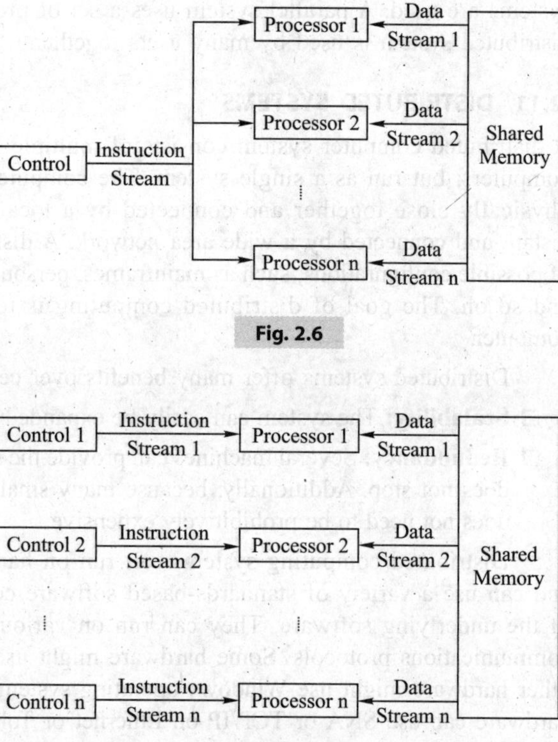

Fig. 2.6

Fig. 2.7

SIMD computers are consisting of 'n' processing units receiving a single stream of instruction from a central control unit and each processing unit operates on a different piece of data. Most SIMD computers operate synchronously using a single global dock. The block diagram of SIMD computer is shown in Fig. 2.6.

MIMD computers are consisting of 'n' processing units; each with its own stream of instruction and each processing unit operate on unit operates on a different piece of data. MIMD is the most powerful computer system that covers the range of multiprocessor systems. The block diagram of MIMD computer is shown in Fig. 2.7.

The SIMD systems are easier to program because it deals with single thread of execution. On the hand, the MIMD machines are more efficient because you can utilize the full machine power.

Parallel operating systems are primarily concerned with managing the resources of parallel machines. A parallel computer is a set of processors that are able to work cooperatively to solve a computational problem. So, a parallel computer may be a supercomputer with hundreds or thousands of processors or may be a network of workstations.

A few years ago, parallel computers could be found only in research laboratories and they were used mainly for computation intensive applications like numerical simulations of complex systems. Today, there are a lot of parallel computers available in the market; used to execute both data intensive applications in commerce and computation intensive applications in science and engineering.

Today, new applications arise and demand faster computers. Commercial applications are the most used on parallel computers. A computer that runs such an application; should be able to process large amount of data in sophisticated ways. These applications include graphics, virtual reality, and decision support, parallel databases, medicine diagnosis and so on. We can say with no doubt that commercial applications will define future parallel computers architecture but scientific applications will remain important users of parallel computing technology.

Concurrency becomes a fundamental requirement for algorithms and programs. A program has to be able to use a variable number of processors and also has to be able to run on multiple processors computer architecture. According to Tanenbaum, a distributed system is a set of independent computers that appear to the user like a single one. So, the computers have to be independent and the software has to hide individual computers to the users. MIMD computers and workstations connected through LAN and WAN are examples of distributed systems. The main difference between parallel systems and distributed systems is the way in which these systems are used. A parallel system uses a set of processing units to solve a single problem A distributed system is used by many users together.

2.11 DISTRIBUTED SYSTEMS

A distributed computer system consists of multiple software components that are on multiple computers, but run as a single system. The computers that are in a distributed system can be physically close together and connected by a local network, or they can be geographically distant and connected by a wide area network. A distributed system can consist of any number of possible configurations, such as mainframes, personal computers, workstations, minicomputers, and so on. The goal of distributed computing is to make such a network work as a single computer.

Distributed systems offer many benefits over centralized systems, including the following:

- **Scalability:** The system can easily be expanded by adding more machines as needed.
- **Redundancy:** Several machines can provide the same services, so if one is unavailable, work does not stop. Additionally, because many smaller machines can be used, this redundancy does not need to be prohibitively expensive.

Distributed computing systems can run on hardware that is provided by many vendors, and can use a variety of standards-based software components. Such systems are independent of the underlying software. They can run on various operating systems, and can use various communications protocols. Some hardware might use UNIX(R) as the operating system, while other hardware might use Windows operating systems. For inter-machine communications, this hardware can use SNA or TCP/IP on Ethernet or Token Ring.

Figure 2.8 shows an example of such a distributed system. This system contains two local area networks (LANs) that are connected to each other. One LAN consists of UNIX workstations from several different manufacturers; the other LAN consists primarily of PCs that are running several different PC operating systems. One of the LANs is also connected to a mainframe by way of an SNA connection.

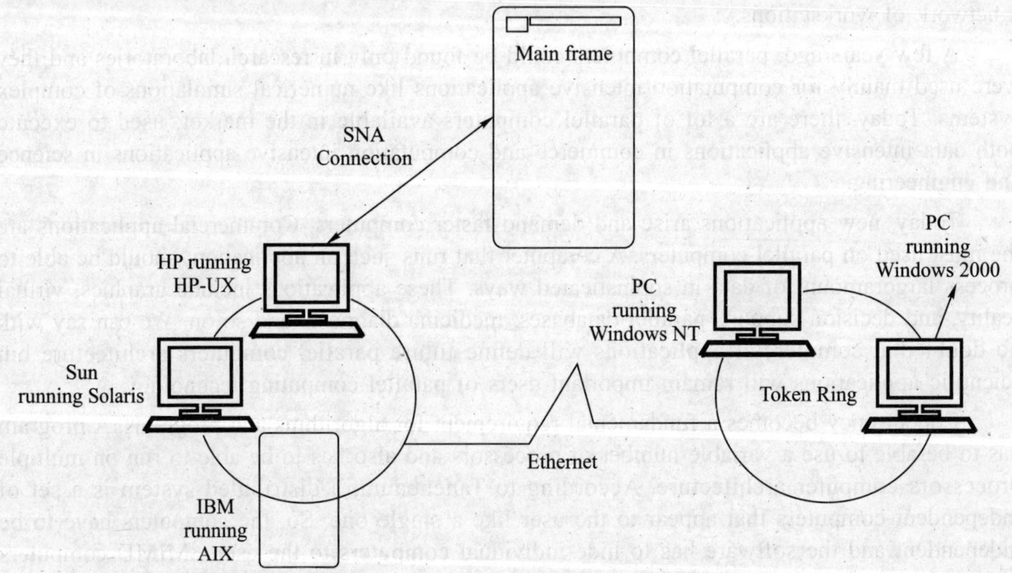

Fig. 2.8 An example open distributed system

REVIEW QUESTIONS

Multiple Choice Questions

1. Where does a computer add and compare data?
(*a*) Hard disk (*b*) Floppy disk (*c*) CPU chip (*d*) Memory chip

2. Computer can not do anything without a:
(*a*) Chip (*b*) Memory (*c*) Output device (*d*) Program

3. The word 'Computer' usually refers to the Central Processor Unit plus:
(*a*) External memory (*b*) Internal memory (*c*) Input devices (*d*) Output devices

4. A computer is a box full of electronic:
(*a*) Switching devices (*b*) Chips (*c*) Circuits (*d*) Registers

5. Processors of all computes, whether micro, mini or mainframe must have:
(*a*) ALU (*b*) Primary storage
(*c*) Control Unit (*d*) All of the above

6. The basic components of a modern digital computers are:
(*a*) Input device (*b*) Output device
(*c*) Central processor (*d*) All of the above

7. Which of the following is a part of the Central Processing Unit?
(*a*) Printer (*b*) Keyboard
(*c*) Mouse (*d*) Arithmetic Logic Unit

8. The term 'memory' applies to which one of the following:
(*a*) Logic (*b*) Storage
(*c*) Control (*d*) Input device

9. Group of instructions that directs a computer is called:
(*a*) Storage (*b*) Memory (*c*) Logic (*d*) Program

10. Which is not true for primary storage?
(*a*) Information must be transferred to primary storage
(*b*) It is relatively more expensive
(*c*) It allows very fast access to data
(*d*) It is not a part of the CPU

11. The Central Processing Unit (CPU) consists of:
(*a*) Input, output and processing
(*b*) Control unit, primary storage, and secondary storage
(*c*) Control unit, arithmetic-logic unit, and primary storage
(*d*) Control Unit, processing, primary storage

12. Primary storage is .... as compared to secondary storage.
(*a*) Slow and inexpensive (*b*) Fast and inexpensive
(*c*) Fast and expensive (*d*) Slow and expensive

13. Which of the following is an example of nonvolatile memory?
(*a*) ROM (*b*) VLSI (*c*) LSI (*d*) RAM

14. Linkage between the CPU and the users is provided by:
(*a*) Storage (*b*) Control Unit (*c*) Peripheral devices (*d*) Software

15. The two kinds of main memory are:
(*a*) ROM and RAM (*b*) Primary and secondary
(*c*) Floppy disk and hard disk (*d*) Direct and sequential

16. RAM is used as short memory because it:
(*a*) Is volatile (*b*) Is very expensive
(*c*) Has small capacity (*d*) Is programmable

17. The silicon chips used for data processing are called:
(*a*) RAM chips (*b*) ROM chips (*c*) Microprocessor (*d*) PROM chips

18. The hardware in which data may be stored for a computer system is called:
(*a*) Registers (*b*) Bus (*c*) Control unit (*d*) Memory

19. Which is the computer memory that does not forget?
(*a*) ROM (*b*) RAM
(*c*) PROM (*d*) All of the above

20. The computer memory used for temporary storage of data and program is called:
(*a*) ROM (*b*) RAM (*c*) EROM (*d*) EPROM

21. Which computer memory is essentially empty?
(*a*) RAM (*b*) ROM (*c*) EPROM (*d*) PROM

22. Everything computer does is controlled by its:
(*a*) RAM (*b*) ROM
(*c*) CPU (*d*) Storage devices

23. A computer consists of:
(*a*) A central processing unit (*b*) A memory
(*c*) Input and output units (*d*) All of the above

24. Which chips are erasable by ultra-violet rays after removing them from the main circuit?
(*a*) EPROM chips (*b*) EEPROM chips
(*c*) PROM chips (*d*) All of the above

25. The memory which is ultraviolet light erasable and electrically programmable is:
(*a*) ROM (*b*) PROM (*c*) RAM (*d*) EPROM

26. Which memory is non-volatile and may be written only once?
(*a*) ROM (*b*) EE-ROM (*c*) RAM (*d*) PROM

27. The memory which is programmed at the time it is manufactured:
(*a*) ROM (*b*) RAM (*c*) PROM (*d*) EPROM

28. Which memory is volatile?
(*a*) RAM (*b*) ROM (*c*) EPROM (*d*) PROM

29. Which of the following statements is wrong?
(*a*) An EPROM can be programmed, erased and reprogrammed by the user with an EPROM programming instrument
(*b*) Magnetic tape is non-volatile
(*c*) Magnetic core and semiconductor memories are used as mass memory medium
(*d*) RAM is a type of volatile memory

ANSWERS

Multiple Choice Questions

1. (*c*)	**2.** (*d*)	**3.** (*b*)	**4.** (*a*)	**5.** (*d*)	**6.** (*d*)	**7.** (*d*)	**8.** (*a*)
9. (*d*)	**10.** (*d*)	**11.** (*c*)	**12.** (*c*)	**13.** (*a*)	**14.** (*c*)	**15.** (*a*)	**16.** (*a*)
17. (*c*)	**18.** (*d*)	**19.** (*a*)	**20.** (*b*)	**21.** (*b*)	**22.** (*c*)	**23.** (*d*)	**24.** (*a*)
25. (*d*)	**26.** (*d*)	**27.** (*a*)	**28.** (*a*)	**29.** (*c*)			

QUESTIONS

1. Show with reference to a block diagram, the structure of a digital computer and the inter-connection of various units. Explain the functions of various units briefly.
2. What are the different sections of CPU? Explain their functions briefly.
3. What is the main purpose of primary storage? Briefly describe various forms of primary storage.
4. Describe the roles that RAM and ROM play within the computer, their main purpose and what distinguishes the two types of memory.
5. What three major units comprise the CPU?
6. Describe an integrated circuit.
7. What is the function of the control unit?
8. Discuss the significance of using MIPS as a gauge of computer speeds.
9. What does the term 'volatile' mean as it pertains to computer memory?
10. What type of memory is volatile?
11. Explain the difference among a ROM chip, a PROM chip, an EPROM chip, and an EEPROM chip.
12. Briefly describe the two cycles involved in the execution of an instruction.
13. What purposes do registers and buffers serve?
14. Explain the Von-Neumann Architectures.
15. What is BIOS? Discuss.
16. What is function of POST?
17. Write short note on CMOS.
18. What is Parallel and Distributed Systems?
19. What is SISD, SIMD, MISD, and MIMD? Explain.

NUMBER SYSTEMS, COMPUTER ARITHMETIC, COMPUTER CODES

The smallest piece of data that can be recognized and used by the computer is the bit, a binary digit. A bit is a single binary value 1 or 0. A grouping of eight bits is a byte. The byte is the basic unit for measuring the size of memory; although with today's memory sizes, it is more common to hear the term kilobyte (KB) or megabyte (MB).

1 Kilobyte = 1024 bytes

1 Megabyte = 1024 × 1024 bytes = 1,048,576 bytes

A number of adjacent bits that can be stored and manipulated as a unit is called a computer word. Some of the newer microcomputers have the ability to manipulate a 32 bit word, while older models have word lengths of 8 and 16 bits. Word lengths for supercomputers range upto 128 bits. The longer the lengths of the computer word that the registers can hold, the faster the computer can process data. Some computers have words of fixed length and some have words of variable length. Each word in the memory is provided its own address. Address may be defined as a means of locating data or communicating with devices connected to a computer.

3.1 NUMBER SYSTEM

In a numbering system, there are only a few symbols which represent different values depending on the position they occupy in the number. The total number of digits applicable to any system is called its radix/base. The actual number of symbols used in a positional system depends on its base. The decimal system has a base of 10 and 10 symbols (0 to 9). In any numbering system, the highest numerical symbol always has a value of one less than the base. Let us have a brief idea of most commonly used numbering systems.

3.2 DECIMAL SYSTEM

Decimal system is a base—10 system which means there are 10 distinct digits—0 through 9. The value that the digits represent depends on the 'weights' or position they hold.

For example:

4th	3rd	2nd	1st	Position
10^3	10^2	10^1	10^0	Weights
1	0	2	4	

$4 \times 10^0 = 4$

$2 \times 10^1 = 20$

$0 \times 10^2 = 0$

$1 \times 10^3 = 1000$

1024_{10}

Many combination of these four digits—1, 0, 2 and 4 can be made but the exact position in which they are placed will determine the final value. To distinguish one number system from the next, a subscript is used to indicate the base/radix.

3.3 BINARY NUMBERING SYSTEM

Every computer stores numbers, letters and other characters in a coded form. As mentioned earlier, every character in storage is represented by a string of 0s and 1s. The numbering system in which these two digits are found is binary numbering system. The binary numbering system uses a base of 2. The possible symbols being 0 and 1. The 0s and 1s can be arranged in various combinations to represent all the numbers, letters, and symbols that can be entered into the computer.

Computers have been designed to use binary numbers because of the following reasons:

(*i*) Computer circuits have to handle only 2 binary digits or bits rather than 10 used in decimal numbering system. This simplifies the design of the circuits, reduces the cost and improves the reliability.

(*ii*) Computer only identifies signals in the form of digital pulses which represent either high voltage or hot state 'on' (1) or a low voltage of cold state 'off' (0).

(*iii*) Everything that can be done with a base of 10 can also be done in binary.

As binary system is a base 2 system, the position weights are used on the powers of 2.

8th	7th	6th	5th	4th	3rd	2nd	1st	Position
$2^7 = 128$	$2^6 = 64$	$2^5 = 32$	$2^4 = 16$	$2^3 = 8$	$2^2 = 4$	$2^1 = 2$	$2^0 = 1$	Weights

3.4 BINARY CALCULATIONS

Addition, subtraction, multiplication and division of binary numbers is carried out in the same way as it is in decimal system. Let us take these operations one by one.

3.4.1 Addition

Rules for carrying out addition of binary numbers are as follows:

$$0 + 0 = 0$$
$$0 + 1 = 1$$
$$1 + 0 = 1$$
$$1 + 1 = 0 \text{ with 1 carry over}$$

Examples (*i*) For adding 110101_2 and 101111_2

Binary	Decimal
110101	53
101111	47
1100100	100

1100100 is equivalent to 100 in decimal system.

(*ii*) For adding 10110_2 and 1101_2

$$\begin{array}{r} 10110 \\ 1101 \\ \hline 100011 \end{array}$$

3.4.2 Subtraction

Rules for subtraction of binary numbers are as follows:

0 – 0 = 0

1 – 0 = 1

1 – 1 = 0

0 – 1 = 1 with one borrow

Examples (*i*) Subtracting 101111 from 110101

Binary	Decimal
110101	53
101111	47
000110	6

110_2 is equivalent to 6 in decimal system.

(*ii*) Subtracting 1101 from 10110

```
 10110
  1101
 -----
  1001
```

3.4.3 Multiplication

Rules for multiplication of binary numbers are as follows:

0 × 0 = 0

0 × 1 = 0

1 × 1 = 1

Examples (*i*) Multiplying 10110 with 1101

```
     10110
      1101
 ---------
     10110
    00000x
   10110xx
  10110xxx
 ---------
 100011110
```

In order to check, let us see the decimal equivalents of these binary numbers.

22 × 13 = 286 which is 100011110_2.

(*ii*) Multiplying 111 with 101

```
    111
    101
 ------
    111
   000x
  111xx
 ------
 100011
```

3.4.4 Division

Division for binary numbers can be carried out by following same rules as those applicable to decimal system.

Examples (*i*) Dividing 100011_2 by 101

```
101 | 100011 | 111
      101
      ---
       111
       101
       ---
        101
        101
        ---
          0  or 35 + 5 = 7
```

(*ii*) Dividing 11110_2 which 110_2

```
110 | 11110 | 101
      110
      ---
        110
        110
        ---
          0
```

3.5 OCTAL SYSTEM

Octal system was issued to provide a shorthand way to deal with the long strings of 1s and 0s created in binary. It is a base 8 system using the digits 0 through 7. The position weights are based on the powers of 8.

8th	7th	6th	5th	4th	3rd	2nd	1st	Position
8^7	8^6	8^5	8^4	8^3	8^2	8^1	8^0	Weights
2097152	262144	32768	4096	512	16	8	= 1	

In the octal numbering system, we write numbers in sequence until all digits in a specific position are exhausted. Then we initialize the given position with 0 and add 1 to the next position. Consider the following pattern in the octal numbering system.

Decimal	Octal	
0	0	
1	1	
2	2	
3	3	
4	4	
5	5	
6	6	
7	7	$7_8 + 1_8 = 10_8$
8	10	
9	11	
10	12	
⋮	⋮	
14	16	
15	17	$17_8 + 1_8 = 20_8$
⋮	⋮	

23	27	$27_8 + 1_8 = 30_8$
24	30	
⋮	⋮	
So on	So on	

Most of the computer manufacturers are using the octal numbering system or base eight system. This numbering system can be used to represent three binary digits as a single octal number. In this way, we can significantly reduce the number of digits required to represent any number and it still maintains the binary concept. Another advantage of Octal system is that we can still utilize the on-off electrical impulse concept of binary numbers.

3.6 HEXADECIMAL SYSTEM

The hexadecimal system is also used to provide a shorthand way to deal with long strings of 1s and 0s created in binary. It contains the digits 0 through 9 and the letters A through F. The letters are used because 16 placeholders are needed and there are only 10 distinct digits in the decimal system. This system is often used in programming as a shortcut to the binary number system.

As we have discussed in the octal numbering system, the computer can group together three binary digits to represent a single digit octal number. In the same manner, we can group together four binary digits to produce a digit in the 16 or hexadecimal numbering system.

In base 10 there are 10 unique digits 0 to 9; In base 16, as we might expect, there are 16 unique digits. Since we are familiar only with 10 digits, the hexadecimal numbering system requires 6 more individual characters to represent numbers 10 to 15. Arbitrarily, the letters A to F were selected to represent these numbers.

Decimal	Hexadecimal
0	0
1	1
2	2
3	3
4	4
5	5
6	6
7	7
8	8
9	9
10	A
11	B
12	C
13	D
14	E
15	F

3.7 RADIX CONVERSIONS

The above mentioned number systems can be converted into one another by following certain steps. Let us take these conversions one by one:

3.7.1 Conversion of Decimal System to Other Systems

3.7.1.1 *Integers*

Decimal system may be converted to other systems by using the following two methods:

1. **Remainder Method:** This is the most commonly used method for carrying out conversions from decimal system to other systems. It involves the following steps:
   (*a*) Dividing the given number of decimal system by the radix R of the proposed system. From this, we'll get a quotient Q_1 and a remainder R_1.
   (*b*) Dividing the quotient Q_1 by the radix R again to get quotient Q_2 and a remainder R_2.
   (*c*) Dividing the quotient Q_2 by the radix R again to get quotient Q_3 and a remainder R_3.

   This process of division of the successive quotients by the radix R of the proposed system should be repeated until the quotients become less than the radix R. Thus, the required number can be obtained by writing the last quotients first and then remainders in the reverse order, *i.e.*,

   $$Q_n\ R_n\ R_{n-1}\ R_{n-2} \ldots R_2\ R_1$$

2. **Power Method:** This method involves the following steps.
   (*a*) Subtracting the highest number which is obtained by raising the radix to the power of the proposed system. R_1 be the remainder.
   (*b*) Subtracting the next highest number from this remainder R_1.
   (*c*) This procedure should be repeated until the remainder is zero.
   (*d*) Write the multiplication factors in the sequential order in such a way that the powers which have been used should be multiplied by 1 and and the ones missing should be multiplied by zero.

3.7.1.2 *Fractions*

The integer part of the fraction can be converted to other systems following the Remainder Method or Power Method. The fraction part can be converted to other systems by following these steps:

1. Finding out the radix of the system to which fraction has to be converted.
2. Multiplying fraction with radix. Let the fraction part of this product be F1 and I_1 resulting integer.
3. Multiplying the resulting fraction part F1 with the radix again, we'll get F2 and I_2.
4. Above steps should be repeatedly done until the fraction part vanishes.
5. The required fraction number in the required system with radix R would be

$$I_1\ I_2\ I_3 \ldots I_n$$

3.8 EXAMPLES

1. Decimal to Binary—(Integers)

(*a*) Using the Remainder Method:

(*i*) 300_{10} $\qquad$ $300_{10} = 100101100_2$

2	300	
2	150	0
2	75	0
2	37	1

2	18	1
2	9	0
2	4	1
2	2	0
2	1	0
	0	1

(*ii*) 1024_{10}

2	1024	
2	512	0
2	256	0
2	128	0
2	64	0
2	32	0
2	16	0
2	8	0
2	4	0
2	2	0
2	1	0
	0	1

$1024_{10} = 10000000000_2$

(*b*) Using Power Method:

(*i*) 300_{10}

Radix of binary system = 2

Powers of radix which are less than 300:

2^8	2^7	2^6	2^5	2^4	2^3	2^2	2^1	2^0
256	128	64	32	16	8	4	2	1

$$
\begin{array}{rl}
300 & \\
-256 & 2^8 = 1 \times 2^8 \\
\hline
44 & \\
-32 & 2^5 = 1 \times 2^5 \\
\hline
12 & \\
-8 & 2^3 = 1 \times 2^3 \\
\hline
4 & \\
-4 & 2^2 = 1 \times 2^2 \\
\hline
0 &
\end{array}
$$

1×2^8	0×2^7	0×2^6	1×2^5	0×2^4	1×2^3	1×2^2	0×2^1	0×2^0
1	0	0	1	0	1	1	0	0

$\therefore$ $300_{10} = 100101100_2$

(*ii*) 1024_{10}

Radix of binary system = 2

Powers of radix which are less than 1024:

2^{10}	2^9	2^8	2^7	2^6	2^5	2^4	2^3	2^2	2^1	2^0
1024	512	256	128	64	32	16	8	4	2	1

$$\begin{array}{r} 1024 \\ -1024 \\ \hline 0 \end{array} \quad 2^{10} = 1 \times 2^{10}$$

1×2^{10}	0×2^9	0×2^8	0×2^7	0×2^6	0×2^5	0×2^4	0×2^3	0×2^2	0×2^1	0×2^0
1	0	0	0	0	0	0	0	0	0	0

$\therefore \quad 1024_{10} = 10000000000_2$

2. Decimal to Binary (Fraction)

(*a*) Converting $(17.35)_{10}$ to binary form.

Integer part = 17.

Using Remainder Method:

2	17	
2	8	1
2	4	0
2	2	0
2	1	0
	0	1

$17_{10} = 10001_2$

Fraction part =.35 Radix = 2

	F	I
.35 × 2 =	0.70	0
.70 × 2 =	1.40	1
.40 × 2 =	0.80	0
.80 × 2 =	1.60	1
.60 × 2 =	1.20	1
.20 × 2 =	0.40	0

$.35_{10} = 011010_{...2}$

$\therefore \quad 17.35_{10} = (10001.010110...)_2$

(*b*) Converting $(0.2)_{10}$ to binary form.

Radix = 2.

	F	I
0.2 × 2 =	0.4	0
0.4 × 2 =	0.8	0
0.8 × 2 =	1.6	1
0.6 × 2 =	1.2	1
0.2 × 2 =	0.4	0

$(0.2)_{10} = (0.00110...)_2$

3. Decimal to Octal (Integer)

(*a*) Converting 119_{10} into octal form.

Radix is 8.

Using Remainder Method:

8	119	
2	14	7
8	1	6
	0	1

$\therefore \quad 119_{10} = 167_8$

4. Decimal to Octal (Fraction)

(*a*) Converting $(634.640625)_{10}$ to Octal equivalent.

Integer part = 634.

Using Remainder Method:

8	634	
8	79	2
8	9	7
8	1	1
0	1	

$634_{10} = 1172_8$

Fraction part = .640625

	F	**I**
0.640625 × 8	5.125	5
0.125 × 8	1.0	1

$0.640625_{10} = 51_8$

$\therefore \quad 634.640625_{10} = 1172.51_8$

5. Decimal to Hexadecimal (Integer)

(*a*) Converting 7551_{10} to hexadecimal equivalent.

Using Remainder Method:

16	7551		
16	471	15	15 = F
16	29	7	
16	1	13	13 = D
	0	1	

$\therefore \quad 7551_{10} = 1D7F_{16}$

6. Decimal to Hexadecimal (Fraction)

(*a*) Converting 3370.75_{10} into hexadecimal form.

Integer = 3370.

Using Remainder Method:

16	3370		
16	210	10	10 = A
16	13	2	
	0	13	13 = D

$\therefore \quad 3370_{10} = \text{D2A}_{16}$

Fraction $= .75$

	F	I
$.75 \times 16$	12.0	12

$\therefore .75 = .\text{C} \quad \therefore 3370.75_{10} = \text{D2A.C}_{16}$

3.8.1 Conversion of Binary System to Other Systems

3.8.1.1 Binary to Decimal (Integer)

We can convert binary to decimal by multiplying each binary digit with its position weight.

Example Converting 11011010_2 to decimal form.

11011010

8th	7th	6th	5th	4th	3rd	2nd	1st	Position
2^7	2^6	2^5	2^4	2^3	2^2	2^1	2^0	Weights
1	1	0	1	1	0	1	0	

$0 \times 2^0 = 0$
$1 \times 2^1 = 2$
$0 \times 2^2 = 0$
$1 \times 2^3 = 8$
$1 \times 2^4 = 16$
$0 \times 2^5 = 0$
$1 \times 2^6 = 64$
$1 \times 2^7 = 128$

$\therefore \quad 11011010_2 = 218_{10}$

3.8.1.2 Binary to Decimal (Fraction)

For converting a fraction of any system with radix R to the decimal system, the following steps should be taken:

1. Multiplying the digits after the points by R^{-1}, R^{-2}, R^{-3}... respectively.
2. Simplifying the resulting fractions and adding them together to get the required fraction of the decimal system.

Example Obtain the decimal/equivalent of $(10101.10101)_2$

Taking the integer part

1 0 1 0 1

$1 \times 2^0 = 1$
$0 \times 2^1 = 0$
$1 \times 2^2 = 4$
$0 \times 2^3 = 0$
$1 \times 2^4 = \underline{16}$
21

Fraction $= .10101$

$1 \times 2^{-1} + 0 \times 2^{-2} + 1 \times 2^{-3} + 0 \times 2^{-4} + 1 \times 2^{-5}$

$$\frac{1}{2}+0+\frac{1}{8}+0+\frac{1}{32} = \frac{21}{32} = .65625$$

$\therefore \quad (10101.10101)_2 = (21.65625)_{10}$

3.8.1.3 Binary to Octal (Integer)

A binary number can be converted into its octal equivalent by using two methods:

Method I: For converting a binary number to its octal equivalents, we need to first convert binary number to decimal form and then convert decimal to octal form.

Example Convert 110011101 to octal form.

Converting 110011101 to decimal form by multiplying each binary digit with its position weights.

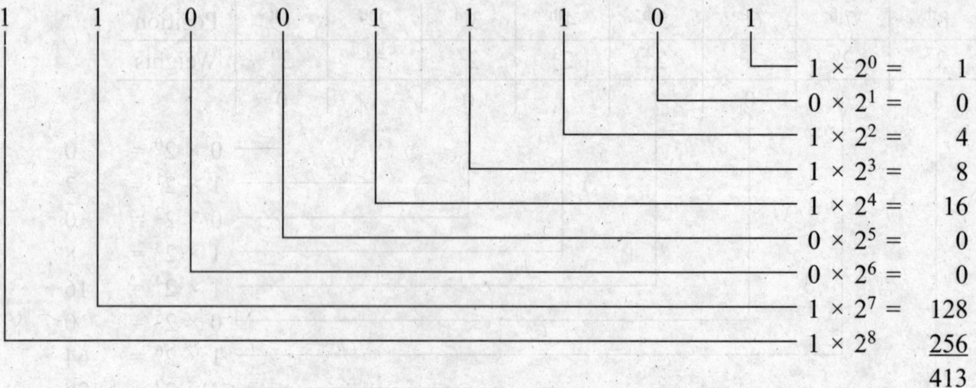

Now converting this decimal to octal form, using Remainder Method.

8	413	
8	51	5
8	6	3
	0	6

$\therefore \quad (110011101)_2 = (413)_{10} = (635)_8$ **Ans.**

Method II: We can also convert the binary number to octal number, by grouping three binary digits to produce a single octal number.

Let us take the same example, The binary number 110 011101 can be represented as:

Binary number (group of three digits)	110	011	101
In exponential form	$2^2\ 2^1\ 2^0$	$2^2\ 2^1\ 2^0$	$2^2\ 2^1\ 2^0$
In decimal form	421	421	421
	$4\times1+2\times1+1\times0=6$	$4\times0+2\times1+1\times1=3$	$4\times1+2\times0+1\times1=5$

$\therefore \quad (110011101)_2 = (635)_8$

3.8.1.4 Binary to Octal (Fraction)

For fraction also, we'll first convert binary number to its decimal equivalent and then convert the resulting decimal number into octal form.

Example Convert 1111111101.111111 into octal form.

Integer = 1111111101. Multiplying each binary digits with its position weights, we get

10th	9th	8th	7th	6th	5th	4th	3rd	2nd	1st	Position
2^9	2^8	2^7	2^6	2^5	2^4	2^3	2^2	2^1	2^0	Weights
1	1	1	1	0	1	1	0	1	0	

$1 \times 2^0 = 1$
$0 \times 2^1 = 0$
$1 \times 2^2 = 4$
$1 \times 2^3 = 8$
$1 \times 2^4 = 16$
$1 \times 2^5 = 32$
$1 \times 2^6 = 64$
$1 \times 2^7 = 128$
$1 \times 2^8 = 256$
$1 \times 2^9 = 512$
1021

Fraction = .111111

$1 \times 2^{-1} + 1 \times 2^{-2} + 1 \times 2^{-3} + 1 \times 2^{-4} + 1 \times 2^{-5} + 1 \times 2^{-6}$

$$\frac{1}{2}+\frac{1}{4}+\frac{1}{8}+\frac{1}{16}+\frac{1}{32}+\frac{1}{64}=\frac{63}{64}=.9843$$

$\therefore \quad (1111111101.111111)_2 = (1021.9843)_{10}$

Now, we can convert this decimal number into octal form.

Integer = 1021

8	1021	
8	127	5
8	15	7
8	1	7
	0	1

$1021_{10} = 1775_8$

Fraction = .9843		**F**	**I**
	.9843 × 8	= 7.8744	7
	.8744 × 8	= 6.9952	6
	.9952 × 8	= 7.9616	7
	.9616 × 8	= 7.6928	7
	.6928 × 8	= 5.5424	5
	.5424 × 8	= 4.3392	4
	.3392 × 8	= 2.7136	2
			⋮

$\therefore \quad (1111111101.111111)_2 = (1021.9843)_{10} = (1775.7677...)_8$

3.8.1.5 *Binary to Hexadecimal (Integer)*

For converting a binary number to hexadecimal form, it should be grouped into fours from the right. An example would make it clear.

Example Convert 11101100111_2 into hexadecimal form.

11101100111

0111, 0110, 0111
↓ ↓ ↓
7 6 7

∴ $(11101100111)_2 = (767)_{16}$

3.8.1.6 *Binary to Hexadecimal (Fraction)*

Example Convert 1101.1111 to hexadecimal form:

Integer = 1101

$1101_2 = 13_{10} = D$

Fraction = .1111

.1111 = .F

∴ $(1101.1111)_2 = (D.F)_{16}$

3.8.2 Conversion of Octal System to Other Systems

3.8.2.1 *Octal to Decimal (Integer)*

For converting octal to decimal, each octal digit should be multiplied by its position weights.

Example Convert 454_8 to decimal form.

3rd	2nd	1st	Position
$8^2 = 64$	$8^1 = 8$	$8^0 = 1$	Weight
4	5	4	

4×8^0 4
5×8^1 40
4×8^2 256
300

∴ $454_8 = 3000_{10}$

3.8.2.2 *Octal to Decimal (Fraction)*

For converting octal fraction into decimal form, we'll follow the same steps as used for converting binary fraction to decimal.

Example Convert $(0.135)_8$ to the decimal system.

Radix = 8 Integer = 0 Fraction =.135

$1 \times 8^{-1} + 3 \times 8^{-2} + 5 \times 8^{-3}$

$= 1/8 + 3/64 + 5/512 = 93/512 = 0.1816406$

$(0.135)_8 = (0.1816406)_{10}$

3.8.2.3 *Octal to Binary (Integer)*

For converting octal to binary form, it should first be converted into decimal and the resulting decimal should be converted to binary.

Example Converting 134_8 to its binary form.

1 3 4

$4 \times 8^0 =$ 4
$3 \times 8^1 =$ 24
$1 \times 8^2 =$ 64
92

$134_8 = 92_{10}$

2	92	
2	46	0
2	23	0
2	11	1
2	5	1
2	2	1
2	1	0
0	1	1

$134_8 = 92_{10} = 1011100_2$

3.8.2.4 Octal to Binary (Fraction)

For converting octal fraction into binary we would first convert it into decimal form and then convert this decimal form into binary form.

Example Convert 3.75_8 to binary systems.

Integer = 3

$3_8 = 3_{10}$

2	3	
2	1	1
	0	1

∴ $3_8 = 3_{10} = 11_2$

Fraction = .75

Converting .75 into decimal form

$7 \times 8^{-1} + 5 \times 8^{2} = 7/8 + 5/64$

$= 61/64 = .953125_{10}$

Now converting $.953125_{10}$ into binary form

Radix = 2

	F	I
.953125 × 2	1.90620	1
.90620 × 2	1.8124	1
.8124 × 2	1.625	1
.625 × 2	1.25	1
.25 × 2	0.50	0
.50 × 2	1.00	1

∴ $(3.75)_8 = (3.953125)_{10}$

$= (11.111101)_2$

3.8.3 Conversion of Hexadecimal System to Other Systems

3.8.3.1 Hexadecimal to Decimal

For converting hexadecimal number to its decimal form, each hexadecimal digit should be multiplied by its position weight as shown below:

Example Convert 1D7F into decimal form.

4th	3rd	2nd	1st	Position
$16^3 = 4096$	$16^2 = 256$	$16^1 = 16$	$16^0 = 1$	Weight
1	D	7	F	

$F \times 16^0 = 15$

$7 \times 16^1 = 112$

$D \times 16^2 = 3328$

$1 \times 16^2 = 4096$

7551

$\therefore \quad 1D7F_{16} = 7551_{10}$

3.8.3.2 Hexadecimal to Binary

A hexadecimal number can be converted to its binary equivalent by using two methods.

Method I: Hexadecimal number, first, should be converted into its decimal equivalent and that decimal number should then be converted into binary form.

Example Converting 2D4AC into decimal form.

Multiplying each hexadecimal digits with its position weights.

2 D 4 A C

$C \times 16^0 = 12$

$A \times 16^1 = 160$

$4 \times 16^2 = 1024$

$D \times 16^3 = 53248$

$2 \times 16^4 = 131072$

185516

$\therefore \quad 2D4AC_{10} = 185516_{10}$

Now, converting this decimal number into binary form by using remainder methods,

2	185516	
2	92758	0
2	46379	0
2	23189	1
2	11594	1
2	5797	0
2	2898	1
2	1449	0
2	724	1
2	362	0
2	181	0
2	90	1
2	45	0
2	22	1

$\therefore 2D4AC_{16} = 185516_{10} = 101101010010101100_2$

2	11	0
2	5	1
2	2	1
2	1	0
2	0	1

This method uses the concept that a hexadecimal digit can be represented by four binary digits.

2	D	4	A	C	Hexadecimal
2	13	4	10	12	Decimal
$2^3\ 2^2\ 2^1\ 2^0$ 8421	$2^3\ 2^2\ 2^1\ 2^0$ 8421	$2^3\ 2^2\ 2^1\ 2^0$ 8421	$2^3\ 2^2\ 2^1\ 2^0$ 8421	$2^3\ 2^2\ 2^1\ 2^0$ 8421	Binary position
0010	1101	0100	1010	1100	Binary Number

$$2D4AC_{16} = 00101101010010101100_2$$

or 101101010010101100_2 which is same as obtained by Method I.

3.9 ARITHMETIC OPERATIONS OF OCTAL NUMBERS

To add two octal numbers, we proceed as we do in the decimal system, keeping in mind, however, that if any addition produces an octal number in excess of 7, we must utilize the next position: $8_{10} = 10_8$, $9_{10} = 11_8$ and so on.

Example 1 $(72)_8 + (25)_8 = (?)_8$

$$\begin{array}{r} 72 \\ +\ 25 \\ \hline 117 \end{array}$$

Ans: $(117)_8$

Example 2 $(337)_8 + (228)_8 = (?)_8$

$$\begin{array}{r} 337 \\ +\ 228 \\ \hline 568 \end{array}$$

Ans: $(567)_8$

We should check out work by connecting each of the octal numbers into the decimal system to determine if, in fact, the addition is correct.

To check, let us take example: –1

$(72)_8$ is equivalent to $(58)_{10}$.

$(25)_8$ is equivalent to $(21)_{10}$.

and total $(117)_8$ is equivalent to $(79)_8$. Hence the addition is correct.

To subtract in the octal numbering system, we may use the complementation and end-around-carry method.

Example 1 $(72)_8 - (25)_8 = (?)_8$

$$\begin{array}{r} 72 \\ -\ 25 \\ \hline \end{array}$$

Step 1: Complement the subtrahend :52

25 + (its complement) = 77

(any no.) + (its complement) = 77

Step 2: Proceed as in addition

$$\begin{array}{r} 72 \\ +\ 52 \\ \hline 144 \end{array}$$

Step 3: End-around carry

$$\begin{array}{r} 144 \\ \rightarrow\ 1 \\ \hline 45 \end{array}$$

Ans: $(45)_8$

Example 2 $(716)_8 - (604)_8 = (?)_8$

$$\begin{array}{r} 716 \\ -\ 604 \\ \hline \end{array}$$

Step 1: Complement the subtrahend :173

604 + (Its complement) = 777

Step 2: Proceed as in addition

$$\begin{array}{r} 716 \\ +\ 173 \\ \hline 1111 \end{array}$$

Step 3: End-around carry

$$\begin{array}{r} 1111 \\ \rightarrow\ 1 \\ \hline 112 \end{array}$$

Ans: $(112)_8$

3.10 ARITHMETIC OPERATIONS OF HEXADECIMAL NUMBERS

Arithmetic operations in hexadecimal are similar to those in other numbering systems. Perform the operation on each column decimally, convert the decimal number to hexadecimal, and proceed.

Example $(BAD)_{16} + (432)_{16}\ (?)_{16}$

$$\begin{array}{ccc} B & A & D \\ 4 & 3 & 2 \\ \hline F & D & F \end{array}$$

11 + 4 = 15 = F

10 + 3 = 13 = D

13 + 2 = 15 = F

Ans: $(FDF)_{16}$

Example $(CAB)_{16} + (627)_{16} = (?)_{16}$

$$\begin{array}{ccc} C & A & B \\ 6 & 2 & 7 \\ \hline 12 & D & 12 \end{array}$$

$12 + 6 = 18_{10} = 12_6$

$11 + 7 = 18_{10} = 12_{16}$ (carry)

Remember: The carrying of hexadecimal numbers to the next position is performed in exactly the same manner as in the decimal numbering system. A sum of 16 results in a carry of $(10_{16} = 16_{10})$.

Example $(74E)_{16} + (F7E)_{16} = (?)_{16}$

```
   74E
 + F7E
  16CC
     └──► 14 + 14 = (28)10 = (1C)16 (Carry 1)
```

Ans: $(16CC)_{16}$

We can subtract hexadecimal numbers by again converting every digit to decimal for each position and then converting the difference obtained back to hexadecimal. Note that the system of borrowing from or exchanging with the next position results in an exchanges of 16 rather that 10.

Example 1 $(26)_{16} - (7)_{16} = (?)_{16}$

```
 26       1   (16 + 6)    (16 borrowed from 2nd position)
 -7  =  –         7
  2               F
```

Ans: $(1F)_{16}$

Example 2 $(28)_{16} - (7)_{16} = (?)_{16}$

```
 28       1   (16 + 8)    (16 borrowed from 2nd position)
 -7  =  –         7
  2               1
                  └──► 24 – 7 = (17)10 = (11)16 (Carry 1)
```

Ans: $(21)_{16}$

3.11 FLOATING POINT NUMBERS

Normalized floating point numbers is also a method of representing data. In this method, a real number is expressed as a combination of a mantissa and exponent.

The mantissa is kept as less than 1 and greater than or equal to 0.1, and the exponent is the power of 10 which multiples the mantissa.

Let us take an example to make it more clear.

94.75×10^5 is represented as 0.9475E7

where E7 is used for 10^7

Here, Mantissa = 0.9475

Exponent = 7

While storing numbers, the leading digit in the mantissa is always made non-zero by approximately shifting it and adjusting the value of the exponent, *i.e.*,

$004642 \rightarrow 0.4642 \times 10^{-2} \rightarrow$ 0.4642E–2

This shifting of the mantissa to the left till its most significant digits is non-zero is called **normalization**. It is done to preserve the maximum number of useful digits.

Let us see how arithmetic operations can be done with normalized floating point numbers.

3.11.1 Addition

For adding two numbers in normalized floating point notation, the exponents of the two numbers must be made equal and the mantissa shifted appropriately.

Example 1 Adding 0.4345E3 to 0.4872E7

Here, exponents of these two numbers are not equal. So, we shift the mantissa of the first operaned 4 places to the right before adding it to the second operated.

0.4872 E7
0.0000 E7
0.4872 E7

Therefore, 0.4345 E3 + 0.48727 = 0.4872 E7

Example 2 Adding 0.6472 E4 to 0.5621 E4

As can be seen, exponents of both numbers are equal. So,

0.6472
0.5621
1.2093

Now, as mantissa has 5 digits and it is greater than 1, mantissa is shifted one place to the right chopping off the last digit, *i.e.*, 3.

Therefore, 0.6472 + 0.5621 = 0.1209.

3.11.2 Subtraction

This process can be treated as addition of one positive number to one negative number.

Example 1 Subtracting 0.5382E-5 from 0.3741E-4

As exponents of numbers are different, we shift the number with smaller exponent to right and increase the exponent by 1 for each right shifts. As 0.5382E-5 has the smaller exponent (in terms of negative values), it becomes.

0.05382E-4

Now subtracting, we get

0.3741E-4
0.0538E-4
0.3203E-4

∴ 0.3741E-4 – 0.5382E-5 = 0.3203E-4

Example 2 Subtracting 0.6565E4 from 0.8854 E4

As in this case, exponents are equals so we subtract the mantissa, *i.e.*,

0.8854E4
0.6565E4
0.2289E4

∴ 0.8854E4 – 0.6565E4 = 0.2289E4

3.11.3 Multiplication

For multiplication of two floating numbers, first their mantissa are multiplied and the exponents are added.

Then the resultant mantissa is normalized and the exponents adjusted accordingly.

Example Multiplying +0.2748E10 with –0.4377E15

+0.2748E10 × –0.4377E15
= –2135196E (10 + (–15))
= –2135196E (10 – 15)
= –2135196E–3

or –2135E–3

∴ +0.2748E10 × (–0.4377E15)
= –2135E–3.

3.11.4 Division

For division of two floating numbers, their mantissa are divided and the exponent of the denominator is subtracted from the numerator exponent. The quotient mantissa is then normalized.

Example Dividing 0.3754E6 by 0.7642E4

$$\frac{0.3754E6}{0.7642E4} = \frac{0.3754E\,(6-4)}{0.7642}$$

$$= \frac{0.3754E2}{0.7642} = 0.4912E2$$

or $$\frac{0.3754E6}{0.7642E4} = 0.4912E2$$

3.12 ENCODING SYSTEMS

Computers must be capable of interpreting more than just numbers. Letters of the alphabets as well as symbols, such as @, #, *, + are used for programming purposes. In fact, any character that is entered into the computer must first be converted into 1s and 0s before it can be used by the computer. To make this conversion, encoding system, which permits alphanumeric characters to be coded in terms of bits using 1 and 0 were developed. The most widely used system are:

1. BCD-Binary Coded Decimal Approach
2. ASCII-American Standard Code for Information Interchange
3. EBCDIC-Extended Binary Coded Decimal Interchange Code

These codes allow the computer to distinguish between a number, letter or symbol. When a computer sees the ASCII bit pattern 1001011, it interprets this pattern as a capital letter 'K', whereas a system using EBCDIC sees the capital letter 'K' as 11010010.

3.12.1 BCD Approach

With BCD, it is possible to convert each decimal number into its binary equivalent rather than convert the entire decimal value into a pure binary form. BCD equivalents of each possible decimal symbol is shown below.

Since 8 and 9 require 4 bits, all decimal digits are represented in BCD by 4 bits. When 4 bits are used, there are only 16 possible configuration (2^4).

As shown in Fig. 3.1, the first 10 of these combinations are used to represent decimal digits. The other six arrangements (1010, 1011, 1100, 1101, 1110, and 1111) have decimal values from 10 to 15.

0	0	0	0	0
1	0	0	0	1
2	0	0	1	0
3	0	0	1	1
4	0	1	0	0
5	0	1	0	1
6	0	1	1	0
7	0	1	1	1
8	1	0	0	0
9	1	0	0	1
	8	4	2	1

Place Value

Fig. 3.1 BCD numeric bit configuration and their decimal equivalents

These arrangements aren't used in BCD coding. That is, 1111 does not represent 15_{10} in BCD. Instead, the proper BCD code for 15_{10} is 0001/0101.

3.12.2 ASCII and EBCDIC

Computer designers first used 6 bits, instead of using 4 bits with only 16 possible characters and then they moved onto 7 or 8 bits to represent characters in alphanumeric versions of BCD.

With 6 bits, its only possible to represent 64 different characters (2^6). Since 64 bit combinations aren't sufficient to provide decimal numbers (10), lowercase letters (26), capital letter (26), and a large number of other characters, designers soon extended the 6 bits BCD code to 7 and 8 bits. With 7 bits, it is possible to provide 128 different arrangements (2^7); and with 8 bits, 256 variations are possible (2^8). In addition to the four numeric place positions, there are three zone bit positions in a 7 bit code and for four zone bit position in an 8 bit code. The 7 bit American Standard Code for Information Interchange is widely used in data communications work and is the code used to represent data internally in personal computers. Figure 3.2 shows the ASCII format and the coding used to represent selected characters.

Character	ASCII
0	011 0000
1	011 0001
2	011 0010
3	011 0011
4	011 0100
5	011 0101
6	011 0110
7	011 0111
A	100 0001
B	100 0010
C	100 0011
D	100 0100
E	100 0101

Fig. 3.2 Bit ASCII format and selected ASCII character codes

Character	EBCDIC	ASCII
0	1111 0000	0101 0000
1	1111 0001	0101 0001
2	1111 0010	0101 0010
3	1111 0011	0101 0011
4	1111 0100	0101 0100
5	1111 0101	0101 0101
6	1111 0110	0101 0110
7	1111 0111	0101 0111
A	1100 0001	1010 0001
B	1100 0010	1010 0010
C	1100 0011	1010 0011
D	1100 0100	1010 0100
E	1100 0101	1010 0101

Fig. 3.3 Selected characters represented by EBCDIC and ASCII-8 bit codes

The 8 bit codes most commonly used are:

(*i*) Extended Binary Coded Decimal Interchange Code (EBCDIC). This is used in IBM mainframe models.

(*ii*) ASCII-8 is an 8 bit version of ASCII that is frequently used in larger machines.

REVIEW QUESTIONS

Multiple Choice Questions

1. Conversion of decimal number 61_{10} to it's binary number equivalent is:
(*a*) 110001_2 (*b*) 111100_2 (*c*) 110011_2 (*d*) 001101_2

2. Conversion of decimal number 61_{10} to it's binary number equivalent is:
(*a*) 110011_2 (*b*) 11001110_2 (*c*) 111101_2 (*d*) 11111_2

3. Conversion of decimal number 71_{10} to it's binary number equivalent is:
(*a*) 110011_2 (*b*) 1110011_2 (*c*) 0110011_2 (*d*) 1000111_2

4. Conversion of decimal number 89_{10} to its binary number equivalent is:
(*a*) 1011011_2 (*b*) 1100111_2 (*c*) 1011001_2 (*d*) 10011_2

5. Conversion of decimal number 99_{10} to it's binary number equivalent is:
(*a*) 1100011_2 (*b*) 100011_2 (*c*) 1110001_2 (*d*) 1111000_2

6. Conversion of decimal number 13_{10} to it's octal number equivalent is:
(*a*) 15_8 (*b*) 17_8 (*c*) 13_8 (*d*) 11_8

7. Conversion of decimal number 28_{10} to it's octal number equivalent is:
(*a*) 32_8 (*b*) 40_8 (*c*) 34_8 (*d*) 36_8

8. Conversion of decimal number 42_{10} to it's octal number equivalent is:
(*a*) 57_8 (*b*) 42_8 (*c*) 47_8 (*d*) 52_8

9. Conversion of decimal number 67_{10} to it's octal number equivalent is:
(*a*) 100_8 (*b*) 103_8 (*c*) 109_8 (*d*) 99_8

10. Conversion of decimal number 99_{10} to it's octal number equivalent is:
(*a*) 121_8 (*b*) 143_8 (*c*) 124_8 (*d*) 119_8

11. Conversion of 1011011_2 to it's decimal equivalent is:
(*a*) 81_{10} (*b*) 91_{10} (*c*) 100_{10} (*d*) 200_{10}

12. Conversion of an octal number 3137_8 to it's decimal equivalent is:
(*a*) 1631_{10} (*b*) 1632_{10} (*c*) 1531_{10} (*d*) 1931_{10}

13. Conversion of an octal number 134_8 to a binary number is:
(*a*) 001011011_2 (*b*) 001101100_2 (*c*) 001011100_2 (*d*) 110011_2

14. Conversion of an octal number 7432_8 to a binary number is:
(*a*) 111100011011_2 (*b*) 111100011010_2 (*c*) 110011010111_2 (*d*) 111111111000_2

15. Conversion of hexadecimal number $1D7F_{16}$ to a decimal number is:
(*a*) 7551_{10} (*b*) 8771_{10} (*c*) 5557_{10} (*d*) 7781_{10}

16. Conversion of hexadecimal number $6B2_{16}$ to it's binary number equivalent is:
(*a*) 111100011011_2 (*b*) 011010110010_2 (*c*) 011001100111_2 (*d*) 1111111_2

17. Conversion of hexadecimal number $93FA_{16}$ to it's binary number equivalent is:
(*a*) 1001001111111010_2 (*b*) 1001001111110111_2
(*c*) 110011111110011_2 (*d*) 111110000111_2

18. Conversion of binary number 1101100011111000_2 to hexadecimal number is:
(*a*) $D8F8_{16}$ (*b*) $A8B9_{16}$ (*c*) 789_{16} (*d*) $D9F8_{16}$

19. Conversion of binary number 101000010111_2 to hexadecimal number is:
(*a*) $D8F9_{16}$ (*b*) $A8B9_{16}$ (*c*) $A17_{16}$ (*d*) $D9F8_{16}$

20. Conversion of binary number 10000000000_2 to decimal number is:
(*a*) 1024_{10} (*b*) 1034_{10} (*c*) 1124_{10} (*d*) 1037_{10}

21. Conversion of binary number 10011_2 to an octal number is:
(*a*) 43_8 (*b*) 47_8 (*c*) 49_8 (*d*) 50_8

22. Conversion of binary number 1100011_2 to an octal number is:
(*a*) 140_8 (*b*) 143_8 (*c*) 147_8 (*d*) 149_8

23. Conversion of binary number 1010000_2 to an octal number is:
(*a*) 119_8 (*b*) 101_8 (*c*) 111_8 (*d*) 120_8

24. Conversion of binary number 11111_2 to an octal number is:
(*a*) 35_8 (*b*) 32_8 (*c*) 37_8 (*d*) 42_8

25. Conversion of binary number 101110_2 to hexadecimal is:
(*a*) 35 (*b*) 46_8 (*c*) 56_8 (*d*) 50_8

26. Conversion of binary number 1100011_2 to hexadecimal is:
(*a*) 63_{16} (*b*) 57_{16} (*c*) 46_{16} (*d*) 40_{16}

27. Conversion of binary number 1100001_2 to hexadecimal is:
(*a*) 57_{16} (*b*) 61_{16} (*c*) 51_{16} (*d*) 43_{16}

28. Conversion of binary number 1001001_2 to hexadecimal is:
(*a*) 40_{16} (*b*) 39_{16} (*c*) 49_{16} (*d*) 42_{16}

29. Conversion of binary number 110000_2 to hexadecimal is:
(*a*) 30_{16} (*b*) 40_{16} (*c*) 43_{16} (*d*) 27_{16}

30. Conversion of binary number 101101_2 to hexadecimal is:
(*a*) 37_{16} (*b*) $2D_{16}$ (*c*) $2E_{16}$ (*d*) 27_{16}

31. Conversion of decimal number 99_{10} to hexadecimal number is:
(*a*) 63_{16} (*b*) 8_{16} (*c*) 61_{16} (*d*) 50_{16}

32. Conversion of decimal number 93_{10} to hexadecimal number is:
(*a*) $2D_{16}$ (*b*) $5D_{16}$ (*c*) 62_{16} (*d*) 31_{16}

33. Conversion of decimal number 81_{10} to hexadecimal number is:
(*a*) $2D_{16}$ (*b*) 51_{16} (*c*) 41_{16} (*d*) 61_{16}

34. Conversion of decimal number 74_{10} to hexadecimal number is:
(*a*) $4A_{16}$ (*b*) $5A_{16}$ (*c*) 41_{16} (*d*) $2D_{16}$

35. Conversion of decimal number 15_{10} to hexadecimal number is:
(*a*) 14_{16} (*b*) 13_{16} (*c*) $0F_{16}$ (*d*) $7F_{16}$

36. Conversion of binary number 11001_2 to its decimal number is:
(*a*) 27_{10} (*b*) 49_{10} (*c*) 39_{10} (*d*) 50_{10}

37. Conversion of binary number 1100011_2 to its decimal number is:
(*a*) 29_{10} (*b*) 97_{10} (*c*) 99_{10} (*d*) 93_{10}

38. Conversion of binary number 1001010_2 to its decimal number is:
(*a*) 74_{10} (*b*) 97_{10} (*c*) 72_{10} (*d*) 63_{10}

39. Conversion of binary number 101101_2 to its decimal number is:
(*a*) 45_{10} (*b*) 43_{10} (*c*) 40_{10} (*d*) 47_{10}

40. Conversion of binary number 1000000 to its decimal number is:
(*a*) 54_{10} (*b*) 57_{10} (*c*) 64_{10} (*d*) 59_{10}

41. Conversion of an octal number 47_8 to its binary number is:
(*a*) 110011_2 (*b*) 100111_2 (*c*) 110011_2 (*d*) 1111011_2

42. Conversion of an octal number 60_8 to binary number is:
(*a*) 110000_2 (*b*) 10011_2 (*c*) 1100111_2 (*d*) 1100110_2

43. Conversion of an octal number 73_8 to binary number is:
(*a*) 110111_2 (*b*) 111100_2 (*c*) 110010_2 (*d*) 111011_2

44. Conversion of an octal number 106_8 to binary number is:
(*a*) 1110010_2 (*b*) 1000110_2 (*c*) 1100110_2 (*d*) 10000110_2

45. Conversion of an octal number 142_8 to binary number is:
(*a*) 1100010_2 (*b*) 110110_2 (*c*) 1100011_2 (*d*) 1101101_2

46. Conversion of a hexadecimal number 63_{16} to binary number is:
(*a*) 1100111_2 (*b*) 1100011_2 (*c*) 111011_2 (*d*) 1100111_2

47. Conversion of a hexadecimal number $4E_{16}$ to binary number is:
(*a*) 1001101_2 (*b*) 1001110_2 (*c*) 1101100_2 (*d*) 110111_2

48. Conversion of a hexadecimal number $3D_{16}$ to binary number is:
(*a*) 111101_2 (*b*) 110011_2 (*c*) 11000110_2 (*d*) 110001_2

49. Conversion of a hexadecimal number $3A_{16}$ to binary number is:
(*a*) 1101101_2 (*b*) 111010_2 (*c*) 100110_2 (*d*) 110011_2

50. Conversion of a hexadecimal number 31_{16} to binary number is:
(*a*) 101010_2 (*b*) 110101_2 (*c*) 110001_2 (*d*) 100101_2

51. Conversion of a octal number 63_8 to its decimal number is:
(*a*) 51_{10} (*b*) 61_{10} (*c*) 57_{10} (*d*) 53_{10}

52. Conversion of an octal number 143_8 to its decimal number is:
(*a*) 90_{10} (*b*) 971_{10} (*c*) 99_{10} (*d*) 107_{10}

53. Conversion of an octal number 125_8 to its decimal number is:
(*a*) 90_{10} (*b*) 85_{10} (*c*) 87_{10} (*d*) 99_{10}

54. Conversion of an octal number 40_8 to its decimal number is:
(*a*) 32_{10} (*b*) 29_{10} (*c*) 39_{10} (*d*) 49_{10}

55. Conversion of an octal number 110_8 to its decimal number is:
(*a*) 70_{10} (*b*) 72_{10} (*c*) 73_{10} (*d*) 110_{10}

56. Conversion of an octal number 143_8 to hexadecimal number is:
(*a*) 63_{16} (*b*) 60_{16} (*c*) 50_{16} (*d*) 57_{16}

57. Conversion of an octal number 136_8 to hexadecimal number is:
(*a*) $7E_{16}$ (*b*) $5E_{16}$ (*c*) $5A_{16}$ (*d*) $5D_{16}$

58. Conversion of an octal number 112_8 to hexadecimal number is:
(*a*) $4A_{16}$ (*b*) $5A_{16}$ (*c*) 15_{16} (*d*) 20_{16}

59. Conversion of an octal number 56_8 hexadecimal number is:
(*a*) $2A_{16}$ (*b*) $3A_{16}$ (*c*) $2E_{16}$ (*d*) F_{16}

60. Conversion of an octal number 20_8 to its binary number is:
(*a*) 10000_{10} (*b*) 10111_{10} (*c*) 10110_{16} (*d*) 11110_{16}

61. Addition of 110101_2 and 101111_2 is:
(*a*) 1100100_2 (*b*) 1101000_2 (*c*) 1110111_2 (*d*) 110011_2

62. Addition of 110101101_2, 111011101_2, 000111111_2, 1001011012, 111110111_2 is:
(*a*) 1011010111010_2 (*b*) 1111011000010_2
(*c*) 1000101000101_2 (*d*) 01001000000010_2

63. Subtraction of 100101100_2 from 1110101010_2 is:
(*a*) 1001011110_2 (*b*) 0110100001_2
(*c*) 1111000001_2 (*d*) 1111011111_2

64. Multiplication of 111_2 by 101_2 is:
(*a*) 110011_2 (*b*) 100011_2 (*c*) 1111002 (*d*) 000101_2

65. Division of 1000112 by 101_2 is:
(*a*) 100_2 (*b*) 111_2 (*c*) 101_2 (*d*) 1010_2

66. Multiplication of 478 by 52_8 is:
(*a*) $(3144)_8$ (*b*) $(4147)_8$ (*c*) $(3146)_8$ (*d*) $(3184)_8$

67. Addition of 102 and 11_2 is:
(*a*) 100_2 (*b*) 101_2 (*c*) 111_2 (*d*) 110_2

68. Addition of 1101_2 and 10102 is:
(*a*) 10111_2 (*b*) 11000_2 (*c*) 11011_2 (*d*) 10111_2

ANSWERS

Multiple Choice Questions

1. (*a*)	**2.** (*c*)	**3.** (*d*)	**4.** (*c*)	**5.** (*a*)	**6.** (*a*)	**7.** (*c*)	**8.** (*d*)
9. (*b*)	**10.** (*b*)	**11.** (*b*)	**12.** (*a*)	**13.** (*c*)	**14.** (*b*)	**15.** (*a*)	**16.** (*b*)
17. (*a*)	**18.** (*d*)	**19.** (*c*)	**20.** (*a*)	**21.** (*a*)	**22.** (*b*)	**23.** (*d*)	**24.** (*c*)
25. (*c*)	**26.** (*a*)	**27.** (*b*)	**28.** (*c*)	**29.** (*a*)	**30.** (*b*)	**31.** (*a*)	**32.** (*b*)
33. (*b*)	**34.** (*a*)	**35.** (*c*)	**36.** (*b*)	**37.** (*c*)	**38.** (*a*)	**39.** (*a*)	**40.** (*c*)
41. (*b*)	**42.** (*a*)	**43.** (*d*)	**44.** (*b*)	**45.** (*a*)	**46.** (*b*)	**47.** (*b*)	**48.** (*a*)
49. (*b*)	**50.** (*c*)	**51.** (*a*)	**52.** (*c*)	**53.** (*b*)	**54.** (*a*)	**55.** (*b*)	**56.** (*a*)
57. (*b*)	**58.** (*b*)	**59.** (*c*)	**60.** (*a*)	**61.** (*a*)	**62.** (*a*)	**63.** (*a*)	**64.** (*b*)
65. (*b*)	**66.** (*c*)	**67.** (*b*)	**68.** (*b*)				

QUESTIONS

1. Define Radix/base of a number system. What is the radix for binary, octal, decimal and hexadecimal number systems?

2. Assuming an arbitrary number system of Radix-3, write down the first ten numbers in this system.

3. Why is the binary number system used for computers?

4. Add the following binary numbers:
(*i*) 011,0111 (*ii*) 1100,101

5. Convert the following binary number to decimal and octal forms:
(*i*) 11011010 (*ii*) 10010011001 (*iii*) 111100111 (*iv*) 101010101
(*v*) 100100101001 (*vi*) 101100110

6. Convert the following hexadecimal numbers to binary form:
(*i*) 2335C (*ii*) 4A467 (*iii*) B5637 (*iv*) B76CA2
(*v*) 363A13 (*vi*) 872DA5

7. Find the decimal equivalents the following octal numbers:
(*i*) 6607 (*ii*) 7576

8. Find the decimal equivalents of the following hexadecimal numbers:
(*i*) 86 (*ii*) 9FC

9. Describe the different coding techniques in computer arithmetic that are available.

10. Find the binary form of the following decimal numbers:
(*i*) 45 (*ii*) 57 (*iii*) 5 (*iv*) 14

11. Find the EBCDIC code for the following:
(*a*) 7 (*b*) Q (*c*) F (*d*) V

12. Find the BCD code for the following:
(*a*) 7 (*b*) Q (*c*) F (*d*) V

13. Determine the decimal equivalents of the following binary numbers:
(*a*) 1001111 (*b*) 11100 (*c*) 110011

14. Determine the decimal equivalents of the following hexadecimal numbers:
(*a*) 6FFE (*b*) 70FD (*c*) 67EE

BOOLEAN ALGEBRA AND LOGIC CIRCUITS

A computer, as we know, is an electrical device or machine which processes information. It uses very primitive ideas such as that wire may at one time be carrying a current and at another time may not. These two states of the wire can be called hot (high) (1) and cold (low) (0) respectively. **Boole** invented two-state algebra to solve logic problems. This new algebra had no practical use until Shannon-applied it to telephone switching circuits. Today boolean algebra is the backbone of computer circuits analysis and design. It is this basic fact that two easily identifiable electrical states exist, which has been exploited to represent information in forms 'understandable' by electrical machines.

The language for computer is based on 1 (high) and 0 (low) values, rather than on decimal symbols or alphabet.

For example, if alternate hot (high) and cold (low) values are introduced to a wire by turning the current on and off, the wire's experiences may be recorded as:

1 0 1 0 1 0 1 0

Here, 1 means hot or high

0 means cold or low

Such sequences ensure the beginning of a language that can be understood by both man and machine.

The **gate** is a circuit with one or more input signals but only one output signal: Gates are digital circuits because the input and output signals are either low or high voltages. Gates are often called **logic circuits** because it can be analyzed with boolean algebra.

It is very helpful to know the first 16 binary numbers. If 0 = Low (L) and 1 = High (H), they are:

Table 4.1

Decimal Number	*Binary Number*
0	L L L L
1	L L L H
2	L L H L
3	L L H H
4	L H L L
5	L H L H
6	L H H L
7	L H H H

Decimal Number	*Binary Number*
8	H L L L
9	H L L H
10	H L H L
11	H L H H
12	H H L L
13	H H L H
14	H H H L
15	H H H H

Note that LLLL(0) is as much a number as any other number.

4.1 INVERTERS (NOT GATES)

An **inverter** (NOT Gate) has one input contact and one output contact. The two contacts always have opposite values. The name NOT is inspired by the fact that the output is hot precisely when the input is not, and vice-versa.

Table 4.2 shows that a low input produces a high output, and a high input results a low output. Similarly, you can interpret same information in binary form also.

Table 4.2

IN	*OUT*
Low(0)	High(1)
High(1)	Low(0)

Figure 4.1 is the symbol for an inverter of any design. Figure 4.2 is the symbol for a non-inverting amplifier. Regardless of the circuit design, the action is always same: a low input voltage produces a low output voltage, and a high output voltage results a high output voltage.

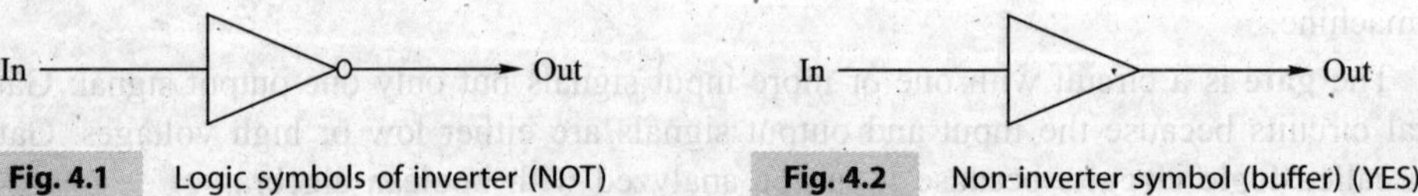

Fig. 4.1 Logic symbols of inverter (NOT) **Fig. 4.2** Non-inverter symbol (buffer) (YES)

Table 4.3

IN	*OUT*
Low	Low
High	High

If you cascade two inverters serially as shown in Fig. 4.3, you get a non-inverter amplifier. The main use of non-inverter amplifier is buffering (isolating) two other circuits.

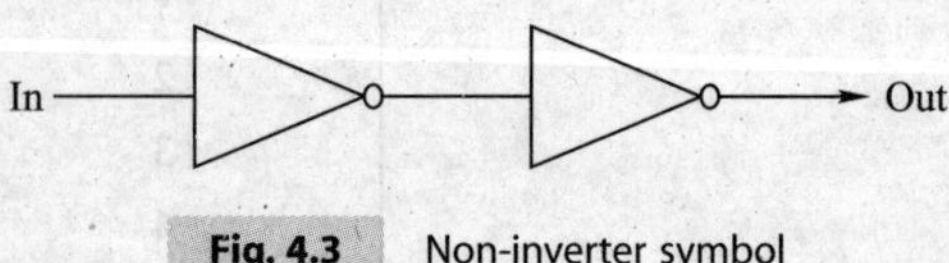

Fig. 4.3 Non-inverter symbol

Note that whenever you see either of these symbols, the output is the complement of the input.

4.2 OR GATES

An OR Gate is a very simple and useful electrical device. It receives input information at two contacts and presents output information at one contact. Its function can be described by stating that the output is low only when both input are low.

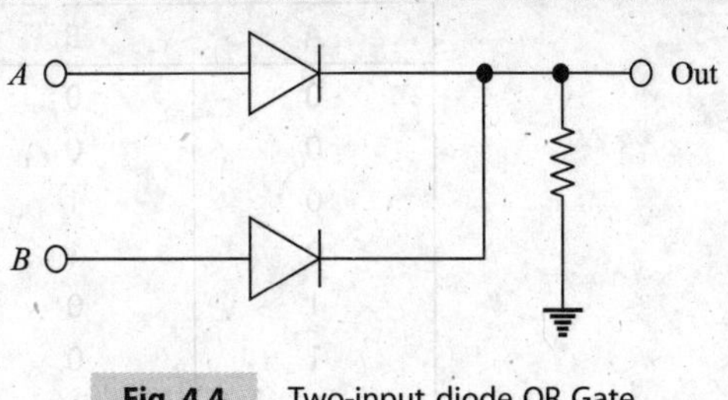

Fig. 4.4 Two-input diode OR Gate

Figure 4.4 shows one way to build an OR Gate. If both input are high, the output is high. If either input is high, the diode with the high conducts and the output is high. If inputs are low, the output is low.

Table 4.4 Two-input OR Gate

A	*B*	*OUT*
0	0	0
0	1	1
1	0	1
1	1	1

The binary 0 stands for low voltage and binary 1 for high voltage. Notice that one or more high inputs produce a high output; this is why the circuit is called an OR Gate.

4.2.1 Truth Table

A table that shows all the input-output possibilities of a logic circuit is called a **truth table**. Table 4.4 is the truth table for an OR Gate.

4.2.2 More than Two Inputs

Figure 4.5 shows a three input OR Gate. The inputs are *A*, *B*, and *C*. When all inputs are low, all diodes are off and the output is low. If *A* or *B* or *C* is high, *Y* will be high because the diode connected to the high input will turn on. Table 4.5 summarises all input possibilities of three input OR Gate. Table 4.6 shows the binary equivalent of Table 4.5.

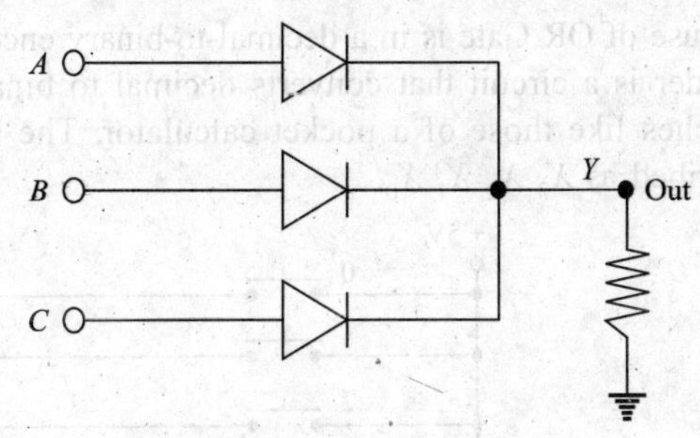

Fig. 4.5 Three-input OR Gate

Table 4.5 Three-input OR Gate

A	*B*	*C*	*OUT*
Low	Low	Low	Low
Low	Low	High	High
Low	High	Low	High
Low	High	High	High
High	Low	Low	High
High	Low	High	High
High	High	Low	High
High	High	High	High

Table 4.6 Three-input OR Gate binary equivalent

A	*B*	*C*	*OUT*
0	0	0	0
0	0	1	1
0	1	0	1
0	1	1	1
1	0	0	1
1	0	1	1
1	1	0	1
1	1	1	1

The number of row in a truth table equal 2^n, where *n* is the number of inputs. For a 2-input OR Gate, the truth table has 2^2, or 4 rows. A 3-input OR Gate has a truth table with 2^3, or 8 rows, while a 4-input OR Gate results in 2^4, or 16 rows, and so on.

An OR Gate can have as many inputs as needed; add one diode for each additional input. Five diodes result in a five-input OR Gate, seven diodes result in a seven-input OR Gate. No matter how many inputs, the action of any OR Gate is same, *i.e.* (one or more high inputs produce a high output). Figure 4.6 shows the logic symbols for two, three, and four-input OR Gates.

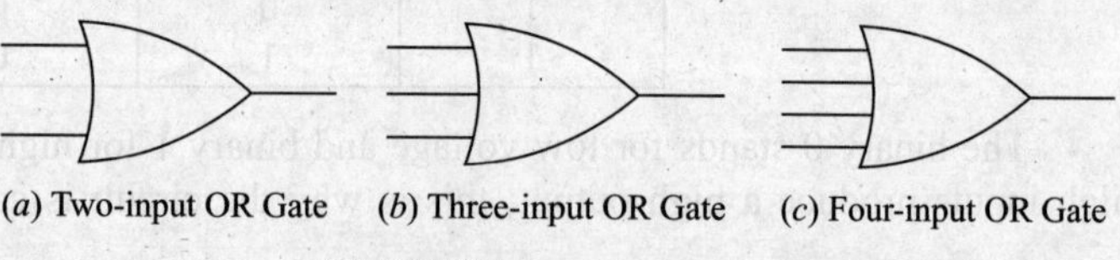

Fig. 4.6 OR Gate symbols

4.2.3 Example of OR Gate

One use of OR Gate is in a decimal-to-binary encoder as shown in Fig. 4.7. A decimal-to-binary encoder is a circuit that converts decimal to binary. The switches of Fig. 4.7 are push button switches like those of a pocket calculator. The bits out of the OR Gates form a 4 bit word, described as $X_3\ X_2\ X_1\ X_0$.

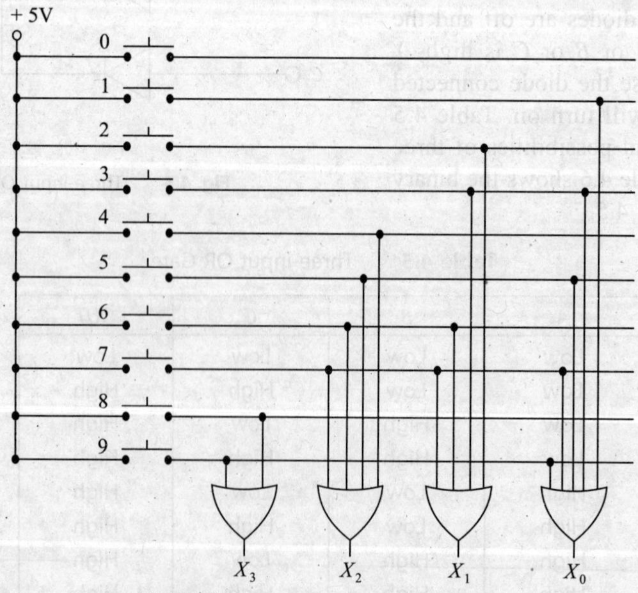

Fig. 4.7 Decimal-to-binary encoder

For instance, if you press 9 push button, then X_3 and X_0 OR Gates have high inputs:

$$X_3\ X_2\ X_1\ X_0 = 1001$$

If you press 7, then X_2, X_1 and X_0 OR Gates have high inputs:

$$X_3\ X_2\ X_1\ X_0 = 0111$$

Similarly, you can check the other push button (input switches) to see the binary equivalent.

4.3 AND GATES

The AND Gate is also simple and useful electrical device. If also receives input information at two contacts and presents output information at one contact. In AND Gate, the output will be high(hot) only when both inputs are high(hot).

Figure 4.8 shows one way to build an AND Gate. With both input voltages low, the cathode of each diode is grounded (low). If one of the inputs is low and the other high, the diode with the low input conducts and this pulls the output down to a low voltage. When both inputs are high, both diodes are nonconducting because the voltage across each is zero. Since the diodes are off, there is no current, and the output is pulled up to the high voltage.

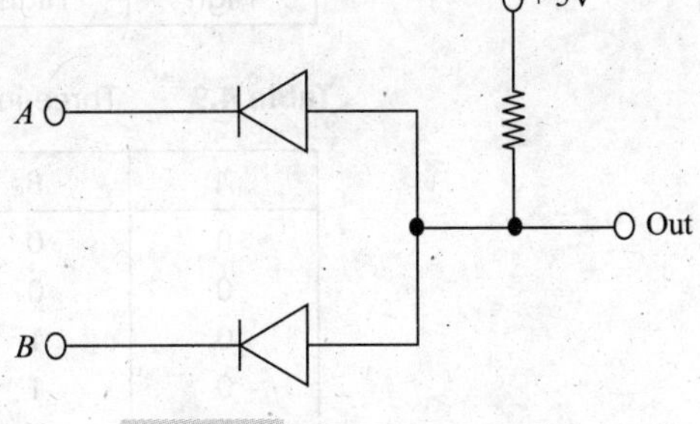

Fig. 4.8 Two-input AND Gate

4.3.1 Truth Table

Table 4.7 shows all the input-output possibilities of two-input AND Gates. Note that the AND Gate has a high output only when both input are high. In other words, the AND Gate is an all-or-nothing Gate; a high output occurs only when all inputs are high.

Table 4.7 Two-input AND Gate

A	*B*	*OUT*
Low (0)	Low (0)	Low (0)
Low (0)	High (1)	Low (0)
High (1)	Low (0)	Low (0)
High (1)	High (1)	High (1)

The AND Gate is named so because of the fact that a high(1) output occurs only when A and B both input contacts are high(1).

4.3.2 More than Two Inputs

Figure 4.9 shows a three input AND Gate. The inputs are *A*, *B*, and *C*, when all inputs are high, all diodes are nonconducting and the supply voltage pulls the output up to a high voltage. If all inputs are low, all diodes conduct and pull the output down to a low voltage. Even one conducting diode will pull the output down to a low voltage. Table 4.8 summarizes all input-out possibilities. Table 4.9 gives the same truth table in binary code.

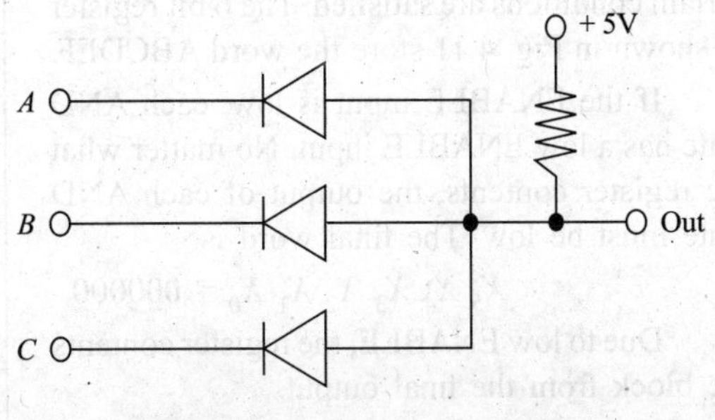

Fig. 4.9 Three-input AND Gate

Table 4.8 Three-input AND Gate

A	*B*	*C*	*OUT*
Low	Low	Low	Low
Low	Low	High	Low
Low	High	Low	Low
Low	High	High	Low
High	Low	Low	Low
High	Low	High	Low
High	High	Low	Low
High	High	High	High

Table 4.9 Three-input AND Gate binary equivalent

A	*B*	*C*	*OUT*
0	0	0	0
0	0	1	0
0	1	0	0
0	1	1	0
1	0	0	0
1	0	1	0
1	1	0	0
1	1	1	1

An AND Gate can have as many inputs as needed; add one diode for each additional input. Five diodes result in a five-input AND Gate. Seven diode result in a seven-input AND Gate. No matter how many inputs an AND Gate has, the action is same, *i.e.*, all inputs must be high to get a high output. Figure 4.10 shows the logic symbols of two, three and four-input AND Gates.

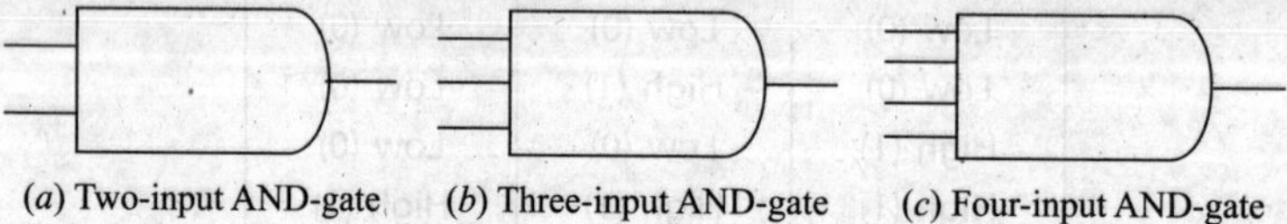
(*a*) Two-input AND-gate (*b*) Three-input AND-gate (*c*) Four-input AND-gate

Fig. 4.10 AND Gate symbols

4.3.3 Example of AND Gate

One use of AND Gates is to transmit data when certain conditions are satisfied. The 6 bit register as shown in Fig. 4.11 store the word ABCDEF.

If the ENABLE input is low, each AND Gate has a low ENABLE input. No matter what the register contents, the output of each AND Gate must be low. The final word is

$$X_5\ X_4\ X_3\ X_2\ X_1\ X_0 = 000000$$

Due to low ENABLE, the register contents are block from the final output.

If the ENABLE input is high, the output of each AND Gate depends on the data inputs;

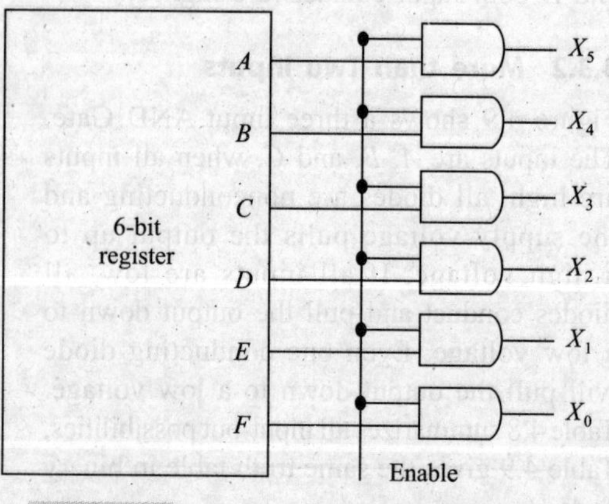

Fig. 4.11 Using AND Gate for transmit data

a low data input results in a low output, and a high data input in a high output. For instance, if $ABCDEF$ = 110010, a high ENABLE gives $X_5\ X_4\ X_3\ X_2\ X_1\ X_0$ = 110010.

Note that a high ENABLE transmits the register contents to the final output to get

$$X_5\ X_4\ X_3\ X_2\ X_1\ X_0 = ABCDEF$$

4.4 NOR GATES

A NOR Gate combines the Gates of OR and NOT as shown in Fig. 4.12—originally called a NOT-OR Gate. Note that in Fig. 4.12 (*b*), the inverter triangle has been deleted and the small circle or bubble moved to the OR-Gate output. The bubble is a reminder of the inversion.

If both inputs are low, the final output is high. If one input is low and other high, the output is low. And if both inputs are high, the output is low. Table 4.10 summarizes the circuit action of the two-input NOR Gate. Table 4.11 summarizes the circuit action of three-input NOR Gate.

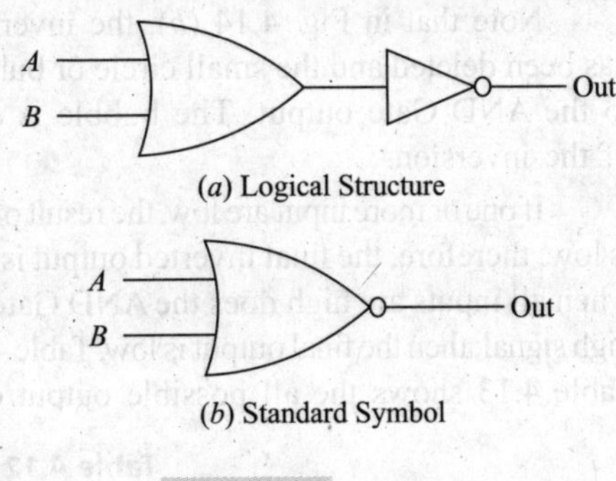

Fig. 4.12 NOR Gate

Table 4.10 Two-input NOR Gate

A	*B*	*OUT*
0	0	1
0	1	0
1	0	0
1	1	0

Figure 4.13 shows the logic symbols of two, three and four-input NOR Gates. The NOR Gate can have as many inputs as needed. No matter how many inputs NOR Gate has, the action is same, *i.e.*, all inputs must be low to get a high output.

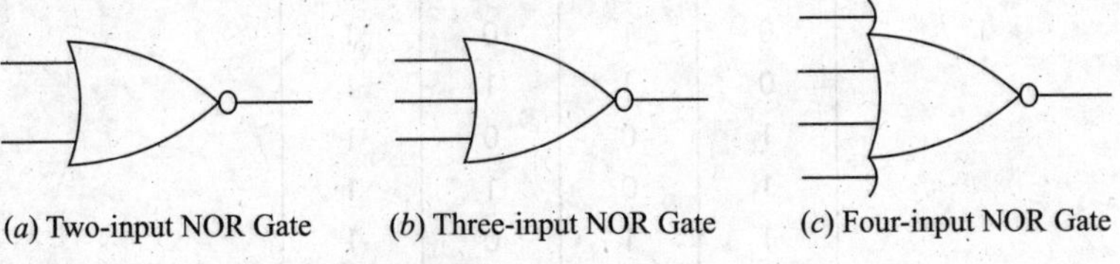

(*a*) Two-input NOR Gate (*b*) Three-input NOR Gate (*c*) Four-input NOR Gate

Fig. 4.13 NOR Gate symbols

Table 4.11 Three-input NOR Gate

A	*B*	*C*	*OUT*
0	0	0	1
0	0	1	0
0	1	0	0
0	1	1	0
1	0	0	0
1	0	1	0
1	1	0	0
1	1	1	0

4.5 NAND GATES

A NAND Gate combines the Gate of AND and NOT as shown in Fig. 4.14—originally called a NOT-AND Gate. The NAND Gate has two or more input signals but only one output signal. All input signals must be high to get a low output.

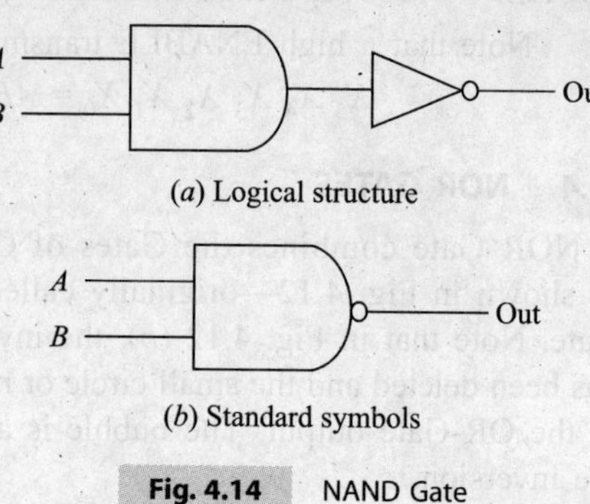

(*a*) Logical structure

(*b*) Standard symbols

Fig. 4.14 NAND Gate

Note that in Fig. 4.14 (*b*), the inverter triangle has been deleted and the small circle or bubble moved to the AND Gate output. The bubble is a reminder of the inversion.

If one or more input are low, the result of AND Gate is low; therefore, the final inverted output is high. Only when all inputs are high does the AND Gate produce a high signal; then the final output is low. Table 4.12 shows the all possible output of two-input NAND Gate. Table 4.13 shows the all possible output of three-input NAND Gate.

Table 4.12 Two-input NAND Gate

A	*B*	*OUT*
0	0	1
0	1	1
1	0	1
1	1	0

Table 4.13 Three input NAND Gate

A	*B*	*C*	*OUT*
0	0	0	1
0	0	1	1
0	1	0	1
0	1	1	1
1	0	0	1
1	0	1	1
1	1	0	1
1	1	1	0

Figure 4.15 shows the logic symbols of two, three and four-input NAND Gates. The NAND Gate can have as many inputs as needed. No matter how many inputs NAND Gate has, the action is same, *i.e.*, one or more inputs produce a high output.

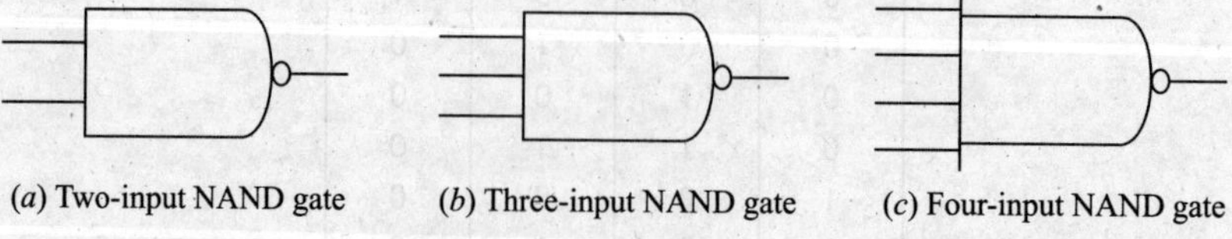
(*a*) Two-input NAND gate (*b*) Three-input NAND gate (*c*) Four-input NAND gate

Fig. 4.15 NAND Gate symbols

There are other two Gates, EXCLUSIVE-OR and EXCLUSIVE-NOR, which will be discussed later in the next chapter because boolean algebra is the backbone of computer circuit analysis and design.

4.6 MULTIPLEXERS

Multiplex means 'may into one'. A multiplexer is a circuit with many inputs but only one output. We can steer any input to the output.

Figure 4.16 (*a*) shows a 16-to-1 multiplexer, which also called a data selector because the output bit depends on the input data bit that is selected. The input bits are labeled D_0 to D_{15}. Only one of these is transmitted to the output—which one depends on the value of *ABCD*, the control unit. Figure 4.16 (*b*) illustrates the general idea.

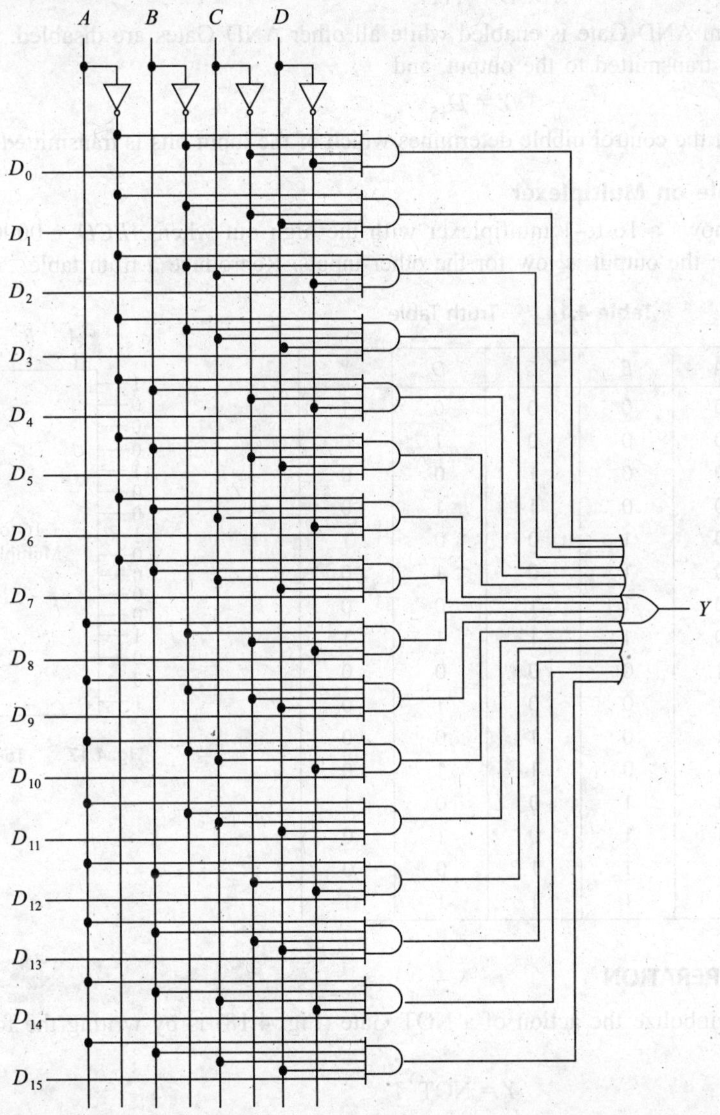

Fig. 4.16 (*a*) Sixteen-to-one multiplexer

For instance, when $ABCD = 0000$ then D_0 is transmitted to the output,

$$Y = D_0$$

Because inverter produce the value of $ABCD = 1111$ and AND Gate produce output high when all the input are high. S_0, $Y = D_0$

If $D_0 = 0$, then $Y = 0$

If $D_0 = 1$, then $Y = 1$.

Therefore, Y depends only on the value of D_0.

If the control nibbles is changed to

$$ABCD = 1111$$

m control signals

n-input signals

10 output signals

Fig. 4.16 (b) Multiplexer

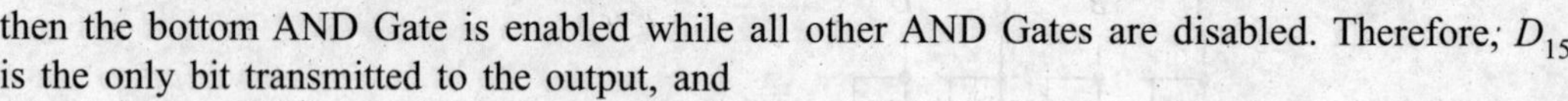

then the bottom AND Gate is enabled while all other AND Gates are disabled. Therefore, D_{15} is the only bit transmitted to the output, and

$$Y = D_{15}$$

☞ Note that the control nibble determines which of the input bits is transmitted to the output.

4.6.1 Example on Multiplexer

Figure 4.17 shows a 16-to-1 multiplexer with the high out when $ABCD = 0000$, 0100, 0111, 1100 and 1111; the output is low for the other inputs. Reproduce a truth table.

Table 4.14 Truth Table

A	B	C	D	Y
0	0	0	0	1
0	0	0	1	0
0	0	1	0	0
0	0	1	1	0
0	1	0	0	1
0	1	0	1	0
0	1	1	0	0
0	1	1	1	1
1	0	0	0	0
1	0	0	1	0
1	0	1	0	0
1	0	1	1	0
1	1	0	0	1
1	1	0	1	0
1	1	1	0	0
1	1	1	1	1

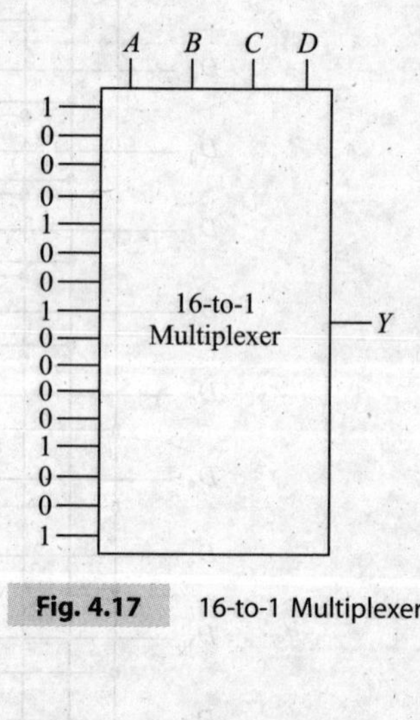

Fig. 4.17 16-to-1 Multiplexer

4.7 NOT OPERATION

One way to symbolize the action of a NOT Gate (Fig. 4.18) is by writing the following word equation:

$$Y = \text{NOT } A \qquad ...(4.1)$$

If $A = 0$, $Y = \text{NOT } 0 = 1$

If $A = 1$, $Y = \text{NOT } 1 = 0$

In boolean algebra, the overbar stands for the NOT operation, and Equation (4.1) can be written as

$$Y = \overline{A} \quad ...(4.2)$$

You can read this equation as 'Y equals the complement of A' or 'Y equals NOT A'.

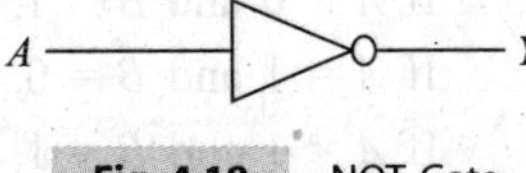

Fig. 4.18 NOT Gate

In boolean algebra, a variable can be either 1 or 0 and this means high or low in digital circuit.

If we use Equation (4.2) and substitute $A = 0$,

$$Y = \overline{A} \Rightarrow Y = \overline{0} \Rightarrow Y = 1$$

Similarly, if we substitute $A = 1$ in NOT equation,

$$Y = \overline{1} \Rightarrow Y = 0$$

because NOT 1 is 0.

4.8 OR OPERATION

One way to symbolize the OR Gate (Fig. 4.19) is by writing the following word equation:

$$Y = A \text{ OR } B \quad ...(4.3)$$

For instance, if we put $A = 0$ and $B = 0$ in Equation (4.3), we get

$$Y = A \text{ OR } B = 0 \text{ OR } 0 = 0$$

In OR Gate, if both the inputs are 0s, then output is 0,

If $A = 0$ and $B = 1$, $\quad Y = A \text{ OR } B = 0 \text{ OR } 1 = 1$

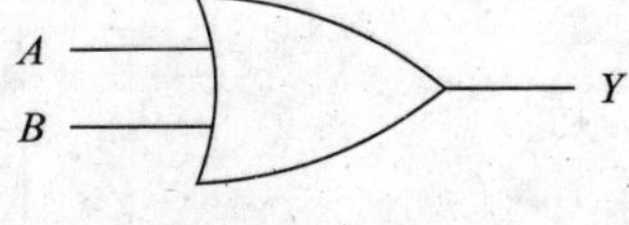

Fig. 4.19 OR Gate

In OR Gate, 1 is the output when either input is 1. Similarly, if $A = 1$ and $B = 0$,

$$Y = A \text{ OR } B = 1 \text{ OR } 0 = 1$$

If $A = 1$ and $B = 1$, $\quad Y = A \text{ OR } B = 1 \text{ OR } 1 = 1$

Because 1 is the output of an OR Gate when both inputs are 1s.

In the boolean algebra, the + sign stands for the OR Operation. Equation (4.3) can be written in boolean form as:

$$Y = A + B \quad ...(4.4)$$

Read this equation as 'Y equals A or B'.

If $A = 0$ and $B = 0$, $\quad Y = A + B = 0 + 0 = 0$

If $A = 0$ and $B = 1$, $\quad Y = A + B = 0 + 1 = 1$

If $A = 1$ and $B = 0$, $\quad Y = A + B = 1 + 0 = 1$

If $A = 1$ and $B = 1$, $\quad Y = A + B = 1 + 1 = 1$

Because OR Gate produces 1 if both input are 1s.

The last result $1 + 1 = 1$ may confuse you, but in boolean algebra the + sign represents OR addition, the action of an OR Gate combining the inputs.

Note that in decimal addition: $1 + 1 = 2$ and OR addition: $1 + 1 = 1$.

4.9 AND OPERATION

One way to symbolize the AND Gate (Fig. 4.20) is by writing the following word equation:

$$Y = A \text{ AND } B \quad ...(4.5)$$

In boolean algebra, the multiplication sign stands for the AND Operation. So, Equation (4.5) can be written as

$$Y = A \cdot B \text{ or } Y = AB \qquad ...(4.6)$$

Read this as 'Y equals A and B'.

If $A = 0$ and $B = 0$, $Y = AB = 0{\cdot}0 = 0$

If $A = 0$ and $B = 1$, $Y = AB = 0{\cdot}1 = 0$

If $A = 1$ and $B = 0$, $Y = AB = 1{\cdot}0 = 0$

If $A = 1$ and $B = 1$, $Y = AB = 1{\cdot}1 = 1$

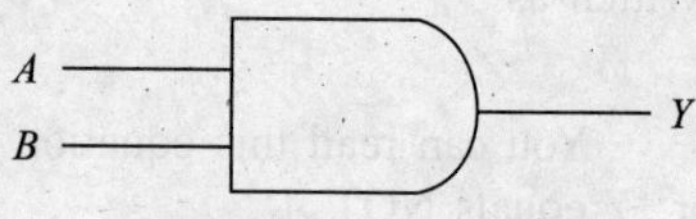

Fig. 4.20 AND Gate

4.10 NOR OPERATION

The boolean equation for a two-input NOR Gate is:

$$Y = \overline{A + B}$$

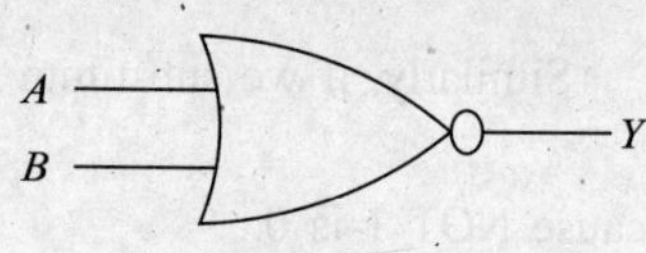

Fig. 4.21 NOR Gate

Read this as 'Y equals NOT A OR B'.

If $A = 0$ and $B = 0$, $Y = \overline{A + B} = \overline{0 + 0} = \overline{0} = 1$

If $A = 0$ and $B = 1$, $Y = \overline{A + B} = \overline{0 + 1} = \overline{1} = 0$

If $A = 1$ and $B = 0$, $Y = \overline{A + B} = \overline{1 + 0} = \overline{1} = 0$

If $A = 1$ and $B = 1$, $Y = \overline{A + B} = \overline{1 + 1} = \overline{1} = 0$

Because the circuit is an OR Gate followed by an inverter, the only way to get a high output is to have both inputs low, as shown in the truth table of Table 4.15.

Table 4.15 Two-input NOR Gate

A	B	$\overline{A + B}$
0	0	1
0	1	0
1	0	0
1	1	0

The boolean equation for three-input NOR Gate is;

$$Y = \overline{A + B + C} \qquad ...(4.8)$$

and the truth table for three-input Gate is described in Table 4.16.

Table 4.16 Three-input NOR Gate

A	B	C	$\overline{A + B + C}$
0	0	0	1
0	0	1	0
0	1	0	0
0	1	1	0
1	0	0	0
1	0	1	0
1	1	0	0
1	1	1	0

4.11 NAND OPERATION

The boolean equation for a 2-input NAND Gate is

$$Y = \overline{AB} \qquad ...(4.9)$$

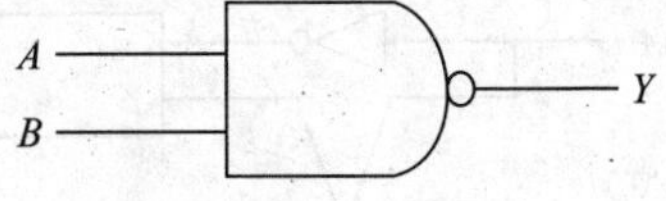

Fig. 4.22 NAND Gate

Read this as 'Y equals NOT AB'.

If $A = 0$ and $B = 0$, $Y = \overline{AB} = \overline{0 \cdot 0} = \overline{0} = 1$

If $A = 0$ and $B = 1$, $Y = \overline{AB} = \overline{0 \cdot 1} = \overline{0} = 1$

If $A = 1$ and $B = 0$, $Y = \overline{AB} = \overline{1 \cdot 0} = \overline{0} = 1$

If $A = 1$ and $B = 1$, $Y = \overline{AB} = \overline{1 \cdot 1} = \overline{1} = 0$

Because the circuit is an AND Gate followed by an inverter, the way to get a high output is to have one or more low inputs, as shown in the truth table (Table 4.17).

Table 4.17 Two-input NAND Gate

A	B	$\overline{AB}$
0	0	1
0	1	1
1	0	1
1	1	0

The boolean equation for three-input NAND Gate is;

$$Y = \overline{ABC} \qquad ...(4.10)$$

and the truth table for three-input NAND Gate is described in Table 4.18.

Table 4.18 Three-input NAND Gate

A	B	C	$\overline{ABC}$
0	0	0	1
0	0	1	1
0	1	0	1
0	1	1	1
1	0	0	1
1	0	1	1
1	1	0	1
1	1	1	0

4.12 EXCLUSIVE-OR GATES

An OR Gate recognizes words with one or more 1s, but EXCLUSIVE-OR Gate recognizes only words that have an odd number of 1. Figure 4.23 shows one way to build a two-input EXCLUSIVE-OR Gate abbreviated XOR. The upper AND Gate forms the product $\overline{A}B$ and the lower AND Gate forms the product $A\overline{B}$. Therefore, the boolean equation is

$$Y = \overline{A}B + A\overline{B} \qquad ...(4.11)$$

If $A = 0$ and $B = 0$, $Y = \overline{A}B + A\overline{B} = \overline{0} \cdot 0 + 0 \cdot \overline{0} = 1 \cdot 0 + 0 \cdot 1 = 0 + 0 = 0$

This implies that two low inputs mean both AND Gates have low outputs; so final output is low.

If $A = 0$ and $B = 1$, $Y = \overline{A}B + A\overline{B} = \overline{0} \cdot 1 + 0 \cdot \overline{1} = 1 \cdot 1 + 0 \cdot 0 = 1 + 0 = 1$

The final output is high. Likewise, a high A and low B result in a final output that is high.

If $A = 1$ and $B = 1$, $Y = \overline{A}B + A\overline{B} = \overline{1} \cdot 1 + 1 \cdot \overline{1} = 0.1 + 1.0 = 0 + 0 = 0$

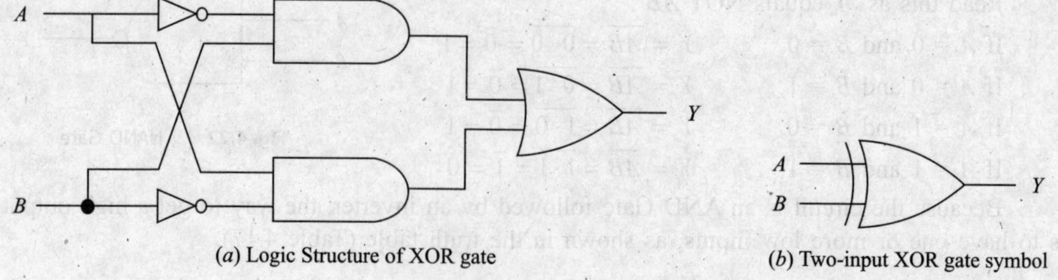

(*a*) Logic Structure of XOR gate (*b*) Two-input XOR gate symbol

Fig. 4.23 XOR Gate

The final output is low if both inputs are high. Table 4.19 shows the truth table for a two-input EXCLUSIVE-OR Gate.

Table 4.19 Two-input XOR Gate

A	B	$\bar{A}B + A\bar{B}$
0	0	0
0	1	1
1	0	1
1	1	0

Note that the output is high when A or B is high but not both, this is why the circuit is known as an EXCLUSIVE-OR Gate.

The word equation for Fig. 4.23 (*b*) is

$$Y = A \text{ XOR } B \quad \text{...(4.12)}$$

In boolean algebra the sign ⊕ standards for XOR addition.

$$Y = A \oplus B \quad \text{...(4.13)}$$

As shown in two-input XOR Gate, the four possible XOR additions are:

$$0 \oplus 0 = 0$$
$$0 \oplus 1 = 1$$
$$1 \oplus 0 = 1$$
$$1 \oplus 1 = 0$$

4.12.1 More Than Two Inputs

An XOR Gate can have as many inputs as needed. No matter how many inputs XOR Gate has, the action is same, *i.e.*, recognizes only words with an odd number of 1s. Figure 4.24 shows the three and six-input XOR Gate. Table 4.20 shows the four-input XOR Gate.

Table 4.20 Four-input XOR Gate

A	*B*	*C*	*D*	*Output*	*Description*
0	0	0	0	0	Even
0	0	0	1	1	Odd
0	0	1	0	1	Odd
0	0	1	1	0	Even
0	1	0	0	1	Odd
0	1	0	1	0	Even

A	B	C	D	Output	Description
0	1	1	0	0	Even
0	1	1	1	1	Odd
1	0	0	0	1	Odd
1	0	0	1	0	Even
1	0	1	0	0	Even
1	0	1	1	1	Odd
1	1	0	0	0	Even
1	1	0	1	1	Odd
1	1	1	0	1	Odd
1	1	1	1	0	Even

The final output of any XOR Gate is;

$$Y = A \oplus B \oplus C \quad ...(4.14)$$

The XOR Gates are used for testing the parity of a word. XOR Gates recognize words with an odd number of 1s. Therefore, the even parity (means a word has an even number of 1s) words produce a low output and odd parity (means a word has an odd number of 1s) words produce a high output.

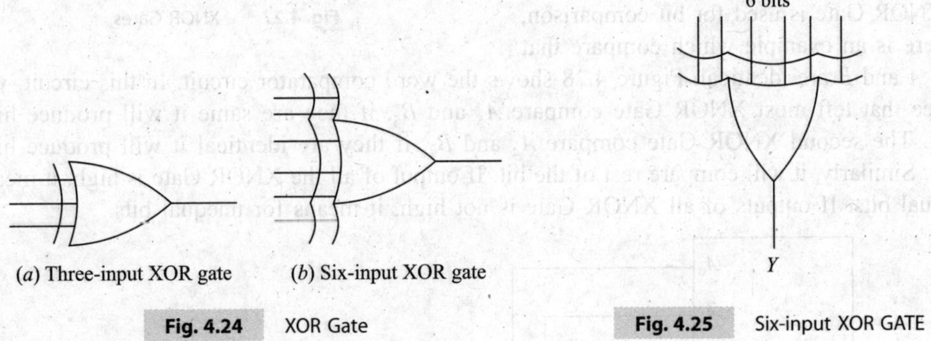

(*a*) Three-input XOR gate (*b*) Six-input XOR gate

Fig. 4.24 XOR Gate

Fig. 4.25 Six-input XOR GATE

4.12.2 Example on XOR Gate

Figure 4.25 shows six-input XOR Gate. What is the output of each of the following word (*i*) 110001 (*ii*) 110011?

(*i*) The word has three 1s, an odd number.

$\therefore$ $Y = 1$ (High)

(*ii*) The word has four 1s, an even number.

$\therefore$ $Y = 0$ (Low)

4.13 EXCLUSIVE-NOR GATES

The EXCLUSIVE-NOR Gate is also denoted by XNOR Gate. XNOR Gate is logically equivalent to an XOR Gate followed by an inverter. Figure 4.26 shows a two-input XNOR Gate.

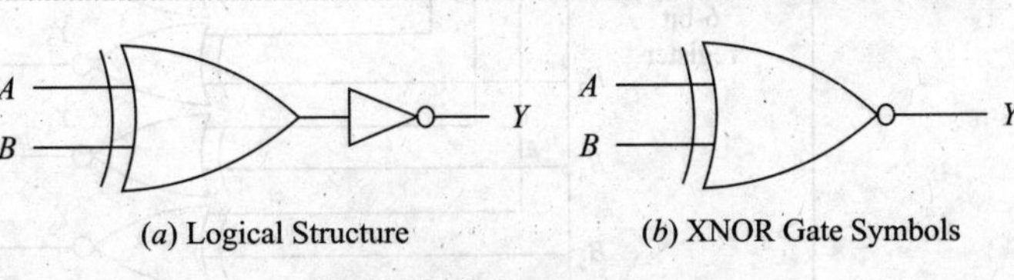

(*a*) Logical Structure (*b*) XNOR Gate Symbols

Fig. 4.26 XNOR Gate

The truth table of XNOR Gate is the complement of an XOR Gate because of the inversion on the output side. Table 4.21 shows the two-input XNOR Gate truth table. The output is high when the inputs are same. For this reason, the XNOR Gate is used for bit comparison, when two input bits are identical.

Table 4.21 Two-input XNOR Gate

A	B	Y
0	0	1
0	1	0
1	0	0
1	1	1

Figure 4.27 shows the three and four-input XNOR Gate. Because of the inversion on the output side, these XNOR Gates perform the complementary function of XOR Gates. Instead of recognizing odd parity words, XNOR recognize even parity words.

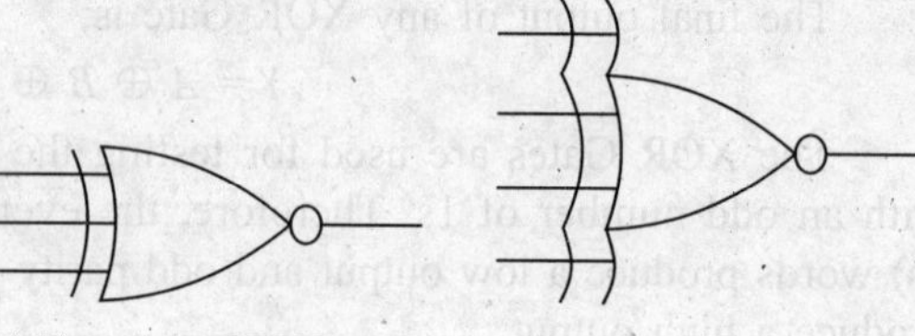

(*a*) Three-input XNOR gate (*b*) Four-input XNOR gate

Fig. 4.27 XNOR Gates

4.13.1 Example on XNOR Gate

The XNOR Gate is used for bit comparison, and here is an example which compare that words *A* and *B* are identical. Figure 4.28 shows the word comparator circuit. In this circuit, you will see that left most XNOR Gate compare A_5 and B_5, if they are same it will produce high output. The second XNOR Gate compare A_4 and B_4, if they are identical it will produce high output. Similarly, it will compare rest of the bit. If output of all the XNOR Gate is high, it means for equal bits. If outputs of all XNOR Gate is not high, it means for unequal bits.

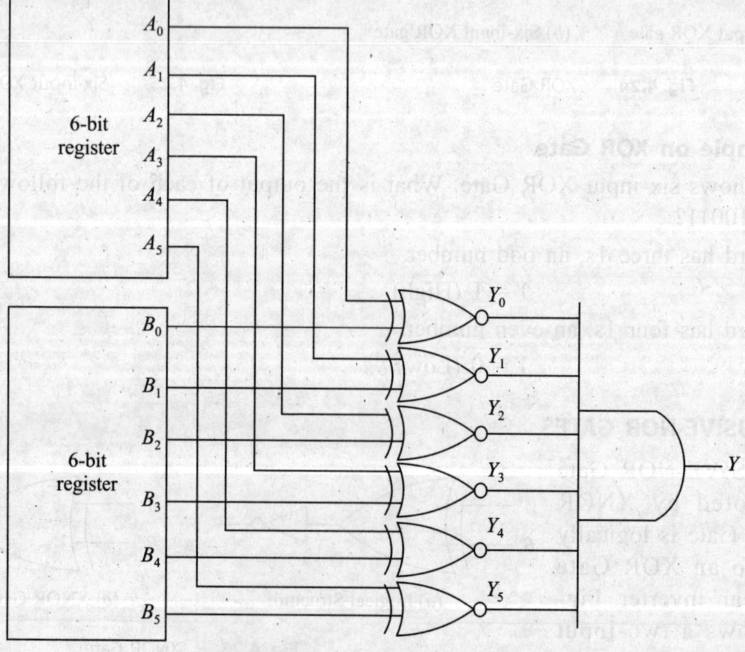

Fig. 4.28 Word comparator circuit

In general, we can say words A and B are equal if all XNOR Gates have high outputs and AND Gate has a Y equal to high. If words A and B differ in any one bit positions, the AND Gate has a Y equal to low.

4.14 DE MORGAN'S FIRST THEOREM

Figure 4.29 shows a two-input NOR Gate and the boolean equation for NOR Gate is:

$$Y = \overline{A + B} \qquad ...(4.15)$$

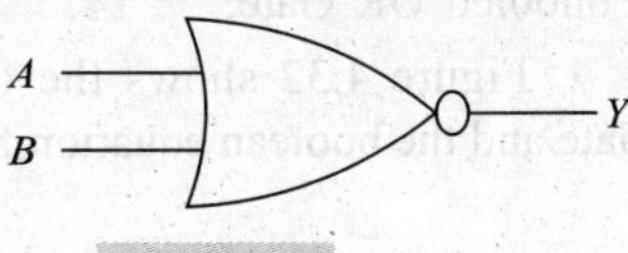

Fig. 4.29 NOR Gate

The truth table for two-input NOR Gate is shown in Table 4.22.

Table 4.22 Two-input NOR Gate

A	B	$\overline{A + B}$
0	0	1
1	0	0
0	1	0
1	1	0

Figure 4.30 has the inputs inverted before they reach the AND Gate. The boolean equation for this is:

$$Y = \overline{A}\overline{B} \qquad ...(4.16)$$

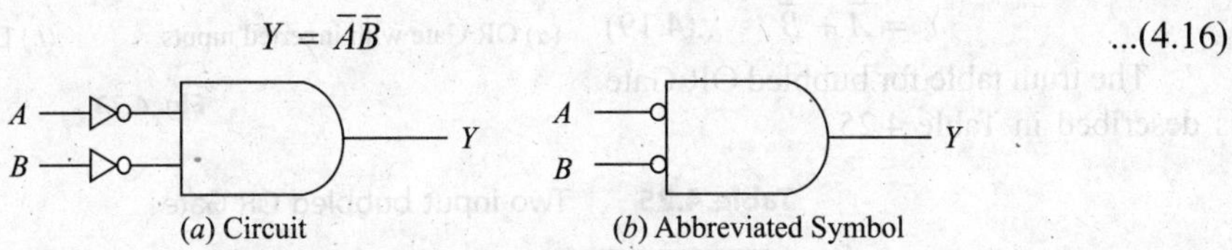

(*a*) Circuit (*b*) Abbreviated Symbol

Fig. 4.30 AND Gate with inverted inputs

The truth table for bubbled AND Gate is shown in Table 4.23.

Table 4.23 Two-input bubbled AND Gate

A	B	$= \overline{A}\overline{B}$
0	0	1
0	1	0
1	0	0
1	1	0

The first equation described a NOR Gate, and the second equation described a bubbled AND Gate. Since the output are equal for the same inputs, we can equate them

$$\overline{A + B} = \overline{A}\overline{B} \qquad ...(4.17)$$

This identity is known as **De Morgan's first theorem**. It says the complement of a sum equals the product of the complements. Figure 4.31 is a graphic summary of De Morgan's first theorem. A NOR Gate and the bubbled AND Gate are equivalent. So you can interchange the circuit very often to reduce complicated circuits to simpler forms.

Fig. 4.31 De Morgan's first theorem

4.15 DE MORGAN'S SECOND THEOREM

In words, the complement of a logical product equals the logical sum of the complements. In terms of circuits, a NAND Gate is equivalent to a bubbled OR Gate.

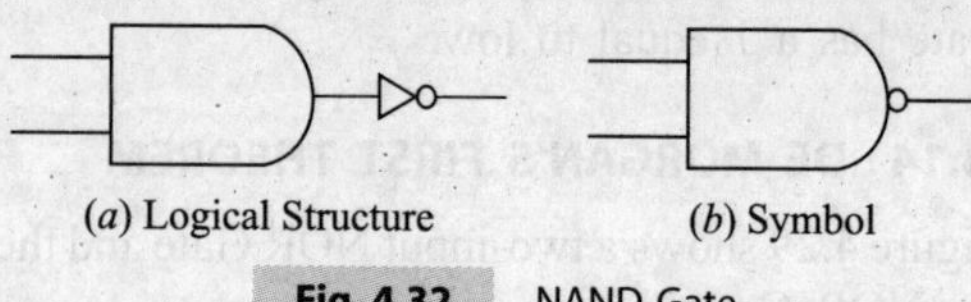

(*a*) Logical Structure (*b*) Symbol

Fig. 4.32 NAND Gate

Figure 4.32 shows the two-input NAND Gate and the boolean equation for NAND Gate is

$$Y = \overline{A} + \overline{B} \qquad \text{...(4.18)}$$

The truth table for two-input NAND Gate is described in Table 4.24.

Table 4.24 Two-input NAND Gate

A	B	$\overline{AB}$
0	0	1
0	1	1
1	0	1
1	1	0

Figure 4.33 shows the OR Gate with inverted inputs (bubbled OR Gate) and the boolean equation for this is;

$$Y = \overline{A} + \overline{B} \qquad \text{...(4.19)}$$

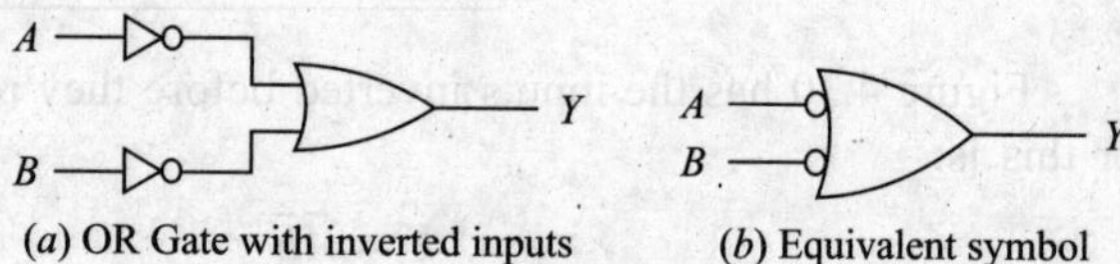

(*a*) OR Gate with inverted inputs (*b*) Equivalent symbol

Fig. 4.33

The truth table for bubbled OR Gate is described in Table 4.25.

Table 4.25 Two-input bubbled OR Gate

A	B	$\overline{A} + \overline{B}$
0	0	1
0	1	1
1	0	1
1	1	0

The first equation describes a NAND Gate, and the second equation describes a bubbled OR Gate. Since the outputs are equals for the same inputs, we equate them

$$\overline{AB} = \overline{A} + \overline{B} \qquad \text{...(4.20)}$$

This identity is known as De Morgan's second theorem. It says the complement of a logical product equals the logical sum of the complements. Figure 4.34 is a graphic summary of De Morgan's second theorem. A NAND Gate is equivalent to a bubbled OR Gate. So you can interchange the circuit very often to reduce complicated circuits to simpler forms.

Fig. 4.34 De Morgan's second theorem

When three inputs are involved, De Morgan's second theorem can be written as

$$\overline{ABC} = \overline{A} + \overline{B} + \overline{C} \qquad \text{...(4.21)}$$

If 4 inputs are used,

$$\overline{ABCD} = \overline{A} + \overline{B} + \overline{C} + \overline{D} \qquad \text{...(4.22)}$$

Figure 4.35 is a visual summary of De Morgan's second theorem, when 3 or 4 inputs are involved, a NAND Gate and a bubbled OR Gate are equivalent.

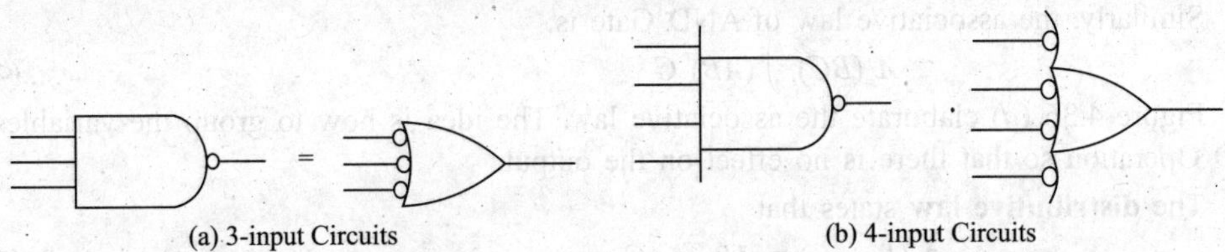

Fig. 4.35 De Morgan's second theorem

4.16 BOOLEAN RELATIONS

You can transpose the input signals to a two-input signals OR Gate without affecting the output [see Fig. 4.36 (*a*)]. The boolean equivalent of this is

$$A + B = B + A \qquad \text{...(4.23)}$$

(*a*) Commutative law with OR operation

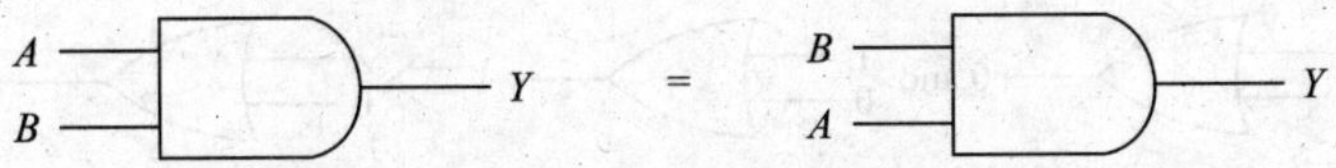

(*b*) Commutative law with AND operation

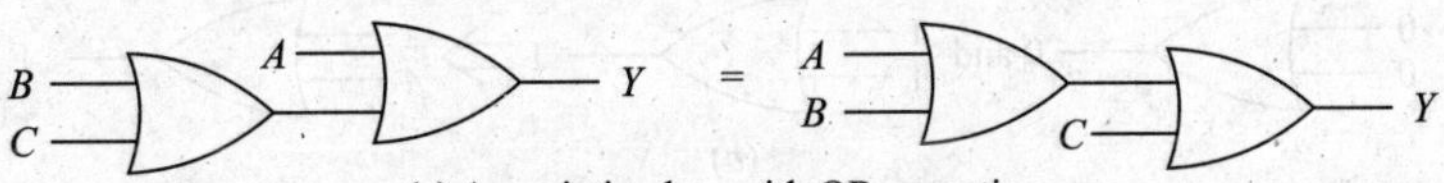

(*c*) Associative law with OR operation

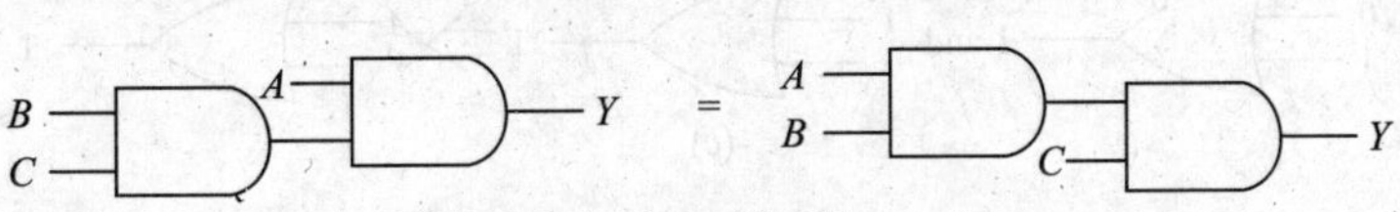

(*d*) Associative law with OR operation

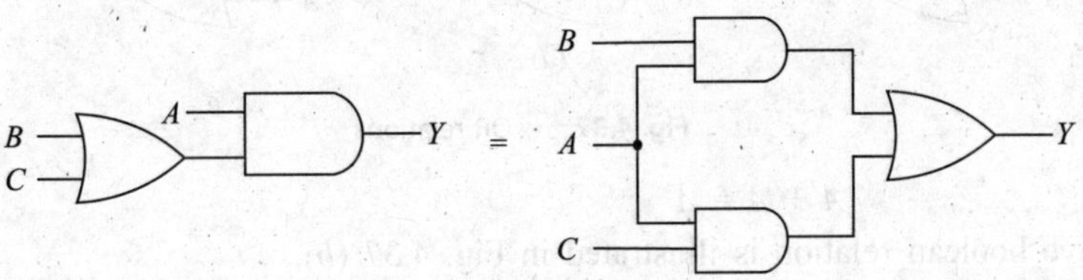

(*e*) Distributuve law

Fig. 4.36 Commutative, Associative and Distributive Laws

Similarly, you can transpose the input signals to a two-input AND Gate without affecting the output [see Fig. 4.36 (*b*)]. In boolean terms

$$AB = BA \qquad \text{...(4.24)}$$

These relations are called **commutative laws.**

The associative law of OR Gate is:

$$A + (B + C) = (A + B) + C \qquad \text{...(4.25)}$$

Figure 4.36 (*c*) elaborate the associative law. The idea is how to group the variables in OR Operation so that no effect on the output.

Similarly, the associative law of AND Gate is:

$$A\,(BC) = (AB)\,C \qquad \text{...(4.26)}$$

Figure 4.36 (*d*) elaborate the associative law. The idea is how to group the variables for AND Operation so that there is no effect on the output.

The **distributive law** states that

$$A\,(B + C) = AB + AC \qquad \text{...(4.27)}$$

Figure 4.36 (*e*) elaborate this rule. It is easy to remember many of these relations because they are identical to ordinary algebra.

4.17 OR OPERATIONS

Now, we will discuss the four boolean relations of OR Operations.

(*i*) $$A + 0 = A \qquad \text{...(4.28)}$$

This means that a variable ORed with 0 equals the variable.

When A is 0, $0 + 0 = 0$

When A is 1, $1 + 0 = 1$

Figure 4.37 (*a*) illustrate this rule.

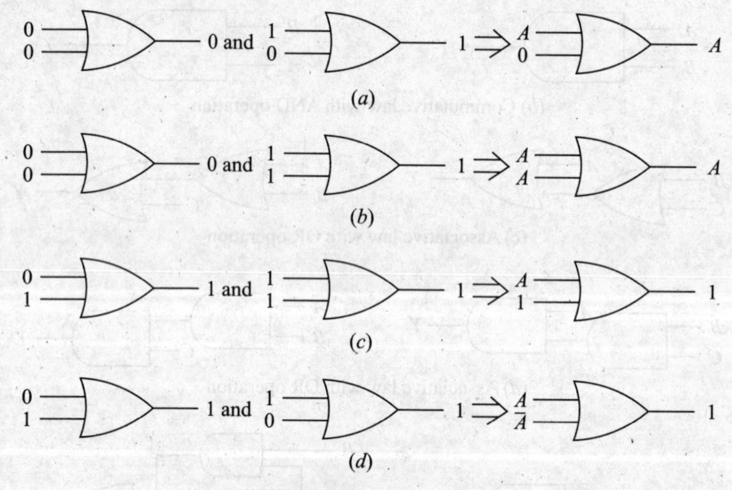

Fig. 4.37 OR relations

(*ii*) $$A + A = A \qquad \text{...(4.29)}$$

The above boolean relation is illustrated in Fig. 4.37 (*b*).

When $A = 0$, $0 + 0 = 0$

When $A = 1$, $1 + 1 = 1$

which is also true because 1 ORed with 1 produces 1. Hence, any variable ORed with itself equals the variable.

(*iii*) $$A + 1 = 1 \qquad \text{...(4.30)}$$

The above boolean relation is illustrated in Fig. 4.37 (*c*).

When $A = 0$, $0 + 1 = 1$

When $A = 1$ $1 + 1 = 1$

This is correct because the plus sign implies OR addition, not ordinary addition.

(*iv*) $A + \bar{A} = 1$ ...(4.31)

Figure 4.37 (*d*) illustrated the above boolean relation. If one input to an OR Gate is high, the output is high no matter what the other input is.

Finally, we get $A + \bar{A} = 1$

When $A = 0$, $0 + 1 = 1$

When $A = 1$ $1 + 0 = 1$

In general, a variable ORed with its complement always equals to 1.

4.18 AND OPERATIONS

Here, we will discuss the three boolean relations of *A*ND operations,

(*i*) $A \cdot 1 = A$ ...(4.32)

(*ii*) $A \cdot A = A$ ...(4.33)

(*iii*) $A \cdot 0 = 0$ ...(4.34)

When $A = 0$, all the foregoing are true. Similarly, when $A = 1$, each is true,

(*iv*) $A \cdot \bar{A} = 0$ ...(4.35)

When $A = 0$, $0 \cdot 1 = 0$

When $A = 1$, $1 \cdot 0 = 0$ which is true.

Equation $A \cdot \bar{A} = 0$, indicates that a variable ANDed with its complement always equals zero.

Figure 4.38 illustrate the visual summary of AND Relations.

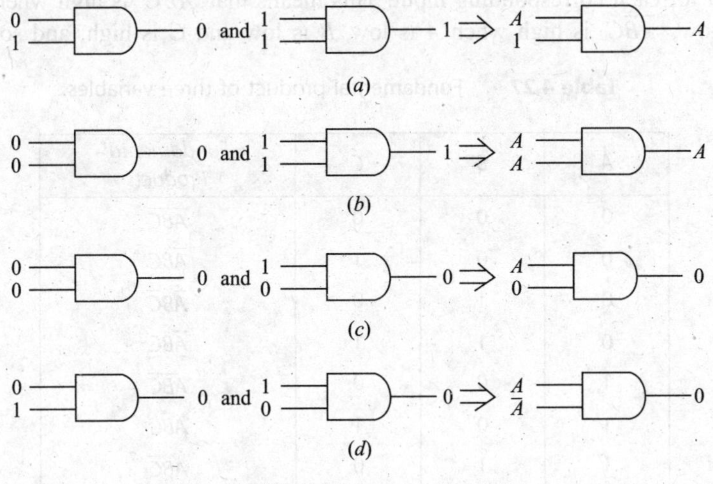

Fig. 4.38 AND Relations

4.19 SUM-OF-PRODUCTS METHOD

As you are aware that digital design often starts by constructing a truth table with a desired output (0 or 1) for each input condition. Once you have a truth table you can transform it to an equivalent logic circuit. Figure 4.39 shows the four possible ways to AND two-input signals that are in complemented and uncomplemented form. These outputs are known as **fundamental products**.

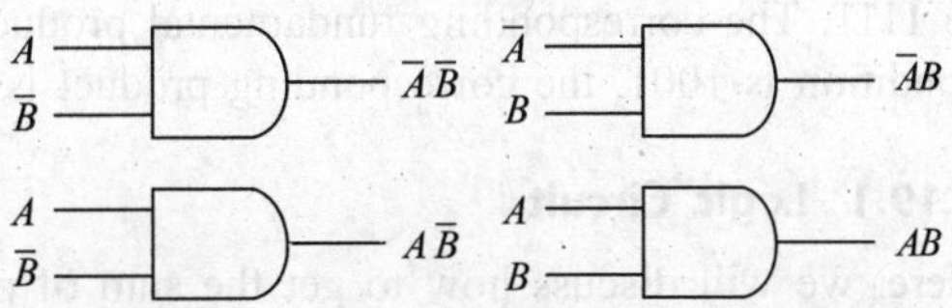

Fig. 4.39 Fundamental products of two variables

Table 4.26 lists the four possible ways to AND two signals in complemented or uncomplemented form. The logical products $\bar{A}\bar{B}$, $\bar{A}B$, $A\bar{B}$, and AB are called fundamental products because they produce a high output.

Table 4.26 Two variables of fundamental products

A	*B*	*Fundamental Products*
0	0	$\bar{A}\bar{B}$
0	1	$\bar{A}B$
1	0	$A\bar{B}$
1	1	AB

For instance, $\bar{A}\bar{B}$ is high when *A* and *B* are low; $\bar{A}B$ is high when *A* is low and *B* is high; and so forth.

Similarly, you can apply the fundamental product idea for three or more variables. For example, assume three input variable *A*, *B*, *C* and their complement. There are eight ways to AND three-input variables and their complements, resulting in fundamental products: $\bar{A}\bar{B}\bar{C}$, $\bar{A}\bar{B}C$, $\bar{A}B\bar{C}$, $\bar{A}BC$, $A\bar{B}\bar{C}$, $A\bar{B}C$, $AB\bar{C}$ and ABC.

Table 4.27 lists each input possibility and its fundamental product. Note that each fundamental product is high for each corresponding input. This means that $\bar{A}\bar{B}\bar{C}$ is high when *A* is low, *B* is low and *C* is low; $\bar{A}\bar{B}C$ is high when *A* is low, *B* is low and *C* is high; and so forth.

Table 4.27 Fundamental product of three variables

A	*B*	*C*	*Fundamental Products*
0	0	0	$\bar{A}\bar{B}\bar{C}$
0	0	1	$\bar{A}\bar{B}C$
0	1	0	$\bar{A}B\bar{C}$
0	1	1	$\bar{A}BC$
1	0	0	$A\bar{B}\bar{C}$
1	0	1	$A\bar{B}C$
1	1	0	$AB\bar{C}$
1	1	1	ABC

Note that here is a quick way to find the fundamental product for any input condition. Whenever an input variable is 0, the same variable is complemented in the fundamental product. For instance, when there are four variables, there are 16 (2^4) possible input condition from 0000 to 1111. The corresponding fundamental products are from $\bar{A}\bar{B}\bar{C}\bar{D}$ through $ABCD$. If the input condition is 1001, the corresponding product is $A\bar{B}\bar{C}D$.

4.19.1 Logic Circuit

Here, we will discuss how to get the sum of product solution from the given truth table. For example, suppose you have a truth table like Table 4.28.

Table 4.28 Truth Table

A	B	C	Y
0	0	0	0
0	0	1	0
0	1	0	0
0	1	1	$1 \rightarrow \overline{A}BC$
1	0	0	0
1	0	1	$1 \rightarrow A\overline{B}C$
1	1	0	$1 \rightarrow AB\overline{C}$
1	1	1	$1 \rightarrow ABC$

Now, you have to locate each output 1 in truth table and write their fundamental product. For instance, the first out 1 occurs for an input of $A = 0$, $B = 1$, and $C = 1$. The corresponding fundamental product is $\overline{A}BC$. The next output 1 is for $A = 1$, $B = 0$, and $C = 1$, the corresponding fundamental product is $A\overline{B}C$; and so on. After getting all the fundamental product for high output you can get the boolean equation by ORing them.

$$Y = \overline{A}BC + A\overline{B}C + AB\overline{C} + ABC \qquad ...(4.36)$$

After you have sum-of-products equation, you can derive the corresponding logic circuit. Equation (4.36) implies four AND Gates driving OR Gate (AND-OR network). The first AND Gate has inputs of $\overline{A}$, B, and C; the second AND Gate has inputs of A, $\overline{B}$, and C; the third AND Gate has A, B, and $\overline{C}$; the fourth AND Gate has A, B, and C. Figure 4.40 shows the corresponding logic circuit. The AND-OR network is equivalent to the truth table.

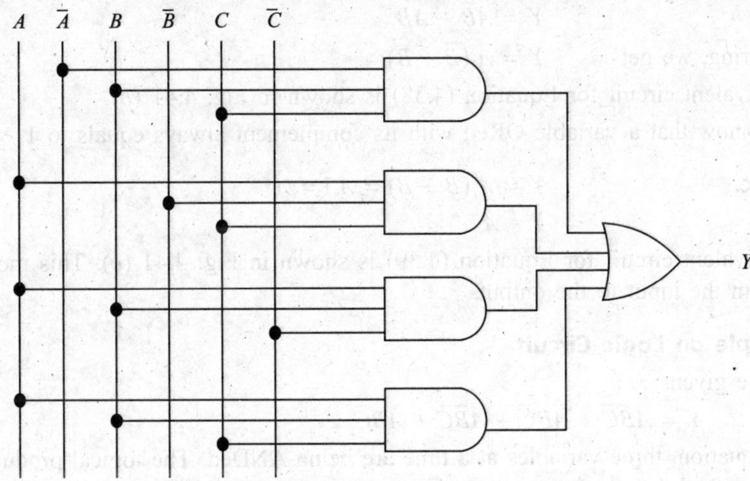

Fig. 4.40 Sum-of-products circuit

The sum-of-products method works always. You OR the fundamental products of each high output in the truth table. This gives an equation which you can transform into an AND-OR network that is the circuit equivalent of the truth table.

4.20 SIMPLIFYING LOGIC CIRCUIT

After obtaining a sum-of-products circuit, the first thing is to simplify the circuit with the help of boolean algebra if possible. Now, question arise as to how you can compare the simplicity of one logic circuit with another. By counting the number of input Gate leads, it means the circuit with fewer input Gate leads is usually easier to build.

Figure 4.40 has a total of 16-input Gate leads (4 on each AND Gate and 4 on the OR Gate). Figure 4.41 (*a*) has a six input Gate leads, which is less than the earlier one.

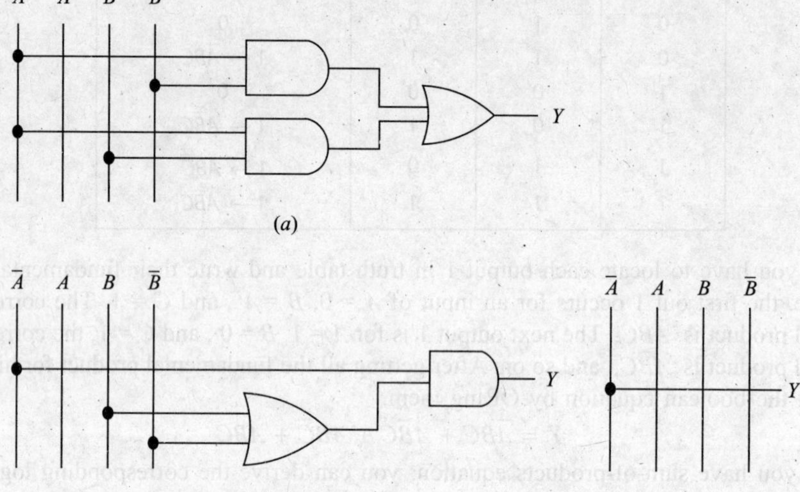

Fig. 4.41 Circuit

For instance, the boolean equation of Fig. 4.41 (*a*) is

$$Y = A\bar{B} + AB \qquad \text{...(4.37)}$$

By factoring, we get

$$Y = A\,(\bar{B} + B) \qquad \text{...(4.38)}$$

The equivalent circuit for Equation (4.38) is shown in Fig. 4.41 (*b*).

As you know that a variable ORed with its complement always equals to 1.

Therefore, $Y = A\,(\bar{B} + B) = A.1 = A$

$$\Rightarrow \quad Y = A \qquad \text{...(4.39)}$$

The equivalent circuit for Equation (4.39) is shown in Fig. 4.41 (*c*). This means, a wire connecting from the input to the output.

4.20.1 Example on Logic Circuit

Suppose we are given

$$Y = \bar{A}\bar{B}\bar{C} + \bar{A}B\bar{C} + A\bar{B}\bar{C} + AB\bar{C} \qquad \text{...(4.40)}$$

In this equation, three variables at a time are being ANDed. The logical products are then ORed to get the final output. Figure 4.42 shows the corresponding logic circuit. It has 16-input Gate leads.

Since $\bar{C}$ is common to each term, factor as follows:

$$Y = (\bar{A}\bar{B} + \bar{A}B + A\bar{B} + AB)\,\bar{C}$$

$$Y = [\bar{A}\,(\bar{B} + B) + A\,(\bar{B} + B)]\,\bar{C}$$

$$Y = [\bar{A}\,(1) + A\,(1)]\,\bar{C}$$

[∴ a variable ORed with its complement always equals 1]

$$Y = [\bar{A} + A]\,\bar{C}$$

$$Y = \overline{C}$$

This means that all you need is a wire connecting input $\overline{C}$ to output Y.

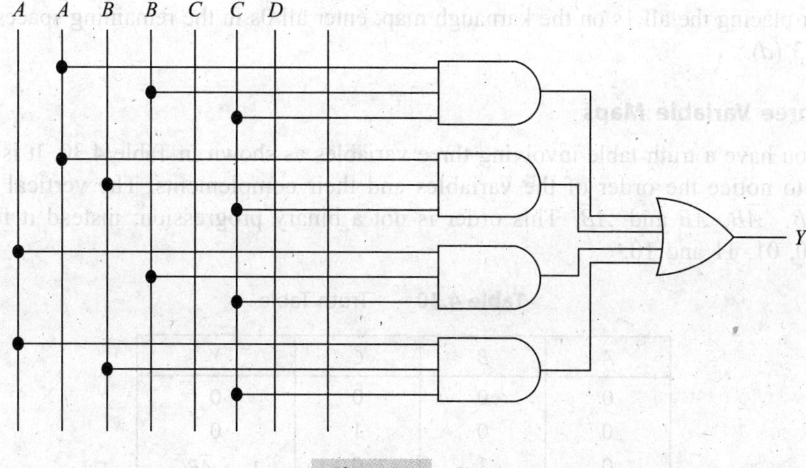

Fig. 4.42 Circuit

4.21 KARNAUGH MAPS

A Karnaugh map is a graphical display of the fundamental products in a truth table. Many engineers don't simplify equation with boolean algebra, they use a method based on Karnaugh maps. First we will discuss how to construct a Karnaugh map for a given truth table.

4.21.1 Two Variable Map

Suppose you have a truth table, involving two variables as shown in Table 4.29. As there are only two variables one variable represent the rows and second variable represents the columns. Note the order of the variables and their complements; the vertical column has $\overline{A}$ followed by A, and the horizontal row has $\overline{B}$ followed by B shown is Fig. 4.43 (*a*).

Table 4.29 Truth Table

A	B	Y
0	0	0
0	1	0
1	0	1
1	1	1

(*a*)

	$\overline{B}$	B
$\overline{A}$		
A		

(*b*)

	$\overline{B}$	B
$\overline{A}$		
A	1	

(*c*)

	$\overline{B}$	B
$\overline{A}$		
A	1	1

(*d*)

	$\overline{B}$	B
$\overline{A}$	0	0
A	1	1

Fig. 4.43 Karnaugh map for two variables

Find the output 1s in the truth table. The first high (1) output to appear is for the input of $A = 1$ and $B = 0$. The fundamental product for this is $A\overline{B}$. Now, enter 1 in the Karnaugh map as shown in Fig. 4.43 (*b*).

Similarly, find the other output 1 in the truth table. The next 1 output to appear is for the input A = 1 and B = 1. The fundamental product for this is AB. Now place the 1 at their corresponding place as shown in Fig. 4.43 (*c*).

After placing the all 1s on the karnaugh map, enter all 0s in the remaining spaces as shown in Fig. 4.43 (*d*).

4.21.2 Three Variable Maps

Suppose you have a truth table involving three variables as shown in Table 4.30. It is especially important to notice the order of the variables and their complements. The vertical column is labeled $\bar{A}\bar{B}$, $\bar{A}B$, AB and $A\bar{B}$. This order is not a binary progression; instead it follows the order of 00, 01, 11 and 10.

Table 4.30 Truth Table

A	B	C	Y
0	0	0	0
0	0	1	0
0	1	0	1 → $\bar{A}B\bar{C}$
0	1	1	1 → $\bar{A}BC$
1	0	0	0
1	0	1	0
1	1	0	0
1	1	1	1 → ABC

Now, look at the output 1s in Table 4.30. The fundamental products of the variable are $\bar{A}B\bar{C}$, $\bar{A}BC$, and ABC. Place these 1s in Karnaugh map as shown in Fig. 4.44 (*b*). The final step is to enter 0s in the remaining space [Fig. 4.44 (*c*)]. This way we get the fundamental products needed for the sum-of-products circuit.

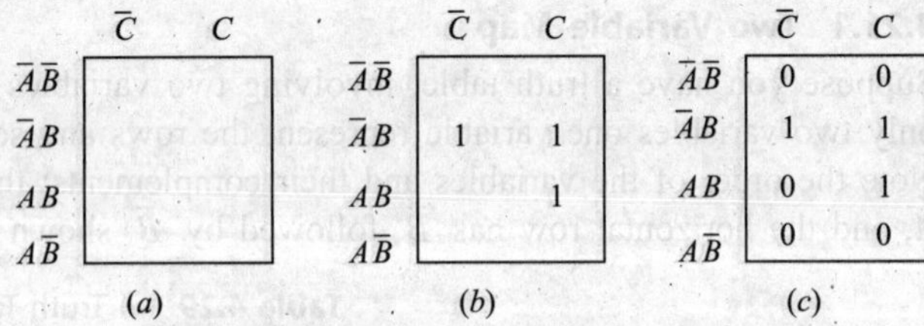

Fig. 4.44 Karnaugh Map for three variables

4.21.3 Four Variable Map

Many MSI circuits process binary words of four bits called nibbles. For this reason, logic circuits are often designed to handle four variables. Suppose you have the truth table of Table 4.31. To obtain the Karnaugh map of four variables, the variables are divided into two groups each containing two variables. The two variables are drawn as rows while other two variables represents the column of the graph. There is no restriction applied to choose the group for rows and columns, but the concatenation of the variables to represent the fundamental product of the variable must be in the same order. The vertical column is labeled $\bar{A}\bar{B}$, $\bar{A}B$, AB and $A\bar{B}$. The horizontal row is labeled $\bar{C}\bar{D}$, $\bar{C}D$, CD and $C\bar{D}$.

Now, look at the output 1s in Table 4.31. The fundamental products of the variable are $\bar{A}\bar{B}\bar{C}D$, $\bar{A}BC\bar{D}$, $\bar{A}BCD$, and $ABC\bar{D}$. Place these 1s in Karnaugh map as shown in Fig. 4.45 (*b*). The final step is to enter 0s in the remaining space [Fig. 4.45 (*c*)]. This represents the four variable Karnaugh map.

Table 4.31 Truth Table

A	B	C	D	Y
0	0	0	0	0
0	0	0	1	$1 \rightarrow \bar{A}\bar{B}\bar{C}D$
0	0	1	0	0
0	0	1	1	0
0	1	0	0	0
0	1	0	1	0
0	1	1	0	$1 \rightarrow \bar{A}BC\bar{D}$
0	1	1	1	$1 \rightarrow \bar{A}BCD$
1	0	0	0	0
1	0	0	1	0
1	0	1	0	0
1	0	1	1	0
1	1	0	0	0
1	1	0	1	0
1	1	1	0	$1 \rightarrow ABC\bar{D}$
1	1	1	1	0

(a)

	$\bar{C}\bar{D}$	$\bar{C}D$	CD	$C\bar{D}$
$\bar{A}\bar{B}$				
$\bar{A}B$				
AB				
$A\bar{B}$				

(b)

	$\bar{C}\bar{D}$	$\bar{C}D$	CD	$C\bar{D}$
$\bar{A}\bar{B}$		1		
$\bar{A}B$			1	
AB				
$A\bar{B}$				

(c)

	$\bar{C}\bar{D}$	$\bar{C}D$	CD	$C\bar{D}$
$\bar{A}\bar{B}$	0	1	0	1
$\bar{A}B$	0	0	1	1
AB	0	0	0	1
$A\bar{B}$	0	0	0	0

Fig. 4.45 Karnaugh map for four variables

4.22 LOGIC CIRCUIT DESIGN

Karnaugh map is used to simplified logic circuits. Consider the Karnaugh map of Fig. 4.46 which contains a **pair** of 1s that are horizontally adjacent. The first 1 represents the product $ABCD$; the second 1 represents the product $ABC\bar{D}$. As we move from the first one from the other 1, only one variable D goes from uncomplement to complement. The other variables remain uncomplemented, *i.e.*, A, B and C. In this case, you can easily eliminate the variable that changes form.

	$\bar{C}\bar{D}$	$\bar{C}D$	CD	$C\bar{D}$
$\bar{A}\bar{B}$	0	0	0	0
$\bar{A}B$	0	0	0	0
AB	0	0	(1	1)
$A\bar{B}$	0	0	0	0

Fig. 4.46 Pair on a Karnaugh map

The sum-of-products equation for Fig. 4.46 is

$$Y = ABCD + ABC\bar{D}$$

$$Y = ABC\,(D + \bar{D})$$

$$Y = ABC \qquad (\because D + \bar{D} = 1)$$

A pair of adjacent 1s always means that the sum-of-products equation will have a variable and a complement that drop out.

Figure 4.47 shows a pair of 1s that are vertically adjacent. These 1s correspond to the product $ABCD$ and $A\bar{B}CD$. Note that only one variable changes from uncomplemented to complemented form (B to $\bar{B}$) and all other variables remain uncomplemented (or their original form).

The sum-of-products for this is:

$$Y = ABCD + A\overline{B}CD$$

$$Y = ACD\,(B + \overline{B})$$

$$Y = ACD \qquad [\because\ B + \overline{B} = 1]$$

This means that the encircled pair of Fig. 4.47 represents ACD.

	$\overline{C}\,\overline{D}$	$\overline{C}D$	CD	$C\overline{D}$
$\overline{A}\,\overline{B}$	0	0	0	0
$\overline{A}B$	0	0	0	0
AB	0	0	1	0
$A\overline{B}$	0	0	1	0

Fig. 4.47 Pair on a Karnaugh map

☞ **Note:** Whenever you see a pair of adjacent 1s eliminate the variable that goes from complemented to uncomplemented form.

Figure 4.48 shows the two pairs on a Karnaugh map. You can OR the simplified product to get the boolean equation. The first pair represent $AB\overline{C}$ and second pair represent ABC. The corresponding boolean equation for this map is

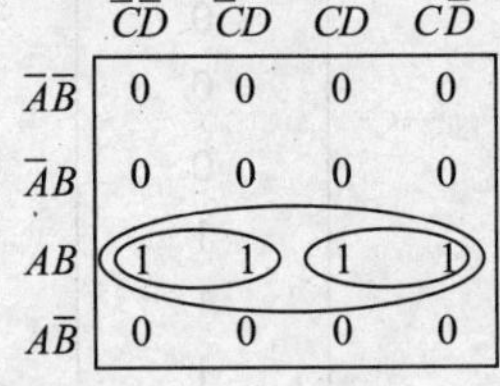

Fig. 4.48 Quads on a Karnaugh map

$$Y = AB\overline{C} + ABC$$

$$Y = AB\,(\overline{C} + C)$$

$$Y = AB$$

So the quads represents a product where two variables and their complements drop out.

There is no need to go through the algebra again. Whenever variables go from complemented to uncomplemented form, these variables are drop out.

In Fig. 4.48, $\overline{C}\,\overline{D}$ is uncomplemented to CD, and $\overline{C}D$ is uncomplemented to $C\overline{D}$. So, these variables ($\overline{C}\,\overline{D}$, CD, $\overline{C}D$, $C\overline{D}$) are dropouts. Therefore, the simplified equation is

$$Y = AB.$$

Here is another example of quads on a Karnaugh map (Fig. 4.49). When you move horizontally, D is the variable that changes form. When you move vertically, B changes form. Therefore, the simplified equation is

	$\overline{C}\,\overline{D}$	$\overline{C}D$	CD	$C\overline{D}$
$\overline{A}\,\overline{B}$	0	0	0	0
$\overline{A}B$	0	0	0	0
AB	0	0	1	1
$A\overline{B}$	0	0	1	1

Fig. 4.49 Quads on a Karnaugh map

$$Y = AC.$$

An **octet** is a group of eight adjacent 1s like those of Fig. 4.50. An octet alway eliminates three variables and their complements. Consider the octets as two quads. The sum-of-products for these two quads is

	$\overline{C}\,\overline{D}$	$\overline{C}D$	CD	$C\overline{D}$
$\overline{A}\,\overline{B}$	0	0	0	0
$\overline{A}B$	0	0	0	0
AB	1	1	1	1
$A\overline{B}$	1	1	1	1

Fig. 4.50 Octets on a Karnaugh map

$$Y = A\overline{C} + AC$$

$$Y = A\,(\overline{C} + C)$$

$$Y = A$$

So the octet reduces three variables and their complements and equation reduces to single variable whose value does not change.

You have to see how a pair eliminates one variable, aquad eliminates two variables, and an octet eliminate three variables. Because of this, you should encircle the octets first, the quads second, and the pairs last. In this way, the greatest simplification takes place.

4.22.1 Example on Karnaugh Map

Example 1: Consider a Karnaugh map as shown in Fig. 4.51. First, we will look for octets. There are none. Next, we will look for quads. These are two. Finally, we look for pairs. There is one. The pair represent the simplified product $\overline{A}\overline{B}D$, the lower quad represent for $A\overline{C}$, and the other quad represent fundamental product $C\overline{D}$.

The boolean equation for the Karnaugh map is

$$Y = \overline{A}\overline{B}D + A\overline{C} + C\overline{D} \qquad \text{...(4.41)}$$

	$\overline{C}\overline{D}$	$\overline{C}D$	CD	$C\overline{D}$
$\overline{A}\overline{B}$	0	1	1	1
$\overline{A}B$	0	0	0	1
AB	1	1	0	1
$A\overline{B}$	1	1	0	1

Fig. 4.51 Karnaugh map

Example 2: Here is an example for the overlapping groups. Consider a Karnaugh map as shown in Fig. 4.52. The simplified equation for the overlapping groups is

$$Y = A + B\overline{C}D \qquad \text{...(4.42)}$$

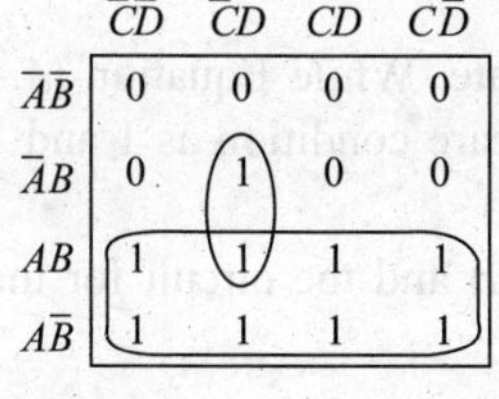

Fig. 4.52 Karnaugh map

	$\overline{C}\overline{D}$	$\overline{C}D$	CD	$C\overline{D}$
$\overline{A}\overline{B}$	0	0	0	0
$\overline{A}B$	0	1	0	0
AB	1	1	1	1
$A\overline{B}$	1	1	1	1

Fig. 4.53 Karnaugh map

It is valid to encircle the 1s as shown in Fig. 4.53, but then the isolated 1 results in a more complicated equation:

$$Y = A + \overline{A}B\overline{C}D \qquad \text{...(4.43)}$$

This needs a more complicated circuit than Equation (4.42). So always overlap groups if possible.

4.23 DON'T-CARE CONDITIONS

There are occasions when it does not matter what the output is for a given input word. To indicate this, we use an X in the truth table instead of a 0 or a 1. For example, consider a truth Table 4.32 having don't-care conditions and the equivalent Karnaugh map as shown in Fig. 4.54 (*a*).

Table 4.32 Truth Table

A	*B*	*C*	*Y*
0	0	0	1
0	0	1	*X*
0	1	0	1
0	1	1	*X*
1	0	0	0
1	0	1	*X*
1	1	0	1
1	1	1	0

☞ Note that first we visualize all Xs and 1s and try to form the largest groups that include the real 1s. This gives us one quads. Second, we visualize all remaining Xs as 0s. In this way, the X's are used to the best advantage. We are free to do this because X's are 0s or 1s.

Figure 4.54 (*b*) implies the boolean equation

$$Y = \overline{A}\overline{C} + B\overline{C} \qquad \text{...(4.44)}$$

	$\overline{C}$	C
$\overline{A}\overline{B}$	1	X
$\overline{A}B$	1	X
AB	1	0
$A\overline{B}$	0	X

(*a*)

	$\overline{C}$	C
$\overline{A}\overline{B}$	1	X
$\overline{A}B$	1	X
AB	1	0
$A\overline{B}$	0	X

(*b*)

	$\overline{C}$	C
$\overline{A}\overline{B}$	1	X
$\overline{A}B$	1	X
AB	1	0
$A\overline{B}$	0	X

(*c*)

Fig. 4.54 Karnaugh Map

Figure 4.54 (*b*) implies the simplified boolean equation

$$Y = \overline{A} + B\overline{C} \qquad ...(4.45)$$

Equation (4.44) needs two AND Gates and one OR Gate. While Equation (4.45) requires one AND Gate and one OR Gate. So by choosing two don't-care condition as 1 and 1 don't-care condition as 0, we reduced one AND Gate.

The circuit for Equation (4.44) is shown in Fig. 4.55 (*a*) and the circuit for the don't-care condition is shown in Fig. 4.55 (*b*).

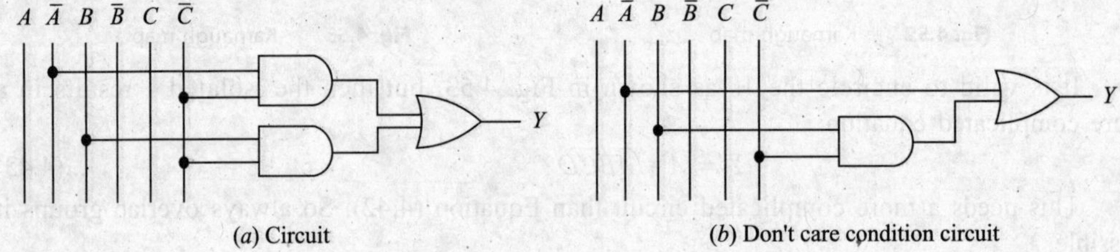

(*a*) Circuit

(*b*) Don't care condition circuit

Fig. 4.55 Comparison of Circuits

Here is another example of four-input variable of truth Table 4.33. Figure 4.56 shows the Karnaugh map for the Table 4.33. Note that first we visualize all X's as 1s and try to form the largest groups that include the real 1s. This gives us three quads. Second, we visualize all remaining Xs as 0s.

Table 4.33 Truth Table

A	B	C	D	Y
0	0	0	0	1
0	0	0	1	0
0	0	1	0	0
0	0	1	1	1
0	1	0	0	1
0	1	0	1	1
0	1	1	0	0
0	1	1	1	1
1	0	0	0	X
1	0	0	1	X
1	0	1	0	X
1	0	1	1	X
1	1	0	0	X
1	1	0	1	X
1	1	1	0	X
1	1	1	1	X

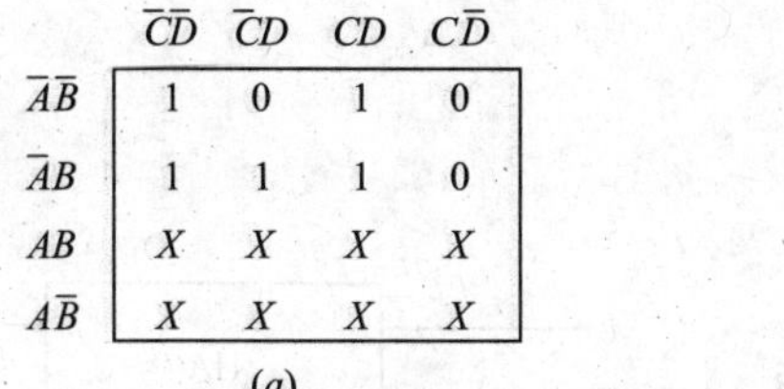

	$\bar{C}\bar{D}$	$\bar{C}D$	CD	$C\bar{D}$
$\bar{A}\bar{B}$	1	0	1	0
$\bar{A}B$	1	1	1	0
AB	X	X	X	X
$A\bar{B}$	X	X	X	X

(*a*)

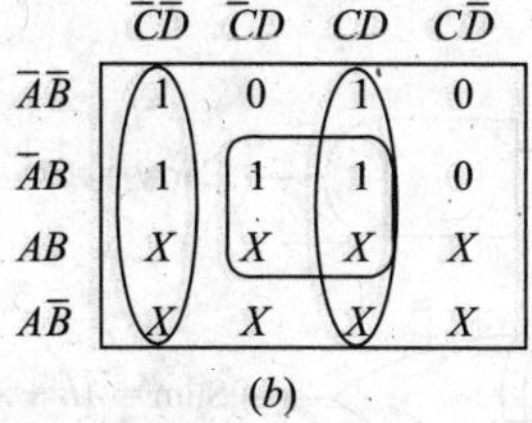

	$\bar{C}\bar{D}$	$\bar{C}D$	CD	$C\bar{D}$
$\bar{A}\bar{B}$	1	0	1	0
$\bar{A}B$	1	1	1	0
AB	X	X	X	X
$A\bar{B}$	X	X	X	X

(*b*)

Fig. 4.56 Don't-care Karnaugh Map

Figure 4.56 implies the simplified boolean equation

$$Y = BD + \bar{C}\bar{D} + CD \qquad ...(4.46)$$

Figure 4.57 shows the simplified logic circuit with AND-OR network having nine input Gate leads.

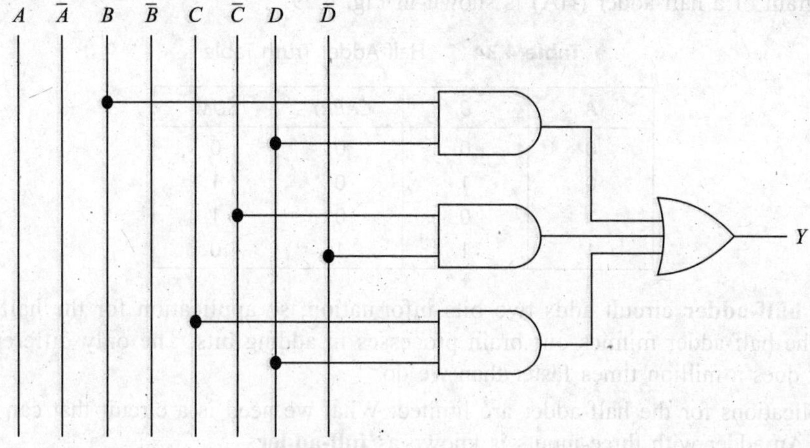

Fig. 4.57 Don't-care logic circuit

4.24 ARITHMETIC LOGIC UNITS

The Arithmetic and Logic Unit (ALU) is that part of CPU where actual data processing occurs. All calculations (mathematical) and all comparisons (logic functions) take place in this unit. A logic function is one where numbers or conditions are compared to each other. Circuits in the ALU are generally used to compare two members by subtracting one from the other. The sign (negative or positive) and the value of the difference tell the processor that the first number is equal to, less than or greater than the second number.

4.25 HALF-ADDERS

A logic circuit that adds 2 bits has two inputs and two outputs. The two inputs are two 1 bit numbers *A* and *B*, and the two output are the SUM of *A* and *B*, and the CARRY bit as shown in Fig. 4.58.

The boolean equations for these outputs are:

$$\text{SUM} = A \oplus B \qquad ...(4.47)$$

$$\text{CARRY} = AB \qquad ...(4.48)$$

The SUM output is *A* XOR *B* and the CARRY output is *A* AND *B*. Therefore, roman SUM = 1, when *A* and *B* are different. CARRY = 1, when *A* and *B* are 1s.

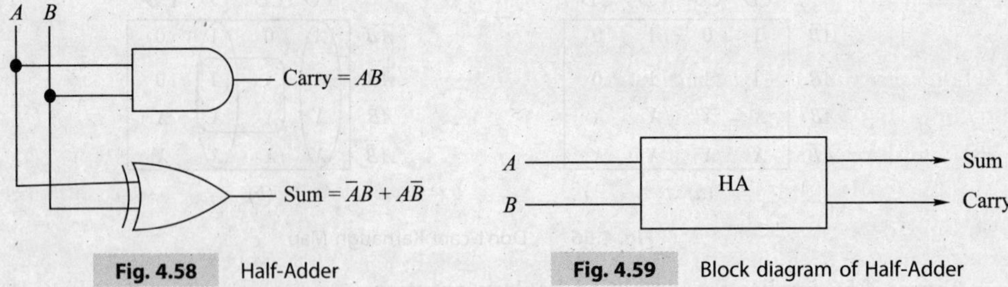

Fig. 4.58 Half-Adder

Fig. 4.59 Block diagram of Half-Adder

Table 4.34 shows the all possible output. When *A* and *B* are 0s, the sum is 0 with a CARRY 0. When *A* is 0 and *B* is 1, then SUM is 1 with CARRY 0. When *A* is 1 and *B* is 0, then SUM is 1 with CARRY 0. When *A* is 1 and *B* is 1, then SUM is 0 with CARRY 1. The block diagram of a half-adder (HA) is shown in Fig. 4.59.

Table 4.34 Half-Adder Truth Table

A	*B*	*CARRY*	*SUM*
0	0	0	0
0	1	0	1
1	0	0	1
1	1	1	0

The **half-adder** circuit adds two bits information, so application for the half-adder are limited. The half-adder mimics our brain processes in adding bits. The only difference is that half-adder does a million times faster than we do.

Applications for the half-adder are limited. What we need is a circuit that can add 3 bits at a time. An adder with three-inputs is known as **full-adder**.

4.26 FULL-ADDERS

A logic circuit that can add 3 bits has three inputs and two outputs. The three-inputs are three 1 bit numbers *A*, *B*, and *C*, and the two outputs are the SUM of *A*, *B*, and *C*, and the CARRY bit as shown in Fig. 4.60.

The boolean equations for these outputs are:

$$\text{SUM} = A \oplus B \oplus C \quad ...(4.49)$$

$$\text{CARRY} = AB + BC + AC \quad ...(4.50)$$

The SUM output is *A* XOR *B* XOR *C* and the CARRY output is *AB* OR *AC* OR *BC*. Therefore, SUM is 1, when the input 1s is odd. CARRY is 1, when two or more inputs are 1s.

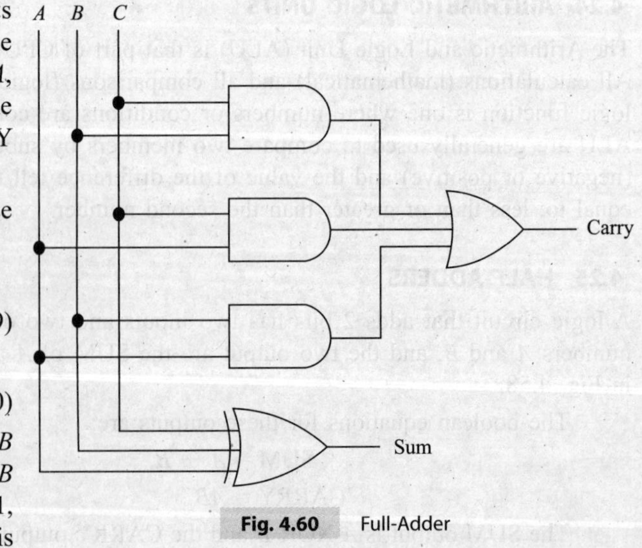

Fig. 4.60 Full-Adder

Table 4.35 shows the all possible output when A, B, and C are 0s, the sum is 0 with a CARRY 0. When $A = 0$, $B = 0$, and $C = 1$, then sum is 1 with CARRY 0. When $A = 0$, $B = 1$ and $C = 0$, then SUM is 1 with CARRY 0. When $A = 0$, $B = 1$ and $C = 1$, then SUM is 0 with CARRY 1. When $A = 1$, $B = 0$, and $C = 0$, then SUM is 1 with CARRY 0. When $A = 1$, $B = 0$, and $C = 1$, then SUM = 0 with CARRY 1. When $A = 1$, $B = 1$ and $C = 1$, then SUM = 0 with CARRY 1. When $A = 1$, $B = 1$, and $C = 1$, then SUM = 1 with CARRY 1.

Table 4.35 Full-Adder Truth Table

A	B	C	CARRY	SUM
0	0	0	0	0
0	0	1	0	1
0	1	0	0	1
0	1	1	1	0
1	0	0	0	1
1	0	1	1	0
1	1	0	1	0
1	1	1	1	1

Figure 4.61 shows the Block diagram of a full-adder.

The full-adder can do more than a million additions per second. Besides that, it never gets tired or bored, or asks for a raise.

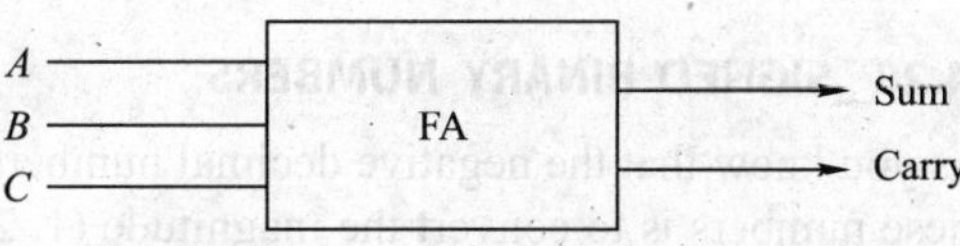

Fig. 4.61 Block diagram of Full-Adder

4.27 BINARY ADDERS

A logic circuit that can add two binary numbers is known as **binary adder**. Figure 4.62 shows a binary adder, which has one half-adder and three half-adders. This will add the two 4 bit word. The half-adder (HA) inputs are A_0 and B_0, and outputs are S_0 (SUM) with C_1 (CARRY). All others are full-adders (FA), each of these has three inputs A_1, B_1, and C_1.

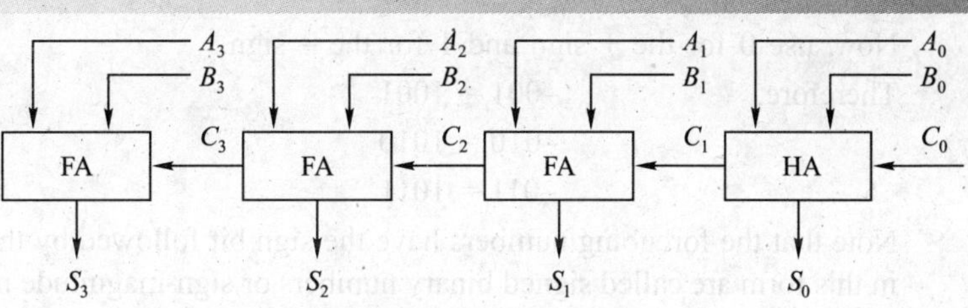

Fig. 4.62 Binary Adder

The circuit add two binary numbers as:

$$\begin{array}{r} A_3A_2A_1A_0 \\ \underline{B_3B_2B_1B_0} \\ \overline{C_4S_3S_2S_1S_0} \end{array}$$

We can build binary adders of any length by using more full-adders. For instance, to add 16 bit numbers, we need 1 half-adder and 15 full-adders. Figure 4.63 shows the abbreviated symbol for binary adder of any length. The words A and B are added to get a SUM plus a final CARRY.

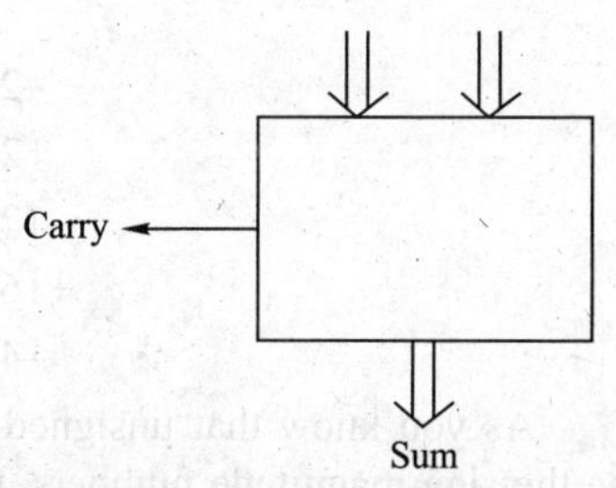

Fig. 4.63 Abbreviated symbol for binary adder of any length

4.27.1 Example on Binary Adders

Consider an example, when A = 1001 and B = 1011, then it carries out the following addition:

$$\begin{array}{r} 1001 \\ +\,1011 \end{array}$$

Figure 4.64 shows the input 1001 and 1011.

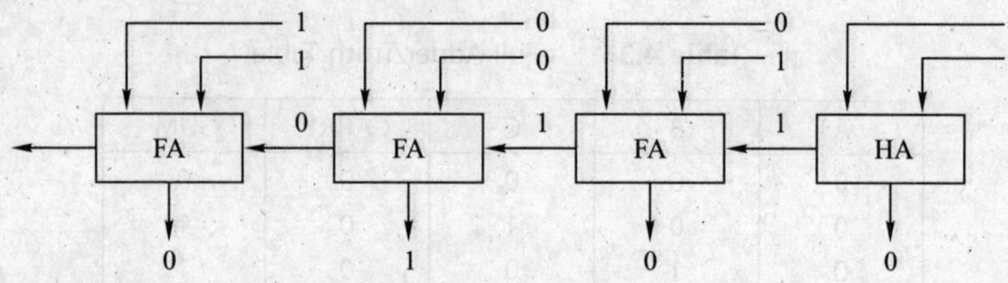

Fig. 4.64 Adding 9 and 11 to get 20

The half-adder produces a SUM = 0 with CARRY 1, the first full-adder produces a SUM = 0 and CARRY 1, the second full-adder produces a SUM = 1 with CARRY 0, and the third full-adder produces a SUM = 0 with CARRY 1. The overall output is 10100 which is equal to 20 in decimal number.

4.28 SIGNED BINARY NUMBERS

As you know that the negative decimal numbers are –1, –2, –3, ... and so on. One way to represent these numbers is to convert the magnitude (1, 2, 3, ...) to its binary equivalent and prefix the sign.

Therefore,
–1 = –001
–2 = –010
–3 = –011

Now, use 0 for the + sign and 1 for the – sign.

Therefore,
–001 = 1001
–010 = 1010
–011 = 1011

☞ Note that the foregoing numbers have the sign bit followed by the magnitude bits. Numbers in this form are called signed binary numbers or sign-magnitude numbers. For larger decimal numbers you need more than 4 bits. But the idea is still the same: the leading bit represents the sign and the remaining bits stand for the magnitude.

Here are some examples of converting sign-magnitude numbers:

+7 = 0000 0111
–25 = 1000 0000 0001 1001
+25 = 0000 0000 0001 1001
–128 = 1000 0000 1000 0000
+165 = 0000 0000 1010 0101
–48 = 1000 0000 0011 0000

As you know that unsigned 8 bit number cover the decimal range of 0 to 255. When you use the sign-magnitude numbers, you reduce the largest magnitude from 255 to 127 because you need to represent both positive and negative quantities. For instance, the negative numbers are 1000 0001 to 1111 1111 (–1 to –127). The positive numbers are 0000 0001 to 0111 1111 (+1 to +127). The largest magnitude is 127, which is approximately half of what unsigned binary numbers.

If the magnitude is greater than 127, then 16 bit arithmetic may work. With 16 bit number, the negative numbers are from

1000 0000 0000 0001 (–1)

to 1111 1111 1111 1111 (–32, 767)

and the positive numbers are from

0000 0000 0000 0001 (+1)

to 0111 1111 1111 1111 1111 (+32, 767)

The largest magnitude is 32, 767, which is approximately half of what unsigned binary numbers.

The main advantage of sign-magnitude numbers is their simplicity. Negative numbers are identical to positive numbers, except for the sign. You can easily find the number after deleting the sign bit and converting the binary number to decimal equivalents. The sign-magnitude numbers have limited use because they require complicated circuit. Sign-magnitude numbers are acceptable, if you don't want to add or subtract the data. For instance, the sign-magnitude numbers are used in analog-to-digital conversion.

4.29 2'S COMPLEMENT REPRESENTATION

As you have seen that the sign-magnitude numbers require complicated arithmetic logic as well as too much hardware because of the range of sign-magnitude numbers. This has led to the widespread use of complement for binary arithmetic.

4.29.1 1's Complement

The 1's complement of a binary number is the number that results when we complement each bit. For instance,

in $A = 1010$

then 1's complement is $\bar{A} = 0101$

For large binary numbers you need more bits. But the idea is still the same: complement each bit to obtain the 1's complement. For instance,

if $A = 1110\ 1100$

then $\bar{A} = 0001\ 0011$

Similarly, if $A = 0011\ 1111\ 0000\ 0110$

then $\bar{A} = 1100\ 0000\ 1111\ 1001$

Figure 4.65 shows how to produce the 1's complement with logic circuits.

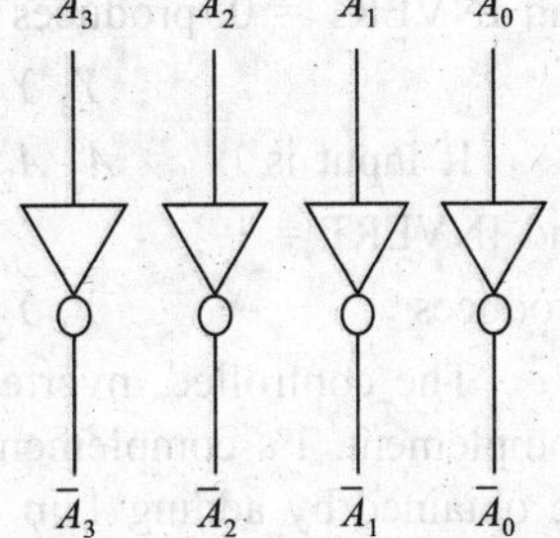

Fig. 4.65 Inverters produce the 1's complements

4.29.2 2's Complement

The 2's complement is the binary number that results when we add 1 to the 1's complement. As a formula:

$$2\text{'s Complement} = 1\text{'s Complement} + 1$$

or $A' = \bar{A} + 1$

where $A' = 2\text{'s Complement}$

$\bar{A} = 1\text{'s Complement}$

For instance, if $A = 1010$

then 1's complement is $\bar{A} = 0101$

and 2's complement is $A' = 0110$

Here is another example, if

$$A = 0011\ 0101\ 1001\ 1100$$
$$\bar{A} = 1100\ 1010\ 0110\ 0011$$
$$A' = 1100\ 1010\ 0110\ 0100$$

4.30 CONTROLLED INVERTER

Figure 4.66 shows a controlled inverter. If INVERT is low, it transmits the 4 bit input to the output. If INVERT is high, it transmits the 1's complement.

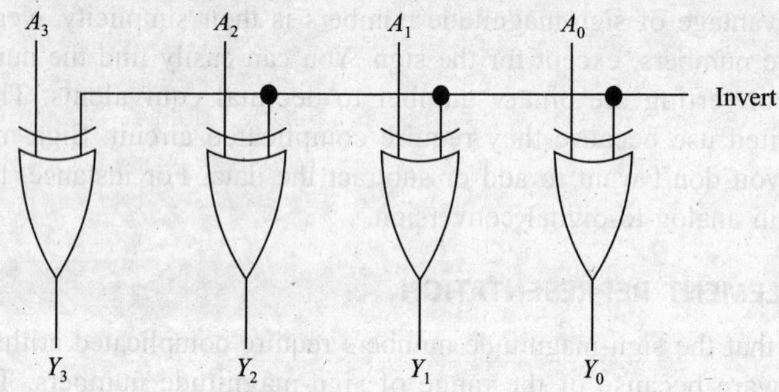

Fig. 4.66 Controlled inverter

For instance, if input is

$$A_3\ A_2\ A_1\ A_0 = 1110$$

and INVERT = 0, produces

$$Y_3\ Y_2\ Y_1\ Y_0 = 1110$$

If input is $A_3\ A_2\ A_1\ A_0 = 1110$

and INVERT = 1

produces $Y_3\ Y_2\ Y_1\ Y_0 = 0001$

The controlled inverter is useful for subtraction, because during subtraction we need 2's complement. 1's complement has been produced by controlled inverter and 2's complement can be obtained by adding 1 in the 1's complement.

4.31 ADDER-SUBTRACTER

In the early stages of computers, the signal binary numbers (positive and negative) are used which led to complicated arithmetic circuits. Then, engineers discovered the 2's complement representation which greatly help to simplify the arithmetic circuits. Adder-subtracter is widely used arithmetic circuit which produces 2's complement.

Figure 4.67 shows the adder-subtracter, as logic circuit that can add or subtract binary numbers. We

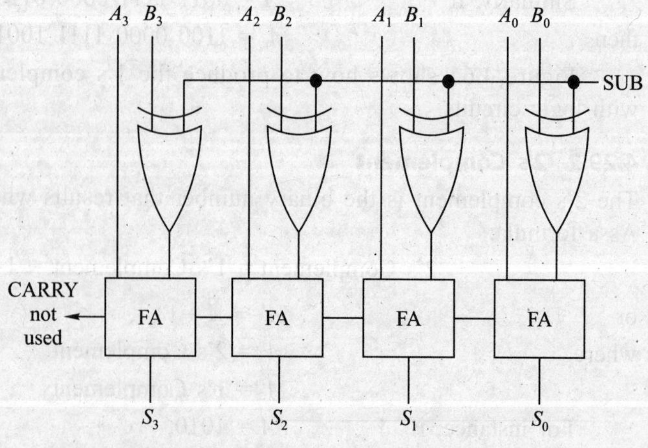

Fig. 4.67 Binary Adder-subtractor (4-bit)

can connect full-adders to add or subtract binary numbers. The circuit is laid out from right to left, similar to the way we add binary numbers. The final CARRY is not used because S_3 is the sign and S_2 roman to S_0 are the numerical bits. The final CARRY has no significance at this time.

4.31.1 Addition

When SUM = 0, the B bits pass through the controlled inverter without inversion. Therefore, the full-adders produce the sum.

$$\text{SUM} = A + B$$

Illustratively,
$$\begin{array}{r} A_3A_2A_1A_0 \\ +\ B_3B_2B_1B_0 \\ \hline S_3S_2S_1S_0 \end{array}$$

For instance, if A = 0001 1000, B = 0001 0000 and SUM = 0, then the output of the adder-subtracter is

$$\begin{array}{r} 0001\ 1000 \\ +\ 0001\ 0000 \\ \hline 0010\ 1000 \\ \hline \end{array}$$

The decimal equivalent of the foregoing addition is

$$\begin{array}{r} 24 \\ +\ 16 \\ \hline 40 \\ \hline \end{array}$$

4.31.2 Subtraction

When SUM = 1, the controlled inverter produces the 1's complement. Furthermore, the high SUM adds a 1 to the first full-adder. This addition of 1 to the 1's complement forms the 2's complement of B.

The output of full-adders is $S = A + B'$ $\qquad (\because B' = \overline{B} + 1)$

which is equivalent to $\qquad S = A - B$

because the 2's complement is equivalent to a sign change.

Here is how subtraction appears:

$$\begin{array}{r} A_3A_2A_1A_0 \\ -\ B_3B_2B_1B_0 \\ \hline S_0S_2S_1S_0 \end{array}$$

or
$$\begin{array}{r} 1 \leftarrow \text{SUM} \\ A_3A_2A_1A_0 \\ -\ \overline{B_3}\overline{B_2}\overline{B_1}\overline{B_0} \\ \hline S_3S_2S_1S_0 \end{array}$$

For instance, if $\qquad A$ = 0001 1000 (24)

B = 0001 0000 (16)

and $\qquad$ SUM = 1

then $\qquad \overline{B}$ = 1110 1111

or $\qquad B'$ = 1111 0010

Therefore, the adder-subtractor subtracts the inputs by adding the 2's complement

$$\begin{array}{rl} 0001\ 1000 & (24) \\ +\ 1111\ 0000 & (-16) \\ \hline 0000\ 1000 & \end{array}$$

The decimal equivalent of the foregoing addition is

$$\begin{array}{r} 24 \\ +\ -16 \\ \hline 8 \\ \hline \end{array}$$

☞ **Note:**

1. Taking the 2's complement of a binary number is the same as changing the sign of the equivalent decimal number.
2. Multiplication is done with addition instructions and division with subtraction instructions. Therefore, an adder-subtracter is all that is needed for addition, subtraction, multiplication, and division.

REVIEW QUESTIONS

Multiple Choice Questions

1. A Gate is a logic circuit with one or more input signals but .... output signal.
   (*a*) two (*b*) double (*c*) one (*d*) more than one
2. An inventor is a Gate with only .... input; the output is always in the opposite state from the input.
   (*a*) one (*b*) two (*c*) more than one (*d*) All of the above
3. An inverter is also called a .... Gate.
   (*a*) NOT (*b*) OR (*c*) AND (*d*) NAND
4. The OR Gate has two or more input signals. If any input is ...., the output is high.
   (*a*) low (*b*) high (*c*) 0 (*d*) All of the above
5. The number of input words in a truth table always equals ...., where n is the number of input bits.
   (*a*) 10^n (*b*) 2^n (*c*) 4^n (*d*) 8^n
6. The .... Gate has two or more input signals. All inputs must be high to get a high output.
   (*a*) OR (*b*) NAND (*c*) AND (*d*) NOR
7. In boolean algebra, the overbar stands for the NOT operation, the plus sign stands for the .... operation.
   (*a*) AND (*b*) OR (*c*) NAND (*d*) NOR
8. In boolean algebra, the times sign stands for the .... operation.
   (*a*) AND (*b*) OR (*c*) NAND (*d*) NOR
9. The inverter OR Gate and AND Gate are called decision-making elements because they can recognize some input .... while disregarding others. A Gate recognizes a word when its output is ....
   (*a*) words, high (*b*) bytes, low (*c*) bytes, high (*d*) character, low
10. How many inputs signals can a Gate have?
    (*a*) one (*b*) more than one (*c*) two only (*d*) both (*a*) and (*b*)
11. How many output signals can a Gate have?
    (*a*) one (*b*) more than one (*c*) two only (*d*) both (*a*) and (*b*)
12. An OR Gate has 6 inputs. How many input words are in its truth table?
    (*a*) 64 (*b*) 32 (*c*) 16 (*d*) 128

13. An OR Gate has 6 inputs. What is the only input word that produces a 0 output?
(*a*) 000000 (*b*) 000111 (*c*) 111000 (*d*) 111111

14. An AND Gate has 7 inputs. How many input word are in its truth table?
(*a*) 64 (*b*) 32 (*c*) 16 (*d*) 128

15. An AND Gate has 7 inputs, what is the only input word that produces a 1 output?
(*a*) 0000000 (*b*) 0001111 (*c*) 1110000 (*d*) 1111111

16. What is the boolean equation for (Fig. 4.68)?
(*a*) $Y = A + B$ (*b*) $Y = AB$ (*c*) $Y = \overline{AB}$ (*d*) $Y = \overline{A + B}$

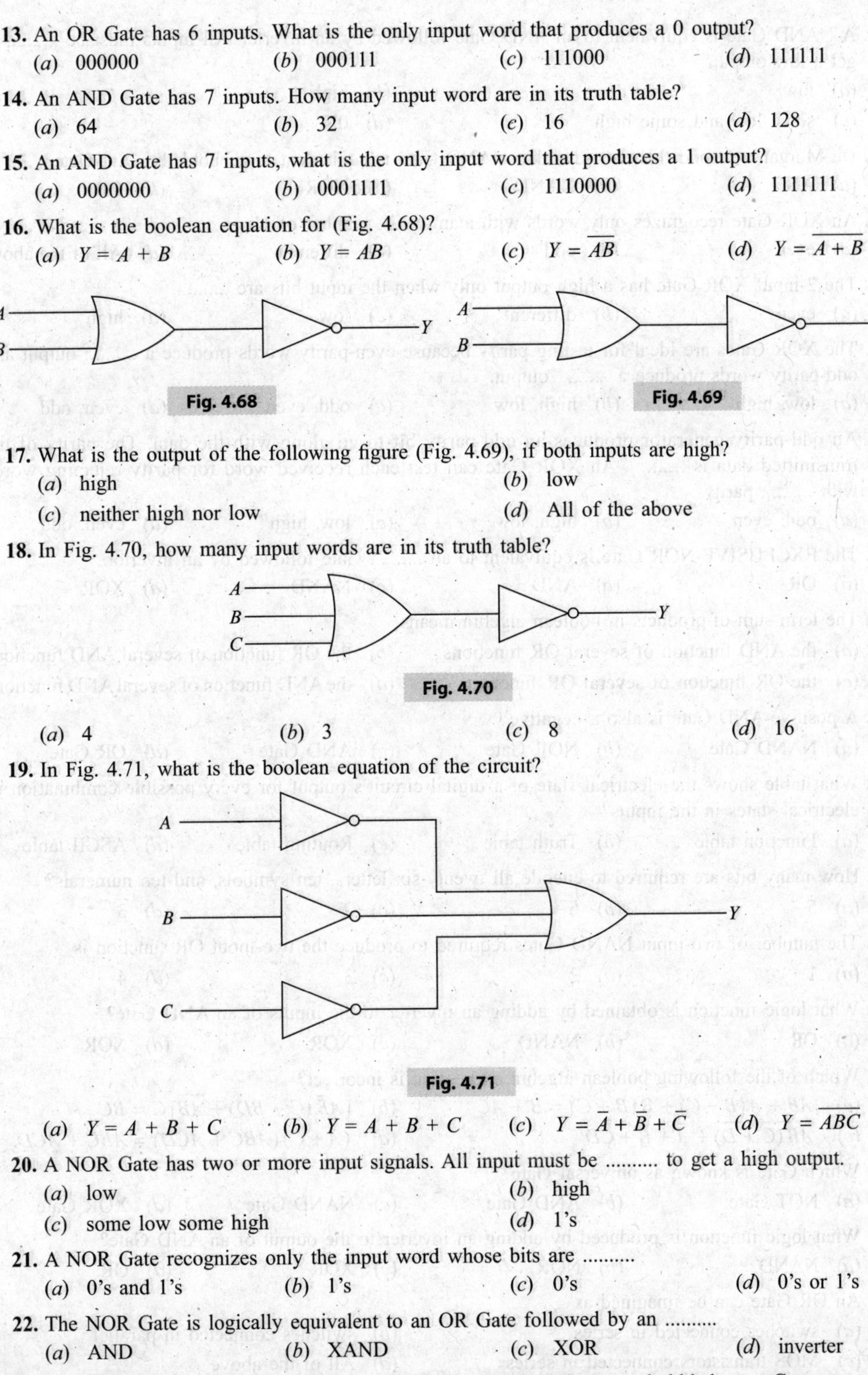

Fig. 4.68

Fig. 4.69

17. What is the output of the following figure (Fig. 4.69), if both inputs are high?
(*a*) high (*b*) low
(*c*) neither high nor low (*d*) All of the above

18. In Fig. 4.70, how many input words are in its truth table?

Fig. 4.70

(*a*) 4 (*b*) 3 (*c*) 8 (*d*) 16

19. In Fig. 4.71, what is the boolean equation of the circuit?

Fig. 4.71

(*a*) $Y = A + B + C$ (*b*) $Y = A + B + C$ (*c*) $Y = \bar{A} + \bar{B} + \bar{C}$ (*d*) $Y = \overline{ABC}$

20. A NOR Gate has two or more input signals. All input must be .... to get a high output.
(*a*) low (*b*) high
(*c*) some low some high (*d*) 1's

21. A NOR Gate recognizes only the input word whose bits are ....
(*a*) 0's and 1's (*b*) 1's (*c*) 0's (*d*) 0's or 1's

22. The NOR Gate is logically equivalent to an OR Gate followed by an ....
(*a*) AND (*b*) XAND (*c*) XOR (*d*) inverter

23. De Morgan's first theorem says that a NOR Gate is equivalent to a bubbled .... Gate.
(*a*) AND (*b*) XAND (*c*) XOR (*d*) NOR

24. A NAND Gate is equivalent to an AND Gate followed by an inverter. All inputs must be .... to get a low output.
(*a*) low (*b*) high
(*c*) some low and some high (*d*) 0's

25. De Morgan's second theorem says that NAND Gate is equivalent to a bubbled .... Gate.
(*a*) AND (*b*) XAND (*c*) XOR (*d*) OR

26. An XOR Gate recognizes only words with a/an .... number of 1's.
(*a*) even (*b*) odd (*c*) different (*d*) All of the above

27. The 2-input XOR Gate has a high output only when the input bits are ....
(*a*) even (*b*) different (*c*) low (*d*) high

28. The XOR Gates are ideal for testing parity because even-parity words produce a .... output and odd-parity words produce a .... output.
(*a*) low, high (*b*) high, low (*c*) odd, even (*d*) even, odd

29. An odd-parity generator produces an odd-parity bit to go along with the data. The parity of the transmitted data is .... An XOR Gate can test each received word for parity rejecting words with .... parity.
(*a*) odd, even (*b*) high, low (*c*) low, high (*d*) even, odd

30. The EXCLUSIVE-NOR Gate is equivalent to an .... Gate followed by an invertor.
(*a*) OR (*b*) AND (*c*) NAND (*d*) XOR

31. The term sum-of-products in boolean algebra means
(*a*) the AND function of several OR functions (*b*) the OR function of several AND functions
(*c*) the OR function of several OR functions (*d*) the AND function of several AND functions

32. A positive AND Gate is also a negative
(*a*) NAND Gate (*b*) NOR Gate (*c*) AND Gate (*d*) OR Gate

33. What table shows the electrical state of a digital circuit's output for every possible combination of electrical states in the inputs?
(*a*) Function table (*b*) Truth table (*c*) Routing table (*d*) ASCII table

34. How many bits are required to encode all twenty-six letters, ten symbols, and ten numerals?
(*a*) 5 (*b*) 6 (*c*) 2 (*d*) 3

35. The number of two-input NAND Gates required to produce the two-input OR function is
(*a*) 1 (*b*) 2 (*c*) 3 (*d*) 4

36. What logic function is obtained by adding an inverter to the inputs of an AND Gate?
(*a*) OR (*b*) NAND (*c*) XOR (*d*) NOR

37. Which of the following boolean algebra expression is incorrect?
(*a*) $AB + A(B + C) + B(B + C) = B + AC$ (*b*) $[A\bar{B}(C + BD) + \overline{AB}]C = B\bar{C}$
(*c*) $\overline{AB(C + D)} + \bar{A} + B + \bar{C}D$ (*d*) $(A + C)(ABC + ACD) = ABC + ACD.$

38. Which Gate is known as universal Gate?
(*a*) NOT Gate (*b*) AND Gate (*c*) NAND Gate (*d*) XOR Gate

39. What logic function is produced by adding an inverter to the output of an AND Gate?
(*a*) NAND (*b*) NOR (*c*) XOR (*d*) OR

40. An OR Gate can be imagined as
(*a*) switches connected in series (*b*) switches connected in parallel
(*c*) MOS transistors connected in series (*d*) All of the above

41. What logic function is produced by adding an inverter to each input and the output of an AND Gate?
(*a*) NAND (*b*) NOR (*c*) OR (*d*) XOR

42. Which of the following boolean algebra statements represent commutative law

(*a*) $(A + B) + CA + (B + C)$ (*b*) $A \cdot (B + C)\ (A \cdot B) + (A \cdot C)$

(*c*) $A + BB + A$ (*d*) $A + AA$

43. For what logic Gate the outputs in complement of the input?

(*a*) NOT (*b*) AND (*c*) OR (*d*) XOR

ANSWERS

1. (*c*) **2.** (*a*) **3.** (*a*) **4.** (*b*) **5.** (*b*) **6.** (*c*) **7.** (*b*) **8.** (*a*)
9. (*a*) **10.** (*d*) **11.** (*a*) **12.** (*a*) **13.** (*a*) **14.** (*d*) **15.** (*d*) **16.** (*d*)
17. (*b*) **18.** (*c*) **19.** (*c*) **20.** (*a*) **21.** (*c*) **22.** (*d*) **23.** (*a*) **24.** (*b*)
25. (*d*) **26.** (*b*) **27.** (*b*) **28.** (*a*) **29.** (*a*) **30.** (*d*) **31.** (*b*) **32.** (*d*)
33. (*a*) **34.** (*b*) **35.** (*c*) **36.** (*d*) **37.** (*b*) **38.** (*c*) **39.** (*a*) **40.** (*b*)
41. (*c*) **42.** (*c*) **43.** (*a*)

QUESTIONS

1. Show the truth table of a 4-input OR Gate.

2. How many input words are in the truth table of an 8-input OR Gate? Which input words produce a high output?

3. Describe the truth table of an 8-input AND Gate.

4. How many input signals can a Gate have? How many output signals?

5. Double inversion occurs when two inverters are cascaded. Does such a connection act like an inverter or noninverter?

6. An OR Gate has 6 inputs. How many input words are in its truth table? What is the only input word that produces a 0 output?

7. If you cascade five inverters, does the overall circuit act like an inverter or noninverter?

8. An AND Gate has 7 inputs. How many input words are in its truth table? What is the only input word that produces 1 output?

9. What do you mean by don't-care conditions. How do you treat don't-care condition in Karnaugh's map?

10. Draw the logic circuit for $Y = A\bar{B}C + ABC$
Use boolean algebra to simplify the equation. Then draw the corresponding logic circuit.

11. Prove that Figs. 4.72 (*a*) and (*b*) are equivalent.

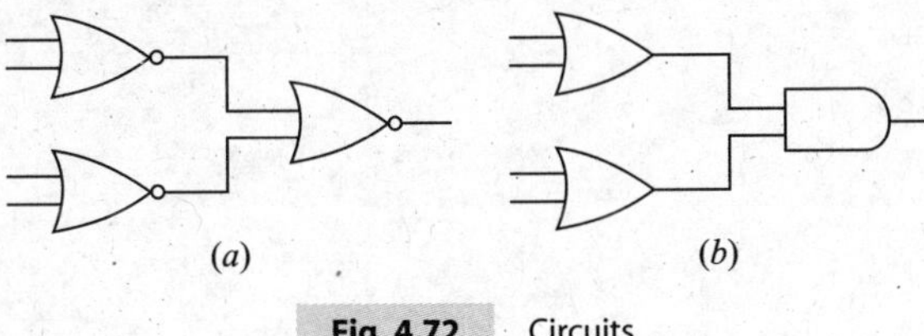

Fig. 4.72 Circuits

12. Prove that Figs. 4.73 (*a*) and (*b*) are equivalent.

13. A NOR has 6-inputs. How many input words are in its truth table? What is the only input word that produces 1 output?

14. How many input words are there in the truth table of an 8-input XOR Gate?

15. Define pairs, quads, and octets.

16. How do you get the boolean equation for the given fundamental products?

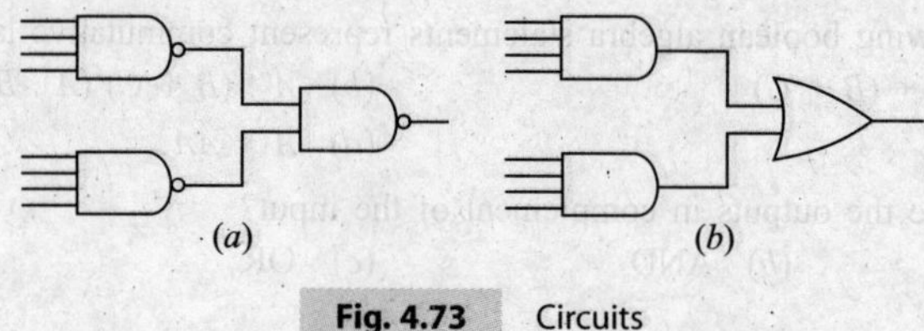

Fig. 4.73 Circuits

17. What are the fundamental products for each of the input words $ABCD$ = 1101, $ABCD$ = 0010, $ABCD$ = 1110?

18. Draw the logic circuit for this boolean equation $Y = A\bar{B}\bar{C}\bar{D} + AB\bar{C}\bar{D} + ABCD$.

19. Why does the carry input has no effect on logic operation?

20. Since sign-magnitude numbers are fairly easy to understand, why has the 2's complement system become so widespread?

21. Suppose that FD34H is the input to a 16 bit controlled inverter. What is the inverted output in hexadecimal notation? In binary?

22. How many inputs does a full-adder have? Explain the circuit diagram along with truth table.

23. Add these 16 bit numbers:

	0000 1111 1010 1100
and	0011 1000 0111 1111

Show the corresponding hexadecimal and decimal numbers

[**Ans:** 0100 1000 0010 1011, 482BH, 18, 475]

24. Show the binary subtraction of 125 and 200.

[**Ans:** 0100 1011]

25. Show how to add 150 and 85 with unsigned 8 bit numbers.

26. What is the 2's complement of each of these?

(*a*) 1111 0000 1111 0000 (*b*) 1011 1110

(*c*) 0101 1010 (*d*) 0000 1111

27. Express each of the following in 8 bit sign-magnitude form?

(*a*) +25 (*b*) –15 (*c*) –56 (*d*) +107

28. What kind of logic circuit can be used to produce the carry output and the sum output of a half-adder?

29. How many bits at the most a half adder can add? Write a truth table for a half-adder.

STORAGE DEVICES

The storage devices are broadly classified into Secondary storage and primary storage. The secondary storage is known as peripheral storage, and is used to stores information of the computer that is not in current use. The secondary storage is typically slower and is of higher capacity than primary storage. The secondary storage is almost non-volatile. The secondary storage is slow due to serial access.

The Primary storage is used to refer for local random access disk storage and is properly called secondary storage. If this type of storage is called primary storage, then the term secondary storage would refer to offline. This usually occurs in the slower, larger forms of storage which is used to develop the vendors to provide secure device management services, authentication services, as well as encryption for data. There is software and application based solutions; however software-based encryption solutions can impact performance during the storage process. Vendors provide hardware based solutions, which are appliances that provide authentication to protect the data. These devices are taken into account for the different requirements of securing data on primary or secondary storage. The primary storage performance and access specifications for the tape environment and requires the encrypting to tape would require integration with backup schemas for primary storage scenarios.

The secondary storage helps in securing the data on media types and storage categories, as data is vulnerable to network attacks, administrative access and media theft. There are many organizations who are working with third parties and disaster recovery efforts. Often data goes offsite and is in the hands of employees that are not authorized to see critical company data. And storage consolidation opens the door to greater administrative access. All of these trends drive the need to ensure the data at rest is secure.

Storage Devices are the data storage devices that are used in the computers to store the data. The computer has many types of data storage devices. Some of them can be classified as the *removable data Storage Devices* and the others as the *non-removable data Storage Devices*.

The data Storage Devices come in many sizes and shapes, and more over the technology used for the storage of the data over them is also altogether different. The storage devices are one of the most important components of the computer system. The memory is of two types; one is the primary memory and the other one is the secondary memory.

The primary memory is the volatile memory and the secondary memory is the non-volatile memory. The volatile memory is the kind of the memory that is erasable and the non-volatile memory is the one where in the contents cannot be erased. Basically when we talk about the data storage devices it is generally assumed to be the secondary memory.

The secondary memory is used to store the data permanently in the computer. The secondary storage devices are usually as follows: hard disk drives—this is the most common type of storage device that is used in almost all the computer systems. The other ones include the 'floppy disk drives', the 'CD ROM', and the 'DVD ROM'. The flash memory, the 'USB data card' etc.

The storage devices are used to record the data over any storage surface. The memories may also be of different types depending upon the architecture and the design like the optical data storage memory, magnetic media storage and the mechanical storage media etc. and also the flash memory devices etc.

The storage devices are actually defined as the peripheral unit which holds the data like the—tape, disk, or flash memory card etc. The most of the drives that are used for the purpose of data storage are fragile and the data can be easily corrupted in them. The data storage devices are the ones that are also used for the backup and the archiving of the data. The data storage devices were at a time in the past used to be too costly and expensive. But these days the data storage devices are becoming cheap day by day. Hence the data storage devices price is falling. So, we are in a position to get a storage device for a comparatively cheaper price than the earlier drive. The technology is improving a lot and now the memory storage capacity has gone up TB.

The data in the storage devices can be in the form of the files, databases, digital video and the audio etc. The storage devices that are called as the non-volatile can store the data permanently until otherwise erased purposely. This is in the case of the hard disk drives or the floppy disk drives.

The other kinds of the storage media like for example the CD and the DVD can even have again two types of the storage; the first one is that in which the data once written cannot be erased. It is stored permanently over it. While the second type of the CD's or the DVD's are called as the rewritable; where in the data that is once written can be erased completely and the same storage device can be used again for storing the different data.

The memory storage device are of two types basically one is the primary memory which is a must in any computer system and the other is the secondary memory. The primary memory is also known as the temporary memory as it cannot hold the data when there is any a kind of disruption of power services. The primary memory is the volatile memory. This means that if the power is switched off or there is a power failure then the data in it is all lost. This is the temporary memory. The other one is the secondary memory or the hard disk, floppy disk or the CD, DVD discs etc. there are called as the non-volatile memories or the permanent storage devices. The RAM is the example of the primary memory or the temporary storage media.

The temporary storage device stores the data only for a period of time. The primary memory or the main memory is a must in any computer system. The primary memory is initiated as soon as the computer is booted. The RAM may be of two types one is the Static RAM and the other is the Dynamic RAM. It is this memory that is actually recognized by the Ms DOS operating system as the base memory. This starts right from the base address.

The read mode is restricted to access only 1 mega bytes of the memory. Consider the booting up of the DOS operating system. The DOS as it boots up the machine, it occupies the first few locations of the base memory or the main memory for the storage of the DOS resident commands or the programs. It is also used for the storage of the vector address of the interrupt routines. After the system gets boot-up, the memory available within the area is called conventional memory. This is the memory that is available for the user to execute the programs. The area of the memory above the conventional memory is called as the upper memory area or the UMA. It is also referred to as the expanded memory. This memory is reserved for the usage of the memory that is reserved for the special use by the BIOS ROM, video and the other hardware devices like the display cards etc. Some of the memory above the conventional memory is empty and some is filled with the RAMs that are used by the adapters of the video terminals and some are filled with the ROMs that contain the low level drivers such as the hard disk controllers, LAN adapters, video adapters etc.

The memory area which is dedicated to the particular device RAMs and the ROMs are called as the reserved memory area. The expanded memory is a system of paging memory within the conventional memory by using the block of memory as a page frame in the expanded memory area. A page frame is an area of the memory map where the expanded pages can be switched in and switched out.

The EMS—Expanded Memory Specification is an alternative definition of the Lotus Intel Microsoft (LIM) standard. The RAM is now available starting from as low as 32 mega bytes to 2 giga bytes. The major manufacturers of the RAM are the Hyundai, and the Hynix. There are also some other brands that are available. This is the most fragile part of the computer that should be handled with care. They certainly increase the speed and the performance of the system.

The Removable Storage Media are the types of storage devices that are used for the storage of the data. The main reason for using the removable storage media is the ease of portability. That is the ease with which the data can be transferred. The data is of importance and is necessary for the movement in some cases.

Here the case of portability of the storage device comes into the picture. The removable storage media serves the same purpose. More over there are many application of the storage of the data over the removable media. The first and the foremost is the portability that is already discussed above. The next is the issue of the backup and archiving of the data that is important and also sensitive in nature. The backup of data is as important as the storage of data is important.

The CD and the DVD are key players in the removable storage types that are used for the purpose of backup and archiving of the data. The main reason for storing the data over the removable devices is that the data can be easily moved physically from one place to another at the time of any disaster or any other casualty.

The floppy disk drive was the removable storage media that was used for the purpose of storing the data over the disk for the backup. This was the case in the 80's; but as the pace has increased in the technology the CD's and the DVD's had gained momentum for the purpose of providing backup to the data. The 'floppy disk drives' that are available even today do not provide enough memory capacity. And now the concept of the 'flash memory devices' is doing rounds for providing data transfer from place to another.

There are some situations where in the normal data transfer through the networking is not possible. But as in the case of the removal storage media the data transfer can be easily done. Hence the main advantage regarding the removal storage media is the data transfer from the computers to the other computers where there is no existence of the network. The data transfer facility is important even in case; when the network actually exists but there is a failure of the network. In such situations the external data transfer is quite useful.

Also in some cases the data from one system is required to be used through the other system. Here the network connections are not at all possible. Hence the data has to be physically moved from one place to the other. The example for this may be the regular video or the audio. If it is so desired that the video or the audio is to be used through the mode of the large panel television; but the digital video or the audio is in the computer. Hence in such a situation it is not possible to connect the two different types of systems that are the computer and the television. In such a situation the removable data storage devices come into the play.

The solution to this problem is that the digital video or the audio should be burned over the CD or the DVD in the format that is supported by the VCD player associated with the television. And after that is done the video could be used through the television. Similar is the case with the audio also. The removable storage media has one more example of the Zip drives.

The acronym for ROM is Read Only Memory. It means that when the data is burnt on a ROM, it cannot be removed nor it cannot be altered, it can only read. ROM can save its contents even when the computer is turned off. Therefore ROM is known as nonvolatile. In most of the personal computers, a ROM stores programs such as the program that boots the computer. ROMs are widely used in calculators and other devices such as laser printers.

There are four basic ROM types—PROM, EPROM, EEPROM and Flash memory. ROM chips are costlier and time-consuming in small quantities. Developers created another type of ROM known as programmable read-only memory PROM. The PROM chips are inexpensively and easily available chips. The PROM chips have a grid aligned along the columns and rows as seen in ordinary ROM. The difference between these two ROM is that at every intersection a PROM chip has a fuse. When a charge is sent between a column, it will pass through the fuse of a cell and indicates a value 1. All the cells have a fuse, to change the value of a cell to 0, we send a specific amount of current to the cell. The higher voltage will breaks the connection by burning out the fuse. This process of burning of fuse is known as burning the PROM. Even though ROM & PROM are inexpensive chip, the cost adds up time to time.

Another improved version known as 'erasable programmable' read-only memory EPROM answers this issue. EPROM chips can be rewritten many times. To Erase an EPROM we require a tool that emits ultraviolet (UV) light. The EPROMs are configured by EPROM programmer that provides voltage depending on the type of EPROM used. The grid of columns and rows in an EPROM consists of a cell at each intersection and has two transistors. These two transistors are separated using thin oxide layer. One transistor is known as the 'floating gate' and the other transistor is known as the 'control gate'. The floating gate only link to the row through the control gate. As long as there is a link is in place, the cell has a value of 1. To change the value to 0 a process called Fowler-Nordheim tunneling. Tunneling is used to alter the placement of electrons. An electrical charge is usually of 10 to 13 volts is applied to the floating gate in order to change the levels. This charge causes the floating gate transistor to act as electron gun. The excited electrons are pushed on the other side of the thin oxide layer, by giving it a negative charge. These negatively charged electrons act as a barrier between the control gate and the floating gate.

The advanced type of ROM known as 'Electrically erasable programmable read-only memory' (EEPROM) chips removes the drawbacks which are present in EPROMs: The chip need not to be removed to be rewritten, the EPROM chip need not have to be completely erased, the contents which has to be changed does not require additional equipment. Instead of using Ultra Violet light, we can simply return the electrons in the cells of an EEPROM to application of an electric field to each cell. This erases the content of EEPROM, which can be used for rewritten.

5.1 COMPUTER STORAGE DENSITY

Computer storage density is the quantity of information that need to be stored on a given length of track of a computer storage medium. The higher computer density is more used and is desirable; it allows more data to be stored on the physical space. Computer storage density has a relation to storage capacity of a medium. The recording density is measured in the following ways.

They are linear recording density:

- The linear recording data is used to store data on concentric tracks of surface of the diskette. The recording density of computer storage density is just 17,434 bits per inch. The computer storage density can also be surface density: The diskette can store 80 tracks of data at a spacing of 135 tracks per inch with the innermost track at approximately 10.5 millimeters radius and the outermost track is at approximately 25.5 millimeters radius. The tracks occupy a surface storage area of approximately 1700 square millimeters. The recording density is 6,940 bits per square millimeter.

- The physical density of computer storage density cans physically measures for a volume of 25,380 cubic millimeters. The physical density of computer storage density is 465 bits per cubic millimeter. The different storage mediums are compared to measure the efficiency of the storage. The modern storage densities are quite high is approximately 5,020,000 bits per cubic millimeter. The computer storage density of digital magnetic tape is usually measured in bytes per length; the other media in bits per square millimeter of surface area.
- The computer storage density media will store data in volumetric space, making volume computations more relevant. Also, storage densities computed for comparison of technologies usually ignore physical containment; that is, memory density is computed based upon the number of bits relative to the surface of the integrated circuit, rather than the surface of the encasement. There is a theoretical upper limit to the amount of information that can be stored in a finite space. This limited information density limits the theoretical maximum information capacity of any given object. Practically speaking, technology is many orders of magnitude away from this limit.
- Computer storage density is a measure of the quantity of information bits that can be stored on a given length of track, area of surface, or in a given volume; of a computer storage medium. The computer storage density is of higher density, it allows greater volumes of data to be stored in the same physical space. Computer storage density has a relationship to storage capacity of a given medium.

  The capacity of a computer storage density could be measured in these ways:
- **The linear recording density** could be able to store on surface of the diskette. The maximum recording density of the computer storage density is of 1 inch for the innermost track is 17,434 bits per inch.
- **The Surface density:** The diskette will store 80 tracks of data at a spacing of 135 tracks per inch (5.05 tracks per millimeter) with the innermost track at approximately 10.5 millimeters The computer storage density of the diskette physically measures 94 × 90 × 3 millimeters. The physical density by volume is 465 bits per cubic millimeter. Computer storage density is compared by density in order to measure the efficiency of the storage.

  Different secondary storage media can be ranked according to the following criteria:

1. **Retrieval speed:** The access time of a storage device is the time it takes to locate and retrieve the stored data. A fast access time is preferable for any storage media.
2. **Storage capacity:** A device's storage capacity is the ability to store data. A large storage capacity is desired.
3. **Cost per bit of capacity:** Low cost is preferred.

Three secondary-storage media used with all sizes of computers are—magnetic tapes; magnetic disks; and optical technology. While these media can hold much more data than primary storage, access to the data is slower.

5.2 CONCEPT DIGITAL DATA STORAGE

The concept of Digital Data Storage is used for storing and backing up computer data on magnetic tape. Digital Data Storage uses tape of 4 millimeters wide and the tape is 60 meters long. Material technology allowed the length to be increased significantly and a Digital Data Storage tape drive uses helical scanning for recording, the same process used by a video cassette recorder. There are two read heads and two write heads which are provided in the drive. The read heads verify the data that has been written and the write heads rewrite the data. In order to keep the drive in the working condition the tape heads should be cleaned to be kept in good conditions.

Digital Data Storage tapes have life of at the maximum of 10 years. The different type of Digital Data Storage is:

- **DDS-1 (Digital Data Storage-1):** This version is used to store up to 1.3 GB compressed on a 60 meter cartridge and 2 GB uncompressed on a 90 meter cartridge.
- **DDS-2 (Digital Data Storage-2):** This version stores up to 4 GB uncompressed on a 120 meter cartridge. Digital Data Storage-2 is best suited for small network servers.
- **DDS-3 (Digital Data Storage-3):** This version stores up to 12 GB uncompressed on a 125 meter cartridge. The Digital Data Storage-3 drive works fine for medium-sized servers. Digital Data Storage-3 uses Partial Response Maximum Likelihood techniques. Partial Response Maximum Likelihood is used to eliminate electronic noise for a cleaner data recording.
- **DDS-4 (Digital Data Storage-4):** This version can stores up to 20 GB uncompressed on a 150 meter cartridge. The businesses of mid-size businesses can get the benefit from DDS-4. DAT 72 Digital Data Storage-72 can stores up to 36 GB uncompressed on a 170 meter cartridge. The Digital Data Storage-72 is backwards compatible with DDS-3 and DDS-4. The data transfer rate is about 7 MB/s.

The digital storage of information has the advantages over analog techniques and are very much similar to the digital communication of information holds advantages over analog communication. This is not to say that digital data storage is unequivocally superior to analog, but it does address some of the more common problems associated with analog techniques and thus finds immense popularity in both consumer and industrial applications.

Digital data storage uses the digital computation technology and find out the natural application of the computers. If we are going to store data regarding the magnitude of a voltage signal then a small chunk in the magnetic material is noticed. Many magnetic materials as we knows are known for strength of magnetization by encoding different types of data into specific binary number schemes, digital storage allows us to archive a wide variety of information that is often difficult to encode in analog form. A wider range of text is encoded using the standard, in like manner. Any kind of numerical data can be represented using binary notation on digital media, and any kind of information that can be encoded in numerical form. The advantage of digital data storage is the data does not get corrupted.

5.3 TAPE DRIVES

The tape drives are the best backup medium which is suitable for average PC user, if you get the right kind and use it properly. The advantages of tape Drives are—First is capacity, as we know, the hard drives keep on getting bigger and bigger, and tape is economical backup medium for similar size. Second is the cost, the tape drives are inexpensive; A normal PC user can buy a drive and reliable backups of several gigabytes of data. The third thing which has been offered is reliability. The tape is a reasonably reliable backup medium which is provided with the media. The fourth advantage is simplicity and universality: There is a support for tape drives and a number of software packages that will support a wide variety of devices.

Tape is perfect backup for the average user. The reliability is good and it is more expensive tape drives. Performance is also less than ideal in many cases, especially when random access is needed to specific files on the tape. A tape drive is also known as a streamer that reads and writes data stored on a magnetic tape. It is used for storage of data stored on hard drives.

Tape drives are sequential access, and must read all preceding data to read any one particular piece of data. The different types of tapes and drives are Digital Data Storage, Digital Linear Tape, Linear Tape-Open, and Advanced Intelligent Tape. Digital Data Storage is a format for storing and backing up computer data on magnetic tape that evolved from Digital Audio Tape technology, which was originally created for CD-quality audio recording.

In 1989, Sony and Hewlett Packard defined the DDS format for data storage using DAT tape. Tapes conforming to the initial DDS format can play on either DAT or DDS tape machines. However, most DDS tape drives cannot be used for the audio storage. DDS uses tape which is initially of 60 or 90 meters long, although advancements in materials technology allowed the length to be increased significantly. A DDS tape drive uses different scanning methods for recording, the same process. There are two read heads and two write heads. The read heads verify the data that has been written. If errors are present, the write heads rewrite the data. A DDS cartridge needs to be retired after 2,000 passes or 100 full backups.

Tape drives should be cleaned regularly to be kept in good working order. DDS tapes have an expected life of at least 10 years. The DDS 1 can stores up to 1.3 GB. The DDS 2 can stores up to 4 GB 120 meter cartridge. The DDS 3 Stores up to 12 GB. The DDS 4 can store upto 20 GB. The DAT 72 can store upto 36 GB uncompressed on a 170 meter cartridge.

Thus, the tape drive is the most economical method, which can be used for the average users who wants to backup their data without any fear of getting damage. Thus, tape drives are more cheaper when compared to other drives and is affordable by the average user without any problem.

5.4 MAGNETIC TAPE

Magnetic tape is a one-half or one-fourth inch ribbon of mylar (a plastic like material) coated with a thin layer of iron-oxide material. It has been used for years as an input/storage medium for batch processing, and it remains a choice today for high speed, large volume applications. It is also a medium that is often selected to store large files that are sequentially accessed and processed. It's data density (the number of characters that can be stored in a given physical space) is high and its transfer rate (the speed with which data can be copied into processor storage) is fast.

Let us have an idea of how does the data get stored and retrieved from the magnetic tape.

Tape, as mentioned above, is coated with a thin layer of iron-oxide material. When the tiny, haphazardly arranged particles of iron-oxide are aligned through magnetization, data are stored as magnetized spots (Fig. 5.1).

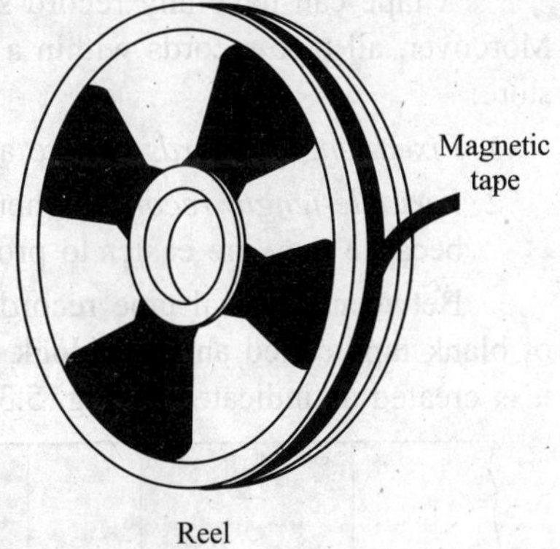

Fig. 5.1 Magnetic tape reel

Tape drive, an input-output device, has an electro-magnetic component, Read/Write head through which the tape passes and data is read and written onto it. Magnetic tape is usually divided into nine separate strips or tracks. Eight of these tracks are used for the codes which represent data characters and the ninth track is reserved for an error-checking bit.

Data is represented on tape in a manner very similar to the CPU's internal code. There are nine longitudinal tracks (Fig. 5.2) or recording surfaces on a tape, each capable of storing one magnetized bit.

The EBCDIC code used for representation of data within a computer also uses nine bits:

- ❒ 4 zone bits
- ❒ 4 digit bits
- ❒ 2 parity bit

The *parity* bit is a check bit to minimize the risk of transmission errors. On even *parity* computers there must always be an even number of bits in one storage area at any time. The parity bit is turned on if, without it, there would be an odd number of bits on; otherwise the parity bit is off. In this way, the loss or gain of a single bit in transmission would be easily detected since that would result in an odd number of bits on. There are odd parity computers as well, which require and *odd* number of bits in each storage location.

Fig. 5.2 Nine-track Representation

Note that millions of characters can be recorded as magnetized bits on a single magnetic tape. The primary reason for this storage capability is the fact that bits are exceedingly small so that hundreds of them can be placed on a very small area of tape. The actual number of characters that can be represented in an inch of tape is called the *density*. Since each character is represented by a series of bits in a specific position, tape densities are measured in bits per inch (bpi). The term bytes per inch would be more appropriate since the density indicates the number of characters per inch. The most common tape densities are 800 bpi, 1600 bpi, or 3250 bpi, but some tapes have densities of 6000 or more characters per inch. Thus, on most tapes 800 to 1600 characters of data or the equivalent of 10 to 20 cards of data can be represented in a single inch of tape. This storage capacity is one reason why magnetic tapes are so frequently used at computer installations.

A tape can have any record size; it is not restricted, like cards, to an 80-column format. Moreover, all tape records within a given file need not have the same length. That is, tapes can store:

1. *Fixed-length records*, where all records are the same size
2. *Variable-length records*, where the lengths differ. We focus on fixed-length tape records because they are easier to process.

Between physical tape records the computer automatically reserves a fraction of an inch of blank tape called an **interblock gap (IBG)**. Thus, when tape is created as computer output, it is created as indicated in Fig. 5.3.

Record 1	IBG	Record 2	IBG	Record 3	IBG

Fig. 5.3 Physical tape records separated by interblock gaps (IBGs)

When a tape record is read at high speeds, it takes a fraction of a second for the drive to physically stop when it senses the end of the record. This delay is analogous to that of applying the brakes on a car: it takes several feet before the automobile physically come to a halt. The interblock gap (IBG) is created so that, when a record is read, the mechanism will not pass over data from the next record in the time it takes to come to a halt.

This interblock gap is usually a fraction of an inch, being as large as 3/4 or 3/5 of an inch. Thus, if small record sizes are used, there will be a significant amount of unused tape between each record (Fig. 5.4).

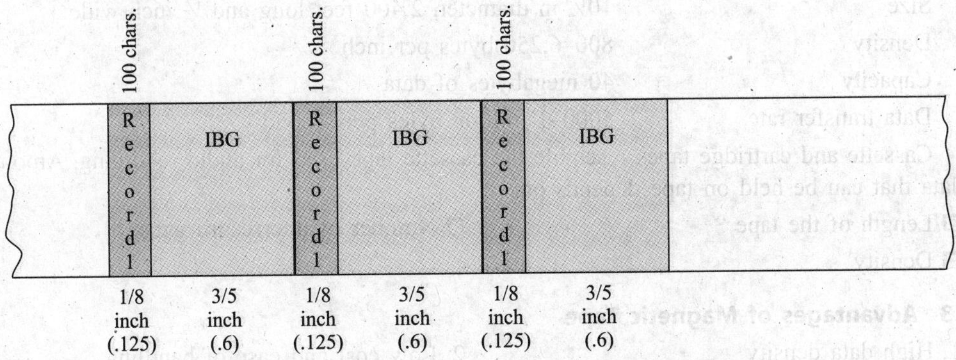

Fig. 5.4 Representation of data showing unused tape (IBGs)

To minimize wasted space, tape records are frequently *blocked* so that several actual or logical tape records are grouped together in a block (see Fig. 5.5). Blocking of logical records maximizes the efficient use of the tape.

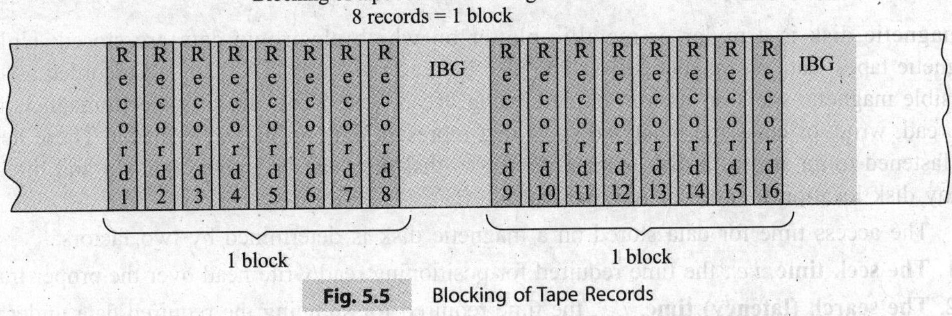

Fig. 5.5 Blocking of Tape Records

5.4.1 Data Storage

The 'write head' aligns the iron oxide particles. If these particles are polarized, *i.e.*, aligned in one direction, the particle represents 1; if they are aligned in opposite direction, iron-oxide particle represents 0.

5.4.2 Data Retrieval

For reading the tape, the drive passes the tape by the 'read head' and the patterns of 1s and 0s are interpreted as pieces of data.

Magnetic tape stores data sequentially, *i.e.*, one after another. Between each record stored on the tape, there is a space called interrecord gap (IRG). These gaps are automatically created when data are written on the tape. When record data are read from a moving tape into the processor, the movement stops when a gap is reached. The tape remains motionless until the present record is processed and then starts moving again to enter the next record into the computer. This procedure is repeated until the file is processed. But what if there are a large number of very short records. To avoid such an inefficient situation, several short records are commonly combined into a block, tape block, and read into the processor as a single unit. This saves tape space and speeds data input.

Magnetic tapes are made in three forms: Reel to Reel forms, Cassette forms and Cartridge forms. Reel to reel tape is most commonly used. It is magnetic tape placed on reels. Its configuration is:

Size	10½ in diameter, 2,400 feet long and ½ inch wide
Density	800–6,250 bytes per inch
Capacity	40 megabytes of data
Data transfer rate	5000–1 million bytes per second

Cassette and cartridge tapes resemble the cassette tape used for audio recording. Amounts of data that can be held on tape depends on:

- ❒ Length of the tape
- ❒ Number of interrecord gaps
- ❒ Density

5.4.3 Advantages of Magnetic Tape

1. High data density
2. Low cost and ease of handling

5.4.4 Limitations of Magnetic Tape

1. Lack of direct access to records
2. Environmental problems-sensitivity to dust, humidity and temperature levels.

5.5 MAGNETIC DISK

A magnetic disk is a mylar or metallic platter on which electronic data are stored. Unlike magnetic tapes, data on magnetic disks can also be read randomly. The data are recorded as tiny invisible magnetic spots on its iron oxide coating. Read/write heads are tiny electromagnets that can read, write, or erase the polarized spots that represent data on magnetic media. These heads are fastened to an arm in a disk storage device so that they can be moved quickly and directly to any disk location to store or retrieve data.

The access time for data stored on a magnetic disk is determined by two factors:

1. **The seek time**, *i.e.*, the time required for positioning read/write head over the proper track.
2. **The search (latency) time**, *i.e.*, the time required for spinning the required data under the head.

Once the data have been accessed, they are copied from the disk to the processor for processing. The transfer rate depends on the density of the stored data and the rotational speed of the disk.

Data is represented on a disk using a 9 bit code similar to the EBCDIC code discussed for tapes. Each byte or character is represented longitudinally along a disk track by a 9 bit configuration. As with tape records, disk records can be any length and can be *blocked* to maximize the efficient use of the disk (See Fig. 5.6).

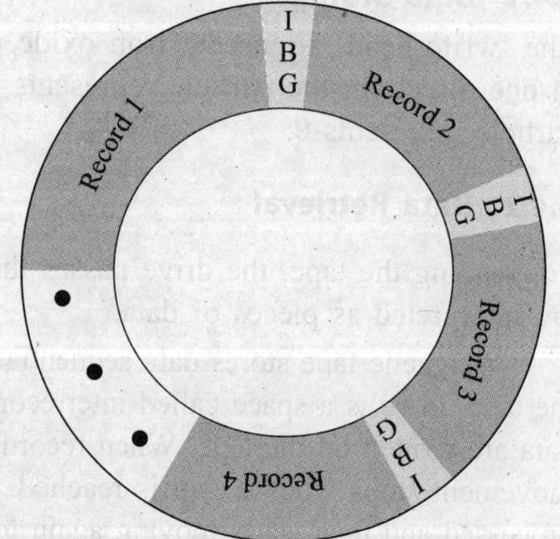

Fig. 5.6 Storing several data records on a disk track

Magnetic disks come in various sizes. They can be portable or permanently mounted in their storage devices, disk drives. They can be made of rigid metal (Hard Disks) or flexible plastic (Floppy Diskettes).

They can be divided into two broad categories:

1. Fixed Disks or Hard Disks
2. Floppy Diskettes

On all disks, there are a number of invisible concentric circles called tracks on which the data are stored. These tracks begin at the outer edge of the disk and continue towards the centre of the disk without touching it. Every track on a disk has a designated number. Each track is divided into portions called sectors.

Storage capacity of a disk depends on:

(i) **disk surface:** The more the disk surface, the greater is its storage capacity

(ii) **bits per inch of track:** Storage capacity depends on the number of bits that can be stored on an inch of track. Both are directly proportional

(iii) **tracks per inch of surface:** The greater the number of tracks that can be placed on an inch of surface, the greater is the storage capacity of the disk.

Now, let us have an idea about the two categories of disks:

5.5.1 Fixed Disk or Hard Disk

A fixed disk or hard disk is made from materials such as aluminium, instead of mylar. The Input/Output device used to transfer data to and from a hard disk is called a hard disk drive. Hard disk may be permanently installed in a drive or may be in the form of a removable cartridge or disk pack that can also be removed from the drive. Let us consider them in detail:

(i) **Larger (14-inch) permanently sealed metal disks:** These disks are permanently housed in sealed contamination free containers, which are usually not removed from their disk drives. Read/Write heads and access mechanisms are also sealed along with the disks they serve. High capacity storage units of all sizes that use such sealed housings are called **Winchester disk drives**. Sealed disks of this size are generally used in larger systems and minicomputers.

(ii) **Larger (14-inch) metal disks in removable cartridges or disk packs:** These disks use one-or-two cartridges or diskpacks containing three or more disks, mounted on a single shaft. These disks are not sealed in contamination free containers. These are used in all mini-sized and larger systems.

(iii) **Rigid disks permanently housed in Winchester drives:** The disks come in 9 inch, 8 inch and 5¼ inch sizes. The larger ones are used in minicomputers while smaller ones are used in PC-systems.

The hard drive, also called the hard disk or fixed disk, is the primary storage unit of the computer. It is always labeled the C drive. Additional drives are labeled after it as the D, E, F, etc. It has several read/write heads that read and record data magnetically on platters, a stack of rotating disks inside the hard drive. Hard drive is important for the following reasons:

- ❐ It stores programs that must be installed to the hard drive before they can be used.
- ❐ It stores data files that can be accessed later.
- ❐ It organizes files like a file cabinet so they can be accessed more easily.

The Hard Drive can store a large amount of computer data on it. Many advancements have made it possible to store a large amounts of data in a small space. The hard drive's speed is discussed in terms of access time. This is the speed at which the hard drive finds data. The average access time is measured in milliseconds. One millisecond equals 1/1000 of a second. The average drives had 9 to 14 ms access time. The lower the access time the faster the hard drive. The capacity, or amount of information that a hard drive can store, is measured in bytes. Today many computers come with 20–80 GB (Giga Byte = 1,000 Mega Bytes) hard drives.

5.6 TYPES OF HARD DRIVES

1. **Bournolli** has a mechanism that acts as a fly wheel. When the HD spins the disk follows gravities course and is lifted up a few centimeters causing the Read/Write heads to touch. When it stops spinning, the HD will fall back down the few centimeters.
2. **Magnetic Optical Drive** has the best storage capacity. It has the same principles as the Bournolli, but is mixed with the Compact Disc technology so that the Read/Write head puts data in order and the laser reads off of it.
3. **Standard Magnetic Drive** is less complex and less expensive than the others. It stores data with a read/write head which sends a pulse of electricity through causing the magnetic films electrons to line up in a certain way.

5.7 HISTORY OF HARD-DISK DRIVES

The hard-disk drive is a wonder of modern technology, consisting of a stack of disk platters, each one an aluminium alloy or glass substrate coated with a magnetic material and protective layers. Readwrite heads, typically located on both sides of each platter, record and retrieve data from circumferential tracks on the magnetic medium. Servo-mechanical actuator arms position the heads precisely above the tracks, and a hydrodynamic air bearing is used to 'fly' the heads above the surface at heights measured in fractions of microinches. A spindle motor rotates the stack at speeds of between 3,600 and 10,000 revolutions per minute.

This basic design traces its origins to the first hard-disk drive-the Random Access Method of Accounting and Control (RAA/IAC)-which IBM introduced in 1956. The RAMAC drive stored data on 50 aluminium platters, each of which was 24 inches in diameter and coated on both sides with magnetic iron oxide. (The coating was derived from the primer used to paint San Francisco's Golden Gate Bridge.) Capable of storing up to five million characters, RAMAC weighed nearly a ton and occupied the same floor space as two modern refrigerators.

In the more than four decades since then, various innovations have led to dramatic increases in storage capacity and equally substantial decreases in the physical dimensions of the drives themselves. Storage capacity has jumped multiple orders of magnitude during that time, with the result that some of today's desktop PCs have disk drives containing more than 80 gigabytes.

According to some analysts the industry has achieved these improvements largely through straightforward miniaturization. 'Smaller heads, thinner disks, smaller fly heights' (the distance between head and platter.)

Many corporations find that the volume of data generated by their computers doubles every year. Extremely large databases containing more than a terabyte—that is, one trillion bytes—are becoming the norm as companies begin to keep more and more of their data on-line, stored on hard-disk drives, where the information can be accessed readily. The benefits of doing so are numerous: with the right software tools to retrieve and analyze the data, companies can quickly identify market trends, provide better customer service, modify manufacturing processes, and so on. Meanwhile individual consumers are using modestly priced PCs to handle a data glut of their own, storing countless emails, household accounting spreadsheets, digitized photographs, and software games.

All this has been enabled by the availability of inexpensive, high-capacity magnetic hard-disk drives. Improvement in the hard disk technology has been quite impressive. The capacity of hard-disk drives grew about 25 to 30 percent each year through the 1980s and accelerated to an average of 60% in the 1990s. By the end of 1999 the annual increase had reached 130 percent. Today disk capacities are doubling every nine months, fast outpacing advances in computer chips, which obey Moore's Law (doubling every 18 months).

5.8 TYPES OF HARD DRIVE CONNECTIONS

Basically there are three types of Hard Drive Connections:

1. Integrated Device Electronics (IDE)
2. Small Computer Interface (SCSI)
3. Enhanced Integrated Drive Electronics (EIDE)

5.9 FLOPPY DISKETTE

Floppy disk drives were originally introduced commercially as a read-only device in the early 1970s. These early floppy disk drives were used to hold microcode and diagnostics for large IBM mainframe computer systems. These disk drives were using 8-inch floppy diskettes recorded on only one side. By changing these diskettes inside the floppy drive, technicians could easily update the microcode to the latest revisions or load diagnostics easily. The storage capacity of these early read-only drives was less than 100 kilobytes.

In 1973 a new upgraded 8 inch drive with read/write capability and a capacity of about 250 kilobytes began shipping which IBM used in data entry systems. This drive incorporated many technical improvements and became a model for drives still in use today. As time went on, designers learned how to reliably record on both sides of the diskette as well as increase the density of the data recorded on the diskette.

In 1976 smaller 5.25 inch size floppy drives were introduced by Shugart Associates. In a cooperative effort, Dysan Corporation manufactured the matching 5.25 inch flexible floppy diskettes. Originally these drives were available in only a single-sided low density format, and like the first 8 inch models, stored less than 100 kilobytes. Later they received many of the same improvements made to the 8 inch models, and eventually 5.25 inch floppy drives settled at a double-sided, 'double density' formatted capacity of about 1.2 megabytes. This drive was used in the IBM-AT personal computer.

Modern floppy drives and diskettes (3.5 inch) have evolved to a much smaller size with larger capacities as well. In 1980, the 3.5 inch floppy drive and diskette was introduced by Sony. During the early 1980's many competing formats were tried to compete with the 3.5 inch drives. Over time the industry settled on the 3.5 inch format which was standardized and manufactured by many companies. Today's standard 3.5 inch diskettes hold a formatted capacity of 1.44 megabytes while still using the same basic technology of the second generation 8 inch drives.

The primary factor that caused engineers to reduce the size and cost of floppies was the introduction and evolution of the personal computer. It was in the personal computer market that the low cost, mass produced floppy drive found its first real home. Very quickly, the floppy became the standard method of exchanging data between personal computers. It also became the popular method of storing moderate amounts of information outside of the computer's hard drive. Floppy diskettes are small, inexpensive, readily available, easy to store, and have a good shelf life if stored properly. It is a round, flat piece of Mylar coated with ferric oxide, a rust like substance containing tiny particles capable of holding a magnetic field, and encased in a protective plastic cover, the disk jacket. Data is stored on a floppy disk by the disk drive's read/write head, which alters the magnetic orientation of the particles. Orientation in one direction represents binary 1; orientation in the other, binary 0.

It is a small flexible mylar disk coated with iron-oxide on which data are stored. These disks are available in three sizes:

1. 8-inch portable floppy (flexible) disk

2. 5¼-inch portable floppy disks

These two diskettes are individually packaged in protective envelopes. Both the floppies are the most popular online secondary storage medium used in PC and intelligent terminal systems.

3. **Compact floppy disks measuring less than 4 inches in diameter:** The 3½ inch diameter miniature diskettes are individually packed in a hard plastic case. This case has a dust-sealing and finger proof shutter which opens automatically once the case is inserted in its disk drive. These disks are popular in desktop and portable personal computers. A floppy disk may be single sided (data can be recorded on one side only) or double sided (data can be recorded on both sides of the disk). All disks have two sides but difference depends on whether the disk has been certified free of errors on one or both sides. Data recorded on a double sided disk by a double sided drive can't be read on a single sided drive because of the way the data are stored. A double-sided drive had 2 read/write heads, one for each side while a single-sided drive has only one read/write head. The most commonly used diskettes are:

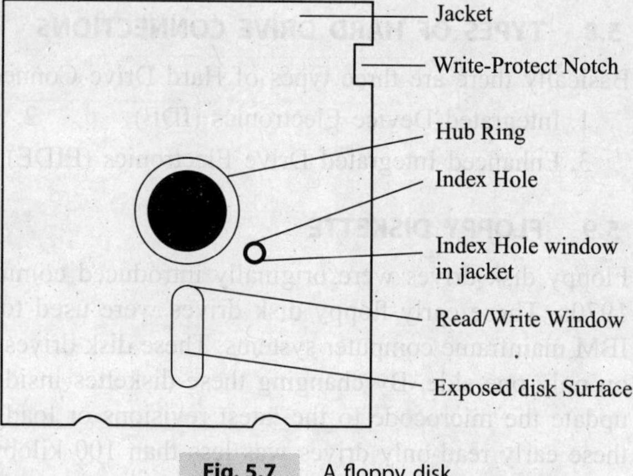

Fig. 5.7 A floppy disk

		Size	Capacity
(*i*)	Double Sided-Double Density (DSDD)	5¼″	360 KB
(*ii*)	Double Sided-Quad Density (DSHD)	5¼″	1.2 MB
(*iii*)	Smaller Double Sided	3½″	1.44 MB

A floppy disk can either be hard-sectored or soft sectored. Earlier hard-sectored disks were used, but now-a-days soft-sectored disks are prevalent. Hard-sectored disks are those disks which are punched with an entire ring of holes so that each hole marks the beginning of a different sector. Whereas in soft-sectored disks, a single hole is punched at the beginning of first sector—the 0 sector.

Each magnetic disk needs to be prepared before it can be used for data storage. This is done by a process called **Formatting**. Formatting a disk involves a process by which the operating system labels each sector of each track with an address so that the computer can go directly to a specified area, rather than starting at the beginning, as in the case of a magnetic tape. It also determines the number of sectors per track and the number of characters that can be stored in each sector.

A Hard Disk is more useful than a floppy disk because:

1. Due to its rigid construction, it is rotated very fast (say 3,600 revolutions per minute) as compared to a floppy disk (360 rpm). Therefore, data can be transferred faster to or from a hard disk as it takes less time to find the storage location.
2. Because of its hard construction, hard disk allows data to be stored more densely. Thus, hard disk has more storage capacity than a floppy disk of the same size.

5.9.1 Data Storage

Disk is rotated at a very high speed (rpms) by a motor. Data are recorded on the tracks of a spinning disk surface and reads from the surface by read/write head(s). In a floppy disk, the head comes in contact with the disk whereas in the case of a hard disk the head remains above its surface without touching it.

In multiple stacked disks, a number of access arms and read/write heads are used. The data on the magnetic disk surface are written as tiny magnetic spots—1-spot magnetized in one direction and 0-spot in another. The BCD codes, 7-or-8 bit discussed in previous chapter are used to represent data.

5.9.2 Data Retrieval

For accessing data on magnetic disks, an access arm, just like pickup arm of a record player, can move a read/write head directly to the track that contains the desired data. It doesn't have to read the outer tracks thereby using direct-access method and not sequential access as in the case of magnetic tape.

Let us have a brief idea about organization and physical storage of data on hard disk and floppy disk.

5.9.3 Data Retrieval-Hard Disk

In the case of stacked disk system, there is an access arm having two read/write heads for each recording surface. All these access arms move in unison in and out of the 152 *Computer Fundamentals* disks. Each hard disk recording surface has specified number of tracks and sectors. A particular track on all the surfaces of multiple disks comprise that particular cylinder of the disks. For example, all the tenth tracks of all surfaces, together from tenth cylinder of the disks. Thus, a cylinder may be defined as all tracks on magnetic disks that are accessible by a single movement of the access mechanism. Track position of a read/write head on top recording surface is the same as track position of other heads on the access arms serving other surfaces.

For accessing a record, its disk address (*i.e.*, the cylinder number, surface number, and record number) must be provided by a computer program. The motor rotates the disk at a high speed and in its one revolution, data on surface of a particular track is read. In the next revolution, data on surface two of the same track is read. A full track of data can be read in a single revolution. This procedure continues down the cylinder with very fast movement of access arms.

After access of the data, they are copied from the disk to the processor, at a rate (transfer rate) which depends on the density of the stored data and the disk's rotation speed.

5.9.4 Data Retrieval-Floppy Disk

As shown in Fig. 5.7, a typical floppy disk jacket has a small hole to the right of the larger center hole, called index-hole window. The disk also has a small hole, called the index-hole which cannot be seen unless it is aligned with the jacket hole. This index hole enables the disk controller to locate disk sectors.

Access of data is carried out in the following steps:

1. Read/Write head moves to the track specified in the disk address (*i.e.*, track number and sector number).
2. Disk-drive controller locates the index reference, *i.e.*, the index-hole for determining sector locations. This takes place with a light passing through the disk once index-hole is aligned with the index-hole window. This light triggers a light-sensing device which marks the hole's location and hence index-hole is detected.
3. The disk controller begins reading data.
4. When the specified sector passes under the head, the controller transmits data to the processor unit.

5.9.5 Advantages of Magnetic Disk

1. Data records can be stored for both sequential and direct-accessing.
2. High speed of access and update as no sorting of transactions.
3. On-line disk records of several related files can be updated simultaneously by a single input transaction.

5.9.6 Limitations of Magnetic Disk

1. **Risk of loss of data:** Records may be lost in case of writing of new records or drive failure. Therefore, special backup procedures are required for disk records protection. This is not so in the case of magnetic tape records.
2. **Data insecurity:** It is easier to maintain the security of magnetic tape files than that of magnetic disk files.

5.9.7 Characteristics of Magnetic Disk Drives

Magnetic disk drives are direct-access devices designed to minimize the access time required to locate specific records. Each drive has not one but a series of access arms that can locate records on specific surfaces. The time it takes to locate specific records will be much less than that required by a tape drive with only one read/write mechanism.

There are several types of disk mechanisms:

1. **Moving-Head Magnetic Disk:** In a moving-head disk system, all the read/write heads are attached to a single movable access mechanism. Thus, the access mechanism moves directly to a specific disk address, as indicated by the computer.

   Because all the read/write heads move together to locate a record, this type of mechanism has a relatively slow access rate as compared to other disks. The access time, however, is still considerably faster than that for tape.
2. **Fixed-Head Magnetic Disk:** Since disks are generally used for high-speed access of records from a file (for example, a railway reservation file), such a method would reduce access time resulting in a substantial benefit. For this reason, fixed-head magnetic disks were developed. These devices do *not* have a movable access arm. Instead, each track has its own read/write mechanism that access a record as it rotates past the arm. The disks in this device are not removable and the capacity of each disk is somewhat less, but the access time is significantly reduced.

   Still other disk devices combine the technologies of both moving and fixed-head access to produce a high-capacity, rapid access device.

5.9.8 Characteristics of Magnetic Disk Processing

1. **Disks are used for High-Volume Files:** Because magnetic disks can be processed very quickly and can store large amounts of data, they are frequently used for high-volume files.
2. **Disks are used for Either Direct-Access or Sequential Processing:** A main advantage of disk processing, as compared to tape, is the ability to directly access records. Because a disk has numerous addressable recording surfaces and numerous read/write heads, records can be accessed directly without the need to search an entire file.

   There are three common methods of processing disks:

   (*i*) Sequential access file

   (*ii*) Direct access file

   (*iii*) Indexed sequential access file

(*i*) **Sequential Access File:** A **sequential access file** is one in which records are stored and accessed one after another as shown in Fig. 5.8. Magnetic tape is a storage medium that is sequential in nature. All preceding records must be read first to access a particular or individual record.

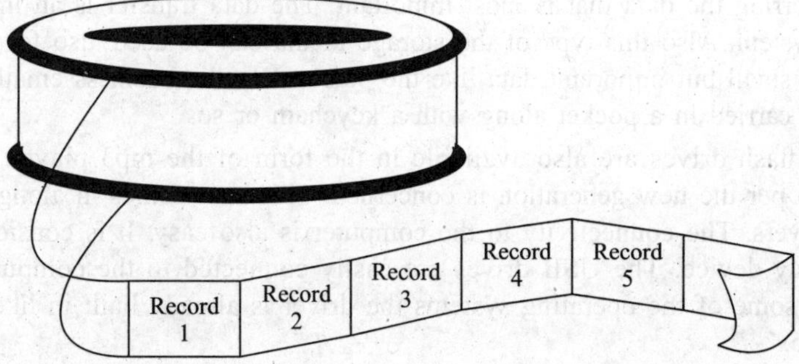

Fig. 5.8 With the sequential access method, records are stored and accessed sequentially. When accessing a record, all preceding records in the file must be accessed first. Here, to access record 5, record 1, 2, 3 and 4 must be accessed first

(*ii*) **Direct Access File:** A **direct access file** is one in which a record is read directly from a disk without reading all preceding records as shown in Fig. 5.9. In direct access method, the order of the storage of records is immaterial. Direct access is the fastest of the three access methods.

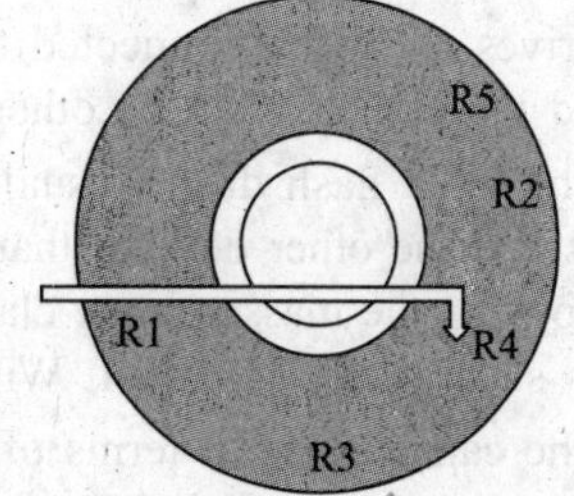

Fig. 5.9 With direct access method, records can be accesed directly without having to access all preceding records. Here record 5 can be accessed directly without having to access any other

(*iii*) **Indexed Sequential Access File:** The most common technique for accessing disk records directly is with the use of an index. During the creation of records, the computer uses file-handling programmed routines to establish an index on the disk itself. The index indicates where each record is located. The concept is similar to that of the index found at the end of a book, which specifies the page where each item of information can be located. The disk index indicates the locations (*i.e.*, track and sector) of each records and where a particular record can be found. A **key data** field in each record must be indicated by the programmer, which is used by the computer as the basis for establishing address information in the index.

For example, if a payroll file is stored on a disk. To access any particular record, the user needs only to supply a particular key data field, such as EMPLOYEE CODE or whatever has been defined at the time of programming. The computer then looks up the corresponding disk location for that particular record in the index and seeks that record directly.

3. **Disk Files may be easily accessed and modified as needed:** Disks have the added advantage over tapes of permitting updates or changes to existing records *on the same disk*. In this way, a new disk need not be created to incorporate the current changes, as is usually required with tape processing. That is, the same disk may be used for *both* input and output. We can read a record from a disk and make changes to that record on the same disk; we can add records to the disk; we can delete records from the disk.

5.9.9 USB Flash Drives

One of the types of storage media, the USB flash drive is playing an important role in dominating the market. A USB flash drive is much popular because of the size and the compactness. It actually behaves as if it is the portable hard drive. It has many provisions that provide you the option of transferring the data that is most important. The data transfer is an important part of any computer system. Also this type of the storage media can be used also for the back up or archiving of the small but important data like the personal or the business emails etc. The ease is that it can be carried in a pocket along with a keychain or so.

The USB flash drives are also available in the form of the mp3 player. The important entertainment as per the new generation is concerned. This also comes in along with the radio and the FM players. The connectivity to the computer is also easy. It is considered as one of the plug and play device. The USB drives are easily connected to the computer through the USB socket. In some of the operating systems the driver is already built in like the Microsoft Windows Xp etc.

Earlier the USB drive needed as software driver that was to be installed in the operating system. The earlier operating systems such as the windows 98 and all; does not have any built in drivers. The drivers need to be installed manually. The USB device's importance is that it can be connected to the computer even when it is already running. In most of the cases where the other drives are to be connected the system is to be switched off prior to the installation. The files and the explorer can be other wise normally seen in the explorer window.

The USB flash drives usually use the protocol for the USB's to interoperate along with the PCs and the other devices that have the USB port. Mostly the USB Flash Drives utilize the technology of the mass storage class drivers. This is the same technique as used in the operating systems such as the Microsoft Windows new versions.

The capacity, of in terms of the storage that is available in the USB flash drives that are currently available is to 2 GB of storage. The USB disk drives are gaining much popularity as comparable to the other devices of the storage media like the DVD or the CD; because of the portability. Also in the case of the CD's or the DVD's if the data is written once then it cannot be erased. Exceptionally in some cases like the rewritable discs, there is the possibility of rewriting the data. The data should be completely erased in order to write it again over the disc. Where as in the USB devices the data can be written or erased easily with out any need of the burner software as in the case of the CD or the DVD discs. The data can be written or removed as if in the case of the floppy disk drives; the only difference is that the data storage capacity is more in terms of the USB flash drives. Also the uploading of the data is much faster than in the case of the other removable devices such as the CD's or the DVD's.

The USB drives are usually fragile and should be handled with care. In case if they are fallen or dropped the device may easily sustain any physical damage. More over the efforts and much research and development is being made in this area for the development of the technology.

5.9.10 Zip Drives

A Zip Drive is a 3.5″ removable disk drive manufactured by Iomega. Zip disks come in various memory capacity models such as 100 MB, 250 MB and 750 MB. The 250 MB drive was introduced in 1998, and also can perform read and can write only on 100 MB disks. The 750 MB drives can read all, but only write only on 250 MB and 750 MB disks. The idea of Zip disks are derived from the floppy technology that uses concepts of design from hard disks. The drive is bundled with software that is used to lock the files for security.

Zip disks were introduced in 1995 and were popularly used. The Zip drive is a medium-capacity removable disk storage system, introduced by Iomega in the year 1994. The Design concept of zip disk is based on Iomega's system; in which both systems have a set of read/write heads mounted over a rapidly spinning floppy disk. The Zip disk uses smaller media generally called as microfloppy, rather than the compact disc sized, and a simplified drive design that reduced its overall cost is formed. This design results in a disk that has an 9 cm floppy convenience, but holds much more data, with performance much more quicker than a standard floppy drive.

The original Zip drive had a data transfer rate of about 1 megabyte/s and the time taken was 28 milliseconds, compared to a standard 1.4 MB floppy of 500 Kbit/s transfer rate and several-hundred millisecond average seek time. The Capacity of Zip system is 100 megabytes. There were plans to construct a lower cost 25 MB version that would work in the same 100 MB drive and the idea was to bring the price of a zip disk closer to that of an ordinary floppy. But it don't seem to have ever been released. The introduction of the 100 megabyte disk made ZIP a success and people used them to store files of 1.44 MB capacity of regular floppy disks. Iomega eventually increases the capacity to 250 and later 750 megabytes, while improving the data transfer rate and seek times.

Zip media is similar in vertical size as of floppy disks, which means the drive slot is large enough to accept such a floppy to prevent drive and disk damage. Higher capacity Zip disks are used in a drive with at least the same capacity ability. Generally, higher capacity drives also handle lower capacity media, the 250 MB drive is much slower than the 100 MB one to write data on a 100 MB disk. The 750 MB drive cannot write to the 100 MB media but it is cheapest and most common.

The Zip's write protection is implemented on the software level instead of mechanically enforced in the hardware. The metadata on the disk indicates the write protection status, which the software driver then enforces to the operating system. This means that the disk must be loaded in a drive and accessed on a computer to turn write protection on or off. It also means that, in theory, a rogue driver could be created which ignores the write protection flag.

The Zip system also introduced the features such as media access protection through a password. Like write protection, this is also implemented other features such as to trick the software into allowing access to a different disk than it believes to be in the drive, thereby bypassing the password protection. Thus, Zip drives are more or less like a floppy and uses concepts of floppy technology.

5.10 OPTICAL TECHNOLOGY

Storage techniques can be based both on the principles of magnetism as well as on the use of light. Optical technology involves the use of laser beams-highly concentrated beams of light. It comes in the form of:

1. Optical laser disk
2. Optical card
3. Optical tape

1. Optical Laser Disk: Sometimes technological developments created for one application will result in an improvement in other areas. **Optical laser disks** (Fig. 5.10) are hard metal disks ranging in size from 5.72 inches to 14-inches; they were originally developed as compact disks for video and audio applications. The same method of using laser beams to encode binary data by burning microscopic 'pits' on audio and video disks to represent 1s and 0s is used to encode the data stored on optical laser disks.

Fig. 5.10 A CD-ROM optical laser disk

Most optical disks are read-only storage devices; however, some of the more expensive optical disks can be written on and erased. A common version of the optical disk is the CD-ROM (compact disk, read-only memory). While not suited to applications where data changes, they are very convenient for storing data that remains constant. The laser technology used gives these devices tremendous storage capacities. For example, *American Academic Encyclopedia*, a nine-million-word (20-volume) encyclopedia is stored on a compact disk less than five inches in diameter with room to spare. Grolier Electronic Publishers sells it to consumers for about $200. A typical 14-inch disk can store as much as 20 reel-to-reel tapes. Libraries have started converting from traditional card catalogues and microfilm to CD-ROM systems. Los Angeles County has one of the largest library systems in the country; it was able to get its more than five million titles on a single disk. The search for references is faster than with either a card catalogue or microfilm.

2. Optical Card: The **optical card**, or laser card, is the size of a credit card and has an optical laser-encoded strip that can store approximately two megabytes of data. These cards have many potential uses, most notably for strong credit records or medical histories. Some people predict that these cards may one day lead to a cashless and checkless society. Optical cards have the potential to store an individual's entire financial history, adding to or subtracting from the appropriate accounts as a person makes, saves, or spends money. These cards might also supply a hospital with the holder's complete medical history. If emergency treatment is required, this information could expedite care.

3. Optical Tape: Continuing developments and refinements in optical technology include optical tape. **Optical tape** is similar in appearance to magnetic tape, but data are stored by optical-laser techniques. Optical tapes which are in cassette form can store over eight gigabytes each, and the tape drives can hold 128 cassettes, providing a total data storage of about one terabyte (1,000 gigabytes). Like other optical methods of data storage, optical tape is read-only. As optical technology develops, higher densities and expanded uses will result.

Data on these secondary storage devices are organized in a hierarchy which includes database, file, record and field designators. A database is a group of related files stored together in a logical fashion. A record is a collection of related items of data treated as a unit. A file is a collection of related records treated as a unit.

5.11 COMPACT DISC DRIVES CD ROM

The CD ROM is the discs that are optical and are used for storage of data. They were introduced by the Philips and the Sony Corporation. The CD–I which stands for the Compact Disk interactive is CD playing device that can be connected directly to a home TV set. It is based on the Motorola 68000 series chip. It provides the home user with the live video and audio interaction.

The CD–I or more commonly referred to as the VCD player has the following components: The CD system, Audio system and the video system. It has the input devices such as the remote control and mouse also. There is also a built in non-volatile RAM. The CD Rom drive is an optical devices and its functional performance considered as the multimedia device. The CR ROM devices can contain the multiple media data in addition to the text. However only one type of the data can be accessed from the drives at a time. To synchronize two types of types of the data that is the audio and the animation one type of the data would have to be copied to the hard disk.

The CD ROM drive is the device that is used to only read the data from the CD disk. The data using the CD ROM cannot be written over to the disk. For this purpose the CD RW is a necessary one.

CD RW is the rewritable drive that can perform both the functions of reading the disk well as writing to the disk. The writing of the data is possible only with help of software that is called as the CD burner software. More over the data cannot be written to the drive as in the case of a normal floppy disk or the hard disk drive. The process of writing the data or any information to the CD is called as the burning. The data once burnt to the CD ROM disk cannot be erased as the name itself suggests. The writing of the data is done only at a time. The data that is already written to the rewritable CD can again be erased with the help of this software. But still there is no such software into existence which can partially erase the data.

All the available CD burner software requires the data to be completely erased and then burnt over the rewritable CD. However the data can be written in the form of multisession. The CD ROM presently is used for the backup of the important data or the information of any kind.

The CD ROM presently has the capacity of about 700 mega bytes. The extended CD ROM has the capacity of the 800 mega bytes. The CD ROM has the speed that is taken into consideration like presently the speed available is that of 52x.

The CD ROM is manufactured by some of the leading names that include the HP, Samsung, LG, Asus, Sony, Phillips, Creative Max, Liteon etc. The CD ROM is the thin optical disk that is used for the storage of the data. Presently after the introduction of the DVD's there is much backdrop in the sales of the CD's.

The CD ROM disks must generally confirm to one additional standard that is the ISO 9660. This is an international standard that defines a file system for the CD ROM disks. This standard comes in two different types: Level One ISO 9660—This provides DOS compatibility. The Level Two ISO 9660—This allows longer file names. It does not allow cross platform compatibility.

5.12 THE CD-ROM TECHNOLOGY

The Compact Disc-CD was invented in 1982 by two well-known companies, Philips and Sony. This was an Audio CD, digital audio. Soon the computer industry recognized that the large amount of digital audio data could be replaced by digital computer data.

CD-ROM (Compact Disc Read-Only Memory) represents a new important tool for the storage, retrieval, and the distribution of information. CD-ROMs can store and play back audio, video, graphic images, digital data, and digitized text. CDs contain computer data in the same way as the hard disk. Compact Disks are usually in the ISO 9660 format. This is a data format that was introduced in 1984 by the International Standards Organization (ISO). Since then it has succeeded in becoming a widely accepted cross-platform.

Because of the digital storage techniques used, CD-ROM can be used to retrieve all types of digitally encoded data. The diameter of a CD disc is 4.7 inches (120 mm or 12 centimeters) and its thickness is 0.047 inches. CDs rotate at a constant linear velocity of 200 to 530 revolutions per minute.

A single Compact Disk can store up to 600–700 MB of data and this is equivalent of:

- ❐ 1500 5.25-inch floppy disks
- ❐ 450 3.5-inch floppy disks
- ❐ 200 books each containing 1,000 pages
- ❐ 10 computer magnetic tapes
- ❐ 275,000 pages of text

5.12.1 Types of Compact Disks

1. **CD-DA:** Audio CD, Digital Audio by Philips and Sony
2. **Photo CD:** Developed by Kodak and Philips
3. **Video CD:** Can hold around 70 minute of video footage
4. **CD Extra:** For Multimedia and developed in 1996
5. **CD-R:** Well known technology for WORM disks
6. **CD-RW:** Rewritable (erasable)-CD, developed in 1995

5.13 THE EVOLUTION OF CD-ROM & DVD-ROM

- **1980:** CD-Audio Philips and Sony create standards for optical disk-based digital audio format.
- **1983:** CD Players Sony introduces the first audio CD player, priced at $1,000. The first CD title is Billy Joel's 52nd Street.
- **1985:** CD-ROM Philips and Sony announce the standard for compact disk-read-only memory for computer data.
- **1987:** CD-ROM Drive The CD-ROM format enters in the PC arena. Drives cost $1,000; the read-only disks hold 650MB of data.
- **1994:** 4X CD-ROM Drive Throughput doubles to 600 KBps. Prices for 4X drives are initially $1,000.
- **1995:** 6X CD-ROM Drive Throughput rises to 900 KBps, with 6X drives initially costing $600, but these models are about to be usurped by 8X drives.
- **1996:** 8X CD-ROM Drive Throughput is up to 1,200 KBps, with the price of an 8X drive initially $400.

  10X and 12X CD-ROM Drives These drives have a claimed throughput of up to 1,800 KBps. They cost around $250.

  CD-R Prices for compact disk-recordable drives drop below $500. This technology lets mainstream.

  PC users create their own 650MB CD-ROMs for data archiving or distribution. The user can write to each blank disk only once.
- **1997:** CD-RW Compact disk-rewritable (also called compact disk-erasable) drives and media let users overwrite files on CDs they have created. CD-RW disks are backward-compatible, letting any standard CD-ROM drive read them.

  DVD-ROM The paradigm shift to DVD disks begins. These read-only disks hold 4.7GB of data, and the format is standard to both the PC and the consumer electronics markets. The drives can read legacy CD-ROM disks.
- **1998:** High-Capacity DVD-ROM Subsequent iterations of the DVD format increase capacities to 8.5 GB for dual-layer designs; to 9.7 GB for double-sided, single-layer implementations; and to 17GB for double-sided, dual-layer designs.

  DVD-RAM DVD-random access memory drives let users create their own 2.6 GB DVDs. The industry will likely skip the write-once format and go straight to designing rewritable disks.

5.14 DIGITAL VERSATILE DISK DVD

The CD ROM was the disk drive that was used for the back up of the data. But as the technology has advanced the DVD has gained momentum to provide the back up of the data and the information that is used to store the data.

DVD was actually used for the videos. It was used for increasing the clarity in the videos. And the name was initially the Digital Video Disk. But the DVD found its application in the computers also. Hence the name is also referred to as the Digital Versatile Disk. The technology is similar to that used in the CD ROM.

Both the CD ROM and the DVD are similar in nature. Both are the optical disks. But the major difference is that in terms of the storage capacity. The DVD has more storage capacity than that of the CD's. The maximum capacity of the storage in the CD that has an extended memory is about the 800 mega bytes of data. But in the case of the DVD the same single DVD that has a physical size as equal to that of the CD that is currently available is 4.7 giga bytes. Even the newly available DVD's has the storage capacity of about 40 giga bytes. Some of the DVD's that are now available are dual sided. That is the information can be stored on both the sides of the disk.

The DVD's are also available in different formats that are the DVD +R, DVD-R, DVD RAM, DVD RW etc. The DVD has superb clarity when it is burnt as Digital Video Disk. The video that is stored over the disk is in the format that is supported by the DVD player. The DVD player that is available for the television sets is quite different from the one that is available for the computer systems.

DVD ROM drive in the computer only supports the reading of the data from the DVD disk. If there is the requirement for burning the data to the DVD then for that the DVD RW or the so called DVD writer should be used. The DVD writer is available for the DVD's that supports almost all the formats of the DVD. The DVD RW is the rewritable format of the DVD. The mini DVD's are also available that can store up to 1.2 giga bytes of the data.

The different formats that are supported by the DVD are briefly explained below:

- The DVD-R/RW means that the disk is recordable once and rewritable. The other format that is the DVD+R/RW also means the same as that of the DVD-R/RW. The DVD-ROM means that the disk is read only memory. The DVD-RAM is the type of disk that is random access rewritable which means that after write checking the integrity of the data is active.
- The types of the DVD include the one like the DVD 5 which is the single sided and also the single layer DVD with the capacity of 4.7 giga bytes. The other is the DVD 9 which is the single sided and the double layer has the capacity of about 8.5 giga bytes. Another is the DVD 10 that is also the double sided and is the single layer on both the sides. Its capacity is about 9.4 giga bytes. The DVD 14 is the double sided disk with the double layer on one of the sides but a single layer on the other side. The capacity of this disk is about 13.3 giga bytes. Finally the DVD 18 is the double sided disk that has double layer on both of the sides. It has the capacity of about 17.1 giga bytes.

5.15 FLASH DRIVES

The type of the memory that is used in the flash drives is the flash memory. The flash memory is a type of chip that is called as the EEPROM. It has the grid that consists of the columns and the rows. It also has a cell. There are two transistors in the cell at each intersection point. The thin oxide layer is responsible for the separation of the two transistors.

The first of the transistors is called as the floating gate. The next or the second transistor is called as the control gate. The only link from the floating gate to the row or the word line is through the other gate that is the control gate. If this is working properly then the cell the value of 1 is there. If the value is to be changed to the 0 then the process known as the tunneling or appropriately known as the Fowler Nordheim tunneling is used. The most useful examples include the following that are listed below: That is these are the things where in you can find the flash memory.

The first one is the BIOS of any computer. The other examples include the compact flash, smartmedia, PCMCIA—used in the solid state disks mostly in the laptops (this is of the type I and also of the type II), the memory stick that is found in the digital cameras etc, USB pen drives and so on. The flash drive is also used in the memory cards of the mobiles etc. The electronic memory is currently available in many forms and many different prices.

The important properties of the flash memory are that it is much fast and very much easier in use. The different types of devices where the services of the flash drive can be utilized also include the computer system. Here the flash drive can be efficiently used for the purpose of data transfer and also for can be used for as if the hard disk drive of any computer is used.

The flash memory is quite expensive as compared to the hard disk drive. But the major advantage of the flash memory over the hard disk is that it is compact and much efficient for the data transfer. The flash memory is also a type of the solid state storage device. That is it means that there are no mobile parts in it. As in the hard disk there are the platters and the read write head moves over it. This is type of mechanism in the hard disk drive is somewhat mechanical in nature but in the consideration with the flash memory this is not the case. There is no such mechanical component in the flash memory drive. Hence it is a purely electronic device.

The other flash types also include the one that is known as the Compact flash card. These compact flash cards were introduced by the Sandisk. This was the case as in the year of 1994. The two things differentiate the compact flash drives from the Smart Media cards: The first one is that they utilize the controller chip in them and the second one is that they are thicker. The Compact flash has small circuit board. This circuit board contains the flash memory chips along with a controller chip. This all is covered in a casing that is much thicker in size than a Smart media card. The concept of the dual voltage is supported by the compact flash. That is they can even operate on a voltage of 3.5 as well as on a voltage of 5 volts.

In comparison to the smart media card the hard casing and the controller chip, its weight and size, all add to the complexity of the compact flash drive. But the storage capacity of the compact flash drive is more then the smart media.

5.16 HOLOGRAPHIC VERSATILE DISC

The holographic versatile disc is designed using advanced optical disc technology, the holographic versatile disc employs a technique known as collinear holography, in which two lasers one red and one blue-green, are used in a single beam. The blue-green laser is used to read data from a holographic layer to the top of the disc and the red laser is used to read servo information from a CD layer near the bottom.

The servo information is used to monitor the position of the read head over the disc and sector information on a hard disk drive. The servo information is interspersed amongst the data. A mirror layer is formed between the holographic data and the servo data letting the red laser to pass through it. This prevents interference from refraction of the blue-green laser off the servo data pits and is an advance over past holographic storage media, which either experienced too much interference, or lacked the servo data entirely, making them incompatible with current CD and the DVD drive technology disks have the capacity to hold up to 3.9 terabytes of information which is eighty times the capacity of Disc.

The holographic versatile disc has a transfer rate of 1 Gbit/s. The holographic versatile disc uses holographic memory around for more than 40 years, several characteristics is difficult to implement in a consumer market. in most of these systems send the reference beam and the information beam are let into the recording medium on different axes.

In holographic versatile disc, the holographic storage systems has no data, the beam carrying data has a change of interfere with the holography process. The holographic memory discs have notably thicker CDs and DVDs. holographic versatile disc is fit for the market.

The holographic versatile disc system has the laser beams which travel in the same axis and strike the recording medium at the same angle. In, the holographic versatile disc test system, the servo data is carried in a red laser. The size and thickness of an holographic versatile disc is compatible with CDs and DVDs.

Holography is a method of recording patterns of light to produce a three dimensional object. The patterns of light are called a hologram. The process of creating a hologram begins with a focused beam of light—a laser beam. This laser beam is split into two separate beams: a reference beam, which remains unchanged throughout much of the process, and an information beam, which passes through an image. When light encounters an image, its composition changes and the image is captured in its waveforms. When these two beams intersect, it creates a pattern of light interference. If you record this pattern of light interference in a layer of a disc you are recording the light pattern of the image.

To retrieve the information stored in a holographic versatile disc, the reference beam is applied directly onto the hologram. When it reflects off the hologram, it holds the light pattern of the image stored there. The holographic memory systems use holograms to store digital instead of analog information. The holographic versatile disc structure has the following: a green writing, Red positioning laser, Hologram, Poly carbon layer, Photo polymeric layer, Distance layers, Diachronic layer, Aluminium reflective layer, Transparent base.

5.17 MEMORY STICK

In October 1998 the Sony Corporation launched a device that is called as the memory stick. This is actually a memory storage chip that is small and compact and which can be used for the storage of data in many different devices. These devices are available in many different formats like the specifications below will explain in detail.

5.17.1 Memory Stick Specifications

The specifications may be in terms of the transfer of the speed. The memory sticks are available in two forms one is the Standard and the other is the PRO. In the Standard the maximum write speed is about 14.4 mega bits per second equivalent to about 1.8 mega bytes per second. And the maximum read speed in the Standard memory stick is about 19.6 mega bits per second that is equivalent to 2.5 mega bytes per second. The same in the PRO is as follows.

The transfer speed is about 160 mega bits per second that is equivalent to the 20 mega bytes per second. And the minimum write speed is about 15 mega bits per second. The form factors for the standard are in the following measurements: 50.0 mm (width) × 21.5 mm (height) × 2.8 mm (depth). And the measurements in the for the Duo are 31.0 mm (width) × 20.0 mm (height) × 1.6 mm (depth).

Some of the formats that are available in the memory sticks are the described below. The white memory stick PRO holds around the data of up to 2GB. This was introduced in year of 2003. The PRO supports the features such as the faster recording that is about 160 Mega bits per second. It also has a protection system of the MagicGate copyright. Before the PRO format, the MagicGate cards that were used had up to 128MB. The memory sticks with MagicGate had similar functions as that of the regular memory sticks. But the only difference is that they supported the Sony's ATRAC3. This is the audio recording format which includes the copyright protection. The copyright protection system is SDMI digital rights. Some of the music players by the Sony Corporation accept MagicGate cards only like the network walkmans.

The memory sticks that are used in the cell phones and the other similar devices, has the 'Duo' that is the smaller card which is inserted into an adapter that is specially made for it. It fits into the regular Memory Stick slot. The Duo card has the feature that it can then be used as the portable device from a memory stick device to a device 'Duo'. The Duo cards have the capacity of up to 128 MB. The PRO Duo still have the capacity of about 512M B.

The memory sticks that are introduces by the Sony Corporation are used in many devices such as the cameras, the PDA's and the mobile hand set phones. They are also used in the mp3 players and the digital radios etc. The memory sticks are also available for the Input and the Output devices such as GPS–Global Positioning Systems and also in the Bluetooth modules.

If the memory stick is required to be connected to the computer, then it should be used through the USB port. The USB port serves as the gateway for the memory sticks. The memory sticks are also used to upgrade the memory in already available memory chips.

5.18 MINI DISKS

The mini disk is a storage device that is popularly used for the storage of the data. Its popularity is based on the fact that it is small and sleek and quite handy as compared to the other storage devices. In the description this is a compact digital audio disk. This mini disk is from the Sony Corporation and comes usually in the read only format. There is also the availability of the rewritable form of the mini disk. This was as said was introduced by the Sony Corporation in the year of 1993. This mini disk is not as much popular in any other country as it is in the Japan.

The physical size of the mini disk is 2.5″ inches. But the memory capacity is about the size of 140 mega bytes. The mini disk is also available for the CD as well as for the DVD. This means that even the CD's and the DVD's both are available in the form of the mini disks.

The maximum capacity in the mini disk CD's that is presently available is about the 192 mega bytes. The same in case of the DVD's is about the size of 1.4 giga bytes. This device can hold the music of about some 74 min. The compression scheme that is used here is that Adaptive Transform Acoustic Coding—ATRAC. This is again from the Sony.

This scheme ATRAC eliminates the inaudible signals. These mini disks can even store the track and the titles that are usually displayed by a media player. In the rewritable mini disks the technology that is used is that of magneto optic. They are usually come in 60 min, 74 min and even the 80 min cartridges.

Apart from the Sony, even now the other market players have introduced the mini disks. They include the HP, Imation which are the leading in this segment; and still many more. The mini disk falls under the category of the pre-mastered disks. The pre-mastered disks are that where there is the usage of the optical playback system and the mastering process. These things are similar also in the CDs. The signals that are recorded are pre-mastered pits and the recordable mini disks are very similar to the CDs except only in the size. The Eight to Fourteen Modulations or the EFM is used in the modification of those CD's. The code known as the Advanced Cross Interleaved Reed Solomon Code or the ACIRC is employed here as the CIRC code.

The mini disk has the data structure and the operation of the functioning similar to that of a computers hard disk drive. That is it can similarly used in the explorer and the data can be read subsequently as if from the hard disk. The permissions like the read only or the write are dependent on the type of the disk; that is whether it is read only or rewritable etc. The bulk of the mini disc may contain the data or the information that is pertaining to the music itself. And a small section may also contain the Table of Contents of the user. This provides the playback device along with some information that is vital to the number and the location of the tracks that are present on the disk. The functioning is similar to the hard disk; because it is possible to rename the tracks. It is also possible to add the tracks or erase them.

5.19 MUTABLE AND IMMUTABLE STORAGE

The other two types of storage are mutable and immutable storage. The data stored in mutable storage can be changed or overwritten, that is the data written could be changed. Whereas the data stored in immutable storage cannot be changed, if the data burnt in the immutable storage device, the data cannot be changed. Data in immutable storage cannot be changed. So it is better to store data in mutable storage because it could be changed.

All programs and data on hard disk drives use the mutable storage devices. Some areas of the hard disk can be logically made immutable such as file system permission. The super user is normally not affected by permissions thus allowing some attacks to succeed. Some operating systems extend logical immutability so data remains immutable even if an attacker gains super user access. Attackers may be able to destroy the data but they can't change it. The mutable storage class is used only on a class data member to make it modifiable even though the member is part of an object declared. You cannot use the mutable with names declared as static or constant members.

The Mutable storage in the past few months are still under development. Mutable storage is far more than software packages: it is indeed a new funda for the development and deployment of applications. The design of a mutable is dealing with songs and videos that never get updated. Thus projects, our design are not aimed to support read and write operations, but also an update facility. This enhancement will greatly enrich the possibilities of peer-to-peer networks.

The goals of Mutable storage are to introduce a overview of related work. Our design of a mutable storage system is having some potential advantages and disadvantages. The web publishing system is highly resistant to censorship. who post information, servers, which host random-looking content, and retrievers, who browse the documents stored in the system. We can able to deal with any kind of static content, for instance, HTML pages and interactive scripting. Most of the research has been related to security issues.

The main contribution of Mutable storage include an automatic tamper checking mechanism, a facility which is used to update and delete published material, for publishing mutually content. Designing a mutable storage system requires the sketch to design of our mutable storage system. The main assumption which was made during the development of the mutable storage devices are that the model that should be based on the users and the users are not be responsible for the allocation of space.

Thus, the immutable storage system could be used to store the systems program and the other back files which have not to undergo the changes and the mutable storage could be used to store the application data where the user continuously refers the data and keeps on changing the data. Thus, the mutable storage system is far more good then immutable storage.

5.20 NETWORK STORAGE DEVICES

The main function of network storage device is to provide a secure access to remote users and other computers on the local network. The use of Intuitive browser interfaces and integrated software systems makes easy the management of network storage devices and avoids the necessity of laborious maintenance. A network storage device if it just not only places a files, it's a powerful when it support the file server appliance with lots of useful features.

There are two test models, they are ReadyNAS 600 and the ReadyNAS X6. The X6 model features uses the expandable RAID and enhanced multimedia support. The ReadyNAS supports RAID levels 0, 1, or 5, so it is very easy for us to balance of speed and reliability that works. The first X6 contained a defective fan which was one of the main disadvantages of those systems. The device used to work with loud, and performed very poorly. There were all sorts of problems and the drive access speed was due to the excessive heat. The results of Infrant representative were that the problems were due to a defect. The Infrant representative was polite, apologetic, and extremely helpful.storage extension.

As we discussed, earlier network storage device is a cost-effective, high performance storage extension device that provides dedicated hardware compression on each client port to deliver maximum compression ratios and minimize latency reducing. The amount of WAN bandwidth required, and the associated recurring bandwidth charges. Network storage devices delivers high efficiency, due to native mapping of storage protocols bypassing intermediate encapsulation protocols, such as IP and ATM.

Network storage device provides plug-and-play deployment and point-and-click management for simplified, easy to manage storage extension. Network storage device allows end users to change supported protocols on each port through a simple software command eliminating the need for additional hardware. The network storage device has significant advantages over other storage extension which are available in the market, including lowest cost of network support which provides, up to 80% less expensive than traditional channel extenders. Dramatically lowers network services costs with per-port hardware based compression.

The features of network storage device is to enables flexible, dynamic multiplexing of multiple channels of application traffic, allowing them to dynamically share network bandwidth, further reducing network services costs. Network storage device has an ability to scale the number of client ports and the WAN connection as data center needs change. Highest Reliability platforms have been hardened from extensive testing. By comparison, the network storage device helps the data networking companies are only enterprise class.

The important feature of network storage device that beat other devices are manageability sets the benchmark for management. network storage device provides the highest level of performance monitoring in the industry. Network storage device helps in attaining maximum Utilization of Bandwidth. Network storage device has the highest concentration capability over individual wavelengths

5.21 NON-REMOVABLE STORAGE MEDIA

The storage media is generally referred to the secondary memory devices such as the hard disk and the floppy disk drive, CD drive, DVD disk drive, USB drives and the flash memory devices and also to the Zip drives. But apart from the hard disk, none of them are the devices that are non removable in nature. It means that the hard disk is the only mentioned device that is considered as the Non-Removable Storage Media. All the rest are the removable storage media.

Another example that can be used for the Non-Removable Storage Media is the RAM. But it is a volatile memory that cannot be used for permanently storing the data. It is just the primary memory that is of utmost importance to the system but at the same time cannot be used for the backup or the archiving of the data.

The non-removable storage media is fixed permanently in to the computer case and can also be used for the backup or the archiving of the data. The hard disk drives are the best suitable example for this type of storage media.

It also important to mention here that the hard disk drive can also either be internal or the external disk drive. In the internal hard disk; the drive is fixed permanently to the computer case. Where as, in the case of the external disk drive the hard drive can be moved from one place to another. Such a drive has a hard casing made over the normal disk drive. It is made to with stand the shocks in case of any physical damage. The external hard disk drive's case acts as shield and a shock absorber in case of any physical damage. The external hard drive is provided with a USB cable that is plugged into the computer case for the ease of usage. Hence this type of the external hard disk becomes the removal type of data storage. The discussion matters here only with the non-removable storage media. Hence the internal hard disks and its types can be discussed elaborately.

The internal hard disk drive is usually fixed in the computer case. The type of hard disk controller gives the name for the different types of the hard disks. The IDE hard disk is the normal hard disk that is used in the regular computers. The IDE controller is used for the purpose of providing connections to this type of the hard disk drive.

The SCSI controllers are used to provide the connections for the SCSI hard disk. The other technology that can be implemented by the internal hard disk drives is the RAID. The RAID is the Redundant Array of Independent (or Inexpensive) disks. In the regular cases the hard disk or mostly the internal hard disk is connected to the motherboard. The motherboard has the IDE connector where in the bus from the hard disk drive is to be plugged in.

If two or more than two hard disk drives are used, then in such case the hard disk drive should clearly be specified as which one is used as the master drive and the other one should also clearly be specified as the slave. The hard disk drive has the jumper settings, by which it can be determined or specified. The internal hard disk is specifically used as the secondary memory. And most importantly the secondary memory that is used in the computer is the non-removable storage media. The removal storage media is not used as the secondary memory.

5.22 ONLINE FILE STORAGE

Online file storage can be used to store a company, service, or application which allows storing computer files on the internet. The online file storage makes the file available through computer with internet access. The online file storage services can be used to offer space on a gigabyte basis, still offer this as a free service.

The online file storage services which are used to download software to make files which is available on computers which have to be software installed. The services of online file storage allow you to retrieve your files through any web browser and can be used for the other online application. The increased inbox space which could be up to 2 GB and is offered by mail sites like Gmail and Yahoo and have started using this as an online drive. The online file storage is used to enable another form of off-site backup that would have been unfeasible to individual and SOHO computer users.

The online file storage could also be used for a company; service allows you to store any computer file on the internet. The file available could also be used by any computer with internet access. The online file storage services offer space on a per Gigabyte Basis, albeit some still offer this as a free service.

The online file storage services are used to require you to download software which will make your files available on computers which have software installed. The other services offered by the online file storage are used to allow you to retrieve your files through any web browser. The inbox space offered by mail sites like Gmail and Yahoo many has started using this as an online drive. This online file storage can be used to enable any form of backup that would have been unfeasible to individual and SOHO computer users. The online file storage is also used to measure the quantity of information that can be stored on a given length of track, area of surface, or in a given volume; of a computer storage medium. The online file storage is used for higher density, which allows you and you can get the greater volumes of data to be stored in the same physical space. Computer storage density has a relationship to storage capacity of a given medium.

The capacity of a computer storage density could be measured in these ways:

- The linear recording density could be able to store on surface of the diskette. The maximum recording density of the computer storage density is of 1 inch for the innermost track is 17,434 bits per inch. The online file storage is used to online file folder as your own personal piece of the Internet. The online file storage can also be used to store, access, and share presentations and even large files like music, photos, and film clips. The online file Folder's generous storage makes it a snap and you can add storage affordably, anytime you need it, all the way up to a whopping 10 GB. The online file storage is easy to use the online file folder. The online file storage can be used to access, share, and manage files and folders right from your desktop. The concept of the online file storage could be used for many other uses which has not been discussed in the following, the concept of the online file storage could also be used for the online transaction and many other uses are formed on this concept.

5.23 SAN-STORAGE AREA NETWORKS

A SAN, or storage area network, is a dedicated network that is separate from LANs and WANs. It generally serves to interconnect the storage-related resources that are connected to one or more servers. It is often characterized by its high interconnection data rates (Gigabits/sec) between member storage peripherals and by its highly scalable architecture. Though typically spoken of in terms of hardware, SANs very often include specialized software for their management, monitoring and configuration (Fig. 5.11).

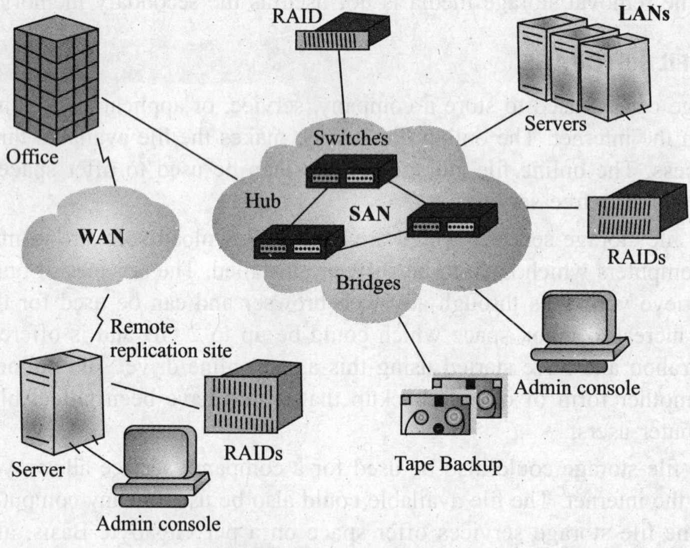

Fig. 5.11 Diagram of SAM

SANs can provide many benefits. Centralizing data storage operations and their management is certainly one of the chief reasons that SANs are being specified and deployed today. Administrating all of the storage resources in high-growth and mission-critical environments can be daunting and very expensive. SANs can dramatically reduce the management costs and complexity of these environments while providing significant technical advantages.

SANs can be based upon several different types of high-speed interfaces. In fact, many SANs today use a combination of different interfaces. Currently, Fibre Channel serves as the de facto standard being used in most SANs. Fibre Channel is an industry-standard interconnect and high performance serial I/O protocol that is media independent and supports simultaneous transfer of many different protocols. Additionally, SCSI interfaces are frequently used as sub-interfaces between internal components of SAN members, such as between raw storage disks and a RAID controller.

Providing large increases in storage performance, state-of-the-art reliability and scalability are primary SAN benefits. Storage performance of a SAN can be much higher than traditional direct attached storage, largely because of the very high data transfer rates of the electrical interfaces used to connect devices in a SAN (such as Fibre Channel). Additionally, performance gains can come from opportunities provided by a SAN's flexible architecture, such as load balancing and LAN-free backup. Even storage reliability can be greatly enhanced by special features made possible within a SAN. Options like redundant I/O paths, server clustering, and run-time data replication (local and/or remote) can ensure data and application availability. Adding storage capacity and other storage resources can be accomplished easily within a SAN, often without the need to shut down or even quiese the server(s) or their client networks. These features can quickly add up to large cost savings, fewer network outages, painless storage expansion, and reduced network loading.

By providing these dedicated and 'very high speed' networks for storage and backup operations, SANs can quickly justify their implementation. Offloading tasks, such as backup, from LANs and WANs is vital in today's IT environments where network loads and bandwidth availability are critical metrics by which organizations measure their own performance and even profits. Backup windows have shrunken dramatically and some environments have no backup windows at all since entire data networks and applications often require 24 × 365 availability.

As with many IT technologies, Sans depend on new and developing standards to ensure seamless interoperability between their member components. SAN hardware components such as Fibre Channel hubs, switches, host bus adapters, bridges and RAID storage systems rely on many adopted standards for their connectivity. SAN software, every bit as important as its hardware, often provides many of the features and benefits that Sans have come to be known for. SAN software can provide or enable foundation features and capabilities, including:

- SAN Management
- SAN Monitoring (including 'phone home' notification features)
- SAN Configuration
- LUN Masking and Assignment
- Data Replication (both local and remote)
- Shared Storage (including support for heterogeneous platform environments)
- Redundant I/O Path Management
- Serverless Backup

5.24 SAN HARDWARE

SANs are built up from unique hardware components. These components are configured together to form the physical SAN itself and usually include a variety of equipment. RAID storage systems, hubs, switches, bridges, servers, backup devices, interface cards and cabling all come together to form a storage system that provides the resources that facilitate the policies of an IT organization (Fig. 5.12).

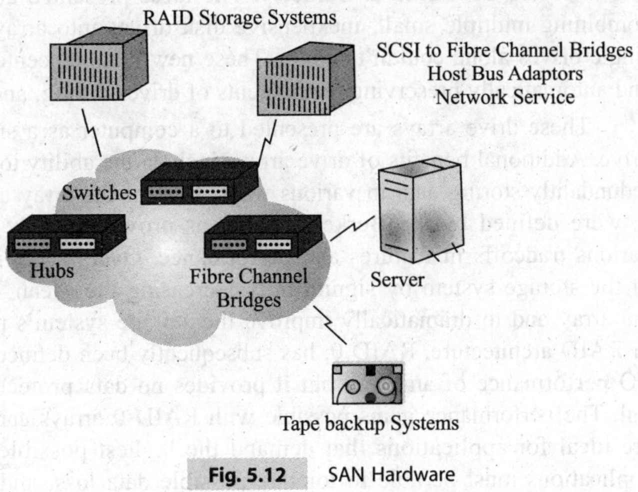

Fig. 5.12 SAN Hardware

It is very important to select the hardware devices (and their configuration) for a SAN with care and consideration. Many of the 'standards' that are involved with SANs are concerned with interoperability. Some of these standards are still evolving and haven't been equally adopted by all manufacturers of equipment used in SANs. This can lead to difficulties when matching up devices from different vendors and suppliers. Since SANs are typically just as dependent upon software for their proper operation, it can be vital to secure the latest version information about software (and firmware) and potential compatibility issues.

Working with companies that specialize in the design, integration and implementation of SAN systems can provide great benefits. Firms that specialize in SANs are often familiar with the latest software and hardware and can speed the process of successfully deploying SAN technology. By working with other vendors, manufacturers and standards bodies, these SAN specialists can help ensure that the promised benefits are realized and successfully integrated into new or existing IT infrastructures.

5.25 RAID SYSTEMS

Most contemporary SANs include RAID systems as their primary data storage devices. These systems have become highly complex. They offer the foundation principles that have come to be the basic modern SAN. First, RAID systems offer data protection, or fault tolerance, in the event of a component or I/O path failure. This is true even if fundamental elements, such as disk drives, fail in the system. Additionally, by way of numerous data striping techniques (described below), and controller configurations, today's RAID systems offer very high performance, storage capacity, scalability, and survivability.
Other reliability features available in today's RAID systems include redundant cooling systems, power supplies, controllers and even monitoring circuitry. These, and other features and characteristics, contribute dramatically to high data availability in a SAN. Modern RAID systems can even permit the direct connection of backup equipment, thus facilitating LANfree and even serverless data backup and replication (Fig. 5.13).

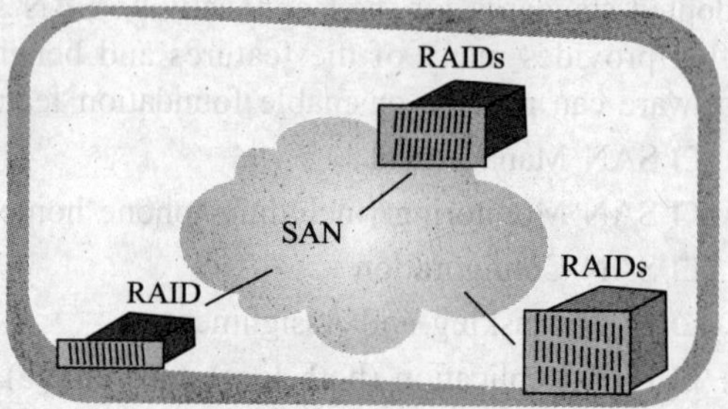

Fig. 5.13 RAID Systems

The roots of RAID technology can be traced back to Patterson, Gibson and Katz at the University of California at Berkeley. The ideas presented and explained in the paper involved combining multiple small, inexpensive disk drives into arrays in order to provide features that single drives alone couldn't supply. These new features centered on improving I/O performance and automatically preserving the contents of drives during, and after, drive or component failures.

These drive arrays are presented to a computer as a single logical storage unit (LUN) or drive. Additional benefits of drive arrays include the ability to make these arrays fault-tolerant by redundantly storing data in various ways. Five of the array architectures, RAID levels1 through 5, were defined by the Berkeley paper as providing disk fault-tolerance with each offering various tradeoffs in features and performance. Overall, the idea was to improve the reliability of the storage system by significantly increasing the Mean Time Between Failure (MTBF) for the array and to dramatically improve the storage system's performance. A sixth common type of RAID architecture, RAID 0, has subsequently been defined that can substantially improve the I/O performance of an array but it provides no data protection should a hardware component fail. The performance gains possible with RAID 0 arrays can be very dramatic. RAID 0 arrays are ideal for applications that demand the highest possible data throughput. Note that these applications must be able to tolerate possible data loss, and service interruption, if a drive or other component in the array fails.

5.25.1 Data Striping in RAID

Fundamental to the RAID concept is 'striping', a method of dividing and distributing data among the arrayed drives and effectively joining multiple drives into one logical storage unit. Striping involves partitioning each drive's storage space into stripes that may be as small as one block

(512 bytes) or as large as several megabytes. These stripes are then interleaved in a round robin fashion, so that the combined space is composed of joined stripes from each drive. In most instances, the application environment determines the suitability of larger vs. smaller stripe sizes.

Most contemporary multi-user operating systems like UNIX, Solaris, NT and Netware support overlapping disk I/O operations across multiple drives. However, in order to maximize throughput for a combined disk subsystem, its I/O load must be balanced between all of its member drives so that each drive can be kept as active as possible. High parallelism during I/O operations generally translates into much greater performance.

In multiple drive systems without striping, the disk I/O load is almost never perfectly balanced. Some drives will contain data that is frequently accessed while other drives will only occasionally be accessed. During intense I/O operations, performance can be optimized by striping the drives in the array with stripes large enough so that each record potentially falls entirely within one stripe segment.

This helps insure that data and I/O operations are evenly distributed across the arrayed drives, thus allowing each drive to work on separate I/O operations at the same time, thereby maximizing the number of simultaneous I/O operations that can be serviced by the array. By contrast, in data intensive applications that access large records, smaller stripe sizes can be used so that each record will span across many, or all, of the drives in an array with each drive storing only part of a record's data. This can allow long record accesses to be performed faster, since the data transfers can occur in parallel on multiple drives in the array. Applications such as digital video editing, audio/video on demand, imaging and data acquisition that employ long record accesses are examples of applications that often achieve optimum performance with smaller stripe sizes. Unfortunately, smaller stripe sizes typically rule out multiple overlapping I/O operations since each I/O will typically involve all of the drives.

5.25.2 Switches, Hubs and Bridges

More and more, the design and deployment of SAN technology involves incorporating specialized interconnection equipment. This category of devices often includes Fibre Channel Hubs, Switches and Bridges. This hardware is generally responsible for linking together the data storage peripherals, such as RAID systems, tape backup units and servers within a SAN.

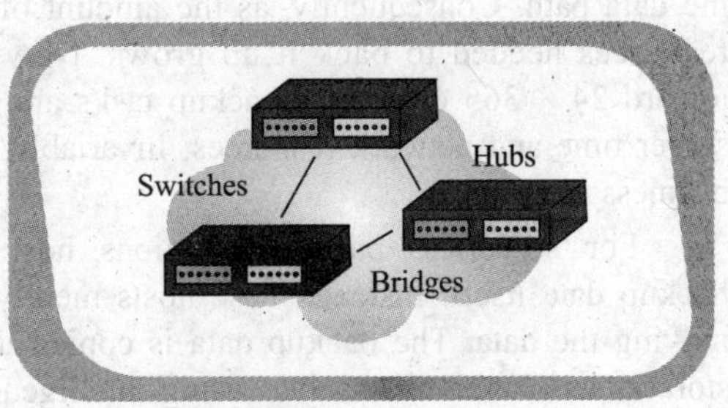

Fig. 5.14 Switches, Hubs and bridges

These interconnection devices are somewhat analogous to their LAN-related counterparts. They perform functions such as data frame routing, media and interface conversion (*i.e.*, copper to optical, Fibre Channel to SCSI), network expansion, bandwidth enhancement, zoning, and they allow concurrent data traffic. Just as customers today are more involved in the design and implementation of their LANs and WANs, they are also looking at these building blocks of SANs to create their own SAN solutions.

Fibre Channel HBAs, hubs, switches, and FC/SCSI bridges are some of the building block components with which IT administrators can develop SAN-based backup solutions, server clusters, enhanced bandwidth, extended distance and other application driven challenges. Selecting the appropriate pieces to address these issues requires an understanding of what each component can do. When, for example, is a fabric switch a better solution than a hub? When should hubs and switches be used in combination? There are no universal answers to these questions, but understanding the architecture and capabilities of switches, hubs and bridges provides a basis for making appropriate choices for SAN designs.

5.25.3 Backup Solutions

One of the most valuable time- and cost-saving features of a SAN architecture is its ability to off load backup operations from a LAN and/ or backup servers. This capability can significantly increase the amount of LAN bandwidth available to network clients and end users during backup operations. When backup servers are relieved from the 'data mover' role, they become more available for other productive tasks (Fig. 5.15).

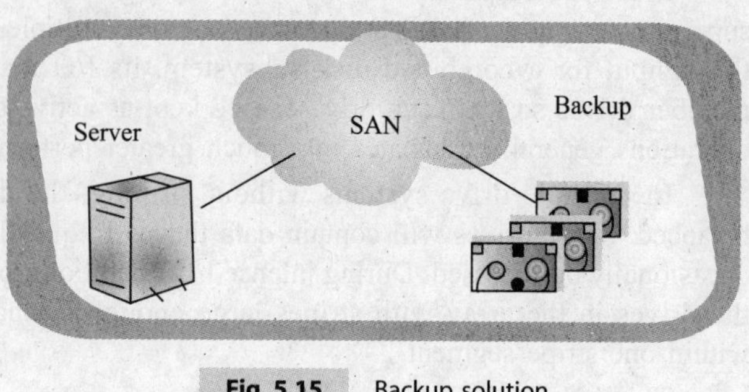

Fig. 5.15 Backup solution

LAN-free and serverless backup solutions optimize backup operations by offloading backup data traffic from a LAN, thereby increasing the amount of LAN bandwidth available to end users. Serverless backup extends these performance gains by removing more than 90 percent of the backup administration overhead that is usually placed on a backup server as backups are performed. This is achieved by incorporating some of the backup intelligence into the data storage or connectivity peripherals themselves. This can significantly free up backup servers by releasing them from large portions of a backup operation's administration and data moving chores. Using these SAN based backup solutions lets administrators optimize network and server utilization.

5.25.4 SANS' Background

Traditional backup operations place the application server, the backup server and the LAN all in the data path. Consequently, as the amount of storage grows, the amount of time and network resources needed to back it up grows. Now that businesses and organizations have moved toward 24 × 365 operation, backup tasks are competing with critical business applications for server time and network resources. Invariably, this causes network congestion and can result in business slowdowns.

For 'serverless' backup operations, host computers (servers) do not 'handle' or touch the backup data itself. Instead, these hosts merely direct and monitor the backup without actually moving the data. The backup data is copied directly from disk to tape, or disk to disk, by the storage peripherals themselves using intelligence that is incorporated into them. Optionally, this intelligence can even be placed inside of other SAN components, such as Fibre Channel switches or hubs. Freed from the routine data transport burden, server resources can be put back to more productive uses. Or, in other words, the backup or tape server is delegated the role of 'backup coordinator,' rather than data mover. Serverless backup takes LAN-free backup a step further since it removes backup traffic from both the LAN and the backup server.

By contrast, with simple 'LAN-free' backup operations, the backup and restore data (traffic) is removed from the LAN but still flows through the administrating server as it moves between data storage and backup devices. The benefit here is still valuable, since backup traffic is taken off of the LAN, reducing LAN congestion. While both serverless and LAN-free backup keep backup data off of the LAN, only the serverless backup frees up the administrating server as well—placing the data movement tasks onto the smart peripherals.

Specifically, smarter peripherals can now perform much of their own backup by supporting newer technologies and APIs—such as the 'extended copy command,' a Storage Networking

Industry Association specification that lets data be moved between storage devices on different buses. The backup server issues the command to a data mover in the SAN, and then removes itself from the data path. This way only the source, destination and SAN devices are involved. The constraints related to the memory, I/O and CPU performance of the backup server itself are eliminated as the data moves through a high-performance copy device or agent that is optimized for data movement. The logic here is fairly obvious since this frees up the backup server for other business-critical applications, and supports server consolidation. The dedicated backup server is no longer needed. Additionally, backups can complete much more quickly over higher speed networks—such as Fibre Channel.

Serverless backup systems can also provide additional cost savings by eliminating expensive, high-end servers. Another advantage unique to the serverless backup architecture is its ability to stream the same data to several tape libraries or other targets simultaneously, even if they are geographically separated, without the need for copying and moving the actual tapes—an important advantage in disaster recovery plans.

5.25.5 Backup Hardware in SANS

Mechanically, backup equipment used in SANs is typically the same as that used in conventional configurations. What is different, however, is how these devices are interfaced to their host servers and client storage systems. Since most contemporary SANs are connected together using Fibre Channel, and since many backup devices use SCSI interfaces, some type of bridge is often required.

These bridges perform the electrical, and any protocol, conversions required between the disparate buses or channels. There are many bridge manufacturers that supply these units, but it is vital to confirm compatibility with the selected backup device(s) before attempting to configure the units together or specifying units for purchase. This SAN topic has many caveats and is often an area that benefits from direct experience. SAN consultants, equipment vendors, and SAN solutions providers can be excellent sources for this type of compatibility information.

If a serverless backup solution is being considered or designed, it is important to note that some of these bridge manufacturers offer 'smart' units that include built-in copy functions. As mentioned above, this set of features is generally required for true serverless backup. In practice, small applications running on a selected server activate and instruct these copy agents remotely, then sit back and monitor progress while the smart bridge, or similar device, moves the data.

These software, or firmware, copy agents can even be found in certain Fibre Channel switches and hubs. There are some software companies that have even developed special programs that can be 'downloaded' into these units to give them these independent copy capabilities. With all of these options available, one can see the importance of selecting components very carefully. First time SAN adopters may want to consider consulting with SAN specialists before purchasing this type of equipment for deployment in a backup solution.

Though SAN backup solutions typically employ a tape server, tape library, and disk-based storage attached together with a Fibre Channel infrastructure, it is becoming fairly common for backup solutions to include disk to disk copies. With today's backup windows shrinking and IT policies calling for remote site replication, backup can now mean much more than just making tapes. Backup can now include data replication to local or remote disk sites via WANs, disk to disk backups that accommodate offline data processing and short backup windows, or all of these at the same time.

REVIEW QUESTIONS

1. The most popular secondary storage today is:
(*a*) magnetic tape (*b*) floppy disk (*c*) mass storage (*d*) semiconductor

2. Magnetic tape can serve as:
(*a*) input media (*b*) output media
(*c*) secondary storage media (*d*) all of these

3. Which is a secondary memory device?
(*a*) CPU (*b*) ALU (*c*) Floppy disk (*d*) Mouse

4. What is the alternative name for a diskette?
(*a*) Floppy disk (*b*) Hard disk (*c*) Flexible disk (*d*) Winchester disk

5. The metal disks which are permanently housed in sealed and contamination free containers are called:
(*a*) hard disk (*b*) floppy disk (*c*) winchester disk (*d*) flexible disk

6. A Winchester disk is a:
(*a*) disk stack (*b*) removable disk (*c*) flexible disk (*d*) all of these

7. Memories in which any location can be reached in a fixed (and short) amount of time after specifying its address is called:
(*a*) sequential-access memory (*b*) random-access memory
(*c*) secondary memory (*d*) mass storage

8. Which of the following isn't used in the storage phase of a computer-based information system?
(*a*) Magnetic (*b*) Keyboard (*c*) Diskette (*d*) Hard disk

9. CD-ROM is a:
(*a*) semiconductor memory (*b*) memory register
(*c*) magnetic memory (*d*) none of these

10. Which of the following is not a primary storage device?
(*a*) Magnetic tape (*b*) Magnetic disk (*c*) Optical disk (*d*) None of these

11. Average access time in the magnetic disk is of the order of:
(*a*) 50 millisecond (*b*) 50 microsecond (*c*) 50 second (*d*) all of these

12. Which of the following is a secondary memory device?
(*a*) Keyboard (*b*) Disk (*c*) ALU (*d*) All of these

13. A floppy disk contains:
(*a*) circular tracks only (*b*) sectors only
(*c*) both circular tracks and sector (*d*) all of these

14. Which of the following is not a sequence storage device?
(*a*) Magnetic disk (*b*) Magnetic tape (*c*) Paper tape (*d*) All of these

ANSWERS

1. (*b*) **2.** (*d*) **3.** (*c*) **4.** (*a*) **5.** (*c*) **6.** (*a*) **7.** (*b*) **8.** (*b*)
9. (*d*) **10.** (*d*) **11.** (*a*) **12.** (*b*) **13.** (*c*) **14.** (*a*)

QUESTIONS

1. What are the various devices used to store data in a computer? Give a classification of storage devices, illustrating their specific application areas.

2. A disk pack has 8 surfaces. There are 128 tracks on each surface over which data can be written. Assume that each has 80 sectors and each sector can store 50 bytes of information.

(*a*) What is the total capacity of disk pack?

(*b*) What is the reason for dividing the pack into surfaces, tracks and sectors?

3. Describe magnetic tape and tell how data are stored on it.

4. What is the relationship of a record to a file?

5. Distinguish between a fixed-length record and variable-length record.

6. Which is the method that allows both sequential and direct access?

7. Which secondary storage medium would be appropriate for a file from which individual records are accessed often?

8. Which data-storage medium allows both sequential and direct access?

9. Which storage medium and which access method would be most appropriate to store data that one frequently accessed, but rarely updated or changed?

10. Describe secondary storage and explain why it is needed?

11. Illustrate the differences between a blocked and an unblocked tape.

12. List three forms of magnetic tape.

13. What are the advantages of magnetic tapes over magnetic disks?

14. What purposes are served by the cutout areas of a floppy diskette jacket?

15. Describe an optical laser disk. How does its storage capacity compare to a magnetic hard disk?

16. Write short notes on the following:

(*a*) USB Flash Drives
(*b*) Holographic Versatile Disc
(*c*) Memory Stick
(*d*) Mini Disks
(*e*) Mutable and Immutable storage
(*f*) Network Storage Devices
(*g*) RAID System
(*h*) Storage Area Networks.

INPUT AND OUTPUT DEVICES

Many traditional ways to input and output data were designed more with the machines in mind than the humans who used them. However, the trend in input and output (I/O) devices is to move toward a more natural means of communication. The most natural way for humans to communicate with a computer is to use the same techniques that people use to communicate with each other. For example, entering data into the computer might be accomplished by speaking, handwriting, or physically pointing at specific objects on the screen. Speech, written text, and visual images such as color graphs are forms of output that humans find easiest to interpret and use. Advances such as voice recognition and speech synthesis have only begun to reach their potential. This chapter will present some basic I/O concepts as well as look at the more common I/O devices.

6.1 INPUT CONCEPTS

For computer processing, data needs to be entered into the computer (input) and the result of processing needs to be communicated to the user (output). Input is the process of entering and translating incoming data into machine readable form. The data to be entered are often referred to as input. Output is the process of translating data in machine—readable form into a form understandable by humans or readable by other machines. The information that is the result of processing is also often referred to as output. Before going into detail, let us recall the meanings of some terms. Hardware is all the physical components of a computer system. Any hardware item which is attached to the main unit of a computer that houses the CPU is referred to as a peripheral device. An input device is a peripheral device through which data are entered and transformed into machine-readable form.

Three things to be concerned with during the input process are:

1. The method of data preparation
2. The type of processing to be used
3. The accuracy of the data being entered

6.1.1 Data Preparation Methods

There are two concepts related to data preparation methods:

(*a*) On-line (*b*) Off-line

(*a*) **On-line** refers to an operation or device in which data are transferred directly to or from a computer.

(*b*) **Off-line** refers to an operation or device in which data are not immediately transferred to or from a computer.

The end product of an off-line input operation may be used as data for an on-line input operation. Now-a-days, on-line devices and operations are most commonly used.

Data for input can be prepared in two ways:

(*i*) Transcriptive data entry (*ii*) Source data entry

***(i)* Transcriptive Data Entry:** The data are prepared on documents at the source of the data. The data must then be transcribed to another medium that can be read and interpreted by a computer.

***(ii)* Source Data Entry:** The data are prepared at the source in a machine readable form that can be used by a computer without a separate intermediate data transcription step. This type of data preparation reduces the number of errors during input process.

6.1.2 Batch and Transaction Processing

The two main data processing methods are:

(*a*) Batch Processing (*b*) Transaction Processing

***(a)* Batch Processing:** Batch processing is a method in which data are gathered and batched through either an on-line or off-line data gathering process and processed periodically without user intervention.

***(b)* Transaction Processing:** Transaction processing is an on-line method in which data are processed immediately, and files are updated as a transaction takes place. This allows the user to communicate with the computer during processing through interactive programs which supply the results of processing so that they can be used when needed to control an operation or modify a process. This procedure is called **real time processing**. It is used in airlines offices to book and prepare a ticket.

6.1.3 Data Accuracy

There are two most commonly used methods which are used to help eliminate errors, at the time of data entry.

(*a*) Verification which is performed by the user

(*b*) Validation which is programmed into the computer

***(a)* Verification:** This can be conducted by corroborating the data entered by checking them against a known source.

***(b)* Validation:** Computer can be programmed to accept only a certain range of data. Checking for data items that deviate from this range is called validation.

6.2 INPUT DEVICES

Before computer processing, data must be entered into the computer by an input device so that they can be translated into a machine readable form. Let us have a look at various input devices available:

6.2.1 Punched Cards and Card Readers

It is a rigid piece of paper containing rows and columns of numbers. These cards are put into a keypunch machine which places holes in the card to represent the data. This pattern of punched holes used to represent characters on the card is called the Hollerith code. These holes are interpreted by a card reader that translates the punched information into a machine readable code, and then sends it to the CPU for processing. Now-a-days, this system is totally replaced by newer, more efficient input device.

Thus, the punched card has numerous uses in industry. It is a widely used file in small-scale computer installations.

Its basic advantages includes the following:

1. Machine and user accessibility, *i.e.*, people, as well as machines, can read card data
2. Relatively low cost
3. Can be used as a turn around document

Its basic disadvantages includes the following:

1. Large volumes of cards becomes difficult to control
2. Mechanical parts of many card devices cause frequent breakdown
3. Low speed of card reader and punch devices
4. Not reusable
5. Inflexibility of the card format—either 80 or 96 columns per card

While cost is minimal, efficiency is limited with punched card processing. Not only can cards be misplaced or missorted rather easily, but machines that read cards are subject to mechanical breakdowns. Moreover, card reader and punch devices are notoriously slow as compared to computer processing speed. The average speed of card devices is far slower than the *billionths* of seconds (nanoseconds) required for actually processing the data. Similarly, the physical limitation of 80 or 96 characters per record is often severely restrictive.

6.2.2 Keyboards

One of the most common and familiar input device is the standard keyboard. The traditional QWERTY typewriter comprises the basic portion of today's computer keyboard. A typical computer keyboard contains all letters, numbers, symbols of a regular typewriter, plus other keys which may include:

(*i*) a numeric keypad which functions like calculator

(*ii*) function keys whose operation can be determined by the user or pre-programmed by the software being used

(*iii*) special keys such as those used to control movement of the cursor (special character or symbol that indicates the user's position on the screen or focuses attention to a specific area, to allow communication and interaction between the user and the program) on the computer screen

A **cursor** is a special character or symbol that indicates the user's position on the screen or focuses attention to a specific area to allow communication and interaction between the user and the program. Cursor movement keys typically include four directional arrow keys which move the cursor one space at a time in either an up, down, left, or right direction. Other keys, typically named Home, End, PgUp (page up), and PgDn (page down), move the cursor over longer distances quickly. The cursor movement keys are often part of the numeric keypad. If this is the case, a key, such as the NumLck, acts as a toggle switching the function of these keys between cursor movement and numeric operations. Other special keys common to many keyboards are ESC (escape), CTRL (control), INS (insert), DEL (delete), and PRT SC (print screen). Many of these keys were added to increase efficiency in programming and in using applications such as word processing packages (Fig. 6.1).

Fig. 6.1 Alphanumeric keyboard

6.2.3 Mouse

A mouse is a pointing device. It usually contains one or three buttons; as the user rolls it on a flat surface, the mouse controls cursor movement on the screen. When the user presses one of the buttons, the mouse either marks a place on the screen or makes selections from data on the screen. It can be used for many applications ranging from games to designing products with graphics. It can be used as an alternative to keyboard or it can be used in combination with a keyboard to enhance input operations. Doug Engelbart developed the mouse as an alternative to the keyboard in the 1960s (Fig. 6.2).

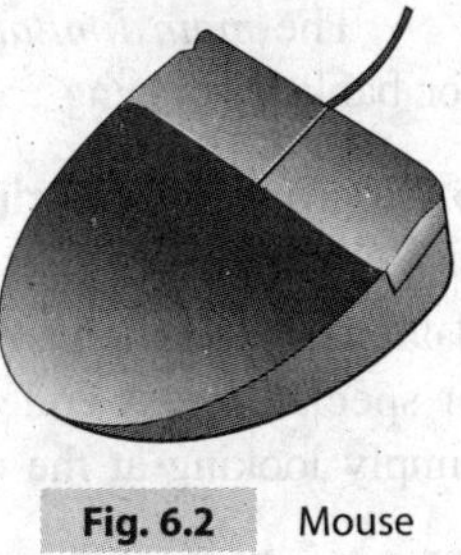

Fig. 6.2 Mouse

6.2.4 Joystick

A joystick, is a most popular input device used to play video games. A joystick uses a level to control the position and speed with which the joystick is moved into digital signals that are sent to the computer to control the cursor movement.

6.2.5 Track Ball

A track ball, uses a hard sphere to control cursor movement. The ball can be rotated by hand in any direction. The track ball translated the sphere's direction and speed of rotation into a digital signal, used to control the cursor.

6.2.6 Touch Screen

A touch screen registers input when a finger or other object comes in beams and ultrasonic acoustic waves. Infrared beams crisscross the surface of the screen and when a light beam is broken, that location is recorded.

6.2.7 Light pen

A light pen is also a pointing device like mouse. It can be used to choose a displayed menu option. The pen contains a photocell placed in a small tube. As the user moves the tip of the pen over the surface of the screen, it detects the light coming from a limited field of view. The light from the screen causes the photocell to respond and this electric response is transmitted to the process which can identify the menu option that is triggering the photocell. Light pen is useful for graphic work, especially for Computer Aided Design (CAD) purposes.

Recall that the data entered directly into a computer system without a transcription process is referred to as source data. Methods of source data input are:

6.2.8 Magnetic Ink Character Recognition (MICR)

MICR is the interpretation by a computer of a line of characters written in a special magnetic ink. These characters can be read by humans as well. For instance, there are a line of numbers and some odd-shaped characters on the bottom of bank's cheques. These magnetic ink characters are bank processing symbols representing the cheque number, customer account number, and bank identification number. When the bank receives the cheque, the amount of the cheque is also printed in magnetic ink. These cheques are sent through a MICR reader to interpret the information, update the appropriate accounts and in some cases, sort the cheques afterwards.

There are several *advantages* associated with the use of MICR:

- ❒ Checks may be roughly handled, folded, smeared, and stamped, but they can still be read with a high degree of accuracy
- ❒ Processing is speeded because checks can be fed directly into the input device
- ❒ People can easily read the magnetic ink characters

The *main limitation* of MICR is that only the 10 digits and 4 special characters needed for bank processing are used. No alphabetic characters are available.

6.2.9 Magnetic Strips

They are thin bands of magnetically encoded data that are found on the back of credit cards. The data stored on the card vary from one application to another, but they include account numbers or special access codes. Data in the form of magnetic strips cannot be seen or interpreted by simply looking at the card and so it can be highly sensitive or personal.

6.2.10 Optical Recognitions

Optical recognition occurs when a device scans a printed surface and translates the image the scanner sees into a machine readable format that is understandable by the computer. Optical recognition can be of the following types:

6.2.10.1 Optical Mark Recognition (OMR)

It employs mark sensing to scan and translate, based on its location which is a series of pen or pencil marks into computer readable form. For instance, the objective type multiple choice question paper we get in the bank recruitment exam. A computerized optical mark reader scores the tests by identifying the position of the mark.

6.2.10.2 Optical Bar Recognition (OBR)

This is a slightly more sophisticated type of optical recognition. Have you seen a series of thin black bars and spaces on the back of few books? They are bar codes or product codes which are arranged to represent data, such as the name of the manufacturer, and the type of product etc. An optical bar reader recognizes and interprets them on the basis of the width of the lines. The bar code is read by a scanner, and the price and product are then matched by the computer.

6.2.10.3 Optical Character Recognition (OCR)

This is the most sophisticated type of optical recognition. An optical card reader works in much the same way as the human eye. It recognizes specially shaped numeric and alphabetic characters.

A set of optical characters may be used to print merchandise tags that can be read using on OCR Reader. To process the sales transaction, the information on the tag, such as item price and the inventory number can be automatically entered at a point of sale terminal. Pertinent data can be saved and transferred to the company's main computer system to be used in activities such as managing inventories and analyzing sales.

The primary *advantage* of OCR is that it eliminates some of the duplication of human effort required to get data into the computer. This reduction in effort can improve data accuracy and can increase the timeliness of the information processed. However, *difficulties* in using OCR equipment may be encountered when documents to be read are poorly typed or have strikeovers or erasures. Also, form design and ink specifications may become more critical than is the case when people key the data from the forms.

6.3 OUTPUT CONCEPTS

An output device is a peripheral device that allows a computer to communicate information to humans or another machine by accepting data from the computer and transforming them into a usable form.

Output is divided into two general categories:

1. Output that can be readily understood and used by humans

2. Output to secondary storage devices that hold the data to be used as input for further processing by computer

Output that can be understood by humans can be in the form of:

1. hard copy
2. soft copy

6.3.1 Hard Copy

It is output on paper and can be read immediately or stored and read later. This is a relatively stable and permanent form of output.

6.3.2 Soft Copy

It is usually a screen displayed output. It is a transient form of output and is lost when the computer is turned off.

6.4 OUTPUT DEVICES

6.4.1 Hard Copy Devices

Hard copy devices can be broadly grouped into two categories: (*a*) Printer and (*b*) Plotter.

6.4.1.1 Printer

A printer produces output usually in the form of text on paper. Before getting into details about the types of printers, let us have an idea of the print quality, an important feature of hard copy devices.

Print quality available from hard copy output can vary considerably.

1. **Near-typeset Quality:** This print is similar in quality to that produced by a type set machine, such as print found in a magazine.
2. **Letter Quality:** This print is made using fully formed (solid line) characters.
3. **Near-letter Quality Print:** Printers that don't produce the fully formed characters can still print high quality documents using this type of print. On some printers, this is done when the print head makes multiple passes over the same letters filling in the spaces between the dots or lines.
4. **Standard-Quality Print:** It is produced when characters composed of dot lines are formed by a single pass of the print head.
5. **Draft-Quality Print:** The characters are formed with a minimum number of dots or lines and are smaller than the standard quality characters.

6.4.1.2 Types of Printers

6.4.1.2.1 Dot-Matrix Printer

It uses printer heads containing 9 to 24 pins. These pins produce patterns of dots on the paper to form the individual characters.

Dot matrix printers are very popular as they are relatively inexpensive and typically print at speed of 100–600 characters per second. These printers can give us draft quality, standard quality and near letter quality prints.

6.4.1.2.2 Daisy Wheel Printer

This printer is used in order to get the quality of type found on type writers. The daisy wheel printer is so called because the print mechanism looks like a daisy. This printer gives us letter quality print but is slow, typically 25–55 characters per second.

The speed of printers, we have discussed above is incredibly slow compared with the processing speed of the computers to which they are connected. The processor while it is sending texts to the printers, cannot normally be used for other productive work until printing is done. There are two approaches which, if used by computer systems, allow users to continue to operate their computers while printing is in progress.

1. **Spooler program (software)**—allows the processor to alternate between processing a user's ongoing activity and controlling the printing process. But for using this approach, disk space or dedicated block of primary storage should be available to store the text to be printed by the spooler.
2. **Printer buffer (hardware)**—It is an additional storage device that can accept text to be printed as fast as the computer can send it. The buffer then slowly releases the text data to match the printer's speed while the computer is free to do other things.

6.4.1.2.3 Line Printer

Line printers, or line-at-a-time printers use special mechanisms mentioned above that can print a whole line at once. They are very fast with speed ranging from 1200 to 6000 lines per minute.

6.4.1.2.4 Ink-Jet Printers

Ink-Jet printers form characters on paper by spraying ink from tiny nozzles through an electrical field that arranges the charged ink particles into characters at the rate of approximately 250 characters per second. The ink is absorbed into the paper and dries instantly. Various colors of ink can also be used. Although this might sound like a messy way of printing, ink-jet printers are reliable, but expensive.

6.4.1.2.5 Thermal-Transfer Printers

An inexpensive alternative to the ink-jet printer is the thermal-transfer printer which uses heat to transfer ink to paper. These printers bond the ink onto the paper by heating pins which press against a special ink ribbon. Thermal-transfer printers can produce color printouts by using a color ribbon.

6.4.1.2.6 Laser Printer

When speed and quality comparable to typeset material are required and cost is no factor, a laser printer is the solution. They produce images on paper by directing a laser beam at a mirror which bounces the beam on to a drum. The laser leaves a negative charge on the drum to which positively charged black toner powder will stick. As the paper rolls by the drum, the toner is transferred to the paper. A hot roller bonds the toner to the paper.

Laser printers use buffers to store an entire page at a time and that is why they print very fast at the rate of approximately 21,000 lines or 437 pages per minute.

6.4.1.3 Features of Printers

6.4.1.3.1 Impact versus Non-impact

An impact printer is one that generally operates by using a hammer to strike a character against an inked ribbon; the impact, then, causes an image of the character to be printed.

Impact printers function just as typewriters do. Their main disadvantage is that they are relatively slow, noisy, and subject to mechanical breakdowns. Despite the disadvantages, most printers in use today are impact devices.

Type of impact printers are:

- ❒ Dot matrix
- ❒ Daisy wheel
- ❒ Line

Non-impact printers were recently developed to meet some of the needs that were not being satisfied by impact technology. Most high-speed page printers, for example, use some form of nonimpact device; but high speed is not the only benefit of nonimpact technology.

Among the nonimpact printers available are:

Laser-xerographic — high speed
Electrosensitive — high speed
Electrophotographic — high speed

Thermal—ideal for lightweight portable terminals; quiet

Ink-jet—for letter—quality printing

6.4.1.3.2 Print Mechanisms for Impact Printers

1. **Wire-Matrix:** Some impact printers print character images out of a series of dots. The pattern of each character is created by extended wires that strike a carbon ribbon leaving the desired image.
2. **Character Printers:**
   (*a*) *Print wheel*: The print wheel rotates until each character moves into the required print position on the line. When all of the characters are in their proper position, a hammer strikes the paper against the wheel and a line is printed.
   (*b*) *Print Chain*: With a chain mechanism, there is one print hammer for each print position on the line. The characters are printed when the hammer presses the paper against the linked ribbon.
   (*c*) *Print drum*: The print drum is a metallic cylinder. Each column on the drum contains all the characters where each array of characters corresponds to a single print position on the line. As the drum rotates, each character that is to print reaches the appropriate position and a hammer then strikes that character.

6.4.1.2 Plotter

A plotter reproduces drawings using pens that are attached to movable arms. The pens are directed across the surface of a stationary piece of paper. High quality bar graphs, pie charts created with a plotter give a very good quality output.

6.4.2 Soft Copy Devices

An output on soft copy devices enables viewing of the work which allows corrections or rearrangement of material to suit specific needs. The most commonly used soft copy device is a monitor.

6.4.2.1 Visual Display Terminal or Terminal

A monitor is a television like device used to display data or information, allowing users to view the results of processing. The combination of monitors with the keyboard is called a **terminal**. Computer industry has divided VDT offerings into three categories.

6.4.2.1.1 Dumb Terminal

The **dumb terminal** is a stand along keyboard and display screen that can send or receive data, but cannot process that data. They are simply devices that immediately transmit each keyed data character to the processor.

6.4.2.1.2 Smart Terminal

They are designed with a microprocessor chip that contains the circuits needed to perform arithmetic logic and control functions, and they also have an internal storage capability. They can move the cursor in all directions to add, delete and change keyed characters. Smart terminals can store and consolidate input data prior to sending them to the processor. But they cannot normally be programmed by users.

6.4.2.1.3 Intelligent Terminal

It combines VDT hardware with built-in microprocessors that can be programmed by the user. They can process small jobs without the need to interact with a larger computer. The intelligent Video Display Terminal is designed with circuits that permit it to communicate with other terminals and larger processors.

The difference between an intelligent terminal and a personal computer is very little. The intelligent terminal is designed with circuits that allow it to communicate with other terminals and larger processor, while most personal computers have been designed primarily to operate alone. But plug in hardware and needed software permit interaction between main frames and personal computer. And other plug in modules are available to convert existing dumb and smart terminals into full fledged microcomputers.

6.4.2.2 Visual Display Unit (Monitor)

A monitor is a television like device used to display input data or information, allowing users to view the results of processing. Quality of the monitor is often judged in terms of resolution which is a measure of the number of picture elements, or pixels, a screen contains. A **pixel** is the smallest increment of a display screen that can be controlled individually. The higher the number of pixels, the clearer and sharper is the image. Screens for monitor are of two types:

6.4.2.2.1 Cathode Ray Tube (CRT)

On this type of screen, a data image can be produced by moving an electron beam across a phosphor-coated screen. By intensifying the strength of the beam, the phosphor-coating glows in certain places, forming the characters. The CRT has a display screen of 25 lines of 80 characters each. it is used in most desk top monitors. Some CRT screens are monochrome (one color) while others produce many colors.

Two types of color monitors are commonly used: composite and red-green-blue. A composite color monitor uses only one electron gun to control the intensity of all three phosphor dots in each pixel. In a red-green-blue (RGB) monitor, three electron guns, one for each dot in a pixel, are used to control the intensity of the phosphor dots. A much sharper picture is produced with the RGB monitor because the three electron guns allow finer control over the intensities of the phosphor dots.

Artists may wonder why red, green, and blue are used as the primary colors instead of red, yellow, and blue. Simply stated, the difference between electronic waves and color pigments requires that green be used instead of yellow to get the appropriate color mixes.

6.4.2.2.2 Flat-Panel Display

A CRT screen is reliable but it is bulky and consumes a lot of power and that is why it is cumbersome to use it with portable computers. For small computers, flat panel display is used. It does not have a picture tube. The most common type of flat panel display is the Liquid Crystal Display (LCD), which produces images by aligning molecular crystals. When a voltage is applied, the crystals line up in a way that blocks light from passing through them and his absence of light is seen as characters on the screen. LCDs are better than CRTs as LCDs don't flicker, thereby avoiding eye strain and fatigue caused by CRTs during prolonged sessions at the computer.

The flat-panel display is still in its infancy; better resolution and contrast, as well as other new features are being developed. One advance is the gas-plasma screen. These displays offer flicker-free viewing and have a much higher contrast than LCDs. Gas-plasma displays contain an ionized gas (plasma) between two glass plates. One glass plate contains a set of horizontal wires; the other has a set of vertical wires. The intersection points of each horizontal and vertical wire identifies a pixel. A pixel is turned on when current is sent through the appropriate vertical and horizontal wires. The plasma at the pixel emits light as the current is applied. Characters are formed by lighting the appropriate pixels.

6.5 CONNECTION

A central processing unit can be connected to its various peripheral devices such as a printer by using a special hardware called **interface**. Two interface standards that have emerged over the years are: Parallel interface and serial interface.

6.5.1 Parallel Interface

A parallel interface is the one that uses 8 wires to transmit all 8 bits in a byte at the same time. Therefore, parallel interfaces are faster and more expensive than serial interfaces. An interface connection is often called a **port**. The program instructions used by the computer to communicate with other devices is called driver program.

6.5.2 Serial Interface

Unlike parallel interface, in a serial interface, the 8 bit bytes are lined up into a single stream of bits for transmission to a peripheral device. That is, a serial interface transmits only one bit at a time and hence it is slow (Fig. 6.3).

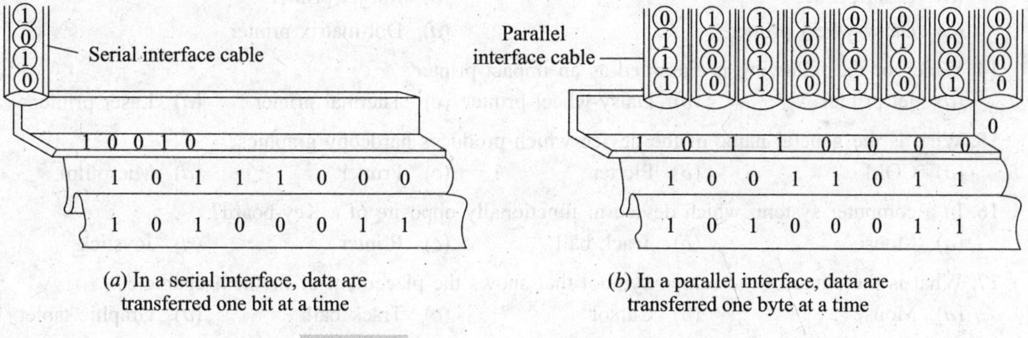

(*a*) In a serial interface, data are transferred one bit at a time

(*b*) In a parallel interface, data are transferred one byte at a time

Fig. 6.3 Serial versus parallel data transfer

REVIEW QUESTIONS

Multiple Choice Questions

1. Which device can produce the final product of machine processing into a form usable by humans?
   (*a*) Storage (*b*) Input device (*c*) Output device (*d*) Control
2. Which can read data and convert them to a form that a computer can use?
   (*a*) Logic (*b*) Storage (*c*) Control (*d*) Input device
3. Which kind of hardware is used the most in the input phase of a computer-based information system?
   (*a*) Keyboard (*b*) Printer (*c*) Monitor (*d*) Hard disk
4. Which kind of devices allows the user to add components and capabilities to a computer system?
   (*a*) System boards (*b*) Storage devices
   (*c*) Input devices (*d*) Expansion slots

5. Which is widely use in academic testing?
(*a*) MICR (*b*) POS (*c*) OCR (*d*) OMR

6. Which is considered a direct entry input device?
(*a*) Optical scanner (*b*) Mouse (*c*) Light pen (*d*) All of the above

7. What is required when more than one person uses a central computer at the same time?
(*a*) Light pen (*b*) Mouse (*c*) Digitizer (*d*) Terminal

8. Large computer system typically use:
(*a*) Line printers (*b*) Ink-jet printers
(*c*) Dot-matrix printers (*d*) Daisy wheel printers

9. Which of the following is not an output device of a computer?
(*a*) Printer (*b*) Keyboard (*c*) VDU (*d*) CRT screen

10. Data entry can be performed with all of the following except:
(*a*) OCR (*b*) OMR
(*c*) COM (*d*) Voice-recognition systems

11. Dot-matrix is a type of:
(*a*) Tape (*b*) Printer (*c*) Disk (*d*) Bus

12. A kind of serial dot-matrix printer that forms characters with magnetically charged ink sprayed dots is called:
(*a*) laser printer (*b*) ink-jet printer (*c*) drum printer (*d*) chain printer

13. Which printer is very commonly used for desk-top publishing?
(*a*) Laser printer (*b*) Ink-jet printer
(*c*) Daisy-wheel printer (*d*) Dot-matrix printer

14. Which of the following is classified as an impact printer?
(*a*) Jet printer (*b*) Daisy-wheel printer (*c*) Thermal printer (*d*) Laser printer

15. What is the general name of the device which produces hardcopy graphics?
(*a*) COM (*b*) Plotter (*c*) Printer (*d*) Microfilm

16. In a computer system, which device in functionally opposite of a Key-board?
(*a*) Mouse (*b*) Track ball (*c*) Printer (*d*) Joystick

17. What is the name of the screen symbol that shows the placement of the next character?
(*a*) Mouse (*b*) Cursor (*c*) Track ball (*d*) Graphic tablet

18. Point out the odd item amongst the following:
(*a*) Computer mouse (*b*) Touch pad (*c*) Light pen (*d*) Printer

19. The barcode which is used on all types of items is read by a scanning device directly into the computer. What is the name of this scanning device?
(*a*) Laser scanner (*b*) Wand (*c*) OCR (*d*) MICR

20. What is the name of the reading device which made use of photosensors and laser technologies to interpret printed, typed or even hand-written data directly from the source documents?
(*a*) MICR (*b*) OCR
(*c*) Mark-sensing device (*d*) ATM

21. Character readers are those devices which read the characters printed on the source documents and then convert them directly into computer-usable input. Which of the following is not a character reader?
(*a*) OCR (*b*) MICR (*c*) OMR (*d*) LCD

22. The OCR stand for?
(*a*) Outsized character reader (*b*) Optical character recognition
(*c*) Operational character reader (*d*) Only character reader

ANSWERS

Multiple Choice Questions

1. (*c*)	**2.** (*d*)	**3.** (*a*)	**4.** (*d*)	**5.** (*d*)	**6.** (*d*)	**7.** (*d*)	**8.** (*a*)
9. (*b*)	**10.** (*c*)	**11.** (*b*)	**12.** (*b*)	**13.** (*a*)	**14.** (*b*)	**15.** (*b*)	**16.** (*c*)
17. (*b*)	**18.** (*d*)	**19.** (*a*)	**20.** (*b*)	**21.** (*d*)	**22.** (*b*)		

QUESTIONS

1. What does it mean to input data into a computer? What is the purpose of an input device?
2. Define output. What is the purpose of an output device?
3. Distinguish between batch and transaction processing?
4. Describe the difference between serial and parallel interfaces.
5. What is the difference between a dumb terminal and a smart terminal?
6. What is the difference between an intelligent terminal and a personal computer?
7. MICR and OCR devices are similar in that both types of machines convert source document data directly into computer—usable input. How do these machines differ?
8. How do resolution and pixels relate to monitors?
9. List two kinds of monitors and tell how they work.
10. What is a Plotter?
11. Output can be divided into two categories. What are they?
12. What is the purpose of an output device?
13. List three types of optical recognition.

PLANNING THE COMPUTER PROGRAM

One major aspect of the data processing function is the logical control of programming elements necessary to ensure that data is read and processed properly and used to produce the required output. In fact, the logical control of element within a program is the single most important aspect of programming. Flowchart is used by computer professionals to indicate the logic that a program is to incorporate.

7.1 FLOWCHART

A flowchart is a pictorial representation of the steps involved in the procedure. It also shows the logical sequence in which the steps are performed.

A flowchart consists of some boxes linked by arrows. In each box, the instruction to be carried out are mentioned. Arrows on the lines connecting the boxes indicate the direction in which we should proceed. These boxes are of different shapes, as shown in Fig. 7.1.

Symbol	Function	Meaning
	Start/Stop Point	Indicates starting points and ending points in a program.
	Input/Output	Indicates when an input or output operation is to be performed.
	Processing Operation	Indicates the movement of data, the editing of data or calculations.
	Decision	Indicates a point in the program at which execution control may be non-consequentially transferred if required conditions are met.
	Connector	Indicates a logic flow from one page of the flowchart to another (in some instances logic flow on the same page).
	Direction of Logic flow	Indicates the direction in which one has to proceed for solving a problem.

Fig. 7.1 Some commonly used program flowchart symbols

A flowchart is drawn before the program is written to ensure that the instructions will be logically integrated. The concept is same as used by architects who prepare pictorial representations prior to the actual design of a building. The pictorial representations are called blue prints, which verify and integrate elements of a building before construction. In the same way, flowcharts verify and integrate elements of a program prior to writing the program. The flowchart is drawn by programmers to ensure the accuracy of their interpretation of the logic required in the program.

The following points may help in drawing the flowcharts:

1. First chart the main line, and then incorporate details
2. Use descriptive titles written in English
3. Do not chart every detail otherwise the chart will only be a pictorial representation of the program
4. Use the flowchart as a genuine reference while writing a program, not as something to be discarded once writing a program has began
5. Do not be afraid to change the flowchart when required during the program writing
6. Try to understand your flowchart while putting yourself in the position of a reader

Let us consider the following problem to see what a program flowchart looks like. Suppose we have a file with the fields, Name, Sex code and Telephone No. The Sex code field will contain either a '1' to denote a male or a '2' to denote a female. We would like the computer to process this file and produce a report that lists the names and telephone numbers of females only.

The logic for this problem consists of the following steps:

7.1.1 Program Logic

1. Read the file
2. Determine if the record pertains to a female, *i.e.*, sex code = 2
3. If sex code is not equal to 2, then do not process this record since it contains data for a male. Instead, read the next record, *i.e.*, go back to step-a
4. If sex code = 2, then print the following fields—Name, and Telephone number
5. Go to step-a to read the next record

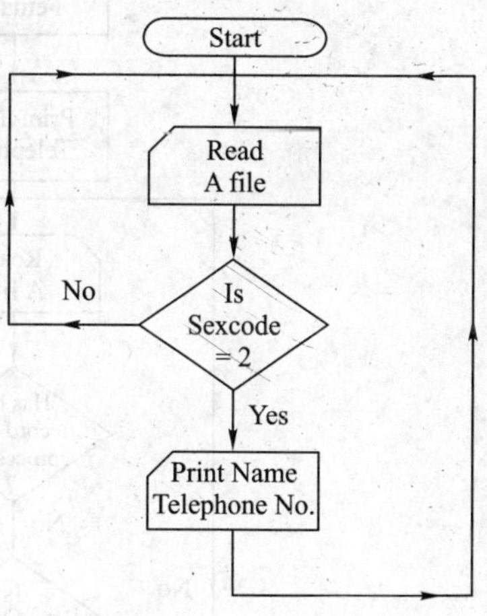

Fig. 7.2 Sample Flowchart

7.1.2 Interpreting the Flowchart

1. File records are read
2. If sex code = 2, then Name and Telephone numbers are printed. Go to step-a
3. If sex code is not equal to 2, then go to step-a
4. The sequence of the steps will be repeated until there is no more data

7.1.3 Flowcharting Conventions

1. Each symbol denotes a type of operation
2. A note is written inside each symbol to indicate the specific function to be performed
3. Flowcharts are read from top to bottom
4. A sequence of operations is performed until a terminal symbol designates the end of the run

For further illustration, suppose we want the report to contain some sort of statistical information such as the total number of Female records processed, title and column heading for identification purposes.

To produce a report with a title and column headings, we can print these items at the beginning of our logic flow as the title and the column headings appear at the beginning of the report.

Now, let us consider the logic necessary to instruct the computer to print the same report but with a message at the end indicating the total number of females processed. Since we want this message to be printed only when all the records have been processed, we must include in our logic a test to see if the last data record has already been processed. In order to print out a count of the number of females, it is necessary for us, at the beginning of our logic, to indicate that a special area must be set up in the CPU. The purpose of this area is to keep a running total of the number of females as the records are being processed. To setup a counter, we must indicate in our program, every time that we want to add to this counter. In this program, we want to find the total number of females, each time the computer finds a female record, then, the COUNT field should be incremented by 1. The flowchart segment that indicates this part of the logic is shown in Fig. 7.3.

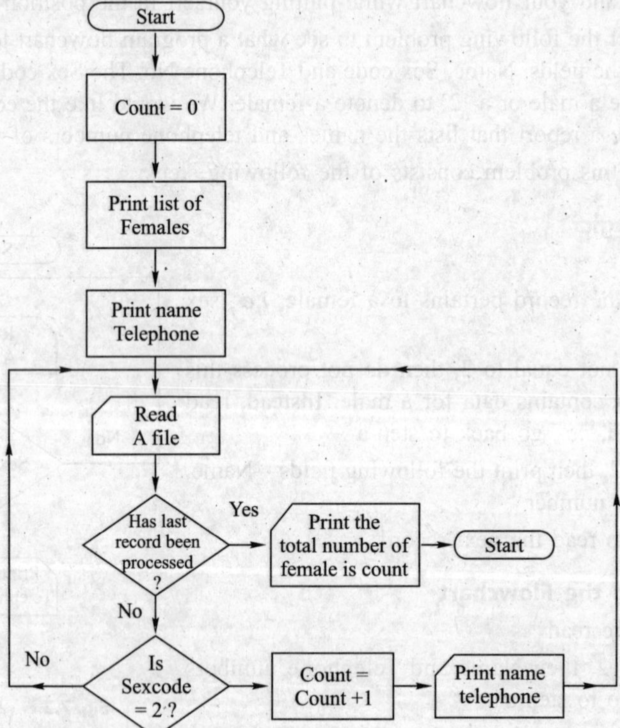

Fig. 7.3 Completed flowchart contains title, heading, names and telephones and number of females processed

7.1.4 Summary of Program Flowchart

1. A flowchart is a pictorial representation of the logical control elements that will be incorporated in a program
2. A flowchart should be written before a program is coded to ensure that all the elements are logically interrelated
3. Flowcharts are read from top to bottom unless a branch alters the normal flow

4. Each symbol in a flowchart represents a specific function
5. The note inside each symbol indicates the specific operation

7.1.5 Advantages of Flowcharts

1. Clarify the program logic
2. Before coding begins, the flowchart assists the programmer in determining the type of logic control to be used in a program
3. Serve as documentation
4. Serve as a guide for program coding or program writing
5. The flowchart is a pictorial representation that may be useful to the business person or user who wishes to examine some facet of the logic used in the program
6. Ensure that all the possible conditions (contingencies) are accounted for
7. Help to detect deficiencies in the problem statement

7.1.6 Limitations of Flowcharts

1. Program flowcharts are cumbersome for the programmer to write. As a result, many programmers do not write the chart until after the program has been completed, which, of course, defeats one of its main purposes
2. It is sometimes difficult for a business person or user to understand the logic depicted in a flowchart
3. Flowcharts are no longer completely standardized tools. The newer structured programming techniques have necessitated changes in the traditional format of a flowchart

7.2 TYPES OF LOGIC USED IN FLOWCHART

In the late 60s, two mathematicians Carrado Bohm and Guiseppe Jacopini, proved that even the most complex logic could be expressed by the following three types of logic which can be represented in a flowchart:

1. Straight Sequential Execution
2. Transfer of Control
3. Looping

Naturally, these general types of program logic and processes may be combined in any fashion or combination to produce a process which, when executed, will yield the desired results.

7.2.1 Straight Sequential Execution

A **Straight Sequential Execution** is a logic which executes statement one after another in a linear fashion as shown in Fig. 7.4.

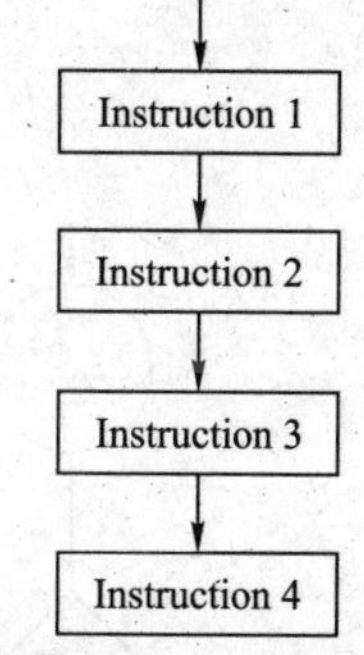

Fig. 7.4 Straight Sequential Execution

7.2.2 Transfer of Control

A **Transfer of Control** is a logic which represents a number of processing options. The option chosen depends on the result of the decision criterion. Figure 7.5 depicts some variations of the Transfer of Control.

7.2.3 Looping

A looping (also called repetition) is a logic which is used to execute an instruction or group of instructions more than once without having to recode them. The two basic variations of this type of structure are DO WHILE and DO UNTIL. If the decision criterion is placed before the statements to be repeated, then it is a DO WHILE loop as shown in Fig. 7.6. A DO UNTIL loop places the decision criterion at the end of the statements to be repeated as illustrated in Fig. 7.7.

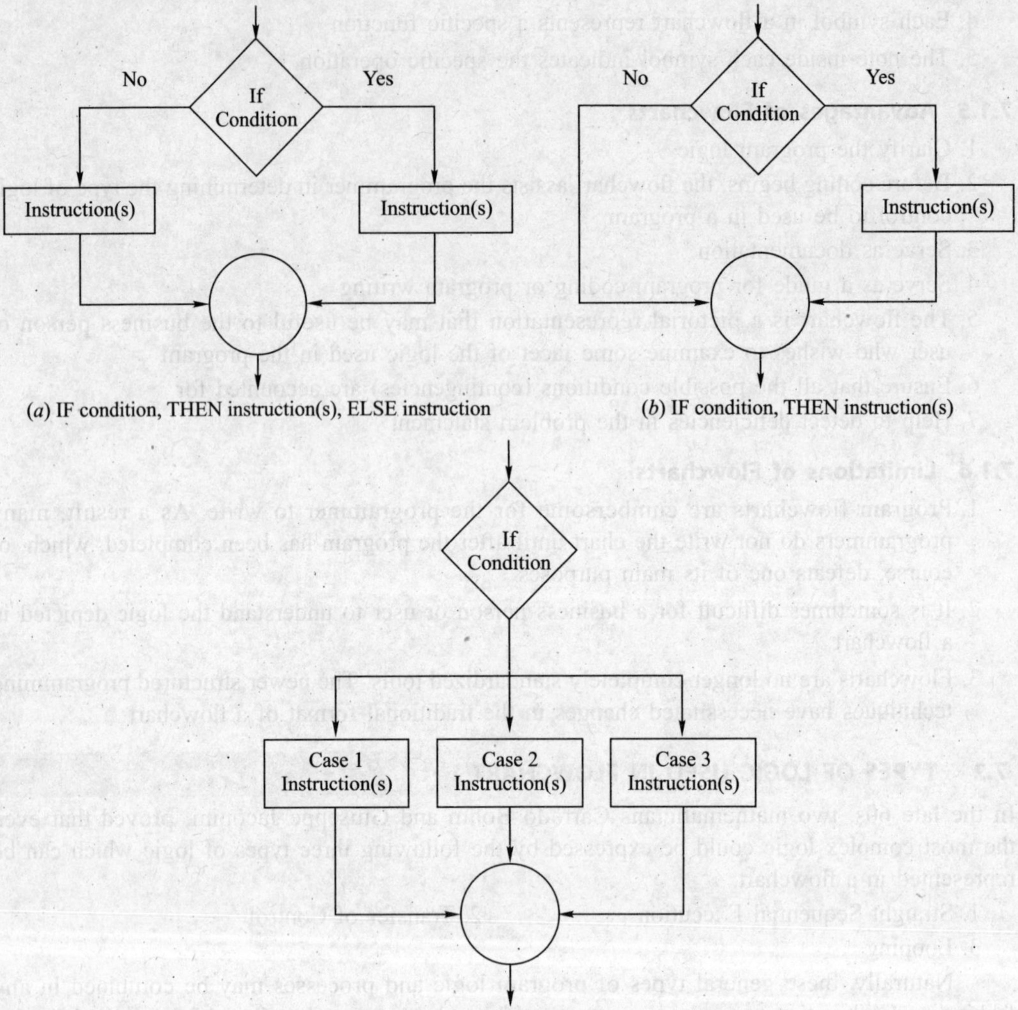

(*a*) IF condition, THEN instruction(s), ELSE instruction

(*b*) IF condition, THEN instruction(s)

(*c*) CASE condition

Fig. 7.5

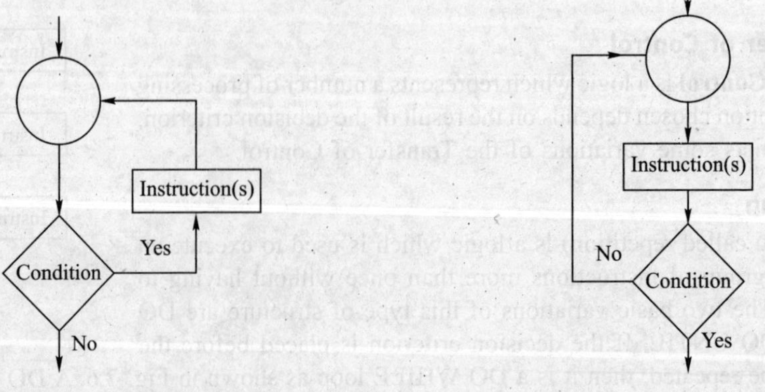

Fig. 7.6 DO WHILE looping

Fig. 7.7 DO UNTIL looping

The general form of looping (repetition) logic is depicted in Fig. 7.8.

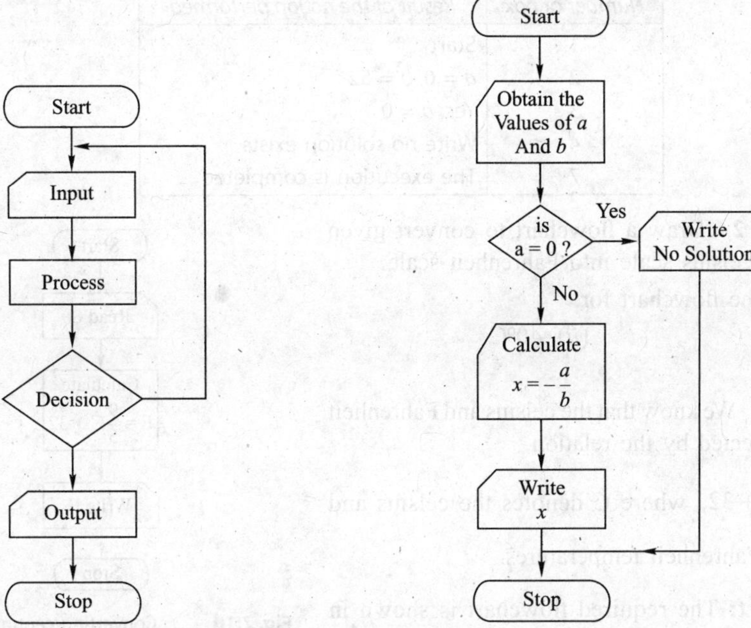

Fig. 7.8 Looping or Repetition Logic

Fig. 7.9 Flowchart to solve the equation $ax + b = 0$

Examples

Example 1 Draw a flowchart to solve the equation $ax + b = 0$. Execute the flowchart using following data.

(*i*) $a = 3$, $b = 6$

(*ii*) $a = 0$, $b = 52$.

Solution Algorithm

The steps are as follows:

Step 1: Obtain the values of a and b

Step 2: If $a = 0$, then write 'No solution exists' and stop; else, calculate $x = -\frac{b}{a}$, write value of x and stop

Flowchart: The required flowchart can be represented as shown in Fig. 7.9.

Execution of flow chart: When $a = 3$, $b = 6$

Number of box	*Result of the action performed*
1	Start
2	$a = 3$, $b = 6$
3	No; $a \neq 0$
5	$x = -6/3 = -2$
6	Write –2
7	The execution is completed

Execution of flowchart: When $a = 0$, $b = 52$

Number of box	*Result of the action performed*
1	Start
2	$a = 0, b = 52$
3	Yes; $a = 0$
4	Write no solution exists
7	The execution is completed

Example 2 Draw a flowchart to convert given temperature in celsius scale into Fahrenheit scale.

Execute the flowchart for:

(*i*) 20ºC (*ii*) 40ºC

(*iii*) 0ºC

Solution We know that the celsius and Fahrenheit scales are connected by the relation.

$F = \frac{9}{5}C + 32$, where C denotes the celsius and F denotes the Fahrenheit temperatures.

Flowchart: The required flowchart is shown in Fig. 7.10.

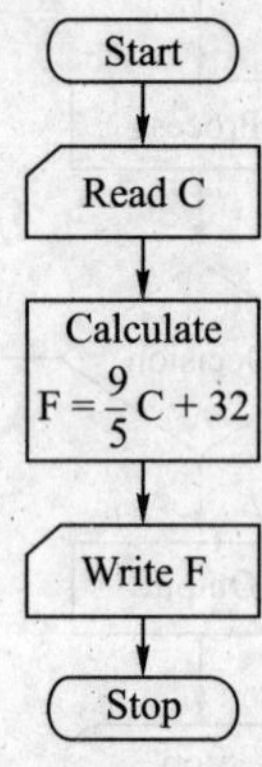

Fig. 7.10 Converting centigrade reading to fahrenheit

7.2.4 Execution of Flowchart

Number of box	*Result Performed when*		
	C = 20ºC	*C = 40º*	*C = 0ºC*
1	Start	Start	Start
2	$C = 20$	$C = 40$	$C = 0$
3	$F = \frac{9}{5} \times 20 + 32$ $F = 68$	$F = \frac{9}{5} \times 40 + 32$ $F = 104$	$= \frac{9}{5} \times 0 + 32$ $F = 32$
4	Write $F = 68$	Write $F = 104$	Write $F = 32$
5	Stop	Stop	Stop

Example 3 Draw a flowchart to obtain H.C.F. of two positive integers, given their L.C.M.

Execute the flowchart when L.C.M. of 12 and 18 is 36.

Solution Let a and b be the two given numbers, then L.C.M. × H.C.F. = $a \times b$

$$\therefore \quad \text{H.C.F.} = \frac{a \times b}{\text{L.C.M.}}$$

Flowchart (Fig. 7.11):

Execution of Flowchart, given

$a = 12$, $b = 18$ and L.C.M. = 36

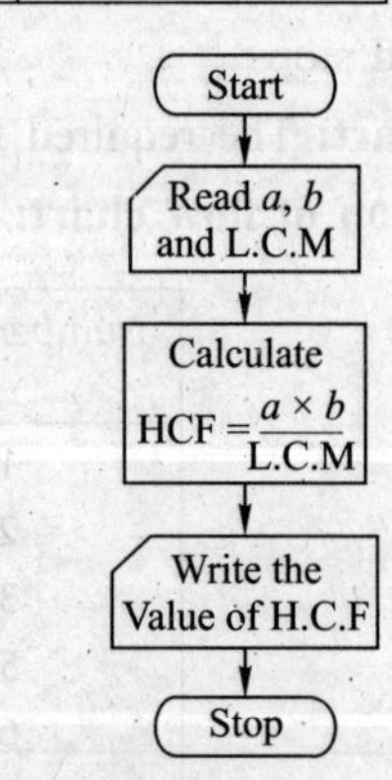

Fig. 7.11 Computing H.C.F.

1. Start
2. Read the value of a, b and L.C.M.
3. Calculate H.C.F. = 12 × 18/36 = 6
4. Write H.C.F. = 6
5. Stop

Example 4 Write a step-by-step procedure and draw a flowchart to find the selling price of an item, given percentage loss or gain and the cost price of an item.

Execute the flowchart with the following data:

(*i*) Gain % = 35, C.P. = ₹ 3,000

(*ii*) Loss % = 25, C.P. = ₹ 300

Solution If there is a gain percentage, then S.P. is given by

$$\text{S.P.} = \frac{\text{C.P.} \times (100 + \text{gain }\%)}{100}$$

and if there is a loss percentage, then

$$\text{S.P.} = \frac{\text{C.P.} \times (100 - \text{loss }\%)}{100}$$

Algorithm

Step 1: Start

Step 2: Input the values of C.P. and Gain % or loss %

Step 3: Decide whether there is a gain % or loss %

Step 4: If the answer is Yes, then

$$\text{S.P.} = \text{C.P.} \times \left(1 + \frac{\text{Gain }\%}{100}\right)$$

Step 5: If the answer is No, then

$$\text{S.P.} = \text{C.P.} \times \left(1 - \frac{\text{Loss }\%}{100}\right)$$

Step 6: Write Selling Price

Step 7: Stop

Flow chart: The required flowchart is shown in Fig. 7.12.

(*i*) Execution of flowchart: When Gain % 35 and C.P. = ₹ 3,000

1. Start
2. Read the value S.P. = 3,000, and Gain % = 35
3. It is gain %
4. Calculate S.P. $= \dfrac{3{,}000 \times (100 + 35)}{100} = 4{,}050$
5. Write S.P. = ₹ 4,050
6. Stop the execution

(*ii*) Execution of flowchart: When Loss % = 25 and C.P. = ₹ 300

1. Start
2. Read the value Loss % = 25 and C.P. = ₹ 300
3. It is gain %; No

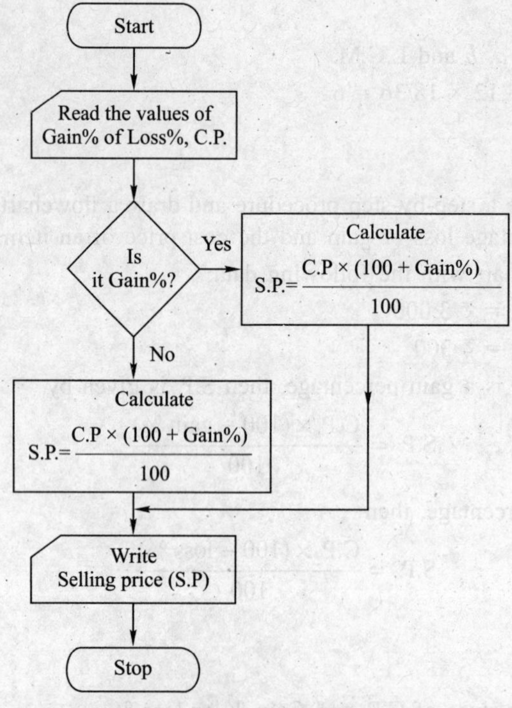

Fig. 7.12 Computing Selling Price

4. Calculate S.P. $= \dfrac{300 \times (100 - 25)}{100} = 225$
5. Write E S.P. = ₹ 225
6. Stop

Example 5 Write an algorithm and draw a flowchart to find the cost price of an item given its selling price and percentage gain or loss incurred.

Execute the flowchart with the following data:

(*i*) Gain % = 20, S.P. = ₹ 3,000 (*ii*) Loss % = 20 S.P. = ₹ 2,000

Solution Algorithm

The steps are as follows:

Step 1: Start

Step 2: Input the selling price and Gain % or Loss %

Step 3: Decide whether it is Gain % or Loss %.

Step 4: If Yes, then

Step 5: Calculate C.P. $= \dfrac{\text{S.P.} \times 100}{100 + \text{Gain }\%}$

Step 6: If No, then

Step 7: Calculate C.P. $= \dfrac{\text{S.P.} \times 100}{100 - \text{Loss }\%}$

Step 8: Stop.

Flowchart: The required flowchart is shown in Fig. 7.13.

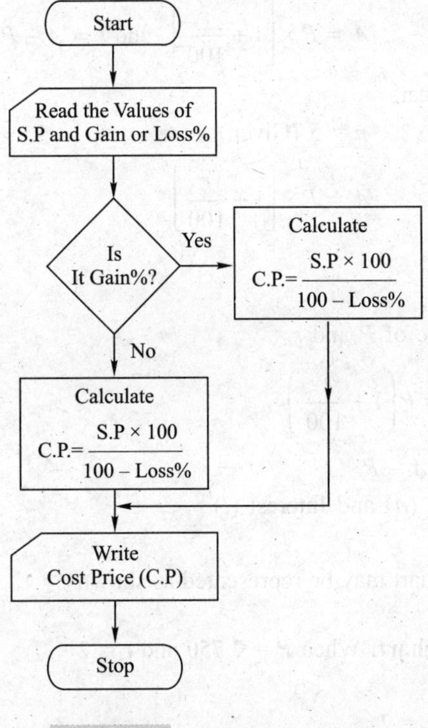

Fig. 7.13 Computing Cost Price

***(i)* Execution of flowchart:** When Gain % = 20 and S.P. = ₹ 3,000

1. Start
2. Read the value S.P. = ₹ 3,000 and Gain % = 20
3. It is Gain %
4. Calculate C.P. $= \dfrac{3,000 \times 100}{100 + 20} = 2,500$
5. Write E C.P. = ₹ 2,500
6. Stop

***(ii)* Execution of flowchart:** When Loss % = 20 and S.P. = ₹ 2,000

1. Start
2. Read the value Loss % = 20 and S.P. = ₹ 2,000
3. It is Loss %
4. Calculate C.P. $= \dfrac{2,000 \times 100}{100 - 20} = 2,500$
5. Write C.P. = ₹ 2,500
6. Stop

Example 6 Write a step-by-step procedure and draw a flowchart to find the compound interest and the amount after 5 years for principal *P* and rate of interest *r* percent.

Execute the flowchart with the following data:

(i) P = ₹ 750, $r = 2$ *(ii)* P = ₹ 2,000, $r = 18$.

Solution We know that compound interest and amount is

$$A = P \times \left[1 + \frac{r}{100}\right]^h \text{ and } I = A - P$$

where n is the number of years.

Here, $n = 5$ (Given)

So, $$A = P \times \left[1 + \frac{r}{100}\right]^5$$

Algorithm

Step 1: Start

Step 2: Read the value of P and r

Step 3: Calculate $A = P\left(1 + \frac{r}{100}\right)^5$

Step 4: Calculate $I = A - P$

Step 5: Write Amount (A) and Interest (I)

Step 6: Stop

Flowchart: The flowchart may be represented as shown in Fig. 7.14.

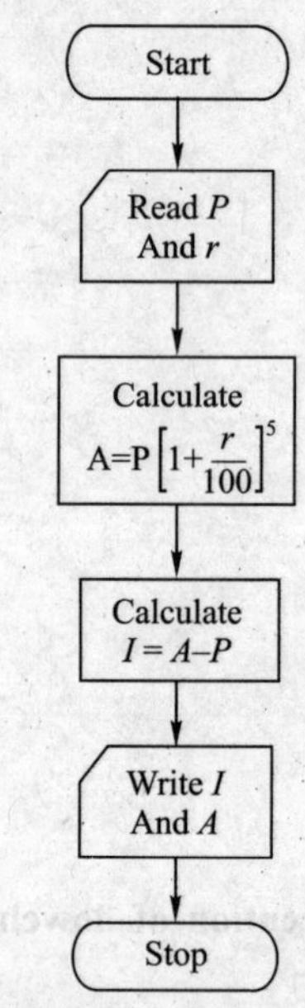

Fig. 7.14 Computing Compound Interest

***(i)* Execution of the flowchart:** When P = ₹ 750 and $r = 2$

1. Start
2. Read P = ₹ 750 and $r = 2$
3. Calculate $A = 750 \times \left[1 + \frac{2}{100}\right]^5 = 828.06$
4. Calculate $I = A - P = 828.06 - 750 = 78.06$
5. Write compound Interest I = ₹ 828.06
6. Write Amount (A) = ₹ 78.06
7. Stop

***(ii)* Execution of the flowchart:** When P = ₹ 2,000, $r = 18$

1. Start
2. Read P = ₹ 2,000, $r = 18$
3. Calculate $A = 2{,}000 \times \left[1 + \frac{18}{100}\right]^5 = 4{,}576$
4. Calculate $I = A - P = 2{,}576$
5. Write compound Interest I = ₹ 2,576
6. Write Amount (A) = ₹ 4,576
7. Stop

Example 7 Write a step-by-step procedure for adding first 100 natural numbers. Draw the flowchart also.

Natural numbers 1, 2, 3, 4, ..., 100

Sum of Natural Numbers 1 + 2 + 3 + 4 + ..., + 100

Solution Algorithm

The steps are as follows:

Step 1: Input last Natural Number, *i.e.*, 100

Step 2: Calculate $X = \dfrac{Nx\ (N+1)}{2}$

Step 3: Print the value of X

Flowchart: The required flowchart is shown in Fig. 7.15.

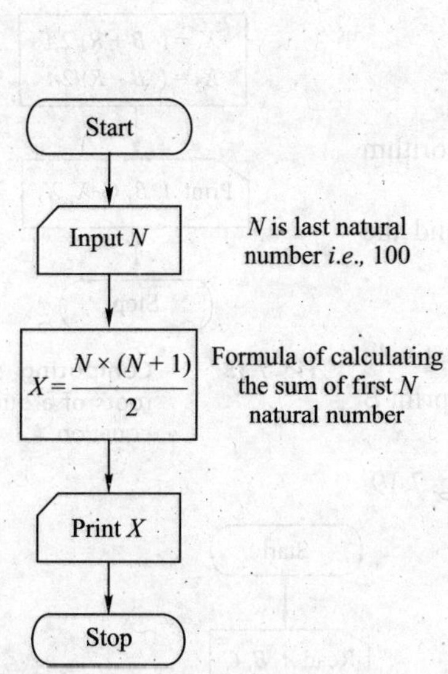

Fig. 7.15 Calculating and printing sum of first 100 natural numbers

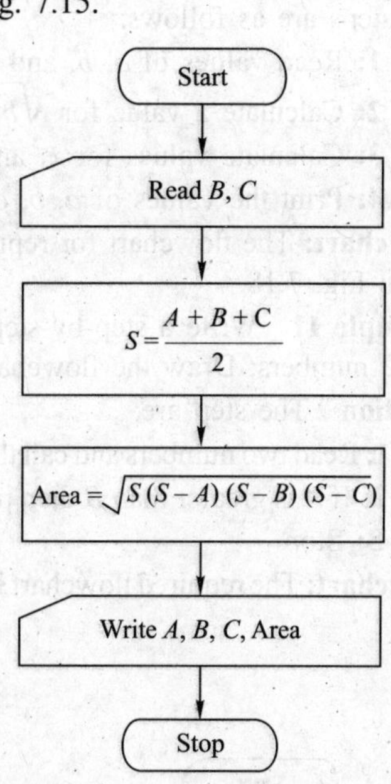

Fig. 7.16 Calculating the area of Trianlge

Example 8 Write a step-by-step procedure to find the area of triangles if their sides are known.

Solution Algorithm

The steps are as follows:

Step 1: Input the values of sides of a triangle

Step 2: Calculate the Area of triangle

Step 3: Print the value of Area of triangle

Flowchart: The required flowchart is shown in Fig. 7.16.

Example 9 Draw a flowchart for calculating the average of three sessional tests of students.

Solution The flowchart may be represented in Fig. 7.17.

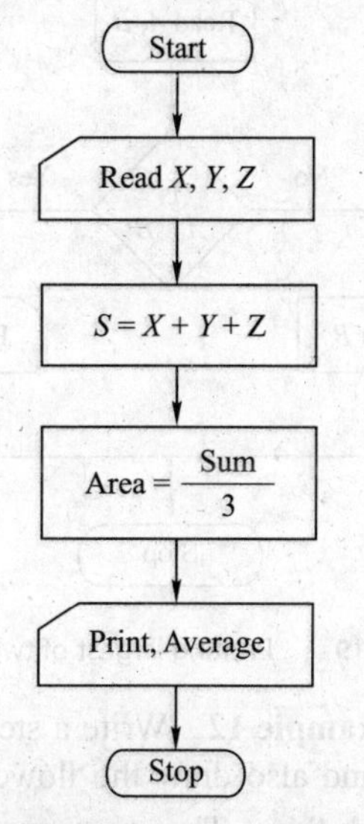

Fig. 7.17 Calculating Average

Example 10 Write a step-by-step procedure to obtain the roots of a quadratic equation by using the well known formulae:

$$x_1 = \frac{-b + \sqrt{b^2 - 4ac}}{2a}$$

$$x_2 = \frac{-b - \sqrt{b^2 - 4ac}}{2a}$$

Draw a flowchart also.

Solution Let us assume that the values of a, b, c are such that $b^2 - 4ac$ will always be positive. Therefore, we need not worry about calculating the square root of a negative number.

The steps are as follows:

Step 1: Read values of a, b, and c

Step 2: Calculate a value for $\sqrt{b^2 - 4ac}$

Step 3: Calculate values for x_1 and x_2

Step 4: Print the values of a, b, c, x_1 and x_2

Flowchart: The flowchart for representing this algorithm is shown in Fig. 7.18.

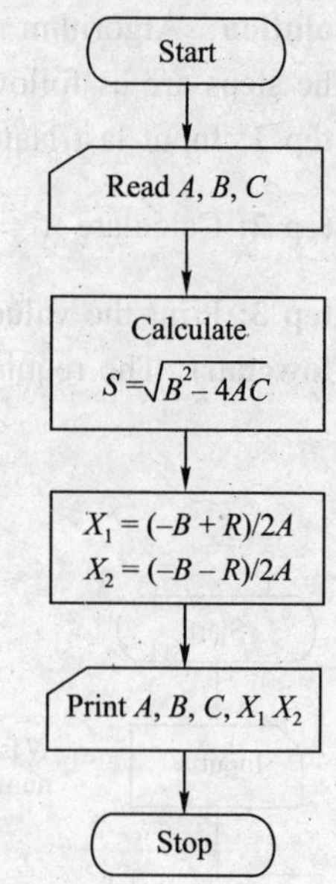

Fig. 7.18 Computing square roots of a quadratic equation

Example 11 Write a step-by-step procedure to find the largest of 2 numbers: Draw the flowchart also.

Solution The step are:

Step 1: Read two numbers and call them A and B respectively

Step 2: If A is greater than B then print A otherwise print B

Step 3: Stop

Flowchart: The required flowchart is shown in the Fig. 7.19.

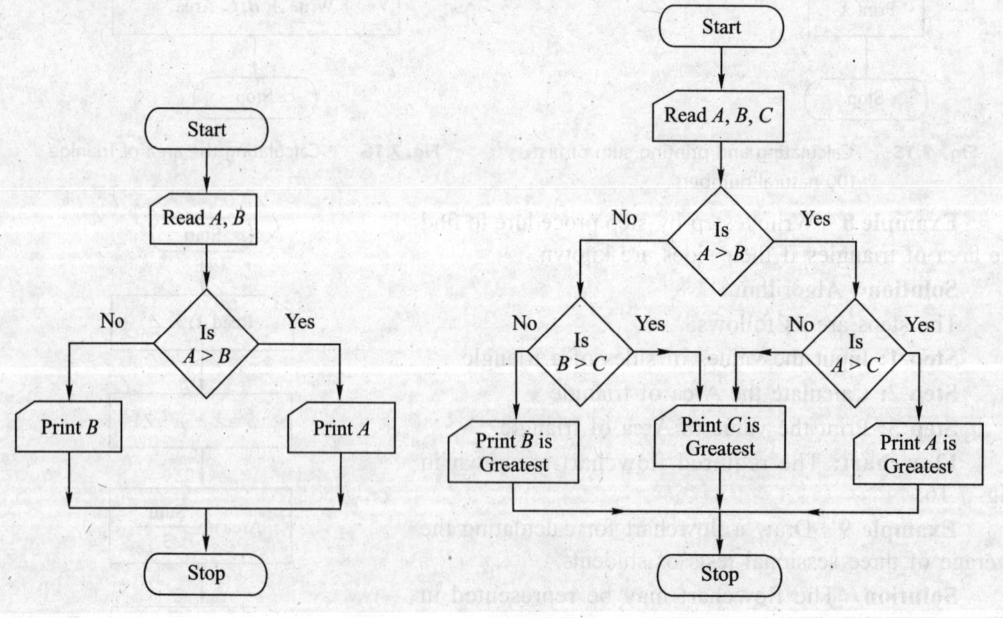

Fig. 7.19 Printing largest of two numbers

Fig. 7.20 Printing the largest of three numbers

Example 12 Write a step-by-step procedure to find out the largest of three numbers given to you and also draw the flowchart.

Solution The steps are as follows:

Step 1: Read three numbers and store them in A, B and C

Step 2: Compare A and B. If A is greater than B then go to step 5 else Step 3

Step 3: Compare *B* and *C*. If *B* is greater than *C* then print '*B* is greatest' and go to Step 7 otherwise go to Step 4

Step 4: Print '*C* is greatest' and go to Step 7

Step 5: Compare *A* and *C*. If *A* is greater than *C* then print *A* is greatest and go to Step 7 otherwise to go Step 6

Step 6: Print '*C* is greatest' and go to Step 7

Step 7: Stop

Flowchart: The required flowchart is depicted in Fig. 7.20.

Example 13 Draw a flowchart to compute and print the grades for an examination. Input is Roll No. and Marks in five subjects out of 100. Grades are allocated on the following basis:

Percentage of Marks	*Grade*
90 and above	*'A'*
80 and less than 90	*'B'*
Less than 80	*'C'*

Short names for memory cells:

R: Roll No.

*S*1, *S*2, *S*3, *S*4, *S*5: Marks in 5 subjects respectively.

T: Total Marks obtained

P: Percentage Marks

Solution The required flowchart may be represented as shown in Fig. 7.21.

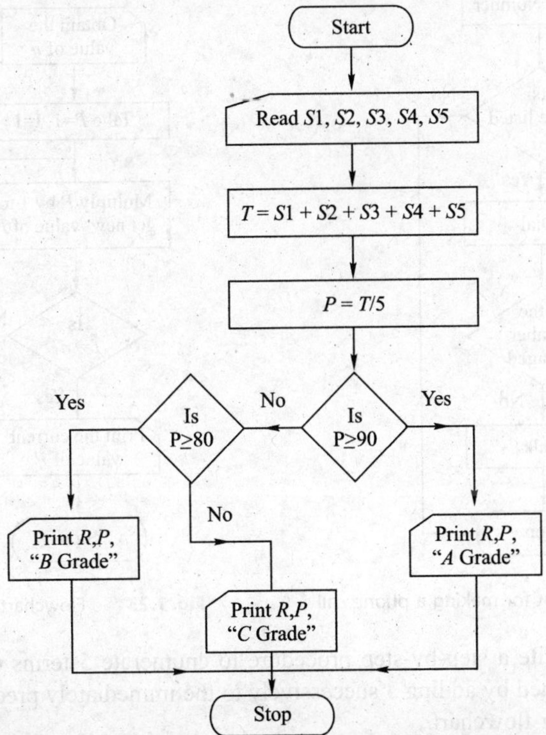

Fig. 7.21 Computing and printing grades obtained in an examination

Example 14 Write an algorithm and draw a simple flowchart for performing the task of making a phone call to a friend.

Solution Algorithm

Step 1: Write the name of the friend

Step 2: Find his phone number from the director or diary

Step 3: Has your friend a phone?

If no, then stop;

else, to Step 4

Step 4: Dial the number

Step 5: If the number is engaged, then go to step 4 (redial),

else, talk to your friend

Step 6: Stop (disconnect the phone)

Flow chart: The flowchart can be represented in Fig. 7.22.

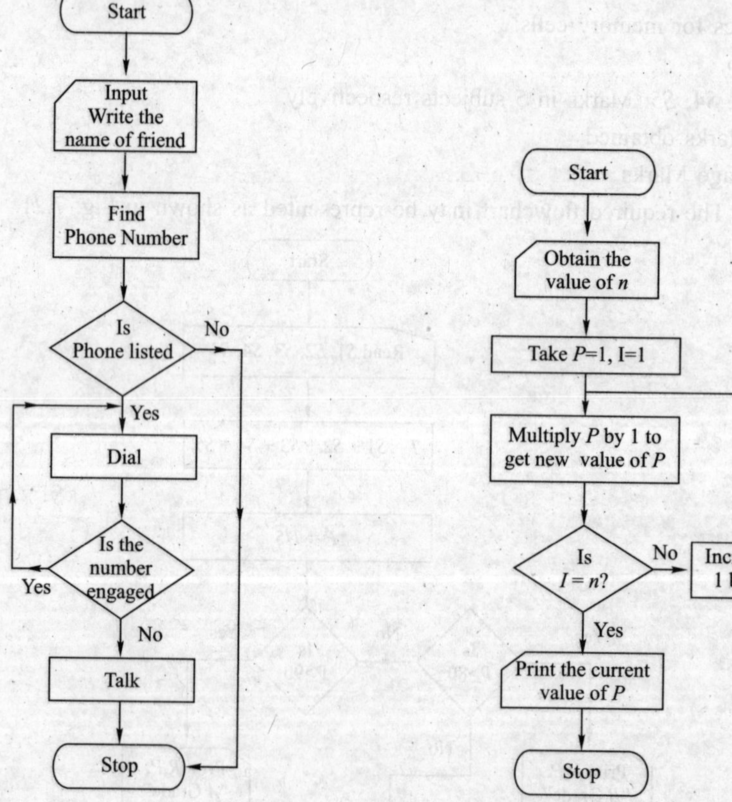

Fig. 7.22 Flowchart for making a phone call

Fig. 7.23 Flowchart for the Example 15

Example 15 Write a step-by-step procedure to enumerate 5 terms the first of which is 4 and the others are obtained by adding 3 successively to the immediately preceding terms obtained. Draw the corresponding flowchart.

Flow chart: The required flowchart is shown in Fig. 7.23.

Execution of Flowchart:

Number of box	*Result of Action Performed*
1.	Start
2.	First term = 4
3.	$n = 1$
5.	4 + 3 = 7
6.	7
7.	$n = 2$
5.	7 + 3 = 10
6.	10
7.	$n = 3$
5.	10 + 3 = 13
6.	13
7.	$n = 4$
5.	13 + 3 = 16
6.	16
7.	$n = 5$
8.	Execution completed

Example 16 Draw a flowchart to calculate the value of X^N, where X is integer and N has to be a +ve integer.

Solution The steps are as follows:

Step 1: Read the value of X and N

Step 2: A is equated to X

Step 3: A is equated to $A^* X$ ($A = A^* X$)

Step 4: Decreases N by 1 ($N = N - 1$) to calculate the value of K^N

Step 5: Compare N is equal to 1 or Not

Step 6: If N is equal to 1, then go to Step 8

Step 7: If N is not equal to 1, then go to Step 3

Step 8: Print the value of A

Flowchart: The required flowchart is shown in Fig. 7.24.

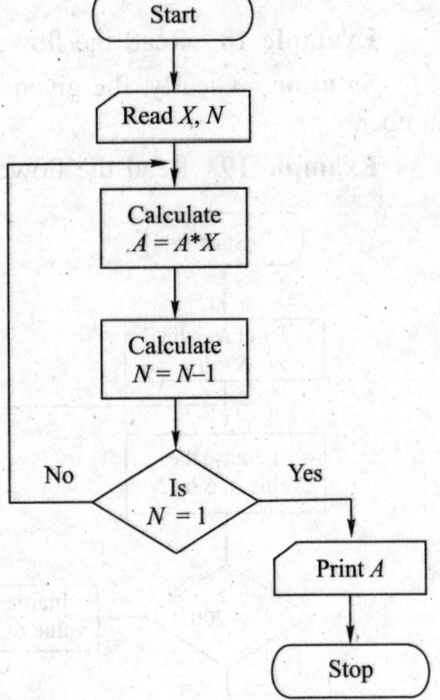

Fig. 7.24 Computing the value of X^N

Example 17 Write a step-by-step procedure to find out the sum of first 50 odd numbers. Draw the flowchart also.

Solution The steps are as follows:

Step 1: N is equated to 1 so that subsequently incrementing with 2 to get the required odd number. X is equated to zero to clear the previous program working location

Step 2: Compute $X = X + N$

Step 3: Compare $N = 99$, because we have to stop the process at the 50th terms which is equal to 99. If $N = 99$, then go to Step 5, else Step 4

Step 4: Increase the value of N by 2 *i.e.*, $N = N + 2$ to get the next odd number

Step 5: Print X

Flowchart: The required flowchart can be represents as shown in Fig. 7.25.

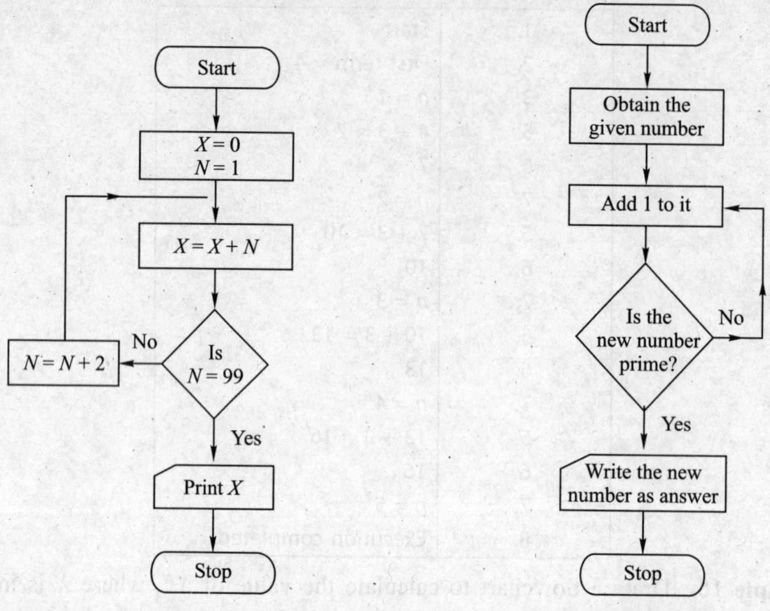

Fig. 7.25 Computing the sum of first 50 odd numbers

Fig. 7.26

Example 18 Read the flowchart (Fig. 7.26) and state what it does?

Solution Clearly, the given flowchart shows to find a prime number greater than a given number.

Example 19 Read the flowchart (Fig. 7.27) and state what it represents?

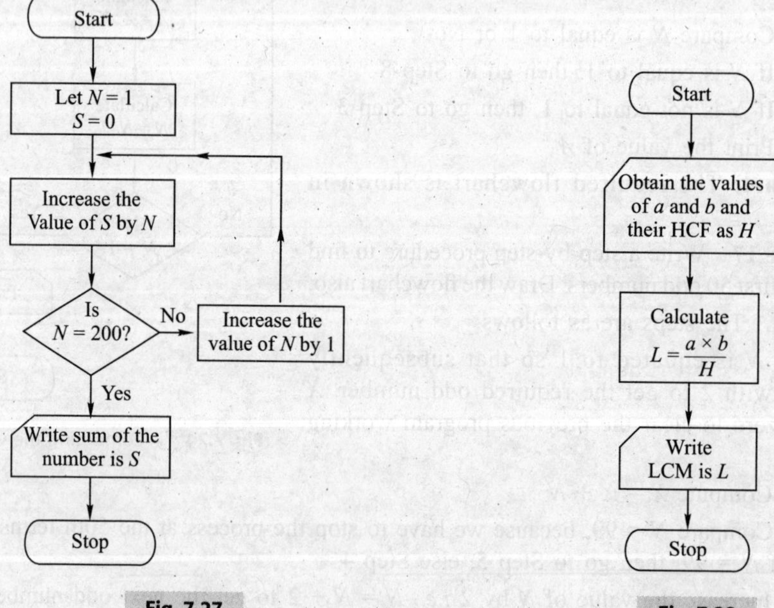

Fig. 7.27

Fig. 7.28

Solution Clearly, the flowchart (Fig. 7.27) shows the summation of all natural numbers upto 200.

Example 20 Study the flowchart (Fig. 7.28) and state what does it do?

Solution Clearly, the given flowchart (Fig. 7.28) shows how to find the L.C.M. of two given numbers a and b when their H.C.F. as H is also given.

REVIEW QUESTIONS

State Whether True or False

1. A flowchart is read sequentially from top to bottom.

2. If a programmer writes a flowchart before he/she writes a program, the program will run flawlessly.

3. There is no standard method for flowcharting.

4. A flowchart is a group of symbols connected by flowlines that depict the logic that will be used in a program.

5. Each decision symbol must be associated with a conditional branch connector.

6. A flowchart is a standard method of representing the flow of data.

7. Each operation denoted in a flowchart converts to a program step during program writing.

8. A flowchart indicates the steps involved in a problem, the sequence or order of these steps, and the number of input records.

Fill in the Blanks

1. A flowchart is a diagram that illustrates the .... of .... in a ....

2. A sequence of steps in a flowchart consists of .... connected by ....

3. The direction of flow in a flowchart is usually from .... to ....

4. A symbol represents ....

5. All symbols must be connected by ....; each symbol contains a .... inside it.

6. Arithmetic operations are coded in .... symbols.

7. Each symbol can generally be used to code a program ....

ANSWERS

True or False

1. T **2.** F **3.** F **4.** T **5.** T **6.** T **7.** T **8.** F

Fill in the Blanks

1. logic (order); functions; program **2.** symbols; flowlines **3.** top; bottom

4. a function **5.** flowlines; note **6.** processing **7.** instruction

QUESTIONS

1. Discuss the advantages and disadvantages of flowcharts.

2. Explain three types of logic used in flowchart.

3. How does the Transfer of Control Logic differ from the Straight Sequential Execution logic?

4. Name and describe the two basic variations of the looping (repetition) logic.

5. What is the function of flowchart?

6. What is Transfer of Control Logic?
7. In a flowchart, what does a cut rectangle represent?
8. In a flowchart, what does the rectangle represent?
9. What is important consideration about what one writes in a flowchart symbol?
10. Write a step-by-step procedure to find the lowest of two numbers. Draw the flowchart also.
11. Write a step-by-step procedure to find the largest of three numbers given to you and also draw the flowchart.
12. If there are three quantities: *X*, *Y*, and *Z*. Draw the flowchart to obtain the highest of these in location *H* and lowest of these in location *L*.
13. Draw a flowchart to compute and print the grades for an examination. Input is Roll. No. and Marks in six subjects out of 100. Grades are allocated on the following basis:

Percentage of Marks	*Grade*
75 and above	'A'
60 and less than 75	'B'
Less than 80	'C'

Short names for memory cells

*S*1, *S*2, *S*3, *S*4, *S*5, *S*6: Marks in 6 subjects respectively

T: Total marks obtained

P: Percentage Marks

14. Draw a flowchart to find the division and percentage of marks obtained by a student in five subjects are:

Hindi	60
English	50
Maths	60
Physics	45
Chemistry	58

Percentage obtained are allocated on the following basis:

Percentage of Marks	*Grade*
60 and above	First
50 and less than 60	Second
33 and less than 50	Third
Less than 33	Fail

15. Draw a flowchart to solve a quadratic equation given as:

$$Ax^2 + Bx + C = 0 \text{ where } A \neq 0.$$

16. Write an algorithm to find the H.C.F. of 18 and 24. Draw the corresponding flowchart.
17. Write an algorithm to obtain the H.C.F. of two given positive integers, their L.C.M. being given. Draw the corresponding flowchart.

    Execute the flowchart for the following data:

    L.C.M. of 24 and 36 is 72.
18. Draw a flowchart to find the marked price of an article which is sold with discount of 10% and still earns a profit of 5%, given the C.P. of that article.
19. Draw a flowchart to find the C.P. of an item, given its S.P. and percentage gain or loss incurred. Execute the flow chart with the following data:

    (*a*) Gain % = 25, S.P. = ₹ 1,000 (*b*) Loss % = 20, S.P. = ₹ 3,000

20. Draw a flowchart for finding the sum of first ten natural numbers.

21. Draw a flowchart for finding the H.C.F. of two given numbers, if their L.C.M. is given. Make provisions that it can be used for more than one pair of numbers, also.

22. Write an algorithm and draw a flowchart to find the first prime number after a given number.

23. Write a step-by-step procedure and draw a flowchart for finding the greatest number less than a given positive integer *n*.

24. Write a step-by-step procedure to find the sum of first 12 natural numbers. Draw the corresponding flowchart.

25. Write an algorithm to enumerate 15 terms, first of which is 10 and others are obtained by multiplying immediately preceding term obtained by 3 successively. Draw the corresponding flowchart also.

COMPUTER LANGUAGES

To some extent, we are all familiar with languages such as English, French, German, and Spanish. People use language to communicate with one another. Each language consists of sounds and symbols and contains grammatical rules that govern its use. Programming languages are similar. A **programming language** is a set of written symbols that instruct the computer hardware to perform specified tasks. Use of these symbols is governed by a set of rules called **syntax.**

Devising programs requires some language (programming language) which can be understood by man as well as machine. A programming language is a set of written symbols that instructs the computer hardware to perform specified tasks. Use of these symbols is governed by a set of rules called **syntax**. Any program regardless of the language in which its written consists of a sequence of instructions which are carried out in a certain order. Design and implementation of a program is characterized by the imposition of a sense of orderlines, a systematic way of doing things. This consists of a set of guidelines, rules, concepts and practices, which taken together are given the name structured programming. The basic purpose of structured programming is to simplify the programming process for production of an easy to formulate and develop program.

There are at least several hundred and possibly several thousand different programming languages. Although each one of them has its own specifications, certain basic instructions are performed by all languages:

- Input/output instructions—transfer instructions and data between the central processing unit and input and output devices
- Arithmetic instructions—perform mathematical operations such as addition, subtraction, multiplication, and division
- Logic instructions—perform comparisons such as equal to, not equal to, less than, greater than, greater than or equal to, and less than or equal to, and test certain conditions. Testing a condition involves evaluating the values or logical relationships of one or more data items.
- Control instructions—alter the order in which the program instructions are to be executed
- Data movement instructions—copy and move data within primary storage
- Specification instructions—specify various parameters such as constants, what portions of memory will be used, file access method, and so on

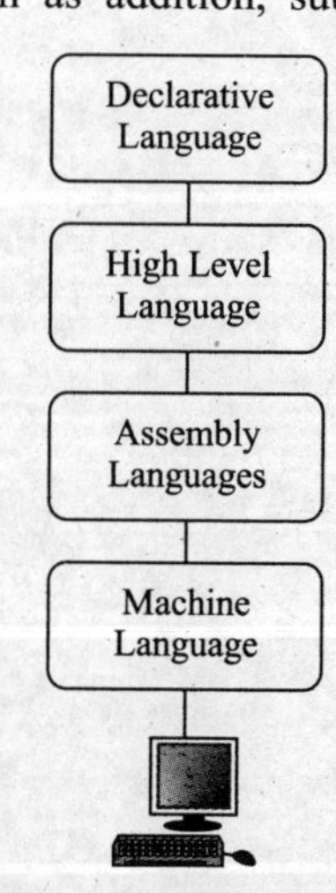

Fig. 8.1 Levels of Programming Languages

8.1 HIERARCHY OF PROGRAMMING LANGUAGES

There are two ways by which programming languages can be viewed, or classified by their level (Fig. 8.1) and by their principal application (Fig. 8.2). Moreover, these views are tempered by historical evolution through which languages drift. There are four distinct levels of programming languages, as shown in Fig. 8.1.

Figure 8.2 shows the hierarchy of programming languages. As you progress from one generation of programming languages to the next, fewer instructions are required to perform a particular programming.

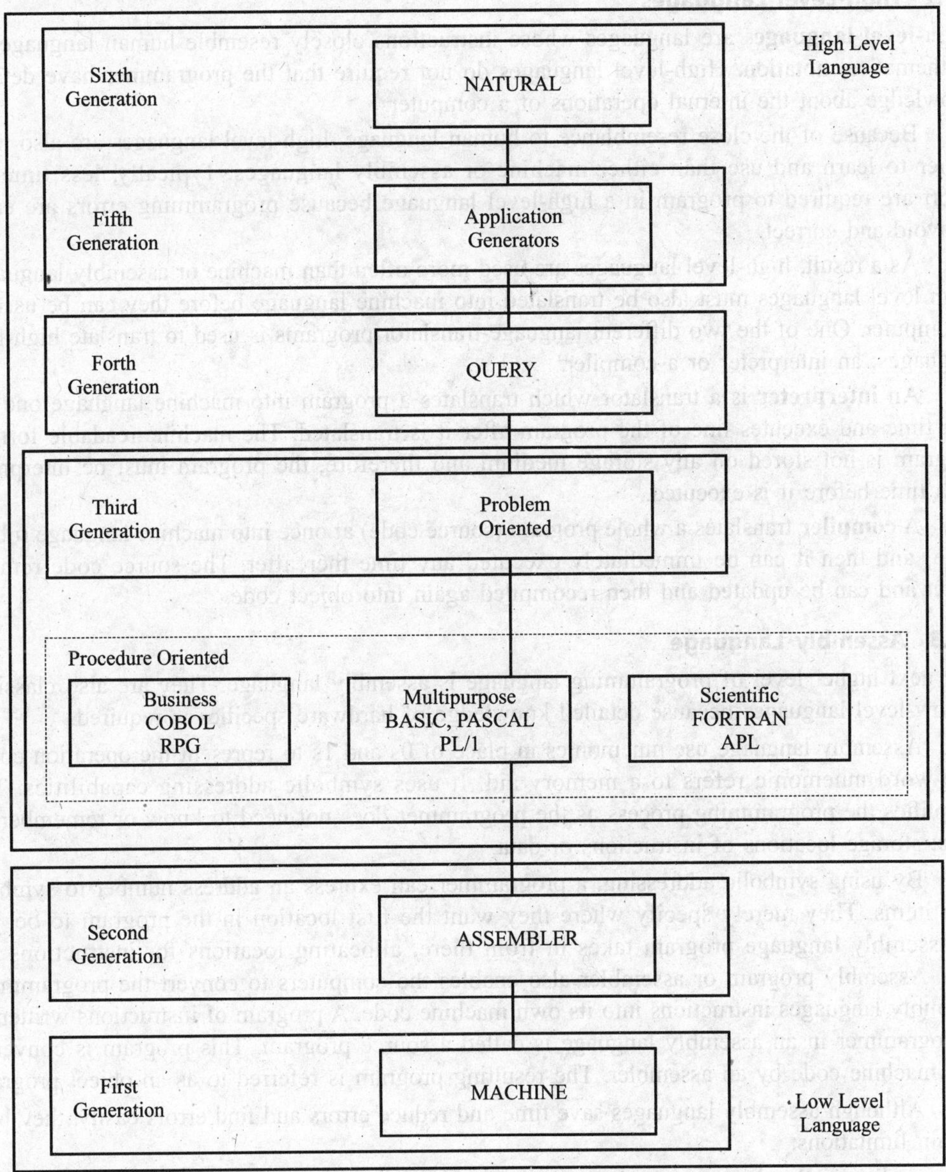

Fig. 8.2 Hierarchy of Programming Languages

8.1.1 Declarative Languages

The **declarative languages** are the most like English in their expressive power and functionality, and, thus are the highest level in comparison with the others. They are fundamentally **command** languages, dominated by statements which express 'what to do' rather than 'how to do it'. Examples include statistical languages like SAS and SPSS and data base retrieval languages like NATURAL and IMS. These languages are developed with the idea that skilled professionals can more quickly assimilate such a language and use it in their work, without the need for programmers or programming skills.

8.1.2 High-Level Languages

High-level languages are languages whose instructions closely resemble human language and mathematical notation. High-level languages do not require that the programmer have detailed knowledge about the internal operations of a computer.

Because of the close resemblance to human language, high-level languages are also much easier to learn and use than either machine or assembly languages. Typically, less time and effort are required to program in a high-level language because programming errors are easier to avoid and correct.

As a result, high-level languages are used more often than machine or assembly languages. High level languages must also be translated into machine language before they can be used by a computer. One of the two different language-translator programs is used to translate high-level languages: an interpreter or a compiler.

An **interpreter** is a translator which translates a program into machine language one line at a time and executes line of the program after it is translated. The machine-readable form of program is not stored on any storage medium and therefore, the program must be interpreted each time before it is executed.

A **compiler** translates a whole program (source code) at once into machine language (object code) and then it can be immediately executed any time thereafter. The source code remains intact and can be updated and then recompiled again into object code.

8.1.3 Assembly Language

The next higher level of programming language is assembly language. They are also classified as low-level languages because detailed knowledge of hardware specifics is required.

Assembly language use mnemonics in place of 0s and 1s to represent the operation codes. The word mnemonic refers to a memory aid. It uses symbolic addressing capabilities. This simplifies the programming process as the programmer does not need to know or remember the exact storage locations of instructions or data.

By using symbolic addressing, a programmer can express an address number to symbolic data items. They merely specify where they want the first location in the program to be, and an assembly language program takes in from there, allocating locations for instructions and data. Assembly program or assembler also enables the computers to convert the programmer's assembly languages instructions into its own machine code. A program of instructions written by a programmer in an assembly language is called a source program. This program is converted into machine code by an assembler. The resulting program is referred to as an object program.

Although assembly languages save time and reduce errors and find errors easily, they have certain limitations:

1. Coding in this language is time-consuming
2. This language is machine-oriented, *i.e.*, they are designed for the specific make and model of processor being used

8.1.4 Machine Language

Machine language is the only programming language that the computer can understand. It is a language made up entirely of 1s and 0s. There is not, however, one universal machine language.

The arrangement of 1s and 0s to represent similar instructions, data, and memory locations differs among computers because of different hardware designs.

Machine language programs have an advantage of very fast execution speeds and efficient use of primary memory. Use of this language is very tedious, difficult and time consuming method of programming. This language is said to be a low-level language. Every detail of an operation to be performed in this language must be specified by the programmer. Thus, a programmer (one who devises programs) should have detailed knowledge of how the machine works. It is easy to make an error and very difficult to debug the machine language program.

To make programming easier and simpler, other easier-to-use programming languages have been developed. These languages must ultimately be translated into machine language before the computer can understand and use them.

8.1.5 Summary of Characteristics of Languages

Language	*Characteristics*
1. Machine Language	1. Machine dependent 2. Uses special codes and the assignment of storage address
2. Assembly Language	1. Machine dependent 2. Uses mnemonics (symbolic operation codes) and operands (symbolic storage addresses) 3. 1-to-1 language, *i.e.*, for one assembly language instruction, one machine language instruction is generated.
3. High-Level Language	1. Machine independent 2. Uses instructions which seem English-like. 3. 1-to-many language, *i.e.*, for one high level instruction, many machine language statements may be generated

8.1.6 Fourth Generation Languages (4GL)

The different categories of languages are sometimes labeled by generations—from lowest to highest. Machine languages are considered first generation; assembly languages are second generation, and high level languages are third generation. Fourth-generation is a term that describes a variety of programming languages that allows users to create programs with much less effort than is required by high level languages.

A high-level language is a procedural language—one which requires the programmers to spell out the steps in the processing procedures needed to achieve the desired result. But a 4GL is a non-procedural language which allows the users to simply specify what the output should be without describing all the details of how the data should be manipulated to produce that result. The **Objectives of 4GL** include;

- Increases the speed of developing programs
- Minimize users efforts to obtain information from computer
- Decrease skill level required of users
- Reduce errors or make programs that are easy to change

Depending on the language, the sophistication of fourth-generation languages varies widely. These languages are usually used in conjuction with a data base and its data dictionary and are often found as part of a MIS or DSS. Fourth-generation languages include: data-base query languages; report generators; and application generators.

A Database Query Language permits formulation of queries that may relate to several records from one or more files. The appropriate records can then be printed or displayed in a suitable format. Example: IBM's SQL.

A Report Generator allows data from a database to be extracted and formatted into reports. It also allows substantial arithmetic and logic operations to be performed on the data before they are displayed or printed.

An Application Generator allows data entry and permits the use to specify how the database will be updated, what calculations will be performed and what output will be created.

8.2 CLASSIFICATIONS OF PROGRAMMING LANGUAGES

There are many terms used to describe an existing or a proposed language, and these classifications are overlapping and many times blurred.

8.2.1 Procedure Oriented Language Vs. Non-Procedure Oriented Language

Programming languages are classified into two different types:

Procedural language and non-procedural languages: A non-procedure oriented language purely describes the task without actually prescribing a set of executable operation to be performed in sequence, to achieve the task, as in the case of procedure oriented languages, *e.g.*, 'Calculate the sum of the first 100 prime numbers' is an example of non-procedure oriented language. However, because of the changing meaning of the term, no language today can be described as purely non-procedural, though levels of non-proceduralness can be raised in some languages. FORTRAN, COBOL, PL/I, Pascal, BASIC are all examples of procedure oriented languages. Another example of non-procedural language sometimes also called problem describing language will be 'Calculate Payroll'. Such languages do not exist at present.

8.2.2 Problem Oriented Language, Problem Defining Language, Problem Solving Language

Any language which is easier for writing a solution to a particular problem than assembly language is called problem oriented language. Thus, any current programming language is problem oriented. A problem defining language defines desired input and output and defines the problem but does not define the execution steps, which are hidden. Therefore, these are not languages in our sense because of their fixed rigid format. Some examples are short and report generators. A problem solving language is one which can be used to specify a complete solution to a problem and thus, all procedure oriented languages are problem solving.

8.2.3 Application Oriented Language

These languages are useful primarily for single application area, *e.g.*, LOGO for civil engineering applications, APT for machine tool control. FORTRAN and COBOL, though widely applicable in numerical, scientific and business calculations, respectively, are far more problem oriented because of their much wider application area.

8.2.4 Reference Language, Publication Language, Hardware Language

A reference language has a unique character for each concept or character in the language; and consists of a fixed set of symbols, while publication language is a well defined variation reference language for printing with reasonable rules to handle subscripts, exponents, spaces and Greek letters. A hardware language is a direct mapping of a reference language into a form which is suitable for direct input of a computer. ALGOL, for example,has all these three forms. A is used in reference language while A is used in publication language, while A**2 is used in hardware language.

8.3 POPULAR PROGRAMMING LANGUAGES

Programming languages are divided into two major categories, low-level and high-level. Low-level languages comprise machine languages and assembly level languages. High-level languages are divided into four classes; scientific, business, specialized and interactive languages. However, there are many hundreds of programming languages and it would be impractical to go into all of them in any detail. Table 8.1 attempts to summarize some of the more common (popular) languages and shows where they are used. Some of the more universal high-level languages from each of the scientific, business, specialized and interactive groups are briefly discussed here. They are called 'universal' simply because most computer manufacturers have taken the precaution to supply the necessary language translators which convert these popular languages into the machine code of their own computers.

Table 8.1 High-Level Programming Languages

Name	*Meaning*	*Main Uses*	*Features*
FORTRAN	Formula Translator	1. Used on small-medium, and large-scale systems	1. Ideal for scientific applications 2. Uses mathematical notation
Pascal	Named after the mathematician Blaise Pascal	1. Used on all types of computers	1. Scientifically oriented 2. Focuses on structured programming techniques
BASIC	Beginner's All purpose Symbolic Instruction Code	1. Used on minis for production runs 2. Used on numerous systems for teaching purposes	1. Interactive 2. Easy to learn 3. Uses mathematical notation 4. Can be used for business and scientific problems
COBOL	Common Business Oriented Language	1. Used on small-medium, and large-scale systems 2. Not available yet for most minis or micros (compiler is too complex)	1. Ideal for business applications 2. Easily handles disk and tape features 3. English-like
APL	A Programming Language	1. Used on minis 2. Used with time-sharing facilities	1. Interactive 2. Requires special graphics keyboard 3. Relatively complex 4 Scientifically oriented
RPG	Report Program Generator	1. Used primarily on minicomputers but can be used on larger systems as well	1. Very simple language 2. Ideally suited for printing reports
PL/1	Programming Language One	1. Used on medium-and large-scale systems	1. Combines the features of COBOL and FORTRAN 2. Somewhat complex in code

8.3.1 FORTRAN (Formula Translator or Translation)

The first high-level language was FORTRAN, developed in 1956 by IBM Development Group for use on an IBM 704 computer. Its prime purpose was to solve mathematical and scientific problems which were allowed to be written in a simple English style with mathematical expressions stated naturally, *e.g.*, $X = Y + Z - W$. Basically it is a scientific language. During the middle 1960s, it became widely used on a number of machines resulting in a variety of 'dialects', the most important being IBM FORTRAN II and IBM FORTRAN IV. By 1962, the American Standards Institute (ASA) set up a working party to produce a specification for the language. Two versions were finally approved in March 1966, ASA FORTRAN (similar to IBM FORTRAN IV) and ASA basic FORTRAN (similar to IBM FORTRAN II). Their popularity grew to such an extent that most manufacturers had to ensure that their dialect of FORTRAN conformed to these standards.

In August, 1966, the ASA changed its name to the United States of American Standards Institute (USASI) and this was changed in October, 1969 to the American National Standards Institute (ANSI). A new 'standard' FORTRAN called **FORTRAN 77** came up in the year 1977. It contains several additional features which are not a part of FORTRAN IV, *e.g.*, character and file handling, constructs related to a more structural approach to programming.

8.3.2 Pascal

Pascal is not an acronym but named after the great French mathematician, Blaise Pascal. Pascal is one of those high-level languages which the enthusiast claims is a joy to use. It was originally designed by Nicklaus Wirth in 1968, belongs to the ALGOL stable and the first operational compiler became available in 1970. One of its more important features is to allow the programmer to structure data in his own way. Standard Pascal was originally developed and implemented on the CDC 6000 series but has been developed for use on other machines. It is well thought of as a programming language for teaching students and has become a highly popular language.

8.3.3 COBOL (Common Business Oriented Language)

The COBOL language is basically a data processing language which is more useful in business. An international business language was inspired by the US Department of Defense in order to handle its many day-to-day commercial problems. COBOL came out around 1958. It attempts to be a subset of English and is meant to be readable by non-programmers. Its data structures, therefore, were devised to facilitate everyday office file procedures. Unfortunately, COBOL has not lived up to the original expectations and cannot be fully understood by the uninitiated (office managers), and its propensity towards English has turned it into a verbose language (from the programmer's point of view), yet it remains the most widely used commercial language.

8.3.4 ALGOL (Algorithmic Language)

Like FORTRAN, the ALGOL language was intended for the solution of numeric and scientific problems, and it differs little in scope from FORTRAN. ALGOL was originally developed in 1958, resulting in ALGOL 58. It was revised in 1960 and the importance of this version (ALGOL 60) lies in the elegance of its structure, something which, historically, will remain long after its demise.

The revised ALGOL 60 report introduced into the computing milieu structural concepts, a precision of language definition, and a certain discipline of programming procedures. These features in FORTRAN had, in contrast, been basically simple. The most recent and more powerful version is ALGOL 68. ALGOL is more popular in Europe than in USA, where IBM, which is influential in the States, has favoured FORTRAN rather than ALGOL.

8.3.5 RPG (Report Program Generator)

RPG offers an example of a popular commercial language which is also a specialized language. Languages such as FORTRAN and COBOL are general purpose languages, *i.e.*, they are used by people who have many types of programs to write and who wish to use the same language for all their programs. RPG, on the other hand, can only be used for generating reports, but reports in a broad sense to include the preparation of invoices and cheque payments, as well as 'normal' reports. The language was developed by IBM as a result of their customer requests for an easy and economic mechanism for producing reports and was launched in 1961 for use on the IBM 1401 computer. Today, RPG is run on IBM 360/370 series and the System 3 as well as on several other makes such as the ICL 2903 and UNIVAC 9000 series. When System 3 was introduced by IBM, it was announced that it would use RPG II. This latter version retains all the features of RPG but contains some additional features such as the ability to work with arrays.

8.3.6 PL/1 (Programming Language 1)

A programmer had a choice of languages in the early 1960s. For numeric work there was FORTRAN or ALGOL; for systems programming some assembly language would be preferred; COBOL was used for commercial applications; there was LISP (List Processing) or SNOBOL. Some installations were beginning to find such a plethora somewhat difficult, not only from an educational aspect but also in the support and maintenance of such a large number of language translators. PL/1 was the intended panacea. PL/1 was developed in the middle 1960s in an attempt to combine the features of these earlier languages. The intention was to create a language which should be adequate for programming any kind of application. This resulted in the production of a language which is enormous by any standards and one that is not easy to learn in its totality. Furthermore, it was developed by IBM and its use is often limited to the equipment of this one manufacturer. Over the past two decades, it has not captured the attention originally anticipated. The current trend in language design is not towards the large language but towards smaller and more elegant ones, *e.g.*, APL. The few features which they possess can be combined by the programmer in such a way as to create, in effect, an individual language for each application.

8.3.7 BASIC (Beginners All-purpose Symbolic Instruction Code)

BASIC language is primarily designed for use on time-sharing computer systems. To understand an interactive programming language like BASIC, it is not necessary to learn complex programming techniques. It is, in fact, intended for those who have no experience with using computers or writing computer programs but still have to use them. It is also very easy to learn and very simple to write. This language can be regarded as a 'General' Higher Level Language which can cope with mathematical and scientific problems as well as commercial routines. BASIC has few grammatical rules and can be said to be the user rather than system-oriented. It resembles FORTRAN in many respects, making use of standard mathematical notation, but serves business applications equally well. It can be learnt in a few hours of concentrated study and, though simple, it is flexible and reasonably powerful. The language was developed by Professors John Kemeny and Thomas Kurtz in the mid-sixties at Dartmouth College in the United States for use on a time-sharing system. Because of its simplicity and bias towards the user, it is a language well suited for use in education, and has become extremely popular with microcomputer users.

8.3.8 APL (A Programming Language)

APL, designed for time-sharing, is derived from the formal mathematical notation invented in 1962 by Kenneth E. Iverson. The notation, developed by Iverson during graduate courses given at Harvard and later at the IBM Systems Research Institute in New York, is described in his book 'A Programming Language, K.E. Iverson; Wiley, 1962'. The APL system, known as APL/360, was developed by Iverson together with Adin D. Falkoff, Larry M. Breed and staff of the IBM/APL Scientific Centre, and released as an experimental time-sharing service for internal IBM use (at the IBM Watson Research Centre) in the autumn of 1966. It was not until 1968 that APL/360 was first released for public use.

Proponents of APL proclaim it as a consistent, concise and very powerful programming language. Much of its power is vested in the rich set of operators available, enabling easy manipulation of matrices and arrays of highest rank. APL programs are capable of handling text as well as numerics. It has been used in most fields of programming, but its less obvious uses include text editing, system simulation and teaching. The APL user utilizes the system from a terminal device in a *conversational* manner.

8.3.9 Autocoder

Once a popular language because of the large number of 1401 installations, this language is one of the more powerful assembly languages. The programming is not structured and being an assembly language, it is difficult to learn. Slowly Autocoder is being replaced by COBOL and other languages as 1401s are being phased out.

8.3.10 Snobol

It stands for String Oriented Symbolic Language. This language was designed by a group led by Griswold in the mid-1960s. It is intended to manipulate strings of characters and for applications in text processing. For example, if it is required to find the frequency of occurrence of certain words and pairs of words in a text, then the basic data to be processed is a text. Operations on strings of characters such as splitting a string, combining strings, matching strings, etc., are required. SNOBOL provides these facilities.

8.3.11 C

The historical development of C parallels that of Unix itself. In 1969, Bell Laboratories sought an alternative to the Multics operating system for the PDP-7 computer. An original version of the Unix operating system was, thus, written in assembly language. During the same period, an experimental language was being developed by Kenneth Thompson. This language was named B. In 1972, the language C was designed as an extension of B; the primary difference was that C had an extensive collection of standard types, while B was essentially a typeless language. In 1973, Unix itself was substantially extended and over 90 per cent of this new version was rewritten in C. Because of this liberation from assembly language, Unix and C became quite portable. In 1976-77, Unix was ported to the VAX system and a new version was independently developed at the University of California at Berkeley. C is primarily used as a systems programming language; however, the C operators, data types and function library are unusually rich and C is very portable, making its applications potentially widespread.

8.3.12 LISP

LISP (List Processing) language was designed by McCarthy in early 1960s. It is used in applications such as game playing, theorem proving and similar non-numeric applications requiring logical rather than numerical operations. It is widely used by researchers working in the areas of pattern recognition and artificial intelligence.

8.3.13 Modula II

In 1977, a project to design an integrated hardware-software computer system began at the Institute for Informatik in Zurich, under the direction of Nicklaus Wirth. The computer system which evolved was called Lilith, and the programming language Modula was designed to support the systems programming requirements of Lilith's software development. The design of Modula was strongly influenced by Pascal. Moreover, Modula was influenced by the special needs of systems programming, especially the need for independent compilation of procedures and the need to control asynchronous processes. Modula II emerged in 1979 as a refinement of Modula. It is considered by many as an exemplary language for systems programming, efficient software development, and effective utilization of machine resources.

8.3.14 Ada

The US Department of Defence (DoD) identified a serious problem of rising software costs for 'embedded' computer systems in the early 1970s, that is, systems which are embedded in various military vehicles. A major cause of this problem was the absence of a single suitable programming language and programming environment for developing and maintaining this software. In 1975, the DoD formed a High Order Language Working Group, whose charge was to identify a complete set of requirements for DoD languages; evaluate the suitability of selected existing languages and make a recommendation that the DoD either adopt one or more existing languages or sponsor the design of a new one. The set of requirements evolved over 1975 to 1978 under the names Strawman, Woodenman, Tinman, Ironman and Steelman. During this time, extensive evaluation of 23 existing languages (including Algol, Pascal, FORTRAN, COBOL and PL/1, but surprisingly excluding C) was made. The final report concluded the need for yet another new language, developed from three 'base languages'—Pascal, Algol and PL/1. Designs for the new language were called for competitively, and finally the design by Honeywell-Bull was selected and named 'Ada', in recognition of Augusta Ada Byron, daughter of the poet Lord Byron. She is considered to be the world's 'first' programmer, working with Charles Babbage, the father of the modern computer.

It is a highly structured language and is now replacing programming work in COBOL and also available on UNIX based systems. Ada is intended for use as a systems programming language, particularly in areas where realtime control of asynchronous events is necessary. However, many feel that Ada is a truly general-purpose language, destined for far wider usage. It is, however, too early to predict the success of Ada, notwithstanding the enormous money that the DoD is committed to pour into it.

8.3.15 Prolog

Prolog was developed in the early 1970s by Philippe Roussel of the Artificial Intelligence Group at the University of Marseilles. Its first interpreter was implemented in 1972. Prolog represents a relatively new style of programming. Designed principally for AI applications, Prolog's style is based on the notion of defining objects and inferential relationships among classes of objects. It has strong theoretical foundations in the propositional calculus. Much recent attention has been paid to Prolog because of its prominent role in Japan's fifth generation computer project. Moreover, Prolog's design represents a dramatic departure from traditional ideas about program behaviour, which are all based on the architecture of the Von Neumann machine.

REVIEW QUESTIONS

Multiple Choice Questions

1. A computer program consists of:
(*a*) System flowchart (*b*) Program
(*c*) Algorithms written in computer's language (*d*) Discrete logical steps

2. The special purpose computer language for process control is:
(*a*) ADA (*b*) COBOL (*c*) BASIC (*d*) PASCAL

3. The transformation of a message into an encoded form is known as:
(*a*) Mnemonics (*b*) Encoding (*c*) Encryption (*d*) Decoding

4. Low level computer language uses:
(*a*) English words (*b*) Mnemonic codes
(*c*) Limited grammar (*d*) Mathematical symbols

5. Computer program writing:
(*a*) Requires high mathematical skills (*b*) Needs a science degree
(*c*) Requires engineering background (*d*) Is more than a science

6. A source program is written in which language?
(*a*) English (*b*) Symbolic (*c*) High-level (*d*) Machine

7. Instructions for execution by a computer are given in which language?
(*a*) Symbolic (*b*) BASIC (*c*) Machine (*d*) Compiler

8. A compiler means:
(*a*) A person who compiles source programs
(*b*) The same thing as a programmer
(*c*) Keypunch operator
(*d*) A program which translates source program into object program

9. An assembler is a:
(*a*) Program (*b*) Person who assembles the parts
(*c*) Symbol (*d*) Language

10. Which of the following languages is not well suited for business applications ?
(*a*) PL/I (*b*) Assembly (*c*) COBOL (*d*) APL

11. Which of the following language is often translated to pseudo code?
(*a*) Assembly (*b*) FORTRAN (*c*) PASCAL (*d*) BASIC

12. Which of the following languages is the most widely used?
(*a*) PL/1 (*b*) BASIC (*c*) FORTRAN (*d*) PASCAL

13. A language which is close to that used within the computer is:
(*a*) High-level language (*b*) Assembly language
(*c*) Low-level language (*d*) All of the above

14. Which language was created by Charles H. Moore at National Radio Astronomy Observatory?
(*a*) BASIC (*b*) FORTH (*c*) dBASE (*d*) COBOL

15. Which was the first available high-level language developed by IBM in 1957?
(*a*) PROLOG (*b*) LEO (*c*) PASCAL (*d*) FORTRAN

16. Which is the short name for Beginner's All-purpose Symbolic Instruction Code?
(*a*) PASCAL (*b*) BASIC (*c*) FORTH (*d*) PL/1

17. The most popular language for interactive use is:
(*a*) COBOL (*b*) PASCAL (*c*) BASIC (*d*) FORTRAN

18. The name of the language which consists of strings of 1s and 0s is called:
(*a*) Assembling language (*b*) High-level language (*c*) Machine language (*d*) 4GL

19. Compilers and interpreters are themselves:
(*a*) High-level language (*b*) Codes (*c*) Programs (*d*) Mnemonics

20. A software used to convert source program instructions to object instruction is known as:
(*a*) Compiler (*b*) Assembler
(*c*) Interpreter (*d*) Language processor

21. Each model of a computer has a unique:
(*a*) Assembly language (*b*) Machine language
(*c*) High level language (*d*) All of the above

ANSWERS

Multiple Choice Questions

1. (*c*) **2.** (*a*) **3.** (*b*) **4.** (*b*) **5.** (*d*) **6.** (*c*) **7.** (*c*) **8.** (*d*)
9. (*a*) **10.** (*b*) **11.** (*c*) **12.** (*c*) **13.** (*c*) **14.** (*b*) **15.** (*d*) **16.** (*b*)
17. (*c*) **18.** (*c*) **19.** (*c*) **20.** (*d*) **21.** (*b*)

QUESTIONS

1. Compare programming in machine, asssembly and in any high-level language.

2. What are the advantages and disadvantages of programming in machine language?

3. What is a compiler? How does it help the user?

4. What is an interpreter? Bring out the differences in a compilerand an interpreter.

5. What is the difference between problem oriented and procedure oriented languages?

6. Describe what is meant by a 4GL and its importance.

7. Write short notes on popular programming languages.

8. What do you understand by the terms: problem oriented language, problem defining language, and problem solving language?

9. Differentiate between Procedure Oriented Language and Non-procedure Oriented Language.

10. What is a declarative language?

11. Briefly describe the salient features of C, PASCAL, FORTRAN, COBOL, ADA, PL/1 and BASIC.

12. Write short notes on the following:

(*a*) SNOBOL (*b*) MODULA (*c*) ALGOL (*d*) RPG
(*e*) PROLOG

PROGRAM DEVELOPMENT PROCESS

Rapid technological advances in computer hardware have heightened the desire by businesses to purchase computers. Once a computer is purchased, a company must either develop or purchase the software to process the input data and produce the desired information.

A problem will never be presented to a computer if it is not realised that the problem is a candidate for a computer solution. In the beginning, therefore, there is an uneasy feeling that something needs attention. A manager may be concerned, for example, that sales are dropping or that the cost of maintaining an inventory of parts is rising. A natural tendency is to 'have a computer to solve the problem'. But what is the problem? Can a computer actually help solve it? Framing the exact problem for the computer to solve is an important step in presenting a job to the computer. It is a must to be aware of what the problem actually is.

Here we are concerned with the various stages of software development and the methods that can be applied at each stage, once there is an awareness of the problem. It is the approach to increasing programmer productivity and ensuring that the programmes are as correct as possible at the end of the program development cycle. The steps include problem definition, program design, coding, debugging, testing, documentation, maintenance, and redesign. In an aid to controlling projects and developing a history of the time necessary to develop a program, and for estimating future programming efforts, each step can be assigned an easily identifiable life.

9.1 CHARACTERISTICS OF A GOOD PROGRAM

Several important general considerations apply to virtually all programming languages. Adherence to the principles below will simplify the process of flowcharting and increase the value of resulting programs.

1. **Simplicity:** Program logic should be as simple and uncomplicated as possible. Avoid tricky, 'cute', or very intricate algorithms.
2. **Testability:** Plan the program for maximum testing case and debugging convenience. Place test points in the program. For example, print out the results of intermediate steps so that they can be checked.
3. **Efficiency** Design the program to use the least amount of primary storage and the fewest devices possible. Avoid reserving excessive storage for tables. Don't place within loops statements that need to be executed only once. Don't read an entire file of data into storage at one time if the data items will be processed singly.
4. **Modularity:** Build programs in blocks or modules. These blocks can be easily modified or expanded later. A library of revisable standardized blocks facilitates preparing other programs or expanding existing ones.

5. **Transferability:** Plan the program to be as machine independent as possible. Such programs are easier to test and debug and easier for others to follow and use as there will be more documentation and literature available for research and debugging. These programs require less conversion and rewriting efforts if they must be transferred to another system. In one system, special features of operating systems, computer hardware, and language extensions may be of great conveniences, while in others they may cause series of problems which are sometimes hard to detect.
6. **Generality:** Design the program to be generalized and flexible, if possible. A program that can process varying amounts of data, or different kinds of data, is more valuable than the one that accepts only a fixed number of items, design plots and sorts to handle a varying number of elements. Read titles and headings as variables instead of as literal text written into the program.
7. **Flexibility:** Account for all possible varieties of data input and processing conditions. Plan the program to handle unpredictable or incorrect data input, such as zero information, no data, values beyond the given range, alphabetic data in numeric fields, and compensating errors. Include provision for handling unexpected situations that arise during processing. Have the program print out error messages indicate the specific problem.

9.2 PROGRAM DEVELOPMENT PROCESS

Coding is mostly confused with software development. Coding is writing programs in a language that is comprehensible to a computer. In fact, coding is usually a small part of software development. Although, very little quantitative research has occurred, a few studies have shown that less than one-fifth of the programming time is spent in coding: the rest is spent in program designing, tests and other stages of software development. An often used rule is that a programmer working on a large software project, will write two to ten fully corrected lines of program per day. Since the writing of even ten lines hardly takes just a few minutes, coding is clearly not the most time-consuming stage of software development.

Software development can be divided into several stages:

1. Problem Definition
2. Program Design
3. Coding
4. Debugging
5. Testing
6. Documentation
7. Maintenance

9.2.1 Problem Definition

This stage is the formal definition of the task. It includes the specification of inputs and outputs processing requirements, system constraints (execution time, accuracy, response time), and error-handling methods.

This step is more critical for the completion of a satisfactory program than any of the following steps. It is impossible to solve a problem by using a computer, without a clear understanding and identification of the problem. Inadequate recognition of a problem is the key element responsible for poor performance of computers. This step is generally difficult, and the programmer should invest a significant portion of his time in problem identification. If he does not spend enough time at this stage, he may find that his well-written program fails to solve the real problem. Depending on the complexity of the problem, the result of a careful analysis may be simply a testing of the factors with which the program must deal, or it may be a formal written statement of the problem, supported by a description of all the considerations necessary to solve the problem.

This step is the process of becoming familiar with the problem that will be solved with a computer program. It starts when the programmer is assigned the task. This step includes the reviewing of the design document that was prepared for the program, as well as any system-wide information that would be helpful. The process ends when all the programmer's questions have been resolved and the requirements of the program are understood.

Problem definition may, thus, include many factors. Input/Output, time constraints, processing requirements, accuracy, memory limitations, error handling, and interfaces with other programs or tables must all be considered.

9.2.2 Program Design

Once the overall problem has been identified, the next stage of software development is program design. A computer is both fast and versatile, but it requires the meticulous specification of what actions it should take. For the user, there is seldom an opportunity to allow the computer to make an undirected decision. Therefore, the programmer must decide, prior to writing his program, exactly which steps the computer should take to solve an identified problem. This should be envisioned as a step-by-step procedure. Such a functional description of the task is either called an algorithm or results in a diagram called a flowchart. An algorithm is similar to a cook-book recipe but is more precisely defined. As the term implies, a flowchart is a chart which depicts the precise flow of computer actions. The flowchart depicts the logic involved in the problem solution and therefore, is a step-by-step sequence which the program will describe to the computer through the higher level language instructions.

Traditionally, program design has been linked with flowcharting. However, flowcharts are probably more useful in documentation than in design. Few programmers draw a detailed flowchart and then write a program from it. In general, programmers find that drawing a detailed flowchart from scratch is just as difficult as describing an initial working program and far less useful. Flowcharting techniques are helpful in describing program structure and in explaining programs. Other techniques, however, are more useful in actually designing programs. They include:

1. **Modular programming:** A method in which long programs are divided into smaller programs or modules that can be designed, coded and debugged separately with a minimum amount of interaction.
2. **Top-down design:** A method in which the overall task is first defined in terms of generalised sub-tasks that, in turn, are subsequently further defined. The process continues downward until the sub-tasks are defined in a form suitable for execution by the computer.

   The opposite method is the **bottom-up design** in which all the subtasks are first coded and then integrated into increasingly larger pieces of the overall design.

   The top-down approach towards program design starts with the specification of the function to be performed by a program and then breaks it down into progressively subsidiary functions. The division of the function progresses with increasing levels of details. Each function at each level is ultimately realised in the form of a module.

   In this approach, the calling module is always designed before the called module. At the time of designing a module, the broad functions to be performed by its immediate subordinate modules are assumed. The details of how a subordinate module can perform the specified functions are not considered until the subordinate module is taken up for design. Thus, the top-down approach represents a successive refinement of functions and this process of refinement is continued until the lowest modules can be designed without further analysis.

   The top-down structure can be viewed as a tree structure, a typical example of which is shown in Fig. 9.1. Each box in this figure is a module. The topmost module denoted by 1 represents the program which can be called the main-line module or main-control module.

In this case, the main-control module is divided into three subordinate modules denoted by 2, 3 and 4. The modules 2 and 4 require further divisions and in this process, the terminal modules are 5, 6, 7 and 8. The functions of these terminal modules are assumed to be simple enough to be easily programmed in the source language.

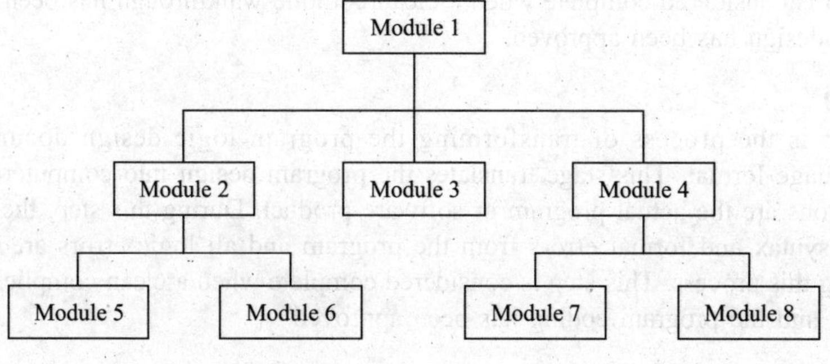

Fig. 9.1 A typical top-down structure

The bottom-up approach is the reverse of the top-down one. The process starts with identification of a set of modules which are either available or to be constructed. An attempt is made to combine the lower level modules to form modules of a high level. This process of combining modules is continued until the program is realized. The basic drawback of the bottom-up approach is the assumption that the lowest level modules can be completely specified beforehand, which in reality is seldom possible. Thus, in the bottom-up approach, quite often it is found that the final program obtained by combining the predetermined lowest level modules does not meet all the requirements of the desired program.

No attempt is made here to compare the advantages and disadvantages of the two approaches. However, program development through top-down approach is widely accepted to be better than the bottom-up approach. The top-down approach has the following advantages:

(*i*) It imitates the human tendency to solve a problem by outlining the broad concepts first and then subsequently going into the details.

(*ii*) The details of a module can be worked out with no (or minimum) change of the previously outlined concepts regarding its functions.

(*iii*) The programmer never loses sight of the assumptions made at the previous levels. The development of modules can take place in parallel.

These advantages suggest that if the top-down approach is taken for program design, the programs can be developed easily and quickly, committing a minimum of errors.

3. **Structured programming:** A method in which programs are written according to specifically defined forms; that is, only certain kinds of program logic are allowed, although the forms involved may be nested within one another to handle complex situations. Structured programming often refers to methods in which sections of a program always have a single entry and a single exit.

This step, thus, consists of preparing documents that will guide the actual coding of the program. Programmers can also prepare a structural chart that shows the hierarchical relationship between program modules. Pseudocode can be used to explain in more detail what each module does.

The software designer can, of course, use a combination of techniques. Flowcharting, top-down design, structured programming and modular programming are not mutually exclusive. The tools used in this step are unimportant. The designer should remember that the real task is to produce a working program, not to follow the tenets of any particular design method. The important aspect is to plan the flow of the program, with a tool that is less rigid than a program language. This allows changes to be made in a more time-efficient manner.

This step is considered complete when a clean compile walkthrough has been held and the program design has been approved.

9.2.3 Coding

The third step is the process of transforming the program logic design documents into a computer language format. This stage translates the program design into computer instructions. These instructions are the actual program or software product. During this step, the programmer eliminates all syntax and format errors from the program and all logic errors are detected and resolved during this process. This step is considered complete when a clean compile walkthrough has been held, and the program coding has been approved.

9.2.3.1 Stylistic Guidelines

This section presents stylistic guidelines on programming style that will be useful, regardless of the particular language or processor involved.

1. **Use meaningful names and labels:** Meaningful names and labels can be helpful in documentation and maintenance as well as in debugging and integrating programs. The names should be as simple and straightforward as possible-PRNTR for the system printer, TTY for a teletypewriter. MAX for the maximum value, START for the beginning of the program. The use of meaningful names will save the programmer endless time and confusion in the various stages of software development.
2. **Clarity and simplicity of expressions:** Expressions play a key role in the programming. It must be clearly understood by the programmers. As far as possible use the standard functions in expressions to improve the readability. There should not be any compromise with the clarity of expressions.
3. **Keep short modules:** Divide long modules into sections. Not only will a shorter module be easier to debug and correct, but it is also more likely to be useful in subsequent programs, since its function will be a small one and is more likely to recur. One or two pages of code (50 to 75 lines) is the maximum size for a module. Modules can be implemented as macros or simply copied into the program in order to avoid a massive number of calls and returns.
4. **Keep names and labels distinct** Distinctive names and labels reduce confusion. The use of numbers 0, 1 and 2, and letter O, I and Z should be kept to a minimum. Certainly the programmer should not, for example, use both MINI and MIN1 as identifiers; the chance for error is too great. Names that, for one reason or another, continually confuse the programmer should be changed; there are always enough errors in programs without inviting additional ones.
5. **Make modules fairly general:** Obviously a module that is too specific (for example, one which sorts precisely 30 elements or searches for the letter S) will find little repeated use. Greater generality can often be achieved with little or no extra code; a sort that will handle any number of elements will be no harder to write than one that handles a specific number. Generality that requires considerable extra code and ingenuity, such as writing a code conversion routine to handle both ASCII and EBCDIC characters, is not worthwhile. Simple ways to achieve generality have already been mentioned—the use of names instead of specific addresses or data, the collection of definitions at the start of the routine, and

the use of meaningful names that suggest the purposes or identities of items. All these techniques can produce a program that can be used frequently and easily modified.

6. **Emphasise simplicity and comprehensibility:** The first objective of programming is to write a program that works. Saving a few microseconds or a few memory locations is seldom important; the code can be optimised later.
7. **Avoid obscure constructions:** Examples include the use of offsets from the program counter in computers that have many multiple-word instructions, the use of complex expressions that depend on the order in which operations are performed or operators that are seldom used, and complex conditional assemblies. Even if the programmer knows the effects of an obscure construction at that moment, surely a few days' or a few months' time will return it to obscurity.
8. **Avoid jumps when possible:** Jumps make programs difficult to follow and debug. Repeating an instruction is often faster and clearer than jumping to a particular instruction. Programs with a series of jumps should be rewritten before the debugging stage.
9. **Place definitions in groups at the start of the program:** Definitions that are grouped at the start of the program can be easily located, checked and changed when necessary. Definitions that are scattered throughout the program can greatly hinder debugging and documentation.
10. **Use names instead of specific addresses or data:** The use of names instead of specific memory addresses, constants, masks, I/O device numbers, or numerical factrs, can not only suggest the actual purpose or meaning of the particular address or data but can also make the program easier to change.
11. **Use comments and indentation:** Comments provide the internal documentation of a program. It makes the program easy to understand. The comments should be included: at the beginning of the program which summarises the purpose of the program, at the beginning of the procedures and functions, and to clarify the global and local variables.

Indentation makes program more clear to understand. The statements should be indented in such a manner that nesting of groups of control statement can be matched (*i.e.*, if ... else). The braces pair {...} should be written in the same column to help in proper matching.

9.2.4 Debugging

This stage is the discovery and correction of programming errors. Few programs run correctly the first time, so debugging is an important and time-consuming stage of software development. Programming theorists often refer to program debugging and testing as verification and validation respectively. Verification ensures that the program does what the programmer intends to do. Validation ensures that the program produces the correct results for a set of test data. There is no clear demarcation line between these stages. The debugging of microprocessor programs is generally quite difficult because of the inability to observe register contents directly, the primitive debugging aids, the close interaction between hardware and software, the frequent dependence of programs on precise timing, and the difficulty of obtaining adequate data for real-time applications. The tools that can be used to debug programs with brief descriptions are given below:

1. **Simulators:** A simulator is a computer program that simulates the execution of programs on another computer.
2. **Logic analysers:** A logic analyser is a test instrument that is the digital bus-oriented version of the oscilloscope. It detects the states of digital signals during each clock cycle and stores them in the memory. It then displays the information on a CRT, much as an oscilloscope does.

3. **Breakpoints:** A breakpoint is a place in a program at which execution can be halted, in order to examine the current contents of registers, memory locations and I/O ports.
4. **Trace routines:** A trace is a program that prints information concerning the status of the processor at specified intervals. Most simulator programs and some microcomputer development systems have trace facilities.
5. **Memory dumps:** A memory dump is a listing of the current contents of a section of the memory. Most simulator programs, microcomputer development systems and monitors can produce memory dumps.
6. **Software interrupts:** The software interrupt or trap instruction is frequently used for debugging purposes. The instruction usually saves the current value of the program counter and then branches to a specified memory location. That memory location can be the starting point of a debugging program that lists or displays status information—breakpoints may be inserted with trap instructions.

Each program has its own unique errors. Nevertheless, some errors are sufficiently common to deserve mention. They include:

1. Failure to initialize variables, particularly counters and pointers. Registers, flags, and memory locations should not be assumed to contain zero at the start of the program.
2. Failure to handle trivial cases, such as an array or table with no elements or only one element.
3. Inverting conditions, such as jumping on zero instead of on not zero.
4. Reversing the order of operands, such as moving *X* to *Y* when *Y* to *X* was meant.
5. Jumping on conditions that have been changed, since they were set to the desired values.
6. Failure to handle fall-through conditions, such as an entry that is never found in a table or a condition that is never met. Such a failure can cause an endless loop.
7. Confusing addresses and values. Memory location 100 does not necessarily contain the number 100.
8. Confusing numbers and characters. ASCII zero or EBCDIC zero is not the same as number zero.
9. Ignoring the direction of noncumulative operations.
10. Ignoring overflow when doing signed arithmetic.

9.2.5 Testing

This stage is the validation of the program. Testing ensures that the program performs correctly the required tasks. Program testing and program debugging are closely related. Testing is essentially a later stage of debugging in which the program is validated by trying it on a suitable set of test cases. Some of the test cases will certainly be the ones used in debugging—the all-zeros case, the various special cases, and other obvious cases that must be checked.

Program testing is, however, more than a simple matter of exercising the program a few times. Exhaustive testing of all possible cases is the best alternative, but this process is usually impractical. Formal validation methods exist, but are only applicable to very simple programs. Thus, program testing requires a choice of test cases. The situation is further complicated by the fact that many microcomputer programs depend on realtime inputs that are difficult to control or simulate; the microprocessor must interact in a precise manner with a large and complex system. How can the necessary data be generated and presented to the microcomputer? Several tools are available to help with this task. Clearly, the debugging tools mentioned earlier will be useful.

Among the rules that can aid in program testing are the following:

1. **Make the test plan part of the program design:** Testing should be one of the factors in the problem definition, program design, and coding stages.
2. **Check all trivial and special cases:** Often the simplest can lead to the most annoying and mysterious errors.
3. **Select test data on a random basis:** Doing so will eliminate any inadvertent bias caused by the programmer selecting test data. Random number tables are widely available, and most computers have random number generators.
4. **Plan and document software testing just like hardware testing:** Obviously, testing can never prove that no errors exist; therefore, good software design, like good hardware design, is an essential part of the testing process.
5. **Use the maximum and minimum values of all variables as test data:** Extreme values are often the source of special errors.
6. **Use statistical methods in planning and evaluating complex tasks:** Methods are available for selecting data and evaluating the significance of results. Optimization of techniques may suggest good choices for system parameters and efficient sets of test data.

There are two goals in preparing a test plan. First, a properly detailed test plan demonstrates that the program specifications are understood completely. Second, the test plan is used during program testing to prove the correctness of the program. During this step, a general approach to the testing of the program is prepared and documented, indicating the number of tests needed and the purpose of each test. In addition, all input test data is defined in detail, and all expected results, including reporting, are determined and documented.

Program testing includes physically running the tests specified in the test plan as well as correcting errors found in the code during the testing. This step is complete when the test results have been reviewed and approved by the project leader.

To build a more consistent history of the time expended to complete each step, the life of the coding step can be defined. The time used in making coding changes needed to correct errors that were detected during the testing step is recorded as test time. This eliminates the question of where to record those hours and facilitates consistent recording of time throughout the programming staff. Similarly, it is not allowed to record time in any step that has been previously completed. However, if a flaw is detected, that forces redesign of all or part of a program, this time can be reported in the earlier phases.

In order to test a program properly, test plan development has to be undertaken at some point in the program development process. It has been experienced that performing this step before any logic is constructed ensures that a usable and exhaustive plan for proving the correctness of a program is available when the coding of the program has been completed. This will most likely provide a more sensible approach to testing all facets of a program with as few test runs as possible. If the development of a test plan is postponed until after the program is coded, it will tend to test only those parts of the program which the programmer has become most concerned with or interested in.

9.2.6 Documentation

This stage is the documentation of the program so that those who use and maintain it can understand it, so that the program can be extended to further applications. Documentation is a stage of software development that is often overlooked. Yet, proper documentation is not only useful in the debugging and testing stages, it is also essential in the maintenance and redesign stages. A properly documented program can easily be used again when needed; an undocumented program usually requires so much extra work that the programmer might as well start from scratch.

Among the techniques commonly found in documentation are flowcharts, comments, memory maps, parameter and definition lists, and program library forms.

Flowcharts are among the few visual aids available for program documentation. A general flowchart can serve as a quick pictorial description of a program. Such a flowchart is a useful part of documentation, although hardly complete in itself. A programmer's detailed flowchart can be invaluable to another programmer who must use or maintain the program. Usually the programmer draws this flowchart after completing the program.

Comments are a basic part of program documentation. They are, however, no substitute for a proper programming style. A program with a clear structure and properly chosen names can be partially self- documenting. Comments should explain the purpose of program instructions; they should not simply repeat the meaning of the instructions. Commenting is a tool that the programmer should learn to use properly. Programmers should ask themselves what explanation they would need to understand the program and should provide it in a reasonable form. Such comments provided in a systematic manner can be of help in all stages of software development.

Memory maps are lists of the memory assignments made in the program. Such maps prevent different routines from interfering with each other, simplifying the passing of parameters, and help in determining the amount of memory needed and finding the locations of subroutines, tables, and temporary storage.

Parameter and definition lists are part of the documentation of any computer program. Besides explaining the function of each parameter and the meaning of the various options, such lists also describe the definitions. The existence of these lists does not mean that parameters should not also be explained in the program.

Program library forms can describe subroutines for use in subsequent programs. Among the information that the programmer should provide is the purpose of the program, the form of input and output data, the requirements of the program, a description of the parameters, and a simple case showing how the program works.

Proper documentation combines all or most of the methods mentioned. Documentation is a time-consuming task that the programmer performs simultaneously with the design, coding, debugging and testing stages of software development. Good design and coding techniques make a program easier to document. Good documentation, in turn, simplifies maintenance and redesign and makes subsequent programming tasks much simpler.

9.2.7 Maintenance

This stage is the updating and correcting of the program to account for changing conditions or field experience. Proper testing and documentation should significantly reduce the frequency and extent of the required maintenance. Unlike student programs, which have a short life (usually one successful run), most large production programs are used for a long time; one to five years is not unusual and ten to fifteen years not unheard of. Events that cause changes to the original program include:

1. **Newly discovered bugs:** Errors that are not detected during the original testing phase may be discovered during the actual program operation.
2. **Specification changes:** The original problem changes because of new laws, user needs, or changing consumer demands. The program must be modified to reflect this change.
3. **Specification expansion:** The original program must be expanded to provide additional information that had not been anticipated.
4. **New equipment:** The program must be rewritten to take advantage of a new computer or compiler.

The costs involved in program maintenance are usually grossly underestimated by most programmers. It has been studied that in a typical programming environment, over 50 per cent of the time is dedicated to maintaining existing programs which means that less than 50 per cent of the time is devoted to designing and coding new programs. A more recent study states that: 'Most programmers with ten years experience have spent at least 60 per cent of their time in program maintenance.' Other statistics related to program development indicate that over the life of a large, complex program, maintenance costs exceed the original development and coding costs, sometimes by as much as five to one.

It is only recently that EDP managers have begun to appreciate the magnitude of maintenance costs. This has led to a demand for techniques that reduce maintenance costs, speed up changes, and minimize the risk of introducing errors. Most of the programming techniques, styles, methods and approaches briefed earlier have been designed for precisely that purpose. In reviewing these techniques, we can now appreciate why they are so critical.

1. **Clarity and Readability:** Program listing is the primary piece of technical documentation. The clarity of the listing significantly affects the time it takes to implement a program change.
2. **Portability and Generality:** Software tends to last longer than hardware. Therefore, a program written with portability in mind will create less havoc when the inevitable new computer arrives. Likewise, when the user needs change, the truly general program will require little or no programmer time to adapt to the new specifications.
3. **Structured Code:** The most common maintenance operation is tracking down bugs that went unnoticed during the testing phase. A program implemented as a series of single entry-single exit blocks will facilitate debugging.
4. **Modularity:** When a change can be localised to a single module, it makes maintenance much easier. We do not need to worry about the effects of that change 'rippling' throughout other modules in the system.
5. **Debugging and Testing:** A formalised debugging and testing scheme reduces the likelihood of undetected bugs in the finished program, thus, reducing the maintenance required on that program.
6. **Documentation:** The technical documentation of a program is necessary because many other programmers will be working with and maintaining that program over its life span.

9.3 ERRORS IN PROGRAMMING

Programming errors generally fall into three categories as follows:

1. **Syntax Errors:** They include mispelled keywords, missing comma, undefined label, etc. and they are detected by the compiler which normally print the error in code form in the output after listing the source program.
2. **Execution Error:** It includes the following type of errors:
   (*i*) division by zero.
   (*ii*) the number calculated exceeds the computer capacity
   (*iii*) loss of signified digits by using integer variables or real variables. Suitable error messages by printing asterisks are then printed by the computer in the output, in order to give the programmer an opportunity to check and realize the mistakes.
3. **Logical Errors:** The sequence of statements or the algorithm may not correctly express the problem and in consequence the results obtained are liable to be incorrect. The computer, however, is incapable or giving any indicating about this type of error.

REVIEW QUESTIONS

Multiple Choice Questions

1. Programming errors generally fall into which category(ies):
   (*a*) Syntax Errors (*b*) Execution Errors (*c*) Logical Errors (*d*) All of the above
2. Syntax errors occurs:
   (*a*) due to mistaken analysis of the problem (*b*) during the execution of a program
   (*c*) at the time of compilation (*d*) All of the above
3. Syntax errors include:
   (*a*) mispelled keywords (*b*) missing comma (*c*) undefined label (*d*) all of the above

ANSWERS

Multiple Choice Questions

1. (*d*) **2.** (*c*) **3.** (*d*)

QUESTIONS

1. Why are logical errors harder to detect?
2. What do you understand by execution errors?
3. What are the characteristics of a good programming?
4. Name the three categories of errors.
5. Write the various guidelines for a stylistic guidelines.
6. Explain the difference between testing and debugging.
7. Write short notes on documentation and program maintenance.
8. Differentiate between commenting and indenting.

OPERATING SYSTEMS

10.1 INTRODUCTION

Computer software, as we know, is basically the set of instructions grouped into programs that make the computer to function in the desired ways. It can be classified into two general categories.

1. Custom-made (specification) programs 2. Pre-written software packages

Figure 10.1, summarizes these categories alongwith their further subdivisions.

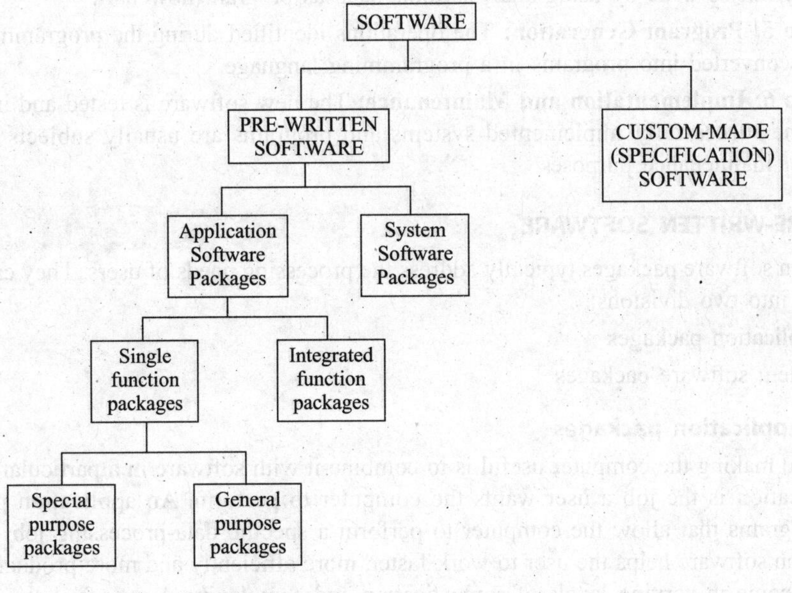

Fig. 10.1 Classifications of software

10.2 CUSTOM-MADE [SPECIFICATION] SOFTWARE

Custom-made programs are usually composed to meet the processing needs of a specific organization or an individual. The need for custom-made programs arises when the specific needs of users are not matched with the capabilities of any of the packages available in the market. The main advantage of such programs is that they can be tailored to the user's exact specifications.

Creation of specification software involves a series of steps to be taken in an ordered manner:

Step 1: Defining the problem: The problem or the need of a new software may result from a number of reasons, say, changing operating conditions. So, the problem should be defined and specific goals outlined.

Step 2: System Analysis: System analysis is the study of existing operations to learn what they accomplish, why they work as they do and what role they may have in future processing activities. A system is a group of parts which are integrated to achieve some objective.

After the need for specific changes is identified, the next step is to analyze data about current processing operations. It involves:

- Data collection
- System Flowchart preparation
- Analysis of findings

Step 3: System Design: It is the process of creating alternative solutions for satisfying the set goals, evaluating different choices available and then drawing up the specifications for the chosen alternative solution. Once the best alternative approach is decided, the new specifications which include the outputs desired, the inputs data needed and the processing procedures requires for converting input data into output results are prepared.

Step 4: Programming Analysis: It is the process in which the new specifications are broken down into four operations.

- Input/Output
- Calculation/text manipulation
- Logic/comparison
- Storage/retrieval operations

This can be done by using analysis tools such as program flowchart.

Step 5: Program Generation: The operations identified during the programming analysis stage are converted into programs in a programming language.

Step 6: Implementation and Maintenance: The new software is tested and implemented. Finally, the successfully implemented systems and programs are usually subjects to continual change for maintenance purposes.

10.3 PRE-WRITTEN SOFTWARE

Pre-written software packages typically address the processing needs of users. They can be further separated into two divisions:

1. Application packages
2. System software packages

10.3.1 Application packages

The key to making the computer useful is to combine it with software in a particular application. An application is the job a user wants the computer to perform. An application package is a set of programs that allow the computer to perform a specific data-processing job for the user. Application software helps the user to work faster, more efficiently and more productively. These packages come in varying levels of sophistication and complexity. A user-friendly package is a package which is 'easy to learn and use'.

Application packages may perform:

(*i*) Single functions (Single-function applications packages)

(*ii*) Integrated functions (Integrated-function applications packages)

10.3.1.1 Single-function Application Packages

These can be further divided into special-purpose packages and general-purpose packages.

Special-Purpose packages are packages designed for a specific class of users. For instance, medical diagnostic packages. A doctor can enter a patient's history and the results of his tests in the computer. A diagnostic package then responds with the most likely diagnosis and recommendations for treatment.

General-Purpose packages are packages that can be applied to a variety of tasks. For instance, Word Processing package, Data Manager, Electronic Spreadsheet Graphics and Electronic Communication.

10.3.1.2 Integrated-function Application Packages

These combine several of general-purpose functions in a single product. They include most of the following functions:

- ❒ processing words
- ❒ manipulating spreadsheet
- ❒ managing database or files
- ❒ preparing graphics

An integrated package makes it possible to use a common set of instructions to share data and move data among several applications. For instance, Word Processing program of an integrated package would allow a user to use the keyboard and display screen of a computer for creating and editing the text of, say, a report. The data organized in columns and rows can be manipulated and also analyzed by using the spreadsheet program of an integrated package. Its graphics program can be used to produce appropriate charts. Thus, it is a single all-in-one package. For example, Microsoft Works. In some integrated packages, overlaid windows are displayed so that the output of the most recent task is positioned on the top and the portions of other current windows are visible below.

These kind of packages are called **multi-function integrated packages**. However, there are other packages which manage to exchange data between the user's separate applications programs. Such packages, known as system integrator (Software Shell) packages, perform integrating functions between the computer's operating system and the user's applications programs. These packages don't have spreadsheet or graphics programs of their own as in the case of multi-function integrated package. Examples of these shell packages are—Windows from Microsoft Corporation and GEM from Digital Research.

10.3.2 System Software Packages

A system software package is a collection of programs designed to operate, control and extend processing capabilities of computers. Intricate system software is almost always supplied by the computer manufacturers and independent software suppliers like microsoft corporation.

There are two components of system software:

10.3.2.1 Operating System (OS)

It is an important system software package found in almost all computer installations. An operating system is a set of programs that controls and supervises a computer system's hardware and provides services to computer users. It permits the computer to supervise its own operations by automatically calling in the applications programs and managing the data needed to produce the output desired by users. It tends to isolate the hardware from the user.

An operating system helps people use computers in many ways. But the functions performed by an OS are generally transparent or invisible to the users.

The computer systems running under OS control range from small personal computers to mainframes and supercomputers For example: MS-DOS, an operating system is generally used for small personal computers. For big computer systems or multiuser systems, operating systems UNIX and XENIX are used.

Operating system programs are generally divided into two categories:

10.3.2.1.1 Control programs

Control programs manage the computer and resources. Major functions of control programs can be listed as:

- resource allocation-control programs allocate the use of computer resources, such as CPU time, input and output devices.
- job management-control programs schedule, control and monitor the programs submitted for execution.
- data management-control programs manage input and output data.

The main program in most operating systems, the supervisor program, is a control program which is also known as the monitor, executor, executive or kernel. It controls all the other operating system programs and application programs. It also controls the activities of all the hardware components of the computer system.

10.3.2.1.2 Service programs

Service programs provide a service to the users of computer system. Example—Language-translator programs and utility programs.

- **Language-translator** programs are programs for converting programs in other languages into machine-language instructions so that they can be executed by the computer. For instance, compilers and interpreters.
- Utility programs, on the other hand, perform routine functions like loading/saving a program and keeping track of the files stored on a disk.

Control and service programs alongwith other essential portions of the supervisor program get loaded into primary storage immediately after the computer is turned on. They reside there throughout the computer's operation. Other programs in the OS are stored in system resident device (hard disk, floppy diskette, or tape) and can be loaded and temporarily stored into the primary storage when they are needed.

10.3.2.2 Translating Programs

These programs transform programming language instructions into the machine-language codes understood by computers. Translating software is essentially invisible to the users who use pre-written applications programs. However, for custom-made software developers, the choice of programming languages and availability of efficient translating software are matters of great concern.

10.4 TYPES OF OPERATING SYSTEMS

There are several types of operating systems, including single-program operating systems, concurrent operating systems, time-sharing operating systems, multiprocessing operating systems, virtual-storage operating systems, real-time operating systems, and virtual-machine operating systems.

Single-program Operating System: A **single-program operating system** allows one program to execute at a time. The program must completely finish executing before the next can begin.

Concurrent Operating System: A **concurrent operating system** allows a single CPU to execute what appears to be more than one program at the same time when, in fact, only one program is being executed. The CPU switches its attention between programs as it receives requests for processing, executing statements from one program, and then from another. This processing happens so fast that it appears that the programs are being executed simultaneously.

Time-sharing Operating System: A **time-sharing operating system** allows multiple users to access a single computer system. The attention of the CPU is switched among users on a timed basis, which is controlled by the operating system. As long as the computer system does not have more users than the operating system can handle, it will appear as if each user has uninterrupted access to the CPU. If the number of users exceeds the operating system's capability, noticeable delays in processing will result.

Multiprocessing Operating System: A **multiprocessing operating system** allows the simultaneous execution of programs on a computer that has several CPUs. Many computer systems such as mainframes and supercomputers have more than one CPU.

Virtual-storage Operating System: A **virtual-storage operating system** allows the use of a secondary-storage device as an extension of primary storage. A problem experienced by some computer users is a lack of sufficient primary storage to meet processing needs. A virtual-storage operating system can resolve this problem. The storage device can be accessed rapidly, *e.g.*, using a hard-disk drive. Portions of a program are swapped between the secondary-storage device and primary storage as needed; this gives the illusion of having the maximum amount of primary storage in the CPU available to each user. With this type of operating system, the user need not worry about how much primary storage is available.

Real-time Operating System: A **real-time operating system** allows a computer to control or monitor tasks performed by other machines and people by responding to the input data in the required amount of time. For controlling processes, immediate response is usually necessary; for simply monitoring processors, periodic response is generally adequate.

Virtual-machine (VM) Operating System: A **virtual-machine (VM) operating system** is a very powerful program that can run several different operating systems at a time. It allows several users of a computer system to operate as if each had the only terminal attached to the computer. To users it appears as if each one were on a dedicated system and had sole use of the CPU and input output devices.

After the VM operating system is loaded, the user chooses the operating system that is compatible with the application he or she plans to run or is familiar with and wants to develop applications for. Other operating systems, such as the virtual-storage operating system, appear as just another application program to the VM operating system. The VM operating system gives users flexibility and allows them to choose an operating system that best suits the needs of a particular application.

10.5 COMPUTER PROCESSING TECHNIQUES

10.5.1 Batch Processing

Batch processing is a method in which data are gathered for a time and collected into a group (or batch) before they are entered into a computer system and processed periodically at specified time intervals (weekly, monthly etc.) without user intervention (Fig. 10.2).

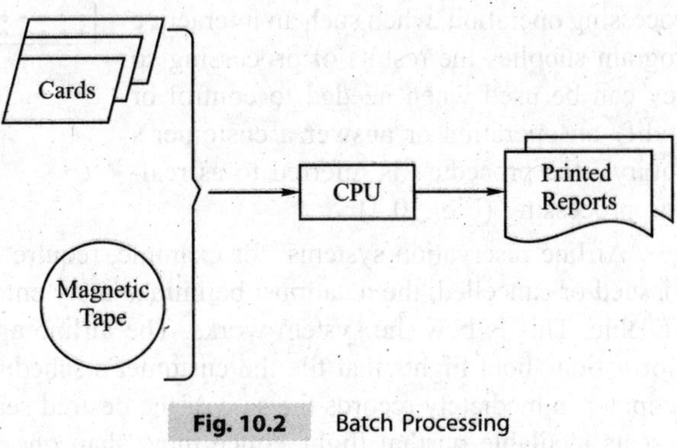

Fig. 10.2 Batch Processing

An example of batch processing is payroll preparation in a business. The number of hours an employee works is maintained throughout the pay period either on paper or punched cards through an off-line data gathering process or in separate employee computer files through an on-line data gathering process. At the end of the pay period, these data are input into the CPU and processed in order to determine the employee's pay amount.

There are several inherent disadvantages to batch processing:

(*i*) It involves accumulating data into batches which causes delay in jobs.

(*ii*) Since it takes a fixed time interval before current data is added, it is not timely. For this reason, a system that utilizes batch processing cannot effectively answer inquiries between processing intervals.

Still, batch processing remains an efficient approach to use in applications, such as processing payrolls, preparing bills etc. After all, we don't expect to get paid every hour, nor do we want to get an electricity bill every time we switch on a light. It makes sense to accumulate data such as hours worked, electricity consumed and then process all the data for a period at once.

10.5.2 On-Line Processing

Batch operations, as described above, frequently process data that has been gathered in batches on punched cards or magnetic tapes. This data is then transported to CPU for processing. This physical transportation of data poses risk of loss of data and is also time consuming.

In some instances, it is more efficient to use terminals at the points where the data are generated. These terminals are directly connected to the CPU. Once the transactions are made, the data are recorded using the terminal. These data are then directly transmitted to the CPU by telephone lines or by cables. This is an on-line operation (Fig. 10.3).

Therefore, an on-line operation is the one which uses devices directly connected to the CPU either for data entry or for inquiry purposes such as status of some record or file that is stored by the computer.

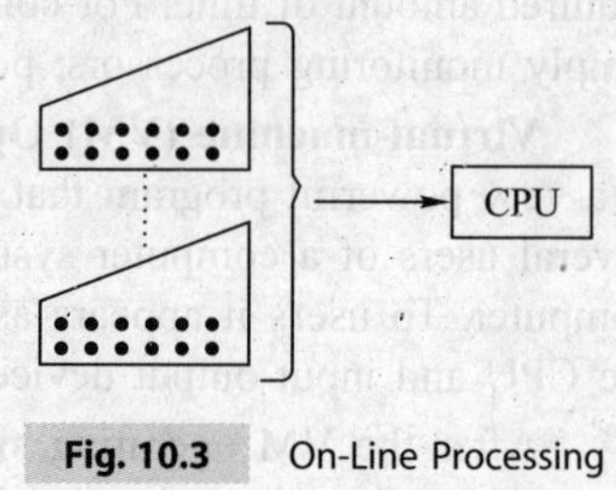

Fig. 10.3 On-Line Processing

10.5.3 Real-Time Processing (Transaction Processing)

Transaction processing is an on-line method in which data are processed immediately and files get updated as soon as a transaction takes place. On-line processing facilitates the use of interactive programs, by which users can communicate with the computer during processing operation, when such an interactive program supplies the results of processing so they can be used when needed to control or modify an operation or answer a customer's inquiry—the procedure is referred to as real-time processing (Fig. 10.4).

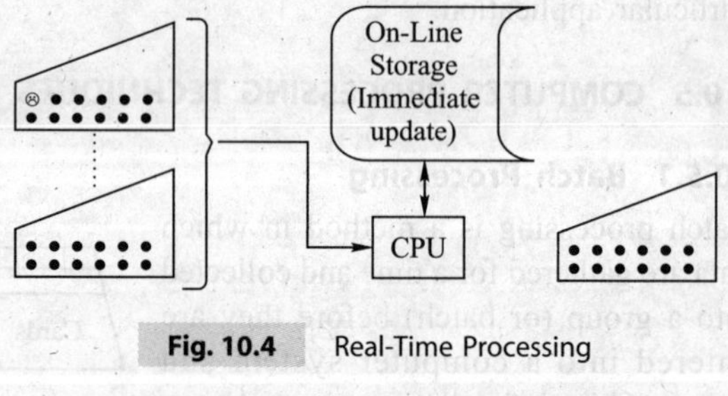

Fig. 10.4 Real-Time Processing

Airline reservation systems, for example, require immediate processing. Each time a ticket is issued or cancelled, the data must be immediately entered into a computer, processed and made available. This is how the system works. The airline agent interacts with the computer and gets information about flights that file the customer's schedule. When an available flight is found, the computer immediately records the sale of the desired seat. This automatically reduces the number of seats available on that flight. Since more than one terminal is used to make reservation for a flight, the ability to record a transaction immediately prevents duplication of a sale that has already been made.

Real-time processing usually uses terminals linked to a CPU via telecommunication lines. When a one-line computer system operates quickly enough to facilitate the decision making process in an organization, it is a real-time system.

10.5.4 Off-Line Processing

Off-line processing is the processing of data that is not directly under the control of the main CPU. A terminal may be used for keying in the data not directly into the CPU but onto a small cassette tape or magnetic disk. This data on tape or disk can later be entered, at high speeds and in batch mode, into the CPU. This key-to-tape or key-to-disk operation is known as an off-line process. This process is used for data entry and data is then batched for reading by the CPU at a future date.

Minicomputers are frequently used to facilitate an off-line procedure. Numerous terminal devices may be linked onto a minicomputer and the data can be keyed onto tape or disk. This validates the data to minimize errors, formats it so that it can be processed quickly. And then the tape or disk can be entered into the main computer system in a batch mode. The minicomputer, thus, controls an off-line procedure as depicted in the Fig. 10.5.

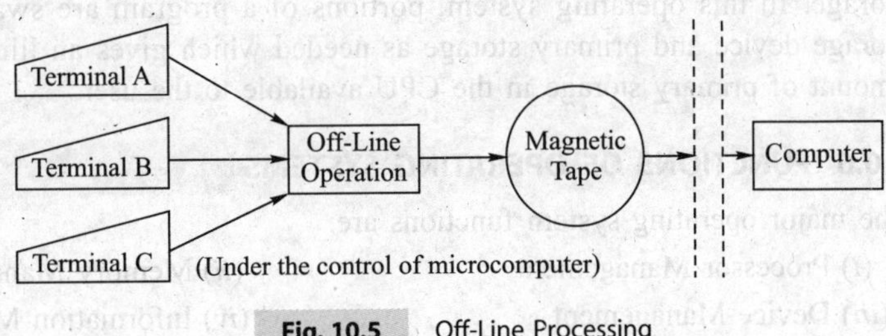

Fig. 10.5 Off-Line Processing

10.5.5 Multiprogramming

The ability of a computer to run more than one program concurrently is referred to as multiprogramming. Although several programs may reside in the memory at a given time, the CPU is capable of executing only one instruction at a time.

In distributed data processing networks with multiple processors, small computers such as minis are often dedicated to handle input/output operations from a variety of terminals. These minicomputers are often referred to as front-end processors. In this way, the mainframe CPU (host computer) needs to access only this minicomputer rather than each of the numerous terminals.

But the supervisor enables the CPU to execute one instruction from one program and then another instruction from a second program and so on. Thus, several programs can be run all concurrently.

Therefore, a program is not usually run continuously from beginning to end, when run in a multiprogramming environment. The net effect is to run numerous programs in far less time than it would take to run them consecutively, *i.e.*, one after another.

Most modern computer systems such as minicomputers usually use this operating system as it allows access of computer by several terminals simultaneously.

10.5.6 Multiprocessing

Multiprocessing is the use of two or more CPUs linked together to optimize data processing. In a multiprocessing environment, more than one instruction can be executed by the CPUs at the same time. In such a system, instructions from different and independent programs can be processed at the same instant of time by different processors, or the processors may simultaneously execute different instructions from the same program. Operating system schedules and balances the input, output and processing capabilities of these systems.

10.5.7 Time Sharing

Time sharing is the ability of a computer to be used by more than one user for more than one application at the same time. It allows multiple users to access a single computer system.This system controls the switching of attention of CPU among users on a time basis. If the number of users is within the number operating system can handle, each user has uninterrupted access to the CPU.

Time sharing operations typically involve the use of terminals. Each terminal provides direct access to the processor. Special programs are used for allowing the processor to switch from one terminal to another and to do a part of each job in an allocated 'time—slice' until the work is completed. This process is so fast that a user has the illusion that nobody else is using the computer.

10.5.8 Virtual Storage

Many computer users face the problem of insufficient memory to meet processing needs. A virtual storage system allows the use of a secondary storage device as an extension of primary storage. In this operating system, portions of a program are swapped between the secondary storage device and primary storage as needed which gives an illusion of having the maximum amount of primary storage in the CPU available to the user.

10.6 FUNCTIONS OF OPERATING SYSTEMS

The major operating system functions are:

(*i*) Processor Management (*ii*) Memory Management

(*iii*) Device Management (*iv*) Information Management

10.6.1 Processor Management

The **process** is basically a program in execution. In a simple case, a single process may be associated with a single user's job. A **processor** is a hardware device which is capable of executing a sequence of instructions. At various times, a process may be in the operating systems, user program, or shared program. Processor management is concerned with the management of physical processors (CPUs), *i.e.*, the allocation of processes (tasks or jobs) to a processor.

Multiprogramming is the interleaved execution of two or more processes by a processor. **Multiprocessing** is the simultaneous execution of two or more processes by a multiple processor computer system.

In the time sharing system, several user's program reside in the computer's memory. Each user is allocated only a fraction of CPU time for their program.

When a program is submitted to the CPU, it may be in one of the three states:

- ❐ Running
- ❐ Ready
- ❐ Blocked (Wait)

Running: A process is running when its instruction sequence is being executed by a processor.

Ready: A process is ready if all conditions are satisfied for the process to be in the running state and it is waiting for a processor.

Blocked: A process is blocked when it is waiting for an event to occur before continuing execution.

Generally, there are two types of programs: One which does a lot of computation but little I/O transactions, others which do a lot of I/O transactions but little computation. The first type of programs are known as compute-bound or CPU-bound programs and second type as I/O-bound programs. See Fig. 10.6.

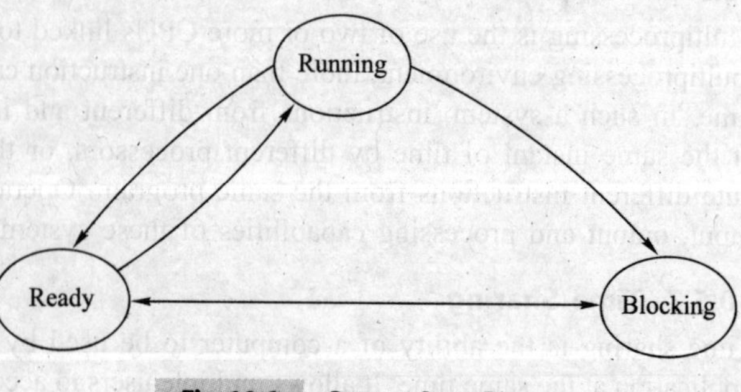

Fig. 10.6 Process State Diagram

For example, a program that computers square root of any number, or log value, is CPU-bound because it will spend considerable time in calculation and little time for writing a block of data on hard disk. In contrast, banking system, inventory system, railway reservation system etc. are I/O-bound programs because it will spend most of its time waiting for a request from the operator. Figure 10.7 shows the behaviour CPU-bound and I/O-bound program.

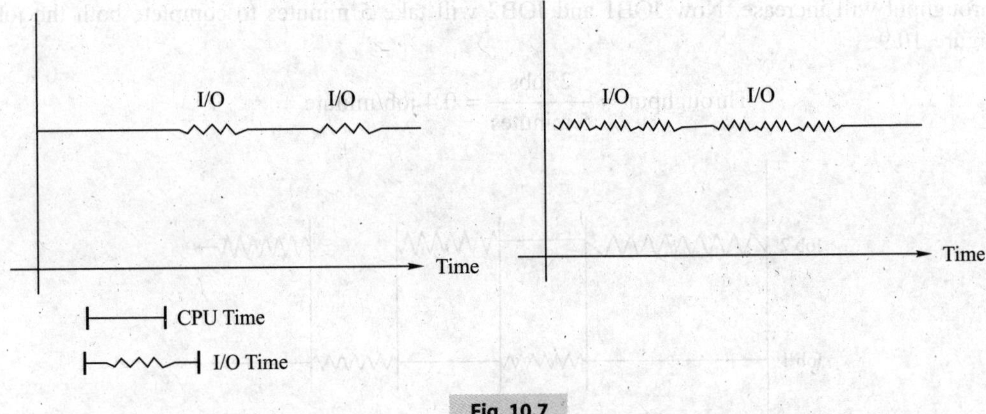

Fig. 10.7

For instance, suppose an I/O-bound program is executed by the CPU then the program will run for a short while and then pass into the wait state. There it will wait for I/O completion, and the CPU will remain idle. The remedy of this problem is multiprogramming. Multiprogramming improves the overall efficiency of the computer system by getting more work done in less time.

Throughput is an important measure of system performance in multiprogramming. It is formulated as:

$$\text{Throughput} = \frac{\text{The number of jobs completed}}{\text{The total time required to complete the jobs}}$$

For instance, JOB 1 and JOB 2 takes 5 minutes each to complete the job. If we execute one job at a time then total time spent in both jobs [*i.e.*, JOB1 and JOB 2 is (Fig. 10.8)]:

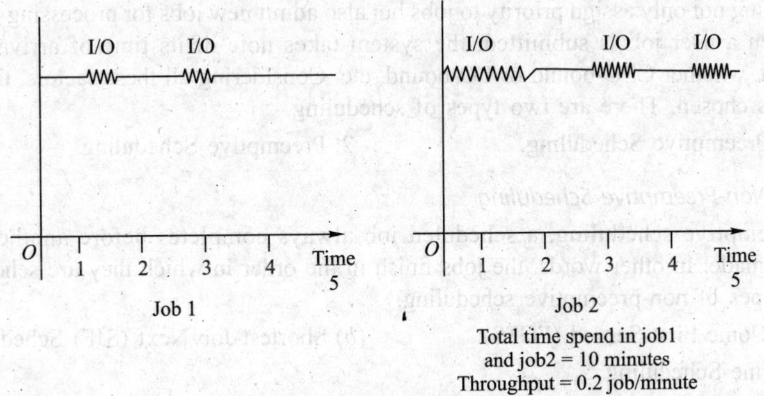

Fig. 10.8 JOB1 and JOB2 are executed independently (without multiprogramming)

$$\text{JOB1} + \text{JOB2} = 5 + 5 = 10 \text{ minutes}$$

$$\therefore \quad \text{Throughput} = \frac{2 \text{ jobs}}{10 \text{ minutes}} = 0.2 \text{ job/minute}$$

A practical strategy is to multiprogram jobs with opposite characteristics (*i.e.*, CPU-bound and I/O-bound) regarding their computational and I/O requirements. When the degree of multiprogramming is two, one job will be CPU-bound while the other one will be I/O-bound. Both jobs will make progress independent of each other, and throughput will be high.

For instance, if we multiprogram JOB1 and JOB2, CPU utilization will be increased as throughput will increase. Now JOB1 and JOB2 will take 5 minutes to complete both the jobs. Figure 10.9.

$$\therefore \quad \text{Throughput} = \frac{2 \text{ jobs}}{5 \text{ minutes}} = 0.4 \text{ job/minute}$$

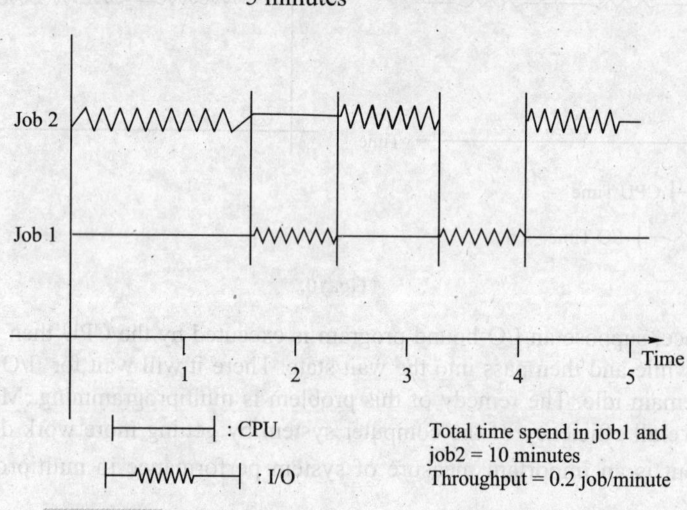

Fig. 10.9 JOB1 and JOB2 are executed with multiprogrammed

☞ When two heavily computational jobs are being multiprogrammed, the throughout would be low because of the idling of I/O channels.

10.6.1.1 *Job Scheduling*

Job scheduling not only assign priority to jobs but also admit new jobs for processing at appropriate times. When a user job is submitted, the system takes note of its time of arrival, processing requirement, whether CPU-bound or I/O-bound, etc. Considering all these factors, the scheduling technique is chosen. There are two types of scheduling.

1. Non-Preemptive Scheduling.
2. Preemptive Scheduling.

10.6.1.1.1 Non-Preemptive Scheduling

In non-preemptive scheduling, a scheduled job always completes before another scheduling decision is made. In other words, the jobs finish in the order in which they are scheduled. There are three types of non-preemptive scheduling.

(*a*) First-Come-First-Served (FCFS)
(*b*) Shortest-Job-Next (SJF) Scheduling
(*c*) Deadline Scheduling

***(a)* First-Come-First-Served (FCS) Scheduling:** The FCFS scheduling is one of the simplest scheduling in the order of their arrival. Its implementation is also straightforward which is maintained by FIFO (First-In-First-Out) queue. The queue

Queue of pending jobs
C *B* *A* → CPU → Job completed

Fig. 10.10 First-in-First-Out Scheduling

of pending jobs is maintained by the scheduler and processes the first one it finds in the queue (Fig. 10.10). **Batch processing** is an obvious example of FCFS scheduling in which all jobs in the batch are executed one by one. In this case, turn-around time (*i.e.*, job arrival time-job completion time) for the very first job in the batch is the best and for the very last job, it is worst.

For instance, consider the processes:

Process	Execution time
P1	22
P2	6

If order of the process is P1 ← P2 then the turn-around times are 22 and 28 (*i.e.*, 22 + 6) units of time respectively. Here P2 must wait for P1 to complete. Then there is an average of 25 [(22 + 28)/2] units of time. The corresponding waiting times are 0 and 22 units of time with the average of 11 time units. However, when the same processes arrive in P2 ← P1 order, the turn-around times are 6 and 28 units of time respectively giving an average of 17 [(6 + 28)/2] units of time and the average waiting time is 3 [(0 + 6)/2] time units. This is substantially reduced. Note that the waiting time could be reduced by putting shorter jobs first. This example shows how short jobs are delayed in the FCFS scheduling. However, the spread of turn-around times and the system throughput would not be affected. The shortest-Job-First scheduling technique solves this problem.

- ❒ A scheduling discipline is non-preemptive if once a process has been given the CPU, the CPU cannot be taken away from the process. A scheduling discipline is preemptive if the CPU can be taken away.
- ❒ In preemptive systems, jobs are made to wait by longer jobs, but the treatment of all processes is fairer.

***(b)* Shortest-Job-First (SJF) Scheduling:** In Shortest-Job-First (SJF) scheduling, a process or job is selected on the basis of its having shortest execution time. If two process have the same execution time, FCFS is used. For instance, consider the following set of process units of time:

Process	Execution Time
P1	4
P2	6
P3	3
P4	7
P5	2
P6	8

By using SJN, these processes would be scheduled in the order:

P5 ← P3 ← P1 ← P2 ← P4 ← P6

$$\therefore \text{ Waiting time (SJF)} = \frac{0+2+5+9+15+22}{6}$$

$$= \frac{53}{6} = 8.83 \text{ units of time}$$

By using FCFS, waiting time will be

$$\therefore \text{ Waiting time (FCFS)} = \frac{0+4+10+13+20+22}{6}$$

$$= \frac{69}{6} = 11.5 \text{ units of time}$$

Hence, waiting time is improved in the Shortest-Job-Next scheduling.

However, the spread of turn-around times and the system throughput remains same as in FCFS scheduling.

☞ It is difficult to implement in practice since the execution time required by a job may not always be known.

***(c)* Deadline Scheduling:** Deadline of a job is the time limit before that a job should be over. In dead-line scheduling, the job with the earliest deadline is selected for scheduling. The motivation of deadline scheduling is to eliminate or minimise the deadline overruns.

No deadline overrun occurs for a particular job if the execution time required by the job is less than or equal to job deadline.

10.6.1.1.2 Pre-emptive Scheduling

In pre-emptive scheduling, a scheduling decision can be made even while the job is executing, whereas in non-preemptive scheduling, a scheduling decision can be made only when some job finishes its execution. The preemptive scheduling may force a job in execution to release the processor so that execution of some other job can take place. There are two types of preemptive scheduling:

(*a*) Round-Robin Scheduling (*b*) Response Ratio Scheduling

***(a)* Round-Robin Scheduling:** This is one of the oldest, simplest and widely used algorithm. Round-Robin scheduling is aimed at giving all programs equal opportunity to make progress. This is implemented by ensuring that no program gets a second opportunity to execute unless all other programs have had at least one opportunity. Basically the CPU time is divided into time slices. Each process is allocated a small time-slice while it is running. No process can run for more than one time slice when there are others waiting in the ready queue. If a process needs more CPU time to complete after exhausting one time-slice, it goes to the end of ready queue to wait the next allocation.

For instance, consider the following set of process units of time:

Process	Execution Time
P1	16
P2	4
P3	8

If the time-slice is equal to 4 units of time, the P1 gets the first 4 units of time. Since P1 requires 12 (16–4) more units of time, it is preempted after the first time slice and the CPU is given to the next process *i.e.*, P2. Since P2 requires only 4 units of time (equal to time-slice, *i.e.*, 4 units of time), it terminates as time-slice expires. The CPU is given to the next process, *i.e.*, P3, which requires 4 (8–4) more units of time. The CPU is returned to P1 for an additional time-slice. The result of round-robin scheduling is:

$$P1 \leftarrow P2 \leftarrow P3 \leftarrow P1 \leftarrow P3 \leftarrow P1 \leftarrow P1$$

However, if it requires I/O operation before δ (duration of time-slice) elapses, it would have to release the processor and another process is scheduled to run. Actual progress made by each program depends upon its capacity to utilize the processor. It implies that the turn around time of a job not only depends on its processor time requirement but also depends on its nature (CPU-bound, I/O-bound). Therefore, a short job may not get better turn-around time than a long job. To overcome with this problem, **Least-Completed Next (LCN)** strategy was mooted. This strategy favours the job which has consumed the least processor time amongst all active jobs in the system. The nature of a job now does influence its turn-around times as drastically. So, another policy known as Shortest-Time-To-Go (STG) scheduling was implemented. In STG scheduling, a job would be scheduled when its remaining processing requirements are smaller than those of all other jobs in the system. This decision would be made at every scheduling moment. The cons of this policy is that it favours any jobs which is near to completion, irrespective of the processing time already consumed by it.

(*b*) Response Ratio Scheduling: The response ratio scheduling was mooted to overcome the drawbacks of LCN and STG scheduling. The response ratio scheduling can be formulated as:

$$\text{Response Ration} = \frac{\text{Elapsed time}}{\text{Execution time received}}$$

The job with the highest response ratio is scheduled for execution at any scheduling moment. Note that the response ratio is very high for a short job, so it is immediately scheduled for execution. A long job which has obtained few execution would continue to have lower response ratio than arriving short jobs, until its elapsed time reaches a large value. At this moment, it would have higher response ratio than other jobs, so it would be scheduled for execution. A longer job would achieve high enough response ratio after a longer wait in the system. Thus, the Highest Response Ratio Next (HRN) policy subsumes the desirable aspects of STG/SJN and LCN scheduling policies. The HRN can also be used for non-preemptive scheduling.

10.6.2 Memory Management

The memory management plays an important role in operating systems. The concepts of multiprogramming is introduced here to illustrate how many management facilitates processor coordination and increased throughput. Some of the important techniques are discussed as follows:

10.6.2.1 Single Contiguous Allocation

In single contiguous allocation, the operating system usually resides in either the upper or lower part of the core memory. A job is assigned all of core although it typically desires and uses only a small fraction. The job has complete control of the CPU until completion. This is wasteful, especially in a system where an operator performs such as loading a tape or card deck. Even in a system with I/O channels, the time in which the CPU remains idle while the I/O channel performs the input and output functions, is appreciable.

A single contiguous allocation technique is shown in Fig. 10.11.

The resources are not managed in an efficient manner in this type of system. There is not enough hardware flexibility to allow effective allocation of memory. This type of allocation is often used for small computing systems. Due to simplicity of the contiguous allocation system, some large computing systems have chosen it to reduce the complexity of programming.

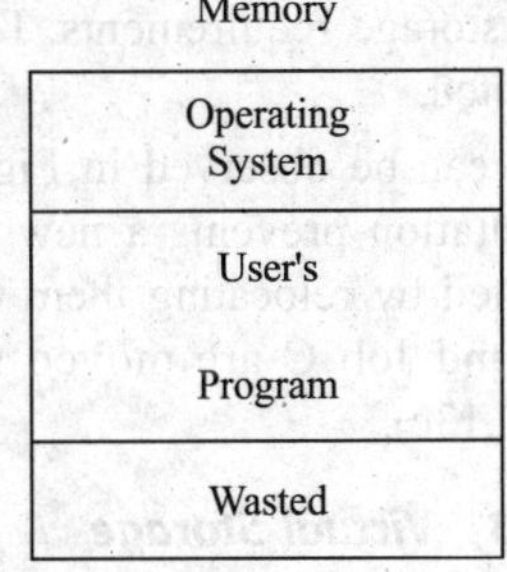

Fig. 10.11 Single Contiguous Allocation

10.6.2.2 Partitioned Allocation

The partitioned allocation technique was introduced to solve the problems of wasted time and wasted memory. This approach is based upon a partitioning of memory to accommodate more programs in the main memory. There are two ways to multiprogrammed storage management in contiguous storage allocation systems.

1. Fixed Size Partitioning Allocation
2. Variable Size Partitioning Allocation (Relocation Allocation)

10.6.2.2.1 Fixed Size Partitioning Allocation

In partitioning allocation, main memory is dividing into a number of partitions, whereas in fixed size partitioning allocation, partitions can be of equal size or different sizes. The number and sizes of partitions are fixed, thus also fixing the degree of multiprogramming. The operator can change the size and the number of partitions only when no programs are executing in the affected partitions. All job step programs of a job run in the same partition. Hence, a user has to be aware of partition sizes and sizes of his various job step programs while specifying the partition in which his program will run. Figure 10.12 show the equal and unequal fixed-size partitioning.

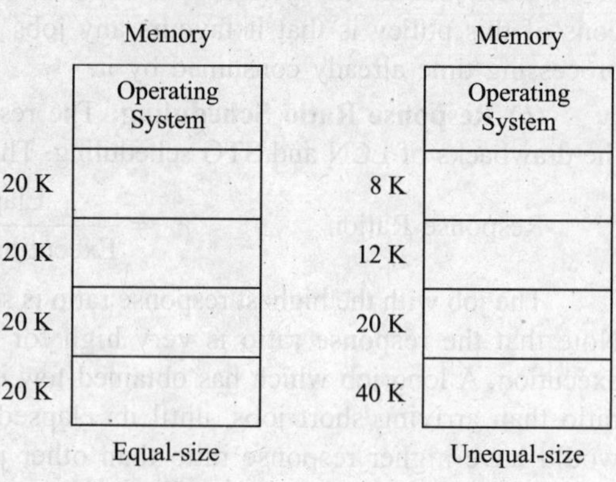

Fig. 10.12 Fixed Size Partitioning Allocation

Case 1: Equal Sized Partitions: In case of equal size partitions, if a program of size is 30 K then it cannot reside in the main memory and therefore, cannot be executed. Similarly, if a program size is 12 K then 8 KB of memory will be wasted.

Case 2: Unequal Sized Partitions: In case of unequal size partitions, for instance, if a program size is 10 KB, then it can be executed if any of the partition except 8 KB. If the 10 KB program is executed in 12 K, or 20 K, or 40 K, then 2 KB or 10 KB or 30 KB of memory will be wasted respectively. To overcome this problem, variable sized partitioning is introduced.

10.6.2.2.2 Variable Size Partitioning Allocation (Relocation Allocation)

In variable size partitioning allocation, a memory of exactly the same size is allocated when a program is brought into the memory.Thus, no wastage of memory. As jobs terminate, the system keeps track of the released storage. When a new job is to be initiated, it creates a partition to suit its storage requirements. Figure 10.13 shows that in due course of time memory becomes fragmented.

It can be observed in Fig. 10.13 that there are four jobs in memory (Fig. 10.13a), when fragmentation prevents a new job from being loaded. The job remain in the memory can be compacted by relocating them upward. Note when Job A and Job D are finished (Fig. 10.13b), Job B and Job C are moved so that Job E can be fitted into the contiguous area formed (Fig. 10.13c).

10.6.2.3 Virtual Storage

Virtual storage is primary storage that does not actually exist. It gives the programmer the illusion of a primary storage, that is, for all practical purposes, unlimited. The computer system itself maintains this illusion through a combination of hardware and software techniques.

Before a program can be executed, each of its instructions must be resident in the real primary storage, but not all instructions of a program have to be resident at the same time. Essentially, virtual storage involves storing in primary storage only those instructions of the program that are

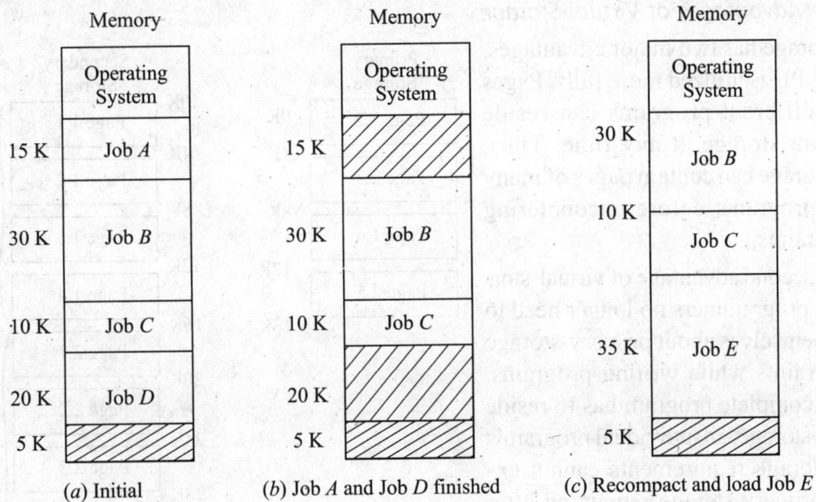

Fig. 10.13 Variable Sized Partitions (dynamically relocation)

currently executing, and storing the remainder on less expensive secondary storage, such as disks. Figure 10.14 illustrates virtual storage. (Virtual storage allows the computer to execute a program even though only a part of the program is in primary storage. The parts of a program are called pages, and they are swapped in and out of primary storage as they are needed for execution).

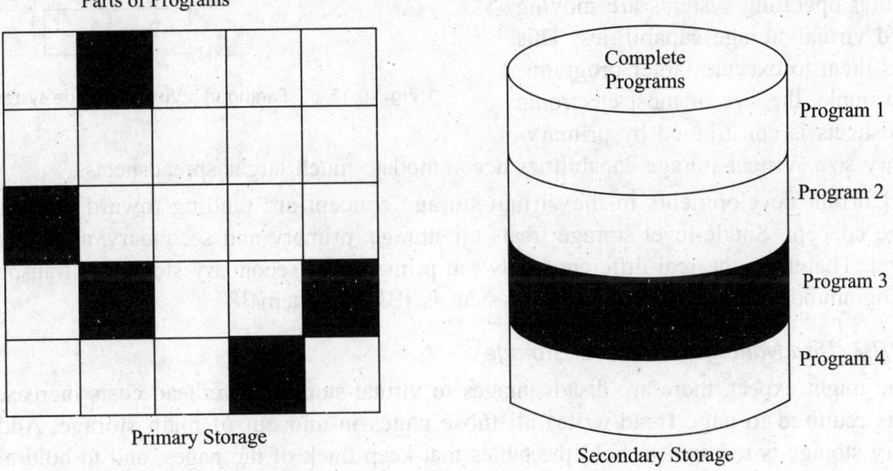

Fig. 10.14 Overview of Virtual Storage

A virtual storage system divides every program into pages, each of which has a size of, let us say, 4 KB. The operating system rolls pages of programs into primary memory as they are needed for execution. Under virtual storage, only the page of the program that is currently executing must be stored in primary storage. All other programs pages can be stored on a peripheral disk unit until each is required for execution. The operating system also maintains tables that tell the CPU where in primary storage each page of a program is located. Figure 10.15 illustrates paging. (Notice that to store all of the three illustrated programs would require 48 KB. However, because of the virtual-storage capability, the CPU can execute all three of these programs concurrently even though there is only 16 KB of primary storage available. For execution of a program to occur, only one page of the program must be in primary storage.

10.6.2.3.1 Advantages of Virtual-Storage

Virtual-storage has two major advantages. First, the CPU is utilized more fully. Pages of many different programs can reside in the main storage at any time. Thus, primary storage can contain pages of many different programs before encountering size constraints.

The second advantage of virtual-storage is that programmers no longer need to concern themselves about primary-storage size constraints while writing programs. When the complete program has to reside in primary storage, an individual program's primary-storage requirements cannot exceed the primary-storage remaining after the operating system's requirements have been met. This is the case with most PC operating systems. Under virtual-storage, there is no practical limit on a program's primary-storage requirements.

As mentioned before, personal computer operating systems are moving toward virtual-storage capabilities. This allows them to execute larger programs. For example, the size of most electronic spreadsheets is constrained by primary-memory size. Virtual-storage capabilities accommodate much larger spreadsheets.

Primary Storage	Address
Page 3.2	0K–4K
Page 2.3	4K–8K
Page 1.4	8K–12K
Page 2.5	12K–16K

Address	Secondary Storage	Program
0K–4K	Page 1.1	Program 1
4K–8K	Page 1.2	Program 1
8K–12K	Page 1.3	Program 1
12K–16K	Page 1.4	Program 1
16K–20K	Page 2.1	Program 2
20K–24K	Page 2.2	Program 2
24K–28K	Page 2.3	Program 2
28K–32K	Page 2.4	Program 2
32K–36K	Page 2.5	Program 2
36K–40K	Page 3.1	Program 3
40K–44K	Page 3.2	Program 3
44K–48K	Page 3.3	Program 3

Fig. 10.15 Paging in a Virtual-storage system

Current developments in the virtual-storage concept are tending toward a single-level storage concept. Single-level storage treats all storage, primary and secondary, as a single unit or level. Therefore, the real difference between primary and secondary storage is transparent to the programmer. An example of such a system is IBM's System/38.

10.6.2.3.2 Disadvantages of Virtual-Storage

As one might expect, there are disadvantages to virtual-storage. Overhead costs increase. CPU time is required to page (read/write) all those pages in and out of main storage. Additional primary storage is required to hold the tables that keep track of the pages, and to hold a virtual storage operating system.

Another potential problem is thrashing, which occurs when one or more pages of a program have to be paged in and paged out of primary storage frequently during execution of the program. Thrashing could reach a point where the CPU is spending too much time on paging in and out as compared to time spent on program execution.

Program structure can have a significant positive impact on the problem of thrashing. Consider the segment of a FORTRAN program illustrated in Fig. 10.16. If, as illustrated, page 2 of the program ends at statement number 40 and page 3 begins at statement number 50, significant thrashing is going to occur when this program is executed. Pages 2 and 3 will have to be paged in and out as many as 100 times each, as the program branches from statement 50 to statement 30. Therefore, when writing a program that is to be executed many times on virtual-storage system, the programmer should minimize the branching within the program. Structured programming (which is sometimes called GOTO-less programming) is a technique that can minimize program branching.

Page 2	15 K = 0 25 N = 100 30 K = k + 1 40 SUMY2 = SUMY + Y(K) **2
Page 3	50 IF (K.LT.N) GO TO 30 60 K = 0

Fig. 10.16 A program that can cause thrashing

If a page has never been referenced before, then it is still in the program file on the auxiliary storage. A page enters the working set only when required. This is called **paging on demand.**

10.6.3 Device Management

A contemporary computer system includes a wide assortment of 'Input/Output' devices, called peripheral devices, such as printers, card readers, magnetic tape units, magnetic disks etc. A large computer installation may put half of the system cost to peripherals, so, it may be used in efficient manner.

10.6.3.1 Device Characteristics

The characteristics of the Device (I/O) management are:

(*i*) The speed of one I/O device is different from another. For instance, cartridge tape is slow than a floppy disk in terms of retrieving data, hard disk is faster than printer, etc.

(*ii*) Data can be represented in different forms on different I/O devices. For instance, some use ASCII code, whereas others use EDCDIC, BCD, etc.

(*iii*) Device are shareable or non-shareable. For example, floppies and hard disks are shareable because they can handle successive requests from different programs, whereas keyboards are non-shareable devices.

(*iv*) Data can be transferred in the various forms, such as characters, words, bytes records, etc.

10.6.3.2 Buffering

Buffering is a method of overlapping input, output and processing of a single job. The idea is quite simple. After data has been read and the CPU is about to start operating on it, the input device is instructed to begin the next input immediately. The CPU ad input device are then both busy. By the time, the CPU is ready for the next data item, the input device will have finished reading it. The CPU can then begin processing the newly read data, while the input device starts to read the following data. Similarly, this can be done for output. In this case, the CPU creates data which is put into a buffer until an output device can accept it. On an average CPU is much faster than an input device, so for input device, most of the time buffer is empty. For the output device, the CPU can proceed at full speed until all system buffers are full, then the CPU must wait for the output device.

10.6.3.3 *Spooling (Simultaneous Peripheral Operation On-Line)*

The spooling is a more sophisticated form of input/output buffering, which essentially use the disk as a very large buffer for reading and for storing output files. Buffering overlaps input, output and processing of a single job whereas spooling allows CPU to overlap the input of one job with the computation and output of other jobs. This approach is better than buffering. Even a simple system, the spooler may be reading the input of one job while printing the output of different job.

10.6.4 Information Management

A computer stores information in the form of files. The operating system provide the convenient ways for storing and accessing the information from files. The information management component of operating system is structured as follows to effectively support these requirements:

(*i*) **Physical IOCS (Input Output Control System):** It is responsible for device management and for ensuring device independence. It provides a basic capability for programs to perform their own IO, without involving themselves with the intricacies of device handling.

(*ii*) **Logical IOCS:** It provides basic capabilities for file definition, choice of data organization, and access methods. It is responsible for efficient organization and access of data on IO devices.

(*iii*) **File System:** It provides for protection and controlled sharing of files existing in the system.

Figure 10.17 illustrates the hierarchy of these modules.

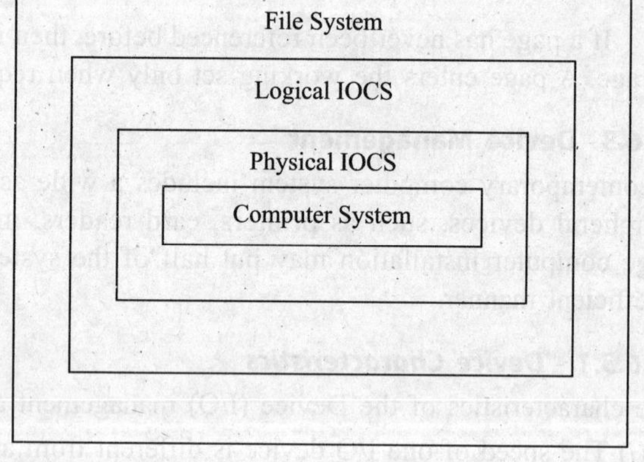

Fig. 10.17 Hierarchy of Information Management Modules

10.6.4.1 *File Organization*

Computers, as we know, operate on data. They accept, process data and communicate results. The data supplied to a computer must generally be organized in a predetermined way to satisfy the numeric, alphabetic or alphanumeric (numeric and alphabetic) forms demanded by the particular program in use.

The basic hierarchy of data organization, going from the general to the specific, is database, file, record and field.

A **database** is a concept of file organization. It is a collection of related files stored together in logical fashion.

A **file** is collection of similar groups of data which fit under one heading. For example, payroll file of a company consists of the salary detail of all employees and all of these records have the same head (*e.g.*, Basic Pay, D.A., H.R.A., C.C.A., Interim relief, G.P.F., etc.)

A file may be further divided into more descriptive subdivisions, called records. The material in a **record** is specific to that particular record but falls under the same topic as that of the file. In other words, a record is a collection of related data items treated as a single unit. For example, in the payroll database of a company, data about a particular employee, such as

Basic Pay, D.A., H.R.A. are an individual record. All the information in the record pertains only to that employee, but all those data are related to pay rolls.

In the record, space needs to be allocated for data. Each individual item of data stored in a record is known as a **field**. Each record may contain one or more than one field. In our payroll example, there are many fields: one for employee's name, one for Basic pay, one for D.A, one for H.R.A and so on.

A record may be of fixed-length or variable-length. A **fixed-length record** is one where each record is set out have a specific number of characters. For instance, if the record length is set at 30 characters, then only 25 characters are used, and 5 empty spaces are stored with the data.

A **variable-length record** is the one in which places are allotted only to data. For instance, if only 25 characters are used, then only 25 characters are used. This method saves storage space.

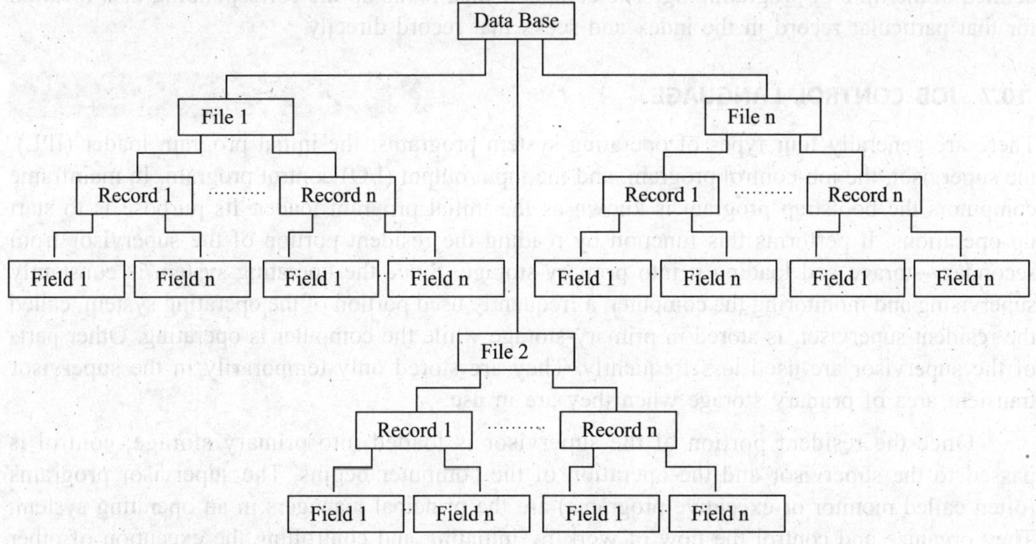

Fig. 10.18 Organization of Hierarchy of Data for Computer Processing

10.6.4.2 File-Access Methods

Data items are organized into files, and these files are recorded on a secondary storage medium such as a disk or tape and accessed. The data items or files' places in secondary storage must be organized in many ways before they can be stored and retrieved. Three common ways are:

1. Sequential access file
2. Direct access file
3. Indexed-sequential access file

10.6.4.2.1 Sequential access file

A **sequential access file** is one in which records are stored and accessed one after another. Magnetic tape is a storage medium that is sequential in nature. All preceding records must be read first to access a particular or individual record.

10.6.4.2.2 Direct access file

A **direct access file** is one in which a record is read directly from a disk without reading all proceeding records. In direct access method, the order of the storage of records is immaterial. Direct access is the fastest of the three access methods.

10.6.4.2.3 Indexed-sequential access file

The most common technique for accessing disk records directly is with the use of an index. During the creation of records, the computer uses file handling programmed routines to establish an index on the disk itself. The index indicates where each record is located. The concept is similar to that of the index found at the end of a book, which specifies the page where each item of information can be located. The disk index indicates the locations (*i.e.*, track and sector) of each records, where a particular record can be found. A **key data** field in each record, must be indicated by the programmer, is used by the computer as the basis for establishing address information in the index.

For example, if a payroll file is stored on a disk. To access any particular record, the user need only supply a particular key data field, such as EMPLOYEE CODE or whatever has been defined at the time of programming. The computer then looks up the corresponding disk location for that particular record in the index and seeks that record directly.

10.7 JOB CONTROL LANGUAGE

There are generally four types of operating-system programs: the initial program loader (IPL), the supervisor, the job-control program, and the input/output (I/O) control program. In mainframe computers the bootstrap program is known as the initial program loader. Its purpose is to start up operations. It performs this function by reading the resident portion of the supervisor from secondary-storage and loading it into primary-storage. Since the operating system is constantly supervising and monitoring the computer, a frequently used portion of the operating system, called the resident supervisor, is stored in primary-storage while the computer is operating. Other parts of the supervisor are used less frequently. They are stored only temporarily in the supervisor transient area of primary storage when they are in use.

Once the resident portion of the supervisor is loaded into primary storage, control is passed to the supervisor and the operation of the computer begins. The supervisor programs (often called monitor or executive programs) are the principal managers in an operating system. They organize and control the flow of work by initiating and controlling the execution of other computer programs.

As operating-system software replaced human operators in the control of mainframe computers, new languages were developed to enable users and programmers to communicate with the operating system. A job-control language (JCL) requires that the user include several job-control statements along with a program. The statements identify the job and its steps, and specify the system resources to be used (for example, expected run time, input/output device to be used, and memory space required). Job-control language also describes the data sets or files that are to be used in the various job steps. (JCL is used with batch processing on mainframe computers to communicate information (about programs and their requirements for system resources) to the operating system. JCL statements must occur before and after each program). Job-control languages are used primarily with the large multiuser computer systems. JCL is not used with personal computers since they are usually single-user systems. The information provided through JCL can be furnished to a personal computer interactively or by defaulting to standard assumptions for the information.

The supervisor and job-control programs acting together issue many instructions to the human operator. Examples of these include instructions to mount or dismount a tape or to load or unload a disk pack. If special forms are needed for printing the output, the programmer specifies these forms through the JCL statements. When the job is ready to be printed, the computer sends a message to the operator to mount the special forms on the printer. A large percentage of the work a computer operator performs is in response to instructions from the operating system. These instructions originate from the JCL that the programmer includes with his program.

Input/output control programs manage the movement of data between primary-storage and peripheral devices such as disk and tape drives. The programs also can check for errors. For example, if an error is detected while a program is reading from a disk, the I/O control program rereads the data several times in an attempt to obtain error-free data. If the error continues to occur, then an appropriate error message is displayed or printed.

10.8 COMPILER, ASSEMBLER AND INTERPRETER

Programming Language is a language that communicates with the computer. Since the communication here is with the machine, a programming language has to be unambiguous and precise. A program is a sequence of instructions to be executed by the computer. An instruction is a command given to the computer to perform a particular function. Essentially, it has to be in a language understandable by the computer. Each instruction produces several lines of machine language instructions.

Computer understands only one language, *i.e.*, Machine Language. The earlier computers had to be programmed in machine language of zeros and ones, which evidently was quite a complicated and tedious process. The procedure was time-consuming, expensive and subject to error.

The difficulties of earlier days led to the development of low level languages also called 'Translating' or assembly programs. They translate the programmers' English-like (symbolic) program called 'Source Program' into a machine language or 'Object Program' for necessary computer processing. The symbols were also referred to as 'Mnemonics'. For instance we use Autocoder in IBM 1401, Plan in ICL and BAL in IBM 360. These languages are machine dependent or machine oriented.

Whereas assembly languages require the programmer to adapt his thinking to the particular computer, high level languages help the programmer by adapting the computer to his thinking. Being machine independent, a program written in compiler language can be run on different computer systems without much difficulty. The use of a high level language would, thus, mean relatively less time spent on program coding, debugging, documentation and maintenance.

Before executing a program written in a high level language, it is necessary to translate them to the machine language. Operating Systems include software called Compilers for translation (or compilation) of the so-called 'higher level languages'. Programs written in higher-level languages are often called Source Programs. Examples of high level languages are COBOL, FORTRAN, BASIC, etc.

Programming in a high-level language or in assembly language, therefore, requires some sort of interface with the machine language at the time the program is to be run. Figures 10.19 (*a*) to 10.19 (*c*) exhibits the three most common such interfaces: an 'assembler', a 'compiler' and an 'interpreter'.

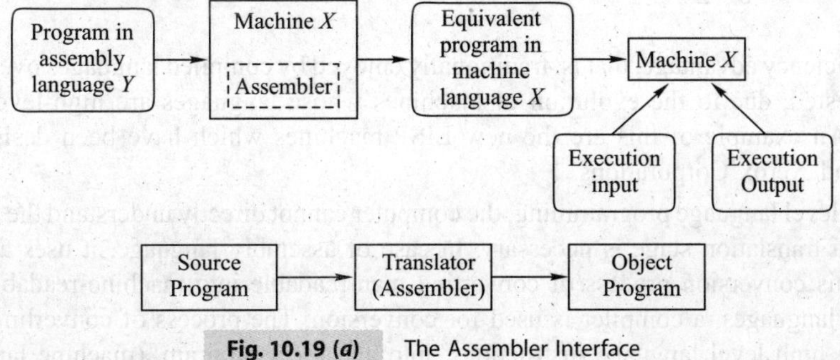

Fig. 10.19 (*a*) The Assembler Interface

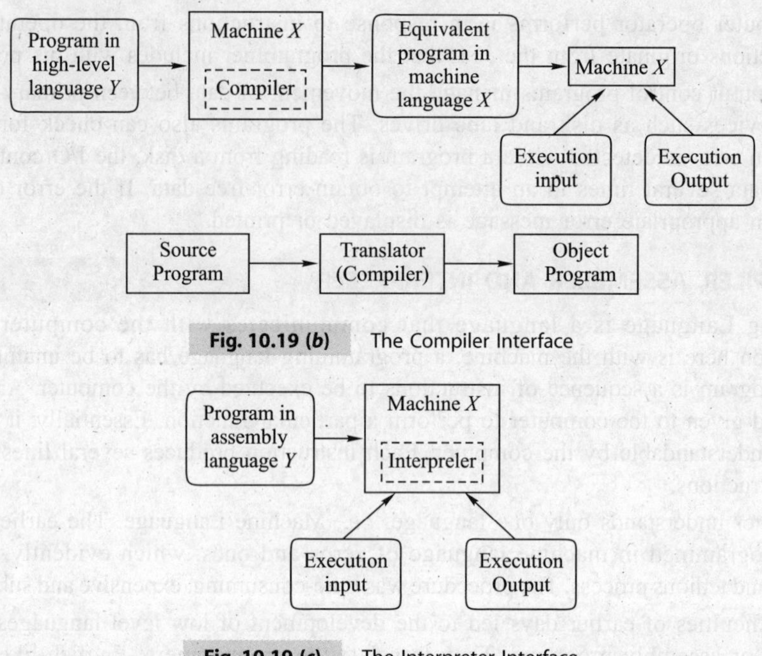

Fig. 10.19 (b) The Compiler Interface

Fig. 10.19 (c) The Interpreter Interface

As shown, the assembler interface and the compiler interface each translates the program into an equivalent program in the 'host' machine's language X as a *separate* step prior to execution. The interpreter, on the other hand, directly executes instructions in the high-level language Y, without a prior processing step.

Compilation is a far more machine-efficient process, in general, than interpretation for most common machine species. This occurs mainly because statements within 'loops' must be reinterpreted each time they are executed by an interpreter. With a compiler, each statement is interpreted and then translated into machine language, only once.

Some languages are mainly interpreted languages, like APL, PROLOG, and LISP while others, for example, Pascal, FORTRAN, COBOL, PL/I, SNOBOL, C, Ada, and Modula-2 are usually compiled languages. In some cases, a compiler will be alternately available for an interpreted language (such as LISP, BASIC), and conversely (such as Bell Laboratories' SNOBOL 4 interpreter).

Interpretation is often preferable to compilation in experimental or educational programming environments, where each new run of a program involves a change in the program text itself. The quality of diagnostic and debugging support for interpreted languages is generally better than that of compiled languages, since error messages are tied directly to statements in the original program text.

The efficiency advantage, that is, traditionally enjoyed by compiled languages over interpreted ones is contested, due to the evolution of machines whose languages are high-level languages themselves. An example of this are the new LISP machines which have been designed by the Symbolics and Xerox Corporations.

In high level language programming, the computer cannot directly understand the instructions, and as such a translation stage is necessary. In case of assembly language, it uses an assembler to perform this conversion process of converting man-readable into machine-readable level, but in high level languages, a compiler is used for conversion. The process of converting the source program, *i.e.*, high level language instructions, into an object program, (machine language) is a basic function of a compiler. Over and above, a compiler reads a source program and scans for errors in its construction. These construction errors are called syntax errors.

The **syntax** of a programming language, broadly speaking, is that set of rules and writing conventions that allow the formation of correct programs in a language, from the point of view of 'presentation' only. That is, syntax has nothing to do with 'meaning' or run-time behaviour of a program. Although syntax is concerned only with the form of a program, it is inextricably tied to **semantics** which is the meaning of the program. Usually, semantics is defined in terms of programs' run-time behaviour: What happens when the program is executed with a certain set of inputs, what statements are executed, what values are assigned to the variables, and what output is produced.

A compiler will also print out the error messages. These error messages are known as diagnostics. Compilers are very large programs which reside permanently on secondary storage devices, or may be on separate storage devices. Whenever required they are copied into the main memory for execution. So the FORTRAN compiler will only be capable of translating source programs which are written in FORTRAN language and each machine will require a compiler for each higher level language which is to be used. Each machine will have to have its own 'personal compiler' because an object program for machine X will not be the same as the object program for machine Y.

In a compiler, the complete source program is usually printed with appropriate notes against each error message, if any, with number of errors shown at the end. When the program is error free, the compiler generates the program in machine code.

An interpreter is nothing but a compiler itself, but the differences between an interpreter and a compiler are further explained. A compiler will take a program as one and compile it. But in case of an interpreter each line is compiled one by one. A compiler will list all the errors in the last, *i.e.*, after going through the program completely. When the program is error free it will generate object code. But an interpreter will check for error in each instruction, and if it does not sense an error, it will go on executing the program. It also immediately prints the error messages and terminates the execution, if any error is found. Compilers are good for a very long program, whereas an interpreter is good for small and short throw-away programs. Compiler converts source program into object program and execution is carried out in the last, but an interpreter will convert and execute a program at the same time, that is, instruction by instruction.

10.9 LOADER AND LINKER

A **loader** is a routine that loads an object program and prepares it for execution. There are various loading schemes: absolute, relocating, and direct-linking. In general, the loader must load, relocate, and link the object program. The **linker** is responsible for an important action, linking, *i.e.*, the process of merging many object modules to form a single machine language program.

REVIEW QUESTIONS

Multiple Choice Questions

1. A software which converts a program in assembly language into machine language is known as:
(*a*) Compiler (*b*) Assembler (*c*) Interpreter (*d*) Loader

2. A software which converts a complete High Level Language program to machine language in one go is known as:
(*a*) Compiler (*b*) Assembler (*c*) Interpreter (*d*) Loader

3. A program which merges many object modules is:
(*a*) Compiler (*b*) Interpreter (*c*) Loader (*d*) Linker

4. An example of system development programs is:
(*a*) operating systems (*b*) performance management systems
(*c*) data-base management systems (*d*) language translators

5. Which of the following is not a part of the operating system?
(*a*) Supervisor (*b*) Performance monitor
(*c*) Job-control program (*d*) Input/output control program

6. If special forms are needed for printing the output, the programmer specifies these forms through:
(*a*) JCL (*b*) IPL (*c*) utility programs (*d*) load modules

7. Which of the following is not an advantage of multiprogramming?
(*a*) Increased throughput (*b*) Shorter response time
(*c*) Decreased operating-system overhead (*d*) Ability to assign priorities to jobs

8. The problem of thrashing is affected significantly by:
(*a*) program structure (*b*) program size
(*c*) primary-storage size (*d*) None of the above

9. Two basic types of operating systems are:
(*a*) sequential and direct (*b*) batch and timesharing
(*c*) sequential and realtime (*d*) batch and interactive

10. Under multiprogramming, turnaround time for short jobs is usually ________ and that for long jobs is slightly ________.
(*a*) lengthened; shortened (*b*) shortened; lengthened
(*c*) shortened; shortened (*d*) shortened; unchanged

11. Remote computing services involve the use of timesharing and ________.
(*a*) multiprocessing (*b*) interactive processing
(*c*) batch processing (*d*) realtime processing

12. Under virtual storage:
(*a*) a signal program is processed by two or more CPUs
(*b*) two or more programs are stored concurrently in primary storage
(*c*) only the active pages of a program are stored in primary storage
(*d*) interprogram interference may occur

13. A front-end processor is usually used in:
(*a*) multiprogramming (*b*) virtual storage (*c*) timesharing (*d*) multiprocessing

14. Which of the following types of software must you have in main memory in order to use your keyboard?
(*a*) word processing (*b*) systems (*c*) spreadsheet (*d*) applications

15. If you want to execute more than one program at a time, the systems software you are using must be capable of:
(*a*) word processing (*b*) virtual memory (*c*) compiling (*d*) multitasking

16. Which of the following is a type of systems software used on microcomputers?
(*a*) Apple DOS (*b*) MS-DOS (*c*) PC-DOS (*d*) UNIX
(*e*) All of the above

17. Which of the following, helpful in evaluating applications software, will best suit your needs?
(*a*) recommendations by other users (*b*) computer magazines
(*c*) objective software reviews (*d*) computer periodicals
(*e*) all of the above

18. Which of the following are loaded into main memory when the computer is booted?
(*a*) internal command instructions (*b*) external command instructions
(*c*) utility programs (*d*) word processing instructions

19. Which of the following software types is used to simplify using system software?
(*a*) spreadsheet (*b*) operating environment
(*c*) timesharing (*d*) multitasking

20. Which of the following is not applications software?
(*a*) word processing (*b*) spreadsheet
(*c*) UNIX (*d*) desktop publishing

21. Which of the following types of software should you use if you often need to create, edit, and print documents?
(*a*) word processing (*b*) spreadsheet
(*c*) UNIX (*d*) desktop publishing

22. Which of the following will determine your choice of systems software for your computer?
(*a*) Is the applications software you want to use compatible with it?
(*b*) Is it expensive?
(*c*) Is it compatible with your hardware?
(*d*) (*a*) and (*c*)

23. Which of the following might be used to convert high-level language instructions into machine language?
(*a*) system software (*b*) applications software
(*c*) an operating environment (*d*) an interpreter

24. Multiprogramming was made possible by:
(*a*) input/output units that operate independently of the CPU
(*b*) operating systems
(*c*) both (*c*) and (*b*)
(*d*) neither (*a*) nor (*b*)

25. A translator which reads an entire program written in a high level language and converts it into machine language code is:
(*a*) assembler (*b*) translator (*c*) compiler (*d*) system software

26. What is the name given to all the programs inside the computer which makes it usable?
(*a*) Application software (*b*) System software (*c*) Firmware (*d*) Shareware

27. Systems software is a program that directs the overall operation of the computer, facilitates its use and interacts with the users. What are the different types of this software?
(*a*) Operating system (*b*) Languages (*c*) Utilities (*d*) All of the above

ANSWERS

1. (*b*)	**2.** (*a*)	**3.** (*d*)	**4.** (*d*)	**5.** (*b*)	**6.** (*a*)	**7.** (*c*)	**8.** (*a*)
9. (*d*)	**10.** (*b*)	**11.** (*c*)	**12.** (*c*)	**13.** (*c*)	**14.** (*b*)	**15.** (*d*)	**16.** (*e*)
17. (*e*)	**18.** (*a*)	**19.** (*c*)	**20.** (*c*)	**21.** (*a*)	**22.** (*d*)	**23.** (*d*)	**24.** (*c*)
25. (*c*)	**26.** (*b*)	**27.** (*d*)					

QUESTIONS

1. What is an operating system? What purpose do the operating system serve to the computer?

2. Differentiate between Online and Offline processing.

3. What do you mean by multiprogramming?
4. What do you understand by the terms 'I/O-bound job' and 'CPU-bound job'?
5. What is meant by turn-around time?
6. Write short note on spooling and buffering.
7. What do you understand by throughout?
8. What do you understand by preemptive and non-preemptive scheduling?
9. What is FCFS and SJN scheduling techniques?
10. What are the advantages and disadvantages of single contiguous allocation?
11. What do you understand by paging?
12. Write short note on partitioning.
13. Write short note on virtual-storage.
14. What is the difference between an interpreter and a compiler?
15. What do you understand by job control language?

11

DATABASE CONCEPTS

A *database* is a concept of file organization; it consists of related files stored together so that groups of data items can be easily accessed or retrieved by those who need them. The data are integrated so that individual datum can be accessed in a variety of ways. A *database management system* (*DBMS*) is the software that functions as the interface between users, other programs, and the database itself. It allows the data to be stored, maintained, manipulated, and retrieved.

Prepackaged DBMSs are available from vendors for both large systems and microcomputers. However, some organizations using extremely large amounts of data and those with special data-handling requirements often must create their own DBMS in-house or hire outside consultants.

11.1 DATABASE DESIGN CONCEPTS

Computers, as we know, operate on data. They accept, process data and communicate results. The data supplied to a computer must generally be organized in a predetermined way to satisfy the numeric, alphabetic or alphanumeric (numeric and alphabetic) forms demanded by the particular program in use.

The basic hierarchy of data organization, going from the general to the specific, is database, file, record and field.

A *database* is a concept of file organization. It is a collection of related files stored together in a logical fashion.

A *file* is a collection of similar groups of data which fit under one heading. For example, payroll file of a company consists of the salary detail of all employees and all of these records have the same heads (*e.g.*, Basic pay, D.A., H.R.A., C.C.A., Interim Relief, G.P.F., etc.)

A file may be further divided into more descriptive subdivisions, called, records. The material in a *record* is specific to that particular record but falls under the same topic as that of the file. In other words, a record is a collection of related data items treated as a single unit. For example, in the payroll database of a company, data about a particular employee, such as Basic Pay, D.A., H.R.A are an individual record. All the information in the record pertains only to that employee, but all those data are related to pay rolls.

In the record, space needs to be allocated for data. Each individual item of data stored in a record is known as a *field*. Each record may contain one or more than one file. In our payroll example, there are many fields: one for employee's name, one for Basic Pay, one for D.A, one for H.R.A and so on.

A record may be of fixed length or variable length. A *fixed-length record* is one where each record is set to have a specific number of characters. For instance, if the record length is set at 30 characters then only 25 characters are used, and 5 empty spaces are stored with the data.

A *variable-length record* is the one in which places are allotted only to data. For instance, if only 25 characters are used then only 25 characters are used. This method saves storage space.

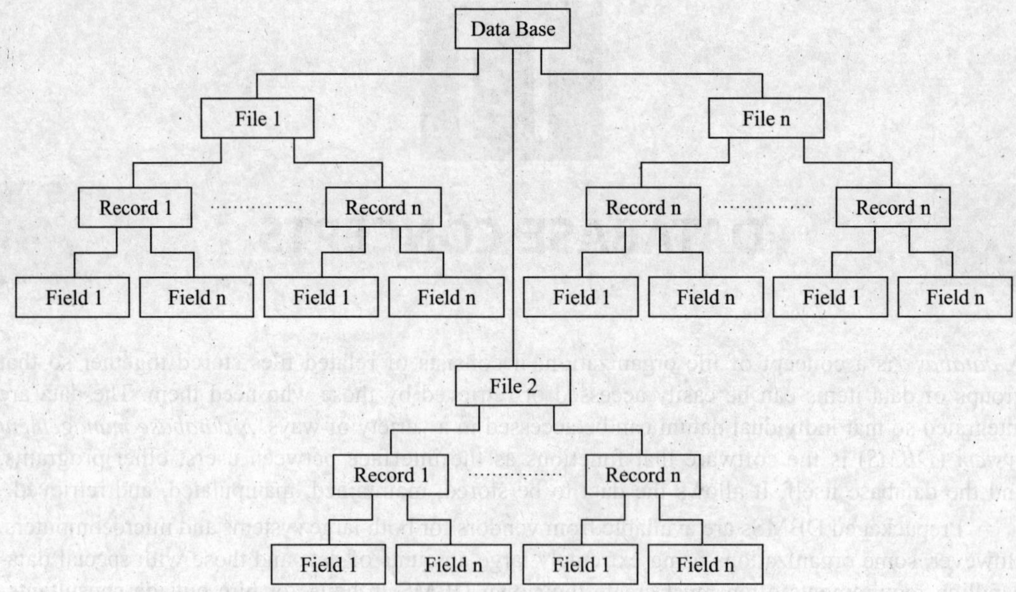

Fig. 11.1 Organization of hierarchy of data for computer processing

11.1.1 Designing a Database

Designing a database in a business environment can be a complex project involving many people. In some companies, the **database administrator** is in charge of designing, implementing, and maintaining the database and all related activities. The data base administrator, along with the users and other specialists, analyze the requirements of the proposed database. Of course, the main factor to be considered is the user's needs.

After determining the database requirements, a schema and subschemas are developed. The **schema** is the conceptual, or logical design showing the relationships among data elements in a database. The schema and subschemas comprise the database's logical design, which is the user's view of how the data appear to be arranged on the secondary storage media.

To help maintain database security, many users will be denied access to some of the information stored in a database; therefore, the logical design must take this into consideration. With the overall schema developed, various subsets of the schema, or **subschemas,** can be designed to limit access of individual users. Users are then limited to accessing only the data in the subschemas that they are authorized to use (Fig. 11.2).

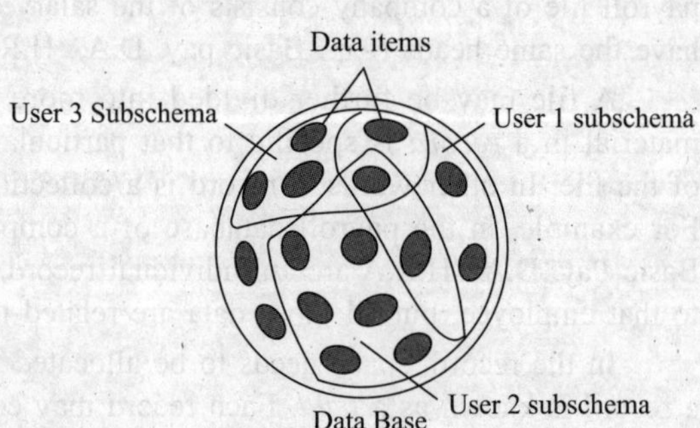

Fig. 11.2 A logical design of a data base showing subschemas, or the individual user's view of what the data base contains

To complete the design of the database, the physical design—how the data are actually stored on a secondary storage media and how data are accessed—has to be determined. Users of prepackaged DBMSs are not concerned with these issues because the physical design is already determined and implemented by the program. With prepackaged DBMSs, the user needs only to make sure that the software's physical design fits that company's needs.

11.2 DATABASE MANAGEMENT SYSTEMS (DBMS)

Database management system is a package that allows users to define data items, place these items in specified records, combine these records into designated files, and then manipulate and retrieve the stored data to fulfill the user's requirements. It supports many separate files and can access appropriate records from two or more files at once (Fig. 11.3).

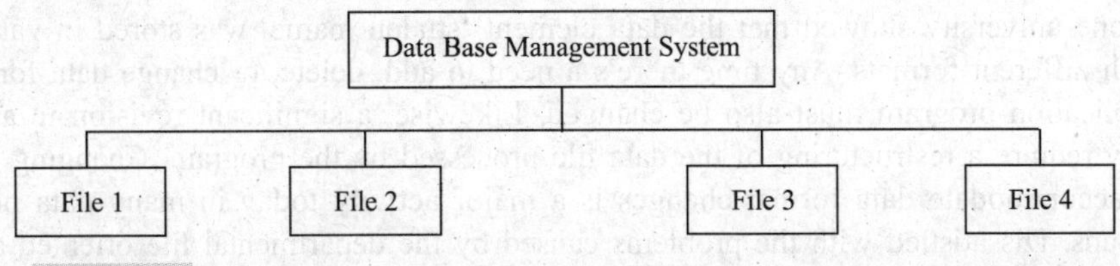

Fig. 11.3 A data base management system can access more than one file at a time

DBMS permits users to search and query database contents in order to extract solution to unplanned and non-recurring problems. The users can use this package to assemble the needed data items from a common database and get solutions to their queries. It is very flexible and easy-to-use package.

DBMS packages are available for all sizes of machines. Mainframe packages are used to develop and maintain scores of applications in an organization. They are controlled by Database Administrators (computer personnel who are responsible for defining, updating and controlling access to a database).

DBMS package for mainframe computers can access database records from several files at once.

DBMS packages for personal computers can be used by an individual for a single purpose, whereas mainframe packages access database records from several files at once. Many PC packages can do this too, but a number of easy-to-use PC programs can only manipulate records from one file at a time.

The first database management package was developed to run on the minicomputer and mainframes of larger organizations. Most of the organisations has originally acquired computers to process a few large volume jobs in a small number of departments. Other applications, treated independently, were added over the years. Each application had its own master file, its own input data, and its own processing program to update the file and supply information. The records in each file were organized according to a single key field, and when the key field of the file wasn't relevant to the information which was required, the entire file had to be searched. For example, a location-wise list of addresses and phones of the customers from a personnel file, organized by the customers' number, required a search of entire file records.

At the same time, new files were being created and data were being duplicated within a department, the same duplication of related field was occurring between various departments. According to the requirements, each department's application and files were often created without any serious thought being given to the total information needs of the organization. The following problems were faced by the departmental file oriented approach.

1. **File updating problems:** When changes occur in a data item, every file which contains that field should be updated to reflect the change. Problem arises when one file is updated while another isn't. For instance, an employee, Sabal Mathur, Account No. 120 has taken a house building loan and it has been entered into the load department file. But this same change may not be carried over to the Account section file, which contains the record of Sabal Mathur, Account No. 312. And, of course, the cost of running different updating programs can be high.

2. **Data redundancy:** The few same data files are often included in many different files. For instance, same data fields such as employee code, name, address, phone, age, etc. may be contained in account file, personal file, loan file, leave-account file. The cost of entering and storing the same data in many files can be high.
3. **Lack of Program:** The programs used with file oriented applications usually contain 'picture', 'format' or 'data' statements that precisely define each data field to be processed. A survey at one university showed that the data element 'student name' was stored in various files with different formats. Any time there's a need to add, delete, or change data formats, the application program must also be changed. Likewise, a significant revision in a program may require a restructuring of the data file processed by the program. Changing programs to accommodate data format changes is a major activity today in many data processing groups. Dissatisfied with the problems caused by the departmental file oriented approach, software designers being looking for ways to integrate activities. The results of their efforts are found today in database management packages.

11.2.1 Features of Database Management System

The basic features of file management systems (a program that stores, manipulates, and prints data stored in separate files) and database management systems permit the user to create, maintain, and manipulate the information stored within a file. These features are common to almost all database packages, but depending on the software packages, the actual commands used to execute them vary.

File management systems are easier to learn and use because the user is manipulating the data in only one file. But with a DBMS, it is possible to manipulate multiple files simultaneously.

11.2.2 Creating File

Let us have a general idea of features of a PC database management system packages with special reference to the most commonly used package—dBASE II PLUS or FoxBASE+ or Fox Pro.

To create a database, we need to type command CREATE, and press the RETURN key, then it first prompts us to

Enter the name of the new file: PIS (any name)

After giving the name PIS to the file, it will ask the information about the fields in each record. For each file, it needs to know the name, type, width, and number of decimal places. The structure of PIS database looks like:

	Field name	Type	Width	Dec
1.	NAME	Char/text	25	
2.	ADDRESS	Char/text	50	
3.	CITY	Char/text	15	
4.	INCOME	NUMERIC	10	2
5.	PIN	Char/text	6	

After entering all field names, just save this file. Now we have created a database file. Every database package allows users to carry out these file-creation activities and the other operations described below.

11.2.3 Entering Database Records

Once file specifications have been set, just type the command APPEND for entering the new data to the database file.

It will bring us a form to fill out on the screen.

Record No.	1
NAME	RAMAN
ADDRESS	47-A, M.I.G. Flats, Ashok Vihar
CITY	DELHI
INCOME	4500.00
PIN	110054

11.2.4 Sorting

Generally, it is easier to read data if they are arranged in some pre-designed order. Sorting records means to arrange them in order. The sort can be numerical or alphabetical, and the data can be arranged in ascending or descending order. The field used in the sorting process are the key fields. Most database packages allow sorting by more than one key field. This would be used, for instance, while sorting names. If the last names are the same, the name might be further sorted by first names. The first key field in the sort is called the primary key, while subsequent fields are the secondary key fields.

11.2.5 Deleting

Removing records from a file is called deleting. It is wise for the user to keep a backup copy of the file to have, in case of accidental deletion. Individual fields within a record can also be deleted. After the data are deleted, those data items are no longer available.

11.2.6 Updating

Updating is the process of changing the content of a record or records in a database file. This updating might be adding, deleting, or changing the contents of a record. By accessing records and changing the field contents, the computer user can keep all the records current.

11.2.7 Searching

Searching a file means to look through a file and to locate data. Searching for data may also be called finding or retrieving by some systems. One file at a time is searched with a file management system, but multiple files can be searched in DBMS. A database management package derives much of its power from the ease with which it can sort records and search for answers to a wide range of questions. Search questions are posed in different ways depending on the type of user interface that's built into the package. Some command-driven packages require users to supply search instructions in cryptic codes. Some menu-driven packages permit users to select words and options appearing in successive menus, until they have built a search command, the program understands.

If a user is uncertain as to exactly what data he or she is looking for, an entire file can be searched, one record at a time. Listing each record in the file permits the use to visually search, sometimes called 'browsing' the file until the right one is located. More often, however, the user knows what data are required. With most data managers, the user can enter the search parameters to locate the specific records containing those data. Those records will be found and displayed.

11.2.8 Merging Database Files

Merging (joining) files is combining records from two or more files. The records found in two files can be merged, only if some logical relationship exists, between the files. For example, in Fig. 11.4, the Personal File and the Account File are merged using the common field 'Emp.Id'.

Personal File

Emp. Id	Name	Address	City	Phone
3707	Pooja	Sadar Apart.,	Delhi	2288855
3708	Semran	Dhruv Apart.,	Delhi	2223432

Account File

Emp. Id	Income	Tax Paid
3707	5675	300
3708	3000	NIL

Account File

Emp. Id	Name	Address	City	Phone	Income	Tax Paid
3707	Pooja	Sadar Apart.,	Delhi	2288855	5675	300
3708	Semran	Dhruv Apart.,	Delhi	2223432	3000	NIL

Fig. 11.4 The Merge Feature allows tables to be combined through a key field

11.2.9 Copying

The copying feature permits the user to make duplicate files to store in another location. For example, a temporary created file from the merging of two files may be copied into a new permanent database file.

11.2.10 Printing

The printing feature permits the user to print the contents of the screen at any time. Sometimes it is required to print only raw data to check the error, occurred at the time of entering data.

11.2.11 Validating

Checking data for appropriateness and accuracy is called validating. Data-entry checks can be built into the database packages to present invalid data from being entered. For instance, in dBASE, format checking (determining if data are in the correct format, *e.g.*, numeric or text) is done automatically because at the time of creating a database file, if you have defined the Type of File as/text, then it will accept only text.

Range checking (determining if the data fall within an acceptable range, *e.g.*, greater than 100 but less than 500) and Accuracy checking (making sure that an entry is possible, *e.g.*, cross-checking an Emp.Id with Emp-Id from the personal file) can be built by writing a simple program in dBASE, FoxBASE+, FoxPro etc.

11.2.12 Converting

Converting data is taking the form in which data are stored in one database package and changing them so they can be used by another database package. This is generally done by a utility program that converts a file from its current format to the desired format. Programs sometimes use different formats for storing data on disk. When this occurs, one database package will not be able to interpret a file created by another database package.

11.2.13 Generating Reports

All database management packages allow the users to print files, and many allow the users to customize the way output will look. This customizing is possible with those database packages that contain a report generator. With a report generator, the user defines how the report will appear when printed. The report generators have following features:

11.2.13.1 Headers

The header part of a report is located at the top of the report page and it contains items such as the date, page, number, heading, column heading, logo, etc.

11.2.13.2 Footers

The footer part of a report is located at the bottom of the report page and it contains page number, user's name, etc.

11.2.13.3 Formatting

The formatting part of a report is located between the headers and footers of the report and it contains margins setting, justifying text, and indicating page length and line spacing.

11.2.13.4 Statistics

Many report generators can perform some simple mathematical functions such as calculating column subtotals, grand totals, averages, and counting.

In dBASE, you can generate a report by just typing

REPORT FORM R_PIS

report file name.

command and defining the field, header ......etc., as desired by dBASE. Finally, the generated report will look like:

Page No. 1
05/11/98

Mailing List by Name

Name	*Address*	*City*	*Phone*
Apoorva Sharma	150, Sadar Apart., Preet Vihar	Delhi	2288 855
Ashish Arora	Punjabi Bagh Apartments	New Delhi	5415 793
Doe Ruth	1421 J.St	New York	31234
Vipul Saxena	M.I.G-189, Jaipur House	Agra	2588 67
Uma Sharma	B-4, Paschim Vihar	New Delhi	5417 283

11.2.14 Structures of Database Management Packages

The structures of Database Management Packages are used to organize the data elements in three basic ways:

1. Hierarchical database structure
2. Network database structure
3. Relational database structure

1. The Hierarchical database structure: resembles an upside-down tree with the root at the top and the branches formed below or resembles an organization chart of a corporation. The president has many vice-presidents, who have many subordinates. There's a superior subordinate relationship in this structure. One might view structure as an upside-down family tree.

At the top level of data is the parent, or root level. Data found under the root level are at the child or subordinate level. Each parent can have numerous children, but each child can have only one parent. Each child level may also be broken down into further levels with the wild becoming the parent for the next level as shown in Fig. 11.5. Each item or branch in this structure below the root has only a single owner. Thus, as we see in Fig. 11.5, a customer record may own street address, credit rating, and invoice elements, and these elements may have subordinate items.

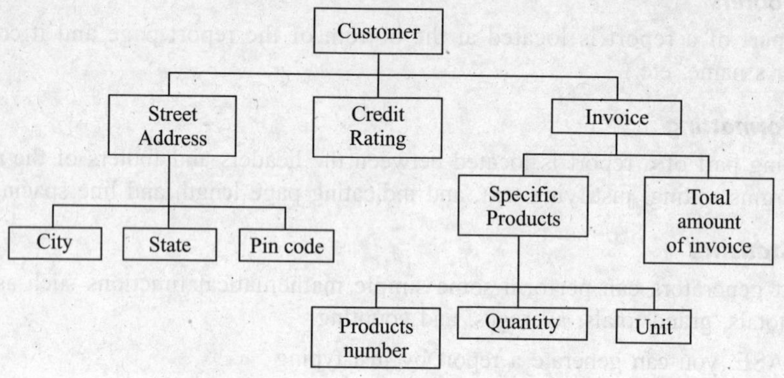

Fig. 11.5 Hierarchical Data Base Structure

2. The Network database structure is similar to the hierarchical structure, it is more complex, but also more flexible in accessing data items. Similar to the hierarchical structure, it is more complex, but also more flexible in accessing data items. Similar to a hierarchical structure, each parent can have more than one child, but in a network database structure each child can have more than one parent. This structure permits the connection of the nodes in a multidirectional manner (Fig. 11.6). Thus, each node may have several owners and may, in turn, own any number of other data units. The network database structure is a more versatile and flexible data-access structure than the hierarchical type because the route of data is not necessarily downward, it can be from any direction.

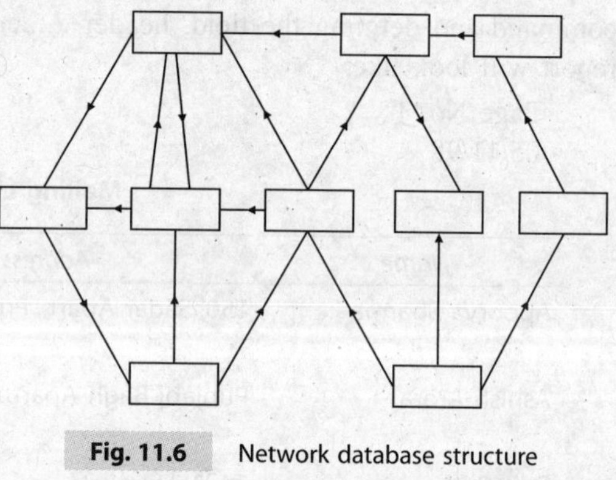

Fig. 11.6 Network database structure

3. The relational database structure manages data in more than one file at once, and these files are treated as tables (Fig. 11.6) with rows and columns, rather than as list of records. Each table column represents a database field, and each row a database record—sometimes called a tuple. Table can be linked to pull various data elements together. The relationship between data items do not have to be defined during the database development. As the information requires, new ways of analyzing data can simply instruct the DBMS to extract and manipulate the desired information. However, the relationships between data items are not predefined, the access time can be relatively slow than the network and hierarchical database structure (Fig. 11.7).

EMPNAM	EMPCODE	EMPDEP	EMPSAL	TAX
Anju	3027	20	5000	500
Neelam	125	23	4050	400
Neeru	3029	20	3025	310
Anjana	1172	17	30000	300
Poonam	2001	13	2500	250

Fig. 11.7 Relational Database Structure

11.3 THE RELATIONAL DATA MODEL

The Relational Data Model (RDM) was formally introduced in 1970. Since that time, it has undergone extensive study. The relational model frees the user from details of storage structures and access methods. It is also conceptually simple and, more importantly, based on sound theoretical principles that provide formal tools to tackle problems arising in database design and maintenance.

The relational data model, after more than a decade, has emerged from the research, the development, test and trial stages as a commercial product. Software systems using this approach are available for all sizes of computer systems. This model has the advantage of being simple in principle; users can express their queries in a powerful query language. It is expected that many existing database applications will be retrofitted to use this approach.

In this mode, the relation is the only construct required to represent the associations among the attributes of an entity as well as the relationships among different entities. One of the main reasons for introducing this model was to increase the productivity of the application programmer by eliminating the need to change application programs when a change is made to the database. Users need not know the exact physical structures to use the database and are protected from any changes made to these structures. They are, however, still required to know how the data has been partitioned into the various relations. While it is possible to infer access paths from the relational mode, as we will see later, the relational approach does require the user to provide logical navigation through the database for the query.

11.4 BASIC OF RELATIONAL DATABASE MANAGEMENT SYSTEMS

The different terms used in the relational database model are being discussed here.

1. **Entities:** An **entity** is simply, a person, place, event, or thing for which we intend to collect data. For example, in a university environment, entities of interest might be students, faculty member, courses, and so on. If you work for an airline, appropriate entities might be pilots, aircraft, routes, suppliers, and any number of additional items for which data must be gathered.
2. **Attributes:** Each entity has certain characteristics known as **attributes**. For instance, the student entity might include the following attributes: Student number, name, grade point average, date of enrollment, date of birth, home address, phone number, major and so on. Similarly, the airline might define these attributes for its aircraft entity: aircraft number, date of last maintenance, total hours flown, hours flown since last maintenance, and so on.

Emp-code	Name	Designation
3727	Anil	Programmer
3728	Kuldeep	DBA
3729	Indra	Manager
3730	Vipul	DBA
3731	Raman	Programmer
3721	Ashish	System Analyst

Fig. 11.8 Employee table

3. **Relation:** The relation is the only data structure used in the relational data model to represent both entities and the relationships between them. A relation may be visualized as a name table. Figure 11.8 shows the two relations EMPLOYEE and DESIGNATION using a tabular structure. Each column of the table corresponds to an attribute of the relation and is named.
4. **Tuple:** Row of a relation is referred to as tuple. A tuple having a set of n numbers of attribute is termed as n-tuple.
5. **Domain:** The values for an attribute or a column are drawn from a set of values known as a **domain**. The domain of an attribute contains the set of values that the attribute may assume. In the relation model, note that no two rows of relation are identical and the ordering of a rows is not significant. For example, the domain for die is {1, 2, 3, 4, 5, and 6}, or domain for coin is {Head, Tail}.

Design_code	Designation
321	Programmer
322	DBA
323	Manager
324	DBA
325	Programmer

Fig. 11.9 Designation Code

6. **Degree:** A relationship's **degree** indicates the number of associated entities or participants. A **unary relationship** exists when an association is maintained within a single entity. A **binary relationship** exists when two entities are associated. A **ternary relationship** exists when three entities are associated. Although higher degrees exist, they are rare and are not specifically named. (For example, an association of four entities is simply described as a *four-entity relationship.*) We have shown a few sample relationships in Fig. 11.10.

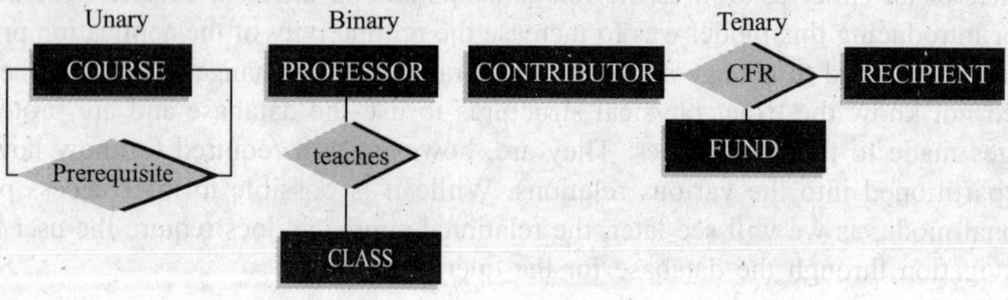

Fig. 11.10 Three Types of Relationships

In the case of the unary relationship shown in Fig. 11.10, a course within the COURSE entity is a prerequisite for another course **within** that entity. In this case, the existence of a course prerequisite means that a **COURSE** requires a COURSE, *i.e.*, COURSE has a relationship with itself. Such a relationship known as a **recursive relationship**.

Binary relationships are most common. In fact, to simplify the conceptual design, most higher-order (ternary and higher) relationships are decomposed into appropriate equivalent binary relationships whenever possible.

Although most relationships are binary, the use of ternary and higher-order relationships does allow the designer some latitude regarding the semantics of a problem. For example, note the relationships (and their consequences) in Fig. 11.10.

(*i*) People or institutions in the CONTRIBUTOR group donate money to a special research FUND. (The research funds may be placed into several categories. For example, if the fund is designed to support medical research, the categories may include cancer, AIDS, heart disease, and so on.

(*ii*) The researchers who are found in the RECIPIENT entity are funded through the FUND CONTENTS.

(*iii*) The relationships are all classified as M:N. For example, contributors can make donations to many funds. A fund can have many donors. A fund may support many researchers who become the FUND recipients, and a researcher may draw support from many funds.

(*iv*) The three entities CONTRIBUTOR, RECIPIENT, and FUND are related through the ternary relationship we have labeled CFR. Because a single verb cannot express a ternary relationship, we elected to use the acronym CFR to indicate its role in defining the relationships between the **C**ONTRIBUTOR, the **F**UND, and the **R**ECIPIENT. Thus CFR enables the database end user to identify the fund's contributors for each recipient, as shown in Database Table 11.1.

Table 11.1 The implementation of a ternary relationships

Table name: CONTRIBUTOR

	CON_ID	CON_NAME
▶	C1	Brown
	C2	Igless
	C3	Smith

Table name: FUND

	FUND_ID	FUND_NAME	CON_ID	FUND_AMOUNT
▶	F1	Heart	C1	$50,000,00
	F1	Heart	C2	$10,000,00
	F2	Cancer	C1	$10,000,00
	F2	Cancer	C2	$5,000,00
	F2	Cancer	C3	$10,000,00

Table name: RECIPIENT

	REC_ID	REC_TYPE
▶	R1	Cancer
	R2	Heart
	R3	Heart

Table name: CFR

	FUND_ID	CON_ID	CFR_AMOUT	REC_ID
▶	F1	C1	$50,000,00	R2
	F1	C1	$10,000,00	R3
	F2	C2	$10,000,00	R2
	F2	C1	$5,000,00	R1
	F2	C2	$10,000,00	R1

As you examine the table contents in Database Table 11.1, note that it is possible to track all transactions. For instance, researcher RI, specializing in cancer research, has received a total of $15,000, divided as follows: $10.000 from contributor C1 (Brown) and $5,000 from contributor C2 (Iglesas). Researcher R2 specializing in heart research, received $40,000; $30,000 of which came from contributor C1 and $10,000 came from contributor C2. In addition, the CFR (ternary) relationship allows us to relate the available funds to the contributors. For example, the table contents indicate that contributor C1 donated $50,000 to heart research; $30,000 of which was received by researcher R2, while the remaining $20,000 was received by researcher R3.

The ternary relationship described here has an effect on the type and extent of the data available to a database query. For example, if 500 people make donations to the *heart* portion of the fund and we do *not* use a ternary relationship, there is no way to identify the specific source of those funds when the recipient receives a *heart* grant. Therefore, if it is necessary to keep track of specific contributors to the fund and the recipients of those funds, the ternary relationship is necessary. As the preceding example demonstrate, you should keep in mind that a ternary relationship is not always equivalent to several I:M relationships. Consequently, the designer must consider the semantics of the problem that is being addressed; desirable simplification may not match end user needs!

7. **Cardinality:** Cardinality expresses the specific number of entity occurrences associated with one occurrence of the related entity. The actual number of associated entities usually is a function of an organization's policy. For example, the Tiny College administration limits the professor to teaching a maximum of three classes per semester. Therefore, the cardinality rule governing the PROFESSOR-CLASS association is expressed as, 'One professor teaches up to three classes per semester'. Similarly, the Tiny College administration may decide to limit a student to a maximum of six classes per semester, and class size may be limited to thirty-five students. The cardinality is indicated by placing the appropriate numbers beside the entities, as shown in Fig. 11.11.

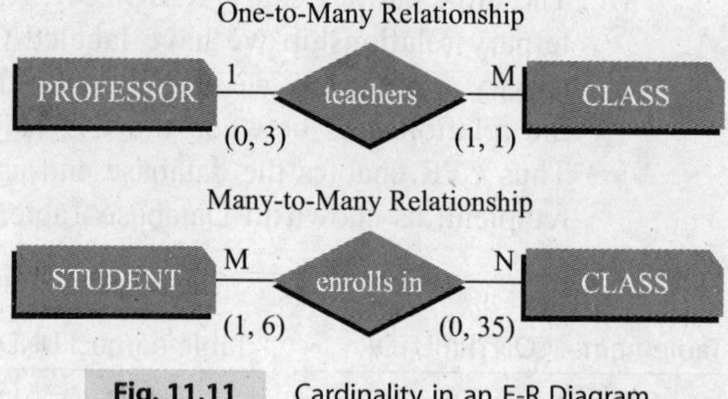

Fig. 11.11 Cardinality in an E-R Diagram

You should realize that the number of associated entities may be variable. For example, a student may enroll in one, two, three, four, five, or six classes. (A student must, however, be enrolled in at least *one* class to be classified as a student.) Similarly, a professor may be assigned to teach one, two, or three classes. (Or, if Tiny College has research professorships, a professor may not teach any classes at all.) Finally, a class may enroll up to thirty-five students, but it is possible for a class to have no currently enrolled students during the first few days of the student registration period.

Figure 11.11 contain all the relevant cardinality information. Note the following features in the PROFESSOR-CLASS relationship:

(*i*) The relationship between PROFESSOR and CLASS is I:M.

(*ii*) The cardinality limits are (0, 3) for PROFESSOR, indicating that a professor may teach a minimum of zero and a maximum of three classes.

(*iii*) The cardinality limits are (1, 1) for the CLASS entity, indicating that the minimum number of professors requires to teach a class is one, as is the maximum number of professors. (Tiny College assigns only one professor to teach a class. If team teaching were an option, the maximum number of professors assigned to teach a class would be something other than one!)

The cardinality constraints in the STUDENT-CLASS relationship may be described as follows:

(*i*) The cardinality limits are (0.35) for the CLASS entity, indicating that a class may contain no students at all or that up to thirty-five students may be enrolled.

(*ii*) The cardinality limits are (1, 6) for the STUDENT entity, indicating that a student must take at least one class but no more than six classes.

8. **Keys:** Tables within the database share common attributes that enable us to link the tables together. Such as attribute is called as a **key**. Keys are central to the use of relational tables. Keys define functional dependencies. That is, other attributes are dependent on the key and can, therefore, be found if the key value is known. A key can be classified according to its characteristics as a super key, a candidate key, a primary key, a secondary key, or a foreign key.

Superkey	An attribute (or combination of attributes) that uniquely identifies each entity in a table.
Candidate Key	A minimal superkey. A superkey that does not contain a subset of attributes that is itself superkey.

Primary Key	A candidate key selected to uniquely identify all other attribute values in any given row. Cannot contain null entries.
Secondary Key	An attribute (or combination of attributes) used strictly for data retrieval purposes.
Foreign Key	An attribute (or combination of attributes) in one table whose values must either match the primary key in another table or be null.

11.5 THE RELATIONAL ALGEBRA

The degree of relational completeness can be defined by the extent to which relational algebra is supported. **Relational algebra** defines the theoretical way of manipulating table contents using the eight relational functions: SELECT, PROJECT, JOIN, INTERSECT, UNION, DIFFERENCE, PRODUCT, and DIVIDE.

☞ To be considered minimally relational, the DBMS must support the key relational functions. SELECT, PROJECT, and JOIN. Very few DBMSs are capable of supporting all eight relational operators.

Although the use of relational algebra functions on existing tables theoretically produces new tables, most of the commercial software implementations of the relational algebra functions yield only listings but not new tables. The use of these relational algebra functions can be illustrated as follows:

11.5.1 Union

UNION combines all rows from two tables. The tables must have the same attribute characteristics (the columns and domains must be identical) to be used in the UNION. When two or more tables share the same columns and domains, they are said to be union **compatible**.

11.5.2 Intersection

INTERSECT produces a listing that contains only the rows that appear in both tables. As was true in the case of UNION, the tables must be union compatible to yield valid results. For example, you cannot use INTERSECT if one of the attributes is numeric and one is character-based.

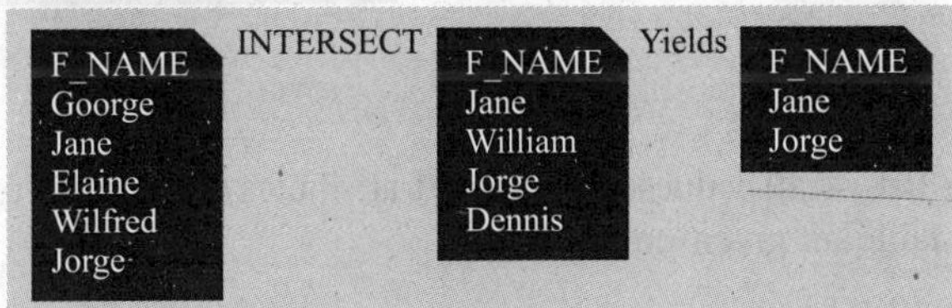

11.5.3 Difference

DIFFERENCE yields all rows in one table that are not found in the other table; that is, it subtracts one table from the other. As was true in the case of UNION, the tables must be *union compatible* to yield valid results.

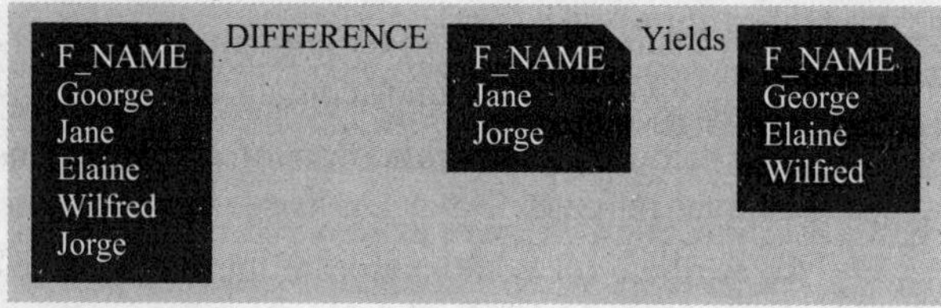

F_NAME
Goorge
Jane
Elaine
Wilfred
Jorge

DIFFERENCE

F_NAME
Jane
Jorge

Yields

F_NAME
George
Elaine
Wilfred

11.5.4 Cartesian Product

PRODUCT produces a list of all possible pairs of rows from two tables. Therefore, if one table has ten rows and the other table has twenty rows, the PRODUCT yields a list composed of $10 \times 20 = 200$ rows.

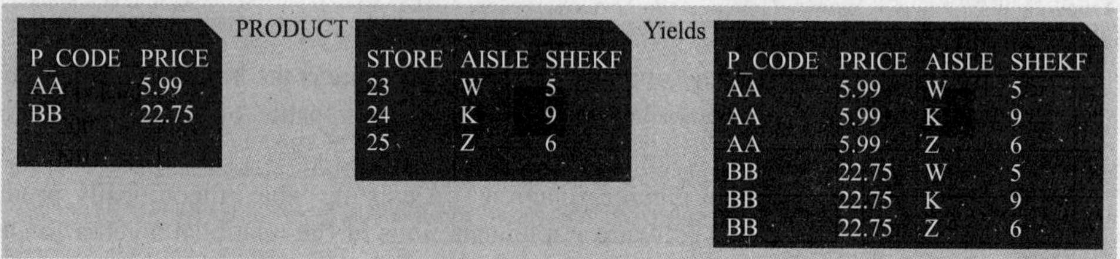

P_CODE	PRICE
AA	5.99
BB	22.75

PRODUCT

STORE	AISLE	SHEKF
23	W	5
24	K	9
25	Z	6

Yields

P_CODE	PRICE	AISLE	SHEKF
AA	5.99	W	5
AA	5.99	K	9
AA	5.99	Z	6
BB	22.75	W	5
BB	22.75	K	9
BB	22.75	Z	6

11.5.5 Select

SELECT yields values for all attributes found in a table. SELECT can be used to list all of the rows values for each attribute or it can yield selected rows' values for each attributes. In other words, SELECT yields a *horizontal subset* of a table.

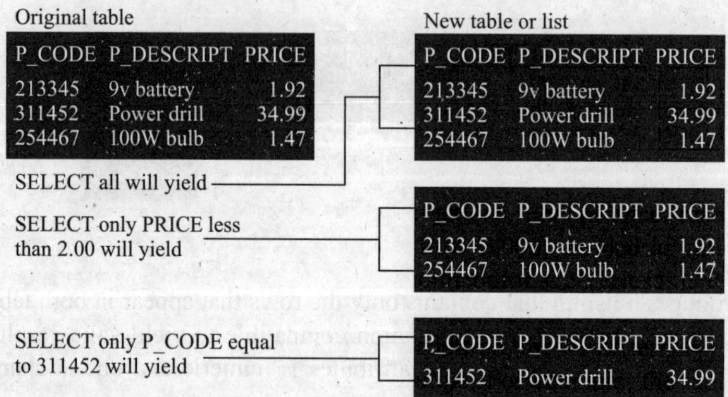

Original table

P_CODE	P_DESCRIPT	PRICE
213345	9v battery	1.92
311452	Power drill	34.99
254467	100W bulb	1.47

New table or list

SELECT all will yield

P_CODE	P_DESCRIPT	PRICE
213345	9v battery	1.92
311452	Power drill	34.99
254467	100W bulb	1.47

SELECT only PRICE less than 2.00 will yield

P_CODE	P_DESCRIPT	PRICE
213345	9v battery	1.92
254467	100W bulb	1.47

SELECT only P_CODE equal to 311452 will yield

P_CODE	P_DESCRIPT	PRICE
311452	Power drill	34.99

11.5.6 Project

PROJECT produces a list of all values for selected attributes. In other words, PROJECT yields a vertical subset of a table as given on next page.

11.5.7 Join

JOIN allows us to combine information from two or more tables. *Join* is the real power behind the relational database, allowing the use of independent tables inked by common attributes. We will use the following CUSTOMER and AGENT tables to illustrate several JOIN versions as given on next page.

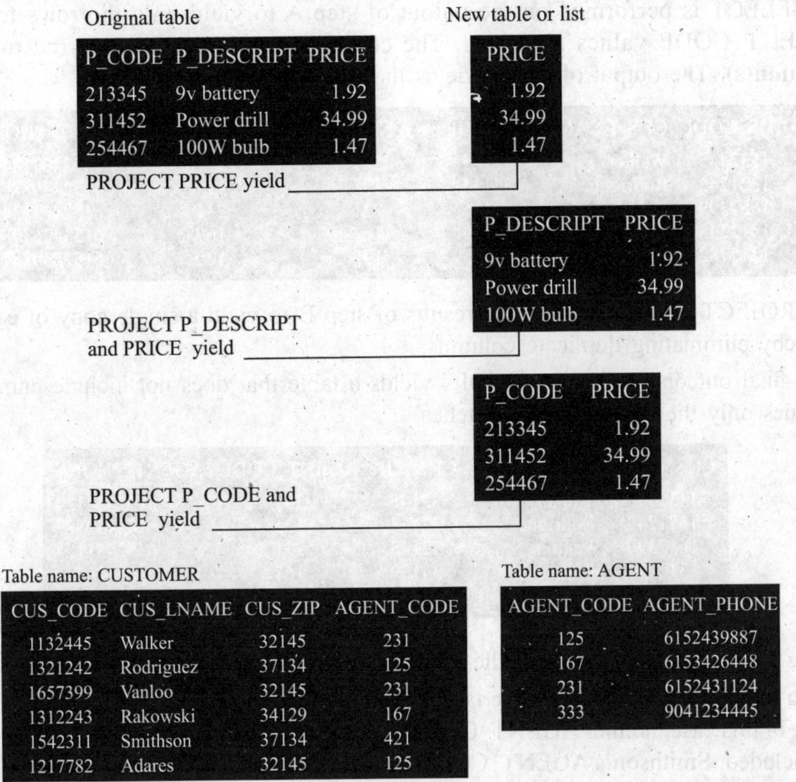

P_CODE	P_DESCRIPT	PRICE
213345	9v battery	1.92
311452	Power drill	34.99
254467	100W bulb	1.47

PRICE
1.92
34.99
1.47

P_DESCRIPT	PRICE
9v battery	1.92
Power drill	34.99
100W bulb	1.47

P_CODE	PRICE
213345	1.92
311452	34.99
254467	1.47

Table name: CUSTOMER

CUS_CODE	CUS_LNAME	CUS_ZIP	AGENT_CODE
1132445	Walker	32145	231
1321242	Rodriguez	37134	125
1657399	Vanloo	32145	231
1312243	Rakowski	34129	167
1542311	Smithson	37134	421
1217782	Adares	32145	125

Table name: AGENT

AGENT_CODE	AGENT_PHONE
125	6152439887
167	6153426448
231	6152431124
333	9041234445

A **natural JOIN** links tables by selecting only the rows with common values in their common attributes(s). A natural join is the result of a three-stage process:

1. A Product of the tables is created, yielding these results.

CUS_CODE	CUS_LNAME	CUS_ZIP	AGENT_CODE	AGENT_CODE	AGENT_PHONE
1132445	Walker	32145	231	125	6152439887
1321242	Rodriguez	37134	125	125	6152439887
1657399	Vanloo	32145	231	125	6152439887
1312243	Rakowski	34129	167	125	6152439887
1542311	Smithson	37134	421	125	6152439887
1217782	Adares	32145	125	125	6152439887
1132445	Walker	32145	231	167	6153426448
1321242	Rodriguez	37134	125	167	6153426448
1657399	Vanloo	32145	231	167	6153426448
1312243	Rakowski	34129	167	167	6153426448
1542311	Smithson	37134	421	167	6153426448
1217782	Adares	32145	125	167	6153426448
1132445	Walker	32145	231	231	6152431124
1321242	Rodriguez	37134	125	231	6152431124
1657399	Vanloo	32145	231	231	6152431124
1312243	Rakowski	34129	167	231	6152431124
1542311	Smithson	37134	421	231	6152431124
1217782	Adares	32145	125	231	6152431124
1132445	Walker	32145	231	333	9041234445
1321242	Rodriguez	37134	125	333	9041234445
1657399	Vanloo	32145	231	333	9041234445
1312243	Rakowski	34129	167	333	9041234445
1542311	Smithson	37134	421	333	9041234445
1217782	Adares	32145	125	333	9041234445

All CUSTOMER rows are JOINed to the 1st row in the AGENT table.

All CUSTOMER rows are JOINed to the 2nd row in the AGENT table.

All CUSTOMER rows are JOINed to the 3rd row in the AGENT table.

All CUSTOMER rows are JOINed to the 4th row in the AGENT table.

2. A SELECT is performed on the output of step A to yield only the rows for which the AGENT_CODE values are equal. The common column(s) are referred to as the **join column(s)**. The output of step 2 yields the following results.

CUS_CODE	CUS_LNAME	CUS_ZIP	AGENT_CODE	AGENT_CODE	AGENT_PHONE
1132445	Walker	32145	231	231	6152431124
1321242	Rodriguez	37134	125	125	6152439887
1657399	Vanloo	32145	231	231	6152431124
1312243	Rakowski	34129	167	167	6153426778
1217782	Adares	32145	125	125	6152439887

3. A PROJECT is performed on the results of step B to yield a single copy of each attribute, thereby eliminating duplicate columns.

The final outcome of a natural JOIN yields a table that does not include unmatched pairs and provides only the copies of the matches.

CUS_CODE	CUS_LNAME	CUS_ZIP	AGENT_CODE	AGENT_PHONE
1132445	Walker	32145	231	6152431124
1321242	Rodriguez	37134	125	6152439887
1657399	Vanloo	32145	231	6152431124
1312243	Rakowski	34129	167	6153426778
1217782	Adares	32145	125	6152439887

Note a few crucial features of the natural JOIN operation.

(*a*) If no match is made between the table rows, the new table does not include the unmatched row. In this case, neither AGENT_CODE 421 nor the customer whose last name is Smithson is included. Smithson's AGENT_CODE 421 does not match any entry in the AGENT table.

(*b*) The column on which we made the JOIN-that is, AGENT_CODE-occurs only once in the new table.

(*c*) If the same AGENT_code were to occur several times in the AGENT table, a customer would be listed for each match. For example, if the AGENT_CODE 167 were to occur three times in the AGENT table, the customer name Rakowski, who is associated with AGENT_CODE, 167, would occur three times in the resulting table. (A good AGENT table cannot, of course, yield such a result because it would contain unique primary key values.

Another form of JOIN, known as equiJOIN, links tables based on an equality condition that compared specified columns of each table. The outcome of the equiJOIN does not eliminate duplicate columns and the condition or criteria to join the tables must be explicitly defined. The equiJOIN takes its name from the equality comparison operator (=) used in the condition. If any other comparison operator is used, the join is called a **theta JOIN**.

In an **outer JOIN** the unmatched pairs would be retained and the valued for the unmatched other table would be left blank or null. For example, the outer JOIN of the CUSTOMER and AGENT tables would yield.

CUS_CODE	CUS_LNAME	CUS_ZIP	AGENT_CODE	AGENT_PHONE
1132445	Walker	32145	231	6152431124
1321242	Rodriguez	37134	125	6152439887
1657399	Vanloo	32145	231	6152431124
1312243	Rakowski	34129	167	6153426778
1542311	Smithson	37134	421	
1217782	Adares	32145	125	6152439887
			333	9041234445

11.5.8 Divide

DIVIDE requires the use of one single-column table and one two- column table. Using the example shown next, note that:

(*a*) Table 1 is 'divided' by Table 2. Tables 1 and 2 both contain the column ODE but do not share LOC.

(*b*) To be included in the resulting Table 3, a value in the unshared column (LOC) must be associated (in the dividing Table 2) with every value in Table 1.

(*c*) The only value associated with both A and B is 5.

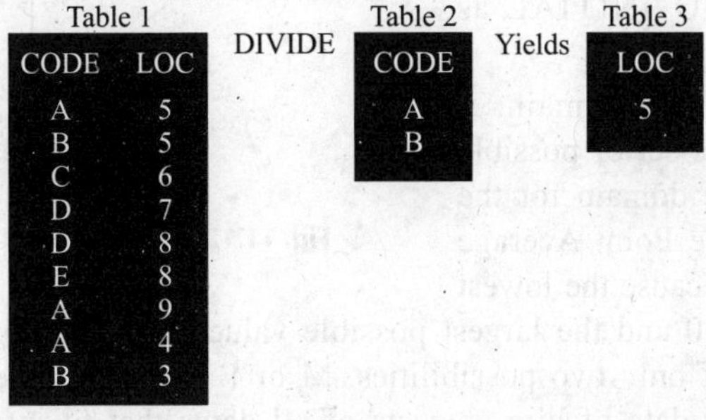

Table 1

CODE	LOC
A	5
B	5
C	6
D	7
D	8
E	8
A	9
A	4
B	3

DIVIDE

Table 2

CODE
A
B

Yields

Table 3

LOC
5

11.6 THE ENTITY RELATIONSHIP (E-R) MODEL

Because the relational model has become dominant in modern database design, we will focus our attention on the layers closest to the conceptual level. Therefore, we will examine the Entity Relationship (E-R) model, a tool that is commonly used to:

- ❐ Translate different views of data among managers, users, and programmers to fit into a common framework.
- ❐ Define data processing and constraint requirements to help us meet the different views.
- ❐ Help implement the database.

The E-R model has been used for several years and is now widely accepted. The E-R approach to conceptual database modeling was first described in 1976 by Peter Chen in a landmark paper entitled. 'The Entity-Relationship Model: Toward a Unified View of Data' Chen's article generated much additional research effort, which yielded the refinements found in the current E-R model.

11.6.1 E-R Model Components

Most of the concepts and definitions used in the E-R model were introduced earlier. For example, entities and attributes are now familiar fare. What is different in this discussion is the graphic depiction of relationships among the entities and the ability, to summarize the wealth of information required to implement a successful design.

The E-R model forms the basis of **E-R diagrams**, which represent the conceptual database as viewed by the end user. These diagrams depict the E-R model's three main components: *entities, attributes, and relationships*. Because an entity represents a real world *object*, the words *entity* and *object* are often used interchangeably. Thus the entities (objects) of Tiny College include students, classes, teachers, classrooms, and so on.

11.6.2 Entities

An entity at the E-R modeling level actually refers to the *entity set* and *not* to a single entity occurrence. *In other words, the word 'entity' in the E-R model corresponds to a* table and not to a row in the relational environment. The E-R model refers to a specific table row as an **entity instance** or **entity occurrence**. An entity is represented by a rectangle containing the entity's name.

11.6.3 Attributes

Attributes are represented by ovals and are connected to the entity with a line. Each oval contains the name of the attribute it represents. For example, the STUDENT entity includes the attributes STU_LNAME, STU_FNAME, and STU_INITIAL as shown in Fig. 11.12.

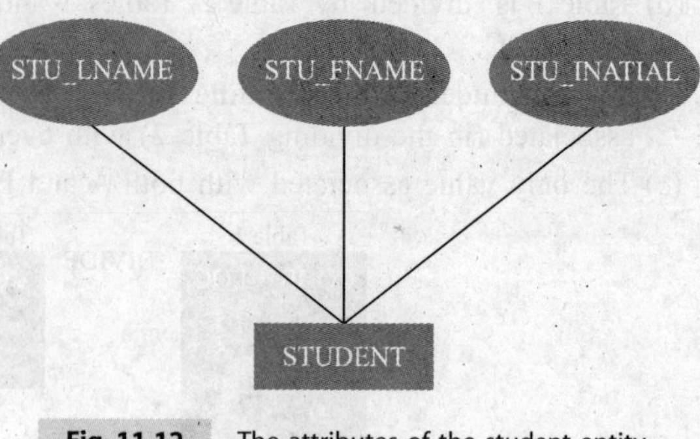

Fig. 11.12 The attributes of the student entity

Attributes also have a domain. A **domain** is the attributes's set of possible values. For example, the domain for the (numeric) attribute Grade Point Average (GPA) is written (0, 4) because the lowest possible (GPA) value is 0 and the largest possible value is 4. The domain for the (character) attribute SEX consists of only two possibilities. M or F (or some other equivalent code). The domain for a company's date of hire consists of all dates that fit into a range (for example, company startup data to current date).

Attributes may share a domain. For instance, a student address and a professor address share the same domain of all possible addresses. In fact, the data dictionary may let a newly declared attribute inherit the characteristics of an existing attribute, if the same attribute name is used. For example, the PROFESSOR and STUDENT entities may each have an attribute named ADDRESS.

Primary keys (key attributes) are underlined in the E-R diagram shown in Fig. 11.13. Key attributes are also underlined in a frequently used table structure shorthand using the format:

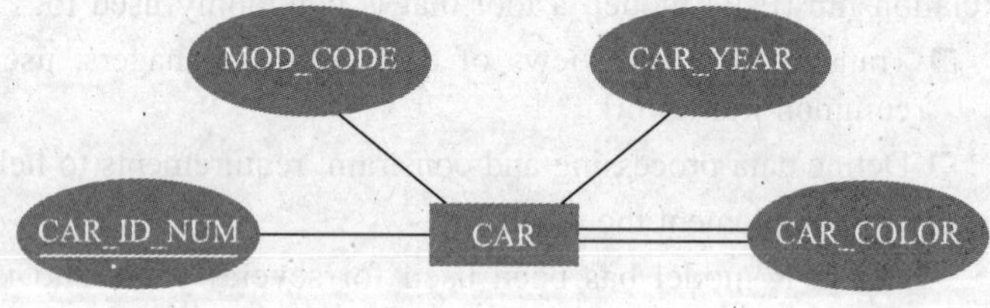

Fig. 11.13 Basic E-R Model Entity Presentation

TABLE NAME (**KEY ATTRIBUTE1**, ATTRIBUTE2, ATTRIBUTE3, ...ATTRIBUTEK)

For example, Fig. 11.13's E-R model may be represented by

CAR (**CAR_ID_NUM**, MOD_CODE, CAR_YEAR, CAR_COLOR)

It is easy to see that the attribute named MOD_CODE is likely to be a foreign key that is used to connect the CAR table to some other table. In this case, the other table probably contains model specific attributes, storing descriptive entities, such as '2-door sports coupe' or '4-door sedan' or 'station wagon'.

Ideally, a primary key is composed of only a single attribute. For example, Database Table 11.2 shows a single-attribute primary key named LASS_MODE. However, it is possible to have **composite keys** that are primary keys composed of more than one attribute. For instance, the Tiny College Database Administrator may decide to identify each CLASS entity instance (occurrence) by using a composite primary key composed of the combination of CRS_CODE and CLASS_SECTION, instead of using CLASS_CODE. Either approach uniquely identifies each entity instance. Given Database Table 11.2's current structure, CLASS_CODE is the primary key and the combination of CRS_CODE and CLASS_SECTION is a proper candidate key. If the

CLASS_CODE attribute is deleted from the CLASS entity, the candidate key (CRS_CODE and CLASS_SECTION) becomes an acceptable composite primary key.

Table 11.2 The class table (entity) components and contents

CLASS_CODE	CRS_CODE	CLASS_SECTION	CLASS_TIME	CLASS_ROOM	PROF_NUM
10012	ACCT-211	1	MWF 8:00-8:50 a.m.	BUS311	105
10013	ACCT-211	2	MWF 9:00-9:50 a.m.	BUS200	105
10014	ACCT-211	3	TTh 2:30-3:45 a.m.	BUS252	342
10015	ACCT-212	1	MWF 10:00-10:50 a.m.	BUS311	301
10016	ACCT-212	2	Th 6:00-8:40 a.m.	BUS252	301
10017	CIS-220	1	MWF 9:00-9:50 a.m.	KLR209	228
10018	CIS-220	2	MWF 9:00-9:50 a.m.	KLR211	114
10019	CIS-220	3	MWF 10:00-10:50 a.m.	KLR209	228

If Database Table 11.2's CLASS_CODE is used as the primary key, the CLASS entity may be represented in shorthand form by:

CLASS (**CLASS_CODE**, CRS_CODE, CLASS_SECTION, CLASS_TIME, CLASS-ROOM, PROF_NUM)

On the other hand, if CLASS_CODE is deleted and the composite primary key is the combination of CRS_CODE and CLASS_SECTION the CLASS entity may be represented by:

CLASS (**CRS_CODE CLASS_SECTION**, CLASS_TIME, CLASS_ROOM, PROF_NUM)

Note that *both* key attributes are underlined in this entity notation.

Attributes are classified, as simple or composite. A **composite attribute**, not to be confused with a composite key, is an attribute that can be further subdivided to yield additional attributes. For example, the attribute ADDRESS can be subdivided into street, city, state, and ZIP code. Similarly, the attribute PHONE_NUMBER can be subdivided into area code and exchange number. A **simple attribute** cannot be subdivided. For example, age, sex, and marital status would be classified as simple attributes. To facilitate detailed queries, it is often appropriate to change composite attributes into a series of simple attributes.

A **single-valued attribute** can have only a single value. For example, a person can have only one social security number, and a manufactured part can have only one serial number. Keep in mind that a single-valued attribute is not necessarily a simple attribute. For instance, the part's serial number SE-08-02-189935 is single-valued, but it is a composite attribute because it can be subdivided into the region in which the part was produced. SE, the plant within that region, 08, the shift, within the plant, 02 and the part number, 189935.

Multivalued attributes can have many values. For instance, a person may have several college degrees, or a household may have several different phones, each with its own number. Similarly, a car's color may be subdivided into colors of roof, body, and trim. In an E-R model the multivalued attributes are shown by a double line connecting the attribute to the entity. The E-R diagram in Fig. 11.13 contains all the components we have introduced thus far. As you examine Fig. 11.13, note that the CAR_ID_NUM is the primary key, and CAR_COLOR is a multivalued attribute of the CAR entity. (We will assume that each car is identified by a unique registration number or CAR_ID_NUM.

Although the conceptual model can handle M:N relationships and multivalued attributes, you should not implement them in the relational DBMS. So, if multivalued attributes exist, the designer must decide on one of two possible courses of action:

1. Within the original entity, create several new attributes. one for each of the original multivalued attributes's components. For example, we can split the CAR entity's attribute CAR_COLOR to create the new attributes, CAR_TOP COLOR, CAR_BODYCOLOR, and CAR_TRIMCOLOR shown in Fig. 11.14 and assign them to the CAR entity.

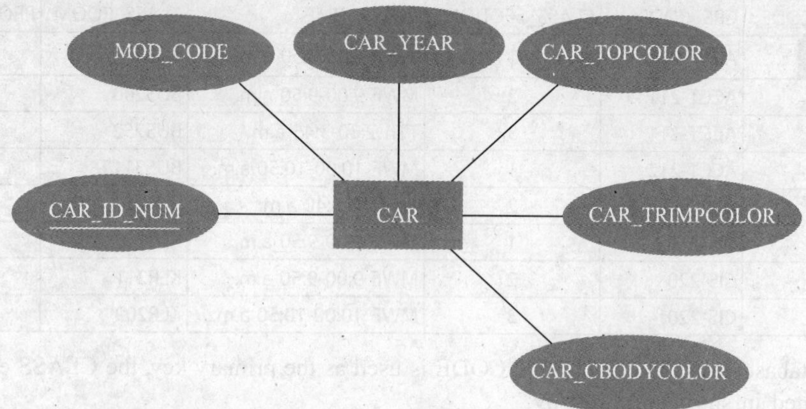

Fig. 11.14 Splitting the multivalued attribute into new attributes

2. Create a new entity composed of the original multivalued attribute's components (See Fig. 11.15).

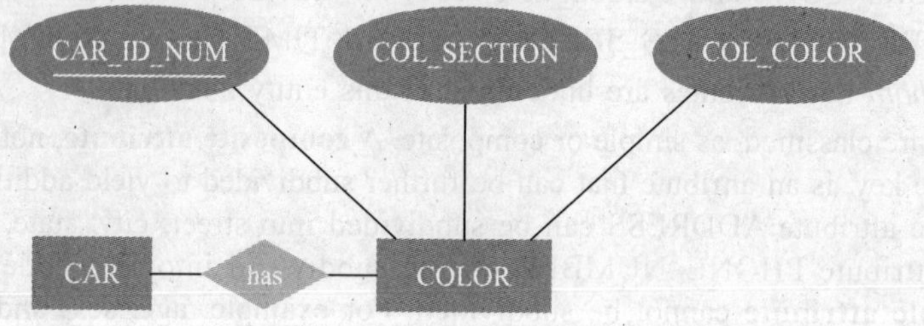

Fig. 11.15 A new entity set composed of a multivalued attribute's components

The new (independent) COLOR entity is then related to the original CAR entity in a 1:M relationship. Note that such a change allows the designer to define color for different sections of the car:

Section	Color
Top	White
Body	Blue
Trim	Green
Interior	Blue

Using this approach, we even get a fringe benefit: We are now able to assign as many colors as necessary, without having to change the table structure.

Finally, an attribute may be classified as a derived attribute. A **derived attribute** need not be physically stored within the database; instead, it is derived by using an algorithm. For example, a person's AGE attribute can be derived by subtracting the date of birth (DOB) from the current date. Similarly, the total cost of an order can be derived by multiplying the quantity ordered by the unit price. Or the estimated average speed can be derived by dividing trip distance by the time spent en route. A derived attribute is indicated by a dotted line connecting the attribute and the entity (See Fig. 11.16).

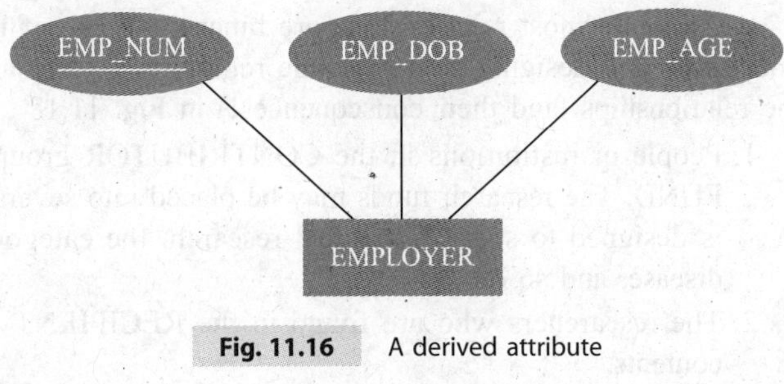

Fig. 11.16 A derived attribute

The decision to use derived attributes depends on processing requirements and the constraints placed on a particular application. The designer should be able to balance the design in accordance with such constraints.

11.6.4 Relationships

A **relationship** is an association between entities. Each relationship is identified so that its name is descriptive of the relationship. Ideally, the relationship name is an active verb, but passive verbs are acceptable, too. Verbs such as takes, eaches, and employs make good relationship names. For example, a student takes a class, professor teaches a class, a department employs a professor, and so on.

Relationships are represented by diamond-shaped symbols. Figure 11.17 repicts a relationship between two entities (also known as the **participants** in the relationship) named PROFESSOR and CLASS, respectively. Lines are used to connect the entities to one another, passing through the diamond-shaped relationship symbol.

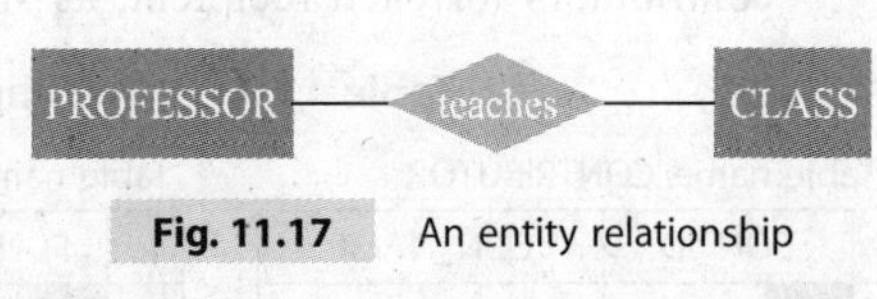

Fig. 11.17 An entity relationship

A relationship's **degree** indicates the number of associated entities or participants. A **unary relationship** exists when an association is maintained with a single entity. A **binary relationship** exists when two entities are associated. A **ternary relationship** exists when three entities are associated. Although higher degrees exist, they are rare and are not specifically named. (For example, an association of four entities is simply described as a *four-entity relationship*). We have shown a few sample relationships in Fig. 11.18.

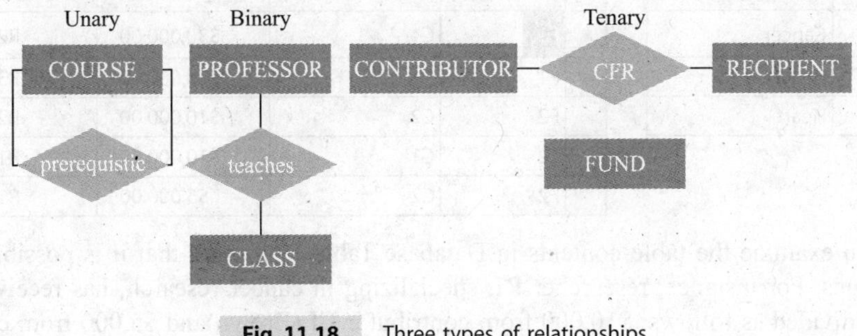

Fig. 11.18 Three types of relationships

In the case of the unary relationship shown in Fig. 11.18, a course within the COURSE entity is a prerequisite for another course *within* the entity. In this case, the existence of a course prerequisite means that a COURSE requires a COURSE, *i.e.*, COURSE has a relationship with itself. Such a relationship is known as a **recursive relationship**.

Binary relationships are most common. In fact, to simplify the conceptual design, most higher-order (ternary and higher) relationships are decomposed into appropriate equivalent binary relationships whenever possible.

Although most relationships are binary, the use of ternary and higher-order relationships does allow the designer some latitude regarding the semantic of a problem. For example, note the relationships (and their consequences!) in Fig. 11.18.

1. People or institutions in the CONTRIBUTOR group donate money to a special research FUND. The research funds may be placed into several categories. For example, if the fund is designed to support medical research, the categories may include cancer, AIDS, heart disease, and so on.
2. The researchers who are found in the RECIPIENT entity are funded through the FUND contents.
3. The relationships are all classified as M:N. For example, contributors can make donations to many funds. A fund can have many donors. A fund may support many researchers who become the FUND recipients, and a researcher may draw support from many funds.
4. The three entities CONTRIBUTOR, RECIPIENT, and FUND are related through the ternary relationship we have labeled CFR. Because a single verb cannot express a ternary relationship, we elected to use the acronym CFR to indicate Table 11.3. The implementation of a ternary relationship its role in defining the relationships between the CONTRIBUTOR, the **F**und, and the **R**ecipient. Thus CFR enables the database end user to identify the fund's contributors for each recipient, as shown in Database Table 11.3.

Table 11.3 The implementation of a ternary relationship

Table name: CONTRIBUTOR

CON_ID	CON_NAME
C1	Brown
C2	Igless
C3	Smith

Table name: FUND

FUND_ID	FUND_NAME	CON_ID	FUND_AMOUNT
F1	Heart	C1	$50,000.00
F1	Heart	C2	$10,000.00
F2	Cancer	C1	$10,000.00
F2	Cancer	C2	$5,000.00
F2	Cancer	C3	$10,000.00

Table name: RECIPIENT

REC_ID	REC_TYPE
R1	Cancer
R2	Heart
R3	Heart

Table name: CFR

FUND_ID	CON_ID	CFR_AMOUNT	REC-ID
F1	C1	$30,000.00	R2
F1	C1	$20,000.00	R3
F2	C2	$10,000.00	R2
F2	C1	$10,000.00	R1
F2	C2	$5,000.00	R1

As you examine the table contents in Database Table 12.3, note that it is possible to track all transactions. For instance, researcher RI, specializing in cancer research, has received a total of $15,000, divided as follows: $10,000 from contributor CI (Brown)and $5,000 from contributor C2 (Iglesas). Researcher R2 specializing in heart research, received $40,000—$30,000 of which came from contributor CI and $10,000 of which came from contributor C2. In addition, the CFR (ternary) relationship allows us to relate the available funds to the contributors. For example, the table contents indicate that contributor CI donated $50,000 to heart research—$30,0000 of which was received by researcher R2, while the remaining $20,000 was received by researcher R3.

The ternary relationship described here has an effect on the type and extent of the data available to a database query. For example, if 500 people make donations to the heart portion of the fund and we do not use a ternary relationship, there is no way to identify the specific source of those funds when the recipient receives a heart grant.

Therefore, it is necessary to keep track of specific contributors to the fund and the recipients of those funds, the ternary relationship is necessary. As the preceding example demonstrates, you should keep in mind that a ternary relationship is not always equivalent to several 1:M relationships. Consequently, the designer must consider the semantics of the problem that is being addressed; desirable simplification may not match end user needs!

11.6.5 Connectivity

Entity relationships may be classified as one-to-one, one-to-many, and many-to-many. The term **connectivity** is used to describe the relationship classification. The E-R diagrams indicate the relationship's connectivity by placing a I, M, or N near the related entities. Figure 11.19 illustrates the use of connectivity.

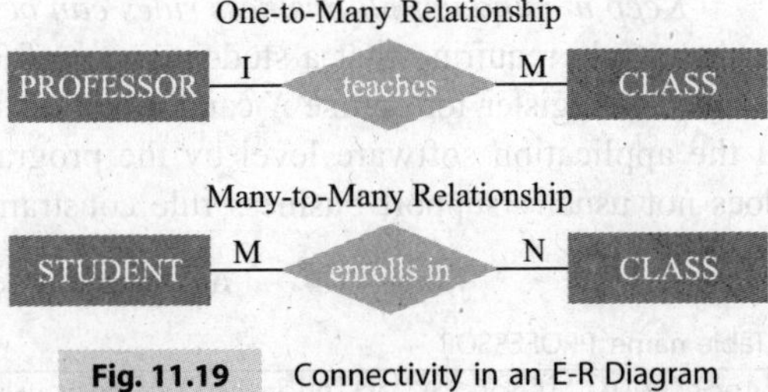

Fig. 11.19 Connectivity in an E-R Diagram

11.6.6 Cardinality

Cardinality expresses the specific number of entity occurrences associated with one occurrence of the related entity. The actual number of associated entities usually is a function of an organization's policy. For example, the Tiny College administration limits the professor to teaching a maximum of three classes per semester. Therefore, the cardinality rule governing the PROFESSOR-CLASS association is expressed as 'One professor teaches up to three classes per semester'. Similarly, the Tiny College administration may decide to limit a student to a maximum of six classes per semester, and class size may be limited to thirty-five students. The cardinality is indicated by placing the appropriate numbers beside the entities, as shown in Fig. 11.20.

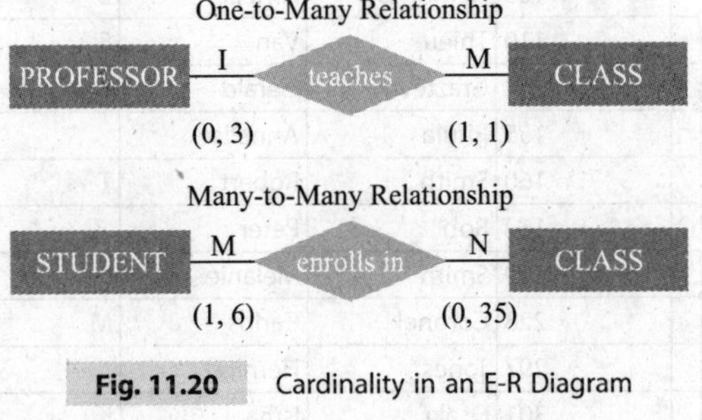

Fig. 11.20 Cardinality in an E-R Diagram

You should realize that the number of associated entities may be variable. For example, a student may enroll in one, two, three, four, five or six classes. (A student must, however, be enrolled in at least one class to be classified as a student). Similarly, a professor may be assigned to teach one, two, or three classes. (Or, if Tiny College has research professorships, a professor may not teach any classes at all). Finally, a class may enroll up to thirty-five students, but it is possible for a class to have no currently enrolled students during the first few days of the student registration period.

The E-R diagram segments in Fig. 11.20 contain all the relevant cardinality information. Note the following features in the PROFESSOR-CLASS relationship:

1. The relationship between PROFESSOR and class is 1:M.
2. The cardinality limits are (0, 3) for PROFESSOR, indicating that a professor may teach a minimum of zero and a maximum of three classes.
3. The cardinality limits are (1, 1) for the CLASS entity, indicating that the minimum number of professors required to teach a class is one, as is the maximum number of professors. (Tiny College assigns only one professor to teach a class. If team teaching were an option, the maximum number of professors assigned to teach a class would be something other than one!)

The cardinality constraints in the STUDENT-CLASS relationship may be described as follows:

1. The cardinality limits are (0, 35) for the CLASS entity, indicating that a class may contain no students at all or that up to thirty-five students may be enrolled.
2. The cardinality limits are (1, 6) for the STUDENT entity, indicating that a student must take at least one class but no more than six classes.

Keep in mind not all business rules can be represented in an E-R diagram. For example, the business rule requiring that a student successfully pass sixty hours of course work before being allowed to register for course *X* cannot be illustrated. Instead, such a rule would be implemented at the application software level by the programmers or program generators. DBMS software does not usually support business rule constraints directly.

Table 11.4 An illustration of the cardinalities (1, 1) and (1, N)

Table name: PROFESSOR

PORF_NUM	PROF_LNAME	PROF_FNAME	PROF_INITIAL	DEPT_CODE	PROF_OFFICE	PROF_EXTENSION
103	Donelly	Ronald	O	HIST	ACK220	6783
104	Yukon	Preston	D	ENG	ACK402E	5561
105	Heffington	Arnelle	B	ACCT	BUS2290	8665
110	Thieu	Van	S	CHEM	PYR200	3412
114	Graztevshi	Gerald	B	CIS	KLR302	4436
155	Ritula	Annelise		MATH	PYR245	4440
160	Smith	Robert	T	ENG	MLL108	2248
162	Rob	Peter		CIS	KLR203E	2359
209	Smith	Melanie	K	CIS	KLR225	3421
228	Coronel	Carlos	M	CIS	KLR203E	2359
297	Jones	Hernine		CHEM	PYR356	1145
301	Osaki	Ismael	K	ACCT	BUS244	4683
335	Okomoto	Ronald	F	ENG	MILL108	3997
342	Smith	Robert	A	ACCT	BUS345	5514
387	Smithson	James	D	ACCT	BUS2290	8665

Table name: CLASS

CLASS_CODE	CRS_CODE	CLASS_SECTION	CLASS_TIME	CLASS_ROOM	PROF_NUM
10012	ACCT-211	1	MWF 8:00-8:50 a.m.	BUS311	105
10013	ACCT-211	2	MWF 9:00-9:50 a.m.	BUS200	105
10014	ACCT-211	3	TTh 2:30-3:45 p.m.	BUS252	342
10015	ACCT-212	1	MWF 10:00-10:50 a.m.	BUS311	301
10016	ACCT-212	2	Th 6:00-8:40 a.m.	BUS252	301
10017	CIS-220	1	MWF 9:00-9:50 a.m.	KLR209	228
10018	CIS-220	2	MWF 9:00-9:50 a.m.	KLR211	114
10019	CIS-220	3	MWF 10:00-10:50 a.m.	KLR209	228
10020	CIS-420	1	W 6:00-8:40 p.m.	KLR209	162
10021	QM-261	1	MWF 8:00-8:50 a.m.	KLR200	114
10022	QM-261	2	TTh 1:00-2:15 p.m.	KRL200	114
10023	QM-362	1	MWF 11:00-11:50 a.m.	KLR200	162
10024	QM-362	1	TTh 2:30-3:45 p.m.	KLR200	162

11.6.7 Existence Dependency

If an entity's existence depends on the existence of one or more entities, it is said to be **existence-dependent**. For example, if you examine Database Table 11.5's 1:M relationship 'COURSE generates CLASS', you see that the CLASS table's foreign key (CRS_CODE) references the COURSE table. Clearly, if the COURSE does not exist, having the CLASS table's foreign key (CRS_CODE) reference a nonexisting table will generate referential integrity violations. Similarly, if a CLASS must be taught by a PROFESSOR, CLASS is existence-dependent on PROFESSOR in the 1:M relationship 'PROFESSOR' teaches CLASS'. (One would assume that a class would be cancelled if there were no professor to teach it).

Table 11.5 An existence-dependent relationship between course and class

Table name: COURSE

CRS_CODE	DEPT_CODE	CRS_DESCRIPTION	CRS_CREDIT
ACCT-211	ACCT	Accounting I	3
ACCT-212	ACCT	Accounting II	3
ACCT-311	ACCT	Managerial Accounting	3
ART-210	ART	Intro to Art	3
ART-340	ART	Jewellery Design	3
BIOL-120	BIOL	Intro to Biology	4
BIOL-220	BIOL	Biology and the Environment	4
CIS-220	CIS	Intro to Microcomputing	3
CIS-320	CIS	Spreadsheet Applications	3
CIS-370	CIS	Intro to Systems Analysis	3
CIS-420	CIS	Database Design and Implementation	4
ECON-240	ECON/FIN	Microeconomics	3
ECON-250	ECON/FIN	Macroeconomics	3
ENG-210	ENG	Writing	3
FIN-220	ENG	Literature	3
FIN-300	ECON/FIN	Money and Banking	3

As you examine the data in Database Table 11.5, keep in mind that existence dependency means that *the order in which the tables are created and loaded is very important*. Because CLASS is existence-dependent on COURSE, the COURSE table must be created *before* the CLASS table. After all, it would not be acceptable to have the CLASS table's foreign key reference a COURSE table that does not yet exist. In some DBMSes, this sequencing problem does not crop up until the data are loaded into the tables.

11.6.8 Relationship Participation

A participating entity in a relationship is either optional or mandatory. The participation is optional if one entity occurrence does not require a corresponding entity occurrence in a particular relationship. For example, suppose that Tiny College employs some professors who conduct research without teaching classes. If we examine the relationship PROFESSOR teaches CLASS, it is quite possible for PROFESSOR not to teach a CLASS. Therefore, CLASS is *optional* to PROFESSOR. On the other hand, a CLASS must be taught by a PROFESSOR. Therefore, PROFESSOR is *mandatory* to CLASS.

An optional entity is shown by drawing a small circle (o) on the side of the optional entity, as shown in Fig. 11.21.

Note also the cardinality rules displayed in Fig. 11.21: A PROFESSOR may teach no classes at all, or may teach as many as three classes. On the other hand, a class a taught by one (and only one) professor.

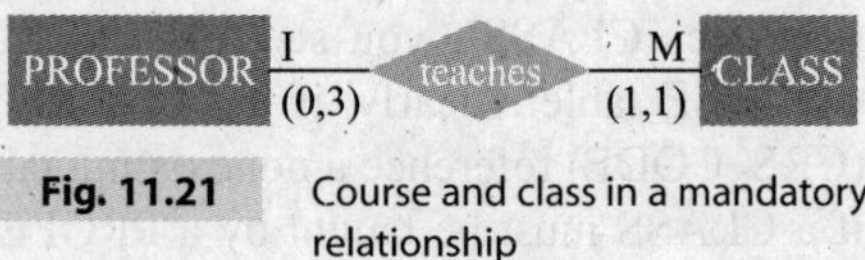

Fig. 11.21 Course and class in a mandatory relationship

Failure to understand the distinction between *mandatory* and *optional* participation in relationships may yield designs in which awkward (and unnecessary) temporary entities must be created just to accommodate the creation of required entities. Therefore, it is important to understand the mandatory and optional concepts clearly.

It is also important to understand that the semantics of a problem may determine the type of participation in a relationship. For example, suppose that Tiny College offers several *courses*; each course has several classes. Note again the distinction between *class* and *course* in this discussion: A CLASS constitutes a specific offering (or section) of a COURSE. Analysing the CLASS entity's contribution to the 'COURSE generates CLASS' relationship, it is easy to see that CLASS is existence-dependent on COURSE because a course's section (CLASS) cannot exist without that course. Therefore, we conclude that the COURSE entity is *mandatory* in the relationship. But we may write two scenarios for the COURSE entity shown in Figs. 11.22 and 11.23. The different scenarios are a function of the semantics of the problem that is, they depend on the business rules that govern the relationship.

Fig. 11.22 Class is optional to course

1. *CLASS is optional*: It is possible for the department to create the entity COURSE first and then create the CLASS entity after making the teaching assignments. In the real world such a scenario is likely; there may be courses for which sections (classes) have not yet been defined. In fact, some courses are taught only once a year and do not generate classes each semester.
2. *CLASS is mandatory*: This condition is created by the constraint that is imposed by the semantics of the statement, 'Each COURSE has one or more CLASSes'. In E-R terms, each COURSE in the 'generates' relationship must have at least one CLASS. Therefore, a CLASS must be created as the COURSE is created, in order to comply with the semantics of the problem.

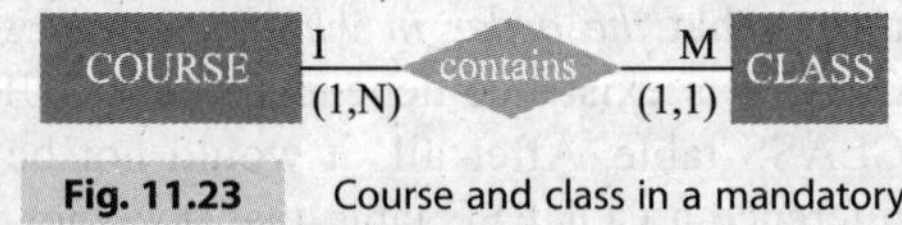

Fig. 11.23 Course and class in a mandatory relationship

Keep in mind the practical aspects of the scenario presented in Fig. 11.23. The system will not accept a course that is not associated with at least one section. Is such a rigid environment desirable from an operational point of view? For example, when we create a new COURSE, the database first updates the COURSE table, thereby inserting a COURSE entity that does not yet have a CLASS associated with it. Naturally, the problems seems to be solved when CLASS entities are inserted into the corresponding CLASS table. However, given the semantics of the mandatory relationship, the system will be in temporary violation of the business rule constraint. A COURSE deletion similarly causes a temporary data integrity problem. For practical purposes, it would be desirable to classify the CLASS as optional in order to produce a more flexible design.

As you examine these scenarios, keep the role of the DBMS in mind. To maintain data integrity, the DBMS must assure that the 'many' side (CLASS) is associated with a COURSE through the foreign key rules. The burden of maintaining data integrity is assigned to the *many* side rather than to the *one* side. The DBMS handles the data integrity constraints imposed by the business rules. (A few DBMS implementations, such as Microsoft's SQL Server and ORACLE, allow the definition of business rules at the DBMS levels.)

Remember that the terms *mandatory* and *optional* refer to the *participation* of an entity within the context of a *relationship* with another entity. The term *optional* refers to a condition in which the other participating entity may or may not be associated with occurrences of the optional entity in the relationship. In contrast, the term **mandatory** refers to a condition in which one participating entity must be associated with one or more occurrences of the other participating entity in the relationship.

11.6.9 Weak Entities

A **week entity** is one that.

1. Is existence-dependent; that is, it cannot exist without the entity with which it has a relationship.
2. Has a primary key that is partially or totally derived from the parent entity in the relationship.

The existence of a weak entity is indicated by a double rectangle, as shown in Fig. 11.24.

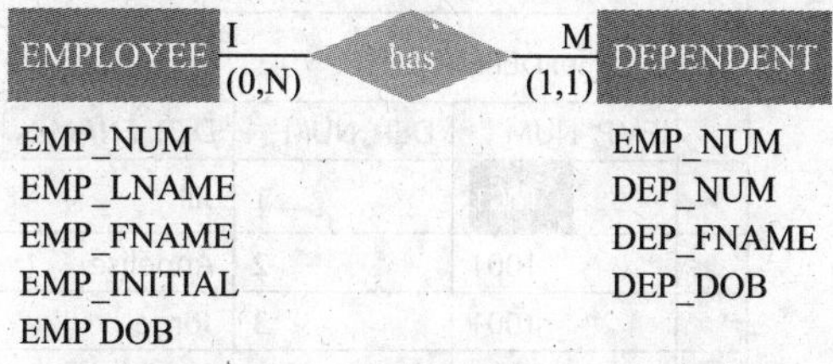

Fig. 11.24 A weak entity in an E-R diagram

For example, a company insurance policy may insure an employee and his/her dependents. For the purpose of describing an insurance policy, an EMPLOYEE may or may not have a DEPENDENT, but the DEPENDENT must be associated with an EMPLOYEE. Moreover, the DEPENDENT cannot exist without the EMPLOYEE; that is, you cannot get insurance coverage at the XYZ Corporation as a *dependent* unless you happen to be a dependent of an employee working for the XYZ Corporation! In other words, DEPENDENT is the weak entity in the relationship 'EMPLOYEE has DEPENDENT'.

The weak entity inherits all or part of its primary key from its strong counterpart. For example, at least part of the DEPENDENT entity's key will be inherited from the EMPLOYEE entity.

EMPLOYEE (EMP_NUM, EMP_LNAME, EMP_FNAME, EMP_INITIAL, EMP_DOB)

DEPENDENT (EMP_NUM, DEP_NUM, DEP_FNAME, DEP_DOB)

Database Table 11.6 illustrates the relationship between the weak entity (DEPENDENT) and its parent or strong counterpart (EMPLOYEE). Note that the DEPENDENT's primary key is composed of two attributes: EMP_NUM and DEP_NUM and that EMP_NUM was inherited from EMPLOYEE. With the help of this relationship, you can determine that Jeanine J. Callifante claims three dependent. Jill, Annelise, and Jorge; William K. Smithson claims to dependents; and Herman H. Washington claims two dependents. Robert and Suzanne.

Keep in mind that *it is the database designer who usually determines whether or* not an entity can be described as weak. For example, an examination of the relationship between COURSE and CLASS any cause you to conclude that CLASS is a weak entity to COURSE. After all, if you examine Database Table 11.5's CLASS rows, it is clear that a CLASS cannot exist without a COURSE, so there is existence dependency. However, note that the CLASS table's primary key is CLASS_CODE, which is not derived from the COURSE *parent entity*. That is, we may represent CLASS by:

CLASS (**CLASS_CODE**, CRS_CODE, CLASS_SECTION, CLASS_TIME, CLASS_ROOM, PROF_NUM)

The second requirements has not been met and, therefore, the CLASS entity may not be classified as weak by definition. On the other hand, if the CLASS entity's primary key has been defined as a composite key, composed of the combination CRS_CODE and CLASS_SECTION, we may represent CLASS by:

CLASS (**CRS_CODE, CLASS_SECTION**, CLASS_TIME, CLASS_ROOM, PROF_NUM)

Table 11.6 An illustration of the weak relationship between dependent and employee

Table name: EMPLOYEE

	EMP_NUM	EMP_LNAME	EMP_FNAME	EMP_INITIAL	EMP_DOB
▸	1001	Callifante	Jeanine	J	3/21/61
	1002	Smithson	William	K	11/23/70
	1003	Washington	Herman	H	8/15/68

Table name: DEPENDENT

	EMP_NUM	DEP_NUM	DEP_FNAME	EMP_DOB
▸	1001	1	Jill	6/21/84
	1001	2	Annelise	12/5/87
	1001	3	Jorge	9/30/92
	1003	1	Robert	11/17/83
	1003	2	Suzanne	10/15/94

In this case, the CLASS primary key is partially derived from COURSE, because the CRS_CODE is the COURSE's primary key. Given this decision, CLASS is a weak entity by definition. In any case, CLASS is always existence-dependent on COURSE, *whether or not it is defined to be weak!*.

11.6.10 Recursive Entities

A **recursive entity** is one in which a relationship can exist between occurrences of the same entity set. (Naturally, such a condition is found within a unary relationship).

For example, a 1:M unary relationship may be expressed by 'an EMPLOYEE may manage many EMPLOYEEs and each EMPLOYEE is managed by one EMPLOYEE'. And, as long as polygamy is not legal, a 1:1 unary relationship may be expressed by 'an EMPLOYEE may be married to one and only one other EMPLOYEE'. Finally, the M:N unary relationship may be expressed by 'a COURSE may be a prerequisite to many other COURSES and each COURSE may have many other COURSEs as prerequisites'. These relationships are shown in Fig. 11.25.

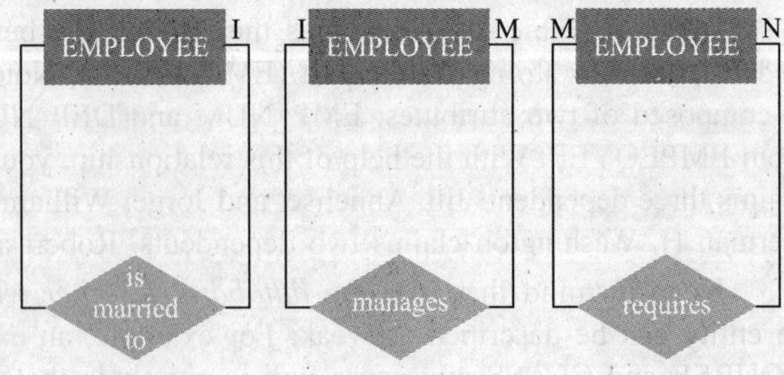

Fig. 11.25 An E–R representation of recursive relationships

The 1:1 relationship shown in Fig. 11.25 can be implemented in the single table shown in Database Table 11.7. Note that we can determine that James Ramirez is married to Louise Ramirez who is married to James Ramirez. And Anne Jones is married to Anton Shapiro, who is married to Anne Jones.

Table 11.7 The 1:1 Recursive relationship 'EMPLOYEE is married to EMPLOYEE'.

EMP_NUM	EMP_LNAME	EMP_FNAME	EMP_SPUSE
345	Ramiez	James	347
346	Jones	Anne	349
347	Ramiez	Louise	345
348	Delaney	Robert	
349	Shapiro	Anton	346

Unary relationship are common in manufacturing industries. For example, Database Table 11.8 illustrates that a rotor assembly (C-130) is composed of many parts but each part is used to create only one rotor assembly. Database Table 11.8 indicates that a rotor assembly is composed of four 2.5 cm. washers, two cotter pins, one 2.5 cm, steel shank, four 10.25 cm. rotor blades, and two 2.5 cm. hex nuts. The relationship implemented in Database Table 11.8, thus enables us to track each part within each rotor assembly we manufacture.

Table 11.8 Another unary relationship: PART contains PART

PART_CODE	PART_DESCRIPTION	PART_IN_STOCK	PART_UNITS_NEEDED	PART_OF_PART
AA216	2.5 cm, washer, 1.0 mm, rim	432	4	C-130
AB-121	Cotter pin, copper	1034	2	C-130
C-130	Rotor assembly	36		
E129	2.5 cm, steel shank	128	1	C-130
X10	10.25 cm, rotor blade	345	4	C-130
X34AW	2.5 cm, hex nut	879	2	C-130

If a part can be used to assemble several different kinds of other parts and is itself composed of many parts, two tables are required to implement the 'PART contains PART' relationship. Database Table 11.9 illustrates such an environment. Part tacking has become increasingly important as managers become more aware of the legal ramifications of producing more complex output. In fact, in many industries, especially those involving aviation, maintaining full parts tracking is mandatory.

The M:N recursive relationships might be more familiar in a school environment. For instance, note how the M:N 'COURSE requires COURSE' relationship illustrated in Fig. 11.25 is implemented in Database Table 11.10. In this Example, MATH-243 is aprerequisite to QM-261 and QM-362, while QM-362 requires both MATH-243 and QM-261 as prerequisites.

Table 11.9 Implementation of the M:N recursive PART/PART relationship

Table name: COMPONENT

COMP_CODE	PART_CODE	COMP_PARTS_NEEDED
C-130	E129	1
C-130	X10	4
C-130	AA21-6	4
C-130	AB-121	2
C-130	X34AW	2
C-131 A2	E129	1
C-131 A2	X10	1
C-131 A2	X34AW	2

Table name: PART

	PART_CODE	PART_DESCRIPTION	PART_IN_STOCK
▸	AA-216	2.5 cm, washer, 1.0 mm. rim	432
	AB-121	Cotter pin, copper	1034
	C-130	Rotor assembly	36
	E129	2.5 cm. steel shank	128
	X10	10.25 cm. rotor blade	345
	X34AW	2.5 cm. hex nut	879

Table 11.10 Implementation of the M:N COURSE requires course recursive relationship

Table name: COURSE

	CRS_CODE	DEPT_CODE	CRS_DESCRIPTION	CRS_CREDIT
▸	ACCT-211	ACCT	Accounting I	3
	ACCT-212	ACCT	Accounting II	3
	CIS-220	CIS	Intro. to Microcomputing	3
	CIS-420	CIS	Database Design and Implementation	4
	MATH-243	MATCH	Mathematics for managers	3
	QM-261	CIS	Intro. to Statistics	3
	QM-362	CIS	Statistical Applications	4

Table name: PREREQ

	CRS_CODE	PRE_TAKE
▸	QM-261	MATH-243
	QM-261	MATH-243
	QM-362	QM-261
	CIS-420	CIS-220

Finally, the 1:M recursive relationship 'Employee manages EMPLOYEE', shown in Fig. 11.25, is implemented in Database Table 11.11.

Table 11.11 Implementation of the I:M EMPLOYEE manages employee recursive relationship

	EMP_CODE	EMP_LNAME	EMP_MANAGER
▸	101	Waddell	102
	102	Orincona	
	103	Jones	102
	104	Reballoh	102
	105	Robertson	102
	106	Deltona	102

11.6.11 Composite Entities

In the original E-R model described by Chen, relationships do not contain attributes. The relational model requires the use of 1:M relationships. If M:N relationships are encountered, we must create a bridge between the entities that display such relationships. The **bridge** is an entity composed of the primary keys of each of the entities to be connected. The bridge entity is known as a **composite entity**.

As you examine Database Table 11.12, note that the composite ENROLL entity is existence dependent on the other two entities; its composition is based on the primary keys of the entities that are connected by the composite entity. The composite entity may also contain additional attributes that play no role in the connective process. For example, although the entity must be composed of at least the STUDENT and CLASS primary keys, it may also include such additional attributes as student grades, absences, and other data uniquely identified by the student's performance in a specific class.

Finally, keep in mind that the ENROLL table's key (CLASS_CODE and STU_NUM) is entirely composed of the primary keys of the CLASS and STUDENT tables. Therefore, no null entries are possible in the ENROLL table's key attributes.

Table 11.12 Converting the M:N relationship into two 1:M relationships

Table name: STUDENT

	STU_NUM	STU_LNAME
▸	324552	Bowser
	324557	Smithson

Table name: ENROLL

	CLASS_CODE	STU_NUM	ENROLL_GRADE
▸	10014	321452	C
	10014	324257	B
	10018	321452	A
	10018	324257	B
	10021	321252	C
	10021	324257	C

Table name: CLASS

	CLASS_CODE	CRS_CODE	CLASS_SECTION	CLASS_TIME	CLASS_ROMM	PROF_NUM
▸	10014	ACCT-211	3	TTh 2:30-3:45 pm	BUS252	342
	10018	CIS-220	2	MWF 9:00-9:50	KLR211	114
	10021	QM-261	1	MWF 8:00-8:50	KLR200	114

Implementing the small database shown in Database Table 11.12 requires that we define the relationships clearly. Specially, we must know the 1 and the M sides of each of the relationships and we must know whether the relationships are mandatory or optional. For example, it is worth noting the following points:

1. A class may exist (at least at the start of registration) even though it contains no students at all. Therefore, If we examine Fig. 11.26 the optional symbol should appear on the STUDENT side of the M:N relationship between STUDENT and CLASS.

Fig. 11.26 The M:N relationship between student and class

However, because the M:N relationship between STUDENT and CLASS is decomposed into two 1:M relationships through ENROLL, the optionality must be transferred to ENROLL (See Fig. 11.27). In other words, *it now becomes possible for some class not to occur in* ENROLL *if no student signs up for that class.* Because a class need not occur in ENROLL, the ENROLL entity becomes optional to CLASS.

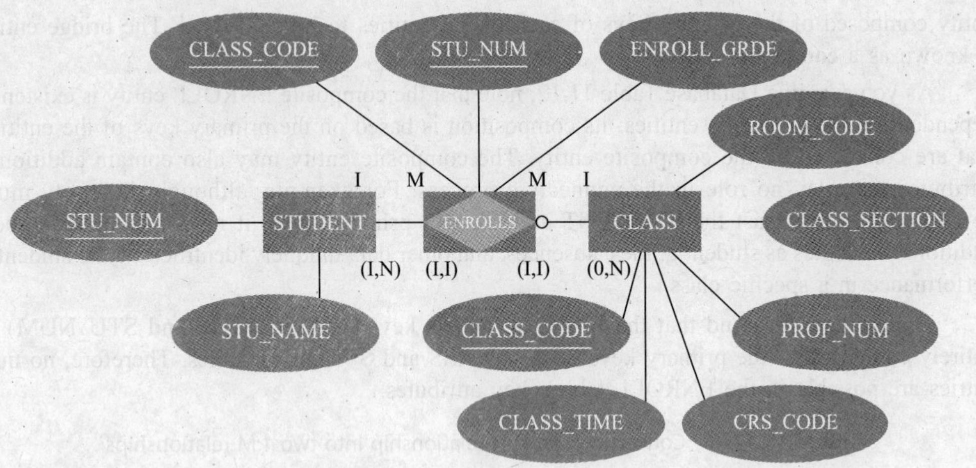

Fig. 11.27 A composite entity in the E-R diagram

2. To be classified as a STUDENT, a person must be enrolled in at least one CLASS. In short, CLASS is mandatory to STUDENT. Therefore, a student must appear at least once in the ENROLL entity. Naturally, if the student takes more than one class, that student may occur more than once in ENROLL. For example, note that STU_NUM = 321452 occurs three times in the ENROLL table in Database Table 11.11. On the other hand, each student occurs only once in the STUDENT entity. (Note that in the STUDENT table in Database Table 11.12 only has one STU_NUM = 321452 entry in it). Therefore, the relationship between STUDENT and ENROLL is shown to be 1:M in Fig. 11.27 with the M on the ENROLL side.
3. If you examine Database Table 11.12, you will see that a class can occur more than once in the ENROLL table. For example, the CLASS_CODE = 10014 occurs twice in the ENROLL table. However, the CLASS_CODE = 10014 occurs only once in the CLASS table, so the relationship between CLASS and ENROLL is 1:M. Note that, in Fig. 11.27, the M is located on the ENROLL side, while the 1 is located on the Class side.

11.6.12 Entity Supertypes and Subtypes

Most business firms employ people with a wide range of skills and special qualifications. For example, an aviation business might employ pilots and many other types of employees. Describing the different types of employees within a single entity would be awkward at best. For one thing, pilots (for example) must meet special requirements such as minimum flight hours, training flight check, and so on, that are not required of other employee. So,if all employee characteristics and special qualifications are described by a single EMPLOYEE entity and stored as shown in Database Table 11.13 you would either have a lot of nulls or you would have to make a lot of needless dummy entries. For example, if employees Lewis, Lange, Williams, Duzak, and Travis are pilots. Database Table 11.13 illustrates that their special pilot characteristics. EMP_LICENSE, EMP_RATINGS, and EMP_MED_TYPE, would cause a large number of nulls for other employees who are not pilots.

Clearly, pilots share common characteristics with other employees, such as a last name (EMP_LNAME) and hire data (EMP_HIRE_DATE). On other hand, there are many characteristics that are not shared. It is there unshared characteristics that create problems when you try to store all employee attributes in the same table. Fortunately, these problems are solved easily by using a generalization hierarchy to represent entity sets that share common characteristics.

Table 11.13 Null created by unique attributes

Table name: EMPLOYEE

EMP_NUM	EMP_LNAME	EMP_LICENSE	EMP_RATINGS	EMP_MED_TYPE	EMP_HIRE_DATE
100	Kolmyez				3/15/85
101	Lewis	ATP	SEL\MEL\Instr/CFII	1	4/25/86
102	Vandam				12/20/90
103	Jones				8/38/94
104	Lange	ATP	SEL\MEL\Instr	1	10/20/94
105	Williams	COM	SEL\MEL\Instr/CFI	2	11/8/94
106	Duzak	COM	SEL\MEL\Instr	2	1/5/89
107	Diante				7/12/94
108	Wiesenbach				11/18/92
109	Travis	COM	SEL\MEL\SES\instr/CFII	1	4/14/89
110	Genkazi				12/1/90

Basically, the **generalization hierarchy** depicts the parent-child relationship. In a relational database context, the generalization hierarchy depicts a relationship between a higher-level supertype entity and a lower-level subtype entity (See Fig. 11.28). In other words, the **supertype** contain the shared attributes. While the **subtype** contain the unique attributes.

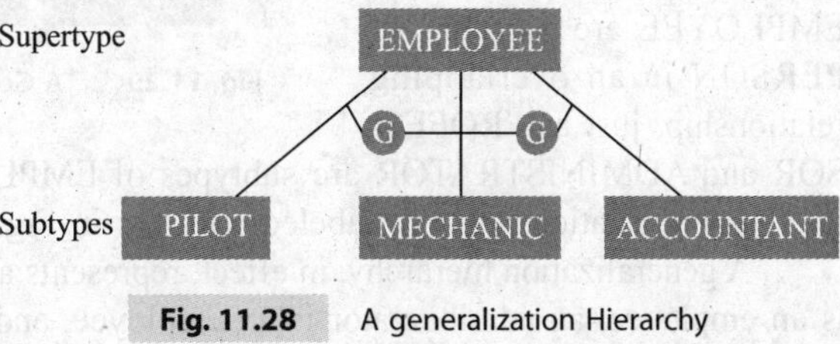

Fig. 11.28 A generalization Hierarchy

As you examine Fig. 11.28, note that its relationship is one of inheritance. That is, a subtype inherits its attributes and its relationships from the supertype entity. For example, pilots, mechanics, and accountants all have names, home addresses, and so on. However, as you discovered earlier, employees can also have attributes that are unique to their craft. In other words, the supertype entity set is usually related to several unique and **disjoint** (non-overlapping) subtype entity sets. Such disjoint relationships are indicated by the symbol G.

The supertype and its subtype(s) maintain a 1:1 relationship. For example, the generalization hierarchy lets us replace the undesirable EMPLOYEE table structure in Database Table 11.13 with two tables, one representing the supertype EMPLOYEE and the other representing the subtype PILOT (See Database Table 11.14).

Table 11.14 The Employee/pilot Supertype/Subtype Relationship

Table name: EMPLOYEE (the supertype)

EMP_NUM	EMP_LNAME	EMP_HIRE_DATE
100	Kolmyez	3/15/85
101	Lewis	4/25/86
102	Vandam	12/20/90
103	Jones	8/38/94
104	Lange	10/20/94
105	Williams	11/8/94
106	Duzak	1/5/89
107	Diante	7/12/94
108	Wiesenbach	11/18/92
109	Travis	4/14/89
110	Genkazi	12/1/90

Table name: PILOT (the subtype)

	EMP_NUM	PIL_LICENSE	PIL_RATINGS	PIL_MED_TYPE
▸	101	ATP	SEL\MEL\Instr/CFII	1
	104	ATP	SEL\MEL\Instr	1
	105	COM	SEL\MEL\Instr/CFI	2
	106	COM	SEL\MEL\Instr	2
	109	COM	SEL\MEL/SES/Instr/CFII	1

Some supertypes contain overlapping subtypes. For example, an employee may be a professor as well as administrator because a department chair may also teach courses. Similarly, a person may be an employee and a student. Because an employee also may be a student, STUDENT and EMPLOYEE are subtypes of PERSON in an overlapping relationship, just as PROFESSOR and ADMINISTRATOR are subtypes of EMPLOYEE in an overlapping relationship. Such overlapping relationships are labeled with **Gs** in Fig. 11.29.

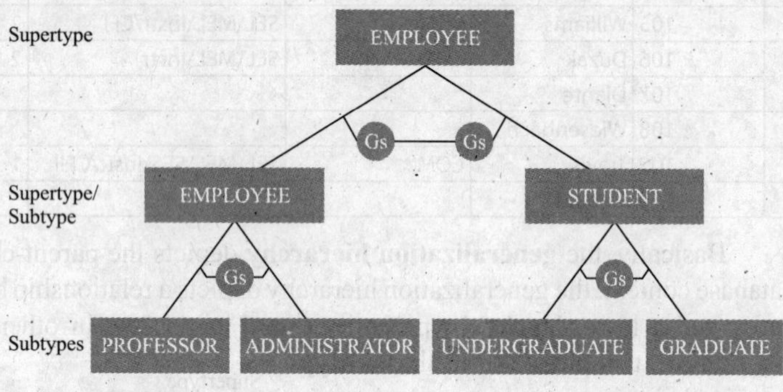

Fig. 11.29 A Generalization Hierarchy with overlapping subtypes

A generalization hierarchy, in effect, represents an 'is-a' relationship. For example, a professor is an employee, an administrator is an employee, and an employee is a person.

11.6.13 E-R Component Summary

We have introduced quite a few E-R components and their graphic representations in the previous sections. Given their importance in mapping the E-R model, it would be wise to review the summary shown in Fig. 11.30. After examining this summary carefully, you should be ready to see how the E-R concepts are used to develop a complete E-R diagram.

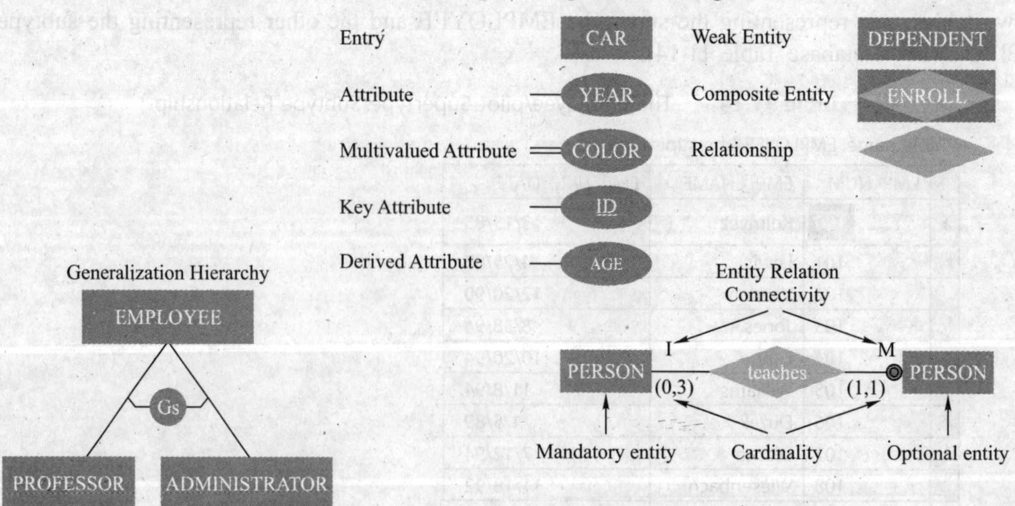

Fig. 11.30 A Graphic summary of E-R model concepts

11.7 NORMALIZATION

Just having good relational database software is not enough to avoid the data redundancy pitfalls. If the database tables are treated as though they were files in a file system, the RDBMS never has a change to demonstrate its superior data-handling capabilities.

The table is a basic building block in the database design process. Consequently, the table's structure is of great interest to us. Ideally, it is possible to create poor table structures even in a good database design. So how do we recognize a poor table structure, and how do we produce a good table? The answer to both questions is based on normalization. **Normalization** is a process for assigning attributes to entities. Normalization reduces data redundancies and, by extension, helps eliminate the data anomalies that result from those redundancies. Normalisation does not eliminate data redundancies; instead, it produces the controlled redundancy that lets us link database tables.

Normalisation works through a series of stages called normal forms. The first three stages are described as **first normal form (INF) second normal form (2NF)**, and **third normal form (3NF)**. From a structural point of view, 2NF is better than INF, and 3NF is better than 2NF. For most business database design purposes, third normal form is as high as we need to go in the normalisation process. However, some very specialized applications may require higher-level normalization.

Although normalization is a very important database design ingredient, you should not assume that the highest level of normalisation is always the most desirable. Generally, the higher the normal form, the more the joins are required to produce a specified output and the slower the database system responds to end user demands. A successful design must also consider end user demand for fast performance. Therefore, you will occasionally be expected to *denormalize* some portions of a database design in order to meet performance requirements. (**Denormalisation** produces a lower normal form; that is, a third normal form would be converted to a second normal form through denormalisation). However, the price you pay for increased performance through denormalisation is a larger amount of data redundancy.

11.7.1 The Need for Normalisation

In order to illustrate the normalisation process, we will examine a simple business application. In this case, we will explore the simplified database activities of a construction company that manages several building projects. Each project has its own project number, name, employees assigned to the project, and so on. Each employee has an employee number, name, and a job classification such as engineer, computer technician, and so on. The company charges its clients by billing the hours spent on each contract. The hourly billing rate is dependent on the employee's position. (For example, one hour of computer technician time is billed at a different rate than one hour of engineer time). Periodically, a report is generated that contains the information displayed in Table 11.15.

Table 11.15 A sample report layout

Proj. Num.	*Project Name*	*Employee Number*	*Employee Name*	*Job Class*	*Chg/Hour*	*Hours Billed*	*Total Charge*
15	Evergreen	103	June E. Arbough	Elect. Engineer	$84.50	23.8	$2,011.10
		101	John G. News	Database Designer	$105.00	19.4	$2,037.00
		105	Alice K Johnson*	Database Designer	$105.00	35.7	$3.748.50
		106	William Smithfield	Programmer	$35.75	12.6	$450.45

Proj. Num.	*Project Name*	*Employee Number*	*Employee Name*	*Job Class*	*Chg/Hour*	*Hours Billed*	*Total Charge*
		102	David H. Senior	Systems Analyst	$96.75	23.8	$2,302.65
				Subtotals			$10,549.70
18	Amber Wave	114	Annelise Jones	Applications Designer	$48.10	24.6	$1,183.26
		118	James J. Frommer	General Support	$18.36	45.3	$831.71
		104	Anne K. Ramoras*	Systems Analyst	$96.75	32.4	$3,134.70
		112	Darlene M. Smithson	DSS Analyst	$45.95	44.0	$2,021.80
				Subtotals			$$7,171.47
22	Rolling Tide	105	Alice Johnson	Database Designer	$105.00	64.7	$6,793.50
		104	Anne K. Ramoras	System Analyst	$96.75	48.4	$4,682.70
		113	Delbert K. Joenbrood*	Applications Designer	$48.10	23.6	$1,135.16
		111	Geoff B. Wabash	Clerical Support	$26.87	22.0	$591.14
		106	William Smithfield	Programmer	$35.75	12.8	$457.60
				Subtotals			$13,660.10
25	Starflight	107	Maria D. Alozo	Programmer	$35.75	24.6	$879.45
		115	Travis B. Bawangi	Systems Analyst	$96.75	45.8	$4,431.15
		115	Travis B. Bawangi	Systems Analyst	$96.75	45.8	$4,431.15
		101	John G. News*	Database Designer	$105.00	56.3	$5,911.50
		114	Annelise Jones	Applications Designer	$48.10	33.1	$1,592.11
		108	Ralph B. Washington	Systems Analyst	$96.75	23.6	$2,283.30
		118	Jame J. Frommer	General Support	$18.36	30.5	$559.98
		112	Darlene M. Smithson	DSS Analyst	$45.95	41.4	$1,902.33
				Subtotals			$17,559.82
				Total			$48,941.09
Note * indicates project leader							

☞ Note Table 11.15 Total Charge is a derived attribute and is not stored in this table.

The easiest short-term way to generate the required report might seem to be a table whose contents correspond to the reporting requirements (See Database Table 11.16).

Table 11.16 A Table Whose Structure Matches the Report Format

PROJ_NUM	PROJ_NAME	EMP_NUM	EMP_NAME	JOB_CLASS	CHG_HOUR	HOURS
15	Evergree	103	June E. Arbough	Elect. Engineer	$84.50	23.8
		101	John G. News	Database Designer	$105.00	19.4
		105	Alice K. Johnson*	Database Designer	$105.00	35.7
		106	William Smithfield	Programmer	$35.75	12.5
		102	David H. Senior	Systems Analyst	$96.75	23.9
18	Amber Wave	114	Annelise Jones	Applications Designer	$48.10	24.6
		118	James J. Frommer	General Support	$18.36	45.3
		104	Anne K. Ramoras*	Systems Analyst	$96.75	32.1
		112	Darlene M. Smithson	DSS Analyst	$45.95	44.0
22	Rolling Tide	105	Alice K. Johnson	Database Designer	$105.00	64.7
		104	Anne K. Ramoras	Systems Analyst	$96.75	48.9
		113	Delbert K. Joenbrood*	Applications Designer	$48.10	23.6
		111	Geoff B. Wabash	Clerical Support	$26.87	22.5
		106	William Smithson	Programmer	$35.75	12.1
25	Staffight	107	Maria D. Alonzo	Programmer	$35.75	24.7
		115	Travis B. Bawangi	Systems Analyst	$96.75	45.8
		101	John G. News*	Database Designer	$105.00	56.3
		114	Annelise Jones	Applications Designer	$48.10	33.1
		108	Ralph B. Washington	Systems Analyst	$96.75	23.9
		118	James J. Frommer	General Support	$18.36	30.2
		112	Darlene M. Smithson	DSS Analyst	$45.95	41.4

Because the total charge is the product of hours billed and charge per hour, it is the only item missing from Database Table 11.16. Unfortunately, Database Table 11.16's structure does not conform to the requirements, nor does it handle data very well 1.

1. The project number (PROJ_NUM) is apparently intended to be a primary key, or at least a part of a primary key, but it contains nulls.
2. The table displays data redundancies, which we will discuss in detail in number 4.
3. The table entries invite data inconsistencies. For example, the JOB_CLASS value 'Elect. Engineer' might be entered as 'Elect.Eng' in some cases, 'EL.ENG'. in others, and 'EE' in still others.
4. The data redundancies yield the following anomalies:
   (*a*) *Update anomalies*: Modifying the JOB_CLASS for employee number (EMP_NUM) 105 requires (potentially) many alterations, one for each EMP_NUM = 105.
   (*b*) *Addition anomalies*: Just do complete a row definition, a new employee must be assigned to a project. If the employee is not yet assigned, a phantom project must be created in order to complete the employee data entry.
   (*c*) *Deletion anomalies*: If employee 103 quits, deletions must be made for every entry in which EMP_NUM = 103. As such deletions are made, other vital data are lost, too.

The table structure appears to work; the report is generated with ease. But suppose Darlene M. Smithson is assigned to work on the Evergreen project and the data entry clerk updates the PROJECT file with the entry

15 Evergreen 112 Darlene M. Smithson DSS Analyst $45.95 0.0

to match the attributes PROJ_NUM, PROJ_NAME, EMP_NUM, EMP_NAME, JOB_CLASS, CHG_HOUR, and HOURS.

Every time another employee is assigned to a project, some repeated information is typed. Imagine the data entry chore when 200 or 300 table entries have to be made. Note that the entry of the employee number should be sufficient to identify Darlene M. Smithson, her job description, and her hourly charge. Because there is only one person identified by the number 112, that person's characteristics (name, job classification, and so on) should not have to be typed in each time the main file is updated. Unfortunately, the structure displayed in Database Table 11.16 does not make allowance for such a possibility.

The data redundancy that is evident in Database Table 11.16 leads to wasted disk space. What's more, data redundancy produces data anomalies.

For example, suppose the data entry clerk had entered the data as:

15 Evergeen 112 Darla Smithson DCS Analyst $45.95 0.0

As first glance the data entry appears to be correct. But is Evergeen the same project as Evergreen? And is DCS Analyst supposed to be DSS Analyst? Is Darla Smithson the same person as Darlene M. Smithson? Such confusion is a data integrity problem, caused by the fact that the data entry failed to conform to the rule that all copies of redundant data must be identical.

The possibility of introducing data integrity problems caused by data redundancy must be considered when a database is designed. The relational database environment is especially well-suited to help the designer overcome these problems.

11.7.2 Conversion to First Normal Form

Because the relational model views the data as party of a table or collection of tables in *which all key values must be identified*, the data depicted in Database Table 11.16 cannot be stored as shown. Note that Database Table 11.16 contains what is known as **repeating groups** because any project number (PROJ_NUM) can have a group of several data entries. For example, the Evergreen project's entries are reproduced in Database Table 11.17.

Table 11.17 The Evergreen Data

PROJ_NUM	PROJ_NAME	EMP_NUM	EMP_NAME	JOB_CLASS	CHG_HOUR	HOURS
15	Evergree	103	June E. Arbough	Elect. Engineer	$84.50	23.8
		101	John G. News	Database Designer	$105.00	19.4
		105	Alice K. Johnson*	Database Designer	$105.00	35.7
		106	William Smithfield	Programmer	$35.75	12.6
		102	David H. Senior	Systems Analyst	$96.75	23.8

A relational table must not contain repeating groups. If repeating groups do exist, they must be eliminated by making sure that each row defines a single entity. The process is simple: just add the appropriate entry is at least the primary key column(s). In other words, the tabulation depicted in Database Table 11.16. must be changed to the layout shown in Database Table 11.18. This change creates a table in first normal form by eliminating repeating groups.

The layout shown in Database Table 11.18 represents much more than a mere cosmetic change. Even a casual observer will note that the PROJ_NUM is not an adequate (primary) key because the project number does not uniquely identify all the remaining entity (row) attributes. For example, the PROJ_NUM value 15 can identify any one of five employees. To maintain a proper primary key that will uniquely identify any attribute value, the new key must be composed of a combination of PROJ_NUM and EMP_NUM.

Table 11.18 Data organization: first normal form

PROJ_NUM	PROJ_NAME	EMP_NUM	EMP_NAME	JOB_CLASS	CHG_HOUR	HOURS
15	Evergree	103	June E. Arbough	Elect. Engineer	$84.50	23.8
15	Evergree	101	John G. News	Database Designer	$105.00	19.4
15	Evergree	105	Alice K. Johnson*	Database Designer	$105.00	35.7
15	Evergree	106	William Smithfield	Programmer	$35.75	12.5
15	Evergree	102	David H. Senior	Systems Analyst	$96.75	23.9
18	Amber Wave	114	Annelise Jones	Applications Designer	$48.10	24.6
18	Amber Wave	118	James J. Frommer	General Support	$18.36	45.3
18	Amber Wave	104	Anne K. Ramoras*	Systems Analyst	$96.75	32.1
18	Amber Wave	112	Darlene M. Smithson	DSS Analyst	$45.95	44.0
22	Rolling Tide	105	Alice K. Johnson	Database Designer	$105.00	64.7
22	Rolling Tide	104	Anne K. Ramoras	Systems Analyst	$96.75	48.9
22	Rolling Tide	113	Delbert K. Joenbrood*	Applications Designer	$48.10	23.6
22	Rolling Tide	111	Geoff B. Wabash	Clerical Support	$26.87	22.5
22	Rolling Tide	106	William Smithson	Programmer	$35.75	12.1
25	Staffight	107	Maria D. Alonzo	Programmer	$35.75	24.7
25	Staffight	115	Travis B. Bawangi	Systems Analyst	$96.75	45.8
25	Staffight	101	John G. News*	Database Designer	$105.00	56.3
25	Staffight	114	Annelise Jones	Applications Designer	$48.10	33.1
25	Staffight	108	Ralph B. Washington	Systems Analyst	$96.75	23.9
25	Staffight	118	James J. Frommer	General Support	$18.36	30.2
25	Staffight	112	Darlene M. Smithson	DSS Analyst	$45.95	41.4
					$0.00	0.0

Dependencies can be identified with the help of the **dependency diagram** shown in Fig. 11.31.

The primary key components are highlighted by the circle. As you examine the dependency diagram in Fig. 11.31, note the following features:

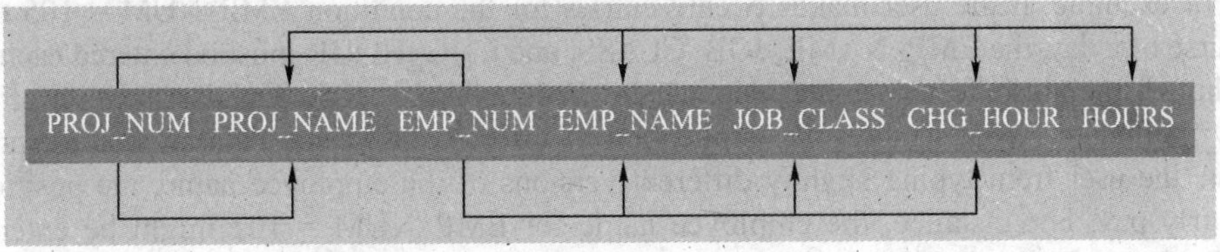

Fig. 11.31 A dependency diagram: first normal form

1. The arrows shown above the entity indicate that the entity's attributes are dependent on the combination of PROJ_NUM and EMP_NUM. In other words, if you know the PROJ_NUM and the EMP_NUM of any row, you can identify all the remaining row values. For example, using the data shown in Database Table 11.18, if you know that PROJ_NUM = 15 and EMP_NUM = 103, the entries for the attributes PROJ_NAME, EMP_NAME, JOB_CLASS, CHG_HOUR,

and HOURS must be Evergreen, June E. Arbough, Elect. Engineer, $84.50, and 23.8 respectively.

2. The arrows below the dependency diagram indicate less desirable dependencies based on only a part of the primary key.

For example, you need to know only the PROJ_NUM to determine the PROJ_NAME, that is, the PROJ_NAME is dependent on only part of the primary key. And you need to know only the EMP_NUM to find the EMP_NAME, the JOB_CLASS, and the CHG_HOUR. Dependencies based on only a part of the primary key are called **partial dependencies**.

In other words, the dependencies in Fig. 11.31 can also be written:

PROJ_NUM, EMP_NUM → PROJ_NAME, EMP_NAME, JOB_CLASS, CHG_HOUR, HOURS

PRJ_NUM → PROJ_NAME

EMP_NUM → EMP_NAME, JOB_CLASS, CHG_HOUR

TABLE NAME (**PRIMARY KEY COMPONENT(S)**, DEPENDENT ATTRIBUTES)

For example, if the preceding table were named CHARGE, the table structure is represented by;

CHARGE (**PROJ_NUM, EMP_NUM**, PROJ_NAME, EMP_NAME, JOB_CLASS, CHG_HOUR, HOURS)

Note that the CHARGE table contains a primary key composed of the attributes PROJ_NUM and EMP_NUM. Any attribute that is at least part of a key is known as a **prime attribute** or a **key attribute**. Therefore, both PROJ_NUM and EMP_NUM are prime (or key) attributes. Conversely, a **nonprime attribute** or a **nonkey attribute** is not even part of a key.

The term *first normal form* (*INF*) *describes the tabular format in which:*

1. All the key attributes are defined.
2. There are no repeating groups in the table. In other words, each row/column intersection can contain one and only one value, rather than a set of values.
3. All attributes are dependent on the primary key.

All relational tables satisfy the INF requirements. The problem with the INF table structure shown in Fig. 11.33, is that it contains partial dependencies; that is, dependencies based on only a part of the primary key.

Partial dependencies cannot be tolerated because a table that contains such dependencies is still subject to data redundancies and, therefore, to various anomalies.

The data redundancies are caused by the fact that every row entry requires duplication of data. For example, if the user makes twenty entries for the condition EMP_NUM = 105 during the course of a day, the EMP_NAME, JOB_CLASS, and CHG_HOUR must be entered each time, even though the attribute values are identical for EMP_NUM = 105. Such duplication of effort is very inefficient. What's more, the duplication of effort helps create data anomalies; nothing prevents the user from typing slightly different versions of the employee name, the position, or the hourly pay. For instance, the employee name for EMP_NUM = 102 might be entered as Dave Senior or D. Senior. Similarly, the project name might be entered correctly as Evergeen or misspelled as Evergeen. Such data anomalies violate the relational database's integrity and consistency rules.

Conversion to Second Normal Form

Fortunately, the relational database design can be improved easily by converting the database into a format known as the second normal form (2NF). The INF-to-2NF conversion is simple: Starting with the INF format displayed in Fig. 11.31 you do the following:

1. Write each key component on a separate line, and then write the original key on the last line:

   PROJ_NUM

   EMP_NUM

   PROJ_NUM   EMP_NUM

   Each component will become the key in a new table. In other words, the original table is now divided into three tables. We'll call these tables PROJECT, EMPLOYEE, and ASSIGN respectively.

2. Write the dependent attributes after each new key (Use Fig. 11.31 to determine which attributes are dependent on which other attributes). The dependencies for the original key components are found by examining the arrows below the dependency diagram shown in Fig. 11.31. In other words, the three new tables, PROJECT, EMPLOYEE, and ASSIGN, are described by

   PROJECT (*PROJ_NUM*, PROJ_NAME)

   EMPLOYEE (*EMP_NUM*, EMP_NAME, JOB_CLASS, CHG_HOUR)

   ASSIGN (*PROJ_NUM, EMP_NUM*, HOURS)

   Because the HOURS attribute is dependent on PROJ_NUM and EMP_NUM, we place HOURS in the ASSIGN table.

The results of this operation are displayed in Fig. 11.32. As you examine Fig. 11.32, note that CHG_HOUR is dependent on JOB_CLASS. Because neither CHG_HOUR nor JOB_CLASS is a prime attribute-that is, neither is at least part of a key-we have a condition known as a **transitive dependency**. And a transitive dependency still yields data anomalies.

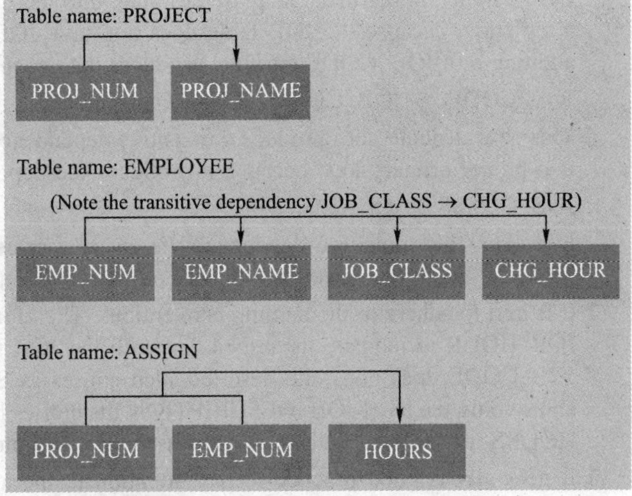

Fig. 11.32 Second normal form (2NF) conversion results

A table is in 2NF if;

1. It is in INF

   and

2. It includes no partial dependencies; that is, no attribute is dependent on only a portion of the primary key. (But it is still possible for a table in 2NF to exhibit transitive dependency; that is, one or more attributes may be functionally dependent on nonkey attributes.

Because a partial dependency can exist only if a table's primary key is composed of several attributes, a table whose primary key consists of only a single attribute must be automatically in 2NF if it is in INF.

11.7.4 Conversion to Third Normal Form

The data anomalies created by the database organization shown in Fig. 11.32 are easily eliminated by breaking off the piece(s) that are identified by the transitive dependency arrow(s) below the dependency diagram and storing them in a separate table. However, JOB_CLASS must be retained in the original 2NF table as a foreign key in order to establish a link between the original table and the newly created table. In other words, after we finish the conversion, our database contains four tables:

PROJECT (*PROJ_NUM*, PROJ_NAME)
ASSIGN (*PROJ_NUM, EMP_NUM*, HOURS)
EMPLOYEE (*EMP_NUM*, EMP_NAME, JOB_CLASS)
JOB (*JOB_CLASS*, CHG_HOUR)

☞ Note that this conversion has eliminated the original EMPLOYEE table's transitive dependency; the tables are now said to be in third normal form (3NF).

A table is in 3NF if;

1. It is in 2NF and
2. It contains to transitive dependencies.

Having cleaned up the table structures to eliminate the troublesome initial particle and transitive dependencies, we can now turn our attention to improving the database's ability to provide information and to enhance its operational characteristics. Therefore, we have made the following changes:

❒ As the number of employees grows, a JOB_CLASS value must be entered each time a new employee is entered into the EMPLOYEE table. Unfortunately, it is too easy to make data entry errors that lead to referential integrity violations. For example, a JOB_CLASS entry of DB Designer, rather than Database designer, into the EMPLOYEE TABLE will trigger such a violation, because the JOB table does not have JOB_CODE entry of DB Designer. The addition of a JOB_CODE attribute produces the dependency.

JOB_CODE → JOB_CLASS, CHARGE

This new attribute does produce a transitive dependency if you assume that the JOB_CODE is a proper primary key, because it produces the dependency.

JOB_CLASS → CHARGE

However, this transitive dependency is an easy price to pay, because the JOB_CODE's presence greatly decreases the likelihood of referential integrity violations.

❒ It is best to adhere to the naming conventions. Therefore, we have changed CHG_HOUR to JOB_HOUR to indicate its association with the JOB table. In addition, the attribute name JOB_CODE does not quite describe such entries as Systems Analyst, Database Designer, and so only the label JOB_DESCRIPTION fits entries better. Similarly, the use of ASSIGN_HOURS, rather than HOURS, lets us associate the hours worked with the ASSIGN table.

❒ It generally is good practice to pay attention to the atomicity requirement; that is, to use attributes that cannot be further subdivided. Clearly, the user of the EMP_NAME in the EMPLOYEE table is not atomic, because EMP_NAME can be decomposed into a last name, a first name, and an initial. By improving the degree of atomicity, we also gain querying flexibility. For example, if we use EMP_LNAME, EMP_FNAME, and EMP_INITIAL, we can easily generate phone lists by sorting last names, first names, and initials. Such a task would be nearly impossible if we keep the name components within a single attribute.

❒ If the EMPLOYEE table were used in a real-world environment, quite a few other attributes would have to be added. For example, year-to-date gross salary payments, social security payments, Medicare payments, etc., are desirable. In our example, we have added an employee hire date. The EMP_HIREDATE can then be used to track employee 'job longevity' and serve as a basis for awarding bonuses to long-term employees and for other moraleenhancing measures.

- The system's ability to supply detailed information about each project's manager is assured by using the EMP_NUM as a foreign key in PROJECT This action ensures that we can access the details of each PROJECT's manager data without producing unnecessary and undesirable data duplication.

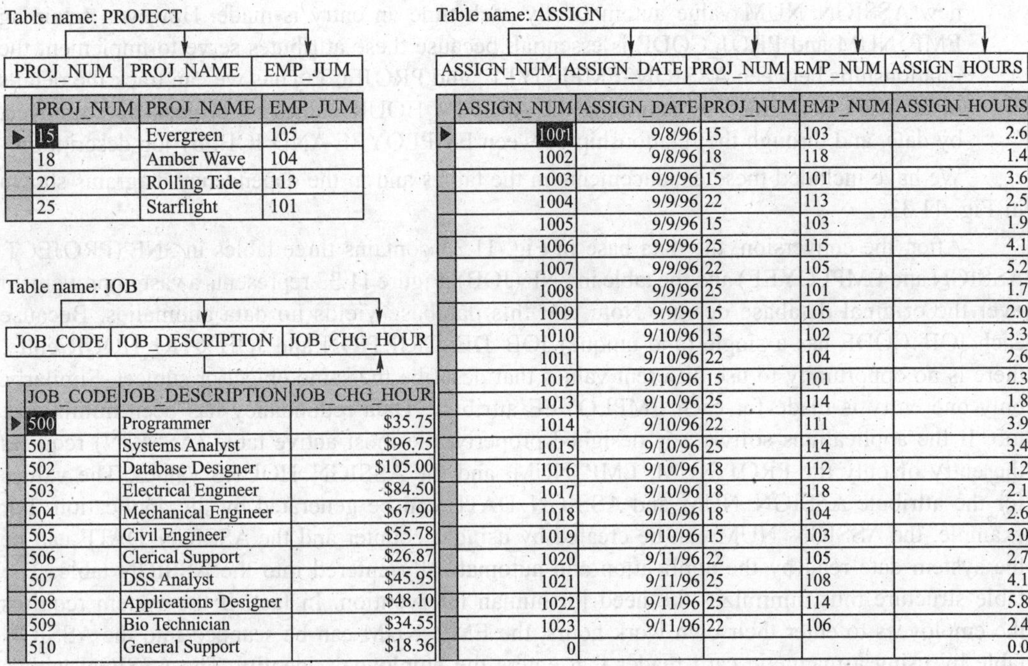

Table name: PROJECT

PROJ_NUM	PROJ_NAME	EMP_JUM

PROJ_NUM	PROJ_NAME	EMP_JUM
15	Evergreen	105
18	Amber Wave	104
22	Rolling Tide	113
25	Starflight	101

Table name: ASSIGN

ASSIGN_NUM	ASSIGN_DATE	PROJ_NUM	EMP_NUM	ASSIGN_HOURS

ASSIGN_NUM	ASSIGN_DATE	PROJ_NUM	EMP_NUM	ASSIGN_HOURS
1001	9/8/96	15	103	2.6
1002	9/8/96	18	118	1.4
1003	9/9/96	15	101	3.6
1004	9/9/96	22	113	2.5
1005	9/9/96	15	103	1.9
1006	9/9/96	25	115	4.1
1007	9/9/96	22	105	5.2
1008	9/9/96	25	101	1.7
1009	9/9/96	15	105	2.0
1010	9/10/96	15	102	3.3
1011	9/10/96	22	104	2.6
1012	9/10/96	15	101	2.3
1013	9/10/96	25	114	1.8
1014	9/10/96	22	111	3.9
1015	9/10/96	25	114	3.4
1016	9/10/96	18	112	1.2
1017	9/10/96	18	118	2.1
1018	9/10/96	18	104	2.6
1019	9/10/96	15	103	3.0
1020	9/11/96	22	105	2.7
1021	9/11/96	25	108	4.1
1022	9/11/96	25	114	5.8
1023	9/11/96	22	106	2.4
0				0.0

Table name: JOB

JOB_CODE	JOB_DESCRIPTION	JOB_CHG_HOUR

JOB_CODE	JOB_DESCRIPTION	JOB_CHG_HOUR
500	Programmer	$35.75
501	Systems Analyst	$96.75
502	Database Designer	$105.00
503	Electrical Engineer	$84.50
504	Mechanical Engineer	$67.90
505	Civil Engineer	$55.78
506	Clerical Support	$26.87
507	DSS Analyst	$45.95
508	Applications Designer	$48.10
509	Bio Technician	$34.55
510	General Support	$18.36

Table name: EMPLOYEE

EMP_NUM	EMP_LNAME	EMP_FNAME	EMP_INITIAL	EMP_HIR_DATE	JOB_CODE

EMP_NUM	EMP_LNAME	EMP_FNAME	EMP_INITIAL	EMP_HIR_DATE	JOB_CODE
101	News	John	G	11/8/92	502
102	Senior	David	H	7/12/87	501
103	Arbough	June	E	12/1/94/	503
104	Ramoras	Anne	K	11/15/85	501
105	Johnson	Alice	K	2/1/91	502
106	Smithfield	William		6/23/90	500
107	Alonzo	Maria	D	10/10/91	500
108	Washington	Ralph	B	8/22/89	501
109	Smith	Larry	W	7/18/95	501
110	Olenko	Gerald	A	12/11/93	505
111	Wabash	Geoff	B	4/4/89	506
112	Smithson	Darlene	M	10/23/92	507
113	Joenbrood	Delbert	K	11/15/94	508
114	Jones	Annelise		8/20/91	508
115	Bawangi	Travis	B	1/25/90	501
116	Pratt	Gerald	L	3/5/95	510
117	Williamson	Angie	H	6/19/94	509
118	Frommer	James	J	1/1/95	510

Fig. 11.33 The completed database

- Although the combination of EMP_NUM and PROJ_CODE may be an acceptable primary key, using a transaction code such as ASSIGN_NUM is more precise and yields greater flexibility.

For example, if the EMP_NUM and PROJ_CODE combination is used as the primary key and an employee makes two 'hours worked' entries in a single day, this action violates the entity integrity requirement. The same data entry yields to problems if the ASSIGN_NUM is used as the primary key, especially if the application software is designed to generate a new ASSIGN_NUM value automatically each time an entry is made. However, retaining EMP_NUM and PROJ_CODE is essential, because these attributes serve to implement the relationships between ASSIGN, EMPLOYEE, and PROJECT. Thus we can track the details of all work performed by summing the ASSIGN_HOUR values by project, by employee, by date, and through the relationship between EMPLOYEE AND JOB, by job description.

We have included these enhancements in the tables and in the dependency diagrams shown in Fig. 11.33.

After, the conversion, the data base in Fig. 11.33 contains three tables in 3NF (PROJECT, ASSIGN and EMPLOYEE) and the table in 2NF (JOB). Figure 11.33 represents a vast improvement over the original database design. Note that this database yields no data anomalies. Because each JOB_CODE has a single (and unique) JOB_DESCRIPTION and JOB_CHG_HOUR entry, there is no opportunity to use different values that describe the same object or subject. Similarly, only one entry is made for each EMPLOYEE attribute. Data redundancy has been minimized, too. If the applications software is designed properly, the most active table (ASSIGN) requires the entry of only the PROJ_NUM, EMP_NUM, and the ASSIGN_HOURS values. The values for the attribute ASSIGN_NUM and ASSIGN_DATE can be generated by the application. For example, the ASSIGN_NUM can be created by using a counter and the ASSIGN_DATE can be the system date read by the application and automatically entered into the ASSIGN table. The table structure thus minimizes the need for human intervention. In fact, if the system requires the employees to enter their own work hours, the EMP_NUM can be scanned into the ASSIGN table by using a magnetic card reader that enters the employee's identity. The ASSIGN table's structure thus can set the stage for maintaining some desired level of security.

11.8 DATA WAREHOUSE

Bill Inmon, the acknowledged father of the Data Warehouse, define it as an *integrated, subject-oriented, time-variant, non-volatile* database that provides support for decision making. To understand what that definition means, let's take a more detailed look at the definition's components.

- **Integrated:** The Data Warehouse is a centralized, consolidated database that integrates data derived from the entire organization. Thus the data warehouse consolidates data from multiple and diverse sources with diverse formats. Data integration implies a well-organized effort to define and standardize all data elements. This integration effort can be time consuming but, once accomplished, it provides a unified view of the overall organizational situation. Data integration enhances decision making and helps managers to better understand the company's operations. This understanding can be translated into a recognition of strategic business opportunities.
- **Subject-oriented:** The Data Warehouse data is arranged and optimized to provide answers to questions coming from diverse functional areas with a company. Therefore, the Data Warehouse contains data organized and summarized by topic; such as sales, marketing, finance, distribution, transportation, and so on. For each one of these topics the Data Warehouse contains specific subjects of interest—products, customers, departments, regions, promotions, and so on. Note that this form of data organization is quite different from that of the more functional or process-oriented organization of typical transaction systems.
- **Time-Variant:** The DSS data include a time element. In contrast to the operational data that focus on current transactions, the Warehouse data represent the flow of data through

time. In short, Data Warehouse contains data that reflect what happened last week, last month, the past five years, and so on. The Data Warehouse can even contain projected data generated through statistical and other models. It is also time-variant in the sense that, once data are periodically uploaded to the Data Warehouse, all time-dependent aggregations are recomputed. For example, when data for previous weekly sales are uploaded to the Data Warehouse, the weekly, monthly, yearly, and other time-dependent aggregates for products, customers, stores, and other variables are also updated.

❒ **Decision support system (DSS):** A decision support system (DSS) is a set of well-integrated, user-friendly, computer-based tools that combine data with various decision-making models (both quantitative and qualitative) to solve semistructured and unstructured problems. Such systems solve a specific problem or a class of problems, such as scheduling, planning, resource allocation, and forecasting. They allow managers to ask ad hoc (nonroutine) queries and receive customized responses. Although DSS were initially targeted for top managers and middle managers, today these systems are being deployed at all levels of the organization.

❒ **Non-Volatile:** Once data enter the Data Warehouse, they are never removed. Because the data in the Warehouse represent the company's entire history, the operational data, representing the near-term history, are always added to it. Because data are never deleted and new data are always added, the Data Warehouse is always growing. That's why the DSS DBMS must be able to support multigigabyte and even multiterabyte databases and multiprocessor hardware.

The four Data Warehouse requirements we have just discussed constitute the key elements of a DSS data repository. If the DSS database is to function properly, the Data Warehouse data must conform to these four requirements.

The Data Warehouse data must be integrated in order to provide a consistent view for all organizational components. Data integration implies that all business entities, data elements, data characteristics, and business metrics are *described in the same way throughout the enterprise.* Although this sounds like a logical requirement, you would be amazed to discover how many different measurements for 'sales performance' can exist within an organization; the same scenario holds true for any other business element. And this is only one small example of the problems that confront DSS database professionals as they encounter the many data integration challenges during the creation of Data Warehouse. In addition to using different definitions to describe the same topic, different departments might have different ways to compute or measure common items. For instance, the status of an order might be indicated with text labels such as 'open', 'received, 'cancel', or 'closed' in one department or as '1', '2', '3', or '4, in another department. A student's status might be defined as 'freshman', 'sophomore', 'Junior', or 'senior' in the Accounting department or as 'FR' 'SO', 'JR', 'SR' in the Computer Information Systems department. To avoid the potential format tangle, the data in the Data Warehouse must conform to a common format acceptable throughout the organization.

Remember that operational systems maintain a *functional* or system orientation; that is, the design focuses on the processes that modify the data. For example, the designer of an invoicing system concentrates on designing normalized data structures (relational tables) to support the business process by storing invoice components in two tables: (INVOICE and INVLINE). In contrast, the Data Warehouse has a subject orientation. (*Subject* refers to the data entities or data elements found within the operational data that concern the data analyst or the organization). Data Warehouse designers focus on the data themselves, rather than on the processes that modify the data. (After all, Data Warehouse data are not subject to numerous real-time data updated). Therefore, instead of storing an invoice, the Data Warehouse stores its product and customer component, because decision support activities require the retrieval of sales summaries by product or customer.

Because Data Warehouse data constitute a snapshot of the company history as measured by its variables, the time component is crucial. Therefore, the Data Warehouse contains a time ID that places the data within a time framework. This time ID is also used to generate appropriate summarizations and aggregations. In other words, the time element allows the data analyst to add a time dimensions to decision analysis, thus permitting the examination of any component by week, month, quarter, and year. Once the data enter the Data Warehouse, the time ID is assigned to the data and cannot be changed.

Table 11.19 summarizes the differences between the Data Warehouse and the operational database.

Table 11.19 A comparison of Data Warehouse and Operational Database Characteristics

Characteristic	*Operational Database Data*	*Data Warehouse Data*
Integrated	Similar data can have different representations or meanings (for example, social security numbers, business metrics, etc.).	Provide a unified view of all data elements with a common definition and representation for all departments.
Subject-Oriented	Data are stored with a functional or process orientation (for example, invoices, credits, debits, etc.)	Data are stored with a subject orientation that facilitates multiple views for data and decision making (for example, sales, products, sales by products, etc.).
Time-Variant	Data represent current transactions (for example, the sales of a product in a given date).	Data are historic in nature. A time dimension is added to facilitate data analysis and time comparisons.
Non-Volatile	Data updates and deletes are very common.	Data cannot be changed. Data are only added periodically from operational systems. Once data are stored, no changes are allowed.

In summary, the Data Warehouse is usually a read-only database optimized for data analysis and query processing. Typically, data are extracted from various sources and are then transformed and integrated—in other words, pass through a data filter—before being loaded into the Data Warehouse. Users access the Data Warehouse via front-end tools and/or end user application software to extract the data in usable form. Figure 11.34, illustrates how a Data Warehouse is created from the data contained in an operational database.

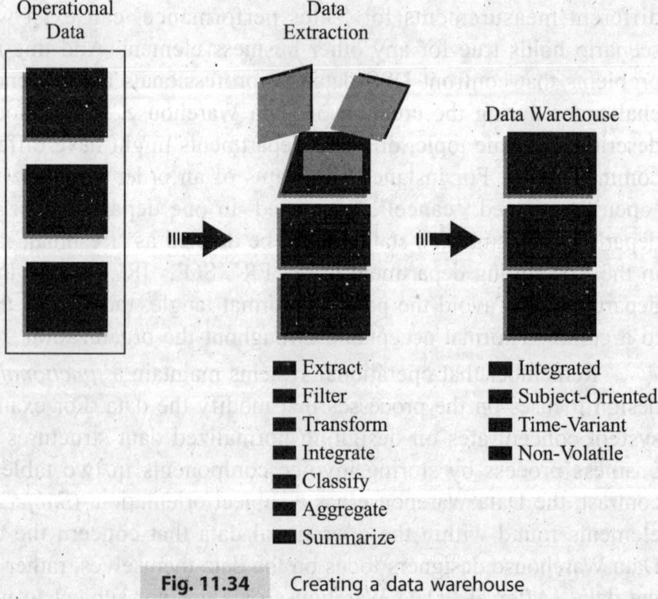

Fig. 11.34 Creating a data warehouse

Creating a good Data Warehouse is seldom simple, because its data are typically derived from a variety of different sources based on different data formats and structure. For example, dates might be stored as strings in one data source and as

Julian date fields in another data source; even like strings might have different formats. Similarly, social security numbers might be stored in one database as a character string containing dashes (xxx-xx-xxxx), in another as a character string without the dashes (xxxxxxxxx), and in yet a third as a numeric field (#########). In addition, the data might be extracted from different types of files and databases, as well as from different platforms. Therefore, integrating the sources, data types, and formats into a homogeneous Data Warehouse framework can be a real challenge.

11.9 DATA MART

Data Warehousing is used to describe all the activities involved in creating and maintaining a Data Warehouse. Data Warehouse creation requires time, money, and considerable managerial effort. Therefore, it is not surprising that many companies begin their foray into Data Warehousing by focusing on more manageable data sets that are targeted to meet the special needs of small groups within the organization. These small data stores are called Data Marts. A **Data Mart** is a small, single subject Data Warehouse subset that provides decision support to a small group of people.

Some organizations are attracted to Data Marts not only because of the lower cost and shorter implementation time, but also because current technological advances and inevitable 'people issue' make Data Marts attractive. Powerful computers allow us to provide a customized DSS to small groups in ways that a centralized system may not be able to. Also, a company's culture may predispose its people to resist major changes, but they may be quick to embrace relatively minor changes that lead to demonstrably improved decision support. In addition, people at different organizational levels are likely to require data with different summarization, aggregation, and presentation formats. Data Marts can serve as a test vehicle for companies exploring the potential benefits of Data Warehouses. By following this gradual Data Mart-to-Data Warehouse migration, managers can solve specific department's decision support needs within a reasonable time frame (six months to one year) as compared to the time usually required to implement a Data Warehouse (one to three years). Information Technology (IT) departments also benefit from this approach because their personnel get the opportunity to learn the issues and develop the skills required to create a Data Warehouse.

11.10 DATA MART VERSUS DATA WAREHOUSE

Keep in mind that the difference between a Data Mart and a Data Warehouse is only the size and scope of the problem being solved. Therefore, the problem definitions and data requirements are essentially the same for both. Whereas a Data Mart addresses local or departmental problems, a Data Warehouse involves a company-wide effort to support decision making at all levels in the organization. Given the size and scope difference, the development of a Data Warehouse requires a greater time, data, and managerial procedures investment than a Data Mart. Fortunately, thanks to client/server technology, the hardware and software components may be common to both the Data Mart and the Data Warehouse, thus making the growth path from one to the other less onerous. We will next examine how client/server technology has helped in the evolution of the Data Warehouse component.

11.11 EVOLUTION OF THE DATA WAREHOUSE

The origins of today's Data Warehouses can be traced to the reporting systems that were popular in the 1980s. These reporting systems provided some basic answers to the end user's questions, although the format wasn't always the most appropriate. The reporting systems that formed the foundation of basic decision support required direct access to the operational data through a menu interface to yield predefined report structures. Typically, the reporting system was front-ended by a text-only presentation tool.

The next development stage produced a sophisticated form of decision support by supplying lightly summarized data extracted for the operational database. Such lightly summarized data were usually stored in an RDBMS and were accessed through SQL statements via a query tool. The SQL-based query tool provided some predefined reports and, better yet, some adhoc query capability. Unfortunately, to use the queries, the end user had to know the details of the underlying data structure. The presentation tool was similar to the one used by the original reporting system, but it did provide additional customization options for *ad hoc* reports. A variation on this theme of greater end user empowerment was the use of spreadsheets or statistical packages to analyze operational data. End users used their own desktop tools to access and manipulate data in order to support their decision-making process.

Primitive as they were by current standards, these reporting systems and their extensions gave IS departments the first major tools with which to solve decision support problems. Given advances in hardware (more capable microprocessors, parallel processing, etc.) and software (relational and client/server technologies) in the late 80s and early to mid-90s, the explosion of available operational data, and the growing sophistication of decision support systems, the current DSS and Data Warehouse developments were almost inevitable.

In a typical Fortune 500 business, the amount of operational data stored in relational databases during the past decade reached into the hundreds of gigabytes. Due to rapidly changing external and internal business forces, such operational data has gained strategic value. In this new business environment, information has become a tool used to develop competitive advantages, to pen new markets, and to create new business opportunities. Unfortunately, from a decision support point of view, operational data can become unusable in a matter of a few months. This is why organizations must ensure that the operational data are reformatted to serve DSS requirements.

Client/server technology has emerged as the dominant force in systems development because it provides an open architecture that yields multiple advantages. The user of client/server architecture, combined with the Data Warehouse, leads to modular systems in which components can be freely interchanged and expanded without requiring the redesign of the entire system. Therefore client/server technology has become a *de facto* standard, and very few managers will venture forth to acquire a DSS tool that is not based on client/server technology. Although it is difficult to assign the primary reason for the development of practical Data Warehousing, client/server technology must be at least near the top of the list of explanations about why DSS databases have evolved so significantly and so quickly.

Client/server architecture also allows us to build systems that adapt better and more quickly to end user needs. Given its modular structure, client/server allows us the luxury of using many off-the-shelf tools from many different vendors with a high degree of integration. Such flexibility yields many benefits to end users—allowing them to use their PC based tools to access and analyse the Data Warehouse data and become productive with minimum training. The modularity of client/server architecture also enables us to develop systems at *different levels* within the organization in order to support end user decision making.

In order to meet decision requirements, a growing number of end users directly access the organization's data to perform appropriate data analysis tasks. The advent of powerful personal computes and maturing client/server technologies have made powerful software applications, such as spreadsheets, statistical packages, and database systems, desktop standards. However, *unless data warehousing*, *data extraction*, and *data integration features are available*, *these applications software packages usually are subject to five major* (and *sometimes crippling*) *limitations in the virtual ocean of data.*

1. They are able to handle only a relatively limited amount of data efficiently (Have you ever tried to import 100,000 data rows in a spreadsheet?)

2. Their recomputation speeds are slow when the data sets are large. Even with the most advanced microprocessing technology, spreadsheet software requires a great deal of time to recompute formulas when there are as many as 100,000 (or more!) data rows.
3. Their data analysis performance tends to be slow when the data sets are large.
4. Data access to external data via a desktop applications package is not necessarily a simple task; the software might not be able to handle some data types or even entire databases.
5. They cannot address problems such as data duplication, end user effort duplication, data inconsistency, and potential lack of data accuracy.

Given these applications software limitations, it is clear why the success of even the early DSS database architecture was built on its three components: a DSS data store, a data extraction and integration filter, and a specialized presentation interface. The data extraction component provides all the tools required to extract data from multiple operational and external sources and to transform, integrate, aggregate, and load the summarized data into the DSS database, usually an RDBMS. The query and presentation tools provide features that allow the end user to analyze and present the properly transformed, integrated and summarized data in many graphical and text formats.

Several DSS database architectural styles are available at this time. These architectures provide advanced decision support features and some are capable of providing access to multidimensional data analysis. The DSS tools that use multidimensional data analysis techniques are known as **On-Line Analytical Processing** (OLAP) tools. (We will discuss OLAP in next Section) Table 11.20 summarizes the main architectural styles that are likely to be encountered in the DSS database environment.

Table 11.20 DSS Architectural Styles

Source Data	*Data Extraction/ Integration Process*	*DSS Data Store*	*End User Query Tool*	*End User Presentation Tool*
Operational Data	None. Reports, reads, and summarizes data directly from operational data.	None. Temporary files used for reporting purposes.	Very basic. Predefined reporting. Basic sorting totals, and averages.	Very basic, menu driven, predefined reports; only text and numbers.
Operational Data	Basic extraction and aggregation: reads, filters, and summarizes operational data into intermediate data store.	Lightly aggregated data in RDBMS.	Same as above plus some ad hoc reporting using SQL.	Same as above plus some ad hoc columnar report definitions.
Operational Data	Data extraction and integration process to populate a DSS, data store; run periodically.	First DSS database generation. Usually RDBMS.	Query tool with some analytical capabilities and predefined reports.	Advanced presentation tools with plotting and graphics capabilities.
Operational Data	Advanced data extraction and integration tools. Features include access to diverse data sources, transformations, filters, aggregations, classifications, scheduling, and conflict resolutions.	Data Warehouse. Integrated DSS database to support entire company. Uses relational database (RDBMS) technology optimized for query purposes. Star schema model.	Same as above. Support for more advanced queries and analytical functions with extensions.	Same as above with some additional multidimensional presentation tools with drill-down capabilities.
Operational Data	Same as above.	Data Warehouse. Stores data using multidimensional database (MDBMS) technology based on data structures referred to as 'cubes' with multiple dimensions.	Same as above but uses different query interface to access MDBMS (proprietary).	Same as above. Uses 'cubes' and multidimensional matrixes, but limited in size of cube.

You may be tempted to think that the Data Warehouse is just a big, summarized database. Actually, our previous discussion indicates that a good Data Warehouse is much more than that. To review, a complete Data Warehouse architecture includes support for a DSS data store, a data extraction and integration filter, and a specialized presentation interface. To be useful, the Data Warehouse must contain a single-image database as the center of a decision support architecture. That is, the Data Warehouse data must conform to uniform structures and formats to avoid data conflicts. In fact, before we can refer to a DSS database as a true Data Warehouse, it must conform to the rules described in the next section.

11.12 TWELVE RULES THAT DEFINE A DATA WAREHOUSE

In 1994, William H. Inmon and Chuck Kelley created a list of twelve rules defining a Data Warehouse. Although, the Inmon/Kelley list summarizes these discussions well:

1. The Data Warehouse and operational environments are separated.
2. The Data Warehouse data are integrated.
3. The Data Warehouse contains historical data over a long time horizon.
4. The Data Warehouse data are snapshot data captured at a given point in time.
5. The Data Warehouse data are subject-oriented.
6. The Data Warehouse contains data with several levels of detail: current detail data, old detail data, lightly summarized, and highly summarized data.
7. The Data Warehouse environment is characterized by read-only transactions to very large data sets. The operational environment is characterized by numerous update transactions to a few data entities at the time.
8. The Data Warehouse data are mainly read-only with periodic batch updates from operational data. No online updates are allowed.
9. The Data Warehouse development life cycle differs from classical systems development. The Data Warehouse development is data driven; the classical approach is process driven.
10. The Data Warehouse environment has a system that traces data sources, transformations, and storage.
11. The Data Warehouses' metadata are a critical component of this environment. The metadata identify and define all data elements. The metadata provide the source, transformation, integration, storage, usage, relationships, and history of each data element.
12. The Data Warehouse contains a charge-back mechanism for resource usage that enforces optimal use of the data by end users.

Note how these twelve rules capture the complete Data Warehouse life cycle, from its introduction as an entity separate from the operational data store, to its components, functionality, and management processes. The current generation of specialized decision support systems provides a comprehensive infrastructure to design, develop, implement, and use decision support systems within an organization.

11.13 ON-LINE ANALYTICAL PROCESSING (OLAP)

The need for more intensive decision support prompted the introduction of a new generation of tools. These new tools, called **On-line Analytical Processing (OLAP)**, refer to an advanced data analysis environment that supports decision making business modeling, and operations research activities. OLAP systems share four main characteristics; they:

1. Use multidimensional data analysis techniques
2. Provide advanced database support

3. Provide easy-to-use end user interfaces
4. Support client/server architecture

Let's examine each of these characteristics

11.13.1 Multidimensional Data Analysis Techniques

This is the most distinguishing characteristic of OLAP tools. Multidimensional data analysis refers to the processing of data in which data are viewed as part of a multidimensional structure.

The interest in the multidimensional aspect of data analysis stems from the fact that business decision makers usually view data from a business perspective. That, they tend to view business data as they relate to other business data.

To better understand this view, let's examine how a business data analyst might investigate sales figures. In this case, (s)he probably is interested in the sales figures as they relate to other business variables such as customers and time. In other words, customers and time viewed as different dimensions of sales. Figure 11.35 illustrates how the operational (one-dimensional) view differs from the multidimensional view.

As you examine Fig. 11.35, note that the tabular view of sales data is not well-suited to decision support, because the relationship INVOICE → Line between INVOICE and LINE does not provide a business perspective of the sales data. On the other hand, the end user's view of sales data *from* a business perspective is more closely represented by the multidimensional view of sales than the tabular view of separate tables. Note also that the multidimensional view allows end users to consolidate or aggregate data at different levels; total sales figures by customers and by date. Finally, the multidimensional view of data allows a business data analyst to easily switch business perspectives (dimensions) from sales by customer to sales by division, by region, and so on.

Operational View of Sales

Table name: INVOICE

Number	Data	Customer	Total Sale
2034	15-May-96	Dartonik	3,500.00
2035	15-May-96	Summer Lake	1,800.00
2036	16-May-96	Dartonik	2,000.00
2037	16-May-96	Summer Lake	800.00

Table name: LINE

Number	Product	Price	Quantity
2034	Serial Mouse	150	20
2035	Floppy drive	50	10

Multidimensional View of Sales

	Time Dimension		
Customer Dimension	15-May-96	16-May-96	Totals
Dartonik	3,500	2,000	3,500
Summer Lake	1,800	800	2,600
Total	5,300	2,800	6,100

Sales figures are located in the intersection of a customer row and time column.

☞Aggregations are provided for both dimensions

Fig. 11.35 Operational vs. Multidimensional view of Sales

Multidimensional data analysis techniques are augmented by the following functions:

- Advanced data presentation functions; 3-D graphics, pivot tables, cross tabs, data rotation, three-dimensional cubes, and so on. Such data presentation facilities are compatible with desktop spreadsheets, statistical packages, and query and report writer packages.

- Advanced data aggregation, consolidation, and classification functions which allow the business data analyst to create multiple data aggregation levels, slice and dice data, and drill-down and roll-up data across different dimensions and aggregation levels. For example, aggregating data across the time dimension (by week, month, quarter, and year) allows the business data analyst to drill-down and roll-up across time dimensions.
- Advanced computational functions: business-oriented variables (market share, period comparisons, sales margins, product margins, percentage changes, etc.) financial and accounting ratios (profitability, overhead, cost allocations, returns etc). statistical and forecasting functions, and so on. These functions are provided automatically and the end user does not need to redefine their components each time they are accessed.
- Advanced data modeling functions: support for 'what-if' scenarios, variable assessment, variable contributions to outcome, linear programming, and other modeling tools.

Because many of the analysis and presentation functions are common to existing desk top spreadsheet packages, most OLAP vendors have closely integrated their systems with desktop spreadsheets such as Microsoft Excel ad Lotus 1-2-3. Using the features available in graphical end user interfaces, such as Windows, the OLAP menu option simply becomes another option within the Lotus or Excel menu bar. This seamless integration is a plus for OLAP systems and for spreadsheet vendors, because end users gain access to advanced data analysis features by using familiar programs and interfaces. Therefore, additional training and development costs are minimized.

11.13.2 Advanced Database Support

In order to deliver efficiency decision support, OLAP tools must have advanced data access features. Such features include:

1. Access to many different kinds of DBMS, flat files, and internal and external data sources.
2. Access to aggregated Data Warehouse data as well as to the detail data found in operational databases.
3. Advanced data navigation features such as drill-down and roll-up.
4. Rapid and consistent query response times.
5. The ability to map end user requests, expressed in either business or model terms, to the appropriate data source and then to the proper data access language (usually SQL). The query code must be optimized to match the data source, regardless of whether the source is operational or Data Warehouse.
6. Support for very large databases. As we already explained, the Data Warehouse can easily and quickly grow to multiple gigabyte and even terabytes.

To provide a seamless interface, OLAP tools map to their own data dictionaries the data elements from the Data Warehouse and from the operational database. These metadata are then used to translate end user data analysis requests into the proper (optimized) query codes, which are then directed to the appropriate data source(s).

11.13.3 Easy-to-Use End Use Interface

Advanced OLAP features become much useful if access to them is kept simple. OLAP tool vendors learned this lesson early and have equipped their sophisticated data extraction and analysis tools with easy-to-use graphical interfaces. Many of the interface features are 'borrowed' from previous generations of data analysis tools that are already familiar to end users. The familiarity makes OLAP easily accepted and readily used.

11.13.4 Client/Server Architecture

Client/server architecture provides a framework within which new systems can be designed, developed, and implemented. (If necessary, review the client/server coverage, which provides an in-depth look at the characteristics of client/server system architecture and principles).

The client/server environment enables us to divide an OLAP system into several components that define its architecture. These components can then be placed on the same computer or they can be distributed among several computers. Thus OLAP is designed to meet ease-of-use, as well as system flexibility, requirements.

11.14 OLAP ARCHITECTURE

Using the client/server concepts and the OLAP operational characteristics provided, we can divide the OLAP system into three main modules:

- ❒ OLAP Graphical User Interface (GUI)
- ❒ OLAP Analytical Processing Logic
- ❒ OLAP Data Processing Logic

These three OLAP modules, residing in the client/server environment, make it possible to use OLAP's three defining characteristics: multidimensional data analysis, advanced database support, and easy-to-use interface. Figure 11.36 illustrates the client/server OLAP components and attributes.

As Fig. 11.36 illustrates, OLAP systems are designed to use both operational and Data Warehouse data. Although Fig. 11.36 shows the OLAP system's components to be located on a single computer, this scenario is only one of many. In fact, one problem with the installation shown here is that each data analyst must have a powerful computer to store and entire OLAP system and perform all data processing. This approach does not provide the benefits of a single business image shared among all users.

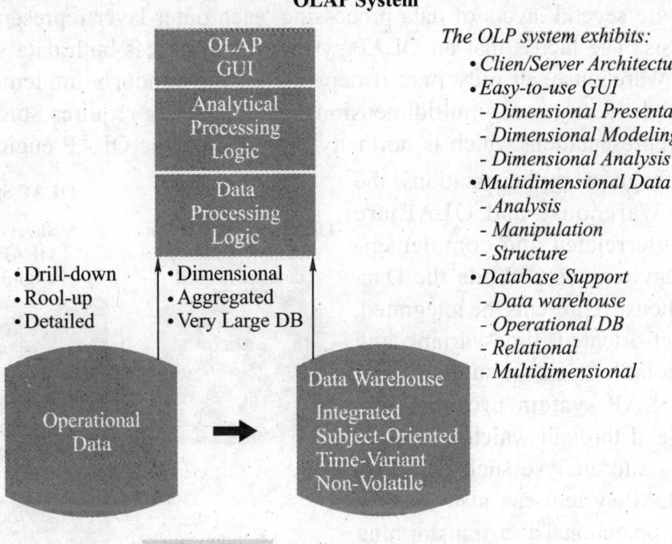

Fig. 11.36 OLAP Client/Server architecture

A more common and more practical architecture is one in which the OLAP GUI runs on client workstations, while the OLAP *engine*, or server, composed of the OLAP Analytical Processing Logic and OLAP Data Processing Logic, runs on a shared computer. In this case, the OLAP server will be a front-end to the Data Warehouse's decision support data. This front-end or middle layer (because it sits between the Data Warehouse and the end user GUI) accepts and processes the data processing requests generated by the many end user analytical tools. The end user GUI might be a custom made program or, more likely, it is a plug-in module that is integrated with Lotus 1-2-3, Microsoft Excel, or some third party analysis and query tool. Figure 11.37 illustrates such an arrangement.

If you examine Fig. 11.37, you will note that the Data Warehouse is created and maintained by a process or software tool that is independent of the OLAP system. This independent software performs the data extraction, filtering, and integration necessary to transform operational data into Data Warehouse data. This scenario reflects that, in most cases, the Data Warehousing and data analysis activities are handled separately.

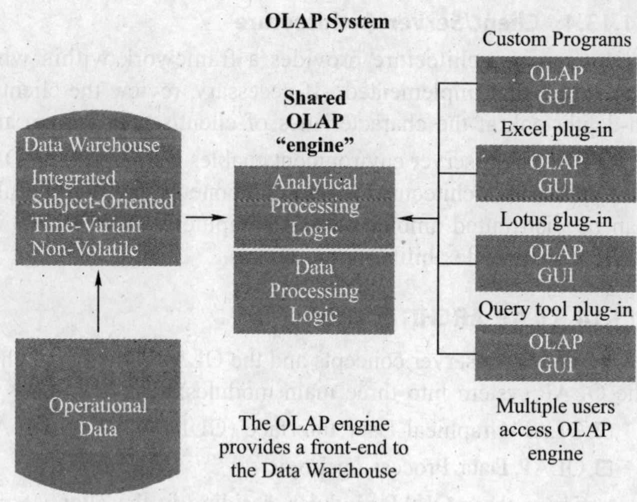

Fig. 11.37 OLAP Server Arrangement

At this point you might ask why you need a Data Warehouse if OLAP provides the necessary multidimensional data analysis of operational data. The answer lies in our definition of OLAP. We defined OLAP as an 'advanced data analysis environment that support decisional making, business modeling, and operation's research activities'. The key word here is *environment*, which includes client/server technology. Environment is defined as 'surroundings or atmosphere'. And an atmosphere surrounds a nucleus. In this case, the nucleus is composed of all business activities within an organization as represented by the operational data. Just as there are several layers within the atmosphere, there are several layers of data processing, each outer layer representing a more aggregated data analysis. The fact is that an OLAP system might access both data storage types (operational or Data Warehouse) or only one; it depends on the vendor's implementation of the product you selected. In any case, multidimensional data analysis requires some type of multidimensional data representation, which is normally provided by the OLAP engine.

In most implementations, the Data Warehouse and OLAP are two interrelated and complementary environments. While the Data Warehouse represents the integrated, subject-oriented, time-variant, and non-volatile decision support data, the OLAP system provides the front-end through which end users access and analyse such data. Yet an OLAP system can also directly access operational data, transforming it an storing it in a multidimensional structure. In other words, the OLAP system can provide a multidimensional store component, as shown in Fig. 11.38.

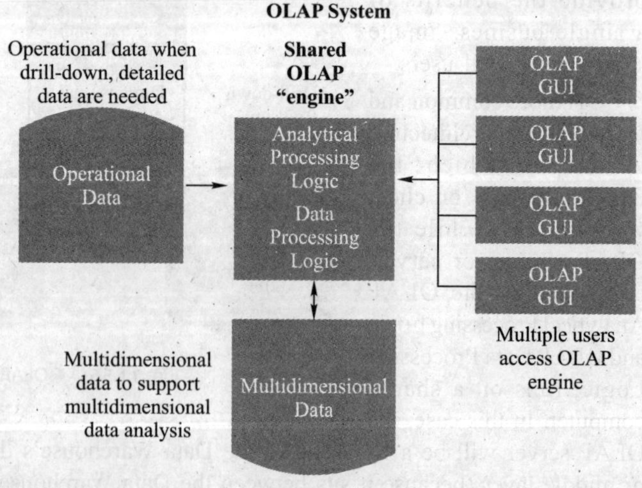

Fig. 11.38 OLAP Server with multidimensional data store arrangement

Figure 11.38 represents a scenario in which the OLAP engine extracts data from an operational database and then stores it in a multidimensional structure for further data analysis. The extraction process follows the same conventions we mentioned in the Data Warehouse section. Therefore, the OLAP provides a mini data Warehouse component that looks remarkably like the Data Mart mentioned in previous sections. In this scenario, the OLAP engine has to perform all the data extraction, filtering integration, classification, and aggregation functions that the Data Warehouse normally provides. In fact, when properly implemented, the Data Warehouse performs all data preparation functions instead of letting OLAP perform those chores, so there is no duplication of functions. Better yet, the Data Warehouse handles the data component much more efficiently than OLAP does, so you can appreciate the benefits of having a central Data Warehouse serve as the *large* enterprise decision support database.

The problem with very large Data Warehouses is that access to them can be time consuming. Therefore, there is a new OLAP system that merges the Data Warehouse and Data Mart approaches by storing small extracts of the Data Warehouse at end user workstations. The objective is to increase the speed of data access and data processing. The logic behind this approach is the assumption that most end users usually work with fairly small, stable Data Warehouse data subsets. For example, the sales analyst is most likely to work with sales data, whereas a customer representative is likely to work with customer data and so on. Figure 11.39 illustrates this scenario.

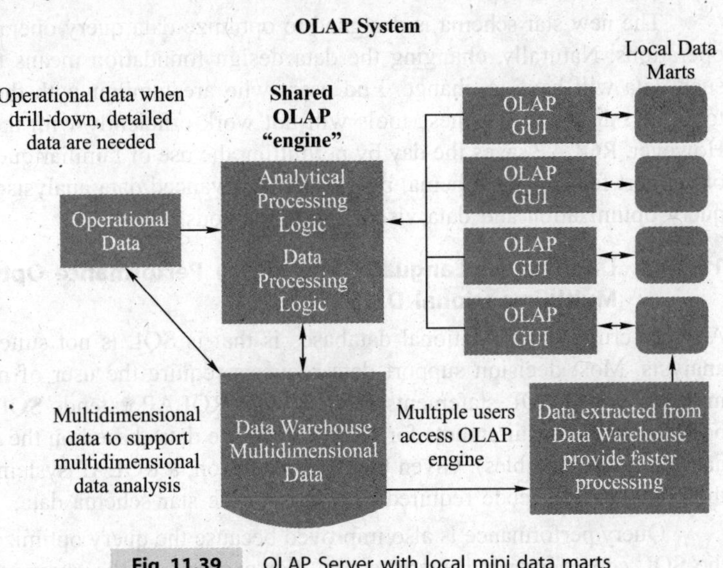

Fig. 11.39 OLAP Server with local mini data marts

We have now summarized the main OLAP architectures you are likely to encounter. Whatever the arrangement of the OLAP components, one thing is certain: multidimensional data must be used. But how are such multidimensional data to be stored and managed best? OLAP proponents are sharply divided: some favour the use of relational databases to store the multidimensional data, whereas other argue the superiority of specialized multidimensional databases to store multidimensional data. We will next examine the basic characteristics of each approach.

11.15 RELATIONAL OLAP

Relational On-line Analytical Processing (ROLAP) provides OLAP functionally by using relational databases and familiar relational query tools to store and analyse multidimensional data. This approach builds on existing relational technologies and represents a natural extension to all those companies that already use relational database management systems within their organizations. ROLAP adds the following extensions to traditional RDBMS technology.

11.15.1 Multidimensional Data Schema Support Within the RDBMS

Relational technology uses normalized tables to store data. The reliance on normalization as the design methodology for relational databases is seen as a stumbling block to its use in OLAP systems. Normalization divides business entities into smaller pieces to produce the normalized tables. For example, sales data components might be stored in four or five different tables. The reason for using normalized tables is to reduce redundancies, thereby eliminating data anomalies, and to facilitate data updates. Unfortunately, for decision support purposes, it is easier to understand data when they are seen with respect to other data (see example in Fig. 11.35). Given this view of the data environment, we have stressed that decision support data tend to be non-normalized, duplicated, and pre-aggregated. These characteristics seem to preclude the user of standard relational design techniques and RDBMS as the foundation for multidimensional data.

Fortunately for those heavily invested in relational technology, ROLAP uses a special design technique to enable the RDBMS technology to support multidimensional data representations. This special design technique is known as a star schema. In effect, the star schema creates the near-equivalent of a multidimensional database schema from the existing relational database.

The new star schema is designed to optimize data query operations rather than data update operations. Naturally, changing the data design foundation means that the tools used to access such data will have to change. End users who are familiar with the traditional relational query tools will discover that these tools will not work efficiently with the new database star schema. However, ROLAP saves the day by permitting the use of familiar query tools through the addition of support for the star schema, by providing advanced data analysis functions, and by improving query optimization and data visualization methods.

11.15.2 Data Access Language and Query Performance Optimized for Multidimensional Data

Another criticism of relational databases is that is SQL is not suited to perform advanced data analysis. Most decision support data requests require the user of multiplepass SQL queries or multiple-nested SQL statements. That is why ROLAP extends SQL so that is can differentiate between access requirements for Data Warehouse data (based on the star schema) and operational data (normalized tables). Given the SQL extension, a ROLAP system is able to properly generate the complex SQL code required to access to the star schema data.

Query performance is also improved because the query optimizer modified so it can identify the SQL code's intended query targets. For example, if the query target is the Data Warehouse, the optimizer passes the requests to the Data Warehouse. However, if the end user performs drill-down queries against operational data, the query optimizer identifies this operation and properly optimizes the SQL requests before passing them through to the operational DBMS. Another source for improved query performance is the user of advanced indexing techniques such as bitmapped indexes within relational databases. Bitmapped indexes are much more efficient at handling large amounts of data than are the b-tree indexes typically found in many relational databases.

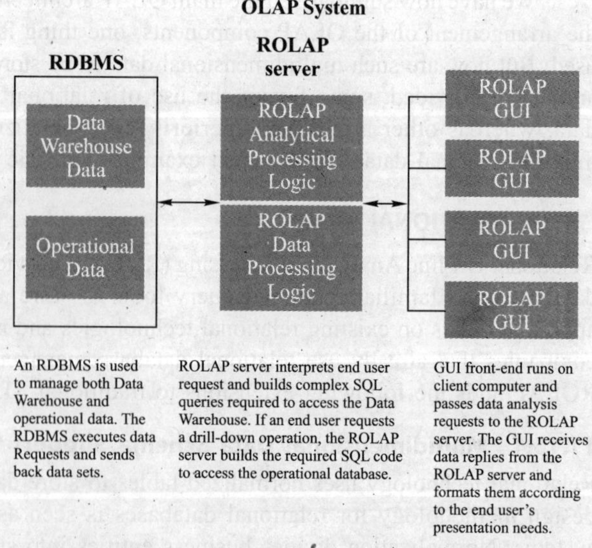

Fig. 11.40 A Typical ROLAP Client/Server Architecture

ROLAP tools are mainly three-tier client/server products in which the end user interface, the analytical processing, and the data processing take place on different computers. Figure 11.40 shows the interaction of the three-tier client/server ROLAP components.

11.15.3 Support for Very Large Database

The relational database is used in a DSS role to store very large amounts of data. Both the storage capability and the process of loading data into the database are crucial. Decision support data are normally loaded in bulk (batch) mode from the operational data. Therefore, the RDBMS must have the proper tools to import, integrate, and populate the Data Warehouse with operational data. Most of the relational data-loading tools perform load operations in batch mode. However, batch operations require that both the source and the destination databases be reserved (locked). The speed of the data-loading operations is important. It is especially important when you realize that most operational systems run twenty-four hours a day, seven days a week, fifty-two weeks a year. Therefore, the window of opportunity for maintenance and batch loading is open only briefly.

Given the existence of an open client/server architecture, ROLAP provides advanced decision support capabilities that are scaleable to the entire enterprise. Clearly, ROLAP is logical choice for companies that already use relational databases for their operational data. Given the size of the relational database market, it is hardly surprising that most current RDBMS vendors have extended their products to support Data Warehouse.

11.16 MULTIDIMENSIONAL OLAP

Multidimensional On-Line Analytical Processing (**MOLAP)** extends OLAP functionality to multidimensional databases (MDBMS) to store and analyse multidimensional data. MOLAP's premise is that multidimensional databases are best suited to manage, store, and analyse multidimensional data. Multidimensional database systems use special proprietary techniques to store data in matrix-like n_dimensional arrays. Most of the proprietary techniques are derived from engineering fields such as Computer-Aided Design/Computer-Aided Manufacturing (CAD/CAM) and Geographic Information Systems (GIS).

Conceptually, MDBMS end users visualize the stored data as a three-dimensional cube known as a **data cube**. The location of each data value in the data cube is a function of the *x*-, *y*- and *z*-axes in a three-dimensional space. The *x*-, *y*-, and *z*-axes represent the dimensions of the data value. The data cubes can grow to *n*-number of dimensions, thus becoming **hypercubes**. Data cubes are created by extracting data from the operational databases or from the Data Warehouse. One important characteristic of data cube is that they are static; that is, they are not subject to change and must be created before they can be used. (In other words, data cubes cannot be created by queries). Therefore, the data cube creation process is critical and requires in depth front-end design work.

This front-end design work may be well-justified by the fact that MOLAP databases are known to be much faster than their ROLAP counterparts, especially when dealing with small to medium data sets. In order to speed data access, data cubes are normally held in memory, in what is called the **cube cache**. Because MOLAP also benefits from a client/server infrastructure, the cube cache can be located at the MOLAP server, at the MOLAP client, or in both locations. Figure 11.41 shows the basic MOLAP architecture.

The ability to capture the data cube in memory provides faster response times, but it also makes the MDBMS more resource-intensive (memory, storage, and processor) than its relational counterpart. In addition, ROLAP proponents argue that the data cube approach limits the flexibility, scalability, and ease of integration.

Because the data cube is predefined with a set number of dimensions, the addition of a new dimension requires that the entire data cube be recreated. This recreation process is a time-consuming operation. Therefore, if data cubes are created tool often, the MDBMS loses some of its speed advantage over the relational database. And, although MDBMSs have performance advantages over relational databases, the MDBMS is best-suited to small and medium data sets. Scalability is somewhat limited, because the size of the data cube is restricted to avoid length data access times. In addition, the MDBMS makes use of proprietary data storage techniques that, in turn, require proprietary data access methods using a multidimensional query language. Relational proponents also argue that using proprietary solutions makes it difficult to integrate the MDBMS with other data sources and tools used within the enterprise. Yet, in spite of the fact that it takes a substantial investment of time and effort to integrate the new technology and the existing information systems architecture, MOLAP may be a good solution for those shops in which small-to to medium-sized databases are the norm and application software speed is critical.

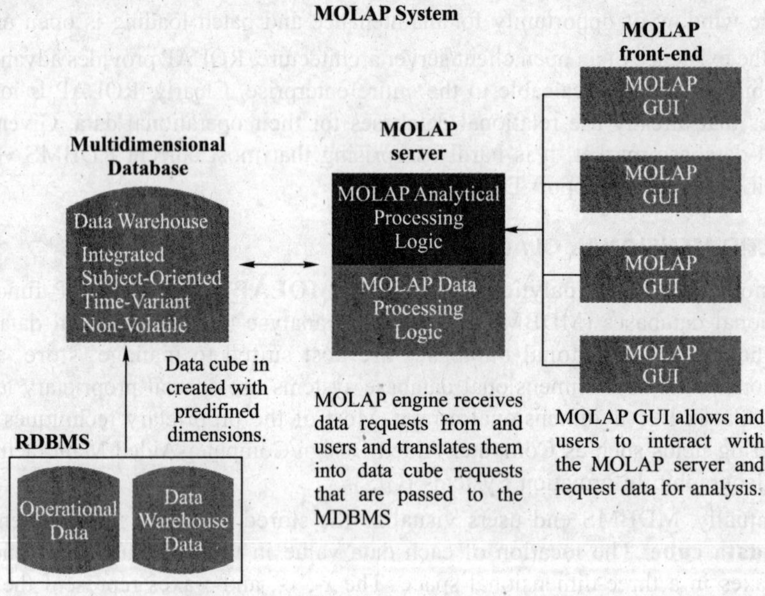

Fig. 11.41 MOLAP Client/Server Architecture

11.17 RELATIONAL VERSUS MULTIDIMENSIONAL OLAP

Table 11.21 summarizes some OLAP and MOLAP pros and cons. However, we should emphasize that some of the advantages of one over the other may be rearranged as technology advances. For example, faster processors and more powerful computers might make the speed and size arguments moot. keep in mind, too, that the selection of one or the other often depends on the evaluator's vantage point. For example, a proper OLAP evaluation must include price, supported hardware platforms, compatibility with the existing DBMS, programming requirements, performance, and availability of administrate tools. Nevertheless, the summary in Table 21.3 provides a useful comparison starting point.

ROLAP and MOLAP vendors are working toward the integration of their respective solutions within a unified decision support framework. As additional features are added to their products, the differences between functionality and capability are reduced. It is quite conceivable that common ground will be found by the RDBMS and MDBMS proponents, thus producing a new kind of DBMS that uses the best features of both ROLAP and MOLAP. Perhaps this new DBMS will be able to handle tabular and multidimensional data with the same ease. In the meantime, relational databases use the star schema design technique successfully to handle multidimensional data, and their market share makes it unlikely that their popularly will fade anytime soon.

Table 11.21 Relational vs. Multidimensional OLAP

Characteristic	*ROLAP*	*MOLAP*
Schema	Uses star schema. Additional dimensions can be added dynamically.	Uses data cubes. Additional dimensions require recreation of cube.
Database size	Medium to large.	Small to medium.
Architecture	Client/Server. Standards-based Open.	Client/Server. Proprietary.
Access	Supports ad hoc requests. Unlimited dimensions.	Limited to predefined dimensions.
Resources	High	Very high
Flexibility	High	Low
Scalability	High	Low
Speed	Good with small data sets; average for medium-large data sets.	Faster for small to medium data sets; average for large data sets.

11.18 GEOGRAPHICAL INFORMATION SYSTEMS

Several years ago, telecommunications carrier GTE tracked the progress of its fiber-optic network by poking pins into maps handed out by a car rental agency. Today, Geographical Information Systems (GIS) provide a much more sophisticated way for companies such as GTE to gather a wide range of information and display it on computer-generated maps. Geography plays an important role in many business decisions, since 85% of corporate data involve geographical elements, such as customers addresses and supplier locations. Also, a number of business decisions, such as store locations, sales territories, sales promotions, and regulatory compliance rely heavily on geographical data. Awareness of this had led many software vendors, such as Lotus, to embed mapping technology in their products so that users can produce maps easily.

Although the term *geographical Information Systems* may conjure up image of software tools for geography majors, they are in fact among the most powerful and versatile tools for the business community and can be used in many different ways in the various functional areas of a business. A *geographical information system* is a computer-based system that stores and manipulates data that are viewed from a geographical point of reference. A GIS has four main capabilities: data input, data storage and retrieval, data communication and analysis, and data output. (Although there are many manual geographical information system, this section focuses on computer-based systems). Note that a GIS should not be confused with cartographic systems, which merely store and generate computer based maps. A GIS is much more versatile and powerful than cartographic system, since it can create information by integrating different data, sometimes from different sources, and display the data in different ways to the end-user.

The number of business applications of GIS has grown significantly in the last few years. For example, Mobil Oil uses a GIS product called MapInfo for crisis management in the event of an oil spill or tank explosion; Levi Strauss uses GIS to match a store's product mix with customer demographics; the *Chicago Tribune* uses GIS for developing new sales territories based on demographics; and Arby's uses GIS for site selection.

The banking industry uses GIS to respond to regulatory pressures and to comply with the Community Redevelopment Act, which requires banks to demonstrate to regulators that their lending practices are nondiscriminatory. A GIS allows a bank to compare deposits with loan approvals in a given area and show that loan approvals meet regulatory standards in areas with high deposits, especially in parts of the country that have heavy minority populations. Essential Information, a Washington-based public- interest group founded by Ralph Nader, recently used a GIS to illustrate its charges that mortgage lenders in some part of the country are violating the Fair Housing and Equal Credit Opportunity acts. Automobile insurers use GIS to estimate the distance travelled between home and work for potential clients, because this is an important factor in determining insurance rates. A recent study by the Industry Research Council showed that many Americans believe it is acceptable to lie about the distance they drive between home and work in order to lower their insurance rates.

In summary, a geographical information system is an excellent decision making tool that integrates geographical data with other business data. For companies with a customer focus, a GIS provides clear profiles of customers and their needs; hence, these tools can be integrated with any of the functional systems discussed above, such as marketing information systems, production information systems, and so on. The ability to integrate different data, analyse their impact on the customer, and integrate the findings in organizational decision making is one of the key factors that separates winners from losers.

11.19 SUMMARY

Data are facts from which a conclusion can be drawn; for this reason, humans record data. Data is required in the operation of any organization, and the same or similar data may be required in various facets of its functioning.

Entity sets are the categories of objects of interest to an organization for which the organization maintains data. To store the data about an entity set, a reasonable model of the entity is made by listing the characteristics or attributes that are of relevance to the database application. In order to uniquely identify a single instance of an entity sét, a primary key is devised either from the attributes that are used to model the entity set or by adding such an attribute. The values for each attribute of an instance of an entity set are grouped together and this collection is called a record type. A file is a collection of identical record type occurrences pertaining to an entity set.

A database system is an integrated collection of related files along with the details about their definition, interpretation, manipulation, and maintenance. It is an attempt to satisfy the data needs of the various applications in an organization without unnecessary duplication. The DBMS not only makes the integrated collection of reliable and accurate data available to multiple applications and users, but also exerts centralized control, prevents fraudulent or unauthorized users from accessing the data, and ensures privacy.

A number of data representation models have been developed over the years. As in the case of programming languages, one concludes that there is no one 'best' choice for all applications. These models differ in their method of representing the associations between entities and attributes.

Traditional data models are hierarchical, network, or relational models. The hierarchical model evolved from the file-based system; the network model is a superset of the hierarchical model. The relational data model is based on the mathematical relational concept. The data model concept evolved at about the same time as the relational data model.

The basic building blocks of a relational database are entities. A grouping of related entities, known as an entity set, is stored in a table. Conceptually speaking, the relational table is composed of intersecting rows (tuples) and columns. Each row represents a single entity, and each column represents the characteristics (attributes) of the entities.

Keys are central to the use of relational tables. Keys define functional dependencies. That is, other attributes are dependent on the key and can, therefore, be found if the key value is known. A key can be classified according to its characteristics as a superkey, a candidate key, a primary key, a secondary key, or a foreign key.

Relational databases can be classified according to the degree to which the relational algebra functions SELECT, PROJECT, JOIN, INTERSECT, UNION, DIFFERENCE, PRODUCT, and DIVIDE are supported and also to the degree that (entity and referential) integrity rules are enforced. A fully relational database supports all eight relational algebra functions and enforces both integrity rules. A relationally complete database lacks only the enforcement of the integrity rules. A minimally relational database supports only SELECT, PROJECT, and JOIN and does not enforce the integrity rules. The tabular database supports only the relational algebra functions supported by the minimally relational database, and it requires that the access paths to the tables be defined. The more relational the relational database is, the greater its user flexibility, and the easier it is to design its applications.

Normalization is a technique used to design tables in which data redundancies are minimized. The first three normal forms (INF, 2NF, and 3NF) are most commonly encountered. From a structural point of view, higher normal forms are better than lower normal forms because higher normal forms yield relatively fewer data redundancies in the database. In other words, 3NF is better than 2NF, which is better than INF. Almost all business designs use the 3NF as the ideal normal, form. A special, more restricted 3nf is known as Boyce-Codd normal form, or BCNF.

A table is in INF when all the key attributes are defined and when all remaining attributes are dependent on the primary key. However; the table in INF can still contain

both partial and transitive dependencies. (A partial dependency is one in which an attribute is functionally dependent on only a part of a multi-attribute primary key. A transitive dependency is one in which one attribute is functionally dependent on another nonkey attribute). Naturally, a table with a single-attribute primary key cannot exhibit partial dependencies.

A table is in 2NF when it is in INF and contains to partial dependencies. Therefore, a INF datable is automatically in 2NF if its primary key is based on only a single attribute. A table in 2NF may still contain transitive dependencies. A table is in 3NF if it is in 2NF and contains no transitive dependencies.

REVIEW QUESTIONS

Multiple Choice Questions

1. In a relational schema, each tuple is divided into fields called:

(*a*) relations (*b*) domains (*c*) queries (*d*) all of these

2. A top-to-bottom relationship among the items in a database is established by a:

(*a*) Hierarchical schema (*b*) Network schema (*c*) Relational schema (*d*) All of these

3. A good query system:

(*a*) can accept English language commands

(*b*) allows non-programmers to access information stored in a database

(*c*) can be accessed only by data processing professionals

(*d*) both (*a*) and (*b*)

4. A list consists of last names, first names, addresses, and pin codes if all people in the list have the same last and the same pin code, a useful key would be:

(*a*) the pin code (*b*) the last name

(*c*) a compound key consisting of the first name and the last name

(*d*) all of these

5. A logical schema:
(*a*) is the entire database
(*b*) is a standard way of organizing information into accessible parts
(*c*) describes how data is actually stored on disk
(*d*) all of these

6. A form defines:
(*a*) where data is placed on the screen (*b*) the width of each field
(*c*) both (*a*) and (*b*) (*d*) all of these

7. A report form:
(*a*) appears on the computer monitor during data entry
(*b*) is used during report generation to format data
(*c*) both (*a*) and (*b*)
(*d*) all of these

8. A command that lets you change one or more fields in a record is
(*a*) insert (*b*) modify (*c*) look-up (*d*) all of these

9. The modify operation is likely to be done after
(*a*) delete (*b*) look-up (*c*) insert (*d*) all of these

10. What is the abbreviation used for a software package that permits the users to create, retrieve and maintain records in a database?
(*a*) DASD (*b*) FMS (*c*) EMMS (*d*) DBMS

11. Which of the following is not a relational database?
(*a*) dBASE IV (*b*) 4th Dimension (*c*) FoxPro (*d*) Reflex

12. If a piece of data is stored in two places in the database, then
(*a*) storage space is wasted
(*b*) changing the data in one spot will cause data inconsistency
(*c*) it can be more easily accessed
(*d*) both (*a*) and (*b*)

13. In order to use a DBMS, it is important to understand
(*a*) the physical schema
(*b*) all subschemas that the system supports
(*c*) one subschema
(*d*) both (*a*) and (*b*)

14. Subschema can be used to
(*a*) create very different, personalized views of the same data
(*b*) present information in different formats
(*c*) hide sensitive information by omitting fields from the subschema's description
(*d*) all of these

15. Data items grouped together for storage purposes are called a
(*a*) record (*b*) title (*c*) list (*d*) string

16. The way a particular application views the data from the database that the application uses is a:
(*a*) module (*b*) relational model (*c*) schema (*d*) subschema

17. A relational database management (RDBM) package manages data in more than one file at once. How does it organize these files? As:
(*a*) tables (*b*) relations (*c*) tuple (*d*) both (*a*) and (*b*)

ANSWERS

Multiple Choice Questions

1. (*b*) **2.** (*a*) **3.** (*b*) **4.** (*c*) **5.** (*b*) **6.** (*c*) **7.** (*b*) **8.** (*b*)
9. (*b*) **10.** (*d*) **11.** (*d*) **12.** (*d*) **13.** (*c*) **14.** (*d*) **15.** (*a*) **16.** (*d*)
17. (*d*)

QUESTIONS

1. What is the difference between a database and a table?

2. What is the function of a database management system?

3. What do you mean by relational database?

4. What is schema?

5. Describe the purpose of developing subschemas.

6. Distinguish between the logical and physical designs of a database.

7. How does the network database structure differ from the hierarchical database structure?

8. Describe the relational database structure.

9. Explain the difference between data and information.

10. What is a database management package? Why were such packages created?

11. How can database management packages reduce the data reducndancy file updating problem?

12. How are files created by using a database management package? How are the database records entered in the package?

13. What is normalization?

14. What is a table in INF?

15. What is a table in 2NF?

16. What is a table in 3NF?

17. What three data anomalies are likely to be the result of data redundancy? How can such anomalies be eliminated?

18. List the three data models. Explain the salient features of each model.

19. What is the function of a database management system?

20. What do you mean by relational database?

21. Define the following:

(a) primary key (b) secondary key (c) foreign key (d) candidate key
(e) alternate key

22. What is relational algebra? What operations are performed in it?

23. What is the need of normalisation?

DATA COMMUNICATIONS AND COMPUTER NETWORKS

A **computer network** is created when several computers and terminal devices are connected together by data communication system. The set of computers may include microprocessors, minicomputers, medium scale computers and large scale computers. The set of terminal devices may include dumb terminals, intelligent terminals, dumb as well as intelligent terminals, etc. and miscellaneous devices such as modems, commonly used for data transmission. Each computer in a network can have its own processing capabilities and can also share computer hardware, programs, software and data files.

The three basic types of computer networks are as follows:

1. Local Area Networks
2. Metropolitan Area Network
3. Wide Area Networks

12.1 LOCAL AREA NETWORKS (LAN)

A local area network (LAN) is two or more computers directly linked within a small, well defined area such as a room, office building, or a campus. A LAN can be made up of only microcomputers or any combination of microcomputer and large system. Main benefit of a LAN is the reduction of hardware and software costs because users can share several computers, peripheral devices such as laser printers, color plotters, hard-disks, modems, LAN platform software. Another benefit is that the users can share the same data.

Famous LANs available for microcomputer users include Ethernet, Novell, PC Network, ARCnet and Omninet. They vary in type and number of computers that may be connected, the speed at which data may be transferred, and the type of software used to control the network.

A LAN generally consists of the following:

1. Two or more computers
2. Software to control the operation of the computers
3. Peripheral devices such as modems, printers, plotters, etc.
4. Coaxial or fiber optic cables are usually used to connect the computers and other devices
5. A plug-in board to handle the data transmissions

Some LANs specifically require all the computers to be of a certain brand, while others allow a variety of brands to be connected. The number of computers in LAN varies widely from small LANs that connect two to twenty-five computers, to large LANs that may connect more than 10,000 computers.

LAN must get the data to its destination, transmit the data correctly, and prevent unauthorized users from gaining access to that data.

The length of the cable connecting to computer through a LAN also varies. Most LANs permit cables of about 1000 feet, but some permit cables of several miles to be used. The speed of data transfer ranges from several thousand bits per second to 10 million bits per second.

12.2 METROPOLITAN AREA NETWORK (MAN)

A *metropolitan area network* (MAN) is a network that is larger than a LAN. It is called metropolitan since it normally covers the area of a city. Different hardware and transmission media are often used in MANs because they must efficiently cover these distances (a few tens to about one hundred kilometers) or because they don't require complete access to locations between the networked sites.

12.3 WIDE AREA NETWORKS (WAN)

A **Wide area network** is two or more geographically dispersed computers, linked by communication facilities such as telecommunication or microwave relays. In other words, one of the most significant aspects of a wide area network while comparing it with the freedom of a local area network, is the involvement of a public telecommunications authority. WAN is usually limited to use by the large organizations and government agencies due to high costs involved in building and maintaining them.

A special designation has also been given to two specific WAN categories:

- **Enterprise:** An *enterprise network* connects all LANs of a single organization. The term is normally used for networks connecting extremely large organizations, or for cross regional boundaries.
- **Global:** By definition, a *global network* is one that spans the earth. While global networks may not cover the entire globe, they cross multiple national boundaries and may include the networks of several organizations.

12.4 NETWORK TOPOLOGY

Each computer or device in a network is called a **node**. The geometrical arrangement of computer resources, remote device, communication facilities is known as **network topology**.

A network can be made in one of the five different topologies:

1. Bus Network	2. Ring Network
3. Star Network	4. Tree Network
5. Mesh Network	6. Star-Ring Network

12.4.1 Bus Network

In a **bus network**, each computer is connected to a single communication cable via an interface, and every computer can directly communicate with every other computer or device in the network as shown in Fig. 12.1. This topology is commonly used alongwith the local area networks.

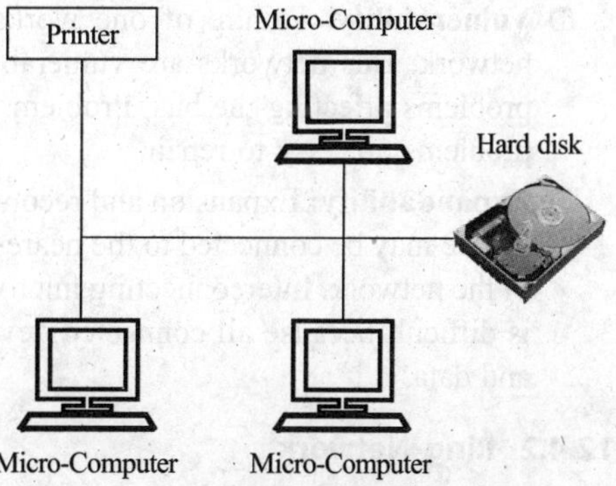

Fig. 12.1 Bus Network

12.4.1.1 *Advantages of the Bus Network*

1. **Short cable length and simple wiring layout:** Because there is a single common data path connecting all nodes, the bus topology allows

a very short cable length to be used. This decreases the installation cost, and also leads to a simple, easy-to-maintain, wiring layout.

2. **Resilient architecture:** The bus architecture has an inherent simplicity that makes it very reliable from a hardware point of view. There is a single cable through which all data passes and to which all nodes are connected.
3. **Easy to extend:** Additional nodes can be connected to an existing bus network at any point along its length. More extensive additions can be achieved by adding extra segments connected by a type of signal amplifier known as a repeater.

12.4.1.2 Disadvantages of the Bus Network

1. **Fault diagnosis is difficult:** Although the simplicity of the bus topology means that there is very little that can go wrong, fault detection is not a simple matter. In most LANs based on a bus, control of the network is not centralised in any particular node. This means that detection of a fault may be performed from many points in the network.
2. **Fault isolation is difficult:** In the star topology, a defective node can easily be isolated from the network by removing its connection at the centre. If a node is faulty on a bus, it must be rectified at the point where the node is connected to the network. Once the fault has been located, the node can simply be removed. In the case where the fault is in the network medium itself, an entire segment of the bus must be disconnected.
3. **Repeater configuration:** When a bus-type network has its backbone extended using repeaters, reconfiguration may be necessary. This may involve tailoring cable lengths, adjusting terminators, etc.
4. **Nodes must be intelligent:** Each node on the network is directly connected to the central bus. This means that some way of deciding who can use the network at any given time must be performed in each node. It tends to increase the cost of the nodes irrespective of whether this is performed in hardware or software.

12.4.1.3 Bus Network Evaluation Factors

- **Application:** Bus networks are a good choice for small networks and networks with low traffic.
- **Complexity:** Bus networks tend to be relatively uncomplex.
- **Performance:** Excellent under light load, may degrade rapidly as load increases.
- **System overhead:** Comparatively low, particularly because much of the hardware is fully developed and readily available. Some redundancy of communication channel is advisable to reduce the vulnerability to channel outrage.
- **Vulnerability:** Failure of one workstation on a bus network does not usually affect the network. Bus networks are vulnerable to failure from damage to the main link and other problems affecting the bus. Problems on the bus are hard to locate. Once located, however, problems are easy to repair.
- **Expandability:** Expansion and reconfiguration of a bus network are easy. A new or relocated device may be connected to the nearest convenient network access point with little disruption of the network. Interconnecting microcomputers and equipment from different manufacturers is difficult because all connected devices must be able to accept the same forms of address and data.

12.4.2 Ring Network

In a **ring network**, several devices or computers are connected to each other in a closed loop by a single communication cable as shown in Fig. 12.2. A ring network is also called loop network.

In the ring network, data must travel around the ring to each station in turn until they arrive at the required station.

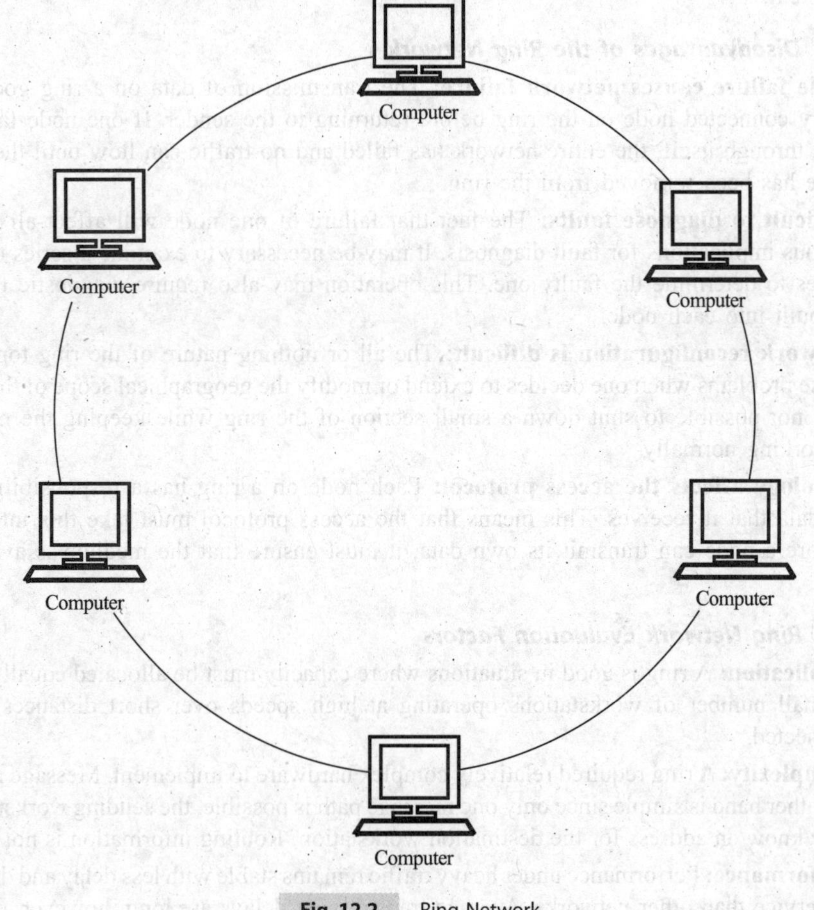

Fig. 12.2 Ring Network

A ring can be unidirectional or bidirectional. In a unidirectional ring, data moves in one direction only, and in a bidirectional ring, data moves in both directions, but in only one direction at a time. In the undirectional ring, a special software is needed if one computer should break down, whereas, in the bidirectional ring, message can be sent in the opposite direction to meet the requirement.

12.4.2.1 Advantages of the Ring Network

1. **Short cable length:** The amount of cabling involved in a ring topology is comparable to that of a bus and is small relative to that of a star. This means that less connections will be needed, which will in turn increase network reliability.
2. **No wiring closet space required:** Since there is only one cable connecting each node to its immediate neighbours, it is not necessary to allocate space in the building for wiring closets.
3. **Suitable for optical fibres:** Optical fibres offer the possibility of very high speed transmission. Because traffic on a ring travels in one direction, it is easy to use optical fibres as a medium of transmission. Also, since a ring is made up of nodes connected by short segments of transmission medium, there is a possibility of mixing the types used for different parts of

the network. Thus, a manufacturing company's network could use copper cables in the office area and optical fibres in the factory areas, where electrical interference may be a problem.

12.4.2.2 *Disadvantages of the Ring Network*

1. **Node failure causes network failure:** The transmission of data on a ring goes through every connected node on the ring before returning to the sender. If one node fails to pass data through itself, the entire network has failed and no traffic can flow until the defective node has been removed from the ring.
2. **Difficult to diagnose faults:** The fact that failure of one node will affect all others has serious implications for fault diagnosis. It may be necessary to examine a series of adjacent nodes to determine the faulty one. This operation may also require diagnostic facilities to be built into each node.
3. **Network reconfiguration is difficult:** The all or nothing nature of the ring topology can cause problems when one decides to extend or modify the geographical scope of the network. It is not possible to shut down a small section of the ring while keeping the majority of it working normally.
4. **Topology affects the access protocol:** Each node on a ring has a responsibility to pass on data that it receives. This means that the access protocol must take this into account. Before a node can transmit its own data, it must ensure that the medium is available for use.

12.4.2.3 *Ring Network Evaluation Factors*

- **Application:** A ring is good in situations where capacity must be allocated equally or where a small number of workstations operating at high speeds over short distances are to be connected.
- **Complexity:** A ring required relatively complex hardware to implement. Message routing, on the other hand is simple since only one message path is possible, the sending workstation need only know an address for the destination workstation. Routing information is not necessary.
- **Performance:** Performance under heavy traffic remains stable with less delay and degradation of service than other networks. Average transmission delays are long, however, even under light traffic. Actual performance is dependent on the control protocols implemented.
- **System overhead:** Duplication of resources or a method of bypassing failure points is needed if the ring is to keep functioning when equipment fails.
- **Vulnerability:** Failure in a single workstation or in the channel can cause system failure because of the interdependence of workstations. Locating a failed repeater is particularly difficult; in a system with wide geographical distribution it may not be possible to immediately repair or circumvent the problem.
- **Expandability:** It is moderately easy to add or delete workstations on a ring network without making numerous connections for each change. Therefore, system modification costs are relatively low. Expansion does disrupt the whole system, even though it may be only briefly.

12.4.3 Star Network

In a **star network**, several devices or computers are connected to one centralized computer as shown in Fig. 12.3. The disadvantage of star network is that none of the other computers can communicate with each other if the central computer breaks down. If it is desired to transmit information from one computer to another, it can be done only by sending the details to the central computer, which in turn sends them to the destination. A star network is used in banking sector for centralized record keeping in an on-line branch office environment.

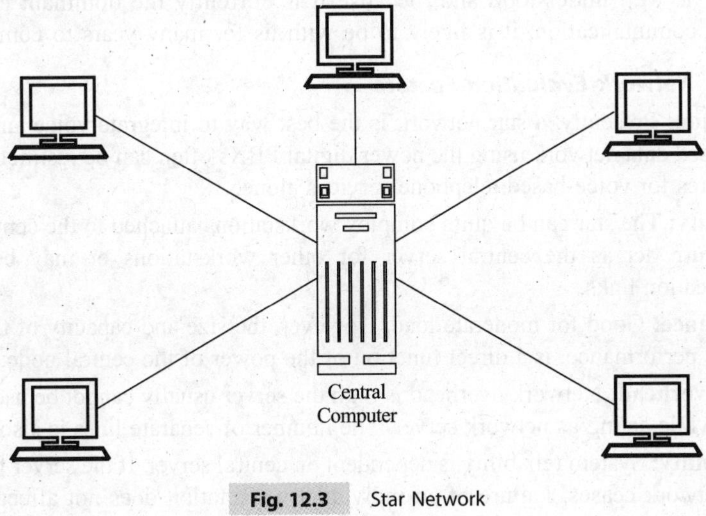

Fig. 12.3 Star Network

12.4.3.1 *Advantages of the Star Network*

1. **Ease of service:** The star topology has a number of concentration points, *i.e.*, at the central node or at intermediate wiring closets. These provide easy access for service of reconfiguration of the network.
2. **One device per connection:** Connection points in any network are inherently prone to failure. In the star topology, failure of a single connection typically involves disconnecting one node from an otherwise fully functional network.
3. **Centralized control/problem diagnosis:** The fact that the central node is connected directly to every other node in the network means that faults are easily detected and isolated. It is a simple matter to disconnect failing nodes from the system.
4. **Simple access protocols:** Any given connection in a star network involves only the central node and one peripheral node. In this situation, contention for who has control of the medium for transmission purposes is easily solved. Thus, in a star network, access protocols are very simple.

12.4.3.2 *Disadvantages of the Star Network*

1. **Long cable length:** Because each node is directly connected to the centre, the star topology necessitates a large quantity of cable. While the cost of the cable is often small, congestion in cable ducts and maintenance and installation problems can increase costs considerably.
2. **Difficult to expand:** The addition of a new node to a star network involves a connection all the way to the central node. Expansion is usually catered for by providing large numbers of redundant cables during the initial wiring. However, problems can arise if a longer cable length is needed or an unanticipated concentration of nodes is required.
3. **Central node dependency:** If the central node in a star network fails, the entire network is rendered inoperable. This introduces heavy reliability and redundancy constraints on this node.

The star topology has found extensive application in areas where intelligence in the network is concentrated at the central node. The tendency in recent computer systems is away from host-based computing power, and the advent of microprocessor-based systems where all nodes possess a high level of processing power has led to a fall off in the use of this topology. Nevertheless, the technology is well understood and, because it is currently the dominant configuration in traditional data communication, it is likely to be with us for many years to come.

12.4.3.3 Star Network Evaluation Factors

- **Application:** Presently, a star network is the best way to integrate voice and data services. A star-based data network using the newer digital PBXs often can be justified by the savings and features for voice-based telephone services alone.
- **Complexity:** The star can be quite complex workstations attached to the central workstation may in turn act as the central server for other workstations or may be connected to communication links.
- **Performance:** Good for moderate load. However, the size and capacity of the network and hence the performance, is a direct function of the power of the central node.
- **System overhead:** Network overhead is high the server usually cannot be used for any other purpose while acting as network server. The number of separate lines is also high.
- **Vulnerability:** System reliability is dependent on central server. If the server fails, all activity on the network ceases. Failure of an individual workstation does not affect the system. In either case, identification of problems and repair is simplified by centralized control.
- **Expandability:** Expandability may be severely restricted; most servers can support a limited number of network interfaces. Bandwidth and data rate limitations are often imposed on each user. The limits are necessary to protect the central processing functions from overload due to the aggregate rate of all the service ports and to keep the cost of each port on the central server low.

12.4.4 Tree Network

In a **tree network**, several devices or computers are linked in a hierarchical fashion as shown in Fig. 12.4. Tree network is also known as **hierarchical network**. This type of distribution system is commonly used in the organization where headquarters communicate with regional offices and regional offices communicate with district offices, and so on.

12.4.4.1 Advantages of the Tree Network

1. **Easy to extend:** Because the tree is, of its very nature, divided into subunits, it is easier to add new nodes or branches to it.
2. **Fault isolation:** It is possible to disconnect whole branches of the network from the main structure. This makes it easier to isolate a defective node.

12.4.4.2 Disadvantages of the Tree Network

1. **Dependent on the root:** If the 'headend' device fails to operate, the entire network is rendered inoperable. In this respect, the tree suffers from the same reliability problems as the star.

12.4.5 Mesh Network

A *mesh* network has point-to-point connections between every device in the network.

Each device requires an interface for every other device on the network, mesh topologies are not usually considered practical. In addition, unless each station frequently sends signals to all the other stations, an excessive amount of network bandwidth is wasted. However, mesh networks are extremely fault tolerant, and each link provides guaranteed capacity (Fig. 12.5).

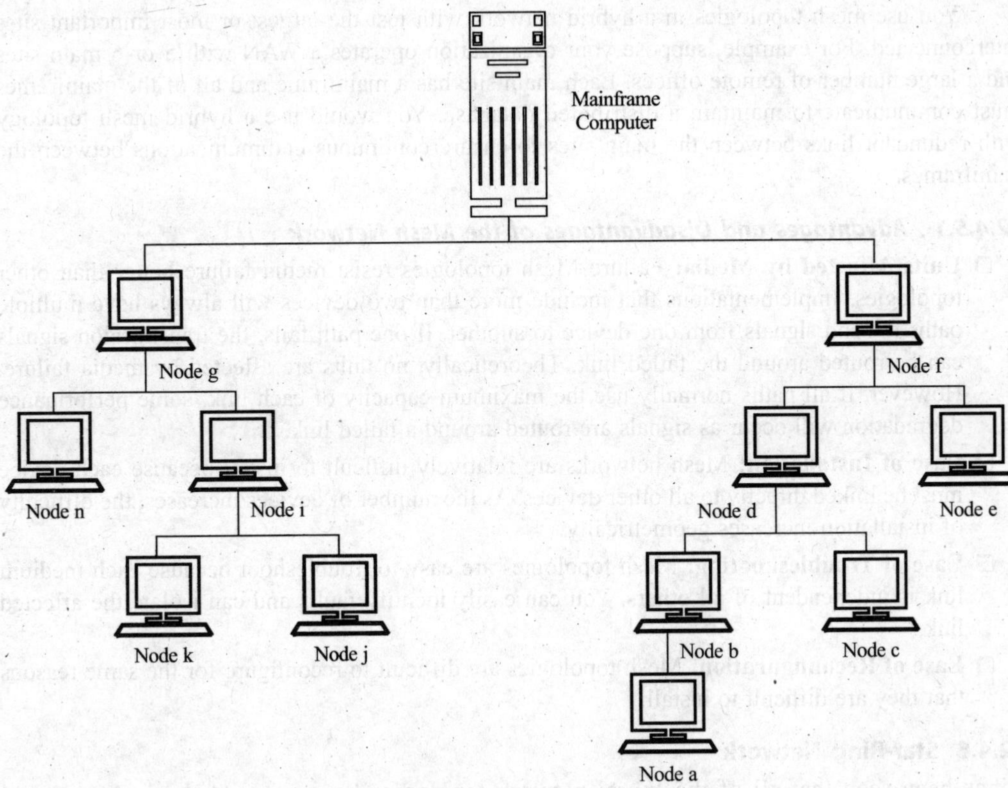

Fig. 12.4 Tree Network

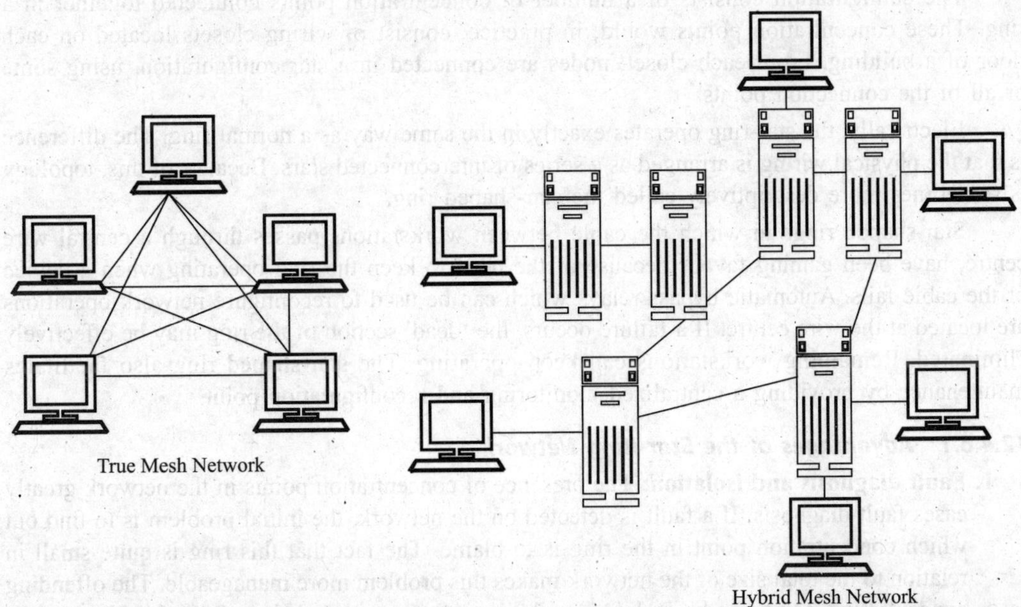

Fig. 12.5 True Mesh Network and Hybrid Mesh Network

You use mesh topologies in a hybrid network with just the largest or most important sites interconnected. For example, suppose your organization operates a WAN with 5 or 6 main sites and a large number of remote offices. Each main site has a mainframe and all of the mainframes must communicate to maintain a distributed database. You would use a hybrid mesh topology with redundant links between the main sites to ensure continuous communications between the mainframes.

12.4.5.1 *Advantages and Disadvantages of the Mesh Network*

- **Units Affected by Media:** Failure Mesh topologies resist media failure better than other topologies. Implementations that include more than two devices will always have multiple paths to send signals from one device to another. If one path fails, the transmission signals can be routed around the failed link. Theoretically, no units are affected by media failure. However, if all paths normally use the maximum capacity of each link, some performance degradation will occur as signals are routed around a failed link.
- **Ease of Installation:** Mesh networks are relatively difficult to install because each device must be linked directly to all other devices. As the number of devices increases, the difficulty of installation increases geometrically.
- **Ease of Troubleshooting:** Mesh topologies are easy to troubleshoot because each medium link is independent of all others. You can easily identify faults and can isolate the affected link.
- **Ease of Reconfiguration:** Mesh topologies are difficult to reconfigure for the same reasons that they are difficult to install.

12.4.6 Star-Ring Network

It has been seen that all of the 'pure' network topologies have associated advantages and disadvantages. In the star-ring, two topologies have been combined with the aim of achieving the best of both.

The configuration consists of a number of concentration points connected together in a ring. These concentration points would, in practice, consist of wiring closets located on each floor of a building. From each closet, nodes are connected in a star configuration, using some or all of the connection points.

Electrically, the star-ring operates exactly in the same way as a normal ring. The difference is that the physical wiring is arranged as a series of interconnected stars. Because of this, topology is sometimes more descriptively called the star-shaped ring.

Star-shaped rings in which the cable between workstations passes through a central wire centre, have been gaining favour because of the need to keep the ring operating when a device or the cable fails. Automatic bypass relays which can be used to reconfigure network operations are located at the wire centre. If a failure occurs, the 'dead' section of the ring may be effectively eliminated. Remaining workstations can keep operating. The star-shaped ring also facilitates maintenance by providing a centralized monitoring and reconfiguration point.

12.4.6.1 *Advantages of the Star-Ring Network*

1. **Fault diagnosis and isolation:** The presence of concentration points in the network greatly eases fault diagnosis. If a fault is detected on the network, the initial problem is to find out which concentration point in the ring is to blame. The fact that this ring is quite small in relation to the total size of the network makes this problem more manageable. The offending concentration point can be isolated easily, leaving the network in a fully functional state while further fault diagnosis is carried out.

2. **Ease of expansion:** The modular construction of a star-ring network means that new sections may be easily added. When designing the network originally, each concentration can have extra, unused lobes which can be called upon later, if needed. The next growth step involves adding a new concentration point and wiring it into the ring.
3. **Cabling:** The concentration points in a star-ring are connected via a single cable. This simplifies wiring between areas in an installation and cuts down on the congestion of cable ducts. Also, the wiring practices involved are very similar to that of telephone system installation. These techniques are well understood by building engineers and lend themselves well to the prewiring of buildings.

12.4.6.2 Disadvantages of the Star-Ring Network

1. **Intelligent concentration points required:** Depending on the implementation used, the concentration points may need to have built in intelligence/processing ability. This will be necessary if it is to assist in network fault diagnosis, node isolation or conversion from one form of transmission medium to another.
2. **Cabling:** The intercloset cabling in a star-ring is critical to its operation. This may mean that redundant cabling in the form of one or more back up rings may be necessary to meet reliability requirements. The largest section of the network (*i.e.*, between the concentration points and the nodes) is laid out in a star. This means that a considerable amount of cable may be required.

12.5 BASIC ELEMENTS IN NETWORKING

All networks require the following three elements:

1. **Network Services:** At least two individuals who have something to *share*
2. **Transmission Media:** A method or *pathway* for contacting each other
3. **Protocols:** Rules so that two or more individual can *communicate*

12.5.1 Network Services

Network services are provided by numerous combinations of computer hardware and software. Depending upon the task, network services require data, input/output resources, and processing power to accomplish their goals.

In the computer industry, the following three types of service providers and requestors are as follows:

- ❒ **Servers:** Servers are only allowed to provide services
- ❒ **Clients:** Clients are only allowed to request services from others
- ❒ **Peers:** Peers may do both concurrently

Computer networks are often classified as one of the following two types:

- ❒ *Peer-to-peer*
- ❒ *Server-Centric*

12.5.1.1 Peer-to-Peer Networks

Peer-to-peer networks allow any entity to both request and provide network services. Peer-to-peer network software is designed so that peers perform the same or similar functions for each other.

12.5.1.2 Server-Centric Networks

Server-centric networks involves strictly defined roles. By definition, a server-centric network places restrictions upon which entity may make requests or service them. Currently, the most popular personal computer networks are server-centric.

12.5.2 Transmission Media

Transmission media is the pathway networked entities use to contact each other. Computer transmission media includes cable and wireless technologies that allow networked devices to contact each another. Transmission media cannot guarantee that other network devices will understand a message. It can, however, guarantee a message delivery path.

12.5.3 Protocols

A protocol can be one rule or a complete set of rules and standards that allow different devices to hold conversations. For example, human communication would be impossible without language, grammar, and cultural rules. The following is an example of set of rules and standards in which network service requestors and service providers can communicate:

- How is the transmission media physically set up?
- How do network entities contact one another?
- How do network entities know how much data can be transmitted?
- How are network entities guaranteed that a message has been received correctly?
- How is a message passed to the intended recipient(s)?
- How are bits transmitted on the media?
- How do network entities, with disparate languages, communicate?
- How do network entities know when to transmit data?

When you formally agree that you will both use the same language in future communications, you have established a communication protocol.

12.6 COMMON NETWORK SERVICES

The following common network services are available:

1. File services
2. Print services
3. Message services
4. Application services
5. Database services

12.6.1 File Services

The network file services improve the efficient storage and retrieval of computer data, they are one of the primary services offered on computer networks. The following file service functions are:

- File transfer—Rapidly move files from place to place
- File storage and data migration—Use storage hardware efficiently
- File update synchronization—Manage multiple copies of the same file
- File archiving—Back up critical data

12.6.1.1 File Transfer

Before computer networks were widely implemented, users physically moved storage media from computer to computer. This inefficient practice has been called 'sneaker-net' (because users hand-carried data from machine to machine). Organizationally, it is relatively expensive and time consuming to employ people to move computer storage media.

The network file service *file transfer* refers to any service that saves, retrieves, or moves files for a network client. This service allows you to handle data much more efficiently.

The major advantage of Computer Networks is, file transfers can be performed with relative ease regardless of file size, distance, and often even the local operating systems. This service increases the organization's efficiency, as well as it also provides access to data and information that were previously inaccessible.

File services may also coordinate access rights because of the increased information access that the file transfer service provides. An organization may allow network transfer of sensitive information, but only by authorized individuals. During file transfer, network file services often use passwords to control access to systems and files. They use data encryption schemes to encode data so that it can only be read by appropriate individuals.

12.6.1.2 File Storage and Data Migration

The rapidly increasing amount of computerized data has caused the development of numerous online, nearline, and offline storage devices. Hard disk drive, tape jukebox, and removable storage is an example of online storage, nearline storage and offline storage respectively. Computers store data on a variety of magnetic and optic disks, diskettes, and tapes. Each storage medium exhibits characteristics that make it suitable for a specific use. Because the efficient use of each storage device requires continuous management of multiple devices, network applications are well suited to control data storage activities on different storage systems.

In addition, if you are working with high-end equipment, such as magnetic tape banks or optical disk libraries, you can use the network's economy of scale to justify the equipment purchase, operation, and maintenance. Using file storage and data migration functions, all networked computers can take advantage of the data storage device that is appropriate for their access time, reliability, and longevity needs.

As data ages and becomes less used, it can be moved from expensive online hard disk drives to less expensive and longer-life offline storage media. Moving data from one storage media or location to another is called **data migration**. Through data migration, you can set up file services to move files based on age, user, size, or various other criteria.

12.6.1.3 File-Update Synchronization

File-update synchronization is a service that compares the time and date corresponding files were saved and determines which is most current. It may also keep track of who has a specific file and if intermediary changes have been made. Using this information, it automatically updates all file locations with the latest version.

For example, mobile computers are not always connected or available to the network. If you are a mobile computer user and you want access to a file that is on a network file server, you would normally save a copy of the file to your computer's hard drive. However, someone else may access and change the original file in the meantime. If that person does make changes, your copy now contains out-of-date information. Somehow you need to recognize when changes have occurred and take the appropriate action.

12.6.1.4 File Archiving

Many organizations create duplicate copies of important data on magnetic tape or some other offline storage media in case of emergency. This practice is called **file archiving** or **file backup**. The original file can be kept in addition to the backup copy, or it can be removed from online storage media so that the offline media contains the only copy. When file storage devices are interconnected on a network, file archiving becomes much easier. Computer operators use the network to traverse great distances, saving the organization time and money.

12.6.2 Print Services

Print services are network applications that control and manage access to printers and fax equipment. Print services accept print job requests, interpret print job formats and printer configurations, manage print queues, and interact with networkable printers and fax equipment for network clients.

The following are print service functions:

- Provide multiple access from limited interfaces—Reduce the number of printers your organization needs
- Eliminate distance constrains—Place printers wherever most convenient
- Handle simultaneous requests—Queue print jobs to reduce the time your computer spends sending a print job
- Share specialized equipment—Share specialized printers efficiently
- Network fax service—Computerize the transmission and reception of fax images

12.6.2.1 Providing Multiple Access from Limited Interfaces

Reducing the total number of printers can save your organization a substantial amount of money. Having fewer printers reduces the number of devices to buy, maintain, and manage.

Most modern printers provide multiple ports or interfaces. However, the number of interfaces is finite and relatively small. Typically, only two or three computers may be directly connected to each printer. On the other hand, a network connection requires only one interface. Through this interface, many computers may send data to the printer. Therefore, print services allow numerous clients to be serviced by a single printer. Managing access to printers, or other devices with limited interfaces, is a major use of modern computer networks.

12.6.2.2 Eliminating Distance Constraints

Printer ports are often based on cable interface specifications that limit the distance between the printer and attached computers. Network cable systems and devices allow longer distances for cable specifications. Organizations can use the network to place printers in strategic locations throughout a building or campus.

12.6.2.3 Handling Simultaneous Requests (Queuing)

Print servers can often handle simultaneous requests for print services. When two user try to send data to a printer at the same time, both applications compete for the printer's limited ability to accept and store print requests. *Queuing* solves this bottleneck problem. A print queue is the part of the print server which captures and stores computer print jobs. Depending upon each implementation's specific features, print queues can hold, prioritize, and manage print jobs.

When printing with network print services, your application sends print requests and data to what it believes is a printer. These requests are actually routed to a print queue. The print requests remain in the queue until the desired printer is available.

Print queuing increases the efficiency of network print services by organizing the interaction between printers and their clients. In addition, because multiple clients may send data simultaneously to the print queue at full network speeds, each may complete print requests rapidly and return to other tasks.

12.6.2.4 Sharing Specialized Equipment

Some printers are designed for specific use, such as high-speed output, large format paper, or color printing. Specialized equipment may be expensive or may not be frequently used by end users. The economies of scale produced by networking each device with numerous clients can reduce the effective cost per user and optimize printer use.

12.6.2.5 Network Fax Service

Network fax allows users to send and receive faxes using special network hardware and software. This service is becoming increasingly popular because it reduces the time and paper handling normally involved in traditional fax transmissions. Traditional fax machines use computer modem, scanner, and printer technologies to send a digital document image to remote locations. Network fax systems use the same computer technologies and computer networks to better integrate fax service with the rest of the network's print and message services.

12.6.3 Message Services

Message services include storing, accessing, and delivering text, binary, graphic, digitized video, and audio data. Message services are similar to file services. However, unlike file services, message services deal actively with the communication interactions between computer users, user applications, network applications, or documents. Instead of simply storing data files, message services transport data from point to point.

The following are the message services functions:

- ❐ Electronic mail
- ❐ Integrated electronic mail and voice mail
- ❐ Object-oriented applications
- ❐ Workgroup applications

12.6.3.1 Electronic Mail

A business depends on the efficient exchange of information between different parts of the business and between the business and the outside world. Much of this exchange has been traditionally carried out through paper documents, delivered by secretary, mail or messenger service. With the growing use of personal computers, a more efficient alternative has emerged: electronic mail.

Electronic mail is usually used to exchange messages and data files. Each user is assigned an electronic mailbox. Using the appropriate command, the user can scan a list of messages in the mailbox, display the contents of a particular message, send a message to another user, and so forth. To send a message, it is not necessary for the recipient to be present at the computer. The message resides in the mailbox until it is read. The sender may restrict delivery of the message to authorised readers by using a password. That is, the recipient must 'sign' for the message by typing his or her identifying password.

Many other features of standard mail delivery are implemented in electronic mail systems. For example, mail can be forwarded, stored for delayed delivery and sent to anyone at a particular phone number. In addition, electronic mail systems implement many new features. An electronic mail system can deliver copies of a message to all individuals listed in a certain file. It also allows merging of standard data (from a data file) with a particular message.

Now-a-days, several companies have started subscription to electronic mail services. These services are accessed through a modem and allow users to communicate with other subscribers to the service. The service may also accept a message and transmit it to its destination city. There the message is printed out and delivered with the next day's mail. This technique can be used to communicate with people who are not subscribers to the network.

12.6.3.2 Integrated Electronic Mail and Voice Mail

Message services that integrate E-mail and voice mail are also being developed. Voice mail is a service offered by specialized computer hardware and software that answers telephone calls and records audio messages. Because voice mail systems are simply specialized computers, they can be incorporated into computer networks. Computer network and voice mail vendors are currently developing ways to make voice mail systems cooperate on computer networks. Eventually, users could retrieve messages from whatever type of device is convenient.

12.6.3.3 Object-Oriented Applications

Object-oriented applications are computer programs that combine smaller applications to accomplish complex tasks. Message services often facilitate communications between objects on a computer network. Messaging applications accomplish this by acting as the object's agent, so every object does not need to contact every other object. The object simply communicates with an agent from the local messaging service. The agent then becomes responsible for communicating the message to the destination object.

12.6.3.4 Workgroup Applications

Message service have also been used to create a new class of applications called **workgroup applications**. The following are common types of workgroup applications:

(*i*) Workflow management (*ii*) Linked-object documents

12.6.3.4.1 Workflow Management

Workflow management applications intelligently route forms, notices, and documents among network clients. These service providers are designed to handle multiuser, distributed business processes. For example, assume that you want to convert a payroll process using workflow management. The old manual process required that employees fill out a paper-based time card. The time card was then signed by a manager and sent to the payroll department. Upon receipt, payroll employees entered the information from the time card, calculated the employee's pay and benefits, and generated a check. At each point along the path, an auditor verified that the steps were completed correctly and that errors did not occur. In addition, all of these steps had to take place hurriedly to meet employee expectations and government regulations.

Message services are ultimately responsible for making workflow routing and delivery decisions. Workflow management can improve this process by intelligently routing electronic forms to each individual. The form can contain data provided previously by other users that is customized to represent the formats required by each individual. In addition, data can now be moved, stored, manipulated, verified, and presented to each user much faster than similar manual processes.

12.6.3.4.2 Linked-Object Documents

The computer industry is moving toward the linked-object model for creating compound documents. Linked-object documents, similar to object-oriented applications, incorporate independent data objects into larger structures. For example, a single electronic document could contain text, spreadsheets, graphics, voice, and video elements which are linked to other files, objects, or parts. Although this technology is still in development, network message services may act as agents on behalf of the data objects that comprise linked-object documents. Conceptually, each object includes the intelligence required to pass messages between a document element and its originating application or file. A single document serves as the integrator of the various pieces.

12.6.4 Application Services

Application services are network services that run software for network clients. They are different from file services because they allow computers to share processing power, not just share data.

The following two other aspects normally associated with application services are:

1. Specialization of servers
2. Scalability and growth

12.6.4.1 Specialization of Servers

The greatest benefit of application servers is that they can employ specialized equipment to increase speed, data integrity, and security. However, how much processing should be handled by a server and how much is left to the client? Application servers have more computing power than user workstations, and they often use special operating systems that have been optimized to perform a specific operation. For example, a personal computer user wants to perform a complex mathematical calculation to create a graph. Using a personal computer (PC), the calculation would take an extremely long time. To accomplish the task more rapidly, the PC sends out the math portion of the calculation to be processed by a mainframe computer. The mainframe quickly processes the request and sends back the results. The PC is only required to collect the resulting data set and generate the graph. What would normally take a very long time can now be accomplished much more rapidly.

12.6.4.2 Scalability and Growth

Network application services can also provide organizations with relatively inexpensive upgrade paths. If more computing power is required, only the network application server is upgraded. For example, assume that you use an extremely complex modeling application and that the application server software currently runs on a minicomputer. As your company grows, the minicomputer becomes overworked and response time gets worse and worse. To improve response times you simply move the application software to a faster computer, or add another server. You can improve the processing power of your computer while leaving other client and server computers totally unaffected.

12.6.5 Database Services

Network *database services* provide server-based database storage and retrieval that allow network clients to control data manipulation and presentation. A special term has been created to describe database applications that allow clients to request data from these specialized servers: *client-server databases*.

Client-server database applications divide and optimize the tasks involved in requesting and providing data. Depending upon the design goal, the client is given a portion of the tasks involved in formulating the request and processing the response, while database servers typically evaluate incoming requests and return data.

Network database provide the following services:

- ❒ Optimize the computers which store, search, and retrieve database records
- ❒ Control where data is stored geographically
- ❒ Organize data logically between organizational departments
- ❒ Provide data security
- ❒ Reduce database-client access time

The following aspects of network database services are:

1. Coordinating distributed data
2. Replication

12.6.5.1 Coordinating Distributed Data

Large organizations often segregate tasks and information between multiple departments. When data access is shared, concerns arise about who controls what data and where it should be stored. Network database services employ a tactic called **distributed data** to achieve seamless data sharing. They divide control over the pieces of the database among the various departments' computer systems. The database management system is responsible for making the database appear as one logical unit while coordinating changes that occur on various computer systems.

12.6.5.2 Replication

Data from local databases may typically be retrieved much more rapidly than from remote databases. Therefore, users prefer to work on local data. However, when more than two copies of a database exist, organizations run the risk of making decisions based upon out-of-data or incorrect information. *Replication* creates and synchronizes multiple copies of a database over the network. Presently, the leading database software uses two different methods to perform replication. One method uses a master database, which is the repository of all additions and changes. The database management system is responsible for making sure that the changes recorded in the master are sent to all copies of the database. The second method gives several local databases responsibility for recording adds and changes. In addition, the local portion of the management system must then coordinate adds and changes with all the other copies.

12.7 PRIVATE NETWORKS

Some networks are designed specifically for and used completely by individual organisations. They are called private networks. The communication equipment that forms the network is purchased or leased in the name of the organisation. The first WAN to be designed and developed was the private network, ARPANET, and United States network. The objective was to make the interesting and unique computer facilities available in some computer centres accessible to a large community of users. It has grown from a four-site experimental network to a nationwide communication system interconnecting more than fifty universities and research centres.

A few computer networks link computer centres in multiple locations. To operate these multicorporate networks, a separate service organisation is usually set up and that organisation will take care of creating and operating the network. A leading example is the SWIFT electronic fund transfer network that passes financial transactions between banks.

SWIFT (Society for Worldwide Interbank Financial Transactions) is a non-profit organisation set up and wholly owned by the banks connected to it. The objective of this network is to replace mail, cable and telex and work for 24 hours a day and 7 days a week. It handles over a million transactions per day. It is used to send money, messages and bank statements at high speed between banks and the transaction time is drastically reduced.

SWIFT connects about 3000 financial institutions in more than 600 countries. Citibank Corp in New York was the first one to opt for the system and over 40 banks in India have joined the network. The computer-based terminals of these banks are hooked with SWIFT's access centre in Bombay, which is maintained by CMC Ltd. From here, messages are relayed to the overseas communication centre of VSNL, and then transmitted to SWIFT's international receiving centres based in London or Singapore, depending on the location of the receiver, through VSNL's GPSS services. The software needed for the operations has been supplied by SWIFT terminal services, a wholly owned subsidiary of SWIFT and the hardware is being supplied by Tata Unisys, Digital Equipment (India) Ltd. The participating banks finance the system and a tariff structure has been built based on the message, connection charge and annual charge.

SITA is another private network that passes messages between airline computers around the world.

Some of the private networks operational in India are the following:

- CMC's INDONET that offers e-mail services on a subscription basis to the customers.
- NIC's NICNET that connects all the district head quarters.
- SBI's SBINET that connects all the branches of the State Bank of India across the country.
- WELCOMNET, that connects the Welcome Group hotels in India.

12.8 VALUE ADDED NETWORKS

Value Added Networks. Another type of network is the value-added network. This is an established data communication network that owns or leases communication facilities and computers to manage communication. The facilities may include microwave antennas and communication satellites. The owners design and maintain the value-added network. They then rent the network simultaneously to many subscribers, who link their own equipment to the facilities. Using a value-added network saves organisations the time and cost of designing and maintaining their own networks.

The concept of value-added common carriers was important in the development of computer networking. A value-added carrier leases communications facilities from conventional common carriers and uses these in conjunction with computers to build a network which offers new types of communications services and tariffs. These are called **Value-Added Networks** (VANs). Graphnet offered services for delivery of documents, often in facsimile form. Telenet built a network for the interconnection of data processing machines, like the ARPA network although the software and hardware mechanisms eventually became substantially different from ARPANET. Telenet delivers packets of data between computers or terminals in a fraction of a second, and charges by the packet. TYMNET offering similar services evolved from a private time-sharing network to a value-added common carrier.

In 1971 the United States Office of Telecommunications Policy recommended a policy of first-tier second-tier common carriers. The first-tier carriers construct and own telecommunications links, and lease channels to their customers. They typically own 50–100% of the channel miles in service and lease the remainder from another carrier. The second-tier carriers are the value-added carriers. They add equipment including multiplexers and computers, to channels leased from first-tier carriers and sell services that they create in this way, including message-delivery services, computer networks, and possibly information retrieval services and computer timesharing devices. It seems likely that second markets will develop in many telecommunications areas. The second-tier carrier may minimize investment in terminals by letting the customer provide these.

Legislation in favour of second-tier carriers has increased the diversity and competitiveness of the telecommunications industry in those countries where it has been passed. In most countries, such legislation does not yet exist.

Telecommunications systems use computers in different ways. Some use them for switching; some for sorting messages which are transmitted; some for processing the data transmitted. At one extreme the computer merely switches the circuits; at the other the circuits are merely links into a data-processing system. The term 'computer utility' became used for describing public access to computer networks, and in 1966 the United States Federal Communications Commission (FCC) initiated a lengthy inquiry to determine whether public computing services should be regulated. Local and remote data processing services are not to be regulated, whereas communications systems are. There is a hybrid service between these two in which a subscriber sends data, which is processed and transmitted to another subscriber. If the data processing is the primary part of this operation, it is not regulated. On the other hand, if the operation is primarily one of communication between the parties, it is regulated. The former is referred to as hybrid data processing and the latter as hybrid communications. There is a gray area between these two about which lawyers will argue. The FCC is now conducting a new inquiry into the subject partly because of the uses of distributed intelligence. It is difficult to say whether certain intelligent functions are 'computing' or 'communications' functions.

Hybrid communication services must be completely tariffed and regulated by the FCC. Common carriers may not offer data processing services (hybrid or otherwise) except through a separate corporation with separate facilities, officers and accounting. AT&T has been excluded from offering any such unregulated services under an earlier consent decree.

Most countries do not have these legislative problems because the state telecommunications authority rigorously enforces its absolute monopoly over all telecommunications, no matter how bad its service may be.

12.9 PUBLIC NETWORKS

During the mid 1970's the need for building a public data network was realised by the telecommunication administration of various countries, with two specified objectives. One was to provide better services to the computer community and the other was to earn revenue which was enormous. This is the revenue from the switches, concentrators, multiplexers polling equipment, line control equipment, etc.—the various devices used in the interconnection of machines. Common carriers operate (this term includes the telecommunications administrations of countries with government-controlled telecommunications—the PTT's) the equipment for switching and routing telephone calls; it seemed natural that they should operate the new equipment for switching routing data.

Once computers were used for switching the desire grew to use them for other functions also. AT&T developed its plans for ACS (Advanced Communications Service) in which the nodes would not only switch data but provide a variety of functions which need processing and storage. The British Post Office created its View data schema (subsequently called *Prestel*) for operating public data bank accessible with television sets in homes or offices, initially via the telephone network.

12.10 CIRCUIT-SWITCHING AND PACKET-SWITCHING NETWORK

There are two main categories of public computer networks:

1. Packet-switching networks and
2. Circuit-switching networks.

12.10.1 Packet-switching Network

Packet-switching network divides the data traffic into blocks, called **packets** which have a given maximum length (for example, 128 bytes). Each packet of user data travels in a data envelope which gives the destination address of the packet and a variety of control information. Each switching node in a minicomputer reads the packet into its memory, examines the address, selects the next node to which it shall transmit the packet, and sends it on its way. The packets eventually reach their destination, where their envelopes are stripped off. Then, they may have to be reassembled to form the original user messages. It is rather like a postal service in which letters in envelopes are passed from one post office to another until they reach their destination. The typical delivery time on today's packet networks is about a tenth of a second.

A packet-switching network contains multiple switches which allow the network load to be distributed to multiple switching sites (Fig. 12.6). Additional communications lines are also attached to the switches. The arrangement allows alternate routing, avoiding failed or busy nodes and channels. For example, in Fig. 12.6, a packet switch can route the packets of one message to more than one packet switch.

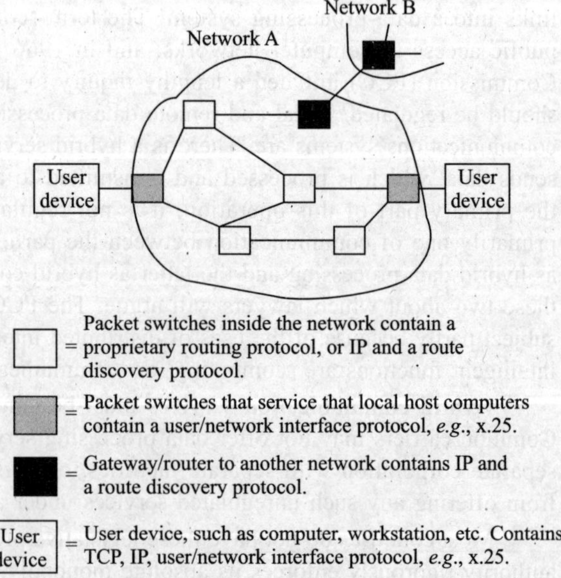

Fig. 12.6 Packet switching network

Packet switching works well with data communications traffic because many devices, such as keyboard terminals, transmit traffic in bursts. The data is sent on the channel, which is then idle while a terminal user inputs more data into the terminal or pauses to think about a problem. The idle channel time could be wasted line capacity, but a packet switch interleaves multiple transmissions from several terminals onto one channel. In effect, packet switching achieves statistical time division multiplexing (STDM) across the communications line. This approach thus provides better use of the expensive communications channel.

Packet switching goes one step further than the simple multiplexing of communications lines. It can also multiplex multiple user sessions onto a single communications port on the computer. Instead of dedicating one port to one user, the system interleaves the bursts of traffic from multiple users across one port.

Packet switching also provides an attractive feature for connecting the terminals and computers together for a session. In a circuit-switched telephone structure, connect time is often slow. A switched telephone call requires that a number be dialed and all resources be set up before the call can be routed to the destination. With a packet-switching system, however, dedicated leased lines are available for multiple users to transmit and receive their data traffic. The lines do not require any circuit setups because they are permanently connected through the system. This technique can improve the slow connect time associated with multiple telephone circuit switches. Of course, leased lines are very expensive and are used only for applications that cannot tolerate dialing delays.

Figure 2.6 also shows the relationship of some of the TCP/IP protocols to the packet-switching components. Note that it shows only one of several configurations that exist in the industry; it is not meant to be all inclusive. Typically, the user device (host) interfaces into a packet-switched network with a user/network interface protocol. The most widely used network interface protocol in the industry today is the ITU-T's X.25 standard. It provides several interface options for connecting the user to the network, including reverse charge, call forwarding, and QOS features such as throughput and delay negotiations. IP is also stored at the host machine because the gateways rely on the IP header to be created by the host computer. Additionally, the transmission control protocol (TCP) resides at the host machine to provide end-to-end integrity for the transmission between the two end-user devices. Inside the network, the packet switches might contain a vendor's proprietary routing protocol, or, in some instances, IP is employed with a companion route discovery protocol.

The gateways in this figure could be configured with IP as in the case with an internet. In a large number of public packet networks, the gateway protocol is often X.75. The X.75 protocol, although a gateway protocol, is quite different from IP because it is connection-oriented.

Many advanced nations now have a public packet-switching network, either working or talked about. These are becoming interconnected into multinational networks so that packets can travel around the world or a least part of it.

The first major public packet-switching network was Telenet. This derived its techniques (and its management) from ARPANET, the first private packet-switching network. Telenet was bought by GT&E, the second largest U.S. telephone company in 1979.

Some of the examples of national packet-switching networks are:

1. Bell Canada's DATAPACK, the X.25 packet switching system of the Trans Canada Telephone System.
2. TYMNET became a value-added common carrier in 1979 and has been growing rapidly ever since. TYMNET competes with Telnet.
3. TRANSPAC, the public packet-switching network of France. Whereas TYMNET and Telenet are private corporations offering value-added service, the networks of European countries

are operated by the government telecommunications organisation like their telephone networks.

4. United Kingdom PSS network.

The public network services available in India are in the form of VSNL's GPSS and DOT's I-Net. These public networks provide value added services to their customers.

Most industrial countries are now building public data networks using the CCITT–X.25 and related standards. These are interconnected via the international record carriers and via EURONET. These networks can add new links and switches quickly.

Many subscribers are a long distance from a switch, so concentrators are used to bring the user traffic to and from the network. The concentrators may form a small start network linked to a packet switch linking many users to the nearest packet switch. Most users are linked to the networks by telephone lines going directly to a switching node or else to a concentrator. This restricts their maximum data rate to that of a telephone line 9600 bits per second. In North America some users can have higher speed digital links into their premises.

User machines connected to a packet switching network need to observe a rigorous set of rules for communication via the network. It is desirable that networks in different countries should follow the same set of rules so that user machines around the world can employ the same software and control mechanisms, and so that packets can pass easily form one network to another. There has been a high degree of international agreement on the rules—the protocols and message formats—for public packet-switching networks, centering around Recommendation X.25 of the CCITT, (Consultative Committee on Internal Telegraphy and Telephony) the international standards organisation for telecommunications.

12.10.1.1 Route Discovery

To forward packets from node to node, packet- and message-switched networks must constantly determine and use the correct path for each piece of data. This path determination task is called **routing**. Using a previous analogy, computer network routing can be compared to the work that is performed by postal carriers.

Before postal carriers can deliver mail, they must identify the locations of addresses in their service area. Once several addresses are identified, the postal carrier logically assigns a route to delivery employees. Similarly, computer networks must identify the location of network layer addresses and determine routes for packet delivery.

Likewise, before a network entity can begin to route, it must discover the route a packet should take to reach the intended destination. Here we, describes the topic of *route discovery* as the process used to identify routes and to maintain *route tables*.

Route tables are lists that indicate the next hop to which packets are directed to reach a destination. Route tables include network addresses, the next address in the data path, and a *cost* to reach the destination network. The cost is calculated using *routing algorithms* and can be stated in the following terms:

- Hop count, which is the number of routers that data must pass through to reach the destination network.
- Tick count, which is the amount of time required to reach the destination network.
- Relative expense, which is an assignable number based upon the amount of money or other criteria required to use a specific path.

Route discovery uses one of the following methods:

(*i*) Distance vector (*ii*) Link-state.

***(i)* Distance Vector Method:** Distance vector routers compile and send network route tables to other routers which are attached to their same media segment. Each router builds its own route table by constantly broadcasting and combining tables from nearby routers. The messages the router sends contain its entire route table.

Since the internetwork can often be large and complex, and since each device can only get update information from its neighbours after they have assimilated the update, the distance vector method can require a relatively large amount of time to change all the address tables throughout the network. Eventually all of the network's routers will become aware of changes, but the complete route tables, including the changes, have to pass from router to router.

Using the distance vector method, cost information is gathered by incrementing the hop, tick, or relative expense information from other tables. In other words, if Router A tells Router B that it can reach network 100 in 6 hops, Router B's table would list network 100 at 7 hops.

***(ii)* Link-State Method:** With the link-state method, routers identify the networks to which they are attached, receiving an initial route table from a local router. After an initial (or an infrequently scheduled update) message is sent out, the router only notifies the others when changes occur. The messages contain information on the state of their network segments. As each router broadcasts this information, the receiving devices build a table of network addresses.

12.10.1.2 Route Selection

Once a router has built a route table, it can use the cost information to calculate the best path through an internetwork. Selection of specific routes can be dynamic, so that the router can constantly adjust to changing network conditions; or it may be static, so that data packets always follow a predetermined path.

12.10.1.2.1 Dynamic route selection

Dynamic route selection uses the routing algorithms to continually gather cost information. Every packet is assigned a route depending upon the latest route discovery costs. Multiple paths may be used to send packets between two devices, depending upon the changing nature of the network. In addition, route selections are made at every router in the network. Each stop along the path can cause the selection of the next stop for every packet.

12.10.1.2.2 Static route selection

On the other hand, static route selection is based upon a path designated by the network administrator or by an assigned network device. In other words, humans create route tables or computers attach route header information that forces all packets along a certain route. Intermediary routers are not allowed to make route selection decisions.

12.10.2 Circuit-switching Network

Circuit-switching network establishes what is in effect, a physical circuit between the communicating machines. The circuit is set up rapidly under computer control; it remains set up while the data passes, which might take a second or less, and may then be disconnected so that other users can employ the same facilities. The reader might think of a copper path, carrying electricity, which is set up for a second or so between the communicating machines and is then disconnected. In fact the path is not a simple copper circuit because time-division switching is used in which many streams of bits flow through an electronic switch, all interleaved with one another. Circuit switching has been used for decades in telephone exchanges and in the worldwide telex network. The difference with computer networks is that the user circuit is set up and disconnected very quickly. The switched connection is often used only for the time it takes one message to pass, or for one message and an interactive response; sometimes it remains connected for the transmission of a batch of data. This rapid computer-controlled switching is sometimes called fast-connect switching.

Circuit switching is arranged in one or a combination of three architectures: concentration (more input lines than output lines), expansion (more output lines than input lines), or connection (an equal number of input and output lines). In its simplest form, a circuit switch is an N × M array of lines that connect to each other at cross points. In a large switching office, the N lines are input from the subscriber (terminals, computers, etc.) and the M lines are output to other switching offices.

Circuit switching simply provides a path for the sessions between data communications components. Error checking, session establishment, frame flow control, frame formatting, and selecting codes and protocols are the responsibility of the users. Little or no care of the data traffic is provided in a pure circuit switching arrangement. Consequently, the telephone network is often used as the basic foundation for a data communications network, and additional facilities are added by the value-added carrier, network vendor, or user organisation. Other switching technologies (*e.g.*, message and packet) often use circuit switching as the basic transmission media and then provide additional value-added functions and facilities, such as store-and-forward services and protocol conversion.

12.11 MESSAGE SWITCHING NETWORK

In the 1960's and 1970's, the pervasive method for switching data communications traffic was message switching. The message switch is typically a specialized computer responsible for accepting traffic from attached terminals and computers (through dial-up or leased lines). It examines the address in the header of the message and switches the traffic to the receiving station or the next switch in the route. Unlike circuit switching in telephone networks, message switching is a store-and-forward technology; the messages are stored temporarily on disk units at the switches. Because the data are usually stored, the traffic is not considered interactive or real-time. Selected traffic can, however, be sent through a message switch at very high speeds by establishing levels of priority for different types of traffic, and this approach could support interactive applications. High-priority traffic is queued for a shorter period than low-priority traffic.

Storing the messages temporarily on disk also helps smooth traffic by queuing the lower-priority traffic during peak periods. Queuing also decreases the chances of traffic being blocked because of network congestion. For example, traffic can be stored temporarily and later routed to stations when the stations are available to accept the traffic.

The message-switching technology may operate in a master relationship. Typically, the switch performs polling and selection functions to manage the incoming and outgoing traffic.

Message switching has served the industry well, but it suffers from three deficiencies. First, because message switching is inherently a master structure, the entire network can be lost if the switch fails because all traffic must go through the switch. Consequently, many organisations install a duplicate (duplexed) switch, which assumes the role of the primary switch in the event of a failure. The second major deficiency stems from the hub arrangement of a message switch. Because all traffic must go through one switch, the switch itself is a potential bottleneck. Degraded response time and decreased throughput can result from such an arrangement. Third, message switching does not use the communications lines as efficiently as other techniques. For these reasons, modern data networks no longer employ message switching.

The advantages of this approach over circuit switching are:

- ❐ Line efficiency is greater, since a single node-to-node channel can be shared by many messages over time. For the same traffic volume, less total transmission capacity is needed.

- Simultaneous availability of sender and receiver is not required. The network can store the message pending the availability of the receiver.
- When traffic becomes heavy on a circuit-switched network, some calls are blocked. On a message-switched network, messages are still accepted, but delivery delay increases.
- A message-switching system can send one message to many destinations. This facility is not easily provided by a circuit-switched network.
- Message priorities can be established.
- Error control and recovery procedures on a message basis can be built into the network.
- A message-switching network can carry out speed and code conversion. Two stations of different data rates can be connected since each connects to its node at its proper data rate. The message-switching network can also easily convert format (*e.g.*, from ASCII to EBCDIC). These features are less often found in a circuit-switched system.
- Messages sent to inoperative terminals may be intercepted and either stored or rerouted to other terminals.

The primary disadvantage of message switching is that it is not suited to real-time or interactive traffic. The delay through the network is relatively long and has relatively high variance. Thus it cannot be used for voice connections. Nor is it suited to interactive terminal-host connections.

12.12 DATA COMMUNICATION

Data communication is the process of sending data electronically from one location to another. Linking one computer to another permits the power and resources of that computer to be tapped. It also makes possible the updating and sharing of data at different locations.

Computers that are located in the same room or office building can communicate data through a direct cable link. For example, in a multiuser system, a single processing unit is linked by several dumb terminals through direct cables. Since multi-user systems link inexpensive terminals instead of the more expensive personal computers used with other systems, multi-user systems provide cost savings for small companies purchasing a complete system or adding users to a system currently in operation. In general, multi-user systems are most appropriate for companies requiring a shared database for extensive data input and output.

Computers located far away from the processor use a special form of data communication-telecommunication or telegraph. For example, teller and point-of-sale terminals are spotted in location away from computers; airlines, car-rentals, railway reservation systems, and hotel reservation systems have thousands of terminals located many miles from the processors. In these cases, the process of using communication facilities such as the telephone system and microwave relays to send data between computers is a form of data communication, sometimes referred to as telecommunication, or tele-processing.

The first linkage of computing and communication devices occurred in 1940, when Dr. George Stibitz used telegraph lines to send data files from Dartmouth College in New Hampshire, USA to a Bell Laboratories' calculator in New York City, USA. An early large-scale business application was the Sabre passenger reservation system, developed in the late 1950s and early 1960s by American Airlines. Hundreds of scattered terminals were linked to the central processing unit.

Communications usage has grown steadily since then. Today, minis and larger machines are in constant communication with outlying terminals. And with available attachments, computers can use telecommunication channels to link up with information retrieval services, banks, and electronic bulletin boards. An electronic-mail message can be sent from one place to another and an answer can be returned by electronic mail as soon as it is received. This service eliminates the hassle of continually trying to return a call, or long mail delays.

12.13 FORMS OF DATA TRANSMISSION

The two forms of data transmission are as follows:

1. Analog data transmission
2. Digital data transmission

12.13.1 Analog data transmission

Analog data transmission is the transmission of data in a continuous wave form as shown in Fig. 12.7. The telephone system, for instance, is designed for analog data transmission.

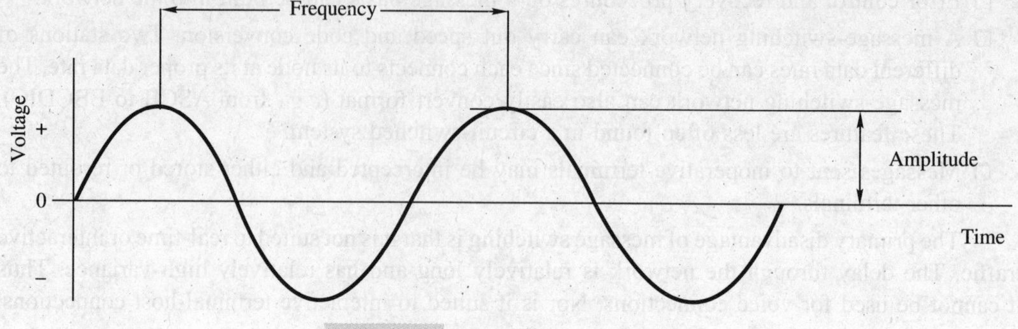

Fig. 12.7 Analog Data Transmission

Waves are measured using one or more of the following three characteristics:

- ❒ Amplitude
- ❒ Frequency
- ❒ Phase

12.13.1.1 Amplitude

You can consider the *amplitude* of a wave as the signal strength compared to some reference value (measured in volts). Analog signals are based upon amplitude, or strength, shifts which vary constantly from positive to negative values. Amplitude is commonly expressed in volts when measuring electrical potential, amps when measuring electrical current, watts when measuring electrical power, and decibels when measuring the ratio between the power of two signals.

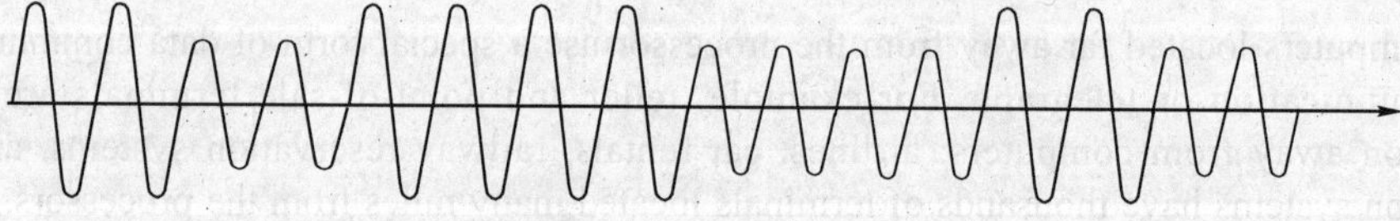

Fig. 12.8 Analog Wave Amplitude

12.13.1.2 Frequency

The *frequency* of a wave is the time it takes for a wave to complete one cycle. In other words, if a signal takes one second to make a transition from high amplitude to low and back to high, the frequency of the wave is one second. Frequency is typically measured in *hertz* (Hz), or cycles per second.

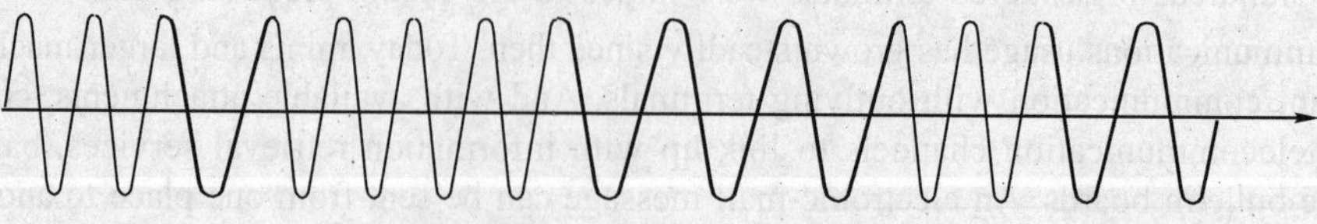

Fig. 12.9 Analog Wave Frequency

12.13.1.3 Phase

The *phase* of a signal refers to the relative state of the wave when timing began. In Fig. 12.10, Signal B crosses zero at a slightly different time than Signal A. Signal phase is measured in *degrees* (the figure shows Signal B shifted 90°, and Signal C shifted 270° relative to Signal A).

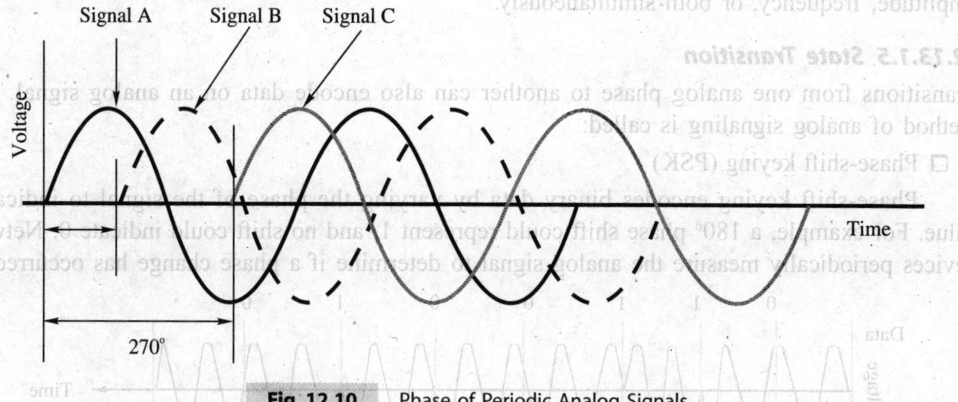

Fig. 12.10 Phase of Periodic Analog Signals

As with digital signals, analog signals can be modulated or encoded to represent binary data (Fig. 12.11).

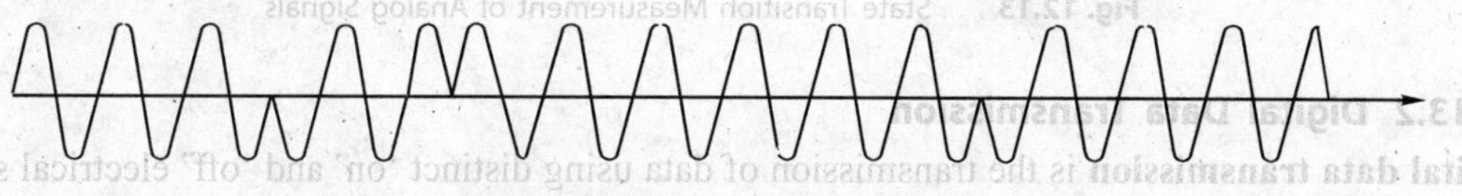

Fig. 12.11 Analog Wave Phase

12.13.1.4 Current State

The most common analog current state strategies use different signal amplitudes or frequencies to represent data. These are two types of analog signal encoding schemes:

- ❐ Amplitude-shit keying (ASK)
- ❐ Frequency-shift keying (FSK)

In Fig. 12.12, *amplitude-shift* keying encodes binary data by varying the singal's amplitude between two or more levels. For example, a binary 0 might be one volt and a binary 1 might be three volts.

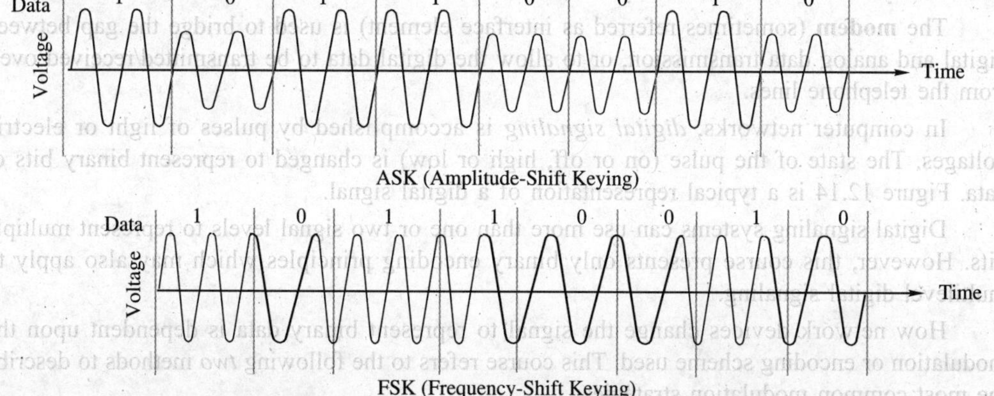

Fig. 12.12 Current State Measurement of Analog Signals

Frequency-shift keying encodes binary data by varying the signal's frequency between two or more values. For example, a binary 0 would be one frequency or group of frequencies, and a binary 1 would be some other frequency or group of frequencies.

Network devices, using current state analog signaling, periodically measure the signal's amplitude, frequency, or both simultaneously.

12.13.1.5 State Transition

Transitions from one analog phase to another can also encode data on an analog signal. This method of analog signaling is called:

❒ Phase-shift keying (PSK)

Phase-shift keying encodes binary data by varying the phase of the signal to indicate a value. For example, a 180º phase shift could represent 1, and no shift could indicate 0. Network devices periodically measure the analog signal to determine if a phase change has occurred.

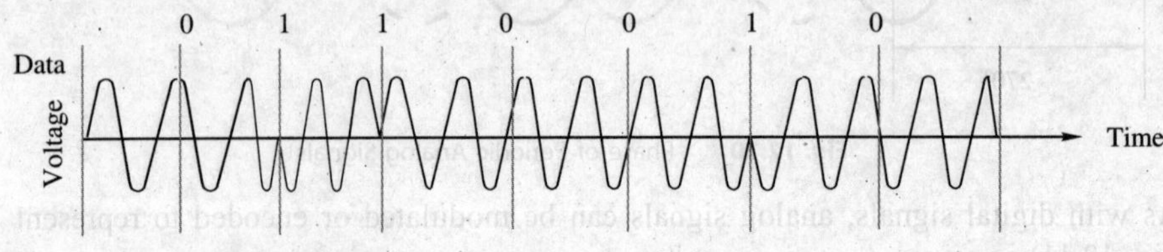

Fig. 12.13 State Transition Measurement of Analog Signals

12.13.2 Digital Data Transmission

Digital data transmission is the transmission of data using distinct 'on' and 'off' electrical states. Computer circuitry represents data as a pattern of 'on' or 'off' electrical states. These two states are represented by a 1 for 'on' and 0 for 'off' Digital data communication as shown in Fig. 12.14 is faster and more efficient than analog. All the data communication between the computers is in digital form as the computers understand and work only in digital forms. However, telephone system, an analog data transmission system, is used for a great percentage of data communication because it is the largest and the most widely used communication system in the world.

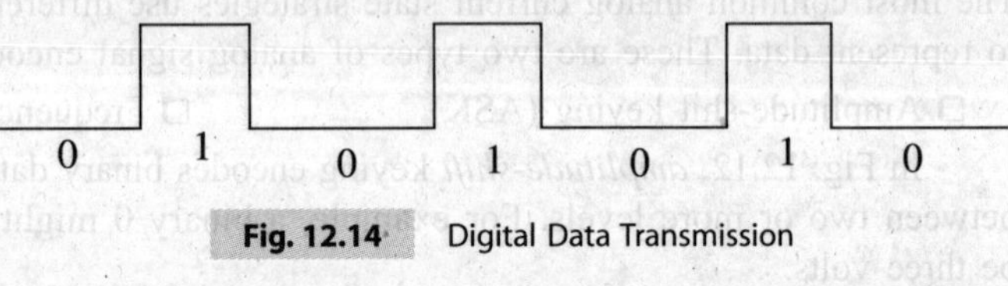

Fig. 12.14 Digital Data Transmission

The **modem** (sometimes referred as interface element) is used to bridge the gap between digital and analog data transmission, or to allow the digital data to be transmitted/received over/from the telephone lines.

In computer networks, *digital signaling* is accomplished by pulses of light or electric voltages. The state of the pulse (on or off, high or low) is changed to represent binary bits of data. Figure 12.14 is a typical representation of a digital signal.

Digital signaling systems can use more than one or two signal levels to represent multiple bits. However, this course presents only binary encoding principles which may also apply to multilevel digital signaling.

How network devices change the signal to represent binary data is dependent upon the modulation or encoding scheme used. This course refers to the following *two* methods to describe the most common modulation strategies:

1. Current state, and
2. State transition.

12.13.2.1 Current State

Current state strategies measure the presence or absence of a state or signal characteristic. For example, fiber optic networks represent data by turning a light source on or off.

Network devices monitor the medium and periodically measure the specific state. The following graphic illustrates periodic voltage measurements. The network device measures the cable's electric voltage at the center of each time slot and associates each measurement with a binary 0 or 1 (Fig. 12.15).

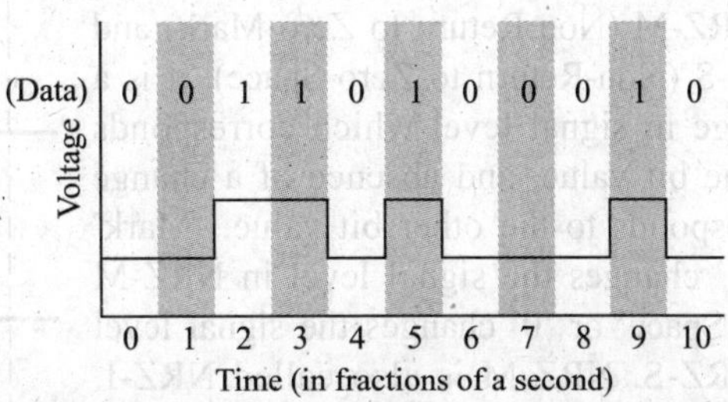

Fig. 12.15 Current state measurement of Digital Signals

In this case, one voltage level indicates a binary 1 while another voltage level represents a binary 0. As long as the voltage (or any other state) can change over time, data can be modulated or encoded on the signal.

The following digital signal encoding schemes use current state measurements:

1. Return-to-Zero (RZ),
2. Biphase,
3. Unipolar, and
4. Polar.

12.13.2.2 State Transition

The *transition* between *states* can also be used to encode data on a digital signal. For example, instead of measuring the absolute voltage on a cable, the transition between two voltages can be measured.

Once again, network devices monitor the medium and make periodic measurements. A transition from one state to another would indicate a binary 0 or 1. In this case, a voltage transition indicates a binary 1 while the absence of a transition represents a binary 0 (Fig. 12.16).

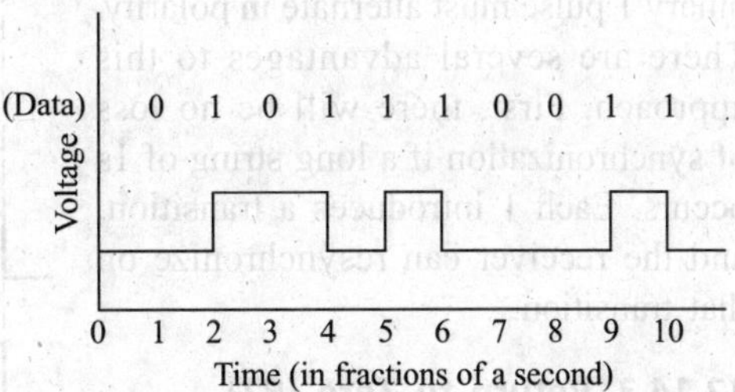

Fig. 12.16 State transition measurement of a digital signals

The following digital signal encoding schemes use state transition measurements:

1. Non-Return-to-Zero (NRZ),
2. Manchester,
3. Differential Manchester,
4. Biphase Space (FM-0), and
5. Bipolar-Alternate Mark Inversion (AMI).

12.14 DIGITAL SIGNAL ENCODING SCHEMES

The following digital encoding schemes are in use:

12.14.1 Non-Return-to-Zero (NRZ) Encoding

The most common and easiest encoding scheme is the Non-Return-to-Zero (NRZ). A 0 is transmitted by raising the voltage level to high and a 1 is transmitted using a low voltage. Thus, any sequence of 0's and 1's is transmitted by alternating appropriately between high and low. The name NRZ refers to the fact the voltage level stays constant *i.e.*, does not return to zero, during the time a bit is transmitted. Figure 12.17 shows a bit sequence 00101101 along with the clock signal and three examples of NRZ encoding. In NRZ-L (Non-Return to Zero-Level), the bit is represented by a voltage level which remains constant during the bit duration. In NRZ-M (Non-Return to Zero-Mark) and NRZ-S (Non-Return to Zero-Space), it is a change in signal level which corresponds to one bit value, and absence of a change corresponds to the other bit value. 'Mark' or '1' changes the signal level in NRZ-M and 'Space' or '0' changes the signal level in NRZ-S. NRZ-M is also called NRZ-I, Non-Return to Zero-Invert on ones.

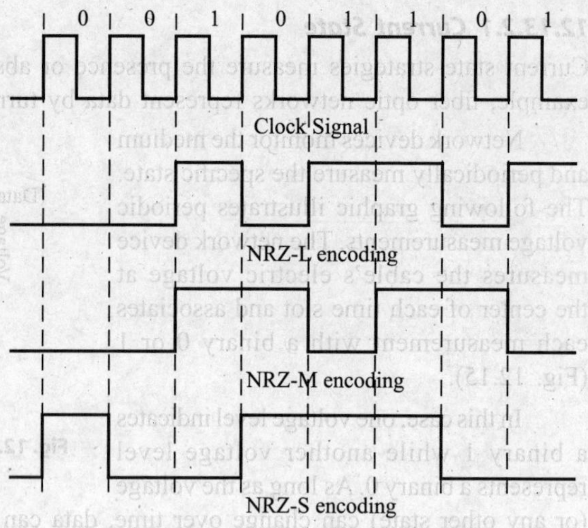

Fig. 12.17 NRZ signal encoding

12.14.2 Bipolar—AMI (Alternative Mark Inversion)

A category of encoding techniques known as multi-level binary address some of the deficiencies of the NRZ codes. These codes use more than two signal levels. Two examples of this scheme are illustrated in Fig. 12.18. In case of **bipolar—AMI**, a binary 0 is represented by no line signal, and a binary 1 is represented by a positive or negative pulse. The binary 1 pulse must alternate in polarity. There are several advantages to this approach. First, there will be no loss of synchronization if a long string of 1s occurs. Each 1 introduces a transition, and the receiver can resynchronize on that transition.

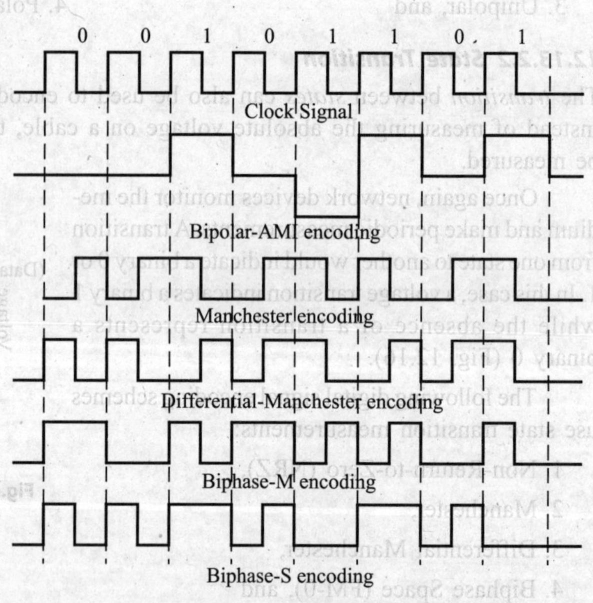

Fig. 12.18 Digital Signal Encoding

12.14.3 Return to Zero (RZ) Encoding

The RZ encoding usually ensure signal transitions for any bit pattern and thus overcome the above limitation of NRZ codes. These codes are essentially a combination of NRZ-L and the clock signal. The following are RZ encoding schemes:

1. Manchester Code,
2. Differential Manchester Code,
3. Biphase-M Code, and
4. Biphase-S Code.

12.14.3.1 Manchester Encoding

There is other set of alternative coding techniques, grouped under the term **biphase**, which overcomes the limitations of NRZ codes. Two of these techniques, Manchester and Differential Manchester, are in common use. In the Manchester encoding, there is a transition at the middle of each bit period. The mid-bit transition serves as a clocking mechanism and also as data: a low-to-high transition represents a 1, and a high-to-low transition represents a 0. Figure 12.18 shows the Manchester encoding transmission of the bit string 00101101. As the figure shows, the signal will never be held constant for a time longer that a single bit interval. Even for a sequence of 0's or 1's, the signals will change in the middle of each interval. This change allows the receiving device's clock to remain consistent with the sending device's clock. A disadvantage in Manchester encoding is that twice the bandwidth is needed. That is, the signals must change twice as frequently as with NRZ encoding.

12.14.3.2 Differential Manchester Encoding

In Differential Manchester, the mid-bit transition is used only to provide clocking. A 0 causes the signal to change at the start of the interval. A 1 causes the signal to remain where it was at the end of the previous interval. Thus, a 0 may go from low to high or high to low depending on the initial value of the signal. Figure 12.18 shows the differential Manchester encoding for the bit string 00101101. In this case, 0's and 1's are distinguished by whether there is a change in the signal at the beginning of the interval. Detecting changes if often more reliable, especially when there is noise in the channel. It is also useful when someone reverses connecting wires, which reverses high and low values. With differential encoding you don't have to mark the wires to indicate which has the high voltage and this, in turn makes the wire less expensive.

12.14.3.3 Biphase-M Encoding

In Biphase-M, there is always a transition at the beginning of a bit interval. Binary 1 has another transition in the middle of the bit interval.

12.14.3.4 Biphase-S Encoding

In Biphase-S, also there is a transition at the beginning of a bit interval. Binary 0 has another transition in the middle of the bit interval.

12.15 DATA TRANSMISSION TECHNIQUES

Data in computer systems are formatted as digital pulses and telephone lines are designed to transmit the human voice. They format data as analog signals. For data communication between computers to take place over a telephone line, the digital pulses must be converted to an analog signal before they are transmitted. After its journey over the telephone lines, the analog signal must be re-converted to digital pulses so that it can be used by the receiving computer. The process of converting digital pulses to an analog signal is called **modulation** (Fig. 12.19). And the process of re-converting an analog signal to digital pulses is called **demodulation** (Fig. 12.20). The device that accomplishes **mo**dulation-**dem**odulation process is called a modem.

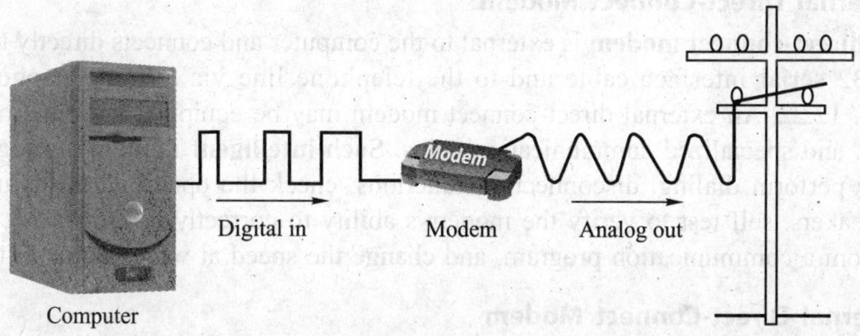

Fig. 12.19 Modulation

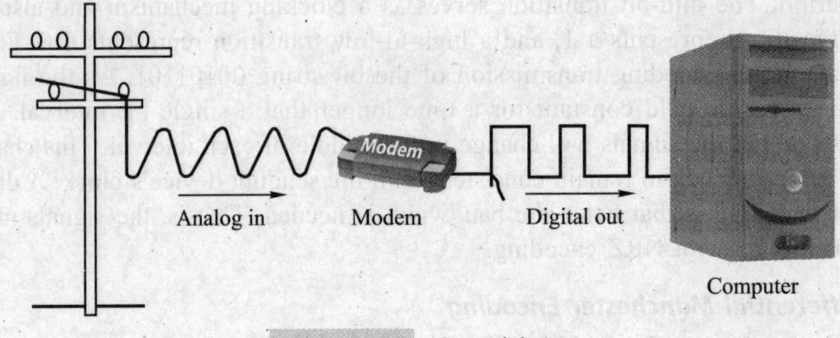

Fig. 12.20 Demodulation

The three basic types of modems used in microcomputers are as follows:

1. Acoustic coupler modem
2. External direct-connect modem
3. Internal direct-connect modem

12.15.1 Acoustic Coupler Modem

An **acoustic coupler modem** is used to provide the necessary interface. The acoustic coupler is attached to a portable terminal, and a standard telephone handset fits into rubber cups located on the coupler. The acoustic coupler modem sends data through the mouthpiece and receives data through the earpiece of the handset. The digital pulses produced by the terminal are converted into audible tones that are picked up by the handset receiver. The signals from these tones are then sent to the processor location where another modem converts them back to digital pulses as shown in Fig. 12.21.

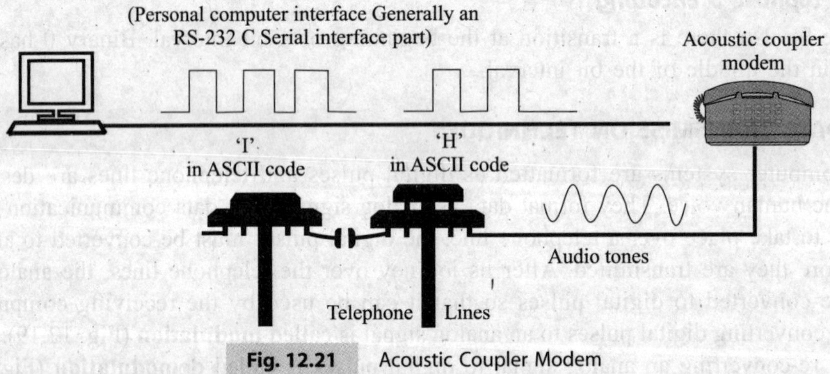

Fig. 12.21 Acoustic Coupler Modem

12.15.2 External Direct-Connect Modem

An **external direct-connect modem** is external to the computer and connects directly to computer via an RS-232 serial interface cable and to the telephone line via a modular phone jack as shown in Fig. 12.22. An external direct-connect modem may be equipped with microprocessors, storage chips, and specialized communication chips. Such **intelligent modem** is programmed to automatically perform dialing, disconnecting functions, check the operating status using status lights and speakers, self test to verify the modem's ability to correctly transmit data, respond to commands from a communication program, and change the speed at which data are transmitted.

12.15.3 Internal Direct-Connect Modem

An internal direct-connect modem has all the needed communication circuitry on a plug-in board that fits into one of the expansion slots inside the computer as shown in Fig. 12.23. Internal direct-connect modem also links directly to the telephone line via a modular phone jack.

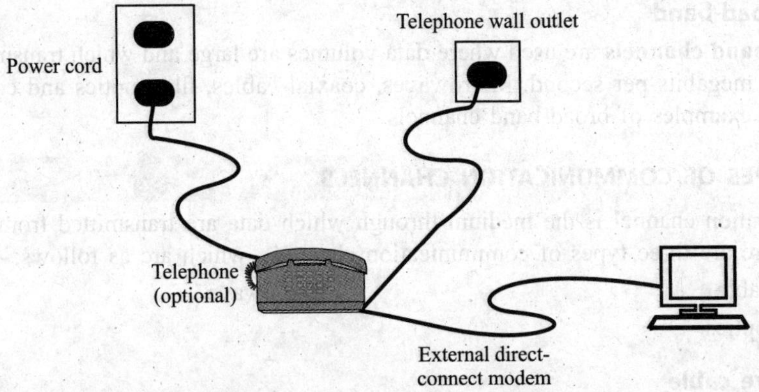

Fig. 12.22 External Direct Connect Modem

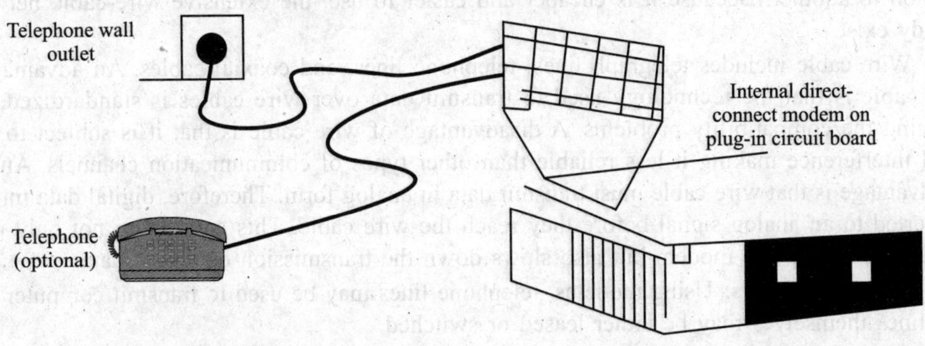

Fig. 12.23 Internal Direct Connect Modem Plug-in Circuit

These modems have many of the same special features as the external direct-connect modems.

12.16 COMMUNICATION CHANNEL BANDWIDTHS

The bandwidth, or grade, of a communication channel determines the rate or speed at which data can be transmitted over a channel. The term 'bandwidth' is often shortened to 'band'. There are three bands for communication channels

1. Narrow-band
2. Voice-band
3. Broad-band or Wide-band

12.16.1 Narrow-band

The **Narrow-band channel** is used where data volume is relatively low and which transmits data at a rate between 40 to 100 bits per second (bps). Telegraph lines are an example of narrow-band channels, and their transmission rate is slow.

12.16.2 Voice-band

The **voice-band channels** are able to speed up the transmission rate between 110 to 9600 bits per second. Telephone lines are an example of voice-band channels.

In many cases, a terminal operator at a remote location uses the regular dial-up telephone switching network, calls a number at the control processor location, and enters the data. For large volumes of data, it is cheaper for an organization to acquire its own dedicated or leased line which can be used for both voice and data transmissions.

12.16.3 Broad-band

The **Broad-band channels** are used where data volumes are large and which transmit data at rate upto several megabits per second. Microwaves, coaxial cables, fiber optics and communication satellites are examples of broad-band channels.

12.17 TYPES OF COMMUNICATION CHANNELS

A communication channel is the medium through which data are transmitted from one place to another. There are three types of communication channels, which are as follows:

1. Wire cable
2. Microwave
3. Fiber optics

12.17.1 Wire cable

Wire cable channels are the most popular and widely used channels to transmit data from one location to another. Because it is cheaper and easier to use, the extensive wire-cable networks already exist.

Wire cable includes telegraph lines, telephone lines, and coaxial cables. An advantage of wire cable is that the technology used to transmit data over wire cables is standardized, thus reducing the compatibility problems. A disadvantage of wire cable is that it is subject to electrical interference making it less reliable than other types of communication channels. Another disadvantage is that wire cable must transmit data in analog form. Therefore, digital data must be converted to an analog signal before they reach the wire cable. This conversion not only needs special hardware, *i.e.*, modem but also slows down the transmission of digital data.

Telephone Lines: Using modems, telephone lines may be used to transmit computer data. The lines themselves may be either leased or switched.

Leased Lines: A leased line is a telephone line that is leased for the express purpose of maintaining a communication channel between two computers. The line is not shared with any other users and is available at all times for data communication between the computers. A leased line is similar to a telephone connection that is always open. Both computers are always listening for a signal to start the communication. Leased lines are used in computer networks where computers or terminals in the network must be in constant contact with one another. For example, leased lines are used in a network employing point-of-sale terminals, as the terminals must be in constant contact with the main computer.

Leased lines are often conditioned to limit the level of noise on the line. Conditioned leased lines are usually necessary to carry on high speed data communication. Security requirements often require that leased lines be shielded from outside interference and unauthorised snooping.

Switched Lines: A switched line can be used for either voice or data communication, and is switched from user to user, as requirements dictate. When switched lines are used, one computer must establish contact with the other by dialing a telephone number. After the transmission has been completed, the connection between the computers is broken, just as if a telephone receiver was hung up.

Twisted Pair Cable: *Twisted pair* (TP) is a common scheme for using coppor wire as telecommunication cable. Because copper is such a good conductor of electrons, copper wires do not constrain electromagnetic signals well. When two copper wires conduct electric signals in close proximity, a certain amount of electromagnetic interference occurs. This type of interference is called **crosstalk**. In addition, because of the electromagnetic range used, TP transmits and receives unwanted signals from other sources. Twisting the copper wires reduces crosstalk and signal emissions. Each intertwined strand conducts a current whose emitted waves are cancelled out by the other wire's emissions.

Twisted pairs are formed by two insulated 22 to 26 gauge copper wires that are twisted about each other. When one or more twisted pairs are combined within a common jacket, they form a twisted pair cable. The two types of TP cable are:

- ❒ Unshielded
- ❒ Shielded

12.17.1.1 Unshielded Twisted Pair Cable

Unshielded twisted pair (UTP) cable is composed of a set of twisted pairs with a simple plastic encasement.

You may be familiar with UTP because it is commonly used in telephone systems. It is widely available and has been largely standardized. The Electrical Industries Association (EIA) popularized a *category* labeling scheme for five different qualities of twisted pair cable. Category 3 and Category 5 UTP are commonly used in computer networking. While Category 3 is suitable for most contemporary computer networks, Category 5 includes some enhancements, such as more twists per foot and a higher grade insulator, to improve the transmission media performance. Category 5 installations also require compatible equipment and more exacting installation techniques.

Due to its voice telecommunication heritage, computer network UTP is often installed in the same manner as most telephone installations. A user device contains a port which accommodates a modular RJ-45 (4-pair) or RJ-11 (2-pair) telephone connector.

The cost of UTP is extremely low compared to other transmission media. It continues to be mass-produced for telecommunications and has become a popular computer network medium. Some network integrators use existing spare wires from telephone cables to significantly reduce the already low implementation costs. However, this practice is not recommended if the existing UTP cable is lower than Category 3, if the cable drops exceed 100 meters, or if significant crosstalk is already present between the voice wires.

UTP installation equipment is also inexpensive, easy to use, and widely available. Installation techniques are so simple that the cable can be adequately installed with very little training. Because voice telecommunication connection techniques have been optimized for easy moves, adds and changes, UTP is easily managed and reconfigured.

Using current and emerging technologies, UTP may support data transfer rates from 1 to 100 Mbps at distances upto 100 m. Ten Mbps is the most common transmission rate in use today.

All copper wire suffers from rapid attenuation when used as a communication medium. UTP is no exception. Current technology restricts the effective range of UTP to hundreds of meters.

The copper cable used in UTP is very susceptible to EMI. Although the twists greatly reduce crosstalk, a certain amount of interference exists between pairs of wires. Also, signals on the pairs are easily influenced by outside emitters of electromagnetic waves. External devices can also be used to intercept signals that are emitted from the pairs, breaching the security of a network.

12.17.1.2 Shielded Twisted Pair Cable

Most TP cable is unshielded, but some forms of *shielded* twisted pair (STP) still exist.

STP is insulated cable which includes bundled pairs wrapped in a foil shielding. Various transmission media specifications from Apple Computer and IBM use STP cable.

STP is more difficult to install than UTP. Like coaxial cable, an electric ground, created by special connectors and installation techniques, must be provided for the shield. However, STP is more difficult to install than coaxial cable. If you use standardized and preconfigured cables, it makes installation simple.

Bulk STP is moderately expensive. It currently costs more than UTP but is less expensive than thick coaxial or fiber optic cable.

With the reduction of outside interference, STP can use higher frequencies and more bandwidth-efficient signaling techniques. It is capable of greater transmission speeds, up to 500 Mbps at 100 m, but has not been widely implemented at data rates higher than 155 Mbps. The most common transmission rate is 16 Mbps.

The biggest difference between UTP and STP is the reduction of interference and EMI emissions provided by STP's shielding. However, STP still suffers from relatively low immunity from interference.

STP suffers from attenuation at a rate similar to UTP. Current technology also restricts the effective range of STP to hundreds of meters.

Coaxial Cables: A coaxial cable consists of many small cables in a protective cover. The cover shields the cable from physical dangers as well as from electromagnetic interference. Within the cover, the various cables are shielded from interference with one another. Coaxial cables are used in communication networks that require many simultaneous communication links. Each coaxial cable can provide more than 5000 links.

The initial installation of coaxial cable is relatively simple. However, current installation techniques usually use a single strand of cable, which may become difficult to manage and reconfigure. Local drops may be connected to the base cable to make device connections easier.

Using current technologies, coax supports data transfer rates between twisted pair and fiber optic cable, although the typical data rate in use today is 10 Mbps. Much greater data rates are available. However, these higher rates are only infrequently used in computer networking. It is important to note that coaxial cable's bandwidth potential increases with the diameter of the inner conductor.

The cost of coaxial cable increases with the diameter and composition of the conductors. The cost of thin coaxial cable is relatively low (less than STP or Category 5 UTP). Thick coaxial cable is moderately expensive (more than STP or Category 5 UTP. Both are more expensive than Category 3 UTP (all comparisons are made in reference to bulk cable with no connectors).

As a copper wire media, coaxial cable suffers from high attenuation, but at a much lower rate than either variety of twisted pair. Using current LAN technology, the effective range of coaxial cable is in the low thousands of meters.

While copper wire generally is a poor resistor to EMI, the shielding provided by coaxial cable greatly reduces its effects.

There are two types of coaxial cables: baseband and broadband. A baseband coaxial cable transmits a single signal at a time at very high speed, while a broadband coaxial cable can transmit many simultaneous signals using different frequencies. A baseband cable transmits a single stream of digital data at a very high communication rate (millions of bits per second) but must be amplified every 1000 feet or so. It is mainly used for local area networks. A baseband coaxial cable can carry only an analog signal, so it must be used in conjunction with a modem. It is more complex to use in a network.

12.17.2 Microwave

Microwave is also a type of analog communication channel. Microwave signals are transmitted through the atmosphere rather than through wire cables, similar to the way radio and television signals are transmitted. Microwave signals must be transmitted in a straight line, and do not bend around corners or around the curve of the earth. Transmitter stations redirect and boost the signals.

The data may be beamed to a communication satellite that acts as a reflector by accepting signals from one point on earth and returning the same signals to some other point on earth. The satellite appears from the earth to be stationary target for the microwave signals because its precisely positioned 22,300 miles above the equator with an orbit speed that matches the earth's rotation.

Dozens of satellites are now in orbit to handle international and domestic data, voice, and video communications. Compared to wire cable, microwave has a much lower error rate, making it more reliable. Also, because there are no physical links between the sending and receiving systems, communication links can be made over large distance and rough terrains.

The only disadvantage is the high cost of ground stations and satellites to support a microwave network.

12.17.3 Fiber Optics

Fiber optics are very reliable communication channels and they transmit data in digital form. They use light impulses that travel through clear flexible tubing (tiny threads of glass or plastic). A single glass fiber is thinner than the size of a human hair and it can transmit all the characters in dozens of books of the same size of this one across the country in a single second. (It would take about 21 hours to send the same information over a copper telephone line). Since thousands of these fibers can be fitted in the same amount of space required for one wire cable, the future cost of broadband transmission capability should be within the reach of small organizations and individuals.

Fiber optics can transmit data at very high speed with no errors. Unlike wire cables, fiber optic cables are not subject to electrical interference. They do, however, require repeaters to read and boost the signal strength because light pulses will lose signal strength over long distances.

Optical fibers support extremely high bandwidths because they are limited by the high-frequency photon properties of light rather than by lower-frequency properties of electrical systems. Current technologies allow data rates from 100 Mbps to over 2 Gbps, at distances from 2 to 25 km. The data rate of a given fiber optic system is dependent upon the fiber composition (glass or plastic), the mode, and the wavelength of the light transmitted. The most common LAN installations include glass multimode fiber and 850 nm wavelength LEDs. This configuration can sustain a transmission rate of 100 Mbps at distances of approximately 20 km.

Historically, bulk fiber and connectors have been relatively expensive compared to copper wire, but these costs are falling rapidly. However, the extreme cost of installation far outpaces the cost of materials.

The nature of fiber optic cable poses installation problems. Every fiber junction, splice, or connection must be made with extreme care to ensure that the light path is unobstructed. Installers must be careful not to excessively stretc.h or bend the fiber.

Fiber optic cables have extremely low attenuation rates. The amount of attenuation varies depending upon the operating wavelength, but effective ranges are usually measured in kilometers. Therefore, fiber optic cable attenuates much less than any copper wire transmission medium.

Due to the use of the light spectrum, fiber optic cables do not leak signals and are immune to electromagnetic interference and eavesdropping. Also, the light spectrum does not require electrical grounds, so fiber optic cables do not suffer from potential shifts to the electrical ground nor do they produce sparks. These characteristics make fiber ideal for hazardous, high voltage, or eavesdropping-sensitive environments.

12.18 METHODS OF DATA TRANSMISSION

There are three methods of data transmission:

- ❒ Asynchronous Transmission
- ❒ Synchronous Transmission
- ❒ Isochronous Transmission

12.18.1 Asynchronous Transmission

In **Asynchronous transmission**, one character is transmitted at a time. The transfer of data is controlled by start bits and stop bits. Each character is surrounded by bits that signal the beginning and end of the character. These characters allow the receiving terminal to synchronize itself with the receipt of data on a character-by-character basis. Asynchronous transmission is often used to low-speed transmission of data in conjunction with narrow-band and few slower speed (less than 1200 bps) voice-band channels where the transmitting device operates manually or intermittently. It is least expensive of the two methods (Fig. 12.24).

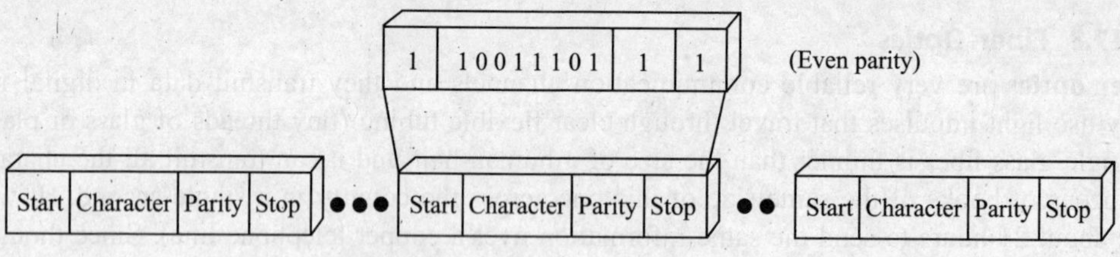

Fig. 12.24 Asynchronous Transmission

Because the bit strings are relatively short, timing errors between the two device's clocks will not cause the receiving device to mistake the start of a frame. This type of transmission is often used when characters are generated at random intervals, such as when a user types at a terminal. The start and stop bits not only indicate when a receiver should measure for the presence of bits, but also indicate the beginning and end of the data stream.

12.18.2 Synchronous Transmission

Synchronous transmission of data is a method in which blocks of characters are transmitted in timed sequences. Rather than using start and stop bits around each character, each block of characters is marked with synchronization characters. The receiving device accepts data until it detects a special ending character or a predetermined number of characters at which time the device knows the message has come to an end. Synchronous transmission commonly uses the faster (greater than 1200 bps) voice-band and broad-band channels and is usually used when data-transfer requirements exceed several thousand bits per second. It is much faster than asynchronous transmission. Synchronous transmission is used in direct computer-to-computer communication for large computer systems because of the high data-transfer speeds required. The special characters used by asynchronous (start/stop bits) and synchronous (synchronization characters) transmission to alert the modem when data are being sent and when the transmissions are finished are called message characters.

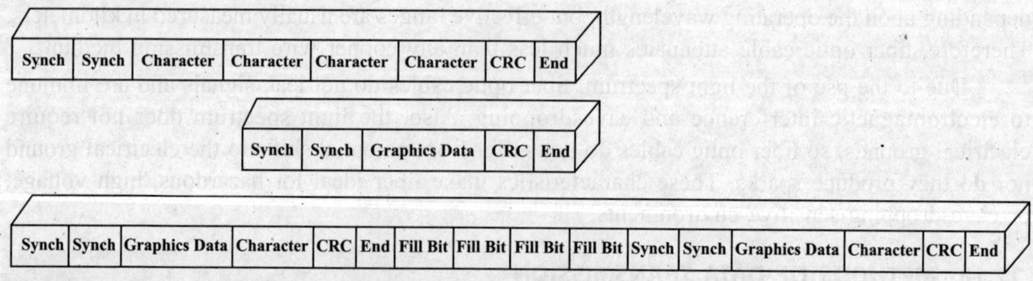

Fig. 12.25 Synchronous Transmission

Synchronized transmissions resist timing errors much better than asynchronous because both the transmitter and receiver use the same clock. To maintain framing when no data is being transmitted, synchronous transmission systems use fill bits. The sender can then maintain the integrity of the transmission timing.

As with asynchronous transmission, synchronous transmission can perform error detection. A method known as Cyclic Redundancy Check (CRC) is often used. The CRC process subjects the block of data to an algorithm. The result of the computation (called the CRC) is appended to the block of data prior to transmission. On the receiving side, the same algorithm is used and the results are compared with the CRC field. Any difference is assumed to mean frame damage occurred during transmission. CRC is less vulnerable to multiple bit errors than asynchronous error-detection methods.

12.18.3 Isochronous Transmission

Isochronous transmission methods use a constant fixed-frequency transmission clock to create set time slots. *A clock signal is generated by a designated network device and is passed to all other devices on the network.*

Using the prescribed media access rules, the network devices monitor the network for free space within the slots and insert data as needed. Multiple frames can be inserted into each slot until the slot is full. By using this method, a clock signal is not provided for every frame like asynchronous, or provided by the sender at the beginning of a string like synchronous. Rather the clock is provided at a constant rate by a single device for all other devices on the network.

12.19 RATE OF DATA TRANSMISSION

The speed at which data travel over a communication channel is called the communication rate. It is also known as the transmission speed. The rate at which the data are transferred is the baud rate. **Baud rate** is the number of times per second that the signal being transmitted changes (modulation or demodulation). Baud is often equated with bits per second (bps), however, this comparison is not entirely accurate because a signal does not always carry one bit. Although higher speeds are possible, typical data transmission speeds are 300, 1200, 2400, 4800, and 9600 bps. Modems used with microcomputers typically use 300, 1200 or 2400 bps. Larger computer systems used for communications in business typically transmit data at speeds of 4800 bps or higher using high-speed modems.

12.20 TRANSMISSION MODES

Data transmission may occur in one of the three modes:

1. Simplex mode
2. Half-duplex mode
3. Full-duplex mode

12.20.1 Simplex Mode

In the **Simplex mode**, data can be transmitted in one direction as shown in Fig. 12.26 (*a*). A device using the simplex mode of transmission can either send or receive data, but it cannot do both. Simplex mode (circuits) are seldom used because a return path is generally needed to send acknowledgment, control, or error signals.

12.20.2 Half-duplex Mode

In the **Half-duplex mode**, data can be transmitted back and forth between two stations, but data can only go in one of the directions at any point of time [Fig. 12.26 (*b*)]. An example is a citizens band radio where the user must either talk or listen, but cannot do both at the same time.

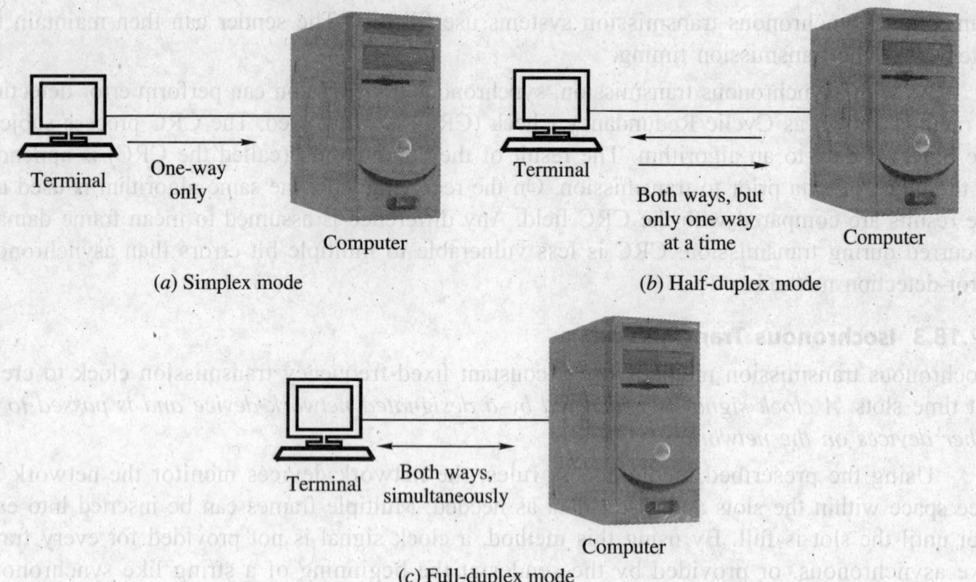

(*a*) Simplex mode (*b*) Half-duplex mode

(*c*) Full-duplex mode

Fig. 12.26 The transfer of data over a communication line can take place in one of the three modes

12.20.3 Full-duplex Mode

The **Full-duplex mode** allows a device to receive and send data simultaneously [Fig. 12.26 (*c*)]. A full-duplex mode is faster, since it avoids the delay that occurs in a half-duplex circuit each time the direction of transmission is changed.

12.21 COMMUNICATION CHANNEL CONFIGURATIONS

The two main communication channel configurations are as follows:

1. Point-to-point
2. Multi-point

In a **point-to-point channel configuration**, a device is connected directly to another device by a dedicated communication channel (Fig. 12.27). This communication channel configuration can be inefficient and costly if a terminal is not active enough to keep the line busy.

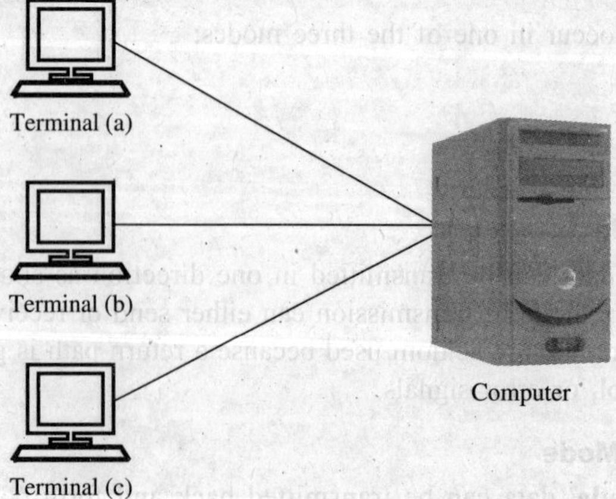

Fig. 12.27 Point-to-Point Channel Configuration

In the **multi-point channel configuration**, three or more devices (*e.g.*, a terminal or computer) are connected to the same line (Fig. 12.28). Compared to point-to-point configuration, multi-point channel configuration is more efficient and less costly because it reduces the amount of intercabling needed.

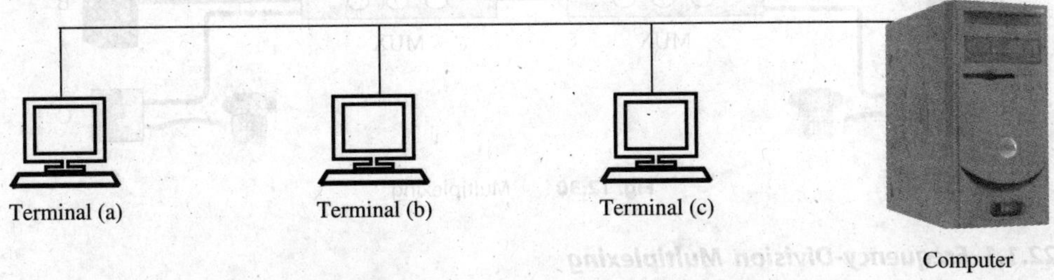

Fig. 12.28 Multi-point-Channel Configuration

12.22 COMMUNICATION PROCESSORS

A number of communication processors are used by network designers to achieve their goals. They increase the efficiency of use of a communication channel. These processors are used for a number of purposes, some of which are as follows:

12.22.1 Multiplexing

Multiplexing is the process of combining the transmission, character by character, from several devices into a single data stream that can be transmitted over a single communication channel. A multiplexer is a device that produces multiplexing. It is also used at the receiving end to separate the transmissions and send them back in their original order for processing (Fig. 12.29). A multiplexer allows the communication channels to transmit much more data, at any one time, than what a single device can send. Multiplexers are more efficient and less expensive.

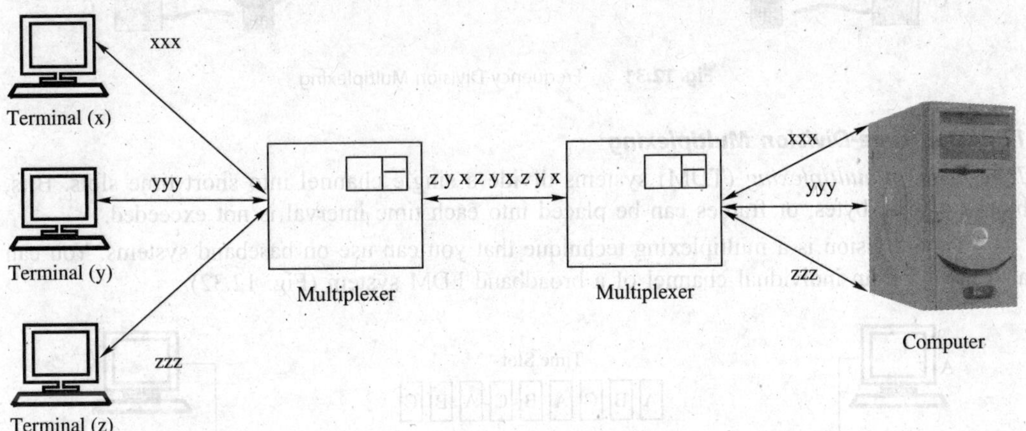

Fig. 12.29 A multiplexer allows several terminals to share a communication channel

The equipment that multiplexes and demultiplexes is sometimes called a **multiplexer** or **mux**.

The following methods are used by Multiplexers to allow multiple devices to communicate concurrently:

- Frequency-Division Multiplexing (FDM)
- Time-Division Multiplexing (TDM)
- Statistical Time-Division Multiplexing (StatTDM)

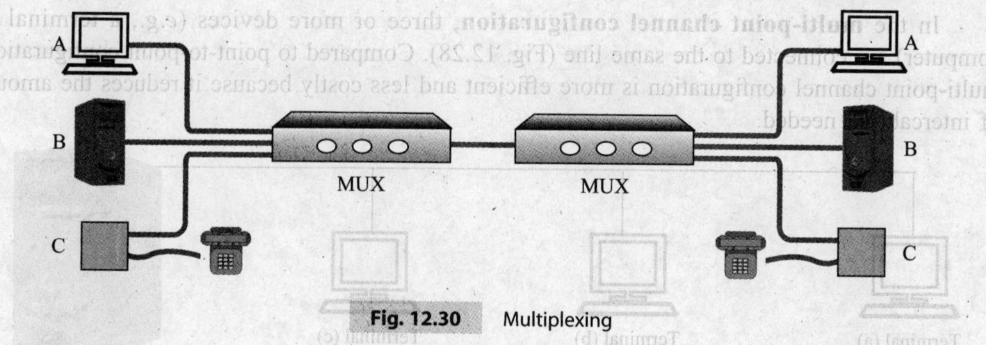

Fig. 12.30 Multiplexing

12.22.1.1 Frequency-Division Multiplexing

Frequency-division multiplexing (FDM) uses separate frequencies to establish multiple channels within a broadband medium. To do this, the mux creates special broadband carrier signals that operate on different frequencies. Data signals are added to the carrier signals and are removed, at the opposite end of the media segment, by another mux.

FDM is used in broadband LANs to separate different direction traffic on the cable and to provide special services like dedicated connections between machines (Fig. 12.31).

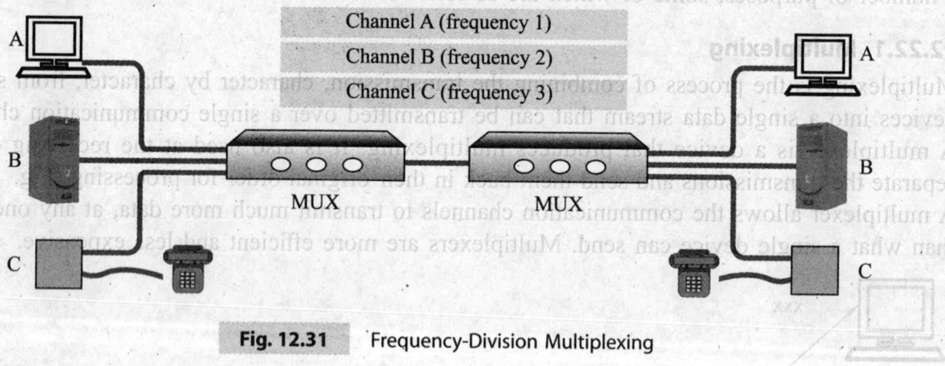

Fig. 12.31 Frequency-Division Multiplexing

12.22.1.2 Time-Division Multiplexing

Time-division multiplexing (TDM) systems divide a single channel into short time slots. Bits, blocks of bits, bytes, or frames can be placed into each time interval is not exceeded.

Time-division is a multiplexing technique that you can use on baseband systems. You can also use it on an individual channel of a broadband FDM system (Fig. 12.32).

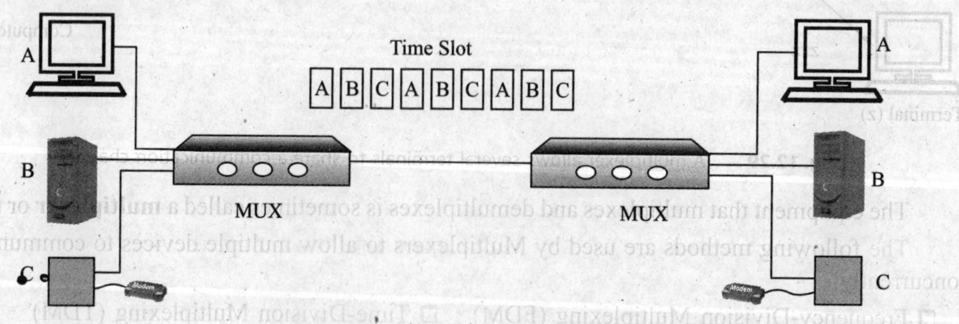

Fig. 12.32 Time-Division Multiplexing

Conventional TDM systems are sometimes called synchronous TDM because the time-divisions are fixed when the muxes are set up. The time slots are always the same length and are assigned in the same order.

12.22.1.3 Statistical Time-Division Multiplexing

Conventional synchronous TDM systems waste bandwidth if many of the time slots are left unused. *Statistical time-division multiplexing* (StatTDM) solves this problem by dynamically allocating time slots to active devices on a first-come, first-served or priority basis. A control field identifies the owners of each slot's data so that the receiving mux can appropriately split out all the individual signals (Fig. 12.33).

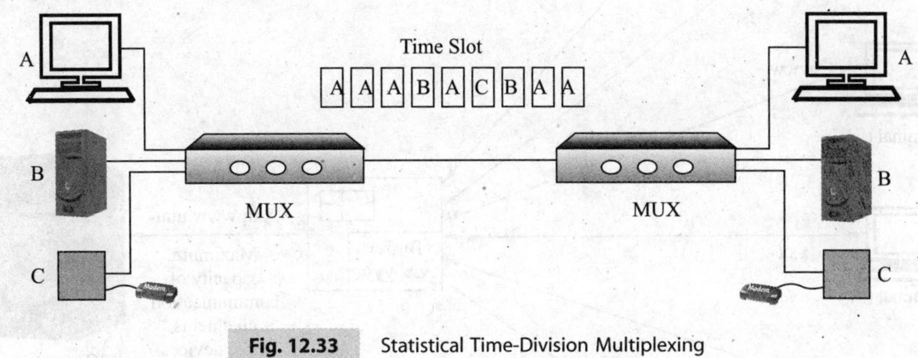

Fig. 12.33 Statistical Time-Division Multiplexing

12.22.2 Concentration

Very often, it is required to connect more devices (or terminals) to a computer so that the communication channel can handle all at once. **Concentration** is the process of connecting and serving these devices. A concentrator is hardware that provides concentration as shown in Fig. 12.34. The data are stored in the buffer of concentrator for later transmission, when the number of devices transmitting exceeds the capacity of the communication channel. However, today's micro-processor equipped multiplexers perform much like concentrators. Compared to concentrators, multiplexers are less expensive.

12.22.3 Message Switching

The **message switcher** receives and analyzes data messages from points in the networks, determines the destination and the proper routing, and then forwards the messages to other network locations. If needed, a message can be stored till an outgoing line is available.

12.22.4 Front-end Processing

The **front-end processor** is a computer, which is usually located at a central computer site. It handles all the data communication control functions (Fig. 12.35) while the Central Processing Unit (CPU) of the front-end processor handles all the communication tasks. Its purpose is to relieve the main computer—called a **host computer**—of a number of the functions required to interact with and control the communications network. The two processors interact only when data need to be passed between them. A typical front-end processor might control scores of communication channels of varying types and speeds coming from a number of diverse remote terminals.

The functions of communications processors differ from one network to another, and there may be an overlapping of functions. A message switching processor, for example, may also function as a remote concentrator; a front-end processor may perform message-switching functions; and, in less complete networks, the host computer may perform most or all of the functions of the front end processor.

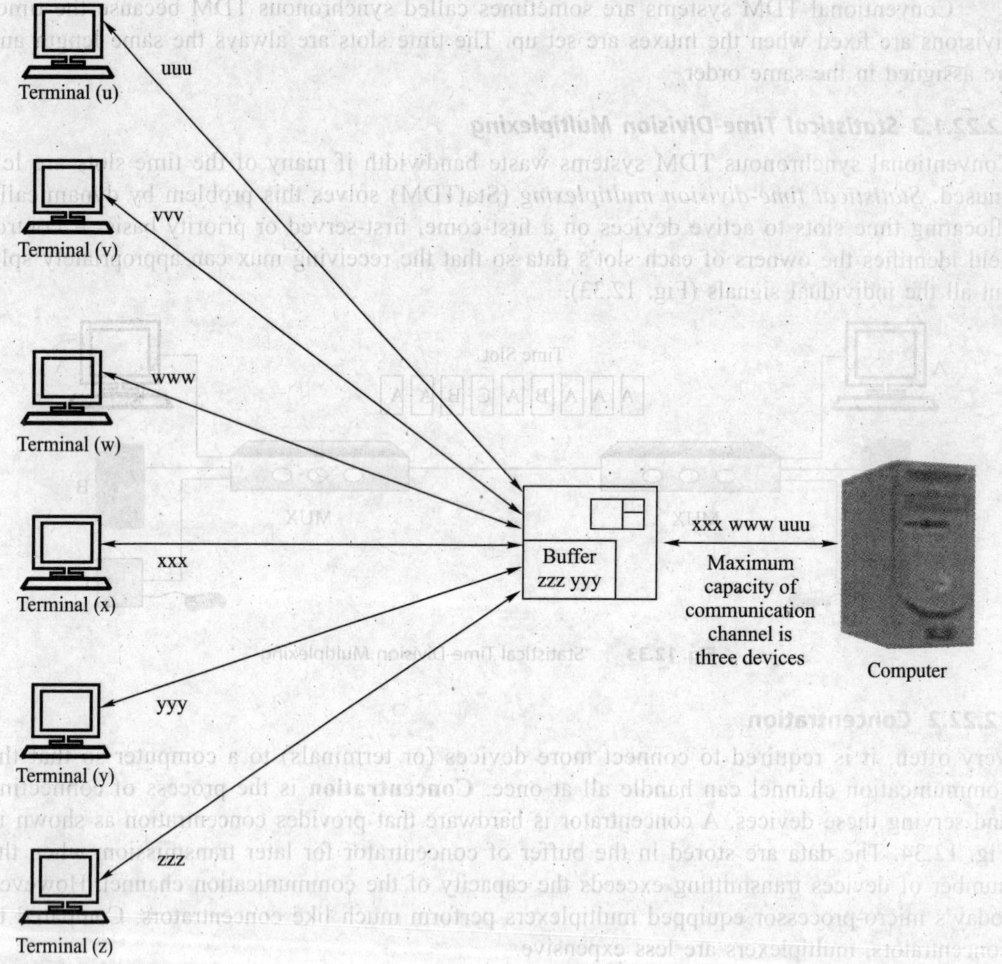

Fig. 12.34 A concentrator allows connection and service to a greater number of devices that the communication channel is capable of transmitting to at one time

12.23 NETWORKING INTERFACE BOARDS

A network interface board includes all of the physical and logical connections between your computer, or other device, and the transmission medium. It is a logic board you install in a computer to connect it to a cable's connector. However, network interface boards may be an interface card, a portion of the device's logic board software and a generic hardware port, or a number of external devices.

The following terms also describe network interface boards, so they will be defined here:

- ❒ Transceiver
- ❒ Network Interface Card (NIC)
- ❒ Transmission media adapter.

12.23.1 Transceivers

All network interface boards include some type of *transceiver*. Transceivers are devices that can transmit as well as receive electric or electromagnetic signals on the transmission media. They come in a variety of different types, but all of them emit electrify, light, or electromagnetic waves. When using cable media, transceivers are often coupled with connectors that are the opposite gender from those directly attached to the media. Using wireless media, transceivers are just transmitting and receiving devices because no mechanical connectors are required.

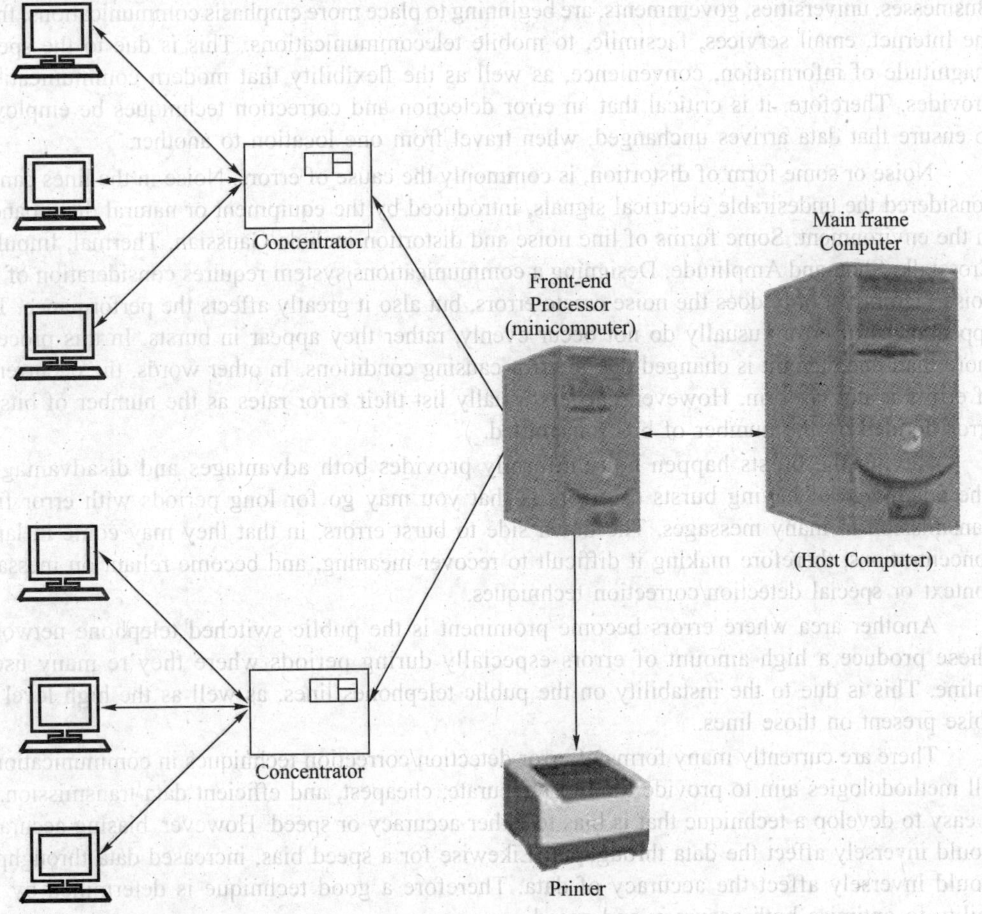

Fig. 12.35 A front-end processor processes and routes all input and output operations

12.23.2 Network Interface Card (NIC)

When the end-user device does not provide a suitable port or network interface board, printed circuit boards called **network interface cards** are used. These cards include the circuitry and mechanical connections to convert the computer's electric signals to be electric or electromagnetic signals used on the medium. A card usually includes a single transceiver but may provide one or more connector types.

12.23.3 Transmission Media Adapter

When a network interface board uses a connector that is different from what is already attached to the transmission medium, a *transmission media adapter* is used. The purpose of this adapter is to receive signals from one type of connector and convert them for use with another type.

12.24 ERROR DETECTION AND CORRECTION

In data communications, errors are usually responsible for information being different at the receiver. To counter this problem error detection/correction techniques have been developed to ensure reliable data via a communications channel. As data communications become more advanced, and widely accessible many different interest groups will utilise its advantages. Businesses, universities, governments, are beginning to place more emphasis communications, from the Internet, email services, facsimile, to mobile telecommunications. This is due to the speed, magnitude of information, convenience, as well as the flexibility that modern communications provides. Therefore, it is critical that an error detection and correction techniques be employed to ensure that data arrives unchanged, when travel from one location to another.

Noise or some form of distortion, is commonly the cause of errors. Noise in the lines can be considered the undesirable electrical signals, introduced by the equipment or natural disturbances in the environment. Some forms of line noise and distortion include Gaussian, Thermal, Impulse, Crosstalk, Shot, and Amplitude. Designing a communications system requires consideration of the noise factor. Not only does the noise create errors, but also it greatly affects the performance. The appearances of errors usually do not occur evenly, rather they appear in bursts. In this process, more than one data bit is changed due to error causing conditions. In other words, the occurrence of errors is not uniform. However, carriers usually list their error rates as the number of bits in error divided by the number of bits transmitted.

Having the bursts happen non-uniformly provides both advantages and disadvantages. The advantage of having bursts of errors is that you may go for long periods with error free transmission in many messages. The down side to burst errors, in that they may come in large concentrations, therefore making it difficult to recover meaning, and become reliant on message context or special detection/correction techniques.

Another area where errors become prominent is the public switched telephone network. These produce a high amount of errors especially during periods where they're many users online. This is due to the instability on the public telephones lines, as well as the high level of noise present on those lines.

There are currently many forms of error detection/correction techniques in communications. All methodologies aim to provide the most accurate, cheapest, and efficient data transmission. It is easy to develop a technique that is bias to either accuracy or speed. However, biasing accuracy would inversely affect the data throughput. Likewise for a speed bias, increased data throughput would inversely affect the accuracy of data. Therefore a good technique is determined by its ability to optimise both accuracy and speed.

12.25 TYPES OF ERRORS

Three types of errors occur in data communication. These types are usually referred to as:

- Single-bit Error,
- Multiple-bit Error, and
- Burst Error.

Of the three, a single-bit error is the most likely to occur and a burst error the least likely.

12.25.1 Single-bit Error

In Single-bit error, one bit of a given data is changed from 1 to 0 or from 0 to 1. For example, 00101010 was sent, but 10101010 was received. Note that one-bit has changed from 0 to 1 (Fig. 12.36).

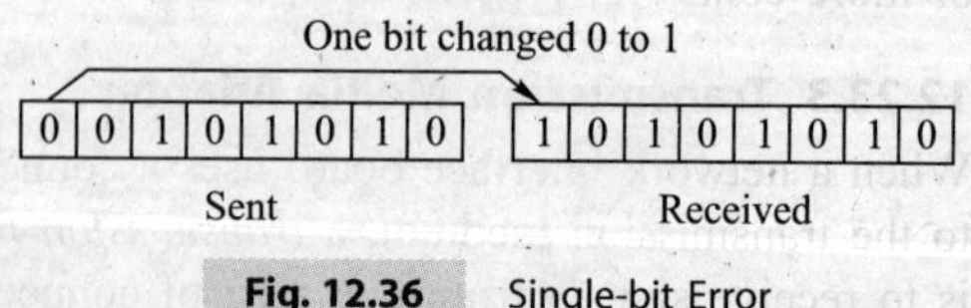

Fig. 12.36 Single-bit Error

12.25.2 Multiple-bit Error

In multiple bit error, two or more non-consecutive bits in a data unit have changed from 1 to 0 or from 0 to 1. For example, 01000010 was sent, but 00001010 was received. Note two non-consecutive bits have changed (Fig. 12.37).

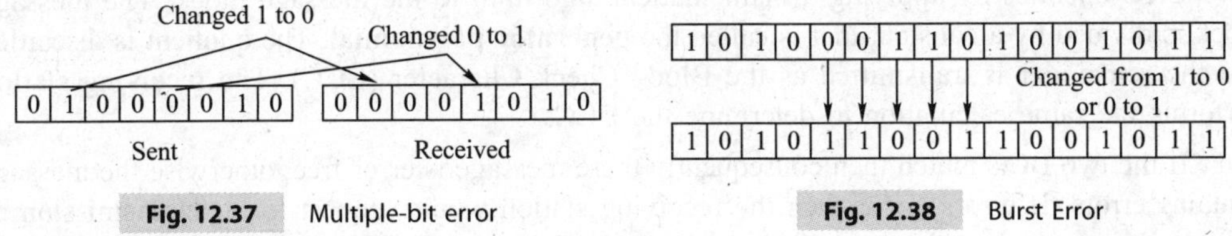

Fig. 12.37 Multiple-bit error

Fig. 12.38 Burst Error

12.25.3 Burst Error

In burst error, two or more consecutive bits in a data unit have changed from 1 to 0 or from 0 to 1. For example, 1010001101001011 was sent, but 1010110011001011 was received. Note that five consecutive bits have changed (Fig. 12.38).

12.26 DIFFERENT CLASSES OF ERROR DETECTION AND CORRECTION

In modern communications, there are many forms of error detection/correction techniques. Before categorising, it is important to establish an understanding, the modes that the techniques operate.

Essentially, there are two modes:

1. Automatic Repeat Request (ARQ)
2. Forward Error Control (FEC)

12.26.1 Automatic Repeat Request (ARQ)

Under an ARQ the data is allowed to flow in two directions. This allows techniques such as:

(*i*) Parity,
(*ii*) Checksum, and
(*iii*) Cyclic Redundancy Check.

All these techniques detect errors in data transmission, and request the data to be retransmitted from the transmitted if faults are detected. This is the characteristic of ARQ techniques.

12.26.2 Forward Error Correction (FEC)

Forward Error Correction (FEC) is used when the data is only allowed to travel in one direction. FEC uses redundant data to prevent errors, as receiver cannot request data to be retransmitted.

Although this section will examine various techniques, guaranteeing the data arriving at the receiving end almost 100 percent intact, there are also many other forms of control that can be used. The method of ignoring errors can still be used. If in a telegram errors have occurred, such as missing characters within a word, retransmitting the word may be pointless. A word can be simply decoded by understanding the context of the message.

These alternatives are options, however the issue of reliability has becoming far more important, and simply ignoring errors can not be accepted.

12.27 CYCLIC REDUNDANCY CHECK

Although the parity still widely used, the preferred checking method for block transmission is called **Cyclic Redundancy Checking** (CRC). The advantage of CRC is the effectiveness of the error checking, and requiring only minimal amounts of hardware.

Cyclic redundancy checking is a method of checking for errors in data that has been transmitted on a communications link. A sending device applies a 16 or 32 bits *polynomial* to a block of data that is to be transmitted and appends the resulting cyclic redundancy code (CRC) to the block. The receiving end applies the same polynomial to the data and compares its result with the result appended by the sender. If they agree, the data has been received successfully. If not, the sender can be notified to resend the block of data.

CRC operates by applying a mathematical algorithm to the message block. The message block is divided by a constant that is called the **generator polynomial**. The quotient is discarded and the remainder is transmitted as the Block Check Character (BCC). The receiving station performs the same calculation to determine the BCC.

If the two BCC match then consequently there message is error free, otherwise the message contains errors. If errors occur then the receiving station would request for a retransmission of the message, or correct the error through some special coding techniques.

Cyclic Redundancy uses a code to detect the errors in the transmission. These codes contain a specific number of bits, which is determined by the size of each character in the message. The commonly used codes are:

- ❒ CRC-12 (12 bits)
- ❒ CRC-16 (16 bits)
- ❒ CRC-CCITT (16 bits).

The BCC for the three cyclic codes is derived from the following generator polynomials, $G(x)$:

- ❒ CRC-12: $G(x) = x^{12} + x^{11} + x^3 + x^2 + x + 1$
- ❒ CRC-16: $G(x) = x^{16} + x^{15} + x^2 + 1$
- ❒ CRC-CCITT: $G(x) = x^{16} + x^{12} + x^5 + 1$.

The ITU-T (CCITT) has a standard for a 16 bit polynomial to be used to obtain the cyclic redundancy code (CRC) that is appended. IBM's SDLC and other protocols use CRC-16, another 16 bit polynomial. A 16 bit cyclic redundancy code detects all single and double-bit error and ensures detection of 99.998% of all possible errors. This level of detection assurance is considered sufficient for data transmission blocks of 4 kilobytes or less. For larger transmissions, a 32 bits CRC is used. The *Ethernet* and *Token Ring* local area network protocols both used a 32 bits CRC.

Example: Polynomials. The CRC generator (the divisor) is most often represented not as a string of 1's and 0's, but as an algebraic polynomial. The polynomial format is useful for two reasons: It is short, and it can be used to prove the concept mathematically.

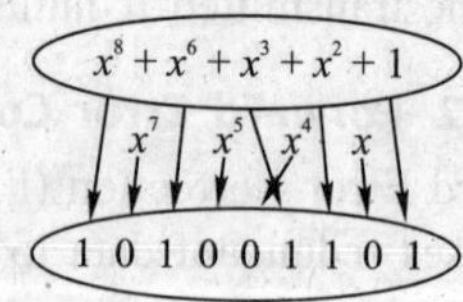

Fig. 12.39 Polynomial and its Binary Representation

Figure 12.39 shows the relationship of a polynomial to its corresponding binary representation.

Given that:

Generator Polynomial, $G(x) = x^5 + x^2 + x + 1 = 100111$

Message Polynomial, $M(x) = x^8 + x^6 + x^3 + x^2 + 1 = 101001101$

To determine the BCC, we perform long division, and the remainder becomes the BCC.

1. Multiply the message, $M(x)$ by x^{n-k}

$$x^{n-k}[M(x)] = x^5 (x^8 + x^6 + x^3 + x^2 + 1) = 10100110100000$$

```
                101111110
101001101 | 10100110100000
                    :
                    :
                -----------
                    11010
```

101111110-This quotient is discarded.

The division gives a remainder 11010 and this is transmitted as the BCC.

The receiver determines the whole transmitted message block, $T(x)$, by adding the BCC to $x^{n-k}[M(x)]$.

$$T(x) = x^{n-k}[M(x)] + BCC$$
$$= 10100110100000 + 11010$$
$$= 10100110111010$$

This number is divided by the same generator polynomial and if the remainder equals 0, then there is no error, otherwise an error has occurred.

CRC-32

$$x^{32}+x^{26}+x^{23}+x^{22}+x^{16}+x^{12}+x^{11}+x^{10}+x^{8}+x^{7}+x^{5}+x^{4}+x^{2}+x+1$$

CRC-16

$$x^{16}+x^{15}+x^{2}+1$$

CRC-12

$$x^{12}+x^{11}+x^{3}+x+1$$

CRC-ITU

$$x^{16}+x^{12}+x^{5}+1$$

Fig. 12.40 Standard polynomials

The standard polynomials used by popular protocols for CRC generation are shown in Fig. 12.40.

12.28 CHECKSUM

A checksum is a count of the number of bits in a transmission unit that is included with the unit so that the receiver can check to see whether the same number of bits arrived. If the counts match, it's assumed that the complete transmission was received. Both TCP and UDP communication layers provide a checksum count and verification as one of their services.

This is the second type of ARQ error detection technique. Checksum is an effective in detecting errors, however this is the techniques problem. The purpose of checksum is to simply detect any errors within the transmission, and ask for retransmission. It does not have the capabilities to identify the precise location of errors.

Checksum functions by addition of the total number of bits in the flow of data to determine the value of Block Check Character (BCC). The BCC is then taken and placed at the end of the message block ready to be transmitted. The process is repeated to determine the BCC of the received data. If the BCC match, then the transfer has occurred error free, otherwise retransmission of the data is required.

12.29 PARITY

In computers, parity refers to a technique of checking whether data has been lost or written over when it's moved from one place in storage to another or when transmitted between computers.

An additional bit, the *parity bit*, is added to a group of bits that are moved together. This bit is used only for the purpose of identifying whether the bits being moved arrived successfully. Before the bits are sent, they are counted and if the total number of data bits is even, the parity bit is set to one so that the total number of bits transmitted will form an odd number. If the total number of data bits is already an odd number, the parity bit remains or is set to 0. At the receiving end, each group of incoming bits is checked to see if the group totals to an odd number. If the total is even, a transmission error has occurred and either the transmission is retried or the system halts and an error message is sent to the user.

Assume an ASCII character that is ready for transmission, consisting of 8 bits. 7 bits in the character itself, plus the parity bit. The transmitting device computes the parity by summing the 1's in the 7 bits character. If even parity is set, then the transmitting device must ensure that the total number of 1's including the parity becomes an even value. Odd parity is exactly the same, except opposite.

The receiving device performs the same calculations on the character, and computes the parity to check it against the transmitted parity. If the parity checks are not the same then an error has occurred, and retransmission must commence.

Data Character	Odd Parity
1001011	1
1101000	0
Data Character	**Even Parity**
1001011	0
1101000	1

Parity checking is also used in communication between modems. Here, parity checking can be selected to be even (a successful transmission will form an even number) or odd. Users may also select *no parity*, meaning that the modems will not transmit or check a parity bit. When no parity is selected (or defaulted), it's assumed that there are other forms of checking that will detect any errors in transmission. No parity also usually means that the parity bit can be used for data, speeding up transmission. In modem-to-modem communication, the type of parity is coordinated by the sending and receiving modems before the transmission takes place.

The description above describes how parity checking works within a computer. Specifically, the PCI bus and the I/O bus controller use the odd parity method of error checking. Parity bit checking is not an infallible error-checking method since it's possible that two bits could be in error in a transmission, offsetting each other. For transmissions within a personal computer, this possibility is considered extremely remote. In some large computer systems where data integrity is seen as extremely important, three bits are allocated for parity checking.

12.29.1 Disadvantages of Checksum

The major problem with parity checking is that it fails to detect errors in multiples of two. This is due to its structure. Parity is calculated using the number of 1 bit present in the character. If 2 bit were not received, then the receiving and would not return a mismatch in the parity, therefore no errors we detected. Also if the number of bits were successfully transmitted, but in the wrong position, the parity would not detect any errors. Clearly errors have occurred, but not detected.

12.29.1.1 Vertical Redundancy Check (VRC)

The idea behind vertical redundancy check (VRC) is based on per character. VRC is essentially another name for the parity bit in the previous section.

12.29.1.2 Longitudinal Redundancy Check (LRC)

Along with calculating the Parity on a per character basis, it can also calculated and inserted at the end of a message block. The parity bit is calculated from the accumulation of the character's Least Significant Bit (LSB) through to the Most Significant Bit (MSB), including the VRC. The resulting word is called *Block Check Character* (BCC).

With the addition of VRC, LRC detection of a single bit error and correction is possible. For example take the message below using VRC and LRC with odd parity checking.

	n	*i*	*C*	*e*	*LRC*
LSB	0	1	1	1	0
	1	0	1	0	1
	1	0	0	1	1
	1	1	0	0	1
	0	0	0	0	1
	1	1	1	1	1
MSB	1	1	1	1	1
VRC	1	1	1	1	1

Say that the LSB for *e*, was transmitted as a 0, instead of a 1, the parity bit would reveal that an error has occurred. For the checking parity bit it would not be able to locate the error using only the LRC. The intersection of the VRC with the LRC, could determine the exact location of the error, and simply invert the value to correct the problem.

Unfortunately, the problem that occurred before in the per character parity, with the detection of errors occurring in multiples of two still exist in this system.

12.30 ERROR CORRECTION

In digital electronic systems, information is represented in binary format (1's and 0's). When binary information is passed from one point to another, there is always some chance that a mistake can be made; a 1 interpreted as a 0 or a 0 taken to be a 1. This can be caused by media defects, electronic noise, component failures, poor connections, deterioration due to age, and other factors. When a bit is mistakenly interpreted, a bit error has occurred.

Error correction is the process of detecting bit errors and correcting them and can be done in software or hardware. For high data rates, error correction must be done in special-purpose hardware because software is too slow.

A group of bits in a computer has conventionally been referred to as a 'word'. Each bit can be thought of as one of two 'letters', 0 or 1. Error correcting systems add extra or 'redundant' letters to computer words. The extra letters (bits) add a certain structure to each word. If that structure is altered by errors, the changes can be detected and corrected.

English words provide an analogy. Not all possible combinations of the English alphabet are legitimate words. The only legitimate words are those listed in a dictionary of the English language. Errors that occur when transmitting or storing English words can be detected by determining if the received word is in the dictionary. If it is not, errors can be corrected by determining which legitimate English word is closest to the received word. Error correcting systems work in a similar fashion.

Around 1947–48, the subject of information theory was created by Claude Shannon. The main result of Shannon's 'Mathematical Theory of Communication' is that the only way to get the most storage capacity in a storage device or the fastest transmission through a communications channel is through the use of very powerful error correcting systems. During the same time period, Richard Hamming discovered and implemented a single-bit error correcting code.

In 1960, researchers, including Irving Reed and Gustave Solomon, discovered how to construct error correcting codes that could correct for an arbitrary number of bits or an arbitrary number of 'bytes' where 'byte' means a group of 'w' bits. Even though the codes were discovered at this time, there still was no way known to decode the codes.

In 1968, Elwyn Berlekamp and James Massey discovered algorithms needed to build decodes for multiple error correcting codes. They came to be known as the Berlekamp-Massey algorithm for solving the key decoding equation.

In the last 30 years, researchers have discovered that the Berlekamp-Massey algorithm is a variation of an ancient algorithm discovered in Egypt around 300 BC by Euclid and known as **Euclid's extended algorithm** for finding the greatest common divisor of two polynomials. Today, numerous variations of the Berlekamp-Massey and Euclid algorithms exist to solve the key decoding equation.

Error correcting encoders and decoders operate on bits or bytes. From a mathematical point of view, each bit or byte is an element in a finite field, which is an abstract algebraic system with a finite number of elements and two operations and their inverses defined. The operations are usually called **multiplication** and addition and their inverses called **division** and **subtraction**.

Error correction is needed to ensure the accuracy and integrity of data and, in some cases, to create fault-tolerance (where components can fail with no loss of performance or data).

No electronic data transmission or storage system is perfect. Each system makes errors at a certain rate. As data transfer rates and storage densities increase, the raw error rate also increases.

If you look at bit error rate in terms of media, some electronic systems experience more errors than others. For instance, optical disk has a higher error rate than magnetic disk. Magnetic tape has a higher error rate than magnetic disk. Fiber optic communications cable and semiconductor memory have a low error rate.

One way to measure bit error rate is in terms of the number of bit errors divided by the total bits transferred. Using magnetic disk as an example, if you were to look at bits coming right off a magnetic disk you would see, on the average, about 1 bit error for every billion bits transferred. If you were to look at bits coming right off an optical disk, you would see a much higher rate of errors, about 1 bit error in every 100,000 bits transferred. Without some form of error detection and correction, most storage devices would be too unreliable to be useful.

Another way to measure bit error rate is in terms of how many bit errors occur in a unit of time. Again, using magnetic disk as an example, if you transfer a million bits per second, on the average, you'd have a bit error every thousand seconds, or every 16.6 minutes. If you transfer a billion bits per second, on the average, you'd have a bit error every second. Currently, some disk drives transfer at the rate of 40 million bits per second, so that a bit error occurs every 25 seconds.

As a general rule, in all electronic devices, transfer rates are increasing as time goes on. Also, errors will occur more frequently in any kind of storage device because manufacturers are squeezing more bits into smaller and smaller spaces. As speed and density increase, error correction becomes a necessity.

Error correction can either be done in hardware or software depending upon how fast it has to be done. In most cases, such as magnetic disk drives or semiconductor memory, errors must be detected and corrected 'on-the-fly', or, at the same rate as data is being read from the disk. The 'on-the-fly' performance requirement usually means the error correction implementation must be done in digital logic (hardware).

In some cases, such as some telecommunications systems where the data rates are relatively low, software implementations of error correction may be fast enough.

If encoded data is written to a storage device in such a way that each byte of the encoded data is recorded on a separate component, then fault-tolerance has been created. If one or more components fail, they can only corrupt the data bytes that are written on them.

As long as the number of component failures is less than or equal to the correction capability of the error correcting code, the failures will not result in any loss of data or performance.

RAID (Redundant Arrays of Inexpensive Devices) is an example of using an error correcting system to create fault-tolerance, even though most RAID systems use a simple single bit erasure correcting system.

Error correction is currently being used to make high capacity storage devices such as magnetic and optical disk and tape reliable. Error correction enables higher density recordings. In magnetic disk drives, for example, inexpensive and reliable 2 to 20 GigaByte capacity drives would not be possible without error correction.

Error correction can be used to decrease the price and increase the reliability of DRAM memory modules (SIMMS) because lower-grade DRAM components can be used.

Error correction can be used to extend the battery life of portable computers and other battery-powered electronic devices by allowing a significant decrease in the DRAM refresh rate.

In communications networks, such a as ATM, error correction can be used to reconstruct lost or missing packets without the need for retransmission and with no loss of performance. For long-haul lines, frequent retransmission causes severe performance degradation.

In RAID (Redundant Arrays of Inexpensive Devices), error correction can be used to create an arbitrary level of fault-tolerance. Multiple devices can fail with no loss of data or performance.

Error correction can also be used to provide fault-tolerant electronic cabling systems, for example, fly-by-wire aircraft.

12.31 ERROR CORRECTION TECHNIQUES

In transmitting data between two terminals, the issue of reliability is critical. Information must arrive in the receiving computer 100% intact for it to be any use to the user. Such an issue has brought about two techniques for resolving this issue. One technique, which is preferred, requests that the data be retransmitted if an error occurs. This method is formally known as **Automatic Repeat Request (ARQ).**

ARQ unlike FEC uses a method of positive acknowledgment and negative acknowledgment. When a receiver receives a message it will return a positive acknowledge to the transmitter, to say that it has received it correctly. If there is an error present in the message, then a negative acknowledgment is returned and the receiver asks for a retransmission of the message. This system is also otherwise referred to as ACK/NCK.

The second method is mainly used in one way (simplex) transmission, where it is impossible to request a retransmission. This technique is called **Forward Error Correction** (FEC). FEC uses redundant pieces of data located within the datastream as an error correction technique. If errors are detected by the receiver, the embedded code is extracted from the message and used to predict and possibly correct the problem.

A common set of codes that are used in FEC, are those developed by the Richard W. Hamming, called **Hamming Code**.

Error correction coding is more sophisticated than error detection coding. Its aim to detect and locate errors in transmission. Once located, the correction is trivial: the bit is inverted. Error correction coding requires lower rate codes than error detection, often markedly so. It is therefore uncommon in terrestrial communication, where better performance is usually obtained with error detection and retransmission. However, in satellite communications, the propagation delay often means that many frames are transmitted before an instruction to retransmit is received. This can make the task of data handling very complex. Realtime transmission often precludes retransmission. It is necessary to get it right first time. In these special circumstances, the additional bandwidth required for the redundant check-bits is an acceptable price. There are *two* principle types: (1) Hamming codes and (2) Convolutional codes.

12.31.1 Hamming Codes

Hamming Codes use redundant bits in the datastream to correct errors that occur on the receiving end. Positioning of the bits is known by the transmitter and the receiver before the transmission. Once errors are detected, the hamming bits located within the message identify the position of the errors. This position is known as **syndrome**, the underlying principle to the Hamming Code.

The number of hamming bits required in the message block is determined by the expression:

$$2^n > m + n + 1$$

- ❑ m is number of bits in the data, and
- ❑ n is number of Hamming bits.

The locations of the Hamming bits are usually located in powers of two, from the right.

Example of Hamming Code:

Character is: 011001

Hamming bits are: HHHH

Thus format of message: 01H100H1HH

1. Take the 1's in the message, convert them to binary form.
2. Add the each position is exclusive OR'd with each other.

Position	*Code*
9	1001
7	0111
3	0011
EX-OR	1101

➤ The hamming bits that are to be embedded in the message is 1101. So the message becomes 0111001101, with the hamming bits included.

Position	*Code*
Hamming	1101
9	1001
7	0111
3	0011
EX-OR	0000

➤ Once the receiver receives the message, it will again perform an exclusive OR with the 1's. The result will produce either an error or no error. If the receiver does not detect an error, then the result will be a zero.

Position	*Code*
Hamming	1101
9	1001
7	0111
4	0100
3	0011
EX-OR	0100

➤ If an error occurs, then the hamming code will detect the position of the error and by simply inverting the value in the cell then the error can be corrected. We use the example from the text, where bit 4 has an error.

➤ The hamming code has detected the error and its location, and simply requires an inversion to correct the error.

12.31.2 Convolution Code

In telecommunication, a convolutional code is a type of error-correcting code in which each *m*-bit information symbol (each m-bit string) to be encoded is transformed into an *n*-bit symbol, where *m*/*n* is the code rate ($n \geq m$) and the transformation is a function of the last *k* information symbols, where *k* is the constraint length of the code. Convolutional codes are used extensively in numerous applications in order to achieve reliable data transfer, including digital video, radio, mobile communication, and satellite communication.

12.32 NETWORKS CONNECTING DEVICES

Internetworks commonly use special devices called repeaters, bridges, routers, and gateways to connect independent networks. Local area networks occasionally use these devices to extend connections within a local area network. Although you don't need to know how each of these devices work, you should understand their function.

12.32.1 Repeater

As its name implies, a **repeater** copies or repeats signals that it receives. However, a repeater also amplifies all received signals before re-transmission. This means a repeater increases the size of analog waveforms it receives. By increasing the size of the waveform (without changing its frequency), a repeater eliminates the signal loss or attenuation that the waveform experienced during its journey to the repeater. In short, a repeater strengthens an incoming signal before sending the signal on its way. By strategically placing repeaters along a network bus, engineers can extend the distance between adjacent computers.

Long-haul networks may contain many repeaters. Ethernets also frequently use repeaters to extend the length of the bus cable within a local area network. That is, network administrators use repeaters to avoid attenuation problems when they connect two pieces of the same network. In other words, although you can use a repeater as part of an internetwork connection, you can also use repeaters within a single, stand-alone network such as a LAN.

12.32.2 Bridge

A **bridge** interconnects two networks that use the same technology (such as Ethernet or ARCNET). A bridge is more sophisticated than a repeater. For example, assume a bridge interconnects two networks called 'Eastside' and 'Westside'. The bridge will examine all packets on each network data bus. When the bridge sees an Eastside packet destined for an address on the Westside network, the bridge transfers the packet from the Eastside network to the Westside network. The bridge will not transmit a packet to the Westside network if the packet's destination address is on the Eastside network.

In other words, a bridge acts like a traffic cop at a busy intersection beside a bridge that crosses a river. The traffic cop (the bridge) asks the occupants of each vehicle (the Eastside packet) where they want to go. If the occupants specify an address on the other side of the river (Westside address), the traffic cop directs the vehicle across the bridge (to the Westside network). If the occupants specify an Eastside address, the traffic cop waves the vehicle through the intersection. The traffic cop (bridge) only redirects traffic (packets) destined for an address located on the other side of the river (a Westside address).

In addition to interconnecting networks, bridges often boost performance, reliability, and security. For example, you have learned that a collision detection system requires a computer to delay transmissions after a data collision occurs. As you add more computers to a network, the number of data collisions rises.

More collisions occur because more computers are trying to transmit data packets at the same time. Like cars on a freeway, packets represent network traffic. As you know, the more cars (packets) you have traveling on the freeway (data bus), the greater the number of collisions. As you attach more computers to a network, data traffic increases. In some cases, traffic can increase to the point that network performance begins to suffer. In effect, traffic jams begin to occur.

Sometimes, you can add a bridge to solve performance problems that result from heavy traffic. In effect, a bridge divides on crowded local area network into two or more networks. For example, suppose the Eastside and Westside networks were originally part of the same local area network. The bridge (traffic cop) keeps Eastside packets on the Eastside network and Westside packets on the Westside network. Eastside packets don't clog the Westside network and Westside packets don't clog the Eastside network. In other words, due to the bridge, the traffic on each network decreases and, as a result, performance increases.

Network administrators often use a bridge to create two or more smaller networks—even if performance is not a problem on their network. As you have learned, in a ring or bus topology, a single break in the data bus stops all network communications. By partitioning a single LAN into multiple LANs (connected by a bridge), network administrators reduce the impact of a break in the data bus.

For example, consider the imaginary Eastside and Westside networks again. Assume that a network administrator added a bridge to a single local area network to create the two networks. A break in the Eastside network data bus would cause all Eastside network communications to stop. However, computers on the Westside network could continue to function normally—except that they could not communicate with any Eastside network computers.

By adding the bridge and dividing a single LAN into two networks, the network administrator improves reliability for the entire network. For example, a single break only affects half the network—not the entire network. Network administrators may repeatedly sub-divide networks until they reach an acceptable level of reliability.

As you have learned, in bus and ring topologies, data passes each computer on the network. As such, any network user can utilize a special electronic device, called a **network analyzer**, to intercept and examine data packets on the network. Depending on the type of network, you can use software to accomplish the same task.

Network analyzers, either hardware or software, help network professionals troubleshoot network problems. Network professionals analyze network traffic for a variety of reasons. For example, they may monitor traffic to help identify traffic problems such as congestion. In other cases, network analyzers monitor packets to help a programmer debug a network program. These are legitimate reasons for monitoring network traffic. Unfortunately, network analyzers can present a security problem for a network administrator if the network carries sensitive information.

A bridge will not prevent unauthorized monitoring. However, a network administrator can use a bridge to divide a local area network into secure and unsecured LANs. In that way, the network administrator can restrict the flow of sensitive data to one LAN and thereby reduce the data's vulnerability to tampering or monitoring.

12.32.3 Router

A **router** transfers or routes data between networks. Although a router can transfer data between networks that use the same technologies, routers commonly transfer data between different technologies such as Ethernet and IBM Token Ring. Since the Internet consists of thousands of networks that use many different technologies, routers are an essential part of the Internet. A router has an address on the network; a bridge does not. This difference is the key to understanding the difference between a bridge and a router. Networks frequently use a router as an intermediate destination.

In other words, a computer can send a packet destined for another network to a router. The router will transfer the packet to the other network. On the other hand, a bridge must examine all data on the bus to determine which packets to transfer between networks. As such, computers never send packets directly to the bridge—doing so is unnecessary. A router never examines a packet on the data bus unless the packet contains the routers's address.

12.32.4 Brouters

Many routers are really *brouters*. Brouters are essentially routers that can also bridge. A brouter will first check to see if it supports the protocol being used by the packet. If not, rather than simply dropping the packet, the packet is bridged using physical address information.

12.32.5 Hub

The network hub is a centralized distribution point for all traffic on a single leg of the actual network. It is like a warehouse distribution center. Data packets from a NIC arrive at hub which receives and rebroadcasts them to other computers connected to it. But a network hub is not smart. It does not know where the destination of data packet is and so, must send a copy to all the connections on the hub.

Hubs can be classified as:

- Stackable versus Non-stackable
- Active versus Passive
- Intelligent versus Non-intelligent (dumb)

12.32.5.1 Stackable versus Non-stackable

Stackable versus non-stackable is one of the two most popular terms vendors use to classify their hubs. Stackable hubs can be stacked and connected (usually through a proprietary interface part) so they appear as a single hub. Non-stackable hubs cannot be interconnected.

12.32.5.2 Active versus Passive

The terms active and passive are used to describe the role of each hub in a stackable set of hubs. The hub that connects to the network backbone is the active hub. Those which connect only to the active hub are passive hubs.

12.32.5.3 Intelligent versus Dumb

Intelligent hubs often cost much more than dumb hubs. However, that higher cost includes SNMP (Simple Network Management Protocol) firmware you can access remotely. SNMP is a polling protocol that allows you to obtain network performance and status data from hubs.

12.32.6 Channel Service Unit/Digital Service Unit (CSU/DSU)

CSU/DSUs are devices that prepare electric pulse signals for transmission on WAN transmission media. These devices make sure that the signal uses the correct signal strength and format. These units protect you, and other public network users, from electrical noise or unsafe electric voltages. In addition, they prepare your data for transmission according to the rules specified for the network. It is advantageous at times to use public transmission media networks. These networks may require that you use *channel service units* and *digital service units* (CSU/DSU) to connect to their media.

12.32.7 A Gateway

Gateway is generic term that can refer to three types of network entities. You can refer to a router as a gateway. When you use the term in this way, a gateway is identical to a router as described in the previous paragraphs. A gateway can also refer to something called an **application gateway**.

Application gateways translate data that specific network programs use. The most common type of application gateway is one that e-mail applications use. For example, you can use MCI Mail to send e-mail to someone on a private company's local area network in another state. Your e-mail message might travel from MCI Mail to the Internet and from the Internet to the destination LAN. At each interconnection, an application gateway (for e-mail) would translate your message into a former suitable for further transmission.

12.32.8 Transmission Media Connectors

Every medium has one or more physical connectors to which you can attach various devices. The first step in using connectivity hardware is to attach the appropriate connectors to each length of transmission media.

12.32.9 Networking Interface Boards

A network interface board includes all of the physical and logical connections between your computer, or other device, and the transmission medium. It is a logic board you install in a computer to connect it to a cable's connector. However, network interface boards may be an interface card, a portion of the device's logic board software and a generic hardware port, or a number of external devices.

The following terms also describe network interface boards, so they will be defined here:

- Transceiver
- Network Interface Card (NIC)
- Transmission Media Adapter

12.32.9.1 Transceivers

All network interface boards include some type of *transceiver*. Transceivers are devices that can transmit as well as receive electric or electromagnetic signals on the transmission media. They come in a variety of different types, but all of them emit electricity, light, or electromagnetic waves. When using cable media, transceivers are often coupled with connectors that are the opposite gender from those directly attached to the media. Using wireless media, transceivers are just transmitting and receiving devices because no mechanical connectors are required.

12.32.9.2 Network Interface Card (NIC)

When the end-user device does not provide a suitable port or network interface board, printed circuit boards called **network interface cards** are used. These cards include the circuitry and mechanical connections to convert the computer's electric signals to be electric or electromagnetic signals used on the medium. A card usually includes a single transceiver but may provide one or more connector types.

12.32.9.3 Transmission Media Adapter

When a network interface board uses a connector that is different from what is already attached to the transmission medium, a *transmission media adapter* is used. The purpose of this adapter is to receive signals from one type of connector and convert them for use with another type.

12.33 THE OPEN SYSTEM INTERCONNECTION (OSI) MODEL

There was a time when there was no such thing as a network architecture. Companies implemented rather rude, crude and socially unacceptable software and hardware communication solutions without any thought as to layering or to the implementation of an architecture. The idea of layering really took off with the introduction of an international standard called the **Open Systems Interconnection** (OSI) model by the International Standards Organization (ISO) in 1982 (International Standard 7498).

In 1978, the ISO Technical Committee 97 (this committee handles standardization of information technology) started subcommittee number 16 (TC97/SC16) to develop an architecture and reference model that would serve as the foundation for future standard activities. From 1978 onwards, they have worked very hard at providing a flexible, reasonable communication architecture that could be implemented on a variety of systems and provide inter-and intra-systems communication capabilities in a variety of environments. Oddly enough, TC97/SC16 has not done most of the work on defining the protocols for each layer of the architecture; other ISO committees have done this, using the model specified by TC97/SC16. All protocols for all layers have not been defined yet, but the model still is highly useful in the definition of how a communication architecture is defined.

In 1978 the International Standards Organization (ISO) proposed a broad model for mainframe wide area network communication, which they titled 'The Reference Model of Open Systems Interconnection'.

Open Systems Interconnection refers to the exchange of information among terminal devices, computers, people, networks and processes. The systems are open to one another by virtue of their mutual use of the standards developed from the original reference model. Openness does not imply any particular implementation, technology or interconnection means.

The Open System Interconnection Reference Model is not, by itself, a standard, nor is it a literal description of computer communication. While it defines where to perform tasks, it does not detail how to perform them. Individual services and protocols are not specified. Within the model, communication functions are addressed from the perspective of computer-to-communication network interconnection.

The Reference Model is intended to provide a common basis for coordinating the development of standards aimed at systems interconnection, while allowing existing standards to be placed in perspective within a common framework.

12.33.1 OSI Layers

The ISO/OSI model uses layers to organize a network into well-defined, functional modules. Network designers use the model's descriptions of these layers to build real network. In a layered network, each module (or layer) provides specific functionality or services to its adjacent layers. In addition, each layer shields layers above it from lower-level implementation details. In other words, each layer only cares about its interface to the next layer in the network. Figure 12.41 shows the layers in the ISO/OSI network model. As an applications programmer, you may not view your software as vertical layers of modularity. However, the concept of one module hiding details from another may not be new to you. For example, your programs probably perform file I/O by calling a function or system service.

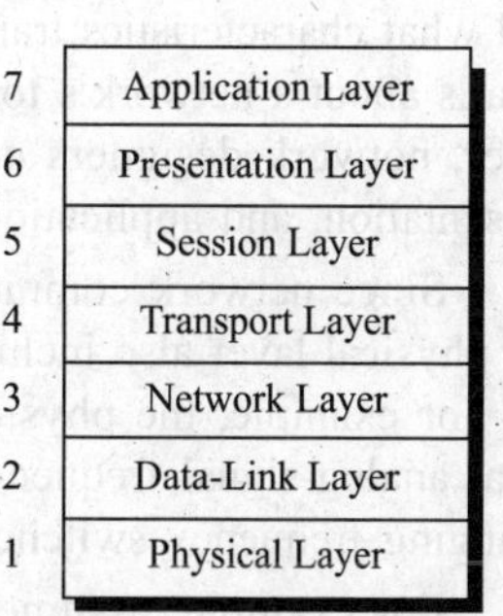

Fig. 12.41 Network layers in the ISO/OSI model

To use the file I/O service, you don't need to understand how the service works. Instead, you simply need to know which parameters pass to and from the service and the possible return values. In short, you treat the service as a black box, not caring what is inside. As a programmer opening a file, you can simply call a function or system service and rely upon the fact that your program will receive a file handle or a pointer to a file. Your program can use the file handle to read or write data. You don't worry about how data passes between your program and the hard disk. Nor do you think much about how the hard disk physically stores your data.

Each network layer provides a communication service to the layer above it. Network professionals design each network layer to hide, from the layer above it, all implementation details related to the layer's services. By building on each layer's services, network designers create functional modules with well-defined interfaces.

The five major principles used to develop the layers in the Open Systems Interconnection reference model:

1. Create a new network whenever the network software needs a different level of abstraction.
2. Each layer should perform a well-defined function.
3. Choose each layer's function with an eye towards defining internationally standardized protocols.

4. Choose layer boundaries to minimize the information flow across the interfaces.
5. The number of layers should be large enough so that the network designers don't need to place dissimilar functions in the same layer. However, the number of layers should not be so large that they become unwieldy.

12.33.1.1 The Physical Layer

The physical layer transmits data through the network's communication channels. The physical layer includes the physical elements (hardware) needed to accomplish this function. As such, the network's transmission lines—the cables that connect all the computers on the network—are part of the physical layer. Data transmission methods, including control signals and timing, are also part of the physical layer. As such, the physical layer also includes network technologies (Ethernet, ARCNET, and token ring) that define parameters for data transmission.

As you have learned, the physical layer transmits data through the network's communication channels. As part of this function, the physical layer determines the mechanical and electrical properties of the network communications channel, as well as procedural details related to these characteristics. For example, the physical layer determines how many electrical pins or wires a network connection uses, what type of cable (coaxial or twisted pair) a transmission line uses, and what characteristics transmission lines have. In a similar fashion, the physical layer contains details about a network's topology. With such design details assigned exclusively to the physical layer, network designers can create the higher layers (data-link, network, session, transport, presentation, and application) without considering the network's topology.

Since network communications at the bit-level (binary data) occur in the physical layer, the physical layer also includes related design issues such as how hardware will represent 1s and 0s. For example, the physical layer determines what analog-signal frequency represents 1 and what analog-signal frequency represents 0. The physical layer will decide the point at which a changing frequency switches from a 1 to a 0 (and vice versa).

For example, assume that the physical layer uses voltage to represent binary data. The physical layer would determine at what point a changing voltage level toggles its logical state to represent the opposite binary number. The physical layer also ensures that the destination host receives each binary digit of data representing a 1 as a 1 and not as a 0. The physical layer also determines whether data transfers use simplex, half-duplex, or full duplex modes of communication.

12.33.1.2 The Data-Link Layer

The data-link layer transfers raw data between the physical layer and the network layer. The network interface card represents the data-link layer in your computer. The data-link layer's primary function is to prevent data corruption within the physical layer. Network newcomers often find the link layer confusing because it seems to contradict what they know about the ISO/OSI model. They know every network layer has a link or interface to layers above and below itself (*e.g.*, the transport layer has a link to the network layer and a link to the session layer). As such, they wonder why the link between the network layer and the physical layer deserves its own layer (the data-link layer) within the ISO/OSI model. You can answer this question by refering back to the five major principles used to derive the ISO/OSI model. In accordance with principle 2, the data-link layer performs a well-defined function. To describe this function, you need a different level of abstraction (principle 1—the data-link layer's function is separate from those of the physical and network layers). Additionally, the data-link layer helps localize the definition of information flowing between the physical and network layers. In other words, the data-link layer minimizes the flow of information across the boundaries between the physical and network layers (principle 4). Finally, the data-link layer lets network designers locate these related functions within their own layer; otherwise, designers would need to arbitrarily place each function in either the physical or the network layer.

The physical layer manages raw data as bits (1's and 0's). The data-link layer formats or transforms raw binary data into something meaningful to the network layer—normally, frames of data. The data-link layer also accepts information from the network layer and translates the data into the correct binary format for the underlying physical layer (for example, FM signals or voltage levels). In all cases, the data-link layer ensures that binary transmissions between network hosts are free from errors.

Network professionals must design a different data-link layer for each different physical network design. For example, you have learned that the physical layer contains details about network technologies such as Ethernet, ARCNET, and token ring. To connect a computer to a network, you must plug a network-interface card into the computer.

Network-interface cards are peculiar to a specific network technology. The design of an Ethernet network-interface card is different from an ARCNET interface card. As such, you can think of the network-interface card within your computer as the data-link layer in most networks. In other words, as previously mentioned, the network card you place in your computer provides the data-link layer.

When the data-link layer formats raw bits, the units of data that result are generally called **frames**. Although the International Organization for Standardization calls these units **physical-layer-service-data-units**, most other network literature simply refers to such data as frames. As you might expect, a data frame's contents depend on the underlying network technology (the physical layer).

For example, assume you attach two personal computers, made by the same manufacturer, to an internetwork. However, suppose that one computer is on an Ethernet network and the other is on a token ring network. At the network layer level, data on these two computers will look identical. At the data-link and physical levels, however, the data format will be completely different. In other words, to package information, the data-link layer creates a very different frame for an Ethernet network than it does for a token ring network. The requirements of the underlying physical layer (network technology) determine the content of the data frame. For example, the physical layer doesn't care (the design is independent of) how (what format) the network layer transmits information to the data-link layer. At the same time, the network layer doesn't care (the design is independent of) how (what format) the data-link layer creates the frames (for the physical layer).

By design, data frames provide error-checking capabilities. You should understand that the primary function of the data-link layer is to prevent data corruption. People often assume that formatting data into frames is the primary purpose of the data-link layer. They miss the real goal of this formatting process. Data frames are simply a means to an end. As described next, the end goal is to prevent data corruption in the communication channel.

You should understand that networks use data frames to detect and correct data corruption in the network communication channel. Figure 12.42 shows the format of an Ethernet frame.

64 Bits	48 Bits	48 Bits	16 Bits	368-12,000 Bits	32 Bits
Preamble	Destination Address	Source Address	Frame Type	Frame Data	Cyclic Redundancy Check (CRC)

Fig. 12.42 The contents of an Ethernet Data Frame

The detect data corruption, the data-link layers of the sender and receiver use a cyclic redundancy check (CRC) value. The 32 bit CRC value is the result of a complex calculation performed on the data contained within the data frame. The sender calculates and then stores the CRC value at the end of the data frame. The receiver re-calculates the CRC, then compares its CRC to the CRC value stored in the data frame. If the CRC value stored in the data frame matches the CRC value calculated by the receiver, the probability that the received data matches the originally transmitted data is extremely high. For all practical purposes, the CRCs guarantee the integrity of transmitted data.

The remainder of the data frame is necessary to properly identify and route the frame. For example, the Preamble field helps receiving hosts synchronize with the sender. In other words, the field identifies which piece of data the frame contains. As you will recall, networks can fragment data (break it into smaller pieces). Data frames must contain destination and source addresses for routing and error-reporting purposes. The receiver uses the Frame Type field to determine which protocol to use as the data passes upward through the network layers.

In short, a key data-link layer operation is to detect and prevent data corruption in the communication channel. As such, because the data-link layer needs an identifiable unit of data with which to calculate a CRC value, the layer formats or encapsulates data to create a finite entity (frame). The CRC value, in turn, ensures data integrity within the physical layer.

12.33.1.3 The Network Layer

The network layer determines the route that data follows to reach its destination on the network. As such, the network layer must handle network traffic, congestion, and transfer rates (speed) across the transmission lines. The network layer must also handle data corruption within the communication channel. You can think of the network layer as the delivery system within a network.

As you have learned, the network layer is the primary delivery system within a network. In a packet-switched network, such as the Internet, the network layer delivers units of data as individual packets. As you might expect, each packet of information contains a destination and source address for routing purposes. As the network delivery system, the network layer defines the interface between host computers and all packet switches located between the source and destination addresses. As such, when network designers create the protocols for the network layer, they must define how much responsibility each network element will have for routing data. In other words, they must decide how to divide the responsibility for data delivery between the host computer and intervening packet switches. The network layer ensures that hosts receive the correct packets. According to the ISO/OSI reference model, the network layer is also responsible for ensuring proper sequencing. As you will learn, however, Internet networks design sequencing into the transport layer instead of the network layer.

To route data, networks commonly use **routing tables**. A routing table is like a look-up database. Using a routing table, routers can look up the correct path from a packet's current location to any destination on the network. Depending on the network's requirements, a designer can implement routing tables as static or dynamic. With a static routing table, the network administrator must update the table. Network software automatically updates dynamic routing tables. A designer can use static routing tables if the network configuration rarely changes (in other words, when the workload to manually update the tables will be minimal). The designer stores routing information in a location that is accessible network-wide. When a network configuration change occurs, network administrators manually update the routing table information. As you might have guessed, network software that uses static routing tables is much easier to implement than network software that uses dynamic routing tables. With dynamic routing table designs, the network software must automatically update the routing tables each time a computer user starts a new network session (login) and possibly each time an application creates a new packet.

As network administrators add more computers to a network or as computer users begin to use a network more frequently, network packet traffic increases. Just as increasing the number of cars on a freeway system can cause traffic congestion, increasing the number of packets on a network can cause network traffic congestion. As a network becomes congested, network packet traffic slows and users experience noticeable degradation in network performance. To reduce such network traffic congestion, the network layer must effectively manage packet routing. As the network layer routes packets through the communication channel, the layer must avoid sending too many packets through the same packet switch. Otherwise, a traffic jam will occur. If the network layer cannot avoid an excessive flow of data, the layer must handle any resulting congestion. One way networks reduce congestion is to manage flow control. The network layer handles flow control problems while routing data. In other words, the network layer must handle problems such as a sender transmitting data faster than the receiver can accept data.

Networks can cross geopolitical boundaries. Many networks, such as the Internet, extend across the borders of two or more countries. In some cases, network professionals must design such networks to supply accounting information for cost and billing purposes. For example, network maintenance costs time, money, and effort. When the flow of data through a communications channel crosses national boundaries, countries may want to share these maintenance costs. For such networks, accounting information that tracks the quantity of data that moves through the network may be essential. The network may track such quantities in terms of numbers of packets, messages, characters, or bits.

Since the network layer has network-wide routing responsibilities, the function of tracking accounting information belongs in the network layer. As such, network professionals must design network layer software that reports accounting information, if required. This type of accounting information rapidly becomes complicated when different billing rates exist on both sides of a national border. Of course, such complications translate into complex network layer software. Fortunately, the Internet does not currently require such accounting information.

12.33.1.4 The Transport Layer

Just as the network layer delivers data packets across the network, the transport layer delivers (or transports) data within a host computer. In other words, after the network layer delivers data to the correct host address, the transport layer delivers data to the correct application within the destination host.

When two computers communicate across the network, two programs actually exchange data. The network layer delivers data to a host computer and then hands the data off to the transport layer. Within the host computer, the transport layer delivers the data to the correct program or application.

As you have learned, peer processes can carry on virtual conversations. For example, given a connection between two host computers, the network layer in the source host carries on a virtual conversation with the network layer in the destination host. Likewise, the source transport layer carriers on a virtual conversation with the destination transport layer.

Figure 12.43 shows the network model that you saw previously. As you have learned, the dotted lines between the corresponding layers in each host indicate a virtual conversation between the layers.

In a packet-switched network, the network layer frequently must route data through packet switches to deliver data between host computers. The network layer delivers data between host computers and handles all traffic management problems related to routing and delivery. In a packet-switched network, the transport layer must break or fragment data it receives from the session layer into the smaller pieces that the network layer requires. On the receiving end, the transport layer must reassemble the fragmented data. As such, the transport layer's design greatly impacts the quantity of packets that flow through the network. In other words, the transport layer produces the packet traffic that the network layer must manage.

Application Layer	◄-------	Application Layer	-------►	Application Layer
Presentation Layer	◄-------	Presentation Layer	-------►	Presentation Layer
Session Layer	◄-------	Session Layer	-------►	Session Layer
Transport Layer	◄-------	Transport Layer	-------►	Transport Layer
Network Layer	◄-------	Network Layer	-------►	Network Layer
Data-Link Layer	◄-------	Data-Link Layer	-------►	Data-Link Layer
Physical Layer	◄-------	Physical Layer	-------►	Physical Layer

Fig. 12.43 Network Model Peer Processes

Within a host computer, multiple programs (processes) may use the network at the same time, in different ways. The transport layer is responsible for getting data from, or sending data to, each network program. In this way, the transport layer must be able to interact with and manage the data for multiple programs at the same time.

As discussed, flow control is how software ensures that a sender does not send data packets faster than the receiver can process the incoming messages. Like the network layer, transport layers must also manage data flow. However, transport layers manage flow control on an end-to-end basis (from process to process) rather than a hop-by-hop basis (from computer to computer). In other words, the network layer handles flow control between end destinations represented by host computers. Likewise, the transport layer controls the data flow between peer processes or programs. Many transport layers, such as the transport layer on the Internet, manage flow control similar to error control. In other words, the transport layers exchange acknowledgement messages. The transport layers include flow control requests in the exchanged messages. For example, one transport layer can tell the other transport layer to either increase or decrease throughput.

12.33.1.5 The Session Layer

As the user's interface to the network, the session layer negotiates connections between processes or applications on different host computers. As such, the session layer handles details such as account names, passwords, and user authorizations. For example, on many networks, you must login (enter your name or user identification and a password) before you can use any network services. In most cases, you must login each time you want to use the network. Network professionals refer to each login as a session. In many cases, you can login to the network more than once. In other words, you can create multiple login sessions on the network. Each time you want to use your computer to communicate with another computer on the network, the session layer handles the negotiations that must occur before the computers can establish a connection.

Before you can establish a connection, both ends of the connection must negotiate options such as data transfer rates, error control, and the expected type of data transfer (simplex, half-duplex, or full-duplex). Either end of the connection can request changes to these options. The session layer must handle requests for a change to a negotiated option. Requests can occur at any time during the login session. The session layer must also authenticate both ends of a connection. In other words, the session layer requires each end of a connection to prove who they are. Both ends of a connection must also establish their authorization to use the specified connection or session.

As discussed, either end of a connection can request changes to a login session. Session changes may also result from problems in the transport layer. For example, if transport layer connections are unreliable, the session layer must recover from broken transports. For example, assume you use a transaction-based, distributed database. Should transport layer errors occur, the session layer might need to rollback (undo) a partially completed transaction. In preparation for such crash recoveries, the session layer may group related messages and either deliver to an application (at one time) all related messages or none of them. By doing so, the session layer prevents an unreliable transport layer from aborting a transport message in the middle of a transaction. Also, when the transport layer does not provide sequencing services, the session layer must do so if an application requires sequencing.

When a network doesn't require application-to-application communication services, network designers may eliminate the session layer. As you will learn, the Internet networks eliminate the session layer completely. Although, in most cases, you must login to use the Internet, the software that verifies Internet user authorizations is not part of the network software design. Instead, such software on the Internet is a program running in the application layer. On the Internet, the transport layer protocols include many functions that the session layer normally handles.

The session layer transforms data packaged for network transmissions into application data. Additionally, the session layer handles application requests for changes to data flow rates and error control. The session layer also verifies that a user or user process has the authority to use the requested connection or computer process on the network. As such, the session layer is the user's interface to a network. In short, the session layer establishes and manages connections between users and network applications. Network designers occasionally merge the session and transport layers. In most cases, the functionality required by a session layer does not disappear. Rather, other network software (either the transport layer or a custom application) assumes responsibility for session-layer functions.

12.33.1.6 The Presentation Layer

The presentation layer consolidates common functions that networks must repeatedly use during network communications. The presentation layer handles details related to the networks' interface to printers, video displays, and file formats. In short, the presentation layer defines how the network presents itself to your hardware and software. To understand the reasons for creating the presentation layer, you can again refer to the five major principles used to derive the OSI model. For example, even though every network application can independently perform all presentation-layer functions, you can also define all presentation-layer functions without reference to an application or any other network layer. To do so, you must create a different level of abstraction and, thus, a new layer. By locating all information related to printers, video displays, and file formats in the same layer, you minimize the flow of such interface information across other layer boundaries.

Well-designed networks let you attach a wide variety of computers. The Internet is an excellent example. Computers on the Internet range from single-user personal computers to minicomputers and large mainframes. Within each of these groups of computers, an even wider variety of video display units and printers exist. Unrelated operating system software on these computers can result in compatible file formats, as well as other incompatibilities. The presentation layer must integrate such diversity in a way that makes these differences transparent to network applications.

Unfortunately, Internet networks do not include a standard presentation layer. As such, application programs perform most presentation-layer functions. As an Internet programmer, you should follow the ISO/OSI design guidelines when you develop presentation-layer functions.

Network professionals often implement the presentation layer in user-callable routines and libraries. As you will learn, the Windows Sockets Application Program Interface (API) forms a kind of session/presentation layer upon which you can build applications. In one way or another, the layers below the presentation layer perform functions required for correct network operations. The presentation layer provides useful but non-essential network services.

12.33.1.7 The Application Layer

The application layer contains details about network-wide applications. As an applications programmer or software developer, you will already be familiar with much of the application layer's functionality. Examples of network-wide applications include electronic mail (e-mail) and distributed databases. Applications that you develop for use across the Internet will be part of the application layer. In fact, all programs for network computer users (the network's end-users) are part of the network's application layer.

For example, networks offer tremendous opportunities for distributed data processing (storing data across multiple host computers). Using a network, you can also connect multiple computer processors and have them simultaneously attack a particular computing problem. However, to develop such programs, you will need to study and learn information that you may not have previously needed to know. You need to learn the basic differences between network applications and non-network applications.

A server is a network device that provides services to intelligent client workstation, such as DOS-and OS/2-based PCs (personal computers), Macintoshes, and Unit-based technical workstations. In a client/server environment, some or all application processing is done on the client machine, while the servers provide access to network resources.

There are many types of servers and services, and they can provide controlled access to files (file service), access to network printers (print service), and access to electronic mail systems (mail service,) to name a few. Computers on a network can be dedicated to providing one or more services, or services can be provided by computers that are also being used for application processing (someone's desktop personal computer, for example).

The heart of a server-oriented LAN system is the file server operating system, also called the LAN operating system or the network operating system. Examples of LAN operating systems include Novell's NetWare, Banyan's VINES, Microsoft's LAN Manager, Sitka's TOPS, and Artisoft's LANtastic. There operating systems include or make provision for other services, such as print service.

A LAN operating system can be a native operating system, interacting directly with the CPU (central processing unit) of the file server computer (Novell's NetWare, for example), or it can be a task or application running on top of a general purpose operating system such as MS-DOS (Microsoft's MS-Net, Artisoft's LANtastic, Webcorp's WEB), OS/2 (Microsoft's LAN Manager), or Unix (Banyan's VINES, Microsoft's LAN Manager, Novell's Portable NetWare). Generally, a native LAN operating system will provide a higher level of performance than a LAN OS operating as a sub-task of another host operating system.

12.34 SUMMARY

Data communication is the process of electronically sending data from one point to another. Using communication facilities such as the telephone system and microwave relays to send data between computers is a type of data communication often referred to as telecommunication.

The transmission of data takes one of two forms: analog or digital. Analog data transmission is the passage of data in distinct on and off pulses.

Modulation is the process of converting a digital signal into an analog signal. Demodulation is the process of connecting the analog signal into a digital signal. A modem (modulator–demodulator) is the device that connects the signals.

A communication channel is the pathway through which data are transmitted between devices. There are three basic types of communication channels: (*i*) wire cable, (*ii*) microwave, and (*iii*) fiber optics. Communication channels are found in two principal configurations: point-to-point and multipoint. Two methods, polling and contention are used to determine which terminal gets access to the communication channel. Polling is the process whereby the computer checks each terminal to see if it is ready to send data. In contention, when the terminal is ready to send a message, it monitors the communication channel to see if the channel is free. The terminal keeps monitoring until the channel is free and then it can send its message.

Multiplexing is the process of combining the transmissions from several computers or other devices so that transmissions can share the same communication channel. A multiplexer is the hard wave that accomplishes multiplexing. Concentration is a process that allows a communication channel to be connected to and serve more devices than the capacity of the channel normally allows. A concentrator is one type of device that accomplishes concentration. A front-end processor is a computer that handles all the data-communication control functions, freeing the CPU of the main computer to work on other tasks.

The baud rate of a communication channel is the number of times per second that the signal being transmitted changes (modulates or demodulates). Typical bps rates are 300, 1200, 2400, 4800, 9600 and more. The band-width or band of a communication channel transmits data. There are three different band-widths: (*i*) narrow-band, (*ii*) voice-band, and (*iii*) broad-band.

Asynchronous transmission transmits data one character at a time. Synchronous transmission transmits data as a block of characters in timed sequences. Message characters alert the model when data are being sent and when they are finished. The exchange of prearranged signals defining the rules to be followed when transmitting and receiving data is known as handshaking. Protocol is the set of rules and procedures defining the technical details for data transfer between two devices.

Data transfer can occur in three modes: (*i*) simplex, (*ii*) half-duplex, and (*iii*) full-duplex.

Data communication has allowed the linking of micro-computer-to-micro-computer and micro-computer-to-mainframe, so data and capabilities can be shared.

Common carriers are companies that are licensed and regulated to transmit the data-communication property of others. Specialized common carriers and value-added carrier are two alternatives to using the major common carrier for data communication.

Ensuring the security and privacy of data are two important challenges facing users of data communication.

Data communication has allowed computers to share data in spite of the boundaries of time or distance and has found many applications in our society, including information services, data-base services electronic funds transfer, electronic mail, telecommuting, reservation systems and other business systems.

Each computer or device in a network is called a **node**. The geometrical arrangement of computer resources, remote device, and communication facilities is known as network topology. A network can be made in one of the five different topologies: Bus, Ring, Star, Tree network and Mesh Network.

In the star-ring, the two topologies have been combined with the aim of achieving the best of both.

Private Networks, Value-Added Networks, and Public Networks, Circuit switching networks, Message switching networks, and Packet switching networks are explained.

TCP/IP runs on both LANs and WANs. Indeed, the TCP/IP logic is unaware of the type of network because it is isolated from the LAN physical and data link layers and any wide area subnetwork logic, such as packet routing.

The ISO/OSI network model describes networks as layers of functionality. Each layer in a network performs a well-defined function and uses one or more protocols to perform its functions. The physical layer transmits data through the network's communication channels and includes all hardware needed to accomplish this function. The data-link layer's primary function is to detect data corruption within the physical layer. The network layer delivers data between host computers on the network. The transport layer delivers data between applications on host computers. The session layer is the user's interface to the network. The presentation layer handles details related to the network's interface to printers, video displays, and file formats. The application layer contains details about all network-wide applications.

REVIEW QUESTIONS

1. Network topology, consisting of nodes attached in a ring, without a host computer, is known as:
(*a*) Star (*b*) Ring (*c*) Bus (*d*) Tree

2. Which of the following is associated with networks?
(*a*) Download, node (*b*) Star topology
(*c*) Point-to-Point (*d*) Both (*a*) and (*b*)

3. WAN hardware includes:
(*a*) Multiplexors and routers (*b*) EDI
(*c*) Bridges and modems (*d*) All of the above

4. E-mail:
(*a*) cannot address many recipients who are part of the e-mail system
(*b*) does not back the privacy protection given to first-class mail
(*c*) always uses an electronic bridge to send a message to someone using another e-mail service
(*d*) none of the above

5. Data transfer rate in modems is measured in:
(*a*) Bits per minute (*b*) Bits per second
(*c*) Bandwidth (*d*) All of the above

6. In half-duplex data transmission:
(*a*) data can be transmitted in one direction only
(*b*) data can be transmitted in both directions
(*c*) data can be transmitted in both directions simultaneously
(*d*) data can not be transmitted

7. A large number of computers in a wide geographical area can be efficiently connected using:
(*a*) twisted pair lines (*b*) coaxial cables
(*c*) communication satellites (*d*) all of the above

8. In MODEMS:
(*a*) several digital signals are multiplexed
(*b*) a digital signal changes some characteristic of a carrier wave
(*c*) digital signal is amplified
(*d*) all of the above

9. Wide area networks ((WANs) always require:
(*a*) high bandwidth communication links
(*b*) high speed processors
(*c*) same type of processors
(*d*) none of the above

10. Ethernet uses:
(*a*) Bus topology
(*b*) Ring topology
(*c*) Star topology
(*d*) Tree topology

11. In a modem using debit phase, encoding has the bit rate:
(*a*) same as the baud rate
(*b*) higher than its baud rate
(*c*) lower than its baud rate
(*d*) independent of its baud rate

12. In FDM every user uses:
(*a*) same frequency band
(*b*) different frequency band
(*c*) a frequency band which he is assigned at random
(*d*) all of the above

13. Typical data transfer rates in LAN are of the order of
(*a*) Bits per sec
(*b*) Kilo bits per sec
(*c*) Mega bits per sec
(*d*) None of the above

14. Which of the following topologies is highly reliable?
(*a*) Star
(*b*) Bus
(*c*) Fully connected mesh
(*d*) All of the above

15. Which of the following topologies is not broadcast type?
(*a*) Star
(*b*) Bus
(*c*) Ring
(*d*) Tree

16. In asynchronous transmission:
(*a*) Inter-character gap is fixed
(*b*) Inter-character gap is variable
(*c*) Inter-character gap is always zero
(*d*) All of the above

17. Data transfer using telephone system is:
(*a*) Time division multiplexing
(*b*) Space division multiplexing
(*c*) Frequency division multiplexing
(*d*) All of the above

18. Synchronous transmission data from various users:
(*a*) reqúire header
(*b*) do not require header
(*c*) sometimes require header
(*d*) all of the above

19. When the time to establish link is large and the size of data is small, the preferred mode of data transfer is:
(*a*) Circuit switching
(*b*) Packet switching
(*c*) Time division multiplexing
(*d*) All of the above

20. In circuit switching:
(*a*) data is stored at intermediate nodes
(*b*) transmission path is set before data transfer
(*c*) dedicated communication link is not required
(*d*) all of the above

21. An electronic device that is capable of accepting encoded data at its input, and generating unencoded data at its output is:
(*a*) Modem
(*b*) Joystick
(*c*) Decoder
(*d*) Plotter

22. Communication using a modulated carrier to apply a data signal to a transmission medium in analog form is:
(*a*) Local area network
(*b*) Modem
(*c*) Base-band networking
(*d*) Broad-band networking

23. A sizeable geographical area with communication based on the telephone system is known as:
(*a*) Local area network (*b*) Wide area network
(*c*) Modulator-Demodulator (*d*) All of the above

24. A number of micro-computers connected together to share peripherals and programs is:
(*a*) Computer graphics (*b*) Local area network
(*c*) Modulator-demodulator (*d*) All of the above

25. A group of parallel lines that connect two or more devices is called:
(*a*) Network (*b*) Bus (*c*) Bound (*d*) Baud

26. The interactive transmission of data within a time sharing system may be best suited to:
(*a*) simplex lines (*b*) half-duplex lines (*c*) full-duplex lines (*d*) biflex-line

27. Coaxial cable has conductors with:
(*a*) equal resistance (*b*) the same diameter (*c*) (*a*) and (*b*) both (*d*) a common axis

28. The cheapest modems can transmit:
(*a*) 300 bits per second (*b*) 1,200 bits per second
(*c*) 2,400 bits per second (*d*) 4,800 bits per second

29. A device that can convert digital signals to analog signals is:
(*a*) a packet (*b*) a modem (*c*) both (*a*) and (*b*) (*d*) a block

30. The physical layer of a network:
(*a*) defines the electrical characteristics of signals passed between the computer and communication devices
(*b*) controls error detection and correction
(*c*) constructs packets of data and sends them across the network
(*d*) all of the above

31. The application layer of a network:
(*a*) establishes, maintains, and terminates virtual circuits
(*b*) defines the user's port into the network
(*c*) consists of software being run on the computer connected to the network
(*d*) all of the above

32. Which layer of international standard organization's OSI model is responsible for creating and recognizing frame boundaries?
(*a*) physical layer (*b*) data link layer
(*c*) transport layer (*d*) network layer

33. The data link layer, in reference to the OSI model, specifies:
(*a*) data link procedures that provide for the exchange of data via frames that can be sent and received
(*b*) the interface between the X.25 network and packet mode device
(*c*) the virtual circuit interface to packet-switched service
(*d*) all of the above

34. In OSI model, which of the following layer provides error-free delivery of data?
(*a*) Data link (*b*) Network (*c*) Transport (*d*) Session

35. In OSI model, which of the following layer transforms information from machine format into the understandable by user?
(*a*) Application (*b*) Presentation (*c*) Session (*d*) Physical

36. Which of the following method is used for dedicated communications path between two devices through one or more intermediate switching node?

(*a*) Switch network (*b*) Circuit switching
(*c*) Packet switching (*d*) (*a*) and (*b*) both

37. Which of the following device is used to connect two systems, especially if the systems use different protocols?
(*a*) Hub (*b*) Bridge (*c*) Gateway (*d*) Repeater

38. Which of the following device copies electrical signals from one Ethernet to another?
(*a*) Bridge (*b*) Repeater (*c*) Hub (*d*) Passive hub

39. A communication network which is used by large organizations over regional, national or global area is called:
(*a*) LAN (*b*) WAN (*c*) MAN (*d*) Intranet

40. Communication between computers is almost always:
(*a*) serial (*b*) parallel (*c*) series parallel (*d*) direct

41. Identify the odd term among the following group.
(*a*) Coaxial cable (*b*) Optical fibre (*c*) Twisted pair wire (*d*) Microwaves

42. What is the name of the network topology in which there are bi-directional links between each possible node?
(*a*) Ring (*b*) Star (*c*) Tree (*d*) Mesh

43. Which of the following is a voice-band channel?
(*a*) Telephone line (*b*) Telegraph line
(*c*) Coaxial cable (*d*) Microwave systems

44. A communications device that combines transmissions from several I/O devices into one line is a:
(*a*) concentrator (*b*) modifier
(*c*) multiplexer (*d*) full-duplex line

45. A distributed data processing configuration in which all activities must pass through a centrally located computer is called a:
(*a*) ring network (*b*) spider network
(*c*) hierarchical network (*d*) data control network

46. In OSI network architecture, the routing is performed by:
(*a*) network layer (*b*) data link layer (*c*) transport layer (*d*) session layer

47. A packet-switching network:
(*a*) is free
(*b*) can reduce the cost of using an information utility
(*c*) allows communication channels to be shared among more than one user
(*d*) both (*b*) and (*c*)

48. Devices on one network can communicate with devices on another network via a:
(*a*) file server (*b*) utility server (*c*) printer server (*d*) gateway

49. A distributed network configuration in which all data/information pass through a central computer is:
(*a*) bus network (*b*) star network
(*c*) ring network (*d*) point-to-point network

50. How many pairs of stations can simultaneously communicate on Ethernet LAN?
(*a*) 1 (*b*) 2 (*c*) 3 (*d*) multiple

51. Which of the following is used for modulation and demodulation?
(*a*) Modem (*b*) Protocols (*c*) Gateway (*d*) Multiplexer

52. Demodulation is the process of:
(*a*) converting digital signals to analog signals

(*b*) converting analog signals to digital signals
(*c*) combining many low speed channels into one high speed channel
(*d*) dividing the high speed signals into frequency bands

53. Which of the following layer protocols are responsible for user and the application program support such as passwords, resource sharing, file transfer and network management?
(*a*) Layer 7 protocols (*b*) Layer 6 protocols
(*c*) Layer 5 protocols (*d*) Layer 4 protocols

ANSWERS

Multiple Choice Questions

1. (*b*)	**2.** (*d*)	**3.** (*a*)	**4.** (*d*)	**5.** (*b*)	**6.** (*b*)	**7.** (*c*)	**8.** (*b*)
9. (*d*)	**10.** (*a*)	**11.** (*b*)	**12.** (*b*)	**13.** (*c*)	**14.** (*c*)	**15.** (*c*)	**16.** (*b*)
17. (*b*)	**18.** (*b*)	**19.** (*b*)	**20.** (*b*)	**21.** (*c*)	**22.** (*d*)	**23.** (*b*)	**24.** (*b*)
25. (*b*)	**26.** (*b*)	**27.** (*d*)	**28.** (*a*)	**29.** (*b*)	**30.** (*a*)	**31.** (*c*)	**32.** (*b*)
33. (*a*)	**34.** (*c*)	**35.** (*b*)	**36.** (*b*)	**37.** (*c*)	**38.** (*b*)	**39.** (*b*)	**40.** (*a*)
41. (*d*)	**42.** (*d*)	**43.** (*a*)	**44.** (*c*)	**45.** (*b*)	**46.** (*a*)	**47.** (*d*)	**48.** (*d*)
49. (*b*)	**50.** (*a*)	**51.** (*a*)	**52.** (*b*)	**53.** (*b*)			

QUESTIONS

1. What is data communication?

2. Describe the difference between analog and digital data transmission.

3. What is a modem's function?

4. Which type of communication channel can transmit data in digital form?

5. Describe and sketc.h how a point-to-point configuration works.

6. Describe the function of a multiplexer.

7. Describe the process of concentration.

8. What is the function of a front-end processor?

9. Describe protocol.

10. What is a common carrier?

11. List and describe three types of modems.

12. Describe the three types of communication channels.

13. What are the three bandwidths for communication channels? Discuss their differences.

14. Describe the three modes in which the transfer of data can occur.

15. List three facts that must be known in order to communicate with a large computer system.

16. What is a computer network?

17. Describe a local-area network.

18. How does a wide-area network differ from a local-area network?

19. Name and describe the four different network topologies.

20. What is the difference between peer-to-peer networks and server-centric networks?

21. Discuss the advantages and disadvantages of Tree Network.

22. What is a repeater?

23. What is the difference between repeater and hub?

24. What is the difference between bridge and Gateway.

25. What do you understand by the term 'Active Hub' and 'Passive Hub'?

26. Write short notes on OSI Layers?

27. What is a WAN?

28. Distinguish among LAN, WAN, MAN.

29. What is a hybrid network? Why are they used?

30. What is a mess network? Discuss.

COMPUTER APPLICATIONS

To meet the today's business requirements with the opening up of the economy and the big thrust being to the exports sector, more and more organizations have begun to display Information Technology (IT) as a strategic tool. Many organizations have already evolved or re-oriented their business on and around information systems. Banks use it for better client serving, manufacturing concerns, for planning, resource allocation and to produce high quality goods; communications has taken a completely new dimension owing to the speed, power, and flexibility that IT offers. An information system is a group of integrated elements—people, procedures, equipment—working together in support decision making and operations within an organization or in a personal setting. The functional information systems of an organisation are its backbone. Understanding the entire information system is impossible without understanding the functional information systems. In this chapter, we will discuss a variety of computer applications.

13.1 COMPUTER APPLICATIONS IN SCIENCE AND TECHNOLOGY

The computer is used to assist man in business organisations, in research and in many other walks of life. Some of these areas are examined so as to give an indication of the very wide range of activities in which the computer is involved. Some of the applications may be surprising, if one considers the limited capabilities of the machine. However, versatility has been provided by man's ability to reduce what are often highly complicated problems to the simple level at which the computer can be used, and to design and implement ingenious computer system which can provide a myriad interplay of the basically simple tasks that the computer can handle. Whatever has been achieved so far has been accomplished in a very short period of time. The first computer was developed as little as forty-five years ago and ten years passed before the industry was established on a firm footing.

13.1.1 Scientific Research

The first computing projects were undertaken in University laboratories and scientific Institutions to develop computers for special purposes. In science, the advent of computers has meant that calculations which were previously beyond contemplation, because of the time-span and drudgery involved in carrying them out, have now become possible. This has greatly accelerated and expanded research in such sciences as Physics, Chemistry, Astronomy and Genetics. Recently there has been an increasing use of computers for research and data analysis in less mathematical areas such as Medicine, the Social Sciences and even the Humanities. Applications in Humanities include concordances, textual criticism and stylistic analysis.

Computers are now a standard feature of life in Universities and industrial laboratories. Almost every branch of science and engineering has benefited from their development. Elementary particle Physics is one field of study which has been broadened considerably. Molecular Biology is another, resulting in spectacular progress in our understanding of the structure of living matter. Because of the immensity of some of the research problems, huge computer complexes are sometimes needed. The CERN Institute in Geneva, researching in high energy Nuclear Physics, is one such centre. It is financed by a number of European Governments, and has become an international pool of scientific brainpower.

13.1.1.1 Mathematics

Although mathematics has had a big impact on the development of computers, the development of many new areas of mathematics has been stimulated by the existence of computers. Numerical mathematics had never so much significance as it has today. Boolean Algebra which was in a state of neglect now plays a central role in logic technology in general and the logic design of computers in particular. Most of the linear programming techniques which involve computations which are long and complex would have had only theorists interest if the fast calculations of computers were not available. Even the development of linear programming techniques would not have received so much attention as they are receiving now. Some of the conjectures in number theory such as Mersenne primes have been disproved by exploiting the power of computers. There is now less incentive for finding formula which generate particular sequences of numbers since the sheer power of computers enables us to enumerate long sequences of numbers which are sufficient for all practical purposes.

13.1.1.2 Genetics

The use of computers in genetics falls mainly into three categories according to the purpose of computations. The first is the use of computers for statistical data analysis. Once a given format of analysis is programmed on a computer, the program can be repeatedly applied on data of similar type. Such cases occur, for example, in the analysis of cyclic selection experiments. The second category is the numerical solution of equations. A genetic problem may be formulated mathematically in order to obtain desired results or certain predictions for the problem. Sometimes, however the resulting formulas are extremely difficult to solve exactly by analytical methods. On other occasions, analytical solutions obtained may be so complex that they still need numerical evaluations. In either event, a computer is indispensable. The last category of applications is simulation of actual biological systems on computers. In many instances, genetic variables, the relationships among these variables, and initial conditions of these variables are known for a particular system, however, the exact mathematical formulations of a system may be extremely messy. One may simulate actual systems on a computer by use of random number generating methods of computer and summarise the results in the form of probability distributions.

13.1.1.3 Molecular Biology

Investigations into large molecules of biological significance now comprise an active research endeavour. Computers have helped in the unravelling of highly complicated organic molecular structures. Nobel Laureate Kendrews's principal contribution in molecular biology seems to be the complete resolution of the structure of the protein myoglobin. This is a molecule with a molecular weight of 18,000 with 1,200 atoms, not counting hydrogen and every one of these atoms was put into its place by a computation which involved fitting 20,000 Fourier coefficients in a million points by least squares. If one had used old-fashioned techniques, it would have taken a few generations to perform the same thing.

Perhaps, the greatest potential problems will be the reproduction of biological history by the Monte Carlo method. Even since Darwin, it was worried many people that homo sapins has appeared too suddenly on the biological scene to be explicable by random mutations and natural selection. Some forty years ago, Sir Ronald Fisher believed that he had answered the question in the affirmative, but his argument is now generally considered unsatisfactory. If we have sufficient knowledge of human genes, it may be possible to play out millions of Monte Carlo games of the development of man by random mutations and natural selection and this may then decide the gigantic dilemma whether there was purpose in man's development or not.

13.1.2 Industrial Applications

In industry, production may be planned, co-ordinated and controlled with the aid of a computer. The computer may also be used to direct the operation of individual machine tools (drills, lathes, saws, etc.) and even to operate assembly machines which piece together parts of equipment (*e.g.*, electrical and mechanical appliances, sections of motor cars and even complete vehicles). The use of numerically controlled (NC) machine tools directed by computer produced tapes can speed up production, ensure greater precision and reduce scrap wastage. In certain industries (*e.g.*, chemical, oil refining) the computer can be used to monitor and regulate total processes (*i.e.*, to perform process control) without human intervention, just as it can to control air conditioning land heating systems in modern multi-story buildings.

The control of a chemical plant by computer can be much safer and more efficient method than by manual control, since changes in conditions which occur during a process can be detected and compensated for immediately. It would, however, be normal for human operators to maintain surveillance over the total process so as to be able to intervene should the need arise.

Computer has been extensively used for oil and natural gas exploration and drilling activities by analysing seismic data. Oil refining, the separation of crude oil into its many component oils, is a continuous process and it depends on the maintenance of certain conditions throughout the process. These two factors make refining a suitable application for computer control. Instruments measure such variables as temperature, flow and pressure. Any deviation from the standard is detected and regulating devices are adjusted to bring back into line.

13.1.2.1 Printing and Paper

Computers are used by the printing trade where they are particularly useful in the production of newspapers and magazines where strict deadlines have to be met and time is short. Articles can be transposed to magnetic tape (or disk) and then rapidly typeset, under computer control, in several type sizes, widths, and depths as necessary. Complete texts may be retained on tape, enabling amendments to be incorporated easily when reprinting. Computers are also used to update the listings in telephone directories, catalogues, parts and price lists so that they can be quickly typeset whenever required. Desk Top Publishing (DTP) systems using personal computers have helped companies to print their leaflets, brochures, etc. in cost-effective way.

13.1.2.2 Engineering Design

The design of any price of engineering, whether an aeroplane, ship, car, bridge, road, building or machine, should not merely be pleasing to look at. The piece of engineering must not only be able to perform the tasks intended for it over its economic or anticipated life, but it must also be able to withstand all foreseeable mishaps during its working life. Engineering designs, however sound they may seem to be on paper, have to be physically tested under simulated or real-life circumstances before becoming operational. Computers can help in calculating that all parts of a proposed design are satisfactory. If modifications are necessary and further calculations are required, the computer can evaluate the alternatives more quickly and more accurately then would otherwise be possible. This means a great saving in time and elimination of technical faults and human error (which could possibly be disastrous), before a design is further developed.

When fitting the structural and spatial requirements of an engineering project into an overall design, the computer can also help with graphical output. The facility to view a design from all angles while it is still on the drawing board, and then to be able to modify it quickly, avoids having to spend time and money building and testing several designs before determining which is the right one. The computer can provide graphical and perspective views to show the shape of a proposed aircraft wing or car body, the slope of a curve for a new road, the visibility that the pilot or motorist will have, or the accessibility of the instruments that he might have to operate. User-friendly Computer Aided Design (CAD) and drafting packages has helped the engineering design considerably.

Computers can also be used in calculations of space and layout as well as strength requirements. This not only helps ensure that engine parts were accessible for maintenance, and bridges and tunnels high and wide enough for unusual traffic; it also ensures that there is enough room for everything—passengers, fuel, cargo, etc. on motorway construction, the computer can calculate the amount of soil, needed to raise an embankment, or the amount of rock to be removed in cutting through a hill, and it can work out the most efficient movement of such materials.

Many engineering design problems require the selection of optimum parameters. The selection of the best parameters is a design choice that must be made. Perhaps, it involves the length and shape of an aeroplane wing or the best position and shape for a radio antenna. These parameters are usually involved in many equations relating to the performance, cost and utility of the major items concerned. Usually, there is no straight way to select the best design, so the engineer uses trial and error or some empirical formulae to explore most of the possibilities and trade-off involved. A computer is a useful tool here when the problem is complex and important decisions must be made.

Computers are also used as an aid to electronic circuit design and Printed Circuit Boards (PCBs), even assisting engineers in designing circuits for other computers.

The application of computers to engineering design seems to have two characteristics; the initial cost is relatively high but the cost/calculation is quite low. The initial high cost is because of the programming and debugging costs of the computer program. However, once a program which is of sufficient generality is developed, the cost of reuse of the program in subsequent projects is nil or negligible. Another factor to be remembered here is that a large variety of mathematical programs required for engineering analysis will be provided by the computer-manufacturer, in the form of a library. This is likely to reduce the program development costs to the user.

13.1.2.3 Electricity

Starting up a power station involves many complex operations which have to follow a strict sequences with set time limits between each operation. This is a laborious, time-consuming task but one for which the computer is well suited. The computer is also used by electricity authorities for load control. Demand for electricity is not constant throughout the day nor throughout the year. Generators have to be phased in and out to meet changing situations. Because of the time lag required to build up the necessary power, fluctuations in the load have to be anticipated in advance.

Under computer control, past records stored in the system, relating to changing hourly demands under various weather conditions, are scanned and compared with the actual, present loads in different parts of the supply network. Predictions are then made and generators are set to start and stop at certain times. This ensures that extra power is transferred to those areas where it is most needed at peak periods. It also ensures that those generators which have to be expensively fuelled with precious natural resources (oil, gas, coal) are not run wastefully when the demand for power drops.

13.1.2.4 Steel

Process control applied to certain parts of steel production has increased efficiency in the industry. One example is in the cutting of the steel into lengths to match the firm's order book. In the rolling mills, which run at great speed, red-hot steel billets are rolled out into strips. The billet size is not known accurately to begin with and, as each is rolled out, the length increases until the required thickness of sheet or diameter of rod is reached. Before the use of computers, the mill would cut the sheets or rods, of varying lengths, into standard sizes or a particular size for one order. The lengths of steel left over would be scrap which would have to be remelted, resulting in a lower grade steel. With the advent of computers the amount of scrap was reduced to a minimum, for it became possible to calculate the lengths that the billets would make whilst still red hot and being rolled out. This information could be matched against a table of orders for the type and quality of steel being rolled, in time for the flying shears (computer controlled) to cut the strips in the best way.

13.1.2.5 Control System

Computerised control systems took considerable time and effort to get started. These applications are inherently more difficult to implement. They place great demands on the computer systems and their programmers. Despite these difficulties, the potential pay-offs justify considerable investment. Speed of response is quite important in these systems. For example, in the operation of a missile guidance system or the operation of a chemical plant or a nuclear reactor, timely response are quite critical. A typical computerised chemical plant may be completely automatic in which case the system is able to sense many variables on a more or less continuous basis. Typical variables might be the purity, temperature, or supply level of various raw materials, the temperature, pressure, or flow rates at different points within the processing mechanism, and levels, rates, and characteristics associated with various products and waste. The computer is expected to control automatically many factors in the production process—flow rates, temperatures, supply of raw materials, cycling procedures etc. It attempts to optimise the overall process. More often the control system is semi-automatic and the computer works in partnership with one or more persons. This is the case with air-traffic control situations in which computers, radars and communication devices are used in conjunction with both ground-based and air-bone personnel. Here rapid response is essential and lives are at risk if the system fails.

13.1.3 Meteorology

Predicting the weather has long been considered something of a mystique based on country signs and folklore. Meteorology, as a science, is relatively new and, with computer assistance, it has become more of an exact science. The problem in meteorology has always been to obtain sufficient data, and to analyse that data quickly enough so that predictions can be made. Satellites, linked directly with computer systems, now provide the meteorologist with information, in addition to the data obtained from weather stations on land and at sea. Armed with more information, the relationship between the variable factors which constitute weather can be analysed in greater depth, and a more accurate prediction of future behaviour can then be made. The computer system is also able to analyse vast quantities of past measurements to test for weather patterns and, based partly on these results, long-range forecasts can be made. Many of the people who depend upon reliable, up-to-the-minute weather forecasts (those concerned with air travel, shipping routes, storm rescue operations, farmers, etc.) do not always realize the extent to which they have become dependent upon computers.

The basic physical equations involved in numerical weather prediction are nonlinear. They presuppose an extremely detailed knowledge of the state of the atmosphere at the beginning of the forecast. The most important weather phenomena have horizontal scales of 10^5 to 10^7 meters and experience has shown that it is necessary to consider conditions over almost an entire hemisphere to predict the weather several days in advance. To deal with difficulties of scale many kinds of approximations in the field of dynamic meteorology have been developed.

They are all concerned with including or omitting certain physical quantities from the model. As a consequence, the solutions of such approximate, discrete systems do not describe all physical phenomena associated with the complete system of differential equations. Such approximations are said to 'filter out' entire ranges of phenomena *e.g.*, sound waves which should not have an effect on the answers of interest such as large-scale cyclonic motion.

Because the partial differential equations for fluid are non-linear and possess difficult initial and boundary conditions, they must be solved by numerical methods for particular physical model under consideration into a form that can be solved by numerical algorithms on a computer.

13.1.4 Space Technology

The development of space technology which culminated in the first moon landing was only possible because of the calculating powers and speed of the computer. Computers were used at the design stage of the project and in all phases of development right through to flight control. For example, they monitored and helped to control the proper functioning of all the equipment; they helped determine the routes (trajectory paths) and kept surveillance during the flight; they plotted courses of action when unforeseen events occurred; and, finally, they processed information relayed from the space vehicles.

The last point is significant because the collection of information is the main reason for putting satellites into orbit. Computer linked space satellites provide previously unavailable information about the universe around us. This information is not merely of interest in scientific research (such as astronomy), but it increases our knowledge of our own planet (in geology and mineralogy), and it is of immediate practical value, for example, in meteorology. Satellites are also used as long-range beacons or microwave reflectors to provide the immediate worldwide coverage of important events by television (TV) and radio that we now take for granted, but which were inconceivable even a generation ago. Satellites are also used to provide worldwide digital communication links for data and voice transmission. The computer has played a leading role in, and continues to be an integral part of, these new wonders of the second half of the twentieth century.

13.1.5 Communication

13.1.5.1 Air Travel

Air Traffic control, which is responsible for organizing the safe movement of overcrowded airlines, depends on a significant amount of computer support. As flying speeds increase, control decisions have to be taken more quickly. This also applies to the pilot who has to react not only to instructions relayed to him from traffic control, but also to changing situations during flight (variations in atmospheric pressure, wind speed and direction). Various instruments, dials and meters indicate the state of the flight and the current weather conditions. These provide the pilot and the flight engineer with the information they need to control the flight and to make navigational calculations. It takes time, however, to scan the instruments and to assimilate the information, and time can be critically precious at the speed at which the plane is flying. Small computers, made possible by the development of compact integrated circuits, can be installed as part of the aeroplane's equipment. These computers are programmed to continuously analyse data, which is relayed direct from the various instruments, and to provide co-ordinated information to the pilot in time for-human decision and action. Control itself can also be invested in the computer so that, when certain conditions arise, automatic corrective action is immediately taken without the need for slower, human intervention.

Besides the many in-flight uses, the computer plays an increasingly vital role in the training of pilots. A flight simulator provides an exact replica of the flight deck and performance of an aircraft, enabling the equivalent of many hours of flying to be undertaken without flying leaving the ground. The computer resolves the tasks, monitors and controls the pilot's action, and maintains a record of the pilot's performance. At ground level, the information needs of a busy airline are extensive. Computers are used for the efficient handling of seat reservations, crew schedules, timetables, tariffs, cargoes, maintenance schedules, personnel records, accounting, and stock control. Large scale air travel has developed quickly in recent years and computers have helped to make it a very reliable and safe form of transport

Computer-controlled seat reservation brings benefit to customers and to the airlines. It is an economic necessity that airlines operate as near to capacity as possible. To avoid overbooking, a complete list of all bookings needs to be maintained and be available for immediate interrogation. This is achieved by using communication networks, covering whole continents, which link the booking offices to a large computer system working in on-line or real-time mode. Communication between continents is established by using transoceanic cables and satellites. A travel agent is able to find out the current status of any flight and can book seats on the basis of the information obtained. This is all done in a matter of seconds and, when a seat is reserved, the information system is automatically updated.

Computer controlled reservations are also applicable to hotel rooms, theatre seats, sporting events at large stadiums and package tour holidays.

13.1.5.2 Transportation

The transport facilities are making increasing use of computers. Computer based railway reservation system for berths and seats has become a boon to travellers by rail. Railways prepare timetables, scheduling at the same time the distribution of the rolling stock to operate their services, and they control busy stretches of track with computer assistance. Computer controlled ticket machines are being used to facilitate the automatic checking of tickets. Shipping companies devise the best method of loading and storing cargo, using computer programs which are designed to take into account such variable factors as size, weight, solidity (the ability to stack in layers), destination and urgency. Computer has been effectively used in traffic and shipping activities in ports. The computer in conjunction with radar and other monitoring equipment can also be used to make increasingly crowded shipping lanes, like the English Channel, safer. Haulage firms and transport concerns may determine optimum routing. If, for example, a vehicle has twenty delivery points, a computer program can consider all the various route options and pin-point the shortest of the best route if other variable factors (such as avoiding travelling empty, combining several deliveries, refuelling) have to be taken into account.

13.1.5.3 Traffic Control

Maintaining the flow of automobile traffic in congested areas is of paramount importance and an ever-increasing problem. The computer already assists with the control of traffic lights in some of the world's major cities, and many more will adopt this method of control. A single computer-based traffic system controls an area of some 200 sq. km in Tokyo and the system is being expanded year by year. A similar system is in operation in London. Results are impressive if not always apparent to the motorist. Individual sets of traffic lights normally change after a set period of time, regardless of the volume of traffic. A network under computer control operates instead on the basis of the volume and flow pattern of the traffic at the time. Information regarding the volume, detected by measuring devices on approaches to all sets of lights as the traffic moves, is transmitted to the computer system. This information, representing a total overall view of the distribution of traffic, is related to permanently stored information regarding distances between lights and the permitted traffic speeds. As a result, the various lights over the whole network are changed to maintain maximum flow. Some computer based traffic systems can even trigger warning signs advising drivers of the optimum speed at which they can maintain continuous movement. It is not unusual for television cameras to be installed at major traffic junctions so that potential trouble spots can be kept under surveillance. With pictures displayed from various vantage points, and a reporting system which indicates when a particular set of traffic lights has broken down, human operators can watch over the network and intervene when the occasion demands, promptly directing police and repair crews to the exact spot(s) where they are required.

13.1.6 Government Departments and States

The computer is used extensively to carry out routine clerical functions, in general supplementing rather than replacing clerical staff, undertaking, for example, the preparation and printing of rate and tax demands, gas, electricity and telephone bills. One national centre is responsible for maintaining all driving licence records and for issuing renewal notices and licences. Similarly the registration of vehicles is handled by computers in regional centres. The computer is also playing an increasingly prominent part in the organization and running of the public health and social services, in the maintenance of law and order, and as an aid to education.

Local authorities, central government departments, and state controlled public utilities all have to maintain extensive records. Indeed, in a socially conscious, heavily populated, industrialized environment, the tasks of official-dom today are of such a scale as to be impossible without computer assistance. The State is the biggest collector and collator of information, and the usefulness of the computer in storing, retrieving and analysing information is greatly increasing the scale on which it is collected. Computerization is also encouraging the centralization of information, for greater convenience and accessibility, in large data banks.

13.1.6.1 Telephone

Computerized telephone exchanges handle an ever-increasing volume of calls. They do so more quickly and with less likelihood of error than would otherwise be possible, and they can be linked-up to other networks/exchanges for wider, prompt use. Cross-country, and even overseas, calls which previously meant a low link-up through several switchboards and/or operators, can now be made directly and quickly. By way of satellites call can also be transmitted at faster speeds than through conventional networks. The computer can also maintain a log of calls for subsequent billing. Computer controlled digital exchanges provides lot more facilities to subscribers than ever before.

13.1.6.2 Medicine

The uses of the computer in the medical field are partly analogous to applications in business and industry. For example, the computer being increasingly used in hospital administration for such tasks as maintaining inventories of drugs, surgical equipment, and linen; for payroll; hospital accounting; and for bed allocation. Information on the condition of patients, details of tests and clinical reports may be stored on a computer systems. This combined information can be used to provide ward and patient summary reports and, where a terminal has been installed for the use of the ward nursing staff, the system can provide instructions and remainders concerning the care of individual patients.

The computer has a important part to play in medical research and in the teaching of doctors and nursing staff. The ability that a computer system has to retain information on a large scale means that detailed records of case histories of particular illnesses can be available for scrutiny in sufficient quantities to assist medical research. 'Models' can be constructed in the computer system to simulate the behaviour of various parts of the body, for example, the lungs and the heart. It is also possible to use computer programs to test the effect that a form of treatment might have on a patient before it is administered.

In Intensive Care Units (ICUs) the computer can be used to monitor a patient's condition. Scanning instruments attached to the patient are linked on-line to the system so that nursing staff can be notified as the patient's condition changes. The computer may print out or display a log of the patient's conditions, drawing attention to measurements that fall outside the critical limits set by the doctor, or the computer itself may trigger directly the necessary corrective action.

In some clinics the computer is used, albeit in an experimental way, to 'interview' patients before or after they see a doctor in order to collect information for the patient's records and even to assist with the diagnostic process. It is suggested that patients are more relaxed, and honest and frank with their replies when faced with an impersonal machine.

These different medical applications are in various stages of development. Some of the ideas discussed are not yet in widespread use, but enough has-been achieved to indicate that the potential benefit of the computer, to both patients and medical profession, is considerable.

13.1.6.3 Medical Diagnosis

The medical diagnostic process may be divided into four general categories:

1. Communication of information about the patent to the physician;
2. Comparison of patient information with the available medical information;
3. Diagnostic decision making;
4. Treatment of the patient.

Information about a patient is obtained by the physician from the patients history, physical examination, laboratory tests. These are regarded as difficult areas in which to apply computer techniques. However, a practicing physician may occasionally need ready access to extensive medical textbook literature or recent medical knowledge to determine the probable courses of signs and symptoms which he has seen in frequently or to reassure himself that he has indeed made the correct diagnosis from a symptom complex. For suçh purposes, a medical information retrieval system is required to aid to practising physician. The diagnostic process for the physician may involve a pattern recognition procedure in the first stages of the diagnosis in order to focus quickly on a group of possible disease and then he may employ his memory of statistics to arrive at a final diagnosis.

The computer programs for different diagnosis should screen out non-pertinent diseases and list out pertinent diseases. A computer can print out a request for further examination when a disease cannot be unambiguously identified. Indeed, what is imagined is that the doctor will use the machine to help guide his examination, based in part on the medical record inside the machine, and in part on other data, such as current epidemic data, for example, the machine will not make the final decisions. Rather, it will print out that it might be one of several things with associated probabilities opposite to each diagnosis.

Computer techniques have been used successfully to implement a number of mathematical and statistical procedures in order to arrive at a medical diagnosis. In these situations use is made of Bayesian conditional probability models, multiple discriminant analysis and principal factor analysis. Bayesian model is used in the diagnosis of: Bone tumours, Epigastric pains, Classification of psychiatric patients, Thyroid function diagnosis, Heart diseases, etc.

The computer may assist in medical diagnosis, for example programs exist which can carry out electro-cardiogram analysis to determine both normal and abnormal heart conditions. The computer system can act as a vast encyclopedia of medical knowledge, providing the doctor with access to an ever-increasing quantity of information which he could not possible hope to carry in his head. Diagnosis itself is a complex process, and the symptoms of a disease are not consistent in all patients. The consultant makes a diagnosis on the basis of information he has gleaned from the patient's condition. He can then carry out a dialogue with the computer system, testing his hypotheses (perhaps referencing other recorded cases) until he is satisfied that his diagnosis is correct. The computer can help, but the experience of the consultant remains all important.

The computer may assist in prescribing the correct dosage and pattern of treatment, for example, in treating cancer by radiotherapy where it is vital that the correct dosage of radium is administered and only to the exact area required. Computers are being used to make these delicate calculations. Using data provided by the consultant, the computer produces a treatment timetable complete with the calculated dosage for the individual patient.

13.1.6.4 Law and Order

The enforcement of law and order depends to an extent on the availability of up-to-date information. Police forces make extensive use of the information retrieval capability of computer systems for this purpose. Records are maintained concerning accidents, vehicle owners, disqualified drivers, traffic tickets, stolen vehicles, fingerprints, criminals, wanted and missing persons, stolen property and drugs. Some of these records are stored on microfiche. It is important for police in all regions to have access to these files of information and for response time to enquiries to be immediate; crime is not local and it does not stand still. A large network of terminals is needed with each terminal linked on-line to large central computer system. Networks can be linked together, *e.g.*, through Interpol, for fast, worldwide investigation of cases of international significance.

Computers are finding their way into solicitors and lawyers offices for the purpose of legal data retrieval as well as for conventional accounting, record keeping and document preparation. Typically an office is provided with a terminal link to a vast data bank of legal information containing statutes, statutory instruments and accounts of past cases. A service organization is responsible for setting up and maintaining the data bank and lawyers who subscribe can conduct searches for information helpful to their clients problems.

13.1.6.5 Libraries and Museums

Increasing use is now being made of computers in library organization. Lists of borrowed books are maintained by the system and reminders for those which are overdue can be generated by computer output. A tally of the number of times books are taken out can be kept. More significant is the number of various ways that the contents of the library may be referenced with computer assistance for the benefit of users. Not only can all the books be classified by subject matter but, by page and paragraph references, information relating to particular topics within the subject can be pin-pointed. This has particular implications, for legal, scientific and technical libraries where detailed references frequently have to be made and cross-references are of considerable value. Some university libraries in America are linked to network so that an obscure document in a distant archive can be quickly located and, in some cases, photocopies can then be faxed/telexed over a wide area.

Museums are also making use of computers to help with cataloguing and indexing. Information about the exhibits in a museum's collection is assembled and retained as a large data base, and the information retrieval capability of the computer can then be exploited to the benefit of staff and visitors. Some museums are linked in a communications network to allow the exchange of information between different computerized museum data bases.

13.1.6.6 Education

The learning process can be enriched in many subjects because of the scale and range of information which a computer data bank can provide. Use is increasingly being made of the computer as a resource in teaching and learning at all levels of education.

Instructional material can be prepared and stored within the computer system in the form of programs which are carefully structured to teach specific lessons. A student could then sit at VDU and call in the program and participate in the lesson. This form of teaching aid has been used successfully to supplement more formal teaching methods and can be particularly useful for remedial purposes. A program can be used by many students, thus freeing the teacher to spend time on more personal tuition.

The computer can also be used to manage the learning process. Programs can be designed to teach for particular skills and knowledge, and then to direct the student to the next learning phase depending on the individual's results. This may mean a step forward or several steps back to repeat a previous lesson. The managed system also records all results and provides up-to-date information for the teacher on each student's progress.

Students, particularly in higher education and those studying science and technology, also benefit from being able to use the computer as a computational tool. They learn programming languages and write programs to solve some of their course work problems, treating the computer as an aid in much the same way as a slide rule or a set of mathematical tables.

Computer programs can be designed to create 'models' for experimental purposes (*e.g.*, simulation of experiments in physics) which a student can use, discovering for himself what happens in given situations. The computer provides the opportunity for experiments to be carried out which would not be feasible in real life, because of dangers, costs, etc. The computer can also be used time and time again with different sets of data so that a variety of conditions can be studied.

The computer can relieve the teacher of some administrative duties, giving him more time to concentrate on teaching. For example, the computer can be used to assist in constructing timetables: to monitor and schedule teaching resources; to build up and maintain comprehensive student records, to provide a complete student profile; and to accumulate information, internal and external for assistance in career guidance.

13.1.6.7 Computer-based Information Systems

Computer-based information services for the general public are now available in the home, using the television screen as an output device. There is a broadcast teletext service, which provide 'pages' of up-to-date information as selected by the viewer by keying-in page numbers on a hand-sized control unit. The services are sent out on the same transmission as conventional TV programmes but a special receiver, or an adaptor, is needed to pick up teletext. The services which are free cover such topics as weather details, travel information, financial news, the industrial news and the exchange rates as they fluctuate, the Financial Times index and the latest trends on the Stock Marker, consumer news, and special events and happenings for the days, as well as important news flashes as they are generated.

There is another and more versatile type of computer-based information system termed viewdata which is based on the telephone as well as the television. Teletext and viewdata systems are sometimes referred to collectively as videotex systems. The British Telecom version of the service is called **Prestel** and this service is based on a number of regional computers situated in various parts of the UK and one master system in London. Within two minutes of updating information on the master system it becomes available through the regional systems. The television is connected to the telephone by way of a jack plug and as with teletext services a key-pad is provided to enable the selection of information. The main difference between the teletext type of service and Prestel is that Prestel is a two-way system which allows the customer to carry on a dialogue with the computer system and the data base of information. For example, it permits a user to make a travel enquiry about a journey to a particular destination on a particular day, or to quiz a mail order catalogue to determine whether a particular item is available and wen to place an order for the article. Unlike the free teletext services, there is normally a charge for accessing a page of information in addition to the standard telephone charge for the communication with the system. Information on Prestel is provided by independent agencies, including government and various business and industrial organizations, who lease space on the system from British Telecom. The information covers similar topics to the teletext services but, in general, does so more extensively.

Another development of significance is Mailbox, an Electronic Mail Service (EMS) which enables subscribers to send messages to each other routed through one of the Prestel computers for as little as the cost of a local telephone call. Other developments include the introduction of special viewdata keyboard terminals and business terminals which can have printing facilities attached to them, enabling the retention of information in printed form. It is possible to connect microcomputers and viewdata services to provide cheap and easy-to-use communication networks for business. It is also possible to connect with the outside world local (that is private) viewdata and electronic mail systems which operate within the businesses themselves.

13.1.7 Simulation

The process of simulation involves the design and study of a model of some physical, economic, or sociological system. The motivation for simulation stems from two sources. First, as an abstract model becomes more realistic, it becomes more and more intractable mathematically. We cannot easily determine the behaviour of systems whose variables are discontinuous, stochastic, and intimately related to many other variables in a multiplicative fashion. Yet, complexities such as these abound in the real world. A person in an administrative position, or an advisor to an administrative person, is completed to depict reality as faithfully as possible. Simulation cannot provide optimal solutions but it can yield very useful insights into the behaviour of a complex system. Second, engineering, economic, and sociological systems are often unavailable for experimentation. In simulation, a computer program depicting some type of system is executed by tracing out the implications of the program's equations over time. Thus, a form of experimentation is provided. The result of the 'experimentation' characterise solely the interaction of the underlying assumptions of the model. Assume that we want to simulate the inventory control in a particular company. We may have available the information about the actual observed withdrawals from stock over the last months. We would like to know what would have happened had we changed our methods of stocking the supplies. In particular, what would have happened if we had changed one or more of the following:

1. the reorder point, that is, when we placed an order for more supplies,
2. the re-order amount that is, how much we ordered at a time.

Variations in these parameters help us in our search for a better strategy of inventory keeping. Small improvements in inventory practice may make a great deal of difference to a company, because inventory represents capital investment not available for other purposes, taxes, storage space, deterioration of goods, obsolescence. A simple simulation may pay off handsomely both the economic returns and quality of service.

Note that experimentation in real life is often not possible, while on machine it is relatively cheap both in time and money. Thus with a good simulation, It is possible to find out the one, or few, that meet our needs, without paying the cost in money and possible social harm of doing the wrong ones to find out that they were wrong.

Simulation has numerous applications; especially worth mentioning are biological phenomena, war-games, flight simulation and weapon-system simulation.

13.1.8 Artificial Intelligence

Mechanical theorem proving is a branch of artificial intelligence. It has been a subject of great interest sine the times of Leibnitz. In 1930 Herbrand proved a very important theorem concerning mechanical proofs of theorems. His method was difficult to apply since it was extremely difficult to carry it out by hand. With the invention of computers logicians regained interest in mechanical theorem proving. In 1960 Herbrand's procedure as implemented by Gilmore on a digital computer, followed shortly by a more efficient procedure proposed by Davis and Putnam. A major breakthrough in mechanical theorem proving was made by J.A. Robinson in 1965. He developed a single inference rule, the resolution principle, which was shown to be highly efficient and very easily implemented on computers. Since then, many improvements of the resolution principle have been made.

Pattern recognition is another problem of artificial intelligence which has some practical uses. The identification of blood samples, the classification of linger prints, particle tracks in high energy physics require the use of pattern recognition and computers can help a great deal in the preliminary. analysis. There are many sophisticated games such as chess and checkers where machines are capable of out-smarting most of the humans and have helped in unearthing new strategies.

13.1.9 Defence Applications

One of the first computerised large-scale command and control systems is SAGE (Semi-Automatic Ground Environment) in the United States. It was designed during 1950's for the air defence of the North America continent. An air defence system must be concerned with all of the air space above the North American continent and far out to sea. This total air space is divided into sectors each of which has a SAGE direction centre housing the computer and related equipment. The primary sources of information are several types of radars situated at strategic spot throughout the sector. The information of interest is the movement of any aircraft, friendly or hostile anywhere in the airspace. To obtain this information the big search radars slowly rotate their beam through 360° providing range and azimuth information on each target. The location of echoes is transmitted automatically over the telephone lines to the direction centre within a few seconds after they occur. Gap filler radars with shorter range capability are employed in a similar manner to improve the low altitude coverage between-search radars. Altitude information is also required, and this is provided by height finder radars. The height finder radars do not search through the entire space, but must be told where to look for a target. In addition to this information about air activity from the various radars, the system also receives information about friendly flight planes and the current status of all air defence weapons, both interceptors and missiles. Summary information is supplied about the situation in adjacent sectors. Information is dynamically changing. Much of it is volatile; it is vitally important for a new minutes, and then it becomes worthless.

The purpose of the system is to aid decision-making at two different levels. At one level it must direct and control individual weapons. It must track aircraft automatically and help identify friendly and hostile aircraft; it must direct height finders, assign weapons to targets, and pass on information to adjacent sectors. These decisions require detailed data and must be made in seconds. At another decision level, the system must be able to present a comprehensive picture of what is happening and how the battle is progressing.

There are many people involved in these decisions at both levels. In a typical direction centre there are over 100 operators communicating with the computer. Much of the output information is presented to the operators in the form of computer-generated electronic display. This permits rapidly changing pictorial displays so that the dynamic situation can be assimilated quickly by a human operator.

There are many other defence-oriented applications where a computer is found to be of enormous help viz., flight dynamic of missiles and aircraft, weapon system analysis, war gaming, missile guidance systems.

13.2 MULTIMEDIA APPLICATIONS

Certain mainstream multimedia applications are used daily by a growing number of people, for example:

- The education sector, for instance, is embracing the collective technology for presentations, Computer-aided Learning (CAL) and reference.
- In the corporate and industrial sectors, multimedia is used extensively for training and business presentations. Renault, for example, use a multimedia program called **Ediris** for training car mechanics.
- Retailers and consumers are benefiting from in-store Point-of-Sale (POS) and Point-of-Information (POI) terminals.

These and many other current applications all share the common function of communicating information. The following subsections discuss some of these, highlighting comparative advantages and what can be expected from them today and in the future.

13.2.1 Education

Multimedia is acknowledged as an environment with great potential in education. It is able to assist both the pupil/student and teacher/lecturer in new ways. For the teacher or lecturer it provides a means of putting across information and ideas, and for the pupil or student it can represent a one-to-one teaching environment which moves at the required pace.

An early pilot program for the Intel platform (for multimedia on IBM and compatible machines) was Palenque, developed with the assistance of Bank Street College of Education, New York. This courseware facilitates the exploration of an ancient Mayan site, giving access to a multimedia database containing audio-visual experiences. Through a joint venture with Shell, Philips also produced an early educational program for its multimedia platform (CD-I). The disc, by SPIN UK, seeks to make mathematics and science more engaging.

At the simplest level, multimedia is harnessed as a presentation tool with which only the teacher or lecturer interacts. Material might represent a pictorial and textual presentation used to enhance a lesson or lecture. In some instances this might be intended as a complete lesson or lecture for dialogue between student/pupil and system, but shortage of systems/terminals restricts this mode of operation.

The true power of multimedia manifests itself through pupil/student interaction, thus, leaving the teacher/lecturer to oversee events and to answer queries. In this guise, multimedia can act like a teacher or lecturer constantly available with expert tuition.

That pupils/students should interact with multimedia is a key aspect of its role in education. An Intel paper on Digital Video Interactive (DVI) states that interactive multimedia can yield as much as 70 percent recall, as opposed to 45 percent for audiovisual aids, and just 25 percent for audio. Many CAL experts are undecided as to the precise improvement such interaction gives. That there is an improvement, however, is agreed.

Distribution of multimedia lessons, lectures and courseware on CD-ROM or CD-I disc adds another dimension to multimedia in education, providing a vehicle for pupils/students to take lessons/lectures at home. For scattered rural communities where schools are inaccessible, and for institutes running distance learning (or correspondence) courses of any kind, the potential is enormous. Indeed a portion of courses run by institutions that depend upon home learning (*e.g.*,

The Open University and The Open College) will certainly be distributed through multimedia in future. Affordable consumer systems such as CD-I players and the Commodore Dynamic Total Vision (CDTV) closely resemble the sort of systems that could provide a basis for this.

It is important to note that multimedia is not poised to replace teachers and lecturers overnight. In addition to current technical constraints, technology is expensive and therefore inaccessible for many educational establishments. With adequate long-term support, however, it will certainly alter the generally accepted study methods of the pupil/student, while transforming traditional teaching methods along the way.

13.2.2 Training

Ranging from simple induction courses to sales techniques, corporate and industry training has in recent years become even-more dependent upon technology. Computer Based Training (CBT) now forms a substantial market. Indeed education and training are the fastest growing markets for multimedia products.

Training requirements often differ from one company to the next and are seldom satisfied through off-the-shelf products. The development of in-house training material is, therefore, common. This is quite different from the education sector, where a higher level of standardisation exists.

Using computers, multimedia represents a powerful solution to training, where employees can interact with video under computer control. Many commercially available authoring systems lend themselves particularly well to the development of CBT courseware. Obtaining the most out of these sometimes demands programming with general purpose languages such as C, *i.e.*, they are script-based environments. Programming is easier where the package includes commonly used library routines.

Such systems must be capable of controlling a videodisc player, should be easy to use, and offer a variety of library routines. Popular authoring systems that fit this profile include TenCORE, TopClass, Authorware Professional, Quest and IBM's Audio Visual Connection (AVC).

Advantages of multimedia in education also apply to corporate and industry training. And because places of work often operate on a 24-hour basis, it can offer the added advantage of constant availability.

13.2.3 Point-of-Information

Traditionally, consumer education has consisted of publishing product brochures, advertising, allowing the potential customer to peruse in a shop or showroom, and product demonstrations. These generally accepted ways in which the consumer chooses an appropriate product can be aided or replaced using multimedia in a point-of-information (POI) guise. POI terminals present the customer with the ability to browse through product ranges, or experience just those items that fit a user-defined profile.

POI can be a powerful marketing and advertising tool providing the means to Display products. The benefits are clear; it gives an opportunity to promote products in a medium that cannot be rivalled by (current) television advertising. It also allows small and medium-sized companies to promote products on terms that only large companies and corporations could previously afford. Furthermore, if products can be demonstrated adequately through multimedia, the need to exhibit them physically becomes unnecessary and so floor space can be saved. Research-also indicates that users of POI terminals Spend more money than those shoppers using conventional means. Finally, the Possibility of fewer sales staff is raised.

With the growing number of multimedia systems in the home and with the falling Price of disc replication, we may well see POI distributed free like 'junk mail'. In the Computer industry, there is also the possibility of distributing short advertisements or Demonstrations containing video sequences on floppy disks. Transmitting such multimedia Directly into the home is also a distinct possibility and is one that is being Researched and developed by several US companies.

Multimedia can also help the consumer in making general decisions. Computer Graphics, combined with video texturing, can help users decide on a colour scheme for the home, for instance. 'Design and Decorate' co-developed by Intel and Videodisc Publishing, Inc., New York, shows how multimedia technology can be used for interior Design. This permits the user to design a living room, choosing everything from the Shape and size of room, to furnishing and accessories.

Museums of various kinds throughout the world have installed POI terminals. These give visitors the opportunity to follow user-defined guided tours. Such an approach also allows visitors to experience interesting items which might otherwise be Catalogued and hidden away from public view. Many other areas such as careers advice, Geographic information systems, surrogate travel (brochures) are also possible through POI.

13.2.4 User-interfaces

It is agreed that computers are generally difficult to use because of the awkward means through which user-interaction takes place. Many users remain enslaved to the QWERTY keyboard, having to enter numerous keyboard commands.

With the introduction of the Macintosh computer, Apple showed that a Graphical User Interface (GUI) and a mouse provides a friendlier interactive environment. Showing Icons and menu items that lead to various applications and features, a GUI simply requires the user to point and click a mouse. Following its commercial success, the GUI concept was made commercially available for all professional personal computers. It can now be seen on the IBM PC, IBM PS/2, Atari ST, Commodore Amiga, workstations and other machines. The PC fraternity was initially given Gem. This shields the user from Disk Operating System (DOS) keyboard commands. For instance, using DOS to run a program called Paradox in the pdox4 directory, it is necessary to enter cd/pdox4 followed by paradox. Gem merely requires the user to point and click on an icon representing the paradox4 directory and then click on an icon for the paradox4 program.

Today, Microsoft Windows and Presentation Manager represent two much—used GUIs for the IBM PC and compatible machines. Microsoft Windows is considerably more popular with a user-base ten times larger than that of Presentation Manager (1992), the GUI front-end for OS/2.

At the simplest level, multimedia can enhance the GUI concept by transforming icons into motion icons (micons). Invented by the Norwegian Hans Peter Brondmo at Massachusetts Institute of Technology (MIT) in 1989, micons consist of a series of frames that are run in a continuous loop. For example, an option on the screen that leads to a flat file database might be represented by a person flicking through a card box. As with icons, micons are often reinforced wit concise descriptions.

Micons manifest more clearly the information, features or applications to which screen options are tagged. It is reasonable to assume that they will consolidate with the current (commercial) user-interface approach, coexisting for some time with the generally accepted 'buttons' and 'icons'.

The pace at which micons will proliferate through business software such as relational databases, word processors and spreadsheets, is likely to be gradual for two reasons. Firstly, when parallels are drawn with icons, few business programs had incorporated these some live years after their commercial introduction. Secondly, business software is traditionally functional with bland screens.

In the longer term, multimedia will have a greater impact on User Interfaces (UIs) than the mere introduction of micons. For example, speech synthesis and audio will be Used to reinforce menu selections, thus, reducing time spent making choices visually. Voice-annotated software for the Macintosh already exists, and you can already incorporate audio and sound into Microsoft Windows with level I Multimedia extensions.

13.2.5 Software Training

The continual introduction of Information Technology, and its pace of change, give rise to a thriving software training industry. This bears testimony to the fact that current commercial software and computers are simply too difficult to use. Evidence of this is seen when a new program is introduced into an office environment; the need for training or retraining emerges instantly. Equally, new employees often have to be trained to use word processors, databases, spreadsheets, integrated packages and so forth.

Depending upon product sophistication, training normally consists of a one- to three-day course, the overall cost of which can be considerable. However, initial high training costs drop off significantly for all but those companies with a high turnover of staff.

There is, however, a feasible and cost-effective multimedia solution to software training as well as to program documentation. The program and documentation could be distributed on a single CD-ROM disc. An installation program (on CD-ROM) can be used to write the program to hard disk, thus, accommodating system configuration, various options chosen, and the type of printer installed.

Multimedia manuals and training material could both be loaded from CD-ROM. A movable and re-sizable window could be used to accommodate such material. The window could even be switched off leaving just verbal instructions. More than this, the interactive text-based, context-sensitive help systems of today could be transformed into motion video and dialogue. Theoretically, then, multimedia could radically alter software training and documentation.

13.3 MARKETING INFORMATION SYSTEM

In many companies with extensive marketing activities, the marketing information system is among the least developed of these companies information systems. One reason for this is that improved information systems for marketing often do not receive priority because they cannot be justified on a cost savings basis, and the benefits of the systems may be largely intangible and not readily observable. These benefits may nevertheless be very real and may include better information for marketing decisions (such as for product pricing) as well as better customer service.

Another reason is the apparent belief of some marketing executives that marketing decision-making is primarily an art and cannot be systematized to the point where decisions can be aided by information analysis. Yet, typically, a wealth of useful information exists and could be made available to marketing managers but is not provided to them. Often information with value is available within one area of the marketing organisation but is not transmitted to the managers who need it.

Marketing managers often rely on reports supplied as by-products of other departments' activities such as those of accounting, production, and inventory control. This information tends to emphasize the past, such as sales in the last period, whereas marketing needs information to help predict the future, including information about market trends. Often, the functional information systems should be drastically revised to accommodate marketing's needs, and marketing also should develop certain information systems for its own purposes.

In some companies with weak marketing information systems, marketing is the most critical activity. Not only is the information that marketing management receives important, but also the information that marketing generates is vital to the rest of the organisation. For example, marketing provides sales forecasts that serve as the basis for production schedules, cash flow projections, and profit plans. Because of this, the impact of ineffective marketing information system is felt throughout the organisation.

Even more important is the marketing's role as a company's revenue generating branch. A well-developed information system for marketing can give a competitive advantage thereby offering better service to customers and better information for market penetration efforts. While even a well-developed marketing information system may provide inadequate information, this information usually is better than no information.

13.4 OVERVIEW OF MARKETING INFORMATION SYSTEM

The discussion here is based on a medium-sized company that produces multiple consumer products grouped into several product lines. The company has sales branches in several locations, each with numerous salespersons in the field whose customers are both wholesalers and retailers. In this company, products are manufactured and placed in inventory to await sale. Thousands of real-life companies fit this description.

The major marketing information subsystems are:

1. The sales information system:
   (*a*) Sales support (*b*) Sales analysis
   (*c*) Customer analysis
2. The market research and intelligence information system:
   (*a*) Customer research (*b*) Market research
   (*c*) Competitor intelligence
3. Promotion and advertising information system
4. New product development information system
5. Sales forecasting information system
6. Product planning information system
7. Product pricing information system
8. Expenditures control information system

Figure 13.1 depicts the major information flows among these systems; not all information flows are shown. These information flows serve to integrate the several marketing systems. In general, the more automated these flows, the more efficient the entire marketing information system and the more rapid the organizations response to market trends and merchandising problems.

Certain information subsystems are shared with other functions. For example, the sales information system is based primarily on the sales order entry information system, which is normally staffed by sales order entry personnel within marketing but which also passes large amounts of information to accounting for accounting reports. Likewise, the sales forecasting Information system may be shared by marketing and accounting. The new product development information system, the product pricing information system, and the new product planning system may serve not only marketing but also other functional areas that participate in product planning, product pricing, and new product development, although these systems are likely to be dominated by the marketing group.

The overall objectives of this integrated set of marketing subsystems are to improve the organization's ability to:

1. Identify and evaluate potentially profitable sales opportunities
2. React rapidly to changes in market conditions
3. Establish profit-maximizing product prices

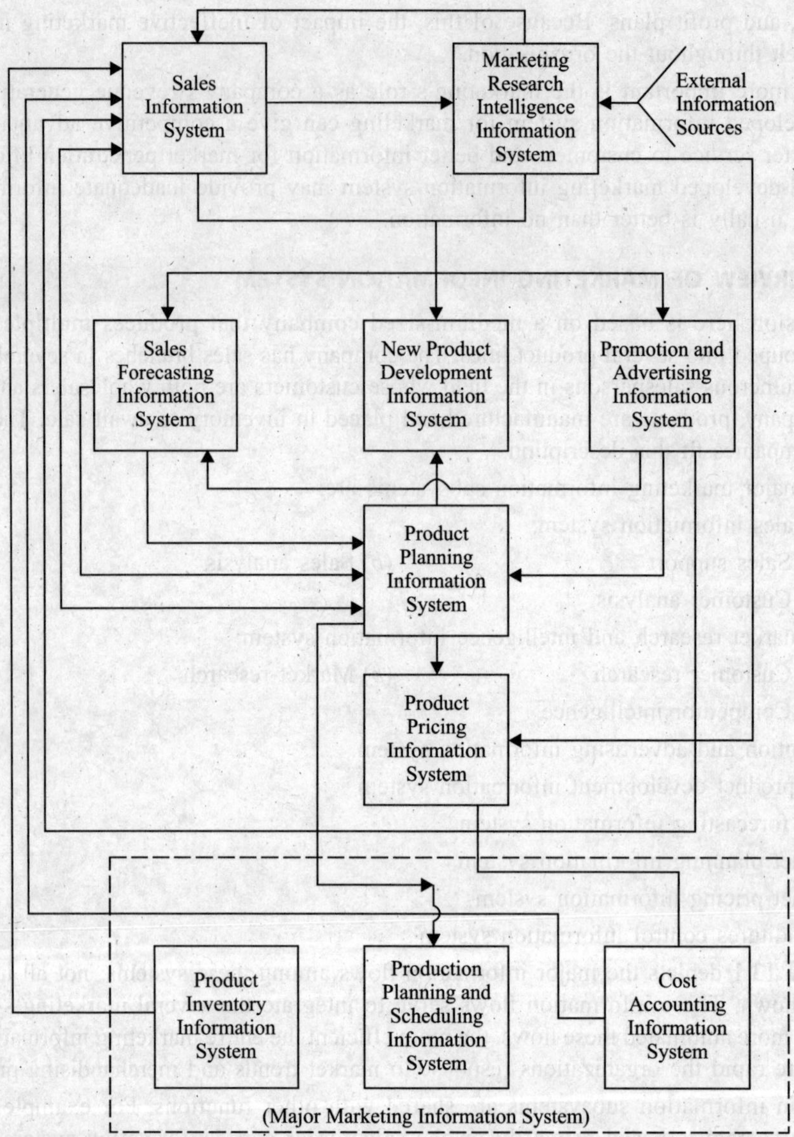

Fig. 13.1 The Major Information Flows within the Marketing Information System

4. Control marketing costs
5. Deploy sales personnel most effectively
6. Assist in allocating expenditures for advertising and other forms of promotion

The major sources of information for these activities are:

1. Sales invoices and other transactions information
2. Salespersons' customer call reports
3. Salespersons' debriefing by marketing managers
4. Sales history files
5. Customer account files
6. The cost accounting system

7. The profit planning (budgeting) system
8. Market research and intelligence-gathering activities
9. Sales forecasts
10. Production schedules
11. Inventory status reports

The following sections examine each marketing subsystem.

13.4.1 Sales Information System

13.4.1.1 Sales Support

Selling is the primary activity of most marketing groups. All the marketing information systems shown in Fig. 13.1 directly or indirectly support this selling activity. However, a specialized sales support information system must provide information to sales personnel about the following:

1. Product descriptions and performance specifications
2. Product prices
3. Quantity discounts and other product discount information
4. Sales incentives for salespersons
5. Sales promotions
6. Financing plans for customers
7. The strengths and weaknesses of competitors' products
8. The histories of customers' relations with the company
9. Sales policies and procedures established by the company
10. Products that have not yet been introduced
11. Product inventory levels

This and other information comes from a variety of sources, most (but not all) of which are mentioned earlier. Product performance specifications, for example, may come from the engineering department.

In many companies the inventory control system must provide extremely accurate and continuously up-to-date information about raw materials and finished goods inventory levels and the approximate dates when additional quantities of each material and Product will be received and placed in inventory. Some companies find that the delivery dates of purchases are a critical concern of customers, who often will not place an order until they are assured that the products they are purchasing are already in inventory or will be available by a specific date.

One approach to providing this inventory information is a periodic report detailing the quantity of each product on hand as of the end of the preceding period (typically the preceding week or month). This report is usually outdated when received, however, since it generally arrives well after the end of the period. The report becomes increasingly out of date until it is replaced by the inventory Status report after the end of the next period. Information from this type of system often is not sufficiently current and may cause a great deal of customer dissatisfaction; often, for example, customers are promised deliveries of their orders on a certain date because the information system indicates that adequate quantities are in inventory, but withdrawals from inventory have already been made that have not yet been recorded in the information system.

A more sophisticated information system can supply the necessary information about product availability. With the OLRT (on line real time) information systems shown in Fig. 13.2, for example, the sales person can inquire directly into the inventory file to determine the quantity of each product on hand. This provides a substantial advantage over competitors who use periodic inventory status reports.

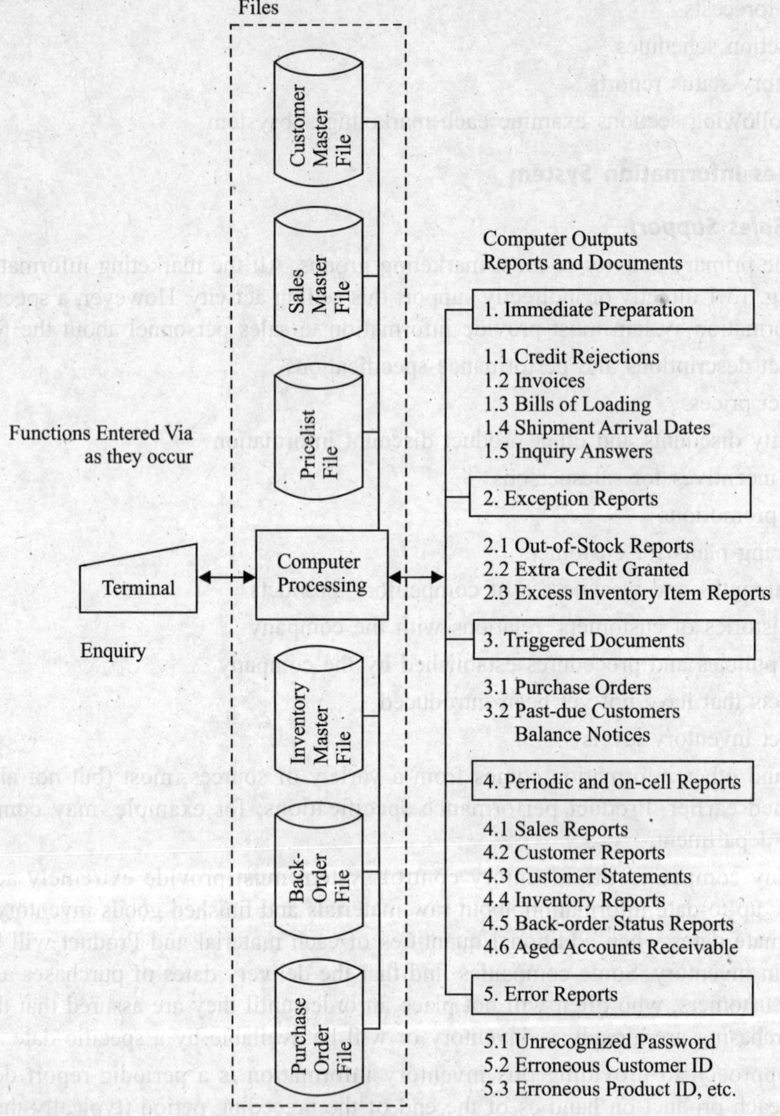

Fig. 13.2 An on-line real time sales order entry system with point-of-sale transaction entry

13.4.1.2 Sales Analysis

The sales analysis information system is one of the most existence and important systems of most companies involved in sales. Its purpose is to provide information for analyses of (1) product sales trends, (2) product profitability on a product-by-product basis, (3) the performance of each sales region and sales branch, and (4) salespersons' performance. Information for sales analysis is derived primarily from the sales order entry system; the majority is information from actual sales transactions and is contained on sales invoices. To fully support the sales analysis system, invoices should contain information about product type, product quantity, price discount terms, customer identity and type, sales region, and sales person.

Information from other sources should also be included in the sales reports. Specifically, the sales reports must contain information about the profitability of products, product lines, sales territories, and individual salespersons. Profitability reporting requires information about product administrative and selling costs—preferably on a marginal cost basis so that contribution margins (marginal contribution to profits) can be determined. As suggested in Fig. 13.1, much of this cost information is supplied by the cost accounting system. Without this information, sales performance may be measured by the rupee volume of sales, and the profitability (or lack of profitability) of these sales will be hidden. With margin analysis information the profit contribution of the profitable products, customers, and salespersons can be identified; the most profitable products are not necessarily those with the highest sales volume. Similarly, unprofitable products, customers, and salespersons can also be identified. This information influences the design of incentive systems that encourage salespersons to concentrate on the more profitable products.

Reports using sales and cost information are usually prepared to emphasize trends in both sales volume and profitability. This information is directly useful to salespersons and is also supplied to the marketing research and intelligence groups for more detailed analysis.

Often, as costs edge upward because of inflation while sales prices remain stable (Perhaps as a result of intense competition), these contribution margin analysis reports show that certain products are no longer profitable, and they prompt the restyling, the re-engineering, or even the elimination of certain products. Alternatively, contribution margin analysis reports may spur management to consider raising the product's price. High contribution margins also may indicate that sales promotions were successful or that certain products should be promoted further or differently.

Similar contribution margin analysis reports are prepared on a sales branch and sales region basis and are used in a similar manner. Additionally, identifying strong and weak sales units enables the company to reward its most effective regional and bran, managers properly.

The sales analysis system also provides most of the information used to evaluate the performance of sales personnel. By reclassifying sales by salesperson rather than by product or sales unit, sales supervisors learn whether each salesperson has met the assigned sales quota. If marginal costs are also assigned, by salesperson, each salesperson's contribution margin can be established as one criterion for performance evaluation.

Each of the above reports involving sales and cost information, such as reports of product Profitability, sales unit profitability, and salesperson profitability, typically would be prepared for the current week or month and the year to date, as well as on the date. For example, sales units should be evaluated relative to the potential in their territory, with this potential indicated by the units profit plans. Direct comparing units in different regions may be invalid because of differing market demand for the various product. These comparisons of planned with actual profitability make possible the calculation of variances for each product, each branch, each salesperson, and so on. Often, the information value of these variances is enhanced if they are split into a price variance (the amount of contribution margin variance caused by not selling all items at the planned price) and a volume variance (the variance due to selling a greater or lesser volume of the product than planned).

The primary types of information used for the sales analysis subsystem are (1) information about customer invoices and back orders that is provided by the sales transaction processing system (as shown in Fig. 13.3), (2) information derived from the oral and written reports of sales personnel, and (3) product cost information obtained from the cost accounting information system. Information about sales transactions may be available from the sales files or the customer files.

The written or oral reports of sales personnel are valuable sources of information which too often are not properly organised. Sales personnel are in direct contact with customers and frequently are the first to be aware of changed market conditions, altered customer expectations, new products in the market, and competitors' actions.

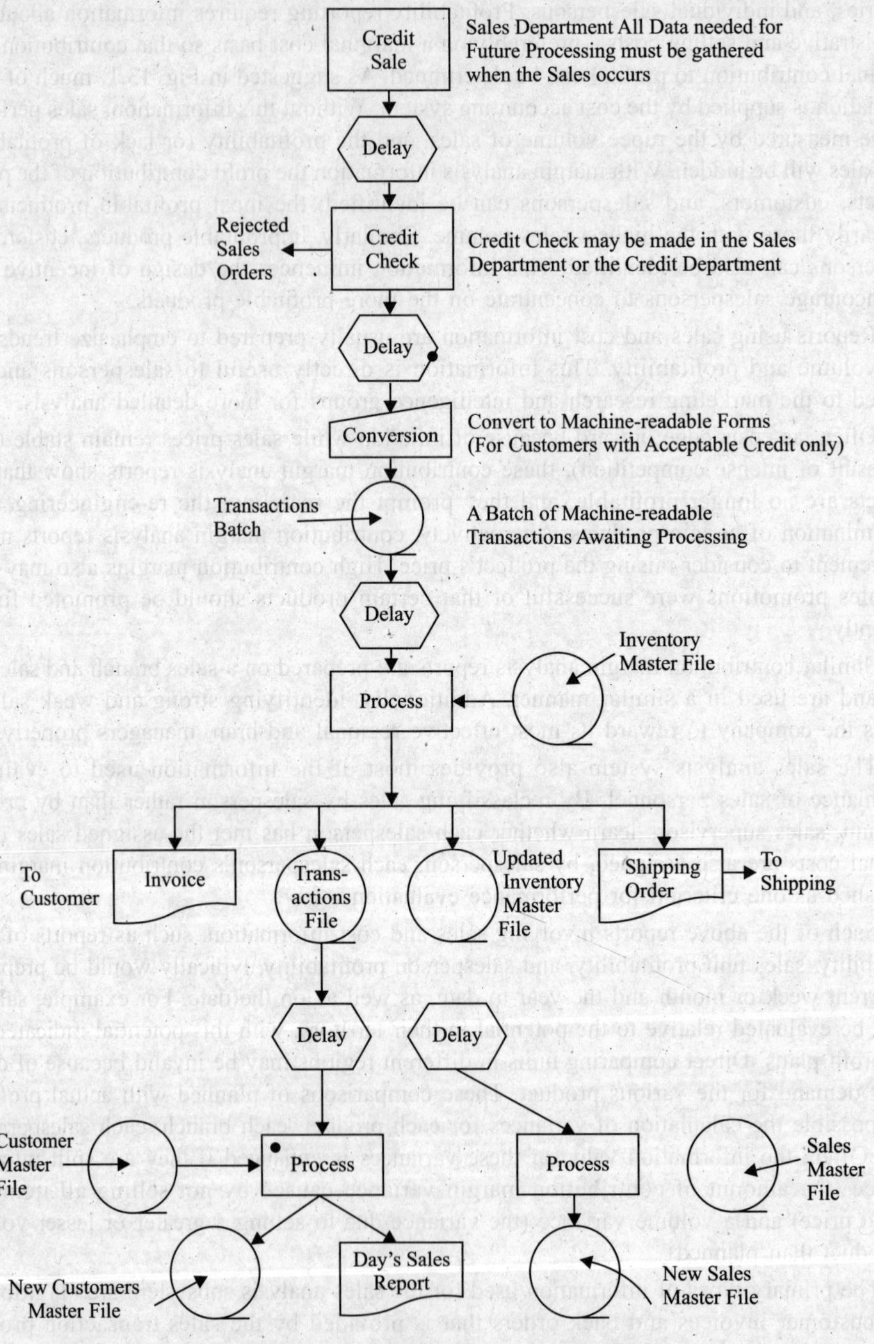

Fig. 13.3 A Batch credit sales order entry system.

Marketing groups should develop a reporting activity that provides analysis with detailed information from salespersons. However, this 'salesperson debriefing' should not burden sales personnel unduly, they often resent paperwork. Some companies accomplish this debriefing by having salespersons complete customer call reports consisting as much as possible of 'yes' or 'no' answers or ratings on a scale. Other companies permit their salespersons to dictate reports for later typing. These reports often supply important contextual information, which may, for example, explain why a branch's or a region's sales are lower than expected or why a particular product has succeeded or failed. Marketing departments cannot afford to ignore this source of grass-roots information.

Grass-roots information from customers is so important that often middle- and senior-level marketing managers call on customers with whom they have good rapport. Because these are clearly information-seeking visits and because the managers' orientation with respect to topics and approach often differs from that of salespersons, the managers will acquire additional information about products or competitors that was not made known to salespersons.

Sales analysis reports are among those most likely to be needed on both an on-call and a key performance indicator basis. For example, a marketing manager may not wish to wait for end-of-period reports to see the sales impact of a major advertising or promotion campaign because an ineffective campaign may need to be altered immediately. On-call or key indicator reports will permit early evaluation of a current campaign. Many OLRT marketing information systems have this capability.

13.4.1.3 Customer Analysis

The purposes of customer analysis are to establish a profile of buying habits and to determine the profitability of each customer on a contribution margin basis. Usually customers are classified into two, three, or four categories by total sales volume; for simplicity, two categories are discussed here.

One category of customers usually includes those who make the largest amount of purchases. These few customers often provide a very substantial proportion of total revenues; for example, 10 per cent of the customers may provide 80 or 90 per cent of total sales revenue. Frequent and detailed reports should be available about each of these major customers, and marketing managers may spend most of their time analyzing these reports to ensure that sales volume and profit margins are up to expectations, to be certain that customer service is good, and to spot trends in the buying habits of these important customers. Special pricing policies may exist for these customers, and marketing managers are quick to reward salespersons who are successful with prime customers and to remove salespersons who are not. Often, these customers demand price concessions based on the volume of their purchases, and marketing must have detailed cost information available to evaluate the reasonableness of their requests.

Information about the low-volume customers in the second category also is useful. The analysis of their purchasing activity tends to focus on determining whether each is a profitable customer so that strategies can be developed for the unprofitable customers to increase prices or reduce services or costs (such as by cutting back on the number of sales calls).

Much of the quantitative information used for customer analyses is extracted from the customer master file, as shown in Figs. 13.2 and 13.3. Additionally, analyses of customer profitability require product cost information from the cost accounting system and information about other costs from other cost data files.

13.4.2 Market Research and Intelligence Information System

Whereas the sales information system is based primarily on sales transactions data plus information about inventory status and product cost, the market research and intelligence information system relies on information from a wide variety of sources. While one principal source is the sales information system, other major sources are outside the organization.

Some organizations split market research and market intelligence functions into separate groups, with the former concentrating on the market, and the latter concerned about only one aspect of the market—the organization's competitors. However, the information that each function requires overlaps, and some comes from the same sources. Additionally, both focus on analyzing the information to discern trends, sudden changes, or threats to the organization. For these reasons, both functions are examined in this section.

13.4.2.1 Customer Research

Customer research is broader and more analytic than the customer analysis associated with the sales information system. Customer analysis reporting involves reporting past customer transactions using information from the sales order entry system. Customer research utilizes this information, provides information about the market environment as a context for it, and also uses information about customers' financial and operating conditions and about their selling and purchasing dealings with the organisation's competitors. Additionally, customer research frequently analyzes potential rather than present customers.

Analyses of this information may offer insights into possible new or better ways in which the organization can serve its present customers and acquire new ones. These analyses can also affect credit terms and discounts extended to customers or can give early warnings that certain competitors pose a major threat with particular customers. Often, these analyses will lead to negotiations between the marketing managers and the senior managers of customers on matters (such as product specifications) that are beyond the Jurisdiction of direct-contact salespersons.

13.4.2.2 Market Research

Market research is broader than customer research in that it focuses on the entire market for the organization's products. One purpose of market research is to assess the overall size of the market for each product line and for each product within a product line. This usually is done on both a short- and a long-term basis. Such 'market definition' can be difficult. Potential market size can change rapidly as economic conditions and technology change.

When market potential is determined and the market is fully defined, the organization's market share can be established, and the roles of competitors within the market can be better evaluated. This information is useful for the product planning function shown in Fig. 13.1 because it helps suggest sales goals and strategies that will yield the desired market penetration. This information is useful too for selecting new products. Analyses of this type also enhance the ability to forecast future sales levels of each product tine and individual product. A market potential analysis is likely to result in a narrative report for input to the marketing planning activity.

The key information needs for a market potential analysis are (1) information about the economy and economic trends and the probable impact of these trends on demand for the product, (2) information about past sales and sales trends for the entire industry, and (3) information about competing 'substitution' products (products that customers can substitute for the product being analyzed). Usually the market research department assumes responsibility for gathering and analyzing this information.

Salespersons often can provide information about potential new markets for products as well as about substitute products. Properly designed sales call reports can supply a wealth of information to the market research group because salespersons often find out much about the market directly through their discussions with clients. Additionally, the accumulated information on sales call reports can offer important hints about shifts in the market's preferences or about the market's perception of the organization's products.

Directly questioning customers or potential customers, such as by means of a consumer survey or interview, can also provide useful information, Many companies employ independent marketing consultants to systematically gather information needed for analyzing market potential. Smaller companies often will ask consultants to undertake a complete analysis of market potential.

13.4.2.3 Competitor Intelligence

A company should gather information about its competitors. This includes information about (1) the specifications of competitors' products, (2) competitors' operating strengths and weaknesses, (3) competitors' customer service levels and customer policies, (4) competitors' financial structure and strength, and (5) competitors' new product plans, marketing goals and strategies, product promotion plans, and probable reactions to the organization's strategies. Ideally, of course, the organization would like to have a complete set of each competitor's long- and short-range plans.

Acquiring the information needed may require continuous surveillance of competitors' activities. Most of this information is not directly available to an organization. A network of sources must be developed, and information, or 'intelligence,' often must be inferred from independent bits of data that are processed and combined within the organization's intelligence activity.

The quantity of data that must be gathered and processed in order to gain a good perspective on competitors can be voluminous. However, extensive information is usually available from public sources and particularly from government regulatory agencies. A well-organized system of reporting by the organization's own salespersons about their observations of competitors' dealing with customers also can be useful. Marketing intelligence from commercial intelligence companies is also widely available.

Marketing intelligence information systems that gather and process information about competitors often are closely affiliated with the intelligence activity of the entire organization; at the same time, they are an integral part of the marketing information systems. Marketing intelligence information systems often provide intelligence that is extremely important in formulating the entire organization's long-range plans.

13.4.3 Promotion and Advertising Information System

The promotion and advertising department within marketing-devotes its attention to planning and executing advertising campaigns and to carrying out various, product promotions such as package coupons, contests, special sales, and trade shows. This department's activities are focussed on increasing sales revenues without an equivalent increase in costs. Accordingly, information about how effective particular advertising and promotion activities are in terms of increasing revenues is sought and used in conjunction with information about possible increased costs associated with the revenue increases.

Figure 13.1 shows the principal information flows to the promotion and advertising information system. A major source of this information is the sales information system, which supplies information about past and present sales activity. This information indicates which products are selling well and which need promotional assistance. Product cost and profitability information, provided via the sales reports, is also important so that the more profitable products can be identified and given greater emphasis.

Sales analyses provided by the sales information system can assist the advertising and promotion group by highlighting trends that may influence the allocation of promotion and advertising expenditures. Additionally, a time-series sales analysis that correlates advertising and promotion activities with subsequent sales will indicate which are the most effective promotion campaigns for particular products.

The market research information system can supply the promotion and advertising information system with information about market size and about characteristics for each product market. This is helpful for tailoring promotion campaigns to specific market segments. The intelligence information system may be able to shed light on competitors' future promotion strategies or the probable effectiveness of competitors' past campaigns,both of which can influence the organisation's promotion and advertising strategy.

The promotion and advertising information system should be a storehouse of information that helps managers build on past experience with promotion and advertising. By systematically organizing and analyzing this information, an organization can eventually establish a body of knowledge about what the market is like and how it responds to each of several types of promotional activities for each product. However, the complexions of markets can change rapidly, and the information systems already described should continuously 'refresh' and modify this promotion and advertising information base in light of the most current information available.

13.4.4 New Product Development Information System

New product research involves analyzing a possible opportunity for a new product and evaluating preferred specifications and probable market success. Often the market research activity initially perceives the opportunity and passes along information about it to the new product development group, as suggested in Fig. 13.1. Alternatively, a salesperson who deals directly with customers may become aware of their need for a new product. A customer call reports system may help elicit information about new products needed in the market. For example, explicit questions on the call report, such as 'Do customer needs exist that our products are not filling completely?' and 'Do customers need a product that is not now available?' encourage salespersons to think about new product possibilities.

During the analysis of new product feasibility, after a probable need has been identified, information from the sales analysis system about past sales of similar or related products may indicate the most desirable characteristics for the new product or the structure of the market for the product. Also, market research can be tailored to gather information about the size and structure of the market for the product, and the marketing intelligence information system may help evaluate the market strength and profitability of similar products produced by competitors. These information flows are outlined in Fig. 13.1.

The product development department uses all this information to develop specifications for a new product. These specifications may then be passed along to engineering and other groups for cost estimating. Risk profiles, which include estimated costs and revenues for the product over its life cycle, are developed as a basis for deciding whether to produce the product.

13.4.5 Sales Forecasting Information System

Sales forecasting is one of the most important activities of many organisations, and for these companies the sales forecasting information system should be as well developed as possible. Of course, forecasting sales deals with the future, about which little concrete information is available; thus the range of error for sales forecasting can be wide, no matter how sophisticated the information system is. Nevertheless, in general, the better information provided for sales forecasting, the more accurate the forecasts will be.

Sales forecasting is important for planning sales and promotion strategies and for post-period evaluation of salespersons' performance. Additionally, other activities vital to the organization depend on reliable sales forecasts. First, sales forecasts are generally the first step in the profit planning cycle of the entire organization; for example, they initiate the short-term financial and marketing planning cycles. If forecasts for the period are seriously in error, the organization's entire budgeting activity will be based upon the wrong level of activity.

Production planning, work-force planning, and production scheduling are based on sales forecasting. Materials are ordered and personnel are employed and reassigned according to the expected sales pattern for the next period. If sales are overestimated, finished product inventory levels or materials inventory levels will be too high, and production labour costs will be excessive, or personnel will have to be laid off. Conversely, if the sales forecast is too low, sales may be lost because of inventory shortages, or higher costs will be incurred as a result of overtime work and the need to secure additional materials in a hurry.

Cash planning is also based on sales forecasts. Usually, weekly or monthly sales forecasts form the basts for estimates of cash position, which in turn form the basis for planning how much cash will have to be borrowed and how much can be invested. Obviously, sales forecasting and the systems that provide sales forecasting information are vital to market-oriented organisations.

The basic information needed for sales forecasting is the following:

1. Past sales, provided by the sales analysis information system
2. Market conditions, provided by the market research information system.
3. Competitors' activities, provided by the competitor intelligence information system.
4. Promotion and advertising plans, provided by the information system for this function.

The general approach of medium-term sales forecasting (3 months to 1 year) is to begin with the last period's sales by product line, individual product, and geographic area and to adjust these for established trends, for newly perceived changes in the economy and the market, and for competitors' new strategies. Then, expected changes that have not yet taken place are considered, such as an anticipated economic downturn or competitors' probable reactions to sales strategies that the organization plans to implement during the period.

All these types of information are merged and weighted according to their relative importance by skilled forecasting specialists. Usually this information is entered into a formal computerized forecasting system, which may accomplish the weighting, compensate for seasonal variations and other variables, and produce a forecast by product line, individual product, and sales territory. This forecast is likely to be passed along to the sales managers who do the product planning, and they may revise the sales strategies in order to modify the forecast sales levels to more acceptable ones. These new strategies, for example, may involve additional promotion and advertising expenses. The revised strategies are likely to be communicated to the sales forecasting information system to serve as the basis for revised sales forecasts.

Shorter-term sales forecasting is usually a less involved activity. A sales forecast for a week, for example, may be primarily a simple projection of the preceding week's sales forecast, adjusted slightly for strong trends and other major forces (such as holidays) that are expected to affect the following week's sales.

13.4.6 Product Planning Information System

Marketing planning usually is done by product line generally results in a long- and a short-range marketing profit plan for each product line. Developing a long-range marketing plan requires information about the organization's overall long-range plans, of which the long-range marketing plan becomes an integral part.

Similarly, the short-range marketing profit plan becomes an integral element in the entire organization's profit plan. As illustrated in Fig. 13.1, most of the marketing information subsystems contribute information either directly or indirectly to the product planning information system. Sales history information, market research information, competitor intelligence information, sales forecasts, and information about the nature and success of promotion and advertising campaigns are all utilized as part of the product planning information system to help formulate both long- and short-range profit plans.

In turn, product planning supplies information to most marketing activities that sets their direction and focus. The most important of these information flows from the planning information system are shown in Fig. 13.1; for example, product planning provides information to the sales activity about sales strategies, and the feedback to the sales forecasting information system has already been noted. In addition to determining pricing strategies, product planning also decides what new products will be introduced and passes along information about this to the new product development information system.

13.4.7 Product Pricing Information System

Product pricing is a complex managerial activity that is affected by product costs, customer demand, market psychology, competitors prices, and various actions taken by competitors, to mention but a few considerations. Because product cost information on a full cost or marginal cost basis is usually seen as the starting point in setting prices, pricing information systems almost always utilize information about product costs.

Cost information is most directly used when price is cost plus a percentage markup. In competitive situations, however, product costs may set a lower limit on product prices. Market research into the strength of demand for each product in the market is also useful for pricing purposes. Of course, a vital ingredient in pricing is information about competitors' prices for similar products.

In many organizations pricing is done on a 'margin maintenance' basis. Gross or contribution margin goals are established for products, and prices are set in accordance with what price will maintain the established margin. Past sales profitability information is useful here to help determine how much prices should be adjusted for changed costs in order to ensure that margins are maintained.

13.4.8 Expenditures Control Information System

Expenditures within marketing include salaries, sales commissions, advertising and promotion costs, market research consulting fees, and the cost of purchased intelligence and market research studies. In some organizations product distribution costs are also controlled by marketing managers. Often, sales discounts, returns and allowances, and profit decreases or increases caused by a mix of sales that is different from what was anticipated are controlled in a manner similar to the way expenditures are controlled.

In most organizations, the control mechanism is the marketing profit plan, which is an integral part of the organization's profit plan. Usually, marketing managers have the responsibility for controlling both expenditures and the other elements under their jurisdiction that influence profits. To accomplish this, they receive regular profit plan reports that show the planned level of expenditures, the actual expenditures, and the spending variances for each expenditure category, as well as additional information that helps explain the reasons for the variances. Some feel that marketing should have its own controller who would apply accounting control and quantitative methods control techniques to the marketing area.

13.5 MANUFACTURING INFORMATION SYSTEMS

The role of production in organizations is to provide a product that the market demands. This means (1) producing the quantity of products needed by customers, (2) maintaining the quality of the products established by the product specifications, and (3) producing within the cost constraints imposed by the production control system. Production activities involve transforming energy, labour, raw materials, and purchased parts and components into finished products by production or assembly activities. For the purposes of this discussion, raw materials and purchased parts and components are all referred to as 'materials', and no distinction is made among them.

There are four general types of production: (1) continuous-flow production, such as is used in oil refineries; (2) repetitive or mass production, which is used in automobile parts production and assembly activities; (3) project production, such as is used in ship manufacturing; and (4) discrete, job-oriented production, in which production activities may be discontinuous or in which a 'batch' of a particular product is produced in a few hours, days, or weeks, after which the 'production run' is terminated.

With continuous-flow and mass production, the focus of attention is on the rate of production, and the emphasis is on achieving an efficient production rate that meets production quotas and quality standards at the lowest possible cost. With project production, the focus is on a group of products that are produced together, and time, quality, materials, and labour usage are all controlled on a product batch basis. Discrete production often uses general-purpose equipment; thus when production of one product is terminated and a different product is started, the equipment must first be 'set up', or modified, to produce the other product. Discrete production is by far the most widespread type of production and probably accounts for more than 75 per cent of total production in the United States. Many companies using discrete production produce several different products, or even thousands of different products.

Discrete production processes offer the greater challenge to the information system. This section assumes that discrete production is the production mode; however, most of the discussion is relevant to all types of manufacturing processes.

Complexity is the dominant characteristic of discrete production activities, and it is the major determinant of the required sophistication of the production information systems. The product structure provides one dimension of production complexity. Figure 13.4 illustrates a 'product structure' which, when recorded in list form rather than the hierarchical form shown, constitutes a bill of materials for the product the relationships between the items are then indicated in each item's record. The product structure displays the relationships between the items that make up the product. By convention, level 0 in the figure is the completed product. At level 1, it can be seen that B and C are the major components of A and that A consists of one each of B and C (in parentheses). In turn, component B consists of D, E (four units), and F (two units), which may be parts, components, raw materials, or a combination, and C consists of G after processing. G, in turn, is composed of E (two units) and H. Note that item E is used in both components B and C.

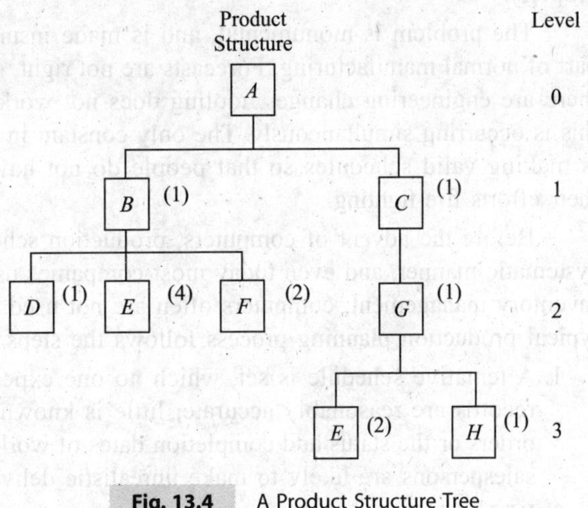

Fig. 13.4 A Product Structure Tree

Where the product structure is complex, production activities are correspondingly complex. An automobile or an airplane, for example, may have 10,000 or more parts in its product structure, resulting in complex production activities and complex information needs.

Another dimension of production complexity is the dynamics of the environment. A stable environment means that, all else being equal, the production activities are less complex and the production information systems can be correspondingly less sophisticated. A roller-coaster market in which customer demand fluctuates rapidly across a broad range means that production activities are complicated by frequent speedups and slowdowns. Rapid technological changes in the industry, such as in the electronics industry, require frequent engineering changes, which can cause continuous chaos in production activities. Dynamic environments greatly increase the amount of information required for production activities.

Large-volume production, especially where many different products are involved, also causes complexity. Thousands of American companies produce hundreds of products, and hundreds of companies produce thousands of products. A few companies produce more than 10,000 different products.

A discrete product in many companies encompasses all the above variables; a complex product structures with many part, a dynamic environment and large production volumes, including large numbers of different parts. In these companies the production information needs are massive, and the information needs are complex.

13.5.1 Present Status of Production Operation

The production problems in a complex situation may appear to be almost insurmountable. Because of the complexity, it has not always been possible to fully understand what needs to be accomplished in terms of organizing production. Production personnel also have not been provided the information tools needed for either production planning or actual production and its control. As a result, production activities have been fragmented, and production Information systems have been partial, inaccurate, and not timely in providing needed information. Additionally, information flows have not been integrated.

A typical company has hundreds or thousands of components to be scheduled. Many components go together to make assemblies. They are made from raw materials and often put into finished goods. There are branch warehouses in many companies that have to be scheduled properly.

The problem is monumental, and is made insurmountable by the constant change that is part of normal manufacturing. Forecasts are not right, machines break down, vendors deliver late, there are engineering changes, tooling does not work, new products are introduced, and all of this is occurring simultaneously. The only constant in manufacturing is change, and the problem is making valid schedules so that people do not have to work to shortage lists and dissipate their efforts fire-fighting.

Before the advent of computers, production scheduling usually was not done in a formal, systematic manner, and even today most companies use computers primarily for better materials inventory management; computers often are not used effectively for production scheduling. The typical production planning process follows the steps outlined below:

1. A tentative schedule is set, which no one expects will be maintained. Even if inventory records are reasonably accurate, little is known about the status of outstanding purchase orders or the status and completion dates of work in process. Lacking accurate information, salespersons are likely to make unrealistic delivery-date promises to customers.
2. With a wide range of uncertainty about current production activities, materials are ordered, but the quantities ordered may be too little or too great, and their arrival time often does not coincide with the date that production is to begin.
3. Inaccurate information about production status, unrealistic schedules, and frequent inventory shortages during production causes chaos. This chaos results in an inability to meet production schedules and customer delivery dates, constant delays in production while awaiting materials, and frequent rescheduling of batches, with the consequences of more machine setup time

and cost and more idle personnel and equipment. This all means that production resources are used less efficiently and that production costs are higher than necessary.

Production departments attempt to control this chaos with two major forms of 'expediting.' The first continuously reallocates resources to try to keep critical jobs, on or close to, schedule. This is usually done by the production supervisor. The second uses 'expediters' to speed up receipt of materials that are not on hand but are critical to the production processes. These expediters may be the supervisor, other employees, or specially hired expediters.

Materials expediting usually begins with a manual analysis of production materials requirements for a product batch already in or about to enter the manufacturing process. Usually all needed materials that are in inventory have already been requisitional for the job in order to permit an accurate assessment of what additional materials are needed. A 'shortage list' is developed that shows materials that are in short supply, and expediters are assigned to secure these materials from whatever source possible.

Materials expediting may consist of, for example, pleading with the vendor to ship materials earlier than planned (perhaps at a premium price or with 'special handling' costs), asking that the materials be shipped by a faster (and more costly) form of transportation such as by air express, or begging, borrowing, or (literally) stealing materials from another department or even another company. Large manufacturing companies may employ hundreds of expediters. It has been seen that 60 per cent of the average production supervisor's time is spent expediting because of inadequate production scheduling.

13.5.2 Production Processes and Information Needs

To understand the information needs of production processes and the nature of the information systems that can fulfill those needs, it is necessary to understand the production planning, production scheduling, and resource procurement and assignment processes. Figure 13.5 illustrates the general nature of the production-related activities and the major information systems of a production activity. The production processes and the associated information systems are shown within the dashed lines in the Fig. 13.5. The leftmost part of the Fig. 13.5 illustrates the interaction of the marketing, cash planning, and personnel information systems with production activities.

The cost/responsibility accounting information system at the top right-hand comer of Fig. 13.5 is a combined production and accounting information system, as illustrated, which provides information for operations and management control by managers in manufacturing. This system also provides product cost information that is used to establish the value of inventories and the cost of sales for financial reporting purposes.

In many companies, particularly smaller ones, production is initiated in response to actual orders received. However, in Fig. 13.5, production is shown to be initiated by a sales forecast, long-range planning information, and short-range planning information that is used for production planning. The resulting plan is developed by the organization's senior managers, including the more senior production managers, and is an aggregate plan that contains no details but establishes rough quantities of each product type to be produced and a general framework for the near- and long-term future production activities. The decisions reached are communicated to the personnel who prepare the master production schedule; the managers involved in this process are likely to be a mix of administrative staff personnel and experienced middle- and senior-level production managers. This group also needs information about current inventory levels of all finished products; if inventory levels of a product are high enough, that product may not need to be produced within the time period under consideration. Production scheduling also utilizes information from the personnel information system about the skills of available employees so that personnel can be assigned to production tasks for which they are qualified.

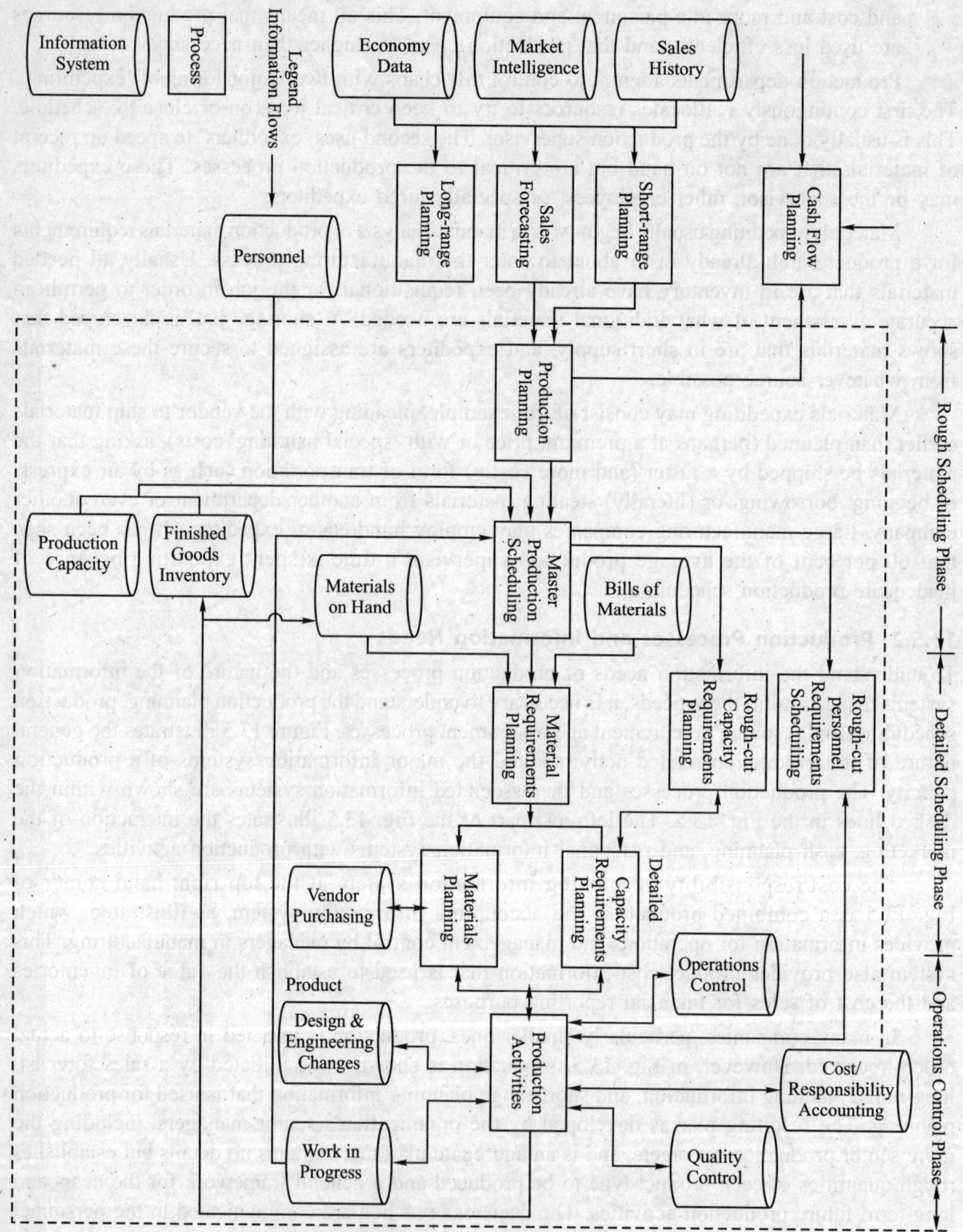

Fig. 13.5 The production process and information systems

Part of production planning is production capacity analysis or capacity planning. Capacity planning establishes the mix and quantities of personnel, machines, and facility resources that will be required to produce a particular batch, and it adjusts the capacity of the production department to those requirements. The information used for this purpose is found in the production capacity file of Fig. 13.5. Production capacity analyses involve balancing production activities with the physical space available, balancing machine utilization by minimizing the amount of machine idle time and by reconcilling conflicting simultaneous needs for the same machinery, and minimizing the total amount of machine setup time when different products are started into production. The production capacity file contains a variety of information relating to these matters; for example, the file may contain setup times for a machine when it is reconfigured from a particular configuration for one product to another configuration for another product, and it may contain machine speeds for each of a variety of tasks. With this information, schedulers can attempt to establish a production schedule that maximizes the usage of available equipment and personnel.

Information provided by master production scheduling is used for four-major purposes, as indicated by the four arrows leaving the master production scheduling process box in Fig. 13.5. First, an overall production schedule is provided for material requirements planning. Also, this schedule is 'costed out' to gain a rough idea of the cash flows that will be required by the production processes during the following periods; this information is forwarded to the treasury department for cash planning. The master production schedule is also used as the basis for determining approximately how much capacity will be needed in various work centers to provide a rough-cut capacity requirements plan and for determining the types of personnel skills that will be needed to establish a rough-cut personnel requirements schedule.

The rough scheduling phase shown at the top of Fig. 13.5 is now completed. For the next process, information about the bill of materials for each product is combined with this master scheduling information for detailed material requirements planning. Each bill of materials contains a detailed listing of the types and quantities of materials, parts, and components required for the manufacture of one unit of the product.

The material requirements for production of a product batch can then be determined automatically from the bill of materials by multiplying the number of products in a batch by the number of each of the line items of the bill of materials that are required for the manufacture of one unit of the product. This step is often referred to as 'exploding the bill of materials.' The bill of materials must be continuously revised to reflect engineering changes that affect the specifications of the product.

Comparing the total requirements for each item with information from the materials-on-hand file, in terms of the quantity on hand of each type of raw material, part, or component, establishes the quantities of each that must be acquired. These can be acquired by purchase (the materials purchasing process) or by production (production activity planning). This step also establishes when each item (material, part, or component) must be ordered or fabricated to be available in time for production to start according to schedule.

The detailed capacity planning process establishes the work load by personnel skill type, machine type, and types of other detailed resources needed for production activities. In effect, this activity assigns resources to workstations. Information from the rough-cut capacity requirements planning processes is used for this activity.

The detailed scheduling and capacity planning activities are now completed in preparation for actual production activities within the operations control phase shown at the top of Fig. 13.5. Production activities require information for physical control over operations, such as production rates and detailed instructions concerning production-step sequences and manufacturing techniques. This information is provided by the operations control information system shown in Fig. 13.5.

A critical aspect of operations control is ensuring that production deadlines will be met. The operations control information system contains information that indicates the quantity of products that should be completed by certain times. Using this information, production personnel can determine when production is behind schedule and can take remedial actions to adjust capacity or estimated completion times. This information also enables the production department to answer customers' inquiries about the progress of their orders.

The work-in-process information system shown in Fig. 13.5 receives information about resources committed to the production process. It contains an open order record for each product that is in production or is on order through purchasing. Each record contains materials requisitions and other related records. Information from this information system is used for the next cycle of master production scheduling as well as for operation control.

In some organizations, shopworkers input data directly into a shop data collection system through terminals, at their workstations. Typically, the worker inserts an employee identification card into the terminal and keys in the batch production number and the number of the task being worked on. The terminal reads the employee number from the identification card and records the start time. A similar process takes place when the employee completes the task. The operations control and work-in-process files may be combined into one information system.

Quality control information must also be gathered from the production processes to monitor the extent to which product quality indicators stay within established tolerances. Quality control checks are built into the production process at each key step in production. The quality control information system contains the product quality specifications and standards and tracks the history of conformance to these standards by, for example, gathering information about scrap levels. This information system also provides information to the purchasing function about defective materials received from vendors so that this can be considered in vendor selection.

The production design and engineering change information system records the original design specifications and production tolerances established for the product and updates this information systematically for what may be dozens or hundreds of engineering changes made to product. These changes must be fed into the flow of production in process, and they may be made to improve the performance of products, reduce their production costs, or increase product safety. Additionally, engineering changes often result from a particular customer's request that the product be altered in a certain manner. This information system is shown in Fig. 13.5.

The shared accounting and production information systems of cost and responsibility accounting shown in Fig. 13.5 provide information about production cost standards for labor and materials, gather information about labor and materials costs of the production batch, and supply cost variances to production managers for cost control. This information permits both determining product costs and assigning cost and quantity variances to the managers who are responsible for them.

At the conclusion of the production process, the finished products and finished parts are placed in physical inventory. At this time, the finished goods inventory and the materials-on-hand (for finished parts) records are updated, as indicated in Fig. 13.5.

An analysis of Fig. 13.5 indicates that even in this greatly simplified schematic, the production information flows are complex. When the complicating factors of perhaps hundreds of products with thousands of different materials required at multiple production and inventory sites are also considered, the information flows become compounded several fold. In so complicated an environment, accurate sales forecasts, accurate materials and finished goods inventories, and accurate purchasing records are essential, but difficult, to achieve. For example, if the finished goods inventory or the materials inventory records for one product are in error, purchase orders may be wrong, and a substantial materials inventory shortage may result. This shortage may cause havoc in production activities or necessitate last-minute juggling of production schedules, either of which causes inefficiencies in the production processes.

With a large number of files to maintain, data processing may be unable to complete all processing on time. This delayed processing may be the cause of a large proportion of the inaccuracies in the data files. Integrating data files so that data is automatically passed from one information system to another as needed enables the files to be processed with less manual intervention and keeps them more up to date. This greatly decreases the differences between the actual status and the recorded status of production activities.

13.5.3 Materials Requirements Planning

How can the production activities and information systems be organized in complex manufacturing environments to avoid costly production inefficiencies? Before the advent of computers, it was impossible to avoid these inefficiencies because manual systems could not process information fast enough. Even during the first 20 years of the computers age, computer systems remained only partially effective in this area.

It is eye-opening to realize that a major cause of production inefficiency is a lack of integrated production planning, production scheduling, and production control information systems. One approach to improved production efficiency is materials requirements planning (MRP), which is a set of computer software programs. MRP integrates several production-related information systems so that MRP programs can access and extract data from these systems to accomplish production scheduling automatically. MRP's purpose is to greatly improve both inventory management and production scheduling.

Several of the MRP systems distributed by a variety of computer program vendors integrate several of the information systems shown in Fig. 13.5 and also provide an automated inventory and production scheduling system that gives accurate and up-to-date information for production management purposes. The scope of many MRP systems is shown in Fig. 13.6. The computer file of planned transfers, distribution requirements, etc., indicates the use by the MRP programs of information about the possible need to transfer completed parts or components to other production locations for further production activity and about the logistic arrangements of distribution of finished goods to the wholesale or other market.

MRP systems probably introduce as much change to an organization as any other major type of systems implementation, and perhaps more. A primary reason for the partial success or outright failure of many MRP systems is that top management does not invest the time necessary to learn the new MRP concepts thoroughly—top-level managers do not perceive the entire manufacturing process as an information system that requires their total commitment for successful implementation. Because MRP is also a system of management, its implementation is not primarily a data processing task; however, lacking a complete understanding of MRP, management is likely to make the error of assigning the task to the data processing department.

To achieve the efficiencies of which they are capable, MRP systems require high levels of discipline—such as not requisitioning materials long before they are needed, proper scrap reporting, and using well-defined procedures for implementing and recording engineering changes promptly. Accurate input data also is absolutely necessary; for example inventory quantity data must be accurate, and interplant transfers must be recorded accurately and promptly.

Production personnel typically do not fully understand computer systems or the need for discipline and for timely and accurate information in computer files. Also, like other personnel, production personnel resist change in general, and sometimes they resist computer systems in particular. Accordingly, the majority of implemented MRP systems have not lived up to expectations. Increasingly, however, an understanding of computer systems and the personal discipline required for successful MRP systems are arriving on the shop floor. Additionally, newer versions of MRP possess enhanced error-detection and error-tracing routines. Because of these changes, more and more MRP systems are now becoming successful.

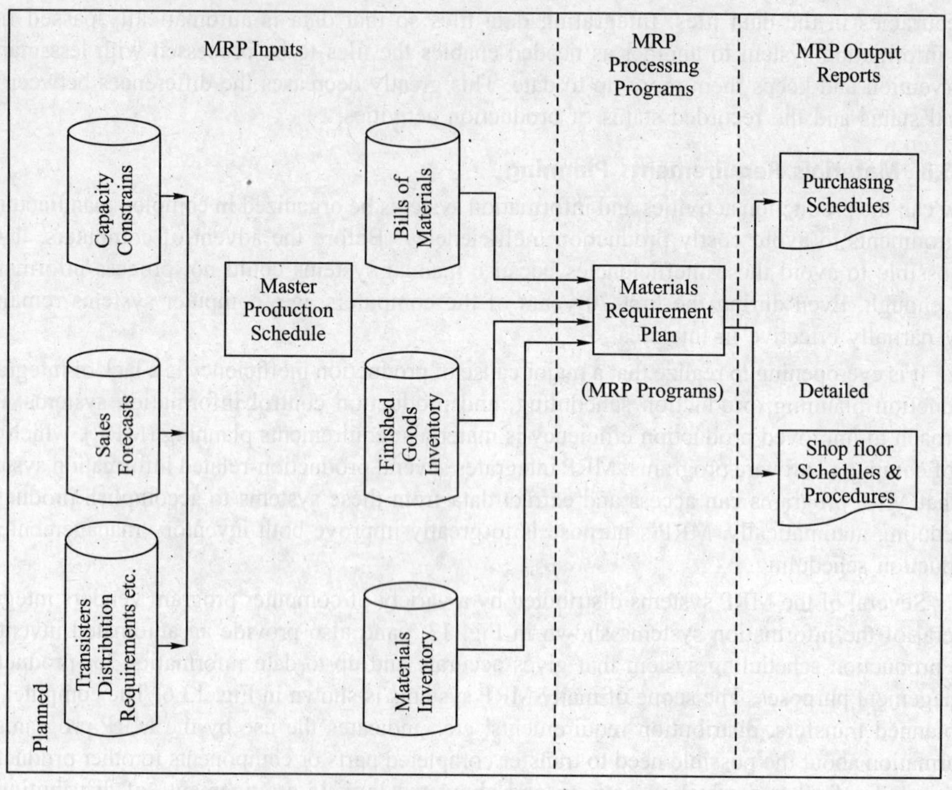

Fig. 13.6 An MRP system

MRP activity shown in Fig. 13.6 usually begins with the development of a master production schedule by family of products. The individual product members of each product line are then assigned quantities and time periods for production. This master production schedule, the bills of materials, and data about inventory levels serve as input to the MRP programs.

MRP programs first determine the materials needs of the individual products by 'exploding' each bill of materials (which describes each product in terms of its individual item components) and by multiplying the quantity of the product scheduled for production by the materials needs per unit of the product. The programs then combine the needs of all products for each type of material and determine net materials requirements by taking into account existing uncommitted materials inventory and inventory due to be received prior to production.

MRP programs prepare two types of reports. The first type, purchase order recommendations, utilizes economic order quantity (EOQ) formulas and considers quantity discount information. Managers may revise the recommendation in light of information known to them which is not considered within the EOQ formula. MRP programs assign a release date to each purchase order so that the materials will be received on time, but not so early as to cause a costly inventory buildup. An effective MRP system can be working several weeks ahead to help prevent shortages of materials. The second type of report, a shop floor schedule, or 'dispatch list', is prepared for each production department. This schedule provides day-to-day plan for shop floor activities and serves as a standard against which to evaluate each department's production activity.

MRP is also utilized when a product is manufactured only after receipt of a customer order. An order and its delivery date can be entered into the MRP system when received, and the bills of materials for the products ordered are exploded so that a materials-needed list is developed automatically. The MRP system then compares these needs with inventory records and creates a purchase order for materials not available from inventory. The MRP program determines what and how many components and products must be produced and when production must be started so that the delivery date can be met.

The benefits of a successful MRP system include:

1. Significantly decreased inventory levels (typically a 20 to 40 per cent reduction) and corresponding decreases in inventory carrying costs.
2. Fewer stock shortages, which cause production interruptions and time-consuming schedule Juggling by managers.
3. Less expediting by a factor of several times, with savings of labor, material costs, and premium transportation charges.
4. Increased effectiveness of production supervisors. Less production chaos and decreased expediting free them to devote more attention to the tasks in their job description, such as personnel relations and operations control.
5. Better customer service—an increased ability to meet delivery schedules and to set delivery dates earlier and more reliably.
6. Greater responsiveness to change. MRP gives manufacturing a better feel for the effects of economic swings, and changes in product demand can be translated into schedule changes quickly.
7. Closer coordination of the marketing, engineering, and finance activities with the manufacturing activities.

However, even as companies are embracing MRP, a new and more comprehensive concept is emerging. Manufacturing resources planning, or MRP-II, is a follow-on and broader information system that not only encompasses inventory management and production scheduling but also includes and integrates production planning and financial planning processes. MRP-II views all manufacturing-related activities as an interactive information network; thus factory automation,' production scheduling, and materials inventory management information systems are integrated. So far, only a few companies have had extensive experience with MRP-II, but for them the benefits appear to exceed those provided by MRP.

13.6 COMPUTER APPLICATIONS IN WAREHOUSING

Around 1960, computers churned out reams of order and shipping papers. In the 1970s, minicomputers controlled automated high-rise storage retrieval systems and high capacity stock-picking machines. As we entered the 1980s, another step in the evolutionary process emerged—computer assisted warehousing systems (CAWS). CAWS concept involves computers that keep track of stock that is received, stored, assembled, sorted, staged, and shipped. The systems provide timely and accurate updating of inventory records, stock locations and quantities, and direct workers' activities to improve productivity and accuracy.

Many variations of the basic CAWS concept are possible. The methods have been applied to conventional fork lift truck operations, mobile equipment from pick vehicles to fixed-path stackers, and to piece-by-piece sorting and picking activities.

First, let us look at a conventional mobile vehicle operation. Communication may originate directly on-line from a central mainframe or host computer, that serves as the central processing unit (CPU). Signals are sent over a line to warehouse video display units and to printers, which produce hard copy printout sheets for signout to the warehouse workers.

More advanced systems eliminate the printout papers and signout sheets. Instead, vehicle operators refer to instructions that appear on special visual terminal units (VTUs) mounted on their vehicles. The display device may be either a light emitting diode (LED), liquid crystal display (LCD), a small cathode ray video tube (CRT), a gas discharge tube, or a small tape printer.

Communication between the central computer and vehicle terminals can be real time or batch method. One system transmits radio signals from computer to vehicle terminals via special FM transceivers. The vehicle terminal includes a transceiver-antenna, LED display and tape printer. The system provides a realtime link with strong discrete signals on each channel to as many as ten mobile units.

A firm specialising in automated warehousing applications offer a data station option. Here, vehicle terminals are microcomputers with logic and memory faculties. Periodically, terminals are plugged into a data station to update the central computer on completed assignments and to receive up to an hour or more of new assignments. The data exchange is made in 30 seconds, with placement of data stations at convenient points in the warehouse minimising the total time required for the process.

Although the on-line (realtime) communication between the central computer and the vehicle operator is sacrificed, the frequent data exchange with this kind of batching technique is adequate for most warehouse needs. It avoids the cost of transceivers and potential blind spots that can affect the quality of radio signals.

A specific task in a series of instructions to a lift truck operator may be displayed on the VTU as follows:

Location .... aisle 5, slot 10,

Pick .... 4 cases #0478

Item .... 8 ounces Premium

After completing the pick, the operator pushes a button on the terminal that indicates the task is done. The computer memory (or microcomputer memory if data-station method is used) is instantly adjusted and the next assignment appears on the display. The process continues until an order is filled or a pallet load assembled. The operator may use the on-vehicle keyboard to key in changes or exceptions or ask for instruction on disposition of the load.

For an inbound product, the computer tells the operator where to take the load and where to store it. Then, on receiving the operator's signal that the job is completed the computer locks it into the memory bank and transmits further instructions.

Because of the high cost of custom designed systems, a trend is developing for use of stock software modules designed for routine functions. Costs can be minimised by selecting a series of these off-the-shelf modules.

13.6.1 Stock Picking Possibilities

Computers can also be used in a warehouse or distribution centre to assist stock pickers along case- or piece-pick lines. Picture a long aisle with racks containing bins of hundreds of items on either side. A conveyor belt runs down the aisle centre.

A central computer reads the complete order, then sends signals over lines to light display panels located at each bin. The lighted displays immediately identify all the bins containing line items called for on the order. Lighted digits on the display tell the workers the number of pieces to pick at each bin.

Following each pick, the worker pushes a button located at the display that turns off the light and signals the computer that the pick is completed. When all bin display lights are turned off, the order has been picked, and the computer stock records adjusted.

A marker, usually a plastic box or basket, is then dropped onto the belt behind the final item to separate it from the next order. The bin display lights then come on again to denote the items to pick for the next order.

13.6.2 Caws for Sorting

One of the most labor-intensive warehouse operations is sorting items into separate piles for truck deliveries. The first step under the computer-assisted design was to get all vendors to affix a label to each case that identifies vendor, item and destination with a bar code. Inbound goods are received and transferred onto a conveyor belt. Then, as each case passes a sort station, a stock clerk checks the label and calls out the name of the store where it is to be shipped. The clerk's voice is picked up by a microphone and fed into a computer that translates the pattern of sound waves into a digital code and locks it into the memory system.

Immediately, a laser scanner reads the bar code of the case, activates a labelling device that prints a label with the pertinent information, and affixes it automatically onto the case. At the same time, another printer out on the shipping dock produces a duplicate or control label for final verification that the item is included in the particular store's shipment at the time of loading. As the case moves along the conveyor belt, the computer's memory system traces it and signals a diverter plate to push it off at the proper accumulation bin on the truck dock. Voice entry systems of this kind are particularly effective for operations in which the employee's hands and eyes are busy, and time does not permit shuffling papers or sending keyboard messages.

The ultimate in human-oriented computer technology, voice entry/voice response, has also found its way into warehousing and shipping operations. A human voice is used to encode anywhere from a few to several hundred isolated words into the computer file. The encoded words, upon command of a microprocessor chip, are reproduced by voice synthesis to carry on a 'conversation' with someone using a microphone at the terminal or calling in from a remote point by telephone.

Warehousing and shipping applications to date have been related mostly to verification of stock availability and order entry. As en example, a salesperson at a buyer's office may wish to determine the stock position of a certain item. After telephoning the central computer number, a computer-synthesized voice asks for the salesperson's identity. The response may be in two ways, depending on the system.

One way is to input a digital code directly, using telephone touch-tone buttons. The other is to speak single words, slowly and distinctly, so the computer can recognise and convert sound patterns into digital codes for the memory system.

The computer voice may then ask a series of questions in sequence such as: Item you want? Color Size? Quantity? etc. The salesperson responds to each question vocally or by touchtone buttons. The 'conversation' may lead to an order entry which includes a designated shipping date.

13.6.3 Portable Terminals

Also growing in use are the small microcomputer-based remote data entry terminals. The hand-held units, which look a lot like electronic hand calculators, have information storage capacity to 64 KB (64,000 bytes or characters) and more.

Commonly used with hand wand scanners to read bar codes for fast input of stock records, most of the devices are batch oriented. Interface to main computers is accomplished via telephone acoustical couplings or direct plug-in at the computer terminal.

The benefits that justify purchase and maintenance of computer-assisted warehousing systems are usually related to productivity improvements and better utilisation of equipment. However, stock control alone may justify systems for some operations, particularly where a large number of stock keeping units (SKUs) or high value items are involved.

The elimination of paper handling by warehouse workers has a notable impact on productivity, especially in piece-picking operations. By making it easier to locate bins and items in stock, the computer-assisted systems can double or triple productivity. Computer-assisted sorting not only reduces the number of employees required, but usually makes possible the handling of peak-hour volumes with the same crew.

Innovative computer-based applications will undoubtedly continue to appear as the concept becomes better known to distribution centre managers. Also, as new material handling and warehousing technology develop, so too will computer adaptations.

For example, an increasing number of high-rack installations are indicated for the future. With the addition of vehicle terminals, operators of the costly high-lift vehicles can be relieved of paper shuffling and checking, and hunting for product locations. Signals between computer and vehicle terminal can be sent over laser beams for fixed-path high-lift trucks.

The new material handling systems that bring the product to the worker, such as rotating carousels and ferris wheel-like paternosters, will also benefit. At the touch of a button, a microcomputer will select the item, rotate it to the worker via the shortest route, and display the quantity of items to pick.

Despite the convincing arguments for bringing computer control onto the warehouse floor, many managers have approached the concept with caution. Management is concerned about how workers will react to a little box intended to get them to work harder. System reliability is also a concern. Adequate provision for backup or contingency planning in event of computer downtime should be included in any system. The costs and benefits of realtime versus batching techniques also demand consideration, particularly in relation to mobile vehicle terminal use. Determining factors are the size of warehouse, the number of SKUs, the distances vehicle operators must travel to signout stations, and the value placed on instant versus periodic update of the central computer files.

REVIEW QUESTIONS

Multiple Choice Questions

1. Which of the following is/are not available currently?
   (*a*) electronic funds transfer system
   (*b*) electronic newspaper
   (*c*) home electronic shopping system
   (*d*) two-way cable system
   (*e*) all of the above are available
2. The advent of personal computers:
   (*a*) could cause us to lose some of our basic skills
   (*b*) will make our lives more productive
   (*c*) ill take way some of the boring tasks that we have to perform
   (*d*) two of the above
   (*e*) all three of the above
3. Which of the following is most responsible for the inability of auditors to uncover computer crimes?
   (*a*) the auditor's lack of knowledge in computer technology
   (*b*) the prohibitively expensive audit procedures needed to detect computer frauds
   (*c*) the relatively small average take of computer frauds
   (*d*) the client's concern that the public will learn of the crime
4. Which of the following is/are true of an artificial intelligence system?
   (*a*) it is a computer application where the computer makes decisions or judgements
   (*b*) it is infallible since it is computer-based
   (*c*) ultimately, it is expected to replace professionals such as doctors

(*d*) two of the above
(*e*) all three of the above

5. Which of the following is most likely to occur in the near future?
(*a*) most workers will choose working at home, so the traditional workplace will disappear.
(*b*) the political issue of establishing an information-assistance program will be raised.
(*c*) the presidential election will be done by pushing buttons at home.
(*d*) automation will reduce job opportunities, thus resulting in a lower standard of living.
(*e*) all of the above.

6. Which of the following is/are true concerning information-system careers?
(*a*) the number of information-system specialists recruited is expected to be greater than any other profession in the 1990s
(*b*) the primary reason for this increase is the declining cost of hardware
(*c*) an information-system career is one of the few areas that is recession proof
(*d*) two of the above
(*e*) all three of the above

7. In which area are job openings expected to decline in the future?
(*a*) computer operator (*b*) data-entry operator
(*c*) system programmer (*d*) application programmer
(*e*) none of the above

8. Which of the following is/are true of system analysts?
(*a*) they are heavily involved with the system-development life cycle
(*b*) their responsibility is to analyze and design system software
(*c*) they may be looked upon as an inter-mediary between users and programmers.
(*d*) two of the above
(*e*) all three of the above

9. A person who has a high-school diploma would be least likely to obtain which of the following Jobs?
(*a*) librarian (*b*) computer operator (*c*) data-entry operator (*d*) programmer

10. The major responsibilities of the data-base administrator are all of the following except:
(*a*) analyzing application systems (*b*) designing data bases
(*c*) developing data dictionaries (*d*) advising programmers
(*e*) all of the above are the responsibilities of the DBA

11. Which of the following abilities is/are required for both the system programmer and the EDP auditor?
(*a*) knowledge in computer science (*b*) knowledge in accounting applications
(*c*) knowledge in information systems (*d*) two of the above
(*e*) all three of the above

12. If you are an information-system manager, which organization is most appropriate for your interest?
(*a*) ACM (*b*) SIM (*c*) IEEE (*d*) ASA
(*e*) all of the above

13. Individuals who intend to pursue a career as an information-system manager should have:
(*a*) technical expertise in information systems (*b*) ability to communicate in written from
(*c*) human-relations skills (*d*) two of the above
(*e*) all three of the above

14. Which of the following is not true of the EDP Auditors' Foundation?
(*a*) It is a professional association of those auditors who specialize in EDP auditing
(*b*) It publishes a journal, the EDP Auditor

(*c*) It sponsors the CISA examination
(*d*) It is a member of the AFIPS
(*e*) All of the above are true

15. Which of the following is/are true of the EDP auditors?
(*a*) they should have computer expertise
(*b*) they will be replaced by traditional auditors in the near future
(*c*) currently, there is a very high demand for them, particularly from firms that use Personal computers
(*d*) two of the above
(*e*) all three of the above
(f) none of the above

16. Logical models form the basis for computing systems that generate information useful in dealing with:
(*a*) uncertain situations (*b*) complex situations
(*c*) dynamic situations (*d*) all of the above
(*e*) none of the above

17. Computing systems designed to supply supervisory information include:
(*a*) payroll systems (*b*) invoicing systems
(*c*) process control systems (*d*) all of the above
(*e*) none of the above

18. Computing systems most often facilitate planning because they:
(*a*) enable an appropriate data processing system to provide answers quickly
(*b*) make it possible to solve complex problems
(*c*) make it possible to take into account many possibilities in an uncertain situation
(*d*) all of the above
(*e*) none of the above

19. Assembly languages are most commonly used to write computing systems that provide:
(*a*) supervisory information (*b*) planning information
(*c*) priority setting information (*d*) all of the above
(*e*) none of the above

20. Corporate modelling languages often do provide for:
(*a*) model definition (*b*) report specification (*c*) DML commands (*d*) editing
(*e*) command files

21. The teleprocessing system appropriate for a probability encoding system is:
(*a*) an on-line batch system (*b*) an interactive time-sharing system
(*c*) a large-scale batch system (*d*) any of the above
(*e*) none of the above

22. An excellent liner programming software package for solving large-scale problems is:
(*a*) MIDAS-2 (*b*) OPHELIE II (*c*) PDQ/LP (*d*) all of the above
(*e*) none of the above

23. The type of information most restricted by a poor interface between generalized data base management systems and special computing system languages is:
(*a*) supervisory (*b*) planning (*c*) priority setting (*d*) none of the above

24. The selection of the solution technique to be implemented by a computing system should be made by:
(*a*) systems analysts (*b*) an operations research expert
(*c*) a computer programmer (*d*) a computing system user
(*e*) none of the above

25. Personnel Administration Data Systems, personnel planning data systems and the payroll system all:
(*a*) update the accounts payable file
(*b*) access the inventory file
(*c*) calculate payroll deductions
(*d*) all of the above
(*e*) none of the above.

ANSWERS

Multiple Choice Questions

1. (*b*)	**2.** (*e*)	**3.** (*b*)	**4.** (*a*)	**5.** (*b*)	**6.** (*d*)	**7.** (*b*)	**8.** (*d*)
9. (*d*)	**10.** (*a*)	**11.** (*a*)	**12.** (*b*)	**13.** (*e*)	**14.** (*d*)	**15.** (*a*)	**16.** (*d*)
17. (*c*)	**18.** (*b*)	**19.** (*a*)	**20.** (*a*)	**21.** (*b*)	**22.** (*b*)	**23.** (*b*)	**24.** (*d*)
25. (*e*)							

SYSTEM ANALYSIS AND DESIGN

14.1 INTRODUCTION

Before one can study the techniques a systems analyst must understand and apply, one must appreciate the system analyst's function in the wider context of the employing organization. Regardless of what purpose the organization serves, a systems analyst must have certain fundamental personal qualities to succeed.

An analyst must be able to discover the fundamental logic of a system, produce sound plans and appreciate the effects of new facts in planning. The analyst must be perceptive, but must not jump to quick conclusions, be persistent to overcome difficulties and obstacles, and maintain a planned course of action in spite of setbacks.

Suitable candidates for systems analysis trainee positions often come from a background of analytical work in the commercial area or computer-oriented work involving programming. Since the systems analyst will need both types of experience, the first step in training must be to develop the area of experience that the trainee lacks. Some trainees must develop communication skills, both oral and written; others must be trained in application areas. The level of experience to be developed may vary from a restricted and detailed knowledge of a specific area such as steel production to an overall understanding of a broad area such as management information systems.

The analyst must also be trained in the use of such relevant hardware as computers and peripheral equipment and must know the types of equipment best suited to the solution parameters, overall methods of computer application strategy, and detailed computer systems techniques. Training in this area must be continuous, because new equipment and techniques arise constantly.

Finally, the analyst must be trained in an appreciation of software and know which packages are currently available, so as to decide which are suitable for the system's needs. There is also a need to understand the principles of programming. It is pointless to specify a system that cannot be programmed with currently available software.

When the systems analyst is to start work on a particular project, an informed awareness of the employer's organization is necessary. This will help during employee interviews and will also assist in placing details of the current system in perspective. Often insufficient time is devoted to this area of training. As a result, the analyst does not comprehend fully the significance of some matters discovered during the fact-finding phase of the work, and may design the new system with the limitations of the old.

There must also be an understanding of the constitution of the organization. This covers the overall arrangement of its constituent parts, and the strength of its affiliations with other organizations. When the organization involved is diversified across more than one location, the analyst should discover the function of each.

The analyst will benefit from a knowledge of the organization's history. By tracing the major milestones in the evolution of the firm, the type of management decisions that were made in the past can be identified. The management's overall policies should be kept in mind. The company's annual reports, employee handbooks, the trade literature, investment reviews and press clippings should be examined. This background will help the analyst to appreciate the precise divisional structures currently existing at each location.

The analyst will also need to detail the departmental structure of the area in which the study is being carried out. If there is a company organization chart, the analyst should ascertain that it reflects current conditions and become acquainted with it. If no chart exists, then one should be prepared. In any case, some clear distinction should be drawn between those operations that involve line management and those that are staff functions.

Conventional organization charts, which show a number of branches from a chief executive or board of directors at the top, represent the pyramid of control found in most organizations. The analyst should superimpose on this structure another one that describes the true lines of communication. This structure may not follow the strict divisional and departmental boundaries implied by the original chart, but it will show the analyst how the proposals introduced in one area may affect the work in others. Probably much of the material mentioned above is recorded in one form or another, and will have to be edited and distilled to obtain a coherent picture of the organization. However, there will probably not be any recorded information about the environment in which the organization operates. This information is needed because the firm itself has little direct influence on its environment, which is constantly changing.

14.2 THE SYSTEM DEVELOPMENT LIFE CYCLE

A **system** is the combination of people, devices, and methods interrelated in working towards a common goal. The focus here is on business systems that include computers to reach the common goal. Because data are being converted into information, these systems are called **information systems**.

An information system is a computer-based business system that provides the data-processing capabilities and information that an organisation need to be informed about various aspects of its operations. Because information is a valuable asset to any business or organization, it must be carefully acquired and organised into a system that is useful.

For a valued useful system, it must:

1. provide accurate information;
2. provide timely information; and
3. be capable of communicating that information to the people in the company who need it.

An organisation can have one or more information systems in operation. Among other tasks, businesses use information systems for sales and order processing, administrative record keeping, and accounting and payroll applications. An insurance company, for example, might use an information system to manage all the data it needs to issue policies and process claims. An oil company might use one information system to process and manage data about oil exploration, another system for refinery management, and yet another for customer accounts.

The **system life cycle** is the life span of an information system from its inception until it is removed or redesigned. It consists of five major stages (Fig. 14.1) which are discussed in more detail throughout the chapter.

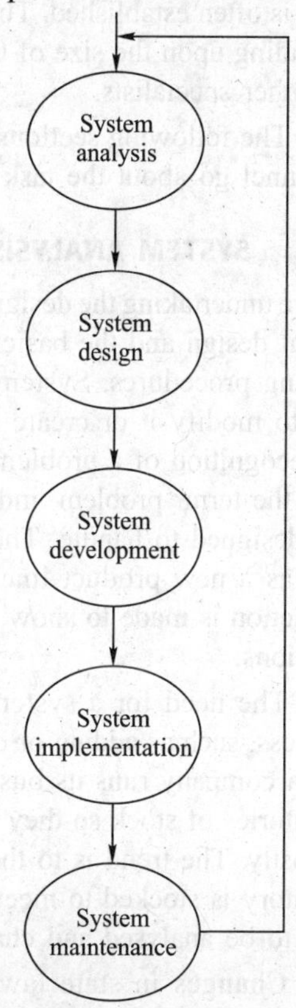

Fig. 14.1 The system life cycle

1. **System analysis**—an evaluation of the current system in response to a problem or new opportunity to determine if the current system should be modified or a new system developed
2. **System design**—a physical design of a proposed system is developed
3. **System development**—creating the new information system from the physical design; the programs of the new or modified system are written
4. **System implementation**—the organisation installs and begins to use a new system.
5. **System maintenance**—the system is continually monitored and adjusted as needed until it is time for a total re-evaluation

Developing an information system throughout the system life cycle involves continual and clear communication among user and system personnel—the people responsible for designing and implementing the information system.

The **user** is the person or persons who will use the information system once it's been installed. For example, users include the operators who run the computers and managers who require information from the system. System personnel include system analysts, system designers, and programmers. A **system analyst** is the person who works with users to determine their information needs. A **system designer** is the specialist who designs a system to fulfill the users' information needs. A **programmer** is the person who codes the instructions that solve a problem in a programming language so that they can be used by the computer. In large organizations, these positions are usually separate and distinct jobs; however, in some companies, particularly the small ones, one person may do all or several parts of these tasks.

To help make the communication process easier and more efficient, a **project management team** is often established. The project management team usually consists of a project manager and, depending upon the size of the project, various number of users, system personnel, programmers, and other specialists.

The following sections explain each stage of the system life cycle and describe how system personnel go about the task of analysing and solving a problem.

14.3 SYSTEM ANALYSIS

Before undertaking the design of a new system, the analyst must understand the precise requirements of that design and the basic problem areas that have caused management to be dissatisfied with existing procedures. System analysis is the process of analysing a system and trying to find a way to modify it or create a new system to meet the user's needs. The process is initiated by the recognition of a problem or new opportunity that the current system cannot handle. As used here, the term 'problem' indicates that the current system is not functioning properly for tasks it was designed to handle. The phrase 'new opportunity' indicates that circumstances have arisen, such as a new product line, that the current system was not originally designed to handle. A distinction is made to show that a system analysis is not always initiated in response to negative situations.

The need for a system analysis may be brought about by the routine business of doing business, such as adding or deleting a new product line. It can also occur because of the particular way a company runs its business. For example, for many years manufacturers would build huge inventories of stock so they would never run out of the product; however, this strategy proved to be costly. The trend is to the Just-In-Time (JIT) method of inventory control where just enough inventory is stocked to meet demands. As a business adopts JIT, its old inventory system would need to be analysed and changed to fit the new method.

Changes in state laws or federal regulations also trigger a need for system analysis. Restructuring of tax laws has caused accounting and tax software packages to become outdated.

Changes in environmental laws may cause a manufacturer to revise some operational aspects which may require changes to its information system.

A business customers may also identify a problem area that needs attention. For example, customers constantly complaining about billing errors should alert a business that its billing system needs to be re-evaluated and possibly re-designed.

Technology-related changes, such as redesigning an information system to include newer, more advanced computer systems, are often suggested by the system analyst.

A problem or new opportunity, however, does not always mean the present system must be scrapped. It may mean simply that new features needed or no system currently exists to perform the functions needed by the business.

At this point, the system analyst is not looking for a solution so much as a clear understanding of the problem or new opportunity. After the area of concern has been recognized, the scope and purpose of the problem or new opportunity should be made clear to all involved parties, including management, system personnel, and the users. Once these parties have agreed on the scope and purpose, management must make the decision of whether or not to proceed with a feasibility study. If it is decided to go ahead with the feasibility study, a system analyst is called upon to conduct it.

14.3.1 Data Gathering

To obtain an adequate understanding of the current objectives, existing procedures, and basic problem areas, the analyst must collect data. The methods used for data collection include:

1. Study procedures or operations manuals if there is an existing system—to determine how the existing system, in principle, is to function.
2. Evaluate current forms and forms distribution—to specify what data is required from the system and to whom the forms are distributed.
3. Interview managers and operating staff—If the analyst is sensitive to the needs and fears of the user, this technique can prove to be the most important one in the data collection phase.
4. Observe users as they perform their jobs—to provide some insight into basic problem areas.
5. Prepare, distribute, and evaluate questionnaires—to supplement information if interviews and observations are inadequate or if more data is required.

14.3.2 Business Systems Elements

Analysis of a system is performed according to a set of procedures that is designed to be as scientific and objective as possible. Figure 14.2 illustrates the elements used to analyse a system and how they relate to one another. We discuss each of these in depth. When designing a new system, one must evaluate and redesign these elements.

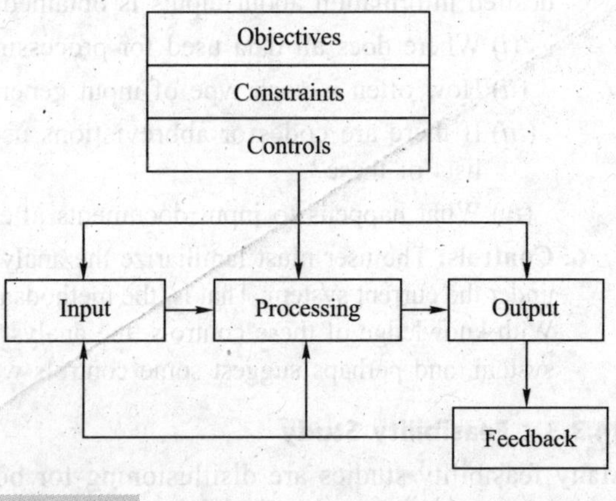

Fig. 14.2 Fundamental structure of a business system

1. **Objectives:** The systems analyst must be aware of exactly what the user requires from a specific system. That is, management's goals or objectives must be fully known and understood. For example, one of a company's objectives for a new design might be

to establish a computerized Accounts Receivable system so that a customer can walk into any branch store and have a clerk immediately determine the customer's balance at that time, based on computer records.

After reviewing the objectives of a current system with the user, the systems analyst may quite possibly recommend a modification to these objectives. The analyst has specialised expertise in data processing. Consequently, he may be aware of computer capabilities that can be utilized to give outstanding performance or to attain broader objectives for some systems. To say to management, 'I can provide you with 96% of what you want for 50% of the cost' is a very persuasive argument.

2. **Constraints:** The analyst *and* the user must both recognize any limitations or constraints that may be imposed when the analyst is designing a computerized system. These are legal constraints, budgetary constraints, and equipment constraints, as discussed below:
   (*i*) Legal: Depending on the specific systems, there are certain legal requirements to which the system must adhere. The user must make the analyst aware of all legal constraints under which the system is to operate.
   (*ii*) Budgetary: Often the management of a company imposes a budgetary constraint on the analyst, limiting the time, and hence money, that can be expended in analyzing and designing a new system.
   (*iii*) Equipment: Computer equipment or hardware devices that are employed within the company represent another type of constraint. Systems Analysts generally attempt to utilize the computer configuration that is currently available at the company. Additional equipment not currently utilized in the company that the analyst considers an asset to the system must be justified from a cost standpoint. In this case, the analyst must perform a **feasibility study** to determine the economic feasibility of acquiring such equipment.
3. **Output:** The analyst must ascertain from the user just exactly what is currently produced as output under the present system. It is the user's job to inform the analyst of all output forms in the new design. The analyst is likely to recommend new or revised reports that can be readily obtained from a computerized system.
4. **Processing:** The analyst must then analyze the processing, or types of operations that are currently performed in order to achieve the desired results. All procedures that are followed and the way in which various computations are made must be understood.
5. **Input:** All input data that serves as the basis for desired outputs must be studied. The analyst will typically seek answers to questions such as the following, to ensure that the desired information about inputs is obtained:
   (*i*) Where does all data used for processing originate?
   (*ii*) How often is each type of input generated?
   (*iii*) If there are codes or abbreviations used for input, does the analyst have complete lists of these?
   (*iv*) What happens to input documents after they have been processed?
6. **Controls:** The user must familiarize the analyst with the ways in which errors are minimized under the current system. That is, the methods used to control or check errors must be specified. With knowledge of these controls, the analyst can then incorporate them in the computerized system, and perhaps suggest some controls with which the user may not be familiar.

14.3.3 Feasibility Study

Many feasibility studies are disillusioning for both users and analysts. First, the study often presupposes that when the feasibility document is being prepared, the analyst is in a position to evaluate solutions. Second, most studies tend to overlook the confusion inherent in system development—the constraints and the assumed attitudes. If the feasibility study is to serve as a decision document, it must answer three key questions:

1. Is the technology available to solve the problem or accommodate the new opportunity?
2. Would the system as proposed be accepted and used by the intended users?
3. Are the benefits of developing the appropriate information system greater than the costs?

The most successful system projects are not necessarily the biggest or most visible in a business but rather those that truly met user expectations. More projects fail because of inflated expectations than for any other reason.

14.3.3.1 Technical Feasibility (Available Technology)

Technical feasibility centers around the existing computer system (hardware, software, etc.) and to what extent it can support the proposed addition. For example, if the current computer is operating at 80 percent capacity—an arbitrary ceiling—then running another application could overload the system or require additional hardware. This involves financial considerations to accommodate technical enhancements. If the budget is a serious constraint, then the project is judged not feasible.

14.3.3.2 Behavioural Feasibility (User Acceptance)

People are inherently resistant to change, and computers have been known to facilitate change. An estimate should be made of how strong a reaction the user staff is likely toward the development of a computerized system. It is common knowledge that computer installations have something to do with turnover, transfers, retraining, and changes in employee job status. Therefore, it is understandable that the introduction of a candidate system requires special effort to educate, sell, and train the staff on new ways of conducting business.

14.3.3.3 Economic Feasibility (Cost/benefit Analysis)

Economic analysis is the most frequently used method for evaluating the effectiveness of a candidate system. More commonly known as cost/benefit analysis, the procedure is to determine the benefits and savings that are expected from a candidate system and compare them with costs. If benefits outweigh costs, then the decision is made to design and implement the system. Otherwise, further justification or alterations in the proposed system will have to be made if it is to have a chance of being approved. This is an ongoing effort that improve in accuracy at each phase of the system life cycle.

14.3.4 Data Analysis and Logical Design Development

After all pertinent data have been gathered by the system analyst, they are analysed and the logical design of the system is developed. A logical design shows the flow of data through a system. There are two general steps in developing the logical design: (*a*) determining the purpose and objectives of an information system; and (*b*) determining the outputs, inputs, and processing requirements of the information system from the user point of view without concern for how the requirements will be physically accomplished. Any anticipated conditions that may cause these to change are also outlined at this time.

14.3.4.1 System Flowchart

A System Flowchart is a diagram that shows a broad overview of the data flow and sequence of operations in a system. This emphasis is placed on input document and output records. Only limited detail is furnished about how a workstation or machine converts input data into the desired output.

System flowcharts use a set of standardized symbols as shown in Figures 14.3 and 14.4.

Preparing flowcharts may help the study team gather data on current operations. Beginning with source-document inputs, each operation step is charted, using the proper symbols. Figure 14.5 is an example of a system flowchart for a Payroll Processing system.

While constructing a logical design, it is usually more productive to first determine what output is needed and then determine the input requirement to produce that output.

The **System analyst** (a person who works with a user to determine his or her data processing needs) determines by working with the users, what output is needed and its format hard copy or soft copy. The users may require output to appear on the display screen or on preprinted forms, such as checks, inventory lists, invoices, or sales receipts. After determining the required output, the system analyst determines what input is required to produce it and the source of that data.

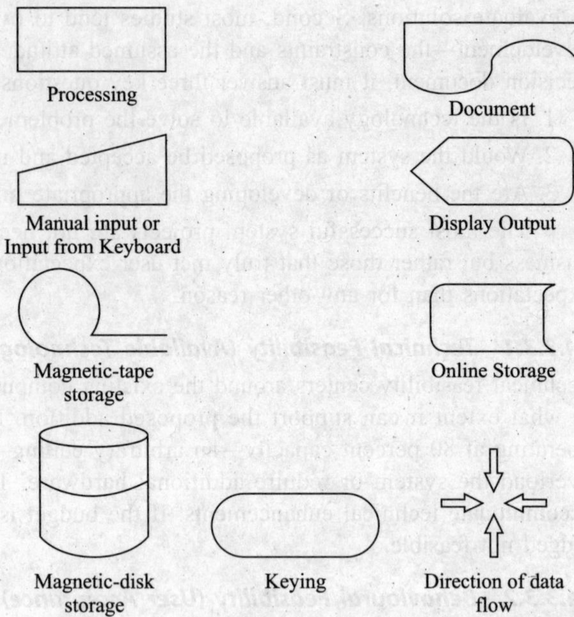

Fig. 14.3 Some commonly used System Flowchart Symbols

Symbol	Meaning
Manual operation	Any off-line process geared to the speed of a human being is represented by this symbol.
Auxilary operation	An operation which supplements the main processing function but which is performed by a machine that is not directly under the control of the processor.
Communication link	Automatic data transmission from one location to another.
Offline storage	A symbol representing data stored in external off line storage. Storage media can be floppy disks, magnetic tapes, paper document etc.
Merge	Used to indicate the combining of two or more sets of items into one set.
Extract	Used to indicate the removal of one or more specific sets of items from a file or other set of items.
Collate	Combining, merging with extracting. two or more files or sets of items ate combined and then two or more files or sets of items are extracted.
Sort	Used to indicate the arranging of file or other set of items into a sequence.

Fig. 14.4 Some additional system flowchart symbols

The system flowcharts are used to record the flow of data in a current procedure from the originating source, through a number of processing operations and machines, to the output report. The flowchart may help a system analyst to acquire a better understanding of the procedure than would otherwise be possible. It can also help point out possible bottlenecks in the data flow of the system. In complex systems, there is likely to be an overall 'macro chart' that describes the general input/processing/output components of the system. There may then be a hierarchy of more detailed 'micro charts, each of which describes a module in a higher-level chart. This decomposition of a system into a series of detailed input/processing/output graphics is a frequently used analysis technique.

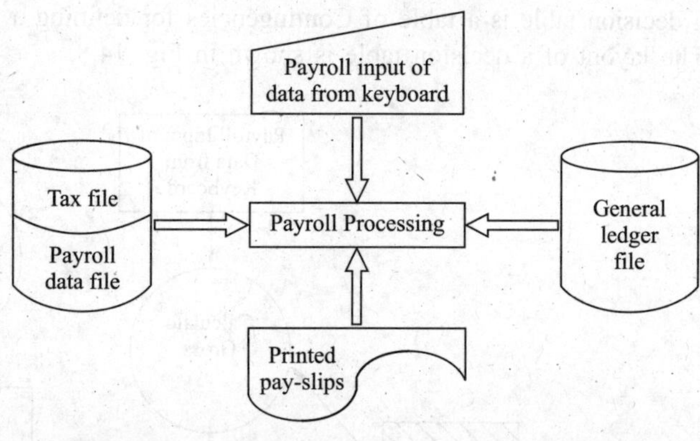

Fig. 14.5 System flowchart for a Payroll Processing System

14.3.4.2 Data Flow Diagram

A newer graphic aid for defining inputs, processes, and outputs is the data flow diagram. Only a few symbols are used, as shown in Fig. 14.6, and these symbols may be located in a rather informal way, as shown in Fig. 14.7. The analyst typically constructs a series of data flow diagrams, beginning with a high level one and then moving to lower-level diagrams that incorporate more details.

Symbol	Function	Meaning
○	Data Transformation	A circle indicates a processing function in which data flowing in are changed in form, value, or location before exiting.
▭	Temporary Data Storage	A box indicate, input to or output from a system.
Open-ended rectangle	Permanent Data Storage	An Open-ended rectangle indicates a data store such as a data base file.
→	Data flow	An arrow indicates data flowing through the system.

Fig. 14.6 Data flow diagram symbols

In Fig. 14.7, data flow diagram shows the general data flow through a payroll process. First, payroll input of data from keyboard. Next, gross pay is calculated using the hourly rate or salary amount retrieved from the payroll data file. Net pay is calculated by subtracting taxes as determined from the data in the tax file deductions contained in the payroll data file. The payroll data are transferred to the general ledger file, and the pay cheques are printed, and finally distributed to the employees.

14.3.4.3 Decision Table

A **decision table** is a diagram which conveniently summarizes complicated decision procedures. More precisely, it is the truth table for a set of logical statements (called actions) which are compounded from a set of simple statements (called conditions). In other words, one can say, a decision table is a table of Contingencies for defining a problem and the actions to be taken. The layout of a decision table is shown in Fig. 14.8.

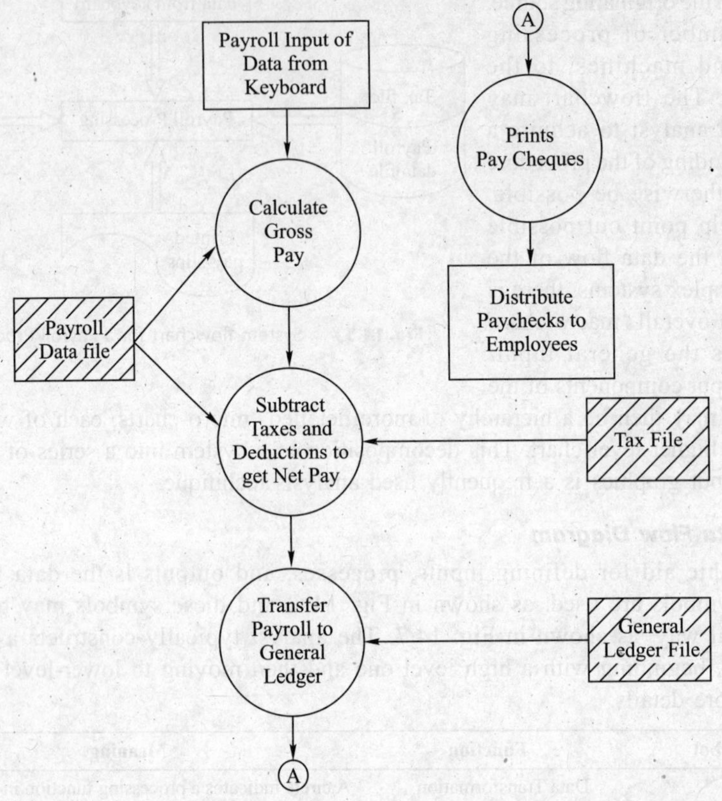

Fig. 14.7 An example of a data flow diagram (taken from a system flowchart for a payroll processing system as shown in Fig. 14.5)

A decision table consists of two parts; **stub** and **entry**. The stub part is divided into a upper quadrant called the **condition stub** and a lower quadrant called the **action stub**. Similarly, the entry part is also divided into an upper quadrant, called the condition entry and a lower quadrant called the action entry.

Condition Stub	Condition
Action Stub	Action

Fig. 14.8 Decision Table

Figure 14.9 shows a decision table that represents our stock policy. The decision table outlines the actions to be taken, given the stated conditions and rules. For instances, if the stock price is low and it is likely to go up, then buy the stock. However if the stock price is low and it is not likely to go up, then don't buy the stock, and so on.

In the Fig. 14.9, the answers are represented by a Y to signify yes, a NO to signify no, or a blank to show that the condition involved has not been tested. In the action entry quadrant, an X indicates the response to the answer(s) entered in the condition entry quadrant. Note that all possible combination of truth and falsity of the two conditions are represented in the $2^2 = 4$ condition columns. (For n conditions there would be 2^n columns). The action stub lists, two possible actions which can be taken regarding a purchase (it is accidental that the number of actions equals the number of conditions here).

Condition	Stub	Condition Entry			
		1	2	3	4
IF (Condition)	Stock price low	Y	Y	N	N
	Stock price likely to rise	Y	N	Y	N
THEN (Action)	Don't buy stock		X	X	X
	Buy stock	X			

Fig. 14.9 Decision table—Stock Policy

The following rules must be followed while making a decision table:

(*a*) A decision should be given a name.

(*b*) The logic of the decision table is independent of the sequence in which the condition rules are written, but the action takes place in the order in which the events occur.

(*c*) Standardized language should be used consistently.

(*d*) Duplication of terms should be eliminated.

14.3.4.3.1 Advantages of Decision Tables

A decision table have following advantages:

(*i*) Decision tables are best suited for dealing with complex branching routines such as calculating discounts or sales commissions or inventory control procedures.

(*ii*) A decision tabe may be easier to construct than a flowchart

(*iii*) It is easy to understand and useful for programmers.

(*iv*) Table users are not required to have computer knowledge.

(*v*) It is very effective for communication between analysts or programmers.

(*vi*) Direct conversion of decision table into a computer program is possible.

(*vii*) It provides a framework for a complete and accurate statement of decision logic.

14.3.4.3.2 Disadvantages of Decision Tables

(*i*) Decision tables does not show the over all picture as presented by flowchart.

(*ii*) For the simple logic, flowcharts are more useful than decision tables.

14.3.4.3.3 Layout Form

A layout form is used to detail, on paper, the setup of the input and output CRT screens and hard-copy reports. This form enables system analysts and users to agree upon the design for the screens and reports before they are actually implemented.

14.3.5 Management

Once the output and input requirements are known, the general processing requirements, including identifying what processing needs to be done and where, how much data will be handled, and how fast the data need to be processed, can be formulated. The specific formulas and procedures to convert input to output are not formulated at this point in the system life cycle.

Once the logical design is complete, a formal report with the system analyst's recommendations is presented to management. This report is often accompanied by an oral presentation to all involved parties. The report is reviewed by management in light of the feasibility study. Management then decides whether to:

(*a*) continue to the system design step: (*b*) repeat the system analysis step:

(*c*) terminate the project. If management decides to continue to the next step, the system analyst or system designer now proceeds with the system design.

14.4 SYSTEM DESIGN

System design involves detailing the physical design of the system; it is the know how of the process. Once the logical design is outlined during system analysis, the system analyst or a system designer determines the physical design, which describes the hardware, the software, and the operating procedures required to make the system operational.

When the analyst gets down to the task of designing the actual processing and computation of the data in his/system, he will face numerous problems. Many of these will be due to constraints imposed by the user or due to limitations in the hardware and software that make up his installation. In the notes which follow, a selection of the matters requiring attention are listed. It is not possible to be comprehensive, as the variety of likely problems is varied, and no two installations are exactly similar. However, the comments made will give the inexperienced analyst a feeling for some situation he may encounter during the design stage.

1. **One-input systems** may be a small routine or a large suite of programs. The stage at which a given function becomes large enough to justify making it a separate procedure is usually determined by the amount of coding involved. Such systems may arise, however, when the function is particularly complex and/or requires specialist knowledge *or* where the appropriate routine or program already exists in usable form.
2. **Two-input systems** almost always imply a matching procedure. This may be by a serial method when both input streams have been put in the same sequence, or by direct access. In the latter case, records will be available on a direct access medium with short access time. Transactions are dealt with on arrival and not necessarily in a predetermined sequence. This method is obligatory in a real-time system. There is a variation of the serial method, which is to take several 'bites' at one file and for each such 'bite', pass the whole of the other file. Each 'bite' is held in store (or, possibly, on a direct access medium) and each pass of the transaction file processes all transactions applying to the records held in the current 'bite'. It may be better to rewrite the transaction file during each pass, dropping off those transactions which have been matched. This method can clearly save on sorting time. Note that, even when it is possible, through the use of direct access media or by the variant described above, to deal with one or both files in random sequence, this may be an erroneous or unacceptable procedure because there is a definite order for several transactions applying to the same record (*e.g.*, one must amend a record before using it to answer an interrogation). In this case, the transaction file must be sorted.
3. **Multiple-input:** Generally, it is not convenient to handle more than three inputs in a single program. In particular cases, however, it may be that a multi-input matching procedure is an attractive method. Often the number of peripheral devices on the computer will establish the limit to the number of input streams which can be handled. Where the method is to be 'two inputs', a system of merges or multi-input sorts will have to be used. Careful consideration may need to be given when deciding whether to mount a large sort-merge system immediately before the two-input run or to sort and merge the several input files progressively as they become available, *e.g.*, daily data capture and validation process leading to a weekly main run.

4. **Spooling and media conversion programs:** 'Spool' = simultaneous peripheral operations off-line (tape-to-printer, cards-to-tape, etc.). The use of these programs will normally impose certain limitations on format and/or sequence. These limitations are usually well worth accepting in view of the benefit obtained from the use of proven programs and the advantages of standardised operating procedures when handling the slow peripherals.
5. **Multi-Programming:** The operating system may impose quite significant constraints on the way in which multi-programming facilities are used. Thus a 'foreground-background' system with a partitioned store may be the basis on which the machine has to work or a full 15-program system may be available or a multi-access system allowing, say, 200 remote users to work concurrently. Even within the manufacturer's constraints, the installation operating management may impose restrictions of their own, designed to ensure that the facilities of the machine are profitably exploited.
6. **Real-time working:** Here input, output, process with access to files must be handled immediately and each procedure is performed once only before going on to another work is by transaction rather than by process (as in batch processing). The approach is usually to deal with all types of input transaction in one message-handling program. This is an input program which accepts, vets and examines the message. The message will define the procedures required and the files to be accessed. The message-handling program then deposits the decoded message data in a standard place and initiates a transfer of control to a processing program. It is this program, or sequence of programs, which deals with the message and then deposits the results in another standard place. An output program then picks it up and passes it to the remote terminal. The processing program may have passed on details of the message for further processing. It is usual for the manufacturer to provide programs, or sets of routines from which programs can be assembled, to handle the communications tasks. These programs will impose certain standards of internal communications on the customer programs. The communications package will deal with context independent checking, line failures, queuing problems, etc.—all of which are specialist topics.
7. **Run segmentation:** The segmentation of the total task is the crucial stage in system design. The basic task is to identify the division of labour between computer and non-computer. Generally, the smaller the number of programs the better. This is, however, a gross over-simplification made essentially from an operational point of view. It will usually be necessary to segment because the program would otherwise be too large to be accommodated in store, and/or the necessity for a sorting function implies a split in procedures (*e.g.*, Data Vet-Sort-Update).
8. **Optimization:** Having completed the initial design scheme, the analyst must examine the proposed design for weaknesses and pay particular attention to questions of peripheral or processor-domination and file design. The most straight forward methods of optimization are those of run combination and run segmentation. Combination of runs reduces set-up time and may enable one or more passes of a file to be saved. If a computer-limited run can be combined with a tape-limited run, this may result in a balanced combined run. Segmentation of runs will tend to increase set-up time but can be used to reduce demand on peripherals. In particular cases of processor-bound runs, it may be possible to effect a reduction in processing time by partitioning into two balanced runs or by moving a particular processing function into the next program.
9. **File design** must be examined carefully to ensure that the right degree of compactness has been achieved. If one or more runs handling a given file are file-limited, it may be worth attempting to reduce the physical sizes of the file records, so reducing file passing time. Such compacting will tend as a secondary effect to increase the processing time, since extra coding

will have to be inserted in the programs concerned to unpack the compacted fields. Conversely, where runs are processor-bound, it may be worth expanding the records, so easing the task of unpacking the record fields, in an attempt to obtain a balance. Where a system is to be run on a multi-programming machine, of course, it is highly desirable to avoid processor-bound runs, since this will tend to limit the flexibility of the system from the operational point of view. Activity distribution on fields should have been considered from the beginning and any '80-20' situation (where 20 percent of the main file records receive 80 percent of the transactions) should have been detected and the file design modified accordingly.

10. **File buffering** may or may not be subject to control by the programmer. Where it is possible to nominate one, two, three or more buffer areas for a file, this may be of use, particularly where a list requires significant processing time but the activity of the file is very low. A large number of buffers can then be employed with advantage to maximize the amount of overlapped file-time, by allowing a queue of blocks to build up while the list is being processed.
11. **Sorting runs** will almost invariably use the standard sort program supplied by the manufacturer. The use of the first and last pass 'own-coding' options should always be borne in mind. In an extreme case, this can save a whole run. If the mechanics of the manufacturer's sort program are fully understood, it may be possible to arrange that the data to be sorted is produced by the preceding program in such a way that the first pass of the sort is made easier and faster. Similarly, if the first pass of the sort is processor-bound, a reduction in the storage used by this pass in forming strings may bring the pass into balance. In critical situations, a pass in Phase II of the sort might be saved by reducing record size and hence *increasing* string length out of the first pass.

Many of the constraints and problems mentioned above are programming-oriented. This is deliberate. They have been included to impress upon the analyst how necessary it is to work closely with the programming team during the design stage. If the analyst ignores the programming implications of his design he does so at his peril, because he is likely to find that many of his pet ideas and theories are not feasible on the equipment at his disposal. A senior programmer, if consulted early enough, when the theory is in embryo, will quickly point out those ideas which will cause programming difficulties. By such liaison, the analyst will save himself much wasted effort.

The **system design process** begins with a functional specification of what the new system is to achieve and ends with a detailed system specification from which programs can be prepared. A well-designed system has the following characteristics:

1. **It achieves the goals set for it:** In day-to-day operation, systems produce a wide variety of outputs for different users. The frequency of these reports ranges from 'daily' to 'annual'. It is therefore very easy to confuse the production of these reports with the goals of the system. At the beginning of the system design process it is very important that we do *not* fall into this trap. A 'system goal' is something that the system will achieve, that is unlikely to change, and that can be expressed in business terms.
2. **It reflects the structure of the business application it serves:** Business application systems usually follow well-defined, structured processes. This is particularly the case in accounting systems for example, where legal constraints and traditional business practice formalize the way in which accounting processes work. In the lifetime of a computer-based system, however, it would be unreasonable to suppose that business demands would remain static and that no changes would be made to the designed system. A well-designed system is therefore able to cope with business change because it is capable of being modified easily. This can often be done when the system design reflects the business procedure and where computer processes mirror the real world.

3. **It is secure, accurate and reliable:** Careful design ensures security against the incorrect use of data, privacy from unauthorized access and a complete audit trail and provides the ability to recover completely after system malfunctions.
4. **It is easy to understand:** Simple solutions are to be preferred in every case. A complex solution which optimizes the use of some technical aspect of the design is more difficult to specify, program, test and modify.

The design process is an iterative activity. As each of the design elements are considered, a re-examination has to be made of the design decisions taken so far and an assessment made of the relationship between these previous design decisions and the element being considered. This repetitive activity continues until every aspect of the proposed system has been considered and the final and complete design has been reached. The basic steps in the overall design process are:

1. the definition of the system
2. the preparation of a conceptual model or logical system design
3. the development of a physical system design
4. the preparation of the system specification

In defining the system's goal it is important to remember that this is not the same thing as providing specific users with specific outputs. We can illustrate the difference between goals and user requirements by taking an accounts receivable system as an example. The goals of an accounts receivable—or sales ledger—system are:

1. To maintain an accurate and timely account of debts owed to the organisation by its customers. To provide internal audit controls that will ensure that debt records are accurate and that the system performs reliably.
2. To provide appropriate management information to support to organization's overall objectives, such as the control of debt and the establishment of customer credit-worthiness.

By definition, these goals are not likely to change. It is not content and format of the inputs and outputs which are variable and which good system design will allow to change. On the other hand, a system designed to produce a specific output format will need to be redesigned each time the content of that format changes.

Preparing a conceptual model or a logical system design requires that the analyst determines how the system will achieve its goals. This takes account of the logical inputs and outputs and of the processes necessary to transform one into the other. No notice is taken at this stage of the organizational constraints within which the system will operate. This is done during physical system design. In the short term, cost performance and reliability figure largely during physical system design. In the long view, the flexibility of the system, the expected growth in usage and its life expectancy may be important: higher performance and reliability may be achieved at a greater cost. In designing the physical system, the analyst must consider the desired performance from the system, its cost and reliability; development time, maintainability and flexibility, potential for growth and life expectancy.

Out of these conflicting requirements will be derived the optimum system capabilities which enable the logical system goals to be achieved within the organisational constraints within which the system must operate.

14.4.1 System Design Tools and Techniques

The following tools and techniques are among those used during system design:

- ❒ **Organisation standards:** Some organisations have standards manuals that specify a consistent design approach. The procedures to follow in designing output reports, input forms, and processing logic may also be spelled out.

- **Special charts and forms:** The charts and forms prepared during the system analysis phase are very helpful in the design stage. Weakness spotted during analysis can now be corrected. And the existing input/processing/output relationships may now be used to design a more integrated system.
- **Top-down design methodology:** The *top-down design* technique requires the early identification of the top-level functions in the proposed system. Each function is then broken down into a hierarchy of understandable lower-level modules and components. After a top-level structure of the system is prepared, lower-level diagrams are created to show the input/processing/output details of each function, module, and component. Several iterations will usually occur in this design and charting process. Designers may start with simple diagrams showing general solutions. This first effort is then refined to produce more complete charts as the design requirements become clearer.
- **Design reviews and walkthroughs:** Periodic sessions may be held so that interested users can review the design progress. Designers can present sample outputs and walk through the input and processing operations to describe the handling of data. Users can be encouraged to interact with designers, look for errors, and make suggestions during this *design walk-through.*
- **Prototyping:** Preliminary prototyping activities may have been carried out during problem definition to get an idea of what's needed. Now, additional prototyping efforts may be made to design the new system. A *working prototype* may be prepared during, or as a result of, the interaction that takes place between users and designers at the design review and walkthrough sessions. The working prototype includes more system features and functions than the preliminary model. Data input screens, menus and other user-interface techniques, and output displays and reports are fully developed. But the prototype is still a model; full-fledged system programs haven't been written. Users and designers may continue to revise and enhance this working model until they have prepared a final set of system specifications. In addition to the benefits cited earlier, the use of prototyping at this stage may reduce (1) the risk of developing a system that doesn't satisfy user needs, and (2) the time required to train users in the operation of the new system.
- **System design workstations:**. A *system design workstation* combines powerful pc hardware with special system design software so that designers can create system specifications in less time and with fewer error. For example, workstation software can monitor all data items, labels, and relationships in a proposed system, and signal when someone tries to use an item or label in violation of design conventions. And graphics-based software allows designers to create flowcharts, other diagrams, screens with windows, and icon-based menus.

14.4.2 Choosing an Alternative

It's assumed at this point that the designers have prepared a detailed set of written and documented system specifications to achieve the system study goals. These specifications should include:

1. **Output requirements:** The form, content, and frequency of output is needed.
2. **Input requirements:** The necessary new input data should be identified along with the stored file data that are required.
3. **File and storage requirements:** The size, contents, storage media, record formats, access restrictions, and degree of permanency of any affected files should be known.
4. **Processing specifications:** The procedures needed for the computer to convert input data into desired output results should be indicated. Manual processing procedures should also be noted.

5. **Control provisions:** The steps required to achieve systems control should be specified, and the later system testing and implementation procedures should be outlined.
6. **Cost estimates:** Preliminary estimates of the costs of different alternatives should be made.

14.4.3 Management

After the file design has been completed, the software design is developed. Software design involves devising programs to ensure that the available inputs will produce the desired output. The design should be easy to understand and maintain by others.

During this stage, work is also begun to design the procedures to be used to test the information system during the development and implementation steps. These procedures are established at this point because, in the development and implementation steps, there is often a great deal of pressure to get a system installed and running as soon as possible. If testing procedures have not already been designed, they are often done haphazardly or not at all.

After the physical design of the system has been determined, a report outlining all the system analysis and design work is submitted to management. This report is again reviewed in light of the original feasibility study. Management may choose to:

(*a*) proceed to the system development phase;
(*b*) redo the system analysis and/or system design; or
(*c*) terminate the project.

14.5 SYSTEM DEVELOPMENT

System development refers to creating the new information system from the physical designs established in the preceding phase.

The system analyst first determines if a suitable prewritten software package exists that can be purchased to implement the physical design or if new programs must be developed.

Depending on the system design and the user's needs, prepackaged software may be available. Prepackaged software is general in nature because it is intended for a wide range of users. If this type of package is chosen, the analyst must make sure it completely fulfills the requirements of the users. Development time is greatly reduced if prewritten software is available.

If a new set of programs is to be written to implement the system, the system designer calls on a computer programmer to write the code. Documentation from the analysis and design processes gives the programmer all the information needed to code the programs. When writing and coding a program, the programmer uses a structured approach to ensure the program can be easily understood and maintained.

Structured programming is a methodology that stresses the systematic design, development, and management of the program development process. Therefore, the purpose and overall goals of structured programming are to:

- ❒ Decrease development time by increasing programmer productivity and reducing the time to test and debug a program
- ❒ Decrease maintenance costs by reducing errors and making programs easier to understand by reducing their complexity
- ❒ Improve the quality of software by providing programs with fewer errors.

Programmers are human beings, just like other people, and being human they are subject to human frailties. Thus, given that most programs are written by human beings, it is inevitable that they will contain errors; in other words, that they will not work correctly. In fact, with our present limited understanding of how best to build programs, it is almost certain that every program of significant size contains at least one undiscovered error, and computers are still unforgiving of our errors. Nevertheless, while it seems that we must accept the inevitability of errors, we need to be able both to build large systems and to rely on their continuing error-free operation. We must therefore use program building techniques which minimize the possibilities for errors, program testing methods which maximize the chances of finding errors, and program design methods which limit the effects of errors. The first step in this process is to recognize that errors can and do exist and, without a valid mathematical proof that the program is correct, will continue to exit. Since the correctness proofs of large programs are also large and complex, the possibility of errors in the proof cannot be ruled out; the possibility of errors remaining in the program exists. Techniques for proving the correctness of programs, and the associated problem of designing programming languages which assist such techniques, are the subject matter of an important current research area; but until that research bears fruit, and the fruit is widely available, practical programming requires the use of indirect methods to try to improve the reliability of software.

The process of minimizing the number of errors in a program follows a law of diminishing returns. Initially, a modest increase in effort will result in a marked decrease in the number of errors remaining in the program. Subsequently, more and more effort must be made to reduce—but not eliminate—these residue errors. The process ends when the number of errors remaining is tolerable, and the limited damage which they can cause is insufficient to justify the costs of eliminating any more of them. All of this may sound somewhat defeatist, but it is the only sensible approach to adopt when perfection is not practicable to achieve. In fact, the rest of this section discusses techniques which help to reduce the incidence of errors and to improve the chances of their detection, hence improving the cost-effectiveness of program testing and debugging.

As in many other situations, prevention of the undesirable is more cost effective than cure, and programs should therefore be written in such a way that the likelihood of errors is minimized, that such errors as remain will be easier to detect, and that the effects of the errors will be contained, that is, both minimized and restricted in range. It is necessary to take this into account at all four of the main stages in programming a project: specification, design, building, and testing, at any of which errors may be introduced.

As we have seen earlier, construction of every program or subprogram must start with a specification which describes how the program is to relate to the real world or a model of the real world. Ideally, and usually, this is a written document, and is used as the initial reference for all the construction work which follows. Sometimes, especially with small, informal programs, the specification is never explicitly set out but remains in the head of the programmer as a mental concept of what he has to do. There are two possibilities for error at this stage. Firstly, the initial specification may be faulty because it is not an accurate description of what the program is to do. This may be a consequence of a misunderstanding by the writer of the specification, or a flaw in the model of the real world that was used. Secondly, the programmer may misinterpret the specification. The result is the same in either case; the program will not perform the tasks required of it—it will solve the wrong problem.

The second stage, of designing a program to satisfy the given specification, can also introduce errors, obviously because the design does not match the specification, or more subtly because it will not function as required in all the circumstances asked of it. It is rather analogous to designing a machine which is perfect in theory, but requires 100% perfection in, say, input materials or operator control if it is to work satisfactorily in an imperfect world. Typical of this class of error is that a program malfunctions because the algorithm on which on which it is based cannot cope with an unexpected combination of input values from which it has not been protected. Most errors, however, arise at the building or coding stage. Errors from this stage can be divided into three main groups. The first group consists of logical errors arising because the programmer misunderstands the language used or the fine detail of the program. Examples of this kind of error are failure to initialize a variable, incorrect initialization of or exit from an iterative loop, and incorrect use of a variable. In the second group are syntax errors which result in code that is unacceptable to the compiler. These generally arise from carelessness in actual coding, but may reflect inadequate understanding of the programming language. In the third group are errors introduced between the programmer and the version of his program which reaches the computer. This group includes transcription and encoding errors, whereby what the programmer intended to write differs from that which appears on the coding sheet or that which is keyed onto cards, tape, disk, or directly into the computer at a terminal. It also includes errors caused by mishandled punched cards, malfunctioning equipment, transmission faults, etc.

The final stage of production also has potential for introducing errors. Disorganised testing can, for example, lead to the use of out-of-date program listings, the wrong identification of errors and what must be done to correct them, and the incorrect amendment of the code. In the resulting confusion, the number of errors in the program can be significantly increased!

At each of the four stages just discussed there are precautions that can be taken to minimize the possibility of errors. The first is to study the initial specification carefully and intelligently. Any peculiarities or ambiguities should be investigated, and unclear passages should be clarified. This will reduce the possibilities for errors and misunderstandings in the specification.

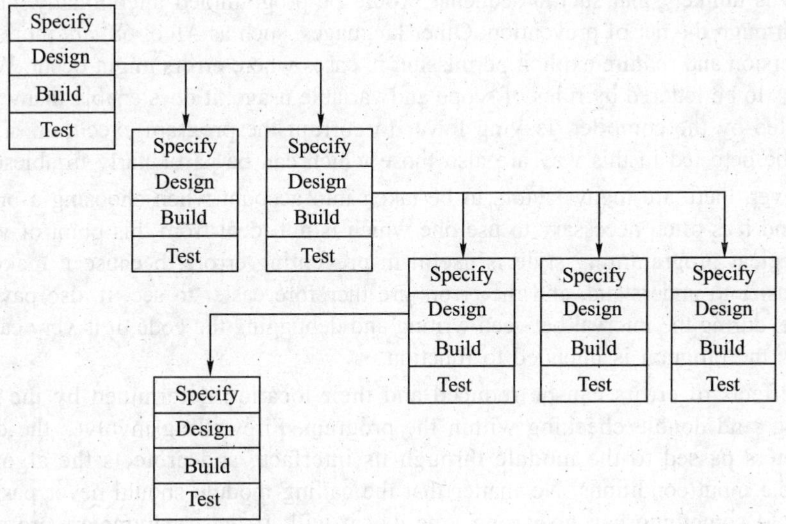

Fig. 14.10 Structured (top down) design

Much successful error prevention stems from the design process, in the selection of the algorithm and of the programming language and style, and from the structure of the design process itself. It has already been indicated that structured design, which implies using a top-down process, is inherently less prone to errors than bottom-up design or monolithic design, and it is time to explain why. The top-down, structured design process, illustrated in Fig. 14.10, follows a cycle of specification, design, building and testing for each of the modules in the program. It starts with the specification and design of the main module. During the design of each module, its requirements for sub-modules become clear, and an exact functional specification can be written for each of these. This offers two main advantages. The specification for each module is fixed during the design process and need not be altered later. With a bottom-up approach, where the specification, design, building, and testing of modules begins at the lowest level, there is always a risk that the completed modules near the bottom of the hierarchy will have to be changed as design problems and change are encountered higher up. The second advantage is in program testing. As we shall see later, it is usually easier to simulate the function of lower modules during the program validation, than to provide an accurate testing environment for an isolated module.

In choosing the algorithm to be used in the program or module, the designer must take care that it will function correctly under all permissible conditions, and then ensure that it is protected from impermissible conditions by validating the data crossing the interface between this module and the rest of the program.

The design of resilient, error-resistant programs also has implications for the choice of programming language. Since the technique of structured programming, with its control over the program flow, reduces the possibility of errors in logic, ideally the language should lend itself to writing structure programs. It is well known that some languages, like Algol 68 and Pascal, have good constructs of expressing the flow of program control, and also allow the programmer to specify and manipulate data structures which reflect the requirements of the problem, whereas other languages, like Fortran and (even more) Basic, are very deficient in these respects. But the differences, as far as reliability and error control are concerned, do not end there. For example, many Fortran implementations are very tolerant of the ways in which typed variables are used. As one instance, a group of Hollerith characters can be stored in an integer variable and then assigned to a real variable with automatic mode conversion and little probability of the fact being signalled. It is unlikely that such a sequence would be programmed intentionally, but this error could slip through the net of prevention. Other languages, such as Algol 68, are more rigid about mode conversion and require explicit permission in cases where errors might occur. While it may seem tedious to be fettered by rules of scope and variable usage, it does enable many more errors to be detected by the compiler, leaving fewer to corrupt the program execution. Those errors which can be detected in this way are also those which can be particularly troublesome later.

However, there are many factors to be taken into account when choosing a programming language, and it is often necessary to use one which is not ideal from this point of view. In any language a clear programming style is useful in preventing errors, because it makes the code clear and easier to understand, and the errors are therefore easier to see. It also pays dividends late because, during the interval between writing and debugging the code, it is very easy to forget exactly how the program is intended to function.

The effects of errors can be reduced and their location determined by the practice of 'fire walling' and double checking within the program. Firewalling involves the checking of the parameters passed to the module through its interface, and protects the algorithm from impermissible input conditions. No matter that the calling module should never pass erroneous parameters; if something can go wrong, one day it will. If these parameters are checked for reasonableness and consistency, then the damage caused by the error cannot propagate through the program, and possible damage to precious files will be avoided. Further, the error will be determined sooner and therefore more accurately. There are often key points within a module where vulnerable variables should be checked. This serves the same purpose as firewalling, locating possible errors and minimizing damage.

Having reached the point where the module has been designed, the next stage is to build or code it. Most of the errors in this process are caused by carelessness or illegible writing. Coding is an exacting task, which should not be hurried. Coding conventions exist so that potentially similar characters can be distinguished, such as the letters O and I from the digits 0 and 1. Since, one some equipment, they also look very similar in the program listing, it is worth while getting them right initially. This may seem too trivial to mention, but many programmers have found to their cost that it does not pay to neglect it.

The code should now be checked, a process in which the computer can be used to complement but not replace the programmer. It is easier to check code from a clear listing with good layout. Another useful machine-generated check is a table of the variables used in each module, showing where each is used and how it is used. The compiler may also carry out checks on variable usage and scope. In languages which require explicit declarations of all the variables, this can help to highlight misspelled variable names and incorrect usage. Invalid transfers of control, such as a branch into the middle of an iterative loop or conditional clause, can also be detected. This is where the choice of language and the compiler used has a significant impact on the early detection of errors..It is all too easy to be tempted to 'switch off' such compiler option (though such switching-off facilities are provided for use with fully developed modules, not programs still under development) or to skimp or skip the task of examining them. Such temptations you should be strong-willed enough to resist if you wish to become a fully competent programmer!

Nevertheless, automatic checking, although useful, does not eliminate the need for desk checking by a programmer: 'a programmer' rather than 'the programmer' because any programmer is limited in his ability to check his own code. He is unlikely to detect any errors due to his own misunderstandings of the specification, of the algorithm, or of the language, because his understanding is unlikely to have improved during the writing of the program. Further, his familiarity with the code he is checking may lead him to overlook errors, however glaring they may be. It is therefore better if another person can desk check the code. There are two main techniques of 'programmer peer review', which is the jargon for this practice. In one, the programmers work in pairs, and each desk checks the modules written by the other. This may be extended so that modules are exchanged for the whole of the testing and debugging process. The other technique requires the programmer to explain his code to a group of other programmers, who offer constructive criticism and point out possible errors. Both techniques offer additional advantages. Firstly, the review, especially if carried out on a group basis, can result in improvements to the module, to improve its accuracy, reliability, or efficiently. Secondly, the programming style diffuses and becomes more uniform throughout the organization. Good ideas are shared, and the intelligibility of the code is improved. Thirdly, because more programmers have studied each module, the problems of later maintenance are reduced: the organisation is less dependent on the continuing availability of the original author.

There are four specific questions that should be asked in desk checking:

1. Is the code both necessary and sufficient? Check that all the steps in the algorithm have been codes and that there are no redundant statements to confuse or produce errors.
2. Is all the non-local data used correctly? Check that the declaration, usage, and range of accepted values for each non-local variable is consistent with its use everywhere else.
3. Is the usage of local data consistent? Check that there are no unexpected variables, that each is used in a consistent way, and that the range of permitted values is acceptable.
4. Is each variable set before it is used? Check that the program does not assume an initial value for any variable, but explicitly sets a value, either at compile time or by assignment before it is used.

Even if you are perforce working alone, without even a friend whom you can ask to look at your program for you, it is worth going through this list as well as you can on your own code, trying as far as possible to pretend it as written by someone else.

When the programs are completed, they are tested using actual data from the users and test data designed by system personnel to test the extremes of the system. To be sure mistakes can be detected by the system, the tests are performed not only with accurate data, but also with data that contain errors. During these tests and, in fact, anywhere in the system life cycle, modifications can be made to the design. However, the later in the cycle that the modification occurs, the more expensive and time-consuming it's likely to be.

The actual specifications of the hardware are also developed during this phrase. For example, if minicomputers were to be used for the system, specific types of minicomputers are selected now. Printers or plotters are chosen, and all the cable needs are finalized. Costs of the equipment are investigated and purchase orders are approved.

Personnel needs, including the users and all support staff to operate the information system, are also determined at this time.

Again, a report of recommendations is compiled and presented to management and the users. After all the involved participants agree, the next stage—system implementation—can begin.

14.6 SYSTEM IMPLEMENTATION

System implementation involves testing the installed system, converting from the old system to the new one, and training the users.

14.6.1 Testing

It is program testing, rather than debugging, which is the central feature of the final stage in the creation of a program. The objective of testing is to verify that the program functions as it should, that it conforms with its specification, and solves the right problem in the real world. This is an uncompromising goal, and is also measurable in that it is possible,at least in principle, to decide when it has been reached. The aim of program debugging, on the other hand, is to remove program errors, and does not necessarily have the same result as testing. Testing may throw up errors which have to be corrected; debugging, in the sense of dealing with errors as they become evident but otherwise 'leaving well alone', may leave at any stage some sections of program untested. Also, since the detection and location of program errors follows a law of diminishing returns, it is reasonable to stop error hunting when only a relatively small number of errors are left and the costs of finding any more are not justified. At this point which can be difficult to determine, the program may still not function correctly under all conditions.

Ideally, the program should be tested with all possible combinations of input, and its output for each case checked against precalculated correct results. However, for almost all programs, even the simplest, there is an infinity of possible input combinations, or at least a number so large as to be effectively infinite. Consider, for example, a program to add three integers together. Each of the integers could range from positive to negative infinity, and hence the number of different input combinations is infinite. Even if the integers are limited to a reasonable range of values, say $\pm 8 \times 10^6$, there are still too many combinations to be checked by hand in a reasonable time. Sceptical readers are invited to carry out the calculations for themselves! Fortunately, the internal operations of the computer system can be considered to have generality: if they work with one set of operands then they will work, within certain limits, for all similar sets of operands. Less fortunately, the same assumption is not valid for programs or parts of programs which contain conditional branches. Testing must therefore be focused on the validation of small, separate parts of the program which do have this kind of generality. It may then be inferred that, if the small part performs correctly with one set of inputs, it will perform correctly with all others. The crux is to decide what constitutes a part simple enough to be validated in this way.

This requirement is provided by the notion of a program path—the sequence of instructions which is performed for a given set of inputs. If this works correctly, then all other sets of inputs which cause the program to follow the same path also yield the correct result. Since most programs contain conditional branches, there will be a number of alternative paths at various parts of the program, and hence very many distinct paths through the code. Exhaustive testing or validation of the program requires that each of these paths should be checked. The total number of paths is determined by the combination of all the alternatives at each stage. Although this is much less then infinity, it may still be unacceptably large for big programs. It is reduced to manageable size by breaking up the programs, validating each part separately, and then using the validated part as single steps in a longer path. The concept of generality ensures that this technique is valid whatever the number of internal paths in the individual parts.

Such a method accords well the techniques of structured design and programming which require that the program should be divided into logical and functional modules. Each of these is validated individually but not in isolation. The testing, like overall construction, proceeds from the top downwards. At each successive stage, the functions of lower modules in the structure are simulated, while the module under test is exercised through all of its logical paths.

Testing of such a modular program starts with the main module in an environment where all the other modules are simulated. As each module is validated it can be added to the structure and its subordinate modules can be investigated. Thus the overall function of the program is apparent from the beginning, and any fundamental problems are uncovered at an early stage.

The production of large quantities of test data can be eased by using the computer itself to format or generate suitable input. Test files of reasonable data can be written by a special program, or by a general purpose generator. Additional cases to test marginal conditions, critical code sequences and error conditions must be added. The 'correct' results for each set should then be determined. This is a potential source of confusion, for errors in the calculation of the expected results will lead the programmer to suspect the veracity of the program under test. After the test shot, the program output must be compared with the precalculated results. Any discrepancies must be investigated, and if the program is at fault then the error must be found and tested. Program testing ends when the program has been run successfully through all of its logical paths.

The testing process is a certification of the program, and must be documented for future credibility. Future users of the program are entitled to more than an unsupported statement that the program works. They should know how and under what conditions it was tested, and what the inputs and results were, so that the tests can be repeated. Retesting will certainly be necessary if the program is ever modified or transferred to another computer system. The documentation should include details of the test procedures, the functions of each test set, the test data, and the calculated results.

14.6.2 Debugging

Knowing that errors exist is one thing; getting rid of them is quite another. The errors in a program or module may manifest themselves in a variety of ways. We have already considered those errors of syntax and internal consistency which can be detected by the compiler. There are also logical errors, broadly of two kinds. There are those which do not cause the program to fail, but cause discrepancies between the expected results and those which are actually produced; and there are those which result in illegal operations such as division by zero, attempting to read past the end of an input file, or attempting to access a non-existent array element, which lead to the premature termination of the program. The division between the two kinds is not clear-cut. In some languages and systems, for example, array bound checking at run-time is automatic, but in others it is not; a Fortran system will normally check array bounds only if this is asked for, if indeed it offers the facility at all. In this case an incorrect access may either result in a premature termination, if the location addressed is outside the range available to the program, or may simply lead to incorrect results. In fact, if you are really unlucky, in a particular case it may not even do that, and the error will not manifest itself! It is important to be aware of which such errors your compiler is capable of detecting, and to provide your own checks for those it will ignore. Also, some compilers incorporate 'recovery' facilities to permit continued processing if an exceptional condition like division by zero arises. If the compiler reports the unexpected occurrence of such a recovery, this must still of course be regarded as an error and treated accordingly.

The diagnosis of logical errors is complicated by the delay which normally exists between the occurrence of the actual error and the appearance of the symptoms. Although it is easy to locate the point at which the first incorrect output was printed or at which the run terminated with an execution error, the real error may have occurred some distance away and may not be so easy to find. The key to efficient debugging is the systematic exploration and elaboration of the symptoms, so that the precise cause of the error can be identified. This process starts with the collection of all the available evidence: what happened; to what extent it happened (if appropriate); when it happened; and where the symptoms appeared. Information about what did *not* happen is as important as the details of what did—as Sherlock Holmes pointed out in *The Hound of the Baskervilles*. From this evidence, the programmer can begin to formulate hypotheses about the cause of the error, and to devise tests of these hypotheses.

The single symptom which originally signalled the error will not usually yield sufficient information on its own; additional information must be extracted from the test run. However, beware of generating too much information, for the relevant facts will then be buried in a morass of useless figures. This, incidentally is the main drawback of post-mortem dumps, which are often provided automatically by the operating system when a premature termination ('abort') occurs as the result of an illegal operation. Undue importance is often attached to the analysis of such dumps, which in most cases should be considered only as a last resort.

A better solution is to trace the execution of the program in the vicinity of the error. Some debugging compilers provide a trace, which can be used simply to follow the program flow from statement to statement, or can include details of each assignment, with the values of relevant expressions. Again there is a risk of producing too much data. The error might not occur until the test run is well advanced, after many thousands of statements have been executed, and several hundred pages of trace output have been printed. Usually the trace can be turned on or off for each module individually, and thus can be used to trace only the module under test. This reduces the output to a more manageable amount. Some compilers offer the option of including a retrospective trace of a program under test. In such systems the trace data is stored during the run in a cyclic buffer so that at any time the trace data is stored for, say, the last 100 statements. If an execution error occurs during the run, the contents of the trace buffer are printed. This provides information about the run in the moments before the catastrophic failure, which (with luck) will contain the prime cause of the error, or at least provide some clues as to its nature and location. It is possible (something which is sometimes overlooked) to press this facility into service even if the program terminates normally (hence producing no retrospective trace) but with incorrect results. The technique is to introduce deliberately an execution error before the end, at a point just past the suspected fault. A suitable statement, for example including an attempt to divide by zero, inserted in the code at the appropriate point, will force an error and generate the trace output. However, this is a once-only device which cannot easily be used to investigate errors occurring in a loop after a number of iterations.

Perhaps the most useful debugging tool is the 'snapshot', which produces a printout of selected variables at key points in the program. The printout may be achieved by a special debugging feature in the language, for example the namelist facility available in some Fortran systems, or more flexibly by print statements set up by the programmer. Again, beware of snapshots used in inner loops which may be executed very many times. If the working of an inner loop is to be investigated, the snapshot can be controlled by code which bypasses it after a small number of iterations, or only activates it after the loop has been executed a given number of times. The amount of detail printed by the snapshot is under the control of the programmer, and can range from a brief message that a given point has been passed, to an appropriately formatted display of the values of chosen variables. All the snapshots should print some identification so that the programmer can relate the output to the point where it was generated. The flexibility and selectivity of the snapshot maximize the amount of useful information which is obtained and minimize the amount of redundant data which surrounds it.

The problems of debugging are not entirely over when the source of an error has been located: the error still has to be corrected. The trouble is that, as has been noted earlier, the correction can itself be a source of additional errors unless care is taken. The offending code must only be altered when it is certain that it is the source of the error and that the alteration will cure the error. It is essential to check that the alteration will not have side effects and cause other problems, perhaps elsewhere in the program. This is particularly difficult when testing and debugging a program interactively at a terminal. The psychological pressure to act immediately and somehow to 'keep up with the computer' is stimulating, but it also tempts the programmer to make hasty and ill-considered decisions which can increase, rather than reduce, the number of errors in the program.

One further aspect of debugging remains to be mentioned: the fact that a working program may on occasion malfunction not through any fault of its own, but because of an external error. Examples of these are errors in a compiler or in system software, faults in the hardware, or mistakes by the operations staff. The novice programmer all too easily jumps to the conclusion that the machine must have made a mistake. One soon learns with experience that the incidence of machine errors is so small that, initially, it is reasonable to assume that the program is at fault. However, the possibility of some external error can never be completely discounted, and must be considered if an error is particularly recalcitrant.

Compilers, being large programs, cannot be expected to be totally error-free. However, except for very new compilers the bugs you are likely to encounter should be known and documented in your installation. Such errors are most likely to affect lesser-used features of the language, and can usually be avoided by treating them as language restrictions. Most system software errors can also be avoided, but in both cases, steps should be taken to rectify the faults if possible. They should certainly be noted documented, as should the steps taken in the program to avoid them, and the reasons for those steps.

Both hardware and operator errors are characterized by being intermittent, or being related to some particular individual or piece of equipment. Good program design, using firewalling between modules, checksums, and batch totals on files, can be used to limit the damage caused by hardware errors, while programs which are sympathetic to their operators will be less prone to human errors. While it is practicable to ask the operator to enter parameters from the console when only one program is running in the machine, this can impose an unreasonable burden in a multiprogramming environment, with the consequent risk of mistakes. The solution lies in easier, more automatic programs with clear and concise operating instructions.

Program testing and debugging lacks the glamour of program design and building, and so is often ignored or only half done. It is tempting, after the while heat of coding, to assume that if the program compiles and runs without any execution errors, then it works. Perhaps it does work, but all it proves is that the program does something—not that it does the right thing. Only thorough testing can validate the program, and demonstrate that it does indeed meet its specification.

14.6.3 Conversion

Conversion means changing from one system to another. The objective is to put the tested system into operation while holding costs, risks, and personnel irritation to a minimum. It involves:

1. creating computer-compatible files, 2. training the operating staff, and
3. installing terminals and hardware.

A critical aspect of conversion is not disrupting the functioning of the organisation.

Conversion should be exciting because it is the last step before the candidate system begins to show results. Unfortunately, the results of conversions have been chaotic and traumatic for many firms. Unforeseen difficulties crop up as the system breaks down, data files are damaged, and tempers grow short. The training package is frequently not complete and people are trying to figure out what to do. Much of this stems from poor planning or no planning at all.

14.6.3.1 Activity Network for Conversion

Several procedures and documents are unique to the conversion phase. They include the following:

1. Conversion begins with a review of the project plan, the system test documentation, and the implementation plan. The parties involved are the user, the project team, programmers, and operators.
2. The conversion portion of the implementation plan is finalised and approved.
3. Files are converted
4. Parallel processing between the existing and the new systems is initiated.
5. Results of computer runs and operations for the new system are logged on a special form.
6. Assuming no problems, parallel processing is discontinued. Implementation results are documented for reference.
7. Conversion is completed. Plans for the post-implementation review are prepared. Following the review, the new system is officially operational.

14.6.3.2 File Conversion

File conversion involves capturing data and creating a computer file from existing files. Problems are staff shortages for loading data and the specialised training necessary to prepare records in accordance with the new system specifications. In most cases, the vendor's staff or an outside agency performs this function for a flat fee.

Copying the 'old' files intact for the new system is the prime concern during conversion. The programs that copy the files should produce identical files to test programs on both systems. At the outset, a decision is made to determine which files need copying. Personnel files must be kept, of course, but an accounts receivable file with many activities might not need copying. Instead, new customer accounts might be put on the new system, while running out the old accounts on the old system.

Once it is determined that a particular file should be transferred, the next step is to specify the data to be converted: current files, year-end files, and so on. The files to be copied must be identified by name, the programmer who will do the copying, and the methods by which the accuracy of the copying will be verified. A file-comparison program is best used for this purpose.

1. **Creating Test Files:** The best method for gaining control of the conversion is to use well-planned test files for testing all new programs. Before production files are used to test live, data, test files must be created on the old system, copied over to the new system, and used for the initial test of each program. The test file should offer the following;

   (*i*) Predictable results

(*ii*) Previously determined output results to check with a sampling of different types of records.

(*iii*) Printed results in seconds.

(*iv*) Simplified error-finding routines.

(*v*) Ability to build from a small number of records out of the production files and then progressively alter the records until they are challenging to the programs.

Selecting the right records for testing is not easy. The user's key staff should get involved in the selection process. The trick is to select a reasonable number of uncomplicated records and also records that have caused problems in the past.

A good test file should show how the new system handles the most difficult tasks. A health insurance test file, for instance, would include an employee with every possible type of insurance: worker's compensation, disability, dental cancer, life and accident insurance. If the new system programs process this file correctly, it is likely to handle the ordinary employee's insurance.

2. **Data Entry and Audit Control:** Many systems are prone to errors because of insufficient attention given to data entry control or protective features such as audit control trails. These items must be part of the overall plan for conversion. Before a data entry clerk begins to enter changes to items in the files, the count of the number of documents to be keyed in should be entered. The data entry program should be designed so that these summary totals are entered first, with the computer keeping a running count of the items entered.

A good audit control trail is the key to detecting fraud and mistakes that might indicate problem entries. At a minimum, the user should have a copy of the additions or deletions to any file. There should be a daily computer-printed entry list with entries and totals before they are entered and a second list showing actual changes after they have been made in the file(s). The detect fraud, many system designs do not allow any records on the file to be deleted easily. Modifications are made by adjustments involving more than one or two operating personnel or similar routines. Preventing records from being deleted makes it more difficult to cover up problems or conceal fraud.

14.6.4 Training

An analysis of user training focuses on two factors: user capabilities and the nature of the system being installed. Users range from the naive to the highly sophisticated. Developmental research provides interesting insights into how naive computer users think about their first exposure to a new system. They approach it as *concrete* learners, learning how to use the system without trying to understand which abstract principles determine which function. The distinction between concrete and formal (student type) learning says much about what one can expect from trainees in general.

There are several user training aids available:

1. **The user manual:** Traditionally, the user manual is prepared reflexively because it is an item that must accompany every system. Yet, there are time when a user manual is discretionary. The important point is that the manual should be prepared only if it will serve the user. A manual is necessary when the user is geographically removed from the project team or when he/she cannot attend all the training sessions. Of course, if the user requests a manual, then one must be prepared.

Probably the best reason for preparing a user manual is on the recommendation of the resident expert. If it will be used, the manual should be written, despite the cost. It should discuss, among other things the functions available to the user and what each can do, how they are executed, and how diagnostic messages should be handled. Above all, the manual should be well organised and indexed for quick reference. Graphics, pictures, and line drawings enhance the teaching value of the material.

2. **Help screens:** This feature is now available in virtually every software package, especially when it is used with a menu. Essentially, the user selects a 'help' option from a menu. The system accesses the necessary description or information for user reference. Then additional 'help' information may be accessed, or the user returns to the menu for further action. HELP offers the advantage of virtually unlimited space and, since it is separate from the program, it does not interfere with system operation.
3. **Data dictionary:** A data dictionary is a separate place for describing data elements. It is more like an electronic 'one-page' sheet available to the user to assure that functions are interpreted and executed properly.
4. **Job aids:** A job aid communicates essential information about certain jobs. It takes a number of forms, for example:
   (*a*) Color printing in forms to accentuate headings.
   (*b*) Color to identify pieces of hardware, cables, etc.
   (*c*) Wall charts to illustrate schematics of processing runs
   (*d*) Flowcharts to guide the user in detecting and handling errors, restarting the system, etc.

It can be seen, then, that training aids help communicate vital information about the new system. To make these aids useful, it is important to consider to whom, when, and why the user will be communicating this information.

14.7 POST IMPLEMENTATION REVIEW

Operational systems are quickly taken for granted. Every system requires periodic evaluation after implementation. A post-implementation review measures the system's performance against predefined requirements. Unlike system testing, which determines where the system fails so that the necessary adjustments can be made, a post implementation review determines how well the system continues to meet performance specifications. It is after the fact—after design and conversion are complete. It also provides information to determine whether major redesign is necessary.

A post-implementation review is an evaluation of a system in terms of the extent to which the system accomplishes stated objectives and actual project costs exceed initial estimates. It is usually a review of major problems that need converting and those that surfaced during the implementation phase. The primary responsibility for initiating the review lies with the user organisation, which assigns special staff for this purpose.

14.8 SYSTEM MAINTENANCE

Maintenance is the enigma of system development. If holds the software industry captive, trying up programming resources. Analysis and programmers spend far more time maintaining programs than they do writing them. Maintenance accounts for 50–80 percent of total system development.

System maintenance is the ongoing process of monitoring and evaluating the new system. Business needs and computer technology are constantly changing; therefore, an information system may need to be updated periodically to keep it current and ensure that it continues to meet the information needs of the business.

System maintenance involves identifying the need for change in the current system and making the appropriate changes. Even the best designed system may some day need to be replaced. When a problem or new opportunity is discovered, the system analysis phase of the system life cycle begins again.

Maintenance can be classified as corrective, adaptive, or perfective. *Corrective maintenance* means repairing processing or performance failures or making changes because of previously uncorrected problems or false assumptions. *Adaptive maintenance* means changing the program function. *Perfective maintenance* means enhancing the performance or modifying the program(s) to respond to the user's additional or changing needs. Of these types, more time and money are spent on perfective than on corrective and adaptive maintenance together.

Maintenance covers a wide range of activities, including correcting coding and design errors, updating documentation and test data, and upgrading user support. Many activities classified as maintenance are actually enhancements. *Maintenance* means restoring something to its original condition. Unlike hardware, however, software does not wear out; it is corrected. In contrast, *enhancement* means adding, modifying, or redeveloping the code to support changes in the specifications. It is necessary to keep up changing user needs and the operational environment.

Although software does not wear out like a piece of hardware, it 'ages' and eventually fails to perform because of cumulative maintenance. Over time, the integrity of the program, test data, and documentation degenerates as a result of modifications. Eventually, it takes more effort to maintain the application than the rewrite it.

A major problem with software maintenance is it labor-intensive nature (and therefore the likelihood of errors). Consider a change in the code. Altering the code, no matter how slight, must be manually introduced into each program because there is no easy way of making sure that the changes will interface with all the programs. Reusing the old codes depends heavily on the programmer's ability to judge what code can and cannot be reused. it is an error-prone process that is still perceived by many as more cost effective than writing programs from scratch.

The work of maintenance is certainly not for neophyte programmers. To put maintenance in its proper perspective requires considerable skill and experience and is an important and ongoing aspect of system development. The ability of the maintenance programmer to make sound judgements depends on his/her technical expertise and ability to identify user needs. This means understanding the operational environment and what the user is trying to accomplish with the software.

An additional factor in the success of the maintenance programmer is the work environment. Maintenance programmers have generally been paid less and received less recognition than other programmers. Little attention has been paid to their training and career plans within the MIS function. Similarly, the need for maintenance programmers to apply standards and methodologies has been overlooked.

Maintenance demands more orientation and training than any other programming activities especially for entry-level programmers. The environment must recognize the needs of the maintenance programmer for tools, methods, and training.

14.9 SUMMARY

The system life cycle is the life span of an information system. The life cycle consists of:

1. System Analysis
2. System Design
3. System Development
4. System Implementation
5. System maintenance

System Analyst is a person who works with a user to determine his or her data processing needs.

System Analysis is the process of analysing an information system to ascertain whether or not it meets the user's current or projected needs.

System Designer is a person who modifies an old system or designs a new one based on the user's information needs.

System Design is the process of detailing the physical layout of a system, such as describing the hardware, software, and operating procedures. This may also include modifying the logical design of the proposed system.

System Development is the process of creating a system from the physical descriptions detailed in the system design.

A type of chart used to graphically illustrate the physical requirements of a system, such as hardware devices and storage media needed to implement the logical design, is known as system flowchart.

System Implementation is the process of testing the new system, converting from an old system to the new one, and training the users on the new system.

The ongoing process of monitoring and evaluating a system is known as system maintenance.

REVIEW QUESTIONS

Multiple Choice Questions

1. A programmer would most likely prepare a:
   (*a*) general system flowchart (*b*) specific system flowchart
   (*c*) general program flowchart (*d*) specific program flowchart
   (*e*) None of the above
2. The first step of the implementation phase is:
   (*a*) implementation planning (*b*) select the computer
   (*c*) announce the implementation project (*d*) prepare physical facilities
   (*e*) None of the above
3. Which of the following is used when a company goes outside its organization to develop a new system?
   (*a*) request for proposal (*b*) data flow diagram (*c*) systems flowchart (*d*) project directory
   (*e*) None of the above
4. At the time of system study, flowcharts are drawn using:
   (*a*) non-standard symbols (*b*) general symbols
   (*c*) abbreviated symbols (*d*) specific symbols
   (*e*) None of the above
5. During system study, data can be collected through:
   (*a*) questionnaires (*b*) interviews (*c*) on-site observations (*d*) All of the above
   (*e*) None of the above
6. In Prototyping:
   (*a*) BASIC is used (*b*) COBOL is used
   (*c*) 4GLs are used (*d*) system is documented
   (*e*) None of the above
7. In Prototyping, the following are used:
   (*a*) screen generators (*b*) input generators
   (*c*) application generators (*d*) All of the above
   (*e*) None of the above
8. The first step to the system study project is to:
   (*a*) define system performance criteria (*b*) describe information needs

(*c*) staff for the study project (*d*) announce the study project
(*e*) None of the above

9. During the system study, analysts determine manager's information needs by:
(*a*) conducting tours of a near by computer center
(*b*) asking questions
(*c*) showing samples of computer reports
(*d*) teaching short courses in programming languages
(*e*) None of the above

10. Which of the following is not a factor in the failure of a systems development project?
(*a*) inadequate user involvement
(*b*) failure of systems integration
(*c*) size of company
(*d*) continuation of a project that should have been cancelled
(*e*) None of the above

11. Environment in systems parlance refers to:
(*a*) a sub-system (*b*) the boundary
(*c*) a part outside the boundaries (*d*) All of the above
(*e*) None of the above

12. Which are the tools not used for System Analysis?
(*a*) System-test data (*b*) Decision table (*c*) Data Flow Diagram (*d*) Flowcharts
(*e*) None of the above

13. A Feasibility study should focus on:
(*a*) technical feasibility (*b*) economic feasibility
(*c*) operational feasibility (*d*) All of the above
(*e*) None of the above

14. The 'big picture' diagram of a system is the:
(*a*) block diagram (*b*) logic diagram
(*c*) system flowchart (*d*) program flowchart
(*e*) None of the above

15. The first step in systems Development Life Cycle is:
(*a*) database design (*b*) system design
(*c*) preliminary investigation and analysis (*d*) graphical user interface
(*e*) None of the above

16. A system design aid should primarily:
(*a*) help analyse both data and activities (*b*) help in documentation
(*c*) generate code (*d*) using a graphical user interface
(*e*) None of the above

17. Which of the following is (are) not a tool for Application Prototyping?
(*a*) Application generators (*b*) third generation language
(*c*) screen generators (*d*) report generators
(*e*) None of the above

18. Coding and testing are done in a:
(*a*) top-down manner (*b*) bottom-up manner
(*c*) ad hoc manner (*d*) cross sectional manner
(*e*) None of the above

19. A feasibility document should contain all of the following except:
(*a*) project name (*b*) problem descriptions
(*c*) feasible alternative (*d*) data-flow diagrams
(*e*) None of the above

20. In data-flow diagrams, an originator or receiver of the data is usually designated by:
(*a*) a circle (*b*) an arrow (*c*) a square box (*d*) a rectangle

21. The first items defined for a new system are its:
(*a*) inputs (*b*) outputs (*c*) storage (*d*) processing

22. A system analyst designs a new system by:
(*a*) identifying sub systems and the interfaces between sub systems
(*b*) adopting a developed system to the present environment
(*c*) developing the system as a large, single unit
(*d*) propose alternatives to the current system
(*e*) None of the above

23. Mistakes made in the system analysis stage show up in:
(*a*) implementation (*b*) system design
(*c*) system developments (*d*) All of the above
(*e*) None of the above

24. Structured design methodology is an approach to design that adheres to rules based on principles such as:
(*a*) top-down refinement (*b*) bottom-up design (*c*) data flow analysis (*d*) All of the above
(*e*) None of the above

25. A Decision-Table is:
(*a*) a way of representing the information flow (*b*) a way of representing multiple conditions
(*c*) a ways to get an accurate picture of the system (*d*) All of the above
(*e*) None of the above

26. Which of the following is not a part of a Data Flow Diagram?
(*a*) disk storage
(*b*) arrow
(*c*) Data store
(*d*) process represented by a bubble circle (circle)
(*e*) None of the above

27. A data flow diagram is:
(*a*) the modern version of flowchart
(*b*) mainly used at the systems specification stage.
(*c*) the primary output of the systems design phase
(*d*) All of the above
(*e*) None of the above

28. A feasibility study:
(*a*) includes a statement of the problems (*b*) considers a single solutions
(*c*) both (*a*) and (*b*) (*d*) a list of alternative solution considered
(*e*) None of the above

29. A graphic representation of an information system is called:
(*a*) flow chart (*b*) pictogram (*c*) data flow diagram (*d*) histogram
(*e*) None of the above

30. During what phase, the requirement analysis is performed?
(*a*) system design phase (*b*) system development phase
(*c*) system analysis phase (*d*) system investigation phase
(*e*) None of the above

31. In functional decomposition, the data flow diagram:
(*a*) is ignored
(*b*) is partitioned according to the 'closeness' of the datagrams and data storage items
(*c*) is partitioned according to the logical 'closeness' of the actigrams
(*d*) both (*a*) and (*c*)
(*e*) None of the above

32. System Study involves:
(*a*) study of an existing system
(*b*) documenting the existing system.
(*c*) identifying current deficiencies and establishing new goals
(*d*) All of the above
(*e*) None of the above

33. A square symbols:
(*a*) defines a source or destination of system data
(*b*) identifies data flow
(*c*) represents a process that transforms incoming data flow(s) into outgoing data flows
(*d*) is a data store-data at rest, or a temporary repository of data
(*e*) None of the above

34. An open rectangle:
(*a*) defines a source or destination of system data
(*b*) identifies data flow
(*c*) represents a process that transforms incoming data flow(s) into outgoing data flows
(*d*) is a data store-data at rest, or a temporary repository of data
(*e*) None of the above

35. The feasibilities studied in preliminary investigation is (are):
(*a*) technical feasibility (*b*) economic feasibility
(*c*) operational feasibility (*d*) All of the above
(*e*) None of the above

36. Which of the following activities, does not belong to the Implementation phase of the SDLC?
(*a*) File conversion (*b*) Program testing (*c*) User training (*d*) All of the above
(*e*) None of the above

37. Structured Programming involves:
(*a*) decentralisation of program activity (*b*) functional modularisation
(*c*) localisation of errors (*d*) All of the above
(*e*) None of the above

ANSWERS

Multiple Choice Questions

1. (*d*) **2.** (*a*) **3.** (*a*) **4.** (*b*) **5.** (*d*) **6.** (*c*) **7.** (*d*) **8.** (*d*)
9. (*b*) **10.** (*c*) **11.** (*c*) **12.** (*a*) **13.** (*d*) **14.** (*c*) **15.** (*c*) **16.** (*a*)

17. (*b*) **18.** (*a*) **19.** (*d*) **20.** (*c*) **21.** (*b*) **22.** (*a*) **23.** (*a*) **24.** (*c*)
25. (*b*) **26.** (*a*) **27.** (*b*) **28.** (*a*) **29.** (*c*) **30.** (*c*) **31.** (*c*) **32.** (*d*)
33. (*a*) **34.** (*d*) **35.** (*d*) **36.** (*b*) **37.** (*b*)

QUESTIONS

1. What are the stages of the system life cycle?

2. What is documentation? Describe its function in the system life cycle

3. Describe the role of the following people in the system life cycle; user; system analyst; system designer; and programmer.

4. What is the purpose of an information system?

5. What is a system.

6. What is the purpose of the system design step?

7. Describe two tools that a system analyst can use to help analyse data.

8. What is the purpose of the system maintenance step?

9. Why is it important that the users be involved in the system life cycle?

10. What is the purpose of the system development step?

11. Describe a file design

12. What is a prototype and why is one developed?

13. What tools and techniques are used during system design?

14. An international airlines initiated a frequent traveler program designed to encourage passengers to fly regularly and earn awards based on miles flown. The airline policy is specified as follows:

15. 'Passengers who fly more than 1,00,000 miles per calender year and, in addition, pay cash for tickets, or have been flying the airline regularly for more than five years are to receive a free round-trip ticket around the world. Passengers who fly less than 1,00,000 miles per calendar year and have been flying the airline regularly for more than five years also get a free round trip ticket around the world'. Draw a decision table for passenger free ticket.

16. Electronic India Ltd., a small manufacturer of electronic calculators, stocks 'ready to ship' units in four warehouses (*A*, *B*, *C*, *D*). Warehouse *A* handles all orders received from foreign customers out of the state of Uttar Pradesh. Warehouse *C* fills orders received from nongovernment customers that operate within the state of Uttar Pradesh. Warehouse *D* handles order received from state or federal government agencies. Develop a decision table to indicate the warehouse from which customers can be accommodated.

15

COMPUTER SECURITY

15.1 INTRODUCTION

This chapter deals with the interaction of computers with society—the issues of computer crime, ethical issues in computer information systems, health and safety issues for people working with computers. We will also outline several important new computer technologies that are likely to change the way we use computers.

You have probably heard a friend or neighbour complain that computers are 'taking over society' and that they 'know too much about us.' Whether you agree with this point of view or not, serious computer professionals recognize that current information processing trends, such as the emergence of-massive credit databases containing the credit history of 150 million Americans can potentially Jeopardize our personal freedoms.

Although there is no reversing the trend toward large credit databases, their existence brings up two important social and organization issues—privacy and security. **Privacy** is an individual concern; people need assurance that their personal information, such as employment and credit history, will be used properly. **Security** is an organizational concern; businesses need safeguards that protect computer systems and data from damage or unlawful use. As a result, security protects hardware, software, and data from natural disasters such as fire, flood, and earthquake; it also guards against sabotage and espionage, as well as, various kinds of theft.

Computer crime, which results from the deliberate tampering with data, has become a costly trend for organizations ranging from small businesses to multinational corporations and the federal government. We will focus on methods that companies use to protect against computer crime; such methods will also help to protect data from natural disasters.

15.2 COMPUTER SECURITY

Computer security includes the policies, procedures, tools, and techniques designed to protect a company's computer assets from accidental, intentional, or natural disasters, including accidental input or output errors, theft, breaking, physical damage, and illegal access or manipulation.

Computer security is a complex and pervasive problem that often stumps many organizations, which struggle to balance proper security against the cost and inconvenience of providing it. It cannot be achieved through automation or sophisticated equipment alone; it also requires the active participation of employees with common sense, good judgement, and high moral values, because security is ultimately the responsibility of the individual using the computer. Therefore, it is not surprising that organizations that promote creativity, innovation, trust, and high ethical standards appear to be more successful in enforcing computer security than organizations with stifling cultures.

15.3 WHY ARE COMPUTER SYSTEMS VULNERABLE?

There are a number of reasons why computer systems are vulnerable to security breaches.

15.3.1 International Breaches by Employees

Unfortunately, among the primary sources of security breaches are employees who are either callous or forgetful about security standards. In some cases, employees intentionally cause breaches, either for financial gain or for the fun of it. One of the best ways to reduce security breaches is to educate employees about security policies and to clearly communicate the penalties for violations.

15.3.2 Increased System Complexity

Today, with the spread of end-user computing, the number of computer systems in the workplace has increased manyfold. Moreover, information systems have gone from being support systems to being the lifelines of many business, so the number of mission-critical systems has also increased significantly. Technological advances in computers have made many systems extremely complex and difficult to manage. A networked systems become the norm, the task of securing computer systems is becoming more and more challenging. Finally, users working on such systems have technical sophistication that can be misdirected.

15.3.3 Choices of System Components

In recent years, the number of hardware, software, and network options available to managers has increased manyfold. As IS managers attempt to integrate this wide variety of tools and techniques, providing system security is often a daunting task. Further, many systems run on different operating systems, and security considerations are often different for different systems. Network components and configurations have also creased, creating the opportunity to 'mix and match' or 'plug 'n play'. It is even more difficult to provide security for a diverse set of systems.

15.3.4 Network Vulnerabilities

Telecommunications, advances in networks and telecommunications have profoundly affected organizational productivity and decision making. The way companies do business has been completely revolutionized by telecommunications. Unfortunately, networks are also among the most vulnerable links in the security chain for computer systems—in fact, in a recent survey of CIOs, more than 90% of the respondents indicated that network security was a **strategic** concern for their organizations.

'Networks' are essentially sieves to anyone with minor technical skills and the desire to retrieve other people's information.

The Internet is a vital link that connects people and organizations all over the world. However, in recent years it has been plagued with security problems as the number of Interest users has increased, the number of security breaches has also increased.

There are many reasons why networks are so prone to security violations. The arrival of cellular phones, radio modems, and sky pagers has created new points of vulnerability in the electronic exchange of information, since many unauthorized parties can tune into a company's voice or data transmissions. Second, in a distributed environment, there are innumerable opportunities for security breaches. 'In contrast to the fortress-like architecture of the mainframe, security exposures in client-server computing almost defy identification'. Third, networks transmit large amounts of data and information around the world and it is difficult to continuously keep track of who is doing what, where, when and how. Fourth, in many organizations network administrators are rewarded for providing easy access to the network, but not for tight security, and obviously the two do not go hand-in-hand. Fifth, many network users are ignorant of network security measures and, intentionally or unintentionally can cause considerable damage. Users often view security policies and procedures are cumbersome and counterproductive, so they try to find short cuts or even to completely bypass security controls.

15.3.5 Sophisticated Hackers

They are given different—hacker, crackers, information warriors, cyberpunks, cyberterrorists, and phone freaks—but they are all people who violate computer security. A **hacker** is an individual who is knowledgeable enough to break into a computer system or facility, although he or she does not cause any harm to the system or the organization. A **cracker**, on the other hand, is a computer thief who breaks into a system with the intent of stealing passwords (sets of characters that allow users to log onto a system or to access a program), mail messages, files, programs, and so on, for fun or for profit. For example, in 1991, Pierre Marion, the former head of French intelligence, admitted that France had been spying on IBM, Corning, and Texas Instruments for almost a decade, causing IBM alone losses of billions of dollars. And why not? Marion asked. After all 'in economics, we are competitors, not allies'.

Crackers can cause financial damages and injure the competitiveness of a firm. For example, in 1991, when a security breach occurred at the research facility of a major U.S. automobile manufacturer, the company lost $500 million worth of designs for future cars and suffered in the marketplace because its designs fell into the hands of competitors.

15.3.6 Complacent Management

In spite of the many highly publicized cases of security violations, top management in many organizations is oblivious to security violations and their ability to bring a corporation to its knees. They are often reluctant to invest in security because they do not believe it has a direct impact on profits. But unless management takes a vigilant and proactive approach to computer security, security breaches are like time bombs waiting to explode.

The challenges of securing computer systems in an organization are summarized as:

- **Intentional breach by employees:** A primary source of security breaches is the intentional or unintentional actions of employees.
- **Increased system complexity:** Open, integrated, mission-critical, and real-time systems are highly complex and difficult to monitor and manage.
- **Too many choice in system components:** The number of hardware, software, and network configurations has increased tremendously.
- **Increased network vulnerabilities:** Networks have become increasingly complex and difficult to manage.
- **More skilled crackers:** Crackers are better educated and more technically skilled, making it easier for them to break into computer systems.
- **Complacent top management:** Top managers often feel that security violations happen at other companies, not at theirs.

15.4 TYPES OF COMPUTER SECURITY BREACHES

The different types of computer breaches can be broadly classified into three categories: accidental or unintentional errors, intentional errors, and natural disasters.

15.4.1 Accidental or Unintentional Errors

Accidents in the workplace can cause security breaches; it is often said that the cost of intentional damage exceeds the cost of computer crime. Accidental security violations can be reduced by education and training, and by establishing and communicating security policies and procedures. Let us look at some types of accidental security violations.

Sometimes hardware components accidentally fail—the memory, keyboards, terminal emulators, LAN connection cards, network cabling, network servers, routers or bridges in networks, WANs, mainframe front-end processors, and a multitude of peripherals and accessories—causing a security breach. Cables, modems, fax machine, and cellular phones are particularly prone to failure. Countless cables installed underground or on building roofs link and support corporate networks; since they are not visible, they are often forgotten during development of security plans. However, cables can be accidentally cut or destroyed during building repairs and maintenance, so measures should be taken to protect them. Software errors—in input, processing, output, or storage—can also cause security violations.

15.4.2 Intentional Errors

Intentional damage to systems is also common. It is widely believed that IS personnel are the greatest threat to system security, because they have intimate knowledge of the workings and the critical elements of a system. Intentional errors may take the form of illicit entry to a system, access to valuable proprietary corporate data, stealing passwords in order to snoop around, reading E-mail, or destroying important files. Regardless of the motives behind such acts, they are serious violations. They may go undetected for days, weeks, or even months, particularly if the violator is good at what he or she does. Let us look at some types of intentional security violations.

15.4.2.1 Cracking Passwords

Cracking, or decoding, passwords, which are the Achilles' heel of computer security, is one of the most common security violations, since hackers and, crackers can easily guess passwords or capture them as they travel over the network. Once the **super-user** (the user, such as a system administrator, who has access to all passwords) password is cracked, the perpetrator has full control of the system and can set up accounts, use the system to uncover more passwords, and gain access to vital information, all without even being detected.

15.4.2.2 Breaking into Computer Hardware

Another type of intentional security breach is breaking into and damaging computer hardware. Modems, fax machine, and cellular phones are particularly vulnerable to this type of damage.

Millions of modems all over the country give employees and other level entities access to a company's computer system. Unfortunately, modems are also highly vulnerable to security breaches. For example, 'demon dialers' are programs that first identify all the phone numbers connected to a modem and then break down passwords to gain illegal access to the system. Two hackers in Seattle used 'demon dialers' to break into a federal court computer, decoded user passwords, and gained access to several files of national importance. Even worse, hackers often share phone numbers and passwords with other hackers for a price, further spreading the results of the crime.

Fax machines, the 'long-distance copiers' of corporate America, are a weak link in computer security. Information sent through fax machines can be intercepted, copied, or rerouted to another machine. Although users rarely hesitate to give out their fax numbers, this practice can be a security threat. A risk management consultant tells the story of two U.S. companies that were negotiating merger terms through their law firms, located in Chicago and in New York. When clerks at the New York firm faxes sensitive contracts to Chicago, they misdialed the Chicago firm's fax number by one digit. The documents, instead of arriving at the Chicago law office, arrive at the office of **The Wall Street Journal**, which made the negotiations public. The merger fell through and one misdialed digit cost the company millions of dollars and irreparable damage to its competitive position.

Experts recommend that you never send anything confidential or proprietary by fax. 'Assume that everything that you fax could go to the local newspaper', says one security expert. Also, documents received by fax should not be treated as original documents. Using a pair of scissors, a little bit of Scotch tape, and a falsified signature' a hacker persuaded a London bank to transfer $600 million into his account! Banks learned an important lesson in the process; today, the U.S. Uniform Commercial Code requires phone-call verification for any fax-based fund transfers.

Cellular phones are the weakest links in communication networks, because they are essentially software devices that can easily be accessed with a $100 scanner. Experts recommend that you should not discuss proprietary information over cellular phones and strongly urge strongly urge callers to use code words when discussing confidential matters.

15.4.2.3 Software Viruses

There are two primary sources of intentional software security breaches: computer viruses and 'sniffer' programs.

The greatest threat to software is a **computer virus**, a program that causes a computer system to behave in unexpected and undesirable ways. Some signs of a virus include unexplainable loss of free memory, unusually long times for program loading or execution, changes in file or program size, print routines that stop working, computers 'freezing up', strange beeps or messages, computer reboots in the middle of a process, and corrupted files. It is estimated that there are more than 2,100 computer viruses and that about 50 new ones are created each month. When a virus is executed, it makes copies of itself and spreads from one system or application to another through networks and diskettes. It is precisely for this reasons that many companies strongly discourage the sharing of diskettes between systems.

Viruses are not easy to isolate and cure. A security manager at Nynex's New York headquarters recalls when a PC on his company's network became infected with the Jerusalem B virus. Every machine on the company's network, and all machines that shared potable disks, had to be examined. Four LAN administrators worked 2 full days plus overtime to isolate and clear the virus; a technician had to spend 9 hours clearing 'trouble tickets;' a security specialist spent 5 hours on followups and reports; 200 users on the LAN each suffered at least 15 minutes of downtime.

15.4.2.4 Legal Implications of Spreading a Virus

Believe it or not, it is still legal in the United States to create a virus and inject any computer system, because the writing of software is protected by the First Amendment, although federal regulatory agencies are working hard to change this situation. There are other reasons why it is difficult to make virus illegal. Researchers often use viruses for scholarly study, such as testing system security; this makes it difficult to ban them. Also, a law that makes it illegal to delete information, would make the popular delete function, DEL *.*, illegal! Further, with no uniform definition of a 'malicious virus', it is difficult to prosecute those who create them. Every state except Vermont has its own definition of what constitutes a computer crime, so catching perpetrators is a legal battle that few are willing to wage.

To further aggravate the problem, when someone is convicted of injecting a system with virus, the punishment is often light. For example, in 1988, Robert Morris actually brought down the Internet and other major networks around the country by injecting a virus into the network. Although this resulted in losses in the millions of dollars and loss of productivity for thousands of workers, he was given only 3 years' probation, a $10,000 fine, and 400 hours of community service. This is because the computer Fraud and Abuse Act of 1986 uses the victims' dollar loss to determine the severity of the crime, rather than considering the larger consequences of the crime. However, a strong and concentrated effort is being made to make the writing of a virus illegal by focusing on the intent of the virus, not just the financial result.

The second type of intentional software security breach is using 'sniffer' programs which explore the system to gather data about network users, their passwords, their access codes and the nature of their work. These programs, which are they useful for network administrators, can dangerous in the hands of a hacker who stealthily monitors data transmissions.

15.4.3 Natural Disasters

The third type of security breach is caused by natural disasters, such as hurricanes, earthquakes, tornadoes, and floods. These can be so devastating that companies, and even entire cities, take a long time to recover from them. In 1992 alone, insurers in the U.S. handled a record $18 billion in natural—disaster claims.

Some less damaging natural disasters include those that affect power supplies, cooling systems, communication networks, alarm systems, lightning protectors, building structures, and other facilities that support computer systems.

Lightning is one form of natural disaster. Keven L. Ervin Consulting Ecologists, a Fort Myres, Florida, firm, lost about $40,0000 worth of personal computer and network equipment when its installed lightning surge protectors failed. It took the firm 2 days to recover from the calamity and more than 6 months to recover from the problems of corrupted data.

Power outages are another common cause of computer downtime and lost productivity. They should not be taken lightly, because a power failure of just 50 milliseconds can result in at least 10 minutes of computer downtime, which can translate into losses of millions per minute for large financial institutions. The average company loses 2% to 3% of its gross sales within 8 days of a sustained power failure; if the outage lasts longer than 10 days, the company may never fully recover from the loss. In fact, almost 50% of companies that suffer prolonged power outages are likely to go out of business within 5 Years.

Telephone outages can cause major havoc and destroy the reputation of a company. For example, the Midwest Stock. Exchange, with security transactions of close to $75 billion last year, knows that even a brief interruption in its telephone service can cause losses in the millions of dollars. The company therefore has a backup exchange. 'We consider the telephone system the highest priority system in the exchange. Even when computers are down, we can continue to do trading manually' provided we have our telephone system operating'.

Although the probability of a disaster is often at the core of cost-benefit analysis for disaster protection and recovery, this may not be the best approach. The first question should be 'What is the probability of a disaster striking?' Instead, it should be 'What is at risk if a disaster does in fact strike'? The following question should drive home the dangers of a disaster much more poignantly and realistically than a cost-benefit model.

- ❐ What will be the loss in revenue if a given disaster strikes?
- ❐ How will the competitive position of the firm be affected?
- ❐ How will suppliers, creditors, and stockholders be affected?
- ❐ How will the firm's customers be affected?
- ❐ What will happen to the financial health of the firm?

Another conventional approach to calculating the expected value of a disaster is to multiply the probability of the disaster by the estimated magnitude of the loss: Expected Value of Damage = Probability of Damage × Estimated Loss in Dollars.

In spite of the alarming statistics about disasters and their effects on a business, very few companies consider disaster avoidance and disaster recovery in their risk management plans. Top management often wrongly believes that the company is immune to disasters.

An ounce of disaster prevention is worth a pound of disaster recovery cure. Physical disasters don't happen randomly. They are caused by preexisting, identifiable, disaster-prone conditions. Clearly, avoiding a corporate heart attack makes a lot more sense than the risk, pain, and expense of an attempt to recover after one strikes.

15.5 SECURITY CONTROL

In this section, we look at some measures that organizations can take to reduce security breaches. Note that we use the word **reduce**, not **eliminate**, since it is impossible to eliminate **all** security violations; crackers always appear to be one step ahead of security experts.

Computer security controls are policies, procedures, tools, and techniques designed to reduce security breaches and system destruction, to prevent errors in data, software and systems, to protect systems from accidental, intentional, and natural disasters, and to continually enhance system security. Controls may be manual or automated. Figure 15.1 shows the four different types of controls: applications controls, development controls, physical facility controls, and personnel controls.

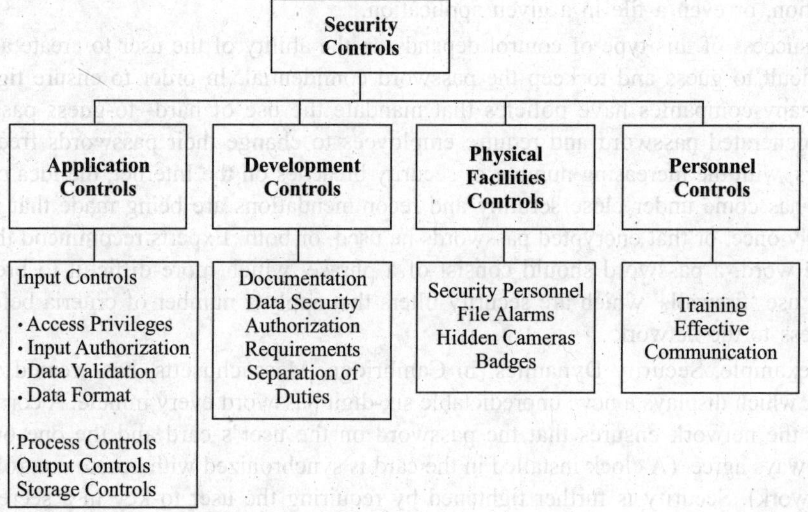

Fig. 15.1 Some types of controls that a company can implement to secure its computer systems

15.5.1 Application Control

Application controls are policies and procedures that ensure the security and quality of system applications in the organization (such as payroll and inventory management). Application controls cover four primary areas of data processing: input, processing, output, and storage.

15.5.1.1 Input Controls

Input controls are designed to prevent users from entering incomplete, erroneous, unauthorized, or inappropriate data there are four different kinds of input controls: access privileges, input authorization, data validation, and data format.

15.5.1.2 Access Privileges

Unique user IDs, aging passwords, smart cards, access control lists, and regular auditing and monitoring of potential security violations are some measures that organizations can take to ensure proper access privileges. Access privileges for vendors should also be closely monitored, since unscrupulous vendors can snoop around and gather intelligence on confidential data. Access privileges should be highly selective, closely guarded, and determined on a user-by-user basis or on a function-by-function basis, since most security breaches are committed by insiders who know the weak points in a company's network.

15.5.1.3 Input Authorization

Data input must be authorized and monitored by appropriate authorities, failing which users with illicit motives may cause financial and legal problems for the company. For example, without proper input control, an unauthorized user can change payroll figures or other vital data.

In batch systems, where source documents are the primary source of data, input controls should monitor the movement of the source documents and the personnel who handle them. The source of each input should also be validated, particularly for critical systems or for those with major financial implications. For online systems, the primary source of input control is passwords.

Passwords, the most common **type** of authorization control, refers to a set of characters that acts like a key to unlock the system. Separate passwords can be used to access a system, an application, or even a file in a given application.

The success of this type of control depends on the ability of the user to create a password that is difficult to guess and to keep the password confidential. In order to ensure tight system security, many companies have policies that mandate the use of hard- to-guess passwords or randomly generated password and require employees to change their passwords frequently. In recent years, with the increasing number of security breaches on the Internet, the idea of reusable passwords has come under close scrutiny and recommendations are being made that passwords be used only once, or that encrypted passwords be used, or both. Experts recommend that instead of a single word, a password should consist of a phrase, which more difficult to break. Some companies use 'firewalls' which are security filters that apply a number of criteria before giving a user access to the network.

For example, Security Dynamics, in Cambridge, Massachusetts, has created a SecurID smart card, which displays a new, unpredictable six-digit password every minute. A corresponding feature on the network ensures that the password on the user's card and the one on the host machine always agree. (A clock installed in the card is synchronized with access control hardware on the network). Security is further tightened by requiring the user to key in a secret personal identification number (PIN) so that in case the card is lost, the PIN will still prevent unauthorized users from gaining access to the system. The company claims that the odds of breaking into a system with SecurID are less than one in 14 billion.

But some experts caution that passwords often convey a false sense of security and recommend that companies use the principles of I&A: identification and authentication. I&A requires the use of three things.

1. **Something you know:** This would include things such as password, a PIN, or a phrase.
2. **Something you own:** This would include such things as a smart card or an ID card.
3. **Something you are:** This would include things like thumb prints, retinal scars, handwriting, and signatures.

These three measures, combined together, can significantly increase the security of a system. Obviously, not all systems require such rigid access controls, but for critical systems they may be a necessity.

15.5.1.4 *Data Validation*

Data should be validated before it is processed. This can be done manually by two employees who compare data, or automatically by a computer comparing the input data with existing master files. There are also programs that automatically compare data values against pre-established values: a long distance phone number should be 10 digits long, and so on. Usually, such checks are made by the DBMS so that the same checks can be applied uniformly to all applications.

Several data validation techniques are commonly used to detect input errors. **Anticipation checks**, which compare input values with expected or anticipated values, are particularly useful for checking for nonblank values, such as an employee name on a payroll check. **Reasonableness checks** are controls that check whether input values are within reasonable limits: for example, hours worked per week cannot be greater than, say, 80. **Arithmetic proof checks** ensure that arithmetic operations are properly executed: numbers cannot be negative, and so on.

15.5.1.5 *Data Format*

Input controls should also check the format of the data, ensuring that there are no missing values and that data are in the right format (integer versus decimal values, for example), the right size, and the right type (for example, telephone numbers should not include alphabetic characters). Though the type and extent of controls vary from organization to organization, and even from application to application, IS managers must establish must establish and implement proper data controls. A distinction should also be made between policies that may be overridden under special circumstances and those that are strictly mandatory.

Controls are also necessary to ensure that all errors are corrected. Cumulative errors lists that identify all errors in a certain application are useful for corrective action. Clearly, only authorized people should be allowed to correct errors and notification of error correction should be documented and forwarded to the proper authority.

15.5.1.6 *Process Controls*

Process controls and procedures that ensure that data are meaningful and reliable. These are designed to catch any errors that may have slipped through the input controls. For example, reasonableness checks can be incorporated into application processing so that any errors that may have gotten past the input controls are detected during processing. Other processing controls include ensuring that the right file or the most recently updated file is being processed and that the processing is accurate and timely.

Earlier in this chapter, we discussed some problems that an organization can face when its system is infected with a virus. What are some process controls that an organization can implement to protect itself from the dreaded virus? One of the most important steps toward eliminating viruses is to educate users about their effects and how to prevent them. In a recent survey of employees at a Fortune 100 company, 98% said that although they had heard about computer viruses, they were not sure as to what viruses do and many indicated that they had little or no knowledge of how to prevent or remove a virus. Education is vital to prevent infection by viruses. Second, a simple yet highly effective measure is to restrict the movement of diskettes from one system to another, this greatly reduces the chances of spreading viruses from one machine to another.

Also, there are many off-the-shelf virus detection programs that can be activated when the computer is first booted up as a way to prevent virus infection. Other steps that organizations can take to prevent virus attack are to mandate that users change their passwords every 30 to 90 days, to establish strict guidelines for the user of 'shareware', and to strictly prohibit access to 'freeware' (software that is available at no charge).

Other process controls include frequent backups of important files. Making backups is creating duplicate copies of a file and storing them on a separate disk or medium, or even in a separate location. It is a way to protect files against accidental deletion, misplacement, and natural or man-made disasters. Take, for example, the case of the Rockland Community Action Council (ROCAC) administrative headquarters in Spring Valley, New York, where a five started on a quiet Sunday morning. When it was put out later that day, seven PCs' had gone up in flames and the CIO was convinced that the organization was ruined because its financial records, stored on those PCs' hard disks, were all gone. He suddenly remembered the fireproof filling cabinets, where some tapes had been stashed away. 'My eyes nearly popped out when I realized the backup tapes were OK'. The backup tapes contained all the vital records of the organization, which saved it from financial ruin.

It is also strongly recommended that the original file be checked for viruses before backups are made. Organizations that are data-intensive keep a long indicating when each backup was made, to avoid any confusion or overwriting. With the spread of end-user computing more and more organizations are shifting the responsibility of backups from the IS department to the end-user. When files are frequently backed up, the losses or damage from a virus are minimized, because only information generated since the last backup is lost or damaged.

Many organizations have written policies on the number and frequency of backups; some even state explicitly the penalty for failing to make backups. Although backups are vital, companies must perform cost-benefit analyses to determine which files are critical and to determine accordingly how frequently these files should be backed up (hourly, daily, weekly, monthly, semiannually, and so on).

15.5.1.7 Output Controls

The third type of application control is **Output Controls,** which ensure that system output is accurate and is disseminated to the right people at the right time and in the right format. The number and rigor of the output controls depend on the critically of the application; for critical or proprietary applications, output controls are likely to be more strict and rigid than for noncritical applications. If the output is confidential, such as nuclear facility designs or medical research findings, controls measures must be taken to secure the output from unauthorized parties.

In most case, output controls include at least a periodic review of system output by authorized individuals who check—the timeliness, accuracy, and format of the output, identify any exceptions (such as overtime being five times the usual value), and make sure that no unauthorized programs were accessed during processing.

15.5.1.8 Storage Controls

The fourth type of application control is **Storage controls**, which ensure that the storage devices on which data and program are stored are safe, secure, and well protected from natural and man-made disasters. Storage controls mechanisms prevent unauthorized access to storage devices, as well as accidental or intentional deletion or manipulation of files. As you may recall, passwords and access privileges are two common and popular control measures that are effective storage controls. Backing up files is another control mechanism that helps organizations recover from damages to storage devices. Clearly, backup files should be stored on different devices from those that hold the original files, and in some cases should even be in a different location. File backups are discussed later in the chapter.

15.5.2 Development Control

Control mechanisms for system security should not be an afterthought, but should be made an integral part of the development process, from product conception to product delivery. **Development**

controls are controls built into each phase of the development cycle. The include measures such as establishing development standards (guidelines for developing systems), creating proper documentation, ensuring the security and reliability of data, establishing proper authorization for changes or additions to requirement specifications, and separation of duties.

15.5.2.1 Documentation

Proper system documentation is one way to control the quality of the development process and consists of detailed record keeping about the system, it logical and physical functions, its features, its interfaces, and any other elements that are essential to its smooth functioning and maintenance. Clear and well-written documentation should be developed for the entire system, for the various programs in the system, and for specific system operations. Documentations is an essential part of security control, because without it security experts may have to guess at the source, or even the indications, of a security breach. Moreover, when developers leave a project or leave the company, documentation is the only way to understand the intricacies and the possible weak links of the system so that proper security measures can be implemented. Though many developers view documentation as a boring task, it is so vital to the continued success of a system that some organizations hire a documentation specialist to ensure that all system are properly documented that the documentation is frequently updated.

15.5.2.2 Data Security and Reliability

Data security and reliability development control mechanism that prevents unauthorized access to data. They are particularly critical in real-time distributed systems. Some measure to secure data are preventing viruses, establishing accessing privileges, securing physical facilities, and implementing user IDs and passwords.

15.5.2.3 Authorization Requirements

Authorization requirements are control mechanisms that allow only authorized users to access and use the system. These control all activities related to input, processing, output, dissemination, storage, and maintenance of data. Any installation of new programs and any system configuration should also require proper authorization.

Authorization controls are particularly essential for System change, so that employees cannot accidentally or intentionally change applications—for example. Payroll or employee benefits.

15.5.2.4 Separation of Duties

Finally, **separation of duties** is another development related control mechanism, which reduces or eliminated conflicts of interest that can compromise the security and reliability of the system. For example, most organizations do not authorize system developers to give the final clearance on the quality and performance of the system. In other words, system testers should not be the same people as the system developers, because system developers have a personal stake in the perceived quality and reliability of the system.

In summary, there are four main types of development controls: documentation, data security and reliability, authorization requirements, and separation of duties. Next, we look at the third type of control—control of physical facilities.

15.5.3 Physical Facilities Control

The primary goal of physical facilities control is to protect the physical facilities that house the computer and other related assets from theft, unauthorized access, natural disasters, and vandalism, through measures such as posting security personnel, installing fire alarms, security alarms, and hidden cameras, and requiring users to wear badges or use smart cards to gain access to the building. Most facilities also include environmental control device that monitor and control the air and the temperature in a building.

Although the reliability of physical support facilities is often overlooked, it is an important part of system security, particularly for real-time systems. Many support facilities were designed in the 1970s, when batch processing was the norm: when a system failed, the computer was simply shut down until the facility was restored. But today, many systems are 24-hour, real-time, mission-critical systems that simply can not be interrupted.

In recent years, many computer failures have been attributable to failure of the support system, rather than of the computer system itself. For example, when an electrical fire broke out in the lower-Manhattan data centre of Securities Industry Automation Corp. (SIAC) a few years ago, the New York and the American stock exchanges (NYSE and AMEX) came to a grinding halt and put transactions worth billions of dollars on hold for several hours. Although news reports attributed the disruption to the fire, the problem was traced to a faulty alarm system, which misinterpreted a blaze in the basement as a fire in the 14th-floor computer room and simply shut down the entire system.

15.5.4 Personnel Controls

Many security breaches are caused by employees within the company, either because they lack knowledge about system security or because they have illicit intentions. Some of the leading security concerns of CIOs in the U.S. are:

- Network security. End-user security awareness
- Winning top management's commitment
- Using access-controlled software
- Distributed computing security
- Integrating security systems
- Monitoring user compliance with security policy

In fact educating end-users about computer security is one of the top three security concerns of CIOs in the U.S.

'There's a bigger security problem with insiders than with terrorists or industrial espionage. You can't worry about protecting against external forces if you have not protected yourself from within. We've seen cases where disgruntled employee has gone in and wiped out all the information on a server', says a security expert at Coopers & Lybrand.

Controls are only as effective as the people who implement them. Training system users and communicating security policies are two types of personnel control.

15.5.4.1 Train system users

Losses from network security breaches are estimated to be, in excess of $2 billion each year. This figure is expected to increase as companies move mission-critical data from mainframes to distributed environments and as the number of mobile users increases. Unfortunately, company employees are among the biggest threats to system data security. 'The hackers you read about are by far the smallest threat. Many security breaches are caused by simple user errors'. Hence, a key ingredient to achieving network security is regular and extensive user training on how to secure systems and data. Also, employees must be educated on the consequences of poor security and the penalties for failing to follow company policies.

15.5.4.2 Establish and Communicate Security Policies and Procedures

Security policies and procedures, combined with extensive user training, should precede any investment in security products. Establishing the security policy for a company is the first and most important step. The security policy should contain a mission statement, identify the security responsibilities of each employee, and address, in very specific terms, the ways to protect system hardware and software.

15.6 SECURING COMPUTER SYSTEMS

One study of 283 businesses and governmental institutions in U.S.A. found that half were victims of computer crime each year. Records show that while a bank robber armed with a gun steals an average of $1,600 from a bank, the white-collar criminal armed with a computer steals an average of $100,000! These statistics for white-collar crimes may in fact be low, because many organizations such as banks, fearing a loss of customer confidence, do not report all the crimes that occur.

Computer crime can be as small-scale as the unauthorized use of business computers for personal purposes, or as large as using computers to send corporate financial assets to a private Swiss bank account. Computer crime can include:

Theft of Computer Time: This common theft may be as simple as students doing term papers on computers at work or as great as someone stealing thousands of dollars of processing time for personal profit.

Manipulation of Computer Programs or Data: Remember the movie War Games, in which the protagonist changed his grades in the high school computer by using a modem at home? Unfortunately, such actions are all too common. Newspapers frequently print stories about computer enthusiasts, or 'hackers', breaking into public and private databases—sometimes just for the technical challenge of it! Some hackers even plant 'computer viruses' that tie up CPUs by commanding them to do such time-consuming tasks as attempting to calculate the precise value of pi—thereby crippling enormous data networks.

Theft of Data and Assets: Legally called embezzlement, computer theft often involves a trusted employee who cannot resist the temptation to steal. All too often, the theft is amazingly easy to carry out. For example, the chairman of the board and some of the executive officers of the Equity Funding Corporation—a publicly held mutual fund and insurance company in U.S.A.—used terminals to enter insurance policies for nonexistent people. By entering bogus data over a period of years, they greatly increased the company's apparent assets of the 97,000 insurance policies maintained by the computer, almost two-thirds were fictitious policies with a face value of $2.1 billion. Because the company appeared to be more profitable than it actually was, the stock of Equity Funding was greatly inflated; consequently, the officers, who were large shareholders, were able to sell their shares at considerable profits. The fraud went undetected because auditors consistently accepted the computer printouts that listed policyholders as beyond question. The crime was discovered by auditors and the police only when a former employee revealed the scheme.

Users Stealing Software: Are you stealing when you make a copy of word processing software for a friend to use? The law says you are. Yet many normally law-abiding people who would not dream of shoplifting see nothing wrong with making a copy of a $500 word processing package and giving it to a friend, despite the fact that it is in violation of the U.S. Copyright Code. **Bootlegging** software is clearly unethical, as well as illegal, yet it is so widespread that estimates suggest there may be as many as ten illegal copies for every legitimate program sold.

To prevent bootlegging, software vendors sometimes copy protect software so that it cannot be copied to other disks—or can only be copied a limited number of times, generally twice. Copy-protected software is becoming rarer, however, as vendors respond to complaints from users that copy protection is a nuisance. Copy protection can make it difficult to do legitimate copying, such as creating backup disks or recovering from hard-disk failure. In fact, the lack of copy protection is often a selling feature for many programs.

15.7 LIMITS OF LEGISLATION TO CONTROL COMPUTER CRIME

Legislators in U.S. have been trying for years to enact laws to curb computer crime at the federal level, without success. The major stumbling block is the lack of a legal definition for 'property' and 'value' as they relate to computerized information. Prosecutors are also reluctant to take computer typically to court because the computer security in an organization is typically so poor and computer crime laws so vague that they find it difficult to build good cases

Because the U.S. federal government has not enacted effective laws in this area, many states are beginning to pass stronger legislation that protects companies from computer theft, deliberate destruction of data, and so on.

15.8 HARDWARE AND SOFTWARE CONTROLS

Precautions and controls can be employed for protecting hardware and software from illegitimate use. Access to a system and its data should be controlled, and secure backup copies maintained. Most electronic network packages include measures for controlling access to sensitive files other ways to reduce the risk of fraud are to rotate personnel in certain Jobs and to separate important tasks so that no one person could complete a fraudulent transaction.

Controlled Access to Hardware and Software: If data or program security is important, system analysts should ensure that unauthorized personnel cannot have physical access to the computer system. The system can be housed in a locked room to protect hardware from theft and to prevent unauthorized people from accessing data or programs. Specific physical and electronic access control techniques include keyboard locks, automatic logs, restricted access to systems, and limited after-hour use' Using passwords that change periodically can also help to keep a system secure.

Backup Copies of Data and Programs: Creating backups consists of making extra copies of programs or data. Backups safeguard against the loss of programs or data in computer memory, on hard disks, or on diskettes. Data should be backed up each time it is updated or changed in any way.

Security for Backup copies: Because backups represent the safety net that will be used if original data or programs are destroyed, the backups must be protected with the same care as the originals. Protection techniques include keeping them under lock and key in a fireproof container and storing them in a location several miles from the original. This protects files from natural disasters as well as computer crime.

Distributed Network Controls: Distributed processing and remote database pose specific control problems for organizations because they are vulnerable to unauthorized access to data from remote locations. For example, a company trying to discover a competitor's confidential data might tap into the competitor's network and monitor transmissions for their own benefit. Two common controls are used for protecting networks: data encryption and callback systems.

- ❐ **Data encryption** involves encoding data so that it cannot be understood unless it is first decoded. To encrypt data, a program uses an algorithm to scramble, or encode, data before it is sent over the network. Another program at the receiving end then decodes the data. If an unauthorized person tapped into the database, the data would not be readable.

  Because data encryption is cumbersome and expensive, it is generally used only for sensitive data. Access to both the encryption and the decoding programs must be tightly controlled as well.

- A **callback system** ensures that a user calling in by phone is calling from an authorized telephone number. After validating user's password, the callback system breaks the phone connection and then immediately calls a previously stored telephone number linked to the password in the system's memory. If this is not the number where the person seeking access is located, entry to the system will not be permitted.

Separation and Rotation of Functions: Another way to ensure the security of computer systems is to segment the work done so that each task requires several different people. This separation of duties minimizes the risk of unauthorized and fraudulent use and/or modification of data as well as programs, because two or more perpetrators within the department would be required to commit a fraud. Separating tasks also reduces the risk of errors since one person can check the work of another.

In addition to separating duties, it is advisable to have duties rotated among individuals within each group from time to time. This arrangement is likely to thwart fraudulent collusion among employees. If, for example a particular data entry operator who enters only payroll data and a programmer who works exclusively on payroll programs intend to work together to commit a computer crime, they may find it difficult to carry it out if their jobs are periodically rotated.

Safeguards such as these help honest people stay honest. Honest computer users often confront ethical challenges as well, and these issues are often not so clearly defined.

15.9 ETHICS IN COMPUTING

Ethical conduct goes beyond merely adhering to laws. All professions have a code of ethics that broadly sets standards for professionals; such ethical standards may not be covered by specific legislation. For example, what should you do if you are an analyst or programmer responsible for a program that invades privacy? Or how responsible are you if you create a software package that produces erroneous results? After all, is it reasonable to expect software packages to be totally free of errors?

There are, of course, no simple answers to questions such as these. Many people with high ethical standards have argued against holding computer professionals totally responsible for their work, because the way a system is used may not be under the programmer's or analyst's control. Some people argue that, just as Alfred Nobel cannot be held accountable for the immoral use of his invention of dynamite, computer professionals should not be held accountable for programs that are used illegally or unethically.

As the debate over these ethical issues goes on, many leaders in the computing field believe that a code of ethics is of primary importance and that it would be far better for professionals to police themselves before the government finds it necessary to pass laws.

15.10 MANAGING THE WORK ENVIRONMENT

The emergence of computers in the workplace has created a number of new organizational issues in such areas as space planning, health, and safety.

Consider what happened to a telephone company that installed an automated telephone system for its operators. Operator productivity suddenly decreased because:

- Light reflecting onto terminal screens from a large bank of windows bothered the operators. While the windows were a much desired change for the operators, the bright, natural light was sometimes so intense that it caused eye strain.
- The operators' workstations were designed for the average operator. There was little, if any, flexibility for changing the position of the screen, keyboard, or desk to satisfy individual tastes and desires.

❒ Each operator was given a U-shaped desk with side panels for privacy. Because the operators were accustomed to seeing their colleagues while they worked, they felt cut off from their peers.

What can be done to help users cope with the physical, mental and social problems caused by new office technologies? **Ergonomics** is the science of adapting machines and work environments to people. Ergonomic studies are designed to provide the best physical arrangement for people using computers and other technology for any length of time.

Reducing Office Glare: Perhaps the most obvious problem in the work environment—and the one easiest to deal with—is office lighting. Improper lighting conditions create glare on video display terminals. There are two common ways to reduce glare: provide indirect lighting, which may almost totally eliminate the problem, and/or provide anti-reflection filters that reduce glare on the screen but also reduce the intensity of the image.

The general trend is toward eliminating all direct overhead lighting, such as fluorescent lights, and substituting softer, indirect lighting in its place.

Reducing Sound Pollution: Well-planned offices eliminate distracting sounds yet make provisions for private conversations. Because office systems commonly result in noise created by keyboards, printers, and even the computer itself, an effective noise control program focusses on three areas: efficient sound-absorbing materials on furniture, walls, ceilings, and floors; sound-masking devices such as printer covers; and well-designed office layouts.

Designing Optimum Workstations: Workstations should be designed to allow users the greatest economy of movement. Factors such as sitting or standing heights, reach lengths, arm angles in keyboarding, and eye viewing angles all contribute to the comfort of performing necessary office tasks. Poor workstation design will ultimately result in user fatigue a high rate of error, and slow task performance.

Reducing Hazards to Health: Many people are concerned that computer systems in businesses can be unhealthy for employees. Consider the experience of data entry operators whose input rate is closely monitored by automated equipment. The system keeps track of the average time it takes an operator to key in an order. If management has set strict standards for acceptable performance, such close monitoring can be devastating to the health of employees. It can induce stress, other health problems, feelings of powerlessness, and even complete apathy. As a result, organizational productivity can plummet.

Another hotly debated issue is whether video display terminals (VDTs) emit harmful radiation. Numerous studies conducted in the 1970s and early 1980s failed to detect radiation above acceptable levels, but these conclusions are now being re-evaluated. Questions center around the long-term biological effects of low-level radiation from VDTs on users, especially on whether prolonged exposure of pregnant women to VDTs can cause birth defects. Until conclusive evidence is available to resolve these issues, a corporate policy requiring periodic testing for malfunctioning video display terminals that emit radiation above safety limits might be appropriate.

Employees' experience with computer systems affects their attitude toward new technology. In a poorly managed computer environment, employees may believe that their computer system displaces workers, affects their health, and limits their freedoms, or they may believe that computers provide new careers, enhance employee control over tasks, and improve their decision-making ability. The perception of the effects of computers in a given business depends on the leadership and vision of the company's managers as well as the computer professionals who plan and create these systems.

15.11 WHERE IS COMPUTING GOING?

The long-term goal of most advanced computer vendors is to create systems that are capable of handling **compound documents** that integrate data from different applications—text, data, spreadsheet, graphic, image and voice information—into a cohesive information system. Compound document systems conceivably allow an architect, for example, to:

1. Turn on the system and orally ask it to display sketches of a new amusement park, which are stored in the database.
2. Combine these sketches with photos of three proposed sites.
3. Attach a written purchase order.
4. Add a short oral note asking for comments.
5. Send the whole package electronically across the country to the client's office.

While such futuristic document systems will not appear overnight, some compound technologies, such as word processing and spreadsheets, are well established. Other technologies such as image and voice processing may not mature for many years.

Following is an overview of areas in which we can expect to see advancements in the next decade.

15.11.1 Image Processing Technology

Beginning computer users are often surprised by how difficult it is to combine drawings, graphics, and photographs into documents. The technical problems arise from the huge amount of storage space required to store graphics: for example, while one page of text requires about two kilobytes of storage, an 8 × 10 inch photograph can require several megabytes—enough computer space to hold two or three thousand pages of text. Image processing systems that allow users to manipulate images in databases and combine them with text are slowly maturing, however, and will become more common throughout this decade.

Current image systems often employ workstations and laser printers; in addition, they may communicate with other devices via local and wide area networks. They often contain specialized devices such as **scanners** (devices that convert pictures and text into machine-readable information), **optical disks** (platters about the size of long-playing records that can contain about 40,000 pages of images and text), and **jukeboxes** that manipulate optical disks to process images. Scanners are now available for microcomputer users for about $200.

A good image processing system also contains software that allows users to index, compress, edit, annotate, cut, paste, and route image information. In addition, image processing systems often contain word processors that allow users to combine text and graphics.

For image systems to work effectively in organizations, three technological hurdles must be overcome: data transfer rates must increase, users must be able to write to optical disks, and software tools capable of integrating images with other office information need to be developed.

Slow Data Transfer: The speed at which data moves between workstations through common LAN wiring such as twisted-pair and coaxial cable is sometimes too slow. These cables cannot accept information faster than 500,00 bits per second (bps), or about 31,000 bytes per second. This may sound fast, but it is too slow for image technologies that commonly use files of several million bytes. However, as LANs begin to use fiber optic cable, which is able to transfer data at much faster rates, image processing will become more practical.

Erasable Optical Disks: For image processing technology to be effective, users must be able to write and erase data on optical disks as easily as on magnetic media. Although it costs about one dollar to store one page of image-based information on magnetic media and only about five cents to store the same information on an optical disk, optical disks are not yet fully practical because these disks can be written to only once but read any number of times (called WORM—write once, read many). Erasable disks that users can write to are becoming more common, however, and are likely to be important storage media for computers in the years ahead.

Manipulation Tools: Traditionally, users have not had the tools to edit, manipulate and integrate images easily with other information such as text, spreadsheets, and databases. However, public standards for using images in compound documents are being developed that allow users to pass graphic pictures, including photographs as well as drawings, back and forth between different systems.

15.11.2 Voice Processing Technologies

Like image processing systems, voice technologies—audio response and voice recognition—are still in the early stages of development. When these technologies mature, researchers expect them to become a major method for users to communicate with each other and with computer system components.

Voice processing technology turns analog, or sound, signals into digital information that machines can understand. This process is called voice input or **recognition**. The technology must then be able to interpret the digital information so that it can be output in a meaningful form. It may then process the output and provide a meaningful **audio response**—that is, turn the digital information into analog signals.

15.11.3 Audio Response Devices

Promising audio response (also called voice output) technologies are voice store-and-forward systems and voice synthesis systems.

Voice Store-and-Forward Systems: Voice store-and-forward systems turn analog voice signals into digital format so that voices can be stored, retrieved, and distributed like any other form of electronic information. A common store-and-forward system is a **voice response system** that turns words into digital information, compresses the digitized words, stores them in libraries of words and phrases, and later uses these words to build responses. The key part of a voice response system is the algorithm used to combine the words and phrases back into meaningful responses.

You have probably used one voice response system many times; most local telephone company directory assistance programs provide digitized directory information. The directory contains a database of telephone numbers and recordings of the first ten digits, zero through nine. To hear a telephone number, the operator identifies the requested number and the system then 'speaks' each digit to you. More sophisticated algorithms can combine phrases from a database of 2,000 to 3,000 words into simple sentences.

Voice Synthesis Systems: Voice synthesis systems turn digital information into sound waves—an audible voice. Unlike voice response systems, which have a limited vocabulary, voice synthesis systems have a potentially unlimited vocabulary. Instead of storing words, a voice synthesis system stores the smallest units of sound used in speech (called phonemes) and uses a set of algorithms to put these basic sound units back together into words. Voice synthesis technology has two basic limitations: currently, the sound quality is poor, and it requires a heavy share of processing memory and secondary storage-space.

15.11.4 Voice Recognition Devices

While voice output technologies are complicated, they are relatively simple when compared to voice recognition systems.

Voice recognition turns human speech into computer-readable code. Because people talk in such hurried and varied ways, voice recognition technologies are extremely complex. Researchers may design voice recognition systems to be speaker—dependent (or independent), to recognize discrete (or continuous) speech, or both.

Speaker-Dependent Systems: Speaker-dependent systems require users to train the system to recognize their specific speech profiles. To train the system, a user speaks into a microphone, pronouncing each word he or she wants the system to recognize. Once trained, such a system recognizes only the intonations of the user it is trained to recognize—a security benefit in some cases, since it limits access to the system. For example, a system trained by an East Indian user who speaks English with a Hindu accent will probably not understand another user who speaks English with a British accent.

Speaker-independent systems allow anyone to use the system without training the system first.

Discrete Recognition Systems: Discrete recognition systems require the user to pause (possibly for only a fraction of a second) between words to help the system identify word breaks. Continuous recognition systems enable users to speak in a normal cadence with words running into one another.

As shown in Fig. 15.2, four different combinations are possible in a voice recognition system. Currently, the most accurate systems are speaker-dependent and discrete; the most inaccurate are independent and continuous. To be effective in computer systems, voice recognition technologies must eventually become independent and continuous.

Voice Recognition Systems

	Independent	Dependent
Recognizes Discrete	**Independent/Discrete** Any user , speaking distinctly	**Dependent/Discrete** One user, speaking distinctly Currently most accurate
Recognizes Continuous	**Independent/Continuous** Any user, speaking naturally Ideal system Currently most inaccurate	**Dependent/Continuous** One user, speaking naturally

Fig. 15.2 Four different combinations of technologies are possible in a voice recognition system

Technical progress is slow in developing these systems because of the numerous complexities involved. Independent and continuous systems need to be able to process large and complex vocabularies, since a literate person's vocabulary may contain 100,000 words. In addition, people talk quickly—generally up to about 145 words a minute—and they often run words and sounds together.

Researchers estimate that a fully independent/continuous system will not be developed until the end of the century at the earliest.

15.11.5 Personal Information Managers

Many computer experts predict that personal information managers (PIMs) will be an exciting breakthrough in software for the 1990s. Currently, most PIMs are used basically as desktop organizers, but more powerful PIMs allow users to enter text information randomly into computers and quickly find it again. Unlike spreadsheets (which take the place of ledgers) or databases (which take the place of filing cabinets), personal information management software has no physical counterpart. It appeals to experienced users who spend most of their time at workstations and who store most of their information in digital form.

Personal information managers are designed to handle the small bits of text information that can get lost in traditional databases. For example, data that is ideal for PIMs include comments that a client made about his or her family during a golf date, or comments that serve as informal leads to potential new clients. The biggest conceptual challenge for those managing this kind of informal text is how to store it so that it can be easily retrieved. Although various personal information managers solve this problem in slightly different ways, they all combine three types of software; text and retrieval programs, free form databases, and hypertext applications.

Text and Retrieval Programs: Text and retrieval programs store the entire contents of a document in a database. These programs retrieve text either by searching from the beginning of a document to the end or by using special search algorithms. What distinguishes full text retrieval from traditional databases is that text can be completely unstructured and undefined—users do not have to remember a document number or name to retrieve information. You simply enter a keyword or phrase that you know is in the document, and the retrieval system tells you which documents in the database contain the specified word or phrase. For example, you can enter a client's name in a PIM record (Shubhag Chand, for example) and the fact that Shubhag likes Anju and has a daughter going to the Indian Institute of Technology. Then, later, in another record, you can make a note to meet Shubhag on Friday. When Friday comes, you can quickly locate all notes pertaining to Suresh.

Freeform Databases: Freeform database documents are structured similarly to the data fields and records of traditional databases: they allow you to sort, search, and manipulate documents as though they were database records. These programs create an actual text database of documents—not simply a collection of text files as in search and retrieval programs. Freeform databases allow users to specify certain words or numbers in a document as data fields, sort by those fields, and use Boolean operators (such as AND, OR, and GREATER THAN) just as you would with a traditional database. For example, using a freeform database containing names and addresses of clients, a stockbroker can make notes like the following:

Krishan Kumar

Likes the railroad and silver industries. Wants
investments with a rate of return GREATER THAN
35 percent.

Gross investment to date: ₹ 1,232,500.

The stockbroker can then calculate the total investments of all his or her clients, create a list of those interested in the railroad, and sort that list by preferred rate of return!

Personal information managers that use freeform database concepts can manipulate text information extensively, but they are difficult to learn and are harder to use than search and retrieval programs. However, once mastered, they are also faster.

Hypertext: Hypertext is a form of DBMS that allows users to link screens of information (text, graphics, images, and even sound) together associatively. Hypertext products mimic our ability to store and retrieve information referentially for quick and intuitive access. Ted Nelson, who coined the term hypertext, defines it as a way of creating documents that can be read in relation to other documents. A common use for hypertext is for in-depth research. While displaying one document, a hypertext application refers readers to other documents, which in turn refer them to still other documents. Readers who want to check a reference might click a mouse button on the item to be referenced, and the referenced text will appear on the screen. In this way, all documents are linked to each other by association.

Many computer novices who use hypertext applications are impressed by its power. Hypercard is a popular hypertext application for the Macintosh. Many applications have been designed to take advantage of Hypercard's capabilities. These range from such business-related tools as medical dictionaries to games.

Personal information managers combine search and retrieval, freeform database, and hypertext techniques to allow systems users to organize the myriad tasks, ideas, and notes—even those created haphazardly—so that they can be retrieved quickly for current projects.

15.12 COOPERATIVE PROCESSING SYSTEMS

Many computer experts are currently combining the strengths of mainframes, minicomputers, and personal computers into cooperative processing systems. A good example of a cooperative system is Prodigy, the subscriber service offered for microcomputer users by IBM and Sears. The Prodigy system consists of a central mainframe, several regional minicomputers, and software on the users' micros. Prodigy is designed so that each element of the system works in cooperation with each other element, and processing tasks are distributed to the most appropriate computer in the system.

For example, one of Prodigy services is to allow users in any part of the country to display a map of the country with local and national weather, and even ski conditions. Rather than store the maps, weather graphics, and current weather information at the central mainframe and then send it over the network to individual users, Prodigy stores the graphics map and menu displays at the users computers; the mainframe sends users only the current weather information via the network, and the users' software overlays it on the resident maps. This substantially reduces processing and access times as well as the amount of storage space required on the mainframe.

Cooperative systems decrease the amount of data traffic and time needed to send data over networks. Each of the system's elements is used to perform the tasks for which it is most effective.

Analysts expect that powerful, multitasking operating system software such as OS/2 will make cooperative processing more common. Multitasking software takes advantage of increasingly powerful microcomputers and enables them to communicate and cooperate with mainframes as equals rather than simply as terminals or network nodes.

15.13 THE CHALLENGE OF COMPUTER SYSTEMS

As a result of the increasing power of image, voice, and expert systems, the day is coming when computer systems will provide many of the services now supplied by managerial support staff. Managers will rely on their computer systems to gather information, analyze it, and present it to workers and decision makers in immediately usable form.

A broad range of tools are converging on computer systems to create this level of support, which is likely to further revolutionize the work environment. These tools include compound documents, electronic messaging, interactive video teleconferencing, and intelligent networks that provide access to thousands of external public databases. They also include specialized workstation technologies such as legal, medical, and engineering expert systems that help professionals better use their creative capacities.

Such developments have significant influences on those who use computer systems, requiring them to change from being merely participants in the system to becoming system designers themselves. Successful users will be those who are able to think and plan strategically, encourage innovation and develop computer solutions to their own business problems.

In many ways, computer systems are at the center of a technological and organizational revolution that is changing today's society. Those at the center of this revolution—those with the vision to see where computer technology is going and its power for constructive change—will be tomorrow's leaders.

15.14 REAL WORLD CASES

1. **Masters of Deception:** The Masters of Deception were five New York hackers who gained illegal access to computers at many major corporations. Companies such as SouthWestern Bell, British Telecom, New York Telephone, Martin Marietta, New York University, and TRW were all victims of this group. A two-year surveillance operation by 150 Secret Service agents, called Operation Sundevil, culminated in 28 search warrants and indictments on 11 charges of security breaches in 14 cities. The damage caused by the group had resulted in almost $50 million in losses. The influence of the group was so widespread that 42 computers and 23,000 disks were confiscated in New York, Chicago, Los Angeles, and 10 other cities.
2. **Internet Security Breaches:** Security breaches on the Internet have increased dramatically in recent years and are causing national concern. The Internet connects 2 million host computers and provides access to a rich and extensive array of data and information to millions of users, whose numbers increase by more than 15% every month. The Internet transmits more than 100 billion bytes of data every day; every country in the world has an Internet connection. It is easy to understand why the Internet is considered an ideal target for 'cyberterrorists'.

   In February 1994, hackers stole thousands of passwords over the internet, allowing them illegal access to government, financial, research, scientific, and defense computers around the country. 'This large-scale digital robbery is in a class by itself for scope, audacity, and potential damage'. The chief of the FBI's Financial Crimes Section Testified that in more than 80% of the FBI's computer-crime investigations, the Internet had been used to gain illegal access to systems.

15.15 SUMMARY

The increase in distributed environments, the exponential growth of information and information-related products, the increase in competitive pressures from all over the world, and advances in technology have all placed data among the most sought-after assets in today's competitive business environment. As our reliance on computers and information systems increases, the task of securing these systems also increases in criticality. A computer security breach is often viewed as a 'corporate heart attack' because it can cause serious damage to the organization. The damage may consists of revenue loss, productivity decline, computer downtime, or loss of competitive status. Hence, computer security is vital to the growth, and even to the survival, of a business. Computer security is defined as a set of policies, procedures, tools, and techniques that an organization establishes to protect its computer assets from theft, security breaches, physical damage, and illegal access or manipulation. Computer security is a broad and encompassing issue that covers all the components of corporate computing: hardware, software, networks, physical facilities, data, and personnel.

There are several reasons why computer systems are vulnerable to security breaches. The increased complexity of information systems has made it difficult for organizations to develop rigorous security measures. The multitude of choices in system configuration is another factor contributing to the security challenge. Today, the number of hardware, software, and network choices is greater than ever before, making the task of the security expert more complex and challenging. Third, because of distributed computing, the number of employees working locally and remotely, nationally and internationally, on homogeneous and heterogeneous systems has increased significantly. It is therefore becoming a Herculean task to prevent illegal access and unauthorized manipulation of files in distributed environments. Fourth, hackers and crackers have become more sophisticated and persistent. A cracker is an individual who illegally breaks into a computer system or facility and steals passwords, mail messages, files, programs, and so on, for fun or for profit. Regardless of a cracker's motive, he or she Computer can cause serious and irreparable damage to a company, its assets, and its reputation. Finally, in spite of all the warnings and horror stories, top management is still often reluctant to invest in system security.

Security breaches can be broadly divided into five categories: hardware, software, networks, personnel and natural or man-made disasters. Hardware breaches can be intentional or accidental cables, fax machines, modems, and cellular phones are particularly vulnerable to security breaches. 'Sniffer' programs and computer viruses are the two primary threats to software. Networks are very vulnerable to security breaches particular weak links on the network include computers, improper access privileges network cables and wires, lack of user training, and lack of well-thought-out security policies and procedures. Finally, disasters can cause security violations. There are three types of disasters: natural, infrastructure, and operational.

Computer security controls are established and implemented in order to reduce security breaches or even system destruction. Effective controls help to prevent system errors and protect systems from accidental, intentional, and natural disasters. There are five types of controls: application controls, development controls, access controls, physical facility controls, and personnel controls.

Application controls are policies and procedures that ensure the security and quality of individual applications in the organization. Some specific types are input, processing, output, ani storage controls. Development controls are established so that the security of the system is addressed during system development itself and not as an after thought. Some specific types of the development controls are standards and documentation, data security, authorization requirements, and separation of duties. Access controls include passwords and other measures to make sure that access to data, programs, and systems is available only to authorized individuals. Physical security controls are measures taken to protect and secure the physical plant and the facilities of an organization. Finally, personnel controls are procedures to educate end users about security measures and their criticality to the organization.

REVIEW QUESTIONS

1. What is the difference between hackers and crackers? Should an organization take measures to protect itself from both or just from one?
2. What is meant by application controls? Briefly describe the four primary areas of data processing that are covered by application controls.
3. What is meant by security controls? Briefly describe the five types of controls.
4. Define computer security. Explain why computer security cannot be achieved through automation alone. Identify any three reasons why computer systems are vulnerable to security breaches. Explain why networks are so prone to security breaches.
5. What are development controls? Identify and describe the four types of development controls.
6. What is meant by access controls? What are some measures that companies must take to ensure that passwords provide the necessary security?
7. What is a computer virus? What are some ways to prevent viruses?
8. What is a backup? Why are backups vital to computer system security?
9. What are some measures that managers can take to protect their networks from security breaches? Describe any two in detail.
10. What are the three types of security breaches? Give an example of each.
11. Why are fax machines and modems particularly vulnerable to security breaches? What measures can an organization take to secure these two types of hardware?
12. What are some data validation controls and how do they help to increase the security of input data?

16

COMPUTER VIRUS

16.1 INTRODUCTION

There are two primary sources of intentional software security breaches: computer viruses and 'sniffer' programs.

The greater threat to software is a **computer virus**, a program that causes a computer system to behave in unexpected and undesirable ways. Some signs of a virus include unexplainable loss of free memory, usually long times for programs loading or execution, changes in file or program size, print routines that stop working computers 'freezing up', strange beeps or messages, computer reboots in the middle of a process, and corrupted files. It is estimated that there are more than 2,100 computer viruses and that about 50 new ones are created each month. When a virus is executed, it makes copies of itself and spreads from one system or application to another through networks and diskettes. It is precisely for this reason that many companies strongly discourage the sharing or distettes between systems.

Viruses are not easy to isolate and cure. A security manager at Nynex's New York headquarters recalls when a PC on his company's network became infected with the Jerusalem B virus. Every machine on the company's network, and all machines that shared portable disks, had to be examined. Four LAN administrators worked 2 full days plus overtime to isolate and clear the virus; a technician had to spend 9 hours clearing 'trouble tickets; a security specialist spent 5 hours on followups and reports; 200 users on the LAN each suffered at least 15 minutes of downtime.

16.2 VIRUS WORKING PRINCIPLES

There has been much mystification on this point, half-spoken rumors, confusion and just plain misunderstanding. Really, there need to be no confusion: virus programs do not differ from any other computer program in any essential way. They are created using common programming tools, using knowledge that can be found in any computer book dealing with technical specifications on DOS. Virus programming demands no special skills; there is no 'black magic' about it. Indeed, many viruses have shown such poor programming skills that it's a wonder they function at all. Yet virus programmers seem to have obtained the reputation of being master programmers. Few things could be further from the truth. In the early virus days, it might have been the mark of a good programmer to be able to write a virus, but hardly so today. A computer never becomes infected in some strange and mysterious fashion that can only be accomplished by a virus. All infections can be traced back to one incident, such as a new program started on your computer or a new disk inserted into the floppy drive. It is important to realize that viruses can only reproduce if they are run. A computer cannot become infected unless an infected program is started on it. For that to occur, they need humans. A virus's true prey is not the computer, but the good will and ignorance of the users. Remember that a virus is always vulnerable to whatever a user of the infected system can think of to combat it. A successful virus must always try to lay low and avoid unnecessary attention drawn to it. A virus's main concern is to remain hidden from the computer user and from various antivirus programs he or she can use to keep a check on the computer system. If spotted, a virus is usually quite easy to get rid of. That is the reason benign viruses are often more successful than destructive ones. Mindless destruction tends to attract attention. Actually, the 'life' of a virus looks more like that of an animal being hunted, desperately trying to keep out of sight from the users, than this fiendishly devious hightech monster, taking over computers while the users are asleep—as it is often depicted.

Once the virus has been executed. It can exploit some weak points in the DOS system,. Everyone seems to come down on DOS these days, so let's see if we can get a kick in while its's down. In my opinion it's possible to make viruses, or viruslike programs, on any existing operating system, but few make it as easy as DOS. One could speculate that if DOS had been more thought through, it would not have been so haunted by the virus ghost. Let's go over some of DOS's weak points that viruses exploit.

- There is no memory protection. Once executed, a virus has free reign on all of the memory—interrupt vector table, normal memory, high memory. This is exploited by viruses in resident state, enabling the virus to spread itself more efficiently.
- File protection is another weak spot. It is possible to hinder either access to programs (like viruses) people to files. It is not possible to protect a file in DOS from unwanted modifications by a virus. Of course, DOS has the file-protection flag, set by the DOS command **attrib r file-name**, but the implementation of this is, as can be seen in the virus examples, almost a joke. It's simply too easy to avoid. Viruses that exploit this DOS weakness are called **file infectors**. They search the disk for files to infect and when one is found, they simply change it to include the virus. It's simple, efficient and could have been avoided with a better DOS.
- Then there are the partition and boot sectors. The partition sector/boot sector is the first part of any disk, hard or floppy. It contains a small program, called the partition record/boot record, which is executed each time the computer is turned on. This program can, like normal files infected by the file infectors, be modified by a virus and thus infected. Viruses targeting the partition or boot sector, are called **partition sector virus/boot-sector viruses.**

16.3 TYPES OF VIRUSES

There are basically three different kinds of these programs:

1. Viruses
2. Trojan horses
3. Worms

Generally, it can be said that these programs gain access to places and/or perform actions not intended by the user, often damaging data in the process. However, the exact phrases often get misused and mixed. That is not surprising, considering the difficulty even experienced computer users can have in obtaining the 'hard' technical information needed to understand the concepts involved. Furthermore, methods that can successfully defend you against one type ay have no effect against another. It is important to known what these 'rouge' programs do, if you are to defend yourself against them.

16.3.1 Viruses

The first computer virus for a personal computer was discovered (and created) around 1980. That means we've had about 15 years to get acquainted with them and used to their presence. Computer viruses are not a short-lived curiosity; they are today and will continue to be here for as long as anyone can foresee. They are sufficiently widespread to be a real danger to most computers, requiring people using computers to have at least a basic knowledge of their workings if they want to avoid infections. And even though the term 'computer virus' is well known even among people with little computer experience, what a computer virus actually signifies remains a mystery to most people. At least this is no mystery, since there is disagreement on what a computer virus is and what it's not, even among people specialized in the computer virus field. There is no general, agreed-upon definition. Still, let's look at some of the basic requirements that must be true before a program can be called a virus.

First, like a biological virus, a computer virus exists to replicate; if it cannot replicate, it's not a virus. A biological virus replicates to spread its DNA; a computer virus replicates to spread its program code. Just as a biological virus changes the cells' own DNA to force them to make new viruses, a computer virus modifies the code on the programs it targets to make new computer viruses. The term 'computer virus' was coined by Fred Cohen in the first paper discussing the theoretical aspects of computer virus programs. His thesis was published as early as 1984, in the days when a virus was still an interesting novelty. However, perhaps because it appeared before many viruses had been discovered, his definition of a virus extends only to viruses that propagate by attaching themselves directly to other programs. This is a bit narrow for today's use and does not contain many of the programs that today we call viruses, namely those that propagate by attaching themselves to floppy/hard disks of specific programs. If we just broaden Cohen's definition to include those disk-infecting viruses, we can cover all of the different virus types in existence today and still have a small group with common characteristics.

1. A virus is a self-replicating program whose main purpose is to propagate itself to as many different places as possible.
2. A virus propagates itself by modifying another program to include itself.
3. A virus can only propagate itself by an (unknowing) act of a user of the system in which it exists.

16.3.2 Trojan Horses

Trojan horses are simply programs that feign, by their name on their documentation, to do one thing, when in fact they do something else entirely, something often very destructive. Trojan horses are not very common and (contrary to viruses) are found mostly on Computer Bulletin Boards. Trojan's spreading potential is not very big, because once they are run they give themselves away (cease to be Trojans) and the only way for a Trojan to propagate itself would be for a user to copy it to somewhere else. Besides the another, few people would knowingly spread them. A typical Trojan horse could simply be a program given the name of another known program, which would be tempting for an unsuspecting user to start. A number of Trojans pretending to be antivirus or anti-Trojan software have been circulated. The name 'Trojan horse' came from the wooden horse the ancient Greek army used to conquer the city of Troy and save the beautiful Helen.

16.3.3 Worms

A *worm* can be defined as a program propagating itself in a network of computers, using bugs, which are unforeseen (by the designers and users) side effects of the operating system, or breaking (guessing) passwords to gain access to other machines in the network. Contrary to viruses, no user interactions are needs in the worm to spread. Worms need no host program to propagate; viruses are parasitic, worms are not. Periodically, rumors surface of worms existing in a DOS environment, using modems to propagate themselves. However, that is just a rumor. No worm has ever spread spreading itself in a network a PCs, few have been spotted, mainly because of the limited size of such networks. There is today only one computer network with sufficient size to enable a worm to be anything but a local menace; the Internet. There have been two major outbreaks of worms on the Internet, the not-so-famous Christmas Exec mail worm of 1967 and the very famous (infamous) Morris Internet of 1998.

16.4 VIRUS DETECTION AND PREVENTION

Detection By Appearance is a purely passive defense method, in that it can only direct an infection after the infection has already taken place. It is nevertheless the most widely used today, not least because of its ease to apply. Detection by appearance involves looking in executable programs for what might be suspicious code. The ideal detection-by-appearance program would be able to sniff out all virus code, while leaving in infected programs alone. However, to achieve such a universal antivirus program, one has to overcome a very large number of difficulties. Basically, there would be no easy road to take. There are a few characteristic many virus programs have, but none that is not also found in numerous other 'normal' programs, and none that is absolutely necessary for a virus. The antivirus program would have to be able to look through and 'understand' the program code, imagining what the original programmer meant it to do and seeing if it does something he did not intend. Even for the most experienced programmer. It is very exhausting work to mentally look through someone else's program and find out what it does not how it does it. A program that could do that automatically would, in short, need artificial intelligence! In fact, in 1984 Fred Cohen proved this to be impossible.

There is another, not so perfect, way to look for impeded virus code. While virus programs as a whole have no general 'stamp' by which they can be found, every unique virus has some code that it, with great probability, shares with no other program. Such code, called *scan strings*, can then be used to scan any program for. The idea is that if the scan string is detected in any program, it's probably infected by the virus from which the string was taken in the first place. Naturally, for the antivirus programmer to know these scan strings, he or she must know the characteristics of particular viruses and as such will always be one step behind the virus writes. It is far from the perfect universal virus detection. New viruses not yet included in the antivirus program, or viruses not programmed for, will not be detected. This does not pose as big a problem, as one could fear—more than 99 percent of all the viruses one is likely to be infected by are old, well-known viruses that any antivirus program should be able to detect. Sadly, an antivirus program using a scan-string search approach is not a one-time investment. To keep pace with the steady flow of new viruses, it needs new scan strings. When buying you antivirus program, you must be certain it is updated on a regular basis and to keep cost down that should be done without extra payment, as a number of such antivirus products already on the market do now. Any antivirus program that is not updated will quickly be outdated and all but useless, if not directly harmful for the false security implied. Scan strings give one more advantage, rarely given by the other methods of detection. It can identify the virus by the scan string and with this information it is often possible to remove the virus from the infected programs, without having to delete them.

Besides the drawbacks already mentioned, there are some limitations the user should be aware of before entrusting his or here disks solely to an antivirus detection-by-appearance approach. To save disk space, programs are often stored in a compressed format. A considerable mount of disk space can be saved by using different compression utilities and with the faster computers the time delay extracting them again is often insignificant. Consequently such disk-saving methods have gained much popularity in recent years. But compression involves some problems for the antivirus software. When compressed the internal code of the programs is changed and consequently the scan strings of any possible virus are changed also. This will prevent an antivirus program from recognizing the scan string and thus detecting the virus. There are three basic ways to store data in a compressed format: disk compression, file compression and executable file compression.

Disk *compression* compresses whole disks at a time. A small program to handle all the compress/extract routines is stored in memory. When a program is loaded from the compressed disk, it's extracted on the fly and stored in an expanded decompressed form in memory. Since the program is decompressed before the antivirus program should be able to detect viruses stored on a disk compressed with a disk-compression utility. Two common disk-compression formats are Stacker and Double Space.

File-compression utilities compress single files at a time and they compress both executable and nonexecutables. File compression is often the most efficient compression format when the smallest size is wanted. It is a much slower process both at compressing and extracting that the other two formats. Also, there is no automatic decompress routine. Before a compressed file can make sense, to you or the computer, it must be manually decompressed. Since the antivirus programs cannot perform this decompression, they will not be able to detect virus infections in programs stored in a compressed format. To scan such compressed programs, they must first be compressed and then scanned. Some common file-compression formats include Pkzip (compressed files with the extension .ZIP), Arj (compressed files with the extension .ARJ) and the Lhz (compressed files with the extension .LZH).

Of course, things get downright depressing from here on. The third compression format, *executable file compression*, referred to as EFC, works only on executable files. Most executable shipped with MS-DOS have been compressed with the executable compression format called the Exepack format. A program compressed with EFC is first compressed and then a small amount of extraction code is added. When executed, the program will automatically be expanded into memory. The program can become infected in two ways, before it's compressed and after it's compressed. If it's infected after it's compressed, the virus itself will not be compressed and should be straightforward to detect by an antivirus tool. If the program becomes infected and then compressed, a scan-string search will not be able to locate the right virus data. Since the program will first decompress itself when executed and scanners do not execute the programs they scan, a scanner will not see the program in the decompressed format. Some antivirus tools have tried to solve this problem, by first decompressing the EFC compressed programs in memory and then scanning them. However, here, as in most places in standard EFC format by which to compress/decompress. Some can scan inside some of the different EFC foremasts, but no scanner can scan inside all the EFC formats.

Another way to deal with this is, like the above file-compression scanning, first to manually decompress the program and then to scan it through. Besides being a time-demanding routine, this might not be a possible option, because, unlike the above file compression method. EFC-compressed programs do not need a separate decompress utility to work properly. If the user did not compress the program, but received it in a compressed format, he or she might not have the EFC tool to decompress it. Or alternatively, if a person wishing to spread a virus makes some small changes to the header that handles the decompress routine, the program may be able to expand itself, but the EFC program that compressed it in the first place will no longer be able to. If you think one of your programs has been infected in an EFC compression and you find yourself unable to decompress it, you will be unable to confirm your suspicion with a detection-by-appearance program. Some common EFCs are Pklite, Lzexe, Diet, Exepack, Tiny and compact.

There are a number of ways a virus can try to elude being identified by scan strings. First, reducing the size of any possible scan string, the virus can hope to make itself too small to be positively identified, to become indistinguishable from normal nonvirus programs. The obvious way to do that would simply be to reduce the size of the virus, thereby reducing the size of any unique code contained therein. But, as shown later, the smallest possible virus is 31 bytes long—a short but ample size for a positive scan string. So virus programmers must try to reduce the unique code is some other way. This is often accomplished by *self encrypting*. The virus will choose a random key to encrypt with and will copy an encrypted version of itself to the target of its infection. The point is that because the outcome of the encrypted data can take many different shapes, it cannot be used as a scan string without first being decrypted. When you encrypt data, it produces some form of semirandom change to the original data; the more like random the change, the better the encryption. A virus does not have to care about good encryption techniques; all it needs is a few hundred different possible encrypted versions of its own code. This is easily decoded by a human, but if all files on a disk should be decrypted by an antivirus program, it would slow the process of scanning the disk to an unacceptable crawl. Encrypting gives the additional advantage, from the virus point of view, of making the debug process harder for the programmer of antivirus software, thereby making the production of antivirus software a more lengthy and costly process, which will give the virus more time to spread before antivirus program become updated to include it. The process of making viruses harder to debug is called **armor** and will be dealt with later. Fortunately, not all of the viruses can be encrypted. It must be able to decrypt itself when run and this decrypting routine can not be copied in encrypted form. Most viruses using self-encrypting can be detected using the virus's own decrypting routine as a scan string.

The natural next step for the virus would be to make it harder for antivirus programs to use the decrypting routine as a scan string. Again, the obvious way to do that would be to reduce the size of the decrypting routine. But even the smallest decrypting routine can still be used as a scan string. This leads up to *polymorphing*, which is the process of using multiple decrypting and encrypting routines, or multiple decrypting routines and just a single encrypting routine. Because only the decrypting part is visible, or useful, to an antivirus program, every different facts of itself—hence the Latin name 'polymorphing' (poly = many, morph = face: many-faced). There is no way antivirus programs can adopt a single general scan string for several decrypting routines. This forces the antivirus program to treat the virus as many different using scan strings always have to 'beware' that their scan strings do not match other nonvirus programs, which will produce irritating false positives. A false positive is when an antivirus program detects a virus where there is none. The more scan strings, the higher the chance of one also matching nonvirus programs. The positive aspect is that polymorphing viruses often makes big viruses, thereby making it easier to detect them by other means.

Another way to elude positive scan strings would be to make each new 'daughter' infection of a 'mother' virus a little bit differently from the 'mother' virus itself and from other 'daughter' infections. This process is called *self-mutating*. It is of course not possible to find any unique code to use as scan-string search useless. One ay to accomplish such a mutating virus could be by replacing an instruction setting a variable to zero (**mov ax,0**) with an instruction subtracting the variable with itself (**sub ax, ax** - or **xor ax, ax;** and **ax, 0;** etc.). Both instructions set the variable to zero, but by different methods. This will change the virus's appearance and leave it still producing the same result. Any scan string containing the changed part will now not be able to detect it. To detect such a mutating virus, we need another, even more complex scan-string search. An antivirus program could have a scan string where each entry is table containing all the different instructions the virus uses interchangeably. For a match to be made, the scan only has to match one instruction in the scan with one of a number of instruction in the table. A well-programmed self-mutating virus can mutate itself into millions and millions of changed 'daughter' viruses, all different from each other. Making an antivirus program using a scan-string search approach on self-mutating viruses is difficult, but so is making a self-mutating virus. The good part of all this is that all viruses can be detected even though not one program can be programmed to detect all viruses. The sad part is that the more complicated the scan-string search becomes, the easier it is to get faulty virus signs where there are no viruses, false positives. False positives have given many a computer user a couple of frenetic hours and can, if he or she tries to disinfect a virus that's not there at all, destroy the program that showed a false positive.

Heuristic detection is basically trying to do what cannot be done and with surprisingly good results. It is a detection by appearance, but instead of looking for already known scan strings, *heuristic detection* looks for characteristics viruses often have. This has been known before as an AI-search (artificial intelligence search). That is not an appropriate term because heuristic detection uses no AI techniques. It does not try to 'understand' the code it searches, rather it looks for typical ways viruses gets things done and for code snippets frequently used in viruses. The trickly part (yes, there is always a tricky part) is the many different ways to program the same code. It cannot expect to find the same string of instructions in many different viruses. The code it looks for cannot be in a fixed order, as in scan strings, because this would be too easy to elude. It cannot even expect to find the same instructions reused in various orders, because as we have seen, there are many instructions for doing the same job. It must use a met hod very much like the scan-string search for self-mutating viruses. If it were only for these difficulties, we might still have a pretty good antivirus program. But as we have already discussed, there are a number of difficulties looking for typical virus code. Basically, they need not be any typical virus code in a virus. It's only slightly harder to program a virus not containing any code that could be called typical for viruses, such as code not also used in numerous other programs. However, because there need not be any typical virus code in a virus does not mean many viruses do not look alike. Many virus programmers are simply too lazy to make their own unique virus code, so they copy it from other viruses. This can be exploited by the antivirus program. Heuristic detection should be used when you suspect you have been infected but a normal scan-string search comes up with nothing.

For a virus to propagate, it needs to perform a number of specific actions, such as reading directory entries, opening files, writing to files, etc. Most of these actions are performed all the time by the system itself and other programs alike, although a few would not be performed under ordinary conditions. *Detection by behaviour* entails monitoring the system, to watch out for such dubious action. A dubious action could be opening (reading) a COM or EXE file in write mode, as one would not expect executable files to be modified. BIOS and DOS comes with a large number of built-in functions, ranging from reading files to formatting disks. All these needed for the system to function properly and are used by both internal and external system commands, such as **dir** and **xcopy**. However, these functions are not restricted for only the system to use; many programs, both virus and nonvirus, use them too. A BIOS/DOS function can be run using the assembler command interrupt (mnemonic: int). Interrupt looks in a table (called the interrupt vector table) containing and addresses of all the different functions to see where the function requested in located and then resumes executing at the address pointed to. It is possible to change the address contained in this table, thereby redirecting the interrupt function to another address (to one's own program). That is called *hooking* the interrupt vector and is how antivirus programs snoop on the system to see if something suspect is going on. Say you had a vile virus on your computer, which will format your hard disk every Sunday. You install and run an antivirus snooper. Come Sunday, the virus will call the DOS interrupt function **format** (ACK!), but luckily the antivirus sunooper had hooked the interrupt to a part of its own code. This code would then be run instead of the DOS format function and could write out 'a format function had been requested' and ask if you wanted to proceed with the format. 'No' would abort the format process and save you hard disk. This is an active defense, because it can detect, and stop, virus infections before they occur (catch the virus in the act, so to speak), while detection by appearance and detection by change are defensive and can only detect infections after they have already taken place. In addition to being able to detect actions related to the virus's spreading, detection by behaviour can also be used to tect and stop action relating to other, secondary, aspects of the virus—the payloads. As already been discussed, a virus payload is a part of the virus designated to other purposes than the main virus purpose of propagating. These can range from harmless, but annoying announcements to total destruction of all data on a disk medium. The format example is an example of such a detection. Beside the apparent good points provided by detection by behaviour, it has some severe shortcomings that make it, at best, a second virus scanner. It must be resident in normal memory, not extended/expanded memory, memory often desperately needed for other programs. Furthermore, it will slow down program executing a bit, not much, but discernible on a slow machine. And not all programs, even should they be clean, may be able to function properly with such a program resident in memory.

Using BIOS/DOS interrupts is an easier way to do things, but by no means the only way. A virus that has its own functions and uses them instead of the BIOS/DOS functions, cannot be detected by hooking interrupt vectors, simply because it does not use them. Also, a virus that does not call BIOS/DOS functions by way of the interrupt vector table, but rather calls them directly (as **Anthrax**, by instructions **call, jmp**, or whatever), will circumvent a detection abased on interrupt hooking. With a small bit of extra work, all partition, and boot-sector viruses can easily adopt such as evasive strategy. There is no counter for a detection-by-behaviour program to these virus defenses, but at lest it forces the viruses to adopt larger and more complicated ways to propagate itself, making them easier to spot in some of the other ways.

Moreover, a virus can include some code that checks the interrupt table. If it finds a hooked interrupt, it can simply unhook it, there by putting the detection by behaviour out of commission.

All the viruses cause some change to the system in which they infect. Detection of this change is called, imagine that, *detection by change*. The change is almost always very easy to spot with normal DOS tools: increase in file length (use DOS command **dir** and a bit of arithmetic), decrease in memory (use **chkdsk** or **mem**), change of time/date stamp (use **dir**), etc. For you to detect any change, it is of course required you have the initial state, file length, respectively mem-size before infection, to compare with, which is not always possible. If you receive a disk from a friend or a commercial program, the size of the programs on the disk before any possible infection is not known. But even if you do not know if your system is virusfree (has the initial state), it is possible to detect any further virus spread, when the virus changes the size of other, until now clean, the files. Sometimes it's not enough just to have the size of the file before infection. There is a group of simple viruses, file overwriting viruses, that just overwrite the targeted program with a copy of itself (thereby destroying the original program). They cannot be detected by their file size increase since they do not necessarily increase it. To detect them, a little more complex method of detecting change must be performed. All computer code can be represented in numbers. By adding up all the code in a file, the results will with a very high probability be a unique number, representing just that file. That is called a *checksum* and it can be used to compare a file before and after a possible infection. If the checksum of a file has changed, but the file size and date/time stamp are the same, the file has been changed. It is very easy for a virus to restore the date/time of a file to what they were before an infection and only slightly harder to, at least seemingly, retain the original file size. It is, however, all but impossible to make a file produce the same checksum before and after an infection.

Keeping account of the file size, time/date and checksums of all files on your system can be hard work. Fortunately, there are a number of antivirus programs that can help you do it. Typically, they must at a minimum be able to save the size of the program, the time/date of last update, the checksum on the file and a copy of the partition and boot sector for partition-/boot-sector infectors. Preferably in one separate file that can be backed up to another disk, this will ensure no virus tries to mess with it to hide its own presence. Today many programs come with their own checksum checker. When run these programs will performs a fast self-test to check for change and if they find any, they will inform the user that the program has been modified. Warning! McAfee's antivirus package SCAN contains a program that performs a checksum on disks. It is implemented in a very unusual (read: lame) way, since it modifies all programs on disks to contain such a self-checker. This will increase the file size of all the executable (EXE and COM) files, thereby messing up other antivirus programs' checksums and any possible self checksum checker. McAfee and associates should not mess with other people's files. But at least this method does not leave thousands of small checksums files lying around all over your hard disk, as many other checksum program do.

A checksum will not be able to detect a companion cirus on the disk, since the companion virus class does not modify the program they infect. The only way to detect a companion is with a detection-by-appearance program.

One of the most common virus protection schemes is called *Stealth*, Stealth is when a crafty virus uses interrupt hooking to run some of its own code that performs according to the virus's wishes. There are numerous ways to use and implement stealth and can, when performed right, be a very cunning way for the virus to hide itself. It is, however, not a new thing. One ofd the earliest viruses, **Brain**, used some stealth techniques. Brain redirected a request to read the boot sector (now infected) to the original boot sector and thus showed no infection. This would fool an antivirus program using a scan-string search and a checksum search. Sealth is an active defense of the virus and requires that the virus have been run. As such it can esasily be defected using a know clean, uninfected, write-protected disk to boot your computer.

We have already stead the need for the uninfected initial state of the programs we want to keep check on. If a program has already been infected when a detection-by-change program first sees it, this infection will not be detected. This is taken advantage of by some viruses, such as **startship**. Startship only infects files in the process of being copied to or from a floppy disk, never files already on floppy or hard disks. The above virus-detection method will not be able to detect such infections, because the modifications of the infected programs occur before the antivirus program obtains the initial state of the infected files.

16.5 NETWORK VIRUSES

Telecommunications, advances in networks and telecommunications have profoundly affected organizational productivity and decision making. The way companies do business has been completely revolutionized by telecommunications. Unfortunately, networks are also among the most vulnerable links in the security chain for computer systems—in fact, in a recent survey of CLOs, more than 90% of the respondents indicated that network security was a *strategic* concern for their organizations.

'Networks are essentially sieves to anyone with minor technical skills and the desire to retrieve other people's information.

The Internet is a vital link that connects people and organizations all over the world. However, in recent years it has been plagued with security problems as the number of Internet users has increased, the number of security breaches has also increased.

There are many reasons why networks are so prone to security violations. The arrival of cellular phones, radio modems, and sky pagers has created new points of vulnerability in the electronic exchange of information, since many unauthorized parties can tune into a company's voice or data transmissions. Second, in a distributed environment, there are innumerable opportunities for security breaches. 'In contrast to the fortess-like architecture of the mainframe, security exposures in client-serve computing almost defy indemnification.' Third, networks transmit large amounts of data and information around the world and it is difficult to continuously keep track of who is doing what, where, when and how. Fourth, in many organizations network administrators are rewarded for providing easy access to the network, but not for tight security, and obviously the two do not go hand-in-hand. Fifth, many network users are ignorant of network security measures and, intentionally or unintentionally, can cause considerable damage,. Users often view security policies and procedures as cumbersome and counterproductive, so they try to find short cuts or even to completely bypass security controls.

Due to LAN, WAN, MAN connectivity the data transmissions from one system to another has increase, so virus also spread along with data transmissions over the network, you must have notice lots of viruses messages while browning and e-mailing. There are lots of company with viruses detection software *i.e.*, Norton, Macfee, Hot do of etc.

REVIEW QUESTIONS

1. How viruses actually work? Explain.

2. What are the kinds of viruses? Illustrate.

3. How do viruses spread on network?

4. Suggest some remedies to prevent the viruses spreading over the network.

DATA STRUCTURES AND PROGRAMMING

17.1 STRUCTURED PROGRAMMING

Data processing managers are increasingly realising the importance of programming function in computer installations. A lot of effort in terms of time, money and manpower is involved in programming and system analysis. In addition, much of the programming effort is directed towards program maintenance, *i.e.*, changes in, or modifications to, existing programs. In such an environment, traditional programming comes into conflict with cost management objectives.

Traditional programming means programming generated as a form of personal art without adherence to established concepts and principles. The traditional way has been to view programming as a personal creation by an individual. It is quite possible for a programmer to write a clever program for solving a problem—the word 'clever' is often synonymous with 'complex' and 'obscure'. The difficulty with such a program is that it is difficult to be understood by persons other than the author and even the author may find it difficult to follow it after a long gap of time.

The recent past has seen a spectacular decrease in the hardware costs. This trend is still continuing. As a result, cost of personnel relative to the hardware costs is increasing at a rapid rate. This call for methods that can increase the personnel performance, thereby reduce the cost of program development. Quite often, the purpose for which a program is developed gets deviated. In such case, there are two alternatives; either the program should be declared obsolete and a new program developed in its place or the program should be modified incorporating the necessary changes.

The cost of personnel being on the increase, the question of discarding a program altogether does not arise. So, the program should be maintained by modifying it. This again calls for methods for program development so that the program is understood and modified easily. Programmers have, therefore, been attempting to find ways and means of writing correct programs which can be maintained easily, modified and debugged; for such factors tend to become very important, especially in a rapidly changing business environment where similar programs have to be run frequently. This effort has led to the development of a programming discipline called structured programming.

As with all new concepts, there is considerable disagreement and misunderstanding as to what structured programming means. In fact, there is no standard definition of structured programming except that it is a disciplined approach to programming. In general, the term 'structured programming' has come to mean a set of principles and practices that are directed towards developing correct programs which are easy to understand and maintain.

Some programmers insist that they have been using this technique for a long time. This may well be true, but the recent emergence of this technique has evolved from an attempt to formalise the process of designing programs in the same manner as the logic design has been formalised. The techniques used are, in general, not new but the formal basis definitely is.

17.1.1 Design Considerations

The process of designing and writing a program can be subdivided into a number of tasks such as:

1. understanding the problem;
2. producing an algorithm to solve the problem;
3. coding the algorithm in a particular programming language;
4. testing the resultant program; and
5. iterating round the above tasks until the program is correct.

In conventional programming, tasks (l) and (2) are undertaken by the systems analyst and (3) and (4) by the programmer, with (5) being shared between both. This process can be though of in a number of ways but structured programming would suggest that it should be looked at as a top-down analysis, *i.e.*, each stage is an elaboration of the previous stage with a greater degree of detail and complexity. This means that the problem is initially specified at a relatively low level of complexity and detail, and that the problem is gradually elaborated to produce the final program by stepwise refinement.

The nature of the difficulties involved in each step depends upon the problem and on the constraints on its solution, such as the resources available. The main difficulty in any problem-solving situation is to contain the complexity of the problem. It is this complexity which provides the intellectual challenge for programming. In structuring the solution, an attempt is made to simplify the complexity and to aid understanding. This approach is more likely to result in a correct solution.

Structured programming offers a number of benefits to its users. Each step is independent of the other steps, thus, allowing separate checks at each step. Each step may be verified by checking the elaboration stage by stage and an error may, therefore, be detected in a systematic manner. At any one time, only a small amount of information has to be remembered and manipulated and the structure evolved is a proof of the correctness of the entire algorithm.

17.1.2 Objective and Principles

The objective of structured programming is to provide methodologies so that:

1. programs are developed quickly and with fewer mistakes;
2. programs are read and understood easily; and
3. a portion of the program can be modified without upsetting the functions of other portions.

In other words, the objective is to meet the challenge offered by the changing trends in data processing. The principles of structured programming are as follows;

1. structuring of control flow;
2. decomposing a program into 'modules' or 'partitions'; and
3. top-down approach towards program designing.

These principles and the methodologies to implement them are outlined below.

17.1.3 Program Structure

A computer program is a set of instructions to the computer. While the instructions are to be executed by the computer, the language in which we communicate these instructions is meant to be comprehensible to people in their direct form and are intended for machine use only indirectly, through the process of compilation. Therefore, a basic principle of good programming is that the program should be easily understood.

A program that can be understood can also be analysed and tested for correctness. Incorrect programs have plagued computing from its early days. Another basic principle of good programming then is to write correct programs. In a more theoretical vein, we talk of proof of program correctness as a reflection of efforts to prove in logical and unambiguous terms that a piece of program code is correct *i.e.*, it does what it is intended to do and nothing else. Theoretical progress has been made only in very limited contexts, and at present we cannot rely on a formal theory to guide us to produce correct programs. Instead, we rely on a number of rules and guidelines that are closer to common sense than they are to a formal theory.

Every program has a structure. If the structure is well-defined, the program is correct and easy to understand and modify. On the other hand, a poorly structured program may have errors that are difficult to detect, may be even, hard to read and troublesome to modify. In cases where a change has to be made, it may become necessary to scrap the whole program and start afresh with a new one. In contrast, a structured program is characterised by clarity and simplicity in its logical flow structure. It reads like ordinary language from the beginning to the end, instead of branching from later paragraph to earlier ones and back again. So, a simple, straight flow of logic is another principle of good programming.

Programming by itself is a complex task and the aim of structured programming is to reduce and control complexity as it is not possible to eliminate the complexity completely. Human intellect can comprehend only a limited amount of data at a given time. When the human mind is faced with a complex task, it tries to manage by breaking it into a series of well connected smaller parts. Each smaller part of module, as it is called, is simple and comprehensible by itself so that within each module, all simplicity and clarity is achieved. So one of the characteristics of a well-structured program is that it consists of a large number of small modular programs. Each modular program is self-contained and performs a single function. Each module can be tested and debugged independently.

This means that every module has only one input and one output point, though within the module there may be branches and loops. Of course, the programmer has to use his common sense in dividing the complex program into a large number of smaller self-contained units or modules. Since each module has a specific independent function, it can be perfected separately without mixing it with the parts of the program. This is indeed a simplification of the programming art.

How is a modular structure developed? In practice, a modular structure is developed by proceeding from the general to the specific, or by using what is widely known as the top-down approach. Starting with the barest specification of the problem, one goes about filling the details. Suppose we are to develop a payroll processing problem utilising the top-down approach. The most abstract statement of the task is 'write pay-roll'. Then one can proceed to break down this general more specific statements, such as:

- ❒ Edit input data
- ❒ Process against master file
- ❒ Output payroll checks and other reports

Each of these broad functions can be subdivided into more specific ones, as for example, we can divide the first job still further as follows:

- ❒ Check the valid employee number
- ❒ Check time card data against job tickets
- ❒ Check for valid department number, and so on.

The first program module which may be called the **Read Module** performs a certain function after making all checks as given by commands or statements within that module. The main point is that the execution of commands or statements within the module has nothing to do with statement in other modules and that is why we say each module can be independently developed, tested and debugged. In the overall structure of the program, each module is taken as a single instruction.

If a problem can be divided into, say, five modular functions, the main program can be considered to be made of five dependent instructions, each instruction performing a module. A program organisation is, therefore, first divided into modular organisation and then each module is further divided into a statement organisation. Just as a government organisation performs the governing function by a hierarchy of officials at different levels, a complex programming task is achieved by dividing the job among different modules organised in a particular hierarchial structure. This is the top-down approach and this seems to work well in all human tasks. Figure 17.1 shows what is called modular level or modular hierarchy diagram of the above problem.

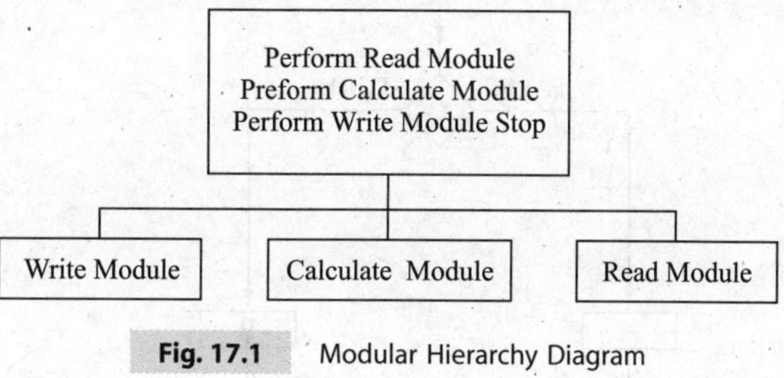

Fig. 17.1 Modular Hierarchy Diagram

It should be noted that no programming language is used while developing a programming structure. The thoughts are simply written in ordinary language with or without graphic aids such as arrows, boxes, brackets, etc., and the whole function is divided into a large number of simpler functions in a logical way. So, structured programming is not concerned with any particular language. It is concerned with programming in general.

17.1.4 Structuring of Control Flow

Except for the most trivial examples, programs are highly complex systems of logic. The ability to design loop operations and to take alternative courses of action depending on a condition can make a program very complex. This is because, quite often, loops are used within alternative paths or loops and alternative paths are used within loops or other alternative paths. The large size of a program and the interconnections between its various parts through the transfer of control also increase the complexity of a program.

The idea behind the structuring of control flow is to keep this complexity under control so that the design and understanding of the program logic become easier. It has been demonstrated that a structured program can be completely developed using three basic forms of program structure, viz., (*i*) sequence structure, (*ii*) decision or selection structure, and (*iii*) loop structure. One may encounter these as special terms which are written: SEQUENCE, IFTHENELSE, DOWHILE.

1. **Sequence structure:** The SEQUENCE structure indicates the sequential flow of program logic. Each block may stand for a statement; it may stand for a whole module or even a collection of modules. In a SEQUENCE structure, the statements are executed one after the other in the order in which they are written. The flowchart of such a structure is shown in Figure 17.2. The flow of control is such that it performs block *A* first, then block *B*, and so on, from top to bottom in the same direction. There is only one entry point and one exit point for the structure and there is no complexity. The flow is in one direction and straight.

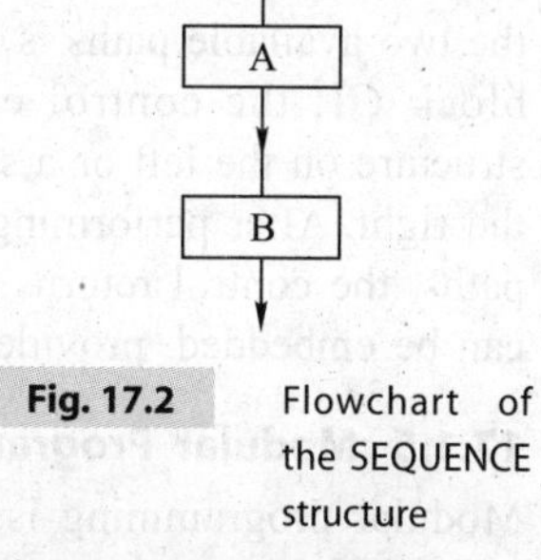

Fig. 17.2 Flowchart of the SEQUENCE structure

2. **Decision structure:** The IFTHENELSE structure indicates a conditional program flow. The program takes one path or another, depending on whether a condition, often referred to as

the predicate, is true or false. The program on entering the test box *C* of Fig. 17.3 makes a decision to go through either of the two paths, *A* or *B*. After performing one of the two paths, the control returns to a single exit point. It can be seen that this structure also has one entry point and one exit point, even though there are multiple exit paths inside the structure.

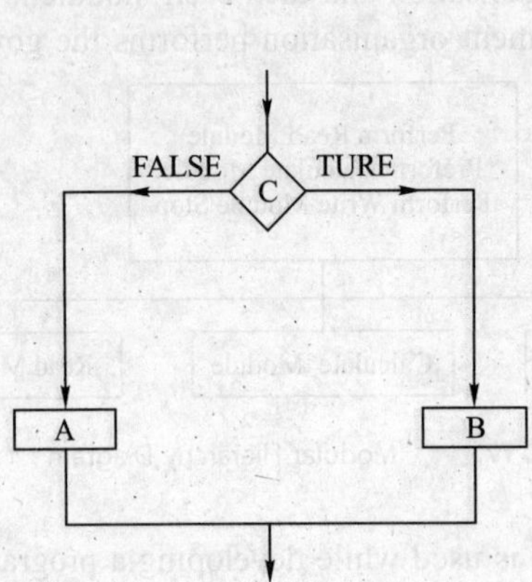

Fig. 17.3 Flowchart of the IFTHENELSE structure

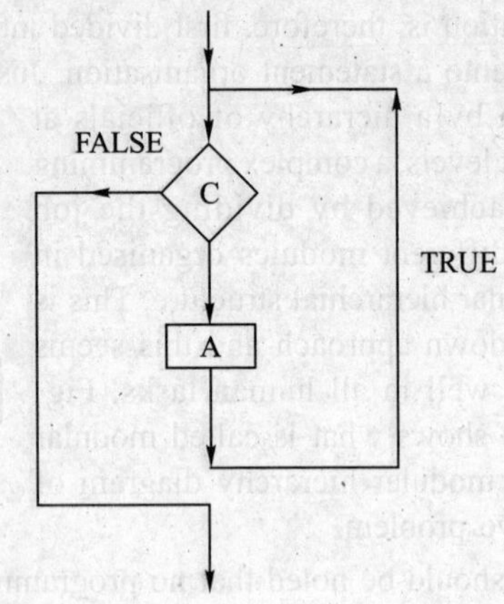

Fig. 17.4 Flowchart of the DOWHILE structure

3. **Loop structure:** The DOWHILE structure provides for a looping operation, *i.e.*, repetitive execution of a program segment. A loop is not infinite if it is correct. The predicate tests for a condition. If the condition holds, we exit from the loop; if not, we execute the instruction. The flowchart of this structure is shown in Fig. 17.4. Whether the operations are to be repeated or stopped is decided in the decision box.

Any program can be written by using these three basic building blocks. In complex programs, one structure may be embedded in the other. For example, in Fig. 17.5, a nested structure is shown. When selection between the two available paths is made in the decision block *C*1, the control enters either a loop structure on the left or a sequence structure on the right. After performing any one of the two paths, the control returns to a single exit point. In a similar manner, any number of structures can be embedded, provided the combination as a whole has one entry point and one exit point.

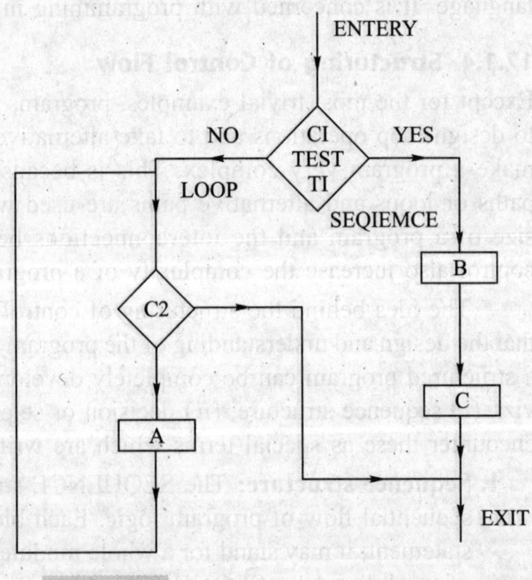

Fig. 17.5 Flowchart of the nested structure

17.1.5 Modular Programming

Modular programming is a programming strategy where a program is divided into a number of identifiable partitions or modules. Thus, a module in itself is a proper program structure. It has one entry and one exit, reads naturally from top to bottom, and may consist of any of the three basic program structures (SEQUENCE, IFTHENELSE, DOWHILE). The module is referenced by a name which should be as descriptive as possible. In COBOL that name is a paragraph or section name. A module should not exceed one page in length so that it is easily read. Finally, each module is executed by reference to it from another part of the program, usually through the verb PERFORM.

Figure 17.6 depicts a general outline of structured programming logic. Note that there is a main logic module and a number of other dependent modules. The main logic part provides a summary of the program, and it is generally short enough so that the essence of the entire program can be understood in the context of the main module. Notice that module *A*, for instance, is executed under control of the main program module. If the name of module *A* is meaningful, say, Compute-total-deductions, we need not bother with the details of module *A*.

It may very well be the case that, as in this example, module *A* is sufficiently large or complex so that we need to break a module *X* out of it. Thus, module *X* is executed under the control of module *A* which in turn is executed under the control of the main module. This nesting of modules is permissible and desirable. We only need to keep in mind that as soon as the end of a module has been reached, we should turn to the module which issued the execute instruction. Thus, when module *X* has been executed, we return to instruction 2 of module *A*, and to the PERFORM MODULE *B* instruction of the main program module, after module *A* has been executed.

```
Begin Main Program Module Instruction 1
  :
  Instruction M
  PERFORM Module A
  PERFORM Module B
  :
  Instruction N
  End Main Program Module
    Begin Module A
    Instruction 1
    PERFORM Module X
    Instruction 2
    :
    Instruction N
    End Module A
  Begin Module B
  Instruction 1
    :
    Instruction N
    End Module B
  Begin Module X
  Instruction 1
    :
    Instruction N
    End Module X
```

Fig. 17.6 A general outline of structured programming logic

The program structure described above is adequate for most data processing. However, there are two conditions that restrict its use. Some tasks are common to more than one program. Repeating the same instructions in each such programme is undesirable. The second case concerns large programming tasks. It is difficult for a team of programmers to work on the same program. At the same time, it is easier to subdivide the composite task into independent program modules that can be written, compiled, and tested by individual programmers working independently of one another.

This latter objective is achieved by using program subroutines, or subprograms. A program subroutine is a program just like any other program, except that it is not executable by itself; it can only be executed under the control of another program. It should be clear, however, that with or without the use of program subroutines, the COBOL programmer can create modular, well-structured programs.

The advantage of modular programming depends on how effectively the modules are designed. Each module must be designed to accomplish a distinct function. This gives the program a rather high modification potential. For example, in a payroll program there may be a module that calculates the dearness allowance from the basic pay using certain rules. If these rules get changed at a later date, the modification will be limited to the said module and/or to its subordinate modules, if any. It has been seen that it is easier to replace a module by a modified one than to make corrections in one particular part of a conventional program without upsetting the functions of the other parts.

17.1.6 Top-Down Approach

The above description of modular programming presupposes a hierarchical structuring of modules. The process of designing a program consisting of a hierarchical structure of modules can be viewed in two ways—top-down, and bottom-up.

The top-down approach towards program design starts with the specification of the function to be performed by a program and then breaks it down into progressively subsidiary functions. The division of the function progresses with increasing levels of details. At every level, each function is ultimately realised in the form of a module.

In this approach, the calling module is always designed before the called module. At the time of designing a module, the broad functions to be performed by its immediate subordinate modules are assumed. The details of how a subordinate module can perform the specified functions are not considered until the subordinate module is taken up for design. Thus, the top-down approach represents a successive refinement of functions and this process of refinement is continued until the lowest modules can be designed without further analysis.

The top-down structure can be viewed as a tree structure, a typical example of which is shown in Fig. 17.7. Each box in this figure is a module. The topmost module denoted by 1 represents the program which can be called the main-line module or main-control module. In this case, the main-control module is divided into three subordinate modules denoted by 2, 3 and 4. The modules 2 and 4 require further divisions and in this process, the terminal modules are 5, 6, 7 and 8. The functions of these terminal modules are assumed to be simple enough to be easily programmed in the source language.

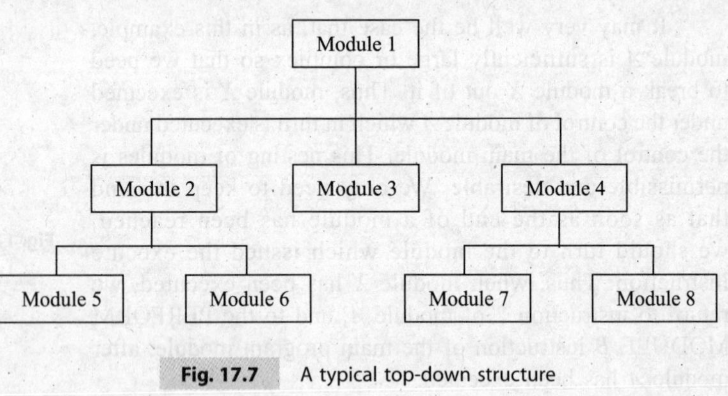

Fig. 17.7 A typical top-down structure

The bottom-up approach is the reverse of the top-down one. The process starts with identification of a set of modules which are either available or have to be constructed. An attempt is made to combine the lower level modules to form modules of a high level. This process of combining modules is continued until the program is realised. The basic drawback of the bottom-up approach is the assumption that the lowest level modules can be completely specified beforehand, which in reality is seldom possible. Thus, in the bottom-up approach, quite often it is found that the final program obtained by combining the predetermined lowest level modules does not meet all the requirements of the desired program.

No attempt is made here to compare the advantages and disadvantages of the two approaches. However, program development through top-down approach is widely accepted to be better than the bottom-up approach. The top-down approach has the following advantages:

1. It imitates the human tendency to solve a problem by outlining the broad concepts first and then subsequently going into the details.
2. The details of a module can be worked out with no (or minimum) change of the previously outlined concepts regarding its functions.
3. The programmer never loses sight of the assumptions made at the previous levels. The development of modules can take place in parallel.

These advantages suggest that if the top-down approach is taken for programs design, the programs can be developed easily and quickly, with a minimum oferrors.

17.1.7 Constrained use of GO TO

The proponents of structured programming appear to be divided on the question of using the GO TO statement in structured programs. While some recommend the total avoidance of GO TOs in structured programs, others favor its constrained use. Without entering into this controversy, it may be stated that the GO TO statements need not be avoided just for the sake of avoiding them. Only when their use requires a compromise with the readability of the program, must they the eliminated.

Some general rules for the constrained use of GO TOs in programs are given below. It may be noted that each rule is more restrictive than the preceding one.

1. Use GO TO to transfer the control within a module without crossing its boundaries. In other words, a short-range GO TO statement whose object is either the name of the paragraph in which it appears or the name of any other paragraph in a series of paragraphs that constitutes a module is allowed according to this rule.
2. Use GO TO to transfer the control in the forward direction within a module. This rule is more restrictive than the previous one as it does not allow the use of the statement to transfer the control in the backward direction.
3. Use GO TO to transfer the control to the exit paragraph of a series of a series of paragraphs constituting a module.

It is worthwhile to note that these rules ensure a localised flow of control so that the readability of the module is not likely to be seriously affected. Moreover, the module as a whole can still be viewed to have single entry and single exit.

17.1.8 Programming Considerations

How do the concepts of structured programming produce better programs? If we take the division of a problem into its programming solution, we see that the programming solution must contain a structure of 'boxes within boxes' in a pictorial representation where boxes within boxes represent the lower level elaboration at the upper level (see Fig. 17.8). This means that we have a modular structure where modules can be tested independently.

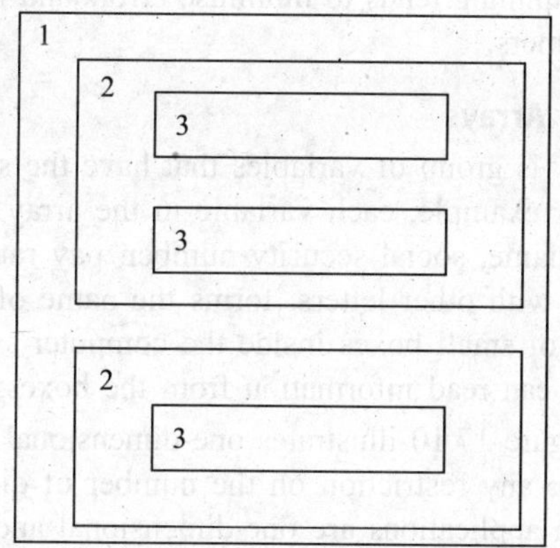

Fig. 17.8 Block structure (numbers represent the levels)

It should be pointed out here that we have a structure which looks, in some respects, similar to a flowchart. It gives a pictorial representation of the program structure. The main difference is that the concepts in structured programming place restraints on the equivalent flowchart representation. The shortcomings of flowcharts are that they are too general and do not constrain the structure to be 'well-formed'. The main problem is the undisciplined use of the GO TO or JUMP instructions which may cause convoluted flowcharts. Here structured flowcharts may be used to good advantage.

17.1.9 Structured Flowcharts

Traditionally, flowcharts have been used for two main purposes; to help the programmer develop the program logic, and to serve as documentation for a completed program. In recent years, there has been some tendency to minimise the need or even the usefulness of flowcharts. A case can be made that if a programmer utilises principles of good program structure, the program is self-documenting and therefore a flowchart is superfluous. Further, there are those who argue that in an environment where program modifications are frequent, redrawing flowcharts becomes cumbersome. Instead of subscribing to the extreme view that flowcharts are useless, flowcharting can be viewed as a very useful tool for program development and documentation. But this programming aid should not be used indiscriminately.

Structured flowcharts are intended to focus on the program logic rather than on the specific tasks to be performed by the program. As such, structured flowcharts tend to do away with special symbols for input, and the like. While there is no standard set of symbols, Fig. 17.9 presents a set of flowcharting symbols adopted to IBM. A complete flowchart can be drawn using these symbols alone, although one may use standard flowcharting symbols as well. In any case, a structured flowchart is clear, simple and easy to understand. It has one clear beginning and one clear end and the advantage of utilising the five basic structure (SEQUENCE, IFTHENELSE, DOWHILE, DOUNTIL, and CASE).

PROCESS OR FUNCTION

DECISION OR PREDICATE

COLLECTOR OR REFERENCE POINT

CASE

ARROW

Fig. 17.9 IBM structured program flowcharting symbols

Structured programming is a good approach for writing correct programs. The strategy behind this technique is: when the variable is formidable, divide and conquer. Such a disciplined approach to programming tends to minimise errors and maximise output, which is the concern of all good programmers.

17.1.10 Arrays

An array is group of variables that have the same name and data type and are related in some way. For example, each variable in the array may contain an inventory quantity, an employee record (name, social security number, pay rate, and so on), or a character that, when grouped together with other letters, forms the name of a state. It may be helpful to picture an array as a group of small boxes inside the computer's memory. You can write information to the boxes and you can read information from the boxes; you just cannot *see* the boxes.

Figure 17.10 illustrates one-dimensional and two-dimensional arrays. Although C++ does, not place any restriction on the number of dimensions an array can have, the commonly used arrays in applications are one-dimensional and two-dimensional.

One-dimensional array is simply a column of variables. Two-dimensional array resembles a table which has rows and columns.

Programmers use arrays to store related data in the internal memory of the computer. By doing so, programmers can increase the efficiency of a program because data stored inside the computer can be

One-dimensional array
9.55
2.65
8.53
6.45
2.24

Two-dimensional array				
9.55	2.65	8.53	6.45	2.24
4.46	2.89	9.76	3.34	8.89
9.87	5.56	8.32	2.24	6.78

Fig. 17.10 Illustrations of one-dimensional and two-dimensional arrays

both written and read much faster than data stored in a file on a disk. The following analogy may help illustrate this point. Think of the computer's internal memory as being comparable to the memory cells in your brain. Now assume that someone asks you to name the first Indian Prime Minister. Because that information is already stored in your brain, you can respond almost immediately with Jawahar Lal Nehru. Similarly, the computer has almost immediate access to the information stored in internal memory—the memory cells in *its* brain.

Now assume that someone asks you to name the eighth Indian president. If that information is not stored in your memory cells, you will need to open a history book, find the page containing the listing of presidents, and then read the eighth name—a much more time-consuming process. Similarly, accessing information that is not stored in the computer's internal memory, but rather in a disk file, takes the computer much longer. The computer must wait for the disk drive to locate the needed information and then read that information into memory.

In addition to speedier access of information, another advantage of using an array is that data can be entered into an array once, usually at the beginning of the program, and can then be used by the program as many times as desired.

17.2 TRAVERSAL

An algorithmic process in which each element in a structure is processed once and only once.

Example 17.1 Let us assume that we have 20 numbers *i.e.*, array MARKS [20] of 20 elements. Now the array MARKS [20] be travelled in such a way that each element of MARKS [20] is visited.

Let *i* be the variable to keep track of the number of elements visited in array MARKS [20]. *i* is initialized to 0 *i.e.* the lower bound of MARKS [20]. Here, at every visit, the count *i* will be increased by one and matched with the upper bound of MARKS [20]. If the value *i* is less than 20 then the steps are repeated otherwise algorithm stops.

The algorithm steps are as follows:

1. `i = 0`
2. `Process Array MARKS [20].`
3. `i = i + 1`
4. `If i < 20 then go to step 2 else step 5`
5. `STOP.`

The C++ implementation of this algorithm is as follows:

```
# include <iostream.h>
void main()
{
int marks [20] = {70, 30, 40, 25, 33, 18, 78, 92, 96, 3, 17, 34,
                   68, 77, 79, 72, 94, 99, 2, 10}
for (int i = 0; i<20; i++)
cout << marks [i] << endl;
}
```

This program prints out each number from the array MARKS [20].

17.3 SEARCHING

In the case of an array, searching means that given a value, we want to find the location of the first element in the array that contains that value. In other words, we can say we are searching for a particular value in the array. Figure 17.11 illustrates the searching concept.

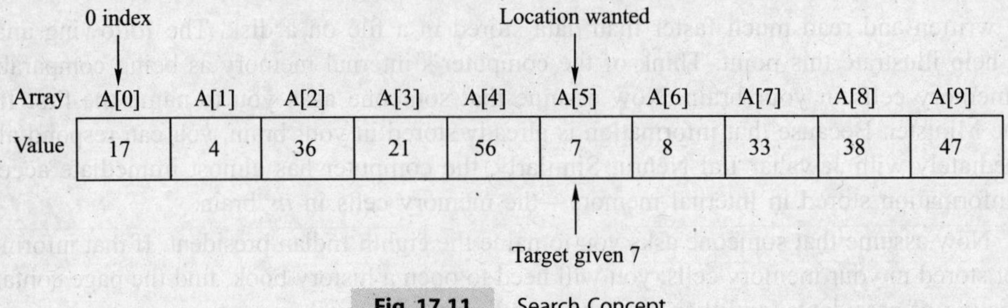

Fig. 17.11 Search Concept

The algorithm used to search a list depends to a large extent on the structure of the list. Since our structure is currently limited to arrays, we will study searches that work with arrays.

There are two basic searches for arrays, the sequential search and the binary search. The sequential search can be used to locate an item in any array. The binary search, on the other hand, requires the list to be sorted.

17.4 SEQUENTIAL SEARCH

In a sequential search (or linear search) we start at the beginning of a list of items and look at each in turn until we either find the one we are looking for or reach the end of the list. Let us take an example of *XYZ* company and its five trucks. Each of *XYZ*'s five trucks has a license plate with a different number. Let us put these licenses in an array, and search through the array to identify which truck has a certain license.

The following program, will start the search at the beginning of the array, and stop searching when we have found what we can looking for or we reach the end of the array.

```
Start at beginning of list
While Item not found and still in list
        Go to next item
if item found
        Acknowledge it
Else
        Indicate failure
```

Example 17.2 The program for the sequential search (or linear search) is as follow:

```
# include <iostream.h>
void search (int&, found, int& location, int licenses [], int n,
    int license);
main()
{
    int licenses [] = {312, 47, 555, 100, 36}, license, found, loc;
    do {
    cout << 'License:';
    cin >> license;
    search (found, loc, licenses, 5, license);
    if (found) cout << license << 'is a license of truck number'
        << loc;
    else cout << license << 'was not found. \n';
    } while (license ! = 0);
}
```

```
void search (int& found, int& location, int licenses [], int n,
    int license)
{
    found = location = 0;
    while (! found && location <n)
        found (licenses [location++] == license);
    -location;
}
```

The outputs of the program is:

```
License: 312
312 is a license of truck number 1
License: 700
700 was not found.
License : 36
36 is a license of truck number 5
```

In each iteration of the search loop, the current element `licences/[location]` is compared with `license`. The loop continues until a match is found or all the elements have been checked. Each iteration increments the index `location`, after it is accessed. So if the loop terminates because a match was found, locator must be decremented to the index where `target` was found.

Note that `search()` function has there 'input parameters' (`licenses`, and `license`) and two 'output parameters' (`found` and `location`).

The **sequential search** is used whenever the list is not ordered. Generally, you will use the technique only for small lists or lists that are not searched often. In other cases, you should first sort the list and then search it using binary search.

17.5 BINARY SEARCH

You have learned how to use a sequential (serial) search to search for a specific value in an array. In a sequèntial search, the program begins the search with the first array element. The program then continues searching, element by element, until either a match is found or the end of the array is encountered. A serial search is useful when the amount of data that must be searched is small. If you have a large amount of data, however, the serial search is extremely inefficient: in those cases, a binary search is a better option. For a binary search to work, the data in the array must be arranged in either alphabetical or numerical order. For example, if you are searching for a last name, then the last names in the array must be sorted in alphabetical order. If you are searching for a zip code, then the zip codes must be sorted in numerical order.

If the items through which we are searching are in order, we can significantly reduce the searching time by using a **binary search.** With such a search, each time we consider an item, we eliminate half the items rather than just the single item. If we are presented with a number from 1 top 10 and guess the one in the middle, 5, and are told that the number is too low, we know the number is between 6 and 10. We have eliminated half the possible range with one guess. We can then repeat the process with the remaining range and so forth until either we have found the correct value, or the range disappears.

To keep track of the range, we can set up two variables, *low* and *high*, as we have done in Fig. 17.12. The middle of the range, *mid*, will be (*low* + *high*)/2. If have value at *mid* is too high, we set *high* to *mid*–1, cutting the range in half, and repeat the process. The search stops when either the correct value is found, or the *low* is greater than the *high*, indicating that there are no more number in the range.

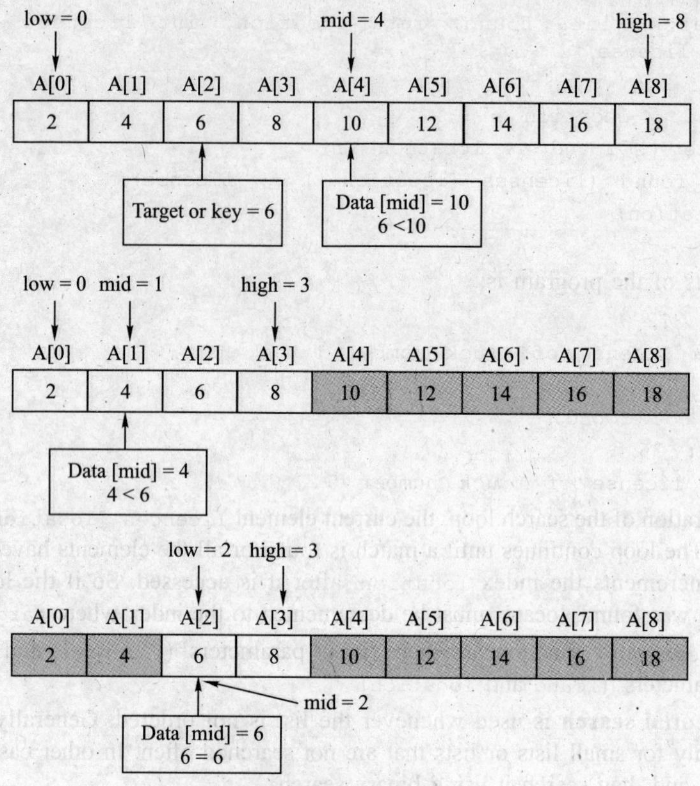

Fig. 17.12 Binary Search

```
          Establish low, high, and initial midpoint
      While range left and key value not found
          If key < mid value
          Limit search to lower end of range
      Else
          Limit search to upper end of range
      Establish new midpoint
```

Notice that *low*, *high*, and *mid* keep track of the indices in the array being searched, not the values in those elements. Since these indices are integers, the result of the midpoint division will also be an integer. For example, (0 + 3)/2 is 1.5, but will be truncated to 1, making the midpoint 1.

Example 17.3 Let us take an example of *XYZ* company and its five trucks. Each of *XYZ*'s five truck has a license plate with a different number. Let us put these licenses in an array, and search through the array to identify, which truck has a certain license.

The program for the binary search is as follows:

```
main()
{
    int licenses[] = {312, 47, 555, 100, 36], license, found, loc;
    do {
        cout << 'License:';
        cin >> license;
        search (found, loc, licenses, 5, license);
```

```
        if (found) cout << license << 'is a license of truck
        number'<< loc;
        else cout << license << 'was not found. \n';
    } while (license ! = 0);
}
void search (int& found, int& location, int
        licenses[], int n, int license)
{
    int low = 0, high = n - 1;
    found = 0;
    while (! found && low < = high)
    {
    location = (low+high) / 2; // midpoint
    found = (licenses[] == license);
    if (licenses [location] < license) low = location +1;
    else high = location - 1;
    }
}
```

The output of the program is:

```
License: 312
312 is a license of truck number 1
License: 700
700 was not found.
License: 36
36 is a license of truck number 5
```

On each iteration of the `while` loop, the middle element `licenses [location]` of the sub-array (from `licenses [low]` to `licenses [high]`) is checked for the `license`. If it is not found there, then either the low half is discarded by resetting low = location + 1, or the high half is discarded by resetting `high = location -1` according to whether (`licenses [location] < license`).

17.6 INSERTION

An insert begins with a set of values in order, and adds one more value to the set. The new value is added so that the set remains in order after the addition. We will store the set of values in an array, which will have to be one element larger than the number of values in the original set, because we are going to add one more value. If we are going to insert a value into a set of 100 values, our array will have to consist of at least 101 elements.

We know that the new value should be inserted in the set where it is greater than the number before and less than the number after. Now all we have to do is explain that to the computer. Let us consider a set of four values 4, 6, 8, 10 and 12–to which we want to add one more –7. As shown in Fig. 17.13, we will declare an array of five variables *A*[*6*], assign the values to the first four variables in the array, and assign the value we wish to insert to *insert*. We will consider each position in the array as a possible insert position and use the variable *position* to keep track of it. The element in that position would be *A*[*position*]. We will either assign our insert value (*insert*) to that element or go on to the next position.

There will already be a blank position at the end of the array, so let's use that as our first possible insert position. (In Fig. 17.13, the possible insert position is represented by a clear area.) If our insert value is greater than the value of the element before our possible insert position (*A* [*position—1*]), then it must belong in this position (*A*[*position*]). (The darker shaded area is the element before the possible insert position.) If it is not greater, then it must belong somewhere above, so let's begin to make space for it by moving a value down one position-assigning the value of *A*[*position*—1] *to A*[*position*]. Then we can move our possible insert position up one element decrementing *position* and repeat the process.

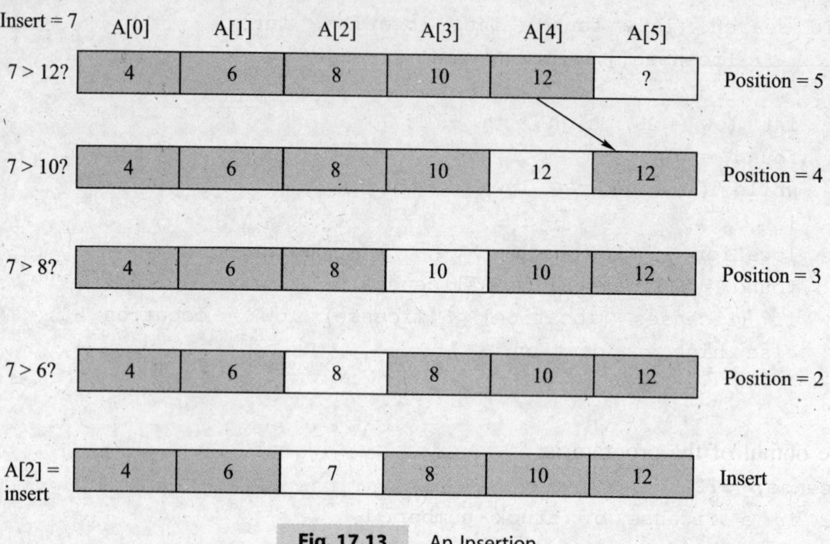

Fig. 17.13 An Insertion

The process will stop when we have either found the proper insert position or considered all the positions back to the second. If it doesn't belong in the second position, it must belong in the first. In either case, if we have decremented our *position* correctly, we can simply insert – assign *insert* to *A*[*position*].

Example 17.4 The following program inserts the item *x* into the sorted array *a* of *n* elements. include <iostream.h>

```
void prnout  (int[], int);
void insert  (int[],  int&,  int);
main()
{
   int a[100]  =  {17,  20,  25,  30,  35,  47,  53,  63,  73,  80};
   int n  =  10,  x;
   prnout  (a,  n);
   cout   << 'Enter  the  value  to  be  inserted:';
   cin   >>  x;
   insert  (a,  n,  x);
   prnout  (a,  n);
}
void prnout  (int a[],  int  n)
{
   for  (int i  =  0;  i  <  n-1;  i++)
        {
          cout  <<  a[i]  <<  ',';
          if  ((i+1)  %  16  ==  0)  cout  <<  endl;
        }
```

```
    cout << a[n-1] << endl;
  }
void insert (int a[], int& n, int x)
  {
    for (int i = n; i > 0 && a[i - 1] > x; i --)
        a[i] = a[i-1];
    a[i] = x;
    ++n;
  }
```

The output of the program is:

```
17, 20, 25, 30, 35, 47, 53, 63, 73, 80
Enter the value to be inserted : 40
17, 20, 25, 30, 35, 40, 47, 53, 63, 73, 80
17, 20, 25, 30, 35, 47, 53, 63, 73, 80
Enter the value to be inserted : 10
10, 17, 20, 25, 30, 35, 47, 53, 63, 73, 80
```

Note that the **insert()** function works from the high end of the array, searching backward for the correct location to put *x*. As it searches, it shifts the elements that are larger than *x* one place to way for *x*.

17.7 DELETION

The **Deletion** is an operation in which a particular element is deleted from an array. To delete the element in the array, first search for it by using either linear search or binary search techniques. If the search is successful, then the element is removed and rest of the elements are shifted to keep the array undisturbed. Suppose if you have deleted an element from the `i`th location of the array then all the elements from the (`i + 1`)th location will be shifted one step towards left. Thus (`i + 1`)th element is copied on `i`th location, (`i + 2`)th element is copied on (`i + 1`)th location, and so on. Figure 17.14 illustrates the deletion concept.

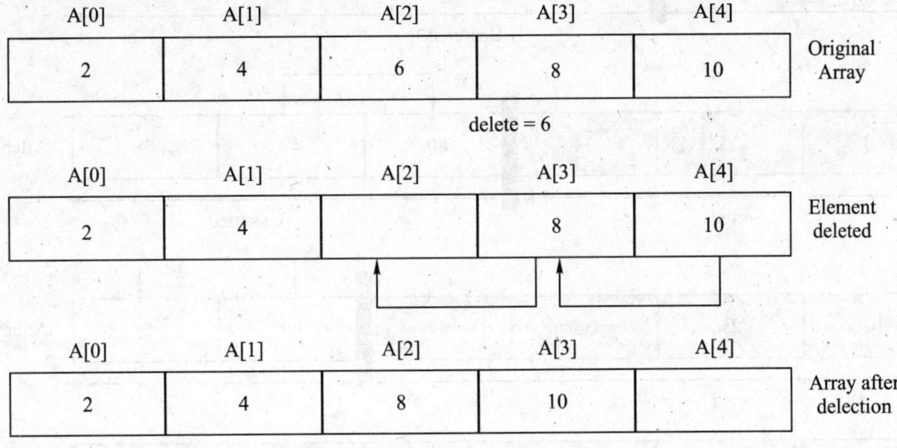

Fig. 17.14 An Deletion

17.8 SORTING

As you learned, arrays let you store related values of the same type. As your programs work with arrays, there will be times when your programs need to sort the array's values, either from lowest to highest (ascending order) or from highest to lowest (descending order). Your programs can use different sorting algorithms to sort arrays: **selection sort, bubble sort, and insertion sort.** One programming concept common to the sorting algorithms is the swapping of data between two elements in a list.

17.9 SELECTION SORT

In the **selection sort,** the list is divided into two sublists, sorted and unsorted, which are divided by an imaginary wall. We find the smallest element from the unsorted sublist and swap it with the element at the beginning of the unsorted data. After each selection and swapping, the wall between the two sublists moves one element ahead, increasing the number of sorted elements and decreasing the number of unsorted ones. Each time we move one element from the unsorted sublist to the sorted sublist, we say that we have completed a **sort pass.** If we have a list of *n* element, we need *n–l* passes to completely rearrange the data.

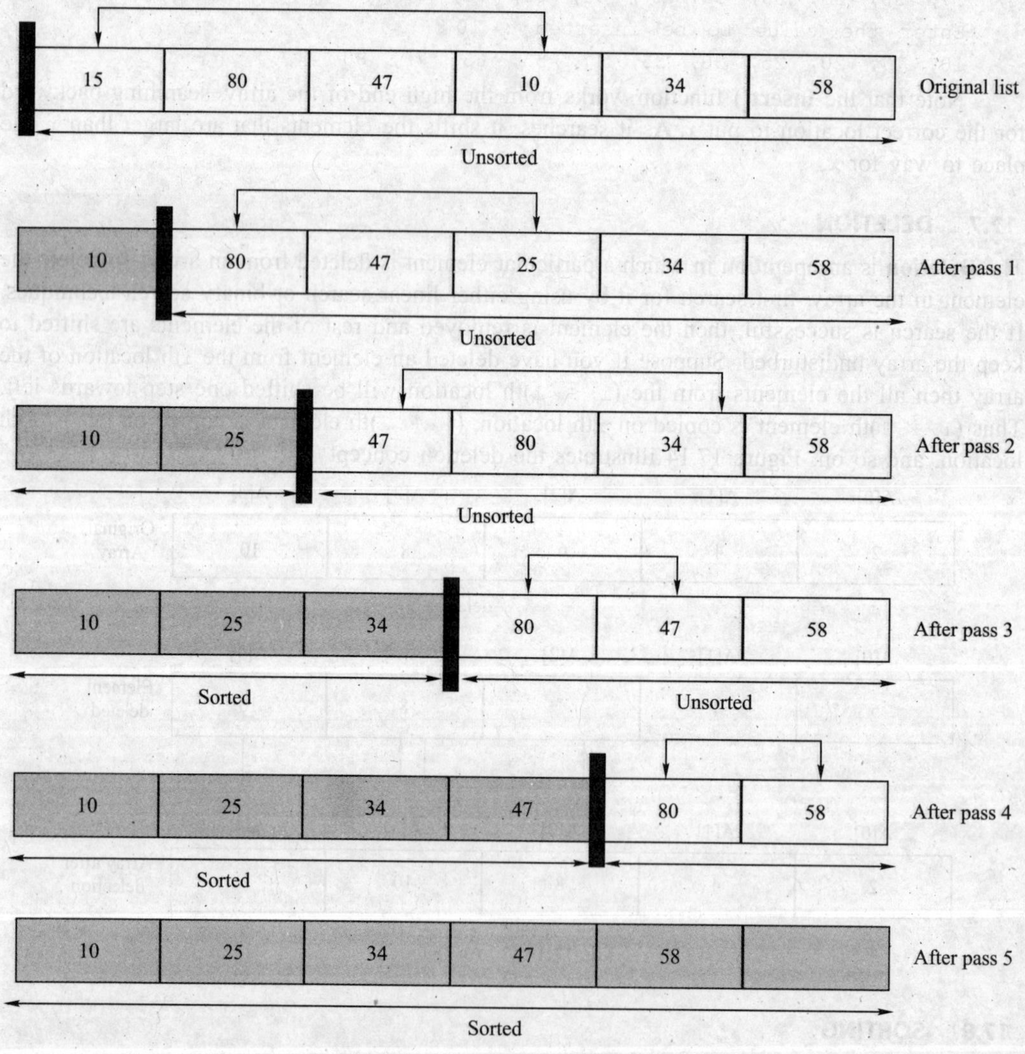

Fig. 17.15 An example of section sort

Figure 17.15 traces a set of six integers as we sort them. It shows how the wall between the sorted and unsorted sublists moves in each pass. As you study the figure, you will see that the array is sorted after five passes, which is one less than the number of elements in the array. This means that if we use a loop to control the sorting, our loop has one less iteration than the number of elements in the array.

Example 17.5 The following program uses selection sort to sort an array containing 30 random values:

```
void selection_sort  (int  array[],  int  size)
   {
      int  temp,  current,  j;
      for  (current  =  0;  current  <size;  current++)
           for  (j  =  current  +1;  j  <  size;  j++)
      if  (array  [current]>  array  [j]);
      {
           temp  =  array  [current];
           array  [current]  =  array[j];
           array  [j]  =  temp;
      }
   }
void  main(void)
   {
      int  values  [30],  i;
      for  (i=0;  i<30;  i++)
      values  [i]  =  rand()  %  100;
      selection_sort  (values,  30);
      for  (i=0;  i<30;  i++)
      cout  <<  values  [i]);
   }
```

Note: The **selection_sort** function sorts values from lowest to highest. To reverse the sort order, simply change the comparison to `if  (array  [current]  <  array[j])`.

17.10 BUBBLE SORT

In the **bubble sort** method, the list is divided into two sublists; sorted and unsorted. The smallest element is *bubbled* from the unsorted sublist and moved to the sorted sublist. After moving the smallest element to the sorted list, the wall moves one element ahead, increasing the number of sorted elements and decreasing the number of unsorted ones. Each time an element moves from the unsorted sublist to the sorted sublist, one sort pass is completed.

Figure 17.16 shows how the wall moves one element in each pass. Looking at the first pass, we start with 58 and compare it to 34. Since 58 is not less than 34, it is not moved and we step down one element. No exchanges take place until we compare 47 to 10. Since 10 is less than 47, the two elements are exchanged and we step down one element. Because 10 was moved down, it is now compared to 80 and these two elements are exchanged. Finally, 10 is compared to 25 and exchanged. This series of exchanges places 10 in the first location and the wall is moved up one position.

The bubble sort was originally written to 'bubble up' the highest element in the list. From an efficiency point of view, it makes no difference whether the high element is bubbled or the low element is bubbled. From a consistency point of view, however, it makes comparisons between the sort easier if all three of them work in the same manner. For that reason, we have chosen to bubble the lowest key in each pass.

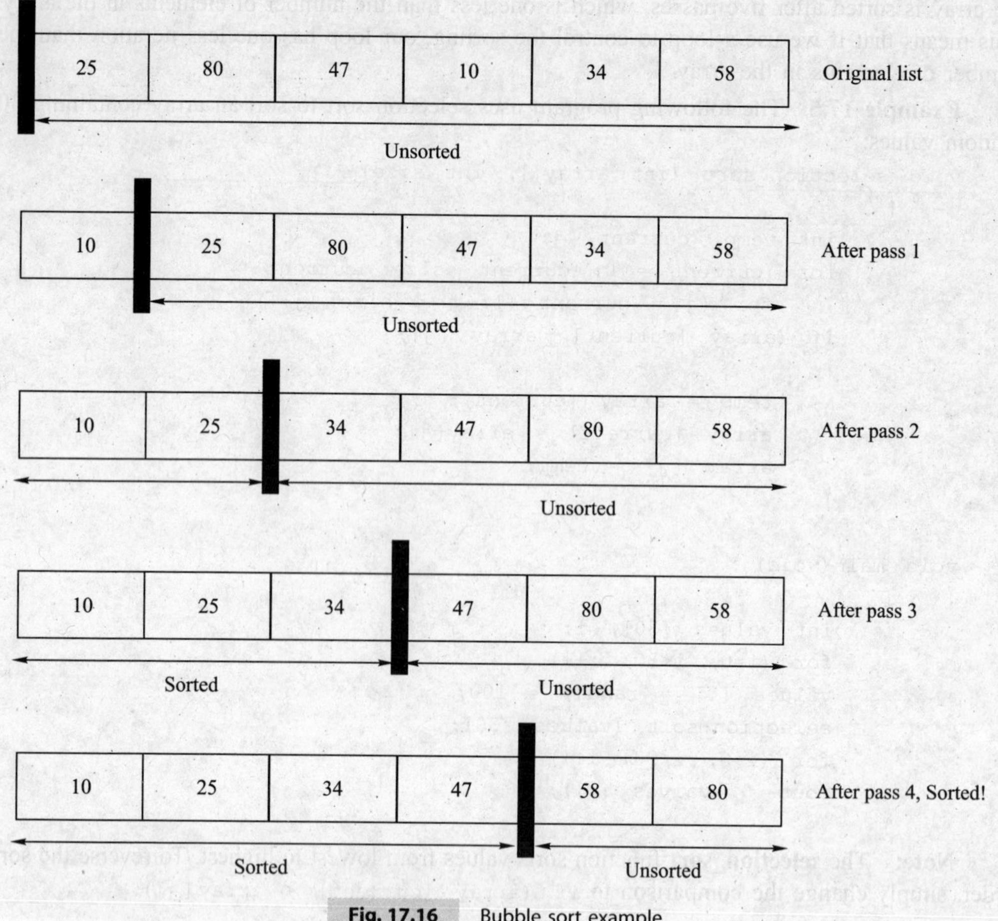

Fig. 17.16 Bubble sort example

Example 17.6 The following program cases the bubble sort an array containing 30 random values:

```
void bubble_sort  (int array[],  int size)
{
   int temp, i, j;
   for  (i = 0; i<size; i++)
   for (j = 0; j<size; j++)
   if  (array  [i]  <array .[j])
      {
         temp = array  [i];
         array [i] = array [j];
         array [j] = temp;
      }
}
void main(void)
   {
   int values  [30], i;
```

```
    for (i=0; i<30; i++)
        values [i] = rand() % 100;
    bubble_sort (values, 30);
    for (i=0; i<3-; i++)
        cout << values [i]);
    }
```

The **bubble-sort** function sorts values from lowest to highest. To reverse the sort order, simply change the comparison to **`if (array[i] > array[j]):`**

17.11 INSERTION SORT

The **insertion sort** algorithm is one of the most common sorting techniques used by card players. As they pick up each card, they insert it into the proper sequence in their hand. As an aside, card sorting is an example of a sort that uses two pieces of data to sort: suit and rank.

In the insertion sort, the list is divided into two parts: sorted and unsorted. In each pass, the first element of the unsorted sublist is picked up and transferred into the sorted sublist by inserting it at the appropriate place. If we have a list of n elements, it will take at most $n - 1$ passes to sort the data.

Figure 17.17 traces the insertion sort through our list of six numbers. Each pass moves the wall as an element is removed from the unsorted sub list and inserted into the sorted sublists.

Example 17.7 The following program uses **insertion sort** to sort an array containing 8 values.

```
        void print (float [], const int);
        void sort (float[], const int);
main()
        {
        float array [8] = {99.9, 44.4, 66.6, 22.2, 33.3, 88.8, 77.7,
                          11.1};
        print(array, 8);
        sort(array, 8);
        print(array, 8);
}
void print (float array[], const int n)
{
        for (int i = 0; i < n-1; i++)
        {
          cout << array[i] << ',';
          if ((i+1) % 16 ==0) cout << endl;
        }
        cout << array[n-1] << endl;
    }
    void sort (float array [], const int n)
    {
       float temp]
       for (int i = 1; i<n; i++)
       {
       temp = array[i];
       for (int j = i; j > 0 && array [j-1] > temp; j--)]
           array[j] = array[j-1];
```

```
        array[j] = temp;
    }
}
```

The printout of above program is:

```
99.9, 44.4, 66.6, 22.2, 33.3, 88.8, 77.7, 11.1
11.1, 22.2, 33.3, 44.4, 66.6, 77.7, 88.8, 99.9
```

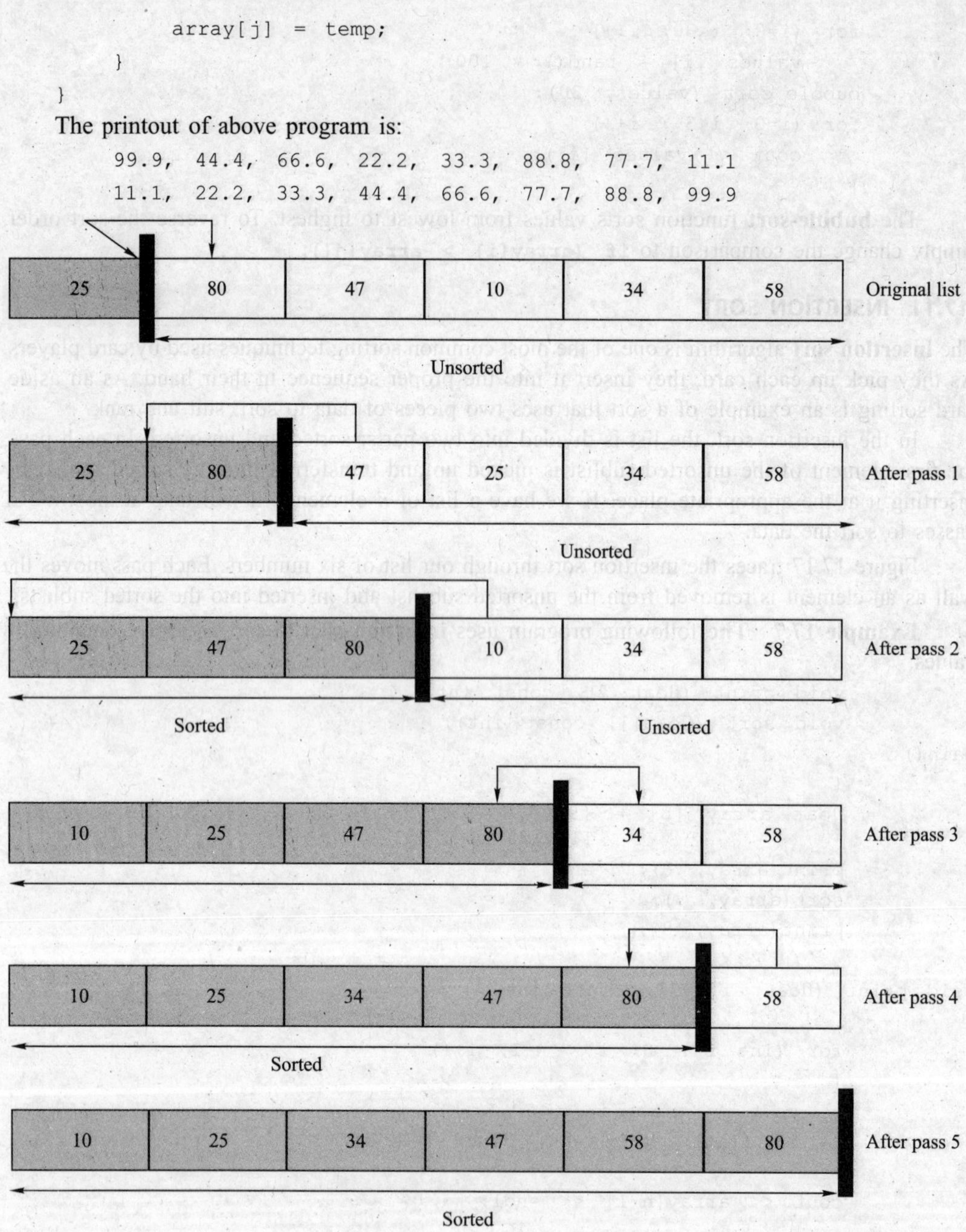

Fig. 17.17 Insertion sort example

17.12 MERGING

Merging is nothing but combining data from the two ordered (ascending or descending) lists into a single ordered list. To merge two sorted lists, we compare successive pairs of elements, one from each list, moving the smaller of each pair to the 'final' list. We can stop when the shorter list runs out of element, and then move all the remaining elements (if any) from the other list to the final list. Figure 17.18 illustrates the general algorithm.

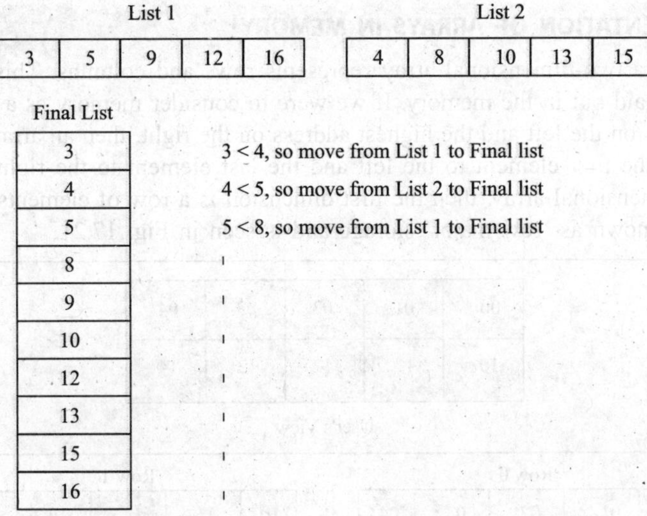

Fig. 17.18 Strategy for merging two sorted lists

Note that the difficult part of the merge design is the end-of-file logic. One of the merge files will end first, but you never know which one. To simplify the end-of-file processing, one can use the maximum value of the integer as define in your C++ software.

17.13 TWO-DIMENSIONAL ARRAYS

As you have learned, a two-dimensional array is best visualized as a table consisting of rows and columns. To reference a specific array element, you must specify the corresponding row and column position. Figure 17.19 illustrates statements that access specific elements within the array table.

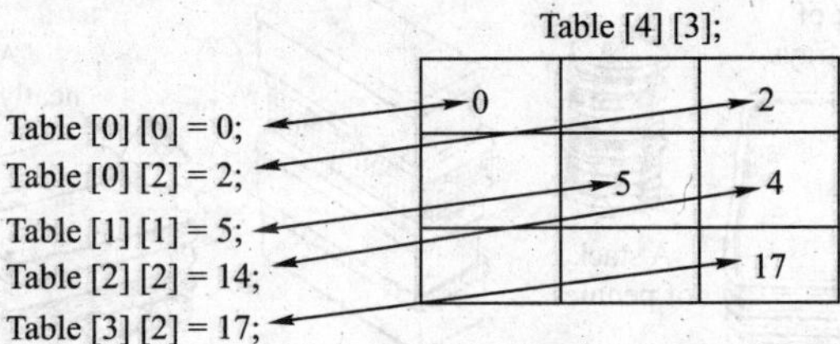

Fig. 17.19 To access elements in a two-dimensional array, you must specify row and column position

In earlier section, you learned that you can initialize array elements by placing the element values within left and right braces following the array declaration. The following statement uses this same technique to initialize a two-dimensional array. However, in this case, the values for each row of the array are specified within their own braces:

```
int table[2] [3] = { {l, 2, 3}, {4, 5, 6} };
```

The C++ compiler will initialize the array elements as shown in Fig. 17.20.

1	2	3
4	5	6

Fig. 17.20 Initializing the elements of a two-dimensional array

17.14 REPRESENTATION OF ARRAYS IN MEMORY

The definition of a two-dimensional array represents rows and columns. This format maps the way the data are laid out in the memory. If we were to consider memory as a row of bytes with the lowest address on the left and the highest address on the right, then an array would be placed in memory with the first element to the left and the last element to the right. Similarly, if the array is a two-dimensional array, then the first dimension is a row of elements that are stored to the left. This is known as 'row-major' storage and is seen in Fig. 17.21.

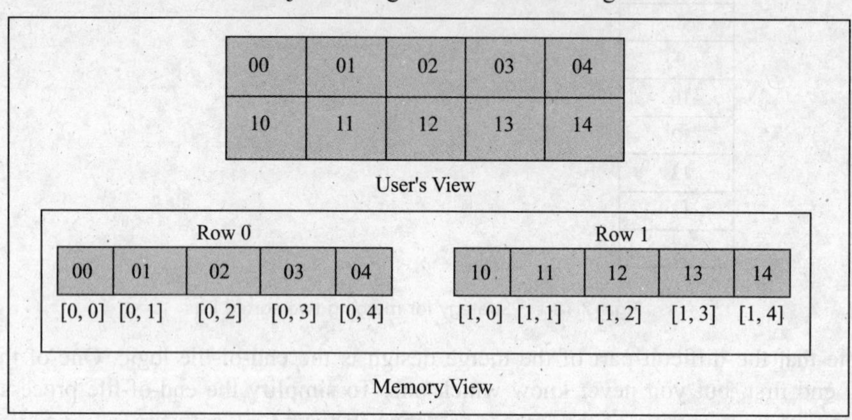

Fig. 17.21 Memory layout

17.14.1 Stack

Consider Fig. 17.22. Although the objects are all different, each illustrates a common concept—the *stack*.

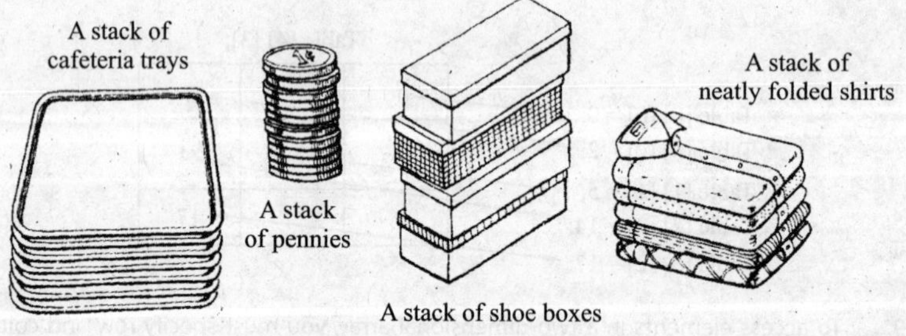

Fig. 17.22 Real-Life stacks

At the logical level, a stack is an ordered group of homogeneous elements. The removal of existing elements and the addition of new elements can take place only at the *top* of the stack. For instance, if your favorite blue shirt is underneath a faded, old, red one in a stack of shirts, you must first remove the red shirt (the top element) from the stack. Only then can you take out the desired blue shirt, which is now the top element in the stack. The red shirt may then be replaced on the top of the stack or thrown away.

The stack is considered an 'ordered' group of items because elements occur in a sequence according to how long they've been in the stack. The items that have been in the stack for the longest duration are on at the bottom; the most recent are at the top. At any time, given any two elements in a stack, one is higher than the other. (For instance, the red shirt was higher in the stack than the blue shirt).

Because items are added and removed only from the top of the stack, the last element to be added is the first to be first to be removed. There is a handy mnemonic to help you remember this rule of stack behaviour. A stack is a **'last in, first out' (LIFO)** structure.

The accessing function of a stack is summarized as follows: Both to retrieve elements and to assign new elements, access only the top of the stack.

17.14.2 Stack Operations

The logical picture of the structure is only half the definition of an abstract data type. The other half is a set of operations that allows the user to access and manipulate the elements stored in the structure. Given the logical structure of a stack, what kinds of operations do we need in order to use a stack?

A stack is a dynamic structure; it changes as elements are added to and removed from it. The operation that adds an element to the top of a stack is usually called *Push*, and the operation that takes the top element off the stack is referred to as *Pop*. When we begin using a stack, it should be empty, so another necessary operation is one that creates an empty stack (a stack containing no elements). We'll call this operation *CreateStack.* We must also be able to tell whether a stack contains any elements before we pop it, so we need a Boolean operation *EmptyStack*. As a logical data structure, a stack is never conceptually 'full', but for a particular implementation, you may need to test whether a stack is full before pushing. We'll call this Boolean operation *FullStack.* We might also want an operation that destroys a stack, getting rid of all the elements left in it and leaving the stack empty. We'll call this operation *DestroyStack*. Figure 17.23 shows how a stack, envisioned as a stack of building blocks, is modified by several Push and Pop operations.

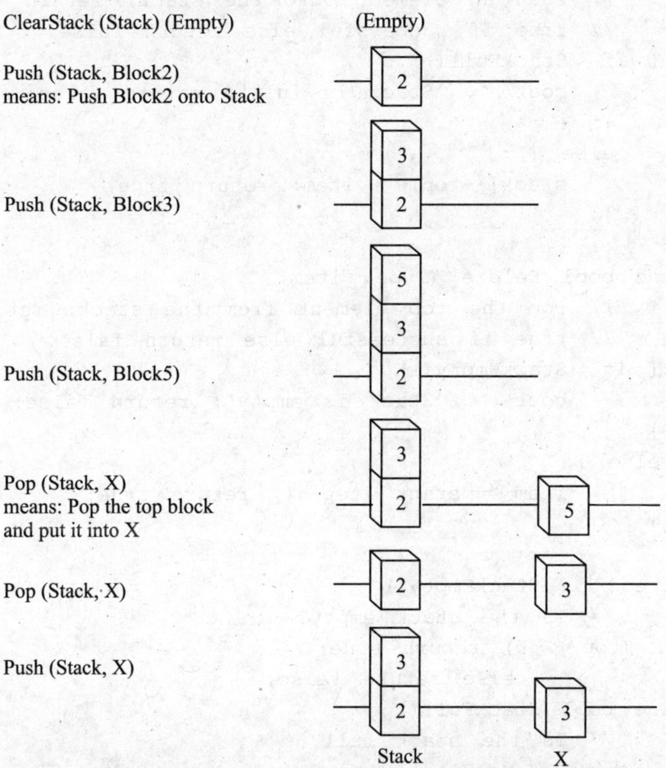

Fig. 17.23 The effects of Push and Pop-Operations

The simplest way to represent a stack is by using a one-dimensional array, say `stack[MaxSize]`, where `MaxSize` is the maximum number of allowable entries. The first or bottom element in the stack is stored at `stack[0]`, the second at `stack[1]`, and the *i*th at `stack [i-1]`. Associated with the array is a variable, typically called top, which points to the top element in the stack. To test whether the stack is empty, we ask if `(top < 0)`. If not, the topmost element is at `stack[top]`. Checking whether the stack is full can be done by asking if `(top >= (Maxsize-1))`.

Two more substantial operations are inserting and deleting elements. A C++ class that includes all these operations is given in Example 17.8.

Example 17.8 A class definition for stack

```
#include<iostream.h>
template<class Type>
class Stack
{
    private:
        int top, MaxSize;
        Type *stack;
    public:
        Stack (int MSize): MaxSize(MSize)
        { stack = new Type[MaxSize]; top=-1;}
        ~Stack()
        { delete [] stack;}
        inline bool Add(const Type item)
            // Push an element onto the stack; return
            // true if successful else return false.
        { if (StackFull()) {
                cout << 'Stack is full'; return false;
            }
            else {
                stack[++top] = item; return true;
            }
    }
    inline bool Delete (Type& item)
            // Pop the top element from the stack; return
            // true if successful else return false.
        { if (StackEmpty()) {
                cout << 'Stack is empty'; return false;
        }
        else {
                item = stack [top--]; return true;
        }
    }
    inline bool StackEmpty()
            // Is the stack empty?
    { if (top < 0) return true;
            <_><~> else return false; }
    inline bool StackFull()
            // Is the stack full?
    { if (top >= MaxSize-1)) return true;
            else return false; }
    };
```

Each execution of `Add` or `Delete` takes a constant amount of time and is independent of the number of elements in the stack. `StackFull()` and `StackEmpty()` are also functions that take $O(1)$ time.

Another way to represent a stack is by using links (or pointers). A *node* is a collection of data and link information. A stack can be represented by using nodes with two fields, possibly called `data` and `link`. The data field of each node contains an item in the stack and the corresponding link field point to the node containing the next item in the stack. The link field of the last node is zero, for we assume that all nodes have an address greater than zero. For example, a stack with the item *A*, *B*, *C*, *D* and *E* inserted in that order, looks as in Fig. 17.24.

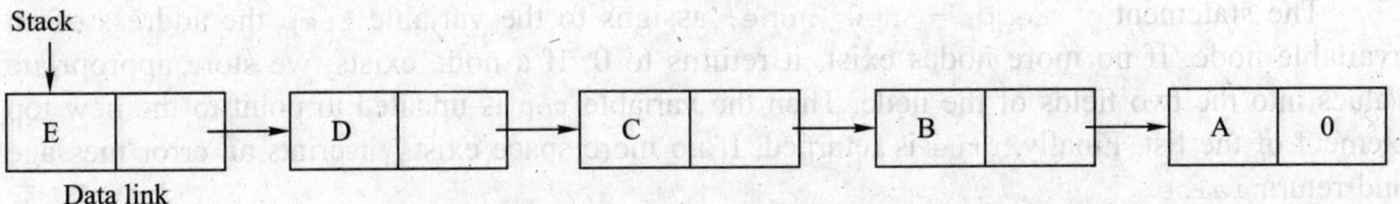

Fig. 17.24 Example of a five-element, linked stack

The variable top points to the topmost node (the last item inserted) in the list. The empty stack is represented by setting top=0. A class definition corresponding to the link representation of a stack is shown below:

Example 17.9 Link representation of a stack.

```
#define NULL 0
#include<iostream.h>
class Stack
{
    private:
        struct node {
            Type data; struct node *link;
        };
        struct node *top;
    public:
        Stack()
        { top = NULL; }
        ~Stack()
        { struct node *temp;
            while (top) {
                temp=top; top=top->link;
                delete temp;
            }
        }
        bool Add(const Type item);
        bool Delete(Type& item);
        inline bool StackEmpty()
                                          // Is the stack empty?
                          { if (top) return false;
                                                  else return true;
                          }
};
```

Because of the way the links are pointing, insertion and deletion are easy to accomplish. For example, to insert an item into the stack, one should write the following:

```
bool Stack::Add(const Type item)
{ struct node *temp = new node;
  if(temp) { temp->data = item; temp->link = top;
     top = temp; return true; }
  else { cout << 'Out of Space!' << endl;
     return false; }
  }
```

The statement `* temp = new node;` assigns to the variable `temp` the address of an available node. If no more nodes exist, it returns to 0. If a node exists, we store appropriate values into the two fields of the node. Then the variable `top` is updated to point to the new top element of the list. Finally, `true` is returned. If no more space exists, it prints an error message and return `false`.

Note that in the `class` definition of Example 17.9, we don't have the operation `StackFull()`. As a result, the program for Add is slightly different from the one in Example 17.8. One way of implementing `StackFull()` in the linked representation is to have the following statement: `struct node *temp = new node;`. If temp is nonnil, we delete temp and return `true`. Otherwise we return `false`. But this makes the Add program inefficient.

Deletion would work as follows:

```
bool Stack::Delete(Type& item)
{ if (StackEmpty()) {
        cout << 'Stack is empty' << endl;
        return false;
    }
    else {
        struct node *temp;
        item=top-> data; temp = top;
        top = top-> link;
        delete temp; return true;
    }
}
```

If the stack is empty, then trying to delete an item produces the error message `Stack is empty` and `false` is returned. Otherwise the top element is stored as the value of the variable `item`, a pointer to the first node is saved, and `top` is updated to point to the next node. The deleted node is returned for future use and finally `true` is returned.

The use of links to represent a stack requires more storage than the sequential array `stack [MaxSize]` does. However, there is greater flexibility when using links, for many structures can simultaneously use the same pool of available space. Most importantly the times for insertion and deletion using either representation are independent of the size of the stack.

17.15 EVALUATION OF EXPRESSIONS

When pioneering computer scientists conceived the idea of higher level programming languages, they were faced with many technical hurdles. One of the biggest was the question of how to generate machine language instructions which would properly evaluate any arithmetic expression. A complex assignment statement such as

$$X \leftarrow A/B^{**}C+D^*E-A^*C \quad ...(1)$$

several might meanings; and even if it were defined uniquely, say by a full use of parentheses, it still seemed a formidable task to generate a correct and reasonable instruction sequence. Fortunately the solution we have today is both elegant and simple. Moreover, it is so simple that this aspect of compiler writing is really one of the more minor issues.

An expression is made up of operands, operators and delimiters. The expression above has five operands: *A*, *B*, *C*, *D* and *E*. Though these are all one letter variables, operands can be any legal variable name or constant in our programming language. In any expression, the values that variables take must be consistent with the operations performed on them. These operations are described by the operators. In most programming languages, there are several kinds of operators which correspond to the different kinds of data a variable can hold. First, there are the basic arithmetic operators: plus, minus, times, divide, and exponentiation (*x*, –, *, /, **). Other arithmetic operators include unary plus, unary minus and **mod, ceil,** and **floor.** The latter three may sometimes be library subroutines rather than predefined operators. A second class are the relational operators: <, <, $\underline{\leq}$, =, $\underline{\geq}$, >>. These are usually defined to work for arithmetic operands, but they can just as easily work for character string data. ('CAT' is less than 'DOG' since it precedes 'DOG' in alphabetical order.) The result of an expression which contains relational operators is one of the two constants: **true** or **false**. Such an expression is called Boolean, named after the mathematical George Boole, the father of symbolic logic.

The first problem with understanding the meaning of an expression is to decide in what order the operations are carried out. This means that every language must uniquely define such an order. For instance, if $A = 4$, $B = C = 2$, $D = E = 3$, then in equation 1, we might want *X* to be assigned the value.

4/(2 ** 2) + (3 * 3) – (4 * 2)

= (4/4) + 9 – 8

= 2.

However, the true intention of the programmer might have been to assign *X* the value

(4/2) ** (2 + 3) * (3 – 4) * 2

= (4/2) ** 5 * – 1 * 2

= (2 ** 5) * – 2

= 32 * –2

= –64.

Of course, he could specify the latter order of evaluation by using parentheses:

X ←((((*A*/*B*) ** (*C* + *D*)) * (*E* – *A*)) * *C*).

To fix the order of evaluation, we assign a priority to each operator. Then within any pair of parentheses we understand that operators with the highest priority will be evaluated first. A set of sample priorities from *PL/I* is given in Fig. 17.25.

Operator	*Priority*
**, unary–, unary+, –	6
*, /	5
+, –	4
<, <, $\underline{\leq}$, =, =, $\underline{\geq}$, >, >	3
and	2
or	1

Fig. 17.25 Priority of arithmetic, Boolean and relational operators

Notice that all of the relational operators have the same priority. Similarly, exponentiation, unary minus, unary plus and Boolean negation all have top priority. When we have an expression where two adjacent operators have the same priority, we need a rule to tell us which one to perform first, For example, do we want the value of $-A$ ** B to be understood as $(-A)$ ** B or $-(A$ ** $B)$? Convince yourself that there will be a difference by trying $A = -1$ and $B = 2$. From algebra, we normally consider A ** B ** C as A ** $(B$ ** $C)$ and so we rule that operators in priority 6 are evaluated right-to-left. However, for expressions such as $A * B/C$ we generally execute left-to-right or $(A * B)/C$. So we rule that for all other priorities, evaluation of operators of the same priority will proceed left to right. Remember that by using parentheses we can override these rules, and such expressions are always evaluated with the innermost parenthesized expression first.

Now that we have specified priorities and rules for breaking ties we know how $X \leftarrow A/B$ ** $C + D * E - A * C$, will be evaluated, namely as

$$X \leftarrow ((A/(B ** C)) + (D * E)) - (A * C).$$

How can a compiler accept such an expression and produce correct code? The answer is given by reworking the expression into a form we call post fix notation. If e is an expression with operators and operands, the conventional way of writing e is called *infix*, because the operators come between the operands. (Unary operators precede their operand). The **postfix** form of an expression calls for each operator to appear before its operands. For example, the infix expression: $A + B$ is written as $+ AB$ in **prefix** form. The **postfix** form of an expression calls for each operator to appear *after* its operand. For example

infix: $A * B/C$ has postfix : $AB * C/$.

If we study the postfix form of $A * B/C$, we see that the multiplication comes immediately after its two operands A and B. Now imagine that $A * B$ is computed and stored in T. Then we have the division operator /, coming immediately after its two arguments T and C.

Let us look at our previous example

infix: $A/B ** C + D * E - A * C$

postfix: $ABC **/DE * + AC * -$

and trace out the meaning of the postfix.

Every time we compute a value, let us store it in the temporary location T_i, $i \geq 1$. Reading left to right, the first operation is exponentiation:

Operator	*Priority*
$T_1 \leftarrow B ** C$	$AT_1/DE * + AC *$
$T_2 \leftarrow A/T_1$	$T_2/DE * + AC * -$
$T_3 \leftarrow D * E$	$T_2T_3 + AC * -$
$T_4 \leftarrow T_2 + T_3$	$T_4AC * -$
$T_5 \leftarrow A * C$	$T_4T_5 -$
$T_6 \leftarrow T_4 - T_5$	T_6

So T_6 will contain the result. Notice that if we had parenthesized the expression, this would change the postfix only if the order of normal evaluation were altered. Thus, $A/(B ** C) + (D * E) - A * C$ will have the same postfix form as the previous expression without parentheses. But $(A/B) ** (C + D) * (E - A) * C$ will have the postfix form $AB/CD + ** EA - * C *$.

Before attempting an algorithm to translate expressions from infix to postfix notation, let us makes some observations regarding the virtues of postfix notation that enable easy evaluation of expression. To begin with, the need for parentheses is eliminated. Secondly, the priority of the operators is no longer relevant. The expression may be evaluated by making a left to right scan, stacking operands, and evaluating operators using as operands the correct number from the stack and finally placing the result onto the stack. This evaluation process is much simpler than attempting a direct evaluation from infix notation.

To see how to devise an algorithm for translating from infix to postfix, note that the order of the operands in both forms is the same. In fact, it is simple to describe an algorithm for producing postfix from infix:

1. fully parenthesize the expression:
2. move all operators so that they replace their corresponding right parentheses:
3. delete all parentheses.

For example, *A*/*B* ** *C* + *D* * *E* – *A* * *C* when fully parenthesized yields

(((*A*/(*B* ** *C*) + (*D* * *E*)) – (*A* * *C*))

The arrows point from an operator to its corresponding right parenthesis. Performing steps 2 and 3 gives

ABC ** /*DE* * + *AC**–

The problem with this as an algorithm is that it requires two passes : the first one reads expression and parenthesizes it while the second actually moves the operators. As we have already observed, the order of the operands is the same in infix and postfix. So as we scan an expression for the first time, we can form the postfix by immediately passing any operands to the output. Then it is just a matter of handling the operators. The solution is to store them in a stack until just the right moment and then to unstack and pass them to the output.

For example, since we want *A* + *B* * *C* to yield *ABC* * +, our algorithm should perform the following sequence of stacking (these stacks will grow to the right):

Next Token	*Stack*	*Output*
none	empty	none
A	empty	*A*
+	+	*A*
B	+	*AB*

At this point, the algorithm must determine if * gets placed on top of the stack or if the + gets taken off. Since * has greater priority, we should stack * producing

*	+*	*AB*
C	+*	*ABC*

Now the input expression is exhausted, so we output all remaining operators in the stack to get

ABC * +

For another example, *A* * (*B* + *C*) * *D* has the postfix form *ABC* + * *D* *, and so the algorithm should behave as:

Next Token	*Stack*	*Output*
none	empty	none
A	empty	*A*
*	*	*A*

Next Token	Stack	Output
(	* (	A
B	* (	AB
++	* (	AB
C	* (+	ABC

At this point, we want to unstack down to the corresponding left parenthesis, and then delete the left and right parentheses; this gives us:

)	*	ABC +
*	*	ABC + *
D	*	ABC + * D*

These examples should motivate the following hierarchy scheme for binary arithmetic operators and delimiters. The general case involving all the operators of Fig. 17.26 is left as an exercise

Symbol	In-Stack Priority	In-Coming Priority
)	–	–
**	3	2
*,/	2	1
binary+,(	1	1
(	0	4

Fig. 17.26 Priorities of Operators for Producing Postfix

Example 17.10

1. Convert $(A - B) * (C / D) + E$ into postfix notation.

The valuation order of given expression will be

$$= ((A - B) * (C/D)) + E$$

Converting expressions in the braces, we get

$$= ((AB -) * (C/D)) + E$$
$$= ((AB -) * (CD/) + E$$
$$= (AB - CD/*) + E$$
$$= AB - CD/* E+$$

Ans.

2. Convert $(A + B) * C/D + E \uparrow F/G$ into postfix notation.

Putting the given expression in evaluation order

$$= ((((A + B) * C)/D) + (E 1\uparrow F))/G$$

Converting expressions, we get

$$= ((((AB +) * C)/D) + (EF \uparrow))/G$$
$$= (((AB + C*)/D) + (EF \uparrow))/G$$
$$= ((AB + C * D/) + (EF \uparrow))/G$$
$$= (AB + C * D/EF \uparrow +)/G$$
$$= AB + C * D/EF \uparrow + G$$

Ans.

3. Convert $X + Y * Z \uparrow P - (X / Y + Z)$ into prefix notation.
Evaluation order of given expression is:

$= (((X + Y) * (Z \uparrow P)) - ((X / Y) + Z))$

Converting expressions in the braces, we get

$= (((XY +) * (ZP \uparrow)) - ((XY /) + Z))$

$= ((XY + ZP \uparrow *) - (XY / Z +))$

$= (XYZP \uparrow * + XY / Z + -)$

$= XYZP \uparrow * + XY / Z + -$ **Ans.**

4. Convert $A * (B + (C + D) * (E + F) / G) * H$ into postfix notation. The evaluation order of the given expression is :

$= (A * (B + ((C + D) * (E + F)) / G)) * H$

Converting expressions in braces, we get

$= (A * (B + ((CD +) * (EF +)) / G)) * H$

$= A * (B + (CD + EF + *) / G) * H$

$= A * (B + (CD + EF + * G /\wedge)) * H$

$= (A * (BCD + EF + * G / +)) * H$

$= (ABCD + EF + * G / + *) * H$

$= ABCD + EF + * G / + * H *$ **Ans.**

5. Convert NOT A OR NOT B NOT C into postfix notation.
The evaluation order of the expression is

= ((NOT A) OR ((NOT B) AND (NOT C)))

Converting expressions in the braces,

= ((A NOT) OR ((B NOT) AND ((C NOT)))

= ((A NOT) OR (B NOT C NOT AND))

= A NOT B NOT C NOT AND OR

6. Convert $(A - B) * (C / D) + E$; into postfix form showing stack status after every step in tabular form.

Step	Scanned	Action	Stack Status	Expression
1	(	Push	(	
2	A	Print	(	A
3	–	Push	(–	A
4	B	Print	(–	AB
5	)	Pop & Print	(	AB –
		Pop	AB –	# (empty)
6	*	Push	*	AB –
7	(	Push	* (	AB –
8	C	Print	* (	AB – C
9	/	Push	* (/	AB – C
10	D	Print	* (/	AB – CD
11	)	Pop & Print	* (	AB – CD/
		Push	*	AB – CD/
12	++	Pop & Print	# (empty)	AB – CD/*
		Push	+	AB – CD/*
13	E	Print	+	AB – CD/*E
		Pop and Print	#	AB – CD/*E+
14	;	Stop		

The output postfix expression

= AB - CD / * E +

7. Convert $A + (B * C - (D / E \uparrow F) * G) * H$; into postfix form showing stack status after every step in tabular form.

Step	Scanned	Action	Stack Status	Expression
1	A	Print	# (empty)	A
2	+	Push	+	A
3	(	Push	+ (	A
4	B	Print	+ (	AB
5	*	Push	+ (*	AB
6	C	Print	+ (*	ABC
7	–	Pop & Print	+ (	ABC *
		Push	+ (–	ABC *
8	(	Push	+ (– (	ABC *
9	D	Print	+ (– (	ABC * D
10	/	Push	+ (– (/	ABC * D
11	E	Print	+ (– (/	ABC * DE
12	↑	Push	+ (– (/↑	ABC * DE
13	F	Print	+ (– (/↑	ABC * DEF
14	)	Pop & Print	+ (– (/	ABC * DEF↑
		Pop & Print	+ (– (	ABC * DEF↑/
		Pop	+ (–	ABC * DEF↑/
15	*	Push	+ (– *	ABC * DEF↑/
16	G	Print	+ (– *	ABC * DEF↑/G
17	)	Pop & Print	+ (–	ABC * DEF↑/G*
		Pop & Print	+ (	ABC * DEF↑/G*–
		Pop	+	ABC * DEF↑/G*–
18	*	Push	+ *	ABC * DEF↑/G*–
19	H	Print	+ *	ABC * DEF↑/G*–H
20	;	Pop & Print	+	ABC * DEF↑/G*–H
		Pop & Print	# (empty)	ABC * DEF↑/G*–H*+
		stop		

8. Evaluate the expression 4 3 10 * + ; in tabular form showing stack status after every step.

Step	Input Element	Action	Stack Status
1	4	Push	4
2	3	Push	4 3
3	10	Push	4 3 10
4	*	Pop (10)	4 3
		Pop (3)	4
		Multiply 10, 3	4
		Push result	4 30
5	+	Pop (30)	4
		Pop (4)	# empty

Step	Input Element	Action	Stack Status
6	;	Add 40, 4 Push result Pop (34) Print result	# empty 34 # empty

17.16 QUEUE

A queue (pronounced like the letter *Q*) is an ordered, homogeneous group of elements in which new elements are added at one end (the 'rear') and elements are removed from the other end (the 'front'). As an example of a queue, consider a line of students waiting to pay for their textbooks at a university bookstore (see Fig. 17.27). In theory if not in practice, each new student gets in line at the rear. When the cashier is ready for a new customer, the student at the front of the line is served.

Fig. 17.27 A FIFO Queue

To add elements to a FIFO queue, we access the rear of the queue; to remove elements, we access the front. The middle elements are logically inaccessible, even if we physically store the queue elements in a random-access structure such as an array. It is convenient to picture the queue as a linear structure with the front at one end and the rear at the other end. However, we must stress that the 'ends' of the queue are *abstractions;* they may or may not correspond to any physical characteristics of the implementation of data structures. The essential property of the queue is its FIFO access.

Like the stack, the queue is a holding structure for data that we will use later. We put a data element on to the queue, and then when we need it we remove it from the queue. If we want to change the value of an element, we must take that element off the queue, change its value, and then return it to the queue. We do not directly manipulate the values of elements that are currently in the queue.

17.17 QUEUE OPERATIONS

The book store example suggests two operations that can be applied to a queue. First, new elements can be added to the rear of the queue, an operation that we will call *Enqueue*. We can also take elements off the front of the queue, an operation that we will call *Dequeue*. Unlike the stack operations Push and Pop, the adding and removing operations on a queue do not have standard names. Enqueue is sometimes called Enq, Add, or Insert; Dequeue is also called Deq, Remove, or Serve.

Another useful queue operation is checking whether the queue is empty. The *EmptyQueue*, function returns True if Queue is empty and False otherwise. We can only Dequeue when the queue is not empty. Theoretically, we can always Enqueue, for in principle a queue is not limited in size. We know from our experience with stacks, however, that certain implementations (an array representation, for instance) require that we test whether the structure is full before we add another element. This real-world consideration applies to queues as well, so we will define a *FullQueue* operation.

We also need an operation to initialize a queue to an empty state, which we will call *CreateQueue*. As with stacks, we might also want an operation to destroy the whole structure, leaving it empty. We will call this operation *DestroyQueue*. Figure 17.28 shows how a series of these operations would affecting a queue.

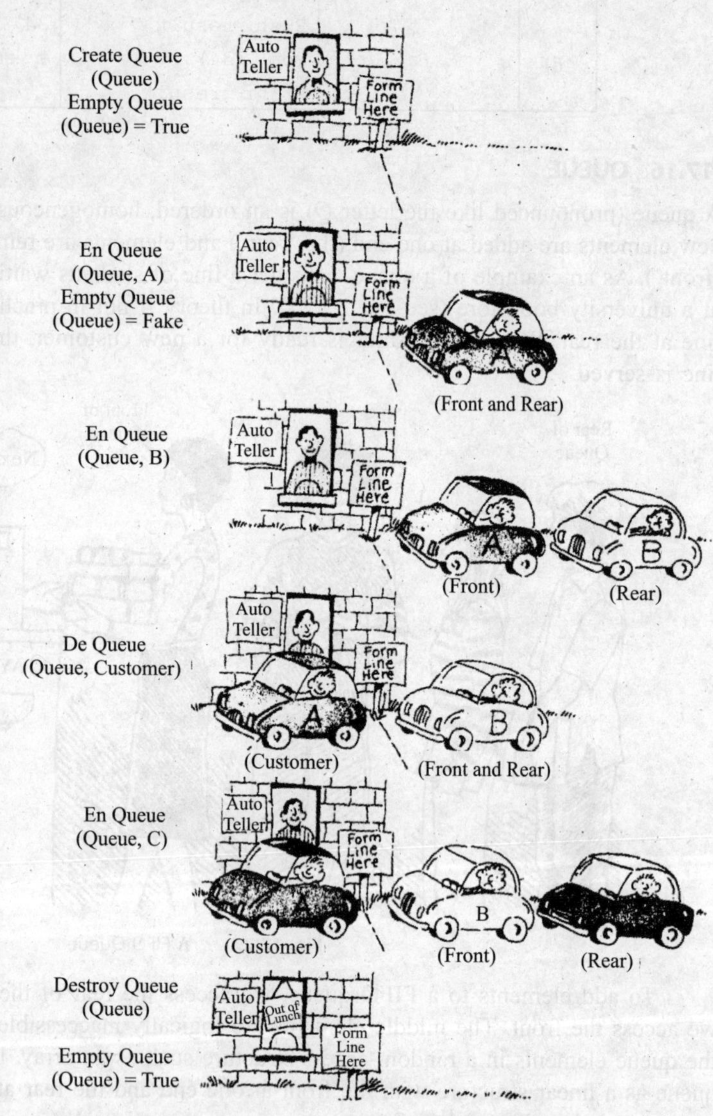

Fig. 17.28 The effects of Queue Operations

An efficient queue representation can be obtained by taking an array `q[MaxSize]`, and treating it as if it were circular. The `class` definition for queue includes three integer variables – `front, rear`, and `MaxSize`-in addition to the array `q []` (See Example 17.10). Elements are inserted by increasing the variable `rear` to the next free position. When `rear== MaxSize-1`, the next element is entered at `q[0] in case that spot is free. The variable front` always points one position counterclockwise from the first element in the queue. `front==rear` if and only if the queue is empty and we initially set `front=rear=0`. Figure 17.29 illustrates two of the possible configurations for a circular queue containing the element *J* / roman to *J 4* with $n > 4$.

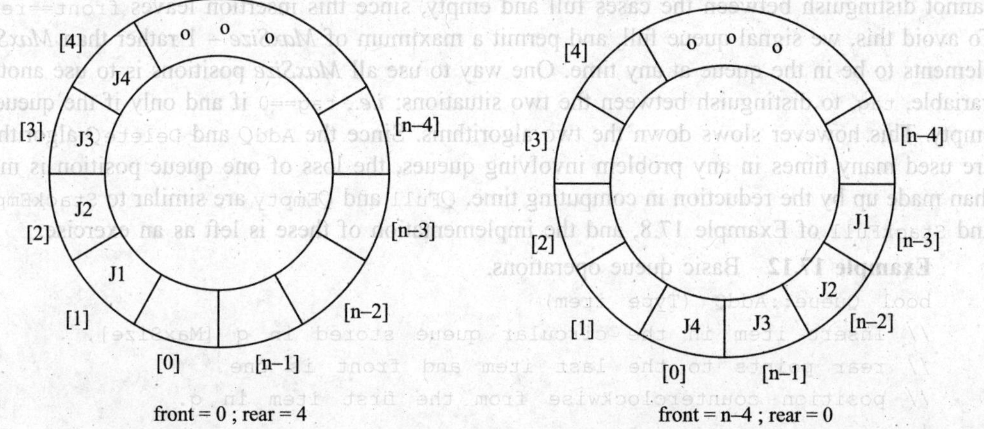

Fig. 17.29 Circular queue of capacity n = MaxSize containing four elements J1, J2, J3 and J4

To insert an element, it is necessary to move rear one position clockwise. This can be done using the code

```
if (rear == MaxSize-1) rear = 0;
else rear++;
```

A more elegant way to do this is to use the built-in modulo operator `%` which computer remainders. Before doing an insert, we increase the rear pointer by saying `rear= (++rear) % MaxSize;`. Similarly, it is necessary to move `front` one position clockwise each time a deletion is made. An examination of the algorithms, Example 17.12 (*a*) and (*b*) indicates that by treating the array circularly, addition and deletion for queues can be carried out in a fixed amount of time or $O(1)$.

Example 17.11 Class definition for queue

```
#define NULLO
#include<iostream>
class Queue
{
    private
        Type* q;
            int front, rear, MaxSize;
    public;
        Queue (int MSize): MaxSize (MSize)
        { q = new Type [MaxSize]; rear=front=0;}
        ~Queue()
        { delete [] q; }
        bool AddQ (Type item);
        bool DeleteQ (Type& item);
        bool QFull ();
        bool QEmpty ();
};
```

One surprise feature in these two algorithms is that the test for queue full in `AddQ` and the test for queue empty in `DeleteQ`, are the same. In the case of `AddQ`, however, when `front==rere`, there is actually one space free, `q[rear]`, since the first element in the queue is not at `q[front]` but is one position clockwise from this point. However, if we insert an item there, then we cannot distinguish between the cases full and empty, since this insertion leaves `front==rear`. To avoid this, we signal queue full, and permit a maximum of *MaxSize* – 1 rather than *MaxSize* elements to be in the queue at any time. One way to use all *MaxSize* positions is to use another variable, `tag`, to distinguish between the two situations; *i.e.*, `tag==0` if and only if the queue is empty. This however slows down the two algorithms. Since the `AddQ` and `DeleteQ` algorithms are used many times in any problem involving queues, the loss of one queue position is more than made up by the reduction in computing time. `QFull` and `QEmpty` are similar to `StackEmpty` and `StackFull` of Example 17.8, and the implementation of these is left as an exercise.

Example 17.12 Basic queue operations.

```
bool Queue::AddQ (Type item)
// Insert item in the circular queue stored in q [MaxSize].
// rear points to the last item and front is one
// position counterclockwise from the first item in q.
{
    rear = (++rear) % MaxSize; // Advance rear clockwise.
    if (front == rear) {
        cout << 'Queue is full' << endl;
        if (!front) rear = MaxSize-1; else rear-;
        // Move rear one position counter clockwise.
        return false;
    }
    else (
        q[rear] = item; // Insert new item.
        return true;
    }
}
```

(a) Addition of an element

```
bool Queue::DeleteQ(Type& item)
// Removes and returns the front element
// of the queue q[MaxSize].
{
    if (front == rear) {
        cout << 'Queue is empty' << endl;
        return false;
    }
    else {
        front = (++front)%MaxSize: // Advance front
            clockwise.
        item = q[front]; // Return front of queue.
        return true;
    }
}
```

(*b*) Deletion of an element

17.18 LINKED QUEUES

Another way to represent a queue is by using links. Figure 17.30 shows a queue with the four elements *A*, *B*, *C* and *D*, entered in that order. As with the linked stack example, each queue is composed of the two fields `data` and `link`. A queue is pointed at by two `front` and `rear`. Deletions are made from the front, and insertions at the rear.

Variable front = 0 signals an empty queue. The procedures for insertion and deletion queues will be discussed in next section.

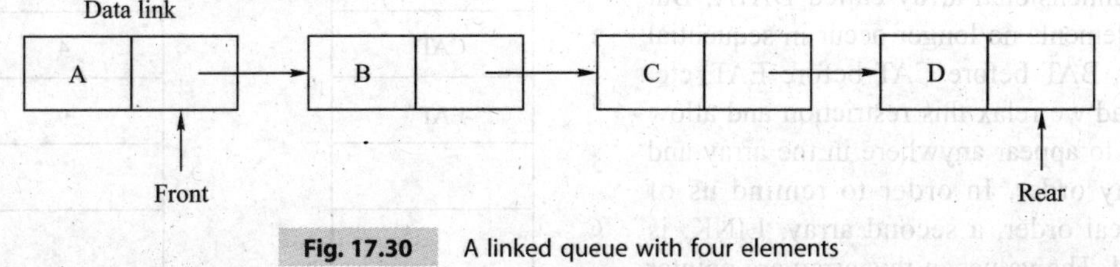

Fig. 17.30 A linked queue with four elements

17.19 LINKED LISTS

A linked list is an ordered collection of data in which each element contains the location of next element; that is, each element contains two parts: **data** and **link.** The data part holds the useful information, the data to be processed. The link is used to **chain** the data together. It contains a pointer that identifies the next node in the list. A pointer variable points to the first node in the list. The name of the list is the same as the name of this pointer variable.

For example, consider the following list of all of the three letter English words ending in AT:

(BAT, CAT, EAT, FAT, HAT, JAT, LAT, MAT,
OAT, PAT, RAT, SAT, TAT, VAT, WAT)

To make this list complete, we naturally want to add the word GAT, which means gun or revolver. If we are using an array to keep this list, then the insertion of GAT will require us to move elements already in the list either one location higher or lower. We must either move HAT, JAT, LAT, ... WAT or else move BAT, CAT, EAT, and FAT. If we have to do many such insertions into the middle, then neither alternative is attractive because of the amount of data movement. On the other hand, suppose we decide to remove the word LAT which refers to the Latvian monetary unit. Then again, we have to move many elements so as to maintain the sequential representation of the list.

When our problem called for several ordered lists of varying sizes, sequential representation again proved to be inadequate. By storing each list in a different array of maximum size, storage may be wasted. By maintaining the lists in a single array, a potentially large amount of data movement is needed. This was explicitly observed when we represented several stacks, queues, polynomials and matrices. All these data objects are examples of ordered lists. Polynomials are ordered by exponent while matrices are ordered by rows and columns. In this section we shall present an alternative representation for ordered lists which will reduce the time needed for arbitrary insertion and deletion.

An elegant solution to this problem of data movement in *sequential* representations is achieved by using *linked* representations. Unlike a sequential representation where successive items of a list are located a fixed distance apart, in a linked representation these items may be placed anywhere in memory. Another way of saying this is that in a sequential representation the order of elements is the same as in the ordered list, while in a linked representation these two sequences need not be the same. To access elements in the list in the correct order, with each element we store the address or location of the next element in that list. Thus, associated with each data item in a linked representation is a pointer to the next item. This pointer is often referred to as a link. In general, a *node* is a collection of data, DATA 1, ...DATA *n* and links LINK 1, ...LINK *m*. Each item in a node is called a *field*. A field contains either a data item or a link.

Figure 17.31 shows how some of the nodes of the list we considered before may be represented in memory by using pointers. The elements of the list are stored in a one-dimensional array called DATA. But the elements no longer occur in sequential order, BAT before CAT before EAT, etc. Instead we relax this restriction and allow them to appear anywhere in the array and in any order. In order to remind us of the real order, a second array, LINK, is added. The values in this array are pointer to elements in the DATA array. Since the list start at DATA(8) = BAT, let us set a variable $F = 8$. LINK(8) has the value 3, which means it points to DATA(3) which contains CAT. The third element of the list is pointed at by LINK(3) which is EAT. By continuing in this way, we can list all the words in the proper order.

We recognise that we have come to the end when LINK has a value of zero.

Some of the values of DATA and LINK are undefined such as DATA(2), LINK(2), DATA(5), etc. We shall ignore this for the moment.

	DATA	LINK
1	HAT	15
2		
3	CAT	4
4	EAT	9
5		
6		
7	WAT	0
8	BAT	3
9	FAT	1
10		
11	VAT	7
	⋮	⋮

Fig. 17.31 Non-sequential list representation

It is customary to draw linked lists as an ordered sequence of nodes with links being represented by arrows as in Fig. 17.32. Notice that we do not explicitly put in the values of the pointers but simply draw arrows to indicate they are there. This is so that we reinforce in our own mind the facts that (*i*) the nodes do not actually reside in sequential locations, and that (*ii*) the locations of nodes may change on different runs. Therefore, when we write a program which works with lists. We almost never look for a specific address except when we test for zero.

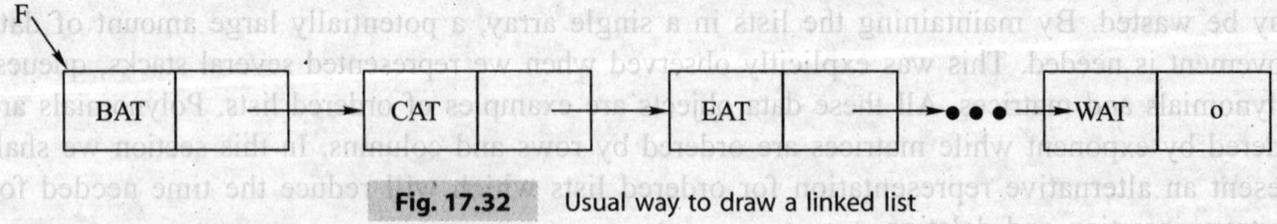

Fig. 17.32 Usual way to draw a linked list

Let us now see why it is easier to make arbitrary insertions and deletions using a linked list rather than a sequential list. To insert the data item GAT between FAT and HAT the following step are adequate:

(*i*) get a node which is currently unused; let its address be *X*:

(*ii*) set the DATA field of this node to GAT;

(*iii*) set the LINK field of *X* to point to the node after FAT which contains HAT.

(*iv*) set the LINK field of the node containing FAT to *X*.

Figure 17.33 (*a*) shows how the arrays DATA and LINK will be changed after we insert GAT. Figure 17.33 (*b*) shows how we can draw the insertion using our arrow notation. The new arrows are dashed. The important thing to notice is that when we insert GAT, we do not have to move any other elements which are already in the list. We have overcome the need to move data at the expense of the storage needed for the second field LINK. But we will see that this is not too severe a penalty.

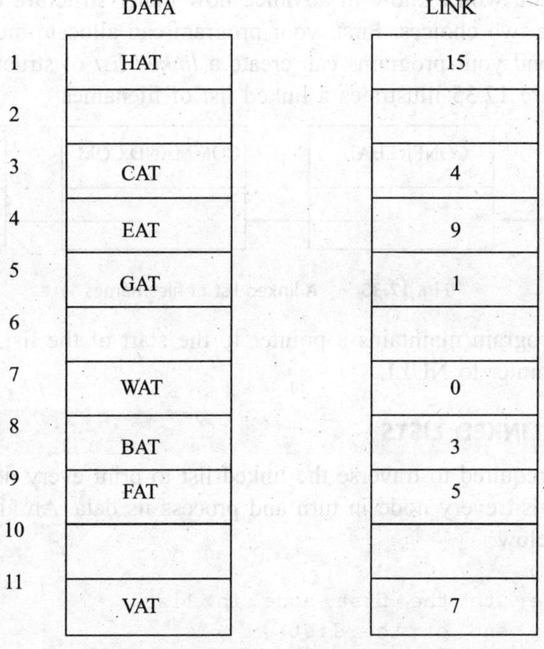

Fig. 17.33 (*a*) Insert GAT Into DATA (5)

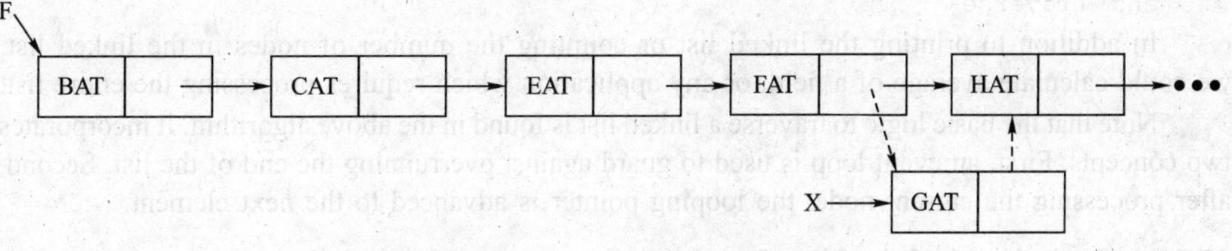

Fig. 17.33 (*b*) Insert Node GAT into List

Now suppose we want to delete GAT from the list. All we need to do is find the element which immediately precedes GAT, which is FAT, and set LINK(9) to the position of HAT which is 1. Again, there is no need to move the data around. Even though the LINK field of GAT still contains a pointer to HAT, GAT is no longer in the list (see Fig. 17.34).

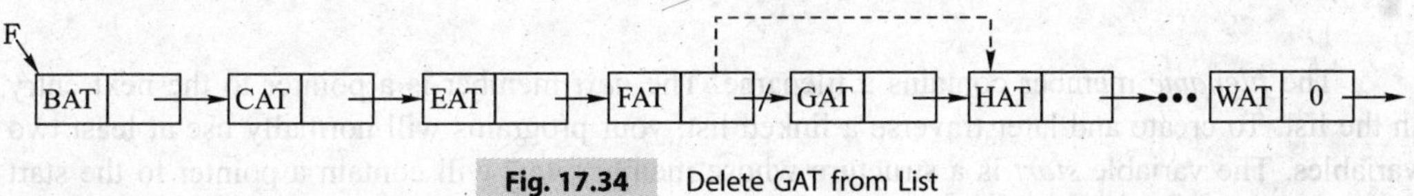

Fig. 17.34 Delete GAT from List

From our brief discussion of linked lists, we see that the following capabilities are needed to make linked representations possible:

(*i*) A means for dividing memory into nodes each having at least one linked field;

(*ii*) A mechanism to determine which nodes are in use and which are free;

(*iii*) A mechanism to transfer nodes from the reserved pool to the free pool and vice-versa.

Example 17.13 By now, you have learned how to group related information into a single variable. If your program needs to work with a fixed number of occurrences of a structure, your program can create an array of structures. As your programs become more complex, there will be many times when you won't know in advance how many structure entries you will need. In such cases, you have two choices. First, your program can allocate memory dynamically for an array structure. Second your programs can create a *linked list* of structures, where one entry points to the next. Figure 17.35 illustrates a linked list of filenames.

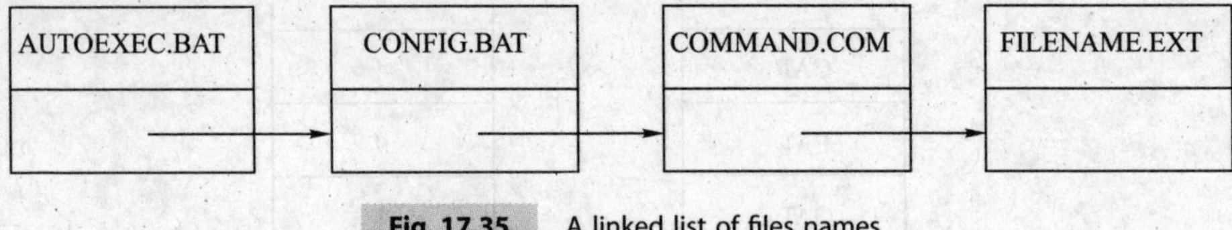

Fig. 17.35 A linked list of files names

In general, the program maintains a pointer to the start of the list. The last entry in the list is indicated by a pointer to NULL.

17.20 TRAVERSING LINKED LISTS

Most of the time, it is required to traverse the linked list to print every node or to count all the nodes in a list *i.e.*, to visit every node in turn and process its data. An algorithm for traversing a linked list is given below:

```
traverse (list)
     set pointer to the first node in list
     While (not end of the list)
          process (current node)
          set pointer to next node
end traverse
```

In addition to printing the linked list or counting the number of nodes in the linked list, we could calculate average of a field, or any application which requires processing the entire list.

Note that the basic logic to traverse a linked list is found in the above algorithm. It incorporates two concepts. First, an event loop is used to guard against overrunning the end of the list. Second, after processing the current node, the looping pointer is advanced to the next element.

17.20.1 Declaring A Linked-list Structure

To create a linked list, one of the structure members is a pointer to a structure of the same type. For example, consider the following structure:

```
struct FileList {
     char filename[64];
     struct FileList *next;
};
```

The *filename* member contains a filename. The *next* member is a pointer to the next entry in the list. To create and later traverse a linked list, your programs will normally use at least two variables. The variable *start* is a structure whose member *next* will contain a pointer to the start of the list or NULL if the list is empty. The variable *node* will be a pointer to the current node.

```
struct FileList start, *node;
```

17.20.2 Building A Linked List

To create a linked list, your programs should perform the following steps:

1. Declare the structure that defines the list entries

2. Declare the variables *start* and **node*
3. Assign start.*next* NULL to signify an empty list.
4. For each list entry
   (*a*) Find the end of the list so that *node->next* is NULL
   (*b*) Allocate memory for the new entry assigning it to *node->next*
   (*c*) Assign node the value of *node->next*
   (*d*) Assign the member values to *node*
   (*e*) Assign *node->next* the value NULL to indicate the end of the list.

Example 17.14 The following program, creates a linked list whose entries contain the numbers 1 through 10:

```
void main(void)
    {
    int i;
    struct ListEntry {
    int number;
    struct ListEntry *next;
    } start, *node;
    start.next = NULL; // Empty list
    node = &start; // Point to the start of the list
    for (i = 1; i <=10; i++)
        node->next= (struct ListEntry *)
            Malloc(sizeof(struct ListEntry));
        node = node->next;
        node->number = i;
        node->next = NULL;
    }
    // Display the list
    node = start.next;
    while (node)
    {
        cout << node->number;
        node = node->next;
    }
}
```

17.21 UNDERSTANDING THE LINKED-LIST TRAVERSAL

Above example created a simple linked list whose entries contained the numbers 1 through 10. The program used the following loop to display the list entries:

```
// Display the list
node = start.next;
while (node)
    {
        cout << node->number;
        node = node->next;
    }
```

As you will recall, the variable *start.next* points to the first entry in the list. As you can see, the code assigns the address of the first entry to *node*. Likewise, as you will recall, the end of the list is indicated by NULL; the loop simply tests the current value of *node* to see if it is NULL. If *node* is not NULL, the loop displays the entry's value and assigns *node* the address of the next list entry.

17.22 BUILDING A MORE INTERESTING LIST

In earlier example, you created a simple linked list that contained the numbers 1 though 10. The following program creates a linked list that contains the names of current directory files.

```
void main(int argc, char *argv[])
    {
        DIR *directory_pointer;
        struct direct *entry;
        struct FileList {
            char filename[64];
            struct FileList *next;
        } start, *node;
        if (( directory_pointer = opendir (argv [1] )) == NULL)
            cout << 'Error opening \n'<< argv[1];
        else
        {
            start.next = NULL;
            node = &start;
            while (entry = readdir(directory_pointer))
            {
                node->next = (struct FileList *)
                    malloc(sizeof(struct FileList));
                node = node->next;
                strcpy(node->filename, entry);
                node->next = NULL;
            }
        closedir(directory_pointer);
        node = start.next;
        while (node)
            {
                cout << node->filename);
                node = node->next;
            }
        }
    }
```

As you can see, the program uses the *readdir* function to read directory entries. The program then allocates memory to hold and entry and copies to the list entry the corresponding filename. After all the files have been added to the list, the program loops through the list, displaying each entry.

17.23 APPENDING A LIST ENTRY

Each of the linked-list programs presented thus far have built the linked list at one time, normally within a *while* or *for* loop. Depending on your program, you will, at some point, probably need to add entries to the list at different times. The easiest way to add an entry is to append it. To append an item to a linked list, you loop through the list until you find the element whose *next* member points to NULL;

```
node = &start;
while (node->next)
    node = node->next;
```

When *node->next* points to NULL, you have found the end of the list, so you can allocate memory for the entry as shown here:

```
node->next = malloc(required_size);
```

Next, you assign the desired entry values and assign the new entry's next field to point to NULL;

```
node = node->next;
node->member = some_value;
node->next = NULL;
```

In some cases, you might want your programs to place elements at specific locations in a list. To perform such processing, see the next section.

17.24 INSERTING A LIST ENTRY

In earlier section, you learned how to append items to a linked list. Depending on your program's function, there will be times when you will want to place items at specific locations in a list. For example, if you want to create a linked list that contains the sorted names of files in the current directory, your program must place each filename into the list at the correct position. To insert an item at a specific location in a list, your programs will normally track the stating node, current node, and the previous node. When your program needs to insert a new element, it will perform the following processing:

```
struct ListNumber start, *node, *previous, *new;
// Code that performs insert of an entry between
// the elements pointed to by node and previous
new = malloc(sizeof(struct ListMember);
new->next = node
previous->next = new;
new->member = some_value;
```

17.25 DISPLAYING A SORTED DIRECTORY

In previous section, you learned that to insert an element in a singly linked list (where each element contains a pointer to the next element), your programs must track the current and previous nodes (list elements). The following program inserts elements into a list to create a list containing the sorted current directory filenames:

```
void main (int argc, char * argv [])
    {
        DIR *directory_pointer;
        struct direct *entry;
        struct FileList {
            char filename[64];
            struct FileList *next;
        } start, *node;
    if ((directory_pointer = opendir(argv[1])) == NULL)
    cout << 'Error opening \n' << argv[1];
```

```
    else
    {
            start.next = NULL;
            while (entry = readdir(directory_pointer))
            {
            // Find the correct location
            previous = &start;
            node = node.next;
            while ((node) && (stromp(entry, node->filename)' > 0))
            }
                node = node->next;
                previous = previous ->next;
            }
            new = (struct FileList *)
                malloc(sizeof(struct FileList));
            if (new == NULL)
            {
                cout<<*Insufficient memory to
                    store list\n*;
                exit (1);
            }
            new->next == node;
            previous->next = new;
            strcpy(new->filename, entry);
        }
        closedir(directory_pointer);
        node = start.next;
        while(node)
        {
            cout << node ->filename;
            node = node->next;
        }
    }
}
```

17.26 DELETING AN ELEMENT FROM A LIST

You have learned how to insert items into a linked list. As your programs manipulate linked lists, there will be times when you need to delete an element from a list. Removing an element from a singly linked list is very similar to an insertion operation, in that you must track pointers to the current and nodes. Once your program locates the list element it wants to delete, it can use code similar to the following to remove the node:

```
previous->next = node->next;
free(node);
```

The following program creates a linked list containing the numbers 1 through 10. The program then searches the list for the element containing the number 5. The program then removes the element:

```
void main (void)
    {
```

```
        int i;
        struct ListEntry {
            int number;
            struct ListEntry *next;
        } start, *node, *previous;
        start.next = NULL; // Empty list
        node = &start; // Point to the start of the
            list
        for (i = 1; i <= 10; i++)
        {
            node->next = (struct ListEntry *)
                malloc(size of (struct ListEntry));
            node = node->next;
            node->number = i;
            node->next = NULL;
        }
        // Remove the number 5
        node = start.next;
        previous = &start;
        while (node)
            if (node->number == 5)
                {
                previous->next = node->next;
                free(node);
                break; // End the loop
                }
            else
                {
                node = node->next;
                previous =previous->next;
                }
        // Display the list
        node = start.next;
        while (node)
    {
    cout<< node->number;
    node = node->next;
    }
}
```

17.27 DOUBLY LINKED LIST

A *singly linked list* is so named because each list element contains a pointer to the next element. You have learned that, to insert elements in a singly linked list, your programs have to maintain pointers—the current and previous elements. To simplify the process of the inserting and removing list elements, your programs can use a *doubly linked list*, for which each element maintains a pointer each to the next and previous list elements. Figure 17.36 illustrates a doubly linked list.

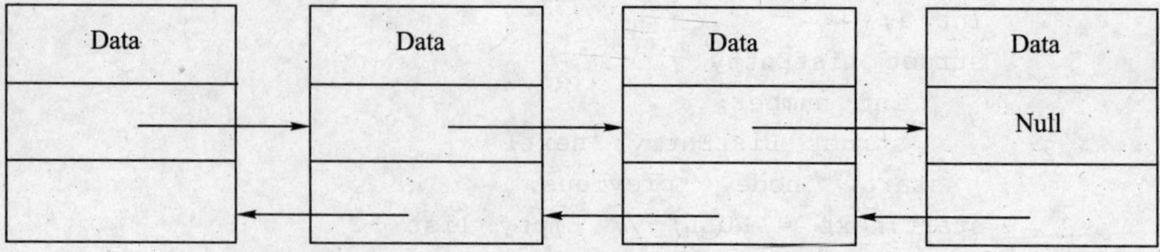

Fig. 17.36 A Doubly Linked list Maintains two Pointers

The following structure illustrates a doubly-linked list structure:

```
struct FileList {
    char filename[64];
    struct FileList *next;
    struct FileList *previous;
} ;
```

When your programs use a doubly-linked list, the program can traverse the list from left to right or right to left. Therefore, two NULL pointers are maintained. When traversing the list from left to right, your program knows it has reached the end of the list when *node→next* is NULL. Likewise, when traversing the list from right to left, the end of the list is indicated when *node→previous* is NULL.

17.28 BUILDING A SIMPLE DOUBLY LINKED LIST

You have learned that a doubly linked list simplifies the process of inserting and removing list elements. The following program uses a doubly linked list to display the numbers 1 to 10 forward and backward:

```
void main(void)
    {
        int i;
        struct ListEntry {
            int number;
            struct ListEntry *next;
            struct ListEntry *previous;
        } start, *node;
        start.next = NULL; // Empty list
        start.previous = NULL;
        node = &start; // Point to the start of the list
        for (i = 1; i <= 10; i++)
            {
                node->next = (struct ListEntry *)
                    malloc(sizeof(struct ListEntry));
                node->next->previous = node;
                node = node->next;
                node->number = i;
                node->next = NULL;
            }
        // Display the list
        node = start. next;
        do {
            cout <<node->number;
```

```
            node = node->next;
        } while (node->next; // Show 10 only one time
        do {
            cout << node ->number;
            node = node->previous;
        } while (node->previous);
}
```

17.29 UNDERSTANDING NODE→PREVIOUS→NEXT

As you have learned, working with doubly linked list simplifies element insert and delete operations. As you examine programs that work with doubly linked lists, you might encounter statements such as the following:

```
node->previous->next = new_node;
```

As you examine such statement, work from left to right. Figure 17.37 illustrates how the Complier resolves the pointer.

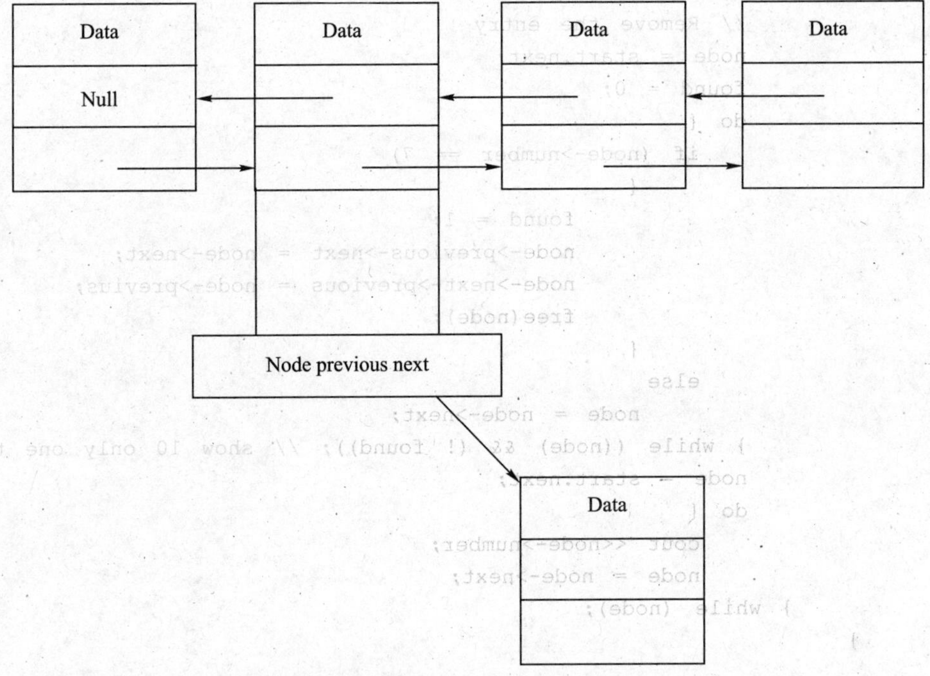

Fig. 17.37 Resolving a complex pointer operation

17.30 REMOVING AN ELEMENT FROM A DOUBLY LINKED LIST

A doubly linked list simplifies the process of inserting and removing list elements. The following program builds a doubly linked list that contains the numbers 1 through 10. The program then searches the list for the entry containing the number 7 and removes the entry:

```
void main(void)
    {
        int i, found;
        struct ListEntry {
```

```
        int number;
        struct ListEntry *next;
        struct ListEntry *previous;
      } start, *node;
      start.next = NULL; // Empty list
      start.previous = NULL;
      node = &start; // Point to the start of the list
      for (i = 1; i <= 10; i ++)
        {
          node->next = (start ListEntry *)
             malloc(sizeof(struct ListEntry));
          node->next->previous = node;
          node = node->next;
          node->number = i;
          node->next = NULL;
        }
        // Remove the entry
        node = start.next;
        found = 0;
        do {
          if (node->number == 7)
             {
                 found = 1;
                 node->previous->next = node->next;
                 node->next->previous = node->previus;
                 free(node);
             {
          else
             node = node->next;
        } while ((node) && (! found)); // show 10 only one time
        node = start.next;
        do {
          cout <<node->number;
          node = node->next;
      } while (node);
  }
```

17.31 INSERTING AN ELEMENT INTO A DOUBLY LINKED LIST

As you have learned, doubly linked lists exists to simplify the insertion and deletion of list elements. The following program builds a list containing the numbers 1, 3, 5, 7 and 9. The program then inserts the numbers 2, 4, 6, 8 and 10 in their correct locations:

```
void main (void)
   {
        int i;
        struct ListEntry {
          int number;
          struct ListEntry *next;
          struct ListEntry *previous;
```

```
} start, *node, *new;
start.next = NULL; // Empty list
start.previous = NULL;
node = &start; // Point to the start of the list
for (i = 1; i < 10; i += 2)
   {
   node->next = (start ListEntry *)
      malloc(sizeof(struct ListEntry));
   node->next->previous = node;
   node = node->next;
   node->number = i;
   node->next = NULL;
}
for (i = 2; i <= 10; i += 2)
{
    int found = 0;
    new = (struct ListEntry *)
       malloc(sizeof(struct ListEntry));
    new->number = i
    node = start.next;
do {
if (node->number -> new ->number)
    {
       new->next = node;
       new->previous = node->previous;
       new->previous->next = new;
       node->previous - new;
       found = 1;
    }
else
    node = node->next;
} while ((node->next) && (! found));
if (! found)
if (node->number -> new ->number)
    {
       new ->next = node;
       new ->previous = node->previous
       new->previous->next = new;
       node->previous = new;
    }
else
{
       new->next = NULL;
       new->previous = node;
       node->next = new;
}
}
    // Display the list
```

```
        node = start.next;
        do {
            cout << node->number;
            node = node->next;
        } while (node);
    }
```

17.32 LINKED STACKS AND QUEUES

We have already seen how to represent stacks and queues sequentially. Such a representation proved efficient if only we had one stack or one queue. However, when several stacks and queues co-exist, there was no efficient way to represent them sequentially. In this section, we present a good solution to this problem using linked lists. Figure 17.38 shows a linked stack and a linked queue.

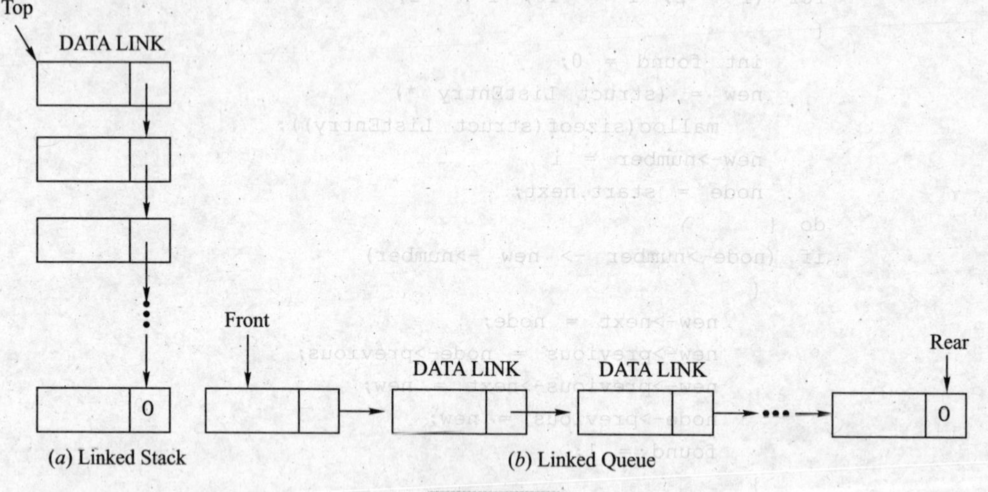

Fig. 17.38

Notice that the direction of links for both the stack and queue are such as to facilitate easy insertion and deletion of nodes. In the case of Fig. 17.38 (*a*), one can easily add a node at the top or delete one from the top. In Fig. 17.38 (*b*), one can easily add a node at the rear and both addition and deletion can be performed at the front, though for a queue we normally would not wish to add nodes at the front.

17.33 CIRCULAR LINKED LISTS

The linked list that we implemented earlier is characterized by a linear (line-like) relationship between the elements: Each element (except the first one) has a unique predecessor, and each element (except the last one) has a unique successor. There is a problem with using linear-linked list: Given a pointer to a node anywhere in the list, we can access all of the nodes that follow, but none of the nodes that precede it. With a singly-linked linear list structure (a list with all its pointers in one direction), we must always have a pointer to the beginning of the list to be able to access all list.

We can, however, change the linear list slightly, making the pointer in the Next field of the last node point back to the first node instead of containing NIL (Fig. 17.39). Now our list is a circular-linked list rather than a linear-linked list. We can start at any node in the list and traverse the whole list. Thus we can make the external pointer of the list point to any node and still be able to access every node in the list. In fact, a truly circular list may not have a first or a last node—just a ring of elements linked to each other.

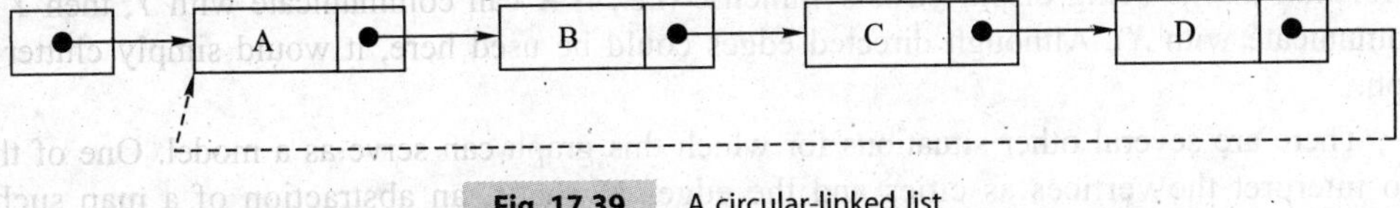

Fig. 17.39 A circular-linked list

A list in which every node has a successor; the 'last' element is succeeded by the 'first' element is called Circular-Linked List.

The advantage of using a circular list with data that is linear in nature (for instance, nodes whose values are ordered smallest to largest) is that we can reach both ends of the list using a single external pointer. It is convenient, but not necessary, to let the external pointer point to the (logical) last node in the list.

17.34 GRAPH—A GENERAL INTRODUCTION

Recall that the following definition of a directed graph was introduced in earlier chapter.

Definition 17.1 ***Directed Graph.*** A directed graph consists of a set of vertices, V and a set of edges, E, connecting certain elements of V. Each element of E is an ordered pair (*i.e.*, an element of $V \times V$). The first entry is the initial vertex of the edge and the second entry is the terminal vertex. In certain cases, there will be more than one edge between two vertices, in which case the different edges are identified with labels.

Despite the set terminology in this definition, we usually think of a graph as a picture, and an aid in visualizing a situation. In the previous chapter, we introduced this concept to help understand relations on sets. Although those relations were principally of mathematical nature, it remains true that when we see a graph, it tells us how the elements of a set are related to one another.

Definition 17.2 ***Simple Graph and Multigraph.*** A simple graph is one for which there is not more than one edge directed from anyone vertex to any other vertex. All other graphs are called multigraphs.

To illustrate the points that we will make in this section, we will introduce the following examples of graphs.

Example 17.15 Figure 17.40 is an example of a simple directed graph. In set terms, this graph is (V, E), where $V = \{s, a, b\}$ and $E = \{(s, a), (s, b), (a, b), (b, a), (b, b)\}$. Note how each edge is labeled either 0 or 1. There are often reasons for labeling even simple graphs. Some labels are to help make a graph easier to discuss; others are more significant. We will discuss the significance of the labels on this graph later.

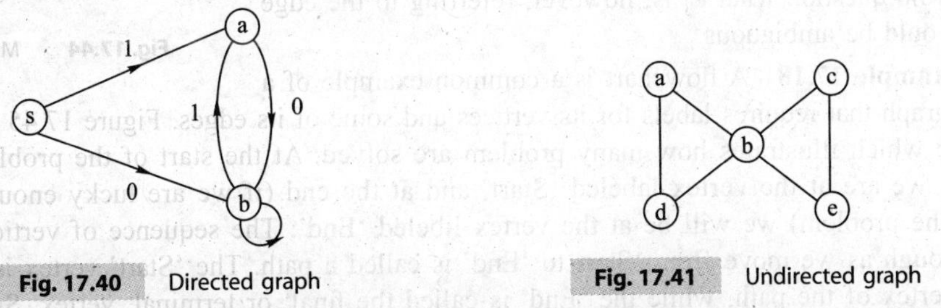

Fig. 17.40 Directed graph

Fig. 17.41 Undirected graph

Example 17.16 An Undirected Graph. A network of computers can be easily described using a graph. Figure 17.41 describes a network of five computers, a, b, c, d and e. An edge between any two vertices indicates that direct two-way communication is possible between the two computers. Note that the edges of this graph are not directed. This is due to the fact that the relation that is being displayed is symmetric (*i.e.*, if *X* can communicate with *Y*, then *Y* can communicate with *X*). Although directed edges could be used here, it would simply clutter the graph.

There are several other situations for which this graph can serve as a model. One of them is to interpret the vertices as cities and the edges as roads, an abstraction of a map such as the one in Fig. 17.42. Another interpretation is as an abstraction of the floor plan of a house (Fig. 17.43). Vertex a represents the outside of the house; all others represent rooms. Two vertices are connected if there is a door between them.

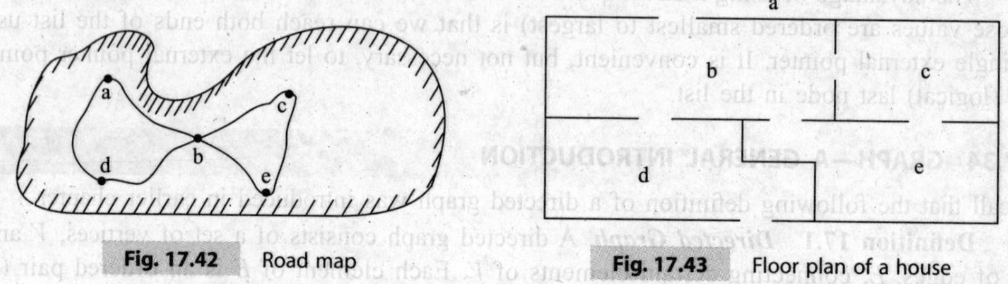

Fig. 17.42 Road map **Fig. 17.43** Floor plan of a house

Definition 17.3 ***Undirected Graph.*** An undirected graph consists of a set *V*, called a vertex set, and a set *E* of two-element subsets of *V*, called the edge set. The two-element subsets are drawn as line connecting the vertices.

The undirected graph of Fig. 17.41 is $V = \{a, b, c, d, e\}$ and $E = \{\{a, b\}, \{a, b\}, \{b, c\}, \{b, d\}, \{c, e\}\}$. A directed graph can be turned into an undirected graph under the condition that if an edge exists from vertex *v* to vertex *w*, then an edge exists from vertex *w* to vertex *v*. In other words, the relation 'is connected by an edge to' is a symmetric relation on the vertices.

Definition 17.4 ***Complete Undirected Graph.*** A complete undirected graph of *n* vertices is an undirected graph with the property that each pair of distinct vertices are connected to one another. Such a graph is usually denoted by K_n.

Example 17.17 A Multigraph. A common occurrence of a multigraph is a road map. This cities and town on the map can be thought of as vertices, while the roads are the edges. It is not uncommon to have more than one road connecting two cities. In order to give clear travel directions, we name or number roads so that there is no ambiguity. We use the same method to describe the edges of the multigraph in Fig. 17.44. There is no question what e_3 is; however, referring to the edge (2, 3) would be ambiguous.

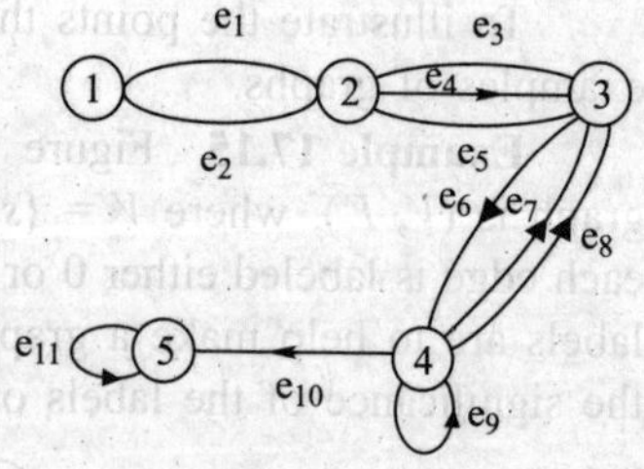

Fig. 17.44 Multigraph

Example 17.18 A flowchart is a common example of a simple graph that requires labels for its vertices and some of its edges. Figure 17.45 is one such example which illustrates how many problem are solved. At the start of the problem-solving process, we are at the vertex labeled 'Start' and at the end (if we are lucky enough to have solved the problem) we will be at the vertex libeled 'End'. The sequence of vertices that we pass through as we move from 'Start to 'End' is called a path. The 'Start' vertex is called the initial vertex of the path, while the 'End' is called the final, or terminal, vertex. Suppose that the problem is solved after two attempts; then the path that was taken is: Start, *R*, *A*, *Q*, *L*, *A*, *Q*, End. An alternate path description would be to list the edges that were used: 1, 2, 3, No. 4,

3 Yes. This second method of describing a path has the advantage of being applicable for multigraphs. In Fig. 17.44, the vertex list 1, 2, 3, 4, 3 does not clearly describe a path between 1 and 3, but e_1, e_4, e_6, e_7 is unambiguous.

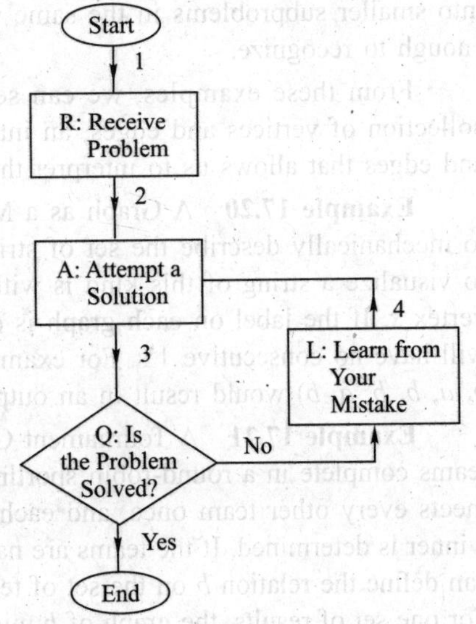

Fig. 17.45 Flowchart for the problem solving process

17.34.1 A Summary of Path Notation and Terminology

If x and y are two vertices of a graph, then a path between x and y describes a motion from x to y along edges of the graph. Vertex x is called the initial vertex of the path and y is called the terminal vertex. A path between x and y can always be described by its edge list, the list of edges that were used : e_1. e_2, ..., e_n), where: (1) the initial vertex of e_1 is x; (2) the terminal vertex of e_i is the initial vertex of e_{i+}, $i = 1, 2, ..., n-1$; and (3) the terminal vertex of e_n is y. The number of edges in the edge list is the path length. A path on a simple graph can also be described by a vertex list. A path of length n will have a list of $n + 1$ vertices (v_0, v_1, ..., v_n), where, for $k = 0, 1, ..., n-1$, (v_k, v_{k+1}) is an edge on the graph. A circuit is a path that terminates at its initial vertex.

Suppose that a path between two vertices has an edge list (e_1, e_2, ..., e_n). A subpath of this graph is any portion of the path described by one or more consecutive edges in the edge list. For example, (3, no, 4) is a subpath of (1, 2, 3, no, 4, 3, yes). Any path is its own subpath; however, we call it an improper subpath of itself. All other subpaths are called *proper subpaths.*

A path or circuit is simple if it contains no proper subpath that is a circuit. This is the same as saying that a path or circuit is simple if it does not visit any vertex more than once except for the common initial and terminal vertex in a circuit. In the problem-solving method described in Fig. 17.45, the path that you take is simple only if you reach a solution on the first try.

Example 17.19 The leadership structure of a corporation is often represented with a graph as in Fig. 17.46. The principle behind such a structure is that everyone but the president has a single immediate supervisor. Any action that anyone takes can reach the president only through a unique 'chain of command'. This chain-of-command property is characteristic of a special type of graph called a tree. Node that me edges of this graph are not directed, but, as in a Hasse diagram, the relation between two connecting vertices is clear. That is, the top vertex is the supervisor of the lower vertex.

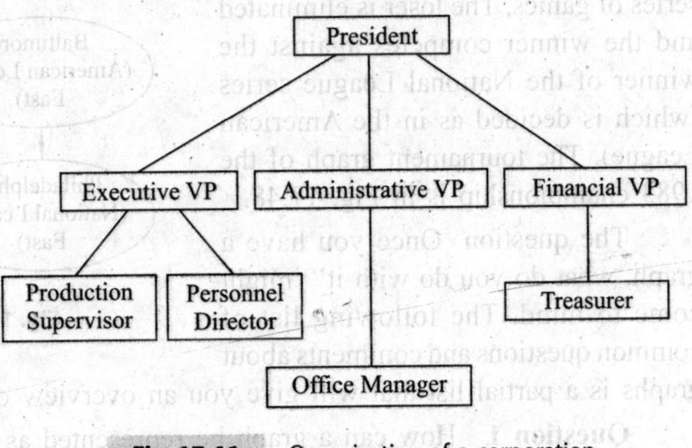

Fig. 17.46 Organization of a corporation

The process of structured (or-top-down) problem solving results in a graph that is similar to this tree. Starting with the top of the tree, which would represent the whole problem, the problem is divided into a sequence of separate subproblems. Each subproblem is divided further into smaller subproblems in the same way until the solutions of the lowest problems are easy enough to recognize.

From these examples, we can see that although a graph can be defined, in short, as a collection of vertices and edges, an integral part of most graphs is the labeling of the vertices and edges that allows us to interpret the graph as a model for some situation.

Example 17.20 A Graph as a Model for a Set of Strings. Suppose that you would like to mechanically describe the set of strings of 0's and 1's having no consecutive 1's. One way to visualize a string of this kind is with the graph in Fig. 17.40. Consider any path starting at vertex *s*. If the label on each graph is considered to be the output of a printer, then the output will have no consecutive 1's. For example, the path that is described by the vertex list (*s*, *a*, *b*, *b*, *a*, *b*, *b*, *a*, *b*) would result in an output of 10010010.

Example 17.21 A Tournament Graph. Suppose that four teams complete in a round-robin sporting event; *i.e.*, each team meets every other team once, and each game is played until a winner is determined. If the teams are named, *A*, *B*, *C* and *D*, we can define the relation *b* on the set of teams by *XbY* if *X* beat *Y*. For one set of results, the graph of *b* might look like Fig. 17.47.

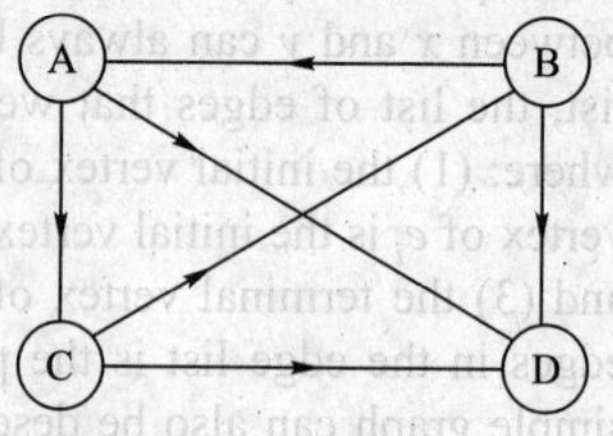

Fig. 17.47 Round-robin graph with four vertices

Definition 17.5 ***Tournament Graph***

(*a*) A tournament graph is a directed graph with the property that no edge connects a vertex to itself, and between any two vertices there is at the most one edge.

(*b*) A completer (or round-robin) tournament graph is a tournament graph with the property that between any two distinct vertices there is exactly one edge.

(*c*) A single-elimination tournament graph is a tournament graph with the properties that: (*i*) one vertex (the champion) has no edge terminating at it and at least one edge initiating from it; (*ii*) every other vertex is the terminal vertex of exactly one edge; and (*iii*) there is a path from the champion vertex to every other vertex.

Example 17.22 The major league baseball championship is decided with a single-elimination tournament. The two divisional champions in the American League (East and West) compete in a series of games. The loser is eliminated and the winner competes against the winner of the National League series (which is decided as in the American League). The tournament graph of the 1983 championship is in Fig. 17.48.

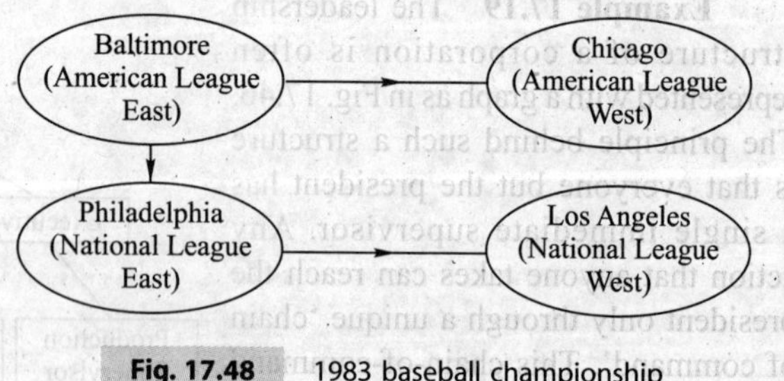

Fig. 17.48 1983 baseball championship

The question 'Once you have a graph, what do you do with it'? might come to mind. The following list of common questions and comments about graphs is a partial list that will give you an overview of the remainder of the chapter.

Question 1 How can a graph be represented as a data structure for use on a computer?

Question 2 Given two vertices in a graph, does there exist a path between them? A related question is: How many paths of a certain type or length are there between two vertices?

Question 3 Is there a path (or circuit) that passes through every vertex (or uses every edge) exactly once? Paths of this kind are called *traversals*.

Question 4 Suppose that a cost is associated with the use of each vertex and/or edge in a path. What is the 'cheapest' path, circuit, or traversal of a given kind?

Question 5 Given the specifications of a graph, or the graph itself, what is the best way to draw the graph? The desire for neatness makes this a reasonable question. Another goal might be to edges of the graph cross one another.

17.34.2 Isomorphic Graph

We will close this section by establishing the relation 'is isomorphic to', a form of equality on graphs. The graphs in Fig. 17.49 obviously share some similarities, such as the number of vertices and the number of edges. It happens that they are even more similar than just that. If the letters *a*, *b*, *c*, and *d* in (*a*) are replaced with the numbers 1, 3, 2, and 4, respectively, and they are moved around so that they appear as in (*b*), you obtain (*b*).

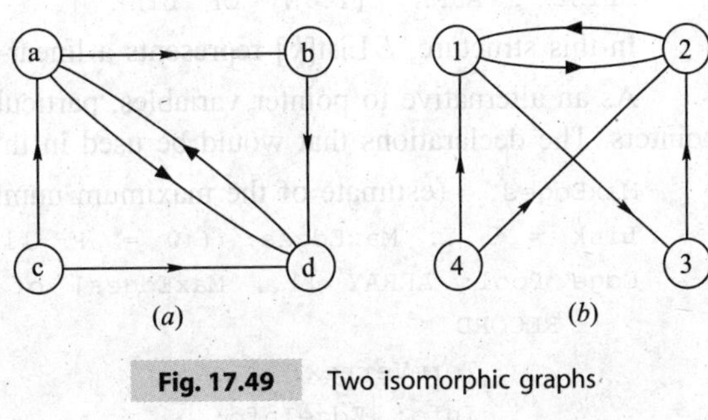

Fig. 17.49 Two isomorphic graphs

Definition 17.6 ***Isomorphic Graphs.*** Let (V, E) and (V', E') be two graphs. They are isomorphic if there exists a bijection, f, from V into V' such that $(v_i, v_j) \in E$, if and only if $(f(v_i), (f(v_j)) \in E'$. For multigraphs, we add that the number of edges connecting v_i to v_j must equal the number of edges from $f(v_i)$ to $f(v_j)$.

17.35 DATA STRUCTURES FOR GRAPHS

In this section, we will represent two methods for representing a graph as a data structure. The structure that you choose for a particular graph depends on the number of vertices and edges and on what you intend to do with the graph. We will give general guidelines for making this decision.

General Assumptions. We will assume that we have a graph with N vertices that can be indexed in some way (possibly arbitrarily) by the sub-range 1...N. In addition, we will assume that each vertex contains information that can be represented as a record of type *V*Info. One common field of this record would contain the name of the vertex. For both of our start with V: ARRAY [1 .. N] OF VInfo. For simplicity, we are separating edge information from this array; however, the edge information could be included in V in all cases.

Data Structure 1: *Adjacency Matrix.* The information about edges in a graph can be summarized with an adjacency matrix. The variable declaration

```
E d g e : ARRAY [1..N, 1..N] OF BOOLEAN
```

is sufficient if no additional information is needed for the edges. To initialize Edge, we would first set each component to FALSE, the input pairs of integer values from 1 .. N that correspond to the edges of the graph. Note that this is the same as the adjacency matrix for a relation, with the exception that we used 0 and 1 for entries instead of FALSE and TRUE.

Data Structure 2: *Linked lists of Edges.* Note that the initializing procedure for an adjacency matrix presumes that a list of edges for the graph exists. This data structure maintains this list form. For each vertex in our graph, there will be a list of edges that initiate at that vertex. This can be accomplished using either Pascal pointer variable or an array of records with integer pointers. For simplicity, we will arrange the edges in a linear linked list; however, in extremely large graphs, the reader should be aware that faster access could be made to the edges with more sophisticated data structures.

Using Pascal pointer variables, we could use the declarations:

```
Link  = ↑Edge;
Edge  = RECORD
```

```
        TermVertex: 1..N;
        Info  : EdgeInfo;  (*Optional*)
        Next  : Link
        END;
    EList  :  ARRAY  [1..N]  OF  Link
```

In this structure, *E* List[*k*] represents a linear-linked list of edges that initiate at vertex *k*.

As an alternative to pointer variables, particularly in other languages, you can use integer pointers. The declarations that would be used in this case are:

```
    MaxEdges  = (estimate of the maximum number of edges that will be needed);
    Link = 0  .. MaxEdges;  (*0  =  No  link*)
    Edge  Pool:  ARRAY  [1..  MaxEdges]  of
        RECORD
            TermVertex:  1..N;
            Info:  EdgeInfo;
            Next:  Link
        END;
    EList:  ARRAY[1..N]  OF  LINK
```

In this structure, EList[*k*] is the index of EdgePool that contains the first edge in the list of edges that initiate from vertex *k*. If EList[*k*] = 0, the no edges initiate at vertex *k*.

A natural question to ask is: Which data structure should be used in a given situation? There are several factors that determine the ideal structure for a given graph.

(*a*) **Memory Needed:** In general, for small graphs, the adjacency matrix structure is the most efficient. This is due to the fact that setting up a list of edges requires a certain amount of overhead memory that is not justified for small graphs. To be more precise, let *n* be the number of vertices in our graph, *e* = the number of edges in the graph (here an undirected edge counts for two edges, one in each direction), *b* = the number of bytes needed to store a Boolean variable (one bit is sufficient, but many systems will use full byte). *z* = the number of bytes needed to store an integer, *p* = the number of bytes needed to store a pointer, and *i* = the number of bytes needed to store additional information for an edge. Under these assumptions, an adjacency matrix will use $M_A = n^2 (b + i)$ bytes, and the edge list structure will require $M_E = np + e (z + i + p)$ bytes.

Sparse and Dense Graphs: If a simple graph has *n* vertices, the maximum number of edges that it can have is n^2. If *e* is small in relation to n^2, then the graph is called sparse. If *e* is nearly n^2, the graph is called dense. The terms small and nearly are vague, but a reasonable interpretation is *e* is small if it is less than $n^2/4$, and it is nearly n^2 if *e* is greater than $3n^2/4$. If a graph is sparse, the term $e (2 + 1 + p)$ in M_E is small, and M_E is likely to be less than M_A. On the other hand, if a graph is dense, $e (z + i + p)$ is large and the adjacency matrix structure is likely to be more efficient.

(*b*) How will you be accessing the edges? If you want to know whether an edge between vertices exists, you can access this information very quickly with an adjacency matrix. To obtain the same information with edge lists, you must examine a list, which could take some time. On the other hand, if you frequently need a list of all edges that initiate at a given vertex, this can be obtained more efficiently using an edge list as opposed to an adjacency matrix.

(*c*) Multigraphs can be represented with edge lists, while the only way to represent a multigraph an adjacency matrix is by making part of each element of the matrix a list.

Example 17.23 Consider the graph in Fig. 17.41 with the interpretation that it represents a floor plan for a house. We might use the following declarations to represent the graph:

RomeType = (Living, Kitchen, Bedroom, Bath, Outside);

```
V: ARRAY [1..5] OF RECORD
     Name: Char;
     RType: Room Type;
END
```

The elements of V could be assigned the values

```
k    V[k]. Name      V[k]. Rtype
1    'A'             Outside
2    'B'             Living
3    'C'             Bath
4    'D'             Kitchen
5    'E'             Bedroom
```

Which data structure should we use for representing the edges of this graph? Suppose that an integer requires two bytes ($z = 2$), a Pascal pointer requires one byte ($p = 1$), a Boolean variable require one byte ($b = 1$, and no additional information is needed for each edge ($i = 0$). The adjacency matrix structure requires $M_A = 5^2\ (1 + 0) = 25$ bytes, while the edge list structure requires $M_E = 5 \times 2 + 12\ (2 + 0 + 2) = 58$ bytes with integer pointers. With Pascal pointers, this can be reduced to $M_E = 5 \times 2 + 12\ (2 + 0 + 1) = 46$ bytes. Using the memory criterion alone, the adjacency matrix structure is preferred. Of course, the memory amounts are so small in this case that other factors might contribute to our decision. For this reason, we will describe both structures.

The adjacency matrix for this graph appears in Fig. 17.50.

	A	B	C	D	E
A	False	True	False	True	False
B	True	False	True	True	True
C	False	True	False	False	True
D	True	True	False	False	False
E	False	True	True	False	False

Fig. 17.50 Adjacency matrix for Fig. 17.41

The use integer pointers, we could declare:

```
MaxEdges  = 12;
Link = 0.. MaxEdges;
EdgePool: ARRAY  [1..12] OF RECORD
                TermVert: 1..5;
                Next  : Link
                END;
EList: ARRAY [1.. 5] OF LINK
```

The contents of EList and EdgePool is not unique.

j	elist[j]	k	EdgePool [k] TermVert	Next
1	4	1	3	5
2	1	2	1	10
3	9	3	5	0
4	2	4	2	6
5	12	5	1	7
		6	4	0
		7	4	8
		8	5	0
		9	2	3

10	2	0
11	3	0
12	2	11

The linked list that this set of values represents appears in Fig. 17.51.

Note that we have come full circle with this figure, which is a graph that helps us picture the data structure that in turn represents a graph.

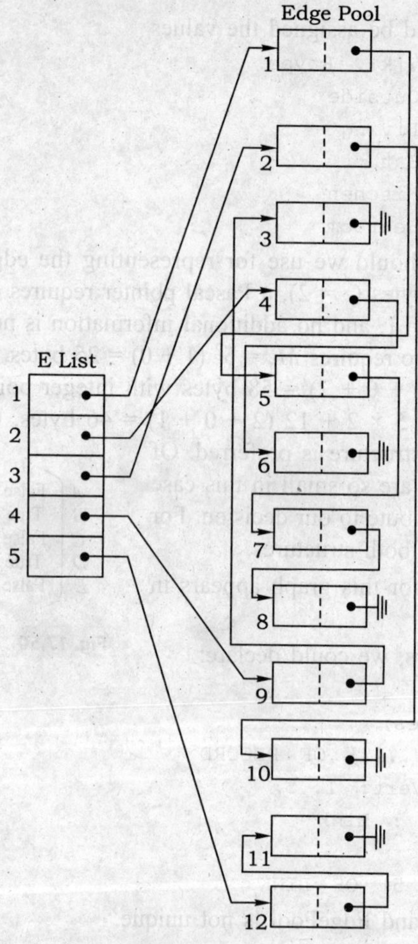

Fig. 17.51 Edge list for graph

If you prefer to use Pascal pointer variables, then the declarations would be

```
Link = ↑ Edge;
Edge = RECORD
         TerrnVert: 1..5;
         Next: Link;
END
```

In this case, we need not specify the number of edges, so that if we cut an extra door between two rooms, the edge that we would create in the graph could easily be accommodated. If the door connects room *i* with room *j*, we could simply create new edge records and add them to the edge lists of vertex *i* and vertex *j*. This can be coded most efficiently by defining the procedure. AddEdge (Fig. 17.52) and then executing AddEdge(*i*, *j*) and AddEdge(*j*, *i*).

```
PROCEDURE AddEdge (I, j: 1..5);
VAR T : Link;
BEGIN
        NEW  (T);
        t ↑.TermVert  := J;
        T ↑.Next  : = EList  [I];
        ELish  [I]  := T
END
```

Fig. 17.52 Procedure for inserting an edge

Example 17.24 Consider an undirected graph represented by the top 200 college football teams in the United States for a given year. If two of the teams play one another, then imagine an edge connecting those two teams. Since the average team plays 11 games, most of which will be other 'Top 200' teams, we could expect up to 11 × 200 edges in our graph (e = 2200). Since 2200 is much smaller than 200^2, we could call this a sparse graph and would expect to find the edge list structure more efficient.

Example 17.25 Consider a timesharing system that consists of a processor and 8 terminals. At any one time, there can be several different terminals competing for processor time. A graph such as in Fig. 17.53 can be used to visualize the current state of the system. Vertex P represents the processor and, unless no terminals are in use, there will be exactly one edge from P that terminates at the terminal that currently has the processor's 'attention'. All active terminals are arranged in a circular pattern. If an edge (T_i, T_j) is labeled F (forward), then T_j precedes T_i in the waiting line for processor time. If an edge is labeled B (backward), then the first vertex precedes the second in the waiting line.

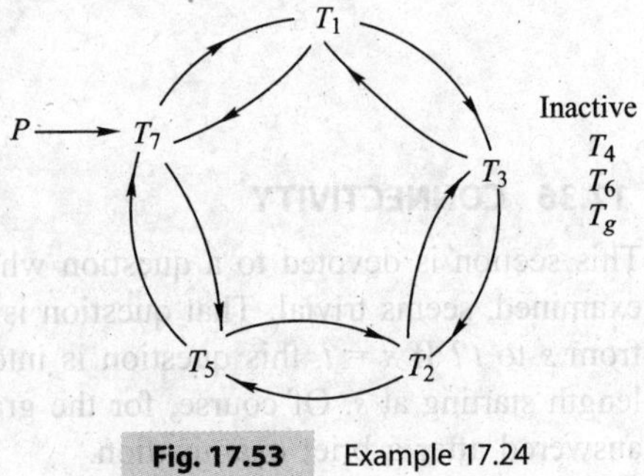

Fig. 17.53 Example 17.24

A declaration for the vertices might be

```
V: ARRAY  [0..8] of Vlnfo,
```

where V [0] represents the processor. We can use a variation on the adjacency matrix to represent the graph:

```
EType  =  (Forward,  Backward,  None);
Edge  =  ARRAY[0..8,  1..8]  OF  EType
```

The situation in Fig. 17.53 would be represented as:

$$Edge = \begin{array}{c} \\ 0 \\ 1 \\ 2 \\ 3 \\ 4 \\ 5 \\ 6 \\ 7 \\ 8 \end{array} \begin{array}{c} \begin{array}{cccccccc} 1 & 2 & 3 & 4 & 5 & 6 & 7 & 8 \end{array} \\ \begin{pmatrix} N & N & N & N & N & N & F & N \\ N & N & F & N & N & N & B & N \\ N & N & B & N & F & N & N & N \\ B & F & N & N & N & N & N & N \\ N & N & N & N & N & N & N & N \\ N & B & N & N & N & N & N & N \\ N & N & N & N & N & N & F & N \\ F & N & N & N & B & N & N & N \\ N & N & N & N & N & N & N & N \end{pmatrix} \end{array}$$

A second representation of this graph would be with a linked list of edges. However, we can use the fact that the maximum number of edges that can initiate from a vertex is two. The edge information can be included in the vertex array by including a backward and a forward pointer:

```
V: ARRAY [0..8] OF RECORD
        Info : Vlnfo;
        Forward, Backward: 0..8
        END
```

Again, a pointer value of 0 represents 'no edge'. The situation in Fig. 17.53 would be represented by the values.

I	V[I].Forward	V[I].Backward
0	7	0
1	3	7
2	5	3
3	2	1
4	0	0
5	7	2
6	0	0
7	1	5
8	0	0

17.36 CONNECTIVITY

This section is devoted to a question which, when posed in relation to the graphs that we have examined, seems trivial. That question is: Given two vertices, *s* and *t* of a graph, is there a path from *s* to *t*? If $s = t$, this question is interpreted as asking whether there is a circuit of positive length starting at *s*. Of course, for the graphs that we have seen up to now, this question can be answered after a brief examination.

There are two situations under which a question of this kind is non-trivial. One is where the graph is very large and an 'examination' of the graph could take a considerable amount of time. Anyone who has tried to solve a maze may have run into a similar problem. The second interesting situation is when we want to pose the question to a machine. If only the information on edges between the vertices is part of the data structure for the graph, how can you put that information together to determine whether two vertices can be connected by path?

Connectivity Terminology. Let *v* and *w* be vertices of a directed graph. Vertex *v* is *connected* to vertex *w* if there is a path from *v* to *w*. Two vertices are *strongly connected* if they are connected in both directions to one another. A graph is connected if, for each pair of distinct vertices, *v* and *w*, *v* is connected to *w* or *w* is connected to *v*. A graph is strongly connected if every pair of its vertices is strongly connected. For an undirected graph, in which edges can be used in either direction, the notions of strongly connected and connected are the same.

Theorem 17.1 If a graph has *n* vertices and vertex *v*, is connected to vertex *w*, then there exist a path from *v* to *w* of length no more than *n*.

Proof (Indirect): Suppose that *v* is connected to *w*, but the shortest path *v* to *w* has is length *m* is greater than *n*. A vertex list for a path of length *m* will have $m + 1$ vertices. This path can be represented as $(v_0, v_1, ..., v_m)$, where $v_0 = v$ and $v_m = w$. Note that since there are only *n* vertices and *m* vertices are listed in the path after v_0, there must be some duplication in the last *m* vertices of the vertex list, which represents a circuit in the path. This means that our path of minimum length can be reduced, which is a contraction?

Method 1: Adjacency Matrix Method. Suppose that the information about edges in a graph is stored (or can be stored) in an adjacency matrix, *E*. The relation, *r*, that *E* defines is

vrw if there is an edge connecting v to w. Recall that the composition of r with itself, r^2, is defined by $vr^2 w$ if there exists a vertex y such that vry and yrw; *i.e.*, v is connected to w by a path of length 2. We could prove by induction that the relation r^k, $k \geq 1$, is defined by $vr^2 w$ if there is a path of length k from v to w. Since the transitive closure, r^+, is the union $r, r^2, r^3, ...,$ we can answer our connectivity question by determining the transitive closure of r, which can be done most easily by keeping our relation in matrix form. Theorem 17.1 is significant in our calculations because it tells us that we need only go as far as E^n to determine the matrix of the transitive closure.

The main advantage of the adjacency matrix method is that the transitive closure matrix can answer all questions about the existence of paths between vertices. Vertex v_i is connected v_j if $E_{ij}^{\ +} = 1$ (or True). A directed graph is connected if $E_{ij}^{\ +} = 1$ or $E_{ji}^{\ +} = 1$ for each $i! = j$. A directed graph is strongly connected if its transitive closure matrix has no zeros.

One disadvantage of answering connectivity questions by the adjacency matrix method is that several matrix multiplications may be needed. If the number of vertices is large, this can be quite time consuming. This is tempered by the fact that adjacency matrices are most often used to represent either small or dense graphs. In a dense graph, the minimum path length between two vertices tends to be small. A second disadvantage is that the transitive closure matrix tells us whether a path exits, but not what the path is.

Method 2: Broadcasting. We will describe this method first with an example.

Example 17.26 The football team at Medicore State University (MSU) has a bad year, 2 win and 9 losses. Thirty days after the end of the football season, the athletic board is meeting to decide whether to rehire the head coach; things look bad for him. However, on the day of the meeting, the coach releases the following list of results from the past year:

Medicore State defeated Local *A&M*
Local *A* & *M* defeated City College
City College defeated Com State *U*.
... (25 results later)
Tough Tech defeated Enormous State University (ESU)
But ESU went on to win the national championship.

The athletic board was so impressed that they hired the coach with a raise in pay. How did the coach come up with such a list?

In reality, such lists exist occasionally and appear in newspapers from time to time. Of course they really don't prove anything that each team they defeated MSU in our example above can produce a similar chain of results. Since college football records are readily available, the coach could have rounded this list by trial and error. All that he needed to start with was that his team won at least one game. Since ESU lost one game, there was some hope of producing the chain.

The problem of finding this list is equivalent to finding a path in the tournament graph for last year's football season that initiates at MSU and ends at ESU (we will ignore tied games). Such a graph is far from complete and would represent using edge lists. To make the coach's problem interesting, let's imagine that only the winner of a game remembers the result of the game. The coach's problem has now taken on the flavor of a maze. To reach ESU, he must communicate with the various team along the path. One way that the coach could have discovered his list in time is by sending the following letters to the two teams that MSU defeated the season.

Dear Football Coach

Please follow these directions exactly:

1. If you are the coach at ESU, call the coach at MSU now and tell him who sent you this letter

2. If you are not the coach at ESU and this is the first letter of this type that you have received then:
   (*a*) Remember who you received this letter from
   (*b*) Send copies of this letter, signed by you, to each of the coaches whose teams you defeated during the past year.
3. Ignore this letter if you have received one like it already.

Signed,

Coach of MSU

Observation: From the conditions of this letter, it should be clear that if everyone cooperates and if mail can be sent and received in one day:

(*a*) If a path of length *n* exists from MSU to ESU, then the each will know about it in *n* days.

(*b*) By making a series of phone calls, the coach can obtain the path that he wants by first calling the coach who defeated ESU (the person who sent ESU's coach that letter). This coach will know who sent him a letter, etc. Therefore, the vertex list of the desired pattern is obtained in reverse order.

(*c*) If a total of *M* football games were played, no more than *M* letters will be sent out.

(*d*) If a day passes without any letter being sent out, no path from MSU to ESU exists.

(*e*) This method could be extended to obtain a list of all teams that a given team can be connected to. Simply imagine a series of letters like the one above sent by each football coach and targeted at every other coach.

The general problem of finding a path between two vertices in a graph, if one exists, can be solved exactly as we solved the problem above. The following algorithm is commonly called the *Breadth-First Search.*

Algorithm 17.1 A Broadcasting Algorithm for Finding a Path between Vertex *i* and Vertex *j* of a Graph Having *n* Vertices. The record *V*[*k*], $k = 1, \ldots, n$, consists of a Boolean field *V*[*k*]. Found and an integer field *V*[*k*]. from. The sets $D_1, D_2, \ldots$, called depth sets, have the property that if *k* is in D_r. then the shortest path from vertex *i* to vertex *k* is of length *r*. In Step 5, a stack is used to put the vertex list for the path from the vertex *i* to vertex *j* in the proper order.

```
1. For k : =1 to n Do V[k]. found: = False
2. r: = 0
3. Do : = {i}
4. While (NOT V[j]. found) and Dr ≠ Φ DO
   4.1 Dr+1 : = Φ
   4.2 For each k in Dr DO
       For each edge (k, t) DO
       If V[t]. found = False then}
       V[t]. found : = True;
       V[t]. from : = k;
       Dr+1 : = Dr+1 U {t}
   4.3 r : = r + 1
5. If V[j]. found = True Then
   5.1 S : = Empty Stack
   5.2 k : = j
```

```
5.3 While V[k]. from ! = i DO
    Push k into S
    k : = V[k]. from
```

Notes on Algorithm 17.1:

(*a*) This algorithm will produce one path from vertex *i* to vertex *j*, if one exists, and that path will be as short as possible. If more than one path of this length exists, then the one that is produced depends on the order in which the edges are examined and the order in which the elements of D_r are examined in Step 4.

(*b*) The condition $D_r = \Phi$ is analogous to the condition that if no mail is sent in a given day, the MSU cannot be connected to ESU.

(*c*) This algorithm can be easily revised to find paths to all vertices that can be reached from vertex *i*. Step 5 would be put off until a specific path to a vertex is needed since the information in *V* contains an efficient list of all paths. The algorithm can also be extended further to find paths between any two vertices.

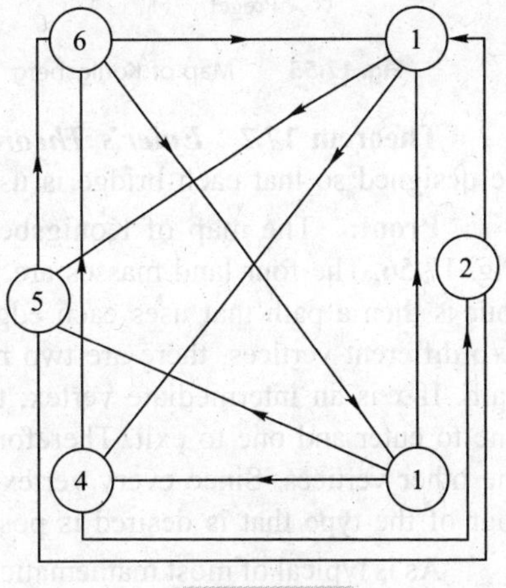

Fig. 17.54

Example 17.27 Consider the graph in Fig. 17.54. The existence of a path from vertex 2 to vertex 3 is not difficult to determine by examination. After a few seconds, you should be able to find two paths of length four, Algorithm 17.1. will produce one of them.

Suppose that the edges from each vertex are sorted in ascending order by terminal vertex. For example, the edges from vertex 3 would be in the order (3, 1), (3, 4), (3, 5). In addition, assume that in the body of Step 4 of the algorithm, the elements of D_r are used in ascending order. Then at the end of Step 4, the value of *V* will be:

k	1	2	3	4	5	6	
V[k] .found	T	T	T	T	T	T	
V[k] .from	2	4	G	1	1	4	
Depth set	1	3	4	2	2	3	(Value of *r* for which $k \in D_r$>

Therefore, the path (2, 1, 4, 6, 3) is produced by the algorithm. Note that if we wanted a path from 2 to 5, the information in *V* produces the path (2, 1, 5) since *V*[5]. from = 1 and *V*[1]. from = 2. A shortest circuit that initiates at vertex 2 is also available by noting that *V*[2]. from = 4, V[4]. from = 1, and *V*[1]. from = 2; thus the circuit (2, 1, 4, 2) is obtained.

17.37 TRAVERSALS: EULERIAN AND HAMILTONIAN GRAPHS

The subject of graph traversals has a long history. In fact, the solution by Leonhard Euler (Switzerland, 1707-83) of the Konigsberg Bridge Problem is considered by many to represent the birth of graph theory).

17.37.1 The Konigsberg Bridge Problem and Eulerian Graphs

The map of the Prussian city of Konigsberg (circa 1735) in Fig. 17.55 shows that there were seven bridges connecting the four land masses that made up the city. The legend of this problem states that the citizens of Konigsberg searched in vain for a walking tour that passed over each bridge exactly once. No one could design such a tour and the search was abruptly abandoned with the publication of Euler's Theorem.

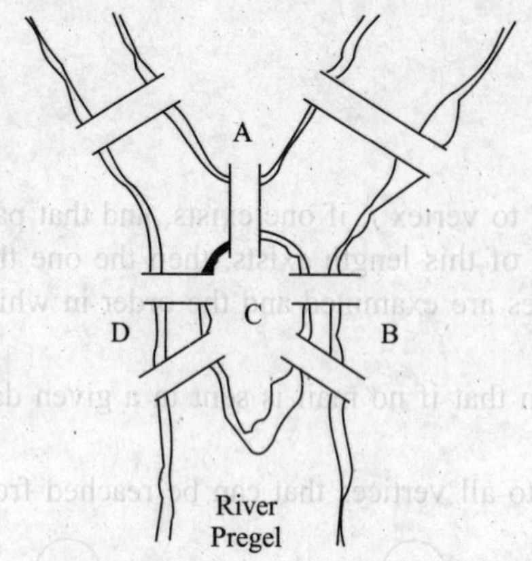

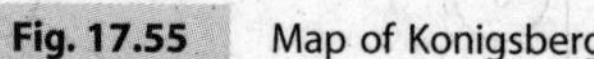

Fig. 17.55 Map of Konigsberg

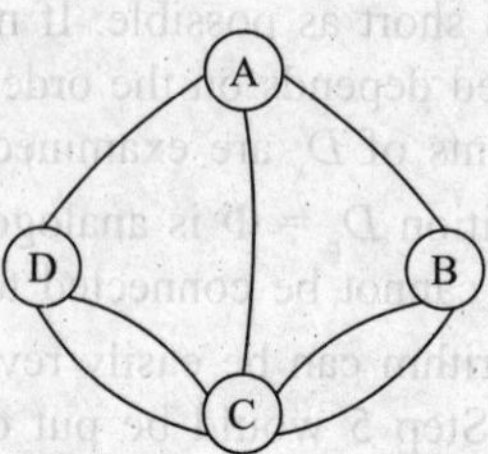

Fig. 17.56 Multigraph representation of Konigsberg

Theorem 17.2 ***Euler's Theorem-Konigsberg Case.*** No walking tour of Konigsberg can be designed so that each bridge is used exactly once.

Proof: The map of Konigsberg can be represented as an undirected multigraph, as in Fig. 17.56. The four land masses are the vertices and each edge represents a bridge. The desired tour is then a path that uses each edge once and only once. Since the path can start and end at two different vertices, there are two remaining vertices that must be intermediate vertices in the path. If x is an intermediate vertex, then every time that you visit x, you must use two edges, one to enter and one to exit. Therefore, there must be an even number of edges connecting x to the other vertices. Since every vertex in the Konigsberg graph has an odd number of edges, no tour of the type that is desired is possible.

As is typical of most mathematicians, Euler wasn't satisfied with solving only the Konigsberg problem. His original theorem, which is paraphrased below, concerned the existence of paths and circuits like those sought in Konigsberg. These paths and circuits have become associated with Euler's name.

Definition 17.7 ***Eulerian Paths, Circuits, Graphs.*** A Eulerian path through a graph is a path whose edge list contains each edge of the graph exactly once. If the path is a circuit, then it is called a Eulerian circuit. A Eulerian graph is one that possesses a, Eulerian path.

In order to state the general theorem efficiently, we must define the degree of a vertex.

Definition 17.8 ***Degree.***

(*a*) Let v be a vertex of an undirected graph. The degree of v (deg (v)) is the number of edges that connect v to the other vertices in the graph.

(*b*) If v is a vertex of a directed graph, then the outdegree of v (outdeg (v)) is the number of edges of the graph that initiate at v. The indegree of v (indeg (v)) is the number of edges that terminate at v.

Example 17.28.

(*a*) The degrees of A, B, C and D in Fig. 17.56 are 3, 3, 5, and 3, respectively.

(*b*) In a tournament graph, *outdeg*(v) is the number of wins for v and *indeg*(v) is number of losses. In a complete (round-robin) tournament graph with n vertices, *outdeg* (v) + *inheg* (v) – n – 1 for each vertex.

Theorem 17.3 ***Euler's Theorem—General Case.*** An undirected graph is Eulerian if and only if it is connected and has either zero or two vertices with an odd degree. If no vertex has an odd degree, then the graph has a Eulerian circuit.

Proof: It can be proven by induction that the number of vertices in an undirected graph that have an odd degree must be even. We will leave the proof of this fact to the reader as an exercise. The necessity of having either zero or two vertices of odd degree is clear from the proof of the Konigsberg case of this theorem. Therefore, we will concentrate on proving that this condition is sufficient to ensure that a graph is Eulerian. Let k be the number of vertices with odd degree.

Phase 1: If $k = 0$, start at any vertex, v_0, and travel along any path, not using any edge twice. Since each vertex has an even degree, this path can always be continued past each vertex that you reach except v_0. The result is a circuit that includes v_0. If $k = 2$, let v_0 be either one of the vertices of odd degree. Trace any path starting at v_0 using up edges until you can go no further, as in the $k = 0$ case. This time, the path that you obtain must end at the other vertex of odd degree.

At the end of Phase 1, we have an initial path that mayor may not be Eulerian. If it is not Eulerian, Phase 2 can be repeated until all the edges have been used. Since the number of unused edges is decreased in Phase 2, a Eulerian path must be obtained in a finite number of steps.

Phase 2: As we enter this phase, we have constructed a path that-uses a proper subset of the edges in our graph. We will refer to this path as the *current path*. Let V be the vertices of our graph, E the edges, and E_u the edges that have been used in the current path. Consider the graph $G' = (V, E - E_u)$. Note that every vertex in G' has an even degree. Select any edge, e, form G'. Let v_a and v_b be the vertices that e connects. Trace a new path starting at v_a whose first edge is e. Be sure that at least one vertex of the new path is also in the current path. This will always bc possible since (V, E) is connected. Starting at v_a, there exists a path in (V, E) to any vertex in the current path. At some point along this path, which we can consider the start of the new path, we will have intersected the current path. Since the degree of each vertex in G' is even, any path that we start at v_a can be continued until it is a circuit. Now, we simply augment the current path with the new path. As we travel along the current path, the first time that we intersect the new path, we travel along it (See Fig. 17.57). Once we complete the circuit, that is the new path, we resume the traversal of the current path.

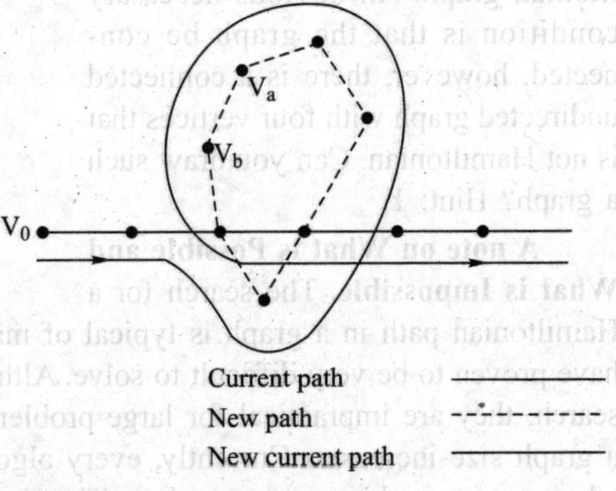

Fig. 17.57 Addition of edges to create a longer current path

If the result of this phase is a Eulerian path, then we are through with it; otherwise, repeat this phase.

Example 17.29 The complete undirected graphs K_2 and K_{2i+1}, $i = 1, 2, 3, ...$, are Eulerian. If i is greater than one, then K_{2i} is not Eulerian.

17.37.2 Hamiltonian Graphs

To search for a path that uses every vertex of a graph exactly once, seems to be a natural next problem after you have considered Eulerian graphs. The Irish mathematician Sir William Hamilton (1805–65) is given credit for defining such paths first.

Definition 17.9 ***Hamiltonian Paths, Circuits, Graphs.*** A Hamiltonian path through a graph is a path whose vertex list contains each vertex of the graph exactly once, except if the path is a circuit, in which case the initial vertex appears a second time as the terminal vertex.

If the path is a circuit, then it is called a Hamiltonian circuit. A Hamiltonian graph is a graph that possesses a Hamiltonian path.

Example 17.30 Figure 17.58 contains graph that is Hamiltonian. In fact, it is the graph that Hamilton used as an example to pose the question of existence of Hamiltonian paths in 1859. In its original form, the puzzle that was posed to readers was called 'Around the World'. The vertices were labeled with names of major cities of the world and the object was to complete a tour of these cities.

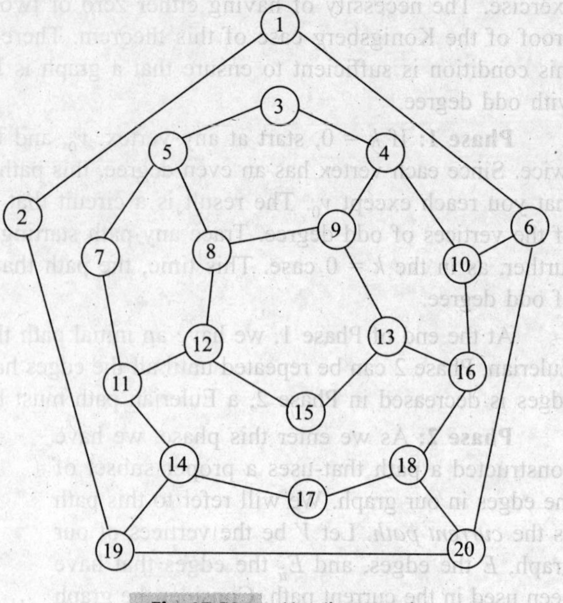

Fig. 17.58 Hamilton graph

Unfortunately, a simple condition doesn't exist that characterizes a Hamiltonian graph. An obvious necessary condition is that the graph be connected, however, there is a connected undirected graph with four vertices that is not Hamiltonian. Can you draw such a graph? Hint: *Y*.

A note on What is Possible and What is Impossible. The search for a Hamiltonian path in a graph is typical of many simple-sounding problems in graph theory that have proven to be very difficult to solve. Although there are simple algorithms for conducting the search, thėy are impractical for large problems because they take such a long time to complete a graph size increases. Currently, every algorithm to search for a Hamiltonian path in a graph takes exponential time to complete.. That is, if $T(n)$ is the time it takes to search a graph of n vertices, then there is a positive real number a, $a > 1$, such that $T(n) > a^n$ for all but possibly a finite number of positive values for n. No matter how close to one we can makes a, a^n will grow at such a fast rate that the algorithm will not be feasible for large values of n. For a given algorithm, the value of a depends on the relative times that are assigned to the steps, but in the search for Hamiltonian paths, the actual execution time for known algorithm is large with 20 vertices. For 1000 vertices, no algorithm is like to be practical, and for 10,000 vertices, no currently known algorithm could be executed.

It is an unproven but widely-held belief that no faster algorithm exists to search for Hamiltonian paths. A faster algorithm would have to be one that takes only polynomial time; that is $T(n) < p(n)$, for some polynomial sequence p.

To sum up, the problem of determining whether a graph is Hamiltonian is certainly possible; however, for large graphs, we consider the problem impossible. Most of the problems that we will discuss in the next section, particularly the Traveling Salesman Problem, are thought to be impossible in the same sense.

The following graphs, which appear in many applications, are all Hamiltonian.

Definition 17.10 ***The n-cube. Let n he greater than or equal to l.*** Let B^n be the set of strings of 0's and 1's with length n. The n-cube is the undirected graph with a vertex for each string in B^n and an edge connecting each pair of strings that differ in exactly one position. The 1-cube, 2-cube, 3-cube and 4-cube are pictured in Fig. 17.59.

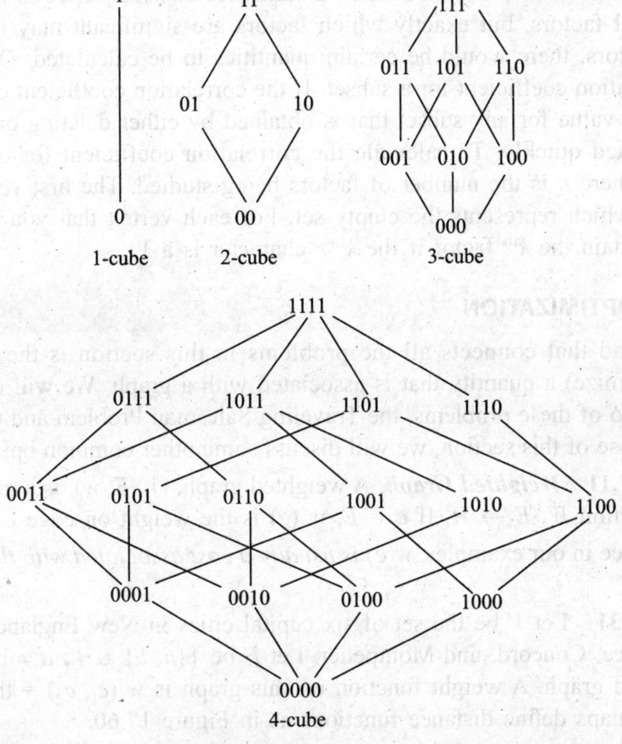

Fig. 17.59 1-, 2-, 3-, and 4-cubes

A Hamiltonian circuit of the *n*-cube can be described recursively. The circuit itself, called the Gray Code, is not the only Hamiltonian circuit of the *n*-cube, but it is the easiest to describe. The standard way to write the Gray Code is as a column of strings, where the last string is followed by the first string to complete the circuit.

Basis (n = 1): The Gray Code for the 1-cube is $G_1 = \begin{pmatrix} 0 \\ 1 \end{pmatrix}$. Note that the edge between 0 and 1 is used twice in this circuit.

Recursion: Given the Gray Code for the *n*-cube, $n \geq 1$, then G_{n+1} is obtained by (1) listing G_n with each string prefixed with 0, and then (2) reversing the list of strings in G_n with each string prefixed with 1. Symbolically, the recursion can be expressed as

$$G_{n+1} = \begin{pmatrix} 0G_n \\ 1G_n^r \end{pmatrix}$$

where G_r^r is the reverse of list G_n.

The Gray Codes for the 2-cube and 3-cube are

$$G_2 = \begin{pmatrix} 00 \\ 01 \\ 11 \\ 11 \end{pmatrix} \quad G_3 = \begin{pmatrix} 000 \\ 001 \\ 011 \\ 010 \\ 110 \\ 111 \\ 101 \\ 100 \end{pmatrix}$$

An Application of the Gray Code: In a statistical analysis, there is often a variable that depends on several factors, but exactly which factors are significant may not be obvious. For each subset of factors, there would be certain quantities to be calculated. One such quantity is the multiple correlation coefficient for a subset. If the correlation coefficient of a given subset, A, is known, then the value for any subset that is obtained by either deleting or adding an element to A can be obtained quickly. To calculate the correlation coefficient for each set, we simply travel along G_n, where n is the number of factors being studied. The first vertex will always be the string of 0's, which represents the empty set. For each vertex that you visit, the set that it corresponds to contain the kth factor if the kth> character is a 1.

17.38 GRAPH OPTIMIZATION

The common thread that connects all the problems in this section is the desire to optimize (maximize or minimize) a quantity that is associated with a graph. We will concentrate most of our attention on two of these problems, the Traveling Salesman Problem and the Maximum Flow Problem. At the close of this section, we will discuss some other common optimization problems.

Definition 17.11 ***Weighted Graph.*** A weighted graph, (V, E, w), is a graph (V, E) together with a weight function $W: E \to \mathbf{R}$. If $e \in E$, $w\ (e)$ is the weight on edge e.

As you will see in our examples, $w(e)$ *is usually a cost associated with the edge e; therefore, will be positive.*

Example 17.31 Let V be the set of six capital cities in New England: Boston, Augusta, Hartford, Providence, Concord, and Montpelier. Let E be $\{\{a, b\} \in V: a \neq \text{b}\}$; *i.e.*, (V, E) is a complete unordered graph. A weight function on this graph is $w\ (c_1, c_2)$ = the distance from c_1 to c_2. Many road maps define distance functions as in Figure 17.60.

	Augusta, ME	*Boston, MA*	*Concord, NH*	*Hartford, CT*	*Montpelier, VT*	*Providence, RI*
Augusta, *ME*	—	165	148	266	190	208
Boston, *MA*	165	—	75	103	192	43
Concord, *NH*	148	75	—	142	117	109
Hartford, *CT*	266	103	142	—	204	70
Montpelier, *VT*	190	192	117	204	—	223
Providence, *RI*	208	43	109	70	223	—

Fig. 17.60 Distance between capital cities of New England

17.38.1 The Traveling Salesman Problem

Given a weighted graph, find a circuit $(e_1, e_2, ..., e_n)$ that visits every vertex at least once and minimizes the sum of the weights,

$$\sum_{i=1}^{n} w(e_1).$$

As such circuit is called an optimal path and is a solution to the *Traveling Salesman Problem.*

Notes:

(*a*) Some statements of the Traveling Salesman Problem require that the circuit be Hamiltonian. In many applications, the graph in question will be complete and this restriction presents no problem.

(*b*) If the weight on each edge is constant, *e.g.*, $w(e) = 1$, then the solution to the Traveling Sales Problem will be any Hamiltonian circuit, if one exists.

Example 17.32 The Traveling Salesman Problem gets its name from the situation of a salesman who wants to minimize the number of miles that he travels in visiting his customers. For example, if a salesman from Boston must visit the other capital cities of New England, then the problem is to find a circuit in the weighted graph. Note that distance and cost are clearly related in this case.

The search for an efficient algorithm that solves the Traveling Salesman Problem, has occupied researchers for years. If the graph in question is complete, then there are $(n - 1)!$ different circuits. As n gets large, it is inefficient to check every possible circuit. The most efficient algorithms for solving the Traveling Salesman Problem take an amount of time that is proportional to $n\, 2^n$. Since this quantity grows so quickly, we can't expect to have the time to solve the Traveling Salesman Problem for large values of n.

Most of the useful algorithms that have been developed have to be heuristic; that is, they find a circuit that should be close to the optimal one. One such algorithm is the "closest neighbor" algorithm, one of the earliest attempts at solving the Traveling Salesman Problem. The general idea behind this algorithm is, starting at any vertex, to visit the closest neighbor to the starting point. At each vertex, the next vertex that is visited is the closest one that has not been reached. This shortsighted approach typifies heuristic algorithms called greedy algorithms, which attempt to solve a minimization (maximization) problem by minimizing (maximizing) the quantity associated with only the first step.

Algorithm 17.2 The Closest Neighbor Algorithm. Let $G = (V, > E, w)$ be a complete weighted graph with $\#V = n$. The *closest neighbour circuit* through G starting at v_1 is $(v_1, v_2, \ldots, v_n)$, defined by the steps:

1. $V_1 := V - \{v_1\}$
2. For k: = 2 to $n - 1$ do:

   2.1 $v_k :=$ the closest vertex in V_{k-1} to v_{k-1};
   i.e., $w(v_{k-1}, v_k) = \min \{w\,(v_{k-1}, v)\colon v \in V_{k-1}\}$.
   In case of a tie for closest, v_k may be chosen arbitrarily.

   2.2 $v_k := V_{k-1} - \{v_k\}$.
3. $v_n :=$ the only element in V_n.

The cost of the closest neighbour circuit is $\sum_{k=1}^{n-1} w(v_k, v_{k+1}) + w(v_n, v_1)$.

Example 17.33 The closest neighbor circuit starting at A in Fig. 17.61 is (A, C, B, D, A), with a cost of 29. The optimal (or cheapest) path is (A, B, C, D, A), with a cost of 27.

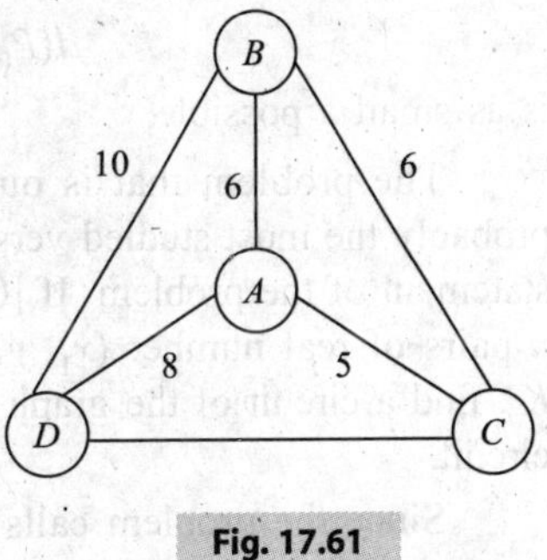

Fig. 17.61

Although the closest neighbor circuit is often not optimal, we may be satisfied if it is close to optimal. If C_{opt} and C_{cn} are the costs of optimal and closest neighbour circuits in a graph, then it is always the case that $C_{opt} \le C_{cn}$, or $C_{cn}/C_{opt} \ge 1$. We can assess how good the closest neighbor algorithm is by determining how small the quantity C_{cn}/C_{opt} gets. If it is always near 1, then the algorithm is good. However, if there are graphs for which it is large, then the algorithm may be discarded. Note that in Example 17.33 C_{cn}/C_{opt} = considered good.

Example 17.34 A salesman must take stops at vertices A, B, (A and C, which are all on the same one-way street. The graph in Fig. 17.62 is weighted by the function $w\,(i, j)$ = the time it takes to drive from vertex i to vertex j. Note that if j is down the street from i, then

$w(i, j)$ is less than $w(j, i)$. The values of C_{opt} and C_{cn} are 20 and 32. Verify that C_{cn} is 32 by using the closest neighbor algorithm. The value of $C_{cn}/C_{opt} = 1.6$ is significant in this case since our salesman would spend 60 percent more time on the road if he used the closest neighbor algorithm.

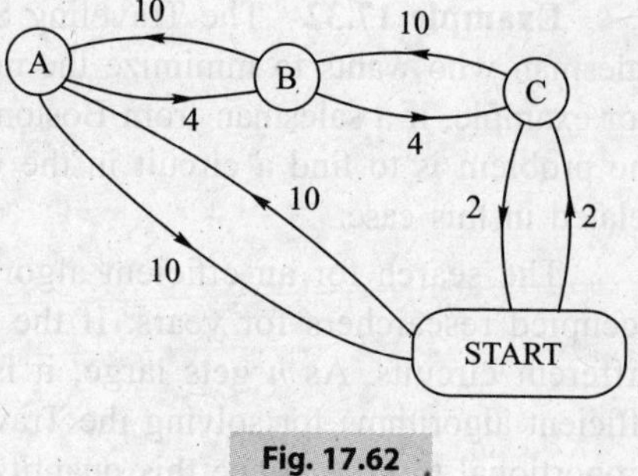

Fig. 17.62

A more general result relating to the closest neighbor algorithm presumes that the graph in question is complete and that the weight function satisfies the conditions (1) $w(x, y) = w(y, x)$ for all x, y in the vertex set, and (2) $w(x, y) + w(y, z) \geq w(x, z)$ for all x, y, z in the vertex set. The first condition is called the symmetry condition and the second is the triangle **inequality**.

Theorem 17.4 If (V, E, w) is a complete weighted graph that satisfies the symmetry and triangle inequality conditions, then

$$C_{cn}/C_{opt} \leq [\log_2 (2n)]/2. \quad \text{...}(i)$$

Notes:

(*a*) If $\#V$ is 8, then this theorem says that C_{cn} can be no larger than twice the size of C_{opt}; however, it doesn't say that the closest neighbor circuit will necessarily be that far from an optimal circuit. The quantity $[\log_2 (2n)]/2$ is called an upper bound for the ratio C_{cn}/C_{opt}. It tells us only that things can't be any worse than the upper bound. Certainly, there are many graph with 8 vertices such that the optimal and closest neighbor circuits are the same. What is left unstated in this theorem is whether there are graphs for which the quantities in 9.5*a* are equal. If there are such graphs, we say that the upper bound is sharp.

(*b*) The value of C_{cn}/C_{opt} in Example 17.34 is 1.6, which is greater than $[\log_2 (8)]/2 = 1.5$; however, the weight function in this example does not satisfy the conditions of the theorem.

17.38.2 Traveling Salesman Problem—Unit Square Version

Example 17.35 A robot is programmed to weld joints on square metal plate. Each plate must be welded at prescribed points on the square. To minimize the time it takes to complete the job, the total distance that the robot's arm moves should be minimized. Let $d(P, Q)$ be the distance between P and Q. Assume that before each plate can be welded, the arm must be positioned at a certain point P_0. Given a list of n points, we want to put them in order so that

$$d(P_0, P_1) + d(P_1, P_2) + \ldots + d(P_n, P_0)$$

is as small a possible.

The problem that is outlined in Example 17.35 is of such obvious importance that is probably the most studied version of the Traveling Salesman Problem. What follows is the usual statement of the problem. If $[0, 1] = \{x \text{ in } \mathbf{R} : 0 \leq x \leq 1\}$, let $S = [0,1]^2$, *the unit square*. Given n pairs of real number (x_1, y_1), (x_2, y_2), ... and (x_n, y_n) in S that represent the n vertices of a K_n, find a circuit of the graph that minimizes the sum of the distances traveled in traversing the circuit.

Since the problem calls for a circuit, it doesn't matter which vertex we start at; assume that we will start at (x_1, y_1). Once the problem is solved, we can always change our starting position. A function can most efficiently describe a circuit in this problem. Every bijection f: $\{1, ..., n\} \rightarrow \{1, ..., n\}$ with $f(1) = 1$ describes a circuit $((x_1, y_1), (x_{f(2)}, Y_{f(n)}), ..., (x_{f(n)}, y_{f(n)}))$. Since there are $(n - 1)!$ such bijections, and examination of all possible circuits is not feasible for large, values of n.

One heuristic algorithm that is popular is the strip algorithm:

Algorithm 17.3 Given n points in the unit square.

Phase 1:

1.1 Divide the square into $[\sqrt{n/2}]$ vertical strips, as in Fig. 17.63. Let d be the width of each strip. If a point lies on a boundary between two strips, consider it part of the left-hand strip.

1.2 Starting from the left, find the first strip that contains one of the points. Locate your starting point by selecting the first point that is encountered in that strip as you travel from bottom to top. We will assume that point is (x_1, y_1).

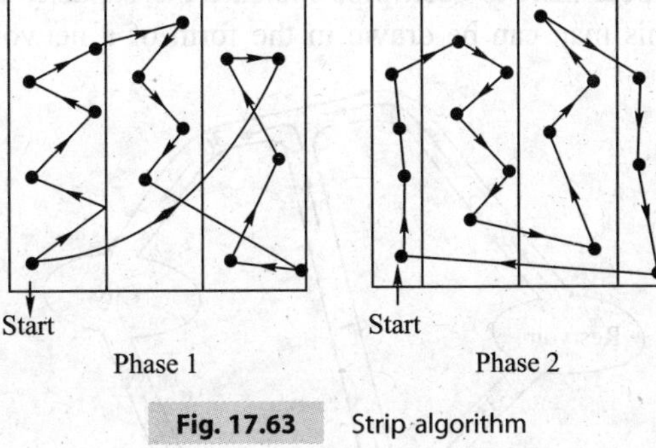

Fig. 17.63 Strip algorithm

1.3 Alternate traveling up and down the strips that contain vertices until all of the vertices have been reached.

1.4 Return to the starting point.

Phase 2:

2.1 Shift all strips $d/2$ units to the right (creating a small strip on the left).

2.2 Repeat Steps 1.2 through 1.4 of Phase 1 with the new strips.

When the two phases are complete, choose the shorter of the two circuits obtained.

Step 1.3 needs a bit more explanation. How do you travel up or down a strip? In most cases, the vertices in a strip will be vertically distributed so that the order in which they are visited is obvious. In some cases, however, the order might not be clear as in the third strip in Fig. 17.63. Within a strip, the order in which you visit the points (if you are going up the strip) is determined thusly: $x_1, y_1)$ precedes $x_2, y_2)$ if $y_1 < y_2$ or if $y_1 = y_2$ and $x_1 < x_2$. In traveling down a strip, replace $y_1 < y_2$ with $y_2 < y_1$.

The selection of $[\sqrt{n/2}]$ strips was made in a 1959 paper by Breadwood, Halton, and Mammersely. It balances the problems that arise if the number of strips is too small or too large. If the square is divided into small strips, some strips may be packed with vertices so that visiting them would require excessive horizontal motion. If too many strips are used, excessive vertical motion tends to be the result. An update on what is known about this algorithm is contained in the paper by K.J. Supowit, E.M Reingold, and D.A. Plaised.

Since the construction of a circuit in the square consists of sorting the given points, it should come as no surprise that the strip algorithm requires a time that is roughly a multiple of $n \log (n)$ time units when n points are to be visited.

The worst case that has been encountered with this algorithm is one in which the circuit obtained has a total distance of $\sqrt{2n}$ approximately (see Sopowit *et al*).

17.38.3 Networks and the Maximum Flow Problem

A *network* is a simple weighted directed graph that contains two distinguished vertices called the source and *sink*. An example of a real situation that can be represented by a network is a city's water system. A reservoir would be the source, while a distribution point in the city to all of the users would be the sink. The system of pumps and pipes that carries the water from source to sink makes up the remaining network. We can assume that the water that passes through a pipe in one minute is controlled by a pump and the maximum rate is determined by the size of the pipe and the strength of the pump. This maximum rate of flow through a pipe is called its *capacity* and is the information that the weight function of network contains.

Example 17.36 Consider the system that is illustrated in Fig. 17.64. The numbers that appear next to each pipe indicate the capacity of that pipe in thousands of gallons per minute. This map can be drawn in the form of a network, as in Fig. 17.65.

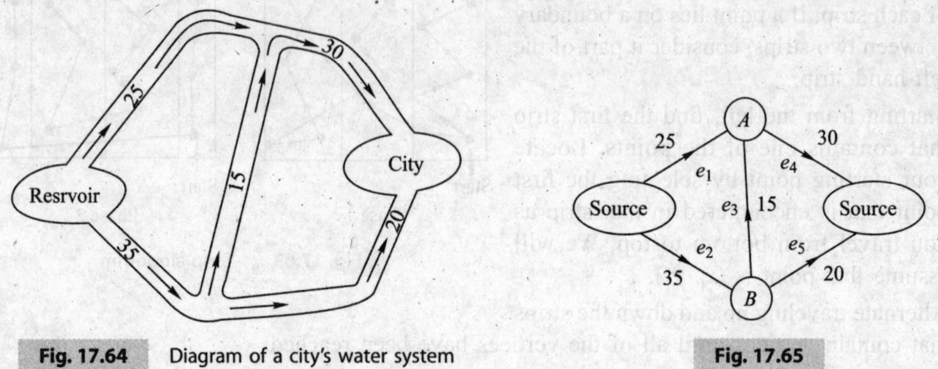

Fig. 17.64 Diagram of a city's water system

Fig. 17.65

Although the material passing through this network is water, networks can also represent the flow automobiles, electricity, and telephone cables.

The maximum Flow Problem is derived from the objective of moving the maximum amount of water of other material from the source to the sink. To measure this amount, we define a *flow* as a function $f: E \rightarrow \mathbf{R}$ such that (1) the flow of material through any edge is non-negative and no larger than its capacity: $0 \leq f(e) \leq w(e)$, for all e in E; and (2) for each vertex other than the source and sink, the total amount of material that is directed into a vertex is equal to the total amount that is directed out:

$$\sum_{(x,v)\in E} f(x,v) = \sum_{(v,y)\in E} f(v,y) \qquad \text{...(17.2)}$$

Flow into v = Flow out of v.

The summation notation on the left of Equation (17.2) represents the sum of the flows, through each edge in E that has v as a terminal vertex. The right-hand side indicates that you should add all of the flow through edges that initiate at v.

Theorem 17.5 If f is a flow, then

$$\sum_{(\text{source},\, v)\in E} f(\text{source}, v)$$

and
$$\sum_{(v,\, \text{sink})\in E} f(v, \text{sink})_f$$

have a common value, which is called the *value of the flow*. We will denote the value of a flow f by $V(f)$. The value of a flow represents the amount of material that passes through the network with that flow.

Proof: Subtract the right-hand side of Equation (17.2) from the left-hand side. The result is: Flow into v – Flow out of v = 0. Now sum up these differences for each vertex in $V' = V$ – (source, sink). The result is

$$\sum_{v\in V}\left(\sum_{(x,v)\in E} f(x,v) - \sum_{(x,y)\in E} f(v,y)\right) = 0 \qquad \text{...(17.3)}$$

Now observe that if an edge connects two vertices in V', its flow appears as both a positive and a negative term in Equation (17.3). This means that the only positive terms that are not cancelled out are the flows out of the source. In addition, the only negative terms that remain are the flows into the sink. Therefore,

$$\sum_{(\text{source}, x)\in E} f(\text{source}, x) - \sum_{(y, \text{sink})\in E} f(y, \text{sink}) = 0.\#$$

17.38.4 Maximal Flows

Since the Maximum How Problem consists of maximizing the amount of material that passes through a given network, it is equivalent to finding a flow with the largest possible value. Any such flow is called a maximal flow.

For the network in Fig. 17.65, one flow is f_1, defined by $f_1(e_1) = 25, f_1(e_2) = 20, f_1(e_3) = 0, f_1(e_4) = 25$, and $f_1(e_5) = 25$. The value of f_1, $V(f_1)$, is 45. Since the total flow into the sink can be no larger than 50 ($w(e_4) + w(e_5) = 30 + 20$), we can tell that f_1 is not very far from the solution. Can you improve on f_1 at all? The sum of the capacities into the sink can't always be obtained by a flow. The same is true for the sum of the capacities out of the source. In this case, the sum of the capacities out of the source is 60, which obviously can't be reached in this network.

A solution of the Maximum How Problem for this network is the maximal flow f_2: $f_2(e_1) = 25, f_2(e_2) = 25, f_2(e_3) = 5, f_2(e_4) = 30$, and $f_2(e_5) = 20$, with $V(f_2) = 50$. The solution is not unique. In fact, there is an infinite number of maximal flows for this problem.

Several algorithms have been developed to solve the Maximal How Problem. One of these is the Ford and Funkerson Algorithm (FFA). The FFA consists of repeatedly finding paths in a network called flow augmenting paths until no improvement can be made in the flow that has been obtained.

Definition 17.12 ***Flow Augmenting Path.*** Given a flow f in a network (V, E), a flow augmenting path with respect to f is a simple path from the source to the sink using edges both in their forward and their reverse directions such that for each edge e in the path, $w(e) - f(e) > 0$ if e used in its forward direction and $f(e) > 0$ if e is used in the reverse direction.

Example 17.37 For f_1 in Example 17.36, a flow augmenting path would be (e_2, e_3, e_4) since

$$w(e_2) - f_1(e_2) = 15, \quad w(e_3) - f_1(e_3) = 15, \text{ and } w(e_4) - f_1(e_4) = 5.$$

These positive differences represent unused capacities, and the smallest value represents the amount of flow that can be added to each edge in the path. Note that by adding 5 to each edge in our path, we obtain f_2, which is maximal. If an edge with a positive flow is used in its reverse direction, it is contributing a movement of material that is counterproductive to the objective of maximizing flow. This is why the algorithm directs us to decrease the flow through that edge.

Algorithm 17.4 The Ford and Funkerson Algorithm.

1. Define the flow function f_0 by $f_0(e) = 0$ for each edge $e \in E$.
2. $i := 0$.
3. Repeat:
   - 3.1 If possible, find a flow augmenting path with respect to f.
   - 3.2 If a flow augmenting path exists, then:
     - 3.2.1 Determine f_{i+1} by

       $d = \min \{\{w(e) - f_i(e) : e \text{ is used in the forward direction}\},$

       $\{f_i(e) : e \text{ is used in the reverse direction}\},$
     - 3.2.2 Define f_{i+1} by

$$f_{i+1}(e) = \begin{cases} f_i(e) \text{ if } e \text{ is not used in the path;} \\ f_i(e) + d \text{ if } e \text{ is used in the forward direction;} \\ f_i(e) - d \text{ if } e \text{ is used in the reverse direction.} \end{cases}$$

3.2.3 $i := i + 1$.
until no flow augmenting path exists.

4. Terminate with a maximal flow f_i

Notes:

(*a*) It should be clear that every flow augmenting path leads to a flow of increased value and that none of the capacities of the network can be violated.

(*b*) The depth-first search should be used to find flow augmenting paths since it is far more efficient than the breadth-first search in this situation. The depth-first search differs from the broadcasting algorithm (a variation of the breadth-first search) in that you sequentially visit vertices until you reach a "dead end" and then backtrack.

A Depth-First Search for the Sink Initiating at the Source: Let E' be the set of directed edges that can be used in producing a flow augmenting path. Add to the network a vertex called start and the edge (start, source).

1. S: = Vertex set of the network.

   2.1 p : = start.

   2.2 p : = Source (Move p along the edge (start, source).)

3. WHILE p is not equal to start or sink DO.

   If an edge in E' exists that takes you from p to another vertex in S, then set p to be that next vertex and delete the edge from E'. Otherwise, reassign p to be the vertex that p was reached from (*i.e.,* backtrack).

4. If p = start, no flow augmenting path exists.

   If p = sink, you have found a flow augmenting path.

(*c*) There have been networks discovered for which the FFA does not terminate in a finite number of steps. These examples have irrational capacities: It has been proven that if all capacities are positive integers, the FFA terminates in a finite number of steps. See Ford and Funkerson, Even, or Berge for details.

(*d*) When you use the FFA to solve the Maximum Flow Problem by hand it is convenient to label each edge of the network with the fraction $f_i(e)/w(e)$.

Example 17.38 Consider the network in Fig. 17.66, where the current flow, f, is indicated by a labeling of the edges. The path (source v_2, v_1, v_3, sink) is a flow augmenting path. Note that (v_1, v_3) is used in the reverse direction, which is allowed because $f(v_1, v_3) > 0$. The value of the new flow is 8. This flow must be maximal since the capacities out of the source add up to 8. This maximal flow is defined by the labeling of Fig. 17.67.

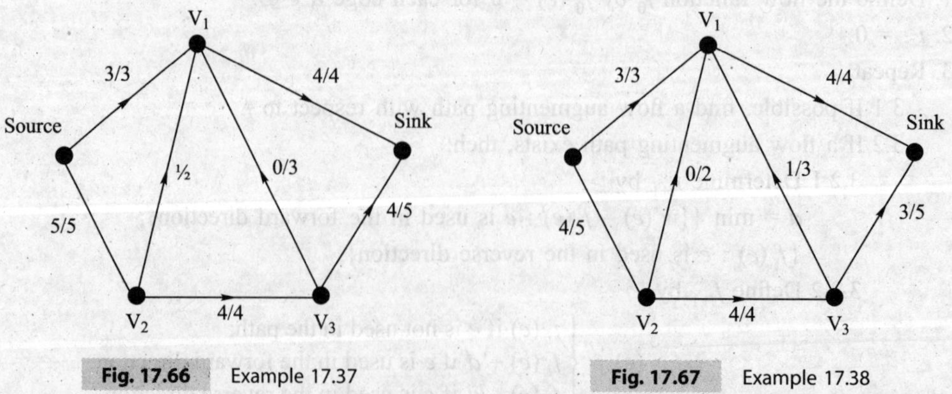

Fig. 17.66 Example 17.37 **Fig. 17.67** Example 17.38

17.39 OTHER GRAPH OPTIMIZATION PROBLEMS

(*a*) *The Minimum Spanning Tree Problem:* Given a weighted graph, (V, E, w), find a subset E' of E with the properties that (V, E') is connected and the sum of the weights of edge in E' are as small as possible.

(*b*) *The Minimum Matching Problem:* Given an undirected weighted graph (V, E, w), with an even number of vertices, pair up the vertices so that each pair is connected by an edge and the sum of these edges is as small as possible. A unit square version of this problem has been studied extensively. See the paper by K.J. Supowit, E.M. Reingold, and D.A. Plaisted for details on what is known about this version of the problem.

(*c*) *The Graph Center Problem:* Given a connected, undirected, weighted graph, find a vertex (the center) in the graph with the property that the distance from the center to every other vertex is as small as possible. 'As small as possible' could be interpreted either as minimizing the sum of the distances to each vertex or minimizing the maximum distance from the center to a vertex.

17.40 TREE

What distinguishes all trees from other types of graphs is the absence of certain paths called *cycles*.

Definition 17.13 *Cycle.* A cycle is a circuit whose edge list contains no duplicates.

The simplest example of a cycle in an undirected graph is a pair of vertices with two edges connecting them. Since trees are cycle-free, we can rule out all multigrades from consideration as trees.

Trees can either be undirected or directed graphs. We will concentrate on the undirected ones for now.

Definition 17.14 *Tree.* An authorized graph is a tree if it is connected and contains no cycles or self-loops.

Example 17.39

(*a*) Graph *a*, *b*, and *c* in Fig. 17.68 are all trees, while graphs *d*, *e*, and *f* are not trees.

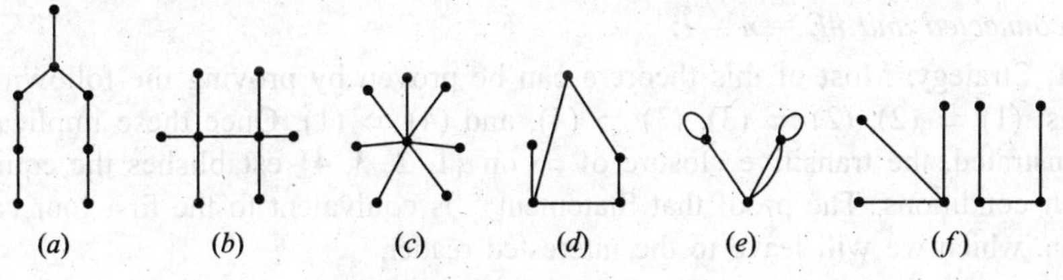

Fig. 17.68 Trees and non-trees

(*b*) A K_2 is a tree. However, if $n \geq 3$, a K_n is not a tree.

(*c*) In a loose sense, a botanical tree is a mathematical tree. There are no cycles in the branch structure of a botanical tree.

(*d*) The structure of some chemical compounds are modeled by a tree. For example, butane [Fig. 17.69 (*a*)] consists of four carbon molecules and ten hydrogen molecules, where an edge between two molecules represents a bond between them. A bond is a force that keeps two molecules together. The same set of molecules can be linked together in a different tree structure to give us the compound isobutane [Fig. 17.69 (*b*)]. There are some compounds whose graphs are not trees. One example is benzene [Fig. 17.69 (*c*)].

One type of graph that is not a tree, but is closely related, is a forest.

(a) (b) (c)

Fig. 17.69 Simple organic compounds

Definition 17.15 ***Forest.*** A forest is an undirected graph whose components are all trees.

Example 17.40 Graph *a*, *b*, and *c* of Fig. 17.68. can be viewed as a forest of three trees.

We will now examine several conditions that are equivalent to the one that defines a tree. The following theorem will be used as a tool in proving that the conditions are equivalent.

Theorem 17.6 Let $G = (V, E)$ be an undirected graph with no self-loops, and let $v_a, v_b \in V$. If two different simple paths exist between v_a and v_b, then there exists a cycle in G.

Proof: Let $p_1 = (e_1, e_2, ..., e_m)$ and $p_2 = (f_1, f_2, ..., f_m)$ be two different simple paths from v_a to v_b. The first step that we will take is to delete the initial edges that are identical from p_2 and p_2. This is, if $e_1 = f_1, e_2 = f_2, ..., e_j = f_j$, and, $e_{j+1} \neq f_{j-1}$, delete the first j edges of both paths. Once this is done, both paths start at the same vertex, call it v_c, and still both end at v_b. Now we construct a cycle by starting at v_c and following what is left of p_1 until we first meet what is left of p_2. If this first meeting occurs at vertex v_d, then the remainder of the cycle is completed by following the portion of p_2 that starts at v_d and ends at v_c.

Theorem 17.7 Let $G = (V, E)$ be an undirected graph with no self-loops and $\#V = n$. The following are all equivalent:

1. *G is a tree.*
2. *For each pair of distinct vertices in V, there exists a unique simple path between them.*
3. *G is connected and if e ∈ E, then (V, E – {e}) is disconnected.*
4. *G contains no cycles, but by adding an edge, you create a cycle.*
5. *G is connected and #E = n – 1.*

Proof: Strategy. Most of this theorem can be proven by proving the following chain of implications: (1) ⇒ (2), (2) ⇒ (3), (3) ⇒ (4), and (4) ⇒ (1). Once these implications have been demonstrated, the transitive closure of ⇒ on {1, 2, 3, 4} establishes the equivalence of the first four conditions. The proof that Statement 5 is equivalent to the first four can be done by induction, which we will leave to the interested reader.

1. ⇒ (2) (Indirect). Assume that G is a tree and that there exists a pair of vertices, v_1 and v_2, between which there is either no path or there are at least two distinct paths. Both of these possibilities contradict the premise that G is a tree. If no path exists, G is disconnected, and if two paths exist, a cycle can be obtained by Theorem 17.6.
2. ⇒ (3). We now use Statement 2 as a premise. Since each pair of vertices in V connected by one path, G is connected. Now if we select any edge e in E, it connects two vertices, v_1 and v_2. By (2), there is no simple path connecting v_1 to v_2 other than (e). In addition, since any path can be reduced to a simple path by deleting some of its edges, no path can exist between v_1 and v_2 in $(V, E - \{e\})$. Hence $(V, E - \{e\})$ is disconnected.
3. ⇒ (4). Now we will assume that Statement 3 is true. We must show that G has no cycles and that adding an edge to G creates a cycle. We will use an indirect proof for this part. Since (4) is a conjunction, by DeMorgan's Law, its negation is a disjunction and we must

consider two cases. First, suppose that G has a cycle. Then the deletion of any edge in the cycle keeps the graph connected, which contradicts (3). The second case is that the addition of an edge to G does not create a cycle. Then there are two distinct paths between the vertices that the new edge connects. By Theorem 17.6, a cycle can then be created, which is a contradiction.

4. $\Rightarrow$ (1). Assume that G contains no cycles and that the addition of an edge creates a cycle. All that we need to prove to verify that G is a tree is that G is connected. If it is not connected, then select any two vertices that are not connected. If we add an edge to connect them, the fact that a cycle is created implies that a second path between the two vertices can be found which is in the original graph, which is a contradiction. The usual definition of a directed tree is based on whether the associated undirected graph, which is obtained by 'erasing' its directional arrows, is a tree.

17.41 SPANNING TREES

The topic of spanning trees is motivated by a graph-optimization problem.

Example 17.41 A map of Atlantis (Fig. 17.70) shows that there are four campuses in its university system. A new phone system is being installed and the objective is to allow communication between any two campuses. To achieve this objective, the university must buy direct lines between certain pairs of campuses. Let G be the graph with a vertex for each campus and an edge for each direct phone line. Total communication is equivalent to G being a connected graph. This is due to the fact that two campuses can communicate over any number of lines. To minimize costs, the university wants to buy a minimum number of lines.

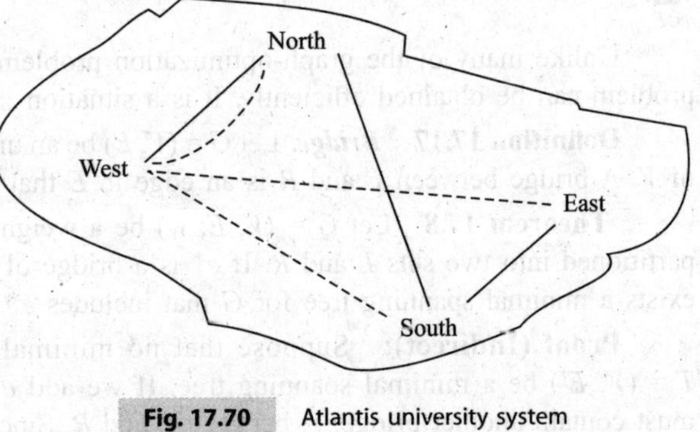

Fig. 17.70 Atlantis university system

The solution is this problem are all trees. Any graph that satisfies the requirements of the university must be connected, and if a cycle does exist, any line in the cycle can be deleted, reducing the cost. Each of the sixteen trees that can be drawn to connect the vertices North, South, East, and solves the problem as it is stated. Note that in each case, three direct lines must be purchased. There are two considerations that can help reduce the number of solutions that would be considered.

Objective 1: Given that the cost of each line depends on certain factors, such as the distance campuses, select a tree whose cost is as low as possible.

Objective 2: Suppose that communication over multiple lines is noisier as the number of lines increase. Select a tree with the property that the maximum number of lines that any pair of campuses must use to communicate is as small as possible.

Typically, these objectives are not compatible; that is, you cannot always simultaneously achieve these objectives in all cases. In the case of the Atlantis university system, the solution with respect to Objective 1 is indicated with solid lines in Fig. 17.70. There are four solutions to the problem with respect to Objective 2: any tree in which one campus is directly connected to the other three. One solution with respect to Objective 2 is indicated with dotted lines in Fig. 17.70. After satisfying the conditions of Objective 2, it would seem reasonable to select the cheapest of the four trees.

Definition 17.16

(*a*) ***Spanning Set.*** Let $G = (V, E)$ be a connected undirected graph. A spanning set for G is a subset E' of E such that (V, E') is connected.

(*b*) ***Spanning Tree.*** If E' is a spanning set for G and $T = (V, E')$ is a tree, then T is called a spanning tree for G.

Notes:

(*a*) If (V, E') is a spanning tree, $\#E' = \#V - 1$.

(*b*) The significance of a spanning tree is that it is a minimal spanning set. A smaller set would not span the graph, while a larger set would have a cycle, which has an edge that is superfluous.

For the remainder of this section, we will discuss two of the many topics that relate to spanning trees. The first is the Minimal Spanning Tree Problem, which is a generalization of Objective 1 above. The second is the Minimum Diameter Spanning Tree Problem, which is a generalization of Objective 2.

17.41.1 The Minimal Spanning Tree Problem

Given a weighted connected undirected graph $G = (V, E, w)$, find a spanning tree (V, E') for $\sum_{e \in E'} w(e)$ which is as small as possible.

Unlike many of the graph-optimization problems that we've examined, a solution to this problem can be obtained efficiently. It is a situation in which a greedy algorithm works.

Definition 17.17 ***Bridge.*** Let $G = (V, E)$ be an undirected graph and let $\{L, R\}$ be a partition of V. A bridge between L and R is an edge in E that connects a vertex in L to a vertex in R.

Theorem 17.8 Let $G = (V, E, w)$ be a weighted connected undirected graph. Let V be partitioned into two sets L and R. If e^* is a bridge of least weight between L and R, then there exists a minimal spanning tree for G that includes e^*.

Proof (Indirect): Suppose that no minimal spanning tree including e^* exists. Let $T = (V, E')$ be a minimal spanning tree. If we add e^* to T, a cycle is created, and this cycle must contain another bridge, e, between L and R. Since $w(e^*) \leq w(e)$, we can delete e and the new tree, which includes e^*, must also be a minimal spanning tree.

Example 17.42 The bridges between the vertex sets $\{a, b, c\}$ and $\{d, e\}$ in Fig. 17.71 are the edges $\{b, d\}$ and $\{c, e\}$. According to the theorem, a minimal spanning tree that includes (b, d) exists. By examination, you should be able to see that this is true. Is it true that only the bridges of minimal weight can be part of a minimal spanning tree? The answer is no.

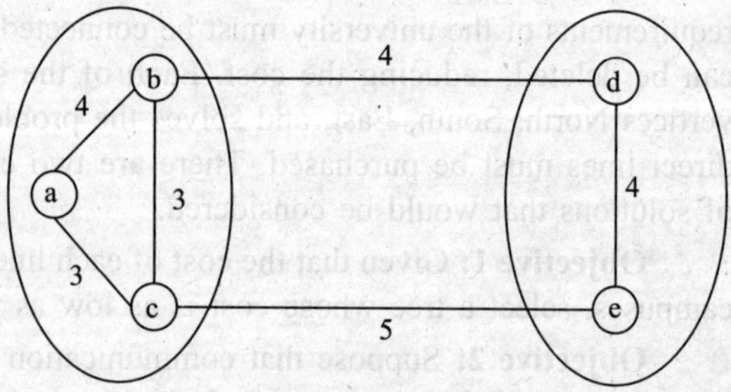

Fig. 17.71

Theorem 17.8 essentially tells us that a minimal spanning tree can be constructed recursively by continually adding minimally weighted bridges to a set of edges.

Algorithm 17.5 Greedy Algorithm for Finding a Minimal Spanning Tree. Let $G = (V, E, w)$ be a connected, weighted, undirected graph, and let v_1 be an arbitrary vertex in V. The following steps lead to a minimal spanning tree for G. L and R will be sets of vertices and E' is a set of edges.

1. (Initialize) $L: = V - \{v_1\}$, $R: = \{v_1\}$, $E : = \varnothing$
2. (Build the tree) While $L \neq \varnothing$ do:
   2.1. Find $e^* = (\{v_L, v_R\})$, a bridge of minimum weight between L and R.
   2.2. (Update sets) $R: = R \cup \{v_L\}$, $L: = L - \{v_L\}$ and E':
   $E = E' \cup \{e^*\}$.
3. Terminate with a minimal spanning tree (V, E').

Notes:

(*a*) If more than one minimal spanning tree exists, then the one that is obtained depends on v_1 and the means by which e^* is selected in Step 2.1 if two minimally weighted bridges exist.

(*b*) Warning: If two minimally weighted bridges exist between L and R, do not try to speed up the algorithm by adding all of them to E'.

(*c*) That Algorithm 17.5. yields a minimal spanning tree can be proven by induction with the use of Theorem 17.8.

(*d*) If it is not known whether G is connected, Algorithm 17.5 can be revised to handle this possibility. The key change (in step 2.1) would be to determine whether any bridge at all exists between L and R. The condition of the while loop in Step 2 must also be changed somewhat.

Example 17.43 Consider the graph in Fig. 17.72. If we apply Algorithm 17.5. starting at a, we obtain the following edge list in the order given: $\{a, f\}$, $\{f, e\}$, $\{e, c\}$, $\{c, d\}$, $\{f, b\}$, $\{b, g\}$. The total of the weights of these edges is 20. The method that we have used (in Step 2.1) to select a bridge when more than one minimally weighted bridge exists is to order all bridges alphabetically by the vertex in L and then, if further ties exist, by the vertex in R. The first vertex in that order is selected in Step 2.1 of the algorithm.

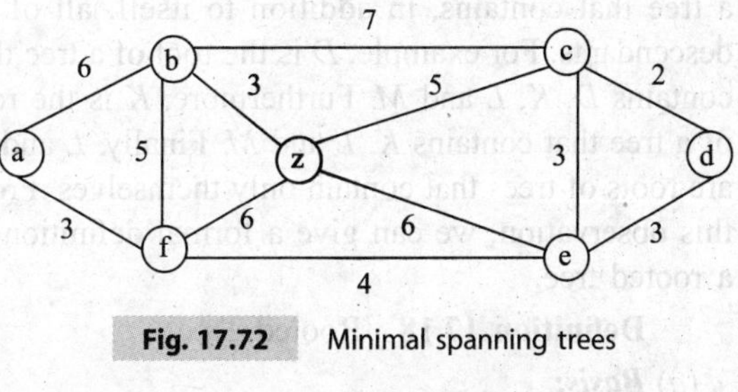

Fig. 17.72 Minimal spanning trees

The Minimum Diameter Spanning Tree Problem

Given a connected undirected graph $G = (V, E)$, find a spanning tree $T = (V, E')$ of G such that the longest path in T is a short as possible.

Example 17.44 The Minimum Diameter Spanning Tree Problem is easy to solve in a K_n. Select any vertex and construct the spanning tree whose edge set is the set of edges that connect v_1 to the other vertices in the K_n. Figure 17.73 illustrates a solution for a K_5.

For incomplete graphs, a two-state algorithm is needed. In short, the first step is to locate a 'center' of the graph. The maximum distance from a center to any other vertex is as small as possible. Once a center is located, a breadth-first search of the graph is used to construct the spanning tree.

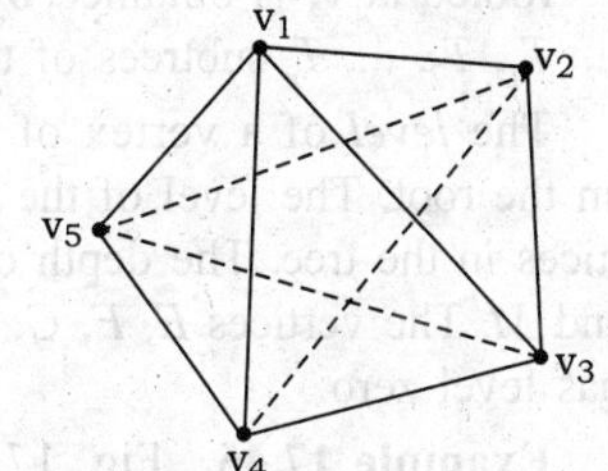

Fig. 17.73 Minimum diameter spanning tree for K_5

17.42 ROOTED TREES

In the next two sections, we will discuss rooted trees. Our primary focuses will be on rooted trees in general and on ordered binary trees in particulars.

Informal Definition and Terminology: What differentiates rooted trees from undirected trees is that a *rooted tree* contains a distinguished vertex, called the *root*. Consider the tree in Fig. 17.74. Vertex *A* has been designated the root of the tree. If we choose any other vertex in the tree, such as *M*, we know that there is a unique path from *A* to *M*. The vertices on this path, (*A*, *D*, *K*, *M*), are described in genealogical terms:

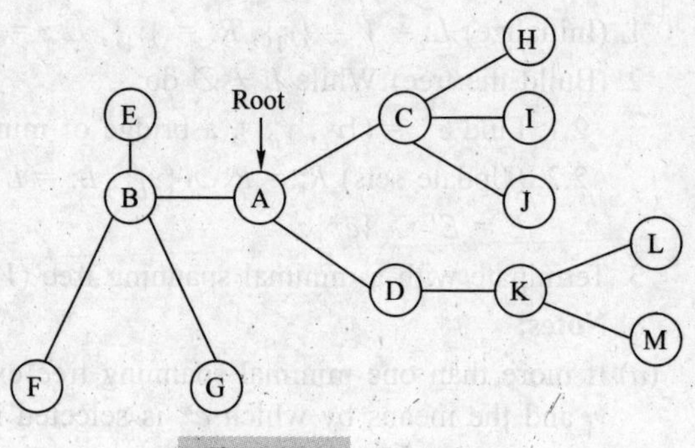

Fig. 17.74 Rooted tree

M is a *child* of *K* (so is *L*).

K is M's parent

A, *D*, and *L* are *M's ancestors*

D, *K*, *L* and *M* are *descendants* of *A*.

These genealogical relationships are often easier to visualize if the tree is rewritten so that children are positioned below their parents, as in Fig. 17.75.

With this format, it is easy to see that each vertex in the tree can be thought of as the root of a tree that contains, in addition to itself, all of its descendants. For example, *D* is the root of a tree that contains *D*, *K*, *L* and *M*. Furthermore, *K* is the root of a tree that contains *K*, *L* and *M*. Finally, *L* and *M* are roots of trees that contain only themselves. From this observation, we can give a formal definition of a rooted tree.

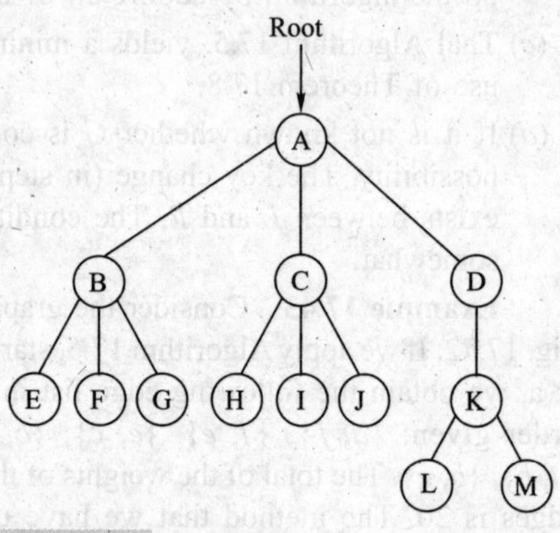

Fig. 17.75 Rooted tree of Fig. 17.74, redrawn

Definition 17.18 Rooted Tree

(*a*) ***Basis:***

(*i*) A tree with no vertices is a rooted tree (the empty tree).

(*ii*) A single vertex with no children is a rooted tree.

(*b*) ***Recursion:*** Let $T_1, T_2, ..., T_r, r \geq 1$, be disjoint rooted trees with roots $v_1, v_2, ..., v_r$, respectively, and v a vertex that does not belong to any of these trees. Then a rooted tree, rooted at v, is obtained by making v the parent of the vertices $v_1, v_2, ...,$ and v_r. We call $T_1, T_2, ..., T_r$ subtrees of the large tree.

The *level* of a vertex of a rooted tree is the number of edges that separate the vertex from the root. The level of the root is zero. The *depth* of the tree is the maximum level of the vertices in the tree. The depth of a tree in Fig. 17.75 is three, which is the level of the vertices *L* and *M*. The vertices *E*, *F*, *G*, *H*, *I*, *J*, and *K* have level two. *B*, *C*, and *D* are at level one and *A* has level zero.

Example 17.45 Fig. 17.74 is a rooted tree, with start as the root. It is an example of what is called a decision tree.

Example 17.46 Pascal note on Record Structure. Frequently, the fields of a record are themselves records. For example, student information can be stored in a Pascal record:

```
Student = RECORD
          Names: RECORD
                 First: String;
```

```
        Middle: Char;
        Last: String
        END;
    Major: String;
    SAT: RECORD
        Math, Verbal: 0..800
    END
END.
```


Fig. 17.76

The organization of this data can be visualized with a rooted tree such as the one in Fig. 17.76.

In general, you can represent a record type, T, as rooted tree with T as the root and a subtree for each field. Those fields that are record are roots of further subtrees, while the non-records (often called elementary fields) have no further children in the tree.

17.42.1 Kruskal's Algorithm

An alternate algorithm for constructing a minimal spanning tree uses a forest of rooted trees. First we will describe the algorithm in its simplest terms. Afterward, we will describe how rooted trees are used to implement the algorithm. Finally, we will describe a simple data type and operations that make the algorithm quite easy to program. In all versions of this algorithm, assume that G (V, E, w) is a weighted undirected graph with $\#V = m$ and $\#E = n$.

17.42.1.1 Kruskal Algorithm–Version 1

1. Sort the edges of G in ascending order according to weight. That is, $i \leq j \Leftrightarrow w(e_i) \leq w(e_j)$.
2. Go down the list obtained in Step 1 and add edges to a spanning set (initially empty) of edges so that the set of edges does not form a cycle. When an edge that would create a cycle is encountered, ignore it. Continue examining edges unit either $m - 1$ edges have been selected or you have come to the end of the edge list. If $m - 1$ edges are selected, these edges make up a minimal spanning tree for G. If fewer than $m - 1$ edges are selected, G is not connected.

Note: Step 1 can be accomplished using one of any number of standard sorting routines. Using the most efficient sorting routine, the time required to perform this step is proportional to $n \log(n)$. The second step of the algorithm, also of $n \log(n)$ time complexity, is the one that uses a forest of rooted trees to test for edge should be added to the spanning set.

17.42.1.2 Kruskal's Algorithm–Version 2

1. Sort the edges as in Version 1.
2. 2.1 Initialize each vertex in V to be root of its own rooted tree.

   2.2 Go down the list of edges until either a spanning tree is completed or the edge list has been exhausted. For each edge $e = \{v_1, v_2\}$ we can determine whether e can be added, to the spanning set without forming a cycle of determining whether the root of v_1's tree is equal to the root of v_2's tree. If the two roofs are equal, then ignore e. If the roots are different, then we can add e to the spanning set. In addition, we merge the trees that v_1 and v_2 belong to. This is accomplished by either making v_1's root the parent of v_2s coot or vice versa.

Notes:

(*a*) Since we start the algorithm with m trees and each addition of an edge decreases the number of trees by one, we end the algorithm with one rooted tree, provided a spanning tree exists.

(*b*) The rooted tree that we obtain is not the spanning tree itself.

(*c*) Suppose that we define the operation merge (r_1, r_2), where r_1 and r_2 are roots of trees, to created a new tree, rooted at r_1, so that the parent of r_2 is r_1. To minimize the time it takes to find the root of a given tree, we want to keep the depths of our trees as small as possible Suppose that the depth of r_1's tree is j and that the depth of r_2's tree is k. If $j = k$, it doesn't matter which way we merge the trees. However, if j is less than k, merge (r_1, r_2) will give us a tree or depth $k + 1$, while merge (r_2, r_1) gives us a tree of depth k. For this reason, we should, if possible, always merge smaller trees in larger trees; that is, the smaller tree's root should be the child of the larger tree's root.

A Data Structure for Kruskal's Algorithm: The important information that we need to maintain about the rooted trees in this algorithm is the identity of each vertex's parent. This can be accomplished quite easily using an array of integers.

Parent: ARRAY [1..m] of 0..m

We interpret the elements of Parent as follows:

If parent [*k*] = 0 then v_k is the root of a tree.

If Parent [*k*] = *j* then v_j is the parent of v_k.

Assume that we have an array of *E* that contains the information on the edges of the graph.

```
E:  ARRAY  [1..  n]  OF  RECORD
       v1,  v2:  1..m;
       wgt:  Real;
       span:  Boolean
       END
```

We will use the span field to keep track of whether an edge is part of the spanning tree that is being constructed. This field is initialized to False at the start of the algorithm.

The following function returns the root of the tree contains vertex *k*.

```
FUNCTION Root  (K:  1..m):  1..m;
BEGIN
If Parent[k]  =  0  THEN  Root:=  k
                               ELSE  Root:=  Root  (Parent  [k])
END;
```

Merge is a very simple procedure that merges two trees as required in the algorithm. Note that our version does not minimize the depth of the resulting tree.

```
PROCEDURE Merge  (VAR  P:  ARRAY[1...m]
    of Integer;  j,  k:1  ..  m);
BEGIN
    P  [k]:  =j
END;
```

17.42.1.3 Kruskal's Algorithm–Version 3

1. Sort the edges in *E* in ascending order according to the weight field.
2. For *i*: = 1 TO *m* DO Parent [*i*]: = 0;
3. For *j*: = 1 TO *n* DO *E*[*j*]. span:= False;
4. *r*: = 0 (*number of edges in the current spanning set*)
5. *q*: = 1 (*index of the current edge to be examined*)
6. While $r \le (m - 2)$ and $q \le n$ DO

    6.1. *j*: ≥ Root (*E*[*q*]. v_1)

6.2. k: = Root ($E[q]$. v_2)

6.3. IF $j = k$

```
THEN q:  =  q  + 1
     ELSE  BEGIN
          Merge  (parent,  j,  k);
          E[q].  span:  =  True;
          r:  =  r  +  1;
          q:  =  q  +  1
     END;
```

The algorithm terminates with a minimum spanning tree if $r = m - 1$; otherwise, the graph is not connected.

17.43 BINARY TREES

An ordered rooted tree is a rooted tree whose subtrees are put into a definite order and are, themselves, ordered rooted trees. An empty tree and a single vertex with no descendants (no subtrees) are ordered rooted

Example 17.47 The trees in Fig. 17.77 are identical rooted trees, but as ordered trees, they are different.

If a tree rooted at v has p subtrees, we would refer to them as the first, second, ..., p^{th} subtrees. If we restrict the number of subtrees of each vertex to be less than or equal to two, we have binary (ordered) tree.

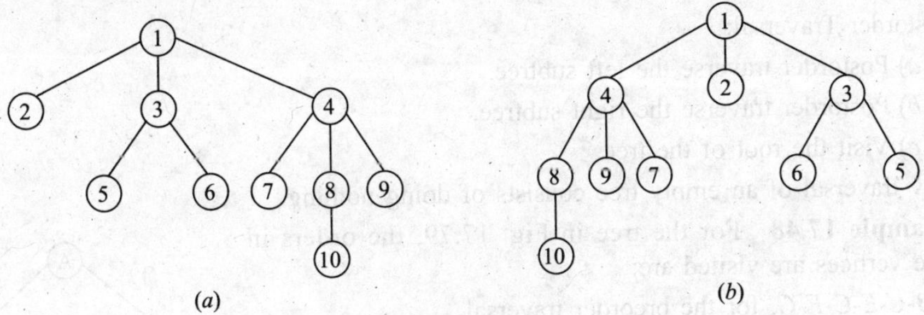

Fig. 17.77

Definition 17.19 **Binary Tree.** A binary tree is

(*a*) a tree consisting of no vertices (the empty tree), or

(*b*) a vertex with two subtrees that are both binary trees. The subtrees are called the left and right subtrees.

The difference between binary trees and ordered trees is that every vertex of a binary tree has exactly two subtrees (one or both of which may be empty), while a vertex of an ordered tree may have any number of subtrees. The two trees in Fig. 17.78 would be considered identical as ordered trees; however, they are different binary trees. Tree *a* has an empty right subtree and Tree *b* has an empty left subtree.

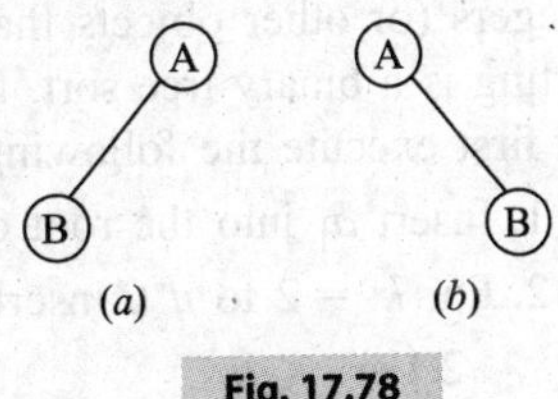

Fig. 17.78

17.43.1 Terminology and General Facts

(*a*) A vertex of a binary tree with two empty subtrees is called a *leaf*. All other vertices are called *internal vertices*.

(*b*) The number of leaves in a binary tree can vary from one up to roughly half the number of vertices in the tree (see Exercise 4 of this section).

(*c*) The maximum number of vertices at level k of a binary tree is 2^k, $k \geq 0$ (see Exercise 5 of this section).

(*d*) A *full binary tree* is a tree in which each vertex has either zero or two empty subtrees. In other words, each vertex has either two or zero children. See Exercise 6 of this section for a general fact about full binary trees.

17.43.2 Traversals of Binary Trees

The traversal of a binary tree consists of visiting each vertex of the tree in some prescribed order. Unlike graph traversals, the consecutive vertices that are visited are not always connected with an edge. The most common binary tree traversals are differentiated by the order in which the root and its subtrees are visited. The three traversals are best described recursively and are:

1. Preorder Traversal:
   (*a*) Visit the root of the tree.
   (*b*) Preorder traverse the left subtree.
   (*c*) Preorder traverse the right subtree.
2. Inorder Traversal:
   (*a*) Inorder traverse the left subtree.
   (*b*) Visit the root of the tree.
   (*c*) In order traverse the right subtree.
3. Postorder Traversal:
   (*a*) Postorder traverse the left subtree.
   (*b*) Postorder traverse the right subtree.
   (*c*) Visit the root of the tree.

Any traversal of an empty tree consists of doing nothing.

Example 17.48 For the tree in Fig. 17.79, the orders in which the vertices are visited are:

A-B-C-E-C-F-G, for the preorder traversal,

D-B-E-A-F-C-G, for the inorder traversal, and

D-E-B-F-G-C-A, for the preorder traversal.

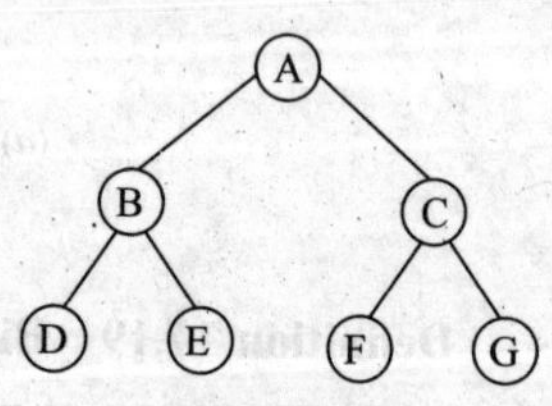

Fig. 17.79

Example 17.49 Binary Tree Sort. Given a collection of integers (or other objects than can be ordered), one technique for sorting is a binary tree sort. If the integers are $a_1, a_2, ..., a_n, n \geq 1$, we first execute the following algorithm that creates a binary tree.

1. Insert a_1 into the root of the tree.
2. For k: = 2 to n (*insert a_k into the tree*)
   2.1. r: = a_1
   2.2. inserted E: = false
   2.3. While not inserted do
   If $a_k < r$ then
   if r has a left child
   then r: = left child of r
   else make a_k the left child of r and

inserted: = true
else (*$ak \geq r$*
if r has a right child
then r: = right child of r
else make a_k the right child of r and
inserted: = true

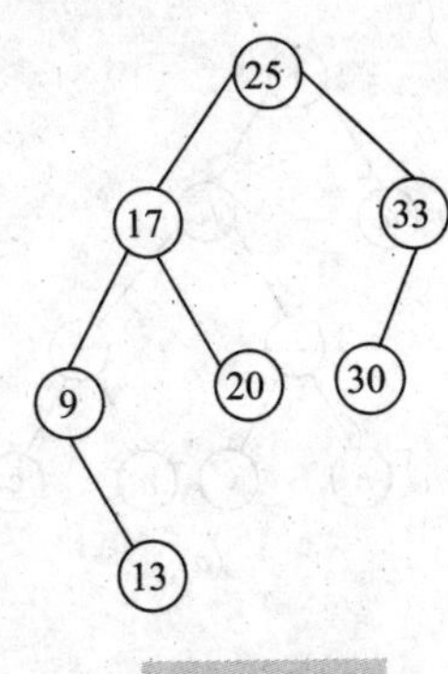

Fig. 17.80

If the integers to be sorted are 25, 17, 9, 20, 33, 13, and 30, then the tree that is created is the one in Fig. 17.80. The inorder traversal of this tree is 9, 13, 17, 20, 25, 30, 33, the integers in ascending order. In general, the inorder traversal of the tree that is constructed in the algorithm above will produce a sorted list. The preorder and postorder traversals of the tree have no meaning.

17.43.3 Expression Trees

A convenient way to represent an algebraic expression is by its expression tree. Consider the expression $X = a*b - c/d + e$. Since it is customary to put a precedence on multiplication/division, X is evaluated as $((a*b)-(c/d))+e$. Consecutive multiplication/division or addition/subtraction are evaluated from left to right. We can analyse X further by noting that it is the sum of two simpler expression $(a*b) - (c/d)$ and e. The first of these expressions can be broken down further into the difference of the expressions $a*b$ and c/d. When the decompose any expression into (left expression) (operation) (right expression), the expression tree of that expression is the binary tree whose root contains the operation and whose left and right subtrees are the trees of the left and right expression, respectively. Additionally, a simple variable or a number has an expression tree which is a single vertex containing the variable or number. The evolution of the expression tree for expression X appears in Fig. 17.81.

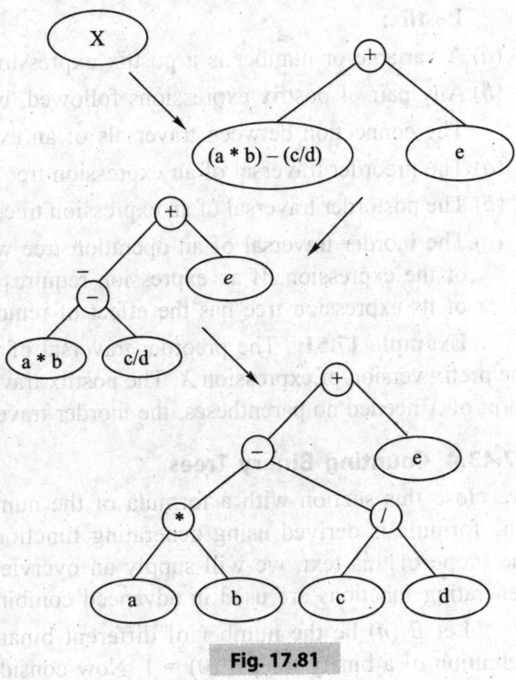

Fig. 17.81

Example 17.50.

(*a*) If we intend to apply the addition and subtraction operations in X first, we would parenthesize * expression to $a*(b - c)/(d + e)$. Its expression tree appears in Fig. 17.82 (*a*).

(*b*) The expression trees for $a^2 - b^2$ and for $(a + b)*\ (a - b)$ appear in Figs. 17.82 (*b*) and 17.82 (*c*).

The three traversals of an operation tree are all significant. A binary operation applied to a pair of numbers can be written in three ways. One is the familiar *infix* form, such as $a + b$ for the sum of a and b. Another form is *prefix*, in which the same sum is written $+\ ab$. The final form is *postfix*, in which the sum is written $ab\ +$ Algebraic expressions involving the four standard arithmetic operations (+, –, *, and /) in prefix and postfix form are defined as follows:

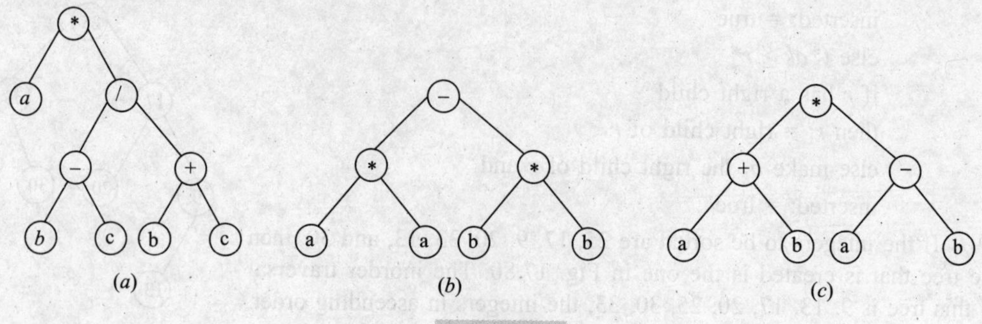

Fig. 17.82

Prefix:

(*a*) A variable or number is a prefix expression.

(*b*) Any operation followed by a pair of prefix expressions is a prefix expression.

Postfix:

(*a*) A variable or number is a postfix expression.

(*b*) Any pair of postfix expressions followed, by an operation is a postfix expression.

The connection between traversals of an expression tree and these forms is simple:

(*a*) The preorder traversal of an expression tree will result in the prefix form of the expression.

(*b*) The postorder traversal of an expression tree will result in the postfix from of the expression.

(*c*) The inorder traversal of an operation tree will not, in general, yield the proper infix form of the expression. If an expression requires parentheses in infix form, an inorder traversal of its expression tree has the effect of removing the parentheses.

Example 17.51 The preorder traversal of the tree in Fig. 17.81 is + – **ab*/*cde*, which is the prefix version of expression *X*. The postfix traversal is *ab***cd*/– *e*+. Note that since the original form of *X* needed no parentheses, the inorder traversal, *a***b* – *c*/*d* + *e*, is the correct infix version.

17.43.4 Counting Binary Trees

We close this section with a formula of the number of different binary trees with *n* vertices. The formula is derived using generating functions. Although the complete details are beyond the scope of this text, we will supply an overview of the derivation in order to illustrate how generating functions are used in advanced combinatorics.

Let $B(n)$ be the number of different binary trees of size *n* (*n* vertices), $n \geq 0$. By our definition of a binary tree, $B(0) = 1$. Now consider any positive integer $n + 1$, $n \geq 0$. A binary tree of size $n + 1$ has two subtrees, the sizes of which add up to *n*. The possibilities can be broken down into $n + 1$ cases:

Case 0: Left subtree has size 0; right subtree has size *n*.

Case 1: Let subtree has size 1: right subtree has size $n - 1$.

⋮

Case *k:* Left subtree has size *k*; right subtree has size $n - k$.

⋮

Case *n*: Left subtree has size *n*; right subtree has size 0.

In case *k*, we can count the number of possibilities by multiplying the number of ways that the left subtree can be filled ($B(k)$) by the number of ways that the right subtree can be filled ($B(n - k)$). Since the sum of these products equals $B(n + 1)$, we obtain recurrence relation.

$$B\,(n+1) = B\,(0)\,B\,(n) + B\,(1)\,B\,(n-1) + \ldots + B\,(n)\,B\,(0)$$
$$= \sum_{k=0}^{n} (k)\,B\,(n-k),\ n \geq 0.$$

Now take the generating function of both sides of this recurrence relation:

$$\sum_{n=0}^{\infty} B\,(n+1)\,z^n = \sum_{n=0}^{\infty}\left[\sum_{k=0}^{n} B\,(k)\,B\,(n-k)\right] z^n$$

or $G\,(B\uparrow;z) = G\,(B{*}B;z) = G\,(B;z)^2$. Therefore, if we abbreviate $G\,(B;z)$ to G, we obtain $(G - B\,(0))/z = G^2$ or $G - 1 = zG^2$, since $B\,(0) = 1$. We can write this final equation in the standard form of a quadratic equation in the unknown $G : zG^2 - G + 1 = 0$. The two solutions of this equation are

$$G_1 = (1 + \sqrt{1-4z})/2z$$

and
$$G_2 = (1 + \sqrt{1-4z})/2z.$$

The gap in our deviation occurs here. By applying calculus techniques, we can eliminate G_2 and so $G\,(B;z) = G_1$. After expanding G_1 by something called its. Taylor series, we can obtain a closed from expression for $B\,(n)$, which is simplified to

$$B\,(n) = \frac{1}{n+1}\binom{2n}{n}.$$

REVIEW QUESTIONS

1. Which of the following statements declares a one-dimensional character array named item that consists of five elements?
   (*a*) `char item [0 to 4] = '';` (*b*) `char item [0 to 5) = '';`
   (*c*) `char item [4] = '';` (*d*) `char item [5) = '';`
2. Which of the following is false?
   (*a*) Data stored in an array can be accessed faster than data stored in a disk file.
   (*b*) Data stored in an array needs to be entered only once, typically at the beginning of the program.
   (*c*) Arrays allow the programmer to store information in the computer's internal memory.
   (*d*) When using arrays, you will have fewer variable names to remember.
   (*e*) None of the preceding statements are false.
3. `Stock [2]` is read
   (*a*) stock 2 (*b*) stock bracket 2
   (*c*) stock bracket 2 (*d*) stock sub 2
   (*e*) 2 sub stock
4. Elements in an array are identified by a unique _______.
   (*a*) data type (*b*) order
   (*c*) subscript (*d*) symbol
5. Which of the following is false?
   (*a*) The elements in an array are related in some way
   (*b*) C++ automatically passes arrays by reference
   (*c*) All of the elements in an array have the same data type
   (*d*) All of the elements in an array have the same subscript
   (*e*) All of the elements in an array have the same name.

Use the following array, named empName, to answer questions 6 through 8. The array was created with the following statement: `char empName [5] = 'Mary';`

M	a	r	y	\0

6. The cout << empName [1] statement will display________.
   (*a*) *M* (*b*) *a* (*c*) *r* (*d*) *y*
   (*e*) the null character
7. The `empName [3] = 'k';` statement will ________.
   (*a*) replace the letter *r* with the letter *k* (*b*) replace the letter *y* with the letter *k*
   (*c*) replace the letter *k* with the letter *r* (*d*) replace the letter *k* with the letter *y*
   (*e*) have no effect on the array.
8. The `empName [0] = empName [2];` statement will________.
   (*a*) replace the letter *M* with the letter *r*. (*b*) replace the letter *r* with the letter *M*
   (*c*) replace the letter *M* with the letters Mr (*d*) result in an error.
9. C++ automatically passes two-dimensional arrays by ________.
   (*a*) reference (*b*) value.
10. The individual elements in a two-dimensional array are identified by a unique________.
    (*a*) combination of two subscripts (*b*) combination of two names
    (*c*) data type (*d*) order
    (*e*) subscript
11. The first element in a two-dimensional array has a row subscript of ________ and a column subscript of.
    (*a*) 0, 0 (*b*) 0, 1 (*c*) 1, 0 (*d*) 1, 1
12. If the `item [2] [3]` element in the item array stores a Short Integer number, then the `item [3] [4]` element in the item array________.
    (*a*) can store either a Short Integer or a Float number
    (*b*) can store either a Short Integer or a Long Integer number
    (*c*) must store a Short Integer number
13. `stock [2] [4]` is read ________.
    (*a*) stock two sub four (*b*) stock array two sub four
    (*c*) stock bracket two bracket four (*d*) stock sub two sub four
    (*e*) stock sub two four.
14. Sorting data means to arrange it in ________order.
    (*a*) alphabetical (*b*) numerical (*c*) either alphabetical or numerical.
15. Data sorted from the largest value to the smallest value is sorted in ________ order.
    (*a*) ascending (b) descending.
16. Value for which you are searching is called the:
    (*a*) binary value (b) key (*c*) search argument (*d*) serial value.
17. If the binary search algorithm determines that the search argument is in the upper half of the array, which of the following statements will set the appropriate variable to the appropriate value?
    (*a*) `startSub = middleSub - 1;` (*b*) `startSub = middleSub + 1;`
    (*c*) `stopSub = middleSub - 1;` (*d*) `stopSub = middleSub + 1;`
18. If the binary search algorithm determines that the search argument is in the lower half of the array, which of the following statements will set the appropriate variable to the appropriate value?
    (*a*) `startSub = middleSub - 1;` (*b*) `startSub = middleSub + 1;`
    (*c*) `stopSub = middleSub - 1;` (*d*) `stopSub = middleSub + 1;`

19. If the which of the following statements is used in the binary search algorithm to halve the array?

(*a*) middleSub = (StartSub + stopSub)/2; (*b*) middleSub = StartSub + stopSub/2;

(*c*) middleSub = middleSub/2; (*d*) middleSub = (stopSub – startSub)/2;

20. Which of the following is false?

(*a*) A binary search begins with the middle element in the array

(*b*) A binary search continues halving the array either until a match is found or until there are no more elements to search

(*c*) If the search argument is greater than the value located in the middle of the array, the binary search continues in the lower half of the array

(*d*) For a binary search to work, the data in the array must be arranged in either alphabetical or numerical order.

21. Which of the following is false?

(*a*) A serial search begins with the first array element

(*b*) A serial search continues searching, element by element, either until a match is found or until the end of the array is encountered

(*c*) A serial search is useful when the amount of data that must be searched is small

(*d*) For a serial search to work, the data in the array must be arranged in either alphabetical or numerical order.

22. Thesort algorithm works by comparing adjacent array elements and swapping ones that are out of order.

(*a*) alphabetic (*b*) bubble (*c*) compare (*d*) list

(*e*) numeric.

23. When you use the bubble sort, the first step in swapping two of the elements in the salary array is to:

(*a*) assign salary [*x*] to temp (*b*) assign salary [*x* + 2] to temp

(*c*) assign salary [*x*] to salary [*x* + 1] (*d*) assign temp to salary [*x*]

(*e*) assign temp to salary [*x* + 1]

24. Evaluate the following prefix expressions:

(*a*) + *2 +/ 14 2 5 1 (*b*) – * 6 3 – 4 1 (*c*) + + 2 6 + – 13 2 4

25. Evaluate the following postfix expressions:

(*a*) 6 4 + 1 3/ (*b*) 1 4 18 6 / 3 + + 5 / +

(*c*) 1 16 8 4 2 / / / + 5 *

26. Convert the following infix expressions to prefix notation:

(*a*) $((A + 2) * (B + 4)) - 1$ (*b*) $Z - ((((X + 1) * 2) - 5)/Y)$

(*c*) $((C * 2) + 1)/(A + B)$

27. True or False:

(*a*) Parenthesis are never needed in prefix or postfix expressions.

(*b*) The relative order of the operators in an infix expression is exactly the reverse of the order of the operators in the equivalent postfix expression.

(*c*) A postfix expression is merely the reverse of the prefix expression.

(*d*) A stack may be used to aid in evaluating a prefix expression.

28. Indicate whether each of the following applications would be suitable for a FIFO queue.

(*a*) An ailing company wants to evaluate employee records in order to lay off some workers on the basis of service time (the most recently hired employees will be laid off first.)

(*b*) A program is to keep track of patients as they check into a clinic, assigning them to doctors on a first-come, first-served basis.

(*c*) A program to solve a maze is to backtrack to an earlier position (the last place were a choice was made) when a dead-end position is reached.

(*d*) An inventory of parts is to be processed by part number.

(*e*) An operating system is to process requests for computer resources by allocating the resources in the order in which they are requested.

(*f*) A grocery chain wants to run a simulation to see how average customer wait time would be affected by changing the number of checkout lines in the stores.

(*g*) A dictionary of words used by a spelling checker is to be created.

(*h*) Customers are to take numbers at a bakery and be served in order when their numbers come up.

(*i*) Gamblers are to take numbers in the lottery and win if their numbers are picked.

29. What is the full form of FIFO?

30. What does 'rear' and 'front' signify in a queue?

31. What is Dequeue and Enqueue?

32. (*a*) Explain the difference between a sequential and a linked representation of a list.

(*b*) Give an example of a problem for which a sequential list would be the better solution.

(*c*) Give an example of a problem for which a linked list would be the better solution.

33. True or False. If you answer False, correct the statement.

(*a*) An array is a random-access structure.

(*b*) A sequential list is a random-access structure.

34. Write a program that reads a list of integers from the keyboard, creates a linked list from them, and prints the result.

35. Write a function that accepts a linked list, traverses it, and returns the data in the node with the minimum key value.

36. Write a function that traverses a linked list and deletes all nodes that are after a node with a negative key.

37. Write a function that traverses a linked list and deletes all nodes that are before a node with a negative key.

38. Write a function that traverses a linked list and deletes all nodes whose key are negative.

39. Write a function that returns a pointer to the last node in a linked list.

40. Write a function that appends two linked lists together.

41. Write a function that appends a linked list to itself.

42. What is the difference between a singly-linked list and a doubly linked list.

43. Name some data structure that use static memory allocation?

44. What is the difference between a linked list and circular link list?

45. Write an algorithm that simulates a stack with the help of a linked list.

46. Write an algorithm that simulates a Queue with the help of a linked list.

47. What is the significance of the fact that there is a path connecting vertex *B* with every other vertex in Fig. 17.41, as it applies to various situations that it models?

48. Draw a graph similar to Fig. 17.40 that represents the set of strings of 0's and l's containing no more than two consecutive 1's.

49. Draw a directed graph which models the set of strings of 0's and 1's where all of the l's must appear consecutively. Assume that the starting vertex has indegree 0.

50. In the NCAA final-four basketball tournament, the East champion plays the West champion, and the champions from the Mideast and Midwest play. The winners of the two games play for the national championship. Draw the eight different single-elimination tournament graphs that could occur.

51. Can a simple undirected graph of eight vertices have forty edges excluding self-loops?

52. Which of the graphs in Fig. 17.83 are isomorphic? What is the correspondence between their vertices?

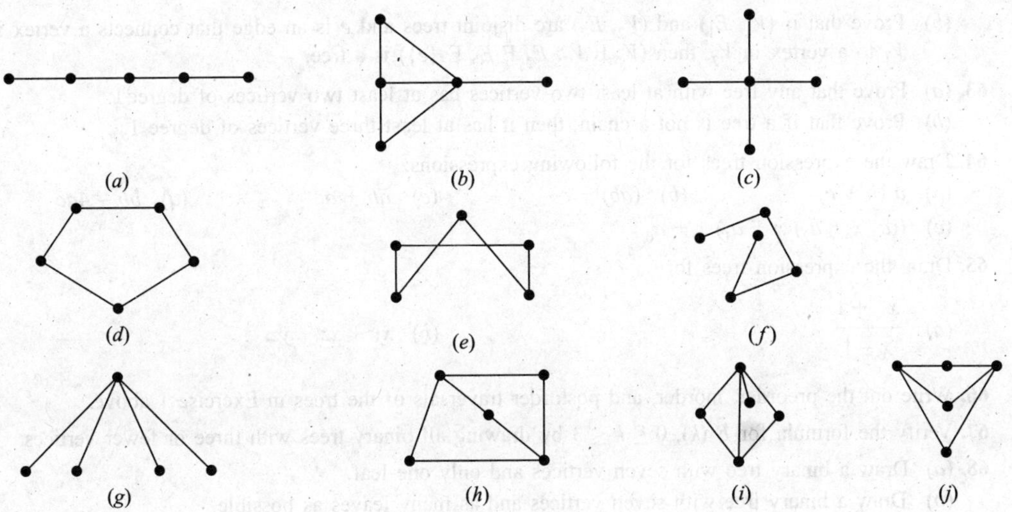

(a) (b) (c)

(d) (e) (f)

(g) (h) (i) (j)

Fig. 17.83

53. (*a*) How many edges does a complete tournament graph with n vertices have?
(*b*) How many edges does a single-elimination tournament graph with *n* vertices have?

54. Draw a complete undirected graph with 1, 2, 3, 4, and 5 vertices. How many edge does a K_n have?

55. Describe appropriate data structures to represent the following graphs. Include information fields that you feel are appro-priate.

(*a*) **Vertices:** Cities of the world that are served by at least one airline. Edges: Pairs of cities that are connected by a regular direct flight.

(*b*) **Vertices:** The top 20 microcomputer systems (in terms of sales). Edges: An edge connects C_A to C_B to C_A has been evaluated to be 'as good as' C_B by an independent evaluating group.

(*c*) **Vertices:** All English words. Edges: An edge connects word *x* to word *y* if *x* is a prefix of *y*.

(*d*) **Vertices:** ASCII characters. Edges: Edges connect characters that differ in their binary code by exactly two bits.

56. Each edge of a graph is colored with one of the four colors red, blue, yellow, or green. How could you represent the edges in this graph using a variation of the adjacency matrix structure?

57. Let *G* be the graph in Fig. 17.84. What is the adjacency matrix for the graph *H* which has vertex set {1, 2, 3, 4} and has an edge from *i* to *j* if *G* has a path of length 2 from *i* to *j*?

58. Write a Boolean-values Pascal function to determine whether vertex 1 is connected to vertex *J* by an edge, where the edge information is stored in edge lists.

59. Given the following vertex sets, draw all possible undirected trees that connect them.

(*a*) V_a = {*right, left*} (*b*) V_b = {+, –, 0}

(*c*) V_c = {*north, south, east, west*}.

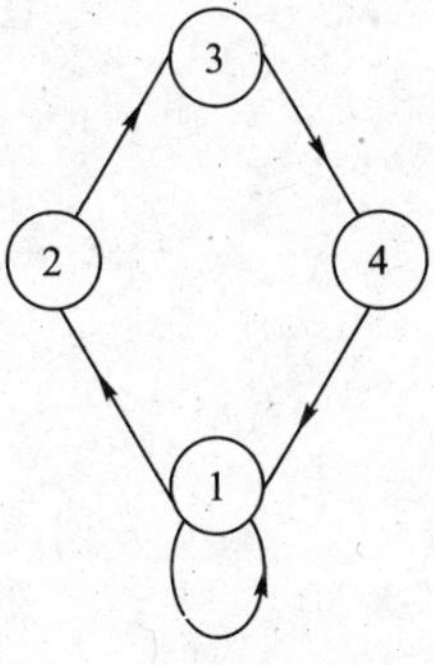

3 2 4 1

Fig. 17.84

60. Are all trees planar? If they are, can you explain why? If they are not, you should be able to find a non-planar tree.

61. Prove that if *G* is a simple undirected graph with no self-loops, then *G* is a tree if and only if *G* is connected and #*E* = #*V* – 1.

62. (*a*) Prove that if *G* = (*V*, *E*) is a tree and *e* Î *E*, then (*V*, *E* – {*e*}) is a forest of two trees.

(*b*) Prove that if (V_1, E_1) and (V_2, E_2) are disjoint trees and e is an edge that connects a vertex in V_1 to a vertex in V_2, then (V_1 È V_2, E_2 È E_2 È $\{e\}$) is a tree.

63. (*a*) Prove that any tree with at least two vertices has at least two vertices of degree 1.

(*b*) Prove that if a tree is not a chain, then it has at least three vertices of degree 1.

64. Draw the expression trees for the following expressions:

(*a*) $a\,(b + c)$ (*b*) $(ab) + c$ (*c*) $ab + ac$ (*d*) $bb - 4ac$

(*e*) $((a_3\,x + a_2)\,x + a_1)\,x + a_0$

65. Draw the expression trees for

(*a*) $\dfrac{x^2 + 1}{x - 1}$ (*b*) $xy + xz + yz$.

66. Write out the preorder, inorder, and postorder traversals of the trees in Exercise 1 above.

67. Verify the formula for $B\,(k)$, $0 \le k \le 3$ by drawing all binary trees with three or fewer vertices.

68. (*a*) Draw a binary tree with seven vertices and only one leaf.

(*b*) Draw a binary tree with seven vertices and as many leaves as possible.

69. Prove that the maximum number of vertices at level k of a binary tree is 2^k and that a tree that many vertices at level k must have at least $2^{k+1} - 1$ vertices.

70. Prove that if T is full binary tree, then the number of leaves of T is one more than the number of internal vertices (non-leaves).

INTRODUCTION TO COMMUNICATION PROTOCOL: TCP/IP

18.1 INTRODUCTION

One of the problems with networks today is that there are many different protocols and network types. The hardware choices are confusing enough, but software protocol suites that run over the various types of network hardware solutions can absolutely boggle the mind. Ethernet, for instance, boasts a vast number of protocol suites such as DDCMP, LAT, MOP, XNS, SCS, TCP/IP, VRP, NRP and a slew of other three-letter acronyms for various protocols that will solve all the problems a customer could possibly have.

Within the scheme of protocols, however, some still seem to rear their ugly heads, no matter how hard the industry tries to put them down or get rid of them. One suite, **Transmission Control Protocol/Internet Protocol (TCP/IP)**, is such an occurrence. Every other vendor of networks will claim that their protocol is better and that TCP/IP is going away. Some will point to the decisions made by the US Department of Defense (DOD) to eventually migrate to internationally recognized and standardized communications hardware and protocols, obviating the need for TCP/IP and eventually replacing it. Some view TCP/IP as a workhorse whose time has come to be put out to pasture.

Then there are the zealots—those that think that the only communications protocol suite for use in the world is TCP/IP and all others are fluff. These folks are dangerous because they not only are vocal about TCP/IP, many times they are UNIX zealots as well.

Somewhere in the middle of the two camps are those who do not know what to do with TCP/IP or, worse, do not even really understand its significance to networks. Unfortunately, these individuals are usually the managers of such diverse camps of attitudes and must make decisions on whether to use TCP/IP on a project or not.

Although it is the ISO open systems protocols which have received most recent publicity, there are other well established protocol sets, particularly on Ethernet, which have a large share of the current LAN market. Some argue that these protocols offer a better alternative to the largely untried and potentially cumbersome ISO set, but most manufacturers indicate a willingness to adopt ISO protocols at some point of time in future.

The non-ISO protocol described in this chapter illustrate different approach from the ISO protocol set to Open Systems working. TCP/IP, is a vendor-independent wide area network protocol set, which has been widely used on LANs for peer-to-peer communications. Here, we will examine the TCP and IP networking protocols and some implementations that have become de-facto standards in the military area as well as academic and UNIX areas.

In recent years, knowledge of the capabilities of Transmission Control Protocol/Internet Protocol (TCP/IP) has spread far in the globe. IT managers in all types of organizations have begun to research its suitability as an internetworking. TCP/IP seems to be a ready-made solution to the commercial information systems requirements of intercommunication and interoperation.

In US, government officials and research communities and many UNIX aficionados are already well versed in the vocabulary and configuration issues of this set of protocols. But for the newcomer to TCP/IP, the existing sources of information are, in many cases, written by developers apparently for developers. Most information is primarily technical with detailed descriptions of the bits, flags and fields of the protocols. But less information is given about the practical problems of implementing TCP/IP from scratch. For example, in a commercial rather than a technical or research environment; here the skills and constraints may be very different. The information needed does exist, but one has to read a considerable quantity of material before finding what one needs.

18.2 ORIGIN OF TCP/IP

A comprehensive set of 'ready-made' communications protocols called TCP/IP became widely available and well-known only when Berkeley Software Distribution released Berkeley UNIX 4.2BSD in September 1983. This was not a coincidence; its inclusion in this release was funded by the US government. TCP/IP protocols are based on standards originally developed for the US government and US research community. With the release of UNIX 4.2BSD, these communications standards emerged from the confines of the US Department of Defense and the US university and research networks; TCP/IP became *the way* to interconnect UNIX systems. Berkeley UNIX 4.2BSD and subsequent releases spread quickly throughout the US university and commercial communities. With UNIX achieving wide popularity as an 'open system', the fame of TCP/IP has continued to spread. But TCP/IP is not and never has been, narrowly confined to UNIX. It was developed to allow free interchange of data among all machines, independent of type, manufacturer, hardware or operating system.

In the late 1980s, TCP/IP received a further boost to its fortunes when Sun Microsystems published the specification for Open Network Computing (ONC), often called the **Network File System (NFS)**. NFS adds important functions to TCP/IP and is now very widely available and regarded as an integral part of the TCP/IP protocol suite. It is particularly valuable for the commercial implementor because of the simple user interfaces that it provides.

TCP/IP was developed to satisfy the need to interconnect various projects that included computer networks and also allow for the addition of dissimilar machines to the networks in a systematic and standardized manner. While it is quite true that smaller defense projects may not have warranted the use of TCP/IP for project aspects, edicts from various DOD concerns such as the Undersecretary of Defense for Research and Development forced many government contractors and in-house developed projects to use the suite to conform with DOD requirements.

The suite of protocols commonly referred to as TCP/IP (US Military Standards 1778 and 1777) was developed by the United States Department of Defense for its A.R.P.A. (Advanced Research Project Agency) network. This is a very large scale wide area network linking many major commercial, university and military establishments. The relevance of TCP/IP to LANs is two-fold. First, as it is a datagram based protocol, it is well suited to LAN access methods, particularly Ethernet. Secondly, it is particularly popular within the UNIX community, giving it a large user base, many of whom wish to use LANs.

Cost-effective implementations of TCP/IP are now available for all types and sizes of machines from the largest mainframe to personal computers and workstations. This has brought TCP/IP and its capabilities to the attention of a very wide audience. Computer managers and users in commercial organizations throughout the world have begun to implement TCP/IP as a way of solving the problems of interworking between machines of different manufacture.

TCP/IP provides all the facilities for two computer systems to exchange information (intercommunication), interpret it properly and present it in a format which can be understood by the local machine and its users (interoperation). NFS gives a simple and locally-familiar representation of a set of remote and possibly unfamiliar computer filing systems; like the original components of the TCP/IP suite, NFS is now available for many different computers.

18.3 TCP/IP LAYER OVERVIEW

Figure 18.1 illustrated TCP/IP four layer and also compare with OSI layer.

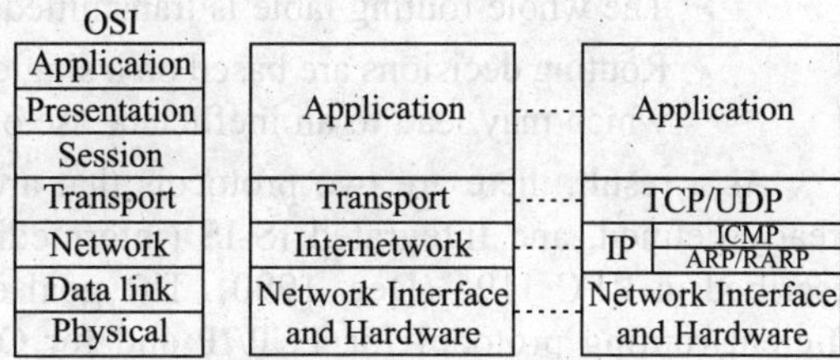

Fig. 18.1 TCP/IP functional layers

18.3.1 Application

Application is a user process cooperating with another process on the same or a different host. Examples are Telnet (protocol for remote terminal connections), FTP (File Transfer Protocol) and SMTP (Simple Mail Transfer Protocol). Other examples will be discussed later.

18.3.2 Transport

Transport provides the end-to-end data transfer. The two protocols at this layer are:

- ❒ **Transport Control Protocol (TCP)**, which is the end-to-end reliable connection-oriented protocol providing flow-controlled, error-free logical connections between pairs of processes.
- ❒ **User Datagram Protocol (UDP)**, which is basically an application interface to IP. It is connectionless, and adds no reliability, flow-control or error recovery to IP. It simply serves as a 'multiplexer/demultiplexer' for sending/receiving IP datagrams. An IP datagram (Internet datagram) is the base transfer packet in the Internet protocol suite. It has a header containing information for IP, and data that is only relevant to the higher level protocols.

18.3.3 Internetwork

Internetwork provides the 'virtual network' image of the Internet. (That is, this layer shields the higher levels from the network architecture below it).

The protocols at this layer are:

- ❒ **Internet Protocol (IP)** is the most important protocol in this group. It is the 'layer' that hides the underlying physical network by creating a virtual network view. It is an unreliable, best-effort connectionless packet delivery protocol that moves data between the intermediate nodes, referred to as routers. It adds no reliability, flow control or error recovery, and also does not assume reliability from the lower layers.
- ❒ **Internet Control Message Protocol (ICMP)** is the protocol used to report errors and control messages at the IP layer. Although ICMP uses IP as if it were a higher level protocol, it is actually part of the IP protocol.
- ❒ **Address Resolution Protocol (ARP)** is the end station to router protocol used to dynamically map Internet addresses to physical (hardware) addresses on local area networks. This protocol is limited to networks that support hardware broadcast.
- ❒ **Reverse Address Resolution Protocol (RARP)** is the protocol that a diskless host (an end node) uses to find its Internet address at startup. RARP maps a physical (hardware) address to an Internet address.

- **Open Shortest Path First (OSPF)**, which is a proposed standard protocol, is an IP routing protocol that uses an algorithm to build a routing table that is used to find the shortest path to every gateway and network the gateway can reach. This protocol uses a link-state algorithm to compute routes, which is more efficient than the vector-distance protocol used by RIP.

  Note: APPN also uses a link-state routing protocol.
- **Routing Information Protocol (RIP)**, which is a vector-distance protocol, is today's most widely used routing protocol for IP networks. It does not, however, have the capability to handle larger internetwork configurations because:
  - The algorithm is run every 30 seconds.
  - The whole routing table is transmitted, which causes network overhead.
  - Routing decisions are based on a single criterion: the number of hops between stations, which may lead to an inefficient use of the network.

As a result, there are two protocols that are vying to replace RIP: OSPF, which we have already defined, and Integrated IS-IS (intermediate system to intermediate system), which is described in RFC 1195 (Dec. 1990). The goal of Integrated IS-IS is to provide a single and efficient routing protocol for TCP/IP and for OSI. Its design extends the OSI IS-IS routing protocol (the ISO-specific protocol for routing within a single routing domain) to encompass TCP/IP. Both OSPF and Integrated IS-IS are link-state protocols, which route information differently than vector-distance protocols, the protocol used by RIP.

18.3.4 Network Interface

Network Interface is the interface to the actual network hardware. This interface may or may not provide reliable delivery, and may be packet or stream-oriented. In fact, TCP/IP does not specify any protocol here, but can use almost any network interface available, which illustrates the flexibility of the IP layer. Examples are IEEE 802.2 (for local area networks, such as the IBM Token-Ring network, or contention-type local area networks, such as Ethernet and CSMA/CD networks), X.25 (which is reliable in itself), and Packet Radio Networks (such as the AlohaNet, which is the granddaddy of broadcast networks).

The actual interactions between the layers are shown by the arrows in Fig. 18.1.

18.4 TCP/IP COMMUNICATIONS ARCHITECTURE

An interconnected set of lines and terminals allowing processing to take place in one or several locations is usually viewed as a network. A network may have several hosts interacting with multiples of terminals. To bring structure to this view of a network, the concept of network architecture is proposed; this is a structured hardware and software design that supports the interconnection of a number of physical and logical components.

A network architecture is a way to define the set of rules to which these interconnecting elements must conform. It is not, however, a definition of how the internal design is made or how the functions in the network operate or how a rule is actually implemented. A network architecture is a statement of what services need to be provided to enable the network to follow one set of rules.

In the past several years the International Organization for Standardization (ISO) has developed a model of network architecture called the Open Systems Interconnection (OSI) model of network architecture. The goal of this model is to promote the interconnecting of networks of all types.

The underlying principle exploited by the OSI model is *layering*. The idea is to create a network architecture with several layers where each layer provides certain unique functions which are not provided by any of the other layer is strictly defined. Based on some standard structuring techniques, the OSI model defines seven distinct layers, as shown in Fig. 18.2. Each layer need only interact with the adjacent layers and has no knowledge about any other layers, as shown in Fig. 18.3. Information flows down through the layers of the sending host and then up through the layers of the receiving host. Because the layers are isolated from each other by strict interfaces, information that is added by a layer in the sending host will only be used by the matching layer in the receiving host. In this sense the matching layers of the sending and receiving hosts communicate with each other in a peer-to-peer relationship, as shown by the dotted lines connecting matching layers in Fig. 18.3.

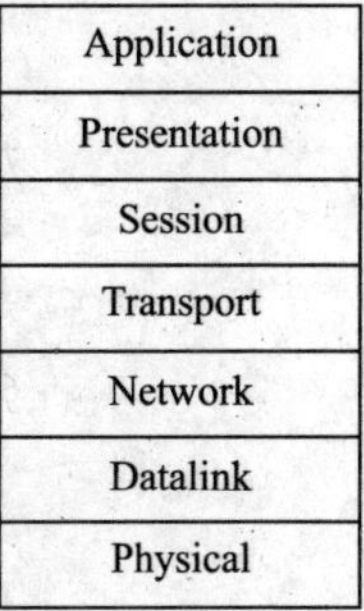

Fig. 18.2 ISO/OSI reference model

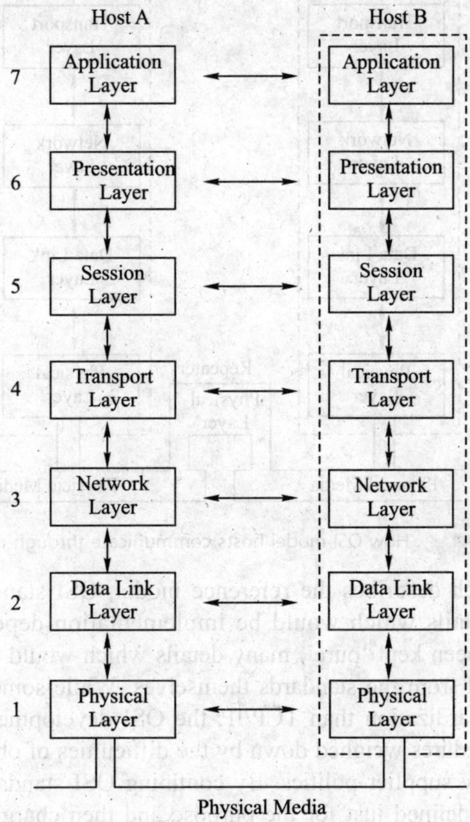

Fig. 18.3 How OSI model hosts communicate on the same network

Each layer adds value to the services provided by the set of lower layers in such a manner that the highest layer is offered the set of services needed to run an application distributed over several networks. Each layer provides services to the layer above and requests services from the layer below. Thus, the total network problem is divided into a set of smaller problems.

Intermediate networks that merely relay information from one network to another will only need to implement some of the lower three layers to act as transferal agents. Figures 18.4, 18.5, 18.6 and 18.7 illustrate this principle of the OSI scheme for differing network problems.

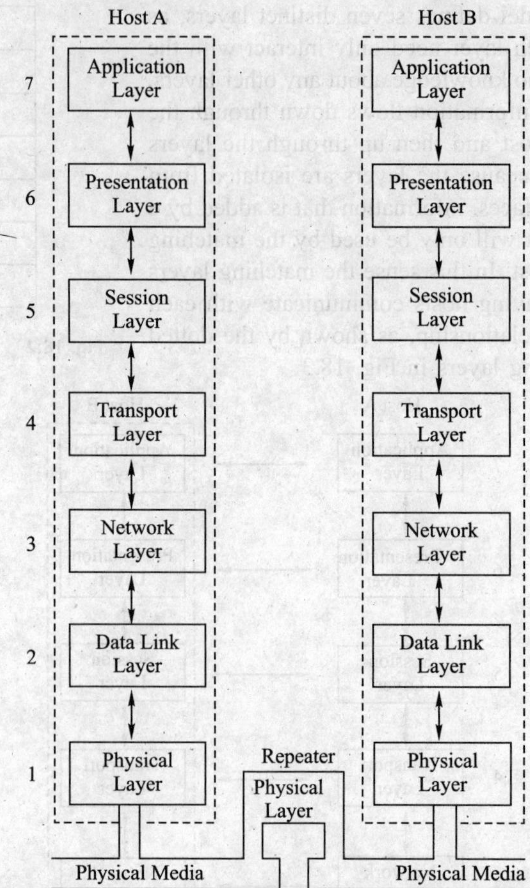

Fig. 18.4 How OSI model hosts communicate through repeaters

In the standard which describes the reference model, OSI standard developers state that they will exclude any details which would be implementation dependent. The result is that while the standards have been kept 'pure', many details which would aid development of viable OSI products are excluded from the standards themselves. While some would argue that OSI is more rigorous in its standardization than TCP/IP, the OSI development process seems to have become enmeshed in procedures weighed down by the difficulties of obtaining consensus in large committees and dogged by supplier politics. By confining OSI standards to abstract definitions in a complex vocabulary, defined just for the purpose and then charging considerable sums for copies of those standards, ISO committees have, undoubtedly, if unintentionally, slowed the OSI development process and the delivery of useful conforming products.

With a more restricted geographic and technical scope, TCP/IP developers adopted a pragmatic approach. TCP/IP standardization was based on the Request For Comments (RFC), a flexible and fast standardizatiion process using electronic mail to publish and exchange comments and ideas and to update drafts. Developers often outlined parts of a standard in a familiar computer language, usually 'C' which, while not intended to be implemented directly, gave a very good starting point for an initial implementation.

TCP/IP standards are freely available on-line from a number of computer systems, originally without full drawings or graphics, but today with all the quality of a laser-printed, desktop-published document as PostScript files. For manufacturers of communications and computing products, the contrast with OSI could not be more stark; it is just so much easier to obtain TCP/IP information than OSI. Standards were produced more quickly and they are written in a readable and comprehensible form by developers for developers.

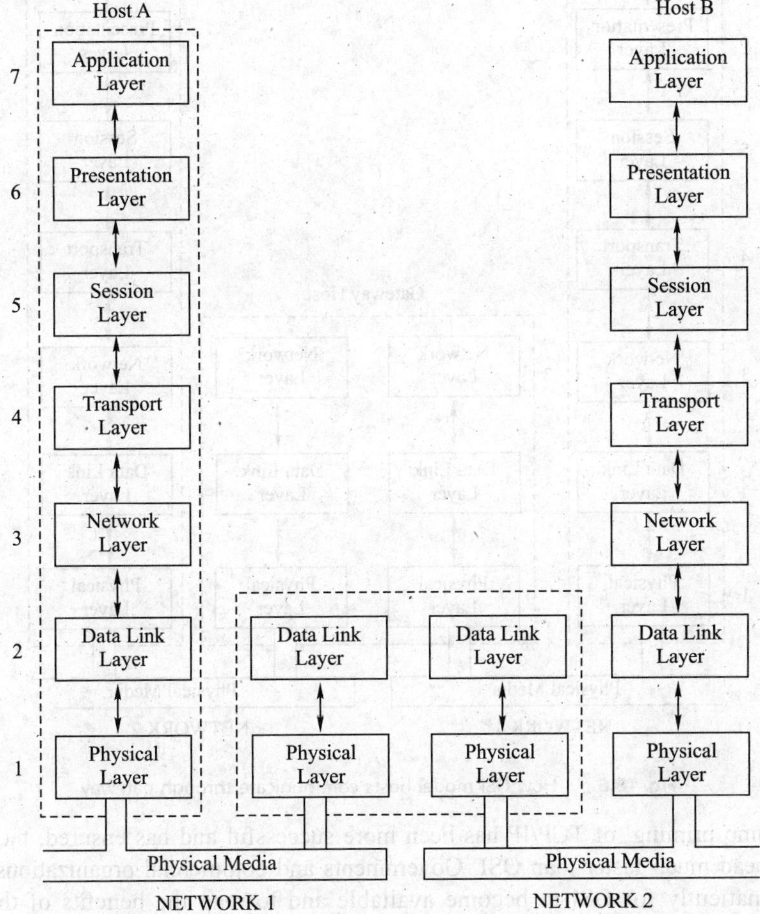

Fig. 18.5 How OSI model hosts communicate through bridge hosts

Ths US government demanded TCP/IP for all systems, thereby ensuring every US government computer supplier provided it. They also funded universities to implement the standards. In the USA, such publicly funded work enters the public domain and, if not of a military nature, is freely available to all citizens. While it may not be used directly for commercial purposes, having a working example in 'C' source code certainly assists future developments by commercial suppliers!

Neither OSI nor TCP/IP has been developed in isolation. There has been a considerable interchange of ideas and techniques, particularly evident in the changes in OSI since the mid-1980s with the development of the connectionless OSI suite. Nor have the OSI standards been ignored by suppliers. As with TCP/IP in the USA, universities have been busy developing OSI implementations and governments have, since the mid-1980s, required OSI-conforming products. But this activity has not as yet created a general market demand and the same level of fully developed OSI computing products, except perhaps with the notable exception of X.25 network equipment.

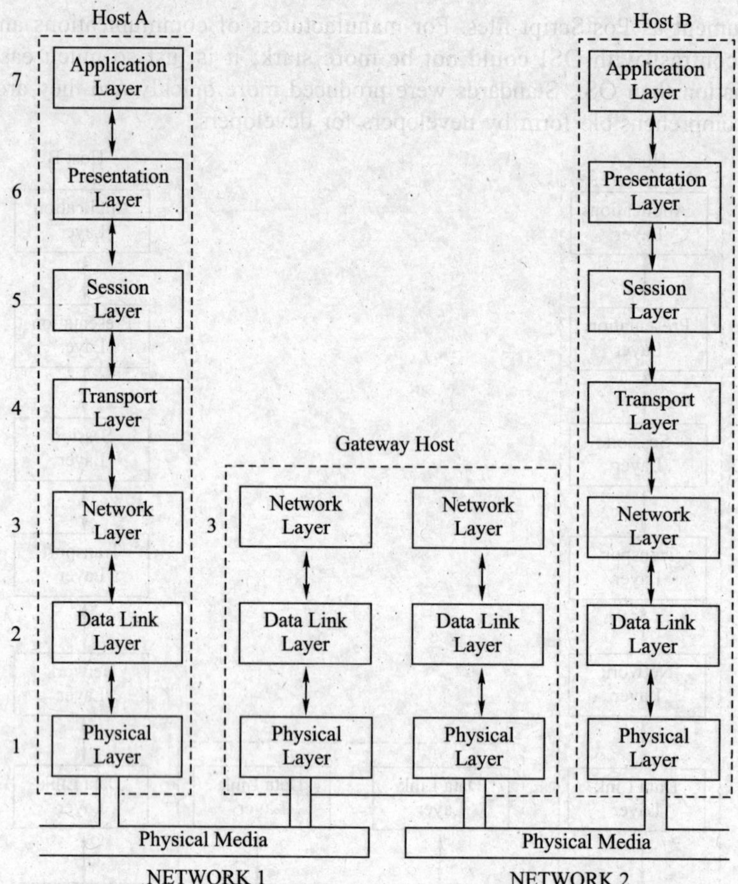

Fig. 18.6 How OSI model hosts communicate through gateway

The 'pump priming' of TCP/IP has been more successful and has ensured, thereby, that it has moved ahead much faster than OSI. Governments and commercial organizations worldwide have waited patiently for OSI to become available and to reap the benefits of the promised flexibility of an international standard for computer communications and inter operation. In short, the development of OSI has lagged considerably behind TCP/IP, despite support from a number of governments (including since 1985, the US government and Department of Defense).

When it comes to breaking down communications barriers between different computer suppliers, information systems managers in commercial companies now see TCP/IP as a fully functional, proven and low-cost alternative to open systems interconnection. OSI is still immature and almost unavailable. This may change in near future but the explosive interest in TCP/IP will, on the one hand, delay OSI implementation and on the other, encourage it as larger organizations come up against some of the known fundamental limitations of TCP/IP.

As with much of the specialist vocabulary which surrounds computers and telecommunications networks, the term TCP/IP will conjure up different concepts to different readers. TCP/IP is used as shorthand for a large set of standards with many different features and functions. The letters 'TCP/IP' stand for two communications protocols, Transmission Control Protocol (TCP) and Internet Protocol (IP). These were developed during the late 1970s and early 1980s as the key communications protocols for the US 'Internet', the collected set of interconnected communications networks (originally comprising ARPAnet, but now including NSFnet, and NYSERnet and the Department of Defense Network among many others). Today these support the US government, Department of Defense, US military, and the university, education and commercial organizations conduct research on behalf of those bodies. (Use of the US Internet for commercial traffic between commercial organizations is not allowed.)

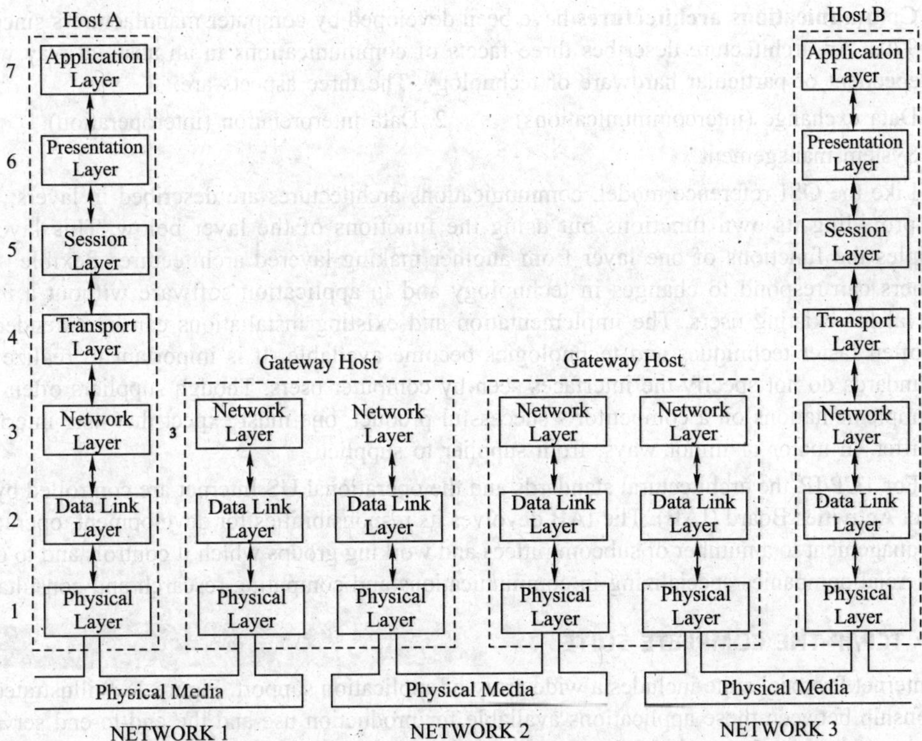

Fig. 18.7 How OSI model hots communicate through routers

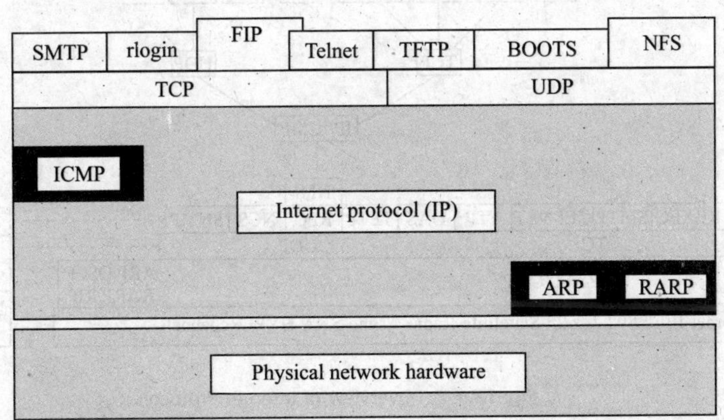

ARP Address Resolution Protocol
RARP Reverse Address Resolution Protocol
ICMP Internet Control Message Protocol
Rologin Remote login
FTP File Transfer Protocol
File Transfer Protocol
Telnet remote terminal login
TFTP Trivial File Transfer Protocol
BOOTP Boot Protocol
NFS Network File System
UDP User Datagram Protocol
TCP Transmission Control Protocol

Fig. 18.8 TCP/IP architecture

TCP and IP, are but two of the building blocks required for a complete communications 'architecture', but the term 'TCP/IP' is most often used as a **shorthand** term of the whole communications 'architecture' specified originally by the US Department of Defense. This architecture is a much bigger set of standards than just TCP and IP. We shall also use 'TCP/IP' to mean the complete architecture, except where this will cause confusion.

Communications architectures have been developed by computer manufacturers since the mid-1970s. An architecture describes three facets of communications in an abstract way which is independent of particular hardware or technology. The three aspects are:

1. Data exchange (intercommunications)
2. Data interpretation (interoperation)
3. System management

Like the OSI reference model, communications architectures are described in layers; each layer providing its own functions but using the functions of the layer below. This layering decouples the functions of one layer from another making layered architectures flexible; their designers can respond to changes in technology and in application software without a major upheaval for existing users. The implementation and existing installations can be extended, as new, often faster techniques and technologies become available. It is important to realize that the standards do not specify the interfaces seen by computer users. Though suppliers often base their implementations on a competitor's successful product, one must expect that user interfaces will differ, in major or minor ways, from supplier to supplier.

For TCP/IP, the architectural standards and the operational US Internet are controlled by the Internet Activities Board (IAB). The IAB devolves its responsibilities for development, operations and management to a number of subcommittees and working groups which it controls and to other commercial companies specializing in communications and computing research and consultancy.

18.5 TCP/IP-THE COMPLETE SUITE

The Internet Protocol suite includes a wide array of application support. Figure 18.9 illustrates the relationship between these applications available for production use and the end-to-end services. Also shown is how they map to the functional layers, discussed above.

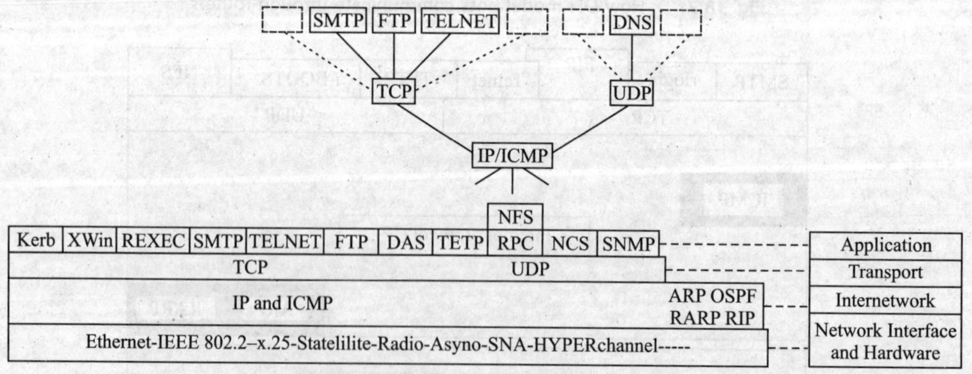

Fig. 18.9 Overview of Internet Protocols

- **Kerberos** is a widely-used, encryption-based, third-party authentication mechanism for network security, which was developed by the Massachusetts Institute of Technology (MIT). It provides mutual security checking between clients and servers in a network environment.
- **X Window System** is a popular windowing system developed by Project Athena at the Massachusetts Institute of Technology and implemented on a number of workstations. It

provides simultaneous views of local or remote programs/processes on a bit-mapped display and allows the application to run independently of terminal technology. For example, X-Windows may run on OS/2, DOS, and X-Windows terminals.

- **Remote Execution Protocol (REXEC)** is a protocol that allows the user to issue remote commands to a destination host implementing the REXEC server. The server performs an automatic login on a local machine to run the command. It is important to note that the command issued cannot be an interactive one; it can only be a batch process with a string output.

  Note: For remote login to interactive facilities, Telnet should be used.
- **Simple Mail Transfer Protocol (SMTP)** is the Internet electronic mail protocol, which provides store-and-forward service for textual electronic mail messages. Mail is sent from the normal local mail application to a background SMTP application that stores the mail and directly contacts the destination host's SMTP application. Thus, mail is kept local until successfully transmitted. RFC822 defines the format of those messages.
- **Telnet** is the Internet virtual terminal protocol, which allows users of one host to log into a remote host and interact as normal terminal users of that host.
- **File Transfer Protocol (FTP)** is the Internet protocol and program, which is used to transfer files between hosts. It uses TCP. The user must be identified to the server with a user ID and a password before any data transfer may proceed.
- **Domain Name System (DNS)** primarily provides mappings between host names and network addresses, and is used extensively in the Internet.
- **Trivial File Transfer Protocol (TFTP)** is a file transfer application implemented over the Internet UDP layer. It is a disk-to-disk data transfer, as opposed to, for example, the VM SENDFILE command, a function that is considered in the TCP/IP world as a mailing function, where you send out the data to a mailbox (or reader in the case of VM). TFTP can only read/write a file to/from a server, and therefore, is primarily used to transfer files among personal computers. TFTP allows files to be sent and received, but does not provide any password protection (or user authentication) or directory capability. TFTP was designed to be small enough to reside in ROM, and thus can be used with BOOTP to boot a diskless workstation.
- **Remote Procedure Call (RPC)** is an API for developing distributed applications, allowing them to call subroutines that are executed at a remote host. It is, therefore, an easy and popular paradigm for implementing the client/server model of distributed computing. A request is sent to a remote system (RPC server) to execute a designated procedure, using arguments supplied, and the result returned to the caller (RPC client). There are many variations and subtleties, resulting in a variety of different RPC protocols.
- **Network File System (NFS)** uses a remote procedure call (RPC) to implement a distributed file system. It was developed by SUN Microsystems, and allows authorized users to access files located on remote systems as if they were local.
- **Network Computing System (NCS)** is a distributed computing environment developed by Hewlett Packard/Apollo Computer. It provides tools for designing, implementing, and supporting applications requiring distributed data and distributed computing. NCS also formed the base for the Open Software Foundation (OSF) Distributed Computing Environment (DCE) definition.
- **Simple Network Management Protocol (SNMP)** is the network management protocol of choice for TCP/IP-based Internets. It is used to communicate management information between the network management applications in the network management station, and the network management agents in the network elements. The network management applications

may alter (set) or request (get) information from the Management Information Base (MIB) defined on each network element. In the other direction, the network element can send alerts (traps) to inform the management application as to the occurrence of asynchronous events.

18.6 INTERNET ARCHITECTURE

Two networks can only be connected by a computer that attaches to both of them. A physical attachment does not provide the interconnection we have in mind, because such a connection does not guarantee that the computer will cooperate with other machines that wish to communicate. To have a viable internet, we need computers that are willing to shuffle packets from one network to another. Computers which interconnect two networks and pass packets from one to the other are called *internet gateways* or *internet routers*.

Consider an example consisting of two physical networks shown in Fig. 18.10. In the figure, machine *G* connects to both network 1 and network 2. For *G* to act as a gateway, it must capture packets on network *1* that are bound for machines on network *2* and transfer them. Similarly, *G* must capture packets on network *2* that are destined for machines on network *1* and transfer them.

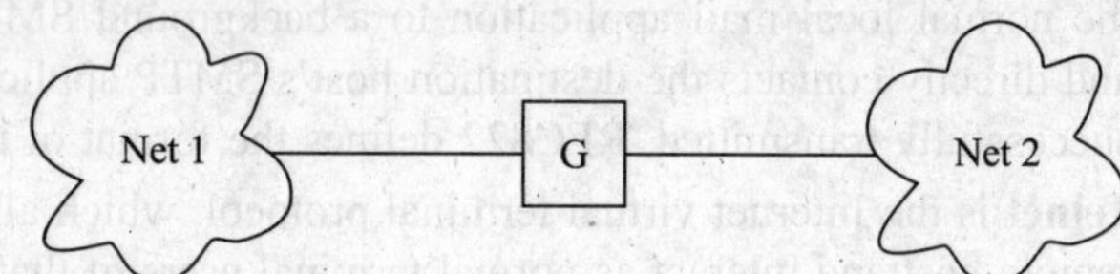

Fig. 18.10 Two networks interconnected by a gateway (G) or router

When internet connections become more complex, gateways need to know about the topology of the internet beyond the networks to which they connect. Figure 18.11 shows an example of three networks interconnected by two gateways.

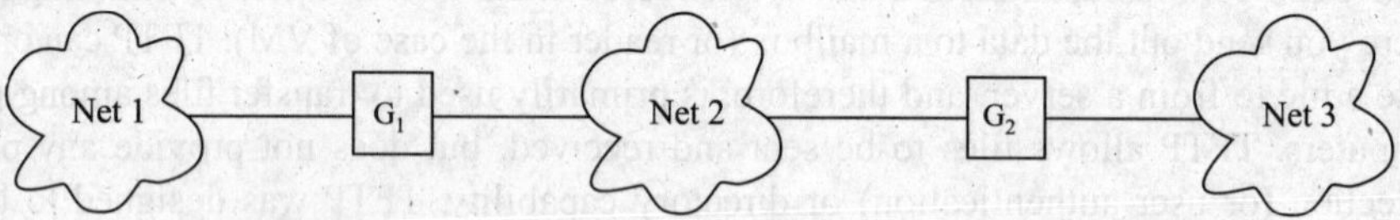

Fig. 18.11 Three networks interconnected by two gateways

In this example, gateway G_1 must move from network *1* to network *2* all packets destined for machines on either network *2* or networks *3*. As the size of the internet expands, the gateway's take of making decisions about where to send packets becomes more complex.

The idea of a gateway seems simple, but it is important because it provides a way to interconnect networks, not just machines.

- Note that in a TCP/IP internet, computers called gateways provide all interconnections among physical networks.

  You might suspect that gateways, which must know how to route packets to their destination are large machines with enough primary or secondary memory to hold information about every machine in the internet to which they attach. However, gateways used with TCP/IP internets are usually minicomputers; they often have little or no disk storage and limited main memories. The concept of building a small internet gateway is gateways route packets based on destination network, not on distinction host.

  If routing is based on networks, the amount of information that a gateway needs to keep is proportional to the number of networks in the internet, not the number of machines.

- Note that TCP/IP is designed to provide a universal interconnection among machines independent of the particular networks to which they attach. Thus, we want the user to view an internet as a single, virtual network to which all machines connect despite their physical connections. In addition to gateways that interconnect physical networks, internet access software is needed on each host to allow application programs to use the internet as if it were a single, real physical network.

The advantage of providing interconnection at the network level now becomes clear. Because application programs that communicate over the internet do not know the details of underlying connections, they can be run without change on any machine. Because the details of each machine's physical network connections are hidden in the internet software, only that software needs to change when new physical connections appear or old ones disappear. It is possible to optimize routing by altering physical connections without event recompiling application programs.

A second advantage of having communication at the network level is more subtle: users do not have to understand or remember how network connect or what traffic they carry. Application programs can be written that operate independent of underlying physical connectivity. In fact, network managers are free to change interior parts of the underlying internet architecture without changing application software in most of the computers attached to the internet.

Figure 18.12 shows that gateways do not provide direct connections among all pairs of networks. It may be necessary for traffic travelling from one machine to another to pass across several intermediate networks. Thus, networks participating in the internet are analogous to highways in the US interstate system: each net agrees to handle transit traffic in exchange for the right to send traffic throughout the internet. Typical users are unaffected and unaware of extra traffic on their local network.

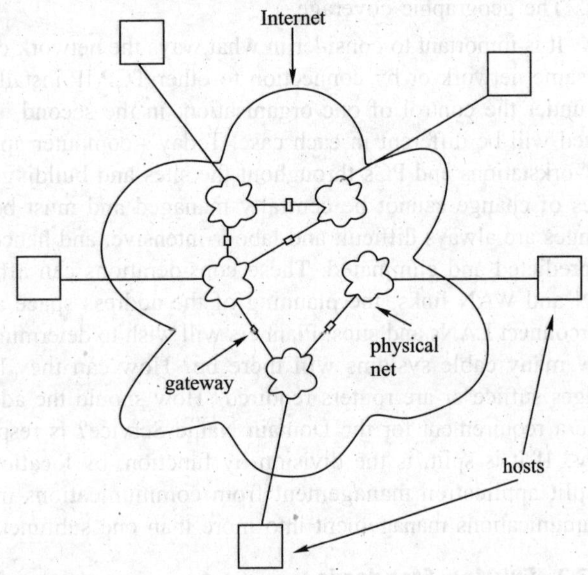

Fig. 18.12 The structure of physical networks and gateways that provide interconnection

It is important to understand a fundamental concept: from the internet point of view, any communication system capable of transferring packets counts as a single network, independent of its delay and throughput characteristics, maximum packet size, or geographic scale. Figure 18.12 uses the same small could to depict all physical networks because TCP/IP treats them equally despite their differences.

❑ Note that the TCP/IP internet protocols treat all networks equally. A local area network like an Ethernet, a wide area network like the NSFNET backbone, or a point-to-point link between two machines each count as one network.

18.7 TCP/IP NETWORK PLANNING

The aim of TCP/IP network planning and design is to provide a communications infrastructure that meets the requirements of the organisation with readily available equipment and skills. It must provide the correct level of performance for different functions within the organisation, at different places, and at acceptable costs. In setting up a local and wide are structure for TCP/IP, the first task of the designer is to consider what each of these terms means for that situation. Each case is unique but the overall size of the organisation and its network requirement will determine the complexity of the problems to be solved.

18.7.1 Growth Rate

Whatever aspect of human communications you consider, it could be said that a measurement of success is often that the size and usage grows rapidly. As a result of experience in road network planning, this has become known as the **motorway** (or **highway**) **effect**. If a system is useful, people change their travel habits and use the system in new ways that the planners never envisaged. Traffic grows to fill the space available. In an organisation a successful network has been seen to grow at a rate which was totally unexpected and to expand rapidly to cover the company.

It is advisable to consider the initial size of the network while planning a TCP/IP installation and have some indication of maximum size and growth rate. This measure of size has two dimensions:

1. The total number of attached ports, that is, computer and router connections to the network.
2. The geographic coverage.

It is important to consider in what ways the network could grow—by addition of devices on the same network or by connection to other TCP/IP installations. In the first case, all the issues are under the control of one organisation; in the second, they may not be. The problems to be solved will be different in each case. Today's computer applications and systems are distributed on workstations and PCs throughout the sites and buildings where the computer users sit. Some types of change cannot be centrally managed and must be carried out at each machine. These changes are always difficult and labour-intensive, and hence costly. As far as possible, they must be predicted and eliminated. These considerations can affect the detailed planning process the LAN and WAN links, the planning of the address space and of the bridges and routers which interconnect LANs and sites. Planners will wish to determine solutions to the following questions. How many cable systems will there be? How can they be interconnected successfully? Will bridges suffice or are routers required? How should the address plan for the network evolve? Is there a requirement for the Domain Name Service? Is responsibility split or with one person or body? If it is split, is the division by function, by location, or by technology? Is there a need to split application management from communications management? Is there a need to split communications management into more than one subfunction?

18.7.2 Existing Standards

To avoid duplication of effort and perhaps more importantly to avoid choosing incompatible solutions to the same TCP/IP options and problems, it is quite important to determine if there are any other existing TCP/IP implementations in the organisation. Some systems may hide their use of TCP/IP; the Banyan VINES resource-sharing LAN or any communications management system which uses the simple network management protocol are current examples. If other examples do exist and will share the same cables or TCP/IP equipment at any time, the developments must be coordinated. In some situations there may already be a central authority for TCP/IP implementation which has set local standards for the use of TCP/IP. These standards should relate to:

- ❒ Addressing conventions
- ❒ Host-naming conventions
- ❒ Local area network
- ❒ Choice of equipment
- ❒ Choice of network software
- ❒ Configuration and management of the network
- ❒ Configuration and management of the applications.

It is easier if these standards can be used rather than starting from scratch.

18.7.3 Traffic Flows and Capacity

While planning the network layout and capacity it is important to know the volume of information which will be carried. At the simplest level, high-performance routes in the network must follow the high traffic flows in the organisation. Faults on those major arterial routes will affect more users, so they, if any, may need to be protected against failure.

Judging future traffic flows is always one of the most difficult estimates in installing new TCP/IP systems. One of the great successes of modern software development techniques is to provide an effective barrier between the application developer and the underlying network. But it leaves the network planners with a major problem. Some people can relate the use of an application to the traffic it will generate.

Given the continued growth in workstation performance, existing LAN implementations already seem slow. For many commercial environments, a single physical LAN can support only 20 to 50 workstations and one or two file servers before the network must be partitioned with bridges or routers. The need for 100 Mbps Fiber Distributed Data Interface (FDDI) or even higher network speeds (1 Gbps–10 Gbps) is evident, particularly for backbone networks and image systems, but the costs of such a system are not yet within the budgets of most network operators.

In the absence of such speeds, planners must ration the limited resource of normal speed LANs. They must understand how particular applications use the network and what the traffic flow between different user groups and applications processors are at different times of the day and business year. Key question are as follows:

- ❒ What will be the total volume of data on different parts of the network at the busiest time of the day? Is this traffic seasonal?
- ❒ How will the traffic grow with time, taking into account the changing and improving user perception of the network services and the increase in number of attached devices and a move towards more demanding applications?
- ❒ How is the traffic distributed among adjacent machines and to more remote machines?

The only way of obtaining such information is to measure the operation of real applications and extrapolate the results. Armed with the traffic information, and its growth, it is time to consider the network structure.

18.8 PARTITION THE NETWORK

'Bridges' and 'routers' partition the network and improve performance for workstations on the same cable. The majority of network traffic should be local to the group of users and a small percentage (15–30%) should cross the bridges into a backbone network which interconnects different user groups. If this traffic split cannot be achieved, then the bridge is not used in the optimum way.

Splitting a network into small pools of users interconnected by routers and bridges is always a poor substitute for that single, reliable, large, high-speed network, for at any time a high proportion of the traffic is less than optimum. By adding bridges and routers to a network the cost per user, the administrative and the technical difficulties all increase and the reliability and performance between some remote portions of the network can fall to unacceptable levels. So why do it? In local area networks it is justified by the **containment of traffic** to physical networks which that traffic must traverse; this reduces the load on the local LAN segment and there is a dramatic improvement in performance for local traffic to local file servers. For long-distance wide-area interconnection, there must be a converter between different link layer technologies. The prime purpose of a bridge in a LAN is to *prevent* traffic flowing where it does not need to, rather than to allow traffic to flow where it will. In many networks, it is only secondary function of the bridge to provide communications where none existed by translating to a different type of cable and extending the cable length limits of the basic LAN specification.

In network partitioning, routers have few advantages and few disadvantages over bridges. They have a more positive role to play. Routers relay only what they are specifically told to relay. They are part of the IP protocol and are designed to interconnect network technologies of different performance. Routers are particularly useful at matching the high speeds of LANs to the much lower speeds of intersite communications circuits that are now available. On the other hand they have a higher cost and lower performance and need more careful management than bridges.

18.9 USING BRIDGES

Bridges filter traffic by Media Access Control (MAC) Address. They must examine each frame received on each port and build a table of frame source addresses with the port on which the frame was received. When the bridge learns that a source and destination are on the same port, it will not pass traffic for that destination to any other cable.

The important performance factors of bridges are described as follows:

- Filtering rate—the ability to examine frames for possible relaying.
- Forwarding rate—the ability to relay frames which have to be relayed.
- 'Routing' algorithm that allows bridges to be connected redundantly in parallel and in loops but prevents frames circulating round the loops.
- Transit delay—normally related to forwarding rate.
- Filter table size.
- Variations in performance with filter table occupancy.

18.9.1 Bridges Filtering Rate

Bridges can filter at the theoretical maximum rate for Ethernet of 14880 frames per second. Even in busy operational networks the offered traffic will not be this demanding, for this figure is based on all minimum-sized frames. The true demand depends on the type of TCP/IP services in use. Networks used mainly for character-by-character TCP/IP Telnet terminal server traffic have a much higher number of small frames that those used for file transfer and NFS. The importance of a bridge operating at this theoretical maximum figure is not that it can examine that number of frames per second but that there is no limitation to the number of successive short frames that can be captured by the bridge, since it can capture at the maximum possible rate.

The frame rates on Token Ring systems are theoretically much higher than on Ethernet (20000 fps on 4 Mbps and 80 000 fps on 16 Mbps Token Ring) but the overheads of TCP/IP mean that the absolute maximum practical frame rates are approximately 7700 and 31000 respectively. Bridges for TCP/IP traffic could be chosen accordingly.

For multi-port hub bridges, one must ensure that each bridge port can examine all frames on every port simultaneously and that the specification does not just give some aggregate figure.

18.10 LIMITED HORIZON

A TCP/IP application working through a bridge has a limited horizon. A bridge isolates two cable segments so that systems have no knowledge of the traffic on the other cable, that is, on the other side of the bridge. A bridge is more likely to be unable to relay all traffic, not because it does not have the power, but because the output cable is continuously busy. Frames will queue in the bridge but bridges eventually throw away any frames that are older than about one second. Most lowlevel protocols—those which carry data over bridges—do not have any error correction or flow control. End stations may retransmit these lost frames from higher level software but, in an extreme case, this may just add to the network congestion that caused the problem in the first place.

It is up to the network manager to design the network so that traffic is distributed correctly and does not concentrate on one work area or in one bridge. Using a high-speed FDDI or Token Ring backbone or a hub bridge may complicate the design of the network. Traffic flows can become more critical, for they may arrive on the high-speed backbone successfully but focus on one work area where a number of key resources are located. High-performance resources, such as ONC (NFS) servers, should either be directly attached to the backbone or must be distributed on a number of feeder work area LANs.

18.11 BROADCASTS, BROADCAST STORMS AND MULTI-CAST FRAMES

TCP/IP protocols use two techniques which impact on the performance of a bridged network. They use 'broadcast' and 'multicast frames' for discovering the locations of resources and for communicating between systems which cooperate to provide a common service.

Multicast frames take capacity on the cable but are not processed by every station. They become a problem only on slower wide area bridged links. 'Slow' is a relative term; for today's LANs, 'slow' could be 256 kbps, 128 kbps or less.

Broadcast frames are much more detrimental to performance. They are generated by ARP, RARP, BOOTP, and RIP. Every system on an Ethernet or Token Ring network must process every broadcast frame. If the number of broadcast frames increases, the performance of every system will degrade noticeably. A frame takes some time to process, independent of its size. Each broadcast frame can reduce the performance of a PC by almost one normal data frame of 1000 to 1450 bytes. PCs slow down noticeably with 10 to 15 broadcast packets per second.

Bridges relay broadcast frames everywhere. To try to filter broadcasts is to destroy the possibility of any-to-any communication. So networks which are interlinked only with bridges reach a size where the percentage of broadcast traffic from all the devices is unacceptable. Unless the broadcast traffic can be reduced, it becomes impossible to manage the network or to grow it further successfully.

It has been known for in-house application programmers who do not appreciate the potential harmful effects to write applications using broadcasts. On more than one occasion, a complete LAN, including powerful minicomputers, has been brought to a standstill by a 'broadcast storm' of about 100 packets per second. Broadcast storms are sometimes attributed to Ethernet design limitations; it is often not realized that the broadcast storm is usually caused by a combination of bad software design and a poor bridged network structure of any type of LAN.

18.11.1 Bridging to a Backbone

As an aid to structuring the distribution of data between work areas it is common practice to use a **backbone** LAN to carry the transit traffic. This backbone may be built with the same technology as the work area, though often on a more robust cable (Thick Ethernet, 10Base5, rather than Thin Ethernet, 10Base2, or Unshielded Twisted Pair, 10BaseT), or it may use a different technology (16 Mbps Token Ring or 100 Mbps FDDI).

Figure 18.13 shows, this topology places a minimum of two bridges in series between any two work areas. Unless application processors or file servers are directly attached to the backbone, the performance for demanding file transfer applications is affected by this double hop. This is most noticeable if the backbone is no faster than the work areas. Those applications using TCP as their transport layer will need an increase in window size; applications which use UDP protocols with a small datagram size may suffer badly.

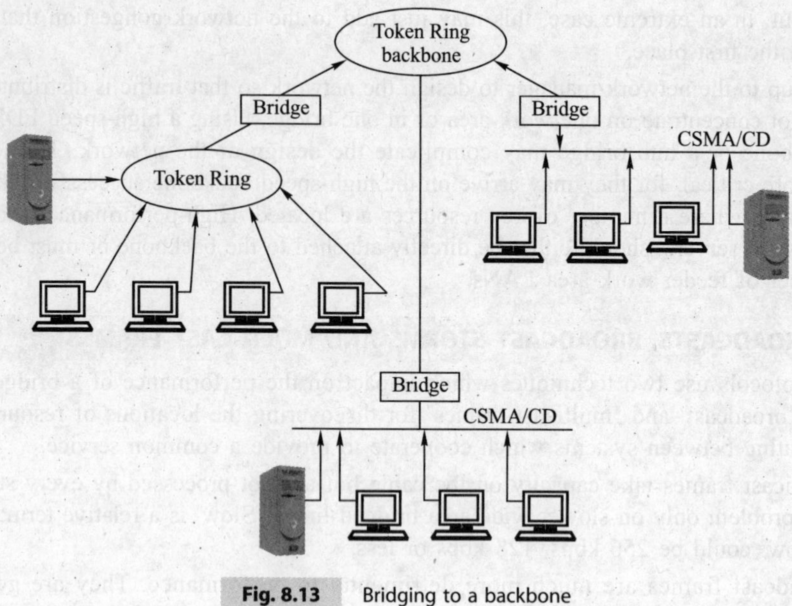

Fig. 8.13 Bridging to a backbone

18.11.2 Hub Bridges

Hub and multiport bridges replace the backbone network with a single internal high-speed bus of greater speed than any LAN. This reduces the double hop effect but requires more extensive cabling and potentially reduces the backbone to a single point of failure (Fig. 18.14).

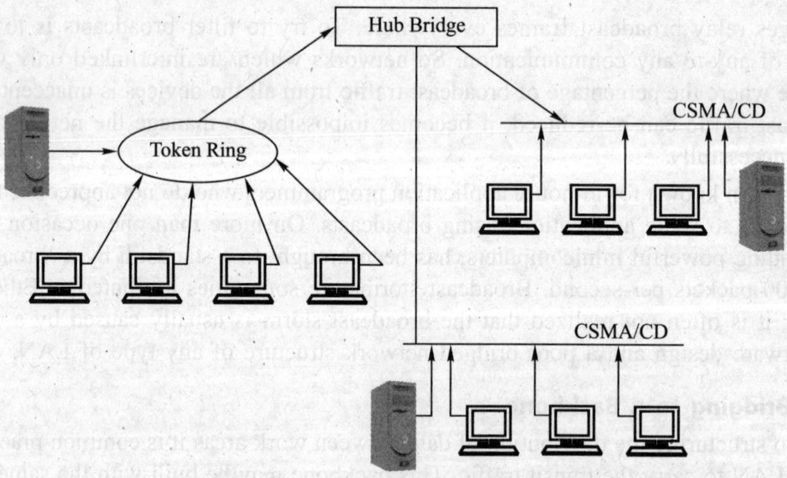

Fig. 18.14 Hub bridge or multiport bridge

18.12 IDENTIFYING A NETWORK CONNECTION

Connections to a TCP/IP network are often known to each other and to users in three different ways, all of which identify the same connection to the network but at different levels of TCP/IP:

- As names: In the **fully qualified host** and **domain** name vax1.icds.com.in
- Using the domain name scheme is often not considered early enough in the planning of commercial networks; users of larger networks will find it invaluable.

- As a group of four numbers separated by full stops. This is the IP or network address used by the IP layer of TCP/IP: 164.120.9.61
- On a shared LAN by its network interface card address the 48-bits MAC address. (Medium Access Control address often called the physical address) 02 60 8C 12 34 56

The three levels of address is required, since they all refer to the same connection to the TCP/IP Internet The reason is that while at any one time these addresses identify the same location, over a period of time a each may change for different reasons. The three types of address allow a degree of flexibility where none would exist if the functions were not separated:

- The host and domain name should remain unchanged for the longest time, for it is completely determined by the system designers and managers, though it will often change if there is a major change in machine location.
- The IP address may change due to network growth and reconfiguration, for instance, if a machine is moved from one location in a building to another.
- The MAC address may change for similar growth or performance reasons, or because the network card is replaced following a card failure. The shortest lived address is likely to be the MAC address.

The fully qualified domain name is for 'human consumption' and consists of a set of identifiers, separated by full stops, which describe a computer in a hierarchical relationship to all others. For example, machine.department.site.organization.org_type.country.

Introducing flexibility brings with it the possibility of error and communications failure if the flexible functions are not managed and controlled correctly.

18.13 PLANNING THE IP ADDRESS SCHEME

To plan an IP addressing scheme you must have the following information:

1. The maximum number of host ports that your organisation could ever wish to interconnect. The whole of your organisation is not just your particular department, but the whole organisational structure, if necessary, worldwide, which may at any time be interconnected.
2. An understanding of the numbers of devices at each location and in each building on each site. Assume one address per member of staff in those buildings and leave some 25% spare.
3. An understanding of the different departments, their geographic locations, and the likelihood that they will need to communicate. An estimate of the amount of information that is exchanged is useful but it has a very short-lived value.
4. A knowledge of any other current users of TCP/IP and any standardization decisions that have been taken already.

In a small organisation of a few hundred people, getting this information is straightforward in comparison to a large corporation; but it is the large corporation that must have accurate figures and which must derive centralized standards that are adhered to everywhere.

18.14.1 Internet Protocol

The Internet Protocol (IP) may be described as the network layer protocol of TCP/IP. IP is operated and interpreted by each intermediate relay in an interconnected set of LANs and WANs which is using the TCP/IP protocol suite to communicate. Such a collection is often called an internetwork and the intermediate relays are routers. IP provides a best efforts delivery service based on a technique called **datagram transmission**; 'best efforts' and 'datagram' because no attempt is made by IP to recover any errors which may occur in transmission. IP supports routing and relaying of information between communicating hosts or end devices according to the Type or quality of Service (TOS) they require. IP allows routing errors to be trapped and reported and their effects on system performance to be minimized. IP does not make assumptions about the underlying network of physical cables, LAN hardware (Ethernet, Token Ring or FDDI) or the point-to-point wide area links (PTT circuits).

18.14.2 IP Addressing

The IP address is one component in the Internet protocol. The IP address is a number that uniquely identifies the connection of a host computer or end system as OSI would call it, to a physical network as it communicates with other computers or end systems. Hosts with more than one connection have a different IP address for each one. IP routers also have their own IP addresses for they can be the source and destination of IP datagrams.

The purpose of the IP address is twofold: to identify each connection to the internetwork in a way that is independent of the underlying physical network (LAN or WAN) technology, and to collect a group of connections together to simplify routing. Internetwork routers use IP addresses to make routing decisions.

IP addresses must be unique in the communicating internetwork. If not, communications will fail erratically. Since TCP/IP protocols do not directly provide any technical means by which IP addresses can be automatically made unique, it is up to network managers to configure and manage them correctly by traditional manual methods aided by database and network management technology.

18.14.3 MAC Addresses

Where TCP/IP systems are connected to a shared cable such as an Ethernet or Token Ring LAN, communication between stations must take place using MAC addresses, normally built into the network adapter card. Since the IP address is configured independently of the MAC address, it remains unchanged even if the network card fails and is replaced.

Every Ethernet or Token Ring card comes with a preconfigured 48-bits MAC address, its universally managed address. LAN standards also allow locally managed addresses; network cards can be loaded with a 48-bits address chosen by the network manager. Locally managed addresses are not normally used in TCP/IP systems. AS IP addresses in TCP/IP must be controlled and managed, there is little value is adding a second layer of management by also configuring and controlling MAC addresses. But the issue of MAC address management does not disappear completely from the TCP/IP story; some of the facilities of TCP/IP such as the Boot Protocol, BOOTP, use the MAC address as a fixed reference point for obtaining other information. If you wish to use these features, you must at least have a record of the MAC address of each computer for which the facility will be used. These addresses appear as a reference point in look-up tables in information servers. But, as discuss above, the MAC address can change if the network card is replaced. In a large network, keeping an up-to-date record of MAC addresses and ensuring that all servers have the correct record can be time-consuming.

Few advanced star wiring systems have management facilities that can record the MAC address attached to each user drop cable. Such systems make it easier to record the location of particular MAC addresses.

18.14 CHARACTERISTICS OF THE IP ADDRESS

The IP address is a 32-bits number which must be unique in internetwork. Devices which must have an IP address include every connection of each application processor and of each network router. As mentioned previously, computers with more than one network connection have a different IP address for each connection. In TCP/IP literature, such computers are referred to as 'multihomed'. These connections are usually on different networks. This is the reason for sizing the networkby-network connections rather than the number of computers, though these numbers will often be very similar.

Unlike some other network addressing schemes, the IP address does not necessarily convey any information about geographic location. Given an IP address you can only deduce a management authority; that authority could manage one corporate network which in itself has global coverage and meshes with many other global networks. This has interesting implications for routing between two worldwide networks. In other way, the IP addressing scheme is not hierarchical unlike the telephone or telex network or for that matter the CCITT X.121 addressing scheme for the X.25 interface to public packet switched networks.

The 32-bits IP address has two components—(1) network number or network identifier and (2) host number or host identifier. Some 'class bits' can be extracted from the network number, but trying to examine these on their own can lead to confusion. It is safer always to think of the network number as containing the class bits.

Class bits + Network number	Host number

Fig. 18.15 Format of the IP address

It is the network number which identifies the controlling organisation and the port number which identifies the particular connection within the authority of that organisation. The term 'host number' is historic and this name could cause confusion for, as we have seen, a multihomed host has more than one IP address and hence more than one host number. For reasons that will become apparent later, it would be unusual for two ports on the same machine to have the same network number (Fig. 18.15).

The terms **net id**. and **host id**. are in common usage for network number and host number. IP addresses are divided into five address classes (A to E). It is important to understand that these divisions were conceived to ease the management of addresses by the Internet Activities Board (IAB); they have less immediate significance for the network manager.

The first three classes, A, B, C, are available for normal allocation and for host-to-host communications. Class D and class E addresses are not for general use; class D is reserved for special use by IAB designated protocols and class E is reserved for future use. One use of class D addresses is by routers, so network managers may encounter them while monitoring router protocols.

There are no practical distinctions in the way in which computer systems with class A, class B or class C addresses use those addresses. With some noted exceptions, which are discussed further below, any address from any class is equivalent for communications purposes. In principle, any host can communicate equally well using an address from any of these three classes. The distinguishing feature of each class of address is the number of network numbers and the number of host connections which each network number can support. The limitations of each class are described as follows:

Network class	*Max. number of network numbers*	*Max. number of hosts on each network number*
A	126	16 777 214
B	16382	382 65 534
C	2 097 150	254
D	Not applicable—reserved for multicast systems	
E	Reserved for IAB use	

18.15 NETWORK NUMBERS AND HOST NUMBERS

The choice of network numbers is most important. Network connections with the same network number should communicate directly on the same physical LAN. Network connections with different network numbers do not communicate directly; they must use the services of a router. This router either is directly connected between the two LANs to which the hosts connect or it in turn knows of a router which can relay the message towards its ultimate destination as shown in Fig. 18.16.

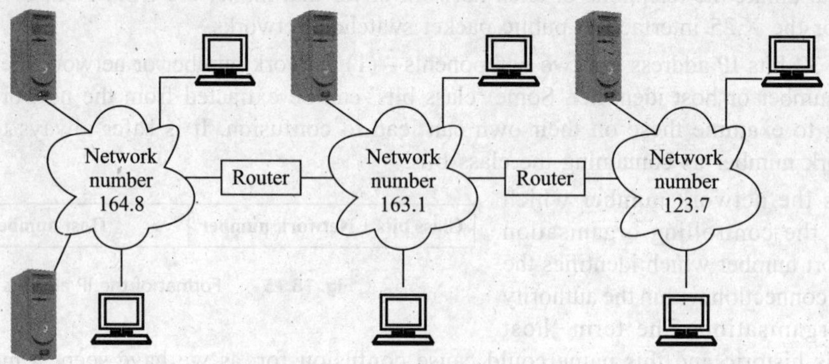

Fig. 18.16 Choosing network numbers

These factors determine the basic rules for choosing network numbers and host numbers. They may alternatively be stated as:

- Computers separated only by bridges or repeaters will have the same network number.
- Computers or workstations separated by routers have different network numbers.

For the network implementor, the most important factor is the choice of IP address for a particular host is affected by the presence of routers. The positioning of routers is determined by the exact geography of the underlying physical networks which connect computers, floors, buildings, sites and countries into a complete internetwork. It is also heavily influenced by organisational needs, traffic flows and traffic volume. The layout will change as the network grows and matures. If a bridge is replaced by a router, the network number on one side of the new router must change.

A TCP/IP addressing scheme evolves as the needs of users are better understood during the design process. Adding a TCP/IP addressing scheme to a LAN must take into account the existing layout of that LAN.

One factor is key. Network planners must attempt to design an addressing scheme that can remain substantially unchanged in a changing environment. This can be achieved using subnetwork addressing.

The convention is the address is written down, or described to software, in dotted decimal notation. Each eight bits of the address (each octet) is converted to a decimal number in the range 0 to 255, and separated by a dot (.). While the US standards initially specified 'dotted decimal notation' some computer staff are more at home with hexadecimal notation. Dotted hexadecimal. (and UNIX or C-style hexadecimal) and octal notations are sometimes used and will be accepted by some (though by no means all) implementations. Occasionally it is useful, if somewhat longwinded, to represent these numbers in binary. Some valid addresses are shown in Table 18.1. Leading zeros in each octet, which have no significance, need not be included. 128.1.0.9 is valid and more usual than 128.001.000.009, though this is also perfectly acceptable; however, 128.1.9 or 128...9 are not valid.

Table 18.1 Distinguishing the class of address

Address class	*Class bits*	*Number of networks bits*	*First usable value*	*Last usable*	*Remark*
A	0	7	1	126	Values 0 and 127 are reserved
B	10	14	128.1	191.254	
C	110	21	192.0.1	233.255.254	
D	1110	—	224.0.0.0	239.255.255.254	Not available for general use
E	1111	—	240.0.0.0	255.255.255.254	Not available for general use

18.15.1 Distinguishing the Class of Address

The five classes of address have already been mentioned. The class of address is determined by certain bits in the first eight bits, that is, in the first decimal number of the four as shown in Table 18.1. The magnitude of the first number that defines the class of the address is given in table.

There are two important features of this system:

1. The division between one class and the next is always at an octet boundary. This simplifies finding the boundaries between the classes of address, since each decimal number represents one octet.
2. When the network number is written down the 'class bits' are always included in the first octet, to ensure that the class of address and hence the true network number are unambiguous.

It is important that users of TCP/IP, planners and implementors should be fully familiar with the different classes of address and the limitations that they place on network growth. Many people new to the subject at first find the technique of dotted decimal notation a little eccentric. But it should become second nature to recognize the class of address, the network number, and the host id. As compared to other network addressing schemes, the TCP/IP addressing range is quite limited. Current work in the IAB is investigating the options for extending the address range.

18.16 IAB AND NETWORK NUMBER REGISTRATION

The addresses in an internetwork must be unique, there has to be a registry which ensures that such a policy can be enforced. TCP/IP was developed for use on the US Internet. This collection of networks is managed by many different authorities, with the IAB as overall design authority. In this environment of devolved management, the network number has two functions. First, since each IP address on the whole set of interconnected networks must be unique, the network number is used to identify one addressing authority, often called an autonomous system, responsible for issuing unique connection ids in that part of the address space. The second function is to support routing.

The IAB ensures that IP addresses on the Internet are unique, by registering and issuing network numbers to organisations that have reasons to connect to the Internet. Such organisations do not choose their own network number, it is issued to them. They agree to undertake certain network management responsibilities when they request an official IAB address allocation. They must then issue host Ids so that they are unique within their own network number address space. If they fail to issue unique host numbers, only the services of that organisation will be affected.

The IAB has devolved the clerical task of registering and issuing IP network numbers to the Internet Registry, part of the Internet Assigned Numbers Authority (IANA) which controls all numbers in the TCP/IP protocol suite, which must be managed if correct operation is to be guaranteed. The Internet Registry is operated by the Department of Defense Network, Network Information Center (DDN NIC), now located in Chantilly, Virginia.

18.17 CONFIGURING THE IP ADDRESS

Every computer, workstation, personal computer, network router and network management station which 'speaks IP' must have a different IP address for each of its connections. The IP address is entered through the normal configuration management processes. IP addresses are usually represented and entered in dotted decimal notation; occasionally dotted hexadecimal notation is accepted. The address is usually stored in non-volatile memory, either RAM or on a disk file when available. Diskless workstations often have no nonvolatile storage. They obtain their IP address across the network at start-up time using BOOTP or RARP. Visiting each device to change the IP address is time-consuming, particularly in dispersed networks. BOOTP provides a mechanism for centralizing the distribution of IP addresses and other useful TCP/IP parameters, even for machines which do have storage. The key to distributing the correct IP address and other information via BOOTP is the MAC address of the interface card. It is then *essential* to record accurately the MAC address used by each machine on the network that uses the BOOTP service. This is excellent policy for fault diagnosis and security in any case, though it is often neglected.

In an operational network, IP addresses become recorded in distributed tables and in software in machines. While this is bad practice, it is unavoidable. Frequent wholesale changes to IP addresses must not occur, so preplanning is essential. Such changes are labour-intensive because of the widespread distribution of addresses; the change introduces errors and has unpredictable consequences for the integrity of operational applications and for the time taken to restore any-to-any communications.

18.18 RESERVED IP ADDRESSES

Certain IP network numbers and host numbers are reserved for the use of particular aspects of TCP/IP communication. Not all these protocols are regularly used. Once you configure a connection with a reserved IP address, the faults caused are likely to be obscure, apparently intermittent and difficult to isolate. Not all host software checks that the IP address it is requested to use in invalid.

The following addresses are reserved:

Network number 127.X.X.X, where X.X.X is any set of numbers. This is used for a local software loopback test.

A network number of all 0's is classless and means 'my current network which I do not know the number of'—sometimes referred to as 'this network'.

- A network number of all 1's.
- Host number 0 is reserved to refer to a particular network number. For example, 192.0.0.1 is the first class C network address which could be allocated.
- Host number 'all 1s' is reserved to broadcast to all hosts on a specific network; it can only be used as a destination address.
- The full address 0.0.0.0 is reserved. It is used in two ways: as a source address when the host does not know its genuine address, for example during bootstrapping of a diskless workstation, and by routers in a list of addresses to advertise the default route, the route to all networks which are not explicitly listed.
- The full address 255.255.255.255 is reserved as a destination address to mean 'broadcast to all hosts on my network'. 0.0.0.0 as a destination is an obsolete form of 255.255.255.255.

18.18.1 IP Addresses with Routers and Dial-up Devices

Few older router implementations need a point-to-point wide-area PTT or dial-up link between two LANs should be identified with its own unique IP network number with only two connections attached. In the larger network this is wasteful of the limited resource of IP network numbers.

Check with your router manufacturer that the most modern techniques, which conserve network and subnetwork numbers, are used in their implementation.

18.19 HOW TCP/IP WORKS?

Most networks provide some sort of connection mechanism to get from point A to point B. Other networks worry about how to get from node A on network X to node B on network Y. If a program wishes to send information from itself on node A to another node on the same network, TCP will provide the packet sequencing, error control, and other services that are required to allow reliable end-to-end communications. This does not mean that IP is required. In fact, some implementations of TCP connect directly to the network services layer and bypass IP altogether. If, however, a program on node A on an Ethernet wished to connect to a destination program on node B on an X.25 network, an internet routing function would be necessary to get data packets sent properly between the two dissimilar network services. IP would take the packet from TCP, pass it through a gateway that would provide conversion services and then send the packet to the IP layer at the remote node for delivery to the remote TCP layer and, subsequently, the destination program. A good comparison would be as follows:

(*a*) Program A on node ALPHA wishes to connect to program B on node BETA on the same network. Program A would send a data packet to TCP with the proper destination address. TCP would then encapsulate the data with the proper header and checksums in accordance with whatever services the program requested and pass the TCP packet to the IP layer. IP would then determine, from network directory information, that the remote node is on the same network as itself and simply pass the packet through to the network services layer for local network routing and delivery.

(*b*) Program A on node ALPHA on network X wishes to connect to program B on node BETA on network Y. In this situation, data would be handled as in case (a) above, but IP would determine that the destination is not on the local network. As a result, the IP layer in node ALPHA would determine the best route to get to the remote node and send the TCP packet to the next IP node in the path to get to the remote. IP does not care which program the source wants to connect to; all it cares about is which node to send the packets to.

IP nodes in the path from node ALPHA to node BETA will examine the packet to determine the destination and will forward the packet to the proper IP until it reaches the destination network IP. That IP determines that the node is on its local network and the packet is handed to the network services layer for the network on which BETA resides for delivery to node BETA.

Once the packet is received at the final destination IP, it is passed up to the TCP layer, which breaks out the packet header to figure out which program on the destination node is to receive the data. First, however, the packet header is examined carefully to insure that it has arrived in the proper sequence and that there are no special handling issues that need to be serviced. Once TCP is satisfied that everything is reasonable, the data is delivered to the destination program.

While all of this seems pretty straightforward, there are some implementation issues that make all of this complex. Since TCP and IP allow many service options such as message priority, security classification, data segmentation at the TCP level, packet segmentation at the IP level and other issues that some network architectures, such as DECnet, need not concern themselves with, there can be some considerable overhead associated with packet processing. As a result, TCP/IP performance varies significantly from network hardware to network hardware as well as from machine implementation to machine implementation.

Now that we have examined the generalized delivery model, let us look at some of the specifics.

18.20 WHAT TCP WAS BUILT TO DO?

One of the base problems that TCP was built to address is the issue of connection from a particular program on a particular node on a particular network to a remote program destination that may or may not be on the same network as the originator. As such, a method of addressing nodes needed to be developed that identified a particular program on a particular node in a particular network. A possible solution is to develop hard addresses for all entities on a particular network. While this solves the problem, it is inflexible and usually does not provide an upwardly-flexible network architecture. Another problem is that some networks have their own proprietary (and sometimes bizarre) addressing scheme that must be considered as TCP/IP are above the local network addressing scheme mechanisms in the network architecture and will need to use the local mechanism on packet delivery. To solve the problem, TCP/IP uses a three-layer addressing mechanism that allows for delivery of packets across dissimilar network architectures.

To begin with, each program (called a PROCESS in TCP) has a unique one-up address on each machine. That unique local program address is combined with a particular node address to form something called a port. The port address is further combined with the local network address, forming a new entity called a socket. There can be many, many sockets on a TCP/IP network but each socket identifies, exactly, one specific application on a specific node on a specific network. Through this mechanism, IP will get the packets to the proper node and TCP will deliver the packet to the proper program on that node. Some nodes provide a standard process type (such as type 23 for remote log-ins) that are 'known' to other network entities and that provide certain standard services. Through this mechanism, TCP provides a multiplexing capability that is essential in the efficient use of the network resource.

18.20.1 From One Socket to Another

As with any network, two sockets that wish to connect to each other must have a mechanism by which this happens. TCP provides this in various ways. One of the more common ways connections are established is via an ACTIVE/PASSIVE network OPEN. A PASSIVE OPEN is when a receptive socket declares itself to be open and available for incoming connections (this would typically be the mode used by something like a database server). A PASSIVE OPEN, however, may be set up in various ways. First, the PASSIVE OPEN may be set up to be FULLY SPECIFIED, which means that the socket issuing the PASSIVE OPEN tells the network exactly which socket may connect to it, including security levels allowed and other related details. Another type of PASSIVE OPEN is the UNSPECIFIED PASSIVE OPEN in which the socket will accept any connection request from any remote socket provided that the remote system requesting connection meets prescribed security and other criteria. In both types of network OPENS, it is pertinent to point out that the socket OPENing the network may also declare timeout values for all data received from the originator of the connection. This allows for the expeditious handling of data as well as providing a means by which 'old' messages are handled in a reasonable fashion and messages requiring special handling (in terms of time) are processed correctly.

Another type of OPEN is the ACTIVE OPEN. Unlike the PASSIVE OPEN, the ACTIVE OPEN aggressively seeks a connection to a particular socket. An ACTIVE OPEN will only be successful if there is a cooperating and corresponding PASSIVE OPEN or other ACTIVE OPEN from the destination socket.

Once a connection has been established between two sockets, data may be transferred between the sockets. TCP provides several mechanisms for data transfer, but the two most popular are segmented data transfer and PUSH mode. Segmented data transfer allows TCP to send user data in chunks across the network. As such, TCP may send the data in such a manner that allows for the best efficiency for the network being used. This means that even if the user has transferred

25 blocks of user data to TCP, TCP may not send it all at once, opting to segment the data in such a manner as to provide optimal flow of data on the network. While this technique is great for data flow issues and network congestion issues, it can be troublesome for transfers in which the data needs to get to the remote system NOW! In such cases, the user may specify the PUSH flag. A PUSH request forces TCP to send whatever has been passed from the user to TCP right away with no consideration for optimal flow control. In addition to the PUSH flag, the user may specify the urgency of the data being transferred to keep the remote system on its toes.

How much data is allowed to be sent from one socket to another is a function of the network and programs involved. Since TCP was developed with multiple network architectures in mind, it allows some level of link negotiation on connection and data transfer that provides for maximum buffer sizes (somewhat dynamically) and maximum buffer allocation.

18.20.2 TCP Sequencing

To insure that everything gets to where it is going and in the proper order, TCP provides packet sequencing services as well as error detection functions utilizing a 16-bit checksum in the TCP header area. It is also interesting to note that TCP presumes the IP layer to be unreliable and, therefore, includes a 96-bit pseudoheader in front of the actual TCP packet header that includes the source address, destination address, protocol being used and segment size. Through the use of the pseudoheader, TCP protects itself from IP delivering the packet to the wrong place (or not at all) by misinterpreting TCP header fields. The checksum in the TCP header also includes the pseudoheader bits to insure that everything is clean when it hits the remote side.

After the connection is established and all data has been transferred, the link may be shut down via user request. This is the clean way. It is very possible that the link may also be abruptly aborted due to link drop or some catastrophic failure of the network or socket-to-socket linkage. TCP provides mechanisms to handle both situations. A CLOSE primitive issuance tells TCP that the user is finished with the network link and to close down the link gracefully by sending all remaining data in local buffers and notifying the remote socket that the sending user wishes to CLOSE the link. The remote TCP socket notifies the user that a CLOSE has been issued. The user may then send any remaining data and issue a CLOSE to the sender. When the sender receives the CLOSE acknowledgement from the receiver, it sends a TERMINATE to the user and notifies the remote TCP that a TERMINATE has been issued. The remote TCP socket sends a TERMINATE to the remote user and the link is closed completely.

If a network link abort occurs, for whatever reason, the ABORT primitive is sent to the remote TCP, which tells the remote user that a TERMINATE has occurred. No more data of any kind is transmitted on the link and the link is closed immediately on both sides. Obviously, a link termination of the ABORT kind is not desirable, as data may be lost and other integrity issues may be involved.

18.20.3 TCP Needs Not an IP

It is important to understand that TCP need not be connected to an IP, although that is frequently the case. TCP provides the essential network connection and data transfer features which a user would require to connect with a particular program on a remote system. Some companies use TCP as the protocol of choice when setting up simple direct-connect network connections (where the remote node is hard-wired to the originating node) or when performing tasks such as downline system loading. In any case, TCP is a powerful and full-featured protocol that provides reasonable network services for user data.

Many times, however, just getting the data from one socket to another may involve the connection to various types of network technologies. A TCP packet coming in from an asynchronous link may need to be routed on to an Ethernet to reach its ultimate destination. Because of the need to connect and properly route data through to its proper network and destination socket, the IP layer was developed.

18.21 WHAT IS AN IP?

IP is a datagram service. It basically provides rudimentary internetwork routing services without any regard to the destination program, TCP formats, error control, packet sequencing, etc. Its function in life is to get the packet to the right network and eventually, to the right node. Further, IP allows for expedited routing of packets that need to get to a destination quicker than other, routine packets. In many respects, with the exception of routing priority, IP functionality is similar to Ethernet packet handling. If a packet arrives that is damaged (there is an IP checksum), the packet is discarded. What is in the data field of the packet is of no interest to IP. IP could be sending a TCP packet or some other protocol for all it cares. As long as the proper SEND (user sending to the network) primitive fields have been filled in, IP will send the packet on its merry way. When the packet reaches the remote node and the checksum figures out OK, IP sends the packet to TCP (or whatever the receptor protocol is) via DELIVER directive and all is well with the universe. If the packet gets trashed in the process of being delivered, so be it. If the packets arrive out of sequence, that is not IP's problem. If a packet is missing, again, IP does not care. IP gets the data packet (usually a TCP packet) from point A on network X to point B on network Y. That is all, nothing more.

18.21.1 Gateways and IP

To provide the internetwork routing function, IP makes use of special nodes called gateways. A gateway, in IP terms, is a machine that allows two dissimilar networks to be connected to each other. The two networks may or may not be the same type (Ethernet, X.25, token ring, etc.), as IP operates above the hardware itself and is only interested in the virtual connection function, not the physical path or hardware used. As such, there may be a need to segment large messages from the upper software layers into sizes that are applicable to the remote network's allowances. To do this, IP will segment large messages into proper-sized chunks (such as when going from 1500 byte Ethernet packets to 128 byte X.25 packets) for the destination network and reassemble them at the remote destination IP layer before delivery to the user. If a packet gets destroyed in the segmented message and the remote IP detects the packet loss, the entire segment is killed off by the remote IP. Obviously, TCP would detect that a segment is missing and request a retransmission from the remote TCP for any missing packets. TCP has the option of forcing IP NOT to segment packets, but this is usually not implemented as it can cause routing problems where differing network technologies are concerned.

IP also provides for proper security classification of packets being sent to a remote site. If an intermediary gateway or network is not at the same security level as the transmitted packet, the packet will not be sent through that network. As a result, some strange routing of data may occur sometimes as IP must contend with the problem of expeditious routing but also the problem of security-oriented routing.

Finally, IP has some different terminology than that typically used in a network. In many networks, the concept of a 'hop' is the routing of a data packet through a node on its way to its final destination point. In IP, a hop is when a data packet goes through a gateway to another network. Therefore, it is quite possible that a packet may wander through various nodes in a local network before it actually gets to the remote network gateway, depending, of course, upon previously discussed variables. If the packet does not incur a route through a gateway, it, in IP terms, has not incurred a hop. If it transverses through two gateways, it would be considered to have incurred two hops on its path to the final destination. Hops, therefore, are not referred to in the same manner as many other popular communications architectures.

As can be seen, TCP and IP are not the same and may actually be implemented totally independent of each other for separate uses. More often than not, however, they are both included in many offerings from various vendors.

18.22 DOMAIN NAME SYSTEM (DNS)

The *Domain name System,* or DNS, is a distributed database that is used by TCP/IP applications to map between hostnames and IP addresses, and to provide electronic mail routing information. We use the term *distributed* because no single site on the Internet knows all the information. Each site (university department, campus, company, or department within a company, for example) maintains its own database of information and runs a server program that other systems across the Internet (clients) can query. The DNS provides the protocol that allows clients and servers to communicate with each other. While these are the main functions of the DNS, it has a more general use. The standard allows the DNS to identify the types of applications that are available on a particular machine (well-known services), to identify gateways to networks and to show which machines are capable of mail relay and to which network. These are some of the functions required from a more general directory service.

To work with names, a general structure has to be defined. Any system where responsibility is devolved to successively lower levels of the structure is 'hierarchical'. The domain name system is hierarchical and uses separate components in a complete name to identify the different levels of management. Like other hierarchical systems, this one can be drawn as an inverted tree, with the trunk (or root as it is more often called) identifying the top level of management, and then spanning out into branches, twigs and leaves that point finally to an individual computer by name (see Fig. 18.17).

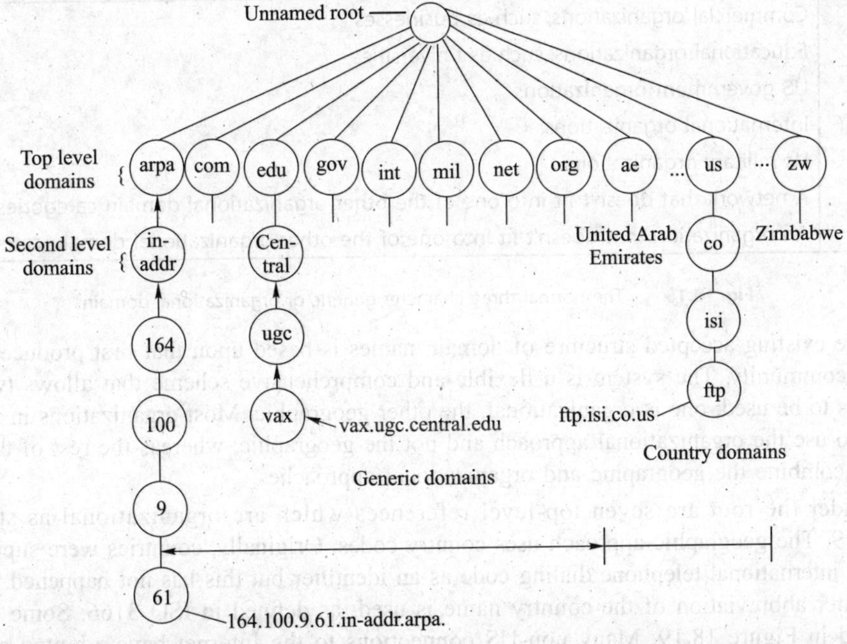

Fig. 18.17 Hierarchical structure of the DNS

Every node circles in Fig. 18.17 has a *label* of up to 63 characters. The root of the tree is a special node with a null label. Any comparison of labels considers uppercase and lowercase characters the same. The *domain name* of any node in the tree is the list of labels, starting at the node, working up to the root, using a period ('dot') to separate the labels. Note that this is different from the Unix filesystem, which forms a pathname by starting at the top and going down the tree. Every node in the tree must have a unique domain name, but the same label can be used at different points in the tree.

A domain name that ends with a period is called an *absolute domain name* or a *fully qualified domain name* (FQDN). An example is a vax.ugc.central.edu.. If the domain name does not end with a period, it is assumed that the name needs to be completed. How the name is completed depends on the DNS software being used. If the uncompleted name consists of two or more labels, it might be considered to be complete; otherwise a local addition might be added to the right of the name. For example, the name vax might be completed by adding the local suffix .ugc.central.edu..

The level immediately below the root of the Internet DNS consists of three top-level domains:

1. *Arpa* is a special Internet domain that maps dotted-decimal IP addresses to domain names rather than domain names to dotted-decimal addresses.
2. The generic or organizational group consists of three-character domain labels such as *com, edu, and gov.*
3. The country or geographical group consists of domain labels that represent two-character country codes that the International Standards Organization defines in the document ISO 3166.

If you've surfed Internet sites in the past, you may be most familiar with the generic or organizational domains. The Internet normally divides this group of domains into seven basic categories. Figure 18.18 identifies the seven basic classifications of the organizational domains.

Domain	*Description*
com,	Commercial organizations, such as businesses
edu,	Educational organizations, such as universities
gov,	US government organizations
int,	International organizations
mil,	Us military organizations
net,	A network that doesn't fit into one of the other organizational domain categories
org,	An organization that doesn't fit into one of the other organizational domain categories

Fig. 18.18 The normal three-character generic or organizational domains

The existing accepted structure of domain names is based upon that first produced by the Internet community. The system is a flexible and comprehensive scheme that allows two basic structures to be used; one is organizational, the other geographic. Most organizations in the USA elected to use the organizational approach and not the geographic, whereas the rest of the world tends to combine the geographic and organizational approaches.

Under the root are seven top-level references which are organizational as shown in Fig. 18.19. The geographic approach uses country codes. Originally, countries were supposed to use their international telephone dialing code as an identifier but this has not happened. Instead, a two-letter abbreviation of the country name is used, as defined in ISO 3166. Some of these are listed in Figure 18.19. Many non-US connections to the Internet have adopted a second tier of domains that closely matches the organization classification used at the top level of the Internet.

Country code	Country name	Additional information
AU,	Australia,	Sometimes OZ.AU or just OZ
BE,	Belgium,	
CA,	Canada,	Some Canadian systems use US conventions
CH	Switzerland	
DE	Germany	
DK	Denmark	
ES	Spain	
FI	Finland	
FR	France	
GR	Greece	
IN	India	
IT	Italy	
JP	Japan	
KW	Kuwait	
NL	The Netherlands	
NO	Norway	
NZ	New Zealand	
SE	Sweden	
US	United States of America	

Fig. 18.3 Some domain name system country codes.

As discussed, the major problem with a flat name-space is the workload it generates for the organization that has to assign names. The hierachical-naming system delegates responsibility for assigning names at different levels of the hierarchy. The Internet Network Information Center (InterNIC) manages the top-level domain names. The InterNIC delegates responsibility for assigning names to different organizations. Each organization is responsible for a specific portion of the DNS tree structure. Internet professionals refer to these areas of responsibility as *zones*. Alternatively, the InterNIC delegates responsibility for assigning names within a specific zone (portion of the DNS tree structure) to specific organizations. The organization responsible for a specific zone can further subdivide the zone and delegate responsibility for assigning names. For example, a business might divide itself into zones based on divisions, and each division might partition itself into zones based on departments. This subdivision normally continues until one person can manage the responsibility for name assignments within a well-defined zone. You refer to such an individual as a DNS administrator. A DNS administrator must set up name servers for his or her zone.

18.23 INTERNET

No discussion of telecommunications would be complete without discussing the Internet, referred to by its millions of users as the Net. The Net evolved from ARPANET, a research network created and subsidized in the 1960s by the Defense Department and the National Science Foundation (NSF) to link research institutions and government agencies around the world to exchange information on a wide range of topics. Although the original ARPANET no longer exists, its design and architecture laid the foundations for the Internet.

The Net, one of the oldest long distance networks in the country, is a network of networks. It links approximately 1.5 million computers, attached to more than 13,000 networks, in 100 or more countries.

Businesses use the Net for a number of tasks, such as sharing files, sending E-mail, and selling goods and services. Fewer than 1% of major companies today are *not* attached to the Internet. In fact, the Internet has become such an integral part of the corporate landscape that it is generating a number of entrepreneurial opportunities and highly specialized jobs: there are Internet explorers, security experts, technicians, librarians, trainers, and other service providers. In fact, the Internet is becoming so common that many employers expect their new hires to have a working knowledge of it.

Think of the Internet as a huge repository of information on almost every topic imaginable. People all over the world can search the net for information, add new information, and exchange views on different topics. The Internet is an electronic web that connects people and businesses that have access to networks and allows them to send and receive E-mail and to participate in a number of other activities, around the clock. In fact, the Internet is so huge, with such a wide variety of features, that there are few, if any, experts in the world who know everything about it.

Thus in spite of its enormous power and potential, no one really owns the Internet, although some segments of it may have their own funding and guidelines.

The primary workings of the Internet are funded by the National Science Foundation (NSF); the Internet Engineering Task Force (IETF), a committee of scientists and experts, provides technical supervision, standards, and guidelines for the Net. Any network (remember, the Internet is simply a network of networks) connected to the Internet must abide by the standards established by the Internet Architecture Board (IAB).

18.24 INFORMATION SUPERHIGHWAY

A network of networks that is fully scalable, with no central controlling entity, and does not determine the user's profile. In recent years, the term **information superhighway** has been used frequently in the media and in the computer literature. Although there is no precise or universally acceptable definition of the information superhighway, it has three primary characteristics:

1. It has no central controlling entity.
2. It is fully capable of handling an increase in the number of users and an increase in the volume of traffic. This is often referred to as the *scalability* of the technology.
3. It does not determine the profile of the user. The user can be a machine, an individual, or any business entity.

Since the Internet has all the above three characteristics, it can be viewed as an excellent model of the information superhighway.

In spite of its many advantages, one of the most-cited disadvantages of the Internet is its inadequate security, because much of the information available over the Net can easily be accessed by dishonest people. The Net was originally used by universities and large corporations to exchange information; 'hackers' were far less numerous. Today, however, with the commercialization of the net, more and more businesses are entering cyberspace—and in their wake come problem of data misuse or theft.

Another problem is that many employees are symbol 'surfing the net' for fun rather than for business purposes. Many companies have established Internet access policies specifying that employees must take *productive* use of the Internet, not waste the time and resources of the organization playing computer games, writing to friends, or accessing information on their favorite topics. Companies are establishing written policies on privacy concerns that employees may have when they realize that they are being monitored by the organization.

Should employees be allowed to surf the Net in search of creative ideas or should they be limited to using the Net strictly for business purposes?

18.25 LINKING TO THE INTERNET

In recent years the Internet has undergone explosive growth, primarily because of the exponential growth in PCs, both at work and in the home. Today, 70% of PC sales are targetted at the home market. Andy Grove, CEO of Intel (which makes Pentium and there chips for the PC market), points out that every 2 years the U.S. makes as many PCs as have existed in all preceding years. Before the spread of PCs, the Internet could be accessed only if an organization was site or node on the Net. Today, one can access the Internet through a company's connection or through commercial online services or simply from a home PC. Further, there are a number of PC-based interfaces that facilitate interaction with the Net. For example, **Cyberdog**, a Macintosh-based tool, allows users to directly access the Internet even without quitting an application, such as word processing. It also allows them to link and update their documents with information from the Internet. Such user- friendly interfaces are another reason for the increased usage of the Internet.

Today, there are a number of commercial online service provides, such as CompuServe, Prodigy, and America Online. It is estimated that there are approximately 6 million users of commercial online services; this number is expected to grow to more than 13 million by 1998. CompuServe claims to have 2 million subscribers, mostly businessmen: Prodigy claims 2 million, including more women and children than CompuServe; America Online claims 1 million subscribers—a younger, more consumer-oriented crowd. (Table 18.2 provides a listing of these online services and their contact numbers.)

Table 18.2 Online Services

Provider	*Number of Subscribers*	*Information Number*
America Online (AOL)	1 million	(800) 827–6364
Prodigy	2 million	(800) 776–3449
CompuServe	2 million	(800) 848–8199
E-World	1 million	(800) 775–4546

18.26 INTERNET ADDRESS

Connection to the Internet opens the door to a vast world of information and communications that resides in files on host computers, including any computer that follows the TCP/IP protocol. (A protocol is a set of rules and standards that ensures the compatibility of different network equipment and components.) Finding a file on the Internet is similar to finding the location of an individual in a city: the user needs the file's address. Addresses are the key to receiving and sending information on the Internet. All individual Internet addresses follow the same two-element pattern: the person's userID, followed by an @, followed by the name of the person's *host computer* (including that of the domain in which it resides). An Internet service provider gives addresses to individuals and organizations that register with it. Let us look closely at the element of an Internet address.

The address uniquely identifies the individual or the organization that the user is trying to reach. For an individual, the name is made up of two parts separated by the character @. For example, if Joe Green is accessing the Net from his home, using his American Online (AOL) account, his internet address might be joe@aol.com. 'aol' identifies the host computer or network; '.com' indicates the domain in which AOL resides. ('.com' stands for commercial sites, '.edu' is for educational institutions. '.mil' is for military ones, and so on.) If Joe Green is connecting to the internet from , say, a machine in the computer science department at New Mexico State University, his address might be jgreen@cs.NMSU.edu.jgreen is his *userID*; cs.NMSU.edu, which identifies the host computer, is known as the *host name*.

Thus, all Internet addresses have the following format or some slight variation thereof:

usrid@name-of-the-computer.name of division/department.name of the institution/organization.type of institution or organization (Note that there are no spaces between the different elements in an Internet address.)

For example, let us take the Internet address

hford@hollywood.fanclub.columbia.com

The userid is *hford* (Harrison Ford); the name of the computer which receives the mail is *hollywood* which is part of the *fanclub* (department) at *Columbia Pictures* (organization), a commercial entity.

18.27 INTERNET TOOLS

Some of the important and popular tools on the Net are discussed below.

These include:

- ❐ Information retrieval tools (ftp and Gopher)
- ❐ Communication tools (E-mail, telnet, Usenet)
- ❐ Multimedia information tools (World Wide Web)
- ❐ Information search tools (WAIS, Archie, Veronica)

Each of these is briefly discussed below:

18.27.1 Information Retrieval Tools

18.27.1.1 ftp

File transfer protocol (ftp) which was one of the first tools on the Internet, allows users to move files, such as text, graphics, sound, and so on, from one computer to another. It is a command that activates a type of client-server relationship. *FTP* works as follows: The user first uses the software on his or her machine (or service provider), called the client, to gain access to the remote machine, called the server. The user's client program communicates with a program on the remote computer, to either *upload*, or *send* to the remote computer or *download* (receive) certain requested files from it.

Another popular way to retrieve files is by using what is called an *anonymous ftp server*. In this case, the user logs on to the server using the special user ID *anonymous*. If the server then asks for a pass-word, the user types in his or her user ID. Freeware and shareware—programs that are available at no cost on the Net—can be obtained through anonymous *ftp* servers. Although it is easy to retrieve the information once the site is located, sometimes it is difficult to locate an *ftp* site or identify the files available on that site.

18.27.1.2 Gopher

The second type of information retrieval tool available on the Internet is **Gopher**, a menu-based interface that provides easy access to information residing on special servers, called Gopher sites. Although Gopher performs primarily the same tasks as the *ftp* command, its interface is much more user-friendly and it provides additional functions, such as links to other Internet services. By selecting an item on the Gopher menu, users can move, retrieve, or display files from remote sites. The menu also allows users to move from one Gopher site to another, where each site provides different information. The entire Gopherspace (which refers to the interconnected Gopher servers) can be easily expanded by adding more servers.

18.27.2 Communication Tools

Communication tools facilitate written communications and in this section we discuss three types of communication tools: E-mail, Telnet and Usenet.

18.27.2.1 E-mail

E-mail, which refers to sending messages or files electronically, was one of the first Internet tools.

18.27.2.2 Telnet

Telnet is a command that connects the user to a remote machine which may be located anywhere on the Internet and the user can then type commands to the remote machine, for example to change directories in search of certain files. While the *ftp* only allows users to move or transfer files, the services that *Telnet* provides depend on the services provided by the host machine, which may include much more than simple file transfers. For example, some servers are dedicated to the playing of board games, such as chess or go.

18.27.2.3 Usenet

The **Usenet** is a network that provides users with discussion groups or forums. A user posts an article to a chosen newsgroup on the Usenet, where each newsgroup is devoted to particular topic such as politics, the environment, gun control, surfing, and so on. The article is routed only to those sites that have expressed an interest in receiving information on the topic.

Many find the Usenet to be helpful for gathering information on a variety of topics. For example, vendors monitor the technical forums on the Usenet closely to answer technical questions that customers may have and to stomp out any misinformation or rumours about their company or its products. For instance, the calculation error in Intel Corp's Pentium microprocessor was first discussed on an Internet Usenet newsgroup. Another popular application on Usenet is downloading new or upgraded software from vendors and obtaining quotes for products and services. IS managers are also tapping into the Usenet to search for potential employees. One IS manager posts particularly thorny technical problems on the Usenet in the relevant discussion groups and then makes an offer to individuals who gave some of the best replies.

18.27.2.4 Multimedia Information Tools

World Wide Web. The **World Wide Web (WWW)** is one of the newest and most popular hypertext-based Internet tool. It allows users to access and display documents and graphics stored on any server on the Internet. In 1989, Tim Berners-Lee, a computer scientist at the CERN particle physics lab in Switzerland, designed WWW as a tool to help an international group of physicists exchange findings and information related to their research. It became popular only in late 1993, when WWW software was delivered for desktops that used popular operating systems, such a Windows, allowing users easy and friendly access to the Internet. Some WWW terms are shown as follows:

CGI: Common gateway interface. A specification for a communication interface between external systems and a Web server.

HTML: Hyper-Text Markup Language. A text formatting language used to create Web pages.

HTTP: Hyper-Text Transport Protocol. The communications protocol between a Web server and a client.

Image Map: A text file that defines regions using graphics files (usually GIF files) that users can click on to navigate.

MIME: Multipurpose Internet Mail Extensions. An Internet standard for sending and receiving multimedia E-mail.

Server-Side: A Web server feature that lets HTML pages be parsed 'on the fly', filling in parts of the page with information from external files.

S-HTTP: Secure Hyper-Text Transport Protocol. An extension of HTTP that provides communication and transaction security for Web clients and servers.

SSL: Secure socket layer. A transport mechanism developed by Netscape Communication for transmitting secure data over a network.

URL: Uniform resource locator. An address that specifies the location of a Web page.

There are many interfaces to the WWW, such as Mosaic, a GUI- based hypertext browser, and Netscape, that allows users to easily navigate the Internet and access it many services. These easy-to-use interfaces are playing an important role in popularizing the Internet, and many companies that once shied away from the Net are now making user of these interfaces to create their own Web pages (discussed below). According to Michael J. Walsh, president of Internet Info., in Falls Church, Virgina, the number of companies with *.com* addresses (which indicate a commercial site) is expected to double within the next year, primarily because it is now easy to use the Internet and gain 24-hour access to customers all over the world.

18.27.2.5 Home page

The World Wide Web has also spawned new services, known as service providers, that provide a multitude of services on the Web. For example, a Web service provider can help a company establish a home page on the Net, an electronic description of the company and its products and services, similar to a catalog or a brochure. Just as catalogs should be attractive and grab the interest of customers, the home page should also be attractive and encourage the user to further explore the company and its products. It can cost from $300 to $10,000 per page of information; for interactive home pages (where the user and the system can interact), the cost per page can be higher.

Basic requirements to set up a home page include an Integrated Services Digital Network (ISDN) line, software to generate Hypertext Markup Language (HTML), which is the graphical interface to the internet, and a PC or Unix Server that has between 16M bytes and 32 M bytes of RAM and runs at 100 Mhz or more.

Many companies are setting up home pages to attract new customers. For example, GE Plastics found that as soon as it set up a Web page, it was getting approximately 12,000 potential inquires each month about its products. Before the page was set up, it took nearly 3 days to respond to customer queries; now customers can get information within a few minutes. The company firmly believes that setting up a Web page has given it a competitive advantage. Further, the cost of setting up a Web page was much lower than that of printing pamphlets and mailing catalogs to customers. The advantages of a Web page are so great that, as one spokesperson said, 'You simply can't lose. There is nothing equivalent to the Net'.

Security APL is an example of another company that relies on the internet to enhance internal and external communications.

In 1995, when statewide elections were held in California, tens of thousands of voters accessed a World Wide Web server that contained poll reports culled every five minutes from the state's Election Web Server. The California Voter Foundation, a nonprofit organization in Sacramento, launched the California Online Voter Guide, a Gopher site that contains biographies, position papers, press releases and E-mail addresses of candidates running for statewide office. Clinton's 1992 presidential campaign was notable for making his E-mail address public, and the White House recently established its own World-Wide Web Home Page (try whitehouse.gov).

United Parcel Service (UPS) is another company that has set up an *electronic storefront* on the Internet—on CompuServe and Prodigy., the commercial online service providers. The home page allows users to arrange for UPS package pickups and deliveries. The company is confident that the page will increase business from existing customers and will also attract new customers who are avid users of the Net. Our competitors aren't online yet, and that gives us an edge where we can generate some allegiance to our service says a UPS spokesperson.

1-800-Flowers, a small business in the flowers-by-wire industry, found that setting up shop on CompuServe not only attracts more business (5% of the firm's $100 million in revenue is generated by online orders), but has also saved the company 10% to 30% by replacing direct mailing and telemarketing.

Although there are many advantages to a home page, some experts are worried that the Internet may simply become a 'de facto national post office', and may become heavily commercialized. As more and more businesses start using the Net to sell their products and services, the Net may not be capable of handling the expanded volume of traffic. Ray Hoving, chairman of the Society for Information Management's (SIM) National Data Highways Advisory Council, is concerned about the technical, administrative, and security issues that will arise as traffic on the Net continues to increase.

18.27.3 Information Search Tools

18.27.3.1 Archie

The tools discussed in this section help users locate information on the Net. For example, **Archie**, one of the first information search tools developed on the Internet, periodically searches anonymous ftp servers that participate in the Archie database and identifies *all* files on these servers. It then creates a central index of all files available on anonymous ftp sites and creates a central database that users can access to locate information.

Users who have the Archie software, or who can use the Telnet command to connect to an Archie server, can access this database. The only disadvantage is that the user must know at least part of the filename in order to be able to search for the file. When the desired file is located, the servicer identifies the file's address and the user can use the ftp command to access and retrieve the file. Though Archie is a very useful tool for locating files, it must be noted that not all anonymous ftp sites participate in the Archie database, and therefore, the database is not a comprehensive one.

18.27.3.2 Veronica

Veronica is a search tool designed specifically to locate all files on Gopher sites and it is listed under *Other Gopher and Information Servers* on the Gopher menu. Users who have access to a Gopher server and a Veronica server can then access the database. Note however, that some Gopher serves may choose not to participate in the Veronica Service. One of the biggest advantages of Veronica over Archie is that the user does not have to know the filename; phrases descriptive of the search area will do.

18.27.3.3 WAIS

WAIS (Wide Area Information Server), pronounced 'ways', is a search system that accesses servers all over the world to locate requested files. The WAIS database has an index of keyboards that helps users to locate files in topic areas of interest to them. When given the keywords, WAIS returns the addresses where the files are located. The user can then user one of the other services discussed above to download the files. If a particular file is not found on a given WAIS server, the server will automatically direct the query to other WAIS servers on the Net.

18.28 SUMMARY

TCP/IP is a serious protocol suite. It provides reasonable network services for most applications and is extensible, well documented, and fairly straightforward to implement. Best, it is capable of connecting dissimilar machines on dissimilar networks together into one big happy network. After all, that is all we really want anyway.

The other Internet resource discovery services that we briefly described, **Archie, WAIS, Gopher**, **Veronica**, and **WWW**, help us locate files and documents across the Internet. Other resource discovery tools are currently being developed.

REVIEW QUESTIONS

1. Find the class of the following host address:
(*a*) 123.56.3.67 (*b*) 197.23.56.23
(*c*) 232.23.67.123 (*d*) 143.23.56.23

2. Find the network address of each host address in the preceding problem.

3. Write the binary form of the following internet addresses:
(*a*) 124.34.6.9 (*b*) 23.67.6.3 (*c*) 0.23.56.0 (*d*) 12.34.67.125

4. Show by calculation how many hosts per network each IP address class (A, B, and C only) can have.

5. Show by calculation how many networks (not hosts) each IP address class (A, B, and C only) can have.

6. Both the DNS and the IP address identify a host computer. Are both identifications necessary? Why or why not?

7. What are the advantages of using UDP over TCP?

8. Why is the domain name reversed when searching for the IP address?

9. Discuss the two connections between client and server that are needed in FTP.

10. How does a manager using SNMP make changes on the network it is managing? Include a discussion of the role of variables.

11. Define the term reliable as used in data communications and relate it to TCP.

12. Define the term connection-oriented as used in data communications and relate it to TCP.

13. Which file transfer protocol uses TCP and establishes two virtual circuits between the local and remote server?
(*a*) FTP (*b*) TFTP (*c*) TELNET (*d*) NFS

14. Which file transfer protocol uses UDP?
(*a*) FTP (*b*) TFTP (*c*) TELNET (*d*) NFS

15. Use the _______ domain functions to find the domain name if the IP address is known.
(*a*) reverse (*b*) generic (*c*) country (*d*) group

16. In DNS, the first-level classification in the _______ domain is based on the organisation type of the host's network.
(*a*) reverse (*b*) generic (*c*) country (*d*) group

17. DNS can obtain the _______ of a host if its domain name is known, and vice-versa.
(*a*) station address (*b*) IP address (*c*) port address (*d*) checksum

18. Which application allows a user to access and change remote files without actual transfer?
(*a*) DNS (*b*) FTP (*c*) NFS (*d*) TELNET

19. Which application allows a user to log in to a remote computer?
(*a*) DNS (*b*) FTP (*c*) TELNET (*d*) RPC

20. Which of the following is an example of a client-server model?
(*a*) DNS (*b*) FTP (*c*) TELNET (*d*) All of the above

21. This transport layer protocol is connectionless.
(*a*) UDP (*b*) TCP (*c*) FTP (*d*) NVT.

22. TCP/IP's _______ layer corresponds to the OSI model's top three layers.
(*a*) application (*b*) presentation (*c*) session (*d*) transport

23. The data unit from the transport layer that uses UDP is called a ________.
(*a*) user datagram (*b*) message (*c*) segment (*d*) frame

24. Which of the following apply to both UDP and TCP?
(*a*) Transport layer protocols (*b*) Port-to-port communication
(*c*) Use services of IP layer (*d*) All of the above

25. Which OSI layer corresponds to the TCP-UDP layer?
(*a*) Physical (*b*) Data link (*c*) Network (*d*) Transport

26. Which OSI layer corresponds to the IP layer?
(*a*) Physical (*b*) Data link (*c*) Network (*d*) Transport

ANSWERS

13. (*a*)	**14.** (*b*)	**15.** (*a*)	**16.** (*b*)	**17.** (*b*)	**18.** (*c*)	**19.** (*c*)	**20.** (*d*)
21. (*a*)	**22.** (*a*)	**23.** (*a*)	**24.** (*d*)	**25.** (*d*)	**26.** (*c*)		

INTERNET PROTOCOL VERSION 6 (IPv6)

19.1 INTRODUCTION

Internet Protocol version 6 (IPv6) is the new generation of the basic protocol of the Internet. IP is the common language of the Internet, every device connected to the Internet must support it. The current version of IP (IP version 4) has several shortcomings which complicate, and in some cases present a barrier to, the further development of the Internet. The coming IPv6 revolution should remove these barriers and provide a feature-rich environment for the future of global networking.

The IPv6 story began in the early nineties when it was discovered that the address space available in IPv4 was vanishing quite rapidly. Contemporary studies indicated that it may be depleted within the next ten years around 2005! These findings challenged the Internet community to start looking for a solution. Two possible approaches were at hand:

1. **Minimal:** Keep the protocol intact, just increase the address length. This was the easier way promising less pain in the deployment phase.
2. **Maximal:** Develop an entirely new version of the protocol. Taking this approach would enable incorporating new features and enhancements in IP.

Because there was no urgent need for a quick solution, the development of a new protocol was chosen. Its original name IP Next Generation (IPng) was soon replaced by IP version 6 which is now the definitive name. The main architects of this new protocol were Steven Deering and Robert Hinden.

The first set of RFCs specifying the IPv6 were released at the end of 1995, namely, RFC 1883: Internet Protocol, Version 6 (IPv6) Specification [RFC1883] and its relatives. Once the definition was available, implementations were eagerly awaited. But they did not come.

The second half of the nineties was a period of significant Internet boom. Companies on the market had to solve a tricky business problem: while an investment in IPv6 can bring some benefits in the future, an investment in the blossoming IPv4 Internet earns money now. For a vast majority of them it was essentially a no-brainer: they decided to prefer the rapid and easy return of investments and developed IPv4-based products.

Another factor complicating IPv6 deployment was the change of rules in the IPv4 domain. Methods to conserve the address space were developed and put into operation. The most important of these was Classless Inter-Domain Routing (CIDR). The old address classes were removed and address assignment rules hardened. As a consequence, newly connected sites obtained significantly less addresses than in previous years.

The use of CIDR may well have delayed the need for IPv6 in the eyes of many people, but not in all. Somewhat perversely, the use of CIDR accelerated the perception of a lack of address space in the eyes of those who were relatively new to the Internet. Since the Internet was booming, requests for new address blocks were increasing, yet the size of assigned address blocks were being reduced. Thus, new or expanding sites had to develop methods to spare this scarce resource. One of these approaches is network address translation (NAT) which allows a network to use an arbitrary number of non-public addresses, which are translated to public ones when the packets leave the site (and vice-versa). Thus, NATs provided a mechanism for hosts to share public addresses. Furthermore, mechanisms such as PPP and DHCP provide a means for hosts to lease addresses for some period of time.

The widespread deployment of NAT solutions weakened the main IPv6 driving force. While IPv6 still has additional features to IPv4 (like security and mobility support), these were not strong enough to attract a significant amount of companies to develop IPv6 implementations and applications. Consequently, the deployment of IPv6 essentially stalled during this period.

Fortunately, the development of the protocol continued. Several experimental implementations were created and some practical experience gained through to operation of the 6bone network. This led to the revisited set of specifications published in the end of 1998 (RFC 2460 and others).

An important player in the IPv6 field has always been the academic networks, being generally keen on new technologies and not that much interested in immediate profit. Many of them deployed the new protocol and provided it to their users for experimentation. This brought a lot of experience and also manpower for further development.

Probably the most important period for IPv6 so far has been the first years of the 21st century, when IPv6 finally gained some momentum. The increasing number of implementations forced remaining hardware/software vendors to react and to enhance their products with IPv6 capabilities.

The new protocol also appeared in a number of real-world production networks. Network providers in Asia seemed to be especially interested in IPv6 deployment. The reason for this is clear—the Internet revolution started later in these countries, so they obtained less IPv4 addresses and the lack of address space is thus considerably more painful here. In short, the rapid growth of Internet connectivity in Asia cannot be served by the relatively miniscule IPv4 address space assigned to the region. This even led to some governments declaring their official support for IPv6.

IPv6 was developed by the Internet Engineering Task Force (IETF) to deal with this long-anticipated IPv4 address exhaustion, and is described in Internet standard document RFC 2460, published in December 1998. Like IPv4, IPv6 is an Internet Layer protocol for packet-switched internetworking and provides end-to-end datagram transmission across multiple IP networks. While IPv4 allows 32 bits for an Internet Protocol address, and can therefore support 2^{32} (4,294,967,296) addresses, IPv6 uses 128 bit addresses, so the new address space supports 2^{128} (*i.e.*, 3.4×10^{38}) addresses. Internet Protocol version 6 (IPv6) greatly improves on IPv4 by vastly increasing the number of available addresses and by enabling more efficient routing, simpler configuration, built-in IP security, better support for real-time data delivery, and other essential enhancements.

It also eliminates the primary need for network address translation (NAT), which gained widespread deployment as an effort to alleviate IPv4 address exhaustion. IPv6 also implements additional features not present in IPv4. It simplifies aspects of address assignment (stateless address auto configuration), network renumbering and router announcements when changing Internet connectivity providers. The IPv6 subnet size has been standardized by fixing the size of the host identifier portion of an address to 64 bits to facilitate an automatic mechanism for forming the host identifier from link layer media addressing information (MAC address). Network security is also integrated into the design of the IPv6 architecture, and the IPv6 specification mandates support for IPsec as a fundamental interoperability requirement.

All in all, after some years of hesitation IPv6 finally leaves the status of a high-tech extravagance and starts to be a usable tool.

19.2 IPv6 ADDRESS STRUCTURE

IPv6 represents a significant update to the Internet Protocol version 4, but the modifications and additions are made without changing the core nature of how IP works. Addressing is the place where most of the differences between IPv4 and IPv6 are seen, but the changes are mostly in how addresses are implemented and used. Some of the general characteristics of the IPv6 addressing are basically the same as in IPv4:

1. **Core Functions of Addressing:** The two main functions of addressing are still network interface identification and routing. Routing is facilitated through the structure of addresses on the internetwork.
2. **Network Layer Addressing:** IPv6 addresses are still the ones associated with the network layer in TCP/IP networks, and are distinct from data link layer also sometimes called physical addresses.
3. **Number of IP Addresses Per Device:** Addresses are still assigned to network interfaces, so a regular host like a PC will usually have one (unicast) address, and routers will have more than one, for each of the physical networks to which it connects.
4. **Address Interpretation and Prefix Representation:** IPv6 addresses are like classless IPv4 addresses in that they are interpreted as having a network identifier part and a host identifier part, but that the delineation is not encoded into the address itself. A prefix length number, using CIDR-like notation, is used to indicate the length of the network ID (prefix length).
5. **Private and Public Addresses:** Both types of addresses exist in IPv6, though they are defined and used somewhat differently.

19.2.1 IPv6 Address Types

One important change in the addressing of IPv6 is the address types supported. IPv4 supported three address types: unicast, multicast and broadcast. Of these, the vast majority of actual traffic was unicast. IP multicast support was not widely deployed until many years after the Internet was established, and continues to be hampered by various issues. Use of broadcast in IP had to be severely restricted for performance reasons (we don't want any device to be able to broadcast across the entire Internet!)

IPv6 also supports three address types, but with some changes:

1. **Unicast Addresses:** These are standard unicast addresses as in IPv4, one per host interface.
2. **Multicast Addresses:** These are addresses that represent various groups of IP devices: a message sent to a multicast address goes to all devices in the group. IPv6 includes much better multicast features and many more multicast addresses than IPv4.
3. **Anycast Addresses:** Anycast addressing is used when a message must be sent to any member of a group, but does not need to be sent to them all. Usually the member of the group that is easiest to reach will be sent the message. One common example of how anycast addressing could be used is in load sharing amongst a group of routers in an organization.

19.2.2 Implications of the Changes to Address Types in IPv6

Broadcast addressing as a distinct addressing method is gone in IPv6. Broadcast functionality is implemented using multicast addressing to groups of devices. A multicast group to which all nodes belong can be used for broadcasting in a network, for example,

An important implication of the creation of anycast addressing is removal of the strict uniqueness requirement for IP addresses. Anycast is accomplished by assigning the same IP address to more than one device. The devices must also be specifically told that they are sharing an anycast address, but the addresses themselves are structurally the same as unicast addresses.

19.2.3 IPv6 Address Size

IPv4 allows 32 bits for an Internet Protocol address, and can therefore support 2^{32} (4,294,967,296) addresses, IPv6 uses 128 bits addresses or sixteen 8 bit octets/bytes, so the new address space supports 2^{128} (*i.e.*, 3.4×10^{38}) addresses.

19.2.4 IPv6 Address Space

IPv6 supports addresses which are four times the number of bits as IPv4 addresses (128 vs. 32). This is 4 Billion times 4 Billion times 4 Billion (2^^96) times the size of the IPv4 address space (2^^32). This works out to be: **340,282,366,920,938,463,463,374,607,431,768,211,456**

This is an extremely large address space. In a theoretical sense this is approximately 665,570,793,348,866,943,898,599 addresses per square meter of the surface of the planet Earth (assuming the earth surface is 511,263,971,197,990 square meters).

19.3 REPRESENTATION OF IPv6 ADDRESS

Increase in the size of IP addresses from 32 bits to 128 bits, makes it very difficult to use in binary and decimal notation. There are various flexible ways to represent the IP addresses.

19.3.1 Dotted Decimal Notation of IPv6

Computers work in binary, and they have no problem dealing with long strings of ones and zeroes, but humans find them confusing. Even the 32 bit addrcsses of IPv4 are very cumbersome, that why we use dotted decimal notation. However, IPv6 addresses are top larger than IPv4 addresses that even using dotted decimal notation becomes problematic. To use this notation, we would split the 128 bits into 16 octets and represent each with a decimal number from 0 to 255. A typical IPv6 address in this notation would appear as follows:

138.81.55.167.230.50.0.0.0.0.242.97.202.100.21.255

The binary and dotted decimal representations of this address are shown at the top of Fig. 19.1. The top two rows show binary and dotted decimal representations of an IPv6 address; not commonly used. The top row of the lower table shows the full hexadecimal representation, while the next two rows illustrate zero suppression and compression. The last row shows mixed notation, where the final 32 bits of an IPv6 address are shown in dotted decimal notation. This is most commonly used for embedded IPv4 addresses.

Binary	1000101001010001001101111010011111100110001100100000000000000000															
	0000000000000000111100100110000111001010011001000001010111111111															
Dotted Decimal	138	81	55	167	230	50	0	0	0	0	242	97	202	100	21	255
Bits	0				32				64				96			128
Hexadecimal																
Straight Hex	8A51		37A7		E632		0000		0000		F261		CA64		15FF	
Leading Zero Suppressed	8A51		37A7		E632		0		0		F261		CA64		15FF	
Zero Compressed	8A51		37A7		E632		::				F261		CA64		15FF	
Mixed Notation	8A51		37A7		E632		::				F261		202	100	21	255

Fig. 19.1 Representations of IPv6 in Binary, Decimal and Hexadecimal

19.3.2 Hexadecimal Notation of IPv6

To make IPv6 addresses shorter, the decision was made to change the primary method of expressing addresses to use hexadecimal instead of decimal. The advantage of this is that it requires fewer characters to represent an address, and that converting from hex to binary and back again is much easier than converting from binary to decimal or vice-versa. The disadvantage is that many people, even computer people, find hexadecimal difficult to comprehend and work with, especially because the notion of 16 values in each digit is a bit strange.

The hexadecimal notation used for IPv6 addresses is similar to the same method used for IEEE 802 MAC addresses, for technologies like Ethernet. There, 48 bits are represented by six octets, each octet being a hexadecimal number from 0 to FF, separated by a dash or colon, like this:

FF-AF-84-17-DB-DF

Since IPv6 addresses are larger, they are instead grouped into eight 16-bit words, separated by colons, to create what is sometimes called *colon hexadecimal notation*, again shown in Fig. 19.1. So, the IPv6 address given in the example above would be expressed as:

8A51:37A7:E632:0000:0000:F261:CA64:15FF

To keep size down, leading zeroes can be suppressed in the notation, so we can immediately reduce this to:

8A51:37A7:E632:0:0:F261:CA64:15FF

Fortunately, there is a short-cut that can be applied to shorten some addresses even further. This technique is sometimes called zero compression. The method allows a single string of contiguous zeroes in an IPv6 address to be replaced by a double-colon. So, for example, the address above could be expressed as:

8A51:37A7:E632::F261:CA64:15FF

Note: To prevent ambiguity, the double-colon can appear only once in any IP address, because if it appeared more than once we could not tell how many zeroes were replaced in each instance. For example, if our address was 8A51:37A7:E632:0:0:F261:0:0, we can replace either the first pair of zeroes or the second, but not both.

For example, if your IP address were 8A51:37A7:0:0:0:0:0:62, then it can be written as 8A51:37A7::62

It works even better on special addresses. The full IPv6 loopback address is:

0:0:0:0:0:0:0:1, with compression, this is simply '::1'

19.3.3 Mixed Notation of IPv6

An alternative notation used in some cases or especially for expressing IPv6 addresses that embed IPv4 addresses. In this case, it is useful to show the IPv4 portion of the address in the older dotted decimal notation. Since embedding uses the last 32 bits for the IPv4 address, the notation has the first 96 bits in colon hexadecimal notation, and the last 32 bits in dotted decimal. For example, IP address:

8A51:37A7:E632::F261:CA64:15FF

Will be written in the mixed notation as:

8A51:37A7:E632::F261:202.100.21.255

This is really a great example of mixed notation, because embedding usually involves long strings of zeroes followed by the IPv4 address. Thus, zero compression comes in very handy here. Instead of seeing something like this:

0:0:0:0:0:0:202.100.21.255

You will typically see:

::202.100.21.255

At first glance this appears to be an IPv4 address; you have to keep a close eye on those colons in IPv6.

19.3.4 Representation of IPv6 Address Prefix Length

Like IPv4 classless addresses, IPv6 addresses are fundamentally divided into a number of network ID bits followed by a number of host ID bits. The network identifier is called the prefix, and the number of bits used is the prefix length. This prefix is represented by following the address by a slash and then putting the prefix length after the slash. This is the same method used for classless IPv4 addressing with CIDR. For example, if the first 48 bits of our example address were the network ID (prefix), then we would express this as:

8A51:37A7:E632::F261:CA64:15FF/48

As in IPv4, specifies for whole networks will typically end in long strings of zeroes. These can be replaced by '::' using zero compression. For example, the 48 bit network ID for the example above is 8A51:37A7:E632::F261:0.0.0.0/48 or 8A51:37A7:E632::F261::/48. You must include the '::' for replacing the trailing zeroes.

Aggregatable global unicast addresses are similar to the IPv4 public addresses and can be routed over an IPv6 Internet. The format prefixes of these addresses are 001::/3. These addresses were designed to support efficient hierarchical addressing and routing. The unique scope of this address scheme is the Internet itself. The lower 3 bits are used to identify the address as globally unique. The next 45 bits are allocated by the ISP of the host, this makes up a prefix of ::/48. The following higher 16 bits determine site topology (subnet) on which the host belongs to. The remaining 64 bits are the unique interface identifier made up of the MAC address and subnet of which it's on.

To create the **Extended Unique Identifier (EUI)** a device's MAC address is used. The value 'fffe' is inserted into the middle of the 48 bit MAC address therefore making it 64 bits. This also means that it becomes a unique identifier for that machine. A MAC address is a global unique identifier for networked machines.

19.4 IPv4 VERSUS IPv6

IPv6 is a new version of the Internet Protocol, designed as a successor to IP version 4. IPv6 is assigned IP version number 6 and is formally called IPv6. Comparison of IPv6 vs IPv4 is shown in Table 19.1.

Table 19.1 Comparison of IPv6 vs IPv4

	IPv4	*IPv6*
Deployed	1981	1999
Address Format	32 Bits Dotted Decimal Notation.	128 Bits Hexadecimal Notation.
Number of Addresses		
Subnetting	Subnet identified by subnet mask.	Subnet identified within the address.
Routing Protocols	RIP, RIPv2, EIGRP	RIP, RIPv2, EIGRP
Classfull/Classless	Classful and Classless.	Classless Addressing Scheme.
Address Configuration	Static, DHCP	Stateless Autoconfiguration, DHCP v6.
Loopback Address	127.0.0.1	::1
Broadcast Address Types	Multicast/Broadcast	Anycast
Header Length	20 bytes	40 bytes
Address Resource Record	Address (A) resource records in DNS to map host names to IPv4 addresses.	Address (AAAA) resource records in DNS to map host names to IPv6 addresses.
Pointer (PTR) Resource Records	Pointer (PTR) resource records in the IN-ADDR.ARPA DNS domain to map IPv4 addresses to host names.	Pointer (PTR) resource records in the IP6.ARPA DNS domain to map IPv6 addresses to host names.
IPsec	Optional	Not Optional

IPv6 was designed to take an evolutionary step from IPv4. It was not a design goal to take a radical step away from IPv4. Functions which work in IPv4 were kept in IPv6. Functions which didn't work were removed. The changes from IPv4 to IPv6 fall primarily into the following categories:

19.4.1 Expanded Routing and Addressing Capabilities

IPv6 increases the IP address size from 32 bits to 128 bits, to support more levels of addressing hierarchy and a much greater number of addressable nodes, and simpler auto-configuration of addresses.

The scalability of multicast routing is improved by adding a 'scope' field to multicast addresses.

A new type of address called a 'anycast address' is defined, to identify sets of nodes where a packet sent to an anycast address is delivered to one of the nodes. The use of anycast addresses in the IPv6 source route allows nodes to control the path which their traffic flows.

19.4.2 Header Format Simplification

Some IPv4 header fields have been dropped or made optional, to reduce the common-case processing cost of packet handling and to keep the bandwidth cost of the IPv6 header as low as possible despite the increased size of the addresses. Even though the IPv6 addresses are four time longer than the IPv4 addresses, the IPv6 header is only twice the size of the IPv4 header.

19.4.3 Improved Support for Options

Changes in the way IP header options are encoded allows for more efficient forwarding, less stringent limits on the length of options, and greater flexibility for introducing new options in the future.

19.4.4 Quality-of-Service Capabilities

A new capability is added to enable the labeling of packets belonging to particular traffic 'flows' for which the sender requests special handling, such as non-default quality of service or 'real-time' service.

19.4.5 Authentication and Privacy Capabilities

IPv6 includes the definition of extensions which provide support for authentication, data integrity, and confidentiality. This is included as a basic element of IPv6 and will be included in all implementations.

The IPv6 protocol consists of two parts, the basic IPv6 header format and IPv6 extension headers.

19.5 IPv6 ADDRESS SPACE ALLOCATION

As was the case with IPv4, the two primary concerns in deciding how to divide the IPv6 address space were address assignment and routing. The designers of IPv6 wanted to structure the address space to make allocation of addresses to ISPs, organizations and individuals as easy as possible.

At first, this perhaps ironically, this led the creators of IPv6 back full circle to the use of specific bit sequences to identify different types of addresses, just like the old 'classful' addressing scheme. The address type was indicated by a set of bits at the start of the address, called the *format prefix* (*FP*). The format prefix was conceptually identical to the 1 to 4 bits used in IPv4 'classful' addressing to denote address classes, but was variable in length, ranging from three to ten bits.

The allocation of different parts of the IPv6 address space still is done based on particular patterns of the first three to ten bits of the address, to allow certain categories to have more addresses than others. The elimination of the specific term denoting this is intended to convey that these bits should not be given 'special attention'.

Table 19.2 shows the allocations of the IPv6 address space, and what fraction of the total address space each represents:

Table 19.2 IPv6 Address Space Alloations

Prefix (Binary)	*Fraction of Total IPv6 Address Space*	*Allocation*
0000 0000	1/256	Unassigned (Includes special addresses such as the Unspecified and Loopback addresses)
0000 0001	1/256	Unassigned
0000 001	1/128	Reserved for NSAP Address Allocation
0000 010	1/128	Reserved for the IPX Allocation
0000 01	1/64	Unassigned
0000 1	1/32	Unassigned
0001	1/16	Unassigned
001	1/8	Global Unicast Addresses
010	1/8	Unassigned
011	1/8	Unassigned
100	1/8	Unassigned
101	1/8	Unassigned
110	1/8	Unassigned
1110	1/16	Unassigned
1111 0	1/32	Unassigned
1111 10	1/64	Unassigned
1111 110	1/128	Unassigned
1111 1110 0	1/512	Unassigned
1111 1110 10	1/1024	Link-Local Unicast Addresses
1111 1110 11	1/1024	Site-Local Unicast Addresses
1111 1111	1/256	Multicast Addresses

This is more complicated than the IPv4 'classful' scheme because there are so many more categories and they range greatly in size, however, most of them are unassigned at the present time.

Subsequent topics in this section provide more information on several of these address blocks. Note that the '0000 0000' reserved block is used for several special address types, including the loopback address, the 'unspecified' address and IPv4 address embedding. The '1111 1111' format prefix identifies multicast addresses; this string is 'FF' in hexadecimal, so any address beginning with 'FF' is a multicast address in IPv6.

This allocation supports the direct allocation of provider addresses, local use addresses, and multicast addresses. Space is reserved for NSAP addresses, IPX addresses, and neutral-interconnect addresses. The remainder of the address space is unassigned for future use. This can be used for expansion of existing use (*e.g.*, additional provider addresses, etc.) or new uses (*e.g.*, separate locators and identifiers). Note that Anycast addresses are not shown here because they are allocated out of the unicast address space.

Approximately fifteen percent of the address space is initially allocated. The remaining 85% is reserved for future use.

19.6 IPv6 GLOBAL UNICAST ADDRESS FORMAT

This is the most important address type because unicast addresses are the 'normal' addresses identifying the common computers, printers and other devices connected to the network. It is anticipated that unicast addressing will be used for the vast majority of Internet traffic under IPv6, just as in the case of IPv4. It is for this reason that the largest of the assigned blocks of the IPv6 address space is dedicated to unicast addressing. A full 1/8th slice of the enormous IPv6 address is assigned to unicast addresses, which are indicated by a '001' in the first three bits of the address.

When IPv4 was first created, the Internet was rather small, and the model for allocating address blocks was based on a central coordinator: IANA. Everyone who wanted address blocks would go straight the central authority. As the Internet grew, this model became impractical. Today, IPv4's classless addressing scheme allows variable-length network IDs and hierarchical assignment of address blocks. Big ISPs get large blocks from the central authority and then subdivide them and allocate them to their customers, and so on. This is managed by today's Internet providers, but there is nothing in the address space that helps manage the allocation process. In turn, each organization has the ability to further subdivide their address allocation to suit their internal requirements.

The designers of IPv6 had the benefit of this experience and realized there would be tremendous advantages to designing the unicast address structure to reflect the overall topology of the Internet. These include:

1. Easier allocation of address blocks at various levels of the Internet topological hierarchy.
2. IP network addresses that automatically reflect the hierarchy by which routers move information across the Internet, allowing routes to be easily aggregated for more efficient routing.
3. Flexibility for organizations like ISPs to subdivide their address blocks for customers.
4. Flexibility for end-user organizations to subdivide their address blocks to match internal networks, much as sub-netting did in IPv4.
5. Greater 'meaning' to IP addresses. Instead of just being a string of 128 bits with no structure, it would become possible to look at an address and know certain things about it.

19.6.1 Generic IPv6 Format of Global Unicast Address Space

The format for dividing up the 128 bits of the unicast address space is into three sections, as shown in Fig. 19.2.

0		128
Global Routing Prefix (n bits)	Subnet ID (m bits)	Interface Identifier (128-n-m bits)

Fig. 19.2 Generic IPv6 Global Unicast Address Format

1. **Global Routing Prefix (n bits):** The network ID or prefix of the address, used for routing.
2. **Subnet Identifier (m bits):** A number that identifies a subnet within the site.
3. **Interface ID (128-n-m bits):** The unique identifier for a particular interface (host or other device). It is unique within the specific prefix and subnet.

The global routing prefix and subnet identifier represent the two basic levels at which addresses need to be hierarchically-constructed: global and site-specific. The routing prefix consists of a number of bits that can be further subdivided according to the needs of Internet Registries and Internet Service Providers, to reflect the topography of the Internet as a whole (we'll discuss this soon). The subnet ID gives a number of bits to site administrators for creating their own internal network structure.

19.6.2 IPv6 Implementation of the Unicast Address Space

In theory, any size for 'n' and 'm' could be used. The implementation chosen for IPv6, however, assigns 48 bits to the routing prefix and 16 bits to the subnet identifier. This means 64 bits are available for interface identifiers, which are constructed based on the IEEE 'EUI-64' format, as described in the next section. Thus, the overall IPv6 unicast address format is constructed as shown in Fig. 19.3.

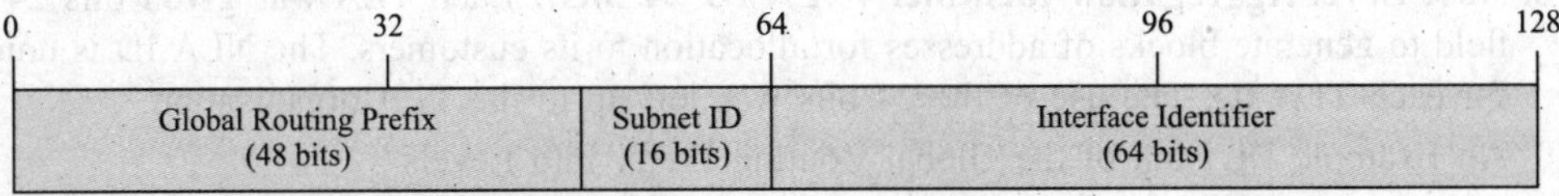

Fig. 19.3 IPv6 Global Unicast Address Format

1. **Global Routing Prefix (48 bits):** The network ID or prefix of the address, used for routing. The first three bits are '001' to indicate a unicast address.
2. **Subnet Identifier (16 bits):** A number that identifies a subnet within the site.
3. **Interface ID (64 bits):** The unique identifier for a particular interface (host or other device). It is unique within the specific prefix and subnet.

Due to this structure, most end sites (regular companies and organizations, as opposed to Internet service providers) will be assigned IPv6 networks with a 48 bit prefix. In common parlance, these network identifiers have now come to be called *48s* or */48s*.

The 16 bits of subnet ID allow each site considerable flexibility in creating subnets that reflect the site's network structure. For example,

1. A smaller organization can just set all the bits in the Subnet ID to zero and have a 'flat' internal structure.
2. A medium-sized organization could use all the bits in the Subnet ID to perform the equivalent of 'straight' sub-netting under IPv4, assigning a different Subnet ID to each subnet. There are 16 bits here, so this allows a whopping 65,536 subnets!
3. A larger organization can use the bits to create a multiple-level hierarchy of subnets, exactly like IPv4's Variable Length Subnet Masking (VLSM). For example, the company could use two bits to create four subnets. It could then take the next three bits to create eight sub-subnets in some or all of the four subnets. There would still be 11 more bits to create sub-sub-subnets and so forth.

19.6.3 Original Division of the Global Routing Prefix

The global routing prefix is similarly divided into a hierarchy, but one that has been designed for the use of the entire Internet, Classless Inter-Domain Routing (CIDR). There are 45 bits available here (48 bits less the first three that are fixed at '001'). When the unicast address structure was first detailed in RFC 2374, that document described a specific division of the 45 bits based on a two-level hierarchical topology of Internet registries and providers. These organizations were described as:

1. **Top-Level Aggregators (TLAs):** The largest Internet organizations, which were to be assigned large blocks of IPv6 addresses from registration authorities.
2. **Next-Level Aggregators (NLAs):** These organizations would get blocks of addresses from TLAs and divide them for end-user organizations (sites).

The 45 bits were split between these two uses, with a few bits reserved in the middle to allow expansion of either field if needed. Thus, the RFC 2374 structure for the 45 bits was as shown follows:

1. **Top-Level Aggregation Identifier (TLA ID 13 bits):** A globally-unique identifier for the Top-Level Aggregator. There are 13 bits so there were a maximum of 8,192 TLAs allowed.
2. **Reserved (RES bits):** These 8 bits were reserved for future use and set to zero. By leaving these 8 bits between the TLA ID and NLA ID unused, they could be later used to expand either the TLA ID or NLA ID fields as needed.
3. **Next-Level Aggregation Identifier (NLA ID 24 bits):** Each TLA was given this 24 bit field to generate blocks of addresses for allocation to its customers. The NLA ID is unique for each TLA ID. The use of the 24 bits was left up to the TLA organization.

An Example Division of the Global Routing Prefix Into Levels

There is no longer any single structure for determining how the 48 bit routing prefix is divided in the global unicast hierarchy. As one example, it might be possible to divide it into three levels, as shown in Figs. 19.4 (*a*) and (*b*).

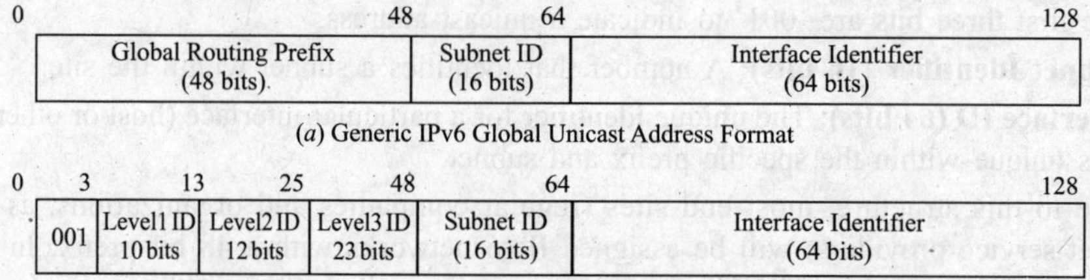

(*a*) Generic IPv6 Global Unicast Address Format

(*b*) Sample Division of Global Routing Prefix into three Hierarchical levels

Fig. 19.4

The details of Fig. 19.4 (*b*) to divide the Global Routing Prefix, into three levels using 10, 12 and 23 bits are shown below:

1. **Unicast Indicator (3 bits):** Each unicast address starts with '001', it used to be called the Format Prefix.
2. **Level 1 Identifier (10 bits):** The identifier of the highest level in the hierarchy. This would be used for assigning to the biggest Internet organizations the largest blocks of addresses in the global hierarchy. The number of Level 1 organizations would be 2^{10} or 1,024. It means 1024 level1 blocks created globally.
3. **Level 2 Identifier (12 bits):** Each block assigned to a Level 1 organization would use 12 bits to create 4,096 address blocks to divide amongst the lower-level organizations it serves.
4. **Level 3 Identifier (23 bits):** Each Level 2 organization has 23 bits to use to divide its Level 2 address block. Thus, it could create over 8 million individual '/48' address blocks to assign to end user sites. Alternately, the 23 bits could be divided further into still lower levels to reflect the structure of the Level 2 organization's customers.

Figure 19.4 (*a*) shows the global IPv6 unicast address format. Fig. 19.4 (*b*) shows one example way to divide the Global Routing Prefix, into three levels using 10, 12 and 23 bits respectively. The third column shows how the first 10 bits are used to create 2^{10} or 1,024 different Level1 blocks, so each of these 13 bit (3 + 10) prefixes, we could have 2^{12} or 4,096 Level2 blocks. Then, within each 25 bits (3 + 10 + 12) Level2 ID, we have 23 bits or 8,388,608 Level3 blocks. A Level3 or '/48' would be assigned to an individual organization.

This is just one possible, theoretical way that the bits in a '/48' network address could be assigned. As you can see, with so many bits there is a lot of flexibility. In the scheme above we can have over 4 million level 2 organizations, ***each of which*** can assign 8 million /48 addresses. And each of those is equivalent in size to an IPv4 Class B address (over 65,000 hosts)!

19.7 IPv6 INTERFACE IDENTIFIERS—MODIFIED EUI-64

Providing 64 bits to identify the interface in the scope of a single subnet seems to be a huge extravagance. For example 48 bits are sufficient for Ethernet addresses which are world-wide unique. Subnets for which 16 bits would not suffice to identify all the nodes are hard to imagine. On the other hand this 64 bit long interface identifier simplifies significantly some auto configuration mechanisms.

RFC 3513 specifies the use of modified EUI-64 identifiers in this part of the IPv6 address. EUI-64 is a network interface identifier defined by the IEEE. The modification deployed in IPv6 is related to 7th bit of the 64 bit identifier. This bit distinguishes global identifiers (world-wide unique) from the local ones (unique only in the scope of single link). The value of this bit is inverted in IPv6 addresses. Hence the value 0 of this bit means a local identifier, while a value of 1 indicates a global ID.

In IPv4, IP addresses have no relationship to the addresses used for underlying data link layer network technologies. A host that connects to a TCP/IP network using an Ethernet network interface card (NIC) has an Ethernet MAC address and an IP address, but the two numbers are distinct and unrelated in any way. IP addresses are assigned manually by administrators without any regard for the underlying physical address.

With the overhaul of addressing in IPv6, an opportunity presented itself to create a better way of mapping IP unicast addresses and physical network addresses. Implementing this superior mapping technique was one of the reasons why IPv6 addresses were made so large. With 128 total bits, as we saw in previous section, even with a full 45 bits reserved for network prefix and 16 bits for site subnet, we are still left with 64 bits to use for the *interface identifier*, which is analogous to the host ID under IPv4.

Having so many bits at our disposal gives us great flexibility. Instead of using arbitrary 'made-up' identifiers for hosts, we can base the interface ID on the underlying data link layer hardware address, as long as that address is no greater than 64 bits in length. Since virtually all devices use layer two addresses of 64 bits or fewer, there is no problem in using those addresses for the interface identifier in IP addresses. This provides an immediate benefit: it makes networks easier to administer, since we don't have to record two arbitrary numbers for each host. The IP address can be derived from the MAC address and the network identifier. It also means we can in the future tell the IP address from the MAC address and vice-versa.

The actual mapping from data link layer addresses to IP interface identifiers depends on the particular technology. It is essential that all devices on the same network use the same mapping technique, of course. By far the most common type of layer 2 addresses in networking are IEEE 802 MAC addresses, used by Ethernet and other IEEE 802 Project networking technologies. As you may already know, these addresses have 48 bits, arranged into two blocks of 24. The upper 24 bits are arranged into a block called the *organizationally unique identifier* (*OUI*), with different values assigned to individual organizations; the lower 24 bits are then used for an identifier for each specific device.

The IEEE has also defined a format called the *64 bit extended unique identifier*, abbreviated *EUI-64*. It is similar to the 48 bit MAC format, except that while the OUI remains at 24 bits, the device identifier becomes 40 bits instead of 24. This provides gives each manufacturer 65,536 times as many device addresses within its OUI. A form of this format, called *modified EUI-64*, has been adopted for IPv6 interface identifiers. To get the modified EUI-64 interface ID for a device, you simply take the EUI-64 address and change the 7th bit from the left (the 'universal/local' or 'U/L' bit) from a zero to a one.

Of course, most devices still use the older 48 bit MAC address format. These can be converted to EUI-64 and then to modified EUI-64 form for creating an IPv6 interface ID. The process is as follows:

We take the 24 bit OUI portion, the left-most 24 bits of the Ethernet address, and put them into the left-most 24 bits of the interface ID. We take the 24 bit local portion (the right-most 24 bits of the Ethernet address) and put it into the right-most 24 bits of the interface ID. In the remaining 16 bits in the middle of the interface ID we put the value '11111111 1111110' ('FFFE' in hexadecimal). The address is now in EUI-64 form. We change the 'universal/local' bit (bit 7 from the left) from a zero to a one. This gives us the modified EUI-64 interface ID.

Let's take as an example the Ethernet address of 48 bits MAC addresses C9-CA-51-64-15-C8 to convert Modified EUI-64 identifiers, as shown in Fig. 19.5.

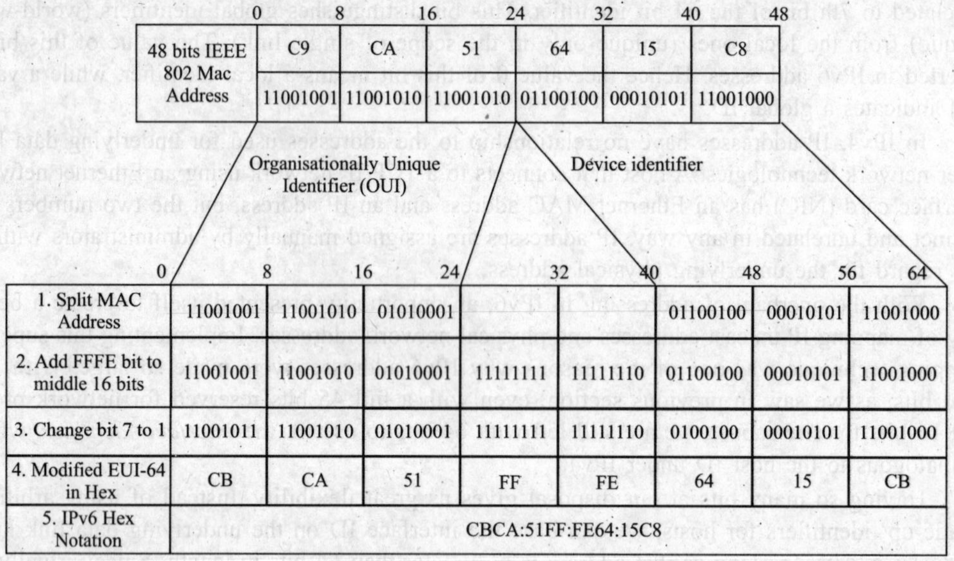

Fig. 19.5 Converting IEEE 802 MAC Addresses To IPv6 Modified EUI-64 Identifiers

1. We take 'C9-CA-51', the first 24 bits of the identifier, and put it into the first (leftmost) 24 bits of the address. The local portion of '64-15-C8' becomes the last 24 bits of the identifier.
2. The middle 16 bits are given the value 'FF-FE'.
3. We change the seventh bit from zero to one, which changes the first octet from 'C9' to 'CB'.
4. The EUI-64 identifier or IPv6 thus becomes 'CB-CA-51-FF-FE-64-15-C8'.
5. The first 64 bits of the device's address are supplied using the global unicast address format.

From a technical point of view this is a perfect working mechanism. But there is a hidden drawback—a threat to privacy. Since a common computer is equipped by some MAC-addressed network card, the second rule is used for the vast majority of computers. But this means that even if the user is traveling and changing the networks used to connect to the Internet, the interface identifier of his/her computer remains constant. In other words the computer can be tracked.

RFC 3041 solves this problem. It recommends the interface to have several identifiers. One of them is a fixed, EUI-64 based identifier. This is used in the 'official' (DNS registered) address and is used mainly for incoming connections. The additional identifiers are randomly generated and their lifetime can be limited to a few hours or days. These identifiers are used for outgoing connections, initiated by the computer itself. Thanks to these short-lived identifiers the systematic long-term tracking of computer activities is much more difficult.

19.8 IPv6 ANYCAST ADDRESSES

The essential idea behind anycast is that there is a group of IPv6 nodes providing the same service. If you use an anycast address to identify this group, the request will be delivered to its nearest member using standard network mechanisms.

An anycast address is hard to distinguish. There is no separate part of the address space dedicated for these addresses, they are living in the unicast space. The local configuration is responsible for identification of anycast addresses.

Common routing methods should be used to maintain the information about the nearest anycast group member. It means that routers inside the network part containing the whole group should have a dedicated entry for this anycast address in their routing tables. This is a serious drawback for largescale anycast deployment, where the anycast group members are spread around the global Internet. Every such anycast address involves a separate entry in global routing tables. It contradicts one of the essential IPv6 addressing design principles: hold the global routing tables as small as possible.

But this is not the sole problem of anycast addresses. Another problem is found in the heart of the anycasting mechanism. Selection of a particular receiver of an anycast-addressed datagram is left to IP, which means it is stateless. In consequence the receiver can change during running communication which can be truly confusing for the transport and application layers.

Yet another problem is related to security. How do we protect anycast groups from intruders falsely declaring themselves to be holders of given anycast addresses and stealing the data or sending false responses. It is extremely inadvisable to use IPSec to secure anycast addressed traffic (it would require all group members to use the same security parameters).

There is a research focused on solving the anycast problem. Until it succeeds, there are serious limitations to the anycast usage. Especially:

1. Anycast addresses must not be used as a sender address in the IP datagram.
2. Anycast addresses may be assigned to routers only. Anycast-addressed hosts are prohibited.

In summary: Anycast addresses represent an experimental area where many aspects are still researched. They are already deployed in limited scope—for example anycast address is used when a mobile node looks for home agent. The scope of this address is limited to its home network only, which makes anycast perfectly usable for such application. RFC 2526 [RFC2526] defines reserved IPv6 anycast addresses with the group span restricted to single subnet.

19.9 IPv6 MULTICAST ADDRESSES

Compared to anycast, multicast is a well-known entity. It is used in the contemporary IPv4 Internet, mainly to transport video/audio data in real time (*e.g.*, videoconferencing, TV/radio broadcast). Multicast in IPv6 is just an evolution of the mechanisms already in use.

There is a separate part of the IPv6 address space dedicated to multicast. It is identified by the prefix ff00::/8. So every multicast address starts with 'ff' or '11111111' which makes them easy to distinguish. The internal structure of the remaining 120 bits is shown in Fig. 19.6.

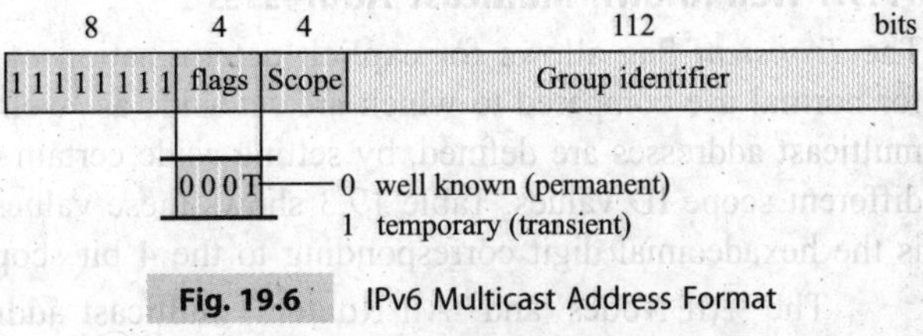

Fig. 19.6 IPv6 Multicast Address Format

The format for multicast addresses is illustrated in Fig. 19.6 and details are as follows:

- **Indicator '11111111' (8 bits):** The first eight bits are always '1111 1111' to indicate a multicast address. This used to be called the 'Format Prefix'. IPv4 supported multicast addressing using the Class D address block in the classful addressing scheme. Under IPv6, multicast addresses are allocated from the multicast block. This is 1/256th of the address space, consisiting of all address that begin with '11111111'. Thus, any address starting with 'FF' in colon hexadecimal notation is an IPv6 multicast address.
- **Flags (4 bits):** Four bits are reserved for flags that can be used to indicate the nature of certain multicast addresses. At the present time the first three of these are unused and set to zero (000). The fourth is the '*T*' (*Transient*) flag. If left as zero, this marks the multicast address as a permanently-assigned, 'well-known' multicast address, as we will see below. If set to one, this means this is a *transient* multicast address, meaning that it is not permanently assigned.
- **Scope ID (4 bits):** These four bits are used to define the scope of the multicast address; 16 different values from 0 to 15 are possible. This field allows multicast address to be created that are global to the entire Internet, or restricted to smaller spheres of influence such as a specific organization, site or lonk. The currently defined values (in decimal) are as follows:

Scope ID Value	*Multicast Address Scope*
0	Reserved
1	Node-Local Scope
2	Link-Local Scope
5	Site-Local Scope
8	Organisation-Local Scope
14	Global Scope
15	Reserved

- **Group ID (112 bits):** Defines a particular group with each scope level.

The notion of explicitly scoping multicast addresses is important. Globally-scoped multicast addresses must be unique across the entire Internet, but locally-scoped addresses are unique only within the organization. This provides tremendous flexibility, as every type of multicast address actually comes in several 'versions': one that multicasts only within a node, one on the local link (local network), one on the local site and so on. The scope also allows routers to immediately determine how broadly they should propagate multicast datagrams, to improve efficiency and eliminate problems with traffic being sent outside the area for which it is intended. Figure 19.7 illustrates the notion of scope graphically.

Figure 19.7 shows how the notion of scope allows IPv6 multicasts to be limited to specific spheres of influence. The 'tightest' scope is node-local scope, with a *Scope ID* value of 1. As the *Scope ID* value increases, the scope expands to cover the local network, site, organization, and finally, the entire Internet.

19.9.1 Well-Known Multicast Addresses

The *Transient* flag allows for explicit determination of which multicast addresses are available for normal use compared to which are set aside as 'well-known'. Several predefined well-known multicast addresses are defined, by setting aside certain Group IDs that are used for a number of different scope ID values. Table 19.3 shows these values; the 'x' in the multicast address pattern is the hexadecimal digit corresponding to the 4 bit scope ID field.

The 'All Nodes' and 'All Routers' multicast addresses enable the equivalent function of what broadcast used to perform in IPv4. Again, the concept of scope is important in a multicast of this type because we don't want to try to send a message to 'all nodes' on the global Internet, for example. So, when the 'all routers' address is used with a scope value of 2, it means 'all routers on the local link'. If it is used with a value of 5, it means 'all routers in this site'.

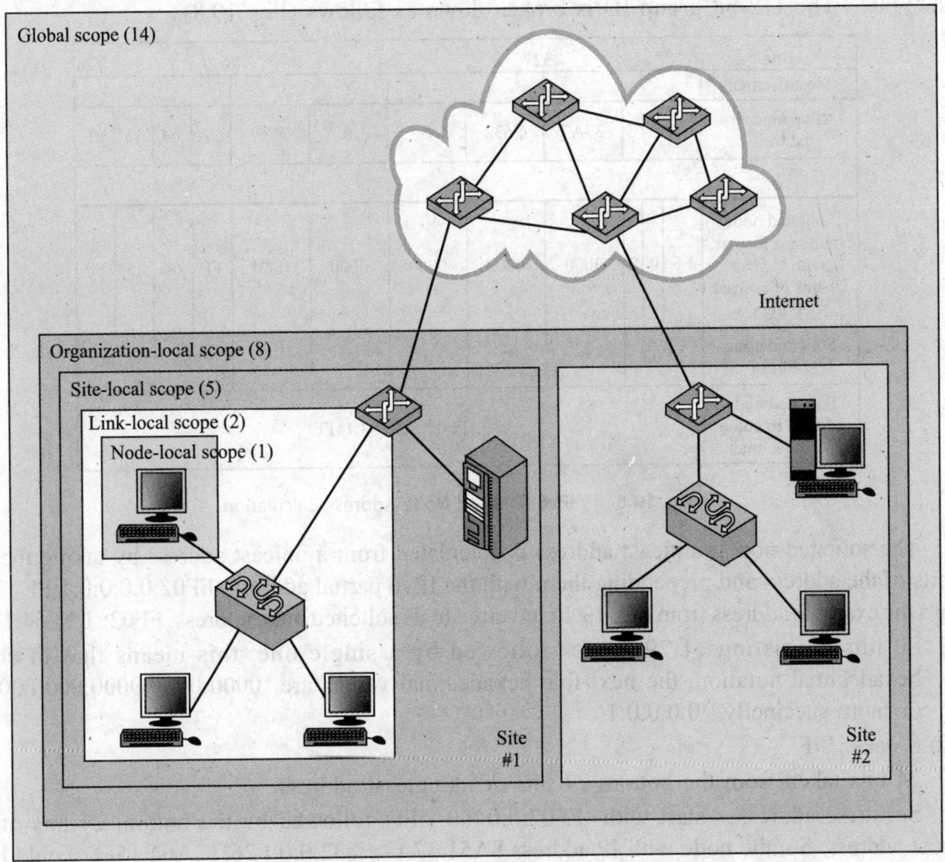

Fig. 19.7 IPv6 Multicast Scope

Table 19.3 Important IPv6 'Well-Known' Multicast Addresses

Multicast Address Pattern	*Valid Scope Values (decimal)*	*Designation*	*Description*
FF0x:0:0:0:0:0:0	0 to 15	Reserved	All multicast addresses where the 112-bit Group ID is zero are reserved.
FF0x:0:0:0:0:0:1	1, 2	All Nodes	When the Group ID is equal to exactly 1, this is a multicast to all nodes. Both node-local (FF01:0:0:0:0:0:1) and link-local (FF02:0:0:0:0:0:1) 'all nodes' multicast addresses are possible.
FF0x:0:0:0:0:0:2	1, 2, 5	All Routers	When the group ID is equal to exactly 2, this designates all routers within a specific scope as the recipients. Valid scope values are node-local, link-local and site-local.

19.9.2 Solicited-Node Multicast Addresses

In addition to the regular multicast addresses, each unicast address has a special multicast address called its *solicited-node address*. This address is created through a special mapping from the device's unicast address. Solicited-node addresses are used by the IPv6 Neighbor Discovery (ND) protocol to provide more efficient address resolution than the ARP technique used in IPv4.

All solicited-node addresses have their *T* flag set to zero and a scope ID of 2, so they start with 'FF02'. The 112-bit group ID is broken down as follows (Fig. 19.8).

Bits	0		32		64		96			128
Hexadecimal										
IPv6 unicast address	8A51	37A7	E632	0	0	F261	CA	64	15	FF
Solicited node multicast format with lowest 24-bits of unicast address	FF 0 2	0000	0000	0000	0000	0001	FF	64	15	FF
Solicited node address	FF02	0	0	0	0	1	FF64		15FF	
Solicited node address in colon hexadecimal	FF02::1:FF64:15FF									

Fig. 19.8 IPv6 Solicited Node Address Calculation

The solicited node multicast address is calculated from a unicast address by taking the last 24 bits of the address and prepending them with the IPv6 partial address 'FF02:0:0:0:0:1:FF'. This shows the example address from Fig. 19.1 converted to its solicited node address, FF02::1:FF64:15FF.

1. 80 bits consisting of 79 zeroes followed by a single one; this means that in colon hexadecimal notation, the next five hexadecimal values are '0000:0000:0000:0000:0001', or more succinctly, '0:0:0:0:1'.
2. 8 ones: 'FF'.
3. 24 bits taken from the bottom 24 bits of its unicast address.

So, these addresses start with 'FF02:0:0:0:0:1:FF' followed by the bottom 24 bits of the unicast address. So, the node with IP address 8A51:37A7:E832:0:0:F261:CA64:15FF would have a solicited-node address of FF02:0:0:0:0:1:FF64:15FF (or FF02::1:FF64:15FF).

19.10 IPV6 AUTOCONFIGURATION AND RENUMBERING

One of the most interesting and potentially valuable addressing features implemented in IPv6 is a facility to allow devices on an IPv6 to actually configure themselves independently. In IPv4 hosts were originally configured manually. Later, host configuration protocols like DHCP enabled servers to allocate IP addresses to hosts that joined the network. IPv6 takes this a step further, by defining a method for some devices to automatically configure their IP address and other parameters without the need for a server. It also defines a method whereby the IP addresses on a network can be renumbered.

19.10.1 IPv6 Stateless Autoconfiguration

Stateless autoconfiguration exploits several other new features in IPv6, including link-local addresses, multicasting, the Neighbor Discovery (ND) protocol, and the ability to generate the interface identifier of an address from the underlying data link layer address. The general idea is to have a device generate a temporary address until it can determine the characteristics of the network it is on, and then create a permanent address it can use based on that information. In the case of multi-homed devices, autoconfiguration is performed for each interface separately, as you would expect.

The following is a summary of the steps a device takes when using stateless autoconfiguration:

1. **Link-Local Address Generation:** The device generates a link-local address. Recall that this is one of the two types of local-use IPv6 addresses. Link-local addresses have '1111 1110 10' for the first ten bits. The generated address uses those ten bits followed by 54 zeroes and then the 64 bit interface identifier (MAC address).
2. **Link-Local Address Uniqueness Test:** The node tests to ensure that the address it generated isn't for some reason already in use on the local network. (This is very unlikely to be an issue if the link-local address came from a MAC address but more likely if it was based on a generated token.) It sends a *Neighbor Solicitation* message using the Neighbor Discovery (ND) protocol. It then listens for a *Neighbor Advertisement* in response that indicates that another device is already using its link-local address; if so, either a new address must be generated, or autoconfiguration fails and another method must be employed.
3. **Link-Local Address Assignment:** Assuming the uniqueness test passes, the device assigns the link-local address to its IP interface. This address can be used for communication on the local network, but not on the wider Internet (since link-local addresses are not routed).
4. **Router Contact:** The node next attempts to contact a local router for more information on continuing the configuration. This is done either by listening for *Router Advertisement* messages sent periodically by routers, or by sending a specific *Router Solicitation* to ask a router for information on what to do next.
5. **Router Direction:** The router provides direction to the node on how to proceed with the autoconfiguration. It may tell the node that on this network 'stateful' autoconfiguration is in use, and tell it the address of a DHCP server to use. Alternately, it will tell the host how to determine its global Internet address.
6. **Global Address Configuration:** Assuming that stateless autoconfiguration is in use on the network, the host will configure itself with its globally-unique Internet address. This address is generally formed from a network prefix provided to the host by the router, combined with the device's identificr as generated in the first step.

Clearly, this method has numerous advantages over both manual and server-based configuration. It is particularly helpful in supporting mobility of IP devices, as they can move to new networks and get a valid address without any knowledge of local servers or network prefixes. At the same time, it still allows management of IP addresses using the (IPv6-compatible) version of DHCP if that is desired. Routers on the local network will typically tell hosts which type of autoconfiguration is supported using special flags in ICMPv6 Router Advertisement messages.

19.10.2 IPv6 Device Renumbering

Renumbering of devices is a method related to autoconfiguration. Like host configuration, it can be implemented using protocols like DHCP, through the use of IP address 'leases' that expire after a period of time. Under IPv6, networks can be renumbered by having routers specify an expiration interval for network prefixes when autoconfiguration is done. Later, they can send a new prefix to tell devices to regenerate their IP addresses. Devices can actually maintain the old 'deprecated' address for a while and then move over to the new address.

19.11 OVERVIEW OF IPv6 DATAGRAM STRUCTURE

The method by which IPv6 encapsulates data received from higher-layer protocols for transmission across the internetwork is basically the same as that used by IPv4. The data received from the transport or higher layers is made the payload of an IPv6 datagram, which has one or more headers that control the delivery of the message. These headers provide information to routers to enable them to move the datagram across the network, and also to hosts so they can tell which datagrams they are intended to receive.

19.11.1 Major Changes to Datagram Structure and Fields in IPv6

While the basic use of datagrams hasn't changed since IPv4, many modifications were made to their structure and format when IPv6 was created. This was done partly out of necessity: IPv6 addresses are different than IPv4 addresses and IP addresses go in the datagram header. The increase in the size of IP addresses from 32 bits to 128 bits adds a whopping extra 192 bits, or 24 bytes of information to the header. This in turn led to an effort to remove fields that weren't strictly necessary, to compensate for the necessary increase in size. However, changes were also made to IPv6 datagrams to add features to them and to make them better suit the needs of modern internetworking.

The following is a list of the most significant overall changes to datagrams in IPv6:

1. **Multiple Header Structure:** Rather than a single header that contains all fields for the datagram (possibly including options), the IPv6 datagram supports a 'main' header and then *extension headers* for additional information when needed.
2. **Streamlined Header Format:** Several fields have been removed from the main header to reduce its size and increase efficiency. Only the fields that are truly required for pretty much ***all*** datagrams remain in the main header; others are put into extension headers and used as needed. Some were removed because they were no longer needed, such as the *Internet Header Length* field; the IPv6 header is of fixed length.
3. **Renamed Fields:** Some fields have been renamed to better reflect their actual use in modern networks.
4. **Greater Flexibility:** The extension headers allow a great deal of extra information to accompany datagrams when needed. Options are also supported in IPv6.
5. **Elimination of Checksum Calculation:** In IPv6, a checksum is no longer computed on the header. This saves both the calculation time spent by every device that packages IP datagrams (hosts and routers) and the space the checksum field took up in the IPv4 header.
6. **Improved Quality of Service Support:** A new field, the *Flow Label*, is defined to help support the prioritization of traffic.

19.11.2 IPv6 General Datagram Structure

Figure 19.9 Shows the IPv6 General Datagram Structure. IPv6 datagrams includes a main header format and zero or more extension headers.

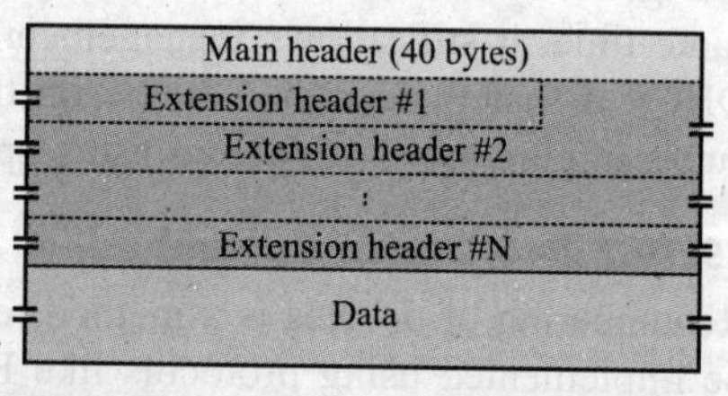

Fig. 19.9 IPv6 General Datagram Structure

The overall structure of the Datagram is described as follows:

1. **Main Header (40 bytes):** Contains the source and destination addresses, and important information required for every datagram and one components per Datagram.
2. **Extension Headers:** Each contains one type of extra information to support various features, including fragmentation, source routing, security and options. Size of the extension headers varies and its have zero or more number of components per datagram.
3. **Data:** The payload from the upper layer to be transmitted in the datagram. It has one component per datagram and size of data varies.

Note that in IPv4, large payloads may be fragmented prior to encapsulation, to ensure that the total size of the datagram doesn't exceed the maximum size permitted on an underlying network. However, the details of fragmentation in IPv6 are different than in IPv4.

19.12 IPv6 HEADER FORMAT

The core of the protocol is naturally the datagram format defined in RFC 2460 [RFC2460]. The datagram design focused mainly on simplicity—to keep the datagram as simple as possible and to keep the size of the headers fixed. The main reason for this decision was to maximize processing performance—simple constant size headers can be processed quickly, at or very close to wire-speed. The IPv4 header format contains a lot of fields including some unpredictable optional ones leading to fluctuating header sizes. IPv6 shows a different approach: the basic header is minimized and a constant size. Only essential fields (like addresses or datagram length) are contained. Everything else has been shifted aside into so called extension headers, which are attached on demand—for example a mobile node adds mobility related extension headers to its outgoing traffic (Fig. 19.10).

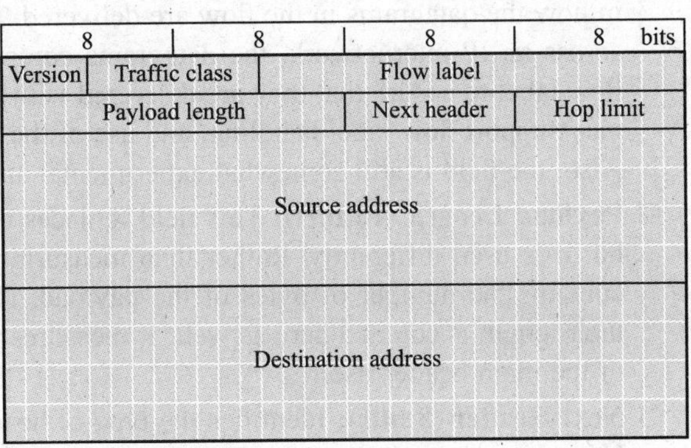

Fig. 19.10 Basic IPv6 Datagram Header

The basic datagram header format of IPv6 is described as follows:

1. **Version (4 bits):** Identifies the version of IP used to generate the datagram. It contains value 6 (0110 binary) to identify IPv6. This field is used the same way as in IPv4.
2. **Traffic Class (8 bits):** This field replaces the *Type Of Service* (*TOS*) field in the IPv4 header. It is used not in the original way that the TOS field was defined (with Precedence, D, T and R bits) but using the new *Differentiated Services* (*DS*) method. It actually specifies Quality Of Service (QOS) techniques for both IPv4 and IPv6.

The 8 bit Traffic Class field in the IPv6 header is available for use by originating nodes and/or forwarding routers to identify and distinguish between different classes or priorities of IPv6 packets. At the point in time at which this specification is being written, there are a number of experiments underway in the use of the IPv4 Type of Service and/or Precedence bits to provide various forms of 'differentiated service' for IP packets, other than through the use of explicit flow set-up. The Traffic Class field in the IPv6 header is intended to allow similar functionality to be supported in IPv6.

It is hoped that those experiments will eventually lead to agreement on what sorts of traffic classifications are most useful for IP packets. Detailed definitions of the syntax and semantics of all or some of the IPv6 Traffic Class bits, whether experimental or intended for eventual standardization, are to be provided in separate documents.

The following general requirements apply to the Traffic Class field:

1. The service interface to the IPv6 service within a node must provide a means for an upper-layer protocol to supply the value of the Traffic Class bits in packets originated by that upper-layer protocol. The default value must be zero for all 8 bits.
2. Nodes that support a specific (experimental or eventual standard) use of some or all of the Traffic Class bits are permitted to change the value of those bits in packets that they originate, forward, or receive, as required for that specific use. Nodes should ignore and leave unchanged any bits of the Traffic Class field for which they do not support a specific use.
3. An upper-layer protocol must not assume that the value of the Traffic Class bits in a received packet are the same as the value sent by the packet's source.

- **Flow Label (20 bits):** This large field was created to provide additional support for real-time datagram delivery and quality of service features. The concept of a *flow* is defined as a sequence of datagrams sent from a source device to one or more destination devices. A unique flow label is used to identify all the datagrams in a particular flow, so that routers between the source and destination all handle them the same way, to help ensure uniformity in how the datagrams in the flow are delivered. For example, if a video stream is being sent across an IP internetwork, the datagrams containing the stream could be identified with a flow label to ensure that they are delivered with minimal latency. Not all devices and routers may support flow label handling, and use of the field by a source device is entirely optional. Also, the field is still somewhat experimental and may be refined over time.
- **Payload Length (16 bits):** This field replaces the *Total Length* field from the IPv4 header, but it is used differently. Rather than measuring the length of the whole datagram, it only contains the number of bytes of the payload. However, if extension headers are included, their length is counted here as well. It measures the length of the datagram less the 40 bytes of the main header itself.
- **Next Header (8 bits):** Identifies the type of header immediately following the IPv6 header. Uses the same values as the IPv4 Protocol field. It identifies the extension header or upper layer protocol (TCP, UDP) data.
- **Hop Limit (8 bits):** This replaces the *Time To Live* (*TTL*) field in the IPv4 header. The sending node assigns some value to this field defining the reach of given datagram. Every forwarding node decreases the value by 1. If decremented to zero, the datagram is dropped and an ICMP message is sent to the sender. It protects the IPv6 transport system against routing loops—in the case of such loop the datagram circulates around the loop for a limited time only.
- **Source Address (128 bits):** Sender identification. It contains the IPv6 address of the node who sent this datagram.
- **Destination Address (128 bits):** Receiver identification. This is the target—the datagram should be delivered to this IPv6 address.

19.12.1 Changes to Main Header Between IPv4 and IPv6

Before we dive deeper into some header specialties let us compare the IPv4 and IPv6 headers (see Fig. 19.11). The result is quite interesting: the total length of the datagram header doubled (from 20 bytes to 40 bytes) although the IPv6 addresses are four times as long. How is it possible? Because just subsets of IPv4 header fields have been adopted by IPv6—the corresponding fields are marked by numbers in Fig. 19.11. The whole second line of the IPv4 datagram, designed for fragmentation, has been moved to an extension header. The CRC (cyclic redundancy check) has been abandoned for two good reasons: First, frame consistency is checked in lower layers, so it is largely redundant. Second, CRC decelerates the datagram processing—every forwarding node decreases the datagram lifetime, so it changes the header and must recalculate the CRC. Thanks to the constant header length the corresponding header length field is not necessary anymore.

To summarize, the IPv6 main header compares to the IPv4 header as follows:

- **Unchanged Fields:** Three fields are used the same way and retain the same name (though they have different content and/or size): *Version*, *Source Address* and *Destination Address*.
- **Renamed Fields:** Two fields are used the same way but renamed: *Traffic Class* and *Hop Limit*.
- **Modified Fields:** Two fields are used in a way similar way to their IPv4 predecessors but are slightly different in meaning and also renamed: *Payload Length* and *Next Header*.
- **Added Fields:** There is one new field: *Flow Label*.

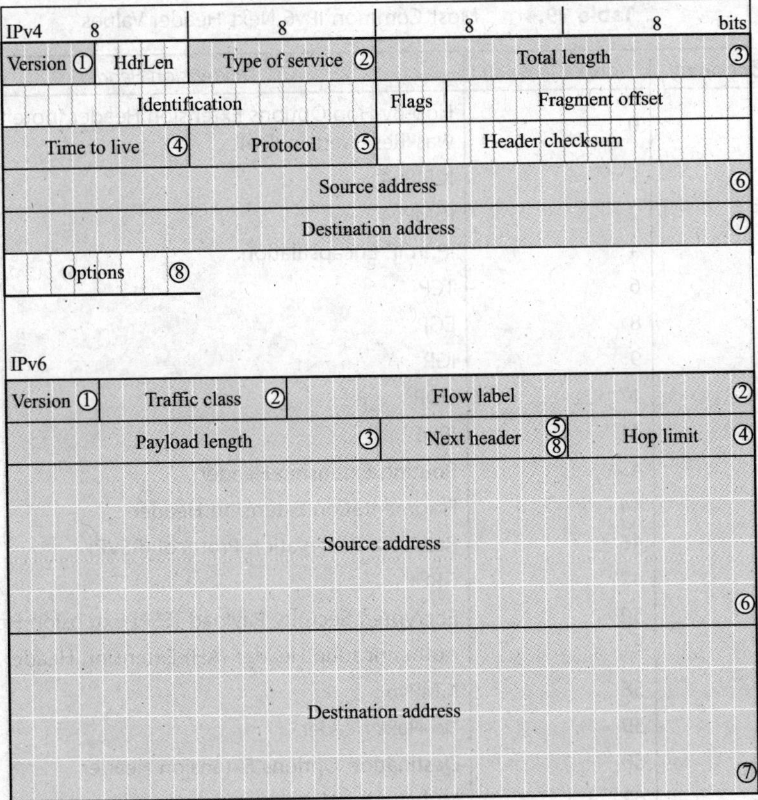

Fig. 19.11 IPv4 and IPv6 Header Comparison

❑ **Removed Fields:** To cut down on header length and unnecessary work, five IPv4 header fields are removed from the IPv6 header:

➢ **Internet Header Length:** No longer needed, as the main IPv6 header is fixed in length at 40 bytes.

➢ **Identification, Flags, Fragment Offset:** These are used for fragmentation, which is done less in IPv6 than IPv4, so these fields are now found only when needed in the Fragmentation extension header.

➢ **Header Checksum:** The decision was made to eliminate header checksum calculations in IPv6. It was viewed as redundant with higher-layer error-checking and data link layer CRC calculations. This saves processing time for routers and 2 bytes in the datagram header.

In addition, while options were formerly considered part of the main header in IPv4, they are separate in IPv6.

19.12.2 IPv6 Next Header Field

The *Next Header* field is one of the most important additions to the IPv6 datagram format. When an IPv6 datagram uses extension headers, this field contains an identifier for the first extension header, which in turn uses its own *Next Header* to point to the next header, and so on. The last extension header then references the encapsulated higher-layer protocol—since the higher-layer protocol's header appears at the start of the IPv6 *Data* field, it is like the 'next header' to the device receiving the datagram. Some of the most common values for *Next Header* in IPv6 are shown in Table 19.4.

Table 19.4 Most Common IPv6 Next Header Values

Value (Hexadecimal)	*Value (Decimal)*	*Extension Header*
00	0	Hop-By-Hop Options Extension Header (note that this value was 'Reserved' in IPv4)
01	1	ICMPv4
02	2	IGMPv4
04	4	IP in IP Encapsulation
06	6	TCP
08	8	EGP
09	9	IGP
11	17	UDP
29	41	IPv6
2B	43	Routing Extension Header
2C	44	Fragmentation Extension Header
2E	46	Resource Reservation Protocol (RSVP)
2F	47	GRE
32	50	Encrypted Security Payload (ESP) Extension Header
33	51	Authentication Header (AH) Extension Header
3A	58	ICMPv6
3B	59	No Next Header
3C	60	Destination Options Extension Header
3E	62	Mobility Header

The total length of the main IPv6 header format is 40 bytes. This is double the size of the IPv4 header without options, largely because of the extra 24 bytes needed for the monstrous IPv6 addresses. There are only 8 bytes of non-address header fields in the IPv6 main header, compared to 12 in the IPv4 header.

19.12.3 IPv6 Header Chaining Using the Next Header Field

The only field common to all extension header types is the *Next Header* field (which actually appears at the end of one header type, the ESP header). The 8 bit *Next Header* field is used to logically link all the headers in an IPv6 datagram as follows:

1. The *Next Header* field in the main header contains a reference number for the first extension header type.
2. The *Next Header* field in the first extension header contains the number of the second extension header type, if there is a second one. If there's a third, the second header's *Next Header* points to it, and so on.
3. The *Next Header* field of the last extension header contains the protocol number of the encapsulated higher-layer protocol. In essence, this field points to the 'next header' within the payload itself.

For example, suppose a datagram that encapsulates TCP has a *Hop-By-Hop Options* extension header and a *Fragment* extension header. Then, the *Next Header* fields of these headers would contain the following values:

1. The main header would have a *Next Header* value of 0, indicating the *Hop-By-Hop Options* header.

2. The *Hop-By-Hop Options* header would have a *Next Header* value of 44 (decimal), the value for the *Fragment* extension header.
3. The *Fragment* header would have a *Next Header* value of 6.

This is illustrated in Fig. 19.12.

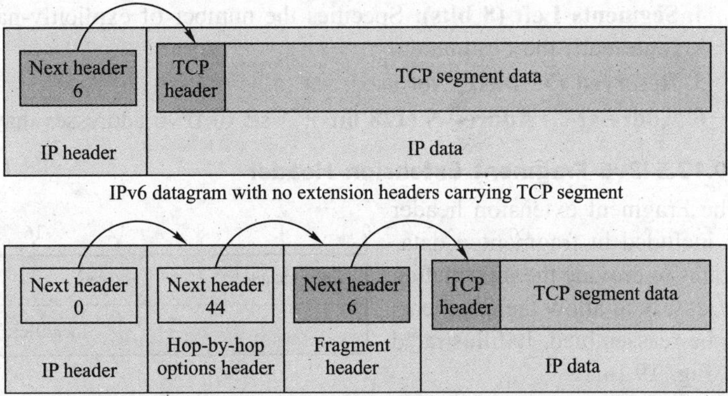

Fig. 19.12 IPv6 Extension Header Linking Using the *Next Header* Field

The *Next Header* field allows a device to more easily process the headers in a received IPv6 datagram. When a datagram has no extension headers, the 'next header' is actually the header at the start of the IP *Data* field, in this case a TCP header with a value of 6. This is the same way the *Protocol* field is used in IPv4. When extension headers do appear, the *Next Header* value of each header contains a number indicating the type of the following header in the datagram, so they logically 'chain together' the headers, as shown in Fig. 19.12.

Note that the *Next Header* value of the IPv6 main header is 41; that of an IPv4 header is 4 (its protocol number). Note that there is also a 'dummy' extension header called *No Next Header* that has a value of 59. This is a placeholder that when found in the *Next Header* field indicates that there is nothing after that extension header.

As I mentioned in the table, the formats for several of the headers are provided in other topics. Two of them I will describe here, however.

19.12.4 IPv6 Routing Extension Header

The *Routing* extension header is used to perform source routing in IPv6 and it is illustrated in Figure 19.13.

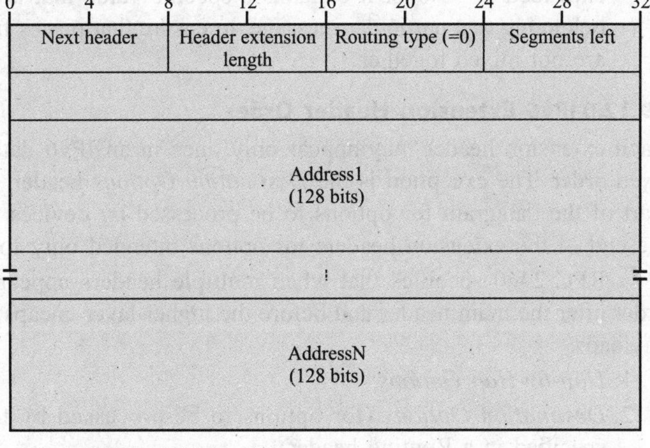

Fig. 19.13 IPv6 *Routing* Extension Header Format

The *Routing* extension header is used to perform source routing in IPv6 and it is described as follows:

1. **Next Header (8 bits):** Contains the protocol number of the next header after the Routing header. Used to link headers together as described above.
2. **Header Extension Length (8 bits):** The length of the Routing header in 8-byte units, not including the first 8 bytes of the header. For a Routing Type of 0, this value is thus two times the number addresses embedded in the header.
3. **Routing Type (8 bits):** This field allows multiple routing types to be defined; at present, the only value used is 0.

4. **Segments Left (8 bits):** Specifies the number of explicitly-named nodes remaining in the route until the destination.
5. **Reserved (32 bits):** Not used; set to zeroes.
6. **Address1 ... AddressN (128 bits):** A set of IPv6 addresses that specify the route to be used.

19.12.5 IPv6 Fragment Extension Header

The Fragment extension header is included in fragmented datagrams to provide the information necessary to allow the fragments to be reassembled. Its illustrated in Fig. 19.14.

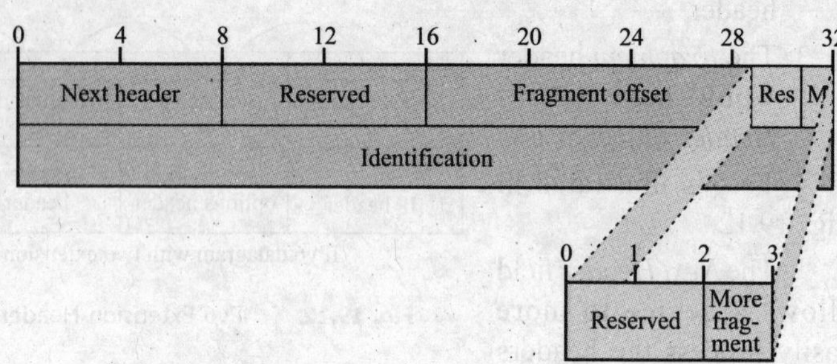

Fig. 19.14 IPv6 Fragment Extension Header Format

The *Fragment* extension header format is described as follows:

1. **Next Header (8 bits):** Contains the protocol number of the next header after the Fragment header. Used to link headers together as described above.
2. **Reserved (8 bits):** Not used; set to zeroes.
3. **Fragment Offset (13 bits):** Specifies the offset, or position, in the overall message where the data in this fragment goes. It is specified in units of 8 bytes (64 bits) and used in a manner very similar to the field of the same name in the IPv4 header.
4. **Reserved (2 bits):** Not used; set to zeroes.
5. **More Fragments Flag (1 bits):** Same as the flag of the same name in the IPv4 header—when set to 0, indicates the last fragment in a message; when set to 1, indicates that more fragments are yet to come in the fragmented message.
6. **Identification (32 bits):** Same as the field of the same name in the IPv4 header, but expanded to 32 bits. It contains a specific value that is common to each of the fragments belonging to a particular message, to ensure that pieces from different fragmented messages are not mixed together.

19.12.6 IPv6 Extension Header Order

Each extension header may appear only once in an IPv6 datagram, and they must appear in a fixed order. The exception is the *Destination Options* header, which may appear twice; near the start of the datagram for options to be processed by devices en route to the destination, and at the end of the extension headers for options intended only for the final destination.

RFC 2460 specifies that when multiple headers appear, they should be in the following order after the main header and before the higher-layer encapsulated header in the IPv6 datagram payload:

1. *Hop-By-Hop Options*
2. *Destination Options* (for options to be processed by the destination as well as devices specified in a Routing header)
3. *Routing*
4. *Fragmentation*
5. *Authentication Header*
6. *Encapsulating Security Payload*
7. *Destination Options* (for options processed only by the final destination)

The only header normally examined by all intermediate devices is the *Hop-By-Hop Options* extension header. It is used specifically to convey management information to all routers in a route. The *Hop-By-Hop Options* extension header must appear as the first extension header if present. Since it is the only one that must be read by every router (which represents a performance drain on routers) it is given 'top billing' to make it easier and faster to find and process.

Finally, note that all extension headers must be a multiple of 8 bytes in length for alignment purposes. Also, remember that the *Next Header* value for a particular extension header appears in the *Next Header* field of the *preceding* header, not the header itself.

19.13 IPv6 DATAGRAM OPTIONS

In IPv4, all 'extra' information required for various purposes is placed into the datagram in the form of options that appear in the IPv4 header. In IPv6, the new concept of extension headers is introduced; these headers take the place of many of the predefined IPv4 options. However, the concept of options is still maintained in IPv6, for a slightly different purpose. Options allow the IPv6 datagram to be supplemented with arbitrary sets of information that aren't defined in the regular extension headers. They provide maximum flexibility, allowing the basic IPv6 protocol to be extended in ways the designers never anticipated, with the goal of reducing the chances of the protocol becoming obsolete.

19.13.1 IPv6 Option Extension Header Types

IPv6 options supplement extension headers; in fact, they are actually implemented as extension headers. There are two different ones used to encode options. These two headers only differ in terms of how the options they contain are to be processed by devices; otherwise, they are formatted the same and used in the same way.

The two extension header types are:

1. **Destination Options:** Contains options that are intended only for the ultimate destination of the datagram (and perhaps a set of routers specified in a Routing header, if present).
2. **Hop-By-Hop Options:** Contains options that carry information for every device (router) between the source and destination

19.13.1.1 IPv6 Option Format

Each of these header types has a one-byte *Next Header* field, and a one-byte *Header Extension Length* field that indicates the header's overall length. The rest of the header has one or more option fields. Figure 19.15 illustrates the overall format of these two headers.

Each of these extension headers begins with two fixed fields, *Next Header* and *Header Extension Length.* The rest of the header consists of a sequence of variable-length options. Each option has the structure shown below, consisting of a type/length/value triplet.The format of each option is similar to that of IPv4 options, and is shown as follows:

1. **Option Type:** 8 bit identifier of the type of option.

   The sequence of options within a header must be processed strictly in the order they appear in the header; a receiver must not, for example, scan through the header looking for a particular kind of option and process that option prior to processing all preceding ones.

   The Option Type identifiers are internally encoded such that their highest-order two bits specify the action that must be taken if the processing IPv6 node does not recognize the Option Type:

   00—skip over this option and continue processing the header.

   01—discard the packet.

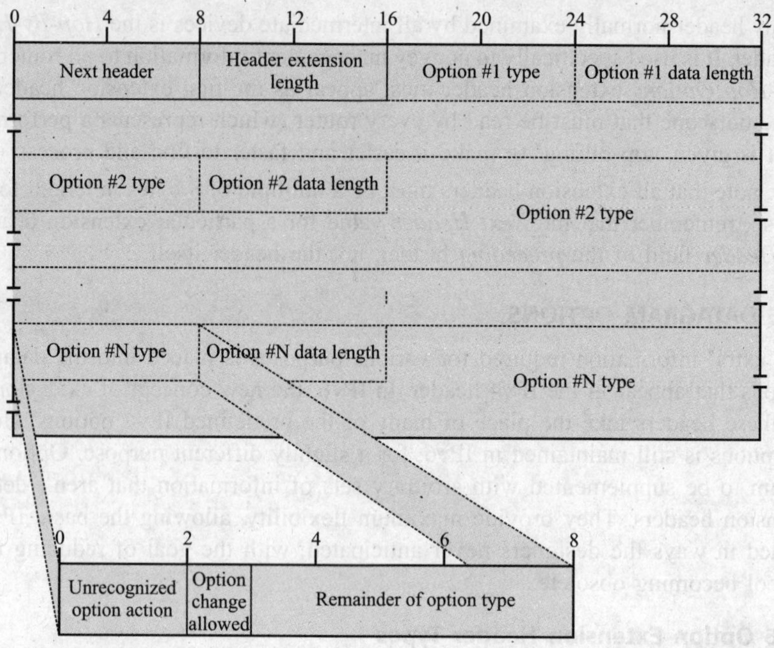

Fig. 19.15 IPv6 Hop-By-Hop Options and Destination Options Header Formats

10—discard the packet and, regardless of whether or not the packet's Destination Address was a multicast address, send an ICMP Parameter Problem, Code 2, message to the packet's Source Address, pointing to the unrecognized Option Type.

11—discard the packet and, only if the packet's Destination Address was not a multicast address, send an ICMP Parameter Problem, Code 2, message to the packet's Source Address, pointing to the unrecognized Option Type.

The third-highest-order bit of the Option Type specifies whether or not the Option Data of that option can change en-route to the packet's final destination. When an Authentication header is present in the packet, for any option whose data may change en-route, its entire Option Data field must be treated as zero-valued octets when computing or verifying the packet's authenticating value.

0—Option Data does not change en-route

1—Option Data may change en-route

The three high-order bits described above are to be treated as part of the Option Type, not independent of the Option Type. That is, a particular option is identified by a full 8 bit Option Type, not just the low-order 5 bits of an Option Type.

The same Option Type numbering space is used for both the Hop-by-Hop Options header and the Destination Options header. However, the specification of a particular option may restrict its use to only one of those two headers.

Individual options may have specific alignment requirements, to ensure that multi-octet values within Option Data fields fall on natural boundaries. The alignment requirement of an option is specified using the notation xn + y, meaning the Option Type must appear at an integer multiple of x octets from the start of the header, plus y octets. For example:

2n means any 2-octet offset from the start of the header.

8n + 2 means any 8-octet offset from the start of the header, plus 2 octets.

There are two padding options which are used when necessary to align subsequent options and to pad out the containing header to a multiple of 8 octets in length. These padding options must be recognized by all IPv6 implementations.

2. Opt Data Len: 8 bit unsigned integer. Length of the Option Data field of this option, in octets.

3. Option Data: Variable-length field. Option-Type-specific data.

19.13.2 Examples of IPv6 Options

These assumptions suggest the following approach to laying out the fields of an option: order the fields from smallest to largest, with no interior padding, then derive the alignment requirement for the entire option based on the alignment requirement of the largest field (up to a maximum alignment of 8 octets). This approach is illustrated in the following examples:

Example 1: If an option X required two data fields, one of length 8 octets and one of length 4 octets, it would be laid out as follows:

		Option Type=X	Opt Data Len=12
4-octet field			
8-octet field			

Its alignment requirement is 8n + 2, to ensure that the 8-octet field starts at a multiple-of-8 offset from the start of the enclosing header. A complete Hop-by-Hop or Destination Options header containing this one option would look as follows:

Next Header	Hdr Ext Len=1	Option Type=X	Opt Data Len=12
4-octet field			
8-octet field			

Example 2: If an option Y required three data fields, one of length 4 octets, one of length 2 octets, and one of length 1 octet, it would be laid out as follows:

			Option Type=Y
Opt Data Len=7	1-octet field	2-octet field	
4-octet field			

Its alignment requirement is 4n+3, to ensure that the 4-octet field starts at a multiple-of-4 offset from the start of the enclosing header. A complete Hop-by-Hop or Destination Options header containing this one option would look as follows:

Next Header	Hdr Ext Len=1	Pad1 Option=0	Option Type=Y
Opt Data Len=7	1-octet field	2-octet field	
4-octet field			
PadN Option=1	Opt Data Len=2	0	0

Example 3: A Hop-by-Hop or Destination Options header containing both options X and Y from Examples 1 and 2 would have one of the two following formats, depending on which option appeared first:

Next Header	Hdr Ext Len=3	Option Type=X	Opt Data Len=12
4-octet field			
8-octet field			

PadN Option=1	Opt Data Len=1	0	Option Type=Y
Opt Data Len=7	1-octet field	2-octet field	
4-octet field			
PadN Option=1	Opt Data Len=2	0	0

Next Header	Hdr Ext Len=3	Pad1 Option=0	Option Type=Y
Opt Data Len=7	1-octet field	2-octet field	
4-octet field			
PadN Option=1	Opt Data Len=4	0	0
0	0	Option Type=X	Opt Data Len=12
4-octet field			
8-octet field			

19.14 IPv6 DATAGRAM SIZE ISSUES, FRAGMENTATION AND REASSEMBLY

IPv6 requires that every link in the internet have an MTU of 1280 octets or greater. On any link that cannot convey a 1280-octet packet in one piece, link-specific fragmentation and reassembly must be provided at a layer below IPv6.

Links that have a configurable MTU (for example, PPP links [RFC-1661]) must be configured to have an MTU of at least 1280 octets; it is recommended that they be configured with an MTU of 1500 octets or greater, to accommodate possible encapsulations (*i.e.*, tunneling) without incurring IPv6-layer fragmentation.

From each link to which a node is directly attached, the node must be able to accept packets as large as that link's MTU.

It is strongly recommended that IPv6 nodes implement Path MTU Discovery [RFC-1981], in order to discover and take advantage of path MTUs greater than 1280 octets. However, a minimal IPv6 implementation (*e.g.*, in a boot ROM) may simply restrict itself to sending packets no larger than 1280 octets, and omit implementation of Path MTU Discovery.

In order to send a packet larger than a path's MTU, a node may use the IPv6 Fragment header to fragment the packet at the source and have it reassembled at the destination(s). However, the use of such fragmentation is discouraged in any application that is able to adjust its packets to fit the measured path MTU (*i.e.*, down to 1280 octets).

A node must be able to accept a fragmented packet that, after reassembly, is as large as 1500 octets. A node is permitted to accept fragmented packets that reassemble to more than 1500 octets. An upper-layer protocol or application that depends on IPv6 fragmentation to send packets larger than the MTU of a path should not send packets larger than 1500 octets unless it has assurance that the destination is capable of reassembling packets of that larger size.

In response to an IPv6 packet that is sent to an IPv4 destination (*i.e.*, a packet that undergoes translation from IPv6 to IPv4), the originating IPv6 node may receive an ICMP Packet Too Big message reporting a Next-Hop MTU less than 1280. In that case, the IPv6 node is not required to reduce the size of subsequent packets to less than 1280, but must include a Fragment header in those packets so that the IPv6-to-IPv4 translating router can obtain a suitable Identification value to use in resulting IPv4 fragments. Note that this means the payload may have to be reduced to 1232 octets (1280 minus 40 for the IPv6 header and 8 for the Fragment header), and smaller still if additional extension headers are used.

In IPv6 fragmentation is only performed by the device sending a datagram, not by routers. If a router encounters a datagram too large to send over a physical network with a small MTU, the router sends an ICMPv6 *Packet Too Big* message back to the source of the datagram. This can be used as part of a process called *Path MTU Discovery* to determine the minimum MTU of an entire route.

19.14.1 IPv6 Fragmentation Process

The actual mechanics of fragmentation in IPv6 are similar to those in IPv4, with the added complication that extension headers must be handled carefully. For purposes of fragmentation, IPv6 datagrams are broken into two pieces:

1. **Unfragmentable Part:** This includes the main header of the original datagram, as well as any extension headers that need to be present in each fragment. This means the main header, and any of the following headers If present: *Hop-By-Hop Options*, *Destination Options* (for those options to be processed by devices along a route) and *Routing*.
2. **Fragmentable Part:** This includes the data portion of the datagram, along with the other extension headers if present—*Authentication Header*, *Encapsulating Security Payload* and/or *Destination Options* (for options to be processed only by the final destination).

The *Unfragmentable Part* must be present in each fragment, while the fragmentable part is split up amongst the fragments. So to fragment a datagram, a device creates a set of fragment datagrams, each of which contains the following, in order:

1. **Unfragmentable Part:** The full *Unfragmentable Part* of the original datagram, with its *Payload Length* changed to the length of the fragment datagram.
2. **Fragment Header:** A *Fragment* header with the *Fragment Offset*, *Identification* and *M* flags set in the same way they are used in IPv4.
3. **Fragment:** A fragment of the *Fragmentable Part* of the original datagram. Note that each fragment must have a length that is a multiple of 8 bytes, because the value in the *Fragment Offset* field is specified in multiples of 8 bytes.

Fragmentation is done in IPv6 in a manner similar to that of IPv4, except that extension headers must be handled specially. Certain extension headers are considered *unfragmentable* and appear in each fragment; others are fragmented along with the data.

19.14.2 IPv6 Fragmentation Example

Figure 19.16 illustrate how IPv6 fragmentation works. Suppose we have an IPv6 datagram exactly 370 bytes wide, consisting of a 40-byte IP header, four 30-byte extension headers, and 210 bytes of data. Two of the extension headers are unfragmentable, while two are fragmentable. (In practice we would never need to fragment such a small datagram but I am trying to keep the numbers simple). Suppose we need to send this over a link with an MTU of only 230 bytes. We would actually require three fragments, not the two you might expect, because of the need to put the two 30-byte unfragmentable extension headers in each fragment, and the requirement that each fragment be a length that is a multiple of 8. Here is how the fragments would be structured (Fig. 19.16).

In this illustration, a 370-byte IPv6 datagram, containing four 30-byte extension headers, is broken into three fragments. The sizes of the fields are shown to scale. The *Unfragmentable Part*, shown in blue, begins each fragment, followed by the *Fragment* header (abbreviated as 'FH' in the figure). Then, portions of the *Fragmentable Part* are placed into each fragment in sequence. The *Authentication* and *Destination Options* extension headers are part of the *Fragmentable Part* so they appear as part of the first fragment.

1. **First Fragment:** The first fragment would consist of the 100-byte *Unfragmentable Part*, followed by an 8-byte *Fragment* header and the first 120 bytes of the *Fragmentable Part* of the original datagram. This would contain the two fragmentable extension headers and the first 60 bytes of data. This leaves 150 bytes of data to send.

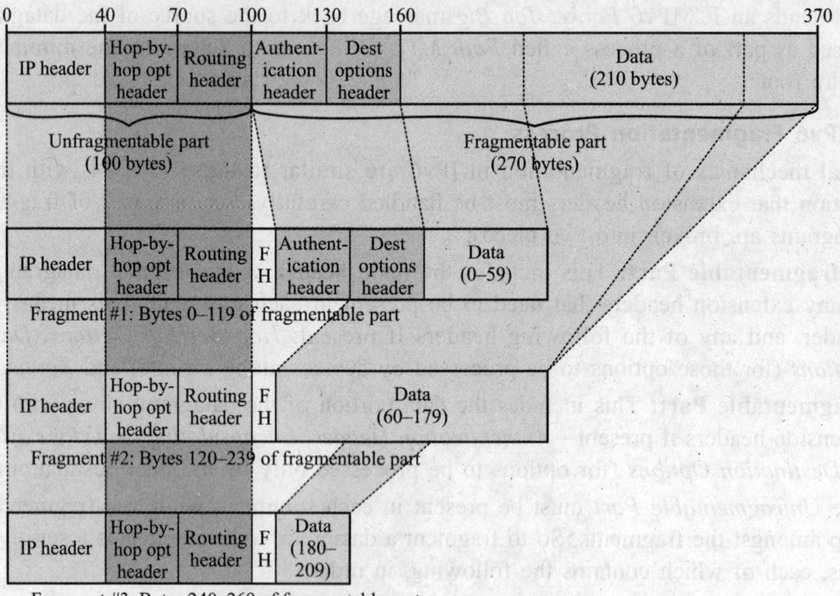

Fig. 19.16 IPv6 Datagram Fragmentation

2. **Second Fragment:** This would also contain the 100-byte *Unfragmentable Part*, followed by a *Fragment* header and 120 bytes of data (bytes 60 to 179). This would leave 30 bytes of data remaining.
3. **Third Fragment:** The last fragment would contain the 100-byte *Unfragmentable Part*, a *Fragment* header and the final 30 bytes of data.

The 'M' (*More Fragments*) flag would be set to one in the first two fragments and zero in the third, and the *Fragment Offset* values would be set appropriately. The receiving device reassembles by taking the *Unfragmentable Part* from the first fragment and then assembling the *Fragment* data from each fragment in sequence.

19.15 UPPER-LAYER PROTOCOL ISSUES

19.15.1 Upper-Layer Checksums

Any transport or other upper-layer protocol that includes the addresses from the IP header in its checksum computation must be modified for use over IPv6, to include the 128 bit IPv6 addresses instead of 32 bit IPv4 addresses. In particular, the following illustration shows the TCP and UDP 'pseudo-header' for IPv6:

Source Address	
Destination Address	
Upper-Layer Packet Length	
zero	Next Header

1. If the IPv6 packet contains a Routing header, the Destination address used in the pseudo-header is that of the final destination. At the originating node, that address will be in the last element of the Routing header; at the recipient(s), that address will be in the Destination Address field of the IPv6 header.

2. The Next Header value in the pseudo-header identifies the upper-layer protocol (*e.g.*, 6 for TCP, or 17 for UDP). It will differ from the Next Header value in the IPv6 header if there are extension headers between the IPv6 header and the upper-layer header.
3. The Upper-Layer Packet Length in the pseudo-header is the length of the upper-layer header and data (*e.g.*, TCP header plus TCP data). Some upper-layer protocols carry their own length information (*e.g.*, the Length field in the UDP header); for such protocols, that is the length used in the pseudo-header. Other protocols (such as TCP) do not carry their own length information, in which case the length used in the pseudo-header is the Payload Length from the IPv6 header, minus the length of any extension headers present between the IPv6 header and the upper-layer header.
4. Unlike IPv4, when UDP packets are originated by an IPv6 node, the UDP checksum is not optional. That is, whenever originating a UDP packet, an IPv6 node must compute a UDP checksum over the packet and the pseudo-header, and, if that computation yields a result of zero, it must be changed to hex FFFF for placement in the UDP header. IPv6 receivers must discard UDP packets containing a zero checksum, and should log the error.

The IPv6 version of ICMP [ICMPv6] includes the above pseudo-header in its checksum computation; this is a change from the IPv4 version of ICMP, which does not include a pseudo-header in its checksum. The reason for the change is to protect ICMP from misdelivery or corruption of those fields of the IPv6 header on which it depends, which, unlike IPv4, are not covered by an internet-layer checksum. The Next Header field in the pseudo-header for ICMP contains the value 58, which identifies the IPv6 version of ICMP.

19.15.2 Maximum Packet Lifetime

Unlike IPv4, IPv6 nodes are not required to enforce maximum packet lifetime. That is the reason the IPv4 'Time to Live' field was renamed 'Hop Limit' in IPv6. In practice, very few, if any, IPv4 implementations conform to the requirement that they limit packet lifetime, so this is not a change in practice. Any upper-layer protocol that relies on the internet layer (whether IPv4 or IPv6) to limit packet lifetime ought to be upgraded to provide its own mechanisms for detecting and discarding obsolete packets.

19.15.3 Maximum Upper-Layer Payload Size

When computing the maximum payload size available for upper-layer data, an upper-layer protocol must take into account the larger size of the IPv6 header relative to the IPv4 header. For example, in IPv4, TCP's MSS option is computed as the maximum packet size (a default value or a value learned through Path MTU Discovery) minus 40 octets (20 octets for the minimum-length IPv4 header and 20 octets for the minimum-length TCP header). When using TCP over IPv6, the MSS must be computed as the maximum packet size minus 60 octets, because the minimum-length IPv6 header (*i.e.*, an IPv6 header with no extension headers) is 20 octets longer than a minimum-length IPv4 header.

19.15.4 Responding to Packets Carrying Routing Headers

When an upper-layer protocol sends one or more packets in response to a received packet that included a Routing header, the response packet(s) must not include a Routing header that was automatically derived by 'reversing' the received Routing header UNLESS the integrity and authenticity of the received Source Address and Routing header have been verified (*e.g.*, via the use of an Authentication header in the received packet). In other words, only the following kinds of packets are permitted in response to a received packet bearing a Routing header:

1. Response packets that do not carry Routing headers.

2. Response packets that carry Routing headers that were NOT derived by reversing the Routing header of the received packet (for example, a Routing header supplied by local configuration).

❐ Response packets that carry Routing headers that were derived by reversing the Routing header of the received packet IF AND ONLY IF the integrity and authenticity of the Source Address and Routing header from the received packet have been verified by the responder.

19.16 IPv6 QUALITY-OF-SERVICE CAPABILITIES

The Flow Label and the Priority fields in the IPv6 header may be used by a host to identify those packets for which it requests special handling by IPv6 routers, such as non-default quality of service or 'real-time' service. This capability is important in order to support applications which require some degree of consistent throughput, delay, and/or jitter. These type of applications are commonly described as 'multi- media' or 'real-time' applications.

(*a*) Flow Labels: The 24 bit Flow Label field in the IPv6 header may be used by a source to label those packets for which it requests special handling by the IPv6 routers, such as non-default quality of service or 'real-time' service.

This aspect of IPv6 is, at the time of writing, still experimental and subject to change as the requirements for flow support in the Internet become clearer. Hosts or routers that do not support the functions of the Flow Label field are required to set the field to zero when originating a packet, pass the field on unchanged when forwarding a packet, and ignore the field when receiving a packet.

A flow is a sequence of packets sent from a particular source to a particular (unicast or multicast) destination for which the source desires special handling by the intervening routers. The nature of that special handling might be conveyed to the routers by a control protocol, such as a resource reservation protocol, or by information within the flow's packets themselves, *e.g.*, in a hop-by-hop option.

There may be multiple active flows from a source to a destination, as well as traffic that is not associated with any flow. A flow is uniquely identified by the combination of a source address and a non-zero flow label. Packets that do not belong to a flow carry a flow label of zero.

A flow label is assigned to a flow by the flow's source node. New flow labels must be chosen (pseudo-)randomly and uniformly from the range 1 to FFFFFF hex. The purpose of the random allocation is to make any set of bits within the Flow Label field suitable for use as a hash key by routers, for looking up the state associated with the flow.

All packets belonging to the same flow must be sent with the same source address, same destination address, and same non-zero flow label. If any of those packets includes a Hop-by-Hop Options header, then they all must be originated with the same Hop-by-Hop Options header contents (excluding the Next Header field of the Hop-by-Hop Options header). If any of those packets includes a Routing header, then they all must be originated with the same contents in all extension headers up to and including the Routing header (excluding the Next Header field in the Routing header). The routers or destinations are permitted, but not required, to verify that these conditions are satisfied. If a violation is detected, it should be reported to the source by an ICMP Parameter Problem message, Code 0, pointing to the high-order octet of the Flow Label field (*i.e.*, offset 1 within the IPv6 packet).

Routers are free to 'opportunistically' set up flow- handling state for any flow, even when no explicit flow establishment information has been provided to them via a control protocol, a hop-by-hop option, or other means. For example, upon receiving a packet from a particular source with an unknown, non-zero flow label, a router may process its IPv6 header and any necessary extension headers as if the flow label were zero. That processing would include determining the next-hop interface, and possibly other actions, such as updating a hop-by-hop option, advancing the pointer and addresses in a Routing header, or deciding on how to queue the packet based on its Priority field. The router may then choose to 'remember' the results of those processing steps and cache that information, using the source address plus the flow label as the cache key. Subsequent packets with the same source address and flow label may then be handled by referring to the cached information rather than examining all those fields that, according to the requirements of the previous paragraph, can be assumed unchanged from the first packet seen in the flow.

(*b*) **Priority:** The 4 bit Priority field in the IPv6 header enables a source to identify the desired delivery priority of its packets, relative to other packets from the same source. The Priority values are divided into two ranges: Values 0 through 7 are used to specify the priority of traffic for which the source is providing congestion control, *i.e.*, traffic that 'backs off' in response to congestion, such as TCP traffic. Values 8 through 15 are used to specify the priority of traffic that does not back off in response to congestion, *e.g.*, 'real-time' packets being sent at a constant rate.

For congestion-controlled traffic, the following Priority values are recommended for particular application categories:

0 Uncharacterized traffic
1 'Filler' traffic (*e.g.*, netnews)
2 Unattended data transfer (*e.g.*, email)
3 (Reserved)
4 Attended bulk transfer (*e.g.*, FTP, HTTP, NFS)
5 (Reserved)
6 Interactive traffic (*e.g.*, telnet, X)
7 Internet control traffic (*e.g.*, routing protocols, SNMP)

For non-congestion-controlled traffic, the lowest Priority value (8) should be used for those packets that the sender is most willing to have discarded under conditions of congestion (*e.g.*, high-fidelity video traffic), and the highest value (15) should be used for those packets that the sender is least willing to have discarded (*e.g.*, low-fidelity audio traffic). There is no relative ordering implied between the congestion-controlled priorities and the non-congestion-controlled priorities.

19.17 IPv6 SECURITY

The current Internet has a number of security problems and lacks effective privacy and authentication mechanisms below the application layer. IPv6 remedies these shortcomings by having two integrated options that provide security services. These two options may be used singly or together to provide differing levels of security to different users. This is very important because different user communities have different security needs.

The first mechanism, called the 'IPv6 Authentication Header', is an extension header which provides authentication and integrity (without confidentiality) to IPv6 datagrams. While the extension is algorithm-independent and will support many different authentication techniques, the use of keyed MD5 is proposed to help ensure interoperability within the worldwide Internet. This can be used to eliminate a significant class of network attacks, including host masquerading attacks. The use of the IPv6 Authentication Header is particularly important when source routing is used with IPv6 because of the known risks in IP source routing. Its placement at the internet layer can help provide host origin authentication to those upper layer protocols and services that currently lack meaningful protections. This mechanism should be exportable by vendors in the United States and other countries with similar export restrictions because it only provides authentication and integrity, and specifically does not provide confidentiality. The exportability of the IPv6 Authentication Header encourages its widespread deployment and use.

The second security extension header provided with IPv6 is the 'IPv6 Encapsulating Security Header'. This mechanism provides integrity and confidentiality to IPv6 datagrams. It is simpler than some similar security protocols (*e.g.*, SP3D, ISO NLSP) but remains flexible and algorithm-independent. To achieve interoperability within the global Internet, the use of DES CBC is being used as the standard algorithm for use with the IPv6 Encapsulating Security Header.

First and foremost it is important to realise that IPv6 is not a super set of IPv4. IPv6 is a whole new protocol suite. Therefore this article will highlight only a few of the most important IPv6 security issues. Believe it or not, the approach to IPv6 security is only marginally better than that of IPv4.

19.17.1 Port Scanning

Firstly let's look at the IPv4 and IPv6 address structure.

The IPv4 address is 32 bits in length, where as the IPv6 address is 128 bits. One main concern for IPv4 network administrators is 'Port Scanning'. Black hat hackers use port scanners to detect open ports on a network node which are associated with well-known vulnerabilities. They then exploit these ports to gain access to the network.

Scanning an IP address of only 32 bits is a relatively simple and quick, which means possible to cover every address within a couple of minutes. However, to scan a whole 128 bit IPv6 address would literally take hundreds of thousands of years. Therefore, Ipv6 makes the option of port scanning nearly impossible, but not completely.

19.17.2 IPSec

One main security feature of IPv4 was IPSec. In brief IPSec provides secure data communication and key exchange. For IPv4 networks IPSec is optional. However, within IPv6 networks IPSec has become mandatory to increase IPv6 security.

19.17.2.1 Authentication Header

The *Authentication Header* (AH) is used to check whether incoming packets have been tampered with. In a typical IPv4 header the AH is stored within the payload of the packet. When it was introduced there was concern about how to integrate this into the new IPv6 header, as the IPv6 header changes in transit. To overcome this problem AH only authenticates and performs integrity checks on parts of the IPv6 header that do not change. Typically AH is located at the end of the header before any higher level extensions such as TCP or UDP.

19.17.2.2 Encapsulating Security Payload

Encapsulating Security Payload (ESP) can also be used to provide authentication, integrity and confidentiality within IPv6. Within the extension EPC a *Security Parameter Index* (SPI) field identifies the group of security the packet sender is using to secure communications. ESP supports multiple encryption methods. However, the default method uses is DES-CBC. While AH authenticates parts of the IPv6 Header which don't change. ESP only authenticates information which follows it. For integrity purposes EPC uses an *integrity check value* (ICV) which is computed once encryption is complete. The ICV uses hash message authentication code such as MD5 for cryptographic purposes.

19.17.3 Neighbour Discovery and Address Auto-Configuration

In brief ND (Neighbour Discovery) is the mechanism responsible for router and prefix discovery, duplicate address and network unreachability detection and also for link layer resolution. Autoconfiguration is responsible for providing a node with either a stateless address or a stateful address. Both work together to make the new protocol more secure as stateful configuration can be provided selectively which reduces the potential for rouge nodes.

IPv6 and IPv4 Dual Stack ·

As the internet slowly migrates to a pure IPv6 network its inevitable that networks will using the old and the new protocol together, this means making use of dual stack technology which supports both protocols. This will without a doubt increase the potential for new security threats. Therefore, network administrators will need to be careful when configuring equipment as most threats will most likely be caused by careless configurations.

19.17.4 Mobility

As IPv6 supports stateless auto-configuration this means that devices can become mobile with the ability to leaving old and enter new networks seamlessly. When entering a new network the device will have two IPv6 addresses, one temporary and one real address. The temporary address is stored within the IPv6 header. This second temporary address can easily be exposed to spoofing attacks. Network administrators should be fully aware of this feature.

This section highlighted a few security issues with the IPv6 protocol. Although significant improvements are made with the new protocol if it is far from solving all problems and difficulties. In fact by introducing the new protocol we are solving some of the old problems with IPv4 while introducing totally new ones. Ultimately the new protocol creates as many problems as it solves. Therefore, becomes no more secure than IPv4. Only the future will tell if the new protocol will offer greater security as we start the migration period.

19.18 TRANSITION MECHANISMS

Unless IPv6 completely supplants IPv4, which is not likely to happen in the foreseeable future, a number of transition mechanisms will be employed to enable IPv4-IPv6 interoperability.

19.18.1 Dual Stack

Since IPv6 is a conservative extension of IPv4, it is relatively easy to write a network stack that supports both IPv4 and IPv6 while sharing most of the code. Such an implementation is called a *dual stack*. Most current implementations of IPv6 provide a dual stack. Some early experimental implementations used independent IPv4 and IPv6 stacks.

19.18.2 Tunneling

In order to reach the IPv6 Internet, an isolated IPv6 host or network must be able to use the existing IPv4 infrastructure to carry IPv6 packets. This is done using a technique known as tunneling, which consists of encapsulating IPv6 packets within IPv4, in effect using IPv4 as a link layer for IPv6.

19.18.3 Automatic Tunneling

Automatic tunneling refers to a technique where the tunnel endpoints are automatically determined by the routing infrastructure. Tunnel endpoints are determined by using a well-known IPv4 anycast address on the remote side, and embedding IPv4 address information within IPv6 addresses on the local side.

19.18.4 Configured Tunneling

Configured tunneling is a technique where the tunnel endpoints are configured explicitly, either by a human operator or by an automatic service known as a Tunnel Broker. Configured tunneling is usually more deterministic and easier to debug than automatic tunneling, and is therefore recommended for large, complex networks.

19.18.5 Proxying and Translation

When an IPv6-only host needs to access an IPv4-only service (for example a web server), some form of translation is necessary. The most widely supported form of translation is the use of a dual-stack application-layer proxy, for example a web proxy. Techniques for application-agnostic translation at the lower layers have also been proposed, but they have been found to be too unreliable in practice due to the wide range of functionality required by common application-layer protocols, and are commonly considered to be obsolete.

The key transition objective is to allow IPv6 and IPv4 hosts to interoperate. A second objective is to allow IPv6 hosts and routers to be deployed in the Internet in a highly diffuse and incremental fashion, with few interdependencies. A third objective is that the transition should be as easy as possible for end- users, system administrators, and network operators to understand and carry out.

The IPv6 transition mechanisms are a set of protocol mechanisms implemented in hosts and routers, along with some operational guidelines for addressing and deployment, designed to make transition the Internet to IPv6 work with as little disruption as possible.

The IPv6 transition mechanisms provides a number of features, including:

1. **Incremental upgrade and deployment:** Individual IPv4 hosts and routers may be upgraded to IPv6 one at a time without requiring any other hosts or routers to be upgraded at the same time. New IPv6 hosts and routers can be installed one by one.
2. **Minimal upgrade dependencies:** The only prerequisite to upgrading hosts to IPv6 is that the DNS server must first be upgraded to handle IPv6 address records. There are no pre-requisites to upgrading routers.
3. **Easy Addressing:** When existing installed IPv4 hosts or routers are upgraded to IPv6, they may continue to use their existing address. They do not need to be assigned new addresses. Administrators do not need to draft new addressing plans.
4. **Low start-up costs:** Little or no preparation work is needed in order to upgrade existing IPv4 systems to IPv6, or to deploy new IPv6 systems. The mechanisms employed by the IPv6 transition mechanisms include:
5. An IPv6 addressing structure that embeds IPv4 addresses within IPv6 addresses, and encodes other information used by the transition mechanisms.
6. A model of deployment where all hosts and routers upgraded to IPv6 in the early transition phase are 'dual' capable (*i.e.* implement complete IPv4 and IPv6 protocol stacks).
7. The technique of encapsulating IPv6 packets within IPv4 headers to carry them over segments of the end-to-end path where the routers have not yet been upgraded to IPv6.
8. The header translation technique to allow the eventual introduction of routing topologies that route only IPv6 traffic, and the deployment of hosts that support only IPv6. Use of this technique is optional, and would be used in the later phase of transition if it is used at all.

The IPv6 transition mechanisms ensures that IPv6 hosts can interoperate with IPv4 hosts anywhere in the Internet up until the time when IPv4 addresses run out, and allows IPv6 and IPv4 hosts within a limited scope to interoperate indefinitely after that. This feature protects the huge investment users have made in IPv4 and ensures that IPv6 does not render IPv4 obsolete. Hosts that need only a limited connectivity range (*e.g.*, printers) need never be upgraded to IPv6.

The incremental upgrade features of the IPv6 transition mechanisms allow the host and router vendors to integrate IPv6 into their product lines at their own pace, and allows the end users and network operators to deploy IPv6 on their own schedules.

19.19 WHY IPv6?

There are a number of reasons why IPv6 is appropriate for the next generation of the Internet Protocol. It solves the Internet scaling problem, provides a flexible transition mechanism for the current Internet, and was designed to meet the needs of new markets such as nomadic personal computing devices, networked entertainment, and device control. It does this in a evolutionary way which reduces the risk of architectural problems.

Ease of transition is a key point in the design of IPv6. It is not something was added in at the end. IPv6 is designed to interoperate with IPv4. Specific mechanisms (embedded IPv4 addresses, pseudo-checksum rules etc.) were built into IPv6 to support transition and compatibility with IPv4. It was designed to permit a gradual and piecemeal deployment with a minimum of dependencies.

IPv6 supports large hierarchical addresses which will allow the Internet to continue to grow and provide new routing capabilities not built into IPv4. It has anycast addresses which can be used for policy route selection and has scoped multicast addresses which provide improved scalability over IPv4 multicast. It also has local use address mechanisms which provide the ability for 'plug and play' installation.

The address structure of IPv6 was also designed to support carrying the addresses of other internet protocol suites. Space was allocated in the addressing plan for IPX and NSAP addresses. This was done to facilitate migration of these internet protocols to IPv6.

IPv6 provides a platform for new Internet functionality. This includes support for real-time flows, provider selection, host mobility, end-to- end security, auto-configuration, and auto-reconfiguration.

In summary, IPv6 is a new version of IP. It can be installed as a normal software upgrade in internet devices. It is interoperable with the current IPv4. Its deployment strategy was designed to not havc any 'flag' days. IPv6 is designed to run well on high performance networks (*e.g.*, ATM) and at the same time is still efficient for low bandwidth networks (*e.g.*, wireless). In addition, it provides a platform for new internet functionality that will be required in the near future.

19.20 IPv6 TUNNELING

The transition period from IPv4 to IPv6 on the Internet will not be an overnight job. This means that for sending IPv6 packets over IPv4 topologies there must be a logical technique. This technique is called *IPv6 Tunneling*, sometimes referred to as encapsulation. Tunneling is

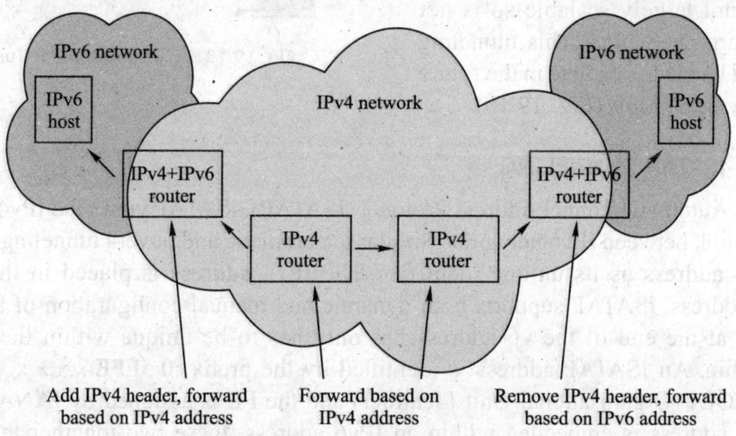

Fig. 19.17 IPv6 Tunneling Diagram

the routing of IPv6 packets over IPv4 topologies. Currently there is six main ways of tunneling IPv6 packets over IPv4 infrastructures (Fig. 19.17).

19.21 IPv6–6 OVER 4 TUNNELING

6-over-4 tunnels are usually used in single organisations. It is also an automatic tunneling technique but solves problems in different ways. It assumes that the IPv4 infrastructure is a single IPv6 subnet. 6-over-4 addresses are mapped to IPv4 multicast addresses, this stateless autoconfiguration. This tunneling technique has not been largely deployed since the use of IPv4 multicasting is not widely used in today's internetworking. 6to4 addresses are a valid prefix for the lower 64 bits in an IPv6 unicast address used for the identifier. This method of tunneling is depreciated in favour of other techniques due to it only working with multicast IPv4 networks.

19.22 IPv6–6 TO 4 TUNNELING

6to4 tunneling allows v6 packets to travel across v4 clouds by using 6to4 gateway routers to configure a special address and prefix. The address prefix 2002: is reserved for 6to4 based addresses. Added to this address is the v4 address which is 32 bits making an end prefix of /48, the next 16 bits are used for v6 subnets which allows 65,536 subnets 6to4 tunneling allows IPv6 packets to travel across v4 clouds by using 6to4 gateway routers to configure a special address and prefix. The address prefix 2002: is reserved for 6to4 based addresses. Added to this address is the v4 address which is 32 bits making an end prefix of /48, the next 16 bits are used for v6 subnets which allows 65,536 subnets

19.23 IPv6–AUTOMATIC TUNNELING

Automatic tunneling means literally that the tunnel does not need to be manually configured. This technique uses IPv4-compatible addresses (fe80::x.x.x.x) where the last 32 bits of the address is a private IPv4 address, the prefix is /96 relating to the zeros before the v4 at the end. For example fe80::5efe:192.168.1.2 Automatic tunneling addresses are supported by Windows XP and some versions of Linux. This tunneling technique is not largely scalable so is not suitable for large networks. This tunneling technique will be made obsolete in the future due to its low scalability (Fig. 19.18).

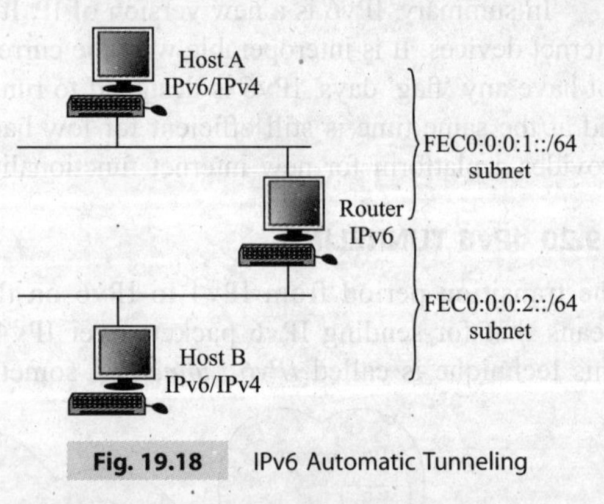

Fig. 19.18 IPv6 Automatic Tunneling

19.24 IPv6–ISATAP TUNNELING

The Intra-Site Automatic Tunnel Address Protocol (ISATAP). ISATAP views the IPv4 infrastructure as one virtual link between IPv6 networks. Similar to automatic and 6over4 tunneling this technique uses an IPv4 address as its unique identifier. The IPv4 address is placed in the last 32 bits of the IPv6 address. ISATAP supports both dynamic and manual configuration of addresses. The IPv4 address at the end of the v6 address has only has to be unique within the network it is deployed within. An ISATAP address is identified by the prefix :0:5EFE:x.x.x.x. The 00-00-5E portion is an OUI (Organisational Unit Identifier) and the FE is assigned by IANA which means that an IPV4 address is embedded within an IPv6 address, these two together make the prefix of 0::5EFE. The IPv4 address is automatically embedded within the v6 address or can also be manually configured. ISATAP addresses can communicate with 6bone hosts through ISATAP routers or even 6-to-4 routers.

19.25 IPv6–MANUAL TUNNELING

A manually configured tunnel is a permanent virtual link between two IPv6 networks connecting over an IPv4 backbone. Manual configured tunnels can carry IPv6 packets only. A v6 address is configured on the tunnel interface, along with this a manual v4 addresses are configured on the source and the destination of the tunnel, configured tunnels must have both v4 and v6 addresses. Routers at the source and destination of the tunnel must have IPv4 and IPv6 dual stack protocols. Because these tunnels have to be configured manually they are not very scalable, so this type of tunneling is only suitable for permanent link. If a change in the network was to occur a manual tunnel does not change, there for they are also high maintenance. Encapsulation of the IPv6 header into the IPv4 header is taken place at the router. Where as 6-over-4 tunnels the encapsulation is taken place at the host. This might lead to a delay or bottle neck in performance over 6-over-4 network topologies. This is one question that could be answered by implementing the tunneling technique in a network simulation.

19.26 IPv6–TEREDO TUNNELING

Teredo is a tunneling technology invented to solve the problem of IPV4 network address translation (NAT). NAT does not work well with tunneling technologies. Since a large number of users on the Internet sit behind a router with a private IP address developers had to come up with a solution to do this NAT does not allow forwarding of many types of payload within the IPV4 header. Since IPv6 is the payload of the IPv4 header this is bound to cause problems. 6to4 tunneling supports NAT as long as the router is running 6to4 and NAT in the same router. NAT was designed to enable more users to connect to the Internet using the same IPv4 address. This helped a lot with IPv4's struggle to assign addresses to the ever growing Internet. An IPv6 network will no longer need this type of technology, but since it is very widely deployed Teredo is a temporary solution to this problem. Teredo works on UDP. Since Teredo was developed to support NAT it has to possess unique global IPv4 addresses. This technique is host-to-host based, which means it is only concerned with end-to-end connections. The global IPv6 prefix for Teredo is 2001:0000:/32. The address contains both the Teredo server and client address. To route IPv6 packets using Teredo, a client needs to send a packet to a Teredo server. The Teredo server then forwards the pack to a Teredo relay, the packet is then sent to the destination node. The 16 bit flag field holds information on the type of NAT that is needed to bypass.

SUMMARY

- IPv6 has unicast and multicast addresses like IPv4. There is, however, no distinct concept of a broadcast address in IPv6. A new type of address, the *anycast* address, has been added to allow a message to be sent to any one member of a group of devices.
- IPv6 addresses are represented using eight sets of four hexadecimal digits, a form called *colon hexadecimal notation*. Additional techniques, called *zero suppression* and *zero compression*, are used to reduce the size of displayed addresses further by removing unnecessary zeroes from the presentation of the address.
- A special mixed notation is defined for IPv6 addresses whose last 32 bits contain an embedded IPv4 address. In this notation, the first 96 bits are displayed in regular colon hexadecimal notation, and the last 32 bits in IPv4-style dotted decimal.

- ❒ In IPv6 the size of an address's prefix is indicating by the prefix length that follows the address, separated with a slash, just as this is done in IPv4 classless addressing.
- ❒ The part of the IPv6 address space set aside for unicast addresses is structured into an address format that uses the first 48 bits for the *routing prefix* (like a network ID), the next 16 bits for a *subnet ID*, and the final 64 bits for an *interface ID* (like a host ID).
- ❒ Multicast addresses are used to send data to a number of devices on an internetwork simultaneously. In IPv6 each multicast address can be specified for a variety of different *scopes*, allowing a transmission to be targeted to either a wide or narrow audience of recipient devices.
- ❒ IPv6 datagrams use a general structure that begins with a mandatory main header 40 bytes in length, followed by optional *extension headers* and then a variable-length *Data* area. This structure was created to allow the main header to be streamlined while allowing devices to add extra information to datagrams when needed.
- ❒ In IPv6 fragmentation is only performed by the device sending a datagram, not by routers. If a router encounters a datagram too large to send over a physical network with a small MTU, the router sends an ICMPv6 *Packet Too Big* message back to the source of the datagram. This can be used as part of a process called *Path MTU Discovery* to determine the minimum MTU of an entire route.
- ❒ Fragmentation is done in IPv6 in a manner similar to that of IPv4, except that extension headers must be handled specially. Certain extension headers are considered *unfragmentable* and appear in each fragment; others are fragmented along with the data.
- ❒ While IPv4 has proven to have tremendous durability in an increasingly networked world, it exhibits some basic limitations that make the features of IPv6 ever more relevant. The most noteworthy of those features is the increased IP address space made possible in the IPv6 addressing scheme. As the installed base of Internet-enabled devices continues to expand worldwide and the high-growth, population-dense regions where IPv4 addresses are in short supply continue to expand, the need for the flexibility offered by IPv6 will become even more important.

REVIEW QUESTIONS

Multiple Choice Questions

1. A very large organization has received its IPv6 address range from its Internet Service Provider and intends to use only IPv6 addresses internally. Employees will access the Internet using port address translation. What is a requirement for their DNS servers?

(*a*) They no longer need DNS servers.
(*b*) Their DNS servers need to support both IPv4 and IPv6 addresses.
(*c*) Their DNS servers need to support only IPv6 addresses.
(*d*) Their DNS servers need to support only IPv4 addresses.
(*e*) They need additional DNS servers in their network just for IPv6 addresses.
(*f*) There are no changes required to their DNS servers.

2. A global corporation has an internal network with the following characteristics:

2,000,000 + hosts
10,000 + routers
Internet connectivity
High traffic volumes with business partners and customers

Which statement best describes what a flexible IPv6 strategy would look like for this corporation?

(*a*) Both hosts and routers would run dual stack.

(*b*) Hosts would run IPv4 and routers would run native IPv6.

(*c*) Hosts would run dual stack and routers would run IPv4 only.

(*d*) Hosts would run IPv6 and routers would run native IPv6.

3. Which two statements about IPv6 addresses are true? (Choose two)

(*a*) Leading zeros are required.

(*b*) Two colons (::) are used to represent successive hexadecimal fields of zeros.

(*c*) Two colons (::) are used to separate fields.

(*d*) A single interface will have multiple IPv6 addresses of different types.

4. Which IPv6 feature enables routing to distribute connection requests to the nearest content server?

(*a*) Link-local (*b*) Site-local (*c*) Anycast (*d*) Multicast

(*e*) Global aggregatable

5. A company is designing a worldwide IPv6 network with duplicated file servers at multiple locations. Each file server contains identical reference information. Which IPv6 address type would be used to allow each end station to send a request to the nearest file server using the same destination address, regardless of the location of that end station?

(*a*) unicast (*b*) anycast (*c*) multicast (*d*) broadcast

6. Which two link state routing protocols support IPv6 routing? (Choose two)

(*a*) BGP4+ (*b*) OSPF (*c*) RIPng (*d*) EIGRP

(*e*) IS-IS

7. Which of the following is the most likely organization from which **an enterprise** could obtain an administrative assignment of a block of IPv6 global unicast IP addresses?

(*a*) An ISP (*b*) ICANN (*c*) An RIR

(*d*) Global unicast addresses are not administratively assigned by an outside organisation.

8. Which of the following is the shortest valid abbreviation for FE80:0000:0000:0100:0000:0000:0000:0123?

(*a*) FE80::100::123 (*b*) FE8::1::123

(*c*) FE80::100:0:0:0:123:4567 (*d*) FE80:0:0:100::123

9. Which of the following answers lists a **multicast** IPv6 address?

(*a*) 2000::1:1234:5678:9ABC (*b*) FD80::1:1234:5678:9ABC

(*c*) FE80::1:1234:5678:9ABC (*d*) FF80::1:1234:5678:9ABC

10. Which of the following answers list either a protocol or function that can be used by a host to **dynamically *learn its own IPv6 address***?

(*a*) Stateful DHCP (*b*) Stateless DHCP

(*c*) Stateless autoconfiguration (*d*) Neighbor Discovery Protocol

11. Which of the following help allow an IPv6 host to learn the **IP address of a default gateway** on its subnet?

(*a*) Stateful DHCP (*b*) Stateless RS

(*c*) Stateless autoconfiguration (*d*) Neighbor Discovery Protocol

12. Which of the following are routing protocols that support IPv6?

(*a*) RIPng (*b*) RIP-2 (*c*) OSPFv2 (*d*) OSPFv3

(*e*) OSPFv4

13. In the following configuration, this router's Fa0/0 interface has a MAC address of 4444.4444.4444. Which of the following IPv6 addresses will the interface use?

ipv6 unicast-routing

ipv6 router rip tag1
interface FastEthernet0/0
ipv6 address 3456::1/64

(*a*) 3456::C444:44FF:FE44:4444 (*b*) 3456::4444:44FF:FE44:4444
(*c*) 3456::1 (*d*) FE80::1
(*e*) FE80::6444:44FF:FE44:4444 (*f*) FE80::4444:4444:4444

14. In the configuration text in the previous question, RIP was not working on interface Fa0/0. Which of the following configuration commands would enable RIP on Fa0/0?
(*a*) network 3456::/64 (*b*) network 3456::/16 (*c*) network 3456::1/128 (*d*) ipv6 rip enable
(*e*) ipv6 rip tag1 enable

15. Which of the following IPv4-to-IPv6 transition methods allows an *IPv4-only host to communicate with an IPv6-only host*?
(*a*) Dual-stack (*b*) 6to4 tunneling (*c*) ISATAP tunneling (*d*) NAT-PT

16. Which two of these statements are true of IPv6 address representation? (Choose two)
(*a*) The first 64 bits represent the dynamically created interface ID.
(*b*) A single interface may be assigned multiple IPV6 addresses of any type.
(*c*) Every IPV6 interface contains at least one loopback address.
(*d*) Leading zeros in an IPV6 16 bit hexadecimal field are mandatory.

17. Which three of the following are IPv6 transition mechanisms? (Choose three)
(*a*) 6to4 tunneling (*b*) GRE tunneling (*c*) ISATAP tunneling (*d*) Teredo tunneling
(*e*) VPN tunneling (*f*) PPP tunneling

18. Which two descriptions are correct about characteristics of IPv6 unicast addressing? (Choose two)
(*a*) Global addresses start with 2000::/3.
(*b*) Link-local addresses start with FF00::/10.
(*c*) Link-local addresses start with FE00:/12.
(*d*) There is only one loopback address and it is ::1.

19. Select the valid IPv6 addresses. (Choose all apply)
(*a*) ::192:168:0:1 (*b*) 2002:c0a8:101::42
(*c*) 2003:dead:beef:4dad:23:46:bb:101 (*d*) ::
(*e*) 2000:: (*f*) 2001:3452:4952:2837::

20. Where will you find IPv6 addresses beginning with 2002 and carrying a /48 prefix?
(*a*) 6to4 tunnel edge routers (*b*) loopback interfaces
(*c*) 6to4 tunnel access routers (*d*) Any link-layer master router
(*e*) Any site-local DR

21. Name three benefits of IPv6. Choose 3.
(*a*) Decreased reliance on multicast (*b*) Elimination of broadcast behavior
(*c*) Enhanced DHCP usage (*d*) Increased security features
(*e*) IP address autoconfiguration

22. Which two statements regarding a link-local address are true? Choose 2.
(*a*) A link-local address is manually configured when needed
(*b*) A link-local address begins FE80
(*c*) A link-local address is assigned by the ISATAP tunnel process
(*d*) A link-local address is based upon an existing Layer 2 address

23. What is the loopback address used in IPv6? Choose 2.
(*a*) 0:0:0:0:0:0:0:1 (*b*) 1:1:1:1:1:1:1:1 (*c*) 1:: (*d*) ::1

24. Which of the following is NOTa feature of Anycast addressing in IPv6?
(*a*) Same IPv6 address assigned to multiple nodes
(*b*) Routing protocol makes the 'nearest' determination
(*c*) Supports many future potential applications
(*d*) Provides an any-to-many communication model

25. Which of the following are invalid IPv6 communication types? (Choose two).
(*a*) Unicast (*b*) Multicast (*c*) Broadcast (*d*) Anycast
(*e*) Cryptocast

26. Which of the following are valid IPv6 addresses? (Choose three.)
(*a*) 2001:0db8:0000:0000:0000:0000:1428:57ab (*b*) 2001:0db8::1428:57ab
(*c*) 2001::1685:2123::1428:57ab (*d*) 2001:99:ab:1:99:2:1:9
(*e*) 2001:1428:57ab:1685:2123:1428:57ab

27. In IPv6, Internet-valid addresses are known by what name?
(*a*) Private (*b*) Public (*c*) Unique (*d*) Unspecified
(*e*) Global

28. In IPv6, a __________ address is used to communicate with hosts on the directly attached network and will never forward beyond the first router hop.
(*a*) Global (*b*) Private (*c*) Link local (*d*) Private restricted
(*e*) Auto-generated

29. Which of the following commands could you use to assign an IPv6 address to your router?
(*a*) Router(config-if)#ip address fe01:3112:abcd::0001 255.255.255.0
(*b*) Router(config-if)#ip address fe01:3112:abcd::0001/48
(*c*) Router(config-if)#ip address 6 fe01:3112:abcd::0001 255.255.255.0
(*d*) Router(config-if)#ip address 6 fe01:3112:abcd::0001/48
(*e*) Router(config-if)#ipv6 address fe01:3112:abcd::0001 255.255.255.0
(*f*) Router(config-if)#ipv6 address fe01:3112:abcd::0001/48

30. Which of the following commands could you use to start a RIPng process on your router?
(*a*) Router(config)#router RIPng (*b*) Router(config)#ipv6 router rip RIPTagNo1
(*c*) Router(config)#routerv6 RIP (*d*) Router(config)#ripv6

31. Which of the following commands enables the IPv6 protocol on a router?
(*a*) Router(config)#ipv6 unicast-routing (*b*) Router(config)#ipv6 enable
(*c*) Router(config)#enable ipv6 (*d*) Router(config)#ipv6
(*e*) Router(config)#router ipv6

ANSWERS

Multiple Choice Questions

1. (*b*) **2.** (*a*) **3.** (*b*), (*d*) **4.** (*c*) **5.** (*b*) **6.** (*b*), (*e*) **7.** (*a*) **8.** (*d*)
9. (*d*) **10.** (*a*), (*c*) **11.** (*a*), (*d*) **12.** (*a*), (*d*) **13.** (*c*), (*e*) **14.** (*e*) **15.** (*d*) **16.** (*b*), (*c*)
17. (*a*), (*c*), (*d*) **18.** (*a*), (*d*) **19.** (*a*), (*b*), (*c*), (*d*), (*f*) **20.** (*a*) **21.** (*b*), (*d*), (*e*)
22. (*b*), (*d*) **23.** (*a*), (*d*) **24.** (*d*) **25.** (*c*), (*e*) **26.** (*a*), (*b*), (*d*) **27.** (*e*) **28.** (*c*)
29. (*f*) **30.** (*b*) **31.** (*a*)

CRYPTOGRAPHY

20.1 INTRODUCTION

In the world where information and communication is the indispensable composition of human activities, where men and technology must communicate or share information in order to make decisions; it therefore behooves that this composite essence of humans should be protected and managed to ensure its sustainability, integrity, accuracy.

Encryption techniques have become the immediate solution to protect information against third parties. These techniques required that data and information should be encrypted with some sort of mathematical algorithm where only the party that shares the information could possible decrypt to use the information. This phenomenon has long existed and is not fully reliable which pose danger to the information sharing. However, many method of encryption emerge to serve the need of the emergent trend of rapid technological advancement. These emergent techniques were more reliable and are fast in operation and performance wise.

Cryptography is the science of writing in secret code and is an ancient art; the first documented use of cryptography in writing dates back to circa 1900 B.C. when an Egyptian scribe used non-standard hieroglyphs in an inscription. Some experts argue that cryptography appeared spontaneously sometime after writing was invented, with applications ranging from diplomatic missives to war-time battle plans. It is no surprise, then, that new forms of cryptography came soon after the widespread development of computer communications. In data and telecommunications, cryptography is necessary when communicating over any un-trusted medium, which includes just about *any* network, particularly the Internet. Cryptography can protect any kind of data, from very sensitive information, such as Internet-based commerce and banking transaction, to harmless messages you would just rather no one else knew about, such as a letter to a friend. Cryptography, also abbreviated as crypto, can provide a great deal of confidentiality and integrity checks for information. However, it is not a silver bullet, and it can lead to a tremendous false sense of security unless used properly.

Within the context of any application-to-application communication, there are some specific security requirements, including:

1. **Authentication:** The process of proving one's identity. (The primary forms of host-to-host authentication on the Internet today are name-based or address-based, both of which are notoriously weak).
2. **Privacy/confidentiality:** Ensuring that no one can read the message except the intended receiver.
3. **Integrity:** Assuring the receiver that the received message has not been altered in any way from the original.
4. **Non-repudiation:** A mechanism to prove that the sender really sent this message.

However, as this new trend of fast and reliable cryptography emerged, there is a very big concern on that issue of using to hide proof of violent scheme as many government authorities see it as impending danger. Since Cryptography has become so powerful that messages scrambled with so-called strong cryptography are virtually undecipherable. Like many powerful technologies, this is a double-edged sword. For good, we know that Encryption can keep email and financial transactions over the Internet secure and private, but law enforcement officials worry those criminals and terrorists could use the same tools to conceal incriminating evidence and violent plots.

This concern has convoked many viewpoint and argument, which has alerted the formation of policies by some law enforcement agencies to regulate the encryption techniques. In this view, we will be discussing popular encryption system, types of cryptography, issues of regulating Encryption technology, social and legal implication, computer ciphers and encryption and other cryptosystems, which will aid the understanding of Encryption Techniques and its advantages and challenges in the electronic age.

20.2 ORIGIN OF ENCRYPTION TECHNIQUE

Encryption is a process of converting messages or data into a form that cannot be read without decrypting or deciphering it. The root of the word encryption—crypt—comes from the Greek word kryptos, meaning 'hidden' or 'secret.'

The study and practice of encryption and decryption is called the *science of cryptography*. Scientists who study different ways to protect and ensure the confidentiality, integrity, and authenticity of information are called cryptologists. Cryptologists also engage in cryptanalysis to find ways to break encryption methods.

For centuries before the age of electronic communication and computers, individuals, Militaries and other groups coded written information. As electronic forms of communication and information storage and processing have developed, the opportunities to intercept, modify, use, disclose, and read confidential information has grown, and the need for powerful encryption techniques has increased.

Government agencies, banks, and many corporations now routinely send a great deal of confidential information from onc computer to another. Such data are usually transmitted via telephone lines or other non-private channels, such as the Internet. Continuing development of secure computer systems and networks will ensure that confidential information can be securely transferred across computer networks.

In the early 1970s, Horst Feistel, a scientist at International Business Machines Corporation (IBM Corporation), developed LUCIFER, a computerized cryptosystem that used both substitution and transposition.

In 1977, the United States National Bureau of Standards (now the National Institute of Standards and Technology [NIST]) developed a cryptographic technique called the Data Encryption Standard (DES). DES was based on LUCIFER and made use of the computer binary code (converting plaintext to bits, or binary digits of 1s and 0s). DES transformed 64 bit segments of information into 64 bit segments of ciphertext using a key that was 56 bits in size. Each user randomly selected a key and revealed it only to those persons authorized to see the protected data. DES was broken in 1998.

In 1978 three American computer scientists, Ronald L. Rivest, Adi Shamir, and Leonard Adleman, who later founded the company RSA Data Security, created the Rivest-Shamir-Adleman (RSA) system. The RSA system uses two large prime numbers, p and q, multiplied to form a composite, n. The formula n = pq, capitalizes on the very difficult problem of factoring prime numbers.

As more and more information is transferred over computer networks, computer scientists continue to develop more secure, complex algorithms. In 1997, the NIST began coordinating development of a replacement for DES called Advanced Encryption Standard (AES). AES will use a more complex algorithm, based on a 128 bit encryption standard instead of the 64 bit standard of DES. This 128 bit algorithm will make AES impossible to decrypt with current technology.

Another encryption system based on 128 bit segments is called International Data Encryption Algorithm, or IDEA. The Swiss Federal Institute of Technology developed the IDEA standard in the 1990s. Computer scientists have also proposed alternatives such as public-key cryptosystems (PKCs), which use two types of keys, a public key and a pri vate key. The public key encrypts data, and a corresponding private key decrypts it. The user gives the public key out to other users, and they can use the public key for encrypting messages to be sent to the user. The user keeps the private key secret and uses it to decrypt received messages. An example of a PKC is the RSA system, described above.

20.3 ENCRYPTION AND DECRYPTION

Data that can be read and understood without any special measures is called *plaintext* or *cleartext.* The method of disguising plaintext in such a way as to hide its substance is called *encryption.* Encrypting plaintext results in unreadable gibberish called *ciphertext*. You use encryption to ensure that information is hidden from anyone for whom it is not intended, even those who can see the encrypted data. The process of reverting ciphertext to its original plaintext is called *decryption.* There are two basic techniques for encrypting information: symmetric encryption (also called secret key encryption) and asymmetric encryption (also called public key encryption). Figure 20.1 illustrates the process.

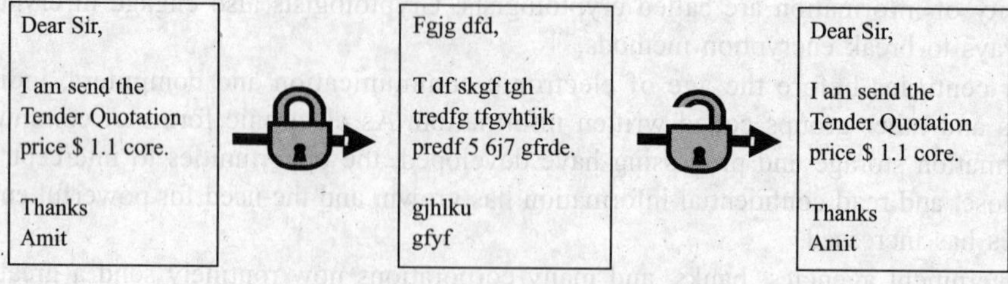

Fig. 20.1 Encryption and Decryption

20.4 HOW ENCRYPTION WORKS

Encryption program uses an encryption algorithm (complex mathematical processes) to encrypt and decrypt the data. Encryption algorithm creates specific strings of data used for encryption-keys that consist of long strings of bits or binary numbers. The more bits in the key, the more the number of possible combinations of binary numbers that makes the code more difficult to break. Then encryption algorithm scrambles data by combining the bits in the key with the data bits. In symmetric encryption, the same key is used to scramble (encrypt) and unscramble (decrypt) data. In asymmetric key encryption, two different keys are required-one for encryption and one for decryption.

20.5 WHY YOU NEED ENCRYPTION?

Nowadays when more and more sensitive information is stored on computers and transmitted over the Internet, we need to ensure information security and safety. One of the most common uses of encryption is encrypting emails. Sending sensitive messages, documents and files over the Internet is like sending a postcard as all emails are transmitted in an unsecured form. It doesn't depend on if you send emails via public and private networks. Your message is totally open to interception by anyone along the way—so anybody—your ISP, your boss, etc. can read your emails. Even if you connect to your server and send your emails via SSL, it only means that your emails can't be seen while transmitting between you and your server. When your email reaches your server, it can be seen by your email service provider. Then your server usually sends your email to the recipient in an unsecured way and your email can also be easily seen by anyone. Private network, where email goes directly to a mail server and resides there until it is retrieved, also doesn't provide necessary security level, as you email can be seen *e.g.*, by network administrator, your boss, etc. Of course, you may believe that your personal email does not contain any private information, but everyone has got something to keep in secret from his family, neighbors or colleagues. It could be financial, sexual, social, political, or professional secrets. There is really only one sure way to protect your email privacy—using encryption.

20.6 DIGITAL SUBSTITUTION (ENCRYPTION)

There are few mathematical operations that are necessary for understanding our subsequent discussion, namely OR, exclusive OR (XOR), and modulo functions.

George Boole, a mathematician in the late 1980s, invented a form of logic algebra that provides the basis for electronic computers and microprocessors chips. His logical operations were a set of truth tables, in which each of the inputs and outputs were either TRUE or FALSE.

The Boolean Exclusive OR (XOR) function is one of the fundamental operations used in cryptography. The output of an XOR is TRUE if exactly one of the inputs is TRUE; otherwise, the output is FALSE. We use 0 for true and 1 for false. The output of an XOR is TRUE if exactly one of the output is a 1 if the two inputs differ.

The properties for XOR are very useful to cryptographers for two reasons. First, any value XORed with itself is 0 (0 + 0 = 0, 1 + 1 = 0). Second, any value XORed with 0 is ust itself (0 + 0 = 0, 1 + 0 = 1).

Suppose Amit has a secret message to sent Sonia, composed of the three character message CAT. This translates to the standard 7-bit ASCII bit stream:

1000011 1000001 1010100 (CAT *i.e.*, C = 1000011, A = 1000001, T = 1010100)

Now, Amit and Sonia have already shared the 21-bit secret key as follows:

1010011 1010010 1001110

Now, Amit convert the plaintext into ciphertext by XORing the message with the key:

```
  1010011 1010010 1001110
+ 1000011 1000001 1010100
=========================
  0010000 0010011 0011010   (Ciphertext by XORing)
```

The output of the algorithm is now become ciphertext *i.e.*, 0010000 0010011 0011010

In the Mathematical Formula, we can write:

$$E_K (M) = C.$$

In these formulas, 'K' would be the secret key. The symbols 'M', 'E' and 'C' represent main text (plaintext), Encryption and Ciphertext.

20.7 DIGITAL SUBSTITUTION (DECRYPTION)

Now, Sonia received the ciphertext from Amit, in turn, XORs it wit the secret key:

```
  1010011 1010010 1001110   (21 bit key)
+ 0010000 0010011 0011010   (Ciphertext)
=========================
  1000011 1000001 1010100   (Plaintext in ASCII i.e., CAT)
     C       A       T
```

The recovered plaintext is Amit's original message. So XOR naturally acts as a cipher: The original message XORed with a key yields a jumble of bits; XORing that jumble with the key again yields the original message.

In the Mathematical Formula, we can write:

$$D_K (C) = M.$$

In these formulas, 'K' would be the secret key. The symbols 'M', 'D' and 'C' represent main text (plaintext), Decryption and Ciphertext.

Note that another Boolean function sometimes seen in cryptography is OR. The output of an OR is TRUE if either of the inputs is TRUE; otherwise the output is FALSE. Using binary digits, the output is a 1 if either or both inputs are a 1; the output is a 0 only if both inputs are 0.

20.8 ARBITRARY SUBSTITUTION

There are two basic methods of encrypting of gabling text are substitution and permutation. A third approach is actually a hybrid, a mixture of both.

Substitution means replacing an element of the plaintext with an element of cipertext. Substitution involves exchanging one character (or byte) for another. Simple substitution schemes use mapping; therefore, one character would be substituted with another to encrypt a message, with decryption being the inverse action. The mapping function is the key; that is, anyone who knows how the characters were mapped to encrypt the message can decrypt the message.

Simple examples for mapping one-to-one mapping are as follows:

Example 1:

Plaintext:	A	B	C	D	E	F	G	H	I	J	K	L	M	N	O	P	Q	R	S	T	U	V	W	X	Y	Z
Ciphertext:	1	2	3	4	5	6	7	8	9	10	11	12	13	14	15	16	17	18	19	20	21	22	23	24	25	26

OR

Example 2:

Plaintext:	A	B	C	D	E	F	G	H	I	J	K	L	M	N	O	P	Q	R	S	T	U	V	W	X	Y	Z
Ciphertext:	q	r	t	y	u	i	o	p	l	k	j	h	g	f	d	s	a	z	x	c	v	b	n	m	w	e

To encrypt the sentence 'meet me when free', Amit would substitute characters and send the string 'guuc gu npuf izuu'. In turn, Sonia, would reverse the substitution to recover the plaintext.

For substitution to work, there must be a unique one-to-one mapping from plaintext character to ciphertext character. A many-to-one or one-to-many mapping would make encryption difficult or impossible. For example, if 'g' replaced both 'm' and 'e', you would still be able to encrypt the message; therefore, 'meet' would become 'gggc'. But if we tried to decrypt it now, we would not know whether the 'g' should be a 'm' or a 'e' because they are both mapped to the same letter.

An example of Multiple Substitution Cipher is as follow:

Key word: cricket

To encode, match up key word letters with letters of message:

Plaintext: M e e t m e w h e n f r e e

Keyword: c r i c k e t c r i c k e t

In example 1, M is 13th letter in the alphabet and c is 3rd, so M + C *i.e.*, 13 + 3 = 16, so, substitute the 16th letter of alphabet: 'o'. Similarly, for the alphabet w + t *i.e.*, 23 + 20 = 43 – 26 = 17 *i.e.*, 'q'.

Ciphertext: ownw xj qkww icjy

These types of encryptions are difficult to decrypt.

20.9 ROTATION SUBSTITUTION

Symmetric encryption is based on simple mathematics that utilizes a single key. Whatever can be encrypted with one key can only be decrypted with the same key. Arbitrary substitution requires mapping for every character in the alphabet. An alternate substitution method does not require mapping is rotation. In this type of substitution, we shift every character a set number of spaces. For example, if we shift A three spaces, it becomes D, B become E, and so on.

Example:

Plaintext: A B C D E F G H I J K L M N O P Q R S T U V W X Y Z
Ciphertext: d e f g h i j k l m n o p q r s t u v w x y z a b c

The Caesar Cipher, invented by Julius Caesar to encode message to his generals, is a famous rotation cipher. If Amit using this 'ROT-3' scheme, he would enrypt his message 'meet' as 'phhw'. In its days, roughly 50–60 BC, the Caesar Cipher was considered good enough to fool almost anyone because very few people could read, even fewer could write, and couriers would rather kill a snooper than let him capture a message. Though the people believe that the Caesar cipher is the earliest cipher, cryptography actually goes back nearly 2000 years earlier to ancient Egypt and China. Caesar did not use just one encryption tool (ROT-3), he also transliterated Latin into Greek and used other form of subterfuge.

If we represent each letter of the alphabet by an integer that corresponds to its position in the alphabet, the formula for re-placing each character 'p' of the plaintext with a character 'C' of the ciphertext can be expressed as

$$C = E(3, p) = (p + 3) \bmod 26$$

A more general version of this cipher that allows for any degree of shift would be expressed by

$$C = E(k, p) = (p + k) \bmod 26$$

The formula for decryption would be

$$p = D(k, C) = (C - k) \bmod 26$$

In these formulas, 'k' would be the secret key. The symbols 'E' and 'D' represent encryption and decryption.

Although character rotation is a trivial scheme, rotation ciphers came back into vogue in the early 1980s, primarily in the form of ROT-13. Shortly USENET newsgroups and electronic mailing lists became popular; subscribers realized they did not always want to see the contents of a message. ROT-13 was never meant to be a strong cipher, it is trivial to break. The point was for the reader to make deliberate effort to decipher the message. ROT-13 eventually became part of newsreader software and a common function of the Unix Operating System. ROT-13 is a symmetric substitution and because of 26 letters in the English alphabet, same implementation will both encode plaintext and decode ciphertext, because performing ROT-13 followed by ROT-13 is actually ROT-26, which would take you back to the original letter.

20.10 PERMUTATION OR TRANSPOSITION CIPHERS

Permutation, also called *Transposition*, shuffles the order in which characters (or bytes) appear rather than substituting one for another. In a transposition cipher, the order of plaintext letters is changed to derive the ciphertext. The message is usually written without word divisions in rows of letters arranged in a rectangular block. The letters are then transposed in a prearranged order, such as by vertical columns, diagonals, or spirals, or by more complicated systems, such as the knight's tour, which is based on the move of the knight in chess. The arrangement of the letters in the enciphered message depends upon the size of the block of code words used and upon the route followed in inscribing and transposing the letters.

A cipher in which every pair of letters is swapped is an example of a transposition cipher. In this case, for example, the ciphertext for elephant would be lepeahtn. The first and second letters are swapped, then the third and fourth letters are swapped, and so on. Transposition ciphers may be combined with substitution ciphers to produce a more complex encoded message.

The best-known transposition ciphers are the route ciphers. In a typical route cipher, the letters of the message are written into a rectangular grid one at a time, going across the rows, something like this

T	H	I	S	I	S	A
R	O	U	T	E	C	I
P	H	E	R			

Then the letters will be read out of the grid in a different order, for example, reading down the columns

TRPHOHIUESTRIESCAI

or diagonally

TRHPOIHUSETIRESCAI

or reading alternately up and down the columns

PRTHOHEUISTREISCIA.

The Union used these types of route ciphers in the US Civil War, and it is believed that they were never broken by the Confederacy. Today, these simple route transpositions make fairly elementary hobbyist ciphers, easily solved by paper and pencil methods.

In the late 19th century the first transposition cipher utilizing a key was developed. It is called a **columnar transposition**, or more precisely, a complete columnar transposition if all of the columns are the same length, and an incomplete columnar transposition otherwise. The letters of the message are written into a rectangular grid, as before, but this time the columns are numbered in some order. This numbering of the columns is the key.

KEY	3	7	1	6	4	8	2	5
	T	H	I	S	I	S	A	C
	O	L	U	M	N	A	R	T
	R	A	N	S	P	O	S	I
	T	I	O	N				

The letters are read out of the grid by reading down the columns, but the columns are taken out in the order specified by the key. In this example, the column numbered 1 is read out first, IUNO, then the column numbered 2, ARS, and so forth.

IUNOARSTORTINPCTISMSNHLAISAO

This is a major improvement over the route transposition, but this type of cipher can still be solved by skilled hobbyists using paper and pencil methods.

The cipher can be made more secure by performing multiple rounds of such permutations.

Double columnar transposition was used by the US, Germany, and other nations from about 1900 to 1945. The message was scrambled by a columnar transposition, and that message was scrambled again by a second columnar transposition, usually using the same key for both steps. The French broke the German version, but it is believed that the Germans did not break the American version. Today advanced hobbyists routinely solve such messages using paper and pencil.

In general, a transposition cipher by itself, no matter how sophisticated, is not secure. However, in the 1890's a French cryptographer named Etienne Bazeries showed that even a simple transposition cipher combined with a simple substitution cipher could provide a decent degree of security. This fact is at the heart of most modern block ciphers, including the AES and GK-Crypt.

20.11 SUBSTITUTION CIPHERS

A substitution cipher is one in which parts of the plaintext are substituted for something else according to the rules of the cipher. The secret message is deciphered using the inverse substitution.

20.11.1 Monoalphabetic Ciphers

A monoalphabetic cipher uses the same substitution across the entire message. For example, if you know that the letter A is enciphered as the letter K, this will hold true for the entire message. These types of messages can be cracked by using frequency analysis, educated guesses and trial and error. The Monoalphabetic Ciphers are as follows:

- ❒ Caesar Cipher
- ❒ Atbash Cipher
- ❒ Keyword Cipher
- ❒ Pigpen/Masonic Ciper
- ❒ Polybius Square

20.11.1.1 Caesar Cipher

A Caesar cipher is one of the simplest (and easiest cracked) encryption methods. It is a Substitution Cipher that involves replacing each letter of the secret message with a different letter of the alphabet which is a fixed number of positions further in the alphabet. Because each letter in the message has a direct translation to another letter, frequency analysis can be used to decipher the message. For example, the letter E is the most commonly used letter in the English language. Thus, if the most common letter in a secret message is K, it is likely that K represents E. Additionally, common word endings such as ING, LY, and ES also give clues.

A brute-force approach of trying all 25 possible combinations would also work to decipher the message.

Example: In this example, each letter in the plaintext message has been shifted 3 letters down in the alphabet.

Plaintext: This is a secret message

Ciphertext: wklv lv d vhfuhw phvvdjh

20.11.1.2 Atbash Cipher

The Atbash cipher is a very specific case of a substitution cipher where the letters of the alphabet are reversed. In other words, all A's are replaced with Z's, all B's are replaced with Y's, and so on. Because reversing the alphabet *twice* will get you actual alphabet, you can encipher and decipher a message using the exact same algorithm.

Example: In this example, alphabets have been reversed to encipher the text.

Plaintext: This is a secret message

Ciphertext: Gsrh rh z hvxivg nvhhztv

20.11.1.3 Keyword Cipher

The Keyword cipher is identical to the Caesar Cipher with the exception that the substitution alphabet used can be represented with a keyword.

To create a substitution alphabet from a keyword, you first write down the alphabet. Below this you write down the keyword (omitting duplicate letters) followed by the remaining unused letters of the alphabet.

ABCDEFGHIJKLMNOPQRSTUVWXYZ
KEYWORDABCFGHIJLMNPQSTUVXZ

To encipher a plaintext message, you convert all letters from the top row to their corresponding letter on the bottom row (A to K, B to E, etc). These types of simple substitution ciphers can be easily cracked by using frequency analysis and some educated guessing.

Example:

Plaintext: This is an example

Ciphertext: qabp bp ki ovkhlgo

20.11.1.4 Pigpen/Masonic Cipher

The pigpen cipher, sometimes called the *masonic* cipher or *Freemasons* cipher, is a simple substitution cipher exchanging letters for symbols based on a grid. The scheme was developed and used by the Freemasons in the early 1700s for record-keeping and correspondence. The example key shows one way the letters can be assigned to the grid (Figs. 20.2 and 20.3).

Fig. 20.2 Letters for symbols based on grid

20.11.1.5 Polybius Square

The Polybius cipher (also called: Polybios cipher) was developed by the Greek author and historian Polybius (200 B.C to 120 B.C.). The principle was especially applied for messages that were transmitted over distances in optical or audible ranges. It was still occasionally used in the twentieth century. Each character is assigned to a specific line and column in a matrix. A character can then be transmitted via knocking signs or with light signals. Interestingly, Julius Caesar used a more primitive cipher approximately 100 years later.

Fig. 20.3 Example of plaintext and ciphertext

A Polybius Square is a table that allows translating letters into numbers. To give a small level of encryption, this table can be randomized and shared with the recipient. In order to fit the 26 letters of the alphabet into the 25 spots created by the table, the letters i and j are usually combined.

	1	2	3	4	5
1	A	B	C	D	E
2	F	G	H	I/J	K
3	L	M	N	O	P
4	Q	R	S	T	U
5	V	W	X	Y	Z

To encipher a message you replace each letter with the row and column in which it appears. For example, D would be replaced with 14.

To decipher a message you find the letter that intersects the specified row and column.

Example:

Plaintext: This is a secret message

Ciphertext: 44232443 2443 11 431513421544 32154343112215

20.11.2 Polyalphabetic Ciphers

In a polyalphabetic cipher, the substitution may change throughout the message. In other words, the letter A may be encoded as the letter K for part of the message, but latter on it might be encoded as the letter W. The Polyalphabetic Ciphers are as follows:

- Vigenère Cipher
- Autokey Cipher
- One-time Pad
- Beaufort Cipher
- Running Key Cipher

20.11.2.1 Vigenère Cipher

The Vigenère cipher was developed in the 16th century by the French cryptologist Blaise de Vigenère. It is based on the usage of the Caesar cipher, but with changing alphabets. For long time this cipher was regarded as unbreakable. Finally, Friedrich Wilhelm Kasiski published a method to decode a text that was encoded with a Vigenère cipher.

In a Caesar Cipher, each letter of the alphabet is shifted along some number of places; for example, in a Caesar cipher of shift 3, A would become D, B would become E and so on. The Vigenere cipher consists of using several Caesar ciphers in sequence with different shift values.

To encipher, a table of alphabets can be used, termed a tabula recta, Vigenère square, or Vigenère table. It consists of the alphabet written out 26 times in different rows, each alphabet shifted cyclically to the left compared to the previous alphabet, corresponding to the 26 possible Caesar ciphers. At different points in the encryption process, the cipher uses a different alphabet from one of the rows. The alphabet used at each point depends on a repeating keyword.

For example, suppose that the plaintext to be encrypted is:

ATTACKATDAWN

The person sending the message chooses a keyword and repeats it until it matches the length of the plaintext, for example, the keyword 'LEMON':

LEMONLEMONLE

Each letter is encoded by finding the intersection in the grid between the plaintext letter and keyword letter. For example, the first letter of the plaintext, A, is enciphered using the alphabet in row L, which is the first letter of the key. This is done by looking at the letter in row L and column A of the Vigenere square, namely L. Similarly, for the second letter of the plaintext, the second letter of the key is used; the letter at row E and column T is X. The rest of the plaintext is enciphered in a similar fashion:

Plaintext: ATTACKATDAWN

Key: LEMONLEMONLE

Ciphertext: LXFOPVEFRNHR

Table 20.1 Vigenère table

	A	B	C	D	E	F	G	H	I	J	K	L	M	N	O	P	Q	R	S	T	U	V	W	X	Y	Z
A	A	B	C	D	E	F	G	H	I	J	K	L	M	N	O	P	Q	R	S	T	U	V	W	X	Y	Z
B	B	C	D	E	F	G	H	I	J	K	L	M	N	O	P	Q	R	S	T	U	V	W	X	Y	Z	A
C	C	D	E	F	G	H	I	J	K	L	M	N	O	P	Q	R	S	T	U	V	W	X	Y	Z	A	B
D	D	E	F	G	H	I	J	K	L	M	N	O	P	Q	R	S	T	U	V	W	X	Y	Z	A	B	C
E	E	F	G	H	I	J	K	L	M	N	O	P	Q	R	S	T	U	V	W	X	Y	Z	A	B	C	D
F	F	G	H	I	J	K	L	M	N	O	P	Q	R	S	T	U	V	W	X	Y	Z	A	B	C	D	E
G	G	H	I	J	K	L	M	N	O	P	Q	R	S	T	U	V	W	X	Y	Z	A	B	C	D	E	F
H	H	I	J	K	L	M	N	O	P	Q	R	S	T	U	V	W	X	Y	Z	A	B	C	D	E	F	G
I	I	J	K	L	M	N	O	P	Q	R	S	T	U	V	W	X	Y	Z	A	B	C	D	E	F	G	H
J	J	K	L	M	N	O	P	Q	R	S	T	U	V	W	X	Y	Z	A	B	C	D	E	F	G	H	I
K	K	L	M	N	O	P	Q	R	S	T	U	V	W	X	Y	Z	A	B	C	D	E	F	G	H	I	J
L	L	M	N	O	P	Q	R	S	T	U	V	W	X	Y	Z	A	B	C	D	E	F	G	H	I	J	K
M	M	N	O	P	Q	R	S	T	U	V	W	X	Y	Z	A	B	C	D	E	F	G	H	I	J	K	L

	A	B	C	D	E	F	G	H	I	J	K	L	M	N	O	P	Q	R	S	T	U	V	W	X	Y	Z
N	N	O	P	Q	R	S	T	U	V	W	X	Y	Z	A	B	C	D	E	F	G	H	I	J	K	L	M
O	O	P	Q	R	S	T	U	V	W	X	Y	Z	A	B	C	D	E	F	G	H	I	J	K	L	M	N
P	P	Q	R	S	T	U	V	W	X	Y	Z	A	B	C	D	E	F	G	H	I	J	K	L	M	N	O
Q	Q	R	S	T	U	V	W	X	Y	Z	A	B	C	D	E	F	G	H	I	J	K	L	M	N	O	P
R	R	S	T	U	V	W	X	Y	Z	A	B	C	D	E	F	G	H	I	J	K	L	M	N	O	P	Q
S	S	T	U	V	W	X	Y	Z	A	B	C	D	E	F	G	H	I	J	K	L	M	N	O	P	Q	R
T	T	U	V	W	X	Y	Z	A	B	C	D	E	F	G	H	I	J	K	L	M	N	O	P	Q	R	S
U	U	V	W	X	Y	Z	A	B	C	D	E	F	G	H	I	J	K	L	M	N	O	P	Q	R	S	T
V	V	W	X	Y	Z	A	B	C	D	E	F	G	H	I	J	K	L	M	N	O	P	Q	R	S	T	U
W	W	X	Y	Z	A	B	C	D	E	F	G	H	I	J	K	L	M	N	O	P	Q	R	S	T	U	V
X	X	Y	Z	A	B	C	D	E	F	G	H	I	J	K	L	M	N	O	P	Q	R	S	T	U	V	W
Y	Y	Z	A	B	C	D	E	F	G	H	I	J	K	L	M	N	O	P	Q	R	S	T	U	V	W	X
Z	Z	A	B	C	D	E	F	G	H	I	J	K	L	M	N	O	P	Q	R	S	T	U	V	W	X	Y

Decryption is performed by finding the position of the ciphertext letter in a row of the table, and then taking the label of the column in which it appears as the plaintext. For example, in row L, the ciphertext L appears in column A, which taken as the first plaintext letter. The second letter is decrypted by looking up X in row E of the table; it appears in column T, which is taken as the plaintext letter.

A **Gronsfeld** cipher is identical to the Vigenere cipher with the exception that only 10 rows are used which allows the keyword to be a number instead of a word.

20.11.2.2 Beaufort Cipher

The cipher was developed in the 17th Century by the Briton Sir Francis Beaufort. He is also known for his development of the Beaufort scale, which is used to measure the wind force. To encrypt a plaintext message using the Vigenère Cipher, one locates the row with the first letter to be encrypted, and the column with the first letter of the keyword. The ciphertext letter is located at the intersection of the row and column. This continues for the entire length of the message.

A Beaufort cipher uses the same alphabet table as the Vigenère cipher, but with a different algorithm. To encode a letter you find the letter in the top row. Then trace down until you find the keyletter. Then trace over to the left most column to find the enciphered letter. To decipher a letter, you find the letter in the left column, trace over to the keyletter and then trace up to find the deciphered letter.

Some people find this easier to do than finding the intersection of a row and column.

Plaintext: ATTACKATDAWN

Key: LEMONLEMONLE

Ciphertext: LLTOLBETLNPR

20.11.2.3 Autokey Cipher

The Autokey cipher was developed by Blaise de Vigenère as well. It is primarily based on the same methods as the Vigenère cipher, but it includes a modification, which increases the security of the cipher. This modification is based on ideas from Gerolamo Cardano.

To encrypt a plaintext message using the Vigenère Cipher, one locates the row with the first letter to be encrypted, and the column with the first letter of the keyword. The ciphertext letter is located at the intersection of the row and column. This continues for the entire length of the message.

An Autokey cipher is identical to the Vigenère cipher with the exception that instead of creating a keyword by repeating one word over and over, the keyword is constructed by appending the keyword to the beginning of the actual plaintext message.

Example:

Plaintext: THIS IS A SECRET TEXT

Keyword: KEY

Key: KEYTHISISASECRETT

Ciphertext: DLGLPASAWCJIVKIQM

Enciphering and deciphering the message is performed using the exact same method as the Vigenère Cipher.

20.11.2.4 Running Key Cipher

To encrypt a plaintext message using the Vigenère Cipher, one locates the row with the first letter to be encrypted, and the column with the first letter of the keyword. The ciphertext letter is located at the intersection of the row and column. This continues for the entire length of the message.

In a Running Key cipher, the keyword is the text of a predetermined book or passage. For example, if the choosed book was 'A Tale of Two Cities' by Charles Dickens, then the keyword would be:

It was the best of times, it was the worst of times...

Enciphering and deciphering the message is performed using the exact same method as the Vigenère Cipher.

If the predetermined passage is a string of random letters that is only used once and then discarded, this is similar to a One-time Pad.

20.11.2.5 One-time Pad

The one-time pad is a long sequence of random letters. These letters are combined with the plaintext message to produce the ciphertext. To decipher the message, a person must have a copy of the one-time pad to reverse the process. A one-time pad should be used only once (hence the name) and then destroyed. This is the first and only encryption algorithm that has been proven to be unbreakable.

To encipher a message, you take the first letter in the plaintext message and add it to the first random letter from the one-time pad. For example, suppose you are enciphering the letter S (the 19th letter of the alphabet) and the one-time pad gives you C (3rd letter of the alphabet). You add the two letters and subtract 1. When you add S and C and subtract 1, you get 21 which is U. Each letter is enciphered in this method, with the alphabet wrapping around to the beginning if the addition results in a number beyond 26 (Z).

To decipher a message, you take the first letter of the ciphertext and subtract the first random letter from the one-time pad. If the number is negative you wrap around to the end of the alphabet.

Example:

Plaintext: SECRETMESSAGE

One-time pad: CIJTHUUHMLFRU

Ciphertext: UMLKLNGLEDFXY

20.11.3 Polygraphic Ciphers

Instead of substituting one letter for another letter, a polygraphic cipher performs substitutions with two or more groups of letters. This has the advantage of masking the frequency distribution of letters, which makes frequency analysis attackes much more difficult. The Polygraphic Ciphers are as follows:

- Playfair Cipher
- Bifid Cipher
- Trifid Cipher
- Four-square Cipher

20.11.3.1 Playfair Cipher

The Playfair cipher was developed by the Briton Sir Charles Wheatstone in 1864. The name of the cipher is derived from the name of his friend Baron Lyon Playfair of St. Andrew. Wheatstone and Playfair often met to discuss ideas regarding cryptography.2 Playfair recommended the usage of this cipher for the British military and it has been in use until the end of the World War I.

The Playfair cipher or Playfair square is a manual symmetric encryption technique and was the first literal digraph substitution cipher. The scheme was invented in 1854 by Charles Wheatstone, but bears the name of Lord Playfair who promoted the use of the cipher.

The Playfair cipher encrypts pairs of letters (digraphs), instead of single letters. This is significantly harder to break since the frequency analysis used for simple substitution ciphers is considerably more difficult.

Memorization of the keyword and 4 simple rules is all that is required to create the 5 by 5 table and use the cipher.

K	E	Y	W	O
R	D	A	B	C
F	G	H	I	J
L	M	N	P	S
T	U	V	X	Z

The Playfair cipher uses a 5 by 5 table containing a key word or phrase. To generate the table, one would first fill in the spaces of the table with the letters of the keyword (dropping any duplicate letters), then fill the remaining spaces with the rest of the letters of the alphabet in order (to reduce the alphabet to fit you can either omit 'Q' or replace 'J' with 'I'). In the example to the right, the keyword is 'keyword'.

To encrypt a message, one would break the message into groups of 2 letters. If there is a dangling letter at the end, we add an X. For example. 'Secret Message' becomes 'SE CR ET ME SS AG EX'. We now take each group and find them out on the table. Noticing the location of the two letters in the table, we apply the following rules, in order.

1. If both letters are the same, add an X between them. Encrypt the new pair, re-pair the remaining letters and continue.
2. If the letters appear on the same row of your table, replace them with the letters to their immediate right respectively, wrapping around to the left side of the row if necessary. For example, using the table above, the letter pair GJ would be encoded as HF.
3. If the letters appear on the same column of your table, replace them with the letters immediately below, wrapping around to the top if necessary. For example, using the table above, the letter pair MD would be encoded as UG.
4. If the letters are on different rows and columns, replace them with the letters on the same row respectively but at the other pair of corners of the rectangle defined by the original pair. The order is important—the first letter of the pair should be replaced first.

For example, using the table above, the letter pair EB would be encoded as WD.

To decipher, ignore rule 1. In rules 2 and 3 shift up and left instead of down and right. Rule 4 remains the same. Once you are done, drop any extra Xs that don't make sense in the final message and locate any missing Qs or any Is that should be Js.

Example:

Paintext: thisisasecretmessage

Ciphertext: vf jp jp cn od dk ul om nc md (omitting Q)

Ciphertext: vf lq lq cp od dk kt on pc nd (Replacing J with I)

20.11.3.2 Bifid Cipher

The Bifid cipher was developed in 1901 by the Frenchman Felix Delastelle. He also developed the Four Square cipher. The Bifid Cipher uses a Polybius Square to encipher a message in a way that makes it fairly difficult to decipher without knowing the secret. This is because each letter in the ciphertext message is dependent upon two letters from the plaintext message. As a result, frequency analysis of letters becomes much more difficult.

	1	2	3	4	5
1	A	B	C	D	E
2	F	G	H	I	K
3	L	M	N	O	P
4	Q	R	S	T	U
5	V	W	X	Y	Z

The first step is to use the Polybius Square to convert the letters into numbers. We will be writing the numbers vertically below the message.

Plaintext: secret message

Ciphertext row no.: 411414 3144121

Ciphertext col no.: 353254 2533125

The numbers are now read off horizontally and grouped into pairs.

Ciphertext: 41 14 14 31 44 12 13 53 25 42 53 31 25

The Polybius Square is used again to convert the numbers back into letters which gives us our ciphertext.

Ciphertext: qddltbcxkrxlk

Since the first letter in the plaintext is encoded into the first and middle letters of the ciphertext, the recipient of the message must have the entire message before they can decode it. This means that if part of the ciphertext is discovered by a third party, it is unlikely that they will be able to crack it.

To decipher a Bifid encrypted message, you first convert each letter into its corresponding number via the Polybius Square. Now, divide the long string of numbers into two equal rows. The digit in the top row and the digit in the bottom row will together reference the decoded letter in the Polybius Square.

The Bifid Cipher can be taken into three dimensions to slightly increase the security of the message. This new cipher is called the Trifid Cipher.

20.11.3.3 Trifid Cipher

The Trifid Cipher is the Bifid Cipher taken to one more dimension. Instead of using a 5 × 5 Polybius Square, you use a 3 × 3 × 3 cube. Otherwise everything else remains the same. As with the Bifid Cipher, the cube can be mixed to add an extra layer of protection, but for these examples we not be using a mixed alphabet cube.

Layer 1			
	1	2	3
1	A	B	C
2	D	E	F
3	G	H	I

Layer 2			
	1	2	3
1	J	K	L
2	M	N	O
3	P	Q	R

Layer 3			
	1	2	3
1	S	T	U
2	V	W	X
3	Y	Z	.

The first step is to use the cube to convert the letters into numbers. We will be writing the numbers vertically below the message in the order of Layer, Column, Row.

Plaintext: secret message

Ciphertext layer no.: 311213 2133111

Ciphertext column no.: 123322 1211112

Ciphertext row no.: 121321 2211132

The numbers are now read off horizontally and grouped into triplets.

311 213 213 311 112 332 212 111 121 213 212 211 132

The cube is used again to convert the numbers back into letters which gives us our ciphertext.

Ciphertext: sppsdxmabpmjf

To decipher a Trifid encrypted message, you first convert each letter into its corresponding number via the cube. Now, divide the long string of numbers into three equal rows. Now, read off each column and use the cube to convert the three numbers into the plaintext letter.

20.11.3.4 Four-square Cipher

The four-square cipher encrypts pairs of letters (digraphs) and is thus less susceptible to frequency analysis attacks. The four-square cipher uses four 5 by 5 matrices arranged in a square. Each of the 5 by 5 matrices contains the letters of the alphabet (usually omitting 'Q' or putting both 'I' and 'J' in the same location to reduce the alphabet to fit). In general, the upper-left and lower-right matrices are the 'plaintext squares' and each contain a standard alphabet. The upper-right and lower-left squares are the 'ciphertext squares' and contain a mixed alphabetic sequence.

a	b	c	d	e	E	X	A	M	P
f	g	h	I	j	L	B	C	D	F
k	l	m	n	o	G	H	I	J	K

p	r	s	**t**	u		N	O	**R**	S	T
v	w	x	y	z		U	V	W	Y	Z
K	E	Y	W	O		a	b	c	d	e
R	D	A	**B**	C		f	g	**h**	i	j
F	G	H	I	J		k	l	m	n	o
L	M	N	P	S		p	r	s	t	u
T	U	V	X	Z		v	w	x	y	z

To generate the ciphertext squares, one would first fill in the spaces in the matrix with the letters of a keyword or phrase (dropping any duplicate letters), then fill the remaining spaces with the rest of the letters of the alphabet in order. The four-square algorithm allows for two separate keys, one for each of the two ciphertext matrices. In the example to the right, 'EXAMPLE' and 'KEYWORD' have been used as keywords.

To encrypt a message you would first split the message into digraphs. 'This is a secret message' would become:

TH IS IS AS EC RE TM ES SA GE

Once that was complete, you would take the first pair of letters and find the first letter in the upper left square and the second letter in the lower right square. In this example we are enciphering TH, so we locate T and H in the grid below (see blue characters). Now, we find the intersections of the rows and columns of the plain text letters. In this example, they have been highlighted in red (R and B). These new letters are the enciphered digraph (RB).

You continue enciphering digraphs in this way until you reach the end of the message. To continue our example, 'This is a secret message' would be enciphered as:

Ciphertext: RB CP CP AL AO TE RI AS NY FE

20.11.4 Transposition Ciphers

Unlike substitution ciphers that replace letters or groups of letters with other letters, a transposition cipher keeps the letters the same, but rearranges their order according to a specific algorithm. The Transposition Ciphers are as follows:

- ❒ Rail Fence
- ❒ Columnar Transposition
- ❒ Route Cipher
- ❒ Double Column Transposition

20.11.4.1 Rail Fence

In the rail fence cipher, the plaintext is written downwards on successive 'rails' of an imaginary fence, starting a new column when the bottom is reached. The message is then read off in rows. For example, if we have 3 rails and a message of 'This is a secret message', you would write out:

T	S	A	C	T	S	G
H	I	S	R	M	S	E
I	S	E	E	E	A	J

The last J is just a random letter to fill in the space. The secret message is then condensed and regrouped.

Ciphertext: TSACTSGHISRMSEISEEEAJ

To decipher a message you must know the number of rails that were used to encipher it. You then break up the letters into equal groups for each rail. For example, if you are using

3 rails, you would break the secret message into 3 equal groups. Now you stack the groups on top of each other and read off the message vertically. If you get gibberish, then there are probably some extra letters tacked on the end of the message that are throwing off the grouping. Try removing one letter from the end and try again.

20.11.4.2 Route Cipher

A Route Cipher is very similar to a Rail Fence cipher with one exception. You still write the message vertically in columns, but instead of reading off the secret message horizontally, you read it off using a predetermined pattern. For example, let's use a spiral pattern for this one:

T	S	A	C	T	S	G
H	I	S	R	M	S	E
I	S	E	E	E	A	J

The last J is just a random letter to fill in the space. If we are using a clockwise spiral to read off the message, then it becomes:

Ciphertext: TSACTSGEJAEEESIHISRMSE

20.11.4.3 Columnar Transposition

In a columnar transposition, the message is written out in rows of a fixed length. The message is then read out by column by column, where the columns are chosen in some scrambled order. The number of columns and the order in which they are chosen is defined by a keyword. For example, the word ZEBRAS is 6 letters long. Therefore, there are 6 columns that will be read of in the following order: 6 3 2 4 1 5. The order is chosen by the alphabetical order of the letters in the keyword.

Regular Case: In a regular columnar transposition cipher, the empty spaces are filled with random letters. For example, suppose we use the keyword ZEBRAS and the message WE ARE DISCOVERED FLEE AT ONCE. Our grid would look like this:

Z	E	B	R	A	S
6	3	2	4	1	5
—	—	—	—	—	—
W	E	A	R	E	D
I	S	C	O	V	E
R	E	D	F	L	E
E	A	T	O	N	C
E	Q	K	J	E	U

The six columns are now written out in the scrambled order defined by the keyword:

EVLNE ACDTK ESEAQ ROFOJ DEECU WIREE

Irregular Case: In the irregular case, the empty letters are not filled in with random letters:

Z	E	B	R	A	S
6	3	2	4	1	5
—	—	—	—	—	—
W	E	A	R	E	D

I	S	C	O	V	E
R	E	D	F	L	E
E	A	T	O	N	C
E					

This results in the following (shorter) ciphertext:

EVLNA CDTES EAROF ODEEC WIREE

To decipher it, the recipient has to work out the column lengths by dividing the message length by the key length. This step is slightly more difficult if the irregular case is used. After determining the number of columns, the message can be written in columns and rearranged back into the plaintext message.

20.11.4.4 Double Column Transposition

To make the message even more difficult to decipher, you can take the ciphertext produced by this algorithm and run it through the encryption again using a different keyword. This transposes the columns twice and makes the message extremely difficult to decipher.

20.12 TYPES OF CRYPTOGRAPHIC ALGORITHMS

In general, there are several ways of classifying cryptographic algorithms. In this chapter, they will be categorized based on the number of keys that are employed for encryption and decryption, and further defined by their application and use. The three types of algorithms (Fig. 20.4 illustrates the Process) that will be discussed are:

1. **Secret Key (or symmetric) Cryptography (SKC):** Uses a single key for both encryption and decryption.
2. **Public Key (or asymmetric) Cryptography (PKC):** Uses one key for encryption and another for decryption.
3. **Hash Functions:** Uses a mathematical transformation to irreversibly 'encrypt' information.

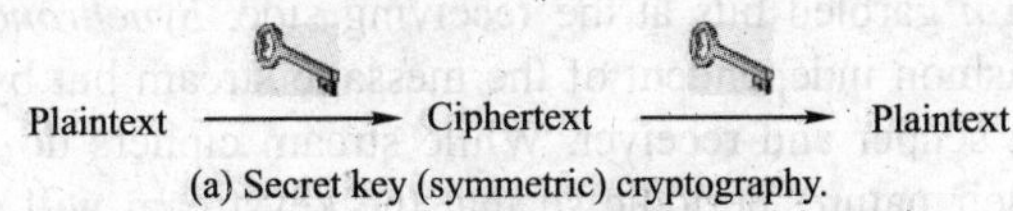

(a) Secret key (symmetric) cryptography.
SKC uses a single key for both encryption and decryption.

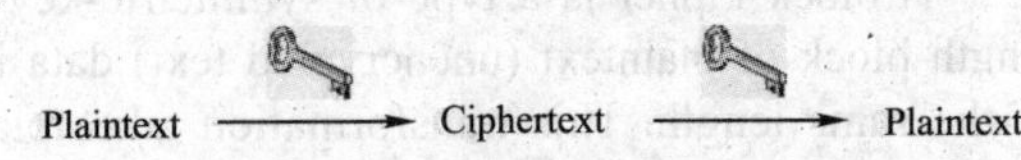

(b) Public key (asym metric) cryptography.
PKC uses two keys, one for encryption and the other for decryption.

hash function

Plaintext → Ciphertext

(c) Hash function (one-way cryptography). Hash functions have no key since the plaintext is not recoverable from the ciphertext.

Fig. 20.4 Three types of cryptography: secret-key, public key, and hash function

20.12.1 Secret Key Cryptography

A single key is used for both encryption and decryption with Secret Key Cryptography, as shown in Fig. 20.2. The sender uses the key (or some set of rules) to encrypt the plaintext and sends the ciphertext to the receiver. The receiver applies the same key (or rule set) to decrypt the message and recover the plaintext. Because a single key is used for both functions, Secret Key Cryptography is also called *symmetric encryption*.

With this kind of cryptography, the Secret key must be known to both the sender and the receiver. The biggest difficulty with this approach is the distribution of the key.

Secret Key Cryptography schemes are generally categorized as being either *stream ciphers* or *block ciphers*. **Stream Ciphers** operate on a single bit (byte or computer word) at a time and implement some form of feedback mechanism so that the key is constantly changing. A **Block**

Cipher encrypts one block of data at a time using the same key on each block. In general, the same plaintext block will always encrypt to the same ciphertext when using the same key in a block cipher whereas the same plaintext will encrypt to different ciphertext in a stream cipher.

A stream cipher is a type of symmetric encryption algorithm. Stream ciphers can be designed to be exceptionally fast, much faster than any block cipher. While block ciphers operate on large blocks of data, stream ciphers typically operate on smaller units of plaintext, usually bits. The encryption of any particular plaintext with a block cipher will result in the same ciphertext when the same key is used. With a stream cipher, the transformation of these smaller plaintext units will vary, depending on when they are encountered during the encryption process.

A stream cipher generates what is called a keystream (a sequence of bits used as a key). Encryption is accomplished by combining the keystream with the plaintext, usually with the bitwise XOR operation. The generation of the keystream can be independent of the plaintext and ciphertext, yielding what is termed a synchronous stream cipher, or it can depend on the data and its encryption, in which case the stream cipher is said to be self-synchronizing. Most stream cipher designs are for synchronous stream ciphers.

Self-synchronizing stream ciphers calculate each bit in the keystream as a function of the previous *n* bits in the keystream. It is termed 'self-synchronizing' because the decryption process can stay synchronized with the encryption process merely by knowing how far into the *n*-bit keystream it is. One problem is error propagation; a garbled bit in transmission will result in *n* garbled bits at the receiving side. *Synchronous stream ciphers* generate the keystream in a fashion independent of the message stream but by using the same keystream generation function at sender and receiver. While stream ciphers do not propagate transmission errors, they are, by their nature, periodic so that the keystream will eventually repeat.

A block cipher is a type of symmetric-key encryption algorithm that transforms a fixed-length block of plaintext (unencrypted text) data into a block of ciphertext (encrypted text) data of the same length. This transformation takes place under the action of a user-provided secret key. Decryption is performed by applying the reverse transformation to the ciphertext block using the same secret key. The fixed length is called the block size, and for many block ciphers, the block size is 64 bits. In the coming years the block size will increase to 128 bits as processors become more sophisticated.

Block ciphers can operate in one of several modes; the following four are the most important:

1. *Electronic Codebook* (*ECB*) *mode* is the simplest, most obvious application: the secret key is used to encrypt the plaintext block to form a ciphertext block. Two identical plaintext blocks, then, will always generate the same ciphertext block. Although this is the most common mode of block ciphers, it is susceptible to a variety of brute-force attacks.
2. *Cipher Block Chaining* (*CBC*) *mode* adds a feedback mechanism to the encryption scheme. In CBC, the plaintext is exclusively-ORed (XORed) with the previous ciphertext block prior to encryption. In this mode, two identical blocks of plaintext never encrypt to the same ciphertext.
3. *Cipher Feedback* (*CFB*) *mode* is a block cipher implementation as a self-synchronizing stream cipher. CFB mode allows data to be encrypted in units smaller than the block size, which might be useful in some applications such as encrypting interactive terminal input. If we were using 1-byte CFB mode, for example, each incoming character is placed into a shift register the same size as the block, encrypted, and the block transmitted. At the receiving side, the ciphertext is decrypted and the extra bits in the block (*i.e.,* everything above and beyond the one byte) are discarded.
4. *Output Feedback* (*OFB*) *mode* is a block cipher implementation conceptually similar to a synchronous stream cipher. OFB prevents the same plaintext block from generating the

same ciphertext block by using an internal feedback mechanism that is independent of both the plaintext and ciphertext bitstreams.

20.12.1.1 Usage of Secret Key Cryptography

Secret key cryptography algorithms that are in use today include:

- **Data Encryption Standard (DES):** The most common SKC scheme used today, DES was designed by IBM in the 1970s and adopted by the National Bureau of Standards (NBS) [now the National Institute for Standards and Technology (NIST)] in 1977 for commercial and unclassified government applications. DES is a block-cipher employing a 56 bit key that operates on 64 bit blocks. DES has a complex set of rules and transformations that were designed specifically to yield fast hardware implementations and slow software implementations, although this latter point is becoming less significant today since the speed of computer processors is several orders of magnitude faster today than twenty years ago. IBM also proposed a 112 bit key for DES, which was rejected at the time by the government; the use of 112 bit keys was considered in the 1990s, however, conversion was never seriously considered.

  Two important variants that strengthen DES are:

  - **Triple-DES (3DES):** A variant of DES that employs up to three 56 bit keys and makes three encryption/decryption passes over the block. It is recommended replacement to DES.
  - **DESX:** A variant devised by Ron Rivest. By combining 64 additional key bits to the plaintext prior to encryption, effectively increases the key length to 120 bits.

- **Advanced Encryption Standard (AES):** In 1997, NIST initiated a very public, 4-1/2 year process to develop a new secure cryptosystem for U.S. government applications. The result, the Advanced Encryption Standard, became the official successor to DES in December 2001. AES uses an SKC scheme called Rijndael, a block cipher designed by Belgian cryptographers Joan Daemen and Vincent Rijmen. The algorithm can use a variable block length and key length; the latest specification allowed any combination of keys lengths of 128, 192, or 256 bits and blocks of length 128, 192, or 256 bits. NIST initially selected Rijndael in October 2000 and formal adoption as the AES standard came in December 2001. FIPS PUB 197 describes a 128 bit block cipher employing a 128-, 192-, or 256 bit key.

- **CAST-128/256:** CAST-128, described in Request for Comments (RFC) 2144, is a DES-like substitution-permutation crypto algorithm, employing a 128 bit key operating on a 64 bit block. CAST-256 (RFC 2612) is an extension of CAST-128, using a 128 bit block size and a variable length (128, 160, 192, 224, or 256 bit) key. CAST is named for its developers, Carlisle Adams and Stafford Tavares and is available internationally. CAST-256 was one of the Round 1 algorithms in the AES process.

- **International Data Encryption Algorithm (IDEA):** Secret-key cryptosystem written by Xuejia Lai and James Massey, in 1992 and patented by Ascom; a 64 bit SKC block cipher using a 128 bit key. Also available internationally.

- **Rivest Ciphers (aka Ron's Code):** Named for Ron Rivest, a series of SKC algorithms.

  - **RC1:** Designed on paper but never implemented.
  - **RC2:** A 64 bit block cipher using variable-sized keys designed to replace DES. It's code has not been made public although many companies have licensed RC2 for use in their products. Described in RFC 2268.
  - **RC3:** Found to be breakable during development.

- **RC4:** A stream cipher using variable-sized keys; it is widely used in commercial cryptography products, although it can only be exported using keys that are 40 bits or less in length.
- **RC5:** A block-cipher supporting a variety of block sizes, key sizes, and number of encryption passes over the data. Described in RFC 2040.
- **RC6:** An improvement over RC5, RC6 was one of the AES Round 2 algorithms.

- **Blowfish:** A symmetric 64 bit block cipher invented by Bruce Schneier; optimized for 32 bit processors with large data caches, it is significantly faster than DES on a Pentium/PowerPC-class machine. Key lengths can vary from 32 to 448 bits in length. Blowfish, available freely and intended as a substitute for DES or IDEA, is in use in over 80 products.
- **Twofish:** A 128 bit block cipher using 128, 192, or 256 bit keys. Designed to be highly secure and highly flexible, well-suited for large microprocessors, 8-bit smart card microprocessors, and dedicated hardware. Designed by a team led by Bruce Schneier and was one of the Round 2 algorithms in the AES process.
- **Camellia:** A secret-key, block-cipher crypto algorithm developed jointly by Nippon Telegraph and Telephone (NTT) Corp. and Mitsubishi Electric Corporation (MEC) in 2000. Camellia has some characteristics in common with AES: a 128 bit block size, support for 128-, 192-, and 256 bit key lengths, and suitability for both software and hardware implementations on common 32 bit processors as well as 8-bit processors (*e.g.*, smart cards, cryptographic hardware, and embedded systems). Also described in RFC 3713. Camellia's application in IPsec is described in RFC 4312 and application in OpenPGP in RFC 5581.
- **MISTY1:** Developed at Mitsubishi Electric Corp., a block cipher using a 128 bit key and 64 bit blocks, and a variable number of rounds. Designed for hardware and software implementations, and is resistant to differential and linear cryptanalysis. Described in RFC 2994.
- **Secure and Fast Encryption Routine (SAFER):** Secret-key crypto scheme designed for implementation in software. Versions have been defined for 40-, 64-, and 128 bit keys.
- **KASUMI:** A block cipher using a 128 bit key that is part of the Third-Generation Partnership Project (3gpp), formerly known as the Universal Mobile Telecommunications System (UMTS). KASUMI is the intended confidentiality and integrity algorithm for both message content and signaling data for emerging mobile communications systems.
- **SEED:** A block cipher using 128 bit blocks and 128 bit keys. Developed by the Korea Information Security Agency (KISA) and adopted as a national standard encryption algorithm in South Korea. Also described in RFC 4269.
- **ARIA:** A 128 bit block cipher employing 128-, 192-, and 256 bit keys. Developed by large group of researchers from academic institutions, research institutes, and federal agencies in South Korea in 2003, and subsequently named a national standard. Described in RFC 5794.\
- **CLEFIA:** Described in RFC 6114, CLEFIA is a 128 bit block cipher employing key lengths of 128, 192, and 256 bits (which is compatible with AES). The CLEFIA algorithm was first published in 2007 by Sony Corporation. CLEFIA is one of the new-generation lightweight blockcipher algorithms designed after AES, offering high performance in software and hardware as well as a lightweight implementation in hardware.
- **SMS4:** SMS4 is a 128 bit block cipher using 128 bit keys and 32 rounds to process a block. Declassified in 2006, SMS4 is used in the Chinese National Standard for Wireless Local Area Network (LAN) Authentication and Privacy Infrastructure (WAPI). SMS4 had been a proposed cipher for the Institute of Electrical and Electronics Engineers (IEEE) 802.11i standard on security mechanisms for wireless LANs, but has yet to be accepted by the

IEEE or International Organization for Standardization (ISO). SMS4 is described in *SMS4 Encryption Algorithm for Wireless Networks* (translated and typeset by Whitfield Diffie and George Ledin, 2008) or in the original Chinese.

- **Skipjack:** SKC scheme proposed for Capstone. Although the details of the algorithm were never made public, Skipjack was a block cipher using an 80-bit key and 32 iteration cycles per 64 bit block.

20.12.1.2 Symmetric Encryption Vulnerabilities

Breaking symmetric encryption: There are two methods of breaking symmetric encryption - brute force and cryptanalysis.

Brute Force Attack is a form of attack in which each possibility is tried until success is obtained. Typically, a ciphertext is deciphered under different keys until plaintext is recognized. No encryption software that is entirely safe from the brute force method, but if the number of possible keys is high enough, it can make a program astronomically difficult to crack using brute force. But the more bits in a key, the more secure it is, so choose software with as many bits as possible.

Cryptanalysis is a form of attack that attacks the characteristics of the algorithm to deduce a specific plaintext or the key used.

Weak passwords: In every kind of encryption software, there is some kind of password that must be created so that the recipients of the information can read it. Creating a strong password that cannot be easily guessed is just as important as choosing a good algorithm or strong encryption software.

Remembering passwords: If you forget your password, you will not be able to decrypt data that you have encrypted. Be sure to make a backup copy of your password and store it in a safe place.

Secret keys exchanging and storing: Symmetric key encryption algorithms require sharing the secret key—both the sender and the receiver need the same key to encrypt or decrypt data. Anyone who knows the secret key can decrypt the message. So it is essential that the sender and receiver have a way to exchange secret keys in a secure manner. The weakness of symmetric encryption algorithms is that if the secret key is discovered, all messages can be decrypted. So, secret key needs to be changed on a regular basis and kept secure during distribution and while using.

20.12.2 Public-Key Cryptography

Public-key cryptography has been said to be the most significant new development in cryptography in the last 300-400 years. Modern PKC was first described publicly by Stanford University professor Martin Hellman and graduate student Whitfield Diffie in 1976. Their paper described a two-key crypto system in which two parties could engage in a secure communication over a non-secure communications channel without having to share a secret key.

PKC depends upon the existence of so-called *one-way functions*, or mathematical functions that are easy to computer whereas their inverse function is relatively difficult to compute. Let me give you two simple examples:

1. **Multiplication vs. factorization:** Suppose I tell you that I have two numbers, 9 and 16, and that I want to calculate the product; it should take almost no time to calculate the product, 144. Suppose instead that I tell you that I have a number, 144, and I need you tell me which pair of integers I multiplied together to obtain that number. You will eventually come up with the solution but whereas calculating the product took milliseconds, factoring will take longer because you first need to find the 8 pairs of integer factors and then determine which one is the correct pair.

2. **Exponentiation vs. logarithms:** Suppose I tell you that I want to take the number 3 to the 6th power; again, it is easy to calculate $3^6 = 729$. But if I tell you that I have the number 729 and want you to tell me the two integers that I used, *x* and *y* so that $\log_x 729 = y$, it will take you longer to find all possible solutions and select the pair that I used.

While the examples above are trivial, they do represent two of the functional pairs that are used with PKC; namely, the ease of multiplication and exponentiation versus the relative difficulty of factoring and calculating logarithms, respectively. The mathematical 'trick' in PKC is to find a *trap door* in the one-way function so that the inverse calculation becomes easy given knowledge of some item of information. (The problem is further exacerbated because the algorithms don't use just any old integers, but very large prime numbers.)

Generic PKC employs two keys that are mathematically related although knowledge of one key does not allow someone to easily determine the other key. One key is used to encrypt the plaintext and the other key is used to decrypt the ciphertext. The important point here is that it **does not matter which key is applied first**, but that both keys are required for the process to work (Figure 1B). Because pair of keys are required, this approach is also called *asymmetric cryptography*.

In PKC, one of the keys is designated the *public key* and may be advertised as widely as the owner wants. The other key is designated the *private key* and is never revealed to another party. It is straight forward to send messages under this scheme. Suppose Alice wants to send Bob a message. Alice encrypts some information using Bob's public key; Bob decrypts the ciphertext using his private key. This method could be also used to prove who sent a message; Alice, for example, could encrypt some plaintext with her private key; when Bob decrypts using Alice's public key, he knows that Alice sent the message and Alice cannot deny having sent the message (*non-repudiation*)

20.12.2.1 Usage of Public Key Cryptography

Public-key cryptography algorithms that are in use today for key exchange or digital signatures include:

1. **RSA:** The first, and still most common, PKC implementation, named for the three MIT mathematicians who developed it—Ronald Rivest, Adi Shamir, and Leonard Adleman. RSA today is used in hundreds of software products and can be used for key exchange, digital signatures, or encryption of small blocks of data. RSA uses a variable size encryption block and a variable size key. The key-pair is derived from a very large number, *n*, that is the product of two prime numbers chosen according to special rules; these primes may be 100 or more digits in length each, yielding an *n* with roughly twice as many digits as the prime factors. The public key information includes *n* and a derivative of one of the factors of *n*; an attacker cannot determine the prime factors of *n* (and, therefore, the private key) from this information alone and that is what makes the RSA algorithm so secure. (Some descriptions of PKC erroneously state that RSA's safety is due to the difficulty in *factoring* large prime numbers. In fact, large prime numbers, like small prime numbers, only have two factors!) The ability for computers to factor large numbers, and therefore attack schemes such as RSA, is rapidly improving and systems today can find the prime factors of numbers with more than 200 digits. Nevertheless, if a large number is created from two prime factors that are roughly the same size, there is no known factorization algorithm that will solve the problem in a reasonable amount of time; a 2005 test to factor a 200-digit number took 1.5 years and over 50 years of compute time. Regardless, one presumed protection of RSA is that users can easily increase the key size to always stay ahead of the computer processing curve. As an aside, the patent for RSA expired in September 2000 which does not appear to have affected RSA's popularity one way or the other.

2. **Diffie-Hellman:** After the RSA algorithm was published, Diffie and Hellman came up with their own algorithm. D-H is used for secret-key key exchange only, and not for authentication or digital signatures.
3. **Digital Signature Algorithm (DSA):** The algorithm specified in NIST's Digital Signature Standard (DSS), provides digital signature capability for the authentication of messages.
4. **ElGamal:** Designed by Taher Elgamal, a PKC system similar to Diffie-Hellman and used for key exchange.
5. **Elliptic Curve Cryptography (ECC):** A PKC algorithm based upon elliptic curves. ECC can offer levels of security with small keys comparable to RSA and other PKC methods. It was designed for devices with limited compute power and/or memory, such as smartcards and PDAs.
6. **Cramer-Shoup:** A public-key cryptosystem proposed by R. Cramer and V. Shoup of IBM in 1998.
7. **Key Exchange Algorithm (KEA):** A variation on Diffie-Hellman; proposed as the key exchange method for Capstone.
8. **LUC:** A public-key cryptosystem designed by P.J. Smith and based on Lucas sequences. Can be used for encryption and signatures, using integer factoring.
9. **ECDSA:** Elliptic Curve DSA (ECDSA) is a variant of the Digital Signature Algorithm (DSA) which operates on elliptic curve groups. As with Elliptic Curve Cryptography in general, the bit size of the public key believed to be needed for ECDSA is about twice the size of the security level, in bits.
10. **XTR:** XTR is an algorithm for asymmetric encryption (public-key encryption). XTR is a novel method that makes use of traces to represent and calculate powers of elements of a subgroup of a finite field. It is based on the primitive underlying the very first public key cryptosystem, the Diffie-Hellman key agreement protocol. From a security point of view, XTR security relies on the difficulty of solving discrete logarithm related problems in the multiplicative group of a finite field. Some advantages of XTR are its fast key generation (much faster than RSA), small key sizes (much smaller than RSA, comparable with ECC for current security settings), and speed (overall comparable with ECC for current security settings).

20.12.2.2 Differences between Symmetric and Asymmetric Encryption Algorithms

Symmetric encryption algorithms encrypt and decrypt with the same key. Main advantages of symmetric encryption algorithms are its security and high speed. Asymmetric encryption algorithms encrypt and decrypt with different keys. Data is encrypted with a public key, and decrypted with a private key. Asymmetric encryption algorithms (also known as public-key algorithms) need at least a 3,000-bit key to achieve the same level of security of a 128 bit symmetric algorithm. Asymmetric algorithms are incredibly slow and it is impractical to use them to encrypt large amounts of data. Generally, symmetric encryption algorithms are much faster to execute on a computer than asymmetric ones. In practice they are often used together, so that a public-key algorithm is used to encrypt a randomly generated encryption key, and the random key is used to encrypt the actual message using a symmetric algorithm. This is sometimes called *hybrid encryption*.

20.12.2.3 Strength of Encryption Algorithms

Strong encryption algorithms should always be designed so that they are as difficult to break as possible. In theory, any encryption algorithm with a key can be broken by trying all possible keys in sequence. If using brute force to try all keys is the only option, the required computing power increases exponentially with the length of the key. A 32 bit key takes 232 (about 109) steps.

This is something anyone can do on his/her home computer. An encryption algorithm with 56 bit keys, such as DES, requires a substantial effort, but using massive distributed systems requires only hours of computing. In 1999, a brute-force search using a specially designed supercomputer and a worldwide network of nearly 100,000 PCs on the Internet, found a DES key in 22 hours and 15 minutes. It is currently believed that keys with at least 128 bits (as in AES, for example) will be sufficient against brute-force attacks into the foreseeable future.

However, key length is not the only relevant issue. Many encryption algorithms can be broken without trying all possible keys. In general, it is very difficult to design ciphers that could not be broken more effectively using other methods.

The keys used in public-key encryption algorithms are usually much longer than those used in symmetric encryption algorithms. This is caused by the extra structure that is available to the cryptanalyst. There the problem is not that of guessing the right key, but deriving the matching private key from the public key. In the case of RSA encryption algorithm, this could be done by factoring a large integer that has two large prime factors. In the case of some other cryptosystems, it is equivalent to computing the discrete logarithm modulo a large integer (which is believed to be roughly comparable to factoring when the module is a large prime number).

20.12.2.4 Symmetric Encryption Advantages

Main advantages of symmetric encryption algorithms are their security and high speed.

20.12.3 Hash Functions

Hash functions, also called *message digests* and *one-way encryption*, are algorithms that, in some sense, use no key (Figure 1C). Instead, a fixed-length hash value is computed based upon the plaintext that makes it impossible for either the contents or length of the plaintext to be recovered. Hash algorithms are typically used to provide a *digital fingerprint* of a file's contents, often used to ensure that the file has not been altered by an intruder or virus. Hash functions are also commonly employed by many operating systems to encrypt passwords. Hash functions, then, provide a measure of the integrity of a file.

Hash algorithms that are in common use today include:

- **Message Digest (MD) algorithms:** A series of byte-oriented algorithms that produce a 128 bit hash value from an arbitrary-length message.
  - **MD2 (RFC 1319):** Designed for systems with limited memory, such as smart cards. (MD2 has been relegated to historical status, per RFC 6149.)
  - **MD4 (RFC 1320):** Developed by Rivest, similar to MD2 but designed specifically for fast processing in software. (MD4 has been relegated to historical status, per RFC 6150.)
  - **MD5 (RFC 1321):** Also developed by Rivest after potential weaknesses were reported in MD4; this scheme is similar to MD4 but is slower because more manipulation is made to the original data. MD5 has been implemented in a large number of products although several weaknesses in the algorithm were demonstrated by German cryptographer Hans Dobbertin in 1996 ('Cryptanalysis of MD5 Compress').
- **Secure Hash Algorithm (SHA):** Algorithm for NIST's Secure Hash Standard (SHS). SHA-1 produces a 160-bit hash value and was originally published as FIPS 180-1 and RFC 3174. FIPS 180-2 (aka SHA-2) describes five algorithms in the SHS: SHA-1 plus SHA-224, SHA-256, SHA-384, and SHA-512 which can produce hash values that are 224, 256, 384, or 512 bits in length, respectively. SHA-224, -256, -384, and -512 are also described in RFC 4634.
- **RIPEMD:** A series of message digests that initially came from the RIPE (RACE Integrity Primitives Evaluation) project. RIPEMD-160 was designed by Hans Dobbertin, Antoon

Bosselaers, and Bart Preneel, and optimized for 32 bit processors to replace the then-current 128 bit hash functions. Other versions include RIPEMD-256, RIPEMD-320, and RIPEMD-128.

- **HAVAL (HAsh of VAriable Length):** Designed by Y. Zheng, J. Pieprzyk and J. Seberry, a hash algorithm with many levels of security. HAVAL can create hash values that are 128, 160, 192, 224, or 256 bits in length.
- **Whirlpool:** A relatively new hash function, designed by V. Rijmen and P.S.L.M. Barreto. Whirlpool operates on messages less than 2^{256} bits in length, and produces a message digest of 512 bits. The design of this has function is very different than that of MD5 and SHA-1, making it immune to the same attacks as on those hashes (see below).
- **Tiger:** Designed by Ross Anderson and Eli Biham, Tiger is designed to be secure, run efficiently on 64 bit processors, and easily replace MD4, MD5, SHA and SHA-1 in other applications. Tiger/192 produces a 192-bit output and is compatible with 64 bit architectures; Tiger/128 and Tiger/160 produce a hash of length 128 and 160 bits, respectively, to provide compatibility with the other hash functions mentioned above.

(Readers might be interested in HashCalc, a Windows-based program that calculates hash values using a dozen algorithms, including MD5, SHA-1 and several variants, RIPEMD-160, and Tiger. Command line utilities that calculate hash values include sha_verify by Dan Mares [Windows; supports MD5, SHA-1, SHA-2] and md5deep [cross-platform; supports MD5, SHA-1, SHA-256, Tiger, and Whirlpool].)

Hash functions are sometimes misunderstood and some sources claim that no two files can have the same hash value. This is, in fact, not correct. Consider a hash function that provides a 128 bit hash value. There are, obviously, 2^{128} possible hash values. But there are a lot more than 2^{128} *possible* files. Therefore, there have to be multiple files—in fact, there have to be an infinite number of files!—that can have the same 128 bit hash value.

The difficulty is *finding* two files with the same hash! What is, indeed, very hard to do is to try to create a file that has a given hash value so as to force a hash value collision—which is the reason that hash functions are used extensively for information security and computer forensics applications. Alas, researchers in 2004 found that *practical* collision attacks could be launched on MD5, SHA-1, and other hash algorithms.

At this time, there is no obvious successor to MD5 and SHA-1 that could be put into use quickly; there are so many products using these hash functions that it could take many years to flush out all use of 128- and 160-bit hashes. That said, NIST announced in 2007 their Cryptographic Hash Algorithm Competition to find the next-generation secure hashing method. Dubbed SHA-3, this new scheme will augment FIPS 180-2. A list of submissions can be found at The SHA-3 Zoo. The SHA-3 standard may not be available until 2011 or 2012.

Certain extensions of hash functions are used for a variety of information security and digital forensics applications, such as:

- *Hash libraries* are sets of hash values corresponding to known files. A hash library of known good files, for example, might be a set of files known to be a part of an operating system, while a hash library of known bad files might be of a set of known child pornographic images.
- *Rolling hashes* refer to a set of hash values that are computed based upon a fixed-length 'sliding window' through the input. As an example, a hash value might be computed on bytes 1-10 of a file, then on bytes 2-11, 3-12, 4-13, etc.
- *Fuzzy hashes* are an area of intense research and represent hash values that represent two inputs that are similar. Fuzzy hashes are used to detect documents, images, or other files that are close to each other with respect to content. See 'Fuzzy Hashing' (PDF | PPT) by Jesse Kornblum for a good treatment of this topic.

20.12.4 Why Three Encryption Techniques?

So, why are there so many different types of cryptographic schemes? Why can't we do everything we need with just one?

The answer is that each scheme is optimized for some specific application(s). Hash functions, for example, are well-suited for ensuring data integrity because any change made to the contents of a message will result in the receiver calculating a different hash value than the one placed in the transmission by the sender. Since it is highly unlikely that two different messages will yield the same hash value, data integrity is ensured to a high degree of confidence.

Secret key cryptography, on the other hand, is ideally suited to encrypting messages, thus providing privacy and confidentiality. The sender can generate a *session key* on a per-message basis to encrypt the message; the receiver, of course, needs the same session key to decrypt the message.

Key exchange, of course, is a key application of public-key cryptography (no pun intended). Asymmetric schemes can also be used for non-repudiation and user authentication; if the receiver can obtain the session key encrypted with the sender's private key, then only this sender could have sent the message. Public-key cryptography could, theoretically, also be used to encrypt messages although this is rarely done because secret-key cryptography operates about 1000 times faster than public-key cryptography.

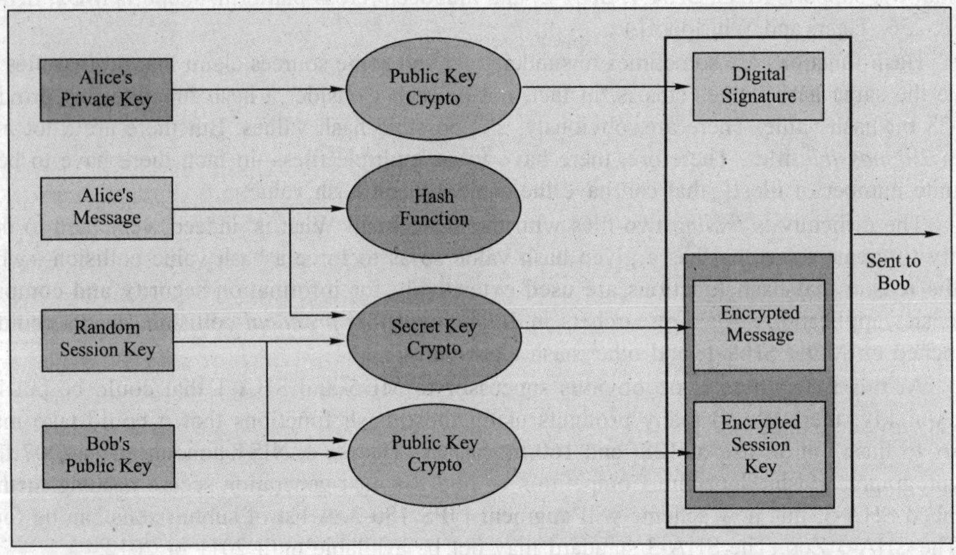

Fig. 20.5 Sample application of the three cryptographic techniques for secure communication

Figure 20.5 puts all of this together and shows how a *hybrid cryptographic* scheme combines all of these functions to form a secure transmission comprising *digital signature* and *digital envelope*. In this example, the sender of the message is Alice and the receiver is Bob.

A digital envelope comprises an encrypted message and an encrypted session key. Alice uses secret key cryptography to encrypt her message using the *session key*, which she generates at random with each session. Alice then encrypts the session key using Bob's public key. The encrypted message and encrypted session key together form the digital envelope. Upon receipt, Bob recovers the session secret key using his private key and then decrypts the encrypted message.

The digital signature is formed in two steps. First, Alice computes the hash value of her message; next, she encrypts the hash value with her private key. Upon receipt of the digital signature, Bob recovers the hash value calculated by Alice by decrypting the digital signature with Alice's public key. Bob can then apply the hash function to Alice's original message, which he has already decrypted (see previous paragraph). If the resultant hash value is not the same as the value supplied by Alice, then Bob knows that the message has been altered; if the hash values are the same, Bob should believe that the message he received is identical to the one that Alice sent.

This scheme also provides non repudiation since it proves that Alice sent the message; if the hash value recovered by Bob using Alice's public key proves that the message has not been altered, then only Alice could have created the digital signature. Bob also has proof that he is the intended receiver; if he can correctly decrypt the message, then he must have correctly decrypted the session key meaning that his is the correct private key.

20.12.5 The Significance of Key Length

In a recent article in the industry literature (circa 9/98), a writer made the claim that 56 bit keys do not provide as sufficient protection for DES today as they did in 1975 because computers are 1000 times faster today than in 1975. Therefore, the writer went on, we should be using 56,000-bit keys today instead of 56 bit keys to provide adequate protection. The conclusion was then drawn that because 56,000-bit keys are infeasible (*true*), we should accept the fact that we have to live with weak cryptography (*false!*). The major error here is that the writer did not take into account that the number of possible key values double whenever a single bit is added to the key length; thus, a 57-bit key has twice as many values as a 56 bit key (because 2^{57} is two times 2^{56}). In fact, a 66-bit key would have 1024 times the possible values as a 56 bit key.

But this does bring up the issue, what is the precise significance of key length as it affects the level of protection?

In cryptography, size does matter. The larger the key, the harder it is to crack a block of encrypted data. The reason that large keys offer more protection is almost obvious; computers have made it easier to attack ciphertext by using brute force methods rather than by attacking the mathematics (which are generally well-known anyway). With a brute force attack, the attacker merely generates every possible key and applies it to the ciphertext. Any resulting plaintext that makes sense offers a candidate for a legitimate key. This was the basis, of course, of the EFF's attack on DES.

Until the mid-1990s or so, brute force attacks were beyond the capabilities of computers that were within the budget of the attacker community. Today, however, significant compute power is commonly available and accessible. General purpose computers such as PCs are already being used for brute force attacks. For serious attackers with money to spend, such as some large companies or governments, Field Programmable Gate Array (FPGA) or Application-Specific Integrated Circuits (ASIC) technology offers the ability to build specialized chips that can provide even faster and cheaper solutions than a PC.

20.12.6 Cryptanalysis

Cryptanalysis refers to the study of ciphers, ciphertext, or cryptosystems (that is, to secret code systems) with a view to finding weaknesses in them that will permit retrieval of the plaintext from the ciphertext, without necessarily knowing the key or the algorithm. This is known as breaking the cipher, ciphertext, or cryptosystem.

Breaking is sometimes used interchangeably with weakening. This refers to finding a property (fault) in the design or implementation of the cipher that reduces the number of keys required in a brute force attack (that is, simply trying every possible key until the correct one is found). For example, assume that a symmetric cipher implementation uses a key length of 2^128 bits

(2 to the power of 128): this means that a brute force attack would need to try up to all 2^128 possible combinations (rounds) to be certain of finding the correct key (or, on average, 2^127 possible combinations) to convert the ciphertext into plaintext, which is not possible given present and near future computing abilities. However, a cryptanalysis of the cipher reveals a technique that would allow the plaintext to be found in 2^40 rounds. While not completely broken, the cipher is now much weaker and the plaintext can be found with moderate computing resources.

There are numerous techniques for performing cryptanalysis, depending on what access the cryptanalyst has to the plaintext, ciphertext, or other aspects of the cryptosystem. Below are some of the most common types of attacks:

1. **Known-plaintext analysis:** With this procedure, the cryptanalyst has knowledge of a portion of the plaintext from the ciphertext. Using this information, the cryptanalyst attempts to deduce the key used to produce the ciphertext.
2. **Chosen-plaintext analysis (also known as differential cryptanalysis):** The cryptanalyst is able to have any plaintext encrypted with a key and obtain the resulting ciphertext, but the key itself cannot be analyzed. The cryptanalyst attempts to deduce the key by comparing the entire ciphertext with the original plaintext. The Rivest-Shamir-Adleman encryption technique has been shown to be somewhat vulnerable to this type of analysis.
3. **Ciphertext-only analysis:** The cryptanalyst has no knowledge of the plaintext and must work only from the ciphertext. This requires accurate guesswork as to how a message could be worded. It helps to have some knowledge of the literary style of the ciphertext writer and/or the general subject matter.
4. **Man-in-the-middle attack:** This differs from the above in that it involves tricking individuals into surrendering their keys. The cryptanalyst/attacker places him or herself in the communication channel between two parties who wish to exchange their keys for secure communication (via asymmetric or public key infrastructure cryptography). The cryptanalyst/attacker then performs a key exchange with each party, with the original parties believing they are exchanging keys with each other. The two parties then end up using keys that are known to the cryptanalyst/attacker. This type of attack can be defeated by the use of a hash function.
5. **Timing/differential power analysis:** This is a new technique made public in June 1998, particularly useful against the smart card, that measures differences in electrical consumption over a period of time when a microchip performs a function to secure information. This technique can be used to gain information about key computations used in the encryption algorithm and other functions pertaining to security. The technique can be rendered less effective by introducing random noise into the computations, or altering the sequence of the executables to make it harder to monitor the power fluctuations. This type of analysis was first developed by Paul Kocher of Cryptography Research, though Bull Systems claims it knew about this type of attack over four years before.

In addition to the above, other techniques are available, such as convincing individuals to reveal passwords/keys, developing Trojan horse programs that steal a victim's secret key from their computer and send it back to the cryptanalyst, or tricking a victim into using a weakened cryptosystem. All of these are valid techniques in cryptanalysis, even though they may be considered unorthodox.

Successful cryptanalysis is a combination of mathematics, inquisitiveness, intuition, persistence, powerful computing resources—and more often than many would like to admit—luck. However, successful cryptanalysis has made the enormous resources often devoted to it more than worthwhile: the breaking of the German Enigma code during WWII, for example, was one of the key factors in an early Allied victory.

Today, cryptanalysis is practiced by a broad range of organizations: governments try to break other governments' diplomatic and military transmissions; companies developing security products send them to cryptanalysts to test their security features and to a hacker or cracker to try to break the security of Web sites by finding weaknesses in the securing protocols. It is this constant battle between cryptographers trying to secure information and cryptanalysts trying to break cryptosystems that moves the entire body of cryptology knowledge forward.

20.12.6.1 Basic Cryptanalysis Techniques

One good method for solving basic substitution ciphers is with frequency counts. A frequency count can be conducted on a cipher to learn what the most and least common characters are in the cipher. The most common letters in the English language are E,T,N,R,O,A,I and S. These eight characters make up around 67% of the words in the English language. Vowels, A,E,I,O, and U make up around 40% of English text. The frequency may vary depending on what the plaintext is. For example, if the message is source code it will use many more symbols than a message that is just written in English. If you conduct a frequency count of this paragraph your results would be: E, T, A, O, and S.

As you can see the results are not exactly the same. This is because the there are approximately 500 characters in the above paragraph. If you use a sample of 1000 characters or more your results will become more accurate. The frequency count of a single character is referred to as a Unigraph. If the frequency of cipher text is actually the same as plaintext then the encoded method is actually a transpositional cipher instead of a substitution cipher. Consider the following example:

Plaintext: IF WE DO NOT PROPERLY PROTECT THE USERS DATA WE CAN SIMPLY HIDE BEHIND THE DMCA IF SOMEONE NOTICES!!

Transpositional: I OOYFDTP O EPW PRRENRLOTTSDWEHEAECERT T SAC U ANPIE LDHTSYEIHI NEMHBD DIM CMFENEC OOSASNT! OEI!

Substitution: RU DV WL MLG KILKVIOB KILGVXG GSV FHVIH WZGZ DV XZM HRNKOB SRWV YVSRMW GSV WNXZ RU HLNVLMV MLGRXVH!!

Top 5 Unigraph Frequency counts:

Plaintext: E, O, T, I and D

Transpositional: E, O, T, I and D

Substitution: V, G, L, R and H

Even though the transpositional cipher is a small sample, it has the top 4 letters used in plaintext with E being the highest.

When dealing with a substitution cipher you should check the frequency of letters and their adjacent letters as well. A pair of letters together is referred to as a Digraph. The common digraphs in the English language are, TH, HE, EN, RE and ER. There are also Trigraphs that consist of frequency of three letters next to each other THE, ING, CON, ENT and ERE.

20.13 SOME TYPES OF ATTACKS ON CRYPTOSYSTEMS

Algebraic attack: A method of cryptanalytic attack used against block ciphers that exhibit a significant amount of mathematical structure.

Algorithmic attack (Formulaic attack): Algorithmic attacks are in some ways much more difficult to perform because they generally require an extremely high degree of knowledge in mathematics. Rather than going after the entire keyspace, the codebreaker will try and find flaws in the algorithm that causes it to be reduced to a problem of decreased complexity.

Birthday attack: A brute-force attack used to find collisions. It gets its name from the surprising result that the probability of two or more people in a group of 23 sharing the same birthday is greater than 1/2.

Brute force attack: Brute Force Attack is a form of attack in which each possibility is tried until success is obtained. Typically, a ciphertext is deciphered under different keys until plaintext is recognized.

Chosen ciphertext attack: An attack where the cryptanalyst may choose the ciphertext to be decrypted.

Chosen plaintext attack: A form of cryptanalysis where the cryptanalyst may choose the plaintext to be encrypted

Ciphertext-only attack: A form of cryptanalysis where the cryptanalyst has some ciphertext but nothing else. Modern cryptosystems are not weak against ciphertext-only attacks, however, in practice it is often possible to guess the plaintext, as many types of messages have fixed format headers. For example, many classical attacks use frequency analysis of the ciphertext, however, this does not work well against modern ciphers.

Dictionary attack: A brute force attack that tries passwords and or keys from a precompiled list of values. This is often done as a pre-computation attack.

Differential cryptanalysis: A chosen plaintext attack relying on the analysis of the evolution of the differences between two plaintexts.

Known plaintext attack: A form of cryptanalysis where the cryptanalyst knows both the plaintext and the associated ciphertext.

Meet-in-the-middle attack: A known plaintext attack against double encryption with two separated keys where the attacker encrypts a plaintext with a key and 'decrypts' the original ciphertext with another key and hopes to get the same value.

Middleperson attack: The idea of Middleperson attack is that when two parties, A and B, are exchanging keys for secure communication, an adversary intercepts the signals that A and B send to each other, and performs a key exchange with A and B separately. A and B will end up using a different key, each of which is known to the adversary. The adversary can then decrypt any communication from A with the key he shares with A, and then resends the communication to B by encrypting it again with the key he shares with B. Both A and B will think that they are communicating securely, but in fact the adversary is hearing everything. The best way to prevent the middleperson attack is to use a public-key cryptosystem capable of providing digital signatures. The parties must know each other's public keys in advance. After the shared secret has been generated, the parties send digital signatures of it to each other.

Precomputation attack: An attack where the adversary precomputes a look-up table of values used to crack encryption or passwords.

20.14 STEGANOGRAPHY

Steganography (abbreviated as stego), not be confused wit stenography, is a means of hiding data in a carrier medium. Steganography means, 'covered writing.' In concept, it dates back to ancient Greece. However, as a means of hiding data electronically, it is a new concept. The modern form of stego can take many forms, although all involve hiding data in something else called a carrier file. This could be the hiding of a document in an image, the hiding of a short message in a document, even hiding an image in a sound file! The applications are only limited by the tool being used, the carrier file and the imagination of the sender.

Stego can be used for a variety of reasons but most often is used to conceal the fact that sensitive information is oeing sent or stored. It can also be used to disguise encrypted data. This helps prevent attacks on encrypted data or in scenarios where encrypted data is inappropriate for transmissions *i.e.*, for example, countries where using encryption tools are against the law.

20.14.1 How Steganography Works?

The principle behind steganography is simple-hiding data within data. This can be oe in many different ways. The only limiter is the steganographer's creativity. Despite the seemingly endless possibilities for steganography, there are some commonalities that can be found in its operation. There are several basic components that are common to all stego and several general types of operations that all stego can be categorized into. There are two general components of standard steganography. The first is the carrier or host file. This is the medium used to hold the hidden data. The carrier can be almost any type of file imaginable. Some popular examples of such hosts are: bmp, gif, and jpeg images files, word documents, sound files, movies files (mpeg), text documents, Html files, etc.

20.14.2 Types of Steganography

Information can be hidden in many ways. In ancient times information was paced on wooden tablets that were then covered with wax to hide the messages. Messages were also tattooed onto messenger's bare heads, or messages were written with invisible inks that appeared only after they were heated. Messages were written with these inks in the margins or between lines in false documents to hide the fact that a hidden message existed.

In the information age, there are many new creative ways to hide information in an electronic carrier. They can be summed in three stego types:

1. Injection
2. Substitution
3. File Generation

20.14.2.1 Injection

There are ways to include information with most file types that will be ignored when the file is processed. This is the basis of injection stego. It Place the information into 'holes', or unused areas of the file. For example, in HTML coding, informational tags tells how it should be processed must precede all characters. While executing the same, Web Browsers *i.e.*, Internet Explorer will ignore data is formatted with certain HTML tags. However, if you examine the same html file in the text editor, the added character will be visible. Another example is the comments can be inserted in the files, such as those cab be placed I a GIF image or MP3 sound file. These comments do not appear when you view the picture or play the music, though the inserted comment is still physically exist in the body of the file. Even Microsoft Word documents contain areas where information can be hidden. This can be demonstrated by creating a large document, saving it, and then by cutting a large portion of the document out. Even after the data is removed the file size is still very large. The slack that is left in the document could also have data inserted into it.

The problem with the injection type of stego is that as data is added; file size of the carrier increases. This makes detection easy if the original file can be found, or if the size is increased outside of the norm for its type. For example, if an MP3 file was injected into a document file, the increased size of the document will most likely be noticed. There is one very popular tool that has been used for the injection type of steganography is 'Snow'. Snow is a command line program that allows the encryption and injection of the hidden message into an ASCII text file as 'white space', which consists of extra spaces ad tabs. Snow uses ICE encryption algorithm which supports upto 1024 bytes encryption key. Snow is an untested tool and should not be used for high security purposes.

20.14.2.2 Substitution

Substitution is the most popular stego method used to hide data in a host file. The concept is that elements are replaced on a bit by bit basis with information that is being hidden in the host document. Because the information is substituted in place of existing information, the file size of the carrier remains the same. However, noticeable file degradation can occur depending on the amount of information placed in the document. The idea with this technique is that only insignificant data should be overwritten to prevent degradation. It is important to have a suitably large carrier file when great amounts of information are being concealed. Generally, insignificant data is replaced with the information to be hidden. This insignificant data can take many forms, but one of the most common forms is the least significant bits (LSB) in the color table of the graphic.

20.14.2.3 File Generation

The most popular stego is the actual generation of a new file from the data to be hidden. This is the only form of stego where carrier isn't needed beforehand. A carrier file is needed, but it is generated on-the-fly by the stego program. The carrier file is actually created from the source information to be concealed. This can be used to generate such output as readable text or fractals. With each unique input file, a completely new and unique output file is generated.

20.15 APPLYING CRYPTOGRAPHY

Cryptography has many applications in information security. The top purposes are confidentiality, integrity, authentication, and non-repudiation. By encrypting information with a key that only the rightful users of the information possess, it can be used to protect the information from prying eyes (confidentiality). It can also be used to detect information tampering (integrity) by cryptographically hashing the information then encrypting the hash. If the information is tampered with, the hash will not match proving that the information has been modified. Cryptography can be used to prove identity (authentication). This can be done by requesting that the user encrypts a test message. The encrypted test message is then decrypted using the user's stored key. If the message decrypts successfully, the user has proven their identity, or at least that they possess the right key. Non-repudiation allows someone to prove in a court of law that someone agreed to a contractual relationship.

20.15.1 Applying Encryption to Network Communications

One of the most common networking uses for cryptography are protecting information as it flows across a network. Information is very exposed when it leaves your PC to travel across a network to another PC or server. At any point between the source and destination of a message, a man-in-the-middle can capture or modify the information contained within the message. An attacker might be able to capture your credit card details as you provide them to an online retailer without encryption.

Potentially more damaging, many network protocols do not encrypt their session information. These protocols transmit your usemame and password information 'in the clear.' An attacker who can listen in on your network conversations when you use one of these unencrypted protocols will be able to impersonate you, gaining access to all of the network resources you have access to through that protocol. As a last example, consider the damage an attacker could cause by simply modifying the contents of the right network conversation. Changing an account number used during a banking transfer or the ship-to address during an online purchase could defraud you of potentially large amounts of money. Cryptography provides a powerful method to protect against these information security risks.

A basic question when protecting network communications is where the protection should be performed. Should each application be responsible for protecting its own network communications, should cryptography be implemented as a service that applications can optionally use, or should it be included at the network level where all communication from and to particular locations can be protected? In practice, all of these methods are currently in use. The following Protocols uses Cleartext:

Protocol		*Purpose*
Telnet		Remote login
R* commands (rlogin, rexec, etc.)		Remote login, and command execution
rsh,		
FTP		File transfer
POP. IMAP		Retrieval of e-mail from mail server
SMTP		Transfer of mail between mail servers

20.15.1.1 Application Specific

Replacing unencrypted protocols like telnet with secure alternatives can be an easy way to improve security, assuming that a secure replacement exists. Examples include replacing post office protocol (POP) with authenticated post office protocol (APOP), Network File System (NFS) with the AlKlrew File System (AFS), and (more commonly) telnet and ftp with Secure Shell. Keep in mind, however, that each application can implement different security enhancements and not all replacements protect all conversations. For example, APOP only improves on POP by protecting the authentication messages, not the e-mail messages themselves. APOP prevents casual eavesdropping of usernames and passwords but does not prevent an attacker from listening in or modifying e-mail conversations.

Secure Shell, on the other hand, provides several security enhancements to the protocols it replaces. Critical is its capability to support strong certificate-based authentication, its capability to encrypt all session traffic providing confidentiality, and its capability to authenticate both sides of a connection, server and client. A high-quality, free version is available from the OpenSSH organization making its use a no-brainer whenever telnet or ftp like services are required.

20.15.1.2 Transport Layer

Another option for protecting information transfer is to provide a secure communications service that many applications can use. The advantage of this method is that each application does not have to re-implement the same security services. This is the approach taken by Transport Layer Security (TLS).

The primary goal of the TLS Protocol is to provide privacy and data integrity between two communicating applications. It is comprised of two protocols: the record protocol, which is used to securely transfer application data, and the handshake protocol, which is used to negotiate the details of a secure session. The combination of these two protocols provide, in an application protocol independent way, confidentiality of the communications using symmetric key encryption, integrity of the communications using a cryptographic message authentication code, and mutual certificate based authentication of client and server.

Many application protocols have been redesigned to utilize TLS security services. Secure Socket Layer (SSL) uses for protecting the transfer of mail from server to server, for the secure retrieval of mail from a mail server, and for authentication of PPP sessions. TLS most common use is to protect and authenticate Web sessions. You most likely have used TLS if you have ever purchased anything from a Web site. Most e-commerce Web sites use TLS to protect communication whenever sensitive information is being requested from you, such as your credit card numbers or your address. You can tell when the Web site you are visiting has activated

TLS because a symbol of a locked padlock appears at the bottom of your browser's window whenever a TLS session has been successfully set up. Even though TLS is application independent, applications must be modified to make use of its services. Just as with application specific cryptography, if the applications you need to use do not support TLS, you cannot make use of its protection.

20.15.1.3 Network Layer

Network layer encryption protects network conversations whether the application using the network supports cryptography or not. Network layer encryption sits in-between the transmitter and receiver. It accepts in cleartext information, and then encrypts it prior to sending it out. At the receiving end, the information is decrypted and forwarded on to its final destination. This type of network encryption is called a virtual private network (VPN).

20.16 SUMMARY

Cryptography, the science of secret writing, is an essential component of computer and network security at all levels. Information security professionals must be comfortable with at least the basic terms and concepts associated with this field so that they can understand products, services, and vendor claims. Cryptography is essential for e-commerce, military communications, and the privacy of individuals on the Internet and other networks. A cryptographic algorithm must provide confidentiality, integrity of data, authentication, and non-repudiation. To achieve these goals, mathematical problems with a suitable computational complexity are used to create a cipher that takes too long to break using brute force methods to be practical.

While the crypto methods used today are vastly stronger and more complex than algorithms used even 35 years ago, the same two fundamental operations still form the basis. of symmetric encryption schemes used to encrypt messages for privacy, namely *substitution* and *permutation.* Substitution is the method of replacing, or substituting, characters in a message with other characters, whereas permutation (transposition) moves characters around within the message.

Crypto schemes that operate on a single bit or byte at one time are usually called *stream ciphers,* whereas those that work on larger collections of bits and bytes are called *block ciphers.* Block ciphers are most common, although there are a number of stream ciphers used in the field. A crypto key governs the transformation of the plaintext into ciphertext. Modem crypto algorithms can be broadly classified into three categories based on the number of keys employed and the goals they accomplish. Each of these methods is used for specific applications. The categories are:

Symmetric encryption algorithms use a single key for both encryption and decryption. Key lengths between 128 and 256 bits are generally thought to be adequate; shorter keys are deemed weak. Common algorithms such as AES, DES, 3DES, IDEA, RC4, and RC5 are used for privacy.

Asymmetric encryption algorithms use a pair of very large, mathematically related keys. Asymmetric encryption uses a two-key system, whereby one of the keys is used to encrypt data, and the other is used for decryption. This depends on the existence of so-called *trapdoor functions* that are easy to calculate whereas the inverse function is very difficult (intractable). With trapdoor functions, one key does not yield knowledge of the other key. One of the keys, therefore, can be widely distributed and is called the *public key;* the other key is kept secret and is called the *private key.* Common schemes such as Diffie-Hellman, Rivest, Shamir, and Adleman (RSA) and Elliptic Curve Cryptography (ECC) may be used for such functions as key exchange, user authentication, and digital signatures.

Hash functions are one-way encryption; they employ no key, and the hash operation cannot be reversed to recover the original plaintext from the hash value. Hash functions such as SHA are used for message integrity.

Symmetric ciphers aren't right for every application. When the two parties, such as a merchant and a customer, have never met, secure key exchange is not easy. Public-key cryptography solves this problem by allowing for separate keys for encryption and decryption. The famous RSA algorithm is one such cipher, and it is used by the Secure Sockets Layer (SSL) to provide secure communications on the Internet. Because symmetric cryptography is much faster, RSA is often used to exchange a session key for Triple DES, which then encrypts the transaction.

REVIEW QUESTIONS

1. What is Cryptography?
2. What are the specific security requirements for application-to-application communication?
3. Write the history of encryption technique.
4. What is Encryption and Decryption? Explain.
5. How encryption works?
6. Why you need encryption?
7. What is Digital Substitution?
8. What is Arbitrary Substitution?
9. What is Rotation Substitution?
10. What is Permutation or Transposition Ciphers?
11. What is Monoalphabetic Ciphers? Also explain the following ciphers: (*a*) Caesar, (*b*) Afbash, (*c*) Keyword, (*d*) Polybuis.
12. What is Polyalphabetic Ciphers? Also explain the following ciphers: (*a*) Vigenere, (*b*) Beaufort, (*c*) Autokey, (*d*) one-time pad, (*e*) Running Key.
13. What is Polygraphic Ciphers? Also explain the following ciphers: (*a*) Playfair, (*b*) Bifid, (*c*) Trifid, (*d*) Four-square.
14. What is Transposition Ciphers? Also explain the following ciphers: (*a*) Rail Fence, (*b*) Route, (*c*) Columnar Transposition, (*d*) Double Column Transposition.
15. What is Secret Key Cryptography and its usage?
16. What is Symmetric Encryption Vulnerabilities?
17. What is Public Key Cryptography and its usage?
18. What are the differences between the Symmetric and Asymmetric encryption Algorithms?
19. What is Hash? Explain.
20. What is the significance of Key length?
21. Write short notes on Cryptanalysis and discuss its techniques.
22. Discuss at least ten types of Attacks on Cryptosystems.
23. What is Steganography and its works?
24. Discuss the types of Steganography.

SECURE COMMUNICATIONS

21.1 INTRODUCTION

Prior to the popularization of VPNs, companies wanting to protect network conversations between different locations purchased dedicated leased lines, frame-relay circuits, ATM connections, or other types of private circuits that provided connectivity between the sites from a telecommunications company. They could be reasonably confident that their information could not be intercepted because these circuits only allow the two sides of the connection to exchange information. No third parties should be able to communicate over the private connection. This assumes that you trust the telecommunications provider, which might or might not be a good bet depending upon where in the world you are. Although secure, these circuits also tend to be slow and expensive and become more expensive as they get faster, or the distance increases between the sites that need to communicate. There is also a large lead-time between the decision to set up one of these connections and getting it running. It can take months for a telecommunications company to fulfill a new circuit order. The disadvantage of the Private Network is dedicated lines are expensive, grow more so with distance, and are underutilized except at peak.

The Virtual Private Network—VPN—has attracted the attention of many organizations looking to both expand their networking capabilities and reduce their costs. The VPN can be found in workplaces and homes, where they allow employees to safely log into company networks. Telecommuters and those who travel often find a VPN a more convenient way to stay connected to the corporate intranet.

21.2 VIRTUAL PRIVATE NETWORK (VPN)

VPNs are a perfect alternative to costly, inflexible private circuits. They give companies the option of setting up virtual circuits across public networks, such as the Internet. Encryption provides the confidentiality needed as the private information flows across the public network. This capability allows VPNs to establish secure communication between different remote offices and can also be used to establish remote access to internal network resources by employees from their homes or while they are on travel.

A VPN supplies network connectivity over a possibly long physical distance. In this respect, a VPN is a form of Wide Area Network (WAN). VPNs enable file sharing, video conferencing and similar network services. Virtual private networks generally don't provide any new functionality that isn't already offered through alternative mechanisms, but a VPN implements those services more efficiently/cheaply in most cases.

A key feature of a VPN is its ability to work over both private networks as well as public networks like the Internet. Using a method called *tunneling*, a VPN use the same hardware infrastructure as existing Internet or intranet links. A VPN technology includes various security mechanisms to protect the virtual, private connections.

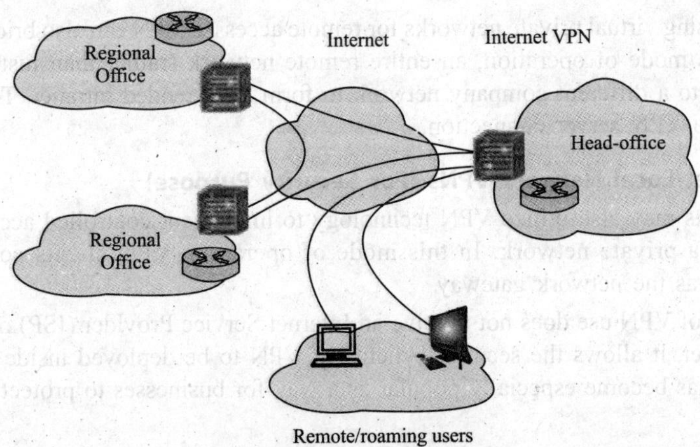

Fig. 21.1 Internet VPN

Specifically, a VPN supports at least three different modes of use:

- Internet remote access client connections (client-to-site VPNs)
- LAN-to-LAN internetworking (site-to-site VPNs)
- Controlled access within an intranet (For security purpose)
- Less common type VPN (client-to-client VPN)

21.2.1 Internet VPNs for Remote Access (Client-to-site)

Client-to-site VPNs provide remote access from a remote client, such as a traveling sales rep or telecommuting employee to the corporate network. Such VPNs are normally established between the client's computer and a gateway device located at the border of the corporate network. The client's computer runs VPN software that allows it to establish the connection to the VPN gateway.

In recent years, many organizations have increased the mobility of their workers by allowing more employees to telecommute. Employees also continue to travel and face a growing need to stay connected to their company networks.

A VPN can be set up to support remote, protected access to the corporate home offices over the Internet. An Internet VPN solution uses a *client/server* design works as follows:

1. A remote host (client) wanting to log into the company network first connects to any public Internet Service Provider (ISP).
2. Next, the host initiates a VPN connection to the company *VPN server*. This connection is made via a *VPN client* installed on the remote host.
3. Once the connection has been established, the remote client can communicate with the internal company systems over the Internet just as if it were a local host.

Before VPNs, remote workers accessed company networks over private leased lines or through dialup remote access servers. While VPN clients and servers careful require installation of hardware and software, an Internet VPN is a superior solution in many situations.

21.2.2 VPNs for Internetworking (Site-to-site)

Site-to-site VPNs provide connectivity to networks, such as headquarters and a remote office. In these connections, gateway devices are located *infront* of both networks. Information needing to flow between the sites is directed to the local gateway, which then encrypts the contents of the message and forwards it to the other site's gateway. The remote site's gateway decrypts the message then sends it onto its final destination.

Besides using virtual private networks for remote access, a VPN can also bridge two networks together. In this mode of operation, an entire remote network (rather than just a single remote client) can join to a different company network to form an extended intranet. This solution uses a VPN server to VPN server connection.

21.2.3 Intranet/Local Network VPNs (For Security Purpose)

Internal networks may also utilize VPN technology to implement controlled access to individual subnets within a private network. In this mode of operation, VPN clients connect to a VPN server that acts as the network gateway.

This type of VPN use does not involve an Internet Service Provider (ISP) or public network cabling. However, it allows the security benefits of VPN to be deployed inside an organization. This approach has become especially popular as a way for businesses to protect their WiFi local networks.

21.2.4 Less Common Type of VPN (Client-to-client)

These VPNs (client-to-client) establish a protected link between two specific computers. As such, they could be considered the most secure of the VPN types, because in the client-to-site, and site-to-site VPNs, part of the path between the transmitter of a message and the receiver of the message is unencrypted. For instance, in client-to-site VPN, the communication from the client's computer to the VPN gateway is protected, but the message travels unencrypted (and unprotected) from the VPN gateway to the internal corporate server, the client is trying to communicate with. If an attacker inserts himself/herself somewhere between the VPN gateway and this server, he/she would be able to eavesdrop or modify the contents of the message.

If client-to-client VPNs are more secure, why are they not used more often? The majority of the reason is the configuration required. Each pair of hosts wanting to communicate must be specifically configured to allow the communication. The most important part of this configuration is key installation. Each host must have a separate unique key that it can use to encrypt information to a particular destination host. Because of this, client-to-client VPNs between every two hosts would quickly become unmanageable as the number of hosts increases, if manual configuration is used, distribution and management of Public Keys are very difficult.

21.3 FLEXIBILITY WITH A VPN

One of the biggest benefits of VPN technology is its flexibility. If you need a secure channel between two hosts only for a day, or even an hour, then a VPN might fit the bill. Once you have all of the components to establish a VPN, setting one up only requires configuration. This makes the technology far more flexible than private circuits, which must be ordered far in advance of their use and might also require additional hardware. This flexibility lends itself to creating new business solutions. For example it's not cost-effective to wire a T1 for every employee who works from home. It is practical, however, to load software on their laptop and let them connect to the home office via a VPN over the Internet. This assumes that the home users already have connections to the Internet.

A VPN—Virtual Private Network—is one solution to establishing long-distance and/or secured network connections. VPNs are normally implemented (deployed) by businesses or organizations rather than by individuals, but virtual networks can be reached from inside a home network. Compared to other technologies, VPNs offers several advantages, particularly benefits for wireless local area networking. For an organization looking to provide a secured network infrastructure for its client base, a VPN offers two main advantages over alternative technologies: cost savings, and network scalability. To the clients accessing these networks, VPNs also bring some benefits of ease of use.

21.4 COST SAVINGS WITH A VPN

Another significant advantage of using VPN technology is the cost savings. It is simple and affordable to get Internet access these days, and in many cases that is all the connectivity that a VPN client will need. A VPN tunnel is then established between two Internet connection points, and the traffic between them is encrypted.

Generally speaking, this provides organizations with more bandwidth for less money (depending on the speed of the remote Internet connection). One downside to this, however, is.that there is no way to offer dedicated bandwidth over the Internet. There are a number of factors that may influence a VPN client connection, most of which are out of the organization's control. Another possible negative aspect of VPN connections is a 1–2 second delay in communications compared to private networks. Although this is acceptable to most organizations, some critical operations may not be able to afford the delay.

1. **VPNs vs leased lines:** Organizations historically needed to rent network capacity such as T1 lines to achieve full, secured connectivity between their office locations. With a VPN, you use public network infrastructure including the Internet to make these connections and tap into that virtual network through much cheaper local leased lines or even just broadband connections to a nearby Internet Service Provider (ISP).
2. **Long distance phone charges:** VPN also can replace remote access servers and long-distance dialup network connections commonly used in the past by business travelers needing to access to their company intranet. For example, with an Internet VPN, clients need only connect to the nearest service provider's access point that is usually local.
3. **Costs:** With VPNs, the cost of maintaining servers tends to be less than other approaches because organizations can outsource the needed support from professional third-party service providers. These provides enjoy a much lower cost structure through economy of scale by servicing many business clients.

21.5 VPN NETWORK SCALABILITY

The cost to an organization of building a dedicated private network may be reasonable at first but increases exponentially as the organization grows. A company with two branch offices, for example, can deploy just one dedicated line to connect the two locations, but 4 branch offices require 6 lines to directly connect them to each other, 6 branch offices need 15 lines, and so on.

Internet based VPNs avoid this scalability problem by simply tapping into the the public lines and network capability readily available. Particularly for remote and international locations, an Internet VPN offers superior reach and quality of service.

21.6 USING A VPN

To use a VPN, each client must possess the appropriate networking software or hardware support on their local network and computers. When set up properly, VPN solutions are easy to use and sometimes can be made to work automatically as part of network sign on.

VPN technology also works well with Wi-Fi local area networking. Some organizations use VPNs to secure wireless connections to their local access points when working inside the office. These solutions provide strong protection without affecting performance excessively.

21.7 LIMITATIONS OF A VPN

Despite their popularity, VPNs are not perfect and limitations exist as is true for any technology. Organizations should consider issues like the below when deploying and using virtual private networks in their operations as given.

1. VPNs require detailed understanding of network security issues and careful installation/configuration to ensure sufficient protection on a public network like the Internet.
2. The reliability and performance of an Internet-based VPN is not under an organization's direct control. Instead, the solution relies on an ISP and their quality of service.
3. Historically, VPN products and solutions from different vendors have not always been compatible due to issues with VPN technology standards. Attempting to mix and match equipment may cause technical problems, and using equipment from one provider may not give as great a cost savings.

21.8 DISADVANTAGES OF VPN

There are also some disadvantages to VPNs, the main one being the lack of performance guarantees. Most private circuits, such as leased-lines or ATM, have the capability to guarantee bandwidth and latency. Similar guarantees have been difficult to achieve with VPNs. TCP/IP, the networking protocol for the Internet, was not designed to provide quality of service (QoS) and improvements have been slow in coming. Providing QoS for VPNs is even more difficult because many QoS solutions require the service provider to look into the messages they are passing on to decide whether the message has higher priority than other messages. If the service provider cannot examine the information in a message (because of encryption), it makes it even more difficult to decide which network traffic should get priority.

There are solutions to these problems. Multiprotocol Label Switching (MPLS), an alternative over traditional layer three routing, is used to address these problems. It allows forwarding of messages across the Internet without requiring examination of the message contents. MPLS based VPNs can be purchased from a wide variety of Internet Service Providers, though they are more expensive than standard IP services.

21.9 SECURITY IMPLICATIONS

Many organizations assume that they have set-up a VPN, so they are secure. This is a bad assumption because VPNs bring their own special security concerns into your network. One frequent error made with VPNs is to overly trust the other side of a VPN connection.

With site-to-site VPNs, it is common to see the VPN connection allowed into the network without applying any security restrictions to it. This might be appropriate if the other side of the VPN belongs to the same organization and is controlled by the same security policies and procedures. If the other side of the connection is another organization, such as a business partner, though, access through the VPN should be restricted. Most VPN gateways include firewall abilities allowing them to limit network traffic across the VPN. It is a best practice to restrict this traffic to the minimum necessary to fulfill the business needs of the connection. Another potential security problem VPNs introduce is caused by the encryption VPNs use to protect the messages they exchange. As mentioned before, this encryption prevents an attacker from eavesdropping, but it also prevents intrusion detection systems and anti-virus tools from examining the packets for malicious or inappropriate content. This reduces or eliminates the effectiveness of these security tools.

Last, client-to-site VPNs suffer from the trusted client problem. Many organizations have strict rules on the type of software allowed on corporate computers. Part of the reason for these controls is that unauthorized software might contain security vulnerabilities.

When allowing employees to use a VPN to access the corporate network, the organization might not be in the same position to dictate a tight configuration. In fact, most home computers are insecurely configured. If an attacker discovers the home computer and takes it over, they might be able to use their access to the computer to leverage access to the corporate network over the employee's VPN connection. For this reason, it is a good idea to recommend, or better yet, enforce the use of a personal firewall product and anti-virus software prior to allowing remote users to access client-to-site VPNs.

21.10 VPN TUNNELING

Virtual private network technology is based on the idea of tunneling. **VPN tunneling** involves establishing and maintaining a logical network connection (that may contain intermediate hops). On this connection, packets constructed in a specific VPN protocol format are encapsulated within some other base or carrier protocol, then transmitted between VPN client and server, and finally de-encapsulated on the receiving side. For Internet-based VPNs, packets in one of several VPN protocols are encapsulated within Internet Protocol (IP) packets. VPN protocols also support authentication and encryption to keep the tunnels secure.

21.10.1 Types of VPN Tunneling

VPN supports two types of tunneling—voluntary and compulsory. Both types of tunneling are commonly used:

1. In voluntary tunneling, the VPN client manages connection setup. The client first makes a connection to the carrier network provider (an ISP in the case of Internet VPNs). Then, the VPN client application creates the tunnel to a VPN server over this live connection.
2. In compulsory tunneling, the carrier network provider manages VPN connection setup. When the client first makes an ordinary connection to the carrier, the carrier in turn immediately brokers a VPN connection between that client and a VPN server. From the client point of view, VPN connections are set up in just one step compared to the two-step procedure required for voluntary tunnels.

Compulsory VPN tunneling authenticates clients and associates them with specific VPN servers using logic built into the broker device. This network device is sometimes called the VPN Front End Processor (FEP), Network Access Server (NAS) or Point of Presence Server (POS). Compulsory tunneling hides the details of VPN server connectivity from the VPN clients and effectively transfers management control over the tunnels from clients to the ISP. In return, service providers must take on the additional burden of installing and maintaining FEP devices.

21.11 VPN TUNNELING PROTOCOLS

Several computer network protocols have been implemented specifically for use with VPN tunnels. The three most popular VPN tunneling protocols listed below continue to compete with each other for acceptance in the industry. These protocols are generally incompatible with each other.

21.11.1 Point-to-Point Tunneling Protocol (PPTP)

Several corporations worked together to create the PPTP specification. People generally associate PPTP with Microsoft because nearly all flavors of Windows include built-in client support for this protocol. The initial releases of PPTP for Windows by Microsoft contained security features that some experts claimed were too weak for serious use. Microsoft continues to improve its PPTP support, though. PPTP—Point-to-Point Tunneling Protocol—extends the Point to Point Protocol (PPP) standard for traditional dial-up networking. PPTP is best suited for the remote access applications of VPNs, but it also supports LAN internetworking. PPTP operates at Layer 2 of the OSI model.

PPTP packages data within PPP packets, then encapsulates the PPP packets within IP packets (datagrams) for transmission through an Internet-based VPN tunnel. PPTP supports data encryption and compression of these packets. PPTP also uses a form of **General Routing Encapsulation (GRE)** to get data to and from its final destination.

21.11.1.1 PPTP Security

PPTP supports **authentication**, **encryption**, and **packet filtering**. PPTP authentication uses PPP-based protocols like EAP, CHAP, and PAP. PPTP supports packet filtering on VPN servers. Intermediate routers and other firewalls can also be configured to selectively filter PPTP traffic.

Extensible Authentication Protocol, or **EAP**, is an authentication framework frequently used in wireless networks and Point-to-Point connections.

Challenge-Handshake Authentication Protocol (CHAP) authenticates a user or network host to an authenticating entity. CHAP provides protection against playback attack by the peer through the use of an incrementally changing identifier and of a variable challenge-value. CHAP requires that both the client and server know the plaintext of the secret, although it is never sent over the network.

A **password authentication protocol (PAP)** is an authentication protocol that uses a password. PAP is used by Point to Point Protocol to validate users before allowing them access to server resources. Almost all network operating system remote servers support PAP. PAP transmits unencrypted ASCII passwords over the network and is therefore considered insecure. It is used as a last resort when the remote server does not support a stronger authentication protocol, like CHAP or EAP. **Password-based authentication** is the protocol that two entities share a password in advance and use the password as the basis of authentication.

21.11.1.2 PPTP and PPP

In general, PPTP relies on the functionality of PPP for these aspects of virtual private networking.

1. authenticating users and maintaining the remote dial-up connection
2. encapsulating and encrypting IP, IPX, or NetBEUI packets

PPTP directly handles maintaining the VPN tunnel and transmitting data through the tunnel. PPTP also supports some additional security features for VPN data beyond what PPP provides.

21.11.1.3 PPTP Pros and Cons

PPTP remains a popular choice for VPNs thanks to Microsoft. PPTP clients are freely available in all popular versions of Microsoft Windows. Windows servers also can function as PPTP-based VPN servers. One drawback of PPTP is its failure to choose a single standard for authentication and encryption. Two products that both fully comply with the PPTP specification may be totally incompatible with each other if they encrypt data differently, for example. Concerns also persist over the questionable level of security PPTP provides compared to alternatives.

21.11.2 Layer Two Tunneling Protocol (L2TP)

The original competitor to PPTP for VPN tunneling was L2F, a protocol implemented primarily in Cisco products. In an attempt to improve on L2F, the best features of it and PPTP were combined to create a new standard called L2TP. Like PPTP, L2TP exists at the data link layer (Layer Two) in the OSI model—thus the origin of its name.

L2F, or **Layer 2 Forwarding**, is a tunneling protocol developed by Cisco Systems, Inc. to establish virtual private network connections over the Internet. L2F does not provide encryption or confidentiality by itself; It relies on the protocol being tunneled to provide privacy. L2F was specifically designed to tunnel Point-to-Point Protocol (PPP) traffic.

21.11.3 Internet Protocol Security (IPsec)

IPsec was developed in conjunction with IPv6 and must be available in all standards-compliant implementations of IPv6 although not all IPv6 implementations include IPsec support, it is optional for IPv4 implementations. However, because of the slow deployment of IPv6, IPsec is most commonly used to secure IPv4 traffic. IPsec protocols were published in 1995. In addition, a mutual authentication and key exchange protocol Internet Key Exchange (IKE) was defined to create and manage security associations. In December 2005, a second version of the Internet Key Exchange standard IKEv2 wa released. These third-generation documents standardized the abbreviation of IPsec to uppercase 'IP' and lowercase 'sec'.

IPsec is actually a collection of multiple related protocols. It can be used as a complete VPN protocol solution or simply as the encryption scheme within L2TP or PPTP. IPsec exists at the network layer (Layer Three) of the OSI model.

Internet Protocol Security (IPsec) is a protocol suite for securing Internet Protocol (IP) communications by authenticating and encrypting each IP packet of a communication session. IPsec also includes protocols for establishing mutual authentication between agents at the beginning of the session and negotiation of cryptographic keys to be used during the session.

IPsec is an end-to-end security scheme operating in the Internet Layer of the Internet Protocol Suite. It can be used in protecting data flows between a pair of hosts (*host-to-host*), between a pair of security gateways (*network-to-network*), or between a security gateway and a host (*network-to-host*).

Some other Internet security systems in widespread use, such as Secure Sockets Layer (SSL), Transport Layer Security (TLS) and Secure Shell (SSH), operate in the upper layers of the TCP/IP model. In the past, the use of TLS/SSL had to be designed into an application to protect the application protocols. In contrast, since day one, applications did not need to be specifically designed to use IPsec. Hence, IPsec protects any application traffic across an IP network. This holds true now for SSL as well with the rise of SSL based VPN revolution with implementations like OpenVPN.

IPsec originally was developed at the Naval Research Laboratory as part of a DARPA-sponsored research project. ESP was derived directly from the SP3D protocol, rather than being derived from the ISO Network-Layer Security Protocol (NLSP). The SP3D protocol specification was published by NIST, but designed by the Secure Data Network System project of the National Security Agency (NSA), IPsec AH is derived in part from previous IETF standards work for authentication of the Simple Network Management Protocol (SNMP).

IPsec is officially specified by the Internet Engineering Task Force (IETF) in a series of Request for Comments documents addressing various components and extensions. It specifies the spelling of the protocol name to be *Ipsec.*

21.11.3.1 Modes of operation

IPsec can be implemented in a host-to-host transport mode, as well as in a network tunnel mode.

21.11.3.1.1 Transport mode

In transport mode, only the payload of the IP packet is usually encrypted and/or authenticated. The routing is intact, since the IP header is neither modified nor encrypted; however, when the authentication header is used, the IP addresses cannot be translated, as this will invalidate the hash value. The transport and application layers are always secured by hash, so they cannot be modified in any way (for example by translating the port numbers). Transport mode is used for host-to-host communications.

21.11.3.1.2 Tunnel mode

In tunnel mode, the entire IP packet is encrypted and/or authenticated. It is then encapsulated into a new IP packet with a new IP header. Tunnel mode is used to create virtual private networks for network-to-network communications (*e.g.*, between routers to link sites), host-to-network communications (*e.g.*, remote user access), and host-to-host communications (*e.g.*, private chat).

21.11.3.2 Session Establishment

There are many options available within IPsec. Before an IPsec connection can be created, the two sides of the connection must agree on what options they are going to use. In addition, many of the options require the exchange of other information, such as session key are sequence numbers. Session establishment negotiates these details. The agreements from these negotiations are called Security Associations. Internet key Exchange (IKE) is the protocol used by IPsec to negotiate the session details of a connection. IKE is a hybrid protocol composed of a key management framework and a key exchange protocol.

21.12 SECURE SOCKETS LAYER (SSL)

The Secure Sockets Layer (SSL) is a commonly-used protocol for managing the security of a message transmission on the Internet. SSL has recently been succeeded by Transport Layer Security (TLS), which is based on SSL. SSL uses a program layer located between the Internet's Hypertext Transfer Protocol (HTTP) and Transport Control Protocol (TCP) layers. SSL is included as part of both the Microsoft and Netscape browsers and most Web server products. Developed by Netscape, SSL also gained the support of Microsoft and other Internet client/server developers as well and became the de facto standard until evolving into Transport Layer Security. The 'sockets' part of the term refers to the sockets method of passing data back and forth between a client and a server program in a network or between program layers in the same computer. SSL uses the public-and-private key encryption system from RSA, which also includes the use of a digital certificate.

TLS and SSL are an integral part of most Web browsers (clients) and Web servers. If a Web site is on a server that supports SSL, SSL can be enabled and specific Web pages can be identified as requiring SSL access. TLS and SSL are not interoperable. However, a message sent with TLS can be handled by a client that handles SSL but not TLS.

21.12.1 SSL History

In 1994 Netscape Corporation designed the Secure Sockets Layer (SSL) protocol to provide a means of safely and securely transporting private data (such as credit card numbers) between a Web Browser and a Web Server. Rather than tie SSL to the http protocol, Netscape wrote it as a protocol for making any TCP/IP connection secure.

At the end of 1994 version 2 of SSL was introduced and this was the first version shipped with a commercial web browser [Netscape Navigator (r)]. In 1995 version 3 of SSL was introduced. At that point an international standards organization (IETF) took over work on SSL and introduced Transport Layer Security (or TLS) protocol (which is based on SSL but has a different handshake protocol). The IETF introduced TLS version 1.0 in 1999.

21.12.2 Secure connections

A secure TCP connection exists between two processes when both agree on the following:

1. A cryptographic algorithm (called a *cipher*) to convert data (plaintext) to encrypted data (ciphertext) and back to plaintext.
2. A secret key to use in the cryptographic algorithm. A secret key is essential since the cryptographic algorithms themselves are well known. There is a distinct key for each direction of data transmission (client to server and server to client).

3. An authentication method used in each packet to ensure that the contents of the packets have not been altered in transit in some way.

These three items are determined via negotiation when the connection is made and the first data is to be sent.

21.12.3 Client/Server

In an SSL connection, one side is the client and the other side is the server. In the http environment, the web browser is the client and the web server is the server. When a secure connection is started, the client starts the negotiation by telling the server all the possible ways that it can communicate securely. The server then chooses one of the possible ways and informs the client. Then the server sends its certificate and possibly other certificates if they are needed to prove that its certificate can be trusted. The important item in the certificate is the public key for the server. The client will use this public key to encrypt a random value which will be used by both the client and server to create the keys needed for the cipher chosen for data transmission.

In theory a certificate isn't necessary if both the client and server side support a key exchange algorithm that can generate a public key on the fly. The SSL libraries we use do not have this capability, thus you must always supply a server certificate.

Once both sides know the keys the other side will use to transmit, the secure data transmission can occur.

21.12.4 Authentication

The SSL protocol also permits each side of the connection to declare who they are. This is done by the exchange of certificates. The server must send a certificate describing itself to the client. The server can request that the client send a certificate to the server (although in the use of SSL on the web this is never done).

21.12.5 Certificates

A certificate is a digital document that stores information about an entity in such a way that it can be verified to be true. The primary use of certificates is to store the public key that can be used to send encrypted messages to the entity.

In the SSL protocol certificates have two uses:

1. Encrpytion—by providing a public key they enable encrypted messages to be sent.
2. Authentication—the certificate proves that the entity on the other end of the socket is who it claims to be.

A certificate contains the following:

1. **A Subject Identifier:** A set of fields describing where the subject is geographically and its role within an organization.
2. **A Subject Public Key:** The key that can be used to encrypt messages that only the Subject can decrypt since only the Subject has the associated private key.
3. **A Valid Time Interval:** The interval of time during which this certificate is valid.
4. **An Issuer Identifier:** Just like the Subject Identifier but describing the entity that certifies that the Subject is who it says it is and that the public key is the correct one for the subject.
5. **An Issuer Signature:** A value which can be used by anyone to verify that the Issuer and only the Issuer signed this document testifying to it being correct.
6. **Various other fields:** Like serial numbers, version numbers, and other minor things.

A certificate is a combination of text and binary data and in order to make it easy to transport certificates they are usually encoded, which turns them into a sequence of printable characters.

When a web browser connects to a site via SSL (which is caused by the use of the 'https:' at the beginning of the url), it checks three things about the certificate:

1. Does it know the Issuer and did the Issuer sign the certificate? A web browser knows about a set of Issuers (called Certificate Authorities) when it's installed on the machine (the Issuer certificates are part of the files that make up the web browser).
2. Is the certificate valid right now or has it expired?
3. Is the certificate for the machine we've contacted? If the url was `https://www.google.com/whatever` then the certificate must be for `www.google.com`. The convention used is to store the name of the server machine in the CommonName slot of the Subject Identifier field of the certificate.

If all three tests pass then the web browser silently accepts the certificate and does a secure web page access. If any of the tests fail then the web browser notifies the user and waits for a response. Each browser displays the failure differently. For example, the Microsoft Internet Explorer shows which of the three tests passed and which failed while the Netscape Navigator just says that it received an invalid certificate. In both cases the person using the web browser is given the option of continuing with the web access. Transmission will still be secure if it is elected to continue. The only issue in doubt is the authenticity of the web server.

21.13 PRETTY GOOD PRIVACY

Pretty Good Privacy (PGP) is a data encryption and decryption computer program that provides cryptographic privacy and authentication for data communication. PGP is often used for signing, encrypting and decrypting texts, e-mails, files, directories and whole disk partitions to increase the security of e-mail communications. Pretty Good Privacy was originally developed by Phillip Zimmerman to provide a means of secure communication in an insecure electronic environment. 'Pretty Good' is an understatement—the framework it is based on, PKI (Public Key Infrastructure) and its encryption standards (it can use Diffie-Helman or RSA algorithms of varying strengths), have been subjected to rigorous cryptanalysis.

PGP has since grown into a more versatile application under the direction of its current owner, Network Associates. Until the most recent release PGP has been completely open source, allowing anyone to review the code and suggest improvements.

21.13.1 How does PGP work?

When someone starts using PGP, they generate a Key Pair. These are really just text files that look like gibberish to a human. The keys can be created at various levels of strength—512, 1024, or 2048 bit strengths are used. The higher the number, the stronger the encryption value of the key. One key of the pair is the Private key—this key should always be kept safe and never given to anyone. The other key is the public key—this key should be given to as many people as possible.

PGP encryption uses a serial combination of hashing, data compression, symmetric-key cryptography, and, finally, public-key cryptography; each step uses one of several supported algorithms. Each public key is bound to a user name and/or an e-mail address. The first version of this system was generally known as a web of trust to contrast with the X.509 system, which uses a hierarchical approach based on certificate authority and which was added to PGP implementations later. Current versions of PGP encryption include both options through an automated key management server.

21.13.2 Uses of PGP

The most commonly used aspect of PGP is the signing and encryption of email or files. 'Signing' a document is a way of verifying the integrity of the original work. The method is as follows:

1. Make a digest or 'hash' of the file or email. A hash is an algorithm that produces (theoretically) a unique output (the hash) from a given input (the message).
2. Add the hash to the end of the message.
3. When someone wants to verify that the message has not been modified, they run the hash algorithm on the message and compare it to the hash at the end of the message. If the signatures match, the message has not been altered.

This is demonstrated in the following example:

The hash algorithm: take every third letter of the message (ignore punctuation), and convert the letter to a number (a = 1, b = 2 ... z = 26). Add the numbers together.

The message:

Hello, This is a sample message to demonstrate signatures.

The hash algorithm in progress:

Hello, **This** is **a** sam**p**le message **to** de**mon**strate sig**nat**ures.

12 +20 +19 +1 +13 +5 +19 +7 +15 +13 +19 +1 +19 +14 +21 +19

= 217 (therefore the hash value is 217)

The message after adding the hash value becomes:

Hello, This is a sample message to demonstrate signatures.

Hash value: 360

If the message is altered, the hash value will not be the same.

Altered message:

Hello, This is an altered message to demonstrate signatures.

Creates a new hash:

Hello, **This** is **an** alt**ered** **m**essage **to** **demon**strate signat**u**res.

12 +20 +19 +1 +12 +18 +13 +19 +5 +4 +15 +20 +20 +9 +1 +18

= 206 (therefore the hash value is 206)

Since the hashes are not equal, the message has been altered.

Actual hashing algorithms are much more complex. Additionally, the hashing algorithm is used in conjunction with the user's private key in such a way that the signature is unique. That is, if different people (thus different private keys) signed the same email, the signatures would be different. Then the public key of the key pair is used to compare the hash created by the private key, and if the hashes match, then two things are assured: (1) The message has not been modified since signing and (2) the signature was not be forged.

Encryption: Encryption is a method of changing plaintext (text that is readable by humans) into ciphertext (text that is meaningless to humans). There are many different ways of encryption, some stronger than others. Two main categories of encryption are symmetric and asymmetric. In symmetric cryptography, the same key that encrypts a file also decrypts it. In asymmetric cryptography, which is what PGP uses, one key (the public key) encrypts the file, and the other key (the private key) decrypts it. So, if user A wants to send an encrypted message to user B, user A would first obtain user B's public key. This is possible because public keys are meant to be widely distributed. Then user A encrypts the message using user B's public key. The encrypted message can now only be decrypted with B's private key, which only he possesses. Not even user A, who wrote the message, can decrypt what he has encrypted, because he does not possess user B's private key. This ensures that the message is unreadable by anyone other than user A.

Encryption and signing are often combined. In this scenario, user A would use user B's public key to encrypt the message, then use his own private key to sign the message. This will ensure that no one but user B can read the message, and when user B receives it, he can be assured that the message was not altered. To read the message, user B would first use user A's public key to verify that the signature matches. Then user B would use his private key to decrypt the message that user A wrote.

21.13.3 Compatibility

As PGP evolves, PGP that support newer features and algorithms are able to create encrypted messages that older PGP systems cannot decrypt, even with a valid private key. Thus, it is essential that partners in PGP communication understand each other's capabilities or at least agree on PGP settings.

21.13.4 Confidentiality

PGP can be used to send messages confidentially. For this, PGP combines symmetric-key encryption and public-key encryption. The message is encrypted using a symmetric encryption algorithm, which requires a symmetric key. Each symmetric key is used only once and is also called a session key. The session key is protected by encrypting it with the receiver's public key thus ensuring that only the receiver can decrypt the session key. The encrypted message along with the encrypted session key is sent to the receiver.

21.13.5 Digital Signatures

PGP supports message authentication and integrity checking. The latter is used to detect whether a message has been altered since it was completed (the *message integrity* property), and the former to determine whether it was actually sent by the person/entity claimed to be the sender (a *digital signature*). In PGP, these are used by default in conjunction with encryption, but can be applied to the plaintext as well. The sender uses PGP to create a digital signature for the message with either the RSA or DSA signature algorithms. To do so, PGP computes a hash (also called a message digest) from the plaintext, and then creates the digital signature from that hash using the sender's private key.

21.13.6 Web of Trust

Both when encrypting messages and when verifying signatures, it is critical that the public key used to send messages to someone or some entity actually does 'belong' to the intended recipient. Simply downloading a public key from somewhere is not overwhelming assurance of that association; deliberate (or accidental) impersonation is possible. PGP has, from its first versions, always included provisions for distributing a user's public keys in an 'identity certificate' which is also constructed cryptographically so that any tampering (or accidental garble) is readily detectable. But merely making a certificate which is impossible to modify without being detected effectively is also insufficient. It can prevent corruption only after the certificate has been created, not before. Users must also ensure by some means that the public key in a certificate actually does belong to the person/entity claiming it. From its first release, PGP products have included an internal certificate 'vetting scheme' to assist with this; a trust model which has been called a web of trust. A given public key (or more specifically, information binding a user name to a key) may be digitally signed by a third party user to attest to the association between someone (actually a user name) and the key. There are several levels of confidence which can be included in such signatures. Although many programs read and write this information, few (if any) include this level of certification when calculating whether to trust a key.

As time goes on, you will accumulate keys from other people that you may want to designate as trusted introducers. Everyone else will each choose their own trusted introducers. And everyone will gradually accumulate and distribute with their key a collection of certifying signatures from other people, with the expectation that anyone receiving it will trust at least one or two of the signatures. This will cause the emergence of a decentralized fault-tolerant web of confidence for all public keys.

The web of trust mechanism has advantages over a centrally managed public key infrastructure scheme such as that used by S/MIME but has not been universally used. Users have been willing to accept certificates and check their validity manually or to simply accept them. No satisfactory solution has been found for the underlying problem.

21.13.7 Certificates

In the (more recent) OpenPGP specification, *trust signatures* can be used to support creation of certificate authorities. A trust signature indicates both that the key belongs to its claimed owner and that the owner of the key is trustworthy to sign other keys at one level below their own. A level 0 signature is comparable to a web of trust signature since only the validity of the key is certified. A level 1 signature is similar to the trust one has in a certificate authority because a key signed to level 1 is able to issue an unlimited number of level 0 signatures. A level 2 signature is highly analogous to the trust assumption users must rely on whenever they use the default certificate authority list (like those included in web browsers); it allows the owner of the key to make other keys certificate authorities.

PGP versions have always included a way to cancel ('revoke') identity certificates. A lost or compromised private key will require this if communication security is to be retained by that user. This is, more or less, equivalent to the certificate revocation lists of centralized PKI schemes. Recent PGP versions have also supported certificate expiration dates.

The problem of correctly identifying a public key as belonging to a particular user is not unique to PGP. All public key/private key cryptosystems have the same problem, if in slightly different guise, and no fully satisfactory solution is known. PGP's original scheme, at least, leaves the decision whether or not to use its endorsement/vetting system to the user, while most other PKI schemes do not, requiring instead that every certificate attested to by a central certificate authority be accepted as correct.

21.13.8 Security Quality

To the best of publicly available information, there is no known method which will allow a person or group to break PGP encryption by cryptographic or computational means. Indeed, in 1996, cryptographer Bruce Schneier characterized an early version as being 'the closest you're likely to get to military-grade encryption.' Early versions of PGP have been found to have theoretical vulnerabilities and so current versions are recommended. In addition to protecting data in transit over a network, PGP encryption can also be used to protect data in long-term data storage such as disk files. These long-term storage options are also known as data at rest, *i.e.*, data stored, not in transit.

The cryptographic security of PGP encryption depends on the assumption that the algorithms used are unbreakable by direct cryptanalysis with current equipment and techniques. For instance, in the original version, the RSA algorithm was used to encrypt session keys; RSA's security depends upon the one-way function nature of mathematical integer factoring. Likewise, the symmetric key algorithm used in PGP version 2 was IDEA, which might, at some future time, be found to have a previously unsuspected cryptanalytic flaw. Specific instances of current PGP, or IDEA, insecurities—if they exist—are not publicly known. As current versions of PGP have added additional encryption algorithms, the degree of their cryptographic vulnerability varies with the algorithm used. In practice, each of the algorithms in current use is not publicly known to have cryptanalytic weaknesses.

New versions of PGP are released periodically and vulnerabilities are fixed by developers as they come to light. Any agency wanting to read PGP messages would probably use easier means than standard cryptanalysis, *e.g.*, rubber-hose cryptanalysis or black-bag cryptanalysis *i.e.*, installing some form of trojan horse or keystroke logging software/hardware on the target computer to capture encrypted keyrings and their passwords. The FBI has already used this attack against PGP in its investigations. However, any such vulnerabilities apply not just to PGP, but to all encryption software.

In 2003, an incident involving seized Psion PDAs belonging to members of the Red Brigade indicated that neither the Italian police nor the FBI were able to decrypt PGP-encrypted files stored on them.

A more recent incident in December 2006 (see *United States v. Boucher*) involving US customs agents and a seized laptop PC which allegedly contained child pornography indicates that US Government agencies find it 'nearly impossible' to access PGP-encrypted files. Additionally, a judge ruling on the same case in November 2007 has stated that forcing the suspect to reveal his PGP passphrase would violate his Fifth Amendment rights *i.e.*, a suspect's constitutional right not to incriminate himself. The Fifth Amendment issue has been opened again as the case was appealed and the federal judge again ordered the defendant to provide the key.

Evidence suggests that as of 2007, British police investigators are unable to break PGP, so instead have resorted to using RIPA legislation to demand the passwords/keys. In November 2009 a British citizen was convicted under RIPA legislation and jailed for 9 months for refusing to provide police investigators with encryption keys to PGP-encrypted files.

21.14 PUBLIC KEY INFRASTRUCTURE (PKI)

A PKI (public key infrastructure) enables users of a basically unsecure public network such as the Internet to securely and privately exchange data and money through the use of a public and a private cryptographic key pair that is obtained and shared through a trusted authority. The public key infrastructure provides for a digital certificate that can identify an individual or an organization and directory services that can store and, when necessary, revoke the certificates. Although the components of a PKI are generally understood, a number of different vendor approaches and services are emerging. Meanwhile, an Internet standard for PKI is being worked on.

The public key infrastructure assumes the use of *public key cryptography*, which is the most common method on the Internet for authenticating a message sender or encrypting a message. Traditional cryptography has usually involved the creation and sharing of a secret key for the encryption and decryption of messages. This secret or private key system has the significant flaw that if the key is discovered or intercepted by someone else, messages can easily be decrypted. For this reason, public key cryptography and the public key infrastructure is the preferred approach on the Internet. (The private key system is sometimes known as *symmetric cryptography* and the public key system as *asymmetric cryptography*.)

In cryptography, a PKI is an arrangement that binds public keys with respective user identities by means of a certificate authority (**CA**). The user identity must be unique within each CA domain. The third-party Validation Authority (**VA**) can provide this information on behalf of CA. The binding is established through the registration and issuance process, which, depending on the level of assurance the binding has, may be carried out by software at a CA, or under human supervision. The PKI role that assures this binding is called the Registration Authority (**RA**). The RA ensures that the public key is *bound* to the individual to which it is assigned in a way that ensures non-repudiation.

A public key infrastructure consists of:

- A certificate authority (CA) that issues and verifies digital certificate. A certificate includes the public key or information about the public key

- ❒ A registration authority (RA) that acts as the verifier for the certificate authority before a digital certificate is issued to a requestor
- ❒ One or more directories where the certificates (with their public keys) are held
- ❒ A certificate management system

21.14.1 How Public and Private Key Cryptography Works?

In public key cryptography, a public and private key are created simultaneously using the same algorithm (a popular one is known as RSA) by a certificate authority (CA). The private key is given only to the requesting party and the public key is made publicly available (as part of a digital certificate) in a directory that all parties can access. The private key is never shared with anyone or sent across the Internet. You use the private key to decrypt text that has been encrypted with your public key by someone else (who can find out what your public key is from a public directory). Thus, if I send you a message, I can find out your public key (but not your private key) from a central administrator and encrypt a message to you using your public key. When you receive it, you decrypt it with your private key. In addition to encrypting messages (which ensures privacy), you can authenticate yourself to me (so I know that it is really you who sent the message) by using your private key to encrypt a digital certificate. When I receive it, I can use your public key to decrypt it. Here's a table that restates it:

To do this	*Use whose*	*Kind of key*
Send an encrypted message	Use the receiver's	Public key
Send an encrypted signature	Use the sender's	Private key
Decrypt an encrypted message	Use the receiver's	Private key
Decrypt an encrypted signature (and authenticate the sender)	Use the sender's	Public key

21.14.2 Who Provides the Infrastructure?

A number of products are offered that enable a company or group of companies to implement a PKI. The acceleration of e-commerce and business-to-business commerce over the Internet has increased the demand for PKI solutions. Related ideas are the virtual private network (VPN) and the IP Security (IPsec) standard. Among PKI leaders are:

- ❒ RSA, which has developed the main algorithms used by PKI vendors
- ❒ Verisign, which acts as a certificate authority and sells software that allows a company to create its own certificate authorities
- ❒ GTE CyberTrust, which provides a PKI implementation methodology and consultation service that it plans to vend to other companies for a fixed price
- ❒ Xcert, whose Web Sentry product that checks the revocation status of certificates on a server, using the Online Certificate Status Protocol (OCSP)
- ❒ Netscape, whose Directory Server product is said to support 50 million objects and process 5,000 queries a second; Secure E-Commerce, which allows a company or extranet manager to manage digital certificates; and Meta-Directory, which can connect all corporate directories into a single directory for security management.

21.14.3 Why Implement a PKI?

The omnipresence of the Internet and e-commerce technologies present many opportunities, but also pose security and integrity issues. For e-commerce to flourish, businesses, customers, vendors, suppliers, regulatory agencies, and other stakeholders must be assured that trusted business relationships are maintained.

An illustration presents the point. If a merchant today has a physical presence at a store, that is, brick and mortar, and customers patronize them for goods and services, the merchant will typically request and receive payment for these directly from either the customers or their agent (*e.g.*, their bank via the presentation of a monetary instrument such as a check), at the time that the goods and services were bargained for and/or provided. The process of exchanging goods and services for value is almost as universal as the rules by which those conversions take place. In many cases those rules are codified, in others they reflect accepted custom.

Whether systematic or custom, the processes in use today provide for the establishment of a trusted business relationship in that the customer and merchant both authenticate one another to the extent that they are willing to undertake the transaction. If an easily recognized monetary instrument like cash is used for transactions, there may be very little authentication which must occur. If a credit card or check is used, then the authentication may include the establishment of the customer's identity to the merchant. In addition, the authentication may also allow for a measure of non-repudiation to be set so that the customer does not deny the transaction occurred.

This traditional face-to-face transaction requires only minimal interaction and normally does not necessitate the use of other security and integrity mechanisms.

However, for e-commerce on the Internet, additional security and integrity mechanisms become necessary. Merchants are typically not willing to ship goods or perform services until a payment has been accepted for them. In addition, authentication can allow for a measure of non-repudiation so the customer cannot deny the transaction occurred. Similarly, consumers need assurance that they are purchasing from a legitimate enterprise, rather than a hacker 's site whose sole purpose is to collect credit card numbers.

With the changes in today's business environments and the shift from the traditional face-to-face business models, mechanisms must be developed to ensure that trusted relationships are maintained and can flourish.

The implementation of a PKI is intended to provide mechanisms to ensure trusted relationships are established and maintained. The specific security functions in which a PKI can provide foundation are confidentiality, integrity, non-repudiation, and authentication.

21.14.4 Uses of PKI

A PKI does not serve a particular business function; rather, a PKI provides a foundation for other security services. The primary function of a PKI is to allow the distribution and use of public keys and certificates with security and integrity. A PKI is a foundation on which other applications and network security components are built. Systems that often require PKI-based security mechanisms include email, various chip card applications, value exchange with e-commerce (*e.g.*, debit and credit cards), home banking, and electronic postal systems.

A PKI has many uses and applications. As discussed later in this article, a PKI enables the basic security services for such varied systems as:

1. SSL, IPsec and HTTPS for communication and transactional security
2. S/MIME and PGP for email security
3. SET for value exchange
4. Identrus for B2B

Some key benefits that PKI and its use of public key cryptography offers for e-commerce and other organizations are as follows:

1. Reduces transactional processing expenses
2. Reduces and compartmentalizes risk

3. Enhances efficiency and performance of systems and networks
4. Reduces the complexity of security systems with binary symmetrical methods

In addition, many other similar solutions rely on the fundamentals of public key cryptography such as:

- Student IDs on college campuses
- Voting
- Anonymous value exchange
- Transit ticketing
- Identification (passports and drivers licenses)
- Notarization (contract, emails, etc.)
- Software distribution
- Symmetric key management

21.14.5 Challenges

There are different challenges in the e-commerce world that a well-planned PKI solution addresses; however, there are also many challenges to consider when attempting the selection of a particular PKI solution. Some of these are technical while others are a question of applicability to a specific business model.

It is important to understand that a PKI is not by itself an authentication, authorization, auditing, privacy, or integrity mechanism. Rather, a PKI is an enabling infrastructure that supports these various business and technical needs. In particular, a PKI only allows for the identification of entities. For example, a PKI does not infer trust by itself, but requires the establishment of a trust base, on which the PKI can rely. This requirement means that the basis of trust must be established on a personal, business, or other level, before it can be accepted by the PKI.

A real world example of this is, suppose you misplace your drivers license and are issued a temporary one which does not have your photograph. A temporary license without a picture does not allow a store clerk to determine if you are the owner of it. Therefore, you may not be able to write a check or use a credit card because your identification mechanism, the temporary license, is not acceptable. This indicates that the trust inferred by identification is a rather subjective matter.

The issue of trust often arises when designing a PKI. From an e-commerce standpoint, a notable predicament of remote business transactions is that of original entity authentication. How an organization identifies and authenticates a customer or entity remotely the first time is a difficult problem. The amount of risk that an organization is willing to endure determines the level of effort they must expend during initial authentication. If high-value transactions or transactions with significant legal consequences occur in your organization, a stringent set of tests should be satisfied for a customer or entity to authenticate their identity. Conversely, if there is little risk to issue certificates to entities, for example, userids to access a public Web site, then those tests may be more simple. In any case, the original entity authentication can occur offline and out of band when more stringent means are needed, or dynamically and online for those needing less robust methods. The original entity authentication or initializing problem is not solved directly by a PKI, but must be addressed operationally in each unique business environment.

In the e-commerce environment, this problem is magnified when organizations move from local to regional and then extra-regional environments. How does a clerk in Denmark determine if a driver's license, temporary or otherwise, is legitimate if it was issued in Japan? How do they determine if they should trust the credentials presented? What mechanism do they use to make that determination? How did the original authority, which issues the credentials, determine the identity of the requestor? Do you trust the original authority to perform its identification tests properly? These are all fundamental issues that a PKI must contend with.

With the rapid expansion of e-commerce, closed proprietary legacy systems that only support binary transactional relationships are giving way to more open Internet-based systems, that support remote, many-to-many relationships. Different threats exist in these two very different business models and thus different security functions must be employed to address them. Prior to considering how a PKI can support your business venture into e-commerce, you must identify and evaluate your business requirements for the different security mechanisms that a PKI can enable. You must also identify the specific threats that exist in your environment.

21.14.6 Planning a PKI Infrastructure

This section briefly discusses how different business opportunities have different needs, and how these differences should be considered when planning a PKI.

21.14.6.1 Defining Business Requirements

A short example will illustrate how different business opportunities have different needs. If a business is a news magazine that freely distributes data over the Internet, the primary concern is maintaining the integrity of the data so it cannot be modified without authorization. Implementing a PKI to simply enable data integrity may not be a cost effective expenditure of resources.

On the other hand, if a business is selling products or services over the Internet, implementing a PKI may be in order. For an e-commerce business, the following must be accounted for when planning a PKI:

- Integrity for the posted prices
- Identification and authentication for a potentially large population of customers
- Confidentiality of customer and transaction information
- Non-repudiation for supporting dispute resolution

Implementing a PKI to enable these various security mechanisms can provide an online merchant with a cost effective approach to risk management.

Other considerations for defining business requirements of a PKI include:

- **Careful planning**—Internet-based e-commerce business solutions are often complex, as are the PKI solutions necessary to support them. Take the time to perform a detailed evaluation of your business and technical environments before taking steps to implement a PKI.
- **Interoperability**—Does your current business model require interoperability? With whom? For what purpose? If your PKI requires interoperability, you should determine which of the different standards and protocols you must adhere. Tangentially, most PKI related standards are in the early stages of development and acceptance. ISO, ANSI, IETF, IEEE, and PKCS are a few examples of standards under development for PKI. Because of the competing standards and protocols and the various interpretations that different vendors have of these, it is critical that organizations determine their interoperability needs.
- **Determining a PKI system and vendor**—There are different PKI and cryptographic systems from competing vendors. Several different protocols, certificate formats, and platforms exist. Some investigation is needed to decide which PKI and vendor is the best for your particular business enterprise. Often a standards compliant solution from one vendor will not integrate with that of another vendor. This may cause problems if you consider a multi-vendor PKI solution.
- **Performance and capacity**—In situations where large amounts of data must be enciphered for confidentiality, public key cryptography may not be suitable because the cryptographic algorithms perform at relatively slow speeds. Symmetric or secret key cryptography is typically used for these applications. Key management is where public key cryptography plays a role in supporting the encryption of large amounts of data for confidentiality. A PKI can be established for the distribution of the symmetric or secret keys that are subsequently used

for the encipherment of data. Public keys and public key certificates can also be significantly larger than symmetric keys and this can affect how they are stored. For example, in the limited memory constraints of a chip card, size can matter.

21.14.7 Structure and Components of a PKI

This section describes the framework of a PKI and how the components of a PKI work together. In addition, this section defines some common terms used in a PKI.

21.14.7.1 PKI Framework

The framework of a PKI consists of security and operational policies, security services, and interoperability protocols supporting the use of public-key cryptography for the management of keys and certificates. The generation, distribution, and management of public keys and associated certificates normally occur through the use of Certification Authorities (CAs), Registration Authorities (RAs), and directory services, which can be used to establish a hierarchy or chain of trust. CA, RA, and directory services allow for the implementation of digital certificates that can be used to identify different entities. The purpose of a PKI framework is to enable and support the secured exchange of data, credentials, and value (such as monetary instruments) in various environments that are typically insecure, such as the Internet.

A PKI enables the establishment of a trust hierarchy. This is one of the primary principles of a PKI. In Internet-based e-commerce, formal trust mechanisms must exist to provide risk management controls. The concept of trust, relative to a PKI, can be explained by the role of the CA. In the Internet environment, entities unknown to each other do not have sufficient trust established between them to perform business, contractual, legal, or other types of transactions. The implementation of a PKI using a CA provides this trust.

In short, a CA functions as follows. Entities that are unknown to one another, each individually establish a trust relationship with a CA. The CA performs some level of entity authentication, according to its established rules as noted in its Certificate Practices Statement or CPS, and then issues each individual a digital certificate. That certificate is signed by the CA and thus vouches for the identity of the individuals. Unknown individuals can now use their certificates to establish trust between them because they trust the CA to have performed an appropriate entity authentication, and the CA's signing of the certificates attests to this fact. A major benefit of a PKI is the establishment of a trust hierarchy because this scales well in heterogeneous network environments.

21.14.7.2 Trust Models

The implementation of a PKI requires an analysis of business objectives and the trust relationships that exist in their environment. The awareness of these trust relationships leads to the establishment of an overall trust model that the PKI enforces. The following three common examples of trust models are presented for comparison purposes.

21.14.7.3 Hierarchical

A hierarchical trust model represents the most typical implementation of a PKI. In its most simple instantiation, this trust model allows end entities' certificates to be signed by a single CA. In this trust model, the hierarchy consists of a series of CAs that are arranged based on a predetermined set of rules and conventions.

For example, in the financial services world, rather than have a single authority sign all end entities' certificates, there may be one CA at a national level that signs the certificates of particular financial institutions. Then each institution would itself be a CA that signs the certificates of their individual account holders. Within a hierarchical trust model there is a trust point for each certificate issued. In this case, the trust point for the financial institution's certificate is the national or root CA. The trust point for an individual account holder is their institution's CA. This approach allows for an extensible, efficient, and scalable PKI.

There are trade-offs to be considered when determining the placement of trust points for end entities in a PKI. In a tiered hierarchy with multiple CAs, compartmentalization of risk can be established, but each CA multiplies the administrative effort necessary to maintain the entire hierarchy. Conversely, a flat hierarchy with a single CA is much easier to administer; however, a failure of that single CA will corrupt the entire trust model and potentially all certificates signed by it.

21.14.7.4 Distributed (Web of Trust)

A distributed Web of trust is one that does not incorporate a CA. No trusted third party actually vouches for the identity or integrity of any end entity. Pretty Good Privacy (PGP) uses this type of trust model in email environments. This trust model does not scale well into the Internet-based e-commerce world because each end entity is left to its own devices to determine the level of trust that it will accept from other entities.

21.14.7.5 Direct (Peer to Peer)

Direct peer-to-peer trust models are used with secret or symmetric key-based systems. A trusted third party does not exist in a direct trust model. Thus, each end entity in a peer-to-peer relationship establishes trust with every other entity on an individual basis. This of course, is rather labor-intensive and similar to the Web of trust model. This trust model does not scale well into the Internet-based e-commerce world.

21.14.7.6 Cross Certification

If PKIs are to be implemented in any widespread fashion, cross certification is another important factor to consider. Instead of using a single global CA, cross certification allows end entities to use a CA based on their particular needs. It is possible that end entities under one CA may need to authenticate end entities under another CA; however, cross certification supports this relatively straightforward process. Essentially, what occurs in a cross certification is that one CA certifies another. As with the generation of an end entity's digital certificate, a CA performs various due diligence tests on the CA it will cross certify. These tests are taken in accordance with the published Certificate Policy and Certificate Practices Statement of the certifying CA.

When a cross-certificate is issued, it extends the trust relationship of a CA. A relying entity, for example, may desire to validate the public key certificate of an end entity whose signing CA's public key it is not aware of. Assuming that the relying entity trusts its own CA, when it sees a cross-certificate signed by that CA, it will then also trust that other CA, and subsequent certificates signed by it.

The net effect of cross certification is to allow many PKI deployments to be both extensible and scalable.

21.14.7.7 Security Services

The principle business objectives and risk management controls that can be implemented by a PKI are summarized in this section. An organization should only consider the implementation of a PKI if they have an actual business need for one or more of the security services described in the following sections. Note that these security services depend on the correct use of accepted certificate formats and signing protocols. Without adherence to accepted certificate formats and signing protocols, relying entities cannot determine the correctness of results from various operations.

21.14.7.8 Confidentiality

Confidentiality means ensuring that the secrecy and privacy of data is provided with cryptographic encryption mechanisms. Customer personal information and legal or contractual data are prime examples of data that should be kept secret by using confidentiality mechanisms. Encryption of data is possible by using either public (asymmetric), or secret (symmetric) cryptography. Since public key cryptography is not as efficient as secret key cryptography for data encipherment, it is normally used to encipher relatively small data objects such as secret keys used by symmetric-based encryption systems. Symmetric cryptographic systems are often incorporated into PKIs for bulk data encryption; thus, they are normally the actual mechanism used to provide confidentiality.

21.14.7.9 Integrity

Integrity means ensuring that data cannot be corrupted or modified and transactions cannot be altered. Public key certificates and digital signature envelopes are good examples of information that must have an assurance of integrity. Often, the content of messages, emails, purchase transactions and contracts, and information that others rely on, also require the assurance of integrity. Integrity can be provided within a PKI by the use of either public (asymmetric), or secret (symmetric) cryptography. An example of secret key cryptography used for integrity is DES in Cipher Block Chaining mode where a Message Authentication Code (MAC) is generated. Note that in the PKI environment, using symmetric cryptographic systems for implementing integrity does not scale particularly well. Public key cryptography is typically used in conjunction with a hashing algorithm such as SHA-1 or MD5 to provide integrity. A well-designed PKI will use protocols that require the use of these algorithms to provide an efficient integrity mechanism.

21.14.7.10 Authentication

Authentication means verifying that the identity of entities is provided by the use of public key certificates and digital signature envelopes. Authentication in the e-commerce environment is performed very well by public key cryptographic systems incorporated into PKIs. In fact, the primary goal of authentication in a PKI is to support the remote and unambiguous authentication between entities unknown to each other, using public key certificates and CA trust hierarchies. Authentication in a PKI environment, relies on the mathematical relationship between the public and private keys. Messages signed by one entity can be tested by any relying entity. The relying entity can be confident that only the owner of the private key originated the message, because only the owner has access to the private key.

21.14.7.11 Non-Repudiation

Non-repudiation means ensuring that data, cannot be renounced or a transaction denied. This is provided through public key cryptography by digital signing. Non-repudiation is a critical security service of any e-commerce application where value exchange, legal, or contractual obligations are negotiated. Non-repudiation is a by-product of using public key cryptography. When data is cryptographically signed using the private key of a key pair, anyone who has access to the public key of that pair can determine that only the owner of the key pair itself could have signed the data in question. For this reason, it is paramount that end entities secure and protect their private keys used for digitally signing data.

21.14.8 PKI Logical Components

Different logical components comprise a PKI. As noted previously, a PKI is a framework of people, processes, policies, protocols, hardware, and software used to generate, manage, store, deploy, and revoke public key certificates. The following outlines the typical logical components in a PKI used in an e-commerce environment. Note that although the security and integrity of the physical infrastructure is important to the successful implementation of a PKI, that subject is beyond the scope of this article. This section discusses the following logical components of a PKI:

- ❒ End entities or subscribers
- ❒ Certificate authorities
- ❒ Certificate policies
- ❒ Certificate practices statement
- ❒ Hardware security modules
- ❒ Public key certificates
- ❒ Certificate extensions
- ❒ Registration authorities
- ❒ Certificate depositories

21.14.8.1 End Entities or Subscribers

An end entity or subscriber is any user or thing, including inanimate objects, such as computers that have a need for a digital certificate to identify them for some reason. The end entity normally must have the capacity to generate a public/private key pair and some means of securely storing and using the private key. By definition, an end entity is not a CA.

21.14.8.2 Certificate Authorities

As noted previously in the discussion on Trust, a Certificate Authority plays a critical role in a PKI. According to the IETF, a CA is 'an authority trusted by one or more users to create and assign public key certificates.' [Internet X.509 Public Key Infrastructure PKIX Roadmap, March 10, 2000].

To elaborate, a CA functions as a trusted third party and provides various key management services. A CA essentially certifies the identity of an end entity. This is accomplished by an entity providing sufficient proof of their identity to the CA, and then having the CA generate a message containing the entity's identity and public key. This message is called a certificate and is cryptographically signed by the CA. The level of trust that a CA has depends on the level of acceptance that other entities have in that CA. This level of acceptance depends on the policies and procedures the CA has established to ascertain the user's identity.

A CA's public keys must be distributed to all entities that trust the CA's certificates. If a CA is a Root CA, that is, at the top of the trust hierarchy and has no superior CA to vouch for it, then the CA must distribute its public keys as self-signed certificates with an acceptable key certificate format and distribution protocol. The CA must also make its cleartext public keys available, so that relying entities can resolve the self-signed certificates. The key management-related functions performed by a CA are:

- ❒ Certificate generation
- ❒ Certificate revocation

A CA works within the context of an overall business policy known as a Certificate Policy (CP) and functions operationally according to a Certificate Practices Statement (CPS). The CP and CPS are discussed briefly in the next section.

21.14.8.3 Certificate Policy

A primary tenet of e-commerce security is the CP statement. The CP statement provides the overall guiding principles that an organization endorses regarding who may do what and how to systems and data. A CP also specifies how controls are managed. In addition, a CP names a set of rules that indicates the applicability of a public key certificate to a particular community or class of applications with common security requirements. For example, a particular CP might indicate applicability of a type of public key certificate to the authentication of electronic data interchange transactions for the trading of goods for monetary value.

Each PKI implementation should reflect the following in a CP statement:

- ❒ Purpose of the PKI

- Specific business requirements the PKI addresses through:
  - Security architecture
  - Associated trust model and threat profile
  - Specific security services the PKI supports

The CP statement should also reflect the specific business realities of a particular customer. For example, e-commerce merchants may desire assurance of timely payment for goods and services rendered through the use of authentication and non-repudiation mechanisms. Alternately, a facilitator of proprietary email services may only require confidentiality of information through the use of encryption facilities.

21.14.8.4 Certificate Practices Statement

The details of a policy statement should be published in a Certificate Practices Statement or CPS. The CPS is a statement of the practices that a CA employs in issuing public key certificates. The CPS document enumerates the procedural and operational practices of a PKI. The CPS should detail all processes within the life cycle of a public key certificate including its generation, issuance, management, storage, deployment, and revocation. The CPS should also specify the original entity authentication process that an end entity must be validated through before participating in a PKI. The objective of the CPS is to instill trust in the PKI such that the user community at large will have sufficient confidence to participate in it.

21.14.8.5 Hardware Security Modules

Hardware Security Modules (HSMs) are another primary component of a CA. A CA must instill trust in not only its client base but also in those who rely upon the certificates issued to subscribers. Since that trust is predicated upon the security and integrity of the CA's private keys used to sign the public key certificates of subscribers, it is necessary that those private keys be secured as best as possible. For this reason, CAs should only store and use their private keys in specialized computer equipment known as HSMs. HSMs are also known as Tamper Resistant Security Modules or (TRSMs) and because of their reliance in the financial services industry, TRSMs are well-defined through various acceptance standards in terms of their features and operational characteristics. The implementation and use of a qualified HSM is critical to any CA and the PKI it supports. Various standards are used to categorize HSMs, for example, FIPS-140-1.

21.14.8.6 Public Key Certificates

As stated previously, a CA's primary purpose is to support the generation, management, storage, deployment, and revocation of public key certificates. A public key certificate demonstrates or attests to the binding of an end entity's identity and its public key. That is, it contains enough information for some other relying entity to validate and verify the identity of the owner of the certificate. The basic constructs of a certificate should include the name of an entity, identifying information about the entity, expiration period for the certificate, and the entity's public key. Normally one would expect a certificate used in the e-commerce world to include additional information and be based upon an accepted format to allow interoperability. Other additional and useful information may be included in a certificate: serial numbers, the CA's name, the CA's public key certificate itself, the type of algorithms used to generate and verify the keys and certificate, and any other information that the CA generating the certificate considers useful.

The most widely used format for digital certificates are those based on the IETF X.509 standards. A detailed semantic profile of X.509 based public key certificates can be found in the IETF RFC 2459 and related documentation. It should be noted that there is no one single definition of a public key certificate defined in the IETF standards. Vendors, integrators, and others offering PKI solutions each have their own ideas as to what extensions and particular data an X.509 certificate should contain. Organizations should evaluate their business needs relative to the constructs of the public key certificates that they wish to issue.

21.14.8.7 Certificate Extensions

Certificate extensions provide additional information within a certificate and allow them to be tailored for the particular needs of an organization. Be aware that certificate extensions can affect the interoperability of certificates if a relying party does not recognize the structure or content of the certificate extensions. The types of information that may be found in a certificate extension include: policy, usage, revocation, and naming data, which provide particular details unique to an organization's PKI.

21.14.8.8 Registration Authorities

A Registration Authority (RA) is an optional but common component of a PKI. An RA is used to perform some of the administrative tasks that a CA would normally undertake. Most importantly, an RA is delegated, with the CA's explicit permission, the authority to perform tasks on behalf of the CA. The primary purpose of an RA is to verify an end entity's identity and determine if an end entity is entitled to have a public key certificate issued. The RA must enforce all policies and procedures defined in the CA's CP and CPS. A typical function of an RA is to interrogate an end entity's certificate request by examining the name, validity dates, applicable constraints, public key, certificate extensions, and related information. The RA may also be responsible for performing due diligence tests on the end entity. This responsibility may be as simple as ensuring the name of the end entity is unique within the scope of the PKI; or, it may be as involved as making credit checks on potential clients.

21.14.8.9 Certificate Depositories

As with an RA, a certificate depository, sometimes referred to as a certificate directory, is also an optional but common component of a PKI. A certificate depository may be an efficient solution for closed systems (*e.g.*, intranet) or those in isolated processing environments (*e.g.*, chipcard-based applications) where the Root CA public key is distributed locally or revocation lists are stored locally. Many other situations warrant the use of a certificate or Certificate Revocation List (CRL) depository. The use of depositories for CRL distribution is discussed later in this article.

Certificate distribution can be accomplished by simply publishing certificates in a directory controlled by a CA or RA. When the directory is controlled by the CA or RA, the certificate distribution process is greatly simplified. Rather than trying to distribute every certificate to a unique point, the CA simply updates the directory. A critical factor is that only the CA must have the authority to update or modify the directory, but the directory must be publicly readable.

LDAP is a good example of a simple and efficient standards based directory format and protocol that can be used for certificate distribution. In particular, LDAP is optimized for easy read access by thin clients that are a necessity in many PKI implementations. Because LDAP defines an API for the application layer used by different clients, users realize a level of scalability and portability, and do not have to contend with the upper layers of the stack. This API also makes it easier for different applications to quickly implement LDAP.

Although LDAP is becoming a de facto standard for certificate distribution, organizations that need an even more robust certificate depository can consider alternatives such as X.500.

21.14.9 PKI Functions

This section discusses the following basic processes which are common to all PKIs:

1. *Public key cryptography*—Includes the generation, distribution, administration, and control of cryptographic keys.

2. *Certificate issuance*—Binds a public-key to an individual, organization, or other entity, or to some other data—for example, an email or purchase order.
3. *Certificate validation*—Verifies that a trust relationship or binding exists and that a certificate is still valid for specific operations.
4. *Certificate revocation*—Cancels a previously issued certificate and either publishes the cancellation to a Certificate Revocation List or enables an Online Certificate Status Protocol process.

21.14.10 Secure Shell (SSH)

Secure Shell (**SSH**) is a network protocol for secure data communication, remote shell services or command execution and other secure network services between two networked computers that it connects via a secure channel over an insecure network: a server and a client (running SSH server and SSH client programs, respectively). The protocol specification distinguishes two major versions that are referred to as SSH-1 and SSH-2.

The best-known application of the protocol is for access to shell accounts on Unix-like operating systems. It was designed as a replacement for Telnet and other insecure remote shell protocols such as the Berkeley rsh and rexec protocols, which send information, notably passwords, in plaintext, rendering them susceptible to interception and disclosure using packet analysis. The encryption used by SSH is intended to provide confidentiality and integrity of data over an unsecured network, such as the Internet.

SSH uses public-key cryptography to authenticate the remote computer and allow it to authenticate the user, if necessary. Anyone can produce a matching pair of different keys (public and private). The public key is placed on all computers that must allow access to the owner of the matching private key (the owner keeps the private key secret). While authentication is based on the private key, the key itself is never transferred through the network during authentication.

SSH only verifies if the same person offering the public key also owns the matching private key. Hence, in all versions of SSH it is important to verify unknown public keys, *i.e.*, associate the public keys with identities, before accepting them as valid. Accepting an attacker's public key without validation will authorize an unauthorized attacker as a valid user.

21.14.11 Serial Line Internet Protocol (SLIP)

The **Serial Line Internet Protocol** (**SLIP**) is an encapsulation of the Internet Protocol designed to work over serial ports and modem connections. It is documented in RFC 1055. On personal computers, SLIP has been largely replaced by the Point-to-Point Protocol (PPP), which is better engineered, has more features and does not require its IP address configuration to be set before it is established. On microcontrollers, however, SLIP is still the preferred way of encapsulating IP packets due to its very small overhead.

SLIP modifies a standard TCP/IP datagram by appending a special 'SLIP END' character to it, which distinguishes datagram boundaries in the byte stream. SLIP requires a serial port configuration of 8 data bits, no parity, and either EIA hardware flow control, or CLOCAL mode (3-wire null-modem) UART operation settings.

SLIP does not provide error detection, being reliant on upper layer protocols for this. Therefore SLIP on its own is not satisfactory over an error-prone dial-up connection. It is however still useful for testing operating systems' response capabilities under load (by looking at flood-ping statistics).

SLIP is also currently used in the BlueCore Serial Protocol for communication between Bluetooth modules and host computers.

A version of SLIP with header compression is called *Compressed SLIP* (*CSLIP*). The compression algorithm used in CSLIP is known as Van Jacobson TCP/IP Header Compression. CSLIP has no effect on the data payload of a packet and is independent of any compression by the serial line modem used for transmission. It reduces the Transmission Control Protocol (TCP) header from 20 bytes to seven bytes. CSLIP has no effect on User Datagram Protocol (UDP) datagrams.

21.14.12 SOCKet Secure (SOCKS)

SOCKet Secure (**SOCKS**) is an Internet protocol that routes network packets between a client and server through a proxy server. SOCKS5 additionally provides authentication so only authorized users may access a server. Practically, a SOCKS server will proxy TCP connections to an arbitrary IP address as well as providing a means for UDP packets to be forwarded.

SOCKS performs at Layer 5 of the OSI model—the session layer (an intermediate layer between the presentation layer and the transport layer). The protocol was originally developed by David Koblas, a system administrator of MIPS Computer Systems. After MIPS was taken over by Silicon Graphics in 1992, Koblas presented a paper on SOCKS at that year's Usenix Security Symposium and SOCKS became publicly available.

21.15 WHAT IS MPLS?

Multi Protocol Label Switching (MPLS) is a switching technology that regulates data traffic and packet forwarding in a complex network. A connection-oriented methodology that traverses packets from source to destination node across networks is what it does for fast packet transmission. It has the feature of encompassing packets in the presence different network protocols.

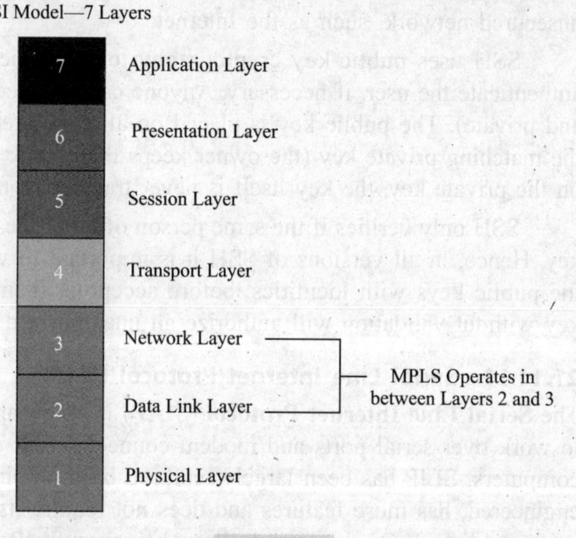

Fig. 21.2

In traditional IP routing, packets undergo analysis at each hop, followed by forwarding decision using network header analysis and then lookup in routing table. In an MPLS network, packets carrying data are assigned with labels on each node and the forwarding decision is totally based on these label headers. This is different from the conventional routing mechanism. Packet header is analyzed only once while they enter the MPLS cloud from then the forwarding decision is 'label-based' that ensures fast packet transmission between local-local and local-remote nodes. For in depth knowledge and familiarity on MPLS switching, find below on MPLS Architecture (Fig. 21.2).

This ensures end-to-end circuits over ANY type of transport medium using ANY network layer protocol. In view of the fact that MPLS supports Internet Protocol revised versions (IPv4 and IPv6), IPX, AppleTalk at Layer 3; Ethernet, Token Ring, Fiber Distributed Data Interface (FDDI), Asynchronous Transfer Mode (ATM), Frame Relay, and PPP (Point to Point Protocol) at Layer 2, it is referred as 'Layer 2.5 protocol'.

The core technology intents to remove protocol-dependency on specific datalink layer technologies such as ATM, Frame Relay, Ethernet, and Synchronous Optical Network (SONET). This avoids the need of multiple layer 2 networks for different types of traffic. It was intended for providing a unified data carrying service for circuit-based and packet switching clients.

An understanding of the basics behind MPLS is required for understanding MPLS based VPNs. MPLS evolved for a number of reasons. The first was that it provided a more scaleable method of allowing IP traffic to travel over an ATM network.

Second, MPLS enhances routing functionality. On a traditional service provider IP Network, traffic is routed via an interior routing protocol such as OSPF. The sum result of relying on traditional Layer 3 routing protocols is that all traffic routes based upon best path. This means that the best paths through service provider cores are used heavily while other, redundant paths, are underutilized. MPLS can be used to move network traffic over these underutilized paths allowing a greater return on redundant architecture investment for the service provider.

Finally, MPLS allows service providers to offer customers enhanced services. Utilizing constraint based outing and MPLS's quality of service features, service providers can provide several layers of service to their customers based upon many factors. Of course, MPLS also allows a service provider to offer value added services such as VPNs.

MPLS is based upon routers, or switches, performing label switching to provide a Label Switched Path (LSP) through a network. Essentially, when an IP packet enters an interface of an MPLS ingress router, that router assigns the packet to a Forwarding Equivalency Class (FEC). FEC assignment can be based on a variety of Access Control List (ACL) matches such as source address, destination address, BGP next hop, application type, and Differentiated Service flag. (Cosine, 2) The router then assigns the packet to an LSP and 'pushes' a label onto the packet header before sending it out the appropriate interface. Since FEC assignment is based upon a number of different factors, rather than just destination, packet forwarding can be policy based providing an advantage over traditional IP networks.

Similar to an ATM VPI/VCI or a Frame Relay DLCI, MPLS labels only have local significance. Intervening Label Switch Routers (LSRs) 'swap' the incoming label with a label defined in their own MPLS forwarding database. When the MPLS egress, or final, router is reached, the label is permanently removed, or 'popped', prior to the egress router forwarding the regular IP packet.

An example of this process is shown in Fig. 21.3. An IP packet arrives at the ingress router with a destination of 192.4.2.10. The ingress router pushes a label of 10 onto the packet and forwards it out a second interface. The intermediary LSR does a lookup on the label of 10 and swaps the 10 with a label of 2. The egress router terminates the LSP by popping the label of 2 and forwarding the regular IP packet onward.

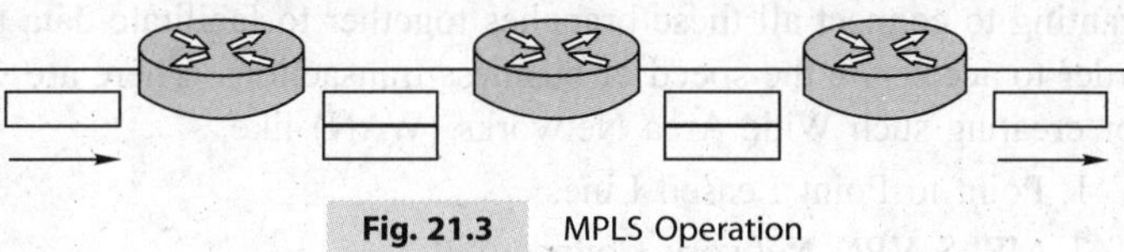

Fig. 21.3 MPLS Operation

When a label is pushed, a MPLS header is added to each packet. MPLS headers contain the following information (Fig. 21.4):

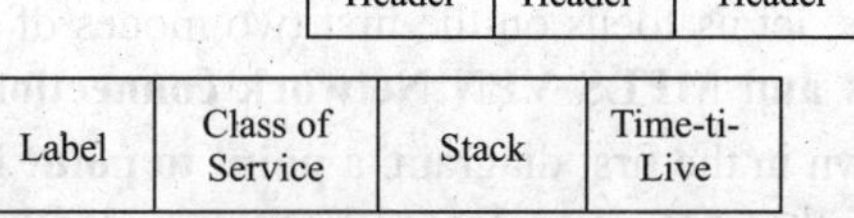

Fig. 21.4 MPLS Header Information

A 20 bit label field that contains the actual label information.

A 3 bit Class of Service field that can have an impact on the packet as it travels the network.

A 1 bit stack field that supports a hierarchical label stack.

An 8 bit Time to Live field which can support conventional IP TTL functionality (Semeria, 13)

LSPs can be setup throughout a network utilizing a variety of methods. LSPs can be manually configured on each LSR that participates within the LSP. Constraint based routing protocols such as Constrained Shortest Path First (CSPF) can also be used to define LSPs. Label Distribution Protocol (LDP), Resource Reservation Protocol (RSVP), and Constraint Based Routing-Label Distribution Protocol (CR-LDP) are signaling methods used to setup the LSP through a network.

21.15.1 MPLS History

The Internet Engineering Task Force (IETF) MPLS working group was formed on 1997 and the first MPLS RFCs had its release on 2001. RFC 3031 specifies MPLS architecture and RFC 3032 specifies its label stack encoding. Label switching allows a device to do the same router operations with performance of ATM switch. ATM switches and label lookups are faster than a conventional IP routing. With advancement in packet switching, MPLS overcomes ATM setbacks with less overhead and connection-oriented services for frames with varying length. This also provides the advantage of maintaining traffic engineering and out-of-band control. Thus Frame Relay and ATM are less in need for installing large-scale networks, as MPLS performance is far superior to previous ones.

Amidst these advantages, there are a few downsides for this label switching technology. First, the management of MPLS is complicated as it is dependent on routing protocols for data transfer. At this instant, any crumples in network can disturb the whole transportation and the redirection of data packets. Initially, the structure of label allows routers to decide and forward IP packets. This was based on label contents instead of a difficult route lookup mechanism based on IP address. With technical progress, Layer 3 switches (ASIC based routers) carry out route lookups at sufficient speed to support interface types.

21.15.2 Advantages of MPLS VPN Network over Point to Point Leased Lines for WAN Connectivity

In this article, we discuss about two important forms of Wide Area Network Connectivity—MPLS VPN Network and Point to Point Leased Lines. We also see how or why MPLS VPN networks have started to gain more popularity for private wide area network connectivity for medium and large organizations having multiple branches.

When you have multiple branches across a state or a country, you would definitely be wanting to connect all these branches together to facilitate data transfer/ access between them in order to accelerate the speed of business transactions. There are various options to be considered for creating such Wide Area Networks (WAN) like,

1. Point to Point Leased Lines
2. MPLS VPN Network Connectivity
3. Internet Leased Lines with Site-to-Site VPN (Virtual Private Network)
4. Broadband/VPN over Broadband
5. Dial-up/CDMA/3G Connectivity/4G Connectivity for small branches
6. Satellite (VSAT) Connectivity for remote locations

Of these, let us focus on the first two modes of connectivity in this article—**Point to Point Leased Lines and MPLS VPN Network connections** (Fig. 21.5).

As shown in the first diagram, a **point to point Leased Line** is formed by connecting every site to every other site using leased lines provided by the service provider network (Or in very large organizations, their own network). This is a private network and is used primarily for site-to-site communications. So for an organization having branches in five locations, four links need to connect each location to all other locations to complete the leased line network. For 'n' locations, the number of links required in each location would be 'n-1'.

An **MPLS Network** is formed by connecting each location with a single link (as shown in the second diagram) to a service provider MPLS network. An MPLS network stands for Multi-Protocol Label Switching and any packet coming to the Label edge routers (from individual locations—source, to the service provider MPLS network) are encapsulated with an MPLS label which is used to identify it and route it through the MPLS network. This label is discarded when the packet comes out of the MPLS network back to individual locations—destination.

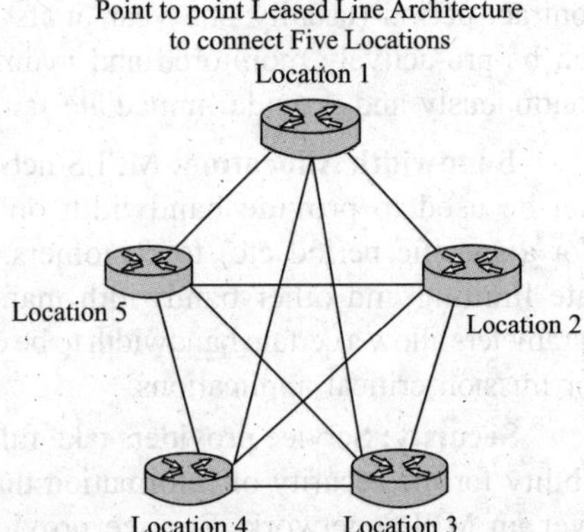

Fig. 21.5 Point to Point Leased Lines for WAN Connectivity—Architecture

In both the above cases, a wide variety of physical hardware is used to carry the information including fiber, copper circuits, wireless connectivity, satellite connectivity etc. The MPLS core service provider network also use high capacity MPLS routers in addition to the MPLS edge routers which send and receive data from the routers located in the individual locations.

Let us now look at the Factors which have enabled MPLS VPN Networks to become more favorable for organizations that want to inter-connect their various branches when compared to Point to Point Leased Lines.

Traffic Engineering: Since the MPLS packets are being added at the MPLS Edge routers, it is possible to set the path that the traffic will have to take through the network. More specifically, each class of traffic (like data, voice, video etc) can be set individual performance characteristics.

Quality of Service: Since MPLS network enables traffic engineering, it is possible to send (for example)—data traffic over a lower priority path and real time delay sensitive voice/video packets over a high priority/ lesser used/shorter path. This enables network convergence (The Wide Area Network becomes more suitable for introduction of new services like voice, video, multi-cast traffic, hosting etc).

Network Redundancy: An MPLS core network is generally designed and built to overcome individual hardware (router) faults or line disconnections. In such cases, the data is re-routed through the next optimum path with a fail-over time of 50 ms or lesser. Even the last mile connections can be backed up using CDMA wireless back up etc, depending upon the options with the service provider.

Easy and Cost effective Expansion: For organizations that are having a lot of branches or expanding with new branches, MPLS network would be very cost effective as each branch needs one MPLS link while each branch would need n-1 links for point to point Leased Lines (n being the total number of branches). MPLS makes it easy for instantaneous addition and deletion of sites.

Protocol Independent forwarding: MPLS networks can carry any type of packets—be it IP, frame relay or ATM using the same infrastructure. This is because, what ever type of packets comes in, MPLS labels would be attached to it for transmitting them over the MPLS network and these labels are protocol independent.

Connection oriented network: MPLS is a connection-oriented network unlike connection less networks like IP. So, it is more reliable.

Service Level Agreement (SLA): Service Providers generally provide an SLA—Service Level Agreement for MPLS networks with a guarantee of very minimum downtime during the contract period (usually one year or its multiples). This is possible because an MPLS network can be pro-actively monitored and maintained. It is possible to analyze the circuit performance continuously and provide immediate fault rectification and support.

Bandwidth Allocation: MPLS networks allow for dynamic bandwidth allocation and hence can be used to provide bandwidth on demand (for a specific period etc) to customers. Further, rate limiting and other bandwidth management parameters allow a certain bandwidth to be dedicated for mission critical applications.

Security: Service providers take full responsibility for the security of information that is sent over an MPLS network. Service providers also create IP tunnels throughout the network without the need for any encryption from user-end.

International MPLS: There are options with service providers to connect individual locations across different countries using MPLS by sharing and inter-connecting their respective MPLS networks.

Lesser Hops: With an MPLS network, there are lesser number of hops between the various network points resulting in improved response times and application performance

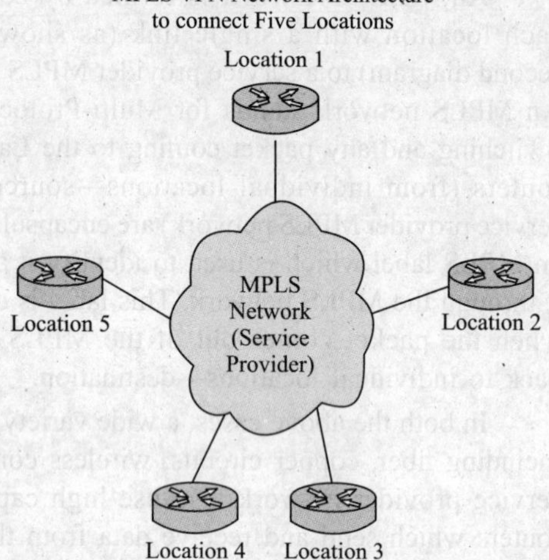

Fig. 21.6 Multi-Label-Protocol-Switching (MPLS) Network Architecture

21.16 SUMMARY

VPNs are a perfect alternative to costly, inflexible private circuits. They give companies the option of setting up virtual circuits across public networks, such as the Internet. Encryption provides the confidentiality needed as the private information flows across the public network. This capability allows VPNs to establish secure communication between different remote offices and can also be used to establish remote access to internal network resources by employees from their homes or while they are on travel.

IP Security (IPSec) is an IEFT standard for establishing virtual private networks. It is slowly replacing proprietary VPN protocols and becoming the industry standard.

SSL is vital to Web security. It provides a strong sense of confidentiality, message integrity, and server authentication to users. The business of e-commerce is tied closely to consumer confidence in the operation of SSL across the net. In the future, SSL termination devices will be able to handle more transactions at a faster rate. The encryption of key lengths and the cipher suites used will also continue to evolve in order to ensure the security of sensitive information over the Web. This way, e-commerce will be able to continue to grow in popularity as users grow more confidant in shopping and banking online, and embracing new online applications.

As standards related to cryptography become more prevalent, there might come a day when almost every piece of information that is processed by a computer system is protected by some form of cryptography. In the meantime, this section has provided a look at some of the current methods for cryptographic protection of our information systems. To organize our discussion, we showed how cryptography could be applied at several levels of a network including the application level, the transport level, and the network level. Each of these levels brings with it advantages and disadvantages.

At the application level, each application must provide its own cryptographic services. This allows the application developers to closely match the services to the needs of the application. The downside is that each application might need to replicate similar cryptographic services and some applications might have implemented the services better than others. Still, replacing insecure applications such as telnet with applications that support cryptography such as SSH can provide an immediate increase in security.

Applying cryptography at the transport level allows many applications to share a uniform set of cryptographic services, reducing the problem of inconsistency. Applications must still be written to use the transport level services, but because the security services themselves are not being duplicated, there is little possibility of irregularity .

If your application neither supports application level nor transport level encryption, you can still take advantage of network level cryptography. Applying encryption at the network level, referred to as virtual private networking, addresses both consistency and availability issues. Any information that flows across the network can be protected. The downside here is that individual application needs might not be taken into account.

This module also included descriptions of current protocols and products that implement cryptographic security. This included a detailed discussion of how IPSec, the current standard for implementing VPNs, can be used to protect all information that flows across an untrusted network. At the application level we described PGP, one of the first widely deployed public key based applications. Finally we discussed what many consider the holy grail of cryptographic protection, PKI systems, and how they can be used to establish trust, even between people who have never interacted with each other before.

Although it will be a long time before we reach a point where all of our information assets are protected at all times by cryptography, there are many current applications and protocols available that support cryptography. Using available applications and protocols such as SSH and IPSec can provide an immediate improvement in your organization's security.

PGP is a great example of an application-specific use of cryptography. The current commercial version ofPGP supports encryption and the creation of digital signatures for files, provides IPSec-compliant VPN capabilities and acts as a host firewall, but PGP's original purpose was to protect e-mail.

PGP provides two main protections for e-mail. First, it supports strong encryption of the e-mail message. This encryption is implemented using a combination of public key and symmetric key cryptography. The second protection is digital signature of e-mail messages, providing non-repudiation and integrity verification.

Public Key Infrastructure (PKI) is the tool most often used for ecommerce and Business-to-business (B2B), and it allows users to exchange encrypted information over an public network. When you purchase goods on the Internet, you privately and securely exchange data and currency (like a credit card number) with an online vendor through the use of a public and a private cryptographic key pair. That cryptographic key pair is obtained and shared through a trusted authority.

A digital certificate is a credential used to help someone decide whether a key is genuine. It works by binding a public key with identification information such as name and e-mail address. This information is then signed by at least one third-party. As long as you trust the opinion of one of the third parties that signed the certificate, you should be able to trust the validity of the certificate.

Digital Certificates bind an individual's identity to the public key. With PKI systems, the purpose is the same, but the process used to produce the certificate is more formal. Most PKI systems do not allow the user to create certificates themselves like PGP does. Instead a certificate authority creates the certificate and issues it to the user. The care at which the CA performs this role directly affects how secure the overall PKI is. If the CA issues a digital certificate to anyone without requesting proof of identity, the confidence you should have in the certificate is low. If instead, the CA requires that you show up, in person, with two forms of government issued ID before issuing you a certificate, your confidence can be high in that CA's certificates.

REVIEW QUESTIONS

1. What is Trusted and Untrusted Networks?
2. What is VPN?
3. What are the different types of VPN?
4. What are the different authentication methods used in VPNs?
5. What are the limitations of VPN?
6. What are the disadvantages of VPN?
7. What is VPN Tunneling?
8. What is VPN Tunneling Protocols? Also explain PPTP, CHAP, PAP?
9. What are the pros and cons of PPTP?
10. What are voluntary and compulsory tunnels?
11. Explain static and dynamic tunnels.
12. What security vulnerabilities are addressed by VPN?
13. What security vulnerabilities are unique to or heightened by VPN?
14. What kind of performance issues does VPN raise?
15. What is the relationship between VPN and firewalls?
16. What firewall issues are relevant to VPN selection and deployment?
17. What are reasonable expectations for a VPN?
18. What are unreasonable expectations for VPN?
19. What kind of policies and procedures need to be developed for VPN?
20. What is IPSec?
21. What is PGP?
22. How secure is PGP?
23. How does PGP work?
24. Has RSA ever been cracked publicly? What is RSA-129?
25. What is the best way to crack PGP?
26. If my secret key ring is stolen, can my messages be read?
27. How do I choose a pass phrase?
28. Why not use RSA alone rather than a hybrid mix of IDEA, MD5, & RSA?
29. Which key size should I use?
30. Why does PGP take so long to add new keys to my key ring?
31. What are the Public Key Servers?
32. Why do SSL certificates expire?
33. Why do some organizations need more than one certificate?
34. Why do certificate providers give out 'child certificates' from 'root certificates' instead of just providing a 'root certificate' copy?
35. What is PKI?
36. What are public and private keys?
37. What about digital signatures?

ELECTRONIC COMMERCE AN OVERVIEW

22.1 INTRODUCTION

Electronic commerce over the Internet is predicted to grow at an ever-increasing rate over the next few years, with on-line sales already heading for several billion. Many companies are using this new sales channel, and a few retailers now have established major on-line sales sites. There have been some successes, particularly in technology, business-to-business and niche markets.

This chapter has been produced to summarise the basics of electronic commerce, covering on-line catalogues and on-line purchasing.

22.2 THE MARKET

The NOP organisation publishes survey results on its Web site. The following quotes are from that source:

1. Home shopping is still at an embryonic stage in all three countries. Approximately 10% of Web users in France, Germany and Britain have shopped on-line in the last four weeks.
2. The NOP findings indicate that, as a proportion of the total adult population, the percentage of people who have used the Web in the past four weeks is highest in Britain and Germany. France currently has the smallest proportion of Internet users with relation to its total adult population-6 per cent (2.87 million people).

The criterion of having purchased in the last four weeks is a little rigid, and most users will purchase less frequently than this. US studies indicate up to 25% of Internet users shop on-line, so the UK 'Internet Shopping' population is probably in the half to one million range.

However the potential figure may be much higher. In a recent survey more than half of those surveyed said they had no qualms about using their credit card over the Internet. So there may be as many as 2–3 million people who would purchase if the sales proposition is right. This research was carried out by leading market research company BMRB, for Internet Monitor.

In mass-market terms this may still be considered low, and merchants selling low-value items may not find that they generate the volume of business to justify a large expensive site. Any projects of this nature, such as supermarket sites, are experimental at this stage.

There are however profitable e-commerce operations in niche areas, business-to-business or export markets. For example, Textor Webmasters Ltd. has been building a successful business intelligence site in partnership with CMS. Initial growth was slow, but now with the benefit of three years of experience and development the enterprise is profitable and has a very respectable turnover.

We recommend that merchants with the right product line and a good business plan start now with this sales channel. In most cases expect slow but steady growth rather than an immediate 'pot of gold'. Establish a beachhead now and grow your Internet presence so that when the market takes off-which it will-you are ready to take advantage of the opportunities that present themselves.

22.3 THE WORLDWIDE MARKET

The total figure worldwide for Internet users is in the region of 200 million. Clearly anyone wishing to export should look at the Internet as a sales channel.

22.4 MARKETING VERSUS SELLING WEB SITES

Most companies with an Internet presence have a straightforward marketing site. The objective of the site is to supplement traditional marketing activities, perhaps give additional information, and generally promote the company. There is often a reluctance to give complete product details because the objective is to induce visitors to call or write to the company for more information and thus establish contact.

A selling site is different. The objective is to close the sale electronically with payment (and sometimes delivery) made over the Internet. This type of site will be designed to include comprehensive product information, as visitors will be expected to make a purchasing decision based on the information presented.

Such sites generally have three sections:

1. **Marketing and added value information:** This is aimed at attracting customers, giving them a feel for the contents, and giving them confidence in the retailer.
2. **The catalogue:** Detailed information on product benefits, specifications, and pricing.
3. **Order processing:** This will include a method for specifying and paying for the order. More advanced systems may have a method for the customer to go back into the system to check progress and delivery of the order.

The true electronic commerce site will have all three components in some degree.

Such sites may be stand-alone, or may form part of a larger retailing site called a 'shopping mall'.

22.5 SHOPPING MALLS

Internet shopping malls were set up early in the development of Internet commerce. A shopping mall has a standardised environment into which several merchants are held in a single Web site. They offer advantages to a new on-line merchant:

- A standard environment for setting up the catalogue and arranging payment.
- Someone else is arranging for promotion of the mall as a whole.
- In the UK, where the payment processing has historically been a problem, it has meant a trouble-free credit card collection mechanism.

However these benefits have not generally materialised. Malls work in the real world because there is something that attracts visitors, generally a large department store. Once visitors arrive, park their cars and start shopping, it is convenient for them to shop at other merchants in that same locality. The Internet is not like this. It is as easy to visit another shop anywhere in the world as the 'next' shop in a virtual mall. People shopping for books are going to search for book sites. If they browse, it is the list of matches to their requirements from a search engine, not an on-line shopping mall.

From the infrastructure point of view, catalogue software and payment processing is now more widely available. Many merchants who started out in a shopping mall have graduated to a stand-alone site.

22.6 BUILDING THE BUSINESS

It is not enough to simply set up the catalogue and electronic commerce programs. 'Build it and they will come' has never been an approach that works on the Internet. The site must be promoted both on the Internet and via traditional means.

The biggest single source of visitors is also the cheapest. Registering with a few major search engines will generate over half, perhaps as much as 75% of your potential total traffic.

Other techniques are:

- ❒ Negotiating links with other Web sites.
- ❒ Traditional marketing and PR.
- ❒ Advertising on search engines and other high traffic sites.
- ❒ Associate programs by which sites that refer visitors get a commission on sales.

Once the site is built and registered, look for other ways of building business such as special offers. Visitors can be tracked through the site and offers customised to their interests. These techniques are in their infancy, but are being developed rapidly.

22.7 IS THIS DIRECT MARKETING?

Direct marketers should also not make the mistake of equating the number of Internet users with a mail shot of that size. If there are 2–3 million potential Internet shoppers in the UK, a Web site is not like a mail shot to 2 million people. Only a tiny fraction of these will ever find your Web site and see it at all. The good news is that they will by and large be people interested in your product.

Direct marketers often have difficulty with handling on-line catalogues. The fact of the matter is that if someone visits a site and decides not to purchase, then that is the end of the matter. If someonc is sent a catalogue or brochure and decides not to purchase, the merchant can re-send the catalogue, follow up by telephone, and so on. Direct marketers are often loath to lose the degree of control implied in traditional methods.

22.8 IS THIS ONE-TO-ONE MARKETING?

Internet selling is not retail, and it is not direct marketing. It has its own characteristics, which are evolving as the technology develops. As we learn more about this area we are finding new innovative ways of building the business, which are unique to this medium. Increasingly we are looking for ways to build a one-to-one relationship with customers using the Internet.

This has to be done carefully. You might be able to tell that you have a repeat visitor, but that person might not like the idea that someone is keeping track of his or her movements. By all means keep records of visitors' preferences so you can present them with the right special offers when they return. But be subtle-or preferably do this by consent.

This new world will require new attitudes and new marketing skills. It may not be right for every business, but when it is appropriate it can offer a low-cost channel with an outlet in virtually every country in the world.

22.9 THE ON-LINE CATALOGUE

The key to a good electronic commerce site is to provide an environment that makes it easy for the customer to navigate through the catalogue of products and ultimately make a purchase. How does this work? In the following section, we take a look at the purchase cycle from the point of view of the customer.

22.10 NAVIGATION

The customer must be able to find the product they need without going through endless levels of indexes or menus. The visitor should be able to get to the product they need with very few clicks.

80% of visitors to any site will take one look at the page they arrive on and then leave. It has been estimated that you lose 20% of visitors every time you ask them to link to a new page. Good navigation is essential.

The information must be comprehensive once the customer has located the product of interest. Provide pictures and diagrams to help the customer understand what is being offered.

22.11 THE SHOPPING CART

When the catalogue is small (say less than 20 items), a simple order form will often do the job. However on larger sites the customer will flag products during this browsing session to be added to an electronic 'shopping cart'. At any point the customer can review the contents of the cart, the cost and so on. This makes it easy for the customer to browse the site selecting products as they go.

When the shopping session is complete, the customer clicks on a hyperlink which takes him or her to the checkout page.

At this stage the customer is presented with a list of the goods marked for purchase, the total cost, shipping, handling, tax, etc. The customer can then add shipping instructions, name, address and so on.

The customer is normally given a range of payment options, and some of the more common are discussed in more detail below. The most common is to use a credit card, and the customer enters the card number, name on the card and expiry date.

At this stage the Web site should switch to secure mode. The technology normally used is called SSL (Secure Socket Layer). This means that all communication with the server is encrypted in such a way that eavesdroppers cannot (without disproportionate difficulty) steal the credit card information. We shall discuss this further later, but it is important for customer confidence that the site switches to secure mode as soon as credit card information is requested.

The customer will get visual warning from his or her Web browser that they are in secure mode, a blue key and blue line in Netscape or a padlock symbol in Internet Explorer. There are some older browsers that don't support SSL but most do.

This technology is widely used and quite well understood by Internet users. Most articles on e-commerce rightly emphasise the need for customers only to give up confidential information in a secure session, and users will look out for it. We believe that it is essential.

It is worth mentioning at this stage that a secure server is not absolutely necessary for bank-approved (and indeed very secure) e-commerce. There is a new British e-commerce product that uses its own Java-based encryption, and therefore does not need a secure server environment.

There are practical benefits here, and the solution is very cost effective and does not require more than a standard Internet server operation. The important issue here in our opinion is that the customer does not get the visual feedback from a secure session (the blue key in Netscape or the padlock symbol in Explorer). So irrespective of the technical merits of this solution, we believe it could adversely affect customer confidence.

22.12 PAYMENT AND ORDER PROCESSING

There are a number of catalogue Web sites being run by UK companies, varying from large sophisticated book retailers to small 'mom and pop' operations. The most popular payment mechanism is payment by credit card, and clearly such payments must be secure. However in a review of a number of such sites, we found that only a minority offered credit card payment over a secure link.

Other options are:

- Credit cards over an insecure link.
- Purchase orders only.
- Purchaser contacted later by phone or post.
- Purchaser prints form and faxes it.

The few sites that accept credit card information over an insecure link are almost certainly in violation of their agreement with the bank that is accepting their payments. They are also taking on the business risk of fraud. The risk does not stop at the bank but gets passed on to the merchant.

Issues for these sites are:

- Perceived non-availability of secure payment methods. We discuss payment methods and security issues below.
- Inability of the design shop that developed the Web site to implement a complex catalogue or secure payment system.
- Difficulty in finding a commercial Web site hosting operation that will offer a suitable secure environment.
- Perceived cost of setting up a merchant server.

Most of these issues are perception rather than reality. There is no reason why a merchant should not be able to offer a fully functional catalogue site with a proper secure payment mechanism. This can be done very, cost-effectively.

22.13 WHAT IS INVOLVED IN CREDIT CARD PROCESSING?

The steps in credit card processing are as follows:

The merchant must first obtain authorisation for the charge from the merchant's credit card processing company. Authorisation simply means that the card has not been reported stolen, and there is sufficient credit on the card. It results in the customer's credit limit being temporarily reduced by the value of the transaction.

There are two ways in which authorisation may be obtained:

1. **Manual:** The merchant downloads details of the sale from the computer that is acting as Web server. The merchant then requests authorisation using their normal method such as a point of sale (POS) terminal or PC program.
2. **Automatic:** The server software communicates directly with the credit card processing company computer and arranges authorisation on-line.

Clearly option 2 is preferred, but this is more complex and the costs are greater.

The final stage is for the credit card to be debited. This can happen at the same time as authorisation, provided that the merchant guarantees that delivery will take place within a certain fixed time. Otherwise capture should take place when the goods are shipped.

If the merchant's business is such that capture can take place immediately, then this can also happen automatically. Otherwise a second manual process is required.

Regretably, there is sometimes a further stage at which the customer is dissatisfied and arranges for the transaction to be cancelled. Because many Internet sales are made to overseas customers, many banks perceive that there is an increased risk of chargebacks. It has been reported that some merchants will not accept orders to Russia because of the frequency of chargeback.

Note that the fact that a payment has been authorised by the bank does not provide any protection against chargeback.

22.14 OTHER PAYMENT METHODS

The discussion above has concentrated on credit card payments because they are the most efficient for most purchases.

However there are a number of alternatives, and you should offer as many of these on your site if you can, for example fax and telephone ordering should almost always be offered.

22.14.1 Fax

Simply printing an order form and faxing it to the merchant is feasible and reasonably secure. The form can be the secure order form-simply offer this as an option in the text.

22.14.2 Telephone Order

Offer customers the option of calling in their order, using the order form as a prompt. Many will prefer this, and the order form will be useful in confirming product codes and prices.

22.14.3 Micro-payments

Whereas credit cards are fine for significant purchases, they are not efficient for a purchase of only a few pence (a micro-payment). There are systems being developed which operate like an electronic purse which can be recharged using traditional payment mechanisms. The purse can be depleted without formality for these small payments. Micro-payment systems are seen as a significant future development. The main players are:

- Mondex—originally developed in the UK but now operated by Master Card. This relies on the use of SmartCards to hold the value, and payments can be made from card to card without any intermediary. This makes the Mondex card a powerful substitute for cash, and with cheap smart card readers becoming available for PCs, a very acceptable Internet payment method.
- Visa Cash has been developed by Visa.
- Cybercash already has an electronic wallet concept to retain credit card information and pass it securely to a merchant (see below). This concept can readily be extended to electronic cash for micro-payments.
- Ecash is an early cash system, which is unlikely to survive in competition with giants like Visa.

Remember that micro-payment systems are often seen as less secure than other payment methods. For example the smart card can be stolen, like a real wallet. A trade off against security is part of the concept. For this reason there will normally be an upper limit to transaction and wallet sizes.

22.14.4 Proprietary Payment Systems

These were developed before secure server technology was widely available. They operate in different ways:

- Cybercash uses an 'electronic wallet' to hold credit card details and to transmit them securely using their own encryption software.
- First Virtual uses a system of e-mail messages to confirm the sale.

The problem with all of these proprietary systems is that they require the user to do something to set themselves up, either to install special software or to register with the organisation.

22.14.5 Electronic Cheques

These are quite possible and are in use in the USA.

22.14.6 Purchase Orders

For business purchases a purchase order would be appropriate.

22.15 SECURITY ISSUES

22.15.1 Introduction to Security

The Internet was started to provide the military with channels of communication that would survive a Nuclear War and to foster communications between research institutions. It has become the most widely used informational tool in the world. Currently, 95% of The Fortune 2000 companies use the Internet in some way. In addition, over 31 million total users are connected to the internet. With the excessive amount of data sharing and the tremendous number of users connected, there are enormous opportunities for unauthorized users to access confidential data.

Since 1992. there have been 1.2 million break-ins and 80% of the intruders gained access via the Internet. Also, 10 billion dollars worth of data are stolen from online thieves in the United States annually. Thus, 60% to 70% of companies refuse to use the Internet for business transactions.

To protect confidential data from intruders, there are several security measures available today. Passwords, Encryption, Firewalls and Virus protection are measures used to secure companies' confidential internal information. If companies want to share data on the Internet, they have to consider security issues:

1. Passwords
2. Viruses
3. Firewalls
4. Encryption

22.15.2 Authentication: Passwords

The most inexpensive and perhaps the easiest method of security is achieved through password protection. There are several different areas in which passwords can be used. Having an internal network strategy where users require a network identification name and a password will protect data internally. In addition requiring a password and user identification for all protocols for remote access via the internet or through telephone dial in, will create a first layer for protection from unauthorized access.

When utilizing a password protection strategy there are several guidelines that should be followed. These guidelines will maximize the benefits of a password protection scheme. The length of a password greatly effects the effort required to break the password. With this in mind, users should be required to make their passwords greater than five characters long. Words that are found in the dictionary should also be avoided when creating a password. People may try to obtain unauthorized access by writing programs that test all dictionary words as possible passwords. Another area that threatens the security of passwords is the use of common passwords like birthdays, social security numbers, and names of relatives. This information is not difficult to obtain, and is very often used as a password.

Firewalls do their authentication using IP addresses which are assigned to each server, client, and network device and can be spoofed. So if you want to give certain users access over the Internet to sensitive internal files and data, you'll want to make sure to authenticate the actual user. *Authentication* simply describes the numerous methods that positively identify a user. Passwords are the most common method of authentication used today, but users are notorious for making poor password choices that can be guessed by an experienced hacker.

In addition to passwords, which are often called 'something you know,' many organizations are turning to solutions that also required 'something you have', such as tokens and smart cards. Tokens are small, credit card-or calculator-size devices that the remote user carries around.

Many of these products use a challenge-response scheme. When the user attempts to connect, an authentication server on the network issues a challenge, which the user keys into the token device. The device displays the appropriate response, which the remote user then sends to the server. Many of these tokens also require the user to type in a PIN. Tokens range from $35 to $65 each, depending on volume. Less expensive software versions of tokens are available.

The market leader in token technology is Security Dynamics, with its SecurID line of token products and ACE/Server. SecurID products are supported by several firewall products, including those from Check Point, Raptor, and Trusted Information Systems. You simply configure the firewall products to forward authentication for certain services to the designated third-party server, or use any included authentication service.

Smart cards used for authentication are similar to tokens, except they require a smart card reader to process the challenge. Though these devices have shrunk in size over the past few years, they're still additional devices that the user has to carry and can find cumbersome. They are also generally more expensive than tokens, ranging in price from $40 to $250 per user. Gemplus and SCM Microsystems are two manufacturers of smart card readers. PC Card devices are also available but more expensive.

Digital certificates, described in the following encryption discussion, are an upand-coming authentication method that holds great promise for messaging and electronic commerce.

22.15.3 Viruses

Viruses are also an important topic in Internet security. A computer virus is a computer program that clones itself when an infected piece of program code is executed. Executable files and all other code that controls your hard disk can be infected. Basically, a computer virus is a piece of code that will copy its code into one or more larger host programs when it is activated. As infected programs are run, the destructive viral code is executed and the virus replicates, causing damage like messages on your screen to wiping out your hard drive. Viruses may spread through modems and networks, and this is of great concern to any organisation wishing to make use of the Internet.

Viruses are mainly transmitted from computer to computer through contaminated diskettes. A problem that is remedied through installation of virus protecting software. The Internet is a different entry point for viruses. Firewalls alone can not protect against virus. There are too many ways of encoding binary files for transfer over networks, and too many different architectures and viruses to try to search for all of them. A firewall cannot protect against a data-driven attack. In other words, attack in which something is mailed or copied to an internal host where it is then executed.

Organization-wide virus control measure should be implemented by companies that are deeply concerned about viruses. Instead of trying to screen viruses out in firewall, make sure that every vulnerable desktop has virus scanning software that is run every time the machine is rebooted. Securing your network with virus scanning software will protect against viruses that come in via floppy disks, modems, and the Internet.

22.15.4 Firewalls

A firewall is a computer or a set of computers that provides a single point of entry into a local network from the outside world of the Internet and which is designed to deny access to any packet that is not known to be authorized. This computer usually sits between the Internet and the local TCP/IP network. The best firewalls start by allowing no packets to pass through them, and then are carefully modified to allow access to only specific categories of known safe packets. Due to the phenomenal growth of computer security violations (over 80% occur via the internet), firewalls are needed to keep interfacing outsiders from destroying information and reading confidential data.

In other word, a firewall is simply a barrier between two networks—in most cases an internal network, often called the *trusted network*, and an external network, called the *untrusted network* (in this case, the Internet). Firewalls examine incoming and outgoing packets and, according to a set of rules defined by the administrator, either let them through or block them. Today, most firewalls use one or more of three packetscreening methods. Many routers use a firewall technique called *packet filtering*, which examines the source and destination addresses and ports of incoming TCP and UDP packets and denies or allows packets to enter based on a set of predefined rules. Packet filters are inexpensive, are transparent to users, and have a negligible impact on network performance. Configuring packet filtering, however, is a relatively complex process. It usually requires precise knowledge of network, transport, and sometimes even application protocols. Another problem with packet filters is that they're susceptible to *IP spoofing*, a trick that hackers use to gain access to a corporate network by changing *Internet Protocol* (*IP*) addresses in packet headers to ones that are acceptable.

A more sophisticated and secure type of firewall is an application gateway. Most application-gateway firewall products, including Raptor's popular eagle line and Trusted Information Systems' Gauntlet, use application proxies. These are programs written for specific Internet services, such as HTTP, FTP, and telnet, that run on a server with two network connections, acting as a server to the application client and as a client to the application server. Since they evaluate network packets for valid application-specific data, application proxies are generally considered more secure than packet filters. Most application-gateway firewalls also have a feature called *network address translation* that prevents internal IP addresses from appearing to users outside the trusted network.

One primary disadvantage of application gateways is performance degradation caused by the proxy function's double processing. Another is the fact that you may have to wait several months for your firewall vendor to supply an application proxy for a newly introduced Internet service, such as RealAudio. If you plan to use a firewall solely as a perimeter defense behind a T1 connection to your ISP, you may not have to worry about performance, the low bandwidth of the connection will become saturated before the firewall.

Many organizations, however, will want to consider using additional firewalls internally to cordon off servers in departments, such as Human Resources, that contain sensitive information. In such cases, performance is a concern, because the connection is likely to be 10-Mbps. Ethernet or 100-Mbps Fast Ethernet. If you plan to use application proxies internally, consider a fast hardware-based solution, such as Cisco's PIX Firewall or Seattle Software's Firebox. Or you may consider installing your firewall software on a system with multiple processors.

22.15.4.1 Types of Firewalls

- There are two types of firewalls—Packet filtering firewalls and proxy application firewalls. Each is used differently depending on the situation. The first type is the **packet filtering firewall**. This type of firewall is used at the border of the TCP/IP protocol and the connection to the Internet. It screens all IP packets (segment of data sent via IP protocol) and allowing in only packets that are authorized to flow through. The firewall knows who is allowed by comparing the IP source and IP destination addresses that accompany each packet. This firewall is fairly common in operations that are doing many information transactions through TCP/IP. This firewall has low startup costs. A typical firewall system that one can purchase consists of a PC server with two ethernet adapters, installation, and training for roughly $15-20,000. Another advantage is that the firewall can appear transparent to the user. Unfortunately, the IP source and destination addresses can be 'spoofed' or forged. Any good hacker could possibly fool the firewall into believing that the hacker truly does have access, however, this does not happen very often, yet! This firewall is also very difficult to configure, requiring someone with vast knowledge of TCP/IP and UDP technologies.

- The other main type of firewall is called an **application level firewall**. These firewalls authenticate all requests at the application layer rather than at the protocol layer. A proxy firewall is set up at either the application or TCP layer. This proxy serves as a middleman to determine what applications have access. The benefits to this type of system are that there is user-level authentication similar to what is in use at the Terry College of Business computer lab. Also, with an application level firewall, a private network is much more transparent to the internet.
- A third type of firewall technology, termed *stateful inspection* by Check Point Software Technologies, is in Check Point's Firewall-1, Cisco's PIX Firewall, ON Technology's ON Guard, and Network-1's Firewall/Plus. Like packet filtering, it first intercepts packets at the network layer, but then it inspects entire packets, comparing them against known bit patterns (states) of friendly packets. Stateful inspection generally results in slightly higher performance than application proxies, but debate remains as to whether it is as secure or marginally less secure. On our tests, we haven't seen any difference in security between the two models. Initially, most firewalls were written for Unix, but last year saw a flood of new Windows NT-based firewall products from vendors, including Check Point, Raptor, Seattle Software Labs, and Trusted Information Systems. If you're comfortable with Unix, a Unix-based firewall gives you the advantage of an operating system that has been around long enough for many security problems to be found and dealt with. If you are more comfortable in the Windows world, however, stick with a Windows NT—based firewall, since security violations are more likely to come from errors in firewall configuration than inherent problems with the products or the operating systems on which they run.

22.15.5 Encryption

As offices and organizations have connected to the Net in droves, many have begun eyeing the Internet infrastructure as an inexpensive vehicle for wide-area and emote connections. To use the Internet for these purposes, however, companies have to protect their information with *encryption*. Encryption is simply the process of using a formula, called an *encryption algorithm*, to translate plain text into an incomprehensible cipher text and then back to plain text again. Essential to encryption is a numeric value called the *key* that becomes part of the encryption algorithm, setting the encryption process in motion.

Many different types of encryption algorithms are available, but the most widely used are DES, a *symmetric* or *secret* key algorithm, and RSA, an *asymmetric* or *public* key algorithm. DES can be used with 40- or 56-bit keys. RSA's key lengths are generally anywhere from 512 to 2,048 bits. A more recent algorithm called Triple DES is a stronger version of DES that uses more than one key. *S/MIME* is an up-and-coming standard for securing e-mail that uses RSA encryption. Microsoft, Netscape, Novel, and Sun all either presently support or have plans to support *S/MIME* in their messaging systems. This will allow the messaging systems to send secure e-mail to each other. They can also address several desktop e-mail encryption packages, including ConnectSoft's EMail Connection, OpenSoft's ExpressMail, and Deming Internet Security's Secure Messenger, support *S/MIME*.

With a symmetric or secrete key algorithm such as DES, the same key is used for encryption and decryption. This technology requires significantly less processing power than asymmetric key encryption. Secret key encryption, however, requires a separate key for each pair of users exchanging information—a significant management burden. It also requires secure establishment and distribution of the secret keys. This is a difficult task in an open environment like the Internet.

RSA's asymmetric encryption uses two separate keys. Each participant in an encrypted transaction has one private key, known only to that person, and one public key, which can be seen by anyone. The same key can't be used for both encryption and decryption. If you need to send me text, I can send you my public key, which you can use to encrypt the text, but only I will be able to decrypt it using my private key.

The advantage here is fewer keys to manage. But RSA requires lots of processing power, resulting in poor performance. So today, most encryped transactions use symmetric keys to encrypt and decrypt the text or transaction. But then that encrypted text is sent to the other party along with the secret key, which itself is encrypted and decrypted using asymmetric RSA encryption.

This combined method of encryption not only assures data privacy, it also enables an authentication mechanism called the *digital signature*. Any value encrypted using the sender's private key authenticates the sender. Any data decrypted using the recipient's private key authenticates the recipient.

Public keys are generally authenticated with *digital certificates*, which accompany transactions and are signed by a *certificate authority*. A certificate authority, officially linking a public key to the user, can exist in an organization using digital certificates internally and with trusted business partners. Netsacape and Xcert offer certificate servers for managing digital certificates. The certificate authority can also be a trusted party among a community of users, or it can be a larger, more public entity such as GTE, Nortel, or Verisign—well known for their stringent processes to verify identifies and assign digital certificates. X.509 is the most widely used industry standard for defining digital certificates. Digital certificates will be one of the primary security techniques used in the credit card and digital cash transactions common in electronic commerce. *Secure Sockets Layer* (*SSL*) is a transport-layer technology developed by Netscape to allow secure transactions between compliant browsers and servers—usually Web servers. The leading browsers from Microsoft and Netscape support SSL, as do many Web servers. SSL uses RSA digital signature algorithms and can use X.509 certificates and several secret key encryption algorithms such as DES and Triple DES.

Ultimately, encryption will become integrated in systems and networks. It will be built into IPv6, the next generation of IP, currently being developed by the IETF. On the hardware side, Intel is currently working on an encryption coprocessor for incorporation onto the motherboards of PCs and servers.

Encryption, which is a new form of Internet security, is used to send confidential information over the Internet or a network. Encryption came about because of the need to send credit card information and things of a confidential nature via the Internet. The three forms of encryption are **Pretty Good Privacy (PGP), Secure Hypertext Transfer Protocol (SHTTP),** and **Secured Socket Layers (SSL).**

22.15.6 Pretty Good Privacy (PGP)

PGP is freeware developed by Philip Zimmerman. The encryption device can be downloaded off the Internet. There is no charge for PGP for personal use but a charge for commercial use. This program requires an export license to be taken out of the United States. The theory behind PGP is that it turns a source message into incomprehensible patterns (encryption). This is used mostly for files and email and may be used on any platform around the world. Another aspect of PGP is that the user signs files with tamper proof signatures that assure that the message has come from a certain sender and not a fictitious one. There are two files associated with PGP. These two files are called unencrypted and encrypted. An unencrypted file is the actual message and the encrypted file is the incomprehensible pattern of the unencrypted message. A single key will decrypt the encrypted file (ciphertext) and turn in into the decrypted file (plaintext).

This is great for simple uses but when information is sent over a large network, like the Internet, public and private keys come into play. A private key is a secret key that only the user knows. A public key is a key that is public to the rest of the world. Both of the keys are mathematically related so that the public key encrypts and the private key decrypts the ciphertext. There is one downfall to a public and private key decoding. The downfall is that depending on the size of the chosen key and the size of the plaintext file, encrypting and decrypting can take a very long time. Another downfall is the lack of sponsorship by the federal government. The federal government will not support this encryption program because it works so well and is able to be used oversees since it is freeware.

22.15.7 Secured Hypertext Transfer Protocol (SHTTP)

Another form of encryption is SHTTP. SHTTP was chosen as the standard for Web-based encryption and authentication by members of the World Wide Web Consortium. It provides the current HTTP (Hyper Text Markup Language) Internet protocol with public key encryption, authentication, and digital signature over a World Wide Web server on the Internet. SHTTP also allows people to send secure data, signatures, and payments over the Internet. SHTTP is unlike other security methods in that it allows for flexibility in the use of different standards for payments methods. The last aspect of SHTTP is that there are different vendors selling this encryption program unlike PGP.

Secure HTTP (S-HTTP) provides secure communication mechanisms between an HTTP client-server pair in order to enable spontaneous commercial transactions for a wide range of applications. Our design intent is to provide a flexible protocol that supports multiple orthogonal operation modes, key management mechanisms, trust models, cryptographic algorithms and encapsulation formats through option negotiation between parties for each transaction.

Secure HTTP is a secure message-oriented communications protocol designed for use in conjunction with HTTP. It is designed to coexist with HTTP's messaging model and to be easily integrated with HTTP applications. Consequently, it mimics much of HTTP's style and syntax.

Secure HTTP provides a variety of security mechanisms to HTTP clients and servers, providing the security service options appropriate to the wide range of potential end uses possible for the World-Wide Web. The protocol provides symmetric capabilities to both client and server (in that equal treatment is given to both requests and replies, as well as for the preferences of both parties) while preserving the transaction model and implementation characteristics of HTTP.

Several cryptographic message format standards may be incorporated into S-HTTP clients and servers. S-HTTP supports interoperation among a variety of implementations, and is compatible with HTTP. S-HTTP aware clients can communicate with SHTTP oblivious servers and vice-versa, although such transactions obviously would not use S-HTTP security features.

S-HTTP does not required client-side public key certificates, as it supports symmetric key-only operation modes. This is significant because it means that spontaneous private transactions can occur without requiring individual users to have an established public key. While S-HTTP is able to take advantage of ubiquitous certification infrastructures, its deployment does not require it.

S-HTTP supports end-to-end secure transactions, in contrast with the original HTTP authorization mechanisms which require the client to attempt access and be denied before the security mechanism is employed. Clients may be 'primed' to nitiate a secure transaction (typically using information supplied in message headers); this may be used to support encryption of fill-out forms, for example. With S-HTTP, no sensitive data need ever be sent over the network in the clear.

S-HTTP provides full flexibility of cryptographic algorithms, modes and parameters. Option negotiation is used to allow clients and servers to agree on transaction modes (*e.g.*, should the request be signed or encrypted or both—similarly for the reply?); cryptographic algorithms (RSA vs. DSA for signing, DES vs. RC2 for encrypting, etc.); and certificate selection (please sign with your 'Blockbuster Video certificate').

22.15.8 Secured Socket Layer (SSL)

The last form of encryption is Secured Socket Layer (SSL). SSL is based on public key encryption. SSL is injected into Netscape Navigator and Windows 95. This encryption tool was developed by RSA Data Security Inc. This is the security protocol of choice in the industry. Microsoft has a product called Private Communication Technology that improves on SSL. There are flaws with Secured Socket Layers. Many of the flaws have occurred because of the wrong implementation of the right technology. Another flaw is that unlike the other two encryption programs, SSL must be licensed by Netscape Communications and is not compatible with non-Netscape products.

22.16 RSA = RIVEST-SHAMIR-ALDEMAN

Name for a cryptographic process developed by those three people. (Ronald Rivest, Adi Shamir and Leonard Adleman from MIT). This process uses a system named 'public key cryptography' because there are created two keys for protect the data. One key, the public key, is listed on a public catalog, and the another, the private key, that has a mathematical relation with the previous, remains on secrecy with the person. The two keys have a mathematical relation, but it is very difficult to derive one from the another (generally they are composed numbers formed by the product from two big prime numbers). When someone wants to send a secure message to this person, go through the catalog and uses the public key to cryptograph the message. Only the person with the private key can decypher the message. The system works like the trap-doors that are easy to open on one way but impossible to open on the opposite way. The multiplication function is a good example. Given two big prime numbers, it is easy multiply them and to obtain a result, but given the result, it is very difficult to know the prime components. Generally the public key is the product from two prime numbers, and the private key is one of them.

22.17 PAYMENT GATEWAYS

You may need authorisation to be made on-line:

- ❒ Because you are delivering the product immediately over the Internet.
- ❒ Because you want to bypass the manual effort of keying the information into your bank terminal.
- ❒ Because you want to protect yourself from fraud. Much credit card fraud happens at the merchant. If the credit card information is handled by the computer, the chance of in-house fraud is reduced.

Generally speaking, connecting your computer directly to the bank is a very expensive option. You can however go through a number of payment gateway services. There is a list of services on the Textor Webmasters Ltd Web site.

These services interface with your Web application in some way to create the link to the bank.

If you are using shopping cart software then it has to be interfaced to the gateway. For example we have interfaced our primary product (Shopsite) to a leading gateway service (DataCash). This is never going to be a straightforward thing to do and it is important that when signing up to a gateway service you are sure that they can interface to the software you need.

22.17.1 Form-based Services

If you are using a simple order form with no shopping cart then the form can possibly be handled by the gateway operation, eliminating the need for a secure server.

22.18 COMMERCE SERVICE PROVIDERS

The most complex type of service is called a Commerce Service Provider (CSP). A CSP offers a complete shopping cart and back-office environment which can be used by a catalogue running on their or another server. The CSP uses complex 'industry strength' software-of which the market leader is Transact, produced by Open Market.

The unique feature of Transact is that the product details can all be held on a catalogue Web site on a non-secure server. They do not have to be held in a product file on the secure server, but can just be built into the Web site. When the customer presses the order button, all the product details are passed to the shopping cart software at that time. What is more, they are passed in a fraud-resistant way guaranteed by security keys.

This has a number of important implications, and is one reason why Transact carries a six-figure price tag. One of these implications is that a company can offer Transact as a utility that can be tapped by merchants without requiring any sort of complex product file-maintenance operation. The merchant needs only a simple piece of software to create a security key against each product offering.

A further implication is that there is no real upper limit on the size of a catalogue, and because of the strong software involved there are no real transaction volume limits.

There are about four Transact-based CSPs in the UK today. Because of the significant investment required these are all major organisations.

Shopsite, offered by Textor Webmasters Ltd., is an Open Market product and an interface between Shopsite and Transact is promised. This gives merchants who purchase Shopsite a good expected upgrade path to Transact if the volume of business warrants or if they feel that a major support organisation is required.

22.19 PLANNING

Planning is an important part of this type of business, as it is with any business venture. We suggest three main stages to the process:

1. **Business Requirements:** Make sure you understand the market, and that you understand the business processes that you need to implement. Select a project manager and ensure that project disciplines are in place. Produce a first-cut budget.
2. **Technical Requirements:** Identify the technical requirements you will need to satisfy. Draw up short lists of products and services. Refine the budget.
3. **Selection/Procurement:** Finally, select the products and services you need to start the project.

It may seem obvious but it is important to procure products and services only after the business and technical investigations have been complete. Businesses that start by (for example) selecting a software product or a service provider before the business requirements are clear are in danger of not meeting those requirements.

22.20 MAJOR PROJECTS IN ELECTRONIC COMMUNICATION

Today, there are two distinct projects underway to continue the advancement of electronic communication. These are:

- ❐ Information Superhighway, and
- ❐ National Information Infrastructure

22.20.1 Information Superhighway

Ten years ago, the information superhighway could not have been built. Many of the core technologies essential to the convergence of computing and communications—a conjunction at the heart of the information superhighway—were simply not ready. The discoveries that initiated or made these technologies possible go back even further—before anyone dared to dream of a world in which scientists could collaborate across continents, in which every school could be connected to the great libraries and museums, and in which ordinary citizens could tap a wealth of digital services and entertainment from their homes.

The true origins of the information superhighway, in fact, include fundamental research on the physics of surfaces in the late 1940s that led to transistors, obscure university work on microwave oscillators in the early 1950s that led to lasers, and a speculative suggestion in an academic journal in the mid-1960s that led to optical fibers. Such research, if proposed today, would be hard to distinguish from hundreds of similar basic research proposals. Yet it produced the seeds of a revolutionary technology that is likely to transform homes and workplaces alike.

Consider one thread in this complex story, that of optical fibers. The idea that laser light could be transmitted over long distances in a glass fiber—and hence used for communications—can be traced to a 1966 article in a scientific journal. The first fibers were relatively crude; they broke easily and defects or impurities in the glass scattered or absorbed enough of the light signal that it couldn't travel very far. But basic research on the chemistry and thermodynamics of glass and on the scattering of light in liquids (glass can be thought of as a cooled liquid) led to steady improvements—purer glasses that reduced losses, for example, and epoxy coatings that made the fibers more flexible and resistant to corrosion. In 1970, Corning Glass Works demonstrated a fiber that could transmit a light signal with losses of only 1 percent per kilometer—a big advance at the time, but not good enough for commercial systems.

Today's fibers have losses of 100-fold less, reduced almost to the theoretical limit, and the result has been an explosion of optical communications. Optical fibers now carry most U.S. long-distance telecommunications and the total traffic over fibers is 1,000 times greater than a decade ago.

But the fiber story is far from finished. Fundamental research into the properties of rare earth elements, such as erbium, has led to a new wave of developments that are transforming fibers from passive to active devices with even greater carrying capacity. When fibers are doped with erbium and powered by a semiconductor laser, they can amplify an optical signal. Spliced directly into a fiber cable, these fiber amplifiers will soon begin to replace the regenerating stations that now detect, amplify, and retransmit optical communications signals every 30 to 100 kilometers. Since the comparatively slow electronic components of regenerating stations are the principal bottlenecks in today's long-distance networks, this change to an all-optical technology will increase the capacity of long-distance communications systems by as much as 100-fold.

The process is a continuing one. Just as commercial deployment of the information superhighway is harvesting earlier investments in the creation of basic knowledge, so the technologies of tomorrow and the commercial competitiveness that goes with them will stem from the science of today.

The **Information Superhighway** is a network that will connect every government agency, business, and citizen. The Information Superhighway is an unprecedented vision of a worldwide electronic communications network that will provide just about any sort of electronic communication imaginable.

The information superhighway provides a potential means of:

❒ Rapid access to information
❒ Electronic communications to every business and citizen
❒ An infrastructure for Electronic commerce.

This vision encompasses an infrastructure of computers, computer data banks, telephones, teleconferencing, document sharing, multimedia applications, and video displays. These devices are connected through highspeed, fiber optic cables capable of transmitting billion of bits of information per second. Some components of the Information Superhighway are already in use. The Internet is the closest infrastructure in existence to the Information Superhighway.

22.20.2 National Information Infrastructure

The National Information Infrastructure (NII) is composed of several components. It is an initiatives that combines communications, computer technologies, digitized information, and individual creativity. The US Administration's initiative to implement the NII is rapidly moving a head. The NII will lick offices, Factories, Libraries, Entertainment sources, Universities, Individuals and Home.

All Americans have a state in the construction of an advanced National Information Infrastructure. This seamless web of communications networks, computers, databases, and consumer electronics will put vast amounts of information at user's finger tips.

Development of the NII can help unleash an information revolution that will change forever the way people live, work, and interact with each other:

- People could live almost anywhere they wanted, without foregoing opportunities for useful and fulfilling employment, by 'telecommuting' to their offices through an electronic highway;
- The best schools, teachers, and courses would be available to all students, without regard to geography, distance, resources, or disability;
- Services that improve America's health care system and respond to other important social needs could be available online, without waiting in line, when and where you needed them.

Ultimately, the value of the NII will be gauged not by the complexity and sophistication of its engineering, but by how people use and benefit from it. Important applications of information technology will occur in areas such as;

- Education and Life-long Learning
- Electronic Commerce
- Environmental Monitoring and Natural Resource Management
- Government Services
- Health Care
- Libraries
- Manufacturing

22.20.2.1 Electronic Commerce Applications of the National Information Infrastructure

The vision of electronic commerce is to enable U.S. companies to increase productivity and adaptability to changing markets. Electronic commerce will provide an integrated collection of low-cost, reliable services to handle tremendous volumes of business and technical transactions and to amass, analyze, and control large quantities of data. Organizations will be able to improve efficiency and accuracy, and reduce costs, while providing faster, more reliable, and more convenient services. U.S. companies will be able to reengineer their business processes, and then use the National Information Infrastructure (NII) to realize the productivity potential of their current and future information technology investments. Smaller firms will be able to enter and participate at lower cost and with greater efficiency in new markets, and large firms will be able to evaluate, select, and more readily work with other companies. New ways of doing business and new forms of economic activities will become commonplace, including telecommuting, global sourcing arrangements, new training and education capabilities, and disaggregated alliances or networks of companies.

22.20.2.1.1 Benefits of Electronic Commerce Applications of the National Information Infrastructure

An advanced NII that supports Electronic Commerce applications will provide benefits in a number of areas:

- *Easier entry into new markets*, especially geographically remote markets, as the playing field becomes more level between companies of different size and locations;

- *Better quality of goods* as specifications are standardized and competition increases, and better variety of goods through expanded markets and the ability to produce customized goods;
- *Faster time to market* as business processes are linked enabling virtual elimination of time delays between steps and the engineering of each subprocess within the whole process for seemingly seamless processing;
- *Reduced time to complete business transactions*, particularly reduced time from delivery to payment;
- *Creation of new markets* through the ability to easily and cheaply reach potential customers;
- *Optimization of resource selection* as businesses quickly form cooperative teams to better tailor capabilities to work opportunities to increase chances of success, to share economic successes more broadly, and to given the customer a mix of capabilities more exactly meeting his requirements. Teaming may happen at either the company or individual level, creating a just-in-time 'virtual' resource for delivery of the right human and business resources for a job. In addition, the workforce can be better utilized by freeing skilled labor from routine activities enabling them to focus instead on customer service and more complex duties;
- *Reduced inventories and a related reduction of risk of obsolete inventories* as the demand for goods and services are electronically linked through just-in-time inventory and integrated manufacturing techniques;
- *Ability to undertake major national programs* such as national health care where the cost and personnel needed to manage a manual or disjoint automated system could be prohibitive or unreasonable;
- *Reduced costs to buyers* from increased competition in procurement as more suppliers are able to compete in an electronically open marketplace;
- *Reduced errors, time, and overhead costs in information processing* by eliminating requirements for re-entering data;
- *Reduced costs to suppliers* by electronically accessing on-line databases of bid opportunities, on-line abilities to submit bids, and on-line review of awards;
- *Reduced overhead costs* through uniformity, automation, and large-scale integration of management processes which enable flatter, wider, more efficient processes, and
- *Reduced use of ecologically damaging materials* through electronic coordination of activities and the movement of information rather than physical objects.

22.21 ELECTRONIC PAYMENTS

Electronic payments are services which allow business parties to pay directly or to debit accounts via telecommunication systems. This area is frequently called *Electronic Funds Transfer* (*EFT*), but that term is best reserved for credit transfers between banks where funds flow directly from one bank account to another. The earliest application of electronic payment systems, and the one most widely used, is the credit card which came into use during the 1950s. Because of the great potential advantages in eliminating physical payments, and the need to integrate payment schemes with electronic sales and other transaction processing applications, new forms of electronic payments are being tried throughout the world.

Electronic Payment technologies can be grouped into three broad application areas. The first involves *retailing payments*, the old familiar credit and charge cards that have been around for half a century. The second involves *Eelectronic banking* (*or e-banking*) applications such as *Electronic Funds Transfer* (*EFT*) and the familiar automated teller machines (ATM). To these familiar banking applications is a newer one which is often referred to as home banking. It provides users, working with a home computer attached by network to their bank, with the ability to authorize payments, reconcile accounts, and access a variety of other banking services. An example of a bank completely oriented to home banking is Security First Network Bank.

A third area of electronic payments involves direct payments between buyer and sellers. For example, in Europe, where credit cards are less widely accepted, *smart cards* can be purchased and used to directly pay for goods and services. Smart cards are used for a wide variety of services such as telephone calls, transportation, and vending machine sales. The wallet-sized cards are embedded with an electronic chip which manages the transactions and carries a value which can be reset. Consumers purchase the cards which are encoded with a certain value, subsequently, the amount is 'debited' until the value of the card is exhausted, at which time the card is recycled or the value reset by some means to add credit. These systems are sometimes referred to as 'electronic wallets' or 'electronic purses'.

Electronic cash systems, such as those provided by the Dutch from DigiCash, or the American based CyberCash permit transactions to be settled through the exchange of electronic cash, referred to as *e-cash*. *E-cash* is similar to smart card technology, but debit and credit typically involves using a customer bank account rather than a card that carries an embedded value.

Electronic checking services are also possible and becoming more popular; these systems *authenticate* the customer's identity and verifies with the bank that funds are available before allowing the purchase to be completed. An example is NetCheque, an electronic payment system for the Internet developed at the Information Sciences Institute of the University of Southern California. Users registered with NetCheque accounting servers are able to write *electronic checks* to other users. These e-checks may be sent through e-mail or as payment for services provided through other network protocols. When deposited, the e-check authorizes the transfer of account balances from the account against which the e-check was drawn to the account to which the check was deposited (Fig. 22.1).

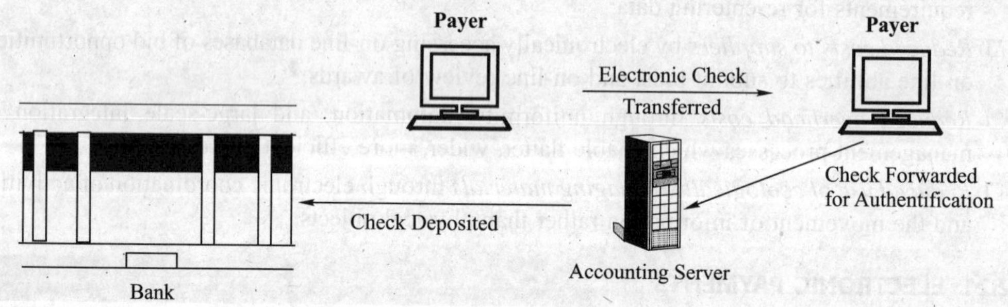

Fig. 22.1 Electronic Check Processing

The use of wide area networks to invoke transactions between an organizations suppliers and customers hightens the concerns about electronic security. These concerns are especially grave when dealing with electronic transfer of funds. Several multi-million dollar frauds concerning EFT have occurred. Furthermore, consumer confidence is dependent upon the public perception that transactions over networks are safe and reliable. Security concerns involve both accidental and deliberate misuses of electronic commerce applications and faculties. These problems are not different than the general concerns about computer and network security, but certainly can increase the magnitude of the problems. Providing public access to organizational computers and networks increases the vulnerability to 'hacker attacks'. Passwords are used to defeat this, but they can often be guessed or stolen. The issuing of passwords to individuals outside of the organization can be troublesome, and enforcing policies concerning the proper use of passwords is just about impossible.

Added to this basic concern about break-ins is the additional concern about detecting imposters who use another individual's identification to invoke a transaction or obtain a service. The passwords and IDs of users can often be easily obtained. Special software known as 'packet sniffers' can be run on networks nodes. As packets are broadcast over the network's transmission media, these sniffers intercept them, where they can be examined to see if they contain user IDs or passwords. Many organizations have adopted the *Kerbros* system which is designed to defeat such attempts.

In Electronic Commerce, one of the first lines of application defense against miscues is the installation of firewalls. Firewalls consists of specialized programs, usually running on dedicated servers, which are configured to examine and filter network traffic. *Proxy servers* are one popular type of firewall. Instead of actually letting the outside client have direct access to the network, the proxy server acts as an intermediary. Requests can be carefully examined, and the outsider never has an opportunity to directly use the internal computers attached to the company networks.

The foil imposters a variety of user *authentication* techniques have been devised. One such technique, endorsed by the federal government, is the *Digital Signature Algorithm* (*DSA*). This technique involves the encryption of a user supplied code, called a 'digital signature'. A problem with this technique is that it requires the sender to supply the key to their 'digital signature' so that it can be verified. It is possible for some other party to obtain the key when it is sent or stored elsewhere.

A more modern type of digital signature, called *public-key cryptography* is now commonly used in electronic commerce. It is a feature built in to many modern web browsers. This techniques uses a pair of keys to provide authentication of signatures. A secret key, known only to the sender, is used to encode the message. A 'public key' which can be given to everyone, is used to decode the message. The public key cannot decode the message unless it has been encoded by the secrete key. As long as the sender carefully guards the secret key, security is very good.

22.22 ELECTRONIC PAYMENT SYSTEMS

The World Wide Web (WWW) has opened up opportunities for commercial organisations to promote and sell their products and services using the Internet. As the Internet continues to transform commerce as we know it, the method of payment is one component which is critical to successfully conducting business across the network. Here we will discuss various **Electronic Payment Systems** available today.

If all that digital cash permits is the ability to trade and store dollars, francs, and other governmental units of account, then we have not come very far. Even the major card associations, such as Visa and MasterCard, are limited to clearing settling governmental units of account. For in an age of inflation and government ineptness, the value of what is being transacted and saved can be seriously devalued. Who wants a hard drive full of worthless 'cash'? True, this can happen in a privately-managed digital cash system, but at least then it is determined by the market and individuals have choices between multiple providers.

True digital cash as an enabling mechanism for electronic commerce depends upon the marriage of economics and cryptography. Independent academic advancement in either discipline alone will not facilitate what is needed for electronic commerce to flourish. There must be a synergy between the field of economics which emphasizes that the market will dictate the best monetary unit of value and cryptography which enhances individual privacy and security to the point of choosing between several monetary providers. It is money, the lifeblood of an economy, that ultimately symbolizes what commercial structure we operate within.

E-cash is our tip for what web-users will be talking about-and perhaps signing up to use-by this time next year.

It is too soon to tell which (if any) of the following products will become widely used. None of them yet provide a simple and elegant solution. Whichever persists, national governments are likely to be concerned about digital cash because they will fear that it makes tax collection harder and tax avoidance easier.

On the consumer side, there is also privacy to consider. Many types of digital cash do not allow anonymous transactions at all, although the user pays a heavy price in invasion of privacy. Others, like Digicash, allow the person paying, but not the receiver, to be anonymous. Even a scheme designed to allow direct peer-to-peer fund transfers, without the intermediation of an entity functioning as a bank, could be configured to keep records of every transaction; perhaps leading to a deluge of junk e-mail in your in-box, or a nasty letter from Customs asking you to pay duty on your imports.

Until large amounts of anonymous currencies or smart-cards are in wide circulation, and these are widely accepted for physical purchases as well as electronic commerce, the owners of electronic cash will need a means of first transferring funds from ordinary cash into electronic cash. The ultimate origin of this ordinary cash—the consumer's wage slip—is likely to remain a local process over which governments will still have punitive tax powers.

Even in Britain, 'a nation of shopkeepers', we are unlikely to see more than a small percentage of consumers becoming semi-pro online merchants or freelance professionals, offering niche goods or services worldwide through the internet, and being paid in untaxed e-cash directly into their offshore accounts. And even these people would need to change e-cash back into local pounds or ecus or dollars, at which point they could be taxed.

Yet the concept of merchant and consumer will inevitably change, we will see much more person-to-person buying, selling, swopping and bartering. The wild success of e-Bay and its imitators is proof of this. The use of the internet and e-cash to oil the wheels of such informal trading might also decrease the ability of a government to monitor some person-to-person transactions and to tax some consumer spending, unless all or almost all governments are able to agree on common worldwide rules. Whatever happens, e-cash will have implications for domestic tax regimes as some trade drifts to low-tax or no-tax locations.

While world governments fret about taxing or not taxing net commerce and e-cash (the US wants a six year moratorium, France wants full sales tax within months), it may be that government attitudes to cryptography will ultimately determine a nation's final share of the vast global e-commerce markets.

Unfortunately—while Ireland sensibly positions itself as a global 'freeport' for e-commerce by deregulating encryption (*i.e.*, the secret codes that you can use to wrap up your files so no-one else can read them)—the British government has been struggling to come to term with the need to deregulate cryptography as a precondition for e-commerce to grow.

22.23 DIGICASH

DigiCash are the leaders in the field, based in the Netherlands, offering truly secure encrypted e-cash. Their technology has been extensively tested and is already in use with The Mark Twain Bank. They have also signed deals with leading German and Australian banks. In 1996 they signed up Deustsche Bank, EUNet in Finland, and the largest banks in Norway and Austria. Beta software has been supplied to a major Australian bank, and Nomura Research in Japan has licenced DigiCash.

DigiCash holds all the patents, but have been incredibly reluctant to license them to others. This may hold them back from keeping their lead in the field. There were also some flaws in the e-cash transfer process.

November 1998, DigiCash collapses, but this might be good—it seems it will force them to open up licencing arrangements in order to generate revenue.

July 1999, DigiCash has been reverse-engineered by a start-up called eCache, who have developed their own client-side software. Led by CityCorp's R&D alumni Steve Shear, eCache says they will release the application from countries like South Africa if they can't get permission to launch officially in the USA.

DigiCash has debit (anonymous digital cash model, stored in PC, needed to be loaded from bank before shopping) facility only.

22.24 CYBERCASH

The CyberCash payment system which provides multiple means for users and merchants to move money on the Internet. One of the critical technologies that must be in place to enable electronic commerce is the ability to move funds between parties. Until now, the only means that has been available have required separate arrangements for payments or very limited use of credit cards. Some have attempted to introduce an integrated electronic mail with facilities for making credit payments within the context of the mail. Open Market, First Virtual and MCI are three examples. Others have attempted to define a more general scheme but have not yet been connected to the banking systems. The CyberCash system is a separate system which can be used by any user, any merchant, and any bank. Moreover, it is introducing a new form of payment, peer-to-peer, which permits individuals to pay each other without requiring the payee to be merchant authorized to accept credit cards.

22.24.1 Customer to Merchant Payments

CyberCash will provide two classes of payment services, customer to merchant and peer to peer. Customer to merchant payments include credit card and debt card. For customer to merchant payments, there are three parties connected to the Internet, the customer, the merchant and the Cyber Cash server. A customer will engage in a dialog with the merchant's web server, eventually arriving at a decision to buy some goods or services. All of the dialog related to the sale is under control of the merchant until it's time to make the payment. At that point, the merchant presents the user with the amount to be paid and a transaction identifier, and then turns control over to the CyberCash payment system.

The CyberCash payment system consists of 'CC user software' on the user's machine, 'CC merchant software' on the merchant's machine, and the CyberCash server (CC server). The user invokes the CC user software, provides his credit card information, and authorizes the sale for a specific amount. Using public key technology, the CC user software encrypts this information under the CC server's key and sends it to the merchant. The merchant thus has a message that it cannot read completely and cannot tamper with but which authorizes the purchase. The merchant adds his identification information and sends it to the CC server. The entire message is digitally signed by the merchant to prevent tampering in transit. The CC server unwraps the message and creates a standard credit card authorization request. The CC server then forwards the request to the appropriate bank or processing house for authorization and returns the result to the merchant.

This is the basic protocol, but there are a number of variations that can be accommodated. As noted, the credit card information is encrypted so the merchant cannot see it. This prevents handling errors such as unauthorized charges originating with the merchant, but some merchants may require the credit card information as part of their record keeping. If the merchant's bank authorizes the merchant to receive the credit card numbers, the CC server will forward the information back to the merchant with the authorization.

Not all transactions will take place via the web. Email and other forms of interaction are possible, and the same protocols are usable in those settings as well.

22.24.2 Peer to Peer Payments

CyberCash enables peer to peer payments between CyberCash account holders and from CyberCash account holders to others. CyberCash accounts are established by users on demand. A user who wishes to open a CyberCash account first obtains the CyberCash software for his machine and then contacts the CyberCash server. As part of this process, the user will generate a public/private key pair. The public key will be known to the CC server and will be identifier for his account. The private key will be known only to the user and will permit the user to sign the instructions he gives to the CyberCash server.

Once the user has opened a CyberCash account, he can 'load' his account by sending an instruction to move money out of his checking account. This instruction has to be digitally signed and accompanied by information which authenticates that the user legitimately has access to that checking account. The funds are then moved from the user's checking account to a CyberCash agency account in the same bank or another bank that is cooperating with the CyberCash service. At the same time, a notation is made on the CyberCash books that the user has those funds in his Cyber-Cash account.

Whenever the user desires to make a payment to another CyberCash account, the user sends the CyberCash server an instruction to do so. The CyberCash server checks that the funds exist in the account and that the instruction is not a duplicate. It then updates both accounts and issues a signed receipt back to the user. The user may then present the receipt to payee to demonstrate that the payment has been made. The receipt is signed by the CC server and can be checked for validity without interacting with the CC server. The payee may also contact the CC server and check the status of his account.

Whenever the user desires to move the money out of his CyberCash account, he sends an instruction to the CC server and the funds are moved out of the CyberCash account into the user's checking account. These funds are then available for any kind transaction, including disbursement in cash.

22.24.3 Security

Security is obviously paramount in this operation. As noted above, public key technology is used, in combination with symmetric algorithms and hash algorithms, to protect the messages in transit and authenticate origins. The public key algorithm is RSA, the symmetric algorithm is DES, and the hash is MD5.

Two other aspects of security are also important. The user must be certain he is using a true copy of the CyberCash code. To provide assurance to the user that he is not using modified code, a third party verification service will be available which provides certificates which convey the correct hash code for the software. Routines which check the hash code will be available from a variety of sources and will be well documented.

Protection of the user's private key is also paramount. User software will keep the user's private key encrypted and available only with a local password. Stron local protection of the password does not protect against loss of a private key, however, and a separate facility is needed in case the user loses access to his private key.

To solve this problem, users will be encouraged to make use of third party data recovery centers will can store encrypted information and make it available only upon successfully completing an interrogatory which had been provided by the user when the data was originally stored.

22.25 SMART CARD

A prepaid smart card contains stored value which the person holding it can spend at retailers. After accepting stored value from cards, retailers are periodically reimbursed with actual money by system providers. A system provider receives money in advance from people and stores corresponding value onto their cards. During each of these three kinds of transactions, secured data representing value is exchanged for actual money or for goods and services.

22.25.1 Card Types

There are in essence only four types of microcircuit card that have been suggested for use in prepaid applications, each based on a particular kind of chip. They are listed here in historical order.

(*i*) **Memory Cards:** The chip in these cards consists only of storage and a little extra hardware that prevents access to the stored data unless certain stored passwords or PINs are input correctly. Most telephone cards are of this type.

(*ii*) **Shared-key Cards:** Secret keys in the chip let the card authenticate its communication with any device sharing the same keys. The chips are standard microcontroller card chips, with masked-in software for the cryptographic authentication algorithms.

(*iii*) **Signature-transporting Cards:** The same chip hardware as in shared-key cards is used, but with different software masked-in. The card stores publicly-verifiable digital signatures created by the system provider and fills them in like blank checks when spending them.

(*iv*) **Signature-creating Cards:** These chips also contain a microcontroller, but in combination with a dedicated co-processor capable of making digital signatures. Instead of spending signatures created by the system provider, they create their own.

22.25.2 Closed or Open Security

Memory cards are suitable only for closed systems where a single company issues the cards and accepts them as payment for goods and services, or for systems with very low fraud incentive. The reason is that defrauding such systems requires only a small computer interposed between an actual card and a cash register. The computer merely has to record the secrets communicated during an initial transaction and can then, as often as desired, be used to play the role of a card having the initial balance.

Shared-key card systems require a tamper-resistant secured module in each vending machine or other point of payment. The module uses the key it shares with a card to authenticate messages during purchases. This lets the card convince the module that it has reduced its stored value by the correct amount and that it is genuine. A card convinces by using the shared key to encrypt a random challenge issued by the module together with an amount, so that the module can decrypt the transmission and compare the result with the expected challenge and amount. Periodically, the module transmits a similarly authenticated message, via telecommunication or manual collection procedure, back to the system provider, who reimburses the retailer.

The secured module in a shared-key system thus needs to store or at least be able to re-create secrete keys of all cards, which gives some problems. If the cards of multiple system providers are to be accepted at the same retailers, all the retailers must have secured modules containing keys of every provider. This means either a mutually trusted module containing the keys of multiple providers, which might be hard to achieve, or one module per provider, which becomes impractical as the number of providers grows. Furthermore, in any shared-key system, if a module is penetrated, not only is significant retailer fraud facilitated, but the entire card base may be compromised.

Signature-transporting and creating card types avoid these problems since they do not require secured modules. Cash registers need no secrete keys, only public ones, in order to authenticate the signatures, which act like guaranteed checks filled in with all the relevant details. These same signatures can later be verified by the system provider for reimbursement. (Although tamper-resistant modules are not needed for verification, they can still be used to aggregate transactions.) Both signature-based card types also allow the cards of any number of issuers to be accepted at all retailers, retailers cannot cheat issuers, and issuers cannot cheat each other. These are the only truly open systems.

22.25.3 Privacy

All cards, except the signature-transporting type, uniquely identify themselves in each transaction. This means that even if the card does not reveal the persons identity, all payments a person makes are linked together by the card identity. As a consequence, if a reload or any one of the payments made by a person is traced to that person, then they all are.

The reason for identification of shared-key cards is that security is thought to be too low if all cards have the master key. Therefore cards are given unique keys, and the cash register needs the card identity each time to re-create the corresponding unique card key from the master key.

The signature-transporting approach avoids the need for identification, since instead of a single key per card, cards use a different signature per payment. When signatures are made by the system provider on blinded checks that are then unblinded by the card, not even the system provider can trace payment to cards.

22.25.4 Card Costs

The overall cost of cards for a system is determined not only by how much each card costs, but also by how long cards last and how much of each card is needed. Nonrefillable memory cards have a very limited card lifetime and are suitable only for a single purpose. But microcontroller cards can last years and are flexible enough to handle a variety of things, not limited to stored value, thereby allowing sharing of card cost among multiple applications.

Bonding chips into modules, assembling them into cards, and printing can cost about the same for all card types, roughly US$ 0.50, 2.00 (plus the cost of the small fraction of chips that are damaged during production). Nonrefillable cards, however, typically use less durable materials and less costly production techniques.

Memory card chips are much smaller, and consequently much less expensive to produce, than those in microcontroller cards. They cost, depending on the type, roughly between US$ 0.10, 0.40 in quantity. Shared-key and signature-transporting cards today use exactly the same chip hardware, only the masked-in software differs. Suitable chips cost about US$ 1.00, 1.20 in quantity. Signature-creating card chips, which need extra circuitry for the co-processor (or a very powerful processor), require more on a chip, are relatively new on the market, and currently cost several times more.

22.25.5 Non-Card Costs

Apart from cards themselves, the other main system costs are card issuing and refilling, retailer equipment, and system provider processing and security measures.

If cards are issued with value on them, as is of course required with nonrefillable memory cards, then they must be transported, stored, and dispensed, using costly security and audit provisions, like those associated with bank notes. Refillable cards can be distributed without value and avoid these costs, but on the other hand require infrastructure for on-line reload transactions with system providers.

Retailer equipment costs may be higher than card costs. Typical ratios of cards to points of sale (about 100 to 1 for cash registers and higher with vending, phones, etc.) and even the price of current terminals (about US$ 150, 1500) suggest that the point-of-sale equipment can be more costly than even a dedicated microcontroller card base.

In the shared-key approach, secured modules trusted by all system providers must be installed in all retailer equipment. In open systems such security modules must be significantly more elaborate and costly than any card, since the security offered by a card is generally considered inadequate to protect the keys of all other cards. But the higher cost of terminals incorporating such modules is at odds with the objective of automating all manner of low value payments, such as in vending. Transaction processing by the system providers also requires tamper-resistant devices. Proper management of keys and auditing of such systems are cumbersome and expensive. If shared-key systems grow, and start to include less trustworthy retailers and more system providers, even the minimum security necessary becomes excessively costly.

With either signature card type, suitable software not tamper-resistant modules is all retailer equipment needs in order to verify payments and later forward the signatures for reimbursement. These can then be verified by any transaction processing computer that has copies of the freely available public keys, thereby reducing exposure while both increasing the quality and reducing the cost of security audit and controls.

22.26 SOCIAL AND ETHICAL ISSUES SURROUNDING ELECTRONIC COMMERCE

Ethical and policy issues include tracking and using information about consumer transactions, corporate espionage, and commercial offerings which are offensive to various communities. Complex legal issues are also raised concerning tax avoidance schemes, money laundering and unauthorized creation of money. While these illegal practices are not specifically limited to electronic commerce, the existence of electronic cash flows provides new opportunities for dishonesty.

Modern computer technology allows organizations to gather extensive data on the purchasing behavior of consumers. Electronic commerce greatly enhances that ability to gather *corporate intelligence*. It is possible for business to share such information, or for private companies to buy and manage such consumer data. Software can then be used to examinc that data and build profiles on these consumers based upon their purchasing patterns. Is this activity ethical? Should it be legal? These are matters of public policy and debate.

Companies can also use communications technologies to monitor the activities of other businesses. Corporate espionage is not new, it has been going on for centuries. Often, there is no clear distinction between legal *corporate intelligence* gathering and illegal espionage activity. The ability to spy on commercial transactions conducted over networks has greatly increased the scope of surveillance. Even the simple act of visiting a web site can help businesses to collect data on the visitor, who may be required to register or who may have a *cookie* inserted in a special file on their computer. A cookie is a record which can contain information concerning the client's web browsing activity. This record can be requested by the web server on subsequent visits to be checked and used to maintain information on the client's activity. Furthermore, governments can also engage in this activity for a variety of purposes. The extent to which such clandestine activity is not known, but some believe it to be considerable. There is debate over when such activity is unethical or should be made illegal.

Ethics involve community standards of acceptable behavior. Electronic commerce links diverse communities of great national and cultural differences; what seems ethical to one community may be deemed unethical in another. A serious concern to electronic commerce is the availability of goods or services over networks which are acceptable in the physical location of the company offering these services but not acceptable, or perhaps even illegal, at the location in which these services are consumed. The sale of medicines, foods, and other products which may be prohibited locally are possible through electronic means, then delivered through conventional means. Gambling and offering of sexually explicity materials are just two types of socially objectionable commercial services which may involve offering electronic versions of copyrighted materials without permission or payment of royalties. The ethical, legal, and policy issues involving electronic commerce are complex and will be the subject of public debate for a long, long time.

22.27 HOW WOULD YOU LIKE TO PAY?

Most online shoppers use credit cards to pay for their online purchases. But debit cards—which authorize merchants to debit your bank account electronically are increasing in use. Your debit card may be an automated teller machine (ATM) card that can be used for retail purchases. To complete a debit card transaction, you may have to use a personal identification number (PIN), some form of a signature or other identification, or a combination of these identifiers. Some cards have both credit and debit features: You select the payment option at the point-of-sale. But remember, although a debit card may look like a credit card, the money for debit purchases is transferred almost immediately from your bank account to the merchant's account. In addition, your liability limits for a lost or stolen debit card and unauthorized use are different from your liability if your credit card is lost, stolen or used without your authorization.

Other electronic payment systems—sometimes referred to as 'electronic money' or 'e-money'—also are now common. Their goal is to make purchasing simpler. For example, 'stored-value' cards let you transfer cash value to a card. They're commonly used on public transportation, at colleges and universities, at gas stations, and for prepaid telephone use. Many retailers also sell stored-value cards in place of gift certificates. Some stored-value cards work offline, say, to buy a candy bar at a vending machine; others work online, for example, to buy an item from a website; some have both offline and online features. Some cards can be 'reloaded' with additional value, at a cash machine; other cards are 'disposable'—you throw them away after you use all their value. Some stored-value cards contain computer chips that make them 'smart' cards: These cards may act like a credit card as well as a debit card, and also may contain stored value.

Some Internet-based payment systems allow value to be transmitted through computers, sometimes called 'e-wallets.' You can use 'e-wallets' to make 'micro payments'—very small online or offline payments for things like a magazine or fast food. When you buy something using your e-wallet, the balance on your online account decreases by that amount. 'E-wallets' may work by using some form of stored value or by automatically accessing an account you've set up through a computer system connected to your credit or debit card account.

22.28 'PAYING' IT SAFE

The FTC encourages you to take steps to make sure your transactions are secure and your personal information is protected. Although you can't control fraud or deception on the Internet, you can take action to recognize it, avoid it and report it. Here's how.

- **Use a secure browser:** Software that encrypts or scrambles the purchase information you send over the Internet-to help guard the security of your information as it is transmitted to a website. Be sure your browser has the post up-to-date encryption capabilities by using the latest version available from the manufacturer. You also can download some browsers for free over the Internet. When submitting your purchase information, look for the 'lock' icon on the browser's status bar, and the phrase 'https' in the URL address for a website, to be sure your information is secure during transmission.
- **Check the site's privacy policy**, before you provide any personal financial information to a website. In particular, determine how the information will be used or shared with others. Also check the site's statements about the security provided for your information. Some websites' disclosures are easier to find than others-look at the bottom of the home page, on

order forms or in the 'About' or 'FAQs' section of a site. If you're not comfortable with the policy, consider doing business elsewhere.

- **Read and understand the refund and shipping policies** of a website you visit, before you make your purchase. Look closely at disclosures about the website's refund and shipping policies. Again, search through the website for these disclosures.
- **Keep your personal information private:** Don't disclose your personal information, your address, telephone number, Social Security number, bank account number or e-mail address—unless you know who's collecting the information, why they're collecting it and how they'll use it.
- **Give payment information only to businesses you know and trust**, and only when and where it is appropriate—like an order form. Never give your password to anyone online, even your Internet service provider. Do not download files sent to you by strangers or click on hyperlinks from people you don't know. Opening a file could expose your system to a computer virus or a program that could hijack your modem.
- **Keep records of your online transactions and check your e-mail** for contacts by merchants with whom you're doing business. Merchants may send you important information about your purchases.
- **Review your monthly credit card and bank statements** for any errors or unauthorized purchases promptly and thoroughly. Notify your credit or debit card issuer immediately if your credit or debit card or checkbook is lost or stolen, or if you suspect someone is using your accounts without your permission.

22.29 REPORT PROBLEMS IMMEDIATELY

The Fair Credit Billing Act (FCBA) and Electronic Fund Transfer Act (EFTA) establish protections against lost or stolen credit or debit cards, and procedures for resolving errors on credit and bank account statements that can include:

- credit charges or electronic fund transfers that you-or anyone you've authorized to use your account-have not made;
- credit charges or electronic fund transfers that are incorrectly identified or show the wrong amount or date;
- computation or similar errors;
- a failure to properly reflect payments or credits, or electronic fund transfers;
- not mailing or delivering credit billing statements to your current address, as long as that address was received by the creditor in writing at least 20 days before the billing period ended; and
- credit charges or electronic fund transfers for which you request an explanation or documentation, because of a possible error.

For credit: The FCBA generally applies to 'open end' credit accounts-that is, credit cards and revolving charge accounts, like department store accounts. It does not apply to loans or credit sales that are paid according to a fixed schedule until the entire amount is paid back, like an automobile loan.

Lost or stolen credit cards: Under the FCBA, your liability for lost or stolen credit cards is limited to $50. If the loss involves only your credit card number (not the card itself), you have no liability for unauthorized use. It's best to notify your card issuer promptly upon discovering the loss. Many companies have toll-free numbers and 24-hour service to deal with such emergencies. Always follow up with a letter and keep a copy for your records.

Billing errors: The FCBA's settlement procedures apply to disputes about 'billing errors' for open-end accounts, including unauthorized charges (you cannot be liable for more than $50 for unauthorized credit charges); charges for goods or services you didn't accept or weren't delivered as agreed; charges that are incorrectly identified or show the wrong amount or date; math errors; a failure to properly reflect payments or credits; not mailing or delivering credit billing statements to your current address, if the address was received by the creditor in writing at least 20 days before the billing period ended; and charges for which you request an explanation or documentation, because of a possible error.

To take advantage of the FCBA's consumer protections for errors on your account, write to the creditor at the address given for 'billing inquiries,' not the address for sending your payments. Include your name, address, account number and a description of the billing error. Send your letter so that it reaches the creditor within 60 days after the first bill containing the error was mailed to you. And if you send your letter by certified mail, return receipt requested, you'll have proof that the creditor received it. Include copies (not originals) of sales slips or other documents that support your position. Keep a copy of your dispute letter.

The creditor must acknowledge your dispute in writing within 30 days after it is received, unless the problem is resolved within that period. The creditor must conduct an investigation and either correct the mistake or explain why the bill is believed to be correct, within two billing cycles (but not more than 90 days), unless the creditor provides a permanent credit instead. You may withhold payment of the amount in dispute and any related finance charges and the creditor may not take any action to collect that amount during the dispute.

For debit: The EFTA applies to electronic fund transfers-transactions involving automated teller machines (ATMs), debit cards and other point-of-sale debit transactions, and other electronic banking transactions that can result in the withdrawal of cash from your bank account.

Lost or stolen debit cards: If someone uses your debit card, or makes other electronic fund transfers, without your permission, you can lose from $50 to $500 or more, depending on when you report the loss or theft. If you report the loss within two business days after you discover the problem, you will not be responsible for more than $50 for unauthorized use. However, if you do not report the loss within two business days after you realize the card is missing, but you do report its loss within 60 days after your statement is mailed to you, you could lose as much as $500 because of an unauthorized withdrawal. And, if you do not report an unauthorized transfer or withdrawal within 60 days after your statement is mailed to you, you risk unlimited loss. That means you could lose all the money in your account and the unused portion of your maximum line of credit established for overdrafts.

Some financial institutions may voluntarily cap your liability at $50 for certain types of transactions, regardless of when you report the loss or theft; because this is voluntary, their policies could change at any time. Ask your financial institution about its liability limits.

EFT errors: The EFTA's error procedures apply to certain problems. This can include:

- Electronic fund transfers that you-or anyone you've authorized to use your account-have not made;
- Incorrect electronic fund transfers;
- Omitted electronic fund transfers;
- A failure to properly reflect electronic fund transfers; and
- Electronic fund transfers for which you request an explanation or documentation, because of a possible error.

To take advantage of the EFTA's error resolution procedures, you must notify your financial institution of the problem not later than 60 days after the statement containing the problem or error was sent. Although most financial institutions have a toll-free number to report the problem, you should follow-up in writing. For retail purchases, your financial institution has up to 10 business days to investigate after receiving your notice of the error. The financial institution must tell you the results of its investigation within three business days of completing its investigation. The error must be corrected within one business day after determining the error has occurred. If the institution needs more time, it may take up to 90 days, in many situations, to complete the investigation-but only if it returns the money in dispute to your account within 10 business days after receiving notice of the error, while it reviews your concerns.

For stored-value: The FCBA and the EFTA may not cover stored-value cards or transactions involving them, so you may not be covered for loss or misuse of the card. However, stored-value cards still might be useful for micropayments and other small purchases online because they can be convenient and-in some cases-offer anonymity. Before you buy a stored-value card or other form of e-money, ask the issuer for written information about the product's features. Find out the card's dollar limit, whether it is reloadable or disposable, if there's an expiration date, and any fees to use, reload or redeem (return it for a refund) the product. At the same time, ask about your rights and responsibilities. For example, does the issuer offer any protection in the case of a lost, stolen, misused, or malfunctioning card, and who do you call if you have a question or problem with the card?

22.30 ELECTRONIC BANKING

For many consumers, electronic banking means 24-hour access to cash through an automated teller machine (ATM) or Direct Deposit of paychecks into checking or savings accounts. But electronic banking now involves many different types of transactions.

Electronic banking, also known as electronic fund transfer (EFT), uses computer and electronic technology as a substitute for checks and other paper transactions. EFTs are initiated through devices like cards or codes that let you, or those you authorize, access your account. Many financial institutions use ATM or debit cards and Personal Identification Numbers (PINs) for this purpose. Some use other forms of debit cards such as those that require, at the most, your signature or a scan. The federal Electronic Fund Transfer Act (EFT Act) covers some electronic consumer transactions.

22.30.1 Electronic Fund Transfers

EFT offers several services that consumers may find practical:

- **Automated Teller Machines or 24-hour Tellers** are electronic terminals that let you bank almost any time. To withdraw cash, make deposits, or transfer funds between accounts, you generally insert an ATM card and enter your PIN. Some financial institutions and ATM owners charge a fee, particularly to consumers who don't have accounts with them or on transactions at remote locations. Generally, ATMs must tell you they charge a fee and its amount on or at the terminal screen before you complete the transaction. Check the rules of your institution and ATMs you use to find out when or whether a fee is charged.
- **Direct Deposit** lets you authorize specific deposits, such as paychecks and Social Security checks, to your account on a regular basis. You also may pre-authorize direct withdrawals so that recurring bills, such as insurance premiums, mortgages, and utility bills, are paid automatically.
- **Pay-by-Phone Systems** let you call your financial institution with instructions to pay certain bills or to transfer funds between accounts. You must have an agreement with the institution to make such transfers.
- **Personal Computer Banking** lets you handle many banking transactions via your personal computer. For instance, you may use your computer to view your account balance, request transfers between accounts, and pay bills electronically.

- **Point-of-Sale Transfers** let you pay for purchases with a debit card, which also may be your ATM card. The process is similar to using a credit card, with some important exceptions. While the process is fast and easy, a debit card purchase transfers money-fairly quickly-from your bank account to the store's account. So it's important that you have funds in your account to cover your purchase. This means you need to keep accurate records of the dates and amounts of your debit card purchases and ATM withdrawals in addition to any checks you write. Your liability for unauthorized use, and your rights for error resolution, may differ with a debit card.
- **Electronic Check Conversion** converts a paper check into an electronic payment at the point of sale or elsewhere, such as when a company receives your check in the mail. In a store, when you give your check to a store cashier, the check is processed through an electronic system that captures your banking information and the amount of the check. Once the check is processed, you're asked to sign a receipt authorizing the merchant to present the check to your bank electronically and deposit the funds into the merchant's account. You get a receipt of the electronic transaction for your records. When your check has been processed and returned to you by the merchant, it should be voided or marked by the merchant so that it can't be used again. In the mail-in situation, you should still receive advance notice from a company that expects to process your check electronically.

Be especially careful in telephone transactions, which also could involve e-checks. A legitimate merchant should explain the process and answer any questions you may have. The merchant also should ask for your permission to debit your account for the item you're purchasing or paying on. However, because telephone e-checks don't occur face-to-face, you should be cautious with whom you reveal your bank or checking account information. Don't give this information to sellers with whom you have no prior experience or with whom you have not initiated the call, or to sellers who seem reluctant to discuss the process with you. Not all electronic fund transfers are covered by the EFT Act. For example, some financial institutions and merchants issue cards with cash value stored electronically on the card itself. Examples include prepaid telephone cards, mass transit passes, and some gift cards. These 'stored-value' cards, as well as transactions using them, may not be covered by the EFT Act. This means you may not be covered for the loss or misuse of the card. Ask your financial institution or merchant about any protections offered for these cards.

22.30.2 Disclosures

To understand your legal rights and responsibilities regarding your EFT account, read the documents you receive from the financial institution that issued your 'access device.' That is, a card, code or other means of accessing your account to initiate electronic fund transfers. Although the means varies by institution, it often involves a card and/or a PIN. No one should know your PIN except you and select employees of the financial institution.

Before you contract for EFT services or make your first electronic transfer, the institution must tell you the following information in a form you can keep.

- A summary of your liability for unauthorized transfers.
- The telephone number and address of the person to be notified if you think an unauthorized transfer has been or may be made, a statement of the institution's 'business days' (which is, generally, the days the institution is open to the public for normal business), and the number of days you have to report suspected unauthorized transfers.
- The type of transfers you can make, fees for transfers, and any limits on the frequency and dollar amount of transfers.
- A summary of your right to receive documentation of transfers, to stop payment on a pre-authorized transfer, and the procedures to follow to stop payment.

- ❐ A notice describing the procedures you must follow to report an error on a receipt for an EFT or your periodic statement, to request more information about a transfer listed on your statement, and how long you have to make your report.
- ❐ A summary of the institution's liability to you if it fails to make or stop certain transactions.
- ❐ Circumstances under which the institution will disclose information to third parties concerning your account.
- ❐ A notice that you may be charged a fee by ATMs where you don't have an account.

In addition to these disclosures, you will receive two other types of information for most transactions: terminal receipts and periodic statements. Separate rules apply to passbook accounts from which pre-authorized transfers are drawn. The best source of information about those rules is your contract with the financial institution for that account. You're entitled to a terminal receipt each time you initiate an electronic transfer, whether you use an ATM or make a point-of-sale electronic transfer. The receipt must show the amount and date of the transfer, and its type, such as 'from savings to checking.' When you make a point-of-sale transfer, you'll probably get your terminal receipt from the salesperson.

You won't get a terminal receipt for regularly occurring electronic payments that you've pre-authorized, like insurance premiums, mortgages, or utility bills. Instead, these transfers will appear on your periodic statement. If the pre-authorized payments vary, however, you should receive a notice of the amount that will be debited at least 10 days before the debit takes place.

You're also entitled to a periodic statement for each statement cycle in which an electronic transfer is made. The statement must show the amount of any transfer, the date it was credited or debited to your account, the type of transfer and type of account(s) to or from which funds were transferred, and the address and telephone number for inquiries. You're entitled to a quarterly statement whether or not electronic transfers were made.

Keep and compare your EFT receipts with your periodic statements the same way you compare your credit card receipts with your monthly credit card statement. This will help you make the best use of your rights under federal law to dispute errors and avoid liability for unauthorized transfers.

22.30.3 Errors

You have 60 days from the date a periodic statement containing a problem or error was sent to you to notify your financial institution. The best way to protect yourself if an error occurs-including erroneous charges or withdrawals from an account, or for a lost or stolen ATM or debit card-is to notify the financial institution by certified letter, return receipt requested, so you can prove that the institution received your letter. Keep a copy of the letter for your records.

If you fail to notify the institution of the error within 60 days, you may have little recourse. Under federal law, the institution has no obligation to conduct an investigation if you've missed the 60-day deadline.

Once you've notified the financial institution about an error on your statement, it has 10 business days to investigate. The institution must tell you the results of its investigation within three business days after completing it and must correct an error within one business day after determining that the error has occurred. If the institution needs more time, it may take up to 45 days, in most situations, to complete the investigation-but only if the money in dispute is returned to your account and you're notified promptly of the credit. At the end of the investigation, if no error has been found, the institution may take the money back if it sends you a written explanation.

An error also may occur in connection with a point-of-sale purchase with a debit card. For example, an oil company might give you a debit card that lets you pay for gas purchases directly from your bank account. Or you may have a debit card that can be used for various types of retail purchases. These purchases will appear on your periodic statement from the bank. In case of an error on your account, however, you should contact the card issuer (for example, an oil company or a bank) at the address or phone number provided by the company. Once you've notified the company about the error, it has 10 business days to investigate and tell you the results. In this situation, it may take up to 90 days to complete an investigation. If no error is found at the end of the investigation, the institution may take back the money if it sends you a written explanation.

22.30.4 Lost or Stolen ATM or Debit Cards

If your credit card is lost or stolen, you can't lose more than $50. If someone uses your ATM or debit card without your permission, you can lose much more.

If you report an ATM or debit card missing to the card issuer before it's used without your permission, you can't be held responsible for any unauthorized withdrawals.

If unauthorized use occurs before you report it, the amount you can be held responsible for depends upon how quickly you report the loss to the card issuer.

- ❒ If you report the loss within two business days after you realize your card is missing, you won't be responsible for more than $50 for unauthorized use.
- ❒ If you fail to report the loss within two business days after you realize the card is missing, but do report its loss within 60 days after your statement is mailed to you, you could lose as much as $500 because of an unauthorized transfer.
- ❒ If you fail to report an unauthorized transfer within 60 days after your statement is mailed to you, you risk unlimited loss. That means you could lose all the money in your account and the unused portion of your maximum line of credit established for overdrafts.

If you failed to notify the institution within the time periods allowed because of an extenuating circumstance, such as lengthy travel or illness, the issuer must reasonably extend the notification period. In addition, if state law or your contract imposes lower liability limits, those lower limits apply instead of the limits in the federal EFT Act.

Once you report the loss or theft of your ATM or debit card, you're no longer responsible for additional unauthorized transfers occurring after that time. Because these unauthorized transfers may appear on your statements, however, you should carefully review each statement you receive after you've reported the loss or theft. If the statement shows transfers that you did not make or that you need more information about, contact the institution immediately, using the special procedures provided for reporting errors.

22.30.5 Limited Stop-Payment Privileges

When you use an electronic fund transfer, the EFT Act does not give you the right to stop payment. If your purchase is defective or your order is not delivered, it's as if you paid cash. That is, it's up to you to resolve the problem with the seller and get your money back.

There is one situation, however, when you can stop payment. If you've arranged for regular payments out of your account to third parties, such as insurance companies, you can stop payment if you notify your institution at least three business days before the scheduled transfer. The notice may be oral or written, but the institution may require a written follow-up within 14 days of the oral notice. If you fail to provide the written follow-up, the institution's responsibility to stop payment ends.

Although federal law provides only limited rights to stop payment, individual financial institutions may offer more rights or state laws may require them. If this feature is important to you, you may want to shop around to be sure you're getting the best 'stop-payment' terms available.

22.30.6 Other Rights

The EFT Act protects your right of choice in two specific situations regarding use of electronic fund transfers: First, the Act prohibits financial institutions from requiring you to repay a loan by electronic transfer. Second, if you're required to receive your salary or government benefit check by EFT, you have the right to choose your institution.

22.30.7 Suggestions

If you decide to use EFT, keep these tips in mind:

- ❒ Take care of your ATM or debit card. Know where it is at all times; if you lose it, report it as soon as possible.
- ❒ Choose a PIN for your ATM or debit card that's different from your address, telephone number, Social Security number, or birthdate. This will make it more difficult for a thief to use your card.
- ❒ Keep and compare your receipts for all types of EFT transactions with your periodic statements. That way, you can find errors or unauthorized transfers and report them.
- ❒ Make sure you know and trust a merchant before you share any bank account information or pre-authorize debits to your account. Be aware that some merchants use electronic processing of your check if you sign a receipt authorizing the transaction.

22.30.8 Where to File Complaints

If you think a financial institution or company has failed to fulfill its responsibilities to you under the EFT Act, speak up. In addition, you may wish to complain to the federal agency that has enforcement jurisdiction over that company.

22.31 EXAMPLES OF TODAY'S E-COMMERCE

We developed a number of examples of today's electronic commerce, with no effort to be inclusive or to weigh significance, in an effort to assure that we had analyzed the important interactions.

22.31.1 Transaction Processing Systems

The most frequent implementation of transaction processing systems has been within an enterprise. However, some enterprise have established external access to their transaction processing systems. Some well-known applications include:

- ❒ airline reservation systems
- ❒ order processing, and
- ❒ stock trading
- ❒ insurance

Variations of this type of processing include credit/debit card verification at the point of purchase and automatically triggered or independent transaction processing after verification.

22.31.2 Facsimile

The standardization of Fax protocols has enabled Fax communications to become a popular means of electronic commerce. The range of transactions is broad and increasing. A few of the many Fax transactions are:

- ❒ correspondence,
- ❒ orders, and
- ❒ confirmations

As the cost of Fax machines have decreased, some of the more novel or suggestive applications are:

- ❐ ordering food from restaurants,
- ❐ catalogue ordering,
- ❐ computer-faxed data
- ❐ grocery lists,
- ❐ fax-back on demand, and

Additional examples enter our business culture and even our language on an almost daily basis.

22.31.3 Commerce at Home

Home-initiated electronic transactions are beginning to appear and much experimentation is being done to test consumer acceptance and develop cost points. Acceptance remains fairly low but this probably reflects the quality and usability of the specific services and the still-nascent ubiquity of the technology in the home.

Video on demand is frequently referenced as a prototypical electronic transaction that will be used in the home. When the infrastructure required for this will be widely available is subject to speculation. The ability of the content providers and carriers to deliver movies on demand at a price acceptable to the computer is also unclear.

The next generation of connection to the home is often expected to depend on the deployment of 'set-top boxes' which terminate the high-bandwidth connection and which deliver some measure of function to the home without personal computers. Considerable debate currently rages over standards and ownership of set-top boxes.

Services offering online shopping are emerging. Some companies are using the Internet as a communication delivery network for this type of service. Shopping on networks will be analogous to catalogue shopping without the printed medium. For this form of shopping to grow substantially, more network security than is generally expected or delivered today must be conceived and deployed.

22.31.4 Electronic Data Interchange

Electronic Data Interchange (EDI) is a traditional form of electronic commerce that is still increasing in popularity and breadth of application. The emergence of industry groups that establish de facto standards for their members has been a motivating factor. Today's EDI transaction set standards that include most of those required between supplier, manufacture and retail enterprises.

The industry groups that are in the 'soft product' business are now becoming active (insurance, banking, health, etc.). Some companies now insist on the use of EDI has a prerequisite for conducting business with them.

A large volume of EDI transactions are exchanged using Value Added Networks (VAN). This relieves the trading partners from having to connect with one another directly. Examples of VANs are provided by Advantis, IVAN, and GE.

22.31.5 Value-Added Networks

The providers of Value-Added Networks will become increasingly challenged to find defensible value in the fabric of electronic commerce as participants establish richer levels of connectivity.

22.31.6 Information Services

The Internet, CompuServe, Prodigy, and America Online are examples of rapidly growing information services with worldwide access, large bases of users, and rich capabilities. They have been a natural locus for early experimentation with consumer-oriented electronic commerce.

Vendors have been using CompuServe Forums for support of product in the Personal Computer and Workstation fields for several years. More recently, they are opening sites on Internet's World Wide Web and Prodigy for these purposes.

Information on demand is being made available in several forms. Owners of large data bases (*e.g., The New York Times*) have for some time offered access to their information. In such services, it is typically the user's responsibility to initiate the search for the desired information. Services are emerging which, with a specified frequency, search the available information on an agreed topic(s) and forward the information to the consumer.

22.31.7 Education and Medical

Access to high bandwidth networks is opening up new opportunities in education. Vast quantities of data are now easily accessible, along with search engines and intelligent 'agents' to find the desired information. We can expect major improvements in the search engines as they evolve into personal intelligent agents for gathering information.

Another opportunity is to use video in the classroom to offer a broader, richer set of courses and maximize access to the best teachers.

The medical field will benefit from the availability of high-bandwidth networks to allow experts to view images from remote locations. Other industries may benefit in a similar fashion.

22.32 SIGNIFICANT ISSUES IN IMPLEMENTING ELECTRONIC COMMERCE

Although it is simple to describe their benefits, it is not nearly as easy to develop and deploy commerce systems. Companies can face significant implementation issues:

- **Cost:** Electronic commerce requires significant investments in new technologies that can touch many of a company's core business processes. As with all major business systems, electronic commerce systems require significant investments in hardware, software, staffing, and training. Businesses need comprehensive solutions with greater ease of use to help foster cost-effective deployment.
- **Value:** Businesses want to know that their investments in electronic commerce systems will produce a return. Business objectives such as lead generation, business-process automation, and cost reduction must be met. Systems used to reach these goals need to be flexible enough to change when the business changes.
- **Security:** The Internet provides universal access, but companies must protect their assets against accidental or malicious misuse. System security, however, must not create prohibitive complexity or reduce flexibility. Customer information also needs to be protected from internal and external misuse. Privacy systems should safeguard the personal information critical to building sites that satisfy customer and business needs.
- **Leverage Existing Systems:** Most companies already use information technology to conduct business in non-Internet environments, such as marketing, order management, billing, inventory, distribution, and customer service. The Internet represents an alternative and complementary way to do business, but it is imperative that electronic commerce systems integrate existing systems in a manner that avoids duplicating functionality and maintains usability, performance, and reliability.
- **Interoperability:** When systems from two or more businesses are able to exchange documents without manual intervention; businesses achieve cost reduction; improved performance; and more dynamic value chains.

Failing to address any of these issues can spell failure for a system's implementation effort.

22.33 FUTURE OF ELECTRONIC COMMERCE

Moving forward, all businesses will be affected by the global move to electronic commerce. Business operations will change, and new processes will be created. Companies that start learning in this new environment today will be leaders in the future.

It is difficult to say the future of e-commerce, in India. They are only now beginning to be aware of the potential and the possibilities of the Internet. It will at least take another few months for Indian companies to adopt to doing business electronically. Most businesses rely on large networks, or efficient networks of partners, suppliers, and customers. If they are interested at all in making their networks more effective, they will consider faster, better ways to communicate and transact. Moreover, in the Information Age, the marketplace is increasingly global. The Internet makes the world much more accessible. A manufacturer in India who sources parts from overseas, and sells its finished product overseas and sells its finished product overseas will be able to use e-commerce to integrate its inventory system and manufacturing system with its supplier's and customer's systems.

22.34 E-COMMERCE TECHNOLOGIES

Many Web store merchants understandably want to concentrate their energies on what they do best-selling-and either ignore the technical aspects or leave them for someone else to worry about.

However, whilst Web store creation software continues to increase in power and ease of use, there is still a requirement for Web merchants to have a sound understanding of the technologies that underpin their stores.

This resource takes you 'under the hood' to explore the key technologies and explain in a straightforward manner how they are used for Web commerce.

22.34.1 Encryption Overview

When you think of encryption, you probably think of some sort of secret code that prevents others from reading your messages. Whilst this privacy aspect of cryptography is important, it is only one of four aspects that are of particular importance in electronic commerce.

- **Authentication** allows customers to be sure that the merchant they are sending their credit card details to is who they say they are. It can also allow merchant's to verify that the customer is the real owner of the credit card being used.
- **Integrity** ensures that the messages have not been tampered with by a third party during transmission.
- **Non-repudiation** prevents customers or merchants denying they ever received or sent a particular message.
- **Privacy** prevents third parties from reading intercepted messages.

22.34.1.1 Elements of an Encryption System

The main elements of an encryption system are the plaintext, the cryptographic algorithm, the key and the ciphertext.

- The **plaintext** is the raw message or data that is to be encrypted.
- A **cryptographic algorithm or cipher** is a mathematical set of rules that defines how the plain text is to be combined with a key.
- The **key** is a string of digits.
- The **ciphertext** is the encrypted message.

These terms are probably best illustrated through a very simple example.

If we take the phrase 'Web store' and add 2 characters to each letter the phrase becomes 'ygd uvqtg'. Here:

'Web store' is the plaintext

'add x characters to each letter' is the cryptographic algorithm

'2' is the key

'ygd uvqtg' is the ciphertext

There are two main types of encryption in common use today: secret-key and public-key.

22.34.2 Secret-key Encryption

Secret-key encryption, also known as single-key or symmetric encryption, involves the use of a single key that is shared by both the sender and the receiver of the message.

After creating the message, the sender encrypts it with their key and passes it to the recipient who then decrypts it by using a copy of the same key used to encrypt it (Fig. 22.2).

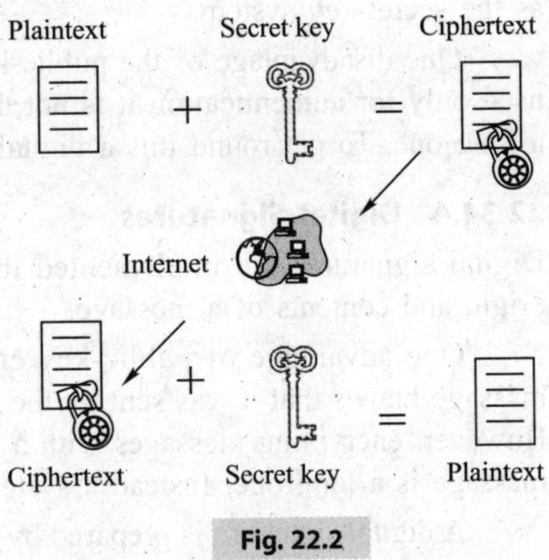

Fig. 22.2

A widely used method of secret-key encryption is the data encryption standard or DES.

Secret-key encryption does have some limitations, particularly with regard to key distribution. For privacy to be maintained, every transmitter of messages would need to provide a different key to everyone they intended to communicate with, otherwise every potential recipient would be able to read all messages whether it was intended for them or not.

Whilst this is manageable where a small number of parties are involved (for example, sending a private e-mail to a friend) it is not practical for Web commerce which can involve communicating with thousands of customers.

Another limitation with secret-key encryption is its inability to support nonrepudiation. As both parties share the same key it is possible for one party to create a message with the shared secret key and falsely claim it had been sent by the other party.

Secret-key encryption on its own is therefore not suitable for Web commerce-instead a system known as public-key encryption is used.

22.34.3 Public-key Encryption

Public-key encryption, or asymmetric encryption involves the use of two keys, one that can be used to encrypt messages (the public key) and one that can be used to either encrypt them or decrypt them (the private key).

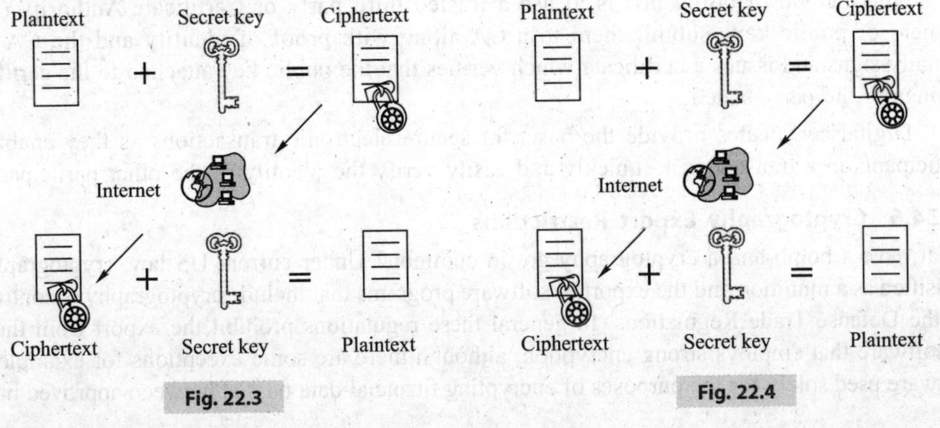

Fig. 22.3

Fig. 22.4

These key pairs can be used in two different ways, to provide privacy or authentication (Fig. 22.3).

Privacy is ensured by encoding a message with the public key as it can only be decoded by the holder of the private key.

Authentication is achieved by encoding a message with the private key. Once the recipient has successfully decrypted it with the public key they can be assured it was sent by the holder of the private key (Fig. 22.4).

As the public key can be made widely available (for example from a server or third party), public-key cryptography does not suffer from the same key distribution and management problems as the secret-key system.

One disadvantage of the public-key system is that it is relatively slow, so when it is being used only for authentication it is not desirable to encrypt the whole message particularly if it is a long one. To get round this a digital signature is used.

22.34.4 Digital Signatures

Digital signatures are implemented through public-key encryption and are used to verify the origin and contents of a message.

One advantage of public-key encryption is that the recipient of successfully decrypted message knows that it was sent by the owner of the private key. This is known as authentication. However, encrypting messages with a private key is a relatively slow process particularly if the message is a long one. Instead a system of digital signatures is used.

A digital signature is prepared by first passing the message through a one-way cryptographic function to calculate the message digest. This digest is much smaller than the original message and can be quickly encrypted with the private key to produce a signature which is then added to the original message.

The recipient of the digital signature can be sure that the message really came from the sender. And, because changing even one character in the message changes the message digest in an unpredictable way, the recipient can be sure that the message was not changed after the message digest was generated.

Authentication can be further strengthened by the use of digital certificates.

22.34.5 Digital Certificates

Before encrypting and transmitting sensitive information it is important to ensure that the public key being used does indeed belong to the intended message recipient and not someone masquerading as them.

One method of doing this is to use a trusted third party or Certificate Authority (CA). Owners of public keys submit them to a CA along with proof of identity and the CA then digitally signs and issues a certificate which verifies that the public key attached to the certificate belongs to the party stated.

Digital certificates provide the basis for secure electronic transactions as they enable all participants in a transaction to quickly and easily verify the identity of the other participants

22.34.6 Cryptography Export Restrictions

What have a bomb and a cryptography got in common? Under current US law, cryptography is classified as a munition and the export of software programs that include cryptography is controlled by the Defense Trade Regulations. In general these regulations prohibit the export from the US of software that employs strong encryption, although there are some exceptions for example, for software used solely for the purposes of encrypting financial data passed between approved banks.

In 1992, the Software Publishers Association reached agreement with the State Department to allow the export of software that contained RSA's RC2 and RC4 encryption algorithms, but only if the key size was limited to 40 bits as opposed to the 128 bit keys available for use within the US.

The security of an algorithm is dependent on the length of the key used. The longer the length the more possible combinations there are and the longer it takes 'crack' the code.

Since 1992 the speed and availability of computers has increased dramatically and although a 40 bit key would still take a considerable amount of time and computer power to 'crack' it is now feasible to do so. It is still much easier and more productive though, for a thief to scan Internet traffic for un-encrypted credit card numbers than it is to try to find and 'crack' encrypted ones. However as computers continue to grow in power the time to decrypt 40 bit codes will continue to drop and 40 bit keys may no longer be deemed secure enough for e-commerce transactions.

The US government has proposed several methods whereby it would allow the export of stronger encryption. These methods are all based on some sort of key escrow or key recovery system which would allow the law enforcement agencies to obtain a copy of a private key to enable it to decrypt messages.

An executive order—the Administration of Export Control on Encryption Products-came in to effect on January 1st 1997. This allows vendors to ship world-wide encryption products using 56 bit keys but only if they agree to add key recovery to their products within two years. However, there is considerable resistance within the industry to the use of key recovery systems because of the potential threat to corporate and individual privacy.

This resolution of this issue is widely regarded as vital to the future of global e-commerce.

22.34.7 Secure Sockets Layer (SSL)

Netscape's Secure Sockets Layer (SSL) protocol is currently the most widely used method for performing secure transactions on the Web and is supported by most Web servers and clients including Netscape Navigator and Microsoft Internet Explorer. The Secure Sockets Layer (SSL) protocol provides several features that make it particularly suitable for use in e-commerce transactions.

Privacy is guaranteed through encryption. Although information can still be intercepted by a third party they will be unable to read them as they have no access to the encryption key.

Integrity is also ensured through encryption. If information is received that will not decrypt properly then the recipient knows that the information has been tampered with during transmission.

Authentication is provided through digital certificates. Digital certificates provide the basis for secure electronic transactions as they enable all participants in a transaction to quickly and easily verify the identity of the other participants.

22.34.7.1 The Encryption Process

Essentially, SSL is secret-key encryption nested within public-key encryption, authenticated through the use of certificates.

The reason that both secret-key and public-key encryption methods are used is because of the relatively slow speed of public-key encryption compared to secret-key encryption. Initially, the client and server exchange public keys, and then the client generates a private encryption key that is used only for this transaction. This is referred to as a session key. The client then encrypts the session key with the server's public key and sends it to the server. Then, for the rest of the transaction, the client and the server can use the session key for private-key encryption.

22.34.7.2 SSL in Action

An SSL connection is initiated by the client (normally a Web browser) by requesting a document to be sent through the HTTPS protocol as proposed to the standard HTTP protocol.

This is done by simply prefixing the URL by 'https' as opposed to 'http'. For example:

http://server.domain.com/index.html

requests the document index.html be sent through the standard HTTP protocol, whilst

https://server.domain.com/index.html

requests the same document be sent using the HTTPS protocol which incorporates SSL.

Here in detail are the steps taken during a SSL transaction:

1. The client sends a request for a document to be transmitted using the HTTPS protocol by prefixing the URL with 'https'.
2. The server sends its certificate to the client.
3. The client checks if the certificate was issued by a Certificate Authority (CA) it trusts. If not, it gives the user the option to continue or to terminate the transaction.
4. The client compares the information in the certificate with the information it just received concerning the site: its domain name and its public key. If the information matches, the client accepts the site as authenticated.
5. The client tells the server what ciphers, or encryption algorithms, it can communicate with.
6. The server chooses the strongest common cipher and informs the client.
7. The client generates a private (or session) key using the agreed cipher.
8. The client then encrypts the session key using the server's public key and sends it to the server.
9. The server receives the encrypted session key and decrypts it with its private key.
10. The client and the server then use the session key for the rest of the transaction.

An alternative secure protocol is the Secure Electronic Transaction (SET) protocol developed by Visa and MasterCard specifically for enabling secure credit card transactions on the Internet. Designed for cardholders, merchants, banks and other card processors, SET uses digital certificates to ensure the identities of all parties involved in a purchase. SET also encrypts credit and purchase information before transmission on the Internet.

22.34.8 Secure Electronic Transactions (SET)

SET is the Secure Electronic Transaction protocol developed by Visa and MasterCard specifically for enabling secure credit card transactions on the Internet. It uses digital certificates to ensure the identities of all parties involved in a purchase and encrypts credit card information before sending it across the Internet.

SET is exempt from the US cryptographic export restrictions and unlike SSL can therefore use strong, 128 bit encryption for credit card numbers world-wide. In order to gain this exemption, the use of strong encryption has to be limited to the financial information only and does not include other elements of the transaction, for example details of the goods being bought and the delivery address.

Like SSL, SET allows for the merchant's identity to be authenticated via digital certificates. However, SET also allows for the merchant to request users authenticate themselves through digital certificates. This makes it much more difficult for someone to use a stolen credit card.

A further advantage of SET is that the merchant has no access to credit card numbers and thus another source of fraud is eliminated.

There are many pilot schemes running using the SET protocol but mainstream adoption has been slower than predicted. The main reasons behind this are the growing acceptance of SSL for secure credit card transactions and the complexity and cost of the SET system.

22.34.8.1 Encryption Process

In a typical SET transaction, there is information that is private between the customer and the merchant (such as the items being ordered) and other information that is private between the customer and the bank (such as the customer's credit card number). SET allows both kinds of private information to be included in a single, digitally signed transaction.

Information intended for the bank is encrypted using the bank's public key whilst information for the merchant is encrypted with the merchant's public key. This means that the merchant has no access to the credit card details and thus a source of fraud is eliminated.

In addition to this encryption, both sets of information are digitally signed. Finally these two signatures are combined to produce one signature that covers the whole transaction

22.34.8.2 SET in Action

There are three parts to the SET system: a software 'wallet' on the user's computer; a commerce server that runs at the merchant's Web site; and the payment server that runs at the merchant's bank.

Although future versions of Microsoft's Internet Explorer and Netscape's Navigator will come with SET wallets pre-installed, currently users need to download and install a wallet on their computers. During the installation process the user provides credit card details and obtains user name and PIN to provide secure access to the wallet. The installation process also produces a public and private key for the user. The user also has to obtain a digital certificate from their bank or certificate agency (CA) for each credit card.

To use SET, users select products from the merchant's Web site and then elect to pay via SET by pressing an on-screen button. This automatically starts the wallet program. The user then selects which credit card they wish to use and the wallet and the merchant's server exchange certificates. If these are accepted, the wallet then encrypts and transmits the purchase details to the merchant.

Although the purchase details include the encrypted credit card information, the merchant can not read them. Instead he passes this on to the bank's payment server which debits the users credit card and passes the payment to the merchant.

22.34.9 Smart Cards

At first glance a smart card looks like a normal credit or debit card. However, closer examination reveals the absence of a magnetic stripe as smart cards store all their information on a chip buried within the card. Compared to conventional magnetic stripe cards, smart cards differ in several important ways:

- ❒ They can store much more data
- ❒ They can be password protected
- ❒ They can incorporate a microprocessor that can perform processes such as encryption

Although relatively unknown in the US, smart cards are by no means a new invention. There use in Europe is widespread for applications such as credit cards, telephone payment cards and the payment of road tolls. France is the leading adopter, having started issuing cards in 1967 and now has some 25 million cards in circulation. However, their use is predicted to grow rapidly world-wide over the next few years on the back of the Internet e-commerce explosion.

The potential for smart card use is enormous, but there are three key functions of interest to the Web store merchant:

- ❒ Storage of encryption keys
- ❒ Electronic purses
- ❒ User profile portability

22.35 SMART CARD APPLICATIONS

22.35.1 Storage of Encryption Keys

Web commerce secure transaction protocols, such as SSL and SET, require that private encryption keys are stored securely.

The most basic storage method is to encrypt the private key using a password and store it on the computer's hard disk-this is what programs such as Netscape's Navigator do. This method although convenient, does have some security risks as anyone who discovers or intercepts the password can use the private key if they have access to the computer where the key is stored. Another vulnerability is that once the key is decrypted it is held within the computer's memory where it could be copied by a rogue program.

Security can be increased by storing the encrypted key on removable media, for example a floppy disk. An attacker would then need access to this media and knowledge of the password before they could use the private key. However, this method still requires the key to be decrypted and held within the computer's memory where again it could be copied by a rogue program.

Smart cards can provide a very secure way of generating, storing and using private keys.

In its most basic implementation, smart cards can be used to store private keys and digital certificates protected with a password. Security can be further enhanced by using a microprocessor within the card to generate the public and private key pairs and to perform the actual encryption. Data to be decrypted or digitally signed is passed to the card where the microprocessor performs the operation and then passes the data back to the computer. That way the key never leaves the card and is therefore not vulnerable to attack by rogue programs scanning the computer's memory for keys.

22.35.2 Electronic Purses

Many applications in place today use a smart card as a replacement for cash because of the higher security they offer over standard credit cards. Although most of these systems (for example Mondex, VisaCash, CLIP and Proton) were developed for point of sales applications, their use is likely to extend to Web commerce as they provide an easy and secure way to handle cash transactions. Many project that smart card readers will become a standard component of PCs-indeed the Intel PC98 specification recommends that Office PCs have a smart card reader installed as standard.

22.35.3 User Profile Portability

One factor that could potentially restrain the growth of Web commerce is restricted access to the Internet. Although the number of home and office computers with Internet access is continually growing, it is still not universally available and even the introduction of low cost access devices (for example Web TV) will not solve this completely. Also, even those with Internet enabled computers are unable to access them when away from their office or desk.

Smart cards could provide an answer to this by providing secure access over public Internet terminals or screen phones. Personal profile information could be stored on the card so no matter what device was being used the appearance would be the same. The on board microprocessor would be able to encrypt all messages thus eliminating security risks.

REVIEW QUESTIONS

1. Why is encrption needed for Web commerce?

   Ans: Enncsrption performs four key functions which enable secure Web transactions to take place:

- **Athentication** allows customers to be sure that the merchant they are sending their credit card details to is who they say they are. It can also allow merchant's to verify that the customer is the real owner of the credit card being used.

- ❒ **Integrity** ensures that the messages have not been tampered with by a third party during transmission.
- ❒ **Non-repudiation** prevents customers or merchants denying they ever received or sent a particular message.
- ❒ **Privacy** prevents third parties from reading intercepted messages.

2. What are the main elements of an encryption system?

Ans: The **plaintext** is the raw message or data that is to be encrypted.

- ❒ A **cryptographic algorithm** or **cipher** is a mathematical set of rules that defines how the plain text is to be combined with a key.
- ❒ The **key** is a string of digits.
- ❒ The **ciphertext** is the encrypted message.

3. What are the main methods of encryption?

Ans: There are two main methods of encryption:

- ❒ Private-key encryption (also known as secret-key or symmetric encryption) in which users share a common key.
- ❒ Public-key encryption (also known as asymmetric encryption) where different keys are used for encryption and decryption.

These systems have their advantages and disadvantages and so secure transaction protocols such as *SSL* and *SET* use a combination of both.

4. What is a digital signature?

Ans: Digital signatures are implemented through public-key encryption and are used to verify the origin and contents of a message.

A digital signature is prepared by first passing the message through a cryptographic function to calculate the message digest. The digest is then encrypted with the private key to produce a signature which is then added to the original message.

The recipient of the digital signature can be sure that the message really came from the sender. And, because changing even one character in the message changes the message digest in an unpredictable way, the recipient can be sure that the message was not changed after the message digest was generated.

5. What is a digital certificate?

Ans: Digital certificates provide the basis for secure electronic transactions as they enable all participants in a transaction to quickly and easily verify the identity of the other participants. They are digitally signed and issued by a Certificate Authority (CA) which verifies that the public key attached to the certificate belongs to the party stated.

6. How does SSL support secure transactions?

Ans: Netscape's Secure Sockets Layer (SSL) protocol is currently the most widely used method for performing secure transactions on the Web and is supported by most Web servers and clients including Netscape's Navigator and Microsoft's Internet Explorer.

The Secure Sockets Layer (SSL) protocol provides several features that make it particularly suitable for use in e-commerce transactions.

- ❒ **Privacy** is guaranteed through encryption. Although data can still be intercepted by a third party they will be unable to read it as they have no access to the encryption key.
- ❒ **Integrity** is also ensured through encryption. If a message is received that ill not decrypt properly then the recipient knows that the information has been tampered with during transmission.

- **Authentication** is provided through digital certificates. Digital certificates provide the basis for secure electronic transactions as they enable all articipants in a transaction to quickly and easily verify the identity of the other participants.

7. How does SET support secure transactions?

Ans: SET is the Secure Electronic Transaction protocol developed by Visa and Master-Card specifically for enabling secure credit card transactions on the Internet. It uses digital certificates to ensure the identities of all parties involved in a purchase and encrypts credit card information before sending it across the Internet.

Like SSL, SET allows for the merchant's identity to be authenticated via digital certificates. However, SET also allows for the merchant to request users authenticate themselves through digital certificates. This makes it much more difficult for someone to use a stolen credit card.

A further advantage of SET is that the merchant has no access to credit card numbers and thus another source of fraud is eliminated.

8. What is a smart card?

Ans: At first glance a smart card looks like a normal credit or debit card. However, closer examination reveals the absence of a magnetic stripe as smart cards store all their information on a chip buried within the card. Compared to conventional magnetic stripe cards, smart cards differ in several important ways:

- They can store much more data.
- They can be password protected.
- They can incorporate a microprocessor that can perform processes such as encryption.

9. How can smart cards be used for Web commerce?

Ans: Smart cards can be used for:

- The secure storage of encryption keys.
- The storage of digital money in an electronic purse.
- Ensuring secure transactions over public Web terminals and screen

ENTERPRISE RESOURCE PLANNING: AN OVERVIEW

ERP (Enterprise Resource Planning) is an industry term for the broad set of activities supported by multi-module application software that help a manufacturer or other business manage the important parts of its business, including product planning, parts purchasing, maintaining inventories, interacting with suppliers, providing customer service, and tracking orders. ERP can also include application modules for the finance and human resources aspects of a business. Typically, an ERP system uses or is integrated with a *relational database system*. In other words, ERP is a software infrastructure that helps to manage the different parts of a company or business. The aim is to improve the cooperation and interaction between all the departments such as the products planning, purchasing, manufacturing, sales and customers service department. In brief, it is the planning of the 4Ms—Man, Money, Machines and Materials. The deployment of an ERP system can involve considerable business process analysis, employee retraining, and new work procedures.

23.1 EVOLUTION OF ERP

In today's business environment, there has to be much greater interaction between the customers and manufacturers. This means that, in order to produce goods tailored to customer requirements and provide faster deliveries, the enterprise must be closely linked to both suppliers and customers. In order to achieve this, improved delivery performance, decreased lead times within the enterprise and, improved efficiency and effectiveness, manufacturers need to have efficient planning and control systems that enable very good synchronisation and planning in all the processes of the organisation. Today, however, the challenge is intense and requires a strong integration across the value chain. In the ever growing business environment the following expectations are placed on the industry:

- ❒ Aggressive Cost control initiatives
- ❒ Need to analyse costs/revenues on a product or customer basis
- ❒ Flexibility to respond to changing business requirements
- ❒ More informed management decision making
- ❒ Changes in ways of doing business.

Enterprise Resource Planning is a strategic tool, which equips the enterprise with the necessary capabilities to integrate and synchronise the isolated functions into streamlines business processes in order to gain a competitive edge in the dynamic business environment.

Prior to 1960s, the business had to rely on the traditional ways of inventory management to ensure smooth functioning of organisation. The most popularly known amongst them is EOQ (*Economic Order Quantity*). In this method, each item in the stock is analysed for its ordering cost and the inventory carrying cost. A trade off is established on a phased out expected demand of one year, and this way the most economic ordering quantity can be decided. This technique in principle is a reactive way of managing inventory. In 1960s, a new technique of Material Requirements Planning, popularly known as MRP, evolved. This was a proactive manner of inventory management. This technique fundamentally explodes the end product demand obtained from the *Master Production Schedule* (MPS) for a specified product structure (which is taken from *Bill of Material*) into a detailed schedule of purchase orders or production orders taking into account the inventory on hand. MRP is a simple logic but the magnitude of data involved in a realistic situation makes it computationally cumbersome. If undertaken manually, the entire process is highly time consuming. It therefore becomes essential to use a computer to carry out the exercise.

The effectiveness of MRP successfully demonstrated in:

- Reduction in production and delivery lead times by improving co-ordination and avoiding delays
- Reduction of inventory
- Increased efficiency, and making commitments more realistic

MRP proved to be a very good technique for managing inventory, but it did not take into account other resources of an organisation. In 1970s, this gave birth to a modified MRP logic, popularly known as *Closed Loop MRP*. In this technique, the capacity of the organisation to produce a particular product is also taken into account by incorporating a module called *Capacity Requirements Planning* (CRP). Hence, a feedback loop is provided from the CRP module to MPS if there is not enough capacity available to produce.

In 1980s, the concept of MRP-II (*Manufacturing Resources Planning*) is an extension of MRP to shop floor and Distribution Management activities. In early 1990s, MRP-II was further extended to cover more areas like Engineering, Finance, Human Resources, Projects Management, etc i.e., the complete gamut of activities within any business enterprise. Hence, the term ERP (Enterprise Resource Planning) was coined. In addition to system requirements, ERP addresses technology aspects like *client/server distributed architecture, RDBMS, object oriented programming*, etc. ERP Systems - Bandwidth ERP solutions address broad areas within any business like Manufacturing, Distribution, Finance, Project Management. Service and Maintenance, Transportation etc. A seamless integration is essential to provide visibility and consistency across the enterprise.

The Enterprise Resource Planning system should be sufficiently versatile to support different manufacturing environments like make-to-stock, assemble-to-order and engineer-to-order. The Customer Order Decoupling Point (CODP) should be flexible to allow the co-existence of these manufacturing environments within the same system. An example here could be any manufacturing company which has businesses spread over all these manufacturing environments. It is also very likely that the same product may migrate from one manufacturing environment to another during its produce life cycle.

The system should be complete enough to support both Discrete as well as Process manufacturing scenario's. The efficiency of an enterprise depends on the quick flow of information across the complete supply chain *i.e.*, from the customer to manufacturers to supplier. This places demands on the ERP system to have rich functionally across all areas like sales, accounts receivable, engineering, planning, Inventory Management, Production, Purchase, account payable, quality management, production, distribution planning and external transportation. *Electronic Data Interchange* (EDI) is an important tool in speeding up communications with trading partners.

Lots of companies are becoming global and focusing on down-sizing and decentralising their business. A typical example here could be ABB and Northern Telecom companies, which have business spread around the globe. For these types of companies to manage their business efficiently, ERP systems need to have extensive multi-site management capabilities. The complete financial accounting and management accounting requirements of the organisation should be addressed. It is necessary to have centralized or de-centralized accounting functions with complete flexibility to consolidate corporate information.

For companies undertaking large scale and complex ERP projects, tools should be available for cost-effective project management, project planning and project control. After-sales service should be streamlined and managed efficiently. A strong Enterprise Information System (EIS) with extensive drill down capabilities should be available for the top management to get a progreess report of their organisation which helps them to analyze, manage, and quick decision making in the key areas.

Difficulty in getting accurate data, timely information and improper interface of the complex natured business functions have been identified as the hurdles in the growth of any business. Time and again depending upon the velocity of the growing business needs, one or the other applications (see Table 23.1) and planning systems (see Table 23.2) have been introduced into the business world for crossing these hurdles and for achieving the required growth.

Table 23.1 Evolution of Business Applications

Abbreviations	*Description*
MIS	Management Information Systems—(No Decision Support)
IIS	Integrated Information Systems—(No Decision Support)
EIS	Executive Information Systems—(Decision Support)
CIS	Corporate Information Systems—(Decision Support)
EWS	Enterprise Wide Systems—(No Decision Support Logistics are considered as a part of system)

Table 23.2 Evolution of Planning Systems

Abbreviations	*Description*
MIP	Material Requirement Planning
IIS	Manufacturing Resource Planning
EIS	Money Resource Planning
CIS	Enterprise Resource Planning

23.2 CHARACTERISTICS OF ERP

An ERP system is not only the integration of various organisation processes. Any system has to possess few key characteristics to qualify for a true ERP solution. These features are:

1. **Flexibility:** An ERP system should be flexible to respond to the changing needs of an enterprise. The client server technology enables ERP to run across various data base back ends through Open Data Base Connectivity (ODBC).
2. **Modular & Open:** ERP system has to have an open system architecture. This means that any module can be interfaced or detached whenever required without affecting the other modules. It should support multiple hardware platforms for the companies having heterogeneous collection of systems. It must support some third party add-ons also.
3. **Comprehensive:** It should be able to support variety of organizational functions and must be suitable for a wide range of business organisations.
4. **Beyond The Company:** It should not be confined to the organisational boundaries, rather support the on-line connectivity to the other business entities of the organisation.

5. **Best Business Practices:** It must have a collection of the best business processes applicable world-wide.
6. **Simulation of Reality:** Last but not the least, it must simulate the reality of business processes on the computers. In no way it should have the control beyond the business processes and it must be able to assign accountabilities to the users controlling the system.

23.3 FEATURES OF ERP

The major features of ERP and what ERP can do for the business system are:

- ERP facilities company-wide Integrated Information System, covering all functional areas like, Manufacturing, Selling and distribution, Payables, Receivables, Inventory, Accounts, Human resources, Purchases, etc.
- ERP performs core corporate activities and increases customer service and thereby augmenting the corporate image.
- ERP eliminates most of the business problems, like Material shortages, Productivity enhancements, Customer service, Cash Management, Inventory problems, Quality problems, Prompt delivery, etc.
- ERP allows automatic introduction of latest technologies, like Electronic Fund Transfer (EFT), Electronic Data Interchange (EDI), Internet, Intranet, Video conferencing, E-Commerce, etc.
- ERP not only addresses the current requirements of the company but also provides the opportunity of continually improving and refining business processes.
- ERP provides business intelligence tools like Decision Support Systems (DSS), Executive Information System (EIS), Reporting, Data Mining and Early Warning Systems for enabling people to make better decisions and thus improve their business processes.
- ERP bridges the information gap across the organisation.
- ERP provides for complete integration of systems not only across the departments in a company but also across the companies under the same management.
- ERP is an effective solution for better Project Management.

23.4 COMPONENTS OF ERP

To enable the easy handling of the system the ERP has been divided into the following core subsystem (see Fig. 23.1):

- Asset Management
- Bill of Materials
- Capacity Requirement Planning
- Financial Accounting
- Logistics
- Master Scheduling
- Material Requirement Planning
- Purchasing
- Sales and Marketing
- Shop floor control

Fig. 23.1 The core Subsystems of ERP

23.5 NEED OF ERP

Most organisations across the world have realised that in a rapidly changing environment, it is impossible to create and maintain a custom designed software package which will cater to all their requirements and also be completely up-to-date. Realizing the requirement of the user organisations, some of the leading software companies have designed, Enterprise Resource Planning software, which will offer an integrated software solution to all the functions of an organisations, such as:

Complete Integration of systems across the departments in a company as well as across the enterprise as a whole.

- ❒ Effective solution for better Project Management
- ❒ Better Customer Service
- ❒ Automatic Introduction of latest technologies
- ❒ Expertise database
- ❒ ERP Vendors

There are various ERP vendors available today, who are very active in the market. Some of the companies offering renowned international ERP products include:

- ❒ SAP
- ❒ Baan
- ❒ Oracle
- ❒ Peoplesoft
- ❒ JD Edwards
- ❒ IBM
- ❒ CODA
- ❒ D&B
- ❒ Marcarn
- ❒ QAD
- ❒ SMI
- ❒ Platinum
- ❒ Software 2000
- ❒ Ramco

These vendors offer slightly differing features in their products; still the major modules are same in all of the products. SAP R/3, which is the market leader in this segment, offers the following modules:

- ❒ Financial Accounting
- ❒ Treasury
- ❒ Controlling
- ❒ Enterprise Controlling
- ❒ Investment Management
- ❒ Production Planning
- ❒ Materials Management
- ❒ Plant Maintenance & Service Management
- ❒ Quality Management
- ❒ Project System
- ❒ Sales & Distribution
- ❒ Human Resources Management
- ❒ Business Information Warehouse

Today SAP is considered to be the most exhaustive ERP system. SAP R/3 also allows the connectivity to Internet and the business through it for the mobile and distantly located users. Other vendors also provide more or less similar functionality in their bundle of product.

23.6 BUSINESS PROCESS REENGINEERING

Business Process Reengineering is a pre-requisite for going ahead with a powerful planning tool, ERP. Since, ERP gets the best out of the available resources, it is very important to reengineer the business processes before, during or immediately after an ERP implementation. If the business processes are not streamlined, the resource allocation will always be sub-optimal. Reengineering also makes it smooth to drive the ERP implementation programme, because the former builds the spirit of competitiveness and adaptation of best practices. An in-depth BPR study has to be done before taking up ERP. Business Process Reengineering brings out deficiencies of the existing system and attempts to maximize productivity through restructuring and reorganizing the human resources as well as divisions and departments in the organisation. Business Process Engineering involves the following steps:

- ❒ Study the current system
- ❒ Design and develop new systems
- ❒ Define Process, organisation structure and procedure
- ❒ Develop customize the software
- ❒ Train people
- ❒ Implement new system

The principle followed for BRP may be defined as USA principle (Understand, Simplify and Automate) *i.e.*, understanding the existing practices, simplifying the processes and automate the process. Various tools used for USA principle are shown in Fig. 23.2.

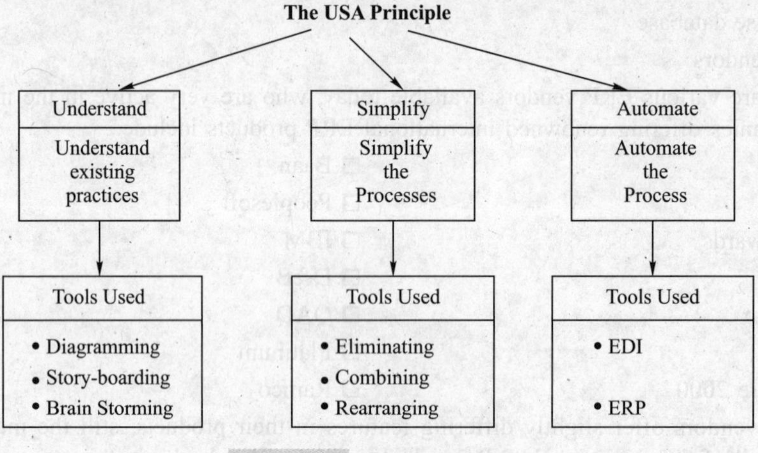

Fig. 23.2 The USA Principle

23.7 EVALUATION CRITERIA FOR ERP PACKAGES

Once the BPR is completed the next task is to evaluate and select a suitable package for implementation. Evaluation of the right ERP package is considered as more crucial step. Evaluation and selection involves:

- ❒ Functional fit with the Company's business processes
- ❒ Degree of integration between the various components of the ERP system
- ❒ Flexibility and scalability
- ❒ Complexity, user friendliness
- ❒ Quick implementation; shorthend ROI period
- ❒ Ability to support multi-site planning and control
- ❒ Technology: client/server capabilities, database independence, security
- ❒ Availability of regular upgrades
- ❒ Amount of customisation required
- ❒ Local support infrastructure
- ❒ Availability of reference sites
- ❒ Total costs, including cost of license, training, implementation, maintenance, customisation and hardware requirements.

23.8 ADVANTAGES OF ERP PACKAGES

The ERP packages have following advantages:

- ❒ Ease to use
- ❒ General purpose
- ❒ Readymade solutions for most of the problems
- ❒ Only customisation required
- ❒ Integration of all functions already established
- ❒ ROI earlier than the software developed in-house
- ❒ Dependency on Human Resources eliminated
- ❒ Easy enterprise wide information sharing
- ❒ Suppliers and customers can be on-line communication
- ❒ Knowledge transfer between industries guarantees innovation
- ❒ Automatic adaptation to new technology.

23.9 IMPLEMENTATION APPROACH OF ERP

Implementation of an ERP package has been done on a phased manner. Step by step method of implementing ERP System will yield a better result. The normal steps involved in implementation of an ERP are as below:

- ❒ Project Planning
- ❒ Business & Operational analysis including Gap analysis
- ❒ Business Process Reengineering (BPR)
- ❒ Installation and configuration
- ❒ Project team training
- ❒ Business Requirement mapping to software
- ❒ Module configuration
- ❒ System modification and interfaces
- ❒ Data conversion
- ❒ Custom Documentation
- ❒ End user training
- ❒ Acceptance testing
- ❒ Post implementation.

The above steps are grouped and sub-divided into four major phases namely

1. Detailed discussions	2. Design & Customisation
3. Implementation and	4. Production.

The phases of implementation, vis-a-vis their tasks and respective deliverables are shown in Fig. 23.3.

Implementation of ERP solutions is one of the largest drivers of growth in the consultancy business. The introduction of a large and complex software like ERP, which enables an oganisation to integrate their manufacturing, finance and marketing operations at all levels, is in itself a challenge, since it calls for technical and functional skills and a change in user mindsets. And therein comes a role of a consultant. Consultant will play a major role in implementation of an ERP solution.

Phase	*Tasks*	*Deliverables*
Detailed Discussions	❒ Project Initialisation	❒ Accepted norms & Conditions
	❒ Evaluation of current processes, business practices, requirements	❒ Project Organisation Chart
	❒ Set-up Project Organisation	❒ Identify Work or Support Teams
Design & Customization	❒ Matp Organisation	❒ Organisation Structure
	❒ Map Business Processes	❒ Design Specification
	❒ Define Functions and Processes	❒ Process Flow Diagrams
	❒ ERP Software Configuration	❒ Function Model
	❒ Build ERP System Modifications	❒ Configuration Recording
		❒ Systems Modification
Implementation	❒ Create Go-Live Plan & Documentation	❒ Testing Environment report
	❒ Integrate Applications	❒ Customisation Test Report
	❒ Test the ERP Customisations	❒ Implementation Report
	❒ Train Users	
Production	❒ Run Trial Production	❒ Reconciliatio Reports
	❒ Maintain systems	❒ Conversion Plan Execution

Fig. 23.3 Implementation Approach of ERP

Assuming a situation where the client has implemented an ERP solution. If the auditor is aware of ERP he can make use of the features of ERP and thereby:

- ❒ ensures that the internal controls and checks are consistently maintained.
- ❒ ensures that the provisions of Income tax or other fiscal laws are not ignored *e.g.*, one can control the payment of cash in excess of ₹ 10,000 for expenses or ₹ 20,000 as loans and advances, TDS deductions and payments are automated etc.
- ❒ ensures that the Accounting Standards are consistently followed across the company.
- ❒ improves the quality of the reporting.

By now, one should be knowing that the ERP is a high end sophisticated software solution that reduces the pressure and work load of the managers and provides accurate, timely information for taking appropriate business decisions. Managers with knowledge of ERP will be able to achieve their targets and goals by proper implementation of ERP system in their organisation. In fact managers are expected to translate the business rules and requirements for mapping them into ERP software. Managers, as representatives of the organisation have to coordinate with vendors, consultants, auditors etc., for a proper implementation of ERP package.

Today, many companies have been benefited a lot by implementing ERP packages. Some of the benefits are listed below:

- ❒ Improved Cost Control
- ❒ Faster response and follow up on customers
- ❒ More efficient cash collection, say, material reduction in delay in payments by customers.
- ❒ Better monitoring and quicker resolution of queries.
- ❒ Enables quick response to change in business operations and market conditions.

- ❐ Helps to achieve competitive advantage by improving its business process.
- ❐ Reduce paper documents by providing on-line formats for quickly entering and retrieving information.
- ❐ Improves timeliness of information by permitting posting daily, instead of monthly.
- ❐ Gives Accounts-Payable personnel increased control of invoicing and payment processing and thereby boosting their productivity and eliminating their reliance on computer personnel for these operations.
- ❐ Greater accuracy of information with detailed content, better presentation, fully satisfactory for the auditors.
- ❐ Improves supply-demand linkage with remote locations and branches in different countries.
- ❐ Improves information access and management throughout the enterprise.
- ❐ Provides solution for problems like Y2K and Single Monitory Unit (SMU) or Euro Currency.
- ❐ Provides unified customer database, usable by all applications.
- ❐ Improves International operations by supporting a variety of tax structures, invoicing schemes, multiple currencies, multiple period accounting and languages.

Today, ERP is being implemented in almost all types of organisations irrespective of its mode and spread of operation. A typical list of segments where ERP systems have been implemented are Aerospace & Defence, Automotive industry, Banking & Insurance, Chemical & pharmaceutical industries, Consumers goods, Healthcare, High-tech & electronics, Mechanical engineering & heavy construction, Oil & gas, Project oriented manufacturing, Public administration & education, Retail, Telecommunications, Utilities etc.

23.10 ENABLING BEST TECHNOLOGY PRACTICES

Thinking of an ERP system without sophisticated information technology infrastructure, is not possible. It is said that, ERP is the finest expression of the inseparability of business and information technology. The incremental improvement in the information technology and the drastic reduction in prices of computers have made it possible even for the small organisation to think about ERP systems. The earlier ERP systems were built only work with huge mainframe computers. The new era of PC, advent of client server technology and scalable Relational Data Base Management Systems (RDBMS) all have contributed for the ease of deployment of ERP systems. Most of the ERP systems exploit the power of Three Tier Client Server Architecture. In a client server environment, the server stores the data, maintaining its integrity and consistency and processes the requests of the user from the client desktops. The load of data processing and application logic is divided between the server and the client. The three tier architecture adds a middle stratum, embodying all application logic and the business rules that are not part of the application, enforcing appropriate validation checks.

It is assumed that the companies implementing ERP solutions have multiple locations of operation and control. Hence, the online data transfer has to be done across locations. To facilitate these transactions, the other important enabling technologies for ERP systems are Workflow, Workgroup, Groupware, Electronic Data Interchange (EDI), Internet, Intranet, Data warehousing, etc.

Companies live or die by IT. When technology investments are perfectly aligned with business goals and work flawlessly, they imbue an enterprise with incredible strength. But when companies fail to identify the right IT-enabled opportunities, deploy ill-conceived systems or mismanage the overall activity. Poorly envisioned an executed IT investments become slow leaks that can burden a company while remaining almost unnoticed—until it's too late. Half of all technology projects fail to meet manager expectations. But instead of figuring out where and why a project fails, business executives sometimes use the Manager as scapegoat, loading to a revolving door atop the IT function and an underlying problem that never gets addressed.

Considering how few business initiatives today can succeed without assistance from IT, executives would be wise to become enlightened partners in the IT process and thus help ensure its overall success. After all, allocating blame becomes irrelevant when—sink or sail—everybody is in the same boat.

Recognizing the need to get involved in IT decision making is one thing, but actually knowing how to do it is another. Many business executives struggle to get their brains around IT. Understandably, they balk at measuring the value and performance of something so intimidatingly complex and, well, so technical. But being a good executive officer requires knowing how to leverage IT to advance business goals. And doing that well means evaluating whether IT is actually living up to its potential.

Once should also keep the following point in consideration while evaluating IT potential in your organisation:

1. Customer satisfaction
2. Enable Business Growth
3. Empower productivity
4. Innovation and learning
5. Running of IS.

1. Customer Satisfaction: IT systems should match business objectives. Otherwise, 'The systems as focused internally on things that are divorced from what really creates value'. And for virtually every successful enterprise, customer satisfaction is a crucial business objective. Indeed, in some commodity-style industries, improving the customer experience offers the best and sometimes the only hope of competitive differentiation.

IT should enable a business to deliver a higher-quality customer experience at a lower cost to the company. While some technologies deliver highly visible forms of customer interaction, customers don't need to see technology to benefit from it-as in the case of a data warehouse that enables a company to tailor its products to customer preferences or a state-of-the art logistics system that allows an organisation to deliver a product two days earlier than the competition.

Companies embrace the goal of improving customer satisfaction to varying degrees. If you're in doubt about your own efforts, look outside your company to see how others do it. At the extreme end of the spectrum are companies like San Jose, Calif-based Cisco Systems Inc. The $6.5 billion Internet networking vendor is loath to approve a new IT project unless it directly affects the customer experience. Cisco claims that this customer-oriented approach saves it at least $290 million per year in operating, organisations competing directly with a Cisco should think hard about making customer satisfaction a priority when designing systems.

But not all customer-focused systems are good customer-focused systems. Don't fall into the trap of creating technology systems just for the sake of having them. The last thing you want is a system that degrades customer satisfaction levels. Better not to invest in an automated customer support hotline at all, for example, if customers with unusual questions get frustrated because they can't talk to a real human. The effect that systems have on the customer experience can be measured by analysing customer surveys or complaints logged into a help desk. If neither of these data points is available, that in itself is a red flag about your company's—and IS department's—commitment to customer satisfaction.

2. Enable Business Growth: An important goal of the IS department should be to enable business growth opportunities. In a merger or acquisition, for instance, IT should clear the path for the unimpeded flow of information and operations. The integration of two companies' technology systems can be the single biggest factor in a merger's success or failure. Yet all too often the IT function isn't factored into initial strategic conversations.

Beyond merely enabling already identified expansion opportunities, the Manager should also pose new ideas for growth. Managers are uniquely qualified to broaden strategic possibilities by proposing new applications of emerging technologies. In fact, information technology can help grow the business to such a degree that it becomes its own line of business. Just look at the Sabre Network, once an application to help American Airlines Inc. keep track of seats, flights and reservations and now the world's largest privately owned real-time computer network. Or look at Amazon com Inc.'s mighty Web bookstore—which is helping to transform an entire industry.

How do you know if IT is fulfilling its potential to help the business grow? First, evaluate the role IT played in the company's major growth moves in the past few years: Was the Manager present at all important conversations about strategy? Did he or she make suggestions about new ways to do things? Can the Manager articulate the long-term vision for the IS department and how it relates to the overall business strategy? Your Manager has a responsibility to communicate new developments to the executive team. If you aren't receiving such updates, you may have cause for concern because the Manager could overlook something important.

3. Empower Productivity: Information technology (IT) can help people do things faster, easier and better. It should empower productivity at the level of both the individual employee and the organisation. Is that happening at your company?

One way to find out is by looking at internal feedback gleaned from steering committees, review boards and councils and surveys of end users. End-user surveys are good for turning up festering problems that impair employee productivity. But they also have their limits, even when users express overall satisfaction, that may not indicate a clean bill of health. You can make customers completely satisfied and still miss new business opportunities across the enterprise.

Again, the trust measure of IT's impact on productivity is the degree of alignment between IS and business strategy. Just because the Manager provides cutting-edge technology tools doesn't mean he's necessarily improving productivity. Someone can be very satisfied with the latest 'gee-whiz' technology, but they are not operating any differently and therefore the organisation is not getting any value from IT. Often organisations go merrily along upgrading to the latest version, but from a business standpoint [this] has a negative impact on productivity because they're making additional capital investments and may not be getting any value out of it. It's also worth noting that productivity is often retarded when people have to climb the next upgrade's learning curve.

The ultimate measure of IT's impact on productivity, however, comes from your own experience. Has your behaviour changed as a result of technology? Are you able to make decisions faster and easier than in the past? What sources of insight do you lack that could help you be a more effective business leader? Do you spend too much time looking for information? Does the Manager know of your frustrations, and is he responding? If the answer to any of these questions is 'no', then you need to sit down with the Manager and hammer out an attack plan to turn the situation around.

4. Innovation and Learning: Technology alone cant's foster innovation. To flourish, innovators need an open, risk-friendly corporate culture. To nurture innovation, IT can develop tools that help employees share information and learn from others. Take a hard look at how your employees research their ideas. Is there an easier way? Can geographically dispersed groups exchange ideas and experiences electronically? Is there a mechanism for capturing institutional knowledge? What about for obtaining and storing ideas from even the lowest-ranking employees? The Manager should play a significant role in both articulating the new space created by technological advancements and providing employees with tools to capitalise on their creative potential.

Benchmarking against other companies is the surest way to answer this question. If competitors are beating you to market with innovations, you need to ramp up your efforts. And such IT tools as intranets, video-conferencing, electronic whiteboards and online training courses play an increasingly important role in stimulating communication and collaboration.

5. **Running of IS:** This is both the most and least important. But it's the one executives have historically concentrated on, sometimes to the detriment of more strategic assessments. At the high level senior business executives are concerned with, you should almost be able to know about the running of Information systems. If your IS department is keeping up-to-date with outside developments, focusing on the customer, aligning properly with business strategy and providing tools to help employees do their jobs better and more creatively, then changes are it's operating effectively. In that case, sticking your nose in the Manager's business is unnecessary, counterproductive and potentially demoralizing.

If, on the other hand, your Manager is untested or appears unable to address the first four questions, then you may want to look inside the department. A malfunctioning Manager is a danger to the organisation, leaving it vulnerable to looming crises like the year 2000 problem and the European Monetary Union convergence as well as to more nimble competitors. Companies that maintain inflexible systems impair their ability to keep up with rivals' innovations and are as good as doomed, even when everyone else but the Manager is doing the right things.

In evaluating IS at the operational level, start with the IT budget-making sure to look at it in the most strategic light: What percentage of the IS budget is spent in furtherance of business objectives? If senior executives focus only on operational details like cost and spending, they can draw the wrong conclusion.

23.11 INFORMATION TECHNOLOGY ASSESSMENT

The Information Technology (IT) plan must be more than a traditional description of technology evolution, more than an ingenious plan scripted to presuade the organisation's financial decision makers to invest. The IT planning effort must move beyond the technical focus to include those issues of particular interest to the ogranisation. A self-serving approach to the development of an IT plan based solely on technical content is unacceptable. Unfortunately, most reports remain unread, tucked away, out of view, in hope of not reminding the author of the questionable expense of the time resource expended. However, a properly structured approach to the research leading up to the creation of the report can be the real value. The end result is not necessarily the benefit, it is the journey, the uncomfortable questions that are asked, and the opportunities that are uncovered that produce the lasting benefit to the organisation.

The information technology assessment methodology sets out to establish two things:

1. To capture the state of deployment of information technology within the organisation.
2. To rank the degree of which the organisation utilizes the existing information technology it has already deployed.

The first benefit in establishing these metrics is that you are able to determine the extent to which information technology is deployed throughout the organisation. As you must have experience that there are probably fewer individuals who appreciate the breath of application of information technology across the organisation. Knowing how widely information technology is deployed throughout an organisation can elicit a strong response from senior managers, who suddenly realize that without information technology, the organisation would virtually come to a standstill. This reality check for senior managers must be controlled and presented in the light of opportunity. You must leverage the fact that the organisation is, to a degree, dependent on information technology. The dependence must be presented as an opportunity to further increase the positive return to the business.

The information technology assessment typically will cover the following areas:

- **Organisational Structure:** The IT Department will take on many forms depending on the organisation's overall structure. Not only are there typical centralized and decentralized structure, there will be matrix structures inherited from the parent organisation.
- **Service Level:** The service level perception of the organisation's information technology users is used to rank the effectiveness of the IT department. This must involve a service level survey, which can take many forms.
- **Budget:** The organisation likely is unaware of the true cost of supporting its information technology resources. The total cost of ownership has been estimated by several industry analysts with some correlation. This study opens the door to opportunity in assigning costs directly to the appropriate business consumer of the technology.
- **Project Mix:** Primarily the assessment is used to identify projects that do not need to be part of the information technology portfolio. These projects are shown to be business initiatives and not technology initiatives.
- **Technology Portfolio:** This resembles a hardware and software inventory.

The fact that your organisation will conduct an information technology assessment should be communicated to the entire business. The communication does not have to be elaborate or highly detailed. The purpose is to inform employees that the organisation values its investment in information technology and that the result will be a status report used to highlight new opportunities to utilize technology even further. The communication can use any medium the organisation currently utilizes. The information posting should include the following information.

- A definition of the assessment
- Who or which group is leading the assessment
- The expected duration
- Any activities in which the employees may be asked to participate
- The expected benefits
- A date when the next communication will be made available.
- A contact for further information or feedback

The assessment is a preliminary measurement exercise. Employees become very interested in measurements because measurements can be used to rank employee performance. The old adage 'what gets measured is what gets done' is both opportunity and risk for the organisation. If the organisation selects the right measurements, then the right things will get done. However, if the organisation selects the wrong measurements, the wrong things will get done.

In the case of the information technology assessment, the measurements help produce the status report, but are more importantly used to identify opportunities in which you can leverage information technology to increase the return of business value.

The second benefit of the information technology assessment is the ability to rank your organisation against industry benchmarks. In large organisations there may be internal corporate benchmarks that can also be used. Table 23.3 provides a sample list of parameters that can be applied in each case.

The information technology assessment is not a trivial exercise for an organisation to complete. Typically, the complexity of the information technology assessment is proportional to the organisation's size. It follows that a large organisation may have several facilities or sites to evaluate and may have to deal with a larger number of personnel. A large organisation would also be challenged to uncover true financial statistics. However, the benefit of a large organisation is that the parameters can be used internally as benchmarks between business units. The comparison will be much more realistic because the underlying definition and calculation of the metrics will be similar across the organisation. A small organisation will have to compare its metrics strictly to external organisations, where the metric definition can vary.

Table 23.3 Metrics Available for the IT Assessment

Area	*Parameters*
Organisation	The following parameters can be used as a measure of compliance that your current organisation exhibits with respect to industry standards.
Organisation	❑ *Number of external contractors or consultants.* Using this measure along with the number of full-time IT personnel will provide a more precise comparison between organisations. ❑ *Number of IT personnel as a percent of total employees.* Typically used as a service metric, but in this context provides a normalized comparison between organisations of varying employee count. ❑ *IT personnel cost as a percent IT budget.* This will provide a normalized measure of the importance placed on human resources over technical resources. ❑ *It personnel cost as a percent of revenue.* This provides a more consistent metric when comparing the human resource importance between organisations of varying revenue levels. ❑ *It spending per total number of employees.* Used occasionally, but only within similar industries. Be cautious; the number of employees can vary dramatically between industries. ❑ *It personnel and contractor/consultant turnover as a percent of total employee turnover.* Use this parameter both alone and as compared to the rest of the organisation. An improvement to this parameter is to gather turnover by reason. The turnover reason can point out various root causes, some under the control of the IT department and some with the organisation. ❑ *Shift in IT personnel capabilities.* Not an absolute measure, but a classification of the skills required to perform the required technical tasks. Over time it is important to develop adequate training programs to meet the emerging technical capability demands.
Service Level	The following service level matrices can be used as a measure of compliance that your current organisation exhibits with respect to industry standards. ❑ *Number of information technology users per IT employee.* A common metric used throughout the industry for intercompany comparisons. This metric is best used to compare organisations in similar industries. Many users on a large, mainframe-based application can be supported by relatively few support personnel, while several distinct client/server applications and fewer end users require relatively more support personnel. ❑ *Support calls per employee and per IT employee.* This can be used as an inter-company comparison, but it primarily used as an internal measure of technical support loading. ❑ *Other support call parameters.* There are dozens of support call metrics that tend to provide better internal measurements than intercompany comparisons. However, these various support call metrics can be averaged to produce an estimation of customer satisfaction.

Area	*Parameters*
Budget	The following financial parameter can be used as a measure of compliance that your current organisation exhibits with respect to industry standards. ❒ *It budget as a percent of sales.* Probably the most widely used parameter when comparing IT departments between companies. ❒ *It versus business unit investment.* A recent trend shows that IT budgets are no longer tightly controlled within the IT Department, but rather each business unit is now being allocated an IT budget. Whether the IT budget is being distributed or the business units are simply allocating more of their existing budget to IT is not entirely clear. This certainly supports the notion that as in increasingly larger portion of technology dollars are controlled outside of the IT department, it follows that the decision making on the target of those budget dollars is being shared proportionally. ❒ *Rate of IT budget change.* Certainly an indicator of your organisation's perception of the value that IT has brought to the business. ❒ *Training as a percent of total IT budget.* Particular to information technology is the increasing rate of change. Developing skills in every emerging technology is not feasible. However, the rate at which training dollars are invested can indicate the optimism an organisation has towards information technology. ❒ *IT spending per technology.* A good comparison to ensure your shift in investment is correlating to the industry and its perception of emerging value-added technology.
Project	The following project parameters can be used as a measure of compliance that your organisation exhibits with respect to industry standards. ❒ *Project completion.* An indicator of whether the IT Department is profit or delivery focused. Primarily an internal benchmark. ❒ *Capital investment.* Also considered an IT budget metric. A relative internal comparison between the dollars invested in organisation capital projects versus those in the IT department. ❒ *R&D investment.* Also considered an IT budget metric. A relative internal comparison between the dollars invested in product research and development and those invested in emerging technology opportunity development. ❒ *Barriers to completion.* A good cross-industry comparison. Determines whether a specific technology. Can be combined with the project completion and the satisfaction with applications metrics to provide a realistic comparison. ❒ *BPR related project rate.* An indication on the value your organisation puts on the efficiency of the underlying business processes. Can be combined with the IT versus business unit investment metric.
Technology Portfolio	The following technology parameters can be used as a measure of compliance that your current organistion exhibits with respect to industry standards. ❒ *Platform distribution.* A ranking of the technologies used in your organisation and the market leadership those technology vendors occupy. ❒ *Rate of growth of client/server.* Combined with the legacy system replacement rate, this metric is a good indicator of the risk level an organisation is willing to accept. ❒ *Package (ERP) systems.* A good indicator of an organisation's willingness to change its thinking from independent business units to a cross-functional model.

A completed information status technology assessment allows the organisation to produce a status report. The review of the status report should serve the entire organistion. The IT status report does not have to be confined to the IT Department. This is an opportunity to alert senior management to any issues that have been identified.

23.12 REVIEWING THE INFORMATION TECHNOLOGY PLAN

IT plans are short lived. Unlike a typical business plan, IT plans do not have a life cycle of four or five years. For example, a personal computer will double in processing capability in 12 months, but can be purchased at the same price as the current model. With this in mind, the IT plan must be reviewed regularly. Typically IT plans can span up to three years.

23.12.1 Reviewing Organisation

Most organisations view the IT Department as a cost of doing business. That view is changing. As the need to carefully craft information technology solutions to support the business processes becomes an absolute necessity to compete, the IT Department is being considered an equal partner in shaping the organisation's direction.

Today, IT leaders are expected to be business leaders first and technologists second. The IT leader must possess the necessary business acumen to participate in the organisation's management process and business planning process. The IT leader must gain the credibility of his or her management peers in order to be trusted with the delivery of the information technology portfolio. An addition to the change in the skill set of the IT leader, is the change required of the IT Department's organizational structure. The change in the IT leader's skill set has brought change in the measurement systems placed against the department from the rest of the organisation. This prompts the IT Department to realign to best meet the new measurements systems.

The organisation's overall structure will have a great deal of influence over the demands placed upon the information technology organisational structure. In a large organisation, the IT Department will tend to be less constrained for resources. This will allow the IT Department to focus some energy on more strategic initiatives. Whereas the small organisation's IT department will likely be resource strained and will need to focus all its available energy on the tactical or operational task.

Utilizing the results of the IT assessment and determining the type of organisation being assessed will show the types of structures available. The intent is not to draw a completely new organisational chart, but to provide an enough influence from the assessment that the current organisational chart has reason to bend to accommodate the findings.

Fundamentally, there are only two structures to apply to organize the IT Department. They are the following:

1. *Centralized*: This structure provides tight control over all strategic, tactical, and operational technology issues. The advantage of the centralized organisation is that it provides a clear source of direction. There is no doubt of this source. In a technical organisation, a centralized structure will provide optimum definition and control of standards, policies, and procedures. This can lead to a better understanding and control of expense or total cost of ownership. Further, with a single set of standards policies, and procedures, the organisation provides itself with some flexibility to change as the need arises.
2. *Decentralized*: This structure provides loose control over all strategic, tactical, and operational technology issues. The advantage of the decentralized organisation increases with overall company size. Although there maybe more than one source of direction, having the input of more than a single source in a large company will provide more visibility to the needs of the organisation. Responsiveness increases as local business units are able to react quickly

to locally changing needs and requirements. Technical decisions can be averaged across the organization to provide a better overall result to the company.

Unfortunately, the optimum organisational structure will exist somewhere in between, typically referred to as a *hybrid* Within the hybrid organisational structure, there are several degrees of freedom that must be understood and defined. These degrees of freedom can include the following:

1. *Information technology steering committee*: In a large organisation where some IT Department decentralisation is expected, the overall information technology direction must be monitored and focused according to the business demands placed on it. A steering committee that includes technical members and key business unit members needs to be formed. There is a distinct need to provide specialized services on a particular set of technology. This could be hardware, software, networking, or communications to name a few. An area of particular interest is the application support.
2. *Competency centers*: The competency center is the notion of distributing responsibility over the ownership of the application process and the underlying infrastructure. The trend in this area continues to be that business units are adopting the application and that the IT Department is retaining control of the infrastructure. This is not meant as a divide and run scenario; it is intended as a partnership. IT will leverage a common infrastructure to keep the business unit from having to have the resources available to provide this service. While the business unit will invest in the process it operates and the IT Department does not have to invest in resources to learn the specific of each business units processes.
3. *Application ownership*: The data center is another functional area that can be organized centrally or be decentralized out to the business units. When the data center is decentralized out to the business units consider both the positive and negatives consequences. Technology consistency is more difficult to maintain. Each data center will tend to make decisions independently of the others, and technology fragmentation can occur. However, multiple data centers offer the opportunity to create redundant or backup data centers. However, there must be sufficient organisation control to mandate data center standards. A slight variation on the decentralized model offers the benefits of both models. The campus model is similar to the decentralized model in that there are multiple centers supporting each business unit able to act as a backup. The campus model capitalizes on the centralized model value to provide consistency in standards. Unfortunately, the campus model is limited to organisations, who themselves are aligned along a campus model. If an organisation locates units independent of each other geographically, then the campus model reduces to the decentralized model.
4. *Hybrid model*: The hybrid organisation model will vary in terms of its implementation in different organisations. This is primarily a result of how the decentralized technical members are viewed. Should they be IT Department members who live in the business unit or members of the business unit who act as technical representatives for the IT Department.

23.12.2 Reviewing Service Level

The service level provided by the IT Department to the technology end users is probably the most interesting parameter to review. The service level is usually estimated by considering the effectiveness of the organisation's technical support help desk. Although this is a very important metric, you must understand that there are other considerations as well.

The IT Department is interested to know how it is perceived from its customer base, the information technology end users. Do the end users view the IT Department as an operational or strategic partner? This dictates the importance the business units will place on the importance of the IT Department. Further, it is proportional to the investment the organisation is willing to make in information technology in general and the IT Department specifically. This will also be concluded from the perception of how the IT Department is perceived to understand the underlying business needs and not just looking to deploy new technology. The IT Department must take a proactive approach to the underlying business needs. It is very important to understand the business that is being supported. This provides the opportunity to determine whether the business is taking full advantage of the available technology.

As part of the IT assessment, try to include an end user survey. Properly structured, replies will provide a wealth of information in a number of areas. This information will help establish some of the parameters previously discussed as well as create awareness. Further, you need to get appreciation for the task at hand. End users need to understand that the IT Department is in a transition and that the final result will provide improved service level to the technology end users. In addition to service level parameters, the survey can capture data that can support cost/benefit calculations leading to identification of new service opportunities. Technology end users need more than help desks. Conducting a survey is one way to accumulate statistics and to produce a customer satisfaction benchmark. Using this benchmark, several opportunities may exist to provide increased support to the end user. For instance, the end users would surely appreciate the fact that the IT Department solicited their input the determine new service offerings.

The IT assessment will attempt to capture information that can lead to conclusions on several issues related to the end user service level.

The first area to get focused feedback is those issues dealing with the end users first priority, that is, technology problem solving and support. This is usually an area where feedback is abundant. Unfortunately, it is usually negative feedback. However, it is the things done poorly that need to be improved. The intent is to categorize the feedback and look for patterns that may point to a particular application or infrastructure element or that may indicate additional training is needed on the part of the help desk technicians. This information could be coupled with reorganisation of the help desk discussed previously.

It is useful to gauge the interest level of the end users to contribute new ideas to the improvement of the information technology portfolio. The use of comment sections provides the opportunity for improvement suggestions. Still better is a comment section that has selections identified. This helps get feedback on specific proposed initiatives and prompts the end users to think of similar needs.

The IT Department can organize itself sufficiently to develop and manage a service level agreement with the end users. There are likely to be several service level agreements in place.

Earlier you learned about the concept of a competency center. The competency center could be used as a vehicle to package and deliver the services included in the end user application service level agreement. The following are various elements to consider with the competency center:

1. *Help desk*: The service level agreement will identify the call resolution rate. That is, how many calls can be responded to in a given time period and what percentage will get resolved in a given time period. The help desk calls must be tacked and documented for several reasons. The two most important reasons are to enable repeat problem identification and to support a claim of meeting the service level agreement.
2. *Application Testing*: Regardless of whether the competency center delivers the enhancements, it should have the capability to test the enhancements in the organisation's production environment.
3. *Customisation*: The competency center is designed to serve the organisation as a whole. It makes little sense to have end users responsible to outsource and project manage application enhancements.

A new release of the application must be tested prior to release into production. The competency center provides an opportunity to utilize the organisation's data and other unique attributes that the application vendor is unable to provide.

4. *Training*: Training can be best organized within a competency center because the application expertise is already present. An external training organisation will not be as familiar with day to day operation of the application, especially if the application has been customized to the organisation.
5. *Marketing*: This is a proactive role for the competency center. The organization cannot afford to have all of its application end users responsible for monitoring new releases of the application for new feature function. The competency center can be responsible for targeting new feature function availability to the specific end users.

The parameters developed in the area of IT Department budget lead to the estimation of the total cost of ownership (TCO). A much touted parameter in the information technology industry, the TCO metric first arose out of the personal desktop computer. The Gartner Group lead the way with TCO studies in the early 1990s. The TCO studies were the first real attempts to consolidate the total investment an organisation must make to support the desktop environment. The TCO parameter accumulate both operational expense and capital investment. The operational expense captures the cost of administration, support, and operations, while the capital investment includes the cost of capital in addition to the acquisition cost. To what extent direct end user costs are included tends to skew the comparison between TCO parameters between organisations.

The intent of the IT assessment in this area is to gather sufficient financial information to formulate the TCO. The IT assessment should focus on the following areas:

1. *Allocation of costs*: It is necessary to determine if a charge back policy exists. Do the end users to the technology have to pay from their departmental budgets or are the funds administered from the IT department budget? What decision cycle or methodology does the organisation use to determine whether a particular information technology investment is appropriate? Is there a particular cost tracking mechanism in place to support the allocation of cost?
2. *Administration costs*: This is a more difficult metric to quantify. However, it is important to understand the amount of time and expense that is invested in developing partnerships and alliances with information technology vendors. The degree to which partnerships are a success can be measured, in part, through the use of compatible technology.
3. *Support costs*: Several areas of interest help develop an idea of support costs. Assess the use of standards, both technology standards (operating systems, network topologies and protocol, and so on) and product standards (brand names, models, and so on). Also determine the extent to which product suites are used.
4. *Purchase costs*: Determine the level to which the organization takes advantage of volume purchasing agreements or has negotiated long-term purchasing agreements.
5. *Operational costs*: Determine the mix of purchase versus leasing of technology. How does older technology get allocated throughout the organisation? Is it recycled, for example, by being trickled down to less demanding applications? How does the IT Department model its software licensing? Is it a concurrent user model or a named user model?

With these parameters, the TCO model will begin to take shape. In some cases it will be a revealing exercise. The TCO is traditionally a Figure that greatly exceeds the purchase price. The purchase price typically is the only metric considered in most organisations.

With the IT assessment results, the IT Department can begin to focus the IT plan with respect to financial planning.

The IT Department budget as a percent of revenue tends to pose a dichotomy to the reviewer. If the actual rate is lower than the industry rate, then it can be perceived that the organisation is well positioned, because it is managing to spend less than its competitor on information technology. It can also be viewed that the organisation is behind the industry and needs to invest more aggressively. If the actual rate is higher than the industry rate, it can be interpreted that the organisation is spending too much on information technology and should consider a more conservative approach. It can also be interpreted that the organisation is being aggressive with respect to its competitors.

The next most popular industry metric is the TCO. However, this parameter is still relatively new in practice. As such, it may be the first time an organisation will be exposed to the TCO. Be well prepared when using this measure in the IT budget. Although the resulting plan may be taking a very aggressive approach to controlling the newly found/allocated costs, the shock of tabling the TCO for the first time may present a barrier to overcome. In this section you will consider some of the ways in which the TCO parameters can be controlled.

To lower the purchase cost of technology, look into preconFigured units, which, in turn, drive the need for standards. If the organisation can leverage many units at a standard configuration, the costs can be lowered. Look to vendors or resellers that can provide a preconfiguration service. The organisation can provide the vendor with a standard profile or image to be installed in each unit. Typically, this is best leverage in the workstation or desktop/laptop area.

To lower support costs, look at your organisation's business model. If the organisation is global, then it follows that the technology vendor must provide a global support model. Attempting to provide service and support across different time zones and different geography involving different languages and cultures can be an enormous challenge. Put simply, the vendor must be where your organisation is located. Of course, product quality should obviate the need for extensive support and service. Ensure the vendor implements quality practices and procedures consistent with your organisation's quality expectations.

To lower operating costs, the organisation must consider the rate at which it wants to refresh technology. Historically, organizations used the trickle down method to reallocate older technology, especially in the computer desktop area. An emerging trend is to consider lease arrangements over capital purchases. Some programs offer the capability to hold the expense constant while replacing the technology as the performance increases.

Another key item to consider closely is the concept of volume license agreements. Historically, the volume required excluded the majority of organisation, however recent trends are clearly bringing the volume barrier to the point where most every company can participate. Be sure to clearly define the model as concurrent use and not per named user. Basically, the concurrent user model requires that you license only active users, while the names user model requires that you license every end user regardless of use. This should be applied to every support (email), productivity (word processor), or production application like SAP, Baan etc.

23.12.3 Reviewing Project Mix

The IT Department has a portfolio of projects it must manage to completion. These projects are typically prioritized relative to the end user's persistence of getting the project delivered. However, the project list must reflect what the IT department should be doing from an organisation perspective and not an individual perspective. The organisation can utilize information technology to do the following:

1. Simply automate existing processes
2. Bring together islands of information
3. Align business processes
4. Reengineer the business
5. Completely redefine the scope of the business.

The level of change the organisation is promoting determines the number and type of projects the IT department must manage.

On the whole, IT Department must manage, there are three broad categories of projects:

1. *Strategic*: The projects are focused on the initiatives in the organisation's business plan that are categorized as capital investment initiatives. These projects will help support the organisation in its new form planned for in the strategic plan.
2. *Tactical*: These project are those initiatives that are currently in place supporting the business in its current or near term form. A tactical project evolves from a planned strategic project or it can be an operational project that may be dealing with infrastructure.
3. *Development*: These projects typically support the strategic initiatives of evolving the technical infrastructure. These projects are coupled with training and development opportunities for the IT personnel. These projects will result in new infrastructure being deployed or new capabilities that can be offered to the organisation.

The IT assessment will attempt to draw out information that will lead to conclusion in the project mix. There are the three categories previously defined: strategic, tactical, and development. Furthermore, you must determine whether the IT Department is leading projects that it should otherwise not be leading. In fact there is a great opportunity to ensure that the business units are taking ownership of the projects that are directly related to their business processes.

The financial parameter related to capital and R & D investment are interesting to calculate and then compare with the organization's overall rate of investment in these categories.

The IT plan must be focused to clearly define the three types of projects and the criteria to determine the type. Project ownership of each type of project must be clearly defined. The fact that all projects must be profit focussed must replace the notion of delivery focused projects. This is not to say that project deadlines are not to be considered at all. Rather, timeliness and milestones are evaluators of progress and really have little to do with success.

The strategic project should have a project leader assigned who resides in the business unit that owns the project. The appropriate business unit, through its understanding of the organization's strategic direction, will likely have initiated this type of project. If the business unit is not willing to manage the project, then the project objective needs to be re-examined. If an initiative is important to a department, that department will certainly provide leadership. It is in that business unit's best interest to take control in order to determine when the project success factor has been reached.

The tactical project is one that is currently in motion to support an existing business need. As with the strategic project, the probable leader for the tactical project is from the sponsoring business unit. This does not preclude the fact that the IT Department may have a major contribution to make to the project. Tactical projects need to complete and deliver the expected benefits in the organisation's near term, typically between 2 and 12 months.

The development project is typically an internal IT Department project. It is tied to strategic initiative, but is separate from the time line of the strategic project. The strategic project may not begin for up to 12 months; however, the technology capabilities need to be understood and developed early and then maintained. As such, the project leader is usually from within the IT Department. The development projects should be organized to provide the majority of training that IT personnel will require. Training does not have to be a separate exercise.

23.12.4 Reviewing Technology Portfolio

Here you will consider the types of information technology and tools typically used and you will define a way in which to group these into manageable families. It tends to look more like an organisational structuring, and in the end this may be the most efficient way to approach the technology classification. The technology portfolio needs to capture several characteristics of the organisation and the technology that is deployed.

From an organisational perspective, deployed application-level technology tends to follow the vertical functions within an organisation. That is to say, certain applications will appear useful only in certain parts of the business. It follows from this that the hardware that supports the application will align along the same application and organisational lines. As you look down into the layers of supporting technology and peer into the infrastructure, the alignment of the technology with the business is less clear. You see this trend continue: The further the technology is from the end user application, the more likely it is to be application independent. The infrastructure will begin to move from a vertical alignment to lay horizontally across the organisation.

From the perspective of managing the technology, you can see that the technology alignment supports with your assumptions of the organisational alignment. Previously, you learned about the requirement of business unit leadership for strategic and tactical projects. It follows that the management or ownership of the technology should follow the same orientation. The business units should own and support the applications they use in their business. That is, as long as it is specific to that business unit. The challenge is then to locate technical resources within the business units, which is not difficult. What is more difficult is to decide if that technical resource is financially supported by the IT Department or is a member of the business unit. The latter is preferred, but is highly dependent on the overall organisational model.

As you move away from the end user application into the infrastructure, the alignment to the business is less and the technology begins to standardize across business units. The technical resource to support the infrastructure will likely be part of the IT Department. The goal is to leverage centralized support for a standard technical infrastructure.

The following technology parameters can be used to gathered or calculated for the IT Department technology portfolio:

1. Platform distribution
2. Rate of growth of client/server
3. Type of computing devices used
4. Type of production systems used
5. Type of productivity tools used
6. Type of collaboration tools used.

The IT assessment will draw primarily on technical personnel to gather data for the infrastructure area. In some cases this can be gathered from existing hardware and software inventories. The survey should include such items as database, collaboration, operating, and network systems, server hardware, and communications. Business unit personnel will have valuable input in the area of production applications, productivity tools, and collaboration needs.

You've reviewed the opportunity for an organisation to focus the IT plan using information recovered from an assessment of the current state. There are probably hundreds of parameters that could be calculated. The success lies with those who understand what they need from the assessment in order to develop a highly focused IT plan.

23.13 THE FUTURE OF ERP SYSTEMS

Enterprise Resource Planning is the latest high end solution, information technology has lent to business application. The ERP solutions seek to streamline and integrate operation processes and information flows in the company to synergise the resources of an organisation namely men, material, money and machine through information. Initially, implementation of an ERP package was possible only for very large multi national companies and infrastructure companies due to high cost involved. ERP implementation in India is picking up very fast. Last few years have seen lot of products coming into the market and the leading companies taking initiatives to implement ERP. But most of these implementation have not yet witness the expected results. However, the experts are hopeful about the success an ERP system. Again, it is not a magic tool, which will transform everything overnight, rather successful implementation is a long journey towards enterprise excellence.

The Internet represents the next major technology enabler which allows rapid supply chain management between multiple operations and trading partners. Most ERP systems are enhancing their products to become 'Internet Enabled' so that customers worldwide can have direct access to the supplier's ERP system. ERP systems are building in the Workflow Management functionally which provides a mechanism to manage and control the flow of work by monitoring logistic aspects like workload, capacity, throughput times, work queue lengths and processing times.

Recognising the need to go beyond the MRP-II all ERP vendors are busy adding to their product portfolio. BaaN for example has already introduced concepts like IRP (Intelligence Resource Planning), MRP-III (Money Resources Planning) and has acquired companies for strategic technologies like Visual Product Configuration, Product Data Management and Finite Scheduling.

23.14 REFERENCES

1. Norbert Welti's Successful SAP R/3 Implementation: Practical Management of ERP Projects.
2. Paul Brislen and K.R. Krishnakumar: Enterprise Resource Planning, www.whatis.com.
3. Shankarnarayanan, S., 'ERP Systems' Using IT to gain a competitive advantage.
4. Sandeep Pal: ERP and Web-based Self Service Application, Sr. Manager (Mktg.), Oracle Software India Ltd.
5. Sudhakar Ram: Enterprise Resource Planning, Director, Mastek Ltd.
6. Polly Schneider: Wanted ERPeople skills, CIO Magazine, March 1st, 1999.
7. CIO Executive Research Center—www.cio.com
8. Cisco Systems Inc.—www.cisco.com
9. ERP Supply Chain Research Center—www.cio.com
10. John Edwards, Emerging Technology, CIO Magazine, July 1st, 1999
11. J.D. Edwards & Co.—www.jdedwards.com
12. Oracle Corp.—www.oracle.com
13. PeopleSoft Inc—www.PeopleSoft.com
14. Polly Schneider, Wanted ERPeople Skills, CIO Magazine, March 1st, 1999
15. SAP AG—www.sap.com
16. The Baan Co.—www.baan.com

24

MOBILE COMMERCE

24.1 INTRODUCTION

E-commerce, or the buying and selling of goods and services on the Internet, has become a part of daily life for many people. The use of the Internet to purchase goods and services has grown along with the popularity of the Internet. Businesses are increasingly turning to the Internet to increase revenue and profits. As the Internet expands to every corner of the globe, it is becoming easier and easier to access it from a wide variety of devices. Cell phones, PDAs, and other mobile devices can now access the Internet from across the globe. Many E-commerce companies have attempted to exploit this rapidly growing segment of the Internet. E-commerce over mobile devices has now been termed M-Commerce. M-Commerce by definition is E-commerce that occurs through the use of wireless solutions such as cell phones, pocket PC's, and PDAs. It allows a user to purchase goods and services on the move, anytime, and anywhere.

Since many businesses used to be conducted in traditional marketplaces, the new innovative market place the Internet and e-Commerce, has provided a huge impact on the global business environment and it has changed the way of conducting business. Regarding the advantages of e-Commerce, firms keep looking for new technology and applications in order to be more competitive and successful. One new business strategy trend is the progress toward mobile computing and the wireless web. This trend is known as mobile computing or nomadic computing, which provides new interest for firms in m-Commerce. M-Commerce is creating entirely new opportunities both for mobile devices and services and it provides the same capabilities, functionalities and mobility of e-Commerce.

There are various mobile devices used in m-Commerce, such as digital cameras, cellular phones, Personal Digital Assistants (PDA) and wireless laptops to name a few. Therefore, users can have unlimited access to all types of information, including music, news, sports, stock trading and financial reports. Wireless and mobile networks have been growing in terms of mobile devices, middle-ware development, standards and network implementation and user acceptance so there is great interest in mobile technology. Demand for mobile devices is increasing throughout the world; there were 720 million people using mobile phones in 2000 and the number is increasing. Such an increase of mobile users will have a huge impact on m-Commerce and it will bring many benefits to firms. This emerging technology has created a new marketplace, called m-Commerce and it has become a new way for many firms to conduct their businesses. This study presents a conceptual understanding of m-Commerce, its four main issues (technological and strategic issues) and their implementation and the substantial benefits of this technology. All of these aspects of m-Commerce may be considered for successfully m-Commerce practices are provided.

Since m-Commerce is a new concept, it is important to first understand the concepts that are associated with it. M-Commerce, also called wireless commerce or mobile e-Commerce does not have one particular definition. In principle, m-Commerce is any monetary business activity conducted via mobile Communication networks. Some studies, however, define m-Commerce in different ways. For example, Tarasewich *et al.* (2002) defined m-Commerce as, all activities related to commercial transaction conducted through communications networks that interface with wireless/mobile devices. Another study defined of m-Commerce as, the use of hand held wireless/mobile devices to communicate, interact and transact via high speed connection to the Internet (Shuster, 2001). This study simplified the definition of m-Commerce as, any activity, including both monetary and non-monetary, conducted through any mobile device. Another important concept that should be defined is mobile devices, since this is how m-Commerce is conducted. It is not easy to present a precise definition of mobile devices (Bardo and Jurgen. 2002). According to Hansmann (2001), mobile devices are defined as electronic appliances that serve communication, data processing and exchange purpose, which can be conducted by its user and which can receive, send or transmit information to other devices. Current mobile devices include mobile phones, mobile-enabled hand held computers, wireless laptops, vehicle-mounted technology and personal pagers. These devices can be interactively used with other devices and can network via wired synchronization.

24.2 MOBILE COMMERCE

Mobile Commerce is any transaction, engaging the transfer of ownership or rights to use goods and services, which is started and completed by using mobile access to computer-mediated networks with the help of an electronic device. Japan and some European countries are much ahead of the United States in using of mobile commerce and mobile payments, and also these countries have already become commonplace.

Mobile Commerce, also known as **M-Commerce** or **mCommerce**, is the ability to conduct commerce using a mobile device, such as a mobile phone, a Personal digital assistantPDA, a smart phone, or other emerging mobile equipment. Mobile Commerce has been defined as follows:

'*Mobile Commerce is any transaction, involving the transfer of ownership or rights to use goods and services, which is initiated and/or completed by using mobile access to computer-mediated networks with the help of an electronic device.*'

Mobile commerce was born in **1997** when the first two mobile-phone enabled **Coca Cola** vending machines were installed in the **Helsinki** area in **Finland**. The machines accepted payment via SMS text messages. The first mobile phone-based banking service was launched in 1997 by Merita Bank of Finland, also using SMS.

Since the launch of the **iPhone,** mobile commerce has moved away from SMS systems and into actual applications. SMS has significant security vulnerabilities and congestion problems, even though it is widely available and accessible. In addition, improvements in the capabilities of modern mobile devices make it prudent to place more of the resource burden on the mobile device.

Mobile Commerce has staged a remarkable come-back. Driven by the technological innovations in the field of telecommunications, it is showing signs of a healthy recovery. The collapse of the dot-com boom in 2001/2002 had dealt a severe blow not only to Electronic Commerce but also to Mobile Commerce, which was just about developing at that time. In addition to a general lack of customer demand for mobile, location-based, services, it suffered heavily under the technical deficiencies of end-devices, slow data transmission and unripe technological standards. These factors in turn had a negative impact on the customer acceptance of mobile services and whatever little demand was available, was rendered useless. Many of the environmental conditions have changed since then. Technology innovations have reduced many barriers to acceptance. Increasing globalization has led to more mobility and therefore to greater demand for mobile, ubiquitous services that can be consumed 'anytime, anywhere'.

24.3 PRODUCTS AND SERVICES AVAILABLE

24.3.1 Mobile Ticketing

Tickets can be sent to mobile phones using a variety of technologies. Users are then able to use their tickets immediately, by presenting their phones at the venue.

Tickets can be booked and cancelled on the mobile device with the help of simple application downloads, or by acccsing the WAP portals of various travel agents or direct service providers.

24.3.2 Mobile Vouchers, Coupons and Loyalty Cards

Mobile ticketing technology can also be used for the distribution of vouchers, coupons, and loyalty cards. These items are represented by a virtual token that is sent to the mobile phone. A customer presenting a mobile phone with one of these tokens at the point of sale receives the same benefits as if they had the traditional token. Stores may send coupons to customers using **location-based services** to determine when the customer is nearby.

24.3.3 Content Purchase and Delivery

Currently, mobile content purchase and delivery mainly consists of the sale of ring-tones, wallpapers, and games for mobile phones. The convergence of mobile phones, portable audio players, and video players into a single device is increasing the purchase and delivery of full-length music tracks and video. The download speeds available with 4G networks make it possible to buy a movie on a mobile device in a couple of seconds.

24.3.4 Location-based Services

The location of the mobile phone user is an important piece of information used during mobile commerce transactions. Knowing the location of the user allows for **location-based services** such:

- ❒ Local discount offers
- ❒ Local weather
- ❒ Tracking and monitoring of people
- ❒ Information services

A wide variety of information services can be delivered to mobile phone users in much the same way as it is delivered to PCs. These services include:

- ❒ News
- ❒ Stock quotes
- ❒ Sports scores
- ❒ Financial records
- ❒ Traffic reporting

Customized traffic information, based on a user's actual travel patterns, can be sent to a mobile device. This customized data is more useful than a generic traffic-report broadcast, but was impractical before the invention of modern mobile devices due to the bandwidth requirements.

24.3.5 Mobile Banking

Banks and other financial institutions use mobile commerce to allow their customers to access account information and make transactions, such as purchasing stocks, remitting money. This service is often referred to as **Mobile Banking**, or M-Banking.

24.3.6 Mobile StoreFront

The reinvention of the mobile phone as a touch sensitive handheld computer has for the first time made mobile commerce practically feasible. 'According to ABI Research, mobile is going to get a lot bigger in the ecommerce market. The research firm is predicting that in 2015, \$119bn worth of goods and services will be purchased via a mobile phone.'

24.3.7 Mobile Brokerage

Stock market services offered via mobile devices have also become more popular and are known as Mobile Brokerage. They allow the subscriber to react to market developments in a timely fashion and irrespective of their physical location.

24.3.8 Auctions

Over the past three years **mobile reverse auction** solutions have grown in popularity. Unlike traditional auctions, the reverse auction (or low-bid auction) bills the consumer's phone each time they place a bid. Many mobile SMS commerce solutions rely on a one-time purchase or one-time subscription; however, reverse auctions offer a high return for the mobile vendor as they require the consumer to make multiple transactions over a long period of time.

24.3.9 Mobile Browsing

Using a mobile browser—a **World Wide Web** browser on a mobile device—customers can shop online without having to be at their personal computer.

24.3.10 Mobile Purchase

Catalog merchants can accept orders from customers electronically, via the customer's mobile device. In some cases, the merchant may even deliver the catalog electronically, rather than mailing a paper catalog to the customer. Some merchants provide **mobile websites** that are customized for the smaller screen and limited user interface of a mobile device.

24.3.11 Mobile Marketing and Advertising

In the context of mobile commerce, **mobile marketing** refers to marketing sent to mobile devices. Companies have reported that they see better response from mobile marketing campaigns than from traditional campaigns. Mobile campaigns must be based on the global Content Generation or what is called Generation C and four other 'C's: Creativity, Casual Collapse, Control, and Celebrity.

24.4 CHARACTERISTICS OF M-COMMERCE

One reason that people adopt m-Commerce may be due to its unique characteristics. It has two fundamental characteristics, Mobility and Reachability. Figure 24.1 shows the characteristics and attributes of m-Commerce.

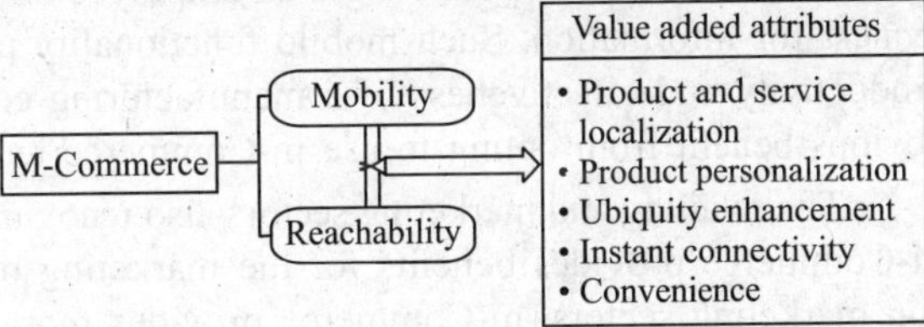

Fig. 24.1 Characteristics and attributes of m-Commerce

Mobility capability of mobile devices provides users with a free of time and location. Reachability is directly related to mobility. Mobile device users can be reached instantly. These two characteristics can solve any geographic or time obstacles of a particular situation. Other characteristics and attributes include: ubiquity, user identity, location awareness and interactivity, security and instant connectivity. Ubiquity is the most obvious advantage of m-Commerce because it can satisfy the need for real-time information and communication anywhere, regardless of a user's location. Furthermore, size and portability would be important reason for potential customers to adopt mobile devices. The desire to buy mobile devices can be easily satisfied by these characteristics.

24.5 ADVANTAGES OF M-COMMERCE

M-Commerce will generate many benefits as has e-Commerce. In the beginning, m-Commerce targeted individual customers rather than businesses. In other words, m-Commerce has mainly been applied to consumer-oriented areas. Such a new type of technology provides individual customers with better data exchange and communication. The current usage of m-Commerce, however, is not only for individuals, but also for organizations. There is now a fast-growing interest in expanding m-Commerce technology into the enterprise market. Now more firms realize that urgent launching of m-Commerce initiative will be a successful strategy for them. A member of firms have launched m-commerce, and each of them has had success m-Commerce, in different ways.

Benefits of m-Commerce are reflected in two aspects; indirect and direct benefits. Regarding indirect, m-Commerce provides more competitive advantages than other firms. M-Commerce initiatives bring the rapid development and deployment of customized-wireless applications, as well as the integration of these applications with an organization's existing communication and data infrastructure, which could create awareness in their business areas. Strategies of a developing market for m-Commerce could enable firms to provide more in-depth comprehensive analysis for its clients. On the other hand, direct benefits are more noticeable in many industry sectors. m-Commerce could improve the efficiency and effectiveness of business activities by distributing information to the workforce remote and by offering new ways in which to interact with customers. Organizations being able to utilize the power of mobile technology in order to automate and make business processes more efficient, may acquire the benefits of enhanced productivity, lowered operational cost, increased customer satisfaction and improved decision-making.

Industry sectors gain substantial benefits from m-Commerce include manufacturing, marketing and retailing. Increasing productivity with efficiency and effectiveness may be the most important assets for manufacturing firms. Mobile devices and m-Commerce are one way to increase productivity. Manufacturing firms utilizing m-Commerce have increased worker productivity. By using mobile devices, such as cell phones, personal digital assistants (PDAs) and laptops with built-in wireless modems, employees can access the company's network and ERP systems or supply-chain integration applications even when they are away from the office. Also, employees can manage their schedules, exchange e-mail and stay in touch with mobile devices on the road. Field operation workers may use mobile devices in order to collect data. Furthermore, the invention of communication standards such as Wireless Access Protocol (WAP) and Bluetooth makes it possible for an employee on the road to quickly respond to a customer's request for information. Such mobile functionality provides great possibilities in improving the productivity and effectiveness of a manufacturing company. Increasing productivity is the most obvious benefit from opting to use m-Commerce technology.

The retailing and marketing sectors also recognize the increased benefits from m-Commerce. M-Commerce provides benefits for the marketing of goods, services and content. In the retail and marketing sectors, m-Commerce provides more opportunity for service differentiation and new routes to promote and sell products to business partners and customers. In other words, m-Commerce is the creation of a new channel for businesses. Five benefits that m-Commerce can provide in the marketing sector: creation of zones, place utility, personalization, promotional utility and interaction. These noticeable benefits of m-Commerce are the systematic, but rapid generation of mobile shopping areas, which are similar real or virtual malls. With e-Commerce, marketing and retailing activities are only possible when customers have the web access. With m-Commerce, firms, however, can market their products and services to customers anytime, anywhere because of mobile devices. With mobility, individual purchasing opportunities will be maximized.

In brief, advantages of m-commerce (Mobile-Commerce) are:

- Providing wider reach
- Reducing transaction cost
- Streamline business processes

- Competitive pricing
- Reducing time to order
- The age of mobile shopping is here to stay, consumers can access millions of products at the palm of their hands and retailers can increase their reach and overall sales.
- Use of graphics unlimited
- Unlimited bandwidth
- WAP and SMS unlimited to small number of characters and text.
- More functionality for mobile Internet over mobile phones and existing generation of handhelds than for mobile computers
- Small screens of most devices still unlimited types of file and data transfer
- The good news is that these mobile sites are an addition of your current contribution but they can also locate on their own
- The mobile sites can be foundation from the same database that your are performing now to make their management very straightforward
- New advanced mobile applications characteristically engage high-speed services being accessed by devices distantly, anywhere, at any time
- M-commerce requests to eradicate even further the intelligence of a consumer having to go to the business for products or services, or requiring to be skilled in multiple technologies or having to preparation whenever they want to contact a business using the Internet
- To allow the development of customer use of data options m-commerce applications and technology that have evolved quickly

24.6 M-COMMERCE TECHNOLOGIES

Mobile devices typically connect through the Internet using one of two technologies, either the Wireless Application Protocol or iMode. Which technology is used depends on location and carrier. Both protocols have security protocols in place to protect data that is transferred. They each also have methods to authenticate the device to the carrier. The following sections will briefly discuss each protocol and then detail the security implementations for each protocol.

24.6.1 Wireless Application Protocol

The Wireless Application Protocol, or WAP, is one of the most widely used standards within M-Commerce. It is a standard created by the WAP forum that dictates a common method for accessing and viewing web content through wireless mobile devices, primarily mobile phones. It has been designed to function on mobile devices that do not have the CPU power, memory, bandwidth, or display abilities that desktop or laptop computers have. The WAP protocol details everything from how the mobile device needs to function when accessing and viewing Internet content, to how the data must be transferred. Every protocol within WAP is optimized for low bandwidth and low power devices. WAP was also developed to be bearer independent. That means that it was designed to work on a variety of mobile network types for example GPRS, EDGE, and CDMA.

WAP allows a user to utilize very basic browser software called a 'micro-browser' to visit web pages that are designed specifically for mobile devices. These sites are usually designed with text and minimum graphics. WAP has also been designed to be flexible and allow devices with varying display abilities, for example screen size or resolution, to all work properly when accessing the same sites.

WAP was initially release in 1998. WAP Version 1.0, as it was called, utilized its own set of wireless protocols in order to communicate with the carrier and remote websites. The following figure shows the different layers of the WAP 1.0 network stack and the stacks utilized by the carrier and a remote web server. The WAP Device is the mobile device, the WAP Gateway is the carrier, and the Web Server is a remote website server. For information on the specific protocols see the WAP Forum documentation for WAP 1.0 (Fig. 24.2).

WAP Device	WAP Gateway		WAP Serve
WAE			WAE
WSP	WSP	HTTP	HTTP
WTP	WTP		
WTLS	WTLS	SSL	SSL
WDP	WDP	TCP	TCP
Bearer	Bearer	IP	IP

Fig. 24.2

This protocol stack was functional for the first incarnation of WAP but it was not very secure and it was not fully functional with all Internet sites. Security in WAP 1.0 was provided through WTLS. WTLS is a scaled down version of the popular TLS protocol. The major security weakness of WAP 1.0 came from a problem called the 'Gap Problem'. When a mobile device attempts to connect to a website it must first connect to the carrier and then the carrier will pass the web request to the remote web site. When using WTLS and WAP 1.0 the mobile device would make a secure connection with the carrier and the carrier would use TLS to make a separate secure connection to the remote website. In the figure above you can see that the Gateway transforms the WTLS connection into a TLS connection with the remote website. The security vulnerability, or Gap Problem, arose when the carrier had to take the data from the mobile device and pass it to the remote server. As a middleman, the carrier would decrypt the data from the mobile device and then reencrypt it using TLS to pass the data to the remote carrier. After the data is unencrypted and before it is passed to the remote website, the data is stored entirely in plain text and visible to anyone who gains access to the carrier's server. The preferred work around to the Gap problem in WAP 1.0 was to not save any transactions to disk and/or, if you were a corporate customer, move the WAP Gateway within the company network so that the data can be better protected. This solution was not thorough enough and is one of many reasons that WAP 2.0 was developed.

WAP 2.0 was released in late 2001 and is fully backwards compatible with WAP 1.0. WAP 2.0 added support for TLS, HTTP, and TCP and introduced the ability to push data from a carrier to a WAP enabled mobile device. WAP 2.0 is also able to support more powerful mobile devices over higher bandwidth connections. From a security perspective the most important addition was the ability to utilize the TCP\IP network stack. The reason being is that TLS could now be used instead of WTLS and common PC Internet technologies could be utilized. The use of TLS instead of WTLS allows a mobile device to make a secure tunnel from the device all the way to the remote website. There is no longer a need to decrypt and reencrypt the data at the carrier's server (WAP Gateway). Therefore there is no longer a Gap Problem. Figure 24.3 shows the protocol stack for WAP 2.0 and the stacks utilized in a typical web connection. The WAP device is the mobile device, the WAP Proxy is the carrier, and the Web Server is the remote website's server.

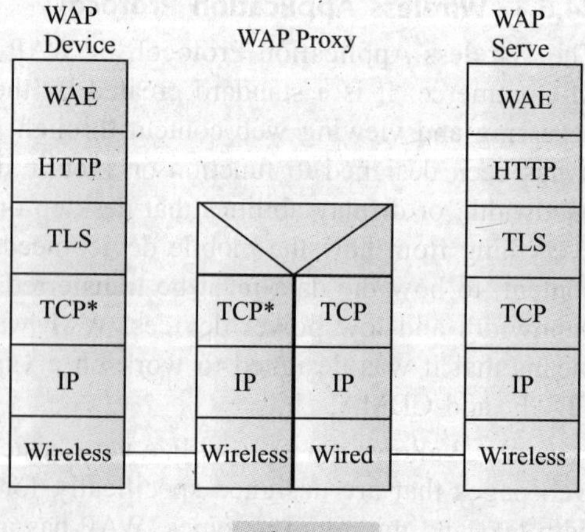

Fig. 24.3

According to the WAP Forums documentation of WAP 2.0, the WAP Gateway from version 1.0 was removed and replaced by the WAP proxy. The Proxy does not perform translation like the WAP Gateway but instead assists by speeding up communications and it can provide services to a mobile device through a WAP push.

Besides the ability to use TLS and make a secure connection from device to website, another major security feature of WAP is the ability to use a WAP Identity Module (WIM). The WIM is a tamper resistant chip that is typically embedded on a users SIM card. The WIM is often referred to as the security module of the SIM chip. The chip contains the user's digital certificate and private key information and it stores the cryptographic functions that can be used with security protocols. The private keys on the WIM can be utilized for authentication and for creating digital signatures. The chip was also designed to be tamper resistant in order to prevent attackers from modifying or extracting the certificates or keys from the chip.

The WIM chip can be utilized within a Wireless Public Key Infrastructure (WPKI). WPKI is the wireless version of typical PKI systems. It allows the use of private and public keys in a M-Commerce environment. WPKI provides confidentiality through cryptography, authentication through digital certificates, integrity through digital signatures, and non-repudiation through the use of digital signatures and certificates. The primary difference between a PKI and WPKI environment is that WPKI has been modified to function with lower powered mobile devices and on lower bandwidth networks. WPKI takes full advantage of the WIM chip by using the user's private keys that are stored within the WIM. The same x.509 certificates that are utilized within standard PKI are also utilized within WPKI and are stored on the WIM.

24.6.2 iMode

iMode is a protocol similar to WAP that allows mobile devices to connect to the Internet. Where as WAP was developed by a forum of vendors and researchers, iMode is a proprietary technology and was developed by NTT DoCoMo, a Japanese telecommunications company. It is extremely popular in Japan and is spreading to Europe and other parts of Asia. At the end of 2004 there were over 35 million users. Many Japanese users send email, access websites, purchase tickets and perform many other online transactions through iMode. Unfortunately, due to the proprietary nature of iMode there does not seem to be the same growth potential that WAP has. iMode requires a user to connect to a NTT DoCoMo owned server in order to access the web. In order for iMode to grow NTT DoCoMo would need to invest a significant amount of money into their infrastructure in order to have enough servers for a larger user base. This differs from WAP where separate vendors can share the cost by implementing their own WAP systems and interconnecting them through the Internet.

Since iMode is proprietary, very little is known about the way security is implemented in the system. It is known that the protocol uses standard HTTP security protocols like TLS and SSL but lower level protocols are all proprietary so no security information is available. It is also known that iMode phones come pre-configured with root CA keys from Verisign or other certificate authorities. This allows for the SSL connection between the device and the remote web sites. As for authentication, iMode uses basic HTTP authentication.

There is reason to worry about the security of iMode because the initial implementation was designed with security as an after thought and the current implementation is vague. The primary goal upon introduction of the product was to provide Internet access and make a profit. Since the initial implementation security features have been added but it is not known exactly how secure the devices really are. I believe in order for iMode to remain competitive with WAP more information about its implementation must be made available to the general public. This is the same debate that exists within the computer world of Open Source vs. Proprietary. While Proprietary may be good for making a profit it is often not the most reliable or secure method.

24.7 ARCHITECTURE AND PROTOCOLS

A mobile-commerce application can be broken down into three parts: the user device, the Web site hosting the application and the payment mechanism. In addition, various gateways come into play. In the simplest model, a Web site would deliver HTML directly to a mobile device, and a protocol such as SSL (Secure Sockets Layer) or TLS (Transport Layer Security) would secure communications. To settle transactions, the Web site would communicate with a financial network either directly or via a third party. This structure merely replaces a standard desktop browser with one operating on a mobile device and a wired link with a wireless link; in fact, HTML browsers are available for Palm and Pocket PC devices. But most deployments are more complicated than this because of slow wireless-link speeds and multiple network and device types.

Most mobile-commerce application developers want to support as many mobile devices as possible. One approach might be to format the content in WML (Wireless Markup Language), which would make the application available to mobile devices with WAP browsers. And WAP browsers are also available for handhelds. What's wrong with this picture? Plenty. Supporting all the different types of available mobile devices requires either an extraordinary amount of development effort or a third-party solution.

Sorting through all the third-party solutions is a project in itself, as we learned through our RFI, but with due diligence, you can find excellent tools that vastly simplify the process of developing mobile applications. Just don't underestimate the amount of work this requires. Installing and evaluating these platforms are comparable in time and difficulty to working with a new computer operating system.

These third-party solutions are middleware platforms that typically translate from XML/HTML format located at the customer site to the appropriate wireless format, whether HDML (a precursor to WAP), HTML, WML or a format understood by interactive pagers. You can deploy these platforms yourself by purchasing a server license, or the vendor can host the platform as an ASP. The platform can also be hosted by a wireless ISP, such as GoAmerica or OmniSky Corp. (The 'Wireless ASP' diagram shows the ASP scenario).

Unfortunately, the conversion from XML or HTML to WML is far from automatic. With nearly all these third-party solutions, the XML or HTML content must be created from the ground up and adhere to strict rules and templates, often in conjunction with SDKs and tools provided by the vendor. Because of a lack of standardization, the rules and templates are specific to each ASP. Thus, if you design using OracleMobile's Portal-to-Go XML, you'll be limited to OracleMobile's platform to translate the content to the various wireless formats.

Converting from XML to mobile formats will be much more reliable and flexible than starting with HTML. HTML conversions essentially involve 'screen scraping,' in which the middleware platform captures portions of the Web page to create mobile content. This approach is highly vulnerable to changes such as new page layouts. With XML, application developers can use specific tags to create mobile content that the middleware can interpret in an unambiguous, consistent fashion.

The middleware can perform other functions as well, such as delivering mobile content using transport protocols better suited to wireless.

This architecture is technically efficient, as it enables standard Internet communications between the middleware platform and the content/application provider. Application developers can deploy their applications on existing Web platforms. The architecture also allows the middleware platform to deliver optimized content to the user with the most appropriate protocols for the connection. However, the solutions are vendor-specific and require a considerable commitment to a middleware platform or ASP. Many of these ASPs are new, and their long-term viability is unproven. In fact, many wireless middleware companies have come and gone over the past five years.

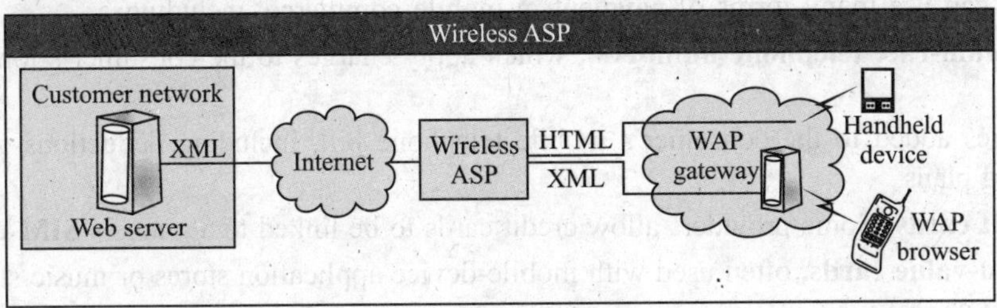

Fig. 24.4

Increasingly, major software vendors are adding capabilities to their Web and database platforms to support mobile formats. This could eventually obviate third-party solutions, though such solutions are likely to have broader network and device support for quite some time.

Watch also for the role that Internet portals will play. These portals are in a strong position to integrate, and eventually subsume, the ASP function. Furthermore, they can provide a place for merchants to situate themselves. America Online, InfoSpace, MSN and Yahoo are ramping up their mobile emphasis and already command intense customer loyalty. For many users, the mobile environment will become an extension of their existing Internet environment. Some wireless portals, such as GoAmerica and OmniSky, are focusing on the mobile environment exclusively. It makes sense for these trailblazers to start providing financial services such as e-wallets or gateways to e-wallets.

Finally, various industry organizations are seeking to standardize mobile-commerce methods and architecture; examples include Fundamo, the Global Mobile Commerce Forum, the Mobey Forum, the Mobile Electronics Transactions initiative, Radicchio and the Wireless Data Forum. So far, these organizations are long on stating the problems and issues involved, and short on delivering actual solutions.

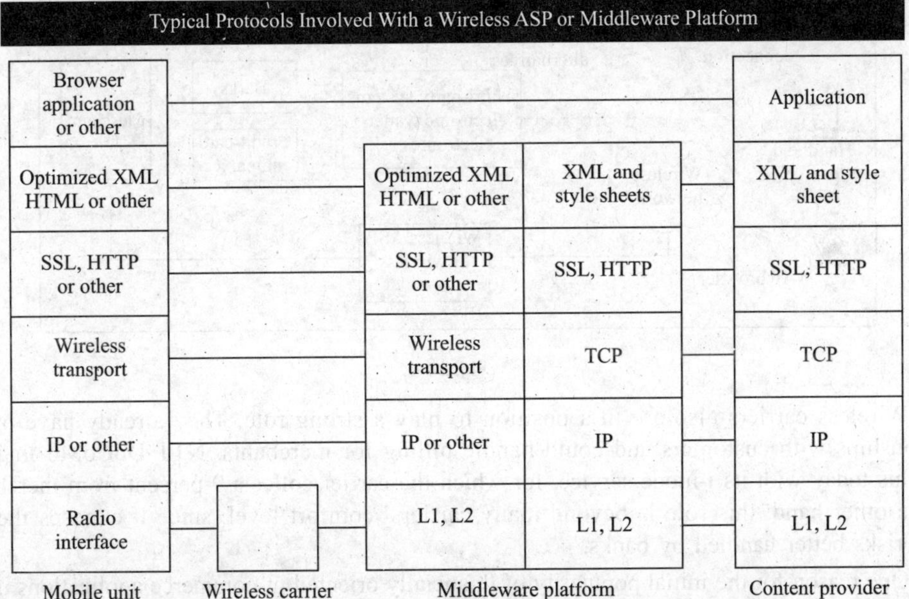

Fig. 24.5

24.8 PAYMENT METHODS & SETTLEMENT

Consumers can use many forms of payment in mobile commerce, including:

- **Premium-rate telephone numbers'**, which apply charges to the consumer's long-distance bill
- Charges added to the consumer's mobile telephone bill, including deductions to pre-paid calling plans
- **Credit cards:** Some providers allow credit cards to be linked to a phone's **SIM card**
- **Stored-value cards,** often used with mobile-device application stores or music stores

Most of today's mobile-commerce applications are extensions of Web-based e-commerce solutions, which typically use credit cards for payment. However, as these applications mature and the variety of mobile-commerce transactions broadens, settlement systems will have to change. Simply put, we need generally available, secure electronic-wallet and electronic-cash mechanisms. This will take years, but many approaches have already been introduced.

To make purchases using many of today's Web-based commerce applications, customers must enter their credit-card information—clearly an unwieldy approach with a mobile device and one that raises security concerns. If the credit card is already on file with a merchant, all the user has to do is authenticate himself or herself. But users don't want to have to register their credit cards with numerous merchants.

Credit-card companies and other organizations are working to solve this problem by developing electronic-wallet mechanisms; these hold users' financial information (such as credit-card accounts) and perhaps shipping info, and may contain funds as well. By supporting a particular wallet system, you can give your customers a convenient way to pay for purchases. Some wireless, host such a wallet mechanism and provide a mobile shopping portal for merchants to plug into. 'The Tangled Web of Settlement Options,' below, shows the various possible interconnections among wireless ASPs, wallet systems, banks and customer networks (Fig. 24.6).

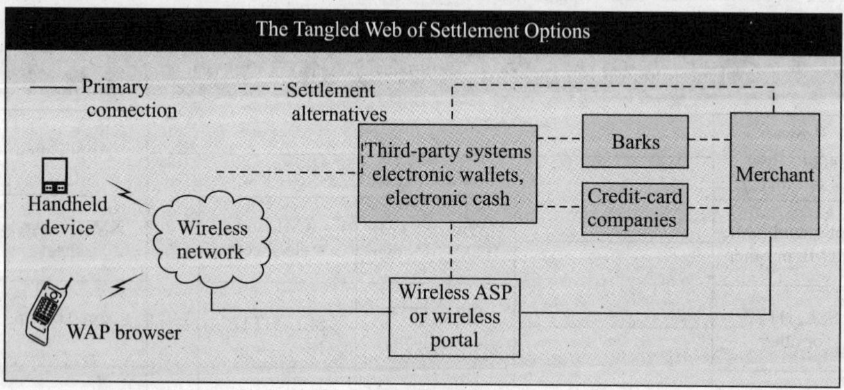

Fig. 24.6

Wireless carriers also are in a position to play a strong role. They already have billing relationships with customers and could handle billing for merchants. NTT DoCoMo in Japan does this today with its i-mode service, for which the carrier collects 9 percent from merchants. On the other hand, this role is beyond many carriers' comfort level, since it exposes them to credit risks better handled by banks.

One reason for the initial popularity of financially oriented m-commerce applications is that the financial institution already has users' account information on file and is simply allowing them to manipulate their accounts—letting them buy or sell stocks, for example, or transfer funds from one account to another. The challenge is to allow a user to easily purchase goods or services from any merchant or institution in a secure and cost-effective manner.

Internet economics demands a reduction in the number of middlemen involved. Today's payment systems—credit-card companies, for instance—involve a number of intermediaries and will not scale to high volumes of smaller transactions. This is where companies such as ECash will play a role. ECash's payment architecture lets banks offer electronic-cash services to customers, who can then spend that cash with participating merchants.

Although in their infancy, such payment infrastructures could truly revolutionize mobile commerce and, in the process, massively disrupt existing financial systems—even making ATMs obsolete. However, this will all take time. Fraud levels in e-commerce are 12 to 18 times higher than in conventional commerce, according to Gartner Group, so banks will proceed cautiously. But if they don't proceed, they will be relegated to irrelevance.

Another significant development that could bypass carriers entirely is local-area wireless connections. In this scenario, customers establish direct connections from their mobile devices to the merchants' point-of-sale systems at the merchants' locations. The infrared link simply replaces the credit-card swipe, and the merchant uses its existing back-end credit-card payment system.

24.9 THE TROUBLE WITH WAP

WAP is getting a bad rap. Originally touted as a panacea for the wireless industry, the Wireless Application Protocol is now getting bad press because of interoperability problems and minuscule market adoption where it's been deployed.

WAP does indeed have interoperability issues. For example, vendors' browser and gateway implementations are inconsistent. But this is being addressed by new interoperability testing programs. Furthermore, some critics dislike having to learn a new markup language, WML (Wireless Markup Language), to work with WAP. But that's exactly what XML (Extensible Markup Language) is all about. WML is based on XML, the very nature of which is extensibility, to allow new markups for particular applications. WAP also delivers on the promise of a network-independent solution. A WAP application does not have to take into account the kind of cellular technology in use nor the underlying network protocols, so long as the network supports WAP.

No, the problem with WAP is that it does not deliver on its fundamental promise: to let application developers develop their content in one format for all wireless networks. Perhaps this promise stemmed from the hubris of the companies that formed the WAP Forum in the first place; they thought they could impose one standard on the entire industry. The result has been far different.

WAP is real, and many operators, particularly in Europe, will support it. But in the United States, most of the big operators, including AT&T Wireless, Sprint PCS and Verizon Wireless, are still using HDML (Handheld Device Markup Language), WAP's predecessor. Why? Because they started working with HDML before WAP was standardized. Also, HDML offers more features and, ironically, better interoperability than WAP, since wireless browsers and gateways come from one company, Openwave Systems. U.S. operators do say they'll eventually move to WAP, but only when a newer version becomes available.

Meanwhile, interactive pagers and handheld devices favor HTML approaches, not WML or HDML. NTT DoCoMo, hugely successful in Japan with its i-mode service (which is based on a subset of HTML), is now trying to export i-mode to the rest of the world. The net result: WAP delivers only to a small slice of the total wireless market. And that's the real trouble with WAP.

24.9.1 User Security

User security is also necessary within a model M-Commerce system. Users must be made aware of the repercussions of their actions when utilizing their mobile devices. They must understand the losses that they may incur if proper precautions are not followed. The best method to provide this is by providing guidance to the user when they purchase the device. One method of providing guidance would be to provide a pamphlet or booklet along with the device that details all the security features on the phone and what settings should be utilized. The booklet should also detail what a user should be aware of when making transactions on their phone. For example they should be shown how to verify that they are making secure connections and they are not being tricked by an attacker. This method of providing guidance may not be followed by all users. In order to ensure that all users receive some sort of guidance, the mobile device should also have warnings appear on screen when a user performs a potentially harmful action. For example, if the user attempts to disable the password feature then the phone should make them aware of the repercussions by displaying a warning on the screen that the user must agree to before continuing on.

24.9.2 Network Security

Of all components of an M-Commerce system the network is currently the most secure. Carriers utilize modern encoding and encryption techniques to ensure that their data is secure when traveling through the air. In order to ensure that this security remains at all times, carriers should ensure that encryption occurs from end to end in a transaction. This means the data is encrypted on the device and is never unencrypted until it arrives at its destination. There should not be a middle man that can read the data.

24.10 SUMMARY

M-Commerce is an interesting and a very recent addition to the way that modem business enterprises conduct business. It w ill become a new frontier for e-Commerce in the near future and it can bring many business opportunities because of its unique characteristics and positive impact in many business sectors. For the past several years, researchers and practitioners have focused more on identifying the issues and challenges of m-Commerce. There is not much research, however, which concentrates on the actual benefits of m-Commerce. This study outlined the potential of m-Commerce and provided information regarding related issues.

Recently, fnms have gained substantial benefits from m-Commerce in many business areas, such as manufacturing, retailing, marketing and finance. Manufacturing firms increased efficiency and effectiveness; firms reduced potential costs, operated business activities more efficiently and improved their competitive position. Furthermore, m-Commerce provides a new channel for retailing and marketing. Business activities are conducted via mobile devices, such as mobile phones and PDAs. In the finance sector, m-Commerce provides better customer service; customers may gain access to data and information anytime, anywhere. Benefits in each sector will bring a potential increase in profits for firms in the future.

With such benefits of m-Commerce, firms should consider tacking the four issues mentioned earlier: measurement, competition, security and standardization, all of which are considered major limitations of m-Commerce. These implementations deal with both technological and managerial issues of m-Commerce and are very important for ensuring long-term success. Since m-Commerce requires infrastructure, applications and *Hardware* and Software, the urgent implementation may focus on technical Issues. M-Commerce, however, is not technology, but it is about discovering innovative ways to define value for customers, as well as to conduct business. Once m-Commerce issues and challenges have been incorporated into the policies of a company, more benefits could be expected. Therefore, in the future, research needs to focus on two aspect; the influences that determine the success of m-Commerce and the benefits themselves.

No longer must a customer be tied to a land line to buy stocks or change an airline reservation. Cell phones, PDAs and devices we haven't yet imagined are getting unwired for commerce. But getting a piece of this growing market is elusive. Obstacles include multiple platforms, lack of payment systems, sketchy security and the need for specialized infrastructure.

Because mobile commerce is still fraught with technical problems, most companies would be wise to seek a service provider. The list of middleware vendors, ASPs and wireless portals is growing rapidly.

A big issue here is security. Although standards are evolving, one—WTLS (Wireless Transport Layer Security)—has taken the lead.

24.11 REFERENCES

1. Bardo, F. and J. Jugen, 2002. *Evaluation of Mobile Applications: Software-technical and Human Aspects*. Proceedings of the 9th European Conference on Information Technology Evaluation (ECITE). Universite Dauphine, Paris, France.
2. Cheskin, 2001. *The Wireless Future: A Look at Youth Unplugged*. September 2001. Retrieved, Dec. 8, 2005 from http://www.ixi.com/PDF/CheskinYouthUnplngged.pdf.
3. Hansmann, U., 2001. *Pervasive Computing Handbook*. Springer. pp. 409.
4. Jukic. N., A. Shanna and B. Jukic 2002. *M-Commerce: Analysis of impact on marketing orientation*. Proceedings of Information Resource Management Association (IRMA) Intl. Conference, Philadelphia, PA.
5. Tarasewich, P., RC. Nickerson and M. Warkentin, 2002. *Issues in Mobile E-commerce*. Commun. Assoc. Inform. Sys., **8:** 41–64.
6. Tarasewich, P. and M. Warkentin, 2000. *Issues in Wireless E-commerce*. ACM SIGecom Exchanges, **1:** 19–23.
7. Tarasewich, P. and M. Warkentin, 2002. *Information Everywhere*. Infor. Sys. Manage., **19:** 8–13.
8. Varshney, U. and R. Vetter, 2001. *A Framework for the Emerging Mobile Commerce Applications*. In: Proceedings of the 34th Hawaii International Conference on System Sciences. Sprague, RH. Jr. (Ed.), Piscataway, New Jersey.
9. Varshney. U., A. Mallow. R. Jain and P. Ahluwalia, 2002. *Wireless in the Enterprise: Requirements and Possible Solutions*. Proceedings of the Workshop on Wireless Strategy in the Enterprise: An International Research Perspective, University of CA, Berkeley, October 15–16.
10. VHA, 2001. *Option for Wireless Technology and Applications in Health Care*. Retrieved April 8, 2006 from https://www.vha.com/research/public/it_whitepaper.pdf.

REVIEW QUESTIONS

1. What is m-commerce?
2. What are the characteristics of m-commerce?
3. What are the advantages of m-commerce?
4. Discuss the m-commerce technologies.
5. What are the payment methods?
6. Discuss the application of m-commerce.
7. What is user and network security?
8. What are the limitation in implementing m-commerce?

25

VIRTUALIZATION AND SECURITY

25.1 INTRODUCTION

When referring to computer systems, most people associate a one-to-one relationship between the software and the hardware. When accessing a physical system we expect there to be a single operating system and set of applications installed on the box. However, with very powerful computer systems there are a lot of wasted resources, and there needs to be a better way to be able to harness the full power of a piece of hardware. In addition, people want to be able to have maximum flexibility in working with software, potentially be able to make changes and recover a previous version if it does not work as planned, and be able to run different versions of a piece of software. This need opened the door for virtualization.

25.2 VIRTUALIZATION

Virtualization allows one to harness the full power of a piece of hardware, no longer limiting it to run a single piece of software. This original idea came about in the 1960's with large mainframes but limited software and programming capability. It has continued to grow in popularity as computers today are becoming more powerful and organizations are looking for cost savings and increases in reliability across their systems. Virtualization can cover an entire computer or individual hardware pieces that make up that system.

The two main components of virtualization are platform and resource virtualization:

25.2.1 Platform Virtualization

Platform virtualization is what most people are familiar with, and that is taking a software platform and running multiple instances on a single piece of hardware. The software can be an operating system such as Windows or Linux, or an application such as a web or e-mail server. This is the area that virtual machines focus mainly on. Now on a hardware server you can run multiple software platforms and each platform has no idea that it is sharing hardware or in a virtualized environment. Each piece of software acts as if it has a one-to-one relationship with the hardware.

25.2.2 Resource Virtualization

While virtualizing a given platform has benefits, you might also want to virtualize hardware resources. One area where this is becoming very popular is with hard drive or storage devices. With a large database you might want to have each application use the same hardware but segment it in a way that the software does not know it is sharing the same external device. In this case, each application is on a separate computer, but they are all using the same external drive or storage area network.

25.3 VIRTUALIZATION TREND

In 2005, virtualization software was adopted faster than anyone imagined, including the experts. There are three areas of IT where virtualization is making head roads, network virtualization, storage virtualization and server virtualization:

- **Network virtualization** is a method of combining the available resources in a network by splitting up the available bandwidth into channels, each of which is independent from the others, and each of which can be assigned (or reassigned) to a particular server or device in real time. The idea is that virtualization disguises the true complexity of the network by separating it into manageable parts; much like your partitioned hard drive makes it easier to manage your files.
- **Storage virtualization** is the pooling of physical storage from multiple network storage devices into what appears to be a single storage device that is managed from a central console. Storage virtualization is commonly used in storage area networks (SANs).
- **Server virtualization** is the masking of server resources (including the number and identity of individual physical servers, processors, and operating systems) from server users. The intention is to spare the user from having to understand and manage complicated details of server resources while increasing resource sharing and utilization and maintaining the capacity to expand later.

Virtualization can be viewed as part of an overall trend in enterprise IT that includes autonomic computing, a scenario in which the IT environment will be able to manage itself based on perceived activity, and utility computing, in which computer processing power is seen as a utility that clients can pay for only as needed. The usual goal of virtualization is to centralize administrative tasks while improving scalability and workloads.

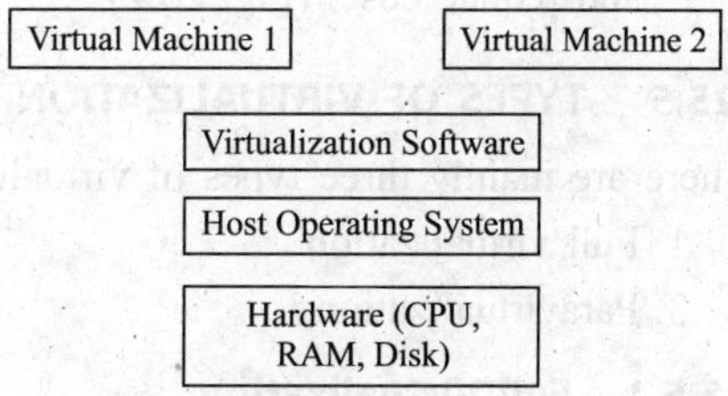

Fig. 25.1 Virtualization

Have you ever think of running an operating system on top of another. If you are a Windows user then you might want some great features of Linux OS. Similarly, if you are Linux user then you might want to work on MS Word. Virtualization will cater all your needs be it software development, running one OS on another, configuration testing and document creation. It will allows you to install new Operating Systems on the same machine and the best thing is that you don't have to worry about hard disk formats and other pre install software or losing any data.

Virtualization is creation of Virtual Machines which can emulate hardware in software or in other words it is the creation of virtual version of something such as a hardware platform, operating system, storage device, or network resources. Virtualization is achieved or created with the help of software and this particular software allows you to install any number of OS on your system without using the available hardware directly.

25.4 HOW VIRTUALIZATION WORKS?

The heart of virtualization is the 'virtual machine' (VM), a tightly isolated software container with an operating system and application inside. Because each VM is completely separate and independent, many of them can run simultaneously on a single computer. A thin layer of software called a hypervisor decouples the VMs from the host, and dynamically allocates computing resources to each VM as needed.

This architecture redefines your computing equation, to deliver:

1. **Many applications on each server:** As each VM encapsulates an entire machine, many applications and operating systems can be run on one host at the same time.
2. **Maximum server utilization, minimum server count:** Every physical machine is used to its full capacity, allowing you to significantly reduce costs by deploying fewer servers overall.
3. **Faster, easier application and resources provisioning:** As self-contained software files, VMs can be manipulated with copy-and-paste ease. This brings unprecedented simplicity, speed, and flexibility to IT provisioning and management. VMs can even be transferred from one physical server to another while running, via a process known as live migration. You can also virtualize business-critical apps to improve performance, reliability, scalability, and reduce costs (Fig. 25.2).

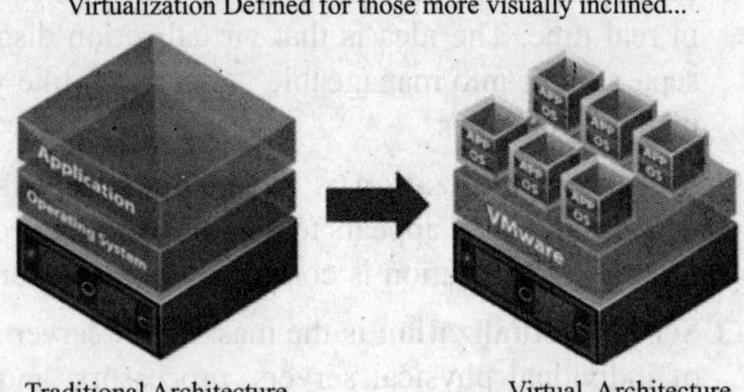

Fig. 25.2 Comparison of Traditional and Virtual Architecture

25.5 TYPES OF VIRTUALIZATION

There are mainly three types of virtualization:

1. Full virtualization
2. OS level virtualization
3. Paravirtualization

25.5.1 Full Virtualization

As the name suggests everything in a system is virtualized which includes the processor, storage, networking components etc. Virtual Box, VMware are example of 'Full Virtualization' solutions.

25.5.2 OS Level Virtualization

In this type of virtualization only applications are run inside the software. In this case the application is given a platform to work. Isolation is created and the application is made to believe that it is the only thing running on the system.

25.5.3 Paravirtualization

It's a semi-virtualized environment created for the guest OS. A modified guest OS is created using a hypervisor. The intent of the modified interface is to reduce the portion of the guest's execution time spent performing operations which are substantially more difficult to run in a virtual environment compared to a non-virtualized environment. The paravirtualization provides specially defined 'hooks' to allow the guest(s) and host to request and acknowledge these tasks, which would otherwise be executed in the virtual domain (where execution performance is worse). A successful paravirtualized platform may allow the virtual machine monitor (VMM) to be simpler (by relocating execution of critical tasks from the virtual domain to the host domain), and/or reduce the overall performance degradation of machine-execution inside the virtual-guest.

25.5.4 Advantages of Virtualization

One of the biggest advantages of virtualization is scalability i.e. the ability to expand. Whenever there is excessive load on some part of application in a server you can easily create a similar virtual environment on a different server and configure the setup.

Hardware maintenance cost is reduced because you don't need many servers to install different applications.

You can save a huge amount of energy by running one physical server instead of many and less power backup is required.

You can get faster and safer backups by taking live snapshot while server is running.

You will get centralized monitoring of your resources as virtualization provides easy way of connecting and maintaining your virtual servers.

One of the main and most obvious benefits is being able to run multiple operating systems on the same computer. Whether you are bringing a laptop to a client and need to run tools on both windows and Unix, or you are a MAC user who wants to be able to access applications that are built for windows operating systems, virtual machines allow you to have one computer run many operating systems at the same time. In the past you would have to either bring multiple computers or set up a dual boot system. Neither one of these is a great option. From a server perspective, instead of having to buy a large number of systems, a small number of higher end systems can run the same number of operating systems with less hardware to maintain.

From a Disaster Recovery Plan (DRP) perspective, instead of having 10 servers each with one OS and no redundancy, you could have 2 systems each with 5 operating systems and 4 failover systems and still have less hardware than before. If a system goes down you do not have to rebuild the system from CD's or restore from backup, you would just load the guest image and can have the system running in minutes. From a security perspective, key components can be isolated and contained to reduce or limit exposure.

25.5.5 Uses of Virtualization

With the main benefits being ease of use and portability, the uses of virtual machines are almost endless. Starting with the most obvious, virtual machines are great for training in which you can bring a single computer and run multiple operating systems that are pre-built by the instructor. Incident response, malicious code analysis, and digital forensics all allow a security professional to have a portable security lab on a single computer with all of the tools and software they need at their fingertips.

25.6 ISSUES SHOULD BE TAKEN SERIOUSLY

The following issues should be consider before going for the virtualization:

1. **Cost of software/Licensing:** One of the biggest problems, which must not be forgotten. Virtualization allows you to easily create new servers, and each of these server environments require a separate license for the software. If you are using the open-source, it will not be a problem, but if you run a paid environment, their deployment could lead to higher license fees.
2. **The effectiveness of planning:** In order to realize the full benefits of virtualization, it is important to match the hardware capabilities of the server with their requirements. In practice, this amounts to setting the maximum number of virtual servers on a physical server without degrading the performance of these servers.
3. **Education:** As with any change, the introduction of virtualization in the IT-environment will require training. Must take the costs (both time and money) into account.
4. **Management:** Despite the fact that the use of virtual servers reduces the amount of physical hardware, virtual machines require management.
5. **High expectations from consolidation:** Consolidation ratio depends on two things: the power of the current physical servers and resource requirements of existing applications. If

existing servers have sufficient capacity, and your applications use them rationally, we can expect a high rate of consolidation. Conversely, if your server is not as powerful, but your applications use so much of the resources, do not expect the high rate of consolidation.

6. **The increasing amount of investment:** This is a potential problem. To realize the full benefits of virtualization, virtual machines must be located on a server with powerful processors. Less powerful hardware reduces the benefits of virtualization. There should be a compromise between the cost of new equipment and reduce the funding of the less powerful computers.
7. **Unavailability of some systems:** Especially in areas such as security, some systems are still not adapted to the peculiarities of virtualization. Many firewalls, for example, continue to believe that an IP-address corresponds to a single unit.

25.7 GUESTS AND HOSTS

A virtual machine (VM) typically has two components: the **host server** and the **guest virtual machine**. The host server is the underlying hardware that provides computing resources, such as processing power, memory, disk and network I/O, and so on. The guest virtual machine is a completely separate and independent instance of an operating system and application software. Guests are the virtual workloads that reside on a host server and share in that server's computing resources.

Virtualization platforms such as VMware vSphere, Microsoft Hyper-V and Citrix Systems' XenServer install a layer of abstraction between the host server and guest virtual machine. This is the virtual machine monitor (VMM), or hypervisor, that isolates each guest from another, enabling multiple guests to reside and operate on the host simultaneously. Abstraction also removes the direct relationship between software and the underlying hardware, so it is possible for a server to host guest virtual machines with different operating systems and application software requirements. For example, one VM with a Windows guest operating system can readily co-exist with a second VM running a Linux guest operating system on the same physical host server at the same time.

The only requirement is that a host server must meet or exceed the minimum hardware requirements for its guest VMs (workload). Since most traditional nonvirtualized servers are woefully underutilized, a host should supply ample computing resources for several guest virtual machines. But as additional guests are added to the host, computing resources—such as memory or processing capacity—may be exhausted. This can create performance problems in one or more guests or can crash guests—even the entire host—leading to numerous simultaneous workload outages, which can undermine user productivity. Guests are usually distributed among several available hosts to better distribute each workload's computing demands.

Although most virtualization relies on the concept of 'isolated guest instances,' some forms of virtualization do not create isolated instances. Instead they create separate areas within the same operating system. Examples of operating system virtualization' or OS virtualization, include Solaris Zones, Parallels Virtuozzo, Linux-VServer, OpenVZ and others. A 'zoned' approach presents certain pros and cons. It is more efficient because there is only one iteration of the OS installed on the host server. However, every guest zone must run an application that supports the operating system; you cannot have one guest run Windows and another run Linux. Further, a security exploit in the operating system will compromise all of the zones, where an exploit in a fully isolated guest virtual machine would only threaten that one guest.

25.8 NETWORK VIRTUALIZATION

Network virtualization is a versatile technology. It allows you to combine multiple networks into a single logical network, parcel a single network into multiple logical networks and even create synthetic, software-only networks between virtual machines (VMs) on a physical server.

Virtual networking typically starts with virtual network software, which is placed outside a virtual server (external) or inside a virtual server—depending on the size and type of the virtualization platform.

Any virtual networking that takes place outside of a virtual server is called external network virtualization. This occurs when multiple physical LANs are aggregated into a single logical LAN, or when a single physical LAN is parceled out into multiple virtual LANs (VLANs). External network virtualization uses virtual network software such as Hewlett-Packard Virtual Connect and involves network switches, network adapters, servers, network storage devices and the Ethernet or Fibre Channel media that interconnects these hardware devices.

In internal network virtualization, virtual network software can emulate network connectivity within the server and allow VMs hosted on that server to exchange data. It might seem trivial, but the isolation that a virtual network provides can be useful. Eliminating the need to pass data on an external network can improve performance and bolster security for associated VMs.

Some virtual platforms support both internal and external network virtualization. VMware is one example; its platform supports internal network virtualization through the native hypervisor and uses additional software to support external virtualization.

Certain vendors tout virtualization and networking as a vehicle for additional services—not just as a way to aggregate and allocate network resources. For example, it's common practice for a network switch to support security, storage, voice over IP (VoIP) and other advanced network services.

Regardless of the approach, managing virtual network software can be extremely challenging. It can be difficult, even impossible, to keep track of the multiple services and virtual networks running within the physical LAN. Careful documentation, clear workflow procedures and comprehensive management tools are vital for proper virtual networking management.

Several initiatives will influence the proliferation of network virtualization in the future. These include, but are not limited to, the Global Environment for Network Innovations, Future Internet Research and Experimentation, the AKARI Architecture Design Project and Federated E-infrastructure Dedicated to European Researchers Innovating in Computing Network Architectures (FEDERICA).

25.9 SERVER CONSOLIDATION

Server consolidation benefits users by allowing one physical server to host multiple virtual machine (VM) instances, which increases the effective utilization of server hardware.

Most traditional non-virtualized servers are only utilized at 5% to 10% of their total computing capacity. By adding a virtualization platform to the server (such as Citrix XenServer, VMware vSphere or Hyper-V in Windows Server 2008 R2), the server can operate its original workload as a virtual machine, and host additional virtual workloads simultaneously—often increasing the total utilization of the physical server from 50% to 80% of its total computing capacity.

But increasing computing efficiency is only one of many server consolidation benefits. With more workloads running on less hardware, power and cooling demands are also lowered. This translates to lower operating costs for the business, and can also forestall capital-intensive facilities projects.

Server consolidation with virtualization allows the flexibility to seamlessly migrate workloads between physical servers—literally moving workloads at-will or as-needed. For example, a traditional server would have to be taken offline for maintenance or upgrades. With virtualization, all of the server's consolidated workloads can be migrated to a spare server or distributed amongst other servers, and then the original server can be shut down without any disruption to the workloads. Once the work is completed, the workloads can be migrated back to the original hardware. Workloads from a failing server can likewise be failed over or restarted on other servers, minimizing the effect of hardware problems.

Virtualization is also a boon to data protection, and workloads consolidated with virtualization can easily be copied with periodic point-in-time snapshots or replicated to off-site storage systems with little (if any) of the performance penalty experienced with traditional tape backup systems.

Even with a wealth of server consolidation benefits, however, successful server consolidation requires a careful server consolidation strategy. First, consolidation should be approached in phases. Start by virtualizing and consolidating non-critical or low-priority workloads. Administrators can gain valuable experience with server consolidation tools. Then With more experience, you can then systematically virtualize and consolidate more important workloads until you tackle the most mission-critical applications.

The distribution of those virtualized workloads can make a tremendous difference in the success of your consolidation project. Since each workload can demand different computing resources, it's important to measure the needs of each workload and allocate workloads so that the underlying host servers are not overloaded—a process known as 'workload balancing.' For example, it's often better to distribute CPU-intensive workloads on different servers rather than putting them on the same server. This prevents resource shortages that can cause workload performance or stability problems.

25.10 STORAGE VIRTUALIZATION

Storage virtualization creates a layer of abstraction between the operating system and the physical disks used for data storage. The virtualized storage is then location-independent, which can enable more efficient storage use and better storage management.

For example, the storage virtualization software or device creates a logical space, and then manages metadata that establishes a map between the logical space and the physical disk space. The creation of logical space allows a virtualization platform to present storage volumes that can be created and changed with little regard for the underlying disks.

The most immediate benefit of storage virtualization is increased storage utilization, which can reduce wasted storage within the enterprise. For example, alogical unit number (LUN) provisioned on a storage area network (SAN) may allocate space that may not be used, or disks may be left unallocated—lost and forgotten on storage arrays scattered across the data center. With virtualization, otherwise-unused storage can be cobbled together into viable LUNs and allocated to applications.

Data storage virtualization also supports migration and replication of LUNs between storage systems. This is particularly useful when one storage system must be taken offline for maintenance or replacement. By simply changing the mapping scheme, virtualization can move the location of data without disrupting disk I/O, allowing for efficient and non-disruptive data movement within an enterprise.

Storage management can be greatly simplified. Rather than managing multiple (often heterogeneous) storage subsystems, a virtualized storage environment can be managed through a single mechanism. In addition, advanced storage management techniques such as thin provisioning and dynamic provisioning can readily be supported. thin provisioning allows the creation of a LUN that is larger than the physical disk space allocated to it. For example, a 1 GB LUN can be created with perhaps 100 MB of storage space to start. As the associated application uses the disk space, more disk space can be allocated periodically (up to the assigned amount) without having to recreate the LUN.

Dynamic provisioning is similar, allowing the size of a LUN to be grown or shrunk as needed, ensuring the size of a LUN is always appropriate for each application. But traditional storage management (such as RAID group creation and maintenance) is still required.

Host-based storage virtualization such as Symantec's Veritas Storage Foundation uses device drivers and additional software to virtualize the physical disks within a host system. Device-based storage virtualization such as Hitachi Data Systems' Universal Storage Platform incorporates and manages virtualization within the storage array itself. Network-based storage virtualization uses a server (appliance) or smart switch like an EMC Invista within a Fibre Channel or iSCSI SAN to implement the abstraction between the network I/O and storage controllers.

25.11 VIRTUAL HARDWARE

A virtual hardware platform is a collection of computing resources allocated from a physical host server to a virtual machine (VM) during the virtualization process.

Virtualization creates a layer of abstraction between the application and the underlying computer hardware. This abstraction allows software—the virtualization hypervisor—to assign, control and monitor the computing resources that form the virtual hardware platform for a workload.

The concept of a virtual hardware platform is crucial to virtualization. It frees a workload from specific physical hardware devices so that the workload can run on any physical host with the proper computing resources available. It also allows key virtualization features, such as live migration, which moves workloads between physical servers with no downtime.

The process of creating a VM assigns a default virtual hardware platform to the VM. Virtual hardware assignments include memory, processor cores, optical drives, network adapters, I/O ports, a disk controller and one or more virtual hard disks (VHDs).

Perhaps the most interesting attribute of a virtual hardware platform is its versatility, because an administrator can adjust the levels of each resource—adding more memory and additional processor cores, allocating another VHD or assigning more network adapter ports, for example. Increasing resource levels will normally boost that workload's performance or responsiveness—especially on older physical servers—or allow the VM to support more users.

Conversely, an administrator can also remove virtual hardware from a VM. For example, an application may not be able to utilize a full 2 GB of memory or two processor cores. Removing excess resources will free those resources for allocation elsewhere, improving the performance of other busy workloads or increasing utilization on the physical server.

Generally speaking, an administrator will need to power down a VM before adding or removing resources.

It is sometimes possible to allocate more memory to a virtual hardware platform than what is actually available from the physical host. For example, it is possible to configure a VM with 16 GB of memory on a physical server with only 8 GB of RAM. This process, called memory overcommit, allows more VMs to reside on a server, because most VMs don't utilize all of their allocated memory space. When physical memory runs short, the virtualization platform implements a virtual memory swap file on the virtual disk.

The practice of memory overcommit is well accepted, but there is still a serious performance penalty when using a swap file. Therefore, it's best to ensure adequate memory on the server.

25.12 VIRTUAL MACHINE

Even though the price of hardware is coming down every day, there are still many reasons why you would not want to purchase or have additional hardware. In addition to hardware becoming less expensive, the processors are becoming more powerful and memory is less expensive.

Therefore, many companies have high-end servers and are only using a small percent of the processing capabilities. For many reasons, being able to run several pieces of software, virtually on the same hardware, has many benefits.

A virtual machine (VM) is a separate and independent software instance that includes a full copy of an operating system and application software. A physical server prepared with a server virtualization hypervisor such as Microsoft Hyper-V, VMware vSphere or Citrix XenServer, can host multiple VMs while maintaining logical isolation between each machine. Each instance can then share the server's computing resources—dramatically increasing physical server hardware usage.

Server consolidation is the most compelling benefit of virtual machines. A typical non-virtualized application server may reach just 5% to 10% utilization. But a virtual server that hosts multiple VMs can easily reach 50% to 80% utilization. The net result is that more VMs can be hosted on fewer physical servers, translating into lower costs for hardware acquisition, maintenance, energy and cooling system usage.

Virtualization also facilitates VM creation and VM management. Unlike conventional servers that host a mixture of an OS, driver and application files, an entire VM exists as a single file, such as a VMDK file. A VM file can be created and duplicated as needed, proliferating virtual machines on servers across an enterprise. These golden images can be modified for each user or application.

Virtual machines in operation are saved to storage non-disruptively using periodic snapshots to a SAN. Troublesome or crashed VMs are quickly reloaded to the server directly from storage, which accelerates recovery times after a server or application crash.

VM tools assist server management by allocating and regulating the computing resources that each VM uses. For example, multiple CPU cores may be allocated to a CPU-intensive application in one VM while other noncritical VMs may share the same CPU core. Similarly, an administrator can reserve the minimum required amount of network bandwidth for a VM running a transactional application. A virtual file or print server may not have this reservation.

Administrators must balance the computing demands of each VM against the total computing resources that each virtual server provides. Instead of supporting multiple memory-intensive VMs on the same server and risking low-memory performance penalties, the VMs can be distributed across multiple physical servers.

The concept of VM workload balancing also relates to CPU and I/O-intensive VMs. Certain tools enable nondistruptive workload migration between servers so that VMs can move from server to server in real time. Migration continues until an acceptable balance of server consolidation and performance is achieved.

25.13 OS LEVEL VIRTUAL MACHINES

The most common form of virtual machines are operating system (OS) virtual machines. This allows multiple operating systems to run independently on the same hardware. This can be used for a laptop that needs to run different operating systems to high-end server farms that need to run many applications with a reduced cost in hardware. The first use is more of a novelty and does not have huge cost savings to an organization. However, it is still a very powerful tool for a network security professional to be able to run Unix tools on an XP or Vista laptop without having to perform a re-install of any components. This is one of the main reasons we are covering virtual machines in this section. The modern security professional must have access to both windows and Unix operating systems since there are some tools that will only run on one OS. Dual-boot machines require reinstallation of key components. Multiple laptops require additional hardware, and bootable CD's have limited read-only capability. Virtual machines are a perfect solution to solving this problem.

25.14 APPLICATION LEVEL VIRTUAL MACHINES

As applications become more powerful, attackers are taking advantage of this increased functionality to find vulnerabilities in the software. Removing these applications is not always an option, yet they are a prime source of malicious code infecting the entire system. An exploit in a web browser can be used to compromise the entire application. One solution is to run application level virtual machines. Now an application runs in a separate virtual machine so if it is exploited or compromised, the scope of the attacker is limited to a separate system and cannot compromise the main operating system in which all of the other applications are running.

25.15 VIRTUAL MACHINE MONITORING

When someone asks if there is a way to monitor their virtual machine (VM), my first question is always, 'What do you want to monitor?' The second question I ask is, 'Do you have any existing server monitoring tools that you can use, and if so, how do they work?' These two questions lead administrators down different VM monitoring paths.

Take, for example, the simple act of monitoring the up/down state of service or virtual machine failure monitoring. There are hundreds of tools that do this with or without the use of agents. If they use agents, the agents install directly within the virtual machine. If they don't use agents, the tools tend to probe the VM for a state to determine if a Web server is running or if the machine can be pinged, for example.

In either case, the agents help you determine if the VM is up or down and whether its services are running. Remember, though, that you can incur license costs for probing a system and installing an agent.

In general, anything you can monitor within a physical system can be monitored within a VM, with one exception: performance. With virtual machine performance monitoring, it is actually better to monitor from outside the VM than from within. This is because data retrieved from within the VM may not be accurate. Although this data can be used as an estimate, you don't know if the raw numbers are correct. When a virtualization host over-commits CPU, the virtualization host scheduler divides the processor between each VM, but not necessarily in a contiguous fashion. In other words, a VM no longer spends all of its time on a CPU.

However, CPU-specific performance counters within a guest operating system are expected to read the CPU for data all the time. The counters then compute this data based on the fact that every nanosecond is spent running a CPU.

When CPUs are over-committed, a VM doesn't spend every nanosecond on a CPU—some nanoseconds are spent idle, waiting for a CPU to run on. Therefore, there is often a discrepancy in the numbers that performance monitoring tools generate and from those within the VM. Since it's difficult for a VM to know when it has been made idle, this information is best retrieved from a hypervisor outside the VM. The hypervisor knows this information and can give accurate numbers for the VM in question.

Therefore, you need a VM performance monitoring tool that works with your hypervisor. There are several available for each hypervisor on the market. If you don't use one specific to your hypervisor, the data you receive will just be an estimate of your current VM performance.

25.16 VIRTUAL SWITCH

The core to the virtual network is the virtual switch. The virtual switch has uplinks from physical switches via physical network interface cards (pNICs) and ports that attach to virtual machines. But what other features define the virtual switch?

Let's start with what a virtual switch is not. Technically speaking, KVM, XenServer, open source Xen and Hyper-V, plus all the hosted virtualization products, use a virtual bridge and not a virtual switch. There is not much difference between a bridge and a switch. They both send data between two different segments of a network and they both verify the data being sent.

However, virtual switch software has many more features available to it and can perform more complex operations, including the implementation of virtual LANs, EtherChannel and other more advanced networking tools.

In either case, the pNICs are placed in bridging mode, and you bridge from a physical switch to a virtual switch. This is just like putting an uplink cable between two physical switches. We are in essence uplinking from the physical switch to the virtual switch. In some cases, it is also possible to have virtual switches that are not connected to any pNIC, thereby creating fully virtualized networks.

Each virtual switch system for each hypervisor has different virtual switch security mechanisms. Currently, VMware vSphere has some of the more advanced capabilities, but this will change when the Xen OpenVSwitch is available.

Connected to the virtual machine side of each virtual switch is a virtual network interface card (vNIC). There can be one or more vNICs per VM. However, it is not possible to layer virtual switches, i.e., one virtual switch cannot directly attach to another virtual switch. To connect a virtual switch to another virtual switch from within the virtual network, you must place a VM between them. These VMs would have at least 2 vNICs and act either as a router, firewall or gateway device. By using VMs that act as these types of devices, it is possible to build very complex virtual networks.

The key to virtual switch configuration is that the switch connects on one side to the physical network through the pNICS, and on the other side a virtual switch connects to the virtual machines via the VM's vNICs. This creates the virtual network.

A full Layer 2 virtual switch (like VMware's vSwitch, Cisco Nexus 1000V and the OpenVSwitch) has its own security and mechanisms to support 802.3ad, 802.1q and other protocols used in today's switching networks.

25.17 VIRTUAL MACHINE DISK

Traditional non-virtualized servers and desktops will load and execute hundreds, even thousands, of individual files such as operating-system kernel files, device drivers, application components and data files. Virtualization abstracts the software from the underlying hardware, and places all of the constituent data for any given virtual machine (VM) into a single disk file.

The Virtual Machine Disk (VMDK) file format is the disk-format specification used with VMware virtual machine files. In essence, a file with a .VMDK file extension is a complete and independent virtual machine using VMware virtualization products or other platforms that support VMDK files such as Sun XVM, QEMU, or VirtualBox.

There are pros and cons to this 'single file' VMDK disk. The principal advantages are simplicity and convenience. A single VMDK file, for example, is easy to move between servers using live migration features in the virtualization platform. Similarly, a single file can easily be protected with snapshots or continuous data protection (CDP) technology. Virtual machine files, in fact, are often copied to the SAN. There, additional resiliency practices such as replication to off-site disaster recovery facilities and RAID within the SAN-storage array can further protect the VMs. By maintaining VM files on a high-performance SAN, recreating VMDK files or restarting troubled VMs on other physical servers is a simple process. This can be crucial when a VMDK file is damaged or corrupted.

The traditional drawback to a 'single file' VMDK disk is the extra effort necessary for recovering lost data. Before the introduction of specialized software tools, it had been impossible to recover only a part of the VM, such as a deleted Word document. The entire VM would have had to be restored, usually to a spare server instead of the actual production server, and the missing or corrupted file could then be retrieved. Today it can be quicker and easier to restore an individual file from a VM than it is to restore an entire VM and extract the desired file(s) from it. But regardless of the available tools, administrators must still develop a sound process for data recovery from VM files.

Since the VMDK format is a central part of VMware's virtual environment, it's critical for any third-party provisioning, management and backup tools to be fully interoperable with disks running VMDK. Third-party developers and organizations developing their own custom applications for a VMware environment can employ the VMware Virtual Disk Development Kit. This includes a C library and command-line utilities that allow developers to create and access VMDK files.

The VMDK file format competes with the Microsoft Virtual Hard Drive (VHD) disk format used with Virtual Server and Hyper-V hypervisors. This can become problematic when moving from VMware to Hyper-V. Since the disk formats are not directly compatible, existing virtual machines cannot operate under a different hypervisor. In many cases, virtual machines would need to be translated onto physical servers first (V2P) to effectively remove virtualization. The new hypervisor would then create new virtual machines using the new disk format. Some third-party tools such as VMDK2VHD claim to convert VMDK to VHD files, smoothing the transition between hypervisors for IT professionals.

25.18 CLUSTERED FILE SYSTEM

Most operating systems include a file system that allows a computer to organize the files and data stored on that system. A file system manages the data storage and retrieval between the operating system (OS) and the storage sub-system. For example, a single personal computer with Windows will usually implement NTFS or FAT on the local disk, while Linux supports a variety of file systems such as ext2, ext3, ext4, XFS, JFS and others.

Storage access is complicated when multiple computers are organized into a cluster, so a Windows clustered file system or a Linux clustered file system may be needed to organize data storage and access across all of the cluster nodes.

The need for a clustered file system depends on the nature of the cluster that is deployed. Many clusters simply provide redundancy. If one server node fails, another server node in the cluster will take over and maintain availability of the workload. Each server operates autonomously in this common configuration, so clustering the file system is usually not necessary.

Some server clusters operate collaboratively, however, and aggregate the processing power of each server to tackle more demanding computing tasks. When servers work together collectively, they must often share access to the same files and data at the same time—which is impossible for individual file systems. This situation requires deployment of a Windows clustered file system or a Linux clustered file system, depending on your environment.

The clustered file system arbitrates and controls each node's access to the shared storage resource (such as a SAN), preventing more than one node from writing data at the same time—a catastrophic phenomenon called a 'write collision.' The actual storage is not important, and clustered file systems can support block-level storage, including SCSI, iSCSI, ATA over Ethernet, Fibre Channel, and Fibre Channel over Ethernet.

Not only does a clustered file system manage simultaneous file access to nodes, it also recognizes and handles node failures that threaten disk consistency. When a node writes bad data or stops sending its changes, it must be fenced off from the other nodes.

Windows clustered file systems can generally isolate a defective node logically, while Linux clustered file systems will employ utilities like STONITH—which stands for 'Shoot The Other Node In The Head'—to actually power down the questionable node.

There are numerous clustered file systems available, and the choice normally depends on the underlying operating system. For example, Linux uses the Global File System (GFS), Oracle provides the Oracle Clustered File System (OCFS) and OCFS2, VMware offers the Virtual Machine File System (VMFS) for ESX servers and Sun Microsystems uses Lustre. Native Windows clustered file systems are available in Microsoft products such as Windows Server 2008 R2, and third-party clustered file systems for Windows are also available.

25.19 LIVE MIGRATION

Virtual machine live migration is a virtualization process that moves a virtual machine (VM) from one physical host server to another. It moves the memory and state of a VM without shutting down the application, so users will generally not detect any significant interruption in application availability.

The process captures the complete memory space occupied by the VM—along with the exact state of all the processor registers currently operating on the VM—then sends that content across a TCP/IP link to memory space on another server. Processor registers are then loaded, and the newly moved VM can pick up its operation without missing a step.

Most VM live migrations occur between similar hypervisors, so the migrated VM retains its name and other unique identifiers. Even though the VM is on a different server, it's the exact same machine as far as the users are concerned.

Live migration is a key benefit of virtualization, allowing workloads to move in real time as server or data center conditions change. Consider the impact on business continuity: A virtual server scheduled for maintenance can migrate its workloads to a spare server or to other servers that have extra computing capacity. Once the maintenance is complete and the server returns to service, these workloads can all migrate back to the original server without disruption.

Live migration helps server consolidation by allowing IT administrators to balance workloads across data center servers, ensuring that each server is used efficiently without being overtaxed. Live migration helps with disaster recovery too because VMs can just as easily be moved from one site to another, relying on spare servers at a remote site to receive and operate the migrated VMs.

All of the major virtualization software platforms include VM live migration tools. These include VMware vMotion (part of vSphere), Microsoft Live Migration (part of Hyper-V R2) and Citrix Systems XenServer live migration.

Migration tools typically allow administrators to prioritize the movement of each VM so that failover and failback processes occur in a predictable and repeatable manner. Mission-critical VMs usually take priority and are often moved to spare servers with ample computing resources.

Secondary VMs can be addressed next, although the migration software may be left to move noncritical VMs automatically based on the computing resources on each available server. Migration audits allow administrators to locate VMs and track their movements to refine and optimize ongoing migration behaviors.

Live migration works between almost all virtual host servers, but it's important to test migration behaviors between servers with various processor manufacturers. Processors from Intel and AMD both include extensions that provide hardware assistance for virtualization tasks, including migration. However, Intel VT and AMD-V processors use different architectures to facilitate migration, and moving VMs between Intel and AMD-based servers may result in unexpectedly poor migration performance.

25.20 MEMORY OVERCOMMIT

Memory overcommit (or overcommitment) is ahypervisor feature that allows a virtual machine (VM) to use more memory space than the physical host has available. For example, virtualization platforms like VMware ESX allow a host server with 2 GB of physical memory to run four guest machines, each with 1 GB of memory space allocated.

The idea of memory overcommit may seem dangerous, because a computer will crash if physical memory is exhausted. In actual practice, however, overcommitment of server computing resources is harmless—most VMs use only a small portion of the physical memory that is allocated to them. For the previous example, a guest machine with 1 GB of physical memory allocated to it might only need 300-400 MB, leaving 600-700 MB of allocated space unused. If all four example machines use 300 MB, the physical server will have 800 MB of its original 2 GB left over.

Still, some VMs may need all (or even more) of the memory that they have been allocated, while some VMs may need considerably less. Hypervisors such as ESX can identify idle memory and dynamically reallocate unused memory from some VMs to others that need more memory. If none of the current guest machines need additional memory, any idle physical memory can be used to host additional guest machines if necessary.

Note that the concept of memory overcommit is not new. For example, operating systems like Windows have been able to operate and execute applications within the confines of limited computer memory for many years by swapping portions of data and program code content between memory and disk as needed. The technology is called virtual memory or memory paging.

Virtual memory or memory paging may prevent a virtual host server from crashing, but it imposes a significant performance penalty on the server, because disk access is far less efficient than with solid-state memory access. The performance hit would simply be too great for servers running multiple VMs.

Ultimately, there must be enough physical memory for optimum virtual server performance. IT professionals will need to exercise due diligence in their assessment of computing resource demands for each VM, then ensure that the prospective host server has adequate computing resources to meet that demand. When memory demands actually approach the server's available memory, an IT professional can choose to add memory to the server (upgrade) or distribute the VMs among various servers to balance computing resource needs (workload balancing).

25.21 SNAPSHOT

Virtual machines are dynamic entities. They exist and run within a portion of the memory space available on a physical host server.

In spite of this dynamic nature, however, virtual machines (VMs) rely on disk for data storage. For example, when a host server boots up, the guest virtual machine must be loaded from the enterprise storage, which is often a high-performance Fibre Channel storage-area network (SAN). But virtual machines also require data-protection technologies in case of system crashes and hardware failures. VM snapshot backup techniques are the most common means of VM protection.

Simply stated, a VM snapshot is a copy of the VM state as it exists in server memory at a particular moment, along with any settings and the state of any virtual disks assigned to the VM. The VM snapshot is saved to disk, typically the SAN.

A regular snapshot backup process can significantly reduce the recovery point objective (RPO) for the protected VM. That is, if you take a VM snapshot every 15 minutes, you stand to lose only up to 15 minutes of data in the event of a failure. If the VM snapshot occurs every five minutes, the RPO is reduced to five minutes, and so on. It's only theoretically necessary to keep the latest VM snapshot, adding less demand for storage.

It may actually take several minutes to write a VM snapshot. During this time, it is impossible to write to the virtual machine disk file (such as a VMware VMDK file). However, an additional VM file will record any differences between the current machine state and the machine state at the start of the VM snapshot. This disk file, called a delta disk file, allows users to continue accessing the VM during the snapshot backup process. It also creates a full and complete copy of the machine state at the moment that the snapshot backup is complete, and the main disk file is available to receive writes again.

Taking a VM snapshot is a simple matter for an administrator. It's usually a feature integrated into the virtualization platform. For example, taking a snapshot in a VMware vSphere environment is as simple as right-clicking the VM, selecting Snapshot, and then choosing Take Snapshot. In the VM snapshot dialog that appears, enter a name and description, capture the VM's memory state, quiesce the VM, and click OK. A snapshot backup can also be scheduled to occur at a certain frequency.

A snapshot backup is an important data-protection tool for VMs, but it should not be the only backup technique. The VM snapshot backup process treats virtual machine disk files as a single file, so the entire instance must be restored to recover a lost text or deleted note. This has long forced administrators to restore the VM snapshot to a lab or other nonproduction server to recover specific files within the VM. However, this is changing with the introduction of more robust and capable tools that can look inside VM snapshots and find specific data.

25.22 VMWARE

VMware is a company that produces a wide range of server products and was formed in 1998. VMware is a very popular product for running multiple OS' on laptops to server consolidation in Fortune 500 data centers. VMware software can be installed on a range of host operating systems and can support a range of guest operating systems. Various distributions of public OS' like Linux have VMware images that can run in both Windows and Linux host operating systems.

25.22.1 VMware File Structure

A virtual machine inside of the VMware application consists of a directory, with several files holding information about that guest operating system installation. The virtual files making up a VMware guest include files with these suffixes:

.vmx = holds the virtual machine's configuration, including hardware and network settings.

nvram = stores the state of the virtual machines BIOS, including the BIOS boot program, clock settings, etc.

.vmdk = stores the virtual disk file, that is, the hard drive image(s) of the virtual machine. A single virtual machine may have multiple virtual drives, so there could be more than one .vmdk file.

.vmss = holds the suspended state file, for a paused virtual machine. This suspended state includes a copy of RAM and the current console screen view.

.vmsn = stores a snapshot file, used for taking a snapshot of the system state for restoring it later. This snapshot feature is immensely useful, especially when analyzing malware. Before you run malware that could be destructive, you should take a snapshot. Then, if the malware hoses the machine entirely, you can roll back to the most recent snapshot, restoring the system easily without having to rebuild!

You can back up the entire contents of a virtual machine, hard drive, and all, by simply creating a directory with a copy of all of these files. You can even zip it up for safe keeping.

25.23 VMWARE PLAYER

With most popular tools, there are free versions of a tool, and as they become popular, commercial companies create separate products with more features and a different interface than the free counterpart. However, with VMware, the company realized that people would want to try out new features and be able to run virtual machines without having to buy a commercial product. Therefore, they created VMware player, which is a free version of VMware that is fully compatible with the commercial versions. This means you can take virtual machines created with any other VMware product and run them in VMware player. Of course, since the product is free there is limited functionality.

25.23.1 Benefits of VMware Player

One of the big reasons for VMware player is it gives people an easy way to evaluate virtual appliances, which are pre-built OS' and applications that someone can run with minimal overhead. For students, or even security professionals, it provides a simplified method of being able to run different operating systems and tools with no additional cost for software. It also provides a great way to create virtualized network environments. With VMware Player you can install multiple operating systems and have them communicate through network protocols as if they were on separate networked machines. This allows you to be able to simulate a lab environment with only one system.

25.23.2 Features of VMware Player

Some of the key features of VMware player are:

- The ability to run 32 and 64 bit operating systems from a standard 32 bit OS. For example, even if you have a standard 32 bit operating system installed, through the virtualization features ofVMware Player you can still run 64 bit operating systems.
- Being able to use multiple CPU's to support more efficient running of virtual machines.
- Ease of backup and portability of operating systems. For example, an instructor can provide an entire operating system image on CD to all of the students and guarantee that everyone has the same environment and tools installed. In addition, if anyone has problems or issues, they can quickly reload the original image.
- The capability to test out new devices. Since VMware Player has full support for USB devices, you can test and run new devices in a virtual machine, minimizing the chances of damaging your host OS.

25.24 SUMMARY

As you can imagine you can use both platform and resource virtualization together. Even 30 years ago, the hardware in some cases out-performed the software and the need for virtualization was born. This need continues to grow and will continue to be popular as the power of hardware continues to increase. One of the most common forms of virtualization that you will use is in the form of virtual machines.

As people recognize the benefits of virtual machines, they are going to continue to grow in popularity. From security professionals running multiple OS' on a laptop, to large corporations saving millions of dollars on hardware, the benefits are obvious. From a network security standpoint it is critical we understand the value and benefit of virtual machines.

When troubleshooting an operating system, it is always important to remember whether you are in a host or guest operating system. While they seem to work the same way, there are subtle differences between the two, since a host operating system is accessing the hardware directly and the guest operating system is accessing virtual hardware through an emulator.

Virtual machines have many benefits from an individual user to a high-end data center. Virtual machines allow security professionals to be able to have access to a wide range of operating systems without having to purchase expensive hardware. This allows us to create virtual security labs with minimal effort. In the early 90's if you wanted a lab, you would have to buy many computer systems with removable drives to be able to have an effective lab. Now, with a few systems and virtual machines, you can simulate an entire corporate network with minimal expense.

The directory structure of VMware is very straightforward. Understanding what information is kept in each file will allow you to be able to rebuilds change, or share your VMware images with other people. From building a virtual lab, to practice running new tools, to performing forensic analysis, VMware offers many benefits to the security professional.

Even with its scaled back capability over commercial VMware solutions, VMware Player provides a simple, easy, free way for you to be able to test and run virtual machines. As you will see, there are many benefits and reasons for using one of the commercial solutions, but VMware Player lets you try before you buy. This allows someone to test and understand how virtual machines work without having to spend any money on the virtual machine product.

REVIEW QUESTIONS

1. What is Server Virtualization?
2. What is a Virtual Machine?
3. How does Virtualization Works?
4. What are the Benefits of Virtualization?
5. Which Issues should be taken seriously? List them.
6. What is the difference between Migration from Physical Server Hosting to Virtual?
7. What operating systems run on virtual servers?
8. What Virtualization Tools are most common?
9. How Many Virtual Machines can one Server Run?
10. What is Platform and Resource Virtualization?
11. What is Host and Guest? Explain.
12. What is Paravirtualization?
13. What is Network Virtualization?
14. What is Virtual Switch? How it is different from traditional switch?
15. What to you understand by the Clustered File System and how it works? Explain.
16. What is Memory Overcommit?
17. What is Snapshot and it usages?

CLOUD COMPUTING AND ITS SECURITY

26.1 INTRODUCTION

Cloud computing is a movement started sometime during the middle of the first decade of the new millennium; the movement is motivated by the idea that information processing can be done more efficiently on large farms of computing and storage systems accessible via the Internet.

Computer clouds support a paradigm shift from local to network-centric computing and network-centric content, when computing and storage resources are provided by distant datacentres. Scientific and engineering applications, data mining, computational financing, gaming and social networking, as well as many other computational and data-intensive activities can benefit from cloud computing. Storing information on the cloud has significant advantages and was embraced by cloud service providers. For example, in 2011 Apple announced the *iCloud,* a network-centric alternative for content such as music, videos, movies, and personal information. Content previously confined to personal devices such as workstations, laptops, tablets, and smart phones need no longer be stored locally, can be shared by all these devices, and it is accessible whenever a device is connected to the Internet.

The appeal of cloud computing is that it offers scalable and elastic computing and storage services. The resources used for these services can be metered and the users can be charged only for the resources they used. Cloud computing is a business reality, as a large number of organizations are adopting this paradigm.

Cloud computing is cost effective because of the multiplexing of resources. Application data is stored closer to the site where it is used in a manner that is device and location independent; potentially, this data storage strategy increases reliability as well as security. The maintenance and security are ensured by service providers; the service providers can operate more efficiently due to economy of scale.

Cloud computing is a technical and social reality and, at the same time, it is an emerging technology. At this time one can only speculate how the infrastructure for this new paradigm will evolve and what applications will migrate to it. The economically, social, ethical, and legal implications of this shift in technology, whereby the users rely on services provided by large data centers and store private data and software on systems they do not control, is likely to be significant.

Cloud computing represents a dramatic shift in the design of systems capable to provide vast amounts of computing cycles and storage space. While, during the previous four decades, one-of-a-kind systems were built with the most advanced components available at the time, at a high cost, the clouds use off-the shelf, low-cost components.

Cloud computing reinforces the idea that computing and communication are deeply intertwined. Advances in one field are critical for the other. Indeed, cloud computing could not emerge as a feasible alternative to the traditional paradigms for high-performance computing before the Internet was able to support high-bandwidth, low-latency, reliable, low-cost communication; at the same time, modern networks could not function without powerful computing systems to manage the network. High performance switches are critical elements of both networks and computer clouds.

A very important question is if under the pressure from the user community the current standardization efforts will succeed. The alternative, the continuing dominance of proprietary cloud computing environments is likely to have a negative impact on the field. The three cloud delivery models, Software as a Service (SaaS), Platform as a Service (PaaS), and Infrastructure as a Service (IaaS) will continue to coexist for the foreseeable future. Services based on SaaS will probably be increasingly more popular because they are more accessible to lay people, while services based on the IaaS will be the domain of computer savvy individuals. If the standardization effort succeeds, then we may see PaaS designed to migrate from one infrastructure to another and overcome the concerns related to vendor lock-in.

26.2 CLOUD COMPUTING

During the last several decades, dramatic advances in computing power, storage, and networking technology have allowed the human race to generate, process, and share increasing amounts of information in dramatically new ways. As new applications of computing technology are developed and introduced, these applications are often used in ways that their designers never envisioned. New applications, in turn, lead to new demands for even more powerful computing infrastructure.

To meet these computing-infrastructure demands, system designers are constantly looking for new system architectures and algorithms to process larger collections of data more quickly than is feasible with today's systems. It is now possible to assemble very large, powerful systems consisting of many small, inexpensive commodity components because computers have become smaller and less expensive, disk drive capacity continues to increase, and networks have gotten faster. Such systems tend to be much less costly than a single, faster machine with comparable capabilities.

Building systems from large numbers of commodity components leads to some significant challenges, however. Because many more computers can be put into a computer room today than was possible even a few years ago, electrical-power consumption, air-conditioning capacity, and equipment weight have all become important considerations for system designs. Software challenges also arise in this environment because writing software that can take full advantage of the aggregate computing power of many machines is far more difficult than writing software for a single, faster machine.

Recently, a number of commercial and academic organizations have built large systems from Commodity computers, disks, and networks, and have created software to make this hardware easier to program and manage. These organizations have taken a variety of novel approaches to address the challenges outlined above. In some cases, these organizations have used their hardware and software to provide storage, computational, and data management services to their own internal users, or to provide these services to external customers for a fee. We refer to the hardware and software environment that implements this service-based environment as a *cloud-computing* environment. Because the term 'cloud computing' is relatively new, there is not universal agreement on this definition. Some people use the terms *grid computing*, *utility computing*, or *application service providers* to describe the same storage, computation, and data-management ideas that constitute cloud computing.

Regardless of the exact definition used, numerous companies and research organizations are applying cloud-computing concepts to their business or research problems including Google, Amazon, Yahoo, and numerous universities.

Cloud computing is a model for enabling convenient, on-demand network access to a shared pool of configurable computing resources (*e.g.*, networks, servers, storage, applications, and services) that can be rapidly provisioned and released with minimal management effort or service provider interaction.

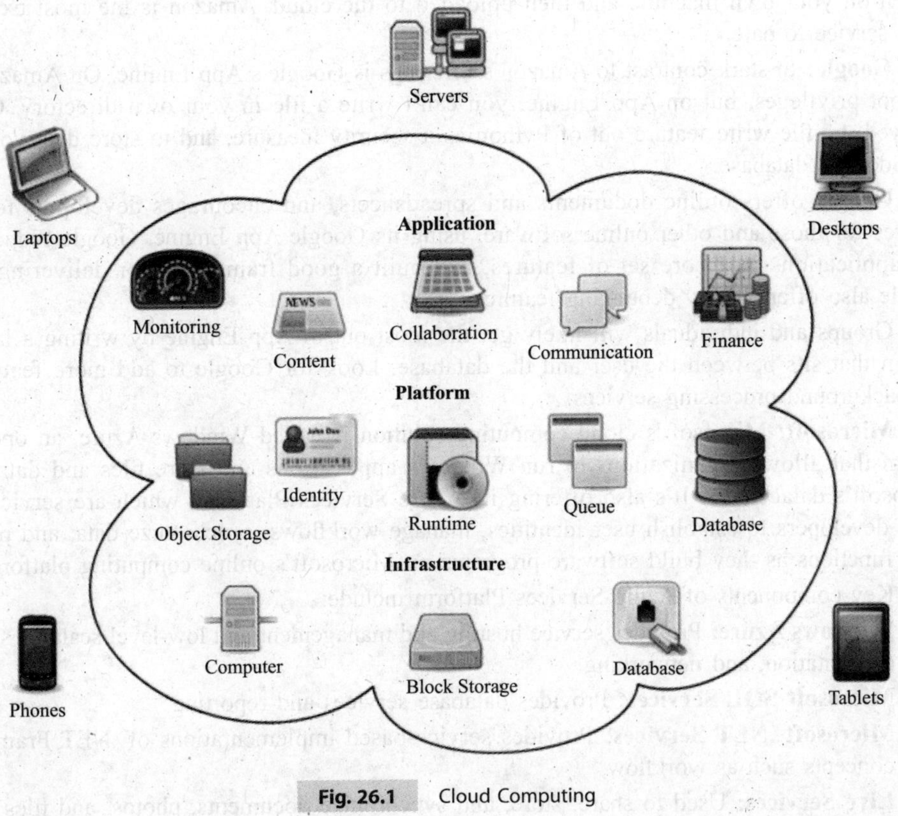

Fig. 26.1 Cloud Computing

There are scores of vendors who offer cloud services. What they have to offer varies based on the vendor and their pricing models are different, as well. Let's take a look at some of the big names in the world of cloud computing and talk, briefly, about what they have to offer.

Cloud computing is a growing field, and there will likely be new players in the market in the foreseeable future. For now, let's look at the names you already know: Amazon, Google, and Microsoft.

Amazon: Amazon was one of the first companies to offer cloud services to the public, and they are very sophisticated. Amazon offers a number of cloud services, including:

1. **Elastic Compute Cloud (EC2):** Offers virtual machines and extra CPU cycles for your organization.
2. **Simple Storage Service (S3):** Allows you to store items up to 5 GB in size in Amazon's virtual storage service.
3. **Simple Queue Service (SQS):** Allows your machines to talk to each other using this message-passing API.
4. **SimpleDB** A web service for running queries on structured data in real time. This service works in close conjunction with Amazon Simple Storage Service (Amazon S3) and Amazon Elastic Compute Cloud (Amazon EC2), collectively providing the ability to store, process, and query data sets in the cloud.

These services can be difficult to use, because they have to be done through the command line. That said, if you are used to working in a command-line environment, you shouldn't have much trouble using the services. Amazon's virtual machines are versions of Linux distributions, so those who are experienced with Linux will be right at home. In fact, applications can be written on your own machine and then uploaded to the cloud. Amazon is the most extensive cloud service to date.

Google: In stark contrast to Amazon's offerings is Google's App Engine. On Amazon you get root privileges, but on App Engine, you can't write a file in your own directory. Google removed the file write feature out of Python as a security measure, and to store data you must use Google's database.

Google offers online documents and spreadsheets, and encourages developers to build features for those and other online software, using its Google App Engine. Google reduced the web applications to a core set of features, and built a good framework for delivering them. Google also offers handy debugging features.

Groups and individuals will likely get the most out of App Engine by writing a layer of Python that sits between the user and the database. Look for Google to add more features to add background processing services.

Microsoft: Microsoft's cloud computing solution is called Windows Azure, an operating system that allows organizations to run Windows applications and store files and data using Microsoft's datacenters. It's also offering its Azure Services Platform, which are services that allow developers to establish user identities, manage workflows, synchronize data, and perform other functions as they build software programs on Microsoft's online computing platform.

Key components of Azure Services Platform include:

1. **Windows Azure:** Provides service hosting and management and low-level scalable storage, computation, and networking.
2. **Microsoft SQL Services:** Provides database services and reporting.
3. **Microsoft .NET Services:** Provides service-based implementations of .NET Framework concepts such as workflow.
4. **Live Services:** Used to share, store, and synchronize documents, photos, and files across PCs, phones, PC applications, and web sites.
5. **Microsoft SharePoint Services and Microsoft Dynamics CRM Services:** Used for business content, collaboration, and solution development in the cloud.

Microsoft plans the next version of Office to offer a browser-based option so that users can read and edit documents online as well as offer the ability for users to collaborate using web, mobile, and client versions of Office. Microsoft is a little late to the cloud party and isn't a leader in cloud computing. That honor goes to Google and Amazon, and more and more companies are offering cloud services, so if Microsoft wants to stay competitive, they're going to have to pick up the pace.

26.3 ESSENTIAL CLOUD CHARACTERISTICS

Cloud computing exhibits the following key characteristics:

1. **Virtualization:** Virtualization technology allows servers and storage devices to be shared and utilization be increased. Applications can be easily migrated from one physical server to another.
2. **Multitenancy:** Multitenancy enables sharing of resources and costs across a large pool of users thus allowing for:
   (*a*) **Centralization:** Centralization of infrastructure in locations with lower costs (such as real estate, electricity, etc.)

(*b*) **Peak-load Capacity:** Peak-load capacity increases (users need not engineer for highest possible load-levels).

(*c*) **Utilisation and efficiency: Utilisation and efficiency** improvements for systems that are often only 10–20% utilised.

3. **Reliability:** Reliability is improved if multiple redundant sites are used, which makes well-designed cloud computing suitable for business continuity and disaster recovery.
4. **Performance:** Performance is monitored, and consistent and loosely coupled architectures are constructed using web services as the system interface.
5. **Security:** Security could improve due to centralization of data, increased security-focused resources, etc., but concerns can persist about loss of control over certain sensitive data, and the lack of security for stored kernels. Security is often as good as or better than other traditional systems, in part because providers are able to devote resources to solving security issues that many customers cannot afford. However, the complexity of security is greatly increased when data is distributed over a wider area or greater number of devices and in multi-tenant systems that are being shared by unrelated users. In addition, user access to security audit logs may be difficult or impossible. Private cloud installations are in part motivated by users' desire to retain control over the infrastructure and avoid losing control of information security.
6. **Maintenance:** Maintenance of cloud computing applications is easier, because they do not need to be installed on each user's computer and can be accessed from different places.
7. **On-demand self-service:** A consumer can unilaterally provision computing capabilities, such as server time and network storage, as needed automatically without requiring human interaction with each service's provider.
8. **Broad network access:** Capabilities are available over the network and accessed through standard mechanisms that promote use by heterogeneous thin or thick client platforms (*e.g.*, mobile phones, tablets, laptops, and workstations).
9. **Resource pooling:** The provider's computing resources are pooled to serve multiple consumers using a multi-tenant model, with different physical and virtual resources dynamically assigned and reassigned according to consumer demand. There is a sense of location independence in that the customer generally has no control or knowledge over the exact location of the provided resources but may be able to specify location at a higher level of abstraction (*e.g.*, country, state, or datacenter). Examples of resources include storage, processing, memory, and network bandwidth.
10. **Rapid elasticity:** Capabilities can be rapidly and elastically provisioned, in some cases automatically, to scale rapidly outward and inward commensurate with demand. To the consumer, the capabilities available for provisioning often appear to be unlimited and can be appropriated in any quantity at any time.
11. **Measured service:** Cloud systems automatically control and optimize resource use by leveraging a metering capability at some level of abstraction appropriate to the type of service (*e.g.*, storage, processing, bandwidth, and active user accounts). Resource usage can be monitored, controlled, and reported, providing transparency for both the provider and consumer of the utilized service.

26.4 CLOUD SERVICES

Cloud providers typically centre on one type of cloud functionality provisioning: Infrastructure as a Service, Platform as a Service or Software/Application as a Service, though there is potentially no restriction to offer multiple types at the same time, which can often be observed in PaaS

(Platform as a Service) providers which offer specific applications too, such as Google App Engine in combination with Google Docs. Due this combinatorial capability, these types are also often referred to as 'components'.

Literature and publications typically differ slightly in the terminologies applied. This is mostly due to the fact that some application areas overlap and are therefore difficult to distinguish. As an example, platforms typically have to provide access to resources indirectly, and thus are sometimes confused with infrastructures. Additionally, more popular terms have been introduced in less technologically centred publications.

The following list identifies the main types of clouds:

26.4.1 Cloud Software as a Service (SaaS)

The capability provided to the consumer is to use the provider's applications running on a cloud infrastructure. The applications are accessible from various client devices through a thin client interface such as a Web browser (*e.g.*, Web-based email), or a program interface. The consumer does not manage or control the underlying cloud infrastructure including network, servers, operating systems, storage, or even individual application capabilities, with the possible exception of limited user-specific application configuration settings.

In the SaaS model, cloud providers install and operate application software in the cloud and cloud users access the software from cloud clients. Cloud users do not manage the cloud infrastructure and platform where the application runs. This eliminates the need to install and run the application on the cloud user's own computers, which simplifies maintenance and support. Cloud applications are different from other applications in their scalability—which can be achieved by cloning tasks onto multiple virtual machines at run-time to meet changing work demand. Load balancers distribute the work over the set of virtual machines. This process is transparent to the cloud user, who sees only a single access point. To accommodate a large number of cloud users, cloud applications can be *multitenant,* that is, any machine serves more than one cloud user organization. It is common to refer to special types of cloud based application software with a similar naming convention: desktop as a service, business process as a service, test environment as a service, communication as a service.

The pricing model for SaaS applications is typically a monthly or yearly flat fee per user, so price is scalable and adjustable if users are added or removed at any point.

Examples of SaaS include: Google Apps, Microsoft Office 365, Onlive, GT Nexus, Marketo, and TradeCard.

26.4.1.1 Benefits (SaaS)

One of the biggest benefits of SaaS is, of course, costing less money than buying the application outright. The service provider can offer cheaper, more reliable applications than organizations can by themselves. Some other benefits include the following:

1. **Familiarity with the World Wide Web:** Most workers have access to a computer and know how to use it on the World Wide Web. As such, the learning curve for using external applications can be much smaller.
2. **Smaller staff:** IT systems require the overhead of salaries, benefits, insurance, and building space. The ability to farm out applications reduces the need for as much IT staff.
3. **Customization:** Older applications were difficult to customize and required tinkering with the code. SaaS applications are much easier to customize and can give an organization exactly what they want.
4. **Better marketing:** A provider who had developed an application for a very narrow market might have had problems marketing that application. However, with SaaS, the entire world is open to the providers.

5. **Web reliability:** We talked earlier about how the World Wide Web can be seen as a source of failure. And while that is sporadically true, the fact of the matter is that the Web is generally quite reliable.
6. **Cost Saving:** Outsourced and public SaaS clouds allow a consumer to begin using an application without the up-front costs of equipment acquisition, but potentially with a recurring usage fee. Additionally, cloud providers should be able to provision their hardware, power, and other computing resources at scale and more efficiently than individual consumers, which may reduce ongoing costs to consumers. This provides a basis for cost savings to consumers. As with any buy vs. rent decision, a careful analysis of all the cost considerations should be performed, including anticipated future prices, before committing to a single approach.
7. **Platform Responsibilities Managed by Providers:** Generally, for outsourced or public SaaS clouds, consumers need not become involved with the management of a provider's infrastructure. For example, consumers need not be distracted by which operating system, hardware devices or configuration choices, or software library versions underlie a SaaS application. In particular, providers have responsibility for operational issues such as backups, system maintenance, security patches, power management, hardware refresh, physical plant security, etc. Providers also have an obligation to field services that guard against known exploits at the application level. Further, consumers are not required to maintain on premises IT support to perform these tasks, with an exception that on premises IT support is still necessary to connect consumer browsers securely to the network. Because SaaS providers implement new application features and provide the server side hardware that runs them, SaaS providers also have advantages in managing the introduction of new features while mitigating the need for consumers to upgrade their hardware systems to use the new features.
8. **Security:** Secure Sockets Layer (SSL) is widely used and trusted. This allows customers to reach their applications securely without having to employ complex back-end configurations, like virtual private networks (VPNs).
9. **More bandwidth:** Bandwidth has increased greatly in recent months and quality of service improvements are helping data flow. This will allow organizations to trust that they can access their applications with low latencies and good speeds.
10. **Efficient Use of Software Licenses:** License management overheads can be dramatically reduced using SaaS. Consumers can employ a single license on multiple computers at different times instead of purchasing extra licenses for separate computers that may not be used and thus over-provisioning the license. Additionally, traditional license management protocols and license servers are not needed to protect the intellectual property of application developers because the software runs in the provider's infrastructure and can be directly metered and billed.
11. **Deployment:** SaaS application deployment has become increasingly convenient and efficient with little or no client-side software required. Unlike shrink-wrapped software applications, SaaS applications can be accessed without waiting for complex installation procedures. Because SaaS applications have very small footprints on client computers, risk of configuration interference between applications on client computers is reduced. Distribution costs for the software are fundamentally reduced.

26.4.1.2 Obstacles (SaaS)

Like anything, SaaS faces obstacles to its implementation and use. The first is that an organization that has a very specific computational need might not be able to find the application available through SaaS. In that case, they may discover that they need to buy the software and install it on their local machines. That said, companies with unique needs may be able to find some of the components in a SaaS.

Portability in SaaS is a concern for transitioning workloads from one SaaS cloud to another. Formats for exporting and importing data may not be fully compatible among SaaS clouds. Customized workflow and business rules, user interface and application settings, support scripts, data extensions, and add-ons developed over time can also be provider specific and not easily transferable.

There is also an element of 'lock-in' with vendors. That is, the customer might pay a provider to use an application, but once they do, they may be unable to port that application to a new vendor. Or, it might be possible to move to a new vendor, but the old vendor might charge a hefty moving fee.

SaaS also faces challenges from the availability of opensource applications and cheaper hardware. If companies are so inclined, they can put their open source applications on hardware that performs better and costs less than it used to.

Although browsers encrypt their communications with cloud providers, subtle disclosures of information are still possible. For example, the very presence or absence of message traffic, or the sizes of messages sent, or the originating locations may leak information that is indirect but still of importance to some consumers. Additionally, even strong cryptography can be weakened by implementation mistakes; a common mistake is to generate keys or passwords in a manner that reduces their strength, thus making the cryptography vulnerable to brute-force guessing attacks. Furthermore, man-in-the-middle attacks on the cryptographic protocols used by browsers can allow an attacker to hijack a consumer's cloud resources. These risks apply to non-cloud environments as well; however in cloud computing, the reliance upon safe, end-user, client applications and networking may be greater.

The availability of a SaaS application depends on a reliable and continuously available network. In the public SaaS cloud scenario, the network's reliability cannot be guaranteed either by the cloud consumer or by the cloud provider because the Internet is not under the control of either one. In outsourced private or community SaaS scenarios, network security and reliability can be achieved using dedicated, protected communications links, but at a cost. Although a SaaS application may include a 'disconnected mode' for continued processing during network outages, the fundamental organization of SaaS, with application logic implemented on the cloud provider's servers, implies that the actual functionality of the application will be dependent on its ability to access a reliable network.

26.4.1.3 Information Security (SaaS)

The following are additional recommendations for SaaS systems:

1. **Data Protection:** Analyze the SaaS provider's data protection mechanisms, data location configuration and database organization/transaction processing technologies, and assess whether they will meet the confidentiality, compliance, integrity and availability needs of the organization that will be using the subscribed SaaS application.
2. **Client Device/Application Protection:** Protect the cloud consumer's client device (*e.g.*, a computer running a Web browser) so as to control the exposure to attacks.
3. **Encryption:** Require that strong encryption using a robust algorithm with keys of required strength be used for Web sessions whenever the subscribed SaaS application requires the confidentiality of application interaction and data transfers. Also require that the same diligence be applied to stored data. Government must employ government-approved cryptographic algorithms for encryption and digital signature, and the implementations need

to be validated. Understand how cryptographic keys are managed and who has access to them. Ensure that cryptographic keys are adequately protected.

4. **Secure Data Deletion:** Require that cloud providers offer a mechanism for reliably deleting data on a consumer's request.

26.4.2 Cloud Platform as a Service (PaaS)

The capability provided to the consumer is to deploy onto the cloud infrastructure consumer-created or acquired applications created using programming languages and tools supported by the provider.3 The consumer does not manage or control the underlying cloud infrastructure including network, servers, operating systems, or storage, but has control over the deployed applications and possibly application hosting environment configurations.

In the PaaS model, cloud providers deliver a computing platform typically including operating system, programming language execution environment, database, and web server. Application developers can develop and run their software solutions on a cloud platform without the cost and complexity of buying and managing the underlying hardware and software layers. With some PaaS offers, the underlying computer and storage resources scale automatically to match application demand such that cloud user does not have to allocate resources manually.

Examples of PaaS include: AWS Elastic Beanstalk, Cloud Foundry, Heroku, Force.com, EngineYard, Mendix, OpenShift, Google App Engine, Windows Azure Cloud Services and OrangeScape.

26.4.2.1 Benefits (PaaS)

PasS shares many of the benefits of SaaS, such as Deployment, Efficient use Licences, Platform Issues Managed by Providers, Cost Savings, Centralized Management, etc.

PaaS provides a low-cost way of developing and deploying applications. A variety of toolkits exist for developing PaaS applications and for supporting them both at the server side via data stores and server-side processing frameworks, and at the client side via thin clients and especially browser-based processing frameworks. These techniques provide a way for organizations to develop and deploy enterprise applications and to maintain centralized control over their operation and the data that is processed with them. PaaS application development frameworks typically provide design patterns supporting a high level of scalability, thus enabling well-written PaaS applications to operate smoothly through large fluctuations in demand. In on-site scenarios, scalability will be limited to the resources provided by consumer data centers; however in outsourced scenarios more resources may be available at the providers' facilities and, particularly in the public scenario, well-written PaaS applications can be quickly deployed to large numbers of consumers and provide very large quantities of data and processing services.

26.4.2.2 PaaS Options

PaaS is found in one of three different types of systems:

1. **Add-on development facilities:** These allow existing SaaS applications to be customized. Often, PaaS developers and users are required to purchase subscriptions to the add-on SaaS application.
2. **Stand-alone environments:** These environments do not include licensing, technical, or financial dependencies on specific SaaS applications and are used for general developments.
3. **Application delivery-only environments:** These environments support hosting- level services, like security and on-demand scalability. They do not include development, debugging, and test capabilities.

26.4.2.3 *Trends Toward Adoption*

PaaS faces the same sorts of factors in its adoption as SaaS did, as it is in its early phase. Some other factors influencing adoption include:

1. The ability of geographically isolated development teams to work together
2. The ability to merge web services from multiple sources
3. The ability to realize cost savings from using built-in infrastructure services for security, scalability, and failover, rather than having to obtain and test them separately
4. The ability to realize cost savings from using higher-level programming abstractions

26.4.2.4 *Obstacles (PaaS)*

There are two main obstacles that developers face when considering PaaS. Because vendors use proprietary services or development languages, some developers are afraid of being locked into a single provider. The vendor may allow the application to be brought to a different provider; however, the costs are typically higher as compared to moving applications between conventional hosts.

26.4.2.5 *Information Security (PaaS)*

The following are additional recommendations for PaaS systems:

1. **Security:** Ensure that a PaaS application can be configured to run in a secure manner (*e.g.*, a dedicated VLAN segment, using cryptography for client-server communications) and can be integrated with existing enterprise/agency security frameworks such as identification and authorization so that enterprise/agency security policies can be enforced.
2. **Secure Data Deletion:** Require that a cloud provider offer a mechanism for reliably deleting data on a consumer's request.
3. **Generic Interfaces:** Before a decision is made to develop new applications on a public PaaS cloud platform, it is recommended to evaluate whether the application infrastructure interfaces (for file, queue, hash table, etc.) provided in that platform are or could be made generic enough to support portability and interoperability of the application. PaaS clouds that support generic interfaces are preferable.
4. **Standard Languages and Tools:** Choose PaaS systems that work with standardized languages and tools unless the only practical options are PaaS systems that are restricted to proprietary languages and tools.
5. **Data Access:** Choose PaaS systems that work with standard data access protocols (*e.g.*, SQL) when practicable.
6. **Data Protection:** Analyze the PaaS provider's data protection mechanisms, data location configuration and database organization/transaction processing technologies, and assess whether they will meet the confidentiality, compliance, integrity and availability needs of the organization that will be using the subscribed PaaS application.
7. **Application Frameworks:** If available, choose PaaS systems that provide application development frameworks that include an architecture and tools for mitigating security vulnerabilities.
8. **Component Testing:** Before a decision is made to deploy a new application on a public PaaS cloud platform (or in some cases composing an application from the building blocks provided by the PaaS cloud provider), ensure that software libraries included in the compilation phase or called during the execution phase behave as intended both in terms of functionality and performance.

26.4.3 Cloud Infrastructure as a Service (IaaS)

The capability provided to the consumer is to provision processing, storage, networks, and other fundamental computing resources where the consumer is able to deploy and run arbitrary software, which can include operating systems and applications. The consumer does not manage or control the underlying cloud infrastructure but has control over operating systems, storage, deployed applications; and possibly limited control of select networking components (*e.g.*, host firewalls).

In the most basic cloud-service model, providers of IaaS offer computers—physical or (more often) virtual machines—and other resources. (A hypervisor, such as Xen or KVM, runs the virtual machines as guests. Pools of hypervisors within the cloud operational support-system can support large numbers of virtual machines and the ability to scale services up and down according to customers' varying requirements.) IaaS clouds often offer additional resources such as images in a virtual-machine image-library, raw (block) and file-based storage, firewalls, load balancers, IP addresses, virtual local area networks (VLANs), and software bundles. IaaS-cloud providers supply these resources on-demand from their large pools installed in data centers. For wide-area connectivity, customers can use either the Internet or carrier clouds (dedicated virtual private networks).

To deploy their applications, cloud users install operating-system images and their application software on the cloud infrastructure. In this model, the cloud user patches and maintains the operating systems and the application software. Cloud providers typically bill IaaS services on a utility computing basis: cost reflects the amount of resources allocated and consumed.

Examples of IaaS providers include: Amazon EC2, Azure Services Platform, DynDNS, Google Compute Engine, HP Cloud, iland, Joyent, LeaseWeb, Linode, NaviSite, Oracle Infrastructure as a Service, Rackspace Cloud, ReadySpace Cloud Services, ReliaCloud, SAVVIS, SingleHop, and Terremark.

HaaS allows you to 'rent' such resources as:

- ❐ Server space
- ❐ Memory
- ❐ Storage space
- ❐ Network equipment
- ❐ CPU cycles

Additionally, the infrastructure can be dynamically scaled up or down, based on the application resource needs. Further, multiple tenants can be on the equipment at the same time. Resources are typically billed based on a utility computing basis, so providers charge by how many resources are consumed.

IaaS involves several pieces:

1. **Service level agreements:** This is an agreement between the provider and client, guaranteeing a certain level of performance from the system.
2. **Computer hardware:** These are the components whose resources will be rented out. Service providers often have this set up as a grid for easier scalability.
3. **Network:** This includes hardware for firewalls, routers, load balancing, and so on.
4. **Internet connectivity:** This allows clients to access the hardware from their own organizations.
5. **Platform virtualization environment:** This allows the clients to run the virtual machines they want.
6. **Utility computing billing:** Typically set up to bill customers based on how many system resources they use.

26.4.3.1 Benefits (IaaS)

As with SaaS and PaaS clouds, in the public and outsourced IaaS scenarios, a cloud provider is free to locate cloud infrastructure in low-cost areas and have consumers access cloud services over the open Internet; cost savings from lower cost infrastructure may be shared with consumers in the form of lower service charges. Furthermore, public and outsourced IaaS clouds allow for savings in up-front costs as do public or outsourced PaaS and SaaS clouds.

In general, IaaS places more system management responsibility on consumers than either SaaS or PaaS; consumers need to manage the VMs and virtualized infrastructure and need to perform system administrator work. Although the provider may offer carefully constructed operating system images and services, replicated storage, cryptography, firewalls, monitoring, demand-based automated VM startup/shutdown, etc., responsibility for the operation of all software layers above the hypervisor rests primarily with the consumer. This can be considered as either a benefit or a concern, depending on the consumer's skill set and special needs.

Consumer access to IaaS cloud resources is typically performed through standard network protocols that use cryptography to prevent eavesdropping or tampering by third parties. Access to cloud resources over the network takes essentially three distinct forms: (1) a consumer issues administrative commands to the cloud provider, such as requests to run virtual machines or to save data on the cloud's servers, (2) a consumer with administrative access to specific running virtual machines (*i.e.*, the consumer who is currently renting them) issues administrative commands to the virtual machines, such as starting a Web server on a virtual machine or installing a new application, and (3) any user, and possibly an anonymous user, with access to the public network interacts with the virtual machines using the network services running on the virtual machines that a consumer has previously enabled.

Fundamentally, cloud computing provides rental of computing resources. These resources, which are typically accessed by consumers over a network, must be measurable in units that can be individually allocated to specific consumers, and paid for based on the length of time a consumer retains a resource. In the case of an IaaS cloud, the primary units of allocation are (administrative access to) VMs, network bandwidth, storage, and IP addresses. Additional resources include monitoring services, firewalls, synchronization mechanisms such as queues, databases, etc. A powerful aspect of having administrative access to a VM is that a consumer can run almost any software the consumer desires, including a custom operating system.

In addition to providing the functionality of raw hardware access, public and outsourced IaaS clouds provide the ability to quickly rent and then release large numbers of VMs or other cloud resources. This gives a consumer the ability to quickly set up large networks of VMs running consumer-selected software to solve large problems without incurring the expense of purchasing and maintaining the necessary hardware.

Because IaaS clouds allow consumers to install and run operating systems of their choosing, a high level of compatibility can be maintained between legacy applications and workloads in an IaaS cloud. For example, nearly any conventional network application (*e.g.*, Web server, email server, database) that a consumer normally runs on consumer-owned server hardware can be run from VMs in an IaaS cloud. Furthermore, many user-facing applications can also be run in an IaaS cloud by virtual desktop technology. While many applications can readily be ported to VMs, however, not all applications can be. For example, applications that require specialized hardware support are not ideal candidates for porting.

26.4.3.2 Obstacles (IaaS)

As with PaaS and SaaS clouds discussed earlier, IaaS clouds depend on a secure and reliable network, and also often depend on a secure and reliable browser for account administration.

In addition, by allowing consumers to run legacy software systems in the providers infrastructures, IaaS clouds expose consumers to all of the security vulnerabilities of those legacy software systems.

IaaS systems allow consumers to create and potentially retain many VMs in various states, *e.g.*, running, suspended, and off. An inactive VM can easily become out of date with respect to important security updates; if an out-of-date VM is activated, such a VM may become compromised. Although, in principle, a provider could update inactive VMs on behalf of consumers, the mechanics of such updating are complex, and the maintenance of security updates typically is a consumer responsibility.

26.4.3.3 Information Security (IaaS)

The following are additional recommendations for IaaS systems:

Multi-tenancy: When an IaaS cloud provider provides computing resources in the form of Virtual Machines (VMs), ensure that the provider has mechanisms in place to protect VMs from attacks (*a*) from other VMs on the same physical host (*b*) from the physical host as well as (*c*) from network originated attacks. Typical attack detection and prevention mechanisms include Virtual Firewalls, Virtual IDS/IPS, and Virtual Private Networks.

Data Protection: Analyze the IaaS provider's data protection mechanisms, data location configuration and processing technologies, and assess whether they will meet the confidentiality, compliance, integrity and availability needs of the organization that will be using the provider's infrastructure.

Secure Data Deletion: Require that a cloud provider offer a mechanism for reliably deleting data on a consumer's request.

Administrative Access: When renting computing resources from an IaaS cloud provider in the form of virtual machines or physical servers, ensure that a limited set of trained/trusted users (from the consumer organization) alone are provided administrative access to those resources.

VM Migration: Formulate a strategy for future migration of Virtual Machines and their associated storage among alternate cloud providers.

26.5 DEPLOYMENT MODELS

Cloud computing is a growing trend that offers an innovative way to deliver software, data storage, and computing services. While the term cloud computing refers in general to the delivery of services on demand over a computer network, the National Institute for Science and Technology (NIST) has defined four different cloud computing deployment models; private cloud, community cloud, public cloud, and hybrid cloud.

26.5.1 Private Cloud

The cloud infrastructure is provisioned for exclusive use by a single organization comprising multiple consumers (*e.g.*, business units). It may be owned, managed, and operated by the organization, a third party, or some combination of them, and it may exist on or off premises.

26.5.2 Community Cloud

The cloud infrastructure is provisioned for exclusive use by a specific community of consumers from organizations that have shared concerns (*e.g.*, mission, security requirements, policy, and compliance considerations). It may be owned, managed, and operated by one or more of the organizations in the community, a third party, or some combination of them, and it may exist on or off premises.

26.5.3 Public Cloud

The cloud infrastructure is provisioned for open use by the general public. It may be owned, managed, and operated by a business, academic, or government organization, or some combination of them. It exists on the premises of the cloud provider (Fig. 26.2).

26.5.4 Hybrid Cloud

The cloud infrastructure is a composition of two or more distinct cloud infrastructures (private, community, or public) that remain unique entities, but are bound together by standardized or proprietary technology that enables data and application portability (*e.g.*, cloud bursting for load balancing between clouds). Such composition expands deployment options for cloud services, allowing IT organization to use public cloud computing resources to meet temporary needs. This capability enables hybrid clouds to employ cloud bursting for scaling across clouds.

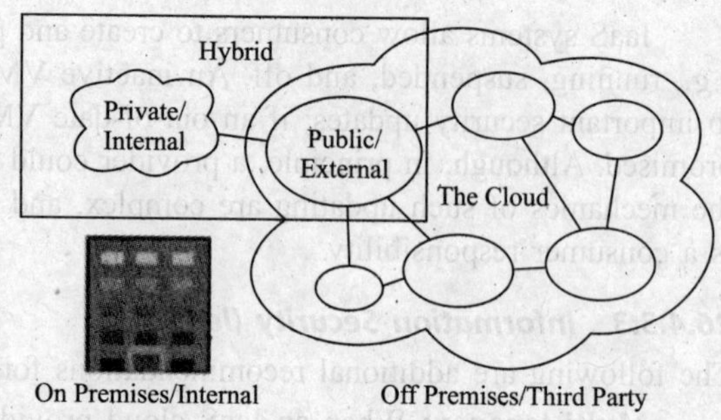

Fig. 26.2 Private Cloud, Public Cloud and Hybrid Cloud

Cloud bursting is an application deployment model in which an application runs in a private cloud or data center and 'bursts' to a public cloud when the demand for computing capacity increases. A primary advantage of cloud bursting and a hybrid cloud model is that an organization only pays for extra compute resources when they are needed.

Cloud bursting enables data centers to create an in-house IT infrastructure that supports average workloads, and use cloud resources from public or private clouds, during spikes in processing demands. By utilizing 'hybrid cloud' architecture, companies and individuals are able to obtain degrees of fault tolerance combined with locally immediate usability without dependency on internet connectivity. Hybrid cloud architecture requires both on-premises resources and off-site (remote) server-based cloud infrastructure.

Hybrid clouds lack the flexibility, security and certainty of in-house applications. Hybrid cloud provides the flexibility of in house applications with the fault tolerance and scalability of cloud based services.

26.6 CLOUD SERVICE AGREEMENT

A consumer's terms of service for a cloud are determined by a legally binding agreement between the two parties often contained in two parts: (1) a service agreement, and (2) a Service Level Agreement (SLA). Generally, the service agreement is a legal document specifying the rules of the legal contract between a consumer and provider, and the SLA is a shorter document stating the technical performance promises made by a provider including remedies for performance failures.

Service Agreements of various types exist. Service agreements are sometimes used internally between the information systems units and other organizational units of an enterprise to ensure that the information technology services provided are aligned with the mission objectives of the organization. Service agreements are normally not used in agreements for services acquired by one government organization from another. Instead, a Memorandum of Understanding (MOU) or Inter-Agency Agreement (IAA) is typically used to codify the terms of service.

Published service agreements between consumers and providers can typically be terminated at any time by either party, either 'for cause' such as a consumer's violation of a cloud's acceptable use policies, or for failure of a consumer to pay in a timely manner. Further, an agreement can be terminated for no reason at all. Consumers should analyze provider termination and data retention policies.

Provider promises, including explicit statements regarding limitations, are codified in their service agreements. A provider's service agreement has three basic parts: (1) Promises: a collection of promises made to consumers, (2) Limitations: a collection of promises explicitly not made to consumers, *i.e.*, limitations, and (3) Obligations: a set of obligations that consumers must accept.

26.6.1 Promises

Generally, cloud service providers make four key promises to consumers:

1. **Availability:** Providers typically advertise availability promises as uptime percentages ranging from 99% to 100.0% or some time 24 × 7 × 365. These are strong claims, and care is needed to understand how these percentages are calculated. Often, the percentage applies to the number of time intervals within a billing cycle (or longer periods such as a year) in which services are not 'up' for the entire interval. Examples of time intervals used by prominent providers are 5 minutes, 15 minutes, and 1 hour. For example, if a provider specifies an availability interval of 15 minutes, and the service is not functional for 14 minutes, 100% availability is preserved using this metric. Generally, the definition of 'up' is intuitively defined as service responsiveness, but in some cases, multiple cloud subsystems must fail before the service is judged as unavailable. Providers may also limit availability promises if failures are specific to particular functions or Virtual Machines (VMs).
2. **Remedies for Failure to Perform:** If a provider fails to give the promised availability, a provider should compensate consumers in good faith with a service credit for future use of cloud services. Service credits can be computed in different ways, but are usually determined by how long the service was unavailable within a specific billing period. Service credits are generally capped not to exceed a percentage of a consumer's costs in the billing period in which downtime occurred. Typical caps range from 10% to 100% of a consumer's current costs, depending on the provider. Responsibility for obtaining a service credit is generally placed on the consumer, who must provide timely information about the nature of the outage and the time length of the outage. It is unclear whether a provider will voluntarily inform a consumer of a service disruption. None of the providers recently surveyed (in their standard service agreements) offer a refund or any other remedy for failure to perform; however, all providers should understand that a poor reputation to perform offers few long-term business benefits.
3. **Data Preservation:** If a consumer's access to cloud services is terminated 'for cause,' *i.e.*, because the consumer has violated the clouds' acceptable use policies or for nonpayment, most providers state that they have no obligation to preserve any consumer data remaining in cloud storage. Further, after a consumer voluntarily stops using a cloud, providers generally state that they will not intentionally erase the consumer's data for a period of 30 days. Some providers preserve only a snapshot of consumer data, or recommend that consumers: (1) backup their data outside that provider's cloud inside another provider's cloud, or (2) back it up locally.
4. **Legal Care of Consumer Information:** Generally, cloud services providers promise not to sell, license, or disclose consumer data except in response to legal requests. Providers, however, usually reserve the right to monitor consumer actions in a cloud, and they may even demand a copy of consumer software to assist in that monitoring.

26.6.2 Limitations

Generally, cloud services provider policies include five key limitations:

1. **Security:** Providers generally assert that they are not responsible for the impacts of security breaches or for security in general, *i.e.*, unauthorized modification or disclosure of consumer data, or service interruptions caused by malicious activity. Generally, service agreements are explicit about placing security risks on consumers. In some cases, providers promise to use best efforts to protect consumer data, but all of the providers surveyed disclaim security responsibility for data breach, data loss, or service interruptions by limiting remedies to service credits for failure to meet availability promises. Further, it is unclear how easy it

would be for a consumer to determine that a service disruption was maliciously induced versus induction from another source.

2. **Service Agreement Changes:** Providers generally reserve the right to change the terms of the service agreement at any time, and to change pricing with limited advanced notice. For standard service agreement changes, notice is generally given by a provider by posting the change to a Web site. It is then the consumer's responsibility to periodically check the Web site for changes. Changes may take effect immediately or after a delay of several weeks. For changes that affect an individual consumer's account, notice may be delivered via email or a delivery service.
3. **Scheduled Outages:** If a provider announces a scheduled service outage, the outage does not count as failure to perform. For some providers, outages must be announced in advance, or must be bounded in duration.
4. **Force majeure events:** Providers generally disclaim responsibility for events outside their realistic control. Examples include power failures, natural disasters, and failures in network connectivity between consumers and providers.
5. **Service API Changes:** Providers generally reserve the right to change or delete service Application Programming Interfaces (APIs) at any time.

26.6.3 Obligations

Generally, consumers must agree to three key obligations:

1. **Acceptable Use Polices:** Consumers generally must agree to refrain from storing illegal content, such as child pornography, and from conducting illegal activities such as: (1) gambling, (2) sending spam, (3) conducting security attacks (*e.g.*, denial of service or hacking), (4) distributing spyware, (5) intrusive monitoring, and (6) attempting to subvert cloud system infrastructures. Acceptable use policies vary among providers.
2. **Licensed Software:** All providers state that third-party software running in their clouds must conform to the software's license terms. In some cases, providers bundle such software and include monitoring to ensure that license restrictions are enforced.
3. **Timely Payments:** Cloud service costs are generally incurred gradually over a billing period, with the fee due to the provider at the period's end. Failure to pay, after a grace period, usually subjects a consumer to suspension or termination 'for cause' which can result in loss of consumer data.

26.6.4 Recommendations

1. **Terminology:** Consumers should pay close attention to the terms that are used in service agreements. Common terms may be redefined by a cloud provider in ways that are specific to that provider's offerings.
2. **Remedies:** Unless a specific service agreement has been negotiated with a provider, remedies for any failures are likely to be extremely limited; consumers may wish to formulate and negotiate remedies that are commensurate with damage that might be sustained.
3. **Compliance:** Consumers should carefully assess whether the service agreement specifies compliance with appropriate laws and regulations governing consumer data.
4. **Security, Criticality, and Backup:** Consumers should carefully examine the service agreement for any disclaimers relating to security or critical processing, and should also search for any comment on whether the provider recommends independent backup of data stored in their cloud.

5. **Negotiated Service Agreement:** If the terms of the default service agreement do not address all consumer needs, the consumer should discuss modifications of the service agreement with the provider prior to use.
6. **Service Agreement Changes:** Be aware that, depending on the details of the service agreement, a provider may change the terms of service with a specified level of advance notice. Changes may affect both price and quality of service. It is prudent to develop a plan to migrate workloads to alternate cloud providers, or back on-premise, in the event that a change in service terms is unacceptable.

26.7 GENERAL CLOUD ENVIRONMENTS

The term 'cloud computing' encompasses a variety of systems and technologies as well as service and deployment models, and business models. A number of claims that are sometimes made about cloud computing, *e.g.*, that it 'scales,' or that it converts capital expenses to operational expenses, are only true for some kinds of cloud systems. To clearly, the cloud computing systems have been categorized into five significant scenarios and, for each scenario, to explain general issues about cloud computing, such as scalability, and how those issues apply in that scenario.

A cloud system is a collection of network-accessible computing resources that cloud consumers can access over a network. In general terms, a cloud system and its consumers employ the client-server model, which means that consumers (the clients) send messages over a network to server computers, which then perform work in response to the messages received.

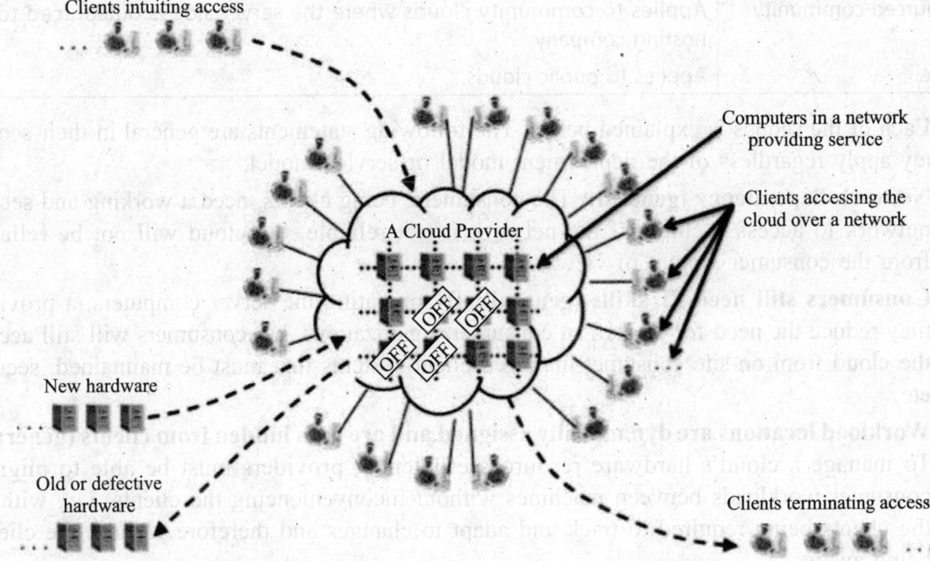

Fig. 26.3 General Cloud Environments and Consumer View

Figure 26.3 gives a general view of a cloud and its clients: the cloud's computing resources are depicted as a grid of computer systems where clients access a cloud over network connections. As shown in the figure, new clients may arrive, existing clients may depart, and the number of clients using a cloud at any one time is variable. Similarly, a cloud maintains a pool of hardware resources that it manages to maximize service and minimize costs. To maintain highly available services despite expected component failures and service life expirations, a cloud incorporates new hardware components as needed and retires old or failing components. To provide services cost-effectively, a cloud will manage the pool of hardware resources for resource efficiency;

one of the strategies that a cloud provider employs during periods of reduced consumer demand is to power off unused components. Whether for power management, or for hardware refresh, migration of customer workloads (data storage and processing) from one physical computer to another physical computer is a key strategy that allows a provider to refresh hardware or consolidate workloads without inconveniencing consumers.

Many statements commonly made about clouds (*e.g.*, that clouds scale for very large workloads or that clouds replace capital expenses with operational expenses), however, are true only for certain types of clouds. From Fig. 26.3, a small number of general statements about cloud computing (*e.g.*, strengths and limitations, performance characteristics) can be inferred; organizations considering the use of cloud computing should consider these general statements as listed below:

Table 26.1 Scope Modifiers for Statements Asserted About Clouds

Scope Name	*Applicability*
general	Applies to all cloud deployment models.
on-site-private	Applies to private clouds implemented at a customer's premises.
outsourced-private	Applies to private clouds where the server side is outsourced to a hosting company.
on-site-community	Applies to community clouds implemented on the premises of the customers composing a community cloud.
outsourced-community	Applies to community clouds where the server side is outsourced to a hosting company.
public	Applies to public clouds.

Each of the scopes is explained below. The following statements are general in their scope, *i.e.*, they apply regardless of the deployment model or service model:

1. **Network dependency (general):** The consumers, being clients, need a working and secure network to access a cloud. If the network is not reliable, the cloud will not be reliable from the consumer's point of view.
2. **Consumers still need IT skills (general):** By operating the server computers, a provider may reduce the need for IT staff in consumer organizations, but consumers will still access the cloud from on-site consumer-managed client systems that must be maintained, secure, etc.
3. **Workload locations are dynamically assigned and are thus hidden from clients (general):** To manage a cloud's hardware resources efficiently, providers must be able to migrate consumer workloads between machines without inconveniencing the clients, *i.e.*, without the clients being required to track and adapt to changes and therefore without the clients being aware.
4. **Risks from multi-tenancy (general):** The workloads of different clients may reside concurrently on the same system and local network, separated only by access policies implemented by a provider's software. A flaw in the implementation or in the provider's management and operational policies and procedures could compromise the security of consumers.
5. **Data import/export, and performance limitations (general):** Because consumers access a cloud over a network, on-demand bulk data import or export may exceed the network's ability to carry the data in a timely manner. Additionally, real-time or critical processing may be problematic because of networking latency or other limitations.

It is sometimes asserted that when compared to traditional on premises computing, cloud computing requires consumers to give up (to providers) two important capabilities:

1. **Control:** The ability to decide, with high confidence, who and what is allowed to access consumer data and programs, and the ability to perform actions (such as erasing data or disconnecting a network) with high confidence both that the actions have been taken and that no additional actions were taken that would subvert the consumer's intent (*e.g.*, a consumer request to erase a data object should not be subverted by the silent generation of a copy).
2. **Visibility:** The ability to monitor, with high confidence, the status of a consumer's data and programs and how consumer data and programs are being accessed by others.

The extent, however, to which consumers may need to relinquish control or visibility depends on a number of factors including physical possession and the ability to configure (with high confidence) protective access boundary mechanisms around a consumer's computing resources.

Figure 26.2 illustrates a key concept from computer security relating to boundaries and control, the security perimeter. As shown in the figure, a security perimeter is a barrier to access: entities that are inside the perimeter may freely access resources inside the perimeter; however entities that are located outside the perimeter may access the resources inside only if allowed by a boundary controller that enforces a policy over access. Although the term is often used to discuss firewalls and networks, the concept of the security perimeter is actually more generic and can be used, for instance, to describe the boundaries between different privilege levels of running software, *e.g.*, between applications and operating systems. By itself, a security perimeter is NOT an adequate security mechanism; however, perimeter controls are an important building block for secure systems.

Typical boundary controllers include firewalls, guards, and Virtual Private Networks. By implementing a security perimeter around its important resources, an organization can achieve both a measure of control over the use of those resources and a means for monitoring access to them. Furthermore, via reconfiguration, an organization can adapt a security perimeter to changing needs (*e.g.*, blocking or allowing protocols or data formats based on changing business circumstances).

The various cloud deployment models have implications for the locations of consumer-controlled security perimeters and hence for the level of control that consumers can exercise over resources that they entrust to a cloud (Fig. 26.4).

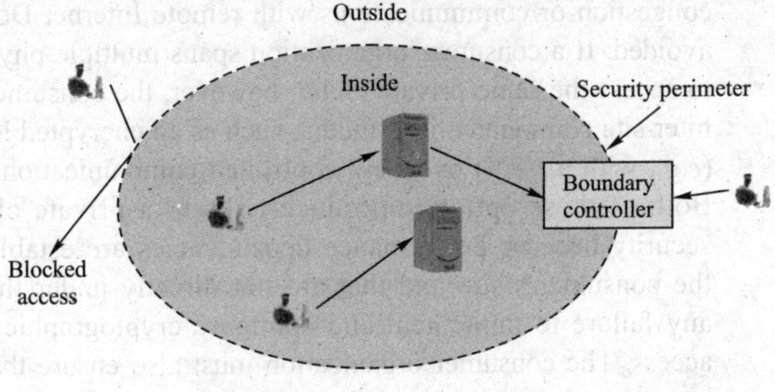

Fig. 26.4 The Security Perimeter

The private and community deployment models, however, admit of two variants that should be discussed separately because they affect the security perimeter: on-site, and outsourced. The hybrid deployment model is a combination of the others and therefore a hybrid deployment may be subject to the implications of all of its building blocks as well as unique implications that arise when multiple systems are composed into more complex integrated systems.

26.8 THE ON-SITE PRIVATE CLOUD SCENARIO

Figure 26.5 presents a simple view of an on-site private cloud. As shown in the figure, the security perimeter extends around both the consumer's on-site resources and the private cloud's resources. The private cloud may be centralized at a single consumer site or may be distributed over several consumer sites. The security perimeter will exist only if the consumer implements it. If implemented, the security perimeter will not guarantee control over the private cloud's resources, but its existence gives an opportunity for a consumer to exercise control over resources entrusted to the on-site private cloud.

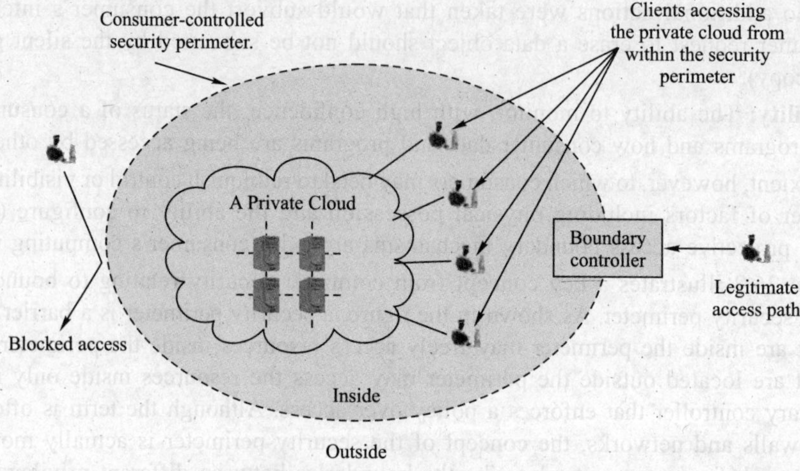

Fig. 26.5 On-site Private Cloud

Although the general implications remain true with an on-site private cloud, the on-site-private scenario allows for additional and more detailed implications that organizations considering the use of an on-site private cloud should consider:

1. **Network dependency (on-site-private):** Depending on the configuration (*e.g.*, single physical site, protected cloud network), the network dependency for an on-site private cloud may be limited to dependence on networking resources over which a consumer has control (*e.g.*, local area networking). In this scenario, larger-scale network problems, such as Internet congestion or communications with remote Internet Domain Name Servers (DNS) may be avoided. If a consumer organization spans multiple physical sites and wishes different sites to access the same private cloud, however, the consumer must either provision a controlled inter-site communications media, such as an encrypted leased line, or must use cryptography (*e.g.*, with a VPN) over less controlled communications media such as the public Internet. Both of these options introduce risks to a private cloud's networking availability and security because performance dependencies are established to resources that exist off of the consumer's site and that are not directly under the consumer's control, and because any failure to implement and configure cryptographic mechanisms could allow outsiders access. The consumer organization must also ensure that remote sites are maintained at an appropriate security level for the private cloud or that boundary devices are installed to prevent inconsistencies in security levels.
2. **Consumers still need IT skills (on-site-private):** Consumer organizations will need the traditional IT skills required to manage user devices that access the private cloud, and will require cloud IT skills as well. Early in the rollout of an on-site private cloud, consumer organizations may wish to maintain parallel cloud and non-cloud operations for an evaluation period. During any such evaluation period, traditional IT skills will be required. Even after an evaluation period, however, traditional IT staff will be needed (perhaps at reduced levels) to manage legacy licensing agreements, special hardware or system requirements, unique security needs for special projects, and legacy investments in equipment and training. In

addition, new skills for working in clouds may be required. For example, an organization that performs compute-intensive jobs may need to eventually reorganize those jobs so that they can run using a higher level of parallelism on the cloud's resources [Dea04]; an organization that processes large data sets in the cloud will need to develop skills with cloud-based storage.

3. **Workload locations are hidden from clients (on-site-private):** As in the general case, to manage a cloud's hardware resources, a private cloud must be able to migrate workloads between machines without inconveniencing clients, *i.e.*, without the clients being aware. In some situations, to avoid creating a single point of failure, it may also be necessary to provision and operate redundant cloud facilities at geographically diverse locations. With an on-site private cloud, however, a consumer organization chooses the physical infrastructure in which the private cloud operates, and hence determines the possible geographical locations of workloads. While individual clients still may not know where their workloads physically exist within the consumer organization's infrastructure at any given time, the consumer organization has both visibility and control over where workloads are allowed to reside.
4. **Risks from multi-tenancy (on-site-private):** As in the general case, the workloads of different clients may reside concurrently on the same systems and local networks, separated only by access policies implemented by a cloud provider's software. A flaw in the implementation or in the provider's management and operational policies and procedures could compromise the security of a consumer organization by exposing client workloads to one another contrary to the consumer's security policy. Logical segregation techniques at the network layer, such as VPN Routing and Forwarding (VRF), can help mitigate risks. An on-site private cloud mitigates these risks somewhat further by restricting the number of possible attackers; all of the clients would typically be members of the consumer organization or authorized guests or partners, but the on-site private cloud is still vulnerable to attack conducted by authorized but also malicious insiders. Different organizational functions, such as payroll, storage of sensitive personally identifiable information, or the generation of intellectual property may be merged as a consequence of such security failures, which can provide access to users who are not authorized to access specific classes of data and who then may disclose data from the on-site private cloud.
7. **Data import/export, and performance limitations (on-site-private):** As with the general case, on-demand bulk data import/export is limited by the on-site private cloud's network capacity, and real-time or critical processing may be problematic because of networking limitations. In the on-site private cloud scenario, however, these limits may be adjusted, although not eliminated, by provisioning high-performance and/or high-reliability networking within the consumer's infrastructure. Particularly if a consumer has only one site that requires access to the on-site private cloud, a consumer may be able to provision local networks that provide higher performance than can practically be achieved via wide area networks.
8. **Potentially strong security from external threats (on-site-private):** In an on-site private cloud, a consumer has the option of implementing an appropriately strong security perimeter to protect private cloud resources against external threats to the same level of security as can be achieved for non-cloud resources. For low-impact data and processing, the security perimeter may consist of commercial firewall rule sets and VPNs. For higher-impact data, security perimeters can be constructed via more restrictive firewall policies, multi-factor authentication, encryption, intrusion detection and prevention, and even physical isolation.
9. **Significant-to-high up-front costs to migrate into the cloud (on-site-private):** An on-site private cloud requires that cloud management software be installed on computer systems within a consumer organization. If the cloud is intended to support process-intensive or

data-intensive workloads, the software will need to be installed on numerous commodity systems or on a more limited number of high-performance systems. Installing cloud software and managing the installations will incur significant up-front costs, even if the cloud software itself is free, and even if much of the hardware already exists within a consumer organization.

Four potential approaches to accomplish, these are:

(*i*) **New Data Center:** The most direct approach is for a consumer to provision a data center in which to deploy the cloud software. In this case, the on-site private cloud incurs up-front costs that are similar to those of a typical data center and the consumer can provision the data center for anticipated workloads.

(*ii*) **Converted Data Center:** As an alternative to provisioning a new data center, a consumer may convert part or all of an existing data center to support the on-site private cloud. This approach, however, may not be compatible with running parallel cloud and non-cloud systems during the initial evaluation period.

(*iii*) **Scavenged Resources:** Another alternative approach, supported by, is for cloud software to be installed primarily on computers that already exist within an organization. In this scenario, cloud systems share hardware resources with other uses of the hardware and essentially can harvest cycles that might otherwise be wasted. This approach offers the advantage that cloud services can be made available on an experimental basis without a large hardware investment; however, the resources available to such a configuration will be limited to the previously-surplus resources in the organization's infrastructure (unless the former uses of the hardware are reduced in favor of the cloud). Additional limitations are that: (*a*) hardware resources must be incorporated into the on-site private cloud from wherever they exist in a consumer organization's infrastructure (via networking) rather than being co-located for efficiency, and (*b*) the available hardware may not be homogeneous and thus may be somewhat more difficult to administer.

(*iv*) **Limited resources (on-site-private):** An on-site private cloud, at any specific time, has a fixed computing and storage capacity that has been sized to correspond to anticipated workloads and cost restrictions. If an organization is large enough and supports a sufficient diversity of workloads, an on-site private cloud may be able to provide elasticity to clients within the consumer organization. Smaller on-site private clouds will, however, exhibit maximum capacity limits similar to those of traditional data centers. An on-site private cloud also requires that some costs, *e.g.*, for equipment, be paid up-front.

26.9 THE OUTSOURCED PRIVATE CLOUD SCENARIO

Figure 26.6 depicts an outsourced private cloud. As shown in the figure, an outsourced private cloud has two security perimeters, one implemented by a cloud consumer (on the right) and one implemented by a provider (left). The two security perimeters are joined by a protected communications link. As is apparent from the figure, the security of data and processing conducted in the outsourced private cloud depends on the strength and availability of both security perimeters and of the protected communication link. The provider thus accepts a responsibility to enforce the provider-implemented security perimeter and to prevent mingling of private cloud resources with other cloud resources that are outside the provider-controlled security perimeter. The suitability of various mechanisms for achieving an appropriate strength of separation between private cloud resources and other cloud resources depends on the consumer's security requirements. A number of possible mechanisms could be used with various tradeoffs between separation strength and cost/convenience (*e.g.*, Virtual Local Area Network (VLAN), VPN, separate network segments or clusters). This scenario, however, should, not merely employ separation mechanisms that are identical to the normal mechanisms (*e.g.*, hardware virtualization, VLANs) that separate customers in a public cloud. If those mechanisms alone were used, this scenario would essentially become the public cloud scenario.

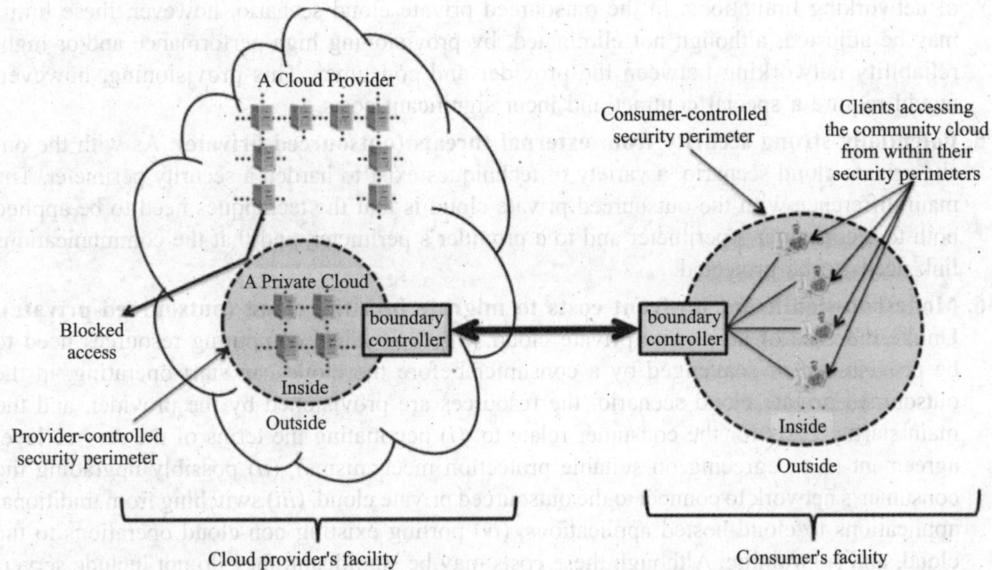

Fig. 26.6 Outsourced Private Cloud

Although the general statements remain true for the outsourced private scenario, the outsourced private scenario also allows for a more detailed understanding of some of the general statements plus additional statements that organizations considering the use of an outsourced private cloud should consider:

1. **Network Dependency (outsourced-private):** In the outsourced private scenario, consumers may have an option to provision dedicated protected and reliable communication links with the provider. Although network dependence does not appear to be avoidable, in this scenario the impact of the network dependency may be ameliorated at a negotiated price (*e.g.*, dedicated leased network connections supporting enhanced performance, reliability, and security).
2. **Workload locations are hidden from clients (outsourced-private):** As in the general case, to manage a cloud's hardware resources, an outsourced private cloud must be able to migrate workloads between machines without inconveniencing the clients, *i.e.*, without the clients being aware of the migrations. The outsourced private cloud scenario, however, provides an opportunity for the consumer's organization to have some visibility and control regarding workload locations. Assuming that the provider faithfully implements the security perimeter agreed upon with the consumer, the consumer organization workloads move only within the agreed-upon security perimeter. Depending on the mechanisms chosen to implement the perimeter, the consumer may know the physical location (*e.g.*, cluster, network segments) of the resources devoted to the outsourced private cloud even though the clients are unaware.
3. **Risks from multi-tenancy (outsourced-private):** The implications are the same as those for an on-site private cloud. FISMA and OMB policy require that external cloud providers

handling federal information or operating information systems on behalf of the federal government meet the same security requirements as federal agencies.

4. **Data import/export, and performance limitations (outsourced-private):** As with the general case, on-demand bulk data import/export is limited by the network capacity between a provider and consumer, and real-time or critical processing may be problematic because of networking limitations. In the outsourced private cloud scenario, however, these limits may be adjusted, although not eliminated, by provisioning high-performance and/or high-reliability networking between the provider and consumer. This provisioning, however, would require a special contract and incur significant costs.
5. **Potentially strong security from external threats (outsourced-private):** As with the on-site private cloud scenario, a variety of techniques exist to harden a security perimeter. The main difference with the outsourced private cloud is that the techniques need to be applied both to a consumer's perimeter and to a provider's perimeter, and that the communications link needs to be protected.
6. **Modest-to-significant up-front costs to migrate into the cloud (outsourced-private):** Unlike the case of an on-site private cloud, where physical computing resources need to be provisioned or scavenged by a consumer before the cloud can start operating, in the outsourced private cloud scenario, the resources are provisioned by the provider, and the main startup costs for the consumer relate to: (*i*) negotiating the terms of the service level agreement (*e.g.*, agreeing on suitable protection mechanisms), (*ii*) possibly upgrading the consumer's network to connect to the outsourced private cloud, (*iii*) switching from traditional applications to cloud-hosted applications, (*iv*) porting existing non-cloud operations to the cloud, and (*v*) training. Although these costs may be significant, they do not include server-side equipment and its supporting infrastructure.
7. **Extensive resources available (outsourced-private):** Unlike the case of an on-site private cloud, in which the resources must be provisioned by a consumer up front, in the case of the outsourced private cloud, a consumer can rent resources in any quantity offered by the provider. Provisioning and operating computing equipment at scale is a core competency of providers. Hence it is likely that a provider can provision relatively large private clouds as needed. As with the on-site private cloud, an outsourced private cloud has a fixed capacity at any given time, and providing elasticity for clients is achievable only if the cloud is large enough and there is sufficient diversity of workloads. As with an on-site private cloud, an outsourced private cloud will exhibit maximum capacity limits similar to those of traditional data centers.

26.10 THE ON-SITE COMMUNITY CLOUD SCENARIO

Figure 26.7 depicts an on-site community cloud. The community depicted in the figure is made up of a set of participant organizations. Each participant organization may provide cloud services, consume cloud services, or both. It is necessary for at least one community member to provide cloud services for a community cloud to be functional. The figure depicts members that provide cloud services (and possibly consume them also) on the left and those that consume-only on the right. Assuming that each organization implements a security perimeter, the participant organizations are connected via links between the boundary controllers that allow access through their security perimeters. Optionally, organizations may implement extra security perimeters to isolate the local cloud resources from other local resources. Many network configurations are possible; the figure shows the extra security perimeter as being inside an organization's 'non-cloud' security perimeter although it could be located outside as well. The boundary controllers in any configuration should grant appropriate access to the cloud resources both to local clients and to clients of other participant organizations. Importantly, providing access to local cloud resources should not grant access to non-cloud resources unless granting such access is a specific policy goal.

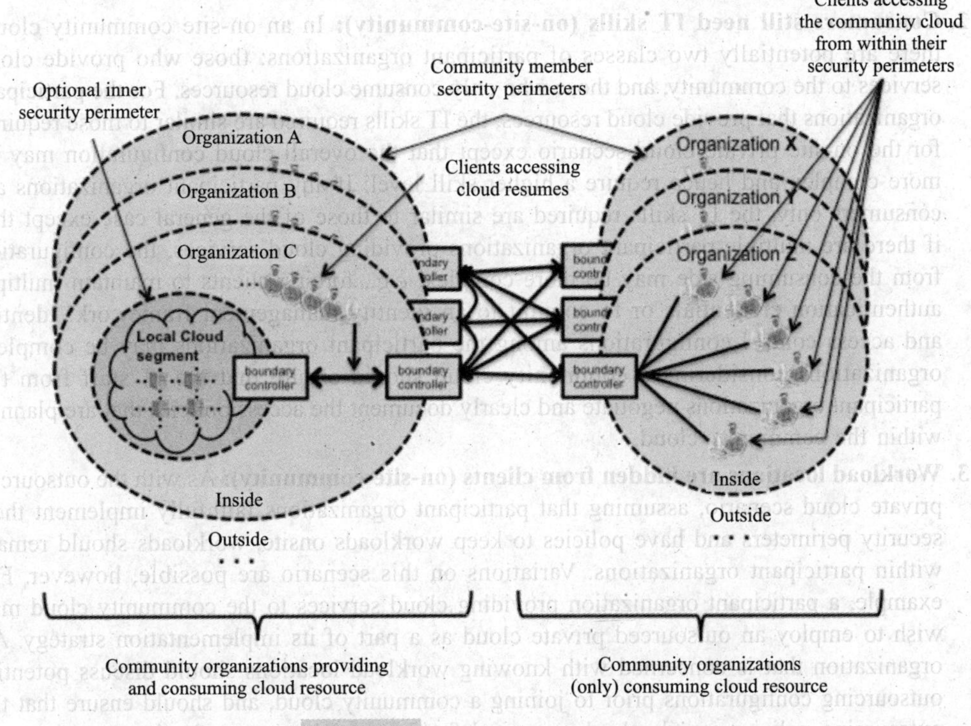

Fig. 26.7 On-site Community Cloud

In Fig. 26.7 it is easy to see that the access policy of a community cloud may be complex: if there are N community members, a decision must be made, either implicitly or explicitly, on how to share a member's local cloud resources with each of the other members. A number of policy specification techniques (*e.g.*, discretionary access control using a standard such as XACML, or following a security model such as role-based access control or attribute-based access control) might be used to express sharing policies. Besides controlling access to resources, identity management is important in this scenario since clients from multiple participant organizations access a common pool of resources.

As with the on-site private cloud and the outsourced private cloud, although the general statements remain true for the on-site community scenario, the on-site community cloud scenario also allows for a more detailed understanding of some of the general statements as well as additional statements that organizations considering the use of an on-site community cloud should consider:

1. **Network Dependency (on-site community):** As with the on-site private scenario, where the organization spans multiple sites, the consumers in an on-site community cloud need to either provision controlled inter-site communication links or use cryptography over a less controlled communications media (such as the public Internet). The reliability and security of the community cloud will depend on the reliability and security of the communication links. Dedicated leased network connections can also be used to support enhanced performance, reliability, and security. In the on-site community case, in addition, care should be taken to understand the actual dependencies between member organizations since there are multiple organizations participating and any subset of them could suffer a cloud infrastructure failure (*e.g.*, going offline). Additionally, local clouds will probably need to be taken offline for

maintenance at various times and therefore two-way communication in advance among the community members is essential to achieving a clear understanding of the service levels that they offer to one another and require from one another.

2. **Consumers still need IT skills (on-site-community):** In an on-site community cloud, there are potentially two classes of participant organizations: those who provide cloud services to the community, and those who only consume cloud resources. For the participant organizations that provide cloud resources, the IT skills required are similar to those required for the on-site private cloud scenario except that the overall cloud configuration may be more complex and hence require a higher skill level. If any participant organizations are consumers only, the IT skills required are similar to those of the general case except that if there are multiple participant organizations providing cloud services, the configuration from the consuming side may be more complex, *e.g.*, forcing clients to maintain multiple authentication credentials or to commit to an identity management framework. Identity and access control configurations among the participant organizations may be complex; organizations considering a community cloud should ensure that the IT staff from the participant organizations negotiate and clearly document the access policies that are planned within the community cloud.
3. **Workload locations are hidden from clients (on-site-community):** As with the outsourced private cloud scenario, assuming that participant organizations faithfully implement their security perimeters and have policies to keep workloads onsite, workloads should remain within participant organizations. Variations on this scenario are possible, however. For example, a participant organization providing cloud services to the community cloud may wish to employ an outsourced private cloud as a part of its implementation strategy. An organization that is concerned with knowing workload locations should discuss potential outsourcing configurations prior to joining a community cloud, and should ensure that the outsourcing policies are clearly documented for the participant organizations.
4. **Risks from multi-tenancy (on-site-community):** As with the on-site private scenario, the on-site community scenario mitigates some of the multi-tenancy risks by restricting the number of possible attackers. In the on-site community scenario, however, the cloud encompasses more organizations and hence may restrict the set of potential attackers less than in the case of the on-site private scenario.
5. **Data import/export, and performance limitations (on-site-community):** The communication links between the various participant organizations in a community cloud can be provisioned to various levels of performance, security and reliability, based on the needs of the participant organizations. The network-based limitations are thus similar to those of the outsourced-private cloud scenario.
6. **Potentially strong security from external threats (on-site-community):** The security of a community cloud from external threats depends on the security of all the security perimeters of the participant organizations and the strength of the communications links. These dependencies are essentially similar to those of the outsourced private cloud scenario, but with possibly more links and security perimeters and greater configuration complexity.
7. **Highly variable up-front costs to migrate into the cloud (on-site-community)**: The up-front costs of an on-site community cloud for a participant organization depend greatly on whether the organization plans to consume cloud services only or also to provide cloud services. For the consume-only scenario, the up-front costs appear to be similar to those for an outsourced private cloud (*i.e.*, modest-to-significant). For a participant organization that intends to provide cloud services within the community cloud, the costs appear to be similar to those for the on-site private cloud scenario (*i.e.*, significant-to-high).

8. **Limited resources (on-site community)**: As with the on-site private cloud scenario, resources for an on-site community cloud must be provisioned or scavenged locally. Therefore the resource limitations appear to be similar to those of the on-site private cloud, *i.e.*, relatively limited.

26.11 THE OUTSOURCED COMMUNITY CLOUD SCENARIO

Figure 26.8 depicts an outsourced community cloud. The community depicted in the figure is made up of a set of participant organizations that consume cloud services. This scenario is very similar to the outsourced private cloud scenario: server-side responsibilities are managed by a cloud provider that implements a security perimeter and that prevents mingling of community cloud resources with other cloud resources that are outside the provider-controlled security perimeter. A significant difference is that the cloud provider may need to enforce a sharing policy among participant organizations in the community cloud.

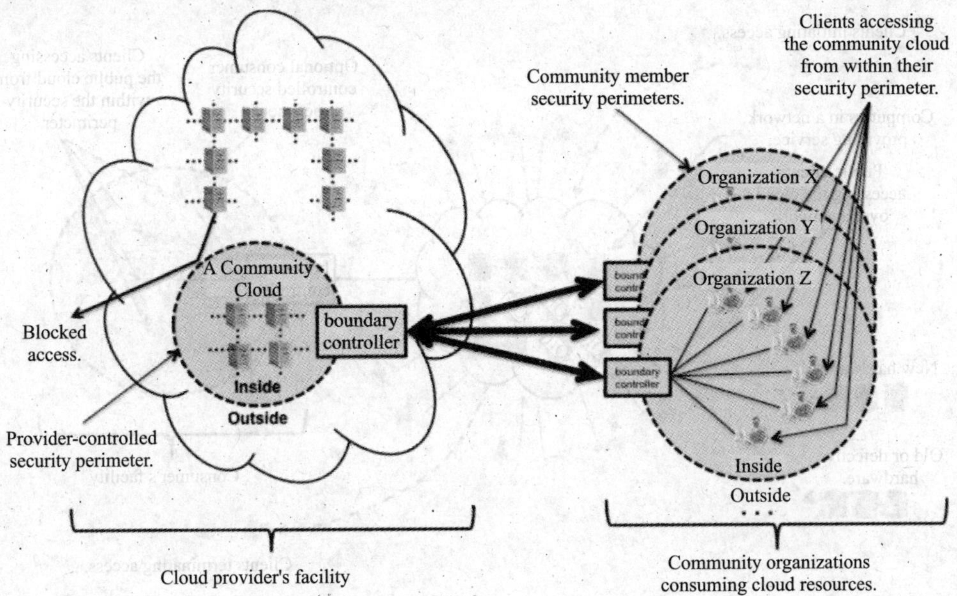

Fig. 26.8 Outsourced Community Cloud

Although the general statements remain true for the outsourced community cloud scenario, the outsourced community cloud scenario also allows for a more detailed view of some of the general statements as follows:

1. **Network dependency (outsourced-community):** As can be seen from Fig. 26.6, the network dependency of the outsourced community cloud is similar to that of the outsourced private cloud. The primary difference is that multiple protected communications links are likely from the community members to the provider's facility.
2. **Workload locations are hidden from clients (outsourced-community):** The implications appear to be the same as for the outsourced private cloud scenario.
3. **Risks from multi-tenancy (outsourced-community):** The implications appear to be the same as for the on-site community cloud scenario.
4. **Data import/export, and performance limitations (outsourced-community):** The implications appear to be the same as for the outsourced private cloud scenario.
5. **Potentially strong security from external threats (outsourced-community):** The implications appear to be the similar to those for the on-site community cloud scenario.

6. **Modest-to-significant up-front costs to migrate into the cloud (outsourced-community):** The implications appear to be the same as for the outsourced private cloud scenario.
7. **Extensive resources available (outsourced-community):** The implications appear to be the same as for the outsourced private cloud scenario.

26.12 THE PUBLIC CLOUD SCENARIO

Figure 26.9 depicts a public cloud. This diagram is essentially similar to Fig. 26.1 except that a consumer facility implementing a security perimeter is shown. In the case of a public cloud, however, more statements can be made based on the diagram than could be made based on Fig. 26.1. For example, in the public setting, the provider's computing and storage resources are potentially large; the communication links can be assumed to be implemented over the public Internet; and the cloud serves a diverse pool of clients (and possibly attackers).

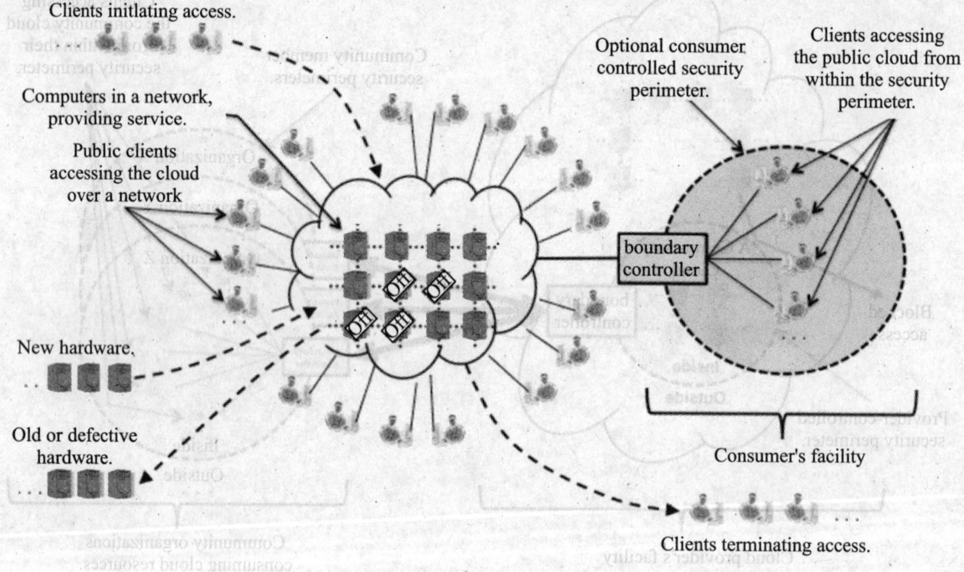

Fig. 26.9 Public Cloud

As with the other scenarios, although the general statements remain true for the public cloud scenario, the public cloud scenario also allows for a more detailed view of some of the general statements:

1. **Network dependency (public):** In the public scenario, consumers connect to providers via the public Internet. The dependability of connections thus depends on the Internet's infrastructure of Domain Name System (DNS) servers, the router infrastructure, and the inter-router links. The reliability of connections can thus be affected by misconfiguration or failure of these components as well as network congestion or attack. Additionally, consumers require a connection via an Internet Service Provider, often designated the 'last mile.' This connection must also be functional for the cloud to be accessible.
2. **Workload locations are hidden from clients (public):** In the public scenario, a provider may migrate a consumer's workload, whether processing or data, at any time. One of the central arguments for cost efficiency in public cloud computing is that data centers (and hence workloads) can be located where costs are low. Generally, workloads in a public cloud may be relocated anywhere at any time unless the provider has offered (optional) location restriction policies and the consumer has configured their account to request

specific location restrictions. Generally, location restrictions in a public cloud are somewhat coarse grained (*e.g.*, the east coast of the US). The confidence that restrictions are actually enforced rests upon protection of consumer credentials (*e.g.*, that the account has not been hijacked and had its location preferences changed) and the faithfulness with which the provider implements the advertised policies. Generally, consumers are not in a position to verify that location restrictions have been enforced.

3. **Risks from multi-tenancy (public):** In a public cloud, a single machine may be shared by the workloads of any combination of consumers. In practice, this means that a consumer's workload may be co-resident with the workloads of competitors or adversaries. As summarized in the general case, this introduces both reliability and security risk. A failure could occur or an attack could be perpetrated by any consumer. Scaling to larger sets of consumers and resources is one of the important strategies for public clouds to achieve low costs and elasticity; if this scaling is achieved, however, it also implies a large collection of potential attackers.
4. **Limited visibility and control over data regarding security (public)**: The details of provider system operation are usually considered proprietary information and are not divulged to consumers. In many cases, the software employed by a provider is proprietary and likely not available for examination by consumers. Consequently, consumers do not (at the time of this writing) have a guaranteed way to monitor or authorize access to their resources in the cloud. Although providers may make strong efforts to carry out the requests of consumers and some may provide monitoring services, consumers must either trust that the provider is performing operations with fidelity or, if the provider has contracted with a third party auditing organization, trust that the auditing is accurate and timely. As an example of this limitation, a consumer cannot currently verify that data has been completely deleted from a provider's systems.
5. **Low up-front costs to migrate into the cloud (public):** The implications appear to be the same as for the outsourced private cloud scenario.
6. **Elasticity:** Illusion of unlimited resource availability (public). Public clouds are generally unrestricted in their location or size. Additionally, they can generally use multi-tenancy without being limited by static security perimeters, which allows a potentially high degree of flexibility in the movement of consumer workloads to correspond with available resources. As a consequence, public clouds have unique advantages in achieving elasticity, or the illusion (to consumers) of unlimited resource availability.
7. **Restrictive default service level agreements (public):** The default service level agreements of public clouds specify limited promises that providers make to subscribers, limit the remedies available to subscribers, and outline subscriber obligations in obtaining such remedies.

26.13 THE HYBRID CLOUD SCENARIO

A hybrid cloud is composed of two or more private, community, or public clouds. As presented in this section, both the private and the community deployment models have two significant variations: on-site and outsourced. The variations are significant because they have different performance, reliability, and security properties, among others. A hybrid cloud, consequently, is a composition of clouds where each constituent cloud is one of the five variants. There are many conceivable configurations of hybrid clouds and it is not realistic to enumerate them. However, the space of possibilities and the potential challenges can be illustrated.

Figure 26.10 depicts a theoretical hybrid cloud composed of a number of constituent clouds representing all of the deployment model variants. The figure depicts access points into the constituent clouds as well as the network connectivity between them. Security policies governing the flow of information and access to resources could be implemented in a wide variety of ways, *e.g.*, based on policies applied by each individual constituent cloud. Additionally, global issues such as identity management and shared standards for authentication and information protection within the hybrid cloud are not shown. A further complication not shown is that a hybrid cloud may change over time with constituent clouds joining and leaving.

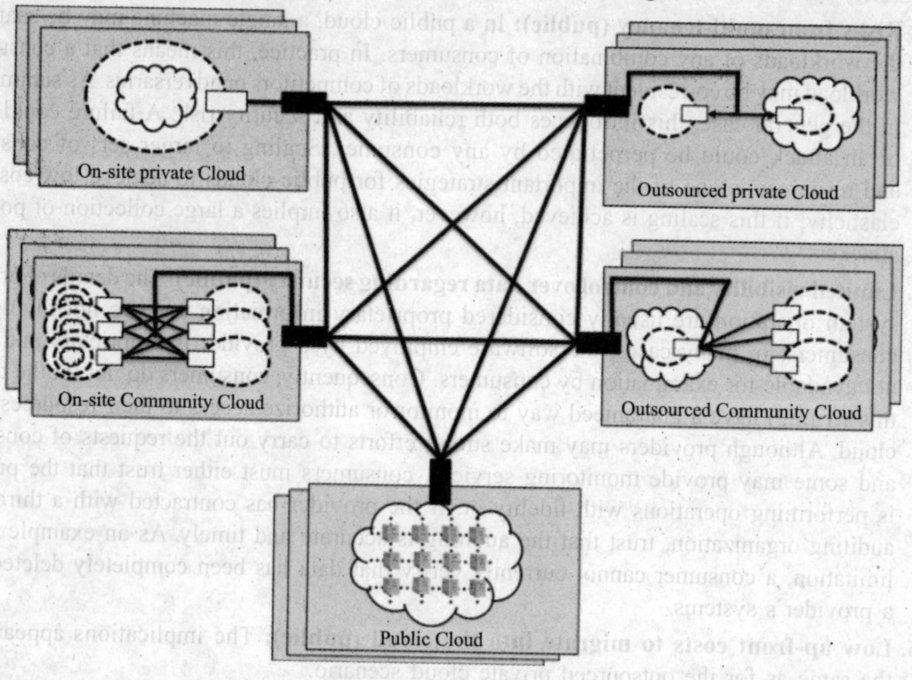

Fig. 26.10 Hybrid Cloud

As depicted in Fig. 26.10, a hybrid cloud can be extremely complex. However many less complex and highly useful hybrid cloud configurations are possible. For example, 'cloud bursting' is an often-discussed concept in which a consumer uses a private cloud for routine workloads, but optionally accesses one or more external clouds during periods of high demand. Using one type of cloud to provide backup resources to another is another hybrid possibility as well as using one cloud for disaster recovery for a second. For new software developed specifically to run on cloud platforms, multi-cloud configurations are possible and even likely. For example, Web request handling platform clouds can be very efficient for making Web applications continuously available at low cost while on-site or community infrastructure clouds may be more suitable for performing necessary background work to support the applications. Different cloud deployment variants may also be appropriate for particular organizational functions or roles; for example, an organization may elect to process sensitive data such as payroll information in an outsourced private cloud but use a public cloud for new software development and testing activities.

26.13.1 Advantages of Cloud Computing

Moving a company towards cloud computing has a variety of advantages, but with these competitive advantages also have some potential risks. The following are the advantages of Cloud Computing:

1. **Lower Cost:** Cloud service providers offer many different ways to purchase their products (one-time-payment, pay-as-you-go and other scalable options) that can often be significantly cheaper than traditional desktop software. *Cloud Computing* is the best cost efficient method

to maintain, use and also to upgrade. Normally desktop software's charge companies a lot. Adding the multiple user licenses to the software is also very costly and increases the company's expenditure. On the other hand, Cloud Technology is cheaper and also reduces the company's expenditure. Here you can pay only for the cloud space you need.

2. **Scalability:** Increase the storage, RAM and CPU capacities as it is needed in a just-in-time (JIT) cloud business model. You need not to worry about the running out of the disk storage or to increase your current storage.
3. **Accessibility:** Once registered, the cloud resources are available anywhere there is an internet connection.
4. **Speedy Deployment:** Cloud deployment can take few minutes depending on what services are being purchased and utilized.
5. **Lower Maintenance Costs:** There is less hardware to maintain and this hardware is maintained by the cloud service provider. Although yours complete data is stored in the cloud it is very easy to take backup and restore of files. It is much easier then storing in the physical drive.
6. **Automatic Software Integration:** In the Cloud software is integrated automatically, that means you need not take much efforts to customize your application. Here just you need to pick up those software and services which is suitable for your business.
7. **Carbon Discharges:** Cloud Computing can also decreases the Company's carbon discharges by 35%.
8. **Backup and Recovery:** Since all your data is stored in the cloud, backing it up and restoring the same is relatively much easier than storing the same on a physical device. Furthermore, most cloud service providers are usually competent enough to handle recovery of information. Hence, this makes the entire process of backup and recovery much simpler than other traditional methods of data storage.

26.13.2 Disadvantages of Cloud Computing

As there are many advantages which are mentioned above, there are disadvantages of cloud computing also, as listed below:

1. **Cost:** Despite the appearance of cheaper software within the cloud, customers should be aware of what they are actually getting before they buy. Will the software provide you with all of the features needed? How important are these features to the company?
2. **Security:** Cloud computing is Internet computing. This means that the information is passing through an unsecure network (the Internet) and the information be transmitted should be monitored and regulated accordingly. However, established and reputable cloud service providers are aware of this concern and offer sophisticated data security systems to combat this potential problem. As you know the data can be accessed by anyone and at any time. The other main problem in the cloud computing is Security. Before implementing this technology, you must know that you are submitting all the company's information to third party cloud provider. This may put your company in to the great risk. So make sure that you choose right and a reliable provider to keep your data totally secure.
3. **Internet Connectivity:** Cloud services do require internet connectivity. No internet connectivity = No cloud services. This issue can be partially remedied by a stable and reputable service provider. However, even the best internet providers will experience down time.
4. **Technical Issues:** Even the best cloud service provider, regardless of how stringent their maintenance standards, will occasionally experience service outages and technical issues. But sometimes this cloud system can have some serious disturbance so you cannot access your files from cloud. This will be rare when you choose a reliable provider.

5. **Prone to Attack:** Storing information in the cloud could make your company vulnerable to external hack attacks and threats. As you are well aware, nothing on the Internet is completely secure and hence, there is always the lurking possibility of stealth of sensitive data.

Each company should carefully consider the potential benefits and repercussions of implementing a cloud based service before moving forward. However, the advantages are continuing to grow and cloud service providers are continually decreasing the risks associated with cloud based services.

As every service, the cloud Technology has its advantages and disadvantages. Implementing this service is a great asset for your company but if you don't know properly to use it, it may harm your files. So make sure to use this technology after understanding the services and how to use it properly.

26.14 ETHICAL ISSUES

Cloud computing is based on a paradigm shift with profound implications on computing ethics. The main elements of this shift are:

1. the control is relinquished to third party services;
2. the data is stored on multiple sites administered by several organizations; and
3. multiple services interoperate across the network.

Unauthorized access, data corruption, infrastructure failure, and service unavailability are some of the risks related to relinquishing the control to third party services; moreover, whenever a problem occurs it is difficult to identify the source and the entity causing it. Systems can span the boundaries of multiple organizations and cross the security borders, a process called *de-perimeterisation*. As a result of de-perimeterisation 'not only the border of the organizations IT infrastructure blurs, also the border of the accountability becomes less clear'.

The complex structure of cloud services can make it difficult to determine who is responsible in case something undesirable happens. In a complex chain of events or systems, many entities contribute to an action with undesirable consequences, some of them have the opportunity to prevent these consequences, and therefore no one can be held responsible, the so-called 'problem of many hands.'

Ubiquitous and unlimited data sharing and storage among organizations test the self determination information, the right or ability of individuals to exercise personal control over the collection, use and disclosure of their personal data by others; this tests the confidence and trust in todays evolving information society. Identity fraud and theft are made possible by the unauthorized access to personal data in circulation and by new forms of dissemination through social networks and they could also pose a danger to cloud computing.

Cloud service providers have already collected petabytes of sensitive personal information stored in data centers around the world. The acceptance of cloud computing therefore will be determined by privacy issues addressed by these companies and the countries where the data centers are located. Privacy is affected by cultural differences; while some cultures favour privacy, other cultures emphasize community and this leads to an ambivalent attitude towards privacy in the Internet which is a global system.

The question of what can be done proactively about ethics of cloud computing does not have easy answers as many undesirable phenomena in cloud computing will only appear in time. However, the need for rules and regulations for the governance of cloud computing are obvious. The term *governance* means the manner in which something is governed or regulated, the method of management, the system of regulations. Explicit attention to ethics must be paid by governmental organizations providing research funding; private companies are less constraint by ethics oversight and governance arrangements are more conducive to profit generation.

Accountability is a necessary ingredient of cloud computing; adequate information about how data is handled within the cloud and about allocation of responsibility are key elements for enforcing ethics rules in cloud computing. Recorded evidence allows us to assign responsibility; but there can be tension between privacy and accountability and it is important to establish what is being recorded, and who has access to the records.

Unwanted dependency on a cloud service provider, the so-called *vendor lock-in*, is a serious concern and the current standardization efforts at NIST attempt to address this problem. Another concern for the users is a future with only a handful of companies which dominate the market and dictate prices and policies.

26.15 CLOUD VULNERABILITIES

As cloud computing continues to gain acceptance corporations must look at each of the existing models to determine which one best suit their specific requirements. Since no single model provides all of the advantages of cost reductions and security protections, the hybrid model remains the most popular.

Cloud computing is a powerful new abstraction for large scale data processing systems which is scalable, reliable and available. In cloud computing, there are large self-managed server pools available which reduces the overhead and eliminates management headache. Cloud computing services can also grow and shrink according to need. Cloud computing is particularly valuable to small and medium businesses, where effective and affordable IT tools are critical to helping them become more productive without spending lots of money on in-house resources and technical equipment. Also it is a new emerging architecture needed to expand the Internet to become the computing platform of the future.

Clouds are affected by malicious attacks and failures of the infrastructure, *e.g.*, power failures. Such events can affect the Internet domain name servers and prevent access to a cloud or can directly affect the clouds. In May, 2009, Google was the target of a serious denial of service attack which took down services like Google News and Gmail for several days.

Lightning caused a prolonged down time at Amazon on June 29–30, 2012; the AWS cloud in the East region of the US which consists of ten data centers across four availability zones, was initially troubled by utility power fluctuations, probably caused by an electrical storm. A June 29, 2012 storm on the East Coast took down some of Virginia based Amazon facilities and affected companies using systems exclusively in this region.

The recovery from the failure took a very long time and exposed a range of problems. For example, one of the ten centers failed to switch to backup generators before exhausting the power that could be supplied by UPS units. AWS uses 'control planes' to allow users to switch to resources in a different region and this software component also failed. The booting process was faulty and extended the time to restart *EC2* and *EBS* services. Another critical problem was a bug in the Elastic Load Balancer (ELB), which is used to route traffic to servers with available capacity. A similar bug affected the recovery process of Relational Database Service (RDS). This event brought to light 'hidden' problems that occur only under special circumstances.

Clustering the resources in data centers located in different geographical area is one of the means used today to lower the probability of catastrophic failures. This geographic dispersion of resources could have additional positive side effects; it can reduce communication traffic and energy costs by dispatching the computations to sites where the electric energy is cheaper, and it can improve performance by an intelligent and efficient load balancing strategy. System's objective, maximize throughput, resource utilization, and financial benefits have to be carefully balanced with the user needs, low cost and response time and maximum availability.

26.16 SUMMARY

As cloud computing continues to gain acceptance corporations must look at each of the existing models to determine which one best suit their specific requirements. Since no single model provides all of the advantages of cost reductions and security protections, the hybrid model remains the most popular.

Cloud computing is a powerful new abstraction for large scale data processing systems which is scalable, reliable and available. In cloud computing, there are large self-managed server pools available which reduces the overhead and eliminates management headache. Cloud computing services can also grow and shrink according to need. Cloud computing is particularly valuable to small and medium businesses, where effective and affordable IT tools are critical to helping them become more productive without spending lots of money on in-house resources and technical equipment. Also it is a new emerging architecture needed to expand the Internet to become the computing platform of the future.

Reaching conclusions on cloud computing is not easy. To some the whole cloud thing may be a bit overwhelming, providing yet more acronyms and complexity; to others the concept of 'the best computer is no computer' sounds very attractive. Although cloud computing combines many existing concepts, it constitutes a fundamental change, comparable to the move from custom made software to standard packages on the application side and as impactful as outsourcing on the operational side.

In general, customers are intrigued by the prospect of using the most economic way to perform computing but not necessarily excited by the idea of moving their data or computing off premise into a cloud environment.

With regard to risk, the most commonly mentioned objection to cloud computing, there are indeed some questions and issues that still need addressing. But the argument that 'our systems are so business critical that we would never risk bringing them under a cloud' is off the mark. If this was the case, companies would never have outsourced or off-shored parts of their operations. It also ignores the enormous investments cloud providers are making to address these still valid concerns.

On the infrastructure side, virtualization and cloud computing add a set of platforms that can significantly increase utilization, scalability and sharing of resources, leading to lower and more variable cost. But in the short term, one should not expect these cloud platforms to replace all current internal platforms, but rather be used in addition.

On the application side, shorter time-to-value and broader functionality at lower initial cost, make Software as a Service very attractive, but the danger of vendor lock-in is also significantly higher here.

The role of IT will certainly change. Technical skills will become less important, as maintaining an overview and achieving synergy will become more important. Cloud computing offers too many possibilities and opportunities to ignore, but given the current media hype around cloud computing there is little chance of anyone being able to do so anyhow.

Several organizations have started building private clouds. Not as a pilot, but as a first real project. Disentangling existing applications is way too expensive and labor intensive to just have a look; we need to build a business case. Others have started using SaaS applications for some less business critical applications, enjoying the fast time-to-value and generally rich functionality. While for others PaaS may be the fastest way to offer a unique, differentiating portfolio of business services.

REVIEW QUESTIONS

1. Which of the following statement is not correct about Hybrid Cloud?
   (*a*) It is a composition of two or more clouds (private, community or public
   (*b*) There must be one private and one public/community cloud in it
   (*c*) It exposes mission-critical applications and data to third-party vulnerabilities
   (*d*) It provides scalability and cost-effectiveness

2. What is not correct about Hyper-V Cloud?
   (*a*) It is launched by Microsoft
   (*b*) It is launched by Amazon
   (*c*) It virtualize existing server hardware assets and move them to a private or public cloud
   (*d*) It provides customers with virtualization and virtualization management software

3. Which of the following characteristics is not exhibited by Cloud computing?
   (*a*) Agility (*b*) Device and location independence
   (*c*) Multitenancy (*d*) Higher cost

4. Rackspace Cloud is an example of:
   (*a*) Infrastructure as a service (IaaS) (*b*) Platform as a service (PaaS)
   (*c*) Software as a service (SaaS) (*d*) None of the above

5. What is not true in relation to cloud computing?
   (*a*) It relies on sharing of resources over a network to achieve coherence and economies of scale
   (*b*) It provides computing and storage capacity to heterogeneous set of users
   (*c*) Publicly available Web search engines that process the same data for every visitor are examples of cloud computing
   (*d*) Cloud based applications can be accessed through a web browser or a light weight desktop or mobile app

6. What is Cloud cartography?
   (*a*) It is a scheme for pinpointing the physical locations of Web servers hosted on a third-party cloud computing service
   (*b*) It is the name of the service provided by Amazon on cloud
   (*c*) It is a schema used by Microsoft for its Windows OS on cloud
   (*d*) It is mechanism to corrupt the data residing on web servers on cloud

7. Windows Azure is:
   (*a*) An upgrade to Microsoft XP OS
   (*b*) Microsoft's operating system for large corporations
   (*c*) Microsoft's operating system for cloud computing
   (*d*) Microsoft's office suite for cloud computing

8. Which of the following service models is not offered by cloud computing?
   (*a*) Infrastructure as a service (IaaS) (*b*) Platform as a service (PaaS)
   (*c*) Software as a service (SaaS) (*d*) Manpower as a service (MaaS)

9. 'Salesforce.com' is an example of
   (*a*) Infrastructure as a service (IaaS) (*b*) Platform as a service (PaaS)
   (*c*) Software as a service (SaaS) (*d*) None of the above

10. What is Amazon S3?
   (*a*) Amazon Simple Storage Service (*b*) Online backup and archiving Service
   (*c*) Both (*a*) and (*b*) above (*d*) None of the above

11. Which of the following is not true about MapReduce?

(*a*) It was developed at Google for indexing Web pages

(*b*) It is a programming model for processing large data sets

(*c*) It is typically used to do distributed computing on clusters of computers

(*d*) It was developed at Amazon for EC2 project

12. Which statement about ZooKeeper is false?

(*a*) It allows distributed processes in large systems to synchronize with each other so that all clients making requests receive consistent data

(*b*) ZooKeeper was a sub project of Lucene

(*c*) It is centralized service for maintaining configuration information, naming, providing distributed synchronization, and providing group services for large distributed systems

(*d*) It is a software project of the Apache Software Foundation

13. What is Amazon EC2?

(*a*) It is Web-based service where subscriber can run their applications in Amazon computing environment

(*b*) It is Amazon Elastic Compute Cloud

(*c*) It enables you to increase or decrease computing capacity based on your requirements

(*d*) All of the above

14. What is not true about Private cloud?

(*a*) It can not be managed by third party and has to be managed internally only

(*b*) It is cloud infrastructure operated solely for a single organization

(*c*) It could be managed by a third-party and hosted internally or externally

(*d*) It provides hosted services to a limited number of people behind a firewall

15. What is grid computing?

(*a*) It is a network of computers that share resources—the network can be local or disributed acrosss the internet

(*b*) It is a physical arrangement of computer terminals that optimize computing power-the computer in the center are the most powerful

(*c*) It is a temporary cloud computer network that only exists as long as single project is active

(*d*) None of these

16. What does SaaS stand for?

(*a*) Secret alternative accounting standards (*b*) Secret alternative accounting standards

(*c*) Software as a service (*d*) None of these

17. What is server virtualization?

(*a*) It is a problem that crops up with cloud computing when servers go offline

(*b*) It is a method of a cloud computing network before you actually build it so that it works properly

(*c*) It is partitioning a normal server so that it behaves as if there are multiple servers

18. What is a redundant system?

(*a*) It is a computer network that duplicates the services already provided by another network

(*b*) it is a system that has multiple data backups across multiple machines to guard against data loss

(*c*) It is a computer network struck with a virus that causes it to perform the same operations repeatedly

19. What is utility computing?

(*a*) It is a cloud computing buisness model-one buisness sells access to its network of computers to other clients (*b*) It is the cloud computing network used by power grids and water companies

(*c*) It is a stripped down computing network that provides only the basic feature of processing power and storage

20. Which of the following companies offers a cloud computing video game service

(*a*) Ubisoft (*b*) Blizzard (*c*) Onlive (*d*) None of these

21. Which of the following is true of cloud computing?

(*a*) It is always going to be less expensive and more secure than local computing

(*b*) You can access your data from any computer in the world, as long as you have an internet connection

(*c*) Only a few small companies are investing in the technology,making it a risky venture

22. What is the name of the backspace cloud service?

(*a*) Cloud on-demand (*b*) Cloud servers (*c*) EC2 (*d*) None of these

23. What is private cloud?

(*a*) A standard cloud service offered via the internet

(*b*) A cloud architecture maintained within an enterprise data center

(*c*) A cloud inaccessible to anyone but the cultural elite

(*d*) None of these

24. Which amazon cloud product recently experienced a massive outage?

(*a*) simpleDB (*b*) EBS (*c*) S3 (*d*) cloudfront

25. What is cloud foundry?

(*a*) A factory that produces cloud components

(*b*) Vmware-led open source PaaS

(*c*) An industry wide PaaS initiative

(*d*) Vmware-led closed source PaaS

26. Which of the following is not an advantage of cloud?

(*a*) No worries about running out of storage (*b*) Easier to maintain a cloud network

(*c*) Immediate access to computing resources (*d*) Paying only for what you use

27. Which company recently shut the doors on its cloud storage service?

(*a*) Hitachi data systems (*b*) Savvies (*c*) Iron mountain (*d*) Symantec

28. Which of these services is not a platform as a service?

(*a*) force.com (*b*) microsoft azure

(*c*) AmazonEC2 (*d*) joyent

29. What feature does not belong in a private cloud?

(*a*) Metered billing (*b*) Self-service portal (*c*) Dial-home support (*d*) Rapid elasticity

30. Match the provider with the cloud based service:

(*a*) Amazon1.Azure (*b*) IBM2.elastic compute cloud

(*c*) EMC3.decho (*d*) Microsoft4.cloudburst

31. Link the cloud-based service on the left with the desktop or server application it is designed to dispace on the right

(*a*) google docs1.intel servers (*b*) salesforce.com2.microsoft office

(*c*) mozy.com3.oracle customer-relationship management

(*d*) amazonEC24.backup disk

32. What august event was widely seen as an example of the risky nature of cloud computing?

(*a*) Spread of conficker virus (*b*) Gmail outage for than an hour

(*c*) Theft of identities over the internet (*d*) Power outages in the midwest

33. Amazon web services is which type of cloud computing distribution model
(*a*) software as a service (*b*) platform as a service
(*c*) infrastructure as a service (*d*) None of these

34. An internet connection is necessary for cloud computing interaction
(*a*) True (*b*) False

35. Which is not a major cloud computing platform?
(*a*) google 101 (*b*) IBM deep blue (*c*) Microsoft azure (*d*) amazon EC2

36. Cloud in cloud computing represents what?
(*a*) Wireless (*b*) Hard drives (*c*) People (*d*) Internet

37. Which of these should a company consider before implementing cloud computing technology?
(*a*) Employee satisfaction (*b*) Potential cost reduction
(*c*) Information sensitivity (*d*) All of the above

38. The term API refers to ________.
(*a*) Application programmable interface (*b*) Application programming interface
(*c*) Application programming interconnect (*d*) None of the above

39. In cloud service model PaaS is based on ________.
(*a*) SaaS (*b*) IaaS (*c*) TaaS (*d*) None of the above

40. The term VPN expands to ________.
(*a*) Viral private network (*b*) Virtual public network
(*c*) Virtual private network (*d*) None of the above

41. The software framework by Google for distributed computing on large data sets is ________.
(*a*) Mapreduce (*b*) Cassandra
(*c*) MongoDB (*d*) None of the above

42. Apache Hadoop is written in which programming language?
(*a*) Java (*b*) PHP
(*c*) Python (*d*) None of the above

43. What is Cloud Computing replacing?
(*a*) Corporate data centers (*b*) Expensive personal computer hardware
(*c*) Expensive software upgrades (*d*) All of the above

44. What is the number one concern about cloud computing?
(*a*) Too expensive (*b*) Security concerns
(*c*) Too many platforms (*d*) Accessability

45. Which of these companies is not a leader in cloud computing?
(*a*) Google (*b*) Amazon (*c*) Blackboard (*d*) Microsoft

46. Google Docs is a type of cloud computing.
(*a*) True (*b*) False

47. Which one of these is not a cloud computing pricing model?
(*a*) Free (*b*) Pay Per Use (*c*) Subscription (*d*) Ladder
(*e*) Perpetual License

48. Which of these is not a major type of cloud computing usage?
(*a*) Hardware as a Service (*b*) Platform as a Service
(*c*) Software as a Service (*d*) Infrastructure as a Service

49. What exactly is cloud computing?
(*a*) A way to organize desktop computers

(*b*) Lightweight software that takes up little space on a hard drive
(*c*) Computing resources that can be accessed on demand, like electricity from a utility
(*d*) The World Wide Web

50. What widely used service is built on cloud-computing technology?
(*a*) Twitter (*b*) Skype (*c*) Gmail (*d*) YouTube
(*e*) All of the above

51. Which of these techniques is vital for creating cloud-computing centers?
(*a*) Visualization (*b*) Transubstantiation
(*c*) Cannibalization (*d*) Insubordination

52. An internal cloud is ...
(*a*) An overhanging threat
(*b*) A career risk for a CIO
(*c*) A cloud that sits behind a corporate firewall
(*d*) The group of knowledge workers who use a social network for water-cooler gossip

53. Cloud computing embraces many concepts that were previously touted as the next big thing in information technology. Which of these is not an antecedent of the cloud?
(*a*) Software as a service (*b*) Utility computing
(*c*) Remote hosted services (*d*) Grid computing
(*e*) Desktop computing

54. The term 'cloud computing' is a metaphor that originated in what?
(*a*) Graphical depiction of computer architectures
(*b*) Meteorological symbolism
(*c*) Worries about an unclear future for computing architectures
(*d*) The idea that computer users trust in magic

55. What is the name of the organization helping to foster security standards for cloud computing?
(*a*) Cloud Security Standards Working (*b*) Cloud Security Alliance
(*c*) Cloud Security WatchDog (*d*) Security in the Cloud Alliance

56. What is cloud computing?
(*a*) It's an intricate weather-mapping system that projects climate patterns over long ranges of time.
(*b*) A model of computing in which your computer acts as a terminal and a network of servers handles the processing power and storage for you.
(*c*) It's just a fancy name for a local area network (LAN).

57. What are the two main sections of a cloud computing system?
(*a*) Terminals and nodes (*b*) Front end and back end
(*c*) Networks and servers

ANSWERS

1. (*c*)	**2.** (*b*)	**3.** (*a*)	**4.** (*a*)	**5.** (*c*)	**6.** (*a*)	**7.** (*c*)	**8.** (*d*)
9. (*c*)	**10.** (*c*)	**11.** (*d*)	**12.** (*b*)	**13.** (*d*)	**14.** (*a*)	**15.** (*a*)	**16.** (*c*)
17. (*b*)	**18.** (*b*)	**19.** (*c*)	**20.** (*c*)	**21.** (*b*)	**22.** (*b*)	**23.** (*b*)	**24.** (*b*)
25. (*b*)	**26.** (*b*)	**27.** (*c*)	**28.** (*b*)	**29.** (*b*)	**30.** (*a*)	**31.** (*a*)	**32.** (*b*)
33. (*c*)	**34.** (*b*)	**35.** (*b*)	**36.** (*d*)	**37.** (*d*)	**38.** (*b*)	**39.** (*b*)	**40.** (*c*)
41. (*a*)	**42.** (*a*)	**43.** (*d*)	**44.** (*b*)	**45.** (*c*)	**46.** (*a*)	**47.** (*d*)	**48.** (*a*)
49. (*c*)	**50.** (*e*)	**51.** (*a*)	**52.** (*c*)	**53.** (*e*)	**54.** (*a*)	**55.** (*b*)	**56.** (*b*)
57. (*b*)							

GLOSSARY

Access Arm: The disk-drive component used to position read/write heads over a specified track.

Access Methods: The technique and/or program code for moving data between main storage and Input/Output devices.

Access Time: The time interval between when data is called for or requested to be stored in a storage device and when delivery or storage is completed.

Access: To locate the desired data.

Accumulator: A register or storage location that forms the result of an arithmetic or logic operation.

Acoustic Coupler: A type of modem which permits data communication over regular telephone lines by means of sound signals.

Acoustic Modem: Also called an acoustic coupler, a type of modem with two rubber cups in which the standard telephone receiver is placed to send and receive data.

Acronym: A word formed from the first letter(s) of the words contained in a phrase or name.

Ada: A programming language named after Augusta Ada Byron, considered the world's first computer programmer. Developed for the US Department of Defense as a standard high-order language.

Adapter: An interface card that allows a PC to connect to a peripheral. These are usually network adapters (usually called network interface cards), but there are also adapters for connecting to monitors, serial devices, and the like.

Adding: The process of entering new records to an existing file or data base.

Add-on-memory: An auxiliary storage device connected to main memory by a communications channel.

Address Bus: The electrical pathway used to transmit the storage locations for data or instructions.

Address Translation: The process of changing the address of an item of data or an instruction to the address in main storage at which it is to be loaded or relocated.

Address: A sequence of bytes representing the logical location of a station, or process within a station, on the network. It is usually prefixed onto the relevant 'onion layer' of the protocol set.

Administrator: The person or persons responsible for managing a local area network—sometimes called the network administrator or network supervisor.

ADP: Automatic data processing.

Advertising-based pricing model: A pricing model whereby services are offered to customers at low or no cost, with the service provider being compensated by advertisers whose ads are delivered to the consumer along with the service.

Algol: Algorithmic Language: An international procedure-oriented language that is widely used in Europe. Like FORTRAN, it was designed primarily for scientific-mathematical applications.

Algorithm: A set of well-defined rules or processes for the solution of a problem in a finite number of steps.

Alphanumeric: A set of well-defined rules for solving a problem in a finite number of operations.

Amazon EC2: Amazon's Elastic Compute Cloud Web service, which provides resizable computing capacity in the cloud so developers can enjoy great scalability for building applications.

Amazon S3: Amazon Simple Storage Services—Amazon's cloud storage service.

Amplifier: A device which regenerates an analogue signal, thus increasing the distance at which the signal can be sent.

Amplitude Shift Keying: The modulation (*i.e.*, modifying) of a signal to carry data by changing the amplitude (*i.e.*, strength) of the signal to reflect the data value.

Analog Computer: A computer that operates on data by measuring changes in continuous physical variables such as voltage, resistance, and rotation. Contrast with Digital computer.

Analog Data Transmission: The transmission of data in a continuous wave form.

Analogue Transmission: The sending of data by using a continuous signal over a medium.

Animation: A feature of some graphic packages that rapidly displays drawings that are slightly different, thereby simulating motion.

ANSI (American National Standards Institute): An organization that develops and approves standards in many fields.

APL (A Programming Language): A mathematically oriented language originated by Kenneth E. Iverson of IBM. Realtime and interactive versions of APL are being utilized in many time-sharing systems.

Appletalk: Apple Computer's proprietary network communications protocol, originally intended to interconnect groups of Macintosh computers. Appletalk is often used when connecting Macintoshes to PC-based LANs, and it can be used to connect PCs (using a PC Appletalk card) to the Appletalk networks. The most common use for Appletalk networks is to connect a group of Macintosh computers to a printer.

Application Software: Programs that specify the information processing activities required for the completion of specific tasks of computer users. Examples are electronic spreadsheet and word processing programs or inventory or payroll programs.

Application: A software program that performs a task such as work processing, spread-sheet or database management. Usually the main use to which a computer in put. Also, the top layer of the OSI model.

Applications Packages: Pre-written computer programs designed for special or general-purpose tasks. Some applications packages perform single functions, while others integrate several functions in a single package.

Application-specific Programs: Application software packages that support specific applications of end users in business, science and engineering, and other areas.

Archiving: Saving backups of software programs and data for future reference or use.

ARCnet: One of the major local area network protocols. ARCnet does not specifically conform to an IEEE standard. However, as one of the most widespread of the LAN protocols, it has evolved into a standard of its own. ARCnet was developed by the Datapoint Corporation for connecting that company's minicomputers, and Datapoint is very active in ensuring that ARCnet standards are maintained. ARCnet is trademark of Datapoint.

Arithmetic And Logic Unit (ALU): The part of the central processing unit (CPU) that performs all mathematical and logical functions.

Artificial Intelligence (AI): A science and technology whose goal is to develop computers that can think, as well as see, hear, walk, talk, and feel. A major thrust is the development of computer functions normally associated with human intelligence, for example, reasoning inference, learning, and problem solving. Major areas of AI research and development includes cognitive science, computer science, robotics, and natural language applications.

Artificial Language: A language based on a set of rules established prior to its usage and without a precise relationship to the user applications for which the language will be used.

ASCII: American Standard Code for Information Interchange, the code used by most PCs to communicate. ASCII codes are used internally by the computer, and they are used in communications between computers in most cases.

Assembler Language: A programming language that utilizes symbols to represent operation codes and storage locations.

Assembler Program: A computer program that takes non machine-language instructions prepared by a programmer and converts them into a form that may be used by the computer.

Assembler: A computer program that translates an assembler language into machine language.

Asynchronous Transmission: The sending of one data character at a time, each preceded by a start bit and terminated by one or more stop bits.

Asynchronous: Involving a sequence of operations without a regular or predictable time relationship. Thus, operations do not happen at regular timed intervals, but an operation will begin only after a previous operation is completed. Data transmission, involves the use of start and stop bits with each character to indicate the beginning and end of the character being transmitted.

Attenuation: The loss of strength of a signal as it passes through a medium.

Attributes: The set of characteristics that are used to describe a data- entry field or to describe how the output will appear. These are often set by the user to fit a particular situation.

Auxiliary Storage: Storage that supplements the primary storage of the computer. Same as secondary storage.

Back-end Processor: A computer, subordinate to the host processor, that handles administrative tasks associated with the retrieval and manipulation of data in database.

Background Processing: The execution under automatic control of lower priority computer programs when higher priority programs are not using the system resources.

Backup File: A duplicate copy of a file.

Backup: The copying of information to provide a means of recovery from lost or corrupt data.

Bandwidth: The range of frequencies offered by a medium for the transmission of signals. Now in common usage as the data rate on a LAN.

Bank-switched Memory: The use of software-controlled switches that allow a central processor to switch between memory locations in primary and supplementary memory banks so that the apparent size of primary storage is increased.

Baseband: The transmission of a signal without modulation. In a LAN, this implies that the whole medium is used to carry one signal at a time.

Baseline: A specification or product that has been formally reviewed and agreed upon, which serves as a basis for further development and can be changed only through formal change procedures.

BASIC (Beginners' All-purpose Symbolic Instruction): A high-level language developed at Dartmouth College as an easy to learn and use language for beginning programmers.

Batch Processing: A category of data processing in which data is accumulated into 'batches' and processed periodically. Contrast with Realtime processing.

Baud Rate: The number of times per second that a transmitted signal changes (modulates or demodulates).

Baud: A unit of measure of the rate of signal modulation. For most data purposes it is equivalent to bits per second.

BCD (Binary-Coded Decimal): A method of representing the decimal digits zero through line by a pattern of binary 1s and 0s (*e.g.*, the decimal number 25 is represented by 0010 0101 in 8-4-2-1 BCD rotation).

Binary Digit: Either of the characters 0 or 1. Abbreviated 'bit'.

Binary Number System: A number system with a base or radix of two.

Binary System: The base 2 numbering system uses the digits 0 and 1. Computer data can be represented by this numbering system.

Binary: Pertaining to characteristic or property involving a selection, choice, or condition in which there are two possibilities, or pertaining to the number system that utilizes a base of two.

Bit: The smallest unit of digital information. Because digital information is expressed using binary states, a bit can be either a 1 or a 0.

Black Box: A process with known inputs, known outputs, and a known function but with an unknown (or irrelevant) internal mechanism.

Block: A grouping of contiguous data records or other data elements that are handled as a unit.

Blocked Tape: A storage technique used where records are grouped together on tape. This provides more storage and faster access by reducing the number of interrecord gaps.

Blocking Factor: The number of logical records combined into one physical record or block.

Bottom-up Testing: Testing a computer program by beginning with individual subroutines or modules and then testing increasingly larger units.

Branch: A transfer of control from one instruction to another in a computer program that is not part of the normal sequential execution of the instructions of the program.

Bridge: A device for linking two or more LANs which may be dissimilar at the physical layer but run the same Link Layer protocols. Usually consisting of both hardware and software.

Broadband Channels: Communication channels such as those made possible by the use of laser beams and microwaves that can transmit data at high speed.

Broadband: The transmission of a signal using modulation. This permits many simultaneous signals on the same medium.

Bubble Memory: A type of nonvolatile memory where data are represented by the presence or absence of magnetized areas (bubbles) formed on a thin piece of garnet.

Buffer: Temporary storage used to compensate for a difference in rate of flow of data, or time of occurrence of events, when transmitting data from one device to another.

Bug: A euphemism for a defect.

Bulletin-board System (BBS): An electronic equivalent of a conventional bulletin board. A BBS is used as part of a communication network where users can post messages, read messages posted by other users, communicate with the system operator, and upload or download programs.

Bus Network: A computer network arrangement where each device is connected to a single communication cable by an interface. Each device can communicate directly with every other device.

Bus: A topology comprising a single linear medium to which all the stations are attached. Also the internal data path of a computer.

Byte: A set of (normally) 8 binary digits (bits).

C: A low-level structural programming language developed by AT&T-Bell Laboratories. It resembles a machine-independent assembler language and is popular for software package development.

Cache Memory: A high-speed temporary storage area in the CPU for storing parts of a program of data during processing.

Cache: A method for reducing the access time to data that is stored in a large, slow medium by retaining the most often accessed data in a smaller, faster medium. A special type of buffer used by fixed disk systems to move data between the computer and the hard disk drive efficiently. Because the cache operates at the computer's clock speed instead of the slower hard disk speed, frequently used data can be held in cache and accessed more quickly than if it were still on the disk. The advent of high speed personal computers has also led to the development of the memory cache, which is a special type of buffer using very fast memory that can keep up with a fast CPU and then feed data into the computer's main memory as it can accept it.

CAI (Computer-Assisted Instruction): A general term that refers to a learning situation in which the student interacts with (and it is guided by) a computer through a course of study aimed at achieving certain instructional goals.

Card Reader: A device that translates the holes in a punched card into machine-readable code

Carrier: A high frequency signal which can be already (modulated) by data do achieve high data rates, carry several data streams, and interconnect several LANs in a backbone. Broadband networks and Ethernet use carriers.

Cartridge Tape: A form of magnetic tape similar to cassette tape but with a much greater storage density. Used mainly with large computer systems.

Cassette Tape: A form of magnetic tape, about one fourth inch wide; generally used for secondary storage with microcomputers.

Cathode Ray Tube (CRT): An electronic tube with a screen upon which information may be displayed.

CDN: Content delivery network—A system consisting of multiple computers that contain copies of data, which are located in different places on the network so clients can access the copy closest to them.

CD-ROM (Compact Disk-Read Only Memory): An optical disk subsystem that can store more than 800 MB of information but cannot be written to, only read. A CD-ROM is very similar to the CD that's used for music reproduction, and many CD-ROM players will also play audio CDs.

Chain Printer: A line-at-a-time impact printer that uses a rotating chain containing all the characters.

Channel: A range of frequencies used to carry a single transmission in a Broadband network.

Check Bit: A binary check digit; for example, a parity bit.

Chip: A tiny sliver (usually made of silicon) on which integrated electronic components are deposited.

Circuit Switching: The provision of a direct, dedicated, physical path between two communicating devices.

Client Server: A model for a particular type of network database management system that splits processing between the workstation and a specialized server called a database server.

Clock: A device that generates periodic signals utilized to control the timing of a synchronous computer. Also, a register whose contents change at regular intervals in such a way as to measure time.

Cloud: A metaphor for a global network, first used in reference to the telephone network and now commonly used to represent the Internet.

Cloud Application: a software application that is never installed on a local machine—it's always accessed over the Internet. The 'top' layer of the Cloud Pyramid where 'applications' are run and interacted with via a web-browser. Cloud Applications are tightly controlled, leaving little room for modification. Examples include: Gmail or SalesForce.com.

Cloud Arcs: short for cloud architectures. Designs for software applications that can be accessed and used over the Internet. (Cloud-chitecture is just too hard to pronounce.)

Cloud as a service (CaaS): A cloud computing service that has been opened up into a platform that others can build upon.

Cloud Bridge: Running an application in such a way that its components are integrated within multiple cloud environments (which could be any combination of internal/private and external/ public clouds).

Cloud Broker: An entity that creates and maintains relationships with multiple cloud service providers. It acts as a liaison between cloud services customers and cloud service providers, selecting the best provider for each customer and monitoring the services.

Cloud client: computing device for cloud computing. Updated version of thin client.

Cloud Computing: A computing capability that provides an abstraction between the computing resource and its underlying technical architecture (*e.g.*, servers, storage, networks), enabling convenient, on-demand network access to a shared pool of configurable computing resources that can be rapidly provisioned and released with minimal management effort or service provider interaction.' This definition states that clouds have five essential characteristics: on-demand self-service, broad network access, resource pooling, rapid elasticity, and measured service. Narrowly speaking, cloud computing is client-server computing that abstract the details of the server away;one requests a service (resource), not a specific server (machine). Cloud computing enables Infrastructure as a Service (IaaS), Platform as a Service (PaaS), and Software as a Service (SaaS). Cloud computing means that infrastructure, applications, and business processes can be delivered to you as a service, over the Internet (or your own network).

Cloud Enabler: A general term that refers to organizations (typically vendors) who are not cloud providers per se, but make available technology, such as cloudware, that enables cloud computing. Vendor that provides technology or service that enables a client or other vendor to take advantage of cloud computing.

Cloud envy: used to describe a vendor who jumps on the cloud computing bandwagon by rebranding existing services.

Cloud governance and compliance: Governance defines who's responsible for what and the policies and procedures that your people or groups need to follow. Cloud governance requires governing your own infrastructure as well as infrastructure that you don't totally control. Cloud governance has two key components: understanding compliance and risk and business performance goals.

Cloud Hosting: A type of internet hosting where the client leases virtualized, dynamically scalable infrastructure on an as-needed basis. Users frequently have the choice of operating system and other infrastructure components. Typically cloud hosting is self-service, billed hourly or monthly, and controlled via a web interface or API.

Cloud Infrastructure: The 'bottom' layer–or foundation–of the Cloud Pyramid is the delivery of computer infrastructure through paravirtualization. This includes servers, networks and other hardware appliances delivered as either Infrastructure Web Services or 'cloudcenters'. Full control of the infrastructure is provided at this level. Examples include GoGrid or Amazon Web Services.

Cloud Manageability: You need a consistent view across both on-premises and cloud-based environments. This includes managing the assets provisioning as well as the quality of service (QOS) you're receiving from your service provider.

Cloud Operating System: A computer operating system that is specially designed to run in a provider's datacenter and be delivered to the user over the Internet or another network. Windows Azure is an example of a cloud operating system or 'cloud layer' that runs on Windows Server

2008. The term is also sometimes used to refer to cloud-based client operating systems such as Google's Chrome OS.

Cloud OS: Also known as platform-as-a-service (PaaS). Think Google Chrome.

Cloud Platform: The 'middle' layer of the Cloud Pyramid which provides a computing platform or framework (*e.g.*, .NET, Ruby on Rails, or Python) as a service or stack. Control is limited to that of the platform or framework, but not at a lower level (server infrastructure). Examples include: Google AppEngine or Microsoft Azure.

Cloud Portability: The ability to move applications (and often their associated data) across cloud computing environments from different cloud providers, as well as across private or internal cloud and public or external clouds.

Cloud provider: A company that provides cloud-based platform, infrastructure, application, or storage services to other organizations and/or individuals, usually for a fee.

Cloud Providers: Computing service providers whose product/platform is based on virtualization of computing resources and a utiliy-based payment model.

Cloud Pyramid: A visual representation of Cloud Computing layers where differing segments are broken out by functionality. Simplified version includes: Infrastructure, Platform and Application layers.

Cloud Security: The same security principles that apply to on-site computing apply to cloud computing security.

Cloud Servers: Virtualized servers running Windows or Linux operating systems that are instantiated via a web interface or API. Cloud Servers behave in the same manner as physical ones and can be controlled at an administrator or root level, depending on the server type and Cloud Hosting provider.

Cloud Service Architecture (CSA): A term coined by Jeff Barr, chief evangelist at Amazon Web Services. The term describes an architecture in which applications and application components act as services on the cloud, which serve other applications within the same cloud environment.

Cloud Sourcing: Outsourcing storage or taking advantage of some other type of cloud service.

Cloud Standards: A standard is an agreed-upon approach for doing something. Cloud standards ensure interoperability, so you can take tools, applications, virtual images, and more, and use them in another cloud environment without having to do any rework. Portability lets you take one application or instance running on one vendor's implementation and deploy it on another vendor's implementation.

Cloud Storage: A service that allows customers to save data by transferring it over the Internet or another network to an offsite storage system maintained by a third party.

Cloud Storm: connecting multiple cloud computing environments. Also called cloud network.

Cloudburst: What happens when your cloud has an outage or security breach and your data is unavailable. The term cloudburst is being use in two meanings, negative and positive:

Cloudburst (negative): The failure of a cloud computing environment due to the inability to handle a spike in demand.

Cloudburst (positive): The dynamic deployment of a software application that runs on internal organizational compute resources to a public cloud to address a spike in demand.

Cloudcenter: A datacenter in the 'cloud' utilizing standards-based virtualized components as a datacenter-like infrastructure; example: a large company, such as Amazon, that rents its infrastructure.

Cloud-Oriented Architecture (COA): A term coined by Jeff Barr at Amazon Web Services to describe an architecture where applications act as services in the cloud and serve other applications in the cloud environment. An architecture for IT infrastructure and software applications that is optimized for use in cloud computing environments. The term is not yet in wide use, and as is the case for the term 'cloud computing' itself, there is no common or generally accepted definition or specific description of a cloud-oriented architecture.

Cloudstorming: The act of connecting multiple cloud computing environments.

Cloudware: A general term referring to a variety of software, typically at the infrastructure level, that enables building, deploying, running or managing applications in a cloud computing environment.

Cloudwashing: Slapping the word 'cloud' on products and services you already have.

Cluster: A group of linked computers that work together as if they were a single computer, for high availability and/or load balancing.

Coaxial Cable: A copper or aluminum wire wrapped with spacers to insulate and protect it. Groups of coaxial cables may also be bundled together in a bigger cable for ease of installation.

COBOL (Common Business-Oriented Language): A high-level language used in business information processing. It was specifically designed to manipulate large data files.

CODASYL (COnference on DAta SYstems Languages): The group of representatives of users and computer manufacturers who developed and maintained the COBOL language.

Coding: The process of writing the computer program instructions in a particular programming language.

Common Carrier: An organization that supplies communication services to other organizations and to the public as authorized by government agencies.

Communication Channel: The medium, or pathway, through which data are transmitted between devices. The pathway may be wire cable, microwave, or fiber optics.

Compiler: A program that translates a high-level programming language into a machine language program.

Computer Generations: Major stages in the historical development of computing.

Computer Network: A processing complex consisting of two or more interconnected computers.

Computer Output Microform (COM): Hard copy in the form of photographic images recorded on microfilm or microfiche.

Computer Program: A serial of instructions or statements, in a form acceptable to a computer, prepared in order to achieve a certain result.

Computer Terminal: Any input/output device connected by telecommunications links to a computer.

Computer Virus: A program that copies its destructive program routines into the computer systems of anyone who accesses computer systems which have used the program, or anyone who uses copies of data or programs taken from such computers. This spreads the destruction of data and programs among many computer users.

Computer: A device that can accept data, perform certain functions on that data, and present the results of those operations.

Computer-aided Design (CAD): The use of computers and advanced graphics hardware and software to provide interactive design assistance for engineering and architectural design.

Concentration: The process of connecting and serving more devices on a communication channel than the channel was designed to handle.

Concentrator: A special-purpose computer that accepts information from many terminals using slow-speed lines and transmits data to main computer system over a high-speed line.

Consumption-based pricing model: A pricing model whereby the service provider charges its customers based on the amount of the service the customer consumes, rather than a time-based fee. For example, a cloud storage provider might charge per gigabyte of information stored. See also Subscription-based pricing model.

Control Bus: The electrical pathway for all timing and controlling functions.

Control Unit: A subunit of the central processing unit that controls and directs the operations of the entire computer system. The control unit retrieves computer instructions in proper sequence, interprets each instruction, and then directs the other parts of the computer system in the implementation of a computer program.

Cursor: A movable point of light displayed on most video display screens to assist the user in the input of data.

Customer self-service: A feature that allows customers to provision, manage, and terminate services themselves, without involving the service provider, via a Web interface or programmatic calls to service APIs.

Cylinder: An imaginary vertical cylinder consisting of the vertical alignment of data tracks on each surface of magnetic disk, which are accessed simultaneously by the read/wire heads of a disk storage device.

Daisy-Wheel Printer: A type of printer that uses a print wheel resembling a daisy. At the end of each 'petal' is a fully formed character.

Data Base Management System (DBMS): The comprehensive software system that builds, maintains, and provides access to a database. Unlike a file management system, a DBMS can access appropriate records from two or more files at once.

Data Bus: The electrical pathway on which program data are transferred.

Data Communication: The process of electronically sending data from one point to another.

Data Dictionary: A repository of definitions of all data flows and data stores in a data flow diagram, in a process specification, or in the data dictionary itself; defines composite data in terms of its components, and elementary data in terms of the meaning of each value that it can assume.

Data Entry: The process of converting data into a form suitable for entry into a computer system. Also called data capture or input preparation.

Data Flow Diagram (allas bubble chart): A graphic tool for depicting the partitioning of a system into a network of activities and their interfaces, together with the origins, destinations, and stores of data. Graphical representation of a system, that shows the sources and processes performed on data, and the flow of data between the nodes.

Data Flow: A pipeline along which information of known composition is passed.

Data in the cloud: Managing data in the cloud requires data security and privacy, including controls for moving data from point A to point B. It also includes managing data storage and the resources for large-scale data processing.

Data Management: Control program functions that provide access to data sets, enforce data storage conventions, and regulate the use of input/output devices.

Data Manipulation: Altering data that enters or exits the computer.

Data Model: A conceptual framework which defines the logical relationships among the data elements needed to support a basic business or other process.

Data Planning: A corporate planning and analysis function that focuses on data resource management. It includes the responsibility for developing an overall information policy and data architecture for the firm's data resources.

Database Administrator: A specialist responsible for maintaining standards for the development, maintenance, and security of an organization's databases.

Data-base Query Language: A fourth-generation language that is used in conjunction with a relational database. Acts as in interface between a user and a DBMS, and helps users to easily access data without the use of complex programming code.

Database: A collection of interrelated data stored together with controlled redundancy to serve one or more applications, so that the data stored are independent of the programs that use them and so that a common, controlled approach can be used for adding, modifying and retrieving data.

Data-entry Operator: The person who enters data into a computer using a keyboard and video display terminal.

Data-flow Diagram: A type of diagram that shows the logical flow of data through a system.

Demodulation: The process of converting an analog signal to a digital signal.

Detection and forensics: Separating legitimate from illegitimate activity.

Digitizer: A device that is used to convert drawing and other graphic images on paper or other materials into digital data that is entered into a computer system.

Disk Operating System (DOS): An operating system for microcomputers in which all or part resides on a disk and must be loaded into the computer; the set of programs that controls and supervises the micro-computer's hardware.

Disk Pack: A removable unit containing several magnetic disks that can be mounted on a magnetic disk storage unit.

Disk: A revolving platter upon which data and programs are stored.

Diskette: A floppy disk. A low-cost magnetic medium used for I/O and secondary storage purposes.

Display: A visual presentation of data.

Disruptive technology: A term used in the business world to describe innovations that improve products or services in unexpected ways and change both the way things are done and the market. Cloud computing is often referred to as a disruptive technology because it has the potential to completely change the way IT services are procured, deployed, and maintained.

Documentation: A collection of documents or information that describes a computer program, information system, or required data processing operations.

Dot-matrix Printer: A type of impact printer that uses a print head containing pins, usually 9 to 24, that produce characters by printing patterns of dots.

Draft-quality Print: Lowest quality print; characters are smaller than standard-quality print and are formed using a minimum number of dots; suitable for rough drafts. Also called compressed print.

Drum Printer: A line-at-a-time impact printer that uses a rotating drum of 80 to 132 print positions with each print position containing a complete set of characters.

Dumb Terminal: A stand-alone keyboard and display screen that can send or receive data, but cannot process that data.

Duplex: In communications, pertaining to a simultaneous two-way independent transmission in both directions.

EBCDIC (Extended Binary Coded Decimal Interchange Code): An eight bit code that is widely used by mainframe computers.

EEPROM: An electronically erasable and programmable read-only memory chip that can be reprogrammed with special electric pulses.

Elastic computing: The ability to dynamically provision and de-provision processing, memory, and storage resources to meet demands of peak usage without worrying about capacity planning and engineering for peak usage.

Elasticity and scalability: The cloud is elastic, meaning that resource allocation can get bigger or smaller depending on demand. Elasticity enables scalability, which means that the cloud can scale upward for peak demand and downward for lighter demand. Scalability also means that an application can scale when adding users and when application requirements change.

Electronic Data Processing (EDP): The use of electronic computers to process data automatically.

Electronic Mail: The transmission, storage, and distribution of text material in electronic form over communications networks.

Encapsulation: Enclosing a packet from one protocol by a header, and sometimes a trailer, of the next protocol down the ISO model.

Encoding System: Where alphanumeric characters are represented by patterns of 1s and 0s so that they can be recognized and used by a computer. The American Standard Code for Information Interchange (ASCII) and Extended Binary Coded Decimal Interchange Code (EBCDIC) are the two most widely used encoding systems.

Encryption: Coding to protect your information assets.

Encryption: The translation of one character string into another by means of a cypher, translation table, or algorithm, in order to render the information contained therein meaningless to anyone who does not possess the decoding mechanism.

External cloud: Public or private cloud services that are provided by a third party outside the organization. A cloud computing environment that is external to the boundaries of the organization.

Facsimile System: A system used to transmit pictures, text, maps, etc., between geographically separated points. An image is scanned at a transmitting point and duplicated at a receiving point.

Facsimile: The transmission of images and their reconstruction and duplication on some form of paper at a receiving station.

Field: A data element that consists of a grouping of characters that describe a particular attribute of an entity. For example, the name field or salary field of an employee.

Fifth-generation Computers: A phrase referring to the next generation of computers, which will incorporate artificial intelligence.

File Maintenance: The activity of keeping a file up-to-date by adding, changing, or deleting data.

File Management System (FMS): A software package that allows users to define data items, place these items into specified records, combine these records into designated files, and then manipulate and retrieve stored data in various ways to achieve user goals. An FMS can typically access records from only one file at a time.

File Processing: Utilizing a file for data processing activities such as file maintenance, information retrieval, or report generation.

File: A collection of related data records treated as a unit. Sometimes called a data set.

File-locking: A file protection procedure that allows only one user to access a file at a time.

File-management System: An application program that can manage (manipulate, store, retrieve, and print) data in separate files. In this system only one file may be accessed at one time.

First-generation Computers: Computers developed and used before 1960 and which employed vacuum tube technology.

Fixed Disk: A hard-disk storage system of one or more nonremovable hard disks protected in a permanently sealed case.

Fixed-length Record: A record in which its data length is set to a specific number of characters. Any unused spaces are stored as blank spaces in the records.

Flat-panel Display: A type of display that does not use a picture tube to display characters. Types include liquid-crystal display (LCD) and gas plasma.

Flip-flop: A circuit or device containing active elements, capable of assuming either one or two states at a given time. Synonymous with toggle.

Floating-point: Pertaining to a number representation system in which each number is represented by two sets of digits. One set represents the significant digits or fixed-point 'base' of the number, while the other set of digits represents the 'exponent,' which indicates the precision of the radix point.

Floppy Diskette: A flexible, mylar magnetic diskette commonly used with microcomputers on which data are magnetically stored.

Flowchart: A graphic tool for depicting the sequence of activities in a system.

FORTRAN (FORmula TRANslator): A high-level language designed to solve complex numerical problems.

Fourth-Generation Computers: (1) Those computers developed and in use from 1971 to the present which make use of large-scale integration (LSI). (2) Programming languages that are easier to use than high-level languages like BASIC, COBOL, or FORTRAN. They are also known as nonprocedural, natural, or very high-level languages.

Front-end Processor: Typically a smaller, general-purpose computer that is dedicated to handling data communications control functions in a communications network, thus relieving the host computer of these functions.

Full- Duplex Mode: A method of transferring data over a communication channel in which data can be transmitted and received at the same time. A full-duplex device can transmit and receive data at the same time.

Full-duplex Transmission: The simultaneous sending and receiving of data over a communication path.

Funnel cloud: discussion about cloud computing that goes round and round but never turns into action (never 'touches the ground').

Gateway: A device which links two or more networks, or a network and a computer, which use different protocols or have different characteristics which prevent normal connection via a bridge.

General-purpose Application Programs: Programs that can perform information processing jobs for users from all application areas. For example, word processing programs, electronic spreadsheet programs, and graphic programs can be used by individuals for home, education, business, scientific, and many other purposes.

General-purpose Computer: A computer that is designed to handle a wide variety of problems. Contrast with special-purpose computer.

Gigabyte: One billion bytes. More accurately, 2 to the 30th power, or 1,073,741,824 in decimal notation.

Google App Engine: A service that enables developers to create and run Web applications on Google's infrastructure and share their applications via a pay-as-you-go, consumption-based plan with no setup costs or recurring fees.

Google Apps: Google's SaaS offering that includes an office productivity suite, email, and document sharing, as well as Gmail, Google Talk for instant messaging, Google Calendar and Google Docs, spreadsheets, and presentations.

HaaS: Hardware as a service; see IaaS.

Half-duplex Mode: A method of transferring data over a communication channel in which data can be transmitted in only one direction at a time. A half-duplex mode device can transmit or receive but not at the same time.

Half-duplex Transmission: The sending and then receiving of data over a communications path during alternating periods of time. Data may not be sent in both directions at the same time.

Hard Copy: A data medium or data record that has a degree of permanence and that can be read by people or machine.

Hard Disk: A rigid metal platter coated with a magnetizable substance. Contrast with floppy disk.

Hexadecimal System: The base 16 numbering system using the digits 0 through 9 and the letters A through F.

Hexadecimal: Pertaining to the number system with a radix of 16. Synonymous with sexadecimal.

High-level Language: A programming language that utilizes macro instructions and statements that closely resemble human language or mathematical notation to describe the problem to be solved or the procedure to be used. Also called a compiler language.

High-resolution Graphics: A method of creating graphic images by turning the pixels that make up the screen display on or off.

HIPO (Hierarchy Plus Input, Processing, Output) Chart: A type of chart where each module's input, output, and processing needs are outlined.

Hollerith Code: A particular type of code used to represent alphanumeric data on 80-column punched cards.

Hollerith: Pertaining to a type of code or punched card utilizing 12 rows per column and usually 80 columns per card. Named after Herman Hollerith, who originated punched card data processing.

Hosted application: An Internet-based or Web-based application software program that runs on a remote server and can be accessed via an Internet-connected PC or thin client. See also SaaS.

Hybrid cloud: A networking environment that includes multiple integrated internal and/or external providers. Hybrid clouds combine aspects of both public and private clouds.

Hybrid Computer: A data processing device using both analog and discrete data representation.

IBM Smart Business: IBM's cloud solutions, which include IBM Smart Business Test Cloud, IBM Smart Analytics Cloud, IBM Smart Business Storage Cloud, IBM Information Archive, IBM Lotus Live, and IBM LotusLive iNotes.

Identity management: Managing personal identity information so that access to computer resources, applications, data, and services is controlled properly.

Index Sequential: A method of data organization in which records are organized in sequential offer and also referenced by an index. When utilized with direct access file devices, it is known as index sequential access method or ISAM.

Index: An ordered reference list of the contents of a file or document together with keys or reference notations for identification or location of those contents.

Indexed-sequential Access: A method of storing and accessing data; has the advantages of both direct and sequential access.

Infrastructure as a Service (IaaS): Cloud infrastructure services or 'Infrastructure as a Service (IaaS)' delivers computer infrastructure, typically a platform virtualization environment, as a service. Rather than purchasing servers, software, data center space or network equipment, clients instead buy those resources as a fully outsourced service. The service is typically billed on a utility computing basis and amount of resources consumed (and therefore the cost) will typically reflect the level of activity. It is an evolution of web hosting and virtual private server offerings.

Ink-jet Printer: A type of nonimpact printer that forms characters on paper by spraying ink through an electrical field that arranges the ink particles in the form of characters.

Input Device: A peripheral device through which data are entered and transformed into machine readable form, such as a keyboard or a mouse.

Internal cloud: A type of private cloud whose services are provided by an IT department to those in its own organization.

Interrecord Gap (IRG): The section of magnetic tape between individual records that allows the tape to attain proper speed for reading or writing.

Job Control Language (JCL): A language for communicating with the operating system of a computer to identify a job and describe its requirements.

Job Management: Preparing, scheduling, and monitoring jobs for continuous processing by a computer system. This is a major system management function of an operating system.

Joystick: A small lever set in a box used to move the cursor on the computer's display screen.

Keyboard: An input device, similar to a typewriter keyboard, that contains letters, numbers, special character keys, keys that control cursor movement, and keys that can be programmed for other uses.

Label: One or more characters used to identify a statement or an item of data in a computer program or the contents of the data file.

LAN: Local area network.

Language: A set of rule and conventions used to convey information.

Language-Translator Program: A program that translates a programming language into machine code for execution by the computer.

Laptop Computer: A portable computer, usually small enough to fit in a briefcase. Named so because it is small enough to fit in a person's lap.

Large-Scale Integration (LSI): A method of constructing electronic circuits in which thousands of circuits can be placed on a single semiconductor chip.

Laser Printer: A nonimpact printer that produces images on paper by directing a laser beam onto a drum, leaving a negative charge in the form of a character to which positively changed toner powder will stick. The toner powder is transferred to paper as it rolls by the drum and is bonded to the paper by hot rollers.

Leased Line: A permanent or semipermanent communications service provided by a common carrier to link sending and receiving units in an organization.

Letter-quality Print: Print of fully formed characters, similar to typewriter print.

Light Pen: A photoelectronic device that allows data to be entered or altered on the face of a video display terminal.

Line Printer: A device that prints all characters of a line as a unit.

Liquid Crystal Displays (LCDS): Electronic visual displays that form characters by applying an electrical charge to selected silicon crystals.

Logo: An interactive graphical language used as a tool or learning a variety of concepts (color, direction, letters, words, sounds, etc.) as well as learning to program and use the computer. Forms and figures are used (sprites and turtles) that a child learns to move around on the screen to accomplish tasks.

Low-level Language: A programming language, such as machine language or assembly; requires the programmer to have detailed knowledge of the internal workings of the computer.

Magnetic Bubble: An electromagnetic storage device that stores and moves data magnetically as tiny magnetic spots that look like bubbles under a microscope as they float on the surface of a special type of semiconductor chip.

Magnetic Core Memory: Small magnetic cores (doughnut-shaped metal rings) with wires through them; cores can be magnetized in different directions to represent data. Preceded semiconductor memory.

Magnetic Disk: A flat circular plate with a magnetic surface on which data can be stored by selective magnetization of portions of the curved surface.

Magnetic Drum: A circular cylinder with a magnetic surface on which data can be stored by selective magnetization of portions of the curved surface.

Magnetic Ink: An ink that contains particles of iron oxide that can be magnetized and detected by magnetic sensors.

Main Frame: (1) Same as central processing unit. (2) A larger-size computer system, typically with a separate central processing unit, as distinguished from microcomputer and minicomputer systems.

Megabyte: One million bytes. More accurately, 2 to the 20th power, or 1,048,576 in decimal notation.

Microcomputer: A very small computer, ranging in size from a 'computer on a chip' to a small typewriter-size unit.

Microsoft Azure: Microsoft cloud services that provide the platform as a service (see PaaS), allowing developers to create cloud applications and services.

Middleware: Software that sits between applications and operating systems, consisting of a set of services that enable interoperability in support of distributed architectures by passing data between applications. So, for example, the data in one database can be accessed through another database.

Mnemonic: Pertaining to a technique used to aid human memory.

Modem: Stands for 'Modulator/Demodulator'. A device which converts the digital output (signals) of a computer into an analog signal capable of being transmitted over a conventional telephone line. It can also receive the same and convert it back into a digital form.

Module: A collection of program statements with four basic attributes; input and output function, mechanics, and internal data.

Monitor: A television-like device used to display data.

Motherboard: The name given to the main circuit board of a microcomputer; contains the microprocessor, memory chips, and chips that handle input, output, and storage.

Mouse: A small device that is electronically connected to a computer and is moved by hand on a flat surface in order to move the cursor on a video screen in the same direction. Buttons on the mouse allow users to issue commands and make responses or selections.

Multiplex: To interleave or simultaneously transmit two or more messages on a single channel.

Multiplexer: An electronic device that allows a single communications channel to carry simultaneous data transmission from many terminals.

Multipoint Channel Configuration: A type of communication channel configuration where three or more devices are connected together and share the same communication channel.

Multiprocessing Operating System: A microcomputer system to which more than one person has access from separate computer terminals.

Multiprocessing: Pertaining to the simultaneous execution of two or more instructions by a computer or computer network.

Multiprocessor: A computer network consisting of two or more central processors under a common control.

Multiprogramming: Pertaining to the concurrent execution of two or more programs by a computer by interleaving their execution.

Multitasking: The concurrent use of the same computer to accomplish several different information processing tasks. Each task may require the use of a different program, or the concurrent use of the same copy of a program by several users.

Near-letter Quality Print: Print made from dots rather than fully formed characters; approaches the appearance of letter-quality print.

Near-typeset Quality Print: Print similar in quality to that produced by commercial typesetting equipment; produced by laser printers.

Network Architecture: A master plan designed to promote an open, simple, flexible, and efficient telecommunications environment through the use of standard protocols, standard communications hardware and software interfaces, and the design of a standard multilevel telecommunications interface between end users and computer systems.

Object: A data element that includes both data and the methods or processes that act on that data.

Octal System: The base 8 numbering system using the digits 0 through 7.

On-demand service: A model by which a customer can purchase cloud services as needed; for instance, if customers need to utilize additional servers for the duration of a project, they can do so and then drop back to the previous level after the project is completed.

Operations System: A basic subsystem of the business firm that constitutes its input, processing, and output components. Also called a physical system.

Optical Card: A small card that stores data on a strip of special material similar to a magnetic strip. However, the data on an optical card are encoded by a laser rather than magnetically as with the magnetic strip.

Optical Character Recognition (OCR): The machine identification of printed characters through the use of high-sensitive devices.

Optical Disks: A secondary storage medium using laser technology to read tiny spots on a plastic disk. The disks are currently capable of storing billions of characters of information.

Optical Laser Disk: A type of storage medium on which data are stored and read by a laser. Optical laser disks have much higher data densities than their magnetic disk counterparts.

Optical Scanner: A device that optically scans characters or images and generates their digital representations.

Optical Tape: A storage medium similar in appearance to magnetic tape, but data are stored by optical-laser techniques.

Optical-Bar Recognition (OBR): A data input method that reads and interprets bar codes.

Optical-Character Recognition (OCR): The most sophisticated form of optical recognition; recognizes letters, numbers, and other optical character sets by their shapes in much the same way as the human eye does.

Optical-Mark Recognition (OMR): A data input method in which a series of pen or pencil marks on a special form are scanned and their position is translated into machine-readable code. For example, computer-scored test answer sheets.

Output Device: A peripheral device that translates machine-readable codes into a form that can be used by humans or another machine.

Packet Switching: A data transmission process that transmits addressed packets such that a channel is occupied only for the duration of transmission of the packet.

Parity Bit: A check bit appended to an array of binary digits to make the sum of all the binary digits, including the check bit, always odd or always even.

Parity Check: A method of checking the accuracy of binary data after those data have been transferred to or from storage. The number of 1 bits in a binary character is controlled by the addition or deletion of a parity bit.

Personal cloud: synonymous with something called MiFi, a personal wireless router. It takes a mobile wireless data signal and translates it to wi-fi. It's pronounced ME-fi, as in 'the personal cloud belongs to me—but if you're nice I'll let you connect.'

Pixel: A picture element on the screen of a visual display used for graphics work that is controlled by the contents of a specific location in storage. By turning each pixel on or off, the processor is able to paint a graphic image.

Platform as a Service (PaaS): Platform as a service—Cloud platform services, whereby the computing platform (operating system and associated services) is delivered as a service over the Internet by the provider. The PaaS layer offers black-box services with which developers can build applications on top of the compute infrastructure. This might include developer tools that are offered as a service to build services, or data access and database services, or billing services.

Point-of-Sale (POS) Terminal: A computer terminal used in retail stores that serves the function of a cash register as well as collecting sales data and performing other data processing functions.

Private clouds: Private clousvirtualized cloud data centers inside your company's firewall. It may also be a private space dedicated to your company within a cloud provider's data center. An internal cloud behind the organization's firewall. The company's IT department provides softwares and hardware as a service to its customers—the people who work for the company. Vendors love the words 'private cloud.'

Programmer: A person mainly involved in designing, writing, and testing computer programs.

PROLOG (PROgramming LOGic): A programming language created for writing programs for expert systems.

PROM (Programmable Read-Only Memory): A read-only storage device that can be programmed after manufacture by external equipment. PROMs are usually integrated circuit chips.

Protocol: A set of rules which govern the interchange of data between two communicating computers.

Public cloud: Services offered over the public Internet and available to anyone who wants to purchase the service.

Random Access Memory (RAM): One of the basic types of semiconductor memory used for temporary storage of data or programs during processing. Each memory position can be directly sensed (read) or changed (write) in the same length of time, irrespective of its location on the storage medium.

Ring Network: A computer network arrangement where each computer or device is connected in a closed loop by a single communication channel. Communication flows through each device in the ring between the source and destination of the data.

Roaming workloads: The backend product of cloudcenters.

RPG (Report Program Generator): A programming language designed for producing reports and processing files.

SaaS Software as a Service: Cloud application services, whereby applications are delivered over the Internet by the provider, so that the applications don't have to be purchased, installed, and run on the customer's computers. SaaS providers were previously referred to as ASP (application service providers). In the SaaS layer, the service provider hosts the software so you don't need to install it, manage it, or buy hardware for it. All you have to do is connect and use it. SaaS Examples include customer relationship management as a service.

Sectors: A pie-shaped division of each magnetic-disk track which further identifies the storage location of data.

Self-service provisioning: Cloud customers can provision cloud services without going through a lengthy process. You request an amount of computing, storage, software, process, or more from the service provider. After you use these resources, they can be automatically deprovisioned.

Semiconductor Memory: A memory type in which electronic circuits are 'etched' onto silicon wafers.

Sequential Access: A method of storing and accessing data in a row, or one after another. To access a record, all preceding records must be read first.

Service level agreement SLA: A contractual agreement by which a service provider defines the level of service, responsibilities, priorities, and guarantees regarding availability, performance, and other aspects of the service.

Service migration: The act of moving from one cloud service or vendor to another.

Service provider: The company or organization that provides a public or private cloud service.

Spooling: The collection of information from several sources at one point, followed by the orderly delivery of that information to a device, *e.g.*, a printer.

Standardized interfaces: Cloud services should have standardized APIs, which provide instructions on how two application or data sources can communicate with each other. A standardized interface lets the customer more easily link cloud services together.

Star: A topology where all of the stations are connected to a central switch.

Subscription-based pricing model: A pricing model that lets customers pay a fee to use the service for a particular time period, often used for SaaS services. See also Consumption-based pricing model.

Super Chip: Larger than many chips and with significantly more circuitry; designed for increased processing capabilities.

Super Computer: A special category of large mainframe computer systems that are the most powerful available. They are designed to solve massive computational problems.

Synchronous: A characteristic in which each event, or the performance of any basic operation, is constrained to start on, and usually to keep in step with signals from a timing clock. Contrast with Asynchronous.

System Analysis: A detailed step-by-step investigation of related procedures to see what must be done and the best way of doing it.

System Design: The creation of alternative solutions to be problems uncovered in system analysis. The final design recommendation is based on cost effectiveness and other factors.

System Implementation: The process of testing the new system, converting from an old system to the new one, and training the users on the new system.

System Life Cycle: The life span of an information system. The life cycle consists of: (a) system analysis; (b) system design; (c) system development; (d) system implementation; and (e) system maintenance.

System Software: Programs that control and support operations of a computer system. System software includes a variety of programs such as operating systems, database management systems, communications control programs, service and utility programs, and programming language translators.

TCP/IP: Transmission Control Protocol/Internet Protocol. A protocol for interconnecting networks or devices on the same network. For example, using TCP/IP is the accepted way to interconnect a DOS LAN with a UNIX system because the DOS and UNIX operating systems normally have no LAN operating software that works on both types of machines.

Top-down Methodology: A disciplined approach to organizing complexity by identifying the top-level functions in a system and then decomposing these functions into a hierarchy of understandable lower-level modules.

Topology: The pattern of wiring connections used in a LAN or shape of the network, *e.g.*, star, bus, ring or tree.

Touch Pad: An input device that uses a pressure sensitive pad to record data input where the pad is touched.

Transaction Processing System: An information system that processes data arising from the occurrence of business transactions.

Transceiver: A device which transmits and receives signals. Usually used in reference to CSMA/CD LANs.

User: A person or group of people who use a computer system.

Utility computing: Online computing or storage sold as a metered commercial service in a way similar to a public utility

VAN (Value Added Network): A network which provides some service as well as interconnection. British Telecom's Prestel is an example.

Vendor lock-in: Dependency on the particular cloud vendor and difficulty moving from one cloud vendor to another due to lack of standardized protocols, APIs, data structures (schema), and service models.

Verification: A method of checking data accuracy by comparing it against a known source.

Vertical cloud: A cloud computing environment that is optimized for use in a particular industry, such as health care or financial services.

Very Large-Scale Integration (VLSI): The process of putting several hundred thousand complete circuits on a single chip.

Virtual Private Cloud (VPC): A term coined by Reuven Cohen, CEO and founder of Enomaly. The term describes a concept that is similar to, and derived from, the familiar concept of a Virtual Private Network (VPN), but applied to cloud computing. It is the notion of turning a public cloud into a virtual private cloud, particularly in terms of security and the ability to create a VPC across components that are both within the cloud and external to it. *e.g.*, the Amazon VPC that allows Amazon EC2 to connect to legacy infrastructure on an IPsec VPN.

Virtual private data center: Resources grouped according to specific business objectives.

Virtual Storage: Descriptive of the capability to use online secondary storage devices and specialized software to divide programs into smaller segments for transmission to and from internal storage in order to significantly increase the effective size of the available internal storage.

Virtual-storage Operating System: An operating system that makes use of a secondary-storage device as an extension of primary storage.

Visual Display Terminal: A device capable of displaying keyed input and processor output on a screen.

VLSI (Very Large-Scale Integration): Semiconductor chips containing hundreds of thousands of circuits.

Volatile: In computers, refers to the loss of data from RAM when power is shut off.

Wide-Area Network (WAN): A computer network where the computers are geographically dispersed.

Zoom: A feature of graphics packages that allows the user to enlarge a specified area of a drawing for viewing or to pull back and view the entire scene.

INDEX

B

C

E

F

G

H

I

N

O

P

Q

R

S

T

U

V

W

Z

NOTES

NOTES